Stanley Gibbons Stamp Catalogue

Southern Balkans

(Albania, Bulgaria, Greece and Macedonia)

1st Edition 2019

STANLEY GIBBONS LTD
London and Ringwood

By Appointment to
Her Majesty The Queen
Philatelists
Stanley Gibbons Ltd,
London

1st edition – 2019

Published by Stanley Gibbons Ltd
Editorial, Publications Sales Offices
7 Parkside, Christchurch Road, Ringwood,
Hants BH24 3SH

© Stanley Gibbons Ltd 2019

Copyright Notice

The contents of this Catalogue, including the numbering system and illustrations, are fully protected by copyright. No part of this publication may be reproduced, stored in a retrieval system, or transmitted in any form or by any means, electronic, mechanical, photocopying, recording or otherwise, without the prior permission of Stanley Gibbons Limited. Requests for such permission should be addressed to the Catalogue Editor. This Catalogue is sold on condition that it is not, by way of trade or otherwise, lent, re-sold, hired out, circulated or otherwise disposed of other than in its complete, original and unaltered form and without a similar condition including this condition being imposed on the subsequent purchaser.

British Library Cataloguing in Publication Data.
A catalogue record for this book is available from the British Library.

Errors and omissions excepted. The colour reproduction of stamps is only as accurate as the printing process will allow.

ISBN-13: 978-1-911304-41-8

Item No. R 1434-19

Printed by
Latimer Trend, Plymouth

Stanley Gibbons Foreign Catalogue

ABOUT THIS EDITION

It is over 35 years since the present split into 'Parts 2 to 22' was announced, dividing up what had up to then been an alphabetical listing of European and Overseas countries over seven large volumes into handy-sized catalogues, bringing together countries or groups of countries, generally united by geography or political affiliations.

Back in 1979 the new 'Parts' catalogues proved to be very popular with collectors, but over time these volumes have grown in size, with the ever increasing numbers of new issues.

In 2015 Stanley Gibbons celebrated 150 years of catalogue production and it seemed the right time to take a look at the structure and break down of our Foreign catalogue range.

- Prices have been thoroughly revised and brought up to date, by leading experts in the field.
- Specimen stamps have been included for the first time

New issue listings have been updated:
- Albania – December 2018
- Bulgaria – December 2018
- Greece – December 2018
- Macedonia – December 2018

The first supplement to this catalogue appeared in *Gibbons Stamp Monthly* for September 2019.

We would like to thank James Bendon for his advice with the Specimen (UPU) lisings.

Addresses for specialist societies for this area are on page iv.

Clare de la Feuillade, Editor
Hugh Jefferies, Consultant
Sue Price, New Issues Listings
Barbara Hawkins, Pricing Assistant
Leslie Fuller, Proof Reader
Emma Fletcher, Designer and page layout

NUMBERS ADDED

ALBANIA
1611a
2779a
3018a/3021a
3065/**MS**3067
MS3070
3129/3140
3142/3149
MS3212
MS3215
3276a
3277
SB10

BULGARIA
51s/60s
2617a
4680a
MS4966a

EASTERN ROUMELIA AND SOUTH BULGARIA
6s/10s

GREECE
45ds, 46s, 55as, 56s, 59s, 61s
D74s/D76s, D78s, D80s/D84s, D85s, D89s, D91s, D94s, D95s
78s, 80s, 81,
175Aa, 175Ab, 175Aba
222a
225a
C343a
340s/402s
594a
C642a
C661, C661a, C661b
1658a
2207a
MS2238a
MS2251a
2692a
MS2278a
MS2278b
2873a
SB35a

BALKAN WAR ISSUES
SAMOS
12a

CRETE
R1a/R4a

MACEDONIA
51a
180a
183a
762a
765a
766a

NUMBERS ALTERED

ALBANIA

OLD	NEW
45a/l	45b/m
SB10/SB12	SB11/SB13

BULGARIA

OLD	NEW
4254/4262	4253/4257
4252a/4262a	4258/4263
4286a/4290a	4286B/4290B
4413a/4416a	4413B/4416B
4475a/4478a	4475B/4478B

GREECE

OLD	NEW
C643	C642

SOUTHERN BALKANS SOCIETIES

Albania Study Circle
Andorran Philatelic Study Circle
Secretary: N. Ames
Email: ames@dircon.co.uk

Contents

Stanley Gibbons Holdings Plc vi
General Philatelic Information and
    Guidelines to the Scope of Stanley
    Gibbons Foreign Catalogues vii
Abbreviations xiv
International Philatelic Glossary xv
List of Catalogues xix
Guide to Entries xx
Stamp Illustrations xxii

ALBANIA   1
   Stamp Booklets 94
   Greek Occupation 94
   Saseno-Italian Occupation 94

BULGARIA   95
   Stamp Booklets 273

EASTERN ROUMELIA and SOUTH BULGARIA   273
   A. Eastern Roumelia 273
   B. South Bulgaria 273
   Bulgarian Occupation 274

EPIRUS   275
   A. Provisional Government 275
   B. Northern Epirus 276

GREECE   277
   Machine Labels 361
   Stamp Booklets 362
   Balkan War Issues 363
   Ikaria 363
   Kavalla 363
   Khios 364
   Lesvos 364
   Limnos 364
   Samos 365
   British Field Office in Salonica 366
   Italian Occupation of Corfu 366
   **Italian Occupation of Corfu
    and Paxos** 366
   Italian Occupation of Cephalonia and
    Ithaca 366
   Italian Occupation of the Ionian
    Islands 367
   German Occupation of Zante 367

CASTERLROSSO   368
   A. French Occupation 368
   B. Italian Occupation 368

CRETE   369
   I. British Administration 369
   II. Russian Administration 369
   III. Provisional Government of Crete 370
   IV. Revolutionary Assembly 372
   Austro-Hungarian Post Offices 373
   French Post Offices 373
   Italian Post Offices 373

DODECANESE ISLANDS   374
   A. Italian Occupation 374
   B. Island Committee for Union with
    Greece 378
   C. Greek Military Administration 378

THRACE   379
   A. Greek Occupation, 1913 379
   B. Autonomous Government of
    Western Thrace 379
   C. Allied Occupation, 1919–1920 380
   D. Greek Occupation, 1920 380

MACEDONIA   381
   A. German Occupation, 1944 381
   B. Independent Republic 381

Stanley Gibbons Holdings Plc

Stanley Gibbons Limited,
Stanley Gibbons Auctions
399 Strand, London WC2R 0LX
Tel: +44 (0)207 836 8444
Fax: +44 (0)207 836 7342
E-mail: help@stanleygibbons.com
Website: www.stanleygibbons.com
for all departments, Auction and Specialist Stamp Departments.
Open Monday–Friday 9.30 am to 5 pm Shop. Open Monday–Friday 9 am to 5.30 pm and Saturday 9.30 am to 5.30 pm

Stanley Gibbons Publications,
Gibbons Stamp Monthly and
Philatelic Exporter
7 Parkside, Christchurch Road, Ringwood, Hampshire BH24 3SH.
Tel: +44 (0)1425 472263
Fax: +44 (0)1425 470247
E-mail: help@stanleygibbons.com
Publications Mail Order.
FREEPHONE 0800 611622
Monday–Friday 8.30 am to 5 pm

Stanley Gibbons Publications Overseas Representation
Stanley Gibbons Publications are represented overseas by the following

Australia
Renniks Publications PTY LTD
Unit 3 37-39 Green Street,
Banksmeadow, NSW 2019, Australia
Tel: +612 9695 7055
Website: www.renniks.com

Canada
Unitrade Associates
99 Floral Parkway, Toronto,
Ontario M6L 2C4, Canada
Tel: +1 416 242 5900
Website: www.unitradeassoc.com

Germany
Schaubek Verlag Leipzig
Am Glaeschen 23, D-04420
Markranstaedt, Germany
Tel: +49 34 205 67823
Website: www.schaubek.de

Italy
Ernesto Marini S.R.L.
V. Struppa, 300, Genova, 16165, Italy
Tel: +3901 0247-3530
Website: www.ernestomarini.it

Japan
Japan Philatelic
PO Box 2, Suginami-Minami,
Tokyo 168-8081, Japan
Tel: +81 3330 41641
Website: www.yushu.co.jp

Netherlands (also covers Belgium
Denmark, Finland & France)
Uitgeverij Davo BV
PO Box 411, Ak Deventer, 7400
Netherlands
Tel: +315 7050 2700
Website: www.davo.nl

New Zealand
House of Stamps
PO Box 12, Paraparaumu,
New Zealand
Tel: +61 6364 8270
Website: www.houseofstamps.co.nz

Philatelic Distributors
PO Box 863
15 Mount Edgecumbe Street
New Plymouth 4615, New Zealand
Tel: +6 46 758 65 68
Website: www.stampcollecta.com

Norway
SKANFIL A/S
SPANAV. 52 / BOKS 2030
N-5504 HAUGESUND, Norway
Tel: +47-52703940
E-mail: magne@skanfil.no

Singapore
C S Philatelic Agency
Peninsula Shopping Centre #04-29
3 Coleman Street, 179804, Singapore
Tel: +65 6337-1859
Website: www.cs.com.sg

South Africa
Peter Bale Philatelics
PO Box 3719
Honeydew 2040
Gauteng
South Africa
Tel: +27 11 462 2463
E-mail: balep@iafrica.com

Sweden
Chr Winther Sorensen AB
Box 43, S-310 20 Knaered, Sweden
Tel: +46 43050743
Website: www.collectia.se

General Philatelic Information and Guidelines to the Scope of Stanley Gibbons Foreign Catalogues

These notes reflect current practice in compiling the Foreign Catalogue.

The *Stanley Gibbons Stamp Catalogue* has a very long history and the vast quantity of information it contains has been carefully built up by successive generations through the work of countless individuals. Philately itself is never static and the Catalogue has evolved and developed during this long time-span. These notes apply to current policy – some of the older listings were prepared using slightly different criteria – and we hope you find them useful in using the catalogue.

THE CATALOGUE IN GENERAL

Contents. The Catalogue is confined to adhesive postage stamps, including miniature sheets. For particular categories the rules are:
(a) Revenue (fiscal) stamps or telegraph stamps are listed only where they have been expressly authorised for postal duty.
(b) Stamps issued only precancelled are included, but normally issued stamps available additionally with precancel have no separate precancel listing unless the face value is changed.
(c) Stamps prepared for use but not issued, hitherto accorded full listing, are nowadays footnoted with a price (where possible).
(d) Bisects (trisects, etc.) are only listed where such usage was officially authorised.
(e) Stamps issued only on first day covers and not available separately are not listed but priced (on the cover) in a footnote.
(f) New printings, as such, are not listed, though stamps from them may qualify under another category, e.g. when a prominent new shade results.
(g) Official and unofficial reprints are dealt with by footnote.
(h) Stamps from imperforate printings of modern issues which also occur perforated are covered by footnotes or general notes, but are listed where widely available for postal use.

Exclusions. The following are excluded:
(a) non-postal revenue or fiscal stamps;
(b) postage stamps used fiscally;
(c) local carriage labels and private local issues;
(d) telegraph stamps;
(e) bogus or phantom stamps;
(f) railway or airline letter fee stamps, bus or road transport company labels;
(g) cut-outs;
(h) all types of non-postal labels;
(i) documentary labels for the postal service, e.g. registration, recorded delivery, airmail etiquettes, etc.;
(j) privately applied embellishments to official issues and privately commissioned items generally;
(k) stamps for training postal officers;
(l) specimen stamps. (except those distributed by the UPU)

Full listing. 'Full listing' confers our recognition and implies allotting a catalogue number and (wherever possible) a price quotation.

In judging status for inclusion in the catalogue broad considerations are applied to stamps. They must be issued by a legitimate postal authority, recognised by the government concerned, and must be adhesives valid for proper postal use in the class of service for which they are inscribed. Stamps, with the exception of such categories as postage dues and officials, must be available to the general public, at face value, in reasonable quantities without any artificial restrictions being imposed on their distribution.

We record as abbreviated Appendix entries, without catalogue numbers or prices, stamps from countries which either persist in having far more issues than can be justified by postal need or have failed to maintain control over their distribution so that they have not been available to the public in reasonable quantities at face value. Miniature sheets and imperforate stamps are not mentioned in these entries.

The publishers of this catalogue have observed, with concern, the proliferation of 'artificial' stamp-issuing territories. On several occasions this has resulted in separately inscribed issues for various component parts of otherwise united states or territories. Stanley Gibbons Publications have decided that where such circumstances occur, they will not, in the future, list these items in the SG catalogue without first satisfying themselves that the stamps represent a genuine political, historical or postal division within the country concerned. Any such issues which do not fulfil this stipulation will be recorded in the Catalogue Appendix only.

For errors and varieties the criterion is legitimate (albeit inadvertent) sale over a post office counter in the normal course of business. Details of provenance are always important; printers' waste and fraudulently manufactured material is excluded.

Certificates. In assessing unlisted items due weight is given to Certificates from recognised Expert Committees and, where appropriate, we will usually ask to see them.

New issues. New issues are listed regularly in the Catalogue Supplement in *Gibbons Stamp Monthly*, then consolidated into the next available edition of the Catalogue.

Date of issue. Where local issue dates differ from dates of release by agencies, 'date of issue' is the local date. Fortuitous stray usage before the officially intended date is disregarded in listing.

Catalogue numbers. Stamps of each country are catalogued chronologically by date of issue. Subsidiary classes (e.g. postage due stamps) are integrated into one list with postage and commemorative stamps and distinguished by a letter prefix to the catalogue number.

The catalogue number appears in the extreme left column. The boldface type numbers in the next column

Information and Guidelines

are merely cross-references to illustrations. Catalogue numbers in the *Gibbons Stamp Monthly* Supplement are provisional only and may need to be altered when the lists are consolidated. Miniature sheets only purchasable intact at a post office have a single MS number; sheetlets – individual stamps available – number each stamp separately. The catalogue no longer gives full listing to designs originally issued in normal sheets, which subsequently appear in sheetlets showing changes of colour, perforation, printing process or face value. Such stamps will be covered by footnotes.

Once published in the Catalogue, numbers are changed as little as possible; really serious renumbering is reserved for the occasions when a complete country or an entire issue is being rewritten. The edition first affected includes cross-reference tables of old and new numbers.

Our catalogue numbers are universally recognised in specifying stamps and as a hallmark of status.

Illustrations. Stamps are illustrated at three-quarters linear size. Stamps not illustrated are the same size and format as the value shown unless otherwise indicated. Stamps issued only as miniature sheets have the stamp alone illustrated but sheet size is also quoted. Overprints, surcharges, watermarks and postmarks are normally actual size. Illustrations of varieties are often enlarged to show the detail.

CONTACTING THE CATALOGUE EDITOR

The editor is always interested in hearing from people who have new information which will improve or correct the Catalogue. As a general rule he must see and examine the actual stamps before they can be considered for listing; photographs or photocopies are insufficient evidence. Neither he nor his staff give opinions as to the genuineness of stamps.

Submissions should be made in writing to the Catalogue Editor, Stanley Gibbons Publications, 7 Parkside, Christchurch Road, Ringwood, Hants BH24 3SH. The cost of return postage for items submitted is appreciated, and this should include the registration fee if required.

Where information is solicited purely for the benefit of the enquirer, the editor cannot undertake to reply if the answer is already contained in these published notes or if return postage is omitted. Written communications are greatly preferred to enquiries by telephone or e-mail and the editor regrets that he or his staff cannot see personal callers without a prior appointment being made.

The editor welcomes close contact with study circles and is interested, too, in finding local correspondents who will verify and supplement official information in overseas countries where this is deficient.

We regret we do not give opinions as to the genuineness of stamps, nor do we identify stamps or number them by our Catalogue.

TECHNICAL MATTERS

The meanings of the technical terms used in the Catalogue will be found in *Philatelic Terms Illustrated*, published by Stanley Gibbons (Price £14.95 plus postage).

1. Printing

Printing errors. Errors in printing are of major interest to the Catalogue. Authenticated items meriting consideration would include background, centre or frame inverted or omitted; centre or subject transposed; error of colour; error or omission of value; double prints and impressions; printed both sides; and so on. Designs *tête-bêche*, whether intentionally or by accident, are listable. *Se-tenant* arrangements of stamps are recognised in the listings or footnotes. Gutter pairs (a pair of stamps separated by blank margin) are excluded unless they have some philatelic importance. Colours only partially omitted are not listed, neither are stamps printed on the gummed side.

Printing varieties. Listing is accorded to major changes in the printing base which lead to completely new types. In recess-printing this could be a design re-engraved, in photogravure or photolithography a screen altered in whole or in part. It can also encompass flat-bed and rotary printing if the results are readily distinguishable.

To be considered at all, varieties must be constant. Early stamps, produced by primitive methods, were prone to numerous imperfections; the lists reflect this, recognising re-entries, retouches, broken frames, misshapen letters, and so on. Printing technology has, however, radically improved over the years, during which time photogravure and lithography have become predominant. Varieties nowadays are more in the nature of flaws and these, being too specialised for a general catalogue, are almost always outside the scope. We therefore do not list such items as dry prints, kiss prints, doctor-blade flaws, blanket set-offs, doubling through blanket stretch, plate cracks and scratches, registration flaws (leading to colour shifts), lithographic ring flaws, and so on. Neither do we recognise fortuitous happenings like paper creases or confetti flaws.

Overprints (and surcharges). Overprints of different types qualify for separate listing. These include overprints in different colours; overprints from different printing processes such as litho and typo; overprints in totally different typefaces, etc.

Overprint errors and varieties. Major errors in machine-printed overprints are important and listable. They include overprint inverted or omitted; overprint double (treble, etc.); overprint diagonal; overprint double, one inverted; pairs with one overprint omitted, e.g. from a radical shift to an adjoining stamp; error of colour; error of type fount; letters inverted or omitted, etc. If the overprint is handstamped, few of these would qualify and a distinction is drawn.

Varieties occurring in overprints will often take the form of broken letters, slight differences in spacing, rising spacers, etc. Only the most important would be considered for footnote mention.

Sheet positions. If space permits we quote sheet positions of listed varieties and authenticated data is solicited for this purpose.

2. Paper

All stamps listed are deemed to be on 'ordinary' paper of the wove type and white in colour; only departures from this are mentioned.

Types. Where classification so requires we distinguish such other types of paper as, for example, vertically and horizontally laid; wove and laid bâtonné; card(board); carton; cartridge, enamelled; glazed; GC (Grande Consommation); granite; native; pelure; porous; quadrillé; ribbed; rice; and silk thread.

The 'traditional' method of indentifying chalk-surfaced papers has been that, when touched with a silver wire, a black mark is left on the paper, and the listings in this catalogue are based on that test. However, the test itself is now largely discredited, for, although the mark can be removed by a soft rubber, some damage to the stamp will result from its use.

The difference between chalk-surfaced and pre-war ordinary papers is fairly clear: chalk-surfaced papers being smoother to the touch and showing a characteristic sheen when light is reflected off their surface. Under good magnification tiny bubbles or pock marks can be seen on the surface of the stamp and at the tips of the perforations the surfacing appears 'broken'. Traces of paper fibres are evident on the surface of ordinary paper and the ink shows a degree of absorption into it.

The various makeshifts for normal paper are listed as appropriate. They include printing on: unfinished banknotes, war maps, ruled paper, Post Office forms, and the unprinted side of glossy magazines. The varieties of double paper and joined paper are recognised.

Descriptive terms. The fact that a paper is hand-made (and thus probably of uneven thickness) is mentioned where necessary. Such descriptive terms as 'hard' and 'soft'; 'smooth' and 'rough'; 'thick', 'medium' and 'thin' are applied where there is philatelic merit in classifying papers.

Coloured, very white and toned papers. A coloured paper is one that is coloured right through (front and back of the stamp). In the Catalogue the colour of the paper is given in italics, thus

black/*rose* = black design on rose paper.

Papers have been made specially white in recent years by, for example, a very heavy coating of chalk. We do not classify shades of whiteness of paper as distinct varieties. There does exist, however, a type of paper from early days called toned. This is off-white, often brownish or buffish, but it cannot be assigned a definite colour. A toning effect brought on by climate, incorrect storage or gum staining is disregarded here, as this was not the state of the paper when issued.

Safety devices. The Catalogue takes account of such safety devices as varnish lines, grills, burelage or imprinted patterns on the front or moiré on the back of stamps.

Modern developments. Two modern developments also affect the listings, printing on self-adhesive paper and the tendency, philatelic in origin, for conventional paper to be reinforced or replaced by different materials. Some examples are the use of foils in gold, silver, aluminium, palladium and steel; application of an imitation wood veneer; printing on plastic moulded in relief; and use of a plastic laminate to give a three-dimensional effect. Examples also occur of stamps impregnated with scent; printed on silk; and incorporating miniature gramophone records.

3. Perforation and Rouletting

Perforation gauge. The gauge of a perforation is the number of holes in a length of 2 cm. For correct classification the size of the holes (large or small) may need to be distinguished; in a few cases the actual number of holes on each edge of the stamp needs to be quoted.

Measurement. The Gibbons Instanta gauge is the standard for measuring perforations. The stamp is viewed against a dark background with the transparent gauge put on top of it. Though the gauge measures to decimal accuracy, perforations read from it are generally quoted in the Catalogue to the nearest half. For example:

Just over perf.
12¾ to just under perf. 13¼ = perf. 13
Perf. 13¼ exactly, rounded up = perf. 13½
Just over perf.
13¼ to just under perf. 13¾ = perf. 13½
Perf. 13¾ exactly, rounded up = perf. 14

However, where classification depends on it, actual quarter-perforations are quoted.

Notation. Where no perforation is quoted for an issue it is imperforate. Perforations are usually abbreviated (and spoken) as follows, though sometimes they may be spelled out for clarity. This notation for rectangular stamps (the majority) applies to diamond shapes if 'top' is read as the edge to the top right.

P 14: perforated alike on all sides (read: 'perf. 14').

P 14×15: the first figure refers to top and bottom, the second to left and right sides (read: 'perf. 14 by 15'). This is a compound perforation. For an upright triangular stamp the first figure refers to the two sloping sides and the second to the base. In inverted triangulars the base is first and the second figure refers to the sloping sides.

P 14-15: perforation measuring anything between 14 and 15: the holes are irregularly spaced, thus the gauge may vary along a single line or even along a single edge of the stamp (read: 'perf. 14 to 15').

P 14 irregular. perforated 14 from a worn perforator, giving badly aligned holes irregular spaced (read 'irregular perf. 14').

Information and Guidelines

P *comp(ound)* 14×15: two gauges in use but not necessarily on opposite sides of the stamp. It could be one side in one gauge and three in the other, or two adjacent sides with the same gauge (Read: 'perf. compound of 14 and 15'). For three gauges or more, abbreviated as 'P 14, 14½, 15 or compound' for example.

P 14, 14½: perforated approximately 14¼ (read: 'perf. 14 or 14½'). It does not mean two stamps, one perf. 14 and the other perf. 14½. This obsolescent notation is gradually being replaced in the Catalogue.

Imperf: imperforate (not perforated).

Imperf×P 14: imperforate at top and bottom and perf 14 at sides.

P 14×*imperf* = perf 14 at top and bottom and imperforate at sides.

Such headings as 'P 13×14 (vert) and P 14×13 (horiz)' indicate which perforations apply to which stamp format – vertical or horizontal.

Some stamps are additionally perforated so that a label or tab is detachable; others have been perforated suitably for use as two halves. Listings are normally for whole stamps, unless stated otherwise.

Other terms. Perforation almost always gives circular holes; where other shapes have been used they are specified, e.g. square holes; lozenge perf. Interrupted perfs are brought about by the omission of pins at regular intervals. Perforations have occasionally been simulated by being printed as part of the design. With few exceptions, privately applied perforations are not listed.

Perforation errors and varieties. Authenticated errors, where a stamp normally perforated is accidentally issued imperforate, are listed provided no traces of perforation (blind holes or indentations) remain. They must be provided as pairs, both stamps wholly imperforate, and are only priced in that form.

Stamps merely imperforate between stamp and margin (fantails) are not listed.

Imperforate-between varieties are recognised, where one row of perfs has been missed. They are listed and priced in pairs:

Imperf between (horiz pair): a horizontal pair of stamps with perfs all around the edges but none between the stamps.

Imperf between (vert pair): a vertical pair of stamps with perfs all around the edges but none between the stamps.

Where several of the rows have escaped perforation the resulting varieties are listable. Thus:

Imperf vert (horiz pair): a horizontal pair of stamps perforated top and bottom; all three vertical directions are imperf – the two outer edges and between the stamps.

Imperf horiz (vert pair): a vertical pair perforated at left and right edges; all three horizontal directions are imperf – the top, bottom and between the stamps.

Straight edges. Large sheets cut up before issue to post offices can cause stamps with straight edges, i.e. imperf on one side or on two sides at right angles. They are not usually listable in this condition and are worth less than corresponding stamps properly perforated all round. This does not, however, apply to certain stamps, mainly from coils and booklets, where straight edges on various sides are the manufacturing norm affecting every stamp. The listings and notes make clear which sides are correctly imperf.

Malfunction. Varieties of double, misplaced or partial perforation caused by error or machine malfunction are not listable, neither are freaks, such as perforations placed diagonally from paper folds. Likewise disregarded are missing holes caused by broken pins, and perforations 'fading out' down a sheet, the machinery progressively disengaging to leave blind perfs and indentations to the paper.

Centering. Well-centred stamps have designs surrounded by equal opposite margins. Where this condition affects the price the fact is stated.

Type of perforating. Where necessary for classification, perforation types are distinguished. These include:

Line perforation from one line of pins punching single rows of holes at a time.

Comb perforation from pins disposed across the sheet in comb formation, punching out holes at three sides of the stamp a row at a time.

Harrow perforation applied to a whole pane or sheet at one stroke.

Rotary perforation from the toothed wheels operating across a sheet, then crosswise.

Sewing-machine perforation. The resultant condition, clean-cut or rough, is distinguished where required.

Pin-perforation is the commonly applied term for pin-roulette in which, instead of being punched out, round holes are pricked by sharp-pointed pins and no paper is removed.

Punctured stamps. Perforation holes can be punched into the face of the stamp. Patterns of small holes, often in the shape of initial letters, are privately applied devices against pilferage. These 'perfins' are outside the scope. Identification devices, when officially inspired, are listed or noted; they can be shapes, or letters or words formed from holes, sometimes converting one class of stamp into another.

Rouletting. In rouletting the paper is cut, for ease of separation, but none is removed. The gauge is measured, when needed, as for perforations. Traditional French terms descriptive of the type of cut are often used and types include:

Arc roulette (percé en arc). Cuts are minute, spaced arcs, each roughly a semicircle.

Cross roulette (percé en croix). Cuts are tiny diagonal crosses.

Line roulette (parcé en ligne or en ligne droite). Short straight cuts parallel to the frame of the stamp. The commonest basic roulette. Where not further described, 'roulette' means this type.

Rouletted in colour or coloured roulette (percé en lignes colorees or en lignes de coleur). Cuts with coloured edges, arising from notched rule inked simultaneously with the printing plate.

Saw-tooth roulette (percé en scie). Cuts applied zigzag fashion to resemble the teeth of a saw.

Serpentine roulette (percé en serpentin). Cuts as sharply wavy lines.

Zigzag roulettes (percé en zigzags). Short straight cuts at angles in alternate directions, producing sharp points on separation. US usage favours 'serrate(d) roulette' for this type.

Pin-roulette (originally *percé en points* and now *perforés trous d'epingle)* is commonly called pin-perforation in English.

4. Gum

All stamps listed are assumed to have gum of some kind; if they were issued without gum this is stated. Original gum (o.g.) means that which was present on the stamp as issued to the public. Deleterious climates and the presence of certain chemicals can cause gum to crack and, with early stamps, even make the paper deteriorate. Unscrupulous fakers are adept in removing it and regumming the stamp to meet the unreasoning demand often made for 'full o.g.' in cases where such a thing is virtually impossible.

Until recent times the gum used for stamps has been gum arabic, but various synthetic adhesives – tinted or invisible-looking – have been in use since the 1960s. Stamps existing with more than one type of gum are not normally listed separately, though the fact is noted where it is of philatelic significance, e.g. in distinguishing reprints or new printings.

The distinct variety of grilled gum is, however, recognised. In this the paper is passed through a gum breaker prior to printing to prevent subsequent curling. As the patterned rollers were sufficient to impress a grill into the paper beneath the gum we can quote prices for both unused and used examples.

Self-adhesive stamps are issued on backing paper from which they are peeled before affixing to mail. Unused examples are priced as for backing paper intact. Used examples are best kept on cover or on piece.

5. Watermarks

Stamps are on unwatermarked paper except where the heading to the set says otherwise.

Detection. Watermarks are detected for Catalogue description by one of four methods:
(1) holding stamps to the light;
(2) laying stamps face down on a dark background;
(3) adding a few drops of petroleum ether 40/60 to the stamp laid face down in a watermark tray; or
(4) by use of the Stanley Gibbons Detectamark, or other equipment, which works by revealing the thinning of the paper at the watermark. (Note that petroleum ether is highly inflammable in use and can damage photogravure stamps.)

Listable types. Stamps occurring on both watermarked and unwatermarked papers are different types and both receive full listing.

Single watermarks (devices occurring once on every stamp) can be modified in size and shape as between different issues; the types are noted but not usually separately listed. Fortuitous absence of watermark from a single stamp or its gross displacement would not be listable.

To overcome registration difficulties the device may be repeated at close intervals (a **multiple watermark**), single stamps thus showing parts of several devices. Similarly a large **sheet watermark** (or all-over watermark) covering numerous stamps can be used. We give informative notes and illustrations for them. The designs may be such that numbers of stamps in the sheet automatically lack watermark; this is not a listable variety. Multiple and all-over watermarks sometimes undergo modifications, but if the various types are difficult to distinguish from single stamps notes are given but not separate listings.

Papermakers' watermarks are noted where known but not listed separately, since most stamps in the sheet will lack them. Sheet watermarks which are nothing more than officially adopted papermakers' watermarks are, however, given normal listing.

Marginal watermarks, falling outside the pane of stamps, are ignored except where misplacement causes the adjoining row to be affected, in which case they may be footnoted.

Watermark errors and varieties. Watermark errors are recognised as of major importance. They comprise stamps intended to be on unwatermarked paper but issued watermarked by mistake, or stamps printed on paper with the wrong watermark. Watermark varieties, on the other hand, such as broken or deformed bits on the dandy roll, are not listable.

Watermark positions. Paper has a side intended for printing and watermarks are usually impressed so that they read normally when looked through from that printed side.

Illustrations in the Catalogue are of watermarks in normal positions (from the front of the stamps) and are actual size where possible.

Differences in watermark position are collectable as distinct varieties. In this Catalogue, however, only normal sideways watermarks are listed (and 'sideways inverted' is treated as 'sideways'). Inverted and reversed watermarks have always been outside its scope: in the early days of flat-bed printing, sheets of watermarked paper were fed indiscriminately through the press and the resulting watermark positions had no particular philatelic significance. Similarly, the special make-up of sheets for booklets can in some cases give equal quantities of normal and inverted watermarks.

6. Colours

Stamps in two or three colours have these named in order of appearance, from the centre moving outwards.

Four colours or more are usually listed as multicoloured.

In compound colour names the second is the predominant one, thus:
orange-red = a red tending towards orange;
red-orange = an orange containing more red than usual.

Standard colours used. The 200 colours most used for stamp identification are given in the Stanley Gibbons Colour Key. The Catalogue has used the Key as a standard for describing new issues for some years. The names are also introduced as lists are rewritten, though exceptions are made for those early issues where traditional names have become universally established.

Determining colours. When comparing actual stamps with colour samples in the Key, view in a good north daylight (or its best substitute: fluorescent 'colour-matching' light). Sunshine is not recommended. Choose a solid portion of the stamp design; if available, marginal markings such as solid bars of colour or colour check dots are helpful. Shading lines in the design can be misleading as they appear lighter than solid colour. Postmarked portions of a stamp appear darker than normal. If more than one colour is present, mask off the extraneous ones as the eye tends to mix them.

Errors of colour. Major colour errors in stamps or overprints which qualify for listing are: wrong colours; one colour inverted in relation to the rest; albinos (colourless impressions), where these have Expert Committee certificates; colours completely omitted, but only on unused stamps (if found on used stamps the information is footnoted).

Colours only partially omitted are not recognised.

Colour shifts, however spectacular, are not listed.

Shades. Shades in philately refer to variations in the intensity of a colour or the presence of differing amounts of other colours. They are particularly significant when they can be linked to specific printings. In general, shades need to be quite marked to fall within the scope of this Catalogue; it does not favour nowadays listing the often numerous shades of a stamp, but chooses a single applicable colour name which will indicate particular groups of outstanding shades. Furthermore, the listings refer to colours as issued: they may deteriorate into something different through the passage of time.

Modern colour printing by lithography is prone to marked differences of shade, even within a single run, and variations can occur within the same sheet. Such shades are not listed.

Aniline colours. An aniline colour meant originally one derived from coal-tar; it now refers more widely to colour of a particular brightness suffused on the surface of a stamp and showing through clearly on the back.

Colours of overprints and surcharges. All overprints and surcharges are in black unless otherwise in the heading or after the description of the stamp.

7. Luminescence

Machines which sort mail electronically have been introduced in recent years. In consequence some countries have issued stamps on fluorescent or phosphorescent papers, while others have marked their stamps with phosphor bands.

The various papers can only be distinguished by ultraviolet lamps emitting particular wavelengths. They are separately listed only when the stamps have some other means of distinguishing them, visible without the use of these lamps. Where this is not so, the papers are recorded in footnotes or headings. (Collectors using the lamps should exercise great care in their use as exposure to their light is extremely dangerous to the eyes).

Phosphor bands are listable, since they are visible to the naked eye (by holding stamps at an angle to the light and looking along them, the bands appear dark). Stamps existing with and without phosphor bands or with differing numbers of bands are given separate listings. Varieties such as double bands, misplaced or omitted bands, bands printed on the wrong side, are not listed.

8. Coil Stamps

Stamps issued only in coil form are given full listing. If stamps are issued in both sheets and coils the coil stamps are listed separately only where there is some feature (e.g. perforation) by which singles can be distinguished. Coil strips containing different stamps *se-tenant* are also listed.

Coil join pairs are too random and too easily faked to permit of listing; similarly ignored are coil stamps which have accidentally suffered an extra row of perforations from the claw mechanism in a malfunctioning vending machine.

9. Booklet Stamps

Single stamps from booklets are listed if they are distinguishable in some way (such as watermark or perforation) from similar sheet stamps. Booklet panes, provided they are distinguishable from blocks of sheet stamps, are listed for most countries; booklet panes containing more than one value *se-tenant* are listed under the lowest of the values concerned.

Lists of stamp booklets are given for certain countries and it is intended to extend this generally.

10. Forgeries and Fakes

Forgeries. Where space permits, notes are considered if they can give a concise description that will permit unequivocal detection of a forgery. Generalised warnings, lacking detail, are not nowadays inserted since their value to the collector is problematic.

Fakes. Unwitting fakes are numerous, particularly 'new shades' which are colour changelings brought about by exposure to sunlight, soaking in water contaminated with dyes from adherent paper, contact with oil and dirt from a pocketbook, and so on. Fraudulent operators, in addition, can offer to arrange: removal of hinge marks; repairs of thins on white or coloured papers; replacement of missing margins or perforations; reperforating in true or false gauges; removal of fiscal cancellations; rejoining of severed pairs, strips and blocks; and (a major hazard) regumming. Collectors can only be urged to purchase from reputable sources and to insist upon Expert Committee certification where there is any doubt.

The Catalogue can consider footnotes about fakes where these are specific enough to assist in detection.

PRICES

Prices quoted in this Catalogue are the selling prices of Stanley Gibbons Ltd at the time when the book went to press. They are for stamps in fine condition for the issue concerned; in issues where condition varies they may ask more for the superb and less for the sub-standard.

All prices are subject to change without prior notice and Stanley Gibbons Ltd may from time to time offer stamps at other than catalogue prices in consequence of special purchases or particular promotions.

No guarantee is given to supply all stamps priced, since it is not possible to keep every catalogued item in stock. Commemorative issues may, at times, only be available in complete sets and not as individual values.

Quotations of prices. The prices in the left-hand column are for unused stamps and those in the right-hand column are for used.

Prices are expressed in pounds and pence sterling. One pound comprises 100 pence (£1 = 100p).

The method of notation is as follows: pence in numerals (e.g. 10 denotes ten pence); pounds and pence up to £100, in numerals (e.g. 4·25 denotes four pounds and twenty-five pence); prices above £100 expressed in whole pounds with the '£' sign shown.

Unused stamps. Prices for stamps issued up to the end of the Second World War (1945) are for lightly hinged examples and more may be asked if they are in unmounted mint condition. Prices for all later unused stamps are for unmounted mint. Where not available in this condition, lightly hinged stamps are often available at a lower price.

Used stamps. The used prices are normally for stamps postally used but may be for stamps cancelled-to-order where this practice exists.

A pen-cancellation on early issues can sometimes correctly denote postal use. Instances are individually noted in the Catalogue in explanation of the used price given.

Prices quoted for bisects on cover or on large piece are for those dated during the period officially authorised.

Stamps not sold unused to the public but affixed by postal officials before use (e.g. some parcel post stamps) are priced used only.

Minimum price. The minimum catalogue price quoted is 10p. For individual stamps prices between 10p and 95p are provided as a guide for catalogue users. The lowest price charged for individual stamps purchased from Stanley Gibbons Ltd. is £1.

Set prices. Set prices are generally for one of each value, excluding shades and varieties, but including major colour changes. Where there are alternative shades, etc, the cheapest is usually included. The number of stamps in the set is always stated for clarity.

Where prices are given for *se-tenant* blocks or strips any mint price quoted is for the complete *se-tenant* strip or block. Mint and used set prices are always for a set of single stamps.

Repricing. Collectors will be aware that the market factors of supply and demand directly influence the prices quoted in this Catalogue. Whatever the scarcity of a particular stamp, if there is no one in the market who wishes to buy it it cannot be expected to achieve a high price. Conversely, the same item actively sought by numerous potential buyers may cause the price to rise.

All the prices in this Catalogue are examined during the preparation of each new edition by expert staff of Stanley Gibbons and repriced as necessary. They take many factors into account, including supply and demand, and are in close touch with the international stamp market and the auction world.

GUARANTEE

All stamps are guaranteed genuine originals in the following terms:

If not as described, and returned by the purchaser, we undertake to refund the price paid to us in the original transaction. If any stamp is certified as genuine by the Expert Committee of the Royal Philatelic Society, London, or by B.P.A. Expertising Ltd, the purchaser shall not be entitled to make claim against us for any error, omission or mistake in such certificate. Consumers' statutory rights are not affected by this guarantee.

The establishment Expert Committees in this country are those of the Royal Philatelic Society, 41 Devonshire Place, London W19 6JY, and B.P.A. Expertising Ltd, PO Box 1141, Guildford, Surrey GU5 0WR. They do not undertake valuations under any circumstances and fees are payable for their services.

Abbreviations

Printers
A.B.N. Co.	American Bank Note Co, New York.
B.A.B.N.	British American Bank Note Co. Ottawa
B.D.T.	B.D.T. International Security Printing Ltd, Dublin, Ireland
B.W.	Bradbury Wilkinson & Co, Ltd.
Cartor	Cartor S.A., La Loupe, France
C.B.N.	Canadian Bank Note Co, Ottawa.
Continental	Continental Bank Note Co. B.N. Co.
Courvoisier	Imprimerie Courvoisier S.A., La-Chaux-de-Fonds, Switzerland.
D.L.R.	De La Rue & Co, Ltd, London.
Enschedé	Joh. Enschedé en Zonen, Haarlem, Netherlands.
Format	Format International Security Printers Ltd., London
Harrison	Harrison & Sons, Ltd. London
J.W.	John Waddington Security Print Ltd., Leeds
P.B.	Perkins Bacon Ltd, London.
Questa	Questa Colour Security Printers Ltd, London
Walsall	Walsall Security Printers Ltd
Waterlow	Waterlow & Sons, Ltd, London.

General Abbreviations
Alph	Alphabet
Anniv	Anniversary
Comp	Compound (perforation)
Des	Designer; designed
Diag	Diagonal; diagonally
Eng	Engraver; engraved
F.C.	Fiscal Cancellation
H/S	Handstamped
Horiz	Horizontal; horizontally
Imp, Imperf	Imperforate
Inscr	Inscribed
L	Left
Litho	Lithographed
mm	Millimetres
MS	Miniature sheet
N.Y.	New York
Opt(d)	Overprint(ed)
P or P-c	Pen-cancelled
P, Pf or Perf	Perforated
Photo	Photogravure
Pl	Plate
Pr	Pair
Ptd	Printed
Ptg	Printing
R	Right
R.	Row
Recess	Recess-printed
Roto	Rotogravure
Roul	Rouletted
S	Specimen (overprint)
Surch	Surcharge(d)
T.C.	Telegraph Cancellation
T	Type
Typo	Typographed
Un	Unused
Us	Used
Vert	Vertical; vertically
W or wmk	Watermark
Wmk s	Watermark sideways

(†) = Does not exist
(–) (or blank price column) = Exists, or may exist, but no market price is known.
/ between colours means 'on' and the colour following is that of the paper on which the stamp is printed.

Colours of Stamps
Bl (blue); blk (black); brn (brown); car, carm (carmine); choc (chocolate); clar (claret); emer (emerald); grn (green); ind (indigo); mag (magenta); mar (maroon); mult (multicoloured); mve (mauve); ol (olive); orge (orange); pk (pink); pur (purple); scar (scarlet); sep (sepia); turq (turquoise); ultram (ultramarine); verm (vermilion); vio (violet); yell (yellow).

Colour of Overprints and Surcharges
(B.) = blue, (Blk.) = black, (Br.) = brown, (C.) = carmine, (G.) = green, (Mag.) = magenta, (Mve.) = mauve, (Ol.) = olive, (O.) = orange, (P.) = purple, (Pk.) = pink, (R.) = red, (Sil.) = silver, (V.) = violet, (Vm.) or (Verm.) = vermilion, (W.) = white, (Y.) = yellow.

Arabic Numerals
As in the case of European figures, the details of the Arabic numerals vary in different stamp designs, but they should be readily recognised with the aid of this illustration.

International Philatelic Glossary

English	French	German	Spanish	Italian
Agate	Agate	Achat	Agata	Agata
Air stamp	Timbre de la poste aérienne	Flugpostmarke	Sello de correo aéreo	Francobollo per posta aerea
Apple Green	Vert-pomme	Apfelgrün	Verde manzana	Verde mela
Barred	Annulé par barres	Balkenentwertung	Anulado con barras	Sbarrato
Bisected	Timbre coupé	Halbiert	Partido en dos	Frazionato
Bistre	Bistre	Bister	Bistre	Bistro
Bistre-brown	Brun-bistre	Bisterbraun	Castaño bistre	Bruno-bistro
Black	Noir	Schwarz	Negro	Nero
Blackish Brown	Brun-noir	Schwärzlichbraun	Castaño negruzco	Bruno nerastro
Blackish Green	Vert foncé	Schwärzlichgrün	Verde negruzco	Verde nerastro
Blackish Olive	Olive foncé	Schwärzlicholiv	Oliva negruzco	Oliva nerastro
Block of four	Bloc de quatre	Viererblock	Bloque de cuatro	Bloco di quattro
Blue	Bleu	Blau	Azul	Azzurro
Blue-green	Vert-bleu	Blaugrün	Verde azul	Verde azzuro
Bluish Violet	Violet bleuâtre	Bläulichviolett	Violeta azulado	Violtto azzurrastro
Booklet	Carnet	Heft	Cuadernillo	Libretto
Bright Blue	Bleu vif	Lebhaftblau	Azul vivo	Azzurro vivo
Bright Green	Vert vif	Lebhaftgrün	Verde vivo	Verde vivo
Bright Purple	Mauve vif	Lebhaftpurpur	Púrpura vivo	Porpora vivo
Bronze Green	Vert-bronze	Bronzegrün	Verde bronce	Verde bronzo
Brown	Brun	Braun	Castaño	Bruno
Brown-lake	Carmin-brun	Braunlack	Laca castaño	Lacca bruno
Brown-purple	Pourpre-brun	Braunpurpur	Púrpura castaño	Porpora bruno
Brown-red	Rouge-brun	Braunrot	Rojo castaño	Rosso bruno
Buff	Chamois	Sämisch	Anteado	Camoscio
Cancellation	Oblitération	Entwertung	Cancelación	Annullamento
Cancelled	Annulé	Gestempelt	Cancelado	Annullato
Carmine	Carmin	Karmin	Carmín	Carminio
Carmine-red	Rouge-carmin	Karminrot	Rojo carmín	Rosso carminio
Centred	Centré	Zentriert	Centrado	Centrato
Cerise	Rouge-cerise	Kirschrot	Color de ceresa	Color Ciliegia
Chalk-surfaced paper	Papier couché	Kreidepapier	Papel estucado	Carta gessata
Chalky Blue	Bleu terne	Kreideblau	Azul turbio	Azzurro smorto
Charity stamp	Timbre de bienfaisance	Wohltätigkeitsmarke	Sello de beneficenza	Francobollo di beneficenza
Chestnut	Marron	Kastanienbraun	Castaño rojo	Marrone
Chocolate	Chocolat	Schokolade	Chocolate	Cioccolato
Cinnamon	Cannelle	Zimtbraun	Canela	Cannella
Claret	Grenat	Weinrot	Rojo vinoso	Vinaccia
Cobalt	Cobalt	Kobalt	Cobalto	Cobalto
Colour	Couleur	Farbe	Color	Colore
Comb-perforation	Dentelure en peigne	Kammzähnung, Reihenzähnung	Dentado de peine	Dentellatura e pettine
Commemorative stamp	Timbre commémoratif	Gedenkmarke	Sello conmemorativo	Francobollo commemorativo
Crimson	Cramoisi	Karmesin	Carmesí	Cremisi
Deep Blue	Blue foncé	Dunkelblau	Azul oscuro	Azzurro scuro
Deep bluish Green	Vert-bleu foncé	Dunkelbläulichgrün	Verde azulado oscuro	Verde azzurro scuro
Design	Dessin	Markenbild	Diseño	Disegno

International Philatelic Glossary

English	French	German	Spanish	Italian
Die	Matrice	Urstempel. Type, Platte	Cuño	Conio, Matrice
Double	Double	Doppelt	Doble	Doppio
Drab	Olive terne	Trüboliv	Oliva turbio	Oliva smorto
Dull Green	Vert terne	Trübgrün	Verde turbio	Verde smorto
Dull purple	Mauve terne	Trübpurpur	Púrpura turbio	Porpora smorto
Embossing	Impression en relief	Prägedruck	Impresión en relieve	Impressione a relievo
Emerald	Vert-eméraude	Smaragdgrün	Esmeralda	Smeraldo
Engraved	Gravé	Graviert	Grabado	Inciso
Error	Erreur	Fehler, Fehldruck	Error	Errore
Essay	Essai	Probedruck	Ensayo	Saggio
Express letter stamp	Timbre pour lettres par exprès	Eilmarke	Sello de urgencia	Francobollo per espresso
Fiscal stamp	Timbre fiscal	Stempelmarke	Sello fiscal	Francobollo fiscale
Flesh	Chair	Fleischfarben	Carne	Carnicino
Forgery	Faux, Falsification	Fälschung	Falsificación	Falso, Falsificazione
Frame	Cadre	Rahmen	Marco	Cornice
Granite paper	Papier avec fragments de fils de soie	Faserpapier	Papel con filamentos	Carto con fili di seta
Green	Vert	Grün	Verde	Verde
Greenish Blue	Bleu verdâtre	Grünlichblau	Azul verdoso	Azzurro verdastro
Greenish Yellow	Jaune-vert	Grünlichgelb	Amarillo verdoso	Giallo verdastro
Grey	Gris	Grau	Gris	Grigio
Grey-blue	Bleu-gris	Graublau	Azul gris	Azzurro grigio
Grey-green	Vert gris	Graugrün	Verde gris	Verde grigio
Gum	Gomme	Gummi	Goma	Gomma
Gutter	Interpanneau	Zwischensteg	Espacio blanco entre dos grupos	Ponte
Imperforate	Non-dentelé	Geschnitten	Sin dentar	Non dentellato
Indigo	Indigo	Indigo	Azul indigo	Indaco
Inscription	Inscription	Inschrift	Inscripción	Dicitura
Inverted	Renversé	Kopfstehend	Invertido	Capovolto
Issue	Émission	Ausgabe	Emisión	Emissione
Laid	Vergé	Gestreift	Listado	Vergato
Lake	Lie de vin	Lackfarbe	Laca	Lacca
Lake-brown	Brun-carmin	Lackbraun	Castaño laca	Bruno lacca
Lavender	Bleu-lavande	Lavendel	Color de alhucema	Lavanda
Lemon	Jaune-citron	Zitrongelb	Limón	Limone
Light Blue	Bleu clair	Hellblau	Azul claro	Azzurro chiaro
Lilac	Lilas	Lila	Lila	Lilla
Line perforation	Dentelure en lignes	Linienzähnung	Dentado en linea	Dentellatura lineare
Lithography	Lithographie	Steindruck	Litografía	Litografia
Local	Timbre de poste locale	Lokalpostmarke	Emisión local	Emissione locale
Lozenge roulette	Percé en losanges	Rautenförmiger Durchstich	Picadura en rombos	Perforazione a losanghe
Magenta	Magenta	Magentarot	Magenta	Magenta
Margin	Marge	Rand	Borde	Margine
Maroon	Marron pourpré	Dunkelrotpurpur	Púrpura rojo oscuro	Marrone rossastro
Mauve	Mauve	Malvenfarbe	Malva	Malva
Multicoloured	Polychrome	Mehrfarbig	Multicolores	Policromo
Myrtle Green	Vert myrte	Myrtengrün	Verde mirto	Verde mirto
New Blue	Bleu ciel vif	Neublau	Azul nuevo	Azzurro nuovo
Newspaper stamp	Timbre pour journaux	Zeitungsmarke	Sello para periódicos	Francobollo per giornali
Obliteration	Oblitération	Abstempelung	Matasello	Annullamento
Obsolete	Hors (de) cours	Ausser Kurs	Fuera de curso	Fuori corso

International Philatelic Glossary

English	French	German	Spanish	Italian
Ochre	Ocre	Ocker	Ocre	Ocra
Official stamp	Timbre de service	Dienstmarke	Sello de servicio	Francobollo di
Olive-brown	Brun-olive	Olivbraun	Castaño oliva	Bruno oliva
Olive-green	Vert-olive	Olivgrün	Verde oliva	Verde oliva
Olive-grey	Gris-olive	Olivgrau	Gris oliva	Grigio oliva
Olive-yellow	Jaune-olive	Olivgelb	Amarillo oliva	Giallo oliva
Orange	Orange	Orange	Naranja	Arancio
Orange-brown	Brun-orange	Orangebraun	Castaño naranja	Bruno arancio
Orange-red	Rouge-orange	Orangerot	Rojo naranja	Rosso arancio
Orange-yellow	Jaune-orange	Orangegelb	Amarillo naranja	Giallo arancio
Overprint	Surcharge	Aufdruck	Sobrecarga	Soprastampa
Pair	Paire	Paar	Pareja	Coppia
Pale	Pâle	Blass	Pálido	Pallido
Pane	Panneau	Gruppe	Grupo	Gruppo
Paper	Papier	Papier	Papel	Carta
Parcel post stamp	Timbre pour colis postaux	Paketmarke	Sello para paquete postal	Francobollo per pacchi postali
Pen-cancelled	Oblitéré à plume	Federzugentwertung	Cancelado a pluma	Annullato a penna
Percé en arc	Percé en arc	Bogenförmiger Durchstich	Picadura en forma de arco	Perforazione ad arco
Percé en scie	Percé en scie	Bogenförmiger Durchstich	Picado en sierra	Foratura a sega
Perforated	Dentelé	Gezähnt	Dentado	Dentellato
Perforation	Dentelure	Zähnung	Dentar	Dentellatura
Photogravure	Photogravure, Héliogravure	Rastertiefdruck	Fotograbado	Rotocalco
Pin perforation	Percé en points	In Punkten durchstochen	Horadado con alfileres	Perforato a punti
Plate	Planche	Platte	Plancha	Lastra, Tavola
Plum	Prune	Pflaumenfarbe	Color de ciruela	Prugna
Postage Due stamp	Timbre-taxe	Portomarke	Sello de tasa	Segnatasse
Postage stamp	Timbre-poste	Briefmarke, Freimarke, Postmarke	Sello de correos	Francobollo postale
Postal fiscal stamp	Timbre fiscal-postal	Stempelmarke als Postmarke verwendet	Sello fiscal-postal	Fiscale postale
Postmark	Oblitération postale	Poststempel	Matasello	Bollo
Printing	Impression, Tirage	Druck	Impresión	Stampa, Tiratura
Proof	Épreuve	Druckprobe	Prueba de impresión	Prova
Provisionals	Timbres provisoires	Provisorische Marken. Provisorien	Provisionales	Provvisori
Prussian Blue	Bleu de Prusse	Preussischblau	Azul de Prusia	Azzurro di Prussia
Purple	Pourpre	Purpur	Púrpura	Porpora
Purple-brown	Brun-pourpre	Purpurbraun	Castaño púrpura	Bruno porpora
Recess-printing	Impression en taille douce	Tiefdruck	Grabado	Incisione
Red	Rouge	Rot	Rojo	Rosso
Red-brown	Brun-rouge	Rotbraun	Castaño rojizo	Bruno rosso
Reddish Lilac	Lilas rougeâtre	Rötlichlila	Lila rojizo	Lilla rossastro
Reddish Purple	Poupre-rouge	Rötlichpurpur	Púrpura rojizo	Porpora rossastro
Reddish Violet	Violet rougeâtre	Rötlichviolett	Violeta rojizo	Violetto rossastro
Red-orange	Orange rougeâtre	Rotorange	Naranja rojizo	Arancio rosso
Registration stamp	Timbre pour lettre chargée (recommandée)	Einschreibemarke	Sello de certificado lettere	Francobollo per raccomandate
Reprint	Réimpression	Neudruck	Reimpresión	Ristampa
Reversed	Retourné	Umgekehrt	Invertido	Rovesciato
Rose	Rose	Rosa	Rosa	Rosa
Rose-red	Rouge rosé	Rosarot	Rojo rosado	Rosso rosa
Rosine	Rose vif	Lebhaftrosa	Rosa vivo	Rosa vivo
Roulette	Percage	Durchstich	Picadura	Foratura
Rouletted	Percé	Durchstochen	Picado	Forato
Royal Blue	Bleu-roi	Königblau	Azul real	Azzurro reale

International Philatelic Glossary

English	French	German	Spanish	Italian
Sage green	Vert-sauge	Salbeigrün	Verde salvia	Verde salvia
Salmon	Saumon	Lachs	Salmón	Salmone
Scarlet	Écarlate	Scharlach	Escarlata	Scarlatto
Sepia	Sépia	Sepia	Sepia	Seppia
Serpentine roulette	Percé en serpentin	Schlangenliniger Durchstich	Picado a serpentina	Perforazione a serpentina
Shade	Nuance	Tönung	Tono	Gradazione de colore
Sheet	Feuille	Bogen	Hoja	Foglio
Slate	Ardoise	Schiefer	Pizarra	Ardesia
Slate-blue	Bleu-ardoise	Schieferblau	Azul pizarra	Azzurro ardesia
Slate-green	Vert-ardoise	Schiefergrün	Verde pizarra	Verde ardesia
Slate-lilac	Lilas-gris	Schierferlila	Lila pizarra	Lilla ardesia
Slate-purple	Mauve-gris	Schieferpurpur	Púrpura pizarra	Porpora ardesia
Slate-violet	Violet-gris	Schieferviolett	Violeta pizarra	Violetto ardesia
Special delivery stamp	Timbre pour exprès	Eilmarke	Sello de urgencia	Francobollo per espressi
Specimen	Spécimen	Muster	Muestra	Saggio
Steel Blue	Bleu acier	Stahlblau	Azul acero	Azzurro acciaio
Strip	Bande	Streifen	Tira	Striscia
Surcharge	Surcharge	Aufdruck	Sobrecarga	Soprastampa
Tête-bêche	Tête-bêche	Kehrdruck	Tête-bêche	Tête-bêche
Tinted paper	Papier teinté	Getöntes Papier	Papel coloreado	Carta tinta
Too-late stamp	Timbre pour lettres en retard	Verspätungsmarke	Sello para cartas retardadas	Francobollo per le lettere in ritardo
Turquoise-blue	Bleu turquoise	Türkisblau	Azul turquesa	Azzurro turchese
Turquoise-green	Vert-turquoise	Türkisgrün	Verde turquesa	Verde turchese
Typography	Typographie	Buchdruck	Tipografia	Tipografia
Ultramarine	Outremer	Ultramarin	Ultramar	Oltremare
Unused	Neuf	Ungebraucht	Nuevo	Nuovo
Used	Oblitéré, Usé	Gebraucht	Usado	Usato
Venetian Red	Rouge-brun terne	Venezianischrot	Rojo veneciano	Rosso veneziano
Vermilion	Vermillon	Zinnober	Cinabrio	Vermiglione
Violet	Violet	Violett	Violeta	Violetto
Violet-blue	Bleu-violet	Violettblau	Azul violeta	Azzurro violetto
Watermark	Filigrane	Wasserzeichen	Filigrana	Filigrana
Watermark sideways	Filigrane couché	Wasserzeichen liegend	Filigrana acostado	Filigrana coricata
Wove paper	Papier ordinaire, Papier uni	Einfaches Papier	Papel avitelado	Carta unita
Yellow	Jaune	Gelb	Amarillo	Giallo
Yellow-brown	Brun-jaune	Gelbbraun	Castaño amarillo	Bruno giallo
Yellow-green	Vert-jaune	Gelbgrün	Verde amarillo	Verde giallo
Yellow-olive	Olive-jaunâtre	Gelboliv	Oliva amarillo	Oliva giallastro
Yellow-orange	Orange jaunâtre	Gelborange	Naranja amarillo	Arancio giallastro
Zig-zag roulette	Percé en zigzag	Sägezahnartiger Durchstich	Picado en zigzag	Perforazione a zigzag

Stanley Gibbons Stamp Catalogues

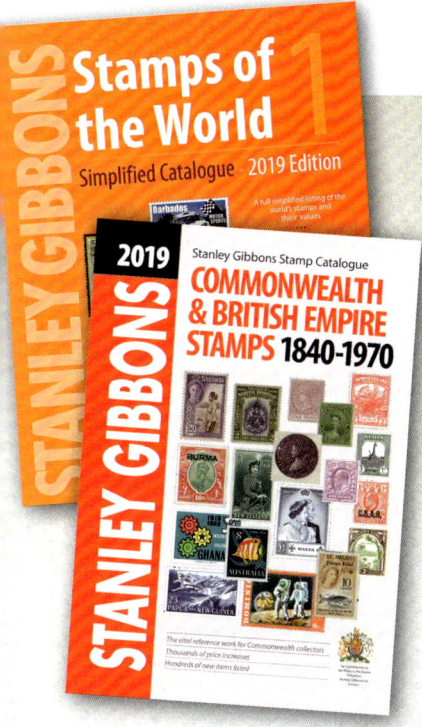

We have catalogues to suit every aspect of stamp collecting

Our catalogues cover stamps issued from across the globe - from the Penny Black to the latest issues. Whether you're a specialist in a certain reign or a thematic collector, we should have something to suit your needs. All catalogues include the famous SG numbering system, making it as easy as possible to find the stamp you're looking for.

Commonwealth & British Empire Stamps 1840–1970 (121st edition, 2019)
King George VI (9th edition, 2018)

Commonwealth Country Catalogues
Australia & Dependencies (11th Edition, 2018)
Bangladesh, Pakistan & Sri Lanka (3rd edition, 2015)
Belize, Guyana, Trinidad & Tobago (2nd edition, 2013)
Brunei, Malaysia & Singapore (5th edition, 2017)
Canada (6th edition, 2016)
Cyprus, Gibraltar & Malta (5th edition, 2019)
East Africa with Egypt & Sudan (4th edition, 2018)
Eastern Pacific (3rd edition, 2015)
Falkland Islands (7th edition, 2016)
Hong Kong (6th edition, 2018)
India (including Convention & Feudatory States) (5th edition, 2018)
Indian Ocean (3rd edition, 2016)
Ireland (7th edition, 2019)
Leeward Islands (3rd edition, 2017)
New Zealand (6th edition, 2016)
Northern Caribbean, Bahamas & Bermuda (4th edition, 2016)
St. Helena & Dependencies (6th edition, 2017)
Southern & Central Africa (2nd edition, 2014)
West Africa (2nd edition, 2012)
Western Pacific (4th edition, 2017)
Windward Islands & Barbados (3rd edition, 2015)

Stamps of the World 2019
Volume 1	Abu Dhabi – Charkhari
Volume 2	Chile – Georgia
Volume 3	German Commands – Jasdan
Volume 4	Jersey – New Republic
Volume 5	New South Wales – Singapore
Volume 6	Sirmoor – Zululand

Great Britain Catalogues
2019 Collect British Stamps (70th edition, 2019)
Collect Channel Islands & Isle of Man (30th edition, 2016)
2019 GB Concise (34th edition, 2019)

Great Britain Specialised
Volume 1	Queen Victoria (16th edition, 2012)
Volume 2	King Edward VII to King George VI (14th edition, 2015)
Volume 3	Queen Elizabeth II Pre-decimal issues (13th edition, 2019)
Volume 4	Queen Elizabeth II Decimal Definitive Issues – Part 1 (10th edition, 2008)
	Queen Elizabeth II Decimal Definitive Issues – Part 2 (10th edition, 2010)

Foreign Countries
Antarctica (2nd edition, 2012)
Arabia (1st edition, 2016)
Austria and Hungary (8th Edition 2014)
Belgium & Luxembourg (1st edition, 2015)
Central America (3rd edition, 2007)
China (12th edition, 2018)
Czech Republic and Slovakia (1st edition, 2017)
Denmark and Norway (1st edition, 2018)
Finland and Sweden (1st edition, 2017)
France, Andorra and Monaco (1st edition, 2015)
French Colonies (1st edition, 2016)
Germany (12th edition, 2018)
Japan & Korea (5th edition, 2008)
Middle East (1st Edition, 2018)
Netherlands & Colonies (1st edition, 2017)
North East Africa (2nd edition 2017)
Poland (1st edition, 2015)
Russia (7th edition, 2014)
South-East Asia (5th edition, 2012)
Southern Balkans (1st edition, 2019)
Spain and Colonies (1st edition, 2019)
United States of America (8th edition, 2015)

STANLEY GIBBONS
LONDON 1856

BY APPOINTMENT TO HER MAJESTY THE QUEEN PHILATELISTS STANLEY GIBBONS LTD LONDON

399 Strand, WC2R 0LX, London
Phone: +44 1425 472 363 | Email: support@stanleygibbons.com
www.stanleygibbons.com

Guide to Entries

(A) Country of Issue – When a country changes its name, the catalogue listing changes to reflect the name change, for example Cambodia was formerly known as Kampuchea, the stamps in South East Asia are all listed under Cambodia, but spilt into Kampuchea and then Cambodia. When a country spilts, for example Czechoslovakia split into Czech Republic and Slovakia, there will be a listing for Czechoslovakia and then separate sections for Czech Republic and Slovakia.

(B) Currency – Details of the currency, and dates of earliest use where applicable, on the face value of the stamps.

(C) Country Information – Brief geographical and historical details for the issuing country.

(D) Illustration – Generally, the first stamp in the set. Stamp illustrations are reduced to 75%, with overprints and surcharges shown actual size.

(E) Illustration or Type Number – These numbers are used to help identify stamps, either in the listing, type column, design line or footnote, usually the first value in a set. These type numbers are in a bold type face – **123**; when bracketed (**123**) an overprint or a surcharge is indicated. Some type numbers include a lower-case letter – **123a**, this indicates they have been added to an existing set. New cross references are also shown in bold.

(F) Date of issue – This is the date that the stamp/set of stamps was issued by the post office and was available for purchase. When a set of definitive stamps has been issued over several years the Year Date given is for the earliest issue. Commemorative sets are listed in chronological order. Stamps of the same design, or issue are usually grouped together, for example one of the French Marianne definitive series' was first issued in 2002 but includes stamps issued to the end of 2004.

(G) Number Prefix – Stamps other than definitives and commemoratives have a prefix letter before the catalogue number.
Their use is explained in the text: some examples are A for airmail, E for East Germany or Express Delivery stamps.

(H) Footnote – Further information on background or key facts on issues.

(I) Stanley Gibbons Catalogue number – This is a unique number for each stamp to help the collector identify stamps in the listing. The Stanley Gibbons numbering system is universally recognised as definitive.
Where insufficient numbers have been left to provide for additional stamps to a listing, some stamps will have a suffix letter after the catalogue number (for example 214a). If numbers have been left for additions to a set and not used they will be left vacant.
The separate type numbers (in bold) refer to illustrations (see **E**).

(J) Colour – If a stamp is printed in three or fewer colours then the colours are listed, working from the centre of the stamp outwards (see **R**).

(K) Design line – Further details on design variations

(L) Key Type – Indicates a design type on which the stamp is based. These are the bold figures found below each illustration, for example listed in Cameroun, in the Germany catalogue is the Key type A and B showing the ex-Kaiser's yacht *Hohenzollern*. The type numbers are also given in bold in the second column of figures alongside the stamp description to indicate the design of each stamp. Where an issue comprises stamps of similar design, the corresponding type number should be taken as indicating the general design. Where there are blanks in the type number column it means that the type of the corresponding stamp is that shown by the number in the type column of the same issue. A dash (–) in the type column means that the stamp is not illustrated. Where type numbers refer to stamps of another country, e.g. where stamps of one country are overprinted for use in another, this is always made clear in the text.

(M) Coloured Papers – Stamps printed on coloured paper are shown – e.g. 'brown/*yellow*' indicates brown printed on yellow paper.

(N) Surcharges and Overprints – Usually described in the headings. Any actual wordings are shown in bold type. Descriptions clarify words and figures used in the overprint. Stamps with the same overprints in different colours are not listed separately. Numbers in brackets after the descriptions are the catalogue numbers of the non-overprinted stamps. The words 'inscribed' or 'inscription' refer to the wording incorporated in the design of a stamp and not surcharges or overprints.

(O) Face value – This refers to the value of each stamp and is the price it was sold for at the Post Office when issued. Some modern stamps do not have their values in figures but instead shown as a letter, shown as a letter, for example Great Britain use 1st or 2nd on their stamps as apposed to the actual value.

(P) Catalogue Value – Mint/Unused. Prices quoted for pre-1945 stamps are for lightly hinged examples.

(Q) Catalogue Value – Used. Prices generally refer to fine postally used examples. For certain issues they are for cancelled-to-order.

Prices
Prices are given in pence and pounds. Stamps worth £100 and over are shown in whole pounds:

Shown in Catalogue as	Explanation
10	10 pence
1·75	£1·75
15·00	£15
£150	£150
£2300	£2300

Prices assume stamps are in 'fine condition'; we may ask more for superb and less for those of lower quality. The minimum catalogue price quoted is 10p and is intended as a guide for catalogue users. The lowest price for individual stamps purchased from Stanley Gibbons is £1.
Prices quoted are for the cheapest variety of that particular stamp. Differences of watermark, perforation, or other details, often increase the value. Prices quoted for mint issues are for single examples. Those in *se-tenant* pairs, strips, blocks or sheets may be worth more. Where no prices are listed it is either because the stamps are not known to exist (usually shown by a †) in that particular condition, or, more usually, because there is no reliable information on which to base their value.
All prices are subject to change without prior notice and we cannot guarantee to supply all stamps as priced. Prices quoted in advertisements are also subject to change without prior notice.

(R) Multicoloured – Nearly all modern stamps are multicoloured (more than three colours); this is indicated in the heading, with a description of the stamp given in the listing.

(S) Perforations – Please see page ix for a detailed explanation of perforations.

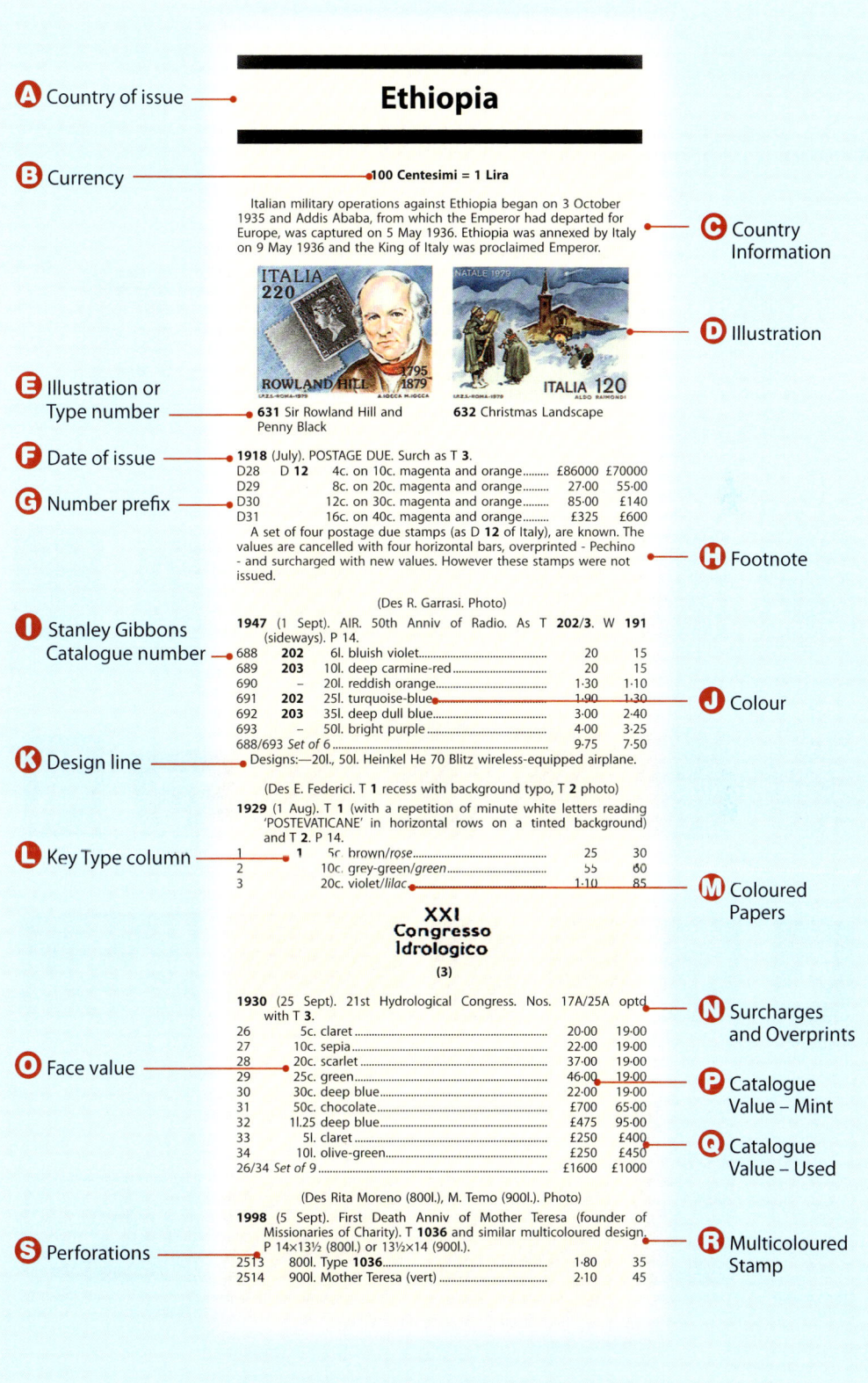

Stamp Illustrations

A number of stamps from other countries are used across the Southern Balkans. The images are included here to aid collectors in identification.

Stamps of France

Commemorative and Definitive Stamps

10 Peace and Commerce   **11** 'Blanc' type   **13** 'Olivier Merson' type   **14** 'Mouchon' type redrawn   **18** Sower, without ground

Stamps of Italy

Commemorative and Definitive Stamps

27   **30**   **31**   **32**   **33**   **34**   **37**

38   **39**   **40**   **41**   **49**   **98** Romulus, Remus and wolf   **99** Julius Caesar

100 Augustus the Great   **102** King Victor Emmanuel III   **103** King Victor Emmanuel III   **110** Pegasus   **114** Ferrucci on Horseback   **115** Ferrucci assassinated by Maramaldo

116 Francesco Ferrucci   **117** Francesco Ferrucci   **118** Helenus and Anchises, *Aeneid* III   **119** Jupiter sending forth Eagle   **121** St Antony's Installation as a Franciscan

Stamp Illustrations

122 The Vision of St Antony **124** Dante, 1265–1321 **125** Leonardo da Vinci's Drawing Flying Man **126** Leonardo da Vinci **127** Leonardo da Vinci

128 Garibaldi and Victor Emmanuel **129** Garibaldi **130** Caprera E **131** Garibaldi (statue), Savoia Marchetti S-55A Flying Boat and Anita Garibaldi (statue) **135** Italian flag

 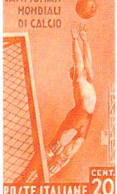   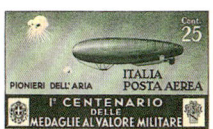

136 Italian flag **143** **144** Savoia Marchetti S-55X Flying Boat over Footballer **146** Military Symbol **147** Italian 'P' Type Airship under Fire

163 Naval Memorial **164** Augustus the Great

Express Letter and Postage Due stamps

E **35** D **141** D **142**

xxiii

Stamp Illustrations

Stamps of Turkey

28 **30** GPO, constantinople **31** Mosque of Selim **38** Mosque of Sultan Ahmed **40** Fountains of Suleiman

69 Howitzer at Sedd el Bahr **72** Mosque at Ortaköy **74** Martyrs Column **78** Pyramids **85** Sentry at Beersheba

Albania

1913. 40 Paras = 1 Piastre or Grosh
1913. 100 Qint = 1 Franc
1947. Leks only
1965. 100 Qint = 1 New Lek

Qint is also expressed as Qintar, Qind or Qindar, the 'ar' meaning gold.

The independence of Albania from Turkish rule was declared on 28 November 1912, during the first Balkan War, and was recognised by the Treaty of London, 30 May 1913.

Austrian Post Offices continued to function in Durrës, Sarandë, Shengjin, Shkodër and Vlórë until 1915 and Italian Post Offices in Ioannina until 1914 (and temporarily in 1917), Shkodër until 1915 and Durrës and Vlórë until 1923. Details of issues are listed under Post Offices in the Turkish Empire in Central Asia of this catalogue and in Austria and Hungary or Italy and Switzerland respectively.

I. Provisional Government

1913–1914

Prior to the June overprinted issues, unoverprinted Turkish stamps were used. From May 1913 handstamped envelopes were made available. The first handstamp used consisted of two concentric circles with a double-eagle shield in the centre and 'MINISTERIA E POST-TELEG E TELEFONEVET' between the circles. This was followed by a handstamp similar to T **2** but without eagle or face value. Cut-outs of both handstamps are known used.

The second handstamp was produced in October 1913 in sheets with 'sewing-machine' perforation.

Types of Turkey

25

(26)

28

Plate I   Plate II

(1)

2

1913 (16 June). Stamps of Turkey handstamped with T **1**.

*A. On issue of 1908 T **25**. P 12*
1	2½pi. brown	£950	£850
	a. Perf 13½	£950	£850

*B. On issue of 1908, T **25** with opt T **26**. P 13½×12*
2	10pa. green	£700	£700

*C. On issue of 1909–1911 T **28** (5pa., 10pa., 20pa., 1pi. Plate II). P 12*
3	2pa. olive-green	£550	£550
4	5pa. yellow-buff	£550	£550
	a. Plate I		
5	10pa. green	£450	£325
	a. Perf 13½×12		
	b. Perf 12×13½		
6	20pa. rose-carmine	£450	£325
	a. Perf 13½×12		
	b. Perf 13½		
7	1pi. ultramarine	£400	£325
	a. *Bright blue* (Plate I) (P 12×13½)		
8	2pi. blue-black	£650	£600
9	5pi. slate-purple	£1600	£1400
	a. Perf 13½		
	b. Perf 12×13½ (handstamp inverted)		
10	10pi. dull red	£6500	£6000

D. As last, but surch '10' in addition
11	10(pa.) on 20pa. rose-carmine	£1600	£1600

*E. On T **28** (10pa., 20pa. Plate II) with opt T **26**.
P 12×13½ (20pa.) or 12 (others)*
12	10pa. green	£1100	£1000
13	20pa. rose-carmine	£1100	£1100
14	1pi. bright blue (Plate I)	£2500	£2250
	a. *Ultramarine* (Plate II)	£2500	£2250
14b	2pi. blue-black	£4500	£4000

*F. On Postage Due stamp of 1908 T **25**. P 12*
15	1pi. black/crimson	£3750	£3250
	a. Perf 13½×12		

*G. On Postage Due stamp of 1910 T **28**, Plate II. P 12*
15b	1pi. black/crimson	£3750	£3250

Stamps are known with handstamp T **1** in red, blue or violet.
2pa. on 5pa. T **28** and 25pi. and 50pi. Types **25** and **28** were not sold at the post office but were distributed to some officials.

Nos. 2/5, 7/9, 13 and 14a exist with handstamp inverted (*Prices*: No. 2, £1800 *used*; No. 4, £1800 *used*; No. 7, £1100 *un or used*; No. 9, £3500 *un*, £2750 *used*; No. 14a, £4500 *un or used*) and No. 3 with handstamp sideways.

There are numerous forgeries of the handstamp.

1913. Handstamped as T **2**. Arms in second colour. Value typewritten in violet. Laid bâtonné paper. With or without gum (10pa.), no gum (others). Imperf.
16	10pa. violet and violet (25.10.13)	19·00	19·00
17	20pa. red and grey (25.10.13)	26·00	22·00
	a. Violet Eagle		
18	1gr. grey and grey (25.10.13)	26·00	26·00
19	2gr. pale blue and violet (21.11.13)	33·00	26·00
20	5gr. violet and pale blue (21.11.13)	39·00	33·00
	a. Grey Eagle		
21	10gr. blue and blue (25.11.13)	39·00	33·00

The Eagle exists inverted, sideways or omitted.
Errors in typewritten value exist, including 1gr. for 10gr, '1 grodh' and '1 grosg'.
Stamps can be found with part of papermaker's watermark, Atlas supporting the World.
Types **2** and **3** postmarked on the back are remainders.

3

4 Skanderbeg (after Heinz Kautsch)

1913 (28 Nov). Independence Anniversary. Issued at Vlórë (Valona). Handstamped from metal stamps. Arms and value in black. Horiz laid paper. P 11½.
22	**3** 10pa. green	6·50	5·25
	a. Vert laid paper	16·00	14·00
	b. Error. 10pa. red	33·00	33·00
	c. Error. 10pa. violet	33·00	33·00
23	20pa. red	9·75	7·75
	a. Vert laid paper	29·00	25·00
	b. Error. 20pa. green	55·00	41·00
24	30pa. violet	9·75	7·75
	a. Vert laid paper	29·00	25·00
	b. Error. 30pa. blue	41·00	41·00
	c. Error. 30pa. red	41·00	41·00
	d. Error. 30pa. black	41·00	41·00
25	1gr. blue	13·00	11·50
	a. Vert laid paper	38·00	34·00
	b. Error. 1gr. green	41·00	41·00
	c. Error. 1gr. violet	41·00	41·00
	d. Error. 1gr. black	41·00	41·00

ALBANIA 1913

26		2gr. black		19·00	13·00
	a. Vert laid paper			50·00	31·00
	b. Error. 2gr. violet			50·00	50·00
	c. Error. 2gr. blue			50·00	50·00

T **3** was produced from separate handstamps for the frame, Eagle and value.

All values exist with Eagle or value, or both, inverted, and with Eagle or value omitted, the 10pa. to 1gr. with frame double or Eagle sideways and the 20pa. to 2gr. with value written in ink (*Prices £60 to £140*).

See final footnote below No. 21.

(Typo Government Printing Office, Turin)

1913 (1 Dec). P 14.

27	**4**	2q. chestnut and yellow	6·50	3·25
28		5q. green and yellow	6·50	3·25
29		10q. carmine and rose	6·50	3·25
30		25q. blue	6·50	3·25
31		50q. mauve and rose	16·00	6·50
32		1f. brown	36·00	19·00
27/32 Set of 6			70·00	35·00

II. Prince William of Wied

1914

Prince William was offered the Crown on 21 February 1914. He left Albania on 3 September.

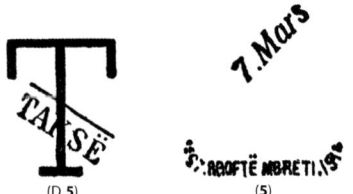

(D **5**)   (**5**)

1914 (23 Feb). POSTAGE DUE. Handstamped with T D **5**.

D33	**4**	2q. chestnut and yellow (V., B. or Blk.)	15·00	6·25
D34		5q. green and yellow (R. or B.)	15·00	6·25
D35		10q. carmine and rose (V.)	21·00	6·25
D36		25q. blue (R.)	25·00	6·25
D37		50q. mauve and rose (Blk.)	38·00	20·00
D33/D37 Set of 5			£100	41·00

Separate handstamps were used for 'T' and 'TAKSË'. Values exist with one or both handstamps inverted or double, or with one handstamp omitted.

1914 (7 Mar). Arrival of Prince William of Wied. Handstamped with T **5**.

33	**4**	2q. chestnut and yellow	95·00	£110
34		5q. green and yellow (V.)	95·00	£110
35		10q. carmine and rose	95·00	£110
36		25q. blue (V.)	95·00	£110
37		50q. mauve and rose	95·00	£110
38		1f. brown	95·00	£110
33/38 Set of 6			£500	£600

Separate handstamps were used for '7. Mars' and rest of overprint. Inverted and double handstamps exist.

5a (*Illustration reduced, actual size 45×45 mm*)   (**5b**)

1914 (19 Mar). Korçë (Koritza) Military Post Issue. Value handstamped in red as in T **5a**. Imperf.

38a		10pa. violet	£325	£250
38b		10pa. black	£450	£425
38c		25pa. violet	£325	£250
38d		25pa. black	£600	£500

Nos. 38a/38d were produced by metal handstamps, the value being applied separately. At first the handstamps were used directly on covers and different kinds of paper are therefore found. Later examples were issued in sheets. Correctly franked covers have two copies of 10pa. or two copies of 25pa.

No. 38a is known with value inverted.

1914 (19 Mar)–**15**. Shkodër (Scutari) Provisional Issue. First Anniversary of Hoisting of Albanian Flag on Fortress of Rozafat, Shkodër.

*(a) POSTAGE. Nos. 40/45 further handstamped as T **5b**, in red*

39		5pa. on 2q. chestnut and yellow	£130	£130
	a. Handstamped in violet		£150	£160
39b		10pa. on 5q. green and yellow	£130	£130
39c		20pa. on 10q. carmine and rose	£130	£130
39d		1gr. on 25q. blue	£130	£130
39e		2gr. on 50q. mauve and rose	£130	£130
39f		5gr. on 1f. brown	£950	£950

All values exist with handstamp inverted.

*(b) POSTAGE DUE. T **4** handstamped with T **5b** in first colour given and further handstamped with large 'T' in second colour given (1915)*

D39g		10q. carmine and rose (Blk.+R.)	£500	£500
D39h		25q. blue (R.+Blk.)	£160	£160
D39i		50q. mauve and rose (R.+Blk.)	£150	£150

The Albanian Post Office in Shkodër (Scutari) was closed from May 1915 following occupation by Montenegro. The Austrians used their own Field Post Office there in 1916–1918, and the Albanian Post Office was re-opened on 15 January 1919.

10	**2**
-**PARA**-	**GROSH**
(**6**)	(**7**)

1914 (2 Apr). Surch as T **6** or T **7**.

40	**4**	5pa. on 2q. chestnut and yellow	4·00	4·00
	a. Surch inverted		£120	
	b. Pair, one with surch omitted, one with surch inverted		£180	
41		10pa. on 5q. green and yellow	4·00	4·00
	a. Surch inverted		£120	
	b. Pair, one with surch omitted		£180	
42		20pa. on 10q. carmine and rose	6·50	5·25
	a. Surch inverted		£120	
43		1gr. on 25q. blue	6·50	5·75
	a. Surch inverted		£120	
	b. Pair, one with surch omitted		£375	
44		2gr. on 50q. mauve and rose	6·50	6·50
	a. Surch inverted		£150	
45		5gr. on 1f. brown	26·00	19·00
	a. Surch inverted		£190	

1914 (16 Apr). POSTAGE DUE. Surch as Types **6** and **7**, and handstamped with word 'TAKSË' only, as in T D **5**.

D46	**4**	10pa. on 5q. green and yellow	7·50	6·25
D47		20pa. on 10q. carmine and rose	7·50	6·25
D48		1gr. on 25q. blue	7·50	6·25
D49		2gr. on 50q. mauve and rose	7·50	6·25

The handstamp is known inverted, double, sideways, double inverted, etc.

1914 (15 Oct). Vlorë (Valona) Provisional Issue. Handstamped with Star within double-lined circle inscr 'POSTE D'ALBANIE' at foot and in Turkish at top.

45b	**4**	2q. chestnut and yellow	£375	£375
45c		5q. green and yellow	£1500	£1500
45d		10q. carmine and rose	50·00	50·00
45e		25q. blue	50·00	50·00
45f		50q. mauve and rose	38·00	38·00
45g		1f. brown	£950	£950
45h		5pa. on 2q. chestnut and yellow	90·00	90·00
45i		10pa. on 5q. green and yellow	90·00	90·00
45j		20pa. on 10q. carmine and rose	75·00	75·00
45k		1gr. on 25q. blue	38·00	38·00
45l		2gr. on 50q. mauve and rose	65·00	65·00
45m		5gr. on 1f. brown	75·00	75·00

III. Provisional Government of Essad Pasha (Central Albania)

1914–1916

From 13 September, 1914, Southern Albania was gradually occupied by Italian forces, and the north by Serbians and Montenegrins. After the defeat of Serbia at the end of 1915, northern Albania was occupied by Austrian troops till the end of 1918. Essad Pasha ruled in Central Albania from January 1914 to 24 February 1916 when the Austrians took control.

(**8**)

1915 ALBANIA

9 Shkodër (Scutari)

10 Tarabosh

1915 (9 Jan). Handstamped with T **8**, in violet, red, blue or black.
46	**4**	2q. chestnut and yellow	31·00	31·00
47		5q. green	70·00	70·00
48		10q. carmine and rose	44·00	44·00
48a		25q. blue	65·00	75·00
48b		50q. mauve and rose	65·00	75·00
49		5pa. on 2q. chestnut and yellow	44·00	44·00
50		10pa. on 5q. green	19·00	19·00
51		20pa. on 10q. carmine and rose	19·00	19·00
52		1gr. on 25q. blue	19·00	19·00
53		2gr. on 50q. mauve and rose	19·00	19·00
54		5gr. on 1f. brown	44·00	65·00
46/54 Set of 11			£400	£425

1915 (9 Jan). POSTAGE DUE. Nos. 46, etc, handstamped with large 'T' in violet or blue-black.
D55	**4**	2q. chestnut and yellow	50·00	50·00
D56		10pa. on 5q. green	31·00	31·00
D57		20pa. on 10q. carmine and rose	31·00	31·00
D58		1gr. on 25q. blue	31·00	31·00
D59		2gr. on 50q. mauve and rose	31·00	31·00
D55/D59 Set of 5			£160	£160

1915 (10 Feb). Unissued stamps handstamped with Crescent and Turkish inscr within circle, in violet or black.
55	**9**	2pa. orange	9·50	10·00
56		5pa. violet	9·50	12·50
57		10pa. green	9·50	10·00
58		20pa. red	9·50	6·25
59		40pa. blue	12·50	6·25
60		100pa. pink	31·00	12·50
61		5pi. black	95·00	38·00
55/61 Set of 7			£160	85·00

Handstamps in gold exist, produced for presentation purposes.

1915 (10 Feb). Same handstamp on fiscals of different type.
62	**10**	10pa. green	11·50	12·50
63		20pa. red	11·50	9·50
64		50pa. blue	7·50	6·25
65		3pi. pink	7·50	6·25
66		6pi. chocolate	19·00	15·00
62/66 Set of 5			50·00	45·00

IV. Autonomous Province of Korçë (Koritza)

1916–1918

French Currency

On 11 December 1916 the French General Sarrail set up the area round Koritza in eastern Albania as an Autonomous Province, to counter Greek and Italian influences. In February 1918 the status of Autonomous Province was abolished and it became French-occupied territory. The area passed into Albanian control when French troops left in June 1920.

(10a)

11

1916 (25 Dec). Nos. 60, 77/78, 82 and 85 of Epirus handstamped as T **10a**.
66a	**36**	10c. on 2l. scarlet	£325	£250
66b	**30**	10c. on 2l. carmine	£1300	£650
66c	**29**	25c. on 3l. vermilion	£550	£325
66d	**30**	25c. on 25l. blue	£700	£450
66e	**31**	25c. on 50l. brown-purple	£7500	£5500

The Eagle on the 25c. handstamp has four wings on each side.
The date given is earliest known cancellation.

(Typo, background litho A. A. Vangheli)

1917 (Jan). P 11½.
67	**11**	1c. brown and green	28·00	19·00
		a. Second 'V' of 'VETQEVERITARE' inverted	£110	
		b. 'S' of 'SHQIPERIE' inverted	90·00	
68		2c. red-brown and green	28·00	19·00
		a. Second 'V' of 'VETQEVERITARE' inverted	£110	
		b. 'S' of 'SHQIPERIE' inverted	95·00	
69		3c. grey and green	28·00	19·00
		a. Second 'V' of 'VETQEVERITARE' inverted	£110	
		b. 'S' of 'SHQIPERIE' inverted	95·00	
70		5c. green and black	25·00	12·50
		a. Second 'V' of 'VETQEVERITARE' inverted	£110	
		b. 'S' of 'SHQIPERIE' inverted	95·00	
71		10c. rose-carmine and black	25·00	12·50
		a. 'S' of 'SHQIPERIE' inverted	75·00	
72		25c. blue and black	25·00	12·50
		a. 'S' of 'SHQIPERIE' inverted	75·00	
73		50c. violet and black	25·00	16·00
		a. 'S' of 'SHQIPERIE' inverted	75·00	
74		1f. brown and black	25·00	16·00
		a. Second 'V' of 'VETQEVERITARE' inverted	£120	
		b. 'S' of 'SHQIPERIE' inverted	90·00	
67/74 Set of 8			£190	£110

Inverted 'S' occurs in position 5 of setting of 12. The inverted 'V' was later corrected.

1917 (May). As last but inscr 'REPUBLIKA SHQIPETARE' at sides. Typo. P 11½.
75		1c. brown and green	4·50	3·75
76		2c. red-brown and green	4·50	3·75
		a. 'CTM' for 'CTS'	£110	£190
77		3c. slate and green	4·50	3·75
		a. 'CTM' for 'CTS'	£130	£225
78		5c. green and black	6·25	6·25
		a. Inscriptions double		
79		10c. red and black	6·25	6·25
80		50c. purple and black	11·50	10·00
81		1f. red-brown and black	31·00	28·00
75/81 Set of 7			60·00	55·00

2c. and 3c. were at first printed with 'CTM' (76a, 77a) in all positions. The error was corrected in later printings.

1918 (2 Apr). No. 78 surch 'QARKU I KORÇËS 25 CTS', in red.
81a		25 on 5c. green and black	£325	£425
		ab. Surch double		

The date given is earliest known cancellation.

1918 (5 Apr). As T **11**, but inscr 'QARKU POSTES I KORÇES'.
82		25c. blue and black	£110	£150
		a. Inverted 'U' in 'QARKU'		
		b. Inverted 'Q' in 'QARKU'		
		c. 'QRAKU'		
		d. 'KORCÊS' (no cedilla on 'C')		
		e. Imperf between (horiz pair)		
		f. Imperf between (vert pair)		

Printed in sheets of 12. In first setting inverted 'U' occurs in position 1, inverted 'Q' in position 6, 'QRAKU' in position 11 and 'KORCÊS' in positions 9 and 12. All errors were corrected in later settings.
Nos. 82e/82f (which come from two vert rows) also have various edges imperf. Completely imperforate pairs have been made from imperf between pairs by trimming perforated edges.
The date given is earliest known cancellation.

The inscription on Nos. 67/74 means 'Koritza: Independent Albania'; that on Nos. 75/81, 'Koritza: Albanian Republic'; and that on Nos. 81a/82, 'Local Post of Koritza'.
T **11** (all inscriptions) overprinted 'TAXE' are fiscal stamps.

From April 1918 until the end of the occupation French stamps were used; the canceller was inscribed 'TRESOR ET POSTES'.

V. Provisional Government

December 1918–February 1920

A Provisional Government under Turkhan Bey was set up in December 1918 with the aim of establishing complete independence and to free the country of Italian troops, who left on 2 September 1920.
Shkodër (Scutari) was governed by an Inter-Allied Commission, as a protection against Serbia, from the end of 1918 till 11 March 1920. Nos. 83/103, 111/113d and 114/122 were for use there.

ALBANIA 1919

| 12 | 13 | 13a |

(Note different types of Eagle)

(Surcharged by Nikaj, Shkodër)

1919 (15 Jan). Fiscal stamps used by the Austrians in Albania with value in heller, as T **12**, surch in black with new value and 'POSTA e Shkodres SHQYPNIS' (Post of Scutari, Albania), and handstamped diagonally with T **13a** in blue (10q.) or red (others). Issued under the joint authority of the British, French and Italian commanders. P 12½.

83	(2)q. on 2h. brown	12·50	12·50
	a. Surch inverted		
84	05q. on 16h. green	12·50	12·50
	a. Surch inverted		
85	10q. on 8h. carmine	12·50	12·50
	a. Surch inverted		
86	25q. on 64h. blue	15·00	15·00
	a. Surch inverted		
	b. Type **13**	£650	£650
87	50q. on 32h. violet	12·50	12·50
	a. Surch inverted		
88	1f. on 1.28k. brown/*blue*	16·00	19·00
	a. 'r' in 'Frank' inverted	36·00	36·00
	b. 'ë' for 'e' in 'Shkodres'	33·00	33·00
	c. Surch inverted		
83/88 Set of 6		75·00	75·00

The surcharge settings consisted of 40 positions (5×8) which were applied twice to the sheets of 80. For the 5q. to 50q. values several different fonts were used for the numerals e.g. wide and narrow figure '0' and letter 'O', '1' and 'I', straight and curly-footed '2', serifed (two sizes) and sans-serif '5'; these occur in various combinations. The 1f. has the figure '1' on the left and the letter 'I' on the right in all positions; Nos. 88a and 88b occur in positions 35 and 36 respectively of the setting.

The date (T **13a**) was handstamped across the stamps to commemorate the re-opening of the Post Office. This is found double, inverted or omitted. It also exists in violet on 2q., 5q. and 25q. and in blue on 2q.

(D **14**)

1919 (15 Jan). POSTAGE DUE. Fiscal stamps with surch as in T **12** (but 'qint' for 'QINT'), without date, handstamped with T D **14**, in violet. P 11½ (4q.) or 12½ (others).

D89	(4)q. on 4h. pink	19·00	15·00
	a. 'qit' for 'qint'		
D90	(10)q. on 10k. red/*green*	19·00	15·00
	a. 'qit' for 'qint'		
D91	20q. on 2k. orange/*lilac*	19·00	15·00
	a. 'qit' for 'qint'		
D92	50q. on 5k. brown/*yellow*	19·00	15·00
	a. 'qit' for 'qint'		
	b. 'nt' of 'qint' at right angle		
D89/D92 Set of 4		70·00	55·00

Most stamps with 'qit' error, which occurs in position 36 of the setting, also have the obliterating bars damaged on the left.

T D **14** exists inverted on all values and sideways on Nos. D89/D91. The handstamp is also found in red or blue; these are believed to be trials.

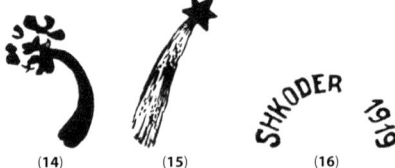

| (14) | (15) | (16) |

1919 (16 Jan). T **12** (without handstamped date) further handstamped with a 'Comet', T **14** (from wooden die), in red or green (10q.).

89	(2)q. on 2h. brown	25·00	25·00
	a. Handstamped in blue	£110	31·00
90	5q. on 16h. green	19·00	19·00
91	10q. on 8h. carmine	19·00	19·00
92	25q. on 64h. blue	£250	£325
	a. Type **13**	80·00	£110
93	50q. on 32h. violet	25·00	25·00
94	1f. on 1.28k. brown/*blue*	25·00	25·00
	a. 'r' in 'Frank' inverted	90·00	90·00
	b. 'ë' for 'e' in 'Shkodres'	90·00	90·00
	c. Surch double		
89/94 Set of 6 (*cheapest*)		£170	£200

The handstamp exists in violet in 1f.

1919 (15 Feb). As Nos. 89/94 but comet with straight tail, T **15**, in violet (from a copper die).

96	(2)q. on 2h. brown	31·00	31·00
97	5q. on 16h. green	31·00	31·00
98	10q. on 8h. carmine	31·00	31·00
99	25q. on 64h. blue	31·00	31·00
	a. Type **13**	£250	£250
100	50q. on 32h. violet	31·00	31·00
	a. Surch double		
101	1f. on 1.28k. brown/*blue*	31·00	31·00
	a. 'r' in 'Frank' inverted	8·75	60·00
	b. 'ë' for 'e' in 'Shkodres'	50·00	50·00
96/101 Set of 6 (*cheapest*)		£170	£170

The handstamp exists in red or blue on 50q., and double on 5q. (both in violet or with one in red).

1919. No. 43 handstamped with T **16**, in violet.

| 103 | **4** | 1gr. on 25q. blue | 45·00 | 34·00 |

No. 103 exists with handstamp inverted or double.

15 QIND 15 **20 QIND 20**
POSTAT **POSTAT**

SHQIPTARE **SHQIPTARE**
||||||||||||||||||||| ////////////
(16a) (16b)

1919 (5 June). Fiscals as Types **12/13**, surch at Durrës (Durazzo). P 12½.

(a) As T **16a**

104	**13**	10q. on 2h. brown	12·50	12·50
105	**12**	15q. on 8h. carmine	12·50	10·50
		a. Surch in violet		
		b. Error. 20q. on 8h.		
		c. Type **13**	£375	£375
106		20q. on 16h. green	12·50	10·50
		a. Perf 11½	12·50	10·50
		b. Error. 25q. on 16h.		
107	**13**	25q. on 64h. blue	12·50	10·50
108	**12**	50q. on 32h. violet	12·50	10·50
		a. Error. 25q. on 32h.		
109		1f. on 96h. orange (P 11½)	12·50	10·50
		a. Type **13** (P 12½)	£350	£325
110	**13**	2f. on 160h. violet	44·00	38·00
		a. Error. 1f. on 160h.		

(b) As T **16b**

111	**13**	10q. on 8h. carmine	12·50	10·50
		a. Type **12**	£400	£375
112		15q. on 8h. carmine (V.)	12·50	10·50
		a. Type **12**	£1300	£750
113	**12**	20q. on 16h. green	12·50	10·50
		a. Perf 11½		
113*b*		25q. on 32h. violet	12·50	10·50
113*c*		50q. on 64h. blue	35·00	25·00
113*d*		1f. on 96h. orange (P 11½)	15·00	12·50
113*e*	**13**	2f. on 160h. violet	25·00	19·00

VI. Regency

February 1920–21 January 1925

17 Prince William I (**18**) **19** Skanderbeg

1920 ALBANIA

(Des Gurschner. Eng F. Schirnböck. Typo Austrian State Ptg Wks, Vienna)

1920 (16 Feb). Optd with T **18** or surch also. P 12½.

114	**17**	1q. grey. (B.)	£130	£150
115		2q. on 10q. rose (Br.)	18·00	38·00
116		5q. on 10q. rose (G.)	18·00	31·00
117		10q. rose	18·00	41·00
118		20q. brown (B.)	55·00	65·00
119		25q. blue	£650	£900
120		25q. on 10q. rose (B.)	18·00	32·00
121		50q. violet	75·00	£110
122		50q. on 10q. rose (Br.)	18·00	55·00

Stamps of T **17** without the overprint were not issued and those offered came from looted stocks.

(Typo Govt Ptg Wks, Paris)

1920 (1 Apr). Optd at Shkodër (Scutari) with Posthorn to obliterate 'SHKODER'. P 14×13½.

123	**19**	2q. orange	13·00	15·00
124		5q. green	22·00	28·00
125		10q. red	41·00	55·00
126		25q. blue	70·00	55·00
127		50q. green	16·00	19·00
128		1f. mauve	16·00	19·00
123/128 Set of 6			£160	£170

D **20** Fortress of Shkodër    (**21**) ('BESA' =Oath of Peace)   D **22**

(Typo Govt Ptg Wks, Paris)

1920 (1 Apr). POSTAGE DUE. Optd with Posthorn. P 14×13½.

D129	D **20**	4q. olive-green	1·70	6·00
D130		10q. rose	3·50	8·75
D131		20q. bistre-brown	3·50	8·75
D132		50q. black	8·75	23·00
D129/D132 Set of 4			16·00	42·00

Nos. 123/128 and D129/D132 were not issued without the overprint.

1921. Handstamped with T **21** at foot.

135	**19**	2q. orange	8·75	12·50
136		5q. green	8·75	12·50
137		10q. red	18·00	21·00
138		25q. blue	31·00	38·00
139		50q. green	18·00	21·00
140		1f. mauves	18·00	21·00
		a. Pair, one with handstamp omitted		
135/140 Set of 6			90·00	£110

The handstamp exists double.
The Oath of Peace was given to observe a truce in a blood feud. A general 'Besa' was proclaimed throughout Albania in February 1920.

1922 (Mar). POSTAGE DUE. Typo. P 12½.

D141	D **22**	4q. black/red	2·30	6·00
		a. Perf 11½		
D142		10q. black/red	2·30	6·00
		a. Perf 11½		
D143		20q. black/red	2·30	6·00
		a. Perf 11½		
D144		50q. black/red	2·30	6·00
D141/D144 Set of 4			8·25	22·00

(**22**)   (**23**)   24

1922. Handstamped with T **22** at foot.

141	**19**	5q. green (10.22)	6·25	10·00
142		10q. red (8.22)	9·50	11·50

The handstamp exists double.

1922 (Oct). No. 135 handstamped with T **23**.

143	**19**	1q. on 2q. orange	8·25	13·00

No. 143 was issued for use on newspapers when the rate was lowered from 2q. to 1q.

(Typo Austrian State Ptg Wks, Vienna)

1923 (Jan). T **24** and similar horizontal views. P 12½.

144		2q. orange (Gjirokastër)	1·30	2·50
		a. Perf 11½	1·80	3·25
145		5q. yellowish green (Kanina)	1·30	1·90
		a. Perf 11½	2·50	3·50
146		10q. carmine (Berat)	1·30	1·90
		a. Perf 11½		
147		25q. blue (Veziri Bridge)	1·30	1·90
148		50q. deep bluish green (Rozafat Fortress, Shkodër)	1·30	1·90
149		1f. deep reddish lilac (Korçë)	1·30	3·50
150		2f. olive-green (Durrës)	7·50	10·50
144/150 Set of 7			14·00	22·00

Nos. 144/150 were released in the Spring of 1922 but were not put on sale at post offices before January 1923.

(**25**)    (**25a**)

1924 (21 Jan). Opening of National Assembly. Nos. 144/148 optd in black with top line of T **25** (on 25q. with T **25a**) and handstamped in violet with rest of T **25**.

151		2q. orange	22·00	28·00
152		5q. yellowish green	22·00	28·00
153		10q. carmine	16·00	22·00
154		25q. blue	16·00	22·00
155		50q. deep bluish green	23·00	28·00
151/155 Set of 5			90·00	£120

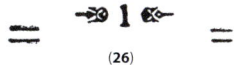

(**26**)

1924 (Apr). No. 144 surch with T **26**.

156		1 on 2q. orange	6·50	11·50
		a. Perf 11½		

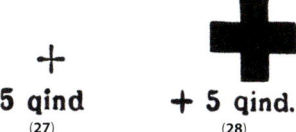

(**27**)   (**28**)

1924. Red Cross.

*(a) Nos. 145 etc surch with T **27** (Cross in red, value in black) (Nov)*

157		5q. +5q. yellowish green	23·00	40·00
		a. Perf 11½		
		b. Perf 12½ ×11½		
158		10q. +5q. carmine	23·00	40·00
159		25q. +5q. blue	23·00	40·00
		a. Surch inverted		
160		50q. +5q. deep bluish green	23·00	40·00

*(b) As last, surch with T **28** in addition (Cross in red, value in black) (Dec)*

161		5q. +5q.+5q. yellowish green	23·00	35·00
		a. Perf 11½		
		b. Perf 12½×11½		
		c. Large red cross of Type **28** omitted		
162		10q. +5q.+5q. carmine	23·00	35·00
		a. '+ 5 qind.' (Type **28**) double		
		b. Large red cross of Type **28** double		
163		25q. +5q.+5q. blue	23·00	35·00
164		50q. +5q.+5q. deep bluish green	23·00	35·00

VII. Republic

21 January 1925–1 September 1928

Triumf' i legalitetit
24 Dhetuer 1924

(**29**)

1925 (5 Mar). Return of Government to Capital in 1924. Nos. 156 and 144/149 optd with T **29**.

164a		1 on 2q. orange	6·50	10·00
165		2q. orange	6·50	10·00

www.robstine-stamps.com

A fantastic array of fine used stamps is now available!

- Good ranges of fine used stamps from Albania, Bulgaria and Greece
- Fine used stamps from other parts of the region, especially the Dodecanese Islands during Italian occupation
- All my stamps are listed on my web site
- Large comprehensive stocks of much of Europe plus Commonwealth and many other places

See also www.robstineextra.com for scans of selected stamps

www.robstine-stamps.com
EXCELLENT QUALITY ♦ PROMPT SERVICE

EVERYTHING FOR THE STAMP COLLECTOR

- **ALBUMS**
  - Peg-fitting • Springback • Ring-fitting
  - Luxury • One-Country • First Day Cover
  - Postcard • Junior

- **CATALOGUES**
  - Great Britain • Commonwealth
  - Foreign • Specialised

- **ACCESSORIES**
  - Microscopes • Watermark Detectors
  - Ultraviolet Lamps • Tweezers
  - Magnifying Glasses • Colour Keys

- **STOCKBOOKS**
  - Wide range of colours and sizes

- **MOUNTS AND HINGES**
  - Huge Selection

- **GIBBONS STAMP MONTHLY**

- **SELECTION OF CHILDREN'S STARTER KITS**

To order, call **01425 472 363** email **orders@stanleygibbons.com** or visit **stanleygibbons.com**

166	5q. yellowish green		6·50	10·00
167	10q. carmine		6·50	10·00
168	25q. blue		6·50	10·00
	a. Perf 11½			
169	50q. deep bluish green		13·50	19·00
170	1f. deep reddish lilac		13·50	25·00
164a/170	Set of 7		55·00	85·00

In the setting of 50, 25 positions are as T **29**, one position (No. 26) has a thin second 'e' in 'Dhetuer' and the remaining 24 positions have some or all of the figures from a thinner fount; 11 of the latter also have a thin 'D'.

Republika Shqiptare
21 Kallnduer 1925
(30)

1925 (11 Apr). Proclamation of Republic. Nos. 156 and 144/149 optd with T **30**.

171	1 on 2q. orange		6·00	11·50
	a. '1921' for '1925'		38·00	44·00
	b. 'Repubiika'		38·00	44·00
	c. 'Républika'		38·00	44·00
172	2q. orange		6·00	11·50
	a. '1921' for '1925'		38·00	44·00
	b. 'Repubiika'		38·00	44·00
	c. 'Républika'		38·00	44·00
173	5q. yellowish green		6·00	11·50
	a. '1921' for '1925'		38·00	44·00
	b. 'Repubiika'		38·00	44·00
	c. 'Républika'		38·00	44·00
174	10q. carmine		6·00	11·50
	a. '1921' for '1925'		38·00	44·00
	b. 'Repubiika'		38·00	44·00
	c. 'Républika'		38·00	44·00
	e. Opt inverted		70·00	75·00
175	25q. blue		6·00	11·50
	a. '1921' for '1925'		38·00	44·00
	b. 'Repubiika'		38·00	44·00
	c. 'Républika'		38·00	44·00
176	50q. deep bluish green		6·00	15·00
	a. '1921' for '1925'		38·00	44·00
	b. 'Repubiika'		38·00	44·00
	c. 'Républika'		38·00	44·00
	d. Opt double, one inverted		70·00	75·00
177	1f. deep reddish lilac		7·75	20·00
	a. '1921' for '1925'		38·00	44·00
	b. 'Repubiika'		38·00	44·00
	c. 'Républika'		38·00	44·00

The 'Republika' error occurs on position 9, 'Repubiika' on position 15, 'République' on position 17 and '1921' on position 31.

(**31**)   (D **32**)

1925 (20 May). Nos. 156 and 144/150 optd with T **31**.

178	1q. on 2q. orange		1·90	2·50
	a. Opt inverted		25·00	31·00
	ab. Perf 11½. Opt inverted*			
	b. 'Republiua'		15·00	24·00
	c. 'Shqiqtare'		15·00	24·00
	d. 'Repuqlika'		15·00	24·00
	e. Opt double, both inverted			
179	2q. orange		1·90	2·50
	a. 'Shqiqtare'		19·00	24·00
	b. 'Republiua'		19·00	24·00
	c. 'Repuqlika'		19·00	24·00
	d. Opt inverted			
	e. Perf 11½			
180	5q. yellowish green		1·90	2·50
	a. 'Repuqlika'		19·00	24·00
	b. Opt inverted			
	c. Perf 11½			
181	10q. carmine		1·90	2·50
	a. 'Repuqlika'		19·00	24·00
	ab. Perf 11½*			
	b. Opt inverted			
182	25q. blue		1·90	2·50
	a. 'Repuqlika'		19·00	24·00
	b. Opt inverted			
	c. Perf 11½			
183	50q. deep bluish green		1·90	2·50
	a. 'Repuqlika'		19·00	24·00
184	1f. deep reddish lilac		8·75	5·75
	a. 'Repuqlika'		35·00	44·00
185	2f. olive-green		13·50	5·75
	a. 'Repuqlika'		35·00	44·00
	b. Opt inverted			

T **31** exists with two types of 'R', in same thickness as rest of overprint or thinner (as in illustration).
The 'Repuqlika' error occurs on position 28.
* 1q. perf 11½ has been seen with overprint inverted only, and 10q. perf 11½ with error 'Repuqlika' only.

1925. POSTAGE DUE. Optd with T D **32**, in white.

D186	D **22**	4q. black/*red*		4·25	6·00
D187		10q. black/*red*		4·25	6·00
D188		20q. black/*red*		4·25	6·00
		a. Perf 11½			
D189		50q. black/*red*		4·25	6·00
		a. Opt inverted			
D186/D189	Set of 4			15·00	22·00

10q. exists with gold overprint, reading up or down. This is believed to be a trial printing.

32   **33**   **34** President Ahmed Zogu, later King Zog I

(Typo State Ptg Wks, Berlin)

1925 (30 May). AIR. Wmk Lozenges. P 14.

186	**32**	5q. green	4·00	4·75
187		10q. carmine	4·00	4·75
188		25q. blue	4·00	4·75
189		50q. deep green	6·50	8·25
190		1f. black and violet	11·50	14·00
191		2f. violet and olive-green	19·00	23·00
192		3f. deep green and chestnut	23·00	23·00
186/192	Set of 7		65·00	75·00

Nos. 186/192 exist imperf; these are proofs.

(Litho Aspiotis, Corfu)

1925 (24 Dec). P 13½×13 or 13½ (25q.).

193	**33**	1q. orange-yellow	40	40
194		2q. red-brown	40	1·40
195		5q. green	35	40
196		10q. rose-red	35	40
		a. Perf 11½	55·00	44·00
		ab. Imperf between (horiz pair)		
197		15q. deep brown	1·70	2·75
198		25q. deep blue	45	40
		a. Perf 13½×11		
199		50q. deep bluish green	1·80	2·10
200	**34**	1f. dull ultramarine and red	3·50	2·75
201		2f. yellow-orange and dull blue-green	4·25	2·75
202		3f. reddish violet and red-brown	8·75	7·00
203		5f. black and reddish violet	10·50	9·50
193/203	Set of 11 (*cheapest*)		29·00	27·00

All values exist imperforate; these are proofs.
The 25q. exists perf 13½×13 in ultramarine, many examples having a double impression. The status of this variety is uncertain but there is no evidence of postal use.
A 1f. blue and brown and 2f. green and brown in a slightly different design were prepared but not issued.

D **35**   (**35**)    Upright 'R'

1925 (24 Dec). POSTAGE DUE. Typo. P 13½×13.

D204	D **35**	10q. blue		1·70	4·75
D205		20q. green		1·70	4·75
D206		30q. red-brown		3·50	9·50
D207		50q. brown		6·00	18·00
D204/D207	Set of 4			11·50	33·00

The above stamps are overprinted 'QINDAR' in red. Large stamps, with double-headed Eagle, inscribed 'SHTETI SHQYPTAR' and 'TAKSE', are purely fiscals.

ALBANIA 1927

1927 (18 Jan). AIR. Optd diag downwards as T **35**.

204	**32**	5q. green	11·00	14·00
		a. Opt double, one inverted	55·00	65·00
		b. Upright 'R'		
205		10q. carmine	11·00	14·00
		a. Opt inverted	50·00	55·00
		b. Opt double, one inverted	55·00	65·00
		c. Upright 'R'		
206		25q. blue	9·25	13·50
		a. Upright 'R'		
207		50q. deep green	6·75	10·50
		a. Opt inverted	50·00	55·00
		b. Upright 'R'		
208		1f. black and violet	6·75	10·50
		a. Opt inverted	50·00	55·00
		b. Upright 'R'	50·00	55·00
		c. No full point after 'Rep' (pos. 38)		
209		2f. violet and olive-green	14·00	14·00
		a. Upright 'R'		
210		3f. deep green and chestnut	19·00	20·00
		a. Upright 'R'		
204/210 Set of 7			70·00	85·00

The upright 'R' variety occurs four times in the sheet, in positions 36, 41, 46 and 47.

(36)

REP. SHQYPTARE
Fluturim' i I-ar
Vlonë–Brindisi
21. IV. 1928
(37)

1927 (1 Feb). Ahmed Zogu's Second Year as President. Optd with T **36**.

211	**33**	1q. orange-yellow (V.)	1·30	1·50
212		2q. red-brown (G.)	60	65
		a. Opt double	44·00	
213		5q. green (R.)	2·75	90
214		10q. rose-red (B.)	60	65
		a. Perf 11½	70·00	38·00
215		15q. deep brown (G.)	16·00	20·00
216		25q. deep blue (R.)	1·30	65
		a. Opt double	44·00	
217		50q. deep bluish green (B.)	1·30	65
218	**34**	1f. dull ultramarine and red	3·00	90
219		2f. yellow-orange and dull blue-green	3·25	1·30
220		3f. reddish violet and red-brown	5·25	2·50
221		5f. black and reddish violet	8·50	4·50
211/221 Set of 11			39·00	31·00

Overprints in different colours are trial printings.

1928 (21 Apr). AIR. Inauguration of Vlörë (Valona) Brindisi Air Service. Optd with T **37**, in violet.

222	**32**	5q. green	11·00	15·00
		a. Opt inverted	38·00	44·00
		b. Error. 'SHQYRTARE'	33·00	39·00
		c. Error. As b, opt inverted	£130	£150
		d. Comma for stop after '21'	33·00	39·00
223		10q. carmine	11·00	15·00
		a. Error. 'SHQYRTARE'	33·00	39·00
		b. Comma for stop after '21'	33·00	39·00
224		25q. blue	11·00	15·00
		a. Error. 'SHQYRTARE'	33·00	39·00
		b. Comma for stop after '21'	33·00	39·00
225		50q. deep green	22·00	29·00
		a. Error. 'SHQYRTARE'	65·00	80·00
		b. Comma for stop after '21'	65·00	80·00
226		1f. black and violet	£120	£150
		a. Error. 'SHQYRTARE'	£200	£425
		b. Comma for stop after '21'	£200	£425
227		2f. violet and olive-green	£120	£150
		a. Error. 'SHQYRTARE'	£200	£425
		b. Comma for stop after '21'	£200	£425
228		3f. deep green and chestnut	£120	£150
		a. Error. 'SHQYRTARE'	£200	£425
		b. Comma for stop after '21'	£200	£425
222/228 Set of 7			£375	£475

Sold at approximately 50 per cent above face value.
The 'SHQYRTARE' error occurs on positions 23 and 48 and the 'Comma' error on positions 13 and 38 in the sheet of 50, the overprint setting of 25 being applied twice.

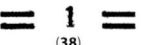
(38)

1928. Nos. 214 and 216, surch as T **38**.

229	**33**	1 on 10q. rose-red	1·30	90
		a. Surch inverted	5·00	5·00
		b. Perf 11½	38·00	25·00
230		5 on 25q. deep blue (R.)	1·30	90
		a. Type **36** inverted	5·00	5·00

39 President Ahmed Zogu, later King Zog I

40

Mbledhjes Kujtim i Kushtetuese
25.8.28
(41)

Mbledhjes Kujtim i Kushtetuese
25.8.28.
(42)

'Dedicated to the memory of the Parliament of 25.8.28'

(Typo Govt Ptg Wks, Paris. Optd locally)

1928. National Assembly. Unissued stamps optd as T **41** or T **42** (1f.). P 14×13½, or 13½×14 (1f.).

231	**39**	1q. red-brown	9·50	15·00
		a. Opt inverted		
232		2q. grey	9·50	15·00
		a. Opt inverted		
233		5q. green	9·50	17·00
		a. Opt inverted		
234		10q. red	9·50	17·00
235		15q. bistre	28·00	65·00
236		25q. blue	11·50	17·00
		a. Opt inverted		
237		50q. lilac-rose	19·00	22·00
238	**40**	1f. black and blue (C.)	14·00	17·00
231/238 Set of 8			£100	£170

This set was sold at a premium of 25 per cent and was on sale for only two days.

VIII. Kingdom

King Zog I.

1 September 1928–7 April 1939

(43) 'Kingdom of Albania. Zog I.I.IX.1928'

(44)

1928 (1 Sept). Accession of King Zog I. Optd as T **43** or T **44**. P 13½×14 (T **40**) or 14×13½ (others).

239	**39**	1q. red-brown	23·00	34·00
240		2q. grey (R.)	23·00	34·00
241		5q. green	19·00	28·00
242		10q. red	19·00	23·00
243		15q. bistre	28·00	39·00

1928 ALBANIA

244		25q. blue (R.)		19·00	23·00
245		50q. lilac-rose		19·00	23·00
246	40	1f. black and blue (R.)		23·00	28·00
247		2f. black and green (R.)		23·00	28·00
239/247 Set of 9				£180	£225

Sold at double face value.

(**45**) 'Kingdom of Albania'

1928. Optd as T **45**. P 13½×14 (T **40**) or 14×13½ (others).

248	39	1q. red-brown		90	1·70
249		2q. grey		90	1·70
250		5q. green		6·00	5·00
251		10q. red		90	1·70
252		15q. bistre		28·00	34·00
253		25q. blue		90	1·70
		a. Pair, one with opt omitted			
254		50q. lilac-rose		1·70	2·75
255	40	1f. black and blue		3·50	3·50
256		2f. black and green		3·50	5·75
257		3f. olive and carmine		14·00	17·00
258		5f. black and violet		14·00	23·00
248/258 Set of 11				65·00	90·00

Mbr. Shqiptare

(**46**)

(**47**) 'Long live the king'

1929. Optd with T **36** and surch as T **46**.

259	33	1 on 50q. deep bluish green (No. 217)		90	90
		a. Surch double			
		b. Surch inverted			
260		5 on 25q. deep blue (No. 216)		90	90
		a. Surch inverted			
		b. Type **36**			
261		15 on 10q. rose-red (No. 214)		1·30	1·50
		a. Perf 11½			
		b. Surch inverted			
		c. Surch double			
		d. Type **36** inverted			
259/261 Set of 3				2·75	3·00

1929 (6 Oct). King Zog's 34th Birthday. Optd with T **47**.

262	33	1q. orange-yellow		14·00	28·00
263		2q. red-brown		14·00	28·00
264		5q. green		14·00	28·00
265		10q. rose-red		14·00	28·00
266		25q. deep blue		14·00	28·00
267		50q. deep bluish green (R.)		19·00	34·00
268	34	1f. dull ultramarine and red		26·00	50·00
269		2f. yellow-orange and dull blue-green		26·00	50·00
262/269 Set of 8				£130	£250

Mbr. Shqiptare

(**48**) 'Kingdom of Albania'

1929 (3 Dec). AIR. Optd with T **48** in brown-red.

270	32	5q. green		13·00	12·50
271		10q. carmine		13·00	12·50
272		25q. blue		13·00	12·50
273		50q. deep green		£250	£250
274		1f. black and violet		£450	£500
275		2f. violet and olive-green		£450	£500
276		3f. deep green and chestnut		£450	£500
270/276 Set of 7				£1500	£1600

Collectors are warned against forgeries of this overprint.

PRINTERS. The following issues to No. 388 were printed in photogravure by the Government Printing Works, Rome.

49 Lake of Butrinto

50 King Zog I

51 Ahmed Zogu Bridge, River Mati

51a Ruins of Zogu Castle

52

D 53 Arms of Albania

1930 (1 Sept). Second Anniversary of Accession. W **52**. P 14×14½ or 14½×14.

277	49	1q. slate		45	35
278		2q. vermilion		45	35
279	50	5q. green		45	35
280		10q. scarlet		45	45
281		15q. sepia		45	45
282		25q. blue		45	45
283	49	50q. blue-green		1·10	80
284	51	1f. violet		1·90	1·40
285		2f. slate-blue		2·50	1·40
286	51a	3f. grey-green		7·00	2·75
287		5f. brown		9·00	5·25
277/287 Set of 11				22·00	12·50

1930 (1 Sept). POSTAGE DUE. W **52**. P 14×14½.

D288	D 53	10q. blue		15·00	29·00
D289		20q. rose		5·50	18·00
D290		30q. violet		5·50	18·00
D291		50q. green		5·50	18·00
D288/D291 Set of 4				28·00	75·00

53 Junkers F-13 over Tirana

(**54**)

1930 (8 Oct). AIR. T **53** (qind values) and similar view. No wmk. P 14×14½.

288		5q. green		2·20	2·50
289		15q. scarlet		2·20	2·50
290		20q. steel-blue		2·20	2·50
291		50q. deep olive		4·50	3·75
292		1f. deep blue		6·50	7·50
293		2f. brown		22·00	25·00
294		3f. violet		33·00	25·00
288/294 Set of 7				65·00	60·00

1931 (6 July). AIR. Tirana–Rome Flight. Nos. 288/294 optd with T **54**.

295		5q. green		11·00	14·00
296		15q. scarlet		11·00	14·00
297		20q. steel-blue		11·00	14·00
298		50q. deep olive		11·00	14·00
299		1f. deep-blue		65·00	80·00
300		2f. brown		65·00	80·00
301		3f. violet		65·00	80·00
		a. Opt inverted		£300	
295/301 Set of 7				£225	£275

(**55**) (D **56**)

1934 (24 Dec). Tenth Anniversary of Revolution. Optd with T **55** (on horiz designs) or similar opt (vert designs).

302	49	1q. slate		13·00	17·00
303		2q. vermilion		13·00	17·00

ALBANIA 1936

304	**50**	5q. green		13·00	13·50
305		10q. scarlet		14·50	17·00
306		15q. sepia		14·50	17·00
307		25q. blue		14·50	17·00
308	**49**	50q. blue-green		19·00	23·00
309	**51**	1f. violet		23·00	28·00
310		2f. slate-blue		31·00	34·00
311	**51a**	3f. grey-green		41·00	50·00
302/311 Set of 10				£180	£200

1936. POSTAGE DUE. Optd with T D **56**.

D312	**50**	10q. carmine		25·00	80·00
		a. Thin 'T'		£150	£200
		b. 'Taksë'		£225	£250

The 'Thin T' occurs 32 times in the sheet of 100. Examples also exist overprinted '– Taksë –' but their status is uncertain.

56 Horse and Flag of Skanderbeg

57 Albania in Chains

1937 (20 Nov). 25th Anniversary of Independence. P 14.

312	**56**	1q. slate-violet		45	45
313	**57**	2q. sepia		65	65
314	–	5q. green		95	75
315	**56**	10q. olive-green		95	1·10
316	**57**	15q. scarlet		1·40	1·40
317	–	25q. pale blue		2·75	2·75
318	**56**	50q. deep blue-green		7·00	4·75
319	**57**	1f. bright violet		18·00	8·50
320	–	2f. chestnut		23·00	13·00
312/320 Set of 9				50·00	30·00
MS320a 140×140 mm. 20q. purple (Type **56**), 30q. olive-brown (Type **57**), 40q. scarlet (as 5q.)				30·00	£200

Design: Vert—5q., 25q., 2f. As T **57**, but Eagle with opened wings (Liberated Albania).

58 Countess Geraldine Apponyi and King Zog

1938 (25 Apr). Royal Wedding. P 14.

321	**58**	1q. deep violet		50	90
322		2q. chestnut		50	90
323		5q. green		50	90
324		10q. olive-green		1·90	1·80
325		15q. scarlet		1·90	1·80
326		25q. bright blue		4·75	3·25
327		50q. deep blue-green		9·75	7·50
328		1f. bright violet		20·00	14·50
321/328 Set of 8				36·00	28·00
MS328a 110×140 mm: 2 each 20q. purple, 30q. olive-brown				55·00	£225

59 National Emblems

60 King Zog

1938 (30 Aug). Tenth Anniversary of Accession. Inscr as in Types **59/60**. P 14.

329	–	1q. deep purple		45	80
		a. Imperf between (vert pair)			
330	**59**	2q. vermilion		45	80
331	–	5q. myrtle green		95	80
332	**60**	10q. chestnut		95	1·40
333	–	15q. scarlet		1·90	1·70
334	**60**	25q. dull ultramarine		2·40	1·90
335	**59**	50q. black		17·00	8·50
336	**60**	1f. deep grey-green		23·00	12·50
329/336 Set of 8				42·00	26·00
MS336a 110×65 mm. 15q. scarlet (No. 333), 20q. grey-green (Type **59**), 30q. violet (Type **60**)				42·00	£160

Design: 1q., 5q., 15q. As T **60**, but Queen Geraldine's portrait. This issue was only on sale for three days (30 Aug-1 Sept).

IX. Italian Occupation

7 April 1939–September 1943

Mbledhja Kushtetuëse 12-IV-1939 XVII
(**61**)

1939 (12 Apr).

*(a) POSTAGE. Optd with T **61**, sideways (reading up) on vert designs*

337	**49**	1q. slate		1·80	1·80
		a. '2' with straight foot		1·80	1·80
338		2q. vermilion		1·80	1·80
339	**50**	5q. green		1·40	1·40
		a. '2' with straight foot		1·40	1·40
340		10q. scarlet		1·40	1·40
341		15q. sepia		3·00	3·75
342		25q. blue		3·25	3·75
343	**49**	50q. blue-green		4·50	5·00
		a. '2' with straight foot			
		ab. Opt inverted		£100	£150
344	**51**	1f. violet		5·75	6·25
345		2f. slate-blue		7·25	8·75
346	**51a**	3f. grey-green		17·00	23·00
347		5f. brown		23·00	31·00

*(b) AIR. Optd horiz with T **61** or (No. 350) additionally surch '20 QIND'*

348	**53**	5q. green		6·50	9·50
349		15q. scarlet		6·50	9·50
350		20q. on 50q. deep olive		11·50	16·00
337/350 Set of 14				85·00	£110

62 Gheg

64 Broken Columns, Botrint

63 King Victor Emmanuel

65 King and Fiat G18V on Tirana–Rome Service

1939–40. P 14.

(a) POSTAGE

351	**62**	1q. slate-blue (1.1.40)		1·20	65
352	–	2q. olive-brown (1.1.40)		1·20	65
353	–	3q. red-brown (1.1.40)		1·20	65
354	–	5q. green (2.11.39)		1·70	40
355	**63**	10q. brown (8.39)		1·70	40
356	–	15q. scarlet (8.39)		1·70	40
357	–	25q. bright blue (8.39)		1·90	1·50
358	–	30q. bright violet (8.39)		2·75	2·75
359	–	50q. slate-violet (1.40)		5·25	3·25
360	–	65q. brown-lake (10.39)		12·00	13·50
361	–	1f. blue-green (24.12.39)		14·00	10·50
362	–	2f. lake (24.12.39)		28·00	24·00
363	**64**	3f. olive-black (24.12.39)		50·00	50·00
364	–	5f. slate-purple (24.12.39)		65·00	65·00

(b) AIR

365	**65**	20q. brown (4.8.39)		£110	23·00
351/365 Set of 15				£275	£180

Designs: As T **62**—2q. Tosk man; 3q. Gheg woman; 50q. Tosk woman. As T **63**—5q., 65q. Profile portrait of King Victor Emmanuel. As T **64**—1f. Krujë Fortress; 2f. Bridge over River Kiri at Mes; 5f. Amphitheatre ruins at Berat.

66 Sheep farming   D **67** Arms of Albania

1940 (20 Mar). AIR. As T **66** (various designs). P 14.
366		5q. green	2·50	2·00
367		15q. scarlet	2·50	2·40
368		20q. blue	5·75	4·50
369		50q. brown	8·00	10·50
370		1f. blue-green	11·00	14·50
371		2f. black	21·00	26·00
372		3f. purple	38·00	39·00
366/372 *Set of 7*			80·00	90·00

Designs: (Savoia Marchetti SM.75 aeroplane and) Horiz—5q. T **66**; 20q. King of Italy and Durrës harbour; 1f. Bridge over River Kiri at Mes. Vert—15q. Aerial route map; 50q. Girl and valley; 2f. Archway and wall, Durrës; 3f. Women in North Epirus.

1940 (1 Mar). POSTAGE DUE. P 14.
D373	D **67**	4q. vermilion	55·00	85·00
D374		10q. bright violet	55·00	85·00
D375		20q. brown	55·00	85·00
D376		30q. blue	55·00	85·00
D377		50q. carmine	55·00	85·00
D373/D377 *Set of 5*			£250	£375

E **67** King Victor Emmanuel   **67** King Victor Emmanuel

1940. EXPRESS LETTER. T E **67** and similar type inscr 'POSTAT EXPRES'. P 14.
E373		25q. bright violet	11·00	13·00
E374		50q. vermilion	23·00	25·00

1942 (Apr). Third Anniversary of Italian Occupation. P 14.
373	**67**	5q. green	2·75	3·25
374		10q. sepia	2·75	3·25
375		15q. scarlet	2·75	3·25
376		25q. blue	2·75	3·25
377		65q. red-brown	9·75	11·50
378		1f. slate-green	9·75	11·50
379		2f. dull purple	9·75	11·50
373/379 *Set of 7*			36·00	43·00

1 QIND.
(**68**)   **69**

1942 (Aug). No. 352 surch with T **68**.
380		1q. on 2q. olive-brown	3·75	5·00

1943 (1 Apr). Anti-Tuberculosis Fund. P 14.
381	**69**	5q. +5q. green	2·40	2·75
382		10q. +10q. olive-brown	2·40	2·75
383		15q. +10q. carmine	2·40	2·75
384		25q. +15q. blue	2·40	3·75
385		30q. +20q. violet	2·40	3·75
386		50q. +25q. orange	2·50	3·75
387		65q. +30q. grey-black	3·50	5·00
388		1f. +40q. brown	5·75	8·25
381/388 *Set of 8*			21·00	29·00

X. German Occupation

September 1943–29 November 1944

14 Shtator 1943 1 Qind.
(**70**)

71 War Refugees

1943.
(a) Nos. 352/363 surch (or optd only as T **70**, in purple-brown (15q.) or red (others).
389	–	1q. on 3q. red-brown	1·90	13·00
		a. '1944' for '1943'	£350	£800
390	–	2q. olive-brown	1·90	13·00
		a. '1643' for '1943'	£350	£800
		b. '1948' for '1943'	£350	£800
391	–	3q. red-brown	1·90	13·00
		a. '1643' for '1943'	£350	£800
		b. '1948' for '1943'	£350	£800
		c. '1944' for '1943'	£350	£800
392	–	5q. green	1·90	13·00
		a. Opt inverted	£550	
		b. '1948' for '1943'	£350	£800
393	63	10q. brown	1·90	13·00
		a. Opt inverted	£550	
		b. '1948' for '1943'	£350	£800
394	–	15q. scarlet	1·90	13·00
		a. '1643' for '1943'	£325	£550
395	–	25q. bright blue	1·90	13·00
		a. '1643' for '1943'	£350	£800
		b. '1948' for '1943'	£350	£800
396	–	30q. bright violet	1·90	13·00
397	–	50q. on 65q. brown-lake	2·50	20·00
		a. '1944' for '1943'	£350	£800
398	–	65q. brown-lake	2·50	20·00
		a. '1944' for '1943'	60·00	£130
399	–	1f. blue-green	17·00	39·00
		a. '1944' for '1943'	£350	£850
400	–	2f. lake	21·00	£130
401	64	3f. olive-black	£140	£325

(b) EXPRESS LETTER. No. E373 optd as in T **70**, in lake-brown
E402	E **67**	25q. bright violet	55·00	50·00
389/E402 *Set of 14*			£225	£600

Designs: Nos. 389, 391 Gheg Women; No. 390 Tosk Man; No. 392 Tosk Woman; Nos. 397/398 Profile portait of King Victo Emmanuel; No. 399 Krujë Fortress; No. 400 Bridge over River Kivi at Mes.
There were several settings of the overprint. One setting contained two errors, '1643' and '1948' on positions 29 and 51; the '1944' error on the qind values is on position 18 of a different setting.
The '1' in '14' and '1943', and also in the surcharge on No. 389, is found in two different fonts: with a horizontal serif at the top or with a shorter oblique serif. Different combinations are found throughout the settings, with the conjunction of two oblique-serifed figures being the least common.

(Photo State Ptg Wks, Vienna)

1944 (22 Sept). War Refugees Relief Fund. P 14.
402	71	5q. +5q. green	7·75	26·00
403		10q. +5q. brown	7·75	26·00
404		15q. +5q. lake	7·75	26·00
405		25q. +10q. blue	7·75	26·00
406		1f. +50q. olive	7·75	26·00
407		2f. +1f. violet	7·75	26·00
408		3f. +1f.50 orange	7·75	26·00
402/408 *Set of 7*			49·00	£160

XI. Independent State

22 October 1944–11 January 1946

QEVERIJA DEMOKRAT. E SHQIPERISE 22-X-1944
= 0 60 =
(**72**)

1943 ÇL. 1945
J.Z. 10 KORRIK SHQ
FR SHQ 2
= =
(**73**)

1945 (4 Jan). Nos. 353/358 and 360/362 surch as T **72** or with similar surch.
409		30q. on 3q. red-brown	6·50	17·00

410		40q. on 5q. green		6·50	17·00
411		50q. on 10q. brown		6·50	17·00
412		60q. on 15q. scarlet		6·50	17·00
413		80q. on 25q. bright blue (R.)		6·50	17·00
414		1f. on 30q. bright violet (R.)		6·50	17·00
415		2f. on 65q. brown-lake		6·50	17·00
416		3f. on 1f. blue-green		6·50	17·00
417		5f. on 2f. lake		6·50	17·00
409/417 Set of 9				55·00	£140

On Nos. 416/417 the second word is spelt in full: 'DEMOKRATIKE'.

1945 (10 July). Second Anniversary of Formation of People's Army. Surch as T **73**. Star in red.

418	**49**	30q. on 1q. slate		4·50	8·50
419		60q. on 1q. slate		4·50	8·50
420		80q. on 1q. slate		4·50	8·50
421		1f. on 1q. slate		8·75	17·00
422		2f. on 2q. vermilion		10·50	19·00
423		3f. on 50q. blue-green		22·00	36·00
424	**51**	5f. on 2f. slate-blue		27·00	55·00
418/424 Set of 7				75·00	£140

(74)

1945 (4 May). Red Cross Week. Surch as T **74**, in carmine.

425	**69**	30q. +15q. on 5q.+5q. green		11·50	18·00
426		50q. +25q. on 10q.+10q. olive-brown		11·50	18·00
427		1f. +50q. on 15q.+10q. carmine		29·00	37·00
428		2f. +1f. on 25q.+15q. blue		40·00	50·00
425/428 Set of 4				85·00	£110

75 Labinot

1945 (28 Nov). Horiz designs as T **75**. Typo. P 11½.

429	**75**	20q. blue-green		65	1·80
430		30q. orange		90	2·75
431	–	40q. brown		90	2·75
432	–	60q. claret		1·30	3·75
433	–	1f. rose-red		3·25	7·75
434	–	3f. blue		22·00	32·00
429/434 Set of 6				26·00	46·00

Designs: 40q., 60q. Bridge at Berat; 1f., 3f. Permet landscape.

Most stamps of this issue on the market are forgeries which can be recognised as they are lithographed and perf 11.

```
QSAMBLEJA
KUSHTETUESE
```

```
10 KALLNUER 1946
```
(76)

1946 (10 Jan). Constitutional Assembly. Nos. 429/434 optd with T **76**.

435	**75**	20q. blue-green		2·00	2·50
436		30q. orange		2·50	3·25
437	–	40q. brown		3·25	3·75
438	–	60q. claret		5·25	6·25
439	–	1f. rose-red		20·00	23·00
440	–	3f. blue		33·00	38·00
435/440 Set of 6				60·00	70·00

Lithographed forgeries exist of this and of Nos. 446/457.

XII. People's Republic

11 January 1946–29 April 1991

77 Globe, Dove and Olive branch   (77a)

1946 (8 Mar). International Women's Congress. Typo.

A. P 11½

441A	**77**	20q. mauve and red		65	1·90
442A		40q. lilac and red		1·30	2·50
443A		50q. violet and red		2·50	3·75
444A		1f. blue and red		5·25	7·50
445A		2f. deep blue and red		6·50	12·50
441A/445A Set of 5				14·50	25·00

B. Imperf

441B	**77**	20q. mauve and red		65	1·90
442B		40q. lilac and red		1·30	2·50
443B		50q. violet and red		2·50	3·75
444B		1f. blue and red		5·25	7·50
445B		2f. deep blue and red		6·50	12·50
441B/445B Set of 5				14·50	25·00

1946 (1 July). Proclamation of Albanian People's Republic. Nos. 429/434 optd with T **77a**.

446	**75**	20q. blue-green		1·30	1·90
447		30q. orange		2·00	2·50
448	–	40q. brown		3·25	5·00
449	–	60q. claret		6·50	9·50
450	–	1f. rose-red		20·00	25·00
451	–	3f. blue		33·00	38·00
446/451 Set of 6				60·00	75·00

Nos. 446/457 were overprinted on a new printing of Nos. 429/434, with slightly different shades and ribbed gum.

```
KONGRESI
K.K.SH.
24-25-11-46
+0.15
```
(78)   **79** Athletes

1946 (16 July). Albanian Red Cross Congress. Nos. 429/434 surch as T **78**. Cross in red.

452	**75**	20q. +10q. blue-green		29·00	44·00
453		30q. +15q. orange		29·00	44·00
454	–	40q. +20q. brown		29·00	44·00
455	–	60q. +30q. claret		29·00	44·00
456	–	1f. +50q. rose-red		29·00	44·00
457	–	3f. +1f.50 blue		29·00	44·00
452/457 Set of 6				£160	£250

1946 (6 Oct). Balkan Games, Tirana. Litho. P 11½.

458	**79**	1q. blackish green		20·00	15·00
459		2q. light green		20·00	15·00
460		5q. brown		20·00	15·00
461		10q. rose-red		20·00	15·00
462		20q. blue		20·00	15·00
463		40q. lilac		20·00	15·00
464		1f. orange		46·00	44·00
458/464 Set of 7				£150	£120

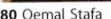

80 Qemal Stafa   **81** Railway Construction

1947 (5 May). Fifth Death Anniversary of Qemal Stafa (Communist activist). Litho. P 13×11½.

465	**80**	20q. brown and yellow-brown	16·00	19·00
466		28q. deep blue and blue	16·00	19·00
467		40q. deep brown and brown	16·00	19·00
465/467 Set of 3			43·00	50·00

MS467*a* 180×210 mm. Nos. 465/467. Imperf. No gum ... £140 £160

1947 (16 May). Durrës–Elbasan Railway. Litho. P 11½×12.

468	**81**	1q. black and drab	6·50	2·10
469		4q. deep green and green	6·50	2·10
		a. Perf 13×12½		
470		10q. black-brown and light brown	6·50	2·50
471		15q. brown-lake and rose-red	6·50	2·50
472		20q. blue-black and slate-blue	13·00	3·25
		a. Perf 13×12½		
473		28q. deep blue and light blue	20·00	3·75
		a. Perf 13×12½		
474		40q. maroon and deep reddish purple	39·00	23·00
		a. Perf 13×12½		
475		68q. deep brown and red-brown (P 13×12½)	47·00	38·00
468/475 Set of 8			£130	70·00

The 1q. is inscribed 'REPUBLIKA ROPULLORE' (instead of 'POPULLORE'); the other values were similarly inscribed but the leg of the 'R' has been erased, although still visible on some values, to form a 'P'.

82 Partisans

83 Enver Hoxha and Vasil Shanto

1947 (10 July). Fourth Anniversary of Formation of People's Army. Designs dated 1943–1947. Litho. P 11½.

476	**82**	16q. brown and orange-brown	13·00	12·50
477	**83**	20q. deep brown and brown	13·00	12·50
478	–	28q. deep blue and blue	13·00	12·50
479	–	40q. brown and mauve	13·00	12·50
476/479 Set of 4			47·00	45·00

Designs: Horiz—28q. Infantry column. Vert—40q. Portrait of Vojo Kushi.

New Currency

84 Ruined Conference Building

85 War Invalids

1947 (16 Sept). Fifth Anniversary of Peza Conference. Litho. P 11½.

480	**84**	2l. purple and mauve	8·50	9·50
481		2l.50 deep blue and blue	8·50	9·50

1947 (17 Nov). First Congress of War Invalids. Photo. P 12½×11½.

482	**85**	1l. red	22·00	19·00

86 Peasants

87 Burning Village

1947 (17 Nov). Agrarian Reform. Various designs as T **86** inscr REFORMA AGRARE. Photo. P 11½×12½ (horiz) or 12½×11½ (vert).

483		1l.50 purple	11·50	12·50
484		2l. brown	11·50	12·50
485		2l.50 grey-blue	11·50	12·50
486		3l. rose-red	11·50	12·50
483/486 Set of 4			41·00	45·00

Designs: Horiz—1l.50, T **86**; 2l. Banquet; 2l.50, Peasants rejoicing. Vert—3l. Soldier being chaired.

1947 (29 Nov). Third Anniversary of the Liberation. Horiz designs as T **87**, inscr '29-XI-1944-1947'. Photo. P 11½×12½.

487	1l.50 red	6·50	6·25
488	2l.50 maroon	6·50	6·25
489	5l. ultramarine and pale blue	13·00	10·00
490	8l. mauve	20·00	15·00
491	12l. brown	33·00	25·00
487/491 Set of 5		70·00	55·00

Designs: 1l.50, T **87**; 2l.50, Riflemen; 5l. Machine-gunners; 8l. Mounted soldier; 12l. Infantry column.

(87*a*)

88 Railway Construction

1948 (22 Feb). Nos. 446/451 surch in 'Lek', as T **87***a*.

492	0l.50 on 30q. orange	65	90
	a. 'Lck' for 'Lek'		
493	1l. on 20q. blue-green	1·30	1·50
494	2l.50 on 60q. claret	3·25	4·50
495	3l. on 1f. rose-red	4·50	5·75
496	5l. on 3f. blue	9·75	9·50
497	12l. on 40q. brown	26·00	25·00
492/497 Set of 6		41·00	42·00

(Litho State Ptg Works, Belgrade)

1948 (1 June). Durrës–Tirana Railway. P 11½.

498	**88**	0l.50 claret and crimson	3·25	1·90
499		1l. green and greenish black	3·25	2·10
500		1l.50 rose and scarlet	5·25	3·25
501		2l.50 pale brown and brown	7·75	4·00
502		5l. light blue and blue	13·00	7·50
503		8l. orange-red and brown	22·00	12·50
504		12l. reddish purple and purple	26·00	15·00
505		20l. grey and black	50·00	31·00
498/505 Set of 8			£120	70·00

89 Parade of Infantrymen

90 Labourer, Globe and Flag

(Litho Belgrade)

1948 (10 July). Fifth Anniversary of People's Army. T **89** and similar type inscr '10 KORRIK 1943–10 KORRIK 1948'. P 11½.

506	**89**	2l.50 reddish brown	6·50	6·25
507		5l. blue	9·00	8·75
508		8l. slate (Troops in action)	17·00	12·50
506/508 Set of 3			29·00	25·00

(Photo State Ptg Wks, Budapest)

1949 (1 May). Labour Day. P 12½×12.

509	**90**	2l.50 sepia	2·00	3·25
510		5l. red	4·00	5·00
511		8l. brown-purple	7·25	8·25
509/511 Set of 3			12·00	15·00

91 Soldier and Map

92 Albanian and Kremlin Tower

93 General Enver Hoxha

ALBANIA 1949

(Photo Budapest)

1949 (10 July). Sixth Anniversary of People's Army. P 12½×12.

512	**91**	2l.50 brown	2·00	3·25
513		5l. blue	4·00	5·00
514		8l. brown-orange	7·25	9·50
512/514 Set of 3			12·00	16·00

(Photo Budapest)

1949 (10 Sept). Albanian–Soviet Amity. P 12½×12.

515	**92**	2l.50 brown	2·00	3·25
516		5l. blue	4·50	6·25

(Eng J. Schmidt. Recess State Ptg Wks, Prague)

1949 (16 Oct). P 12½.

517	**93**	0l.50 reddish violet	40	40
518		1l. blue-green	40	40
519		1l.50 rose-carmine	65	40
520		2l.50 brown	1·30	40
521		5l. ultramarine	2·50	1·30
522		8l. brown-purple	5·25	3·75
523		12l. bright purple	13·00	6·25
524		20l. grey-blue	16·00	8·75
517/524 Set of 8			36·00	19·00

94 Soldier and Flag   **95** Street Fighting   **96** Joseph Stalin

(Photo Prague)

1949 (29 Nov). Fifth Anniversary of Liberation. P 12×12½ (horiz), 12½×12 (vert).

525	**94**	2l.50 brown	1·30	1·90
526	**95**	3l. brown-red	1·30	3·75
527	**94**	5l. violet	4·00	5·00
528	**95**	8l. black	7·75	9·50
525/528 Set of 4			13·00	18·00

(Photo Prague)

1949 (21 Dec). 70th Birthday of Joseph Stalin. P 12½×12.

529	**96**	2l.50 yellow-brown	1·30	2·50
530		5l. blue	3·25	4·50
531		8l. lake	8·50	10·50
529/531 Set of 3			11·50	16·00

97   **98** Sami Frashëri

(Photo Prague)

1950 (1 July). 75th Anniversary of Universal Postal Union. P 12×12½.

532	**97**	5l. blue	3·25	8·25
533		8l. purple	6·50	11·50
534		12l. black	13·00	21·00
532/534 Set of 3			20·00	37·00

(Photo Prague)

1950 (5 Nov). Literary Jubilee. T **98** and portraits inscr '1950–JUBILEU I SHKRIMTAREVE TE RILINDJES'. P 14.

535		2l. blue-green (Type **98**)	2·00	1·90
536		2l.50 brown (A. Zako (Çajupi))	2·50	3·25
537		3l. brown-red (N. Frashëri)	5·25	6·25
538		5l. blue (K. Kristoforidhi)	6·50	7·50
535/538 Set of 4			14·50	17·00

99 Vuno-Himarë   **100** Stafa and Shanto

(Eng B. Housa (0l.50l., 5l.), J. Schmidt (2l., 20l.), B. Roule (1l., 10l.).Recess Prague)

1950 (15 Dec). AIR. Horiz designs as T **99**. P 12½.

539	**99**	0l.50 black	90	1·30
540	–	1l. brown-purple	90	1·30
541	–	2l. blue	2·00	2·50
542	**99**	5l. blue-green	6·50	5·00
543	–	10l. greenish blue	17·00	8·75
544	–	20l. violet	33·00	12·50
539/544 Set of 6			55·00	28·00

Designs: Douglas DC-3 aeroplane over—1l., 10l. Rozafat-Shkodër; 2l., 20l. Kështjellë-Butrinto.

(Des S. Toptani. Photo Budapest)

1950 (25 Dec). Albanian Patriots. Portraits as T **100** inscr 'LAVDI HERONJVE TE POPULLIT'. P 14.

545	2l. green	1·30	1·30
546	2l.50 violet	2·00	1·90
547	3l. scarlet	4·00	3·75
548	5l. blue	6·50	6·25
549	8l. brown	13·00	12·50
545/549 Set of 5		24·00	23·00

Portraits: 2l. Ahmet Haxhia, Hydajet Lezha, Naim Gjylbegu, Ndoc Mazi and Ndoc Deda; 2l.50, Asim Zeneli, Ali Demi, Kajo Karafili, Dervish Hekali and Asim Vokshi; 3l. Abaz Shehu, Baba Faja, Zoja Çure, Mustafa Matohiti and Gjok Doçi; 5l. Perlat Rexhepi, Koci Bako, Vojo Kushi, Reshit Çollaku and Misto Mame; 8l. T **100**.

101 Arms and Flags   **102** Skanderbeg

(Des and eng S. Toptani. Recess Budapest)

1951 (11 Jan). Fifth Anniversary of Republic. P 14.

550	**101**	2l.50 carmine	2·50	3·75
551		5l. blue	5·25	7·50
552		8l. black	8·50	11·50
550/552 Set of 3			14·50	20·00

(Recess Budapest)

1951 (1 Mar). 483rd Anniversary of Death of Skanderbeg (patriot). P 14.

553	**102**	2l.50 brown	2·50	3·25
554		5l. violet	5·25	6·25
555		8l. bistre	8·50	9·50
553/555 Set of 3			14·50	17·00

103 General Enver Hoxha and Assembly

(Photo Budapest)

1951 (24 May). Seventh Anniversary of Permet Congress. P 12.

556	**103**	2l.50 brown	1·30	1·90
557		3l. carmine-lake	1·30	2·50
558		5l. blue	3·25	4·50
559		8l. mauve	5·75	7·50
556/559 Set of 4			10·50	15·00

104 Child and Globe   **105** Enver Hoxha and Meeting-house

1951 ALBANIA

(Des S. Toptani. Photo Budapest)

1951 (1 June). International Children's Day. T **104** and horiz type inscr 'DITA NDERKOMBETARE E FEMIJES'. P 12.

560	**104**	2l. green	3·25	2·50
561	–	2l.50 brown	4·50	3·25
562	–	3l. scarlet	5·75	3·75
563	**104**	5l. blue	9·00	4·50
560/563 Set of 4			20·00	12·50

Design: 2l.50, 3l. Nurse weighing baby.

(Photo Budapest)

1951 (8 Nov). Tenth Anniversary of Foundation of Albanian Communist Party. P 14.

564	**105**	2l.50 yellow-brown	90	1·30
565		3l. brown-lake	90	1·60
566		5l. deep blue	2·10	2·50
567		8l. grey-black	4·00	4·00
564/567 Set of 4			7·00	8·50

106 Young Partisans   (**107**)

(Photo Budapest)

1951 (23 Nov). Tenth Anniversary of Albanian Young Communists' Union. T **106** and similar types inscr '1941–1951'. P 12.

568	2l.50 sepia	1·30	1·90
569	5l. blue	2·50	3·25
570	8l. reddish purple	5·75	6·25
568/570 Set of 3		8·50	10·50

Designs: 2l.50, T **106**; 5l. Schoolgirl, railway, tractor and factories; 8l. Miniature portraits of Stafa, Spiru, Mame and Kondi.

1952 (26 Dec)–**53**. AIR. Nos. 541/543 surch as T **107**.

571	0.50l. on 2l. blue	£275	£225
572	0.50l. on 5l. blue-green (14.3.53)	60·00	43·00
573	2l.50 on 5l. blue-green	£450	£250
574	2l.50 on 10l. greenish blue (14.3.53)	70·00	55·00
571/574 Set of 4		£750	£500

108 Factory   **109** Soldiers and Flags

(Photo Budapest)

1953 (1 Aug). Various designs as T **108**. P 12.

575	0l.50 Venetian red	65	40
576	1l. deep green	1·30	40
577	2l.50 sepia	1·30	65
578	3l. brown-carmine	2·00	1·30
579	5l. blue	3·25	1·90
580	8l. deep olive	4·00	2·50
581	12l. reddish purple	6·50	3·75
582	20l. indigo	9·00	8·25
575/582 Set of 8		25·00	17·00

Designs: Horiz—0l.50, T **108**; 1l. Canal; 2l.50, Girl and cotton mill; 3l. Girl and sugar factory; 5l. Film studio; 8l. Textile worker and machinery; 20l. Hydro-electric dam. Vert—12l. Pylon and hydro-electric station.

1954 (29 Nov). Tenth Anniversary of Liberation. Photo. P 12½×12.

583	**109**	0l.50 deep lilac	40	40
584		1l. yellow-green	90	90
585		2l.50 yellow-brown	1·30	1·30
586		3l. carmine	2·50	2·50
587		5l. indigo	4·00	3·75
588		8l. brown-purple	6·50	6·25
583/588 Set of 6			14·00	13·50

110 First Albanian School   **111**

(Photo Budapest)

1956 (23 Feb). 70th Anniversary of Albanian Schools. T **110** and another horiz design inscr '1886 1956'. P 12×12½.

589	**110**	2l. reddish purple	65	65
590	–	2l.50 dull green	90	1·30
591	–	5l. blue	2·30	2·50
592	**110**	10l. turquoise-blue	7·75	4·50
589/592 Set of 4			10·50	8·00

Design: 2l.50, 5l. Portraits of P. Sotiri, P. N. Luarasi and N. Naci.

(Recess Prague)

1957 (1 June). 15th Anniversary of Albanian Workers' Party. T **111** and similar horiz designs inscr 'VJETORI I THEME-LIMIT P. P SH. 1941 1956'. P 11½.

593	2l.50 brown	70	65
594	5l. violet-blue	2·00	90
595	8l. reddish purple	2·75	3·50
593/595 Set of 3		5·00	4·50

Designs: 2l.50, T **111**; 5l. Party headquarters, Tirana; 8l. Marx and Lenin.

112 Congress Emblem   **113** Lenin and Cruiser *Aurora*

(Des S. I. Murati. Recess Prague)

1957 (4 Oct). Fourth World Trade Unions Congress, Leipzig. P 12×11½.

596	**112**	2l.50 dull slate-purple	70	40
597		3l. rose-red	70	40
598		5l. blue	70	50
599		8l. deep green	3·50	3·25
596/599 Set of 4			5·00	4·00

(Des S. Toptani. Photo State Ptg Wks, Tirana)

1957 (7 Nov). 40th Anniversary of Russian Revolution. P 10½.

600	**113**	2l.50 chocolate	70	65
601		5l. deep violet-blue	2·00	1·90
602		8l. olive-black	2·00	1·90
600/602 Set of 3			4·25	4·00

> **PRINTERS**. The following issues were printed at the State Printing Works, Tirana by lithography, *unless otherwise stated*.

114 Raising the Flag   **115** N. Veqilharxhi   **116** L. Gurakuqi

(Des S. Toptani)

1957 (28 Nov). 45th Anniversary of Proclamation of Independence. P 10½.

603	**114**	1l.50 reddish purple	70	65
604		2l.50 bistre-brown	1·40	65
605		5l. blue	2·00	1·90
606		8l. green	5·50	2·50
603/606 Set of 4			8·75	5·25

(Des S. Toptani)

1958 (1 Feb). 160th Birth Anniversary of Veqilharxhi (patriot). P 10½.

607	**115**	2l.50 deep brown	70	65
608		5l. deep violet-blue	1·40	65
609		8l. reddish purple	4·00	1·90
607/609 Set of 3			5·50	3·00

(Des S. Toptani)

1958 (15 Apr). Removal of Ashes of Gurakuqi (patriot). P 10½.

610	**116**	1l.50 slate-green	70	40
611		2l.50 deep brown	70	50
612		5l. blue	70	65
613		8l. blackish brown	4·00	1·60
610/613 Set of 4			5·50	2·75

ALBANIA 1958

117 Freedom Fighters   **118** Soldiers in Action

(Des S. Toptani)

1958 (1 July). 50th Anniversary of Battle of Mashkullore. T **117** and similar vert design. P 10½.

614	117	2l.50 brown-ochre	70	40
615	–	3l. green	70	40
616	117	5l. Prussian blue	2·00	65
617	–	8l. chestnut	3·50	1·80
614/617	Set of 4		6·25	3·00

Design: 3l., 8l. Tree and buildings.

(Des S. Toptani)

1958 (10 July). 15th Anniversary of Albanian People's Army. T **118** and similar horiz design. P 10½.

618	118	1l.50 blue-green	40	40
619	–	2l.50 chocolate	40	40
620	118	8l. rose-carmine	1·20	1·10
621	–	11l. pale blue	2·75	2·50
618/621	Set of 4		4·25	4·00

Design: 2l.50, 11l. Tank-driver, sailor, infantryman and tanks.

119 Bust of Apollo and Butrinto Amphitheatre   **120** F. Joliot-Curie and Council Emblem

1959 (25 Jan). Cultural Monuments Week. P 10½.

622	119	2l.50 chocolate	70	65
623		6l.50 turquoise-green	1·40	1·30
624		11l. blue	4·00	2·50
622/624	Set of 3		5·50	4·00

1959 (1 July). Tenth Anniversary of World Peace Council. P 10½.

625	120	1l.50 rose-carmine	2·75	65
626		2l.50 reddish violet	5·50	1·90
627		11l. blue	13·50	6·25
625/627	Set of 3		20·00	8·00

121 Basketball   **122** Soldier

1959 (20 Nov). First National Spartacist Games. T **121** and similar vert designs inscr 'SPARTAKIADA 1959' etc. P 10½.

628		1l.50 reddish violet	1·40	40
629		2l.50 emerald	1·40	40
630		5l. carmine	2·75	1·10
631		11l. ultramarine	8·00	4·50
628/631	Set of 4		12·00	5·75

Designs: 1l.50, T **121**; 2l.50, Football; 5l. Running; 11l. Runners with torches.

1959 (29 Nov). 15th Anniversary of Liberation. T **122** and similar vert designs inscr '1944–1959'. P 10½.

632		1l.50 rose-carmine	1·40	40
633		2l.50 red-brown	1·80	40
634		3l. blue-green	2·50	55
635		6l.50 red	5·00	4·50
632/635 Set of 4			9·75	5·25
MS635a 141×96 mm. Nos. 632/635 but in rose-carmine. Imperf.			13·00	18·00

Designs: 1l.50, T **122**; 2l.50, Security guard; 3l. Harvester; 6l.50, Laboratory workers.

123 Mother and Child   **124**

1959 (5 Dec). Tenth Anniversary of Declaration of Human Rights. P 10½.

636	123	5l. greenish blue	6·75	3·75
MS636a 72×65 mm. No. 636. Imperf			9·00	13·00

1960 (8 Mar). 50th Anniversary of International Women's Day. P 10½.

637	124	2l.50 chocolate	1·40	65
638		11l. claret	4·75	1·90

125 Congress Building   **126** A. Moisiu

1960 (25 Mar). 40th Anniversary of Lushnjë Congress. P 10½.

639	125	2l.50 bistre-brown	70	45
640		7l.50 Prussian blue	2·00	1·60

1960 (20 Apr). 80th Birth Anniversary of Moisiu (actor). P 10½.

641	126	3l. chocolate	70	65
642		11l. deep bluish green	2·75	1·30

127 Lenin   **128** Vaso Pasha

1960 (22 Apr). 90th Birth Anniversary of Lenin. P 10½.

643	127	4l. deep turquoise-blue	2·00	1·10
644		11l. crimson	6·75	5·00

1960 (5 May). 80th Anniversary of Albanian Alphabet Study Association. T **128** and similar vert designs. P 10½.

645		1l. deep olive	70	40
646		1l.50 brown	70	40
647		6l.50 blue	2·00	75
648		11l. red	6·00	2·50
645/648	Set of 4		8·50	3·75

Designs: 1l. T **128**; 1l.50, Jani Vreto; 6l.50, Sami Frashëri; 11l. Association statutes.

129 Frontier Guard   **130** Family with Policeman

1960 (12 May). 15th Anniversary of Frontier Force. P 10½.

649	129	1l.50 cerise	70	65
650		11l. greenish blue	3·50	1·90

1960 (14 May). 15th Anniversary of People's Police. P 10½.

651	130	1l.50 green	70	65
652		8l.50 brown	4·00	1·90

131 Normal School, Elbasan   **132** Soldier and Cannon

1960 ALBANIA

1960 (30 May). 50th Anniversary of Normal School, Elbasan. P 10½.
653	**131**	5l. bluish green	2·75	1·90
654		6l.50 purple	2·75	1·90

1960 (2 Aug). 40th Anniversary of Battle of Vlörë. P 10½.
655	**132**	1l.50 sepia	70	65
656		2l.50 brown-purple	1·40	1·10
657		5l. deep blue	2·75	1·30
655/657	Set of 3		4·25	2·75

133 Tirana Clock Tower, Kremlin and Tupolev Tu-104A Jetliner

134 Federation Emblem

1960 (18 Aug). Second Anniversary of Tirana–Moscow Jet Air Service. P 10½.
658	**133**	1l. brown	1·40	1·00
659		7l.50 greenish blue	4·00	5·25
660		11l.50 deep grey	6·75	9·00
658/660	Set of 3		11·00	13·50

1960 (10 Nov). 15th Anniversary of World Democratic Youth Federation. P 10½.
661	**134**	1l.50 ultramarine	70	65
662		8l.50 scarlet	2·75	1·30

135 Ali Kelmendi

136 Flags of Albania and Russia, and Clasped Hands

1960 (5 Dec). 60th Birth Anniversary of Ali Kelmendi (Communist). P 10½.
663	**135**	1l.50 olive	70	65
664		11l. maroon	2·75	1·30

1961 (10 Jan). 15th Anniversary of Albanian–Soviet Friendship Society. P 10½.
665	**136**	2l. violet	70	65
666		8l. brown-purple	2·75	1·30

137 Marx and Lenin

138 Malsi e Madhe (Shkodër) Costume

1961 (13 Feb). Fourth Albanian Workers' Party Congress. P 10½.
667	**137**	2l. rose-red	70	65
668		8l. ultramarine	2·75	1·30

1961 (28 Apr). Provincial Costumes. T **138** and similar vert designs. P 10½.
669	1l. black	1·40	65
670	1l.50 brown-purple	1·40	90
671	6l.50 bright blue	5·50	2·30
672	11l. scarlet	8·00	5·75
669/672	Set of 4	14·50	8·75

Costumes: 1l. T **138**; 1l.50, Malsi e Madhe (Shkodër) (female); 6l.50, Lume; 11l. Mirdite.

139 European Otter

140 Dalmatian Pelicans

1961 (25 June). Albanian Fauna. T **139** and similar horiz designs. P 10½.
673	2l.50 grey-blue (Type **139**)	5·50	1·30
674	6l.50 deep bluish green (Eurasian Badger)	11·00	2·50
675	11l. chocolate (Brown Bear)	24·00	10·00
673/675	Set of 3	36·00	12·50

1961 (30 Sept). Birds. T **140** and similar vert designs. P 14.
676	7l.50 carmine/*pink* (Type **140**)	6·75	1·30
677	7l.50 violet/*blue* (Grey Heron)	9·50	3·75
678	11l. red-brown/*pink* (Little Egret)	17·00	4·50
676/678	Set of 3	30·00	8·50

141 Cyclamen

142 M. G. Nikolla

1961 (27 Oct). Albanian Flowers. T **141** and similar vert designs. P 14.
679	1l.50 bright purple and greenish blue (Type **141**)	2·75	65
680	8l. orange and bright reddish purple (Forsythia)	8·75	3·25
681	11l. carmine and blue-green (Lily)	11·00	3·75
679/681	Set of 3	20·00	7·00

1961 (30 Oct). 50th Birthday of Nikolla (poet). P 14.
682	**142**	0l.50 chocolate	70	65
683		8l.50 slate-green	2·00	1·90

143 Lenin and Marx on Flag

144

1961 (8 Nov). 20th Anniversary of Albanian Workers Party. P 14.
684	**143**	2l.50 red	80	65
685		7l.50 purple-brown	1·90	1·50

1961 (23 Nov). 20th Anniversary of Albanian Young Communists' Union. P 14.
686	**144**	2l.50 ultramarine	70	65
		a. Perf 10½		
687		7l.50 dull magenta	2·75	2·50

145 Yuri Gagarin and *Vostok 1*

POSTA AJRORE
(**146**)

1962 (15 Feb). World's First Manned Space Flight. P 14.
(a) POSTAGE
688	**145**	0l.50 blue	1·40	1·90

17

ALBANIA 1962

689		4l. bright purple	5·50	5·75
690		11l. deep grey-green	13·50	14·00
688/690 Set of 3			18·00	19·00

(b) AIR. Nos. 688/690 optd with T **146** in red and printed on toned paper (20 Mar)

691	**145**	0l.50 blue/*cream*	41·00	65·00
		a. Opt in black	£140	£225
692		4l. bright purple/*cream*	41·00	65·00
		a. Opt in black	£140	£225
693		11l. deep grey-green/*cream*	41·00	65·00
		a. Opt in black	£140	£225
691/693 Set of 3			£110	£180
691a/693a Set of 3			£375	£600

147 P. N. Luarasi **148** Campaign Emblem **149** Camomile

1962 (28 Feb). 50th Death Anniversary of Petro N. Luarasi (patriot). P. 14.

694	**147**	0l.50 greenish blue	70	65
695		8l.50 olive-brown	5·50	1·90

> **IMPERFORATE STAMPS.** Many Albanian stamps and miniature sheets from No. 696 onwards exist imperforate and/or in different colours from limited printings.

1962 (30 Apr). Malaria Eradication. P. 14.

696	**148**	1l.50 blue-green	70	40
697		2l.50 brown-red	70	40
698		10l. bright purple	1·40	1·30
699		11l. greenish blue	1·40	1·30
696/699 Set of 4			3·75	3·00
MS699a 90×106 mm. Nos. 696/699			41·00	50·00

1962 (10 May). Medicinal Plants. T **149** and similar vert designs. P. 14.

700		0l.50 yellow, green and blue	70	65
701		8l. green, yellow and grey	2·75	1·30
702		11l.50 violet, green and ochre	4·75	1·90
700/702 Set of 3			7·50	3·50

Designs: 0l.50, T **149**; 8l. Silver Linden; 11l.50, Sage.

150 Throwing the Javelin **151** *Sputnik 1* in orbit

1962 (31 May). Olympic Games, Tokyo (1964) (1st issue). T **150** and similar designs inscr 'TOKIO 1964'. P. 14.

703		0l.50 black and light greenish blue	40	40
704		2l.50 sepia and light brown	40	40
705		3l. black and blue	55	40
706		9l. deep purple and reddish purple	2·75	1·60
707		10l. black and greyish olive	2·75	1·60
703/707 Set of 5			6·25	4·00
MS707a 81×63 mm. 15l. (as 3l.)			47·00	70·00

Designs: Vert—0l.50, Diving; 2l.50, Pole-vaulting; 9l. T **150**; 10l. Putting the shot. Horiz—3l. Olympic flame.
See also Nos. 754/MS758a, 818/MS821a and 842/MS851a.

1962 (28 June). Cosmic Flights. T **151** and similar vert designs. P. 14.

708		0l.50 yellow-orange and bluish violet	70	80
709		1l. brown and deep bluish green	1·40	1·10
710		1l.50 red and yellow	2·00	2·30
711		20l. blue and reddish purple	13·50	7·00
708/711 Set of 4			16·00	10·00
MS711a 101×76 mm. 14l. (+6l.) brown and blue (Rocket)			80·00	95·00

Designs: 0l.50, T **151**; 1l. Dog Laika and *Sputnik 2*; 1l.50, Artificial satellite and Sun; 20l. *Lunik 3* photographing Moon.

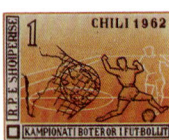 

152 Footballer and Ball in Net **153** 'Europa' and Albania Maps

1962 (3 July). World Football Championships, Chile. T **152** and similar horiz designs. P. 14.

712	**152**	1l. violet and orange	70	65
713	–	2l.50 turquoise-blue and light green	1·40	1·90
714	**152**	6l.50 bright purple and yellow-brown	1·40	2·50
715	–	15l. brown-purple and turquoise-green	4·00	3·25
712/715 Set of 4			6·75	7·50
MS715a 82×66 mm. 20l. red-brown and green (as No. 713 but larger). P 14			55·00	95·00

Design: 2l.50, 15l. As T **152** but with Globe in place of ball in net.

1962 (Aug). Tourist Publicity. T **153** and similar vert design. P. 14.

716	**153**	0l.50 red, yellow and blue-green	70	1·30
717	–	1l. red, deep purple and bright blue	1·40	3·25
718	–	2l.50 red, purple and light blue	11·00	15·00
719	**153**	11l. red, yellow and grey	15·00	22·00
716/719 Set of 4			25·00	37·00
MS719a 82×63 mm. 7l. red, yellow and violet-grey (Type **153**), 8l. carmine and violet-grey (as No. 717). P 14			55·00	95·00

Design: 1l., 2l.50, Statue and map.

154 Dardhë Woman **155** Chamois

1962 (Sept). Costumes of Albania's Southern Region. Vert designs as T **154**. P. 14.

720		0l.50 carmine-red, deep purple and blue	70	40
721		1l. purple-brown and orange-buff	70	65
722		2l.50 black, bluish violet and yellow-green	2·00	1·50
723		14l. brown-red, red-brown and light green	8·75	4·50
720/723 Set of 4			11·00	6·25

Costumes of: 0l.50, T **154**; 1l. Devoll man; 2l.50, Lunxheri woman; 14l. Gjirokastër man.

1962 (24 Oct). Albanian Animals. T **155** and similar designs. P. 14.

724		0l.50 deep purple and grey-green	70	65
725		1l. black and orange-yellow	2·75	1·30
726		1l.50 black and red-brown	3·50	1·90
727		15l. brown-red and light yellow-green	27·00	6·25
724/727 Set of 4			31·00	9·00
MS727a 72×89 mm. 20l. red-brown and yellow-green (as No. 727 but larger). P 14			£180	£225

Animals: Horiz—1l. Lynx; 1l.50, Wild Boar. Vert—0l.50, T **155**; 15l. Roe Deer.

156 Golden Eagle **157** Revolutionaries

1962 (28 Dec). 50th Anniversary of Independence. T **156** and similar vert designs. P. 14.

728		1l. red-brown and red	70	65
729		3l. black and light brown	4·75	1·30
730		16l. black and magenta	8·00	4·50
728/730 Set of 3			12·00	5·75

Designs: 1l. T **156**; 3l. Ismail Qemali; 16l. Golden Eagle over 'RPSH' fortress.

1963 ALBANIA

1963 (15 Jan). 45th Anniversary of October Revolution. T **157** and similar vert design. P 14.

731	5l. slate-violet and yellow (Type **157**)		1·60	90
732	10l. black and orange-red (Statue of Lenin)		3·75	2·30

158 Henri Dunant and Globe

159 Stalin and Battle

1963 (25 Jan). Centenary of Red Cross. Cross in red. P 14.

733	**158**	1l.50 black and claret	70	65
734		2l.50 black and light blue	1·40	65
735		6l. black and yellow-green	2·75	1·30
736		10l. black and ochre-yellow	4·75	3·25
733/736 Set of 4			8·75	5·25

1963 (2 Feb). 20th Anniversary of Battle of Stalingrad. T **159** and similar horiz design. P 14.

(a) POSTAGE

737	8l. black and deep grey-green	13·50	5·00

(b) AIR. Inscr 'AJRORE'

738	7l. crimson and deep green	13·50	5·00

Designs: 7l. 'Lenin' flag, map and tanks, etc; 8l. T **159**.

160 Nikolaev and *Vostok 3*

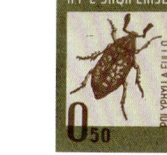

161 Crawling Cockchafer (*Polyphylla fullo*)

1963 (28 Feb). First Team Manned Space Flights. T **160** and similar designs. P 14.

739	2l.50 purple-brown and ultramarine		70	65
740	7l.50 black and light blue		2·00	1·30
741	20l. purple-brown and violet		5·50	4·50
739/741 Set of 3			7·50	5·75
MS741*a* 88×73 mm. 25l. ultramarine and purple-brown (Popovich and Nikolaev)			55·00	50·00

Designs: Horiz—7l.50, *Vostoks* 3 and 4 encircling Globe. Vert—2l.50, T **160**; 20l. Popovich and *Vostok 4*.

1963 (20 Mar). Insects. T **161** and similar vert designs. P 14.

742	0l.50 brown and yellow-green	1·60	65
743	1l.50 red-brown and light blue	2·75	1·30
744	8l. blackish purple and red	11·50	3·25
745	10l. black and greenish yellow	15·00	4·50
742/745 Set of 4		28·00	8·75

Insects: 0l.50, T **161**; 1l.50, Stag Beetle (*Lucanus cervus*); 8l. *Procerus gigas* (Ground Beetle); 10l. *Cicindela albanica* (Tiger Beetle).

162 Policeman and Allegorical Figure

163 Great Crested Grebe (*Podiceps cristatus*)

1963 (20 Mar). 20th Anniversary of State Security Police. P 14.

746	**162**	2l.50 black, purple and carmine	1·40	1·30
747		7l.50 black, lake and vermilion	4·75	3·25

1963 (20 Apr). Birds. T **163** and similar vert designs. Multicoloured. P 14.

748		0l.50 Type **163**	2·00	40
749		3l. Golden Eagle (*Aquila crysaetus*)	4·00	75
750		6l.50 Grey Partridge (*Perdix perdix*)	10·00	2·00
751		11l. Capercaillie (*Tetrao urogallus*)	13·50	3·25
748/751 Set of 4			27·00	5·75

164 Official Insignia and Postmark of 1913

165 Boxing

1963 (5 May). 50th Anniversary of First Albanian Stamps. T **164** and similar horiz design. P 14.

752	5l. brown, black, light blue and yellow	2·75	65
753	10l. green, black and carmine	4·75	2·50

Designs: 5l. T **164**; 10l. Albanian stamps of 1913, 1937 and 1962.

1963 (25 May). Olympic Games, Tokyo (1964) (2nd issue). T **165** and similar vert designs. P 12½×12.

754	2l. deep bluish green, red and yellow	80	1·30
755	3l. light brown, deep blue and orange-buff	95	2·50
756	5l. dull purple, light brown and light grey-blue	1·60	3·75
757	6l. black, grey and green	2·00	6·25
758	9l. blue and red-brown	3·50	10·00
754/758 Set of 5		8·00	21·00
MS758*a* 61×82 mm. 15l. multicoloured (Torch, rings and map). P 14.		20·00	33·00

Designs: 2l. T **165**; 3l. Basketball; 5l. Volleyball; 6l. Cycling; 9l. Gymnastics.

166 General Enver Hoxha and Labinoti Council Building

167 Yuri Gagarin

1963 (10 July). 20th Anniversary of Albanian People's Army. T **166** and similar horiz designs. P 12.

759	1l.50 yellow, black and red	70	65
760	2l.50 yellow-brown, chocolate and blue	1·40	1·30
761	5l. black, drab and blue-green	2·00	1·90
762	6l. blue, buff and red-brown	2·75	2·50
759/762 Set of 4		6·25	5·75

Designs: 1l.50, T **166**; 2l.50, Soldier with weapons; 5l. Soldier attacking; 6l. Peacetime soldier.

1963 (30 July). Soviet Cosmonauts. T **167** and similar horiz designs. Portraits in yellow and brown. P 12.

763	3l. reddish violet (Type **167**)	1·40	50
764	5l. dark blue (Titov)	1·40	65
765	7l. deep blue and grey (Nikolaev)	2·00	65
766	11l. deep blue and reddish-purple (Popovich)	4·00	1·30
767	14l. deep blue and blue-green (Bykovsky)	6·00	1·90
768	20l. blue (Tereshkova)	9·50	4·50
763/768 Set of 6		22·00	8·50

168 Volleyball (Rumania)

169 Celadon Swallowtail (*Papilio podulirius*)

1963 (31 Aug). European Sports Events, 1963 T **168** and similar horiz designs inscr '1963'. P 12×12½.

769	2l. vermilion, black and yellow-olive	70	40
770	3l. bistre, black and carmine-red	70	65
771	5l. yellow-orange, black and green	1·40	1·30
772	7l. light green, black and rose-pink	2·00	1·50
773	8l. rose, black and blue	4·75	1·90
769/773 Set of 5		8·50	5·25

Designs: 2l. T **168**; 3l. Weightlifting (Sweden); 5l. Football (European Cup); 7l. Boxing (Russia); 8l. Ladies' Rowing (Russia).

ALBANIA 1963

1963 (23 Sept). Butterflies and Moths. T **169** and similar vert designs. P 12×12½.

774		1l. black, pale greenish yellow and scarlet	70	35
775		2l. black, scarlet-vermilion and greenish blue	1·40	40
776		4l. black, greenish yellow and deep purple	2·75	1·30
777		5l. multicoloured	4·00	1·30
778		8l. black, scarlet and brown-ochre	6·75	2·50
779		10l. salmon, reddish brown and turquoise-blue	8·75	3·75
774/779 Set of 6			22·00	8·75

Designs: 1l. T **169**; 2l. Jersey Tiger Moth (*Callimorpha hera*); 4l. Brimstone (*Gonepteryx rhamni*); 5l. Death's-head Hawk Moth (*Acherontia atropos*); 8l. Orange-tip (*Euchloe cardamines*); 10l. Peacock (*Vanessa io*).

170 Lunik 1

171 Food Processing Works

1963 (31 Oct). AIR. Cosmic Flights. T **170** and similar horiz designs. P 12.

780		2l. deep olive, yellow and orange	70	50
781		3l. vermilion, greenish yellow, mauve and deep bluish green	1·40	55
782		5l. deep olive, greenish yellow, and reddish purple	2·00	65
783		8l. red, greenish yellow and slate-violet	3·50	1·30
784		12l. orange-red, orange and blue	6·75	4·50
780/784 Set of 5			13·00	6·75

Designs: 2l. T **170**; 3l. *Lunik 2*; 5l. *Lunik 3*; 8l. *Venus 1*; 12l. *Mars 1*.

1963 (15 Nov). Industrial Buildings. T **171** and similar designs. P 14.

785		2l.50 rose-red/pale pink	1·40	65
786		20l. green/pale green	5·50	2·50
787		30l. reddish purple/pale blue	13·00	5·75
788		50l. yellow-brown/pale cream	13·50	6·25
785/788 Set of 4			30·00	13·50

Designs: Vert—20l. Naphtha refinery; 30l. Fruit-bottling plant. Horiz—2l.50, T **171**; 50l. Copper-processing works.

172 Shield and Banner

173 Young Men of Three Races

1963 (24 Nov). First Army and Defence Aid Association Congress. P 12½×12.

789	**172**	2l. deep blue, red, ochre and turquoise-blue	70	65
790		8l. deep blue, red, ochre and light blue	2·75	1·90

1963 (10 Dec). 15th Anniversary of Declaration of Human Rights. P 12.

791	**173**	3l. black and yellow-ochre	70	65
792		5l. blue and yellow-ochre	1·40	1·30
793		7l. violet and yellow-ochre	3·50	2·50
791/793 Set of 3			5·00	4·00

174 Bobsleighing

175 Lenin

1963 (25 Dec). Winter Olympic Games, Innsbruck. T **174** and similar designs. P 14.

794	0l.50 black and light blue	70	40
795	2l.50 black, red and grey	95	65
796	6l.50 black, yellow and grey	1·80	90
797	12l.50 red, black and yellow-green	3·50	3·25
794/797 Set of 4		6·25	4·75

MS797*a* 56×75 mm. 12l.50, black, grey-green and blue (Ski jumper) (49×31 *mm*) .... 38·00 65·00

Designs: Vert—2l.50, Skiing; 12l.50, Figure-skating. Horiz—0l.50, T **174**; 6l.50, Ice-hockey.

1964 (21 Jan). 40th Death Anniversary of Lenin. P 12½×12.

798	**175**	5l. deep olive and yellow-bistre	1·40	90
799		10l. deep olive and yellow-bistre	3·00	1·60

176 Hurdling

177 Sturgeon

1964 (21 Jan). GANEFO Games, Djakarta (1963). T **176** and similar designs. P 12½×12 (vert) or 12×12½ (horiz).

800	2l.50 ultramarine and lilac	70	40
801	3l. red-brown and green	1·40	65
802	6l.50 lake and blue	2·00	1·50
803	8l. ochre and light blue	3·50	2·50
800/803 Set of 4		6·75	4·50

Designs: Horiz—3l. Running; 6l.50, Rifleshooting. Vert—2l.50, T **176**; 8l. Basketball.

1964 (26 Feb). Fish. T **177** and similar horiz designs. Multicoloured. P 14.

804	0l.50 Type **177**	70	40
805	1l. Gilthead	1·40	45
806	1l.50 Striped Mullet	2·00	50
807	2l.50 Carp	2·75	1·30
808	6l.50 Mackerel	4·00	2·50
809	10l. Salmon	6·75	3·75
804/809 Set of 6		16·00	8·00

178 Red Squirrel (*Sciurus vulgaris*)

179 Lighting Olympic Torch

1964 (28 Mar). Forest Animals. T **178** and similar horiz designs. Multicoloured. P 12½×12.

810	1l. Type **178**	70	35
811	1l.50 Beech Marten (*Martes foina*)	1·40	40
812	2l. Red Fox (*Canis vulpes*)	1·40	45
813	2l.50 East European Hedgehog (*Erinaceus rumunicus*)	2·00	65
814	3l. Brown Hare (*Lepus europaeus*)	2·75	90
815	5l. Golden Jackal (*Canis aureus*)	2·75	95
816	7l. Wild Cat (*Fells silvestris*)	5·50	1·00
817	8l. Wolf (*Canis lupus*)	6·75	1·50
810/817 Set of 8		21·00	5·50

1964 (18 May). Olympic Games, Tokyo (3rd issue). T **179** and similar vert designs. P 12½×12.

818	3l. greenish yellow, buff and yellow-green	70	35
819	5l. blue, violet and red	95	1·30
820	7l. light blue, blue and greenish yellow	1·40	1·90
821	10l. blue, violet, orange and black	2·00	3·25
818/821 Set of 4		4·50	6·50

MS821*a* 81×91 mm. 15l. buff, light blue and violet (as No. 820) (49×62 *mm*) .... 34·00 50·00

Designs: 3l. T **179**; 5l. Torch and globes; 7l. Olympic Flag and Mount Fuji; 10l. Olympic Stadium, Tokyo.

180 Soldiers and hand clutching Rifle, and Inscription

1964 ALBANIA

1964 (24 May). 20th Anniversary of Permet Congress. T **180** and similar horiz designs. P 12½×12.

822		2l. sepia, red and orange-red	2·00	1·30
823		5l. black, red, yellow and light emerald	4·75	2·50
824		8l. black-purple, red and lake-red	10·00	7·50
822/824 Set of 3			15·00	10·00

Designs: (each with different inscription at right)—2l. T **180**; 5l. Albanian Arms; 8l. General Enver Hoxha.

181 Revolutionaries with Flag

Rimini
25·VI·64
(182)

1964 (10 June). 40th Anniversary of Revolution. P 12½×12.

825	**181**	2l.50 black and red	70	50
826		7l.50 black and magenta	2·00	1·60

1964 (25 June). Verso Tokyo Stamp Exhibition, Rimini (Italy). No. 821 optd with T **182** in deep green.

827		10l. blue, violet, orange and black	11·00	10·00

183 Full Moon **184** Winter Wren (*Troglodytes troglodytes*)

1964 (27 June). Moon's Phases. T **183** and similar horiz designs. P 12×12½.

828		1l. yellow and reddish violet	70	40
829		5l. yellow and ultramarine	1·40	90
830		8l. yellow and blue	3·50	1·30
831		11l. yellow and deep bluish green	8·00	5·00
828/831 Set of 4			12·00	6·75
MS831a 67×78 mm. 15l. yellow and violet-blue (New Moon) (34×39 mm). P 12×imperf			23·00	44·00

Phases: 1l. T **183**; 5l. Waxing Moon, 8l. Half-Moon, 11l. Waning Moon.

1964 (31 July). Albanian Birds. T **184** and similar vert designs. Multicoloured. P 12×12½.

832		0l.50 Type **184**	70	35
833		1l. Penduline Tit (*Remiz pendulinus*)	1·40	40
834		2l.50 Green Woodpecker (*Picus viridis*)	2·00	50
835		3l. Treecreeper (*Certhia familiaris*)	2·75	65
836		4l. European Nuthatch (*Sitta europaea*)	3·50	1·10
837		5l. Great Tit (*Parus major*)	4·00	1·30
838		6l. Goldfinch (*Carduelis garulus*)	4·75	1·90
839		18l. Golden Oriole (*Oriolus oriolus*)	8·00	4·50
832/839 Set of 8			24·00	9·75

Riccione
23-8-1964
(185)

186 Running and Gymnastics

1964 (23 Aug). AIR. Riccione (Italy) Space Exhibition. Nos. 780, 783, optd with T **185** in violet.

840		2l. deep olive, yellow and orange	13·50	25·00
841		8l. red, greenish yellow and slate-violet	27·00	38·00

1964 (25 Sept). Olympic Games, Tokyo (4th issue). T **186** and similar vert designs. P 12×12½.

842		1l. red, light blue and light green	35	30
843		2l. yellow-brown, light blue and violet	35	35
844		3l. orange-brown, violet and yellow-olive	40	40
845		4l. yellow-olive, turquoise-green and ultramarine	65	55
846		5l. blue-green, reddish purple and carmine	70	65
847		6l. ultramarine, light blue and orange	1·00	95
848		7l. yellow-green, orange and deep blue	1·10	1·00
849		8l. grey, light green and greenish yellow	1·30	1·10
850		9l. light blue, yellow and bright purple	1·40	1·30
851		10l. yellow-brown, yellow-green and blue-green	2·00	1·90
842/851 Set of 10			8·25	7·75
MS851a 70×96 mm. 20l. violet and yellow-bistre (Winners on Dais) (40×67 mm)			23·00	38·00

Designs: 1l. T **186**; 2l. Weightlifting and judo, 3l. Horse-jumping and cycling; 4l. Football and water-polo; 5l. Wrestling and boxing; 6l. Various sports and hockey; 7l. Swimming and yachting; 8l. Basketball and volleyball; 9l. Rowing and canoeing; 10l. Fencing and pistol-shooting.

187 Chinese Republican Emblem **188** Karl Marx

1964 (1 Oct). 15th Anniversary of Chinese People's Republic. T **187** and similar design. P 11½×12 (7l.) or 12×11½ (8l.).

852		7l. red, black and yellow	10·00	4·75
853		8l. black, red and yellow	10·00	6·50

Designs: Vert—7l. T **187**. Horiz—8l. Mao Tse-tung.

1964 (5 Nov). Centenary of First International. T **188** and similar horiz designs. P 12.

854		2l. black, red and lavender	1·40	65
855		5l. greenish grey	3·50	1·90
856		8l. black, red and olive-yellow	6·75	2·50
854/856 Set of 3			10·50	4·50

Designs: 2l. T **188**; 5l. St Martin's Hall, London; 8l. F. Engels.

189 J. de Rada **190** Arms and Flag

1964 (15 Nov). 150th Birth Anniversary of Jeronim de Rada (poet). P 12½×12.

857	**189**	7l. green	2·00	1·20
858		8l. violet	3·50	1·90

1964 (29 Nov). 20th Anniversary of Liberation. T **190** and similar designs. P 12 (vert) or 12×11½ (horiz).

859		1l. black, orange-red, yellow and magenta	70	55
860		2l. ultramarine, red and yellow	1·40	1·10
861		3l. brown-purple, red and yellow	2·00	1·70
862		4l. deep bluish green, red and yellow	2·75	2·30
863		10l. black, red and blue	6·75	5·75
859/863 Set of 5			12·00	10·50

ALBANIA 1964

Designs: Horiz—2l. Industrial scene; 3l. Agricultural scene; 4l. Laboratory worker. Vert—1l. T **190**; 10l. Hands holding Constitution, hammer and sickle.

191 Mercury

192 Chestnut

1964 (15 Dec). Solar System Planets. T **191** and similar horiz designs. Multicoloured. P 12×12½.
864	1l. Type **191**	35	35
865	2l. Venus	40	40
866	3l. Earth	60	55
867	4l. Mars	70	65
868	5l. Jupiter	1·40	1·00
869	6l. Saturn	2·00	1·30
870	7l. Uranus	2·30	1·60
871	8l. Neptune	2·75	1·90
872	9l. Pluto	3·00	2·20
864/872	Set of 9	12·00	9·00
MS872a	88×72 mm. 15l. multicoloured (Solar system and rocket) (61×51 mm). P 12×imperf	41·00	55·00

1965 (25 Jan). Winter Fruits. T **192** and similar vert designs. Multicoloured. P 11½×12.
873	1l. Type **192**	35	30
874	2l. Medlars	70	35
875	3l. Persimmon	95	40
876	4l. Pomegranate	1·40	50
877	5l. Quince	2·75	90
878	10l. Orange	5·50	1·50
873/878	Set of 6	10·50	3·50

193 Industry

194 Buffalo grazing

1965 (20 Feb). 20th Anniversary of Albanian Trade Unions. T **193** and similar vert designs inscr 'B.P.SH. 1945–1965'. P 11½×12.
879	2l. carmine, pink and black	8·50	7·50
880	5l. black, grey and yellow-ochre	12·00	11·50
881	8l. ultramarine, light blue and black	15·00	14·00
879/881	Set of 3	32·00	30·00

Designs: 2l. T **193**; 5l. Set square, book and dividers (Technocracy); 8l. Hotel, trees and sunshade (Tourism).

1965 (Mar). Water Buffalo. T **194** and similar horiz designs. P 12.
882	1l. multicoloured	1·40	65
883	2l. multicoloured	2·75	1·30
884	3l. multicoloured	4·00	1·90
885	7l. multicoloured	9·50	2·50
886	12l. multicoloured	16·00	3·25
882/886	Set of 5	30·00	8·75

Designs: 1l. T **194**; 2l. to 12l. As T **194** showing different views of Buffalo.

1965 (Apr). Scenery. T **195** and similar designs. Multicoloured. P 12½×12 (horiz) or 12×12½ (vert).
887	1l.50 Type **195**	2·00	65
888	2l.50 Mountain forest, Valbona	4·50	1·10
889	3l. Lugina Peak, Thethi Valley (*vert*)	4·75	1·30
890	4l. White River, Thethi (*vert*)	6·00	1·90
891	5l. Dry Mountain, Valbona	7·50	2·50
892	9l. Lake of Flowers, Lure	20·00	5·00
887/892	Set of 6	40·00	11·00

1965 (25 Apr). 20th Anniversary of Frontier Force. P 12.
893	**196** 2l.50 multicoloured	2·00	1·30
894	12l.50 multicoloured	11·50	5·00

197 Rifleman

198 ITU Emblem and Symbols

1965 (10 May). European Shooting Championships, Bucharest. T **197** and similar horiz designs. P 12×12½.
895	1l. brown-purple, cerise and reddish violet	55	35
896	2l. brown-purple, ultramarine and light blue	70	40
897	3l. red and pink	1·40	50
898	4l. brown-purple, black, grey and ochre	2·75	65
899	15l. brown-purple, black, orange-brown and turquoise-green	8·00	3·25
895/899	Set of 5	12·00	4·75

Designs: 1l. T **197**; 2l., 15l. Rifle-shooting (*different*); 3l. 'Target' map; 4l. Pistol-shooting.

1965 (17 May). Centenary of International Telecommunications Union. P 12½×12.
900	**198** 2l.50 magenta, black and blue-green	1·40	65
901	12l.50 blue, black and bright violet	8·00	2·10

199 Belyaev

200 Marx and Lenin

1965 (15 June). Space Flight of *Voskhod 2*. T **199** and similar vert designs. P 12½×12.
902	1l.50 brown and light blue	35	30
903	2l. blue, deep blue and lilac	40	40
904	6l.50 brown and reddish violet	55	50
905	20l. yellow, black and grey-blue	5·50	3·25
902/905	Set of 4	6·00	4·00
MS906	71×86 mm. 20l. yellow, black and light blue (as No. 905 but larger, 59×51 mm). P 12×imperf	18·00	38·00

Designs: 1l.50, T **199**; 2l. *Voskhod 2*; 6l.50, Leonov; 20l. Leonov in space.

1965 (21 June). Postal Ministers' Congress, Peking. P 12½×12.
907	**200** 2l.50 sepia, red and greenish yellow	1·10	65
908	7l.50 bronze green, orange-red and greenish yellow	4·25	2·50

195 Coastal View

196 Frontier Guard

201 Mother and Child

202 Wine Vessel

1965 (29 June). International Children's Day. T **201** and similar designs. Multicoloured. P 12×12½ (3l.) or 12½×12 (others).

909	1l. Type **201**	35	30
910	2l. Children planting tree	40	40
911	3l. Children and construction toy (*horiz*)	55	50
912	4l. Child on beach	1·40	1·30
913	15l. Child reading book	5·50	5·00
909/913 Set of 5		7·50	6·75

1965 (20 July). Albanian Antiquities. T **202** and similar designs. Multicoloured. P 12.

914	1l. Type **202**	35	30
915	2l. Helmet and shield	55	40
916	3l. Mosaic of animal (*horiz*)	80	50
917	4l. Statuette of man	2·10	1·30
918	15l. Statuette of headless and limbless man	5·00	2·50
914/918 Set of 5		8·00	4·50

203 Fuchsia

(**204**)

1965 (11 Aug). Albanian Flowers. T **203** and similar vert designs. Multicoloured. P 12½×12.

919	1l. Type **203**	40	30
920	2l. Cyclamen	1·00	40
921	3l. Lilies	1·60	50
922	3l.50 Iris	2·10	95
923	4l. Dahlia	2·20	1·00
924	4l.50 Hydrangea	2·75	1·10
925	5l. Rose	3·00	1·10
926	7l. Tulips	4·25	1·30
919/926 Set of 8		16·00	6·00

Currency revaluation. 100 Oint = 1 Lek.

1 New Lek = 10 Old Leks

1965 (16 Aug). Nos. 786/788 surch as T **204**.

927	5q. on 30l. reddish purple/*pale blue*	1·10	1·00
928	15q. on 30l. reddish purple/*pale blue*	1·40	1·30
929	25q. on 50l. yellow-brown/*pale cream*	1·80	1·70
930	80q. on 50l. yellow-brown/*pale cream*	4·00	3·75
931	1l.10 on 20l. green/*pale green*	5·75	5·50
932	2l. on 20l. green /*pale green*	9·50	8·75
927/932 Set of 6		21·00	20·00

205 White Stork (*Ciconia ciconia*)

206 War Veterans (after painting by B. Sejdini)

1965 (31 Aug). Migratory Birds. T **205** and similar vert designs. Multicoloured. P 12½×12.

933	10q. Type **205**	70	55
934	20q. European Cuckoo (*Cuculus canorus*)	1·40	65
935	30q. Hoopoe (*Upupa epops*)	2·00	1·00
936	40q. European Bee-eater (*Merops apiaster*)	2·75	1·30
937	50q. European Nightjar (*Caprimulgus europaeus*)	3·50	1·50
938	1l.50 Common Quail (*Coturnix coturnix*)	10·00	4·50
933/938 Set of 6		18·00	8·50

1965 (26 Sept). War Veterans Conference. P 12×12½.

939	**206** 25q. deep olive-brown and black	3·50	65
940	65q. indigo and black	10·00	2·50
941	1l.10 black	13·50	5·00
939/941 Set of 3		24·00	7·25

207 Hunter stalking Capercaillie

208 *Nerium oleander*

1965 (6 Oct). Hunting. T **207** and similar horiz designs. P 12×12½.

942	10q. multicoloured	80	30
943	20q. lake-brown, sepia and yellow-green	1·40	35
944	30q. multicoloured	1·60	40
945	40q. reddish purple and emerald	2·75	50
946	50q. chestnut, grey-blue and black	3·00	1·00
947	1l. olive-brown, bistre and green	6·75	1·90
942/947 Set of 6		14·50	4·00

Designs: 10q. T **207**; 20q. Shooting Roe Deer; 30q. Ring-necked Pheasant; 40q. Shooting Mallard; 50q. Dogs chasing Wild Boar; 1l. Hunter and Brown Hare.

1965 (26 Oct). Mountain Flowers. T **208** and similar vert designs. Multicoloured. P 12½×12.

948	10q. Type **208**	40	30
949	20q. *Myosotis alpestris*	70	35
950	30q. *Dianthus glacialis*	95	40
951	40q. *Nymphaea alba*	1·40	50
952	50q. *Lotus corniculatus*	2·00	90
953	1l. *Papaver rhoeas*	5·50	2·50
948/953 Set of 6		9·75	4·50

209 Tourist Hotel, Fier

210 Freighter *Teuta*

1965 (27 Oct). Public Buildings. T **209** and similar horiz designs. P 12×12½.

954	5q. black and light blue	25	20
955	10q. black and buff	35	25
956	15q. black and dull green	40	30
957	25q. black and violet	70	35
958	65q. black and light red-brown	1·80	40
959	80q. black and yellow-green	2·75	65
960	1l.10 black and reddish purple	3·75	80
961	1l.60 black and light violet-blue	5·50	2·10
962	2l. black and pink	6·75	2·50
963	3l. black and light grey	12·00	4·50
954/963 Set of 10		31·00	11·00

Buildings: 5q. T **209**; 10q. Peshkopi Hotel; 15q. Sanatorium, Tirana; 25q. 'House of Rest', Pogradec; 65q. Partisans Sports Palace, Tirana; 80q. 'House of Rest', Dajti Mountain; 1l.10, Palace of Culture, Tirana; 1l.60, Adriatic Hotel, Durrës; 2l. Migjeni Theatre, Shkodër; 3l. 'A. Moisiu' Cultural Palace, Durrës.

1965 (16 Nov). Evolution of Albanian Ships. T **210** and similar horiz designs. P 12×12½.

964	10q. olive-green and bright green	35	30
965	20q. bistre and olive-green	40	35
966	30q. ultramarine and new blue	55	40
967	40q. violet and light violet	70	50
968	50q. carmine-red and rose	2·00	90
969	1l. red-brown and yellow-ochre	4·75	1·50
964/969 Set of 6		8·00	3·50

Designs: 10q. T **210**; 20q. Punt; 30q. 19th-century sailing ship; 40q. 18th-century brig; 50q. Freighter *Vlora*; 1l. Illyrian galliots.

211 Head of Brown Bear

212 Championships Emblem

1965 (7 Dec). Brown Bear. T **211** and similar designs each showing a Bear. P 11½×12 (vert) or 12×11½ (horiz).

970	10q. brown and yellow-brown	65	30
971	20q. brown and yellow-brown	70	35
972	30q. brown, red and yellow-brown	1·40	40
973	35q. brown and yellow-brown	1·60	45

ALBANIA 1965

974	40q. brown and yellow-brown	2·00	45
975	50q. brown and yellow-brown	3·50	65
976	55q. brown and yellow-brown	4·00	90
977	60q. brown, red and yellow-brown	7·50	3·25
970/977	Set of 8	19·00	6·00

The 10q. to 40q. are vert, remainder horiz.

1965 (15 Dec). Seventh Balkan Basketball Championships, Tirana. T **212** and similar vert designs. Multicoloured. P 12½×12.

978	10q. Type **212**	35	30
979	20q. Competing players	40	35
980	30q. Clearing ball	55	40
981	50q. Attempted goal	2·00	50
982	1l.40 Medal and ribbon	4·00	1·30
978/982	Set of 5	6·50	2·50

213 Arms on Book   **214** Cow

1966 (11 Jan). 20th Anniversary of Albanian People's Republic. T **213** and similar vert designs. Arms in gold. P 12.

983	10q. rosine and brown	35	30
984	20q. light new blue and bright blue	40	40
985	30q. yellow and brown	95	65
986	60q. apple-green and blue-green	2·30	1·30
987	80q. rosine and brown	2·75	1·90
983/987	Set of 5	6·00	4·00

Designs: Arms and—10q. T **213**; 20q. Chimney stacks; 30q. Ear of corn; 60q. Hammer, sickle and open book; 80q. Industrial plant.

1966 (25 Feb). Domestic Animals. T **214** and similar designs. Animals in natural colours; inscriptions in black; frame colours given. P 12½×12 (horiz) or 12×12½ (vert).

988	10q. turquoise-green (Type **214**)	40	30
989	20q. apple-green (Pig)	70	35
990	30q. light violet-blue (Sheep)	1·40	40
991	35q. lavender (Goat)	2·00	50
992	40q. pink (Dog)	2·75	55
993	50q. light yellow (Cat) (vert)	3·00	65
994	55q. light blue (Horse) (vert)	3·50	90
995	60q. yellow (Ass) (vert)	6·75	1·30
988/995	Set of 8	18·00	4·50

215 Football   **216** A. Z. Çajupi

1966 (20 Mar). World Cup Football Championship, England (1st series). T **215** and similar vert designs. P 12½×12.

996	5q. red-orange, greenish grey and pale buff	25	15
997	10q. deep reddish lilac, light blue, ochre and pale buff	30	15
998	15q. blue, greenish yellow and pale buff	35	20
999	20q. greenish blue, ultramarine, yellow-orange and pale buff	40	25
1000	25q. sepia, orange-red and pale buff	50	25
1001	30q. brown, yellow-green and pale buff	70	40
1002	35q. yellow-green, blue and pale buff	95	45
1003	40q. brown, rose and pale buff	1·10	50
1004	50q. red, bright purple, light green and pale buff	1·40	75
1005	70q. multicoloured	2·00	1·00
996/1005	Set of 10	7·25	3·75

Designs: Footballer and map showing—5q. T **215**; 10q. Montevideo (1930); 15q. Rome (1934); 20q. Paris (1938); 25q. Rio de Janeiro (1950); 30q. Berne (1954); 35q. Stockholm (1958); 40q. Santiago (1962); 50q. London (1966); 70q. World Cup and Football.

See also Nos. 1035/1042.

1966 (27 Mar). Birth Centenary of Andon Çajupi (poet). P 12½×12.

1006	**216**	40q. indigo and slate-blue	1·40	65
1007		1l.10 bronze-green and grey-green	4·00	2·50

217 Painted Lady (*Pyrameis cardui*)   **218** WHO Building

1966 (21 Apr). Butterflies and Dragonflies. T **217** and similar vert designs. Multicoloured. P 11½×12.

1008	10q. Type **217**	65	25
1009	20q. *Calopteryx virgo*	70	30
1010	30q. Pale Clouded Yellow (*Colias hyale*)	95	35
1011	35q. Banded Agrion (*Calopteryx splendens*)	1·40	40
1012	40q. Banded Agrion (*different*)	2·00	55
1013	50q. Swallowtail (*Papilio machaon*)	2·75	65
1014	55q. Danube Clouded Yellow (*Colias myrmidone*)	3·50	90
1015	60q. Hungarian Glider (*Neptis lucilla*)	8·75	1·50
1008/1015	Set of 8	19·00	4·50

The 20q., 35q. and 40q. are Dragonflies, remainder are Butterflies.

1966 (3 May). Inauguration of WHO Headquarters, Geneva. T **218** and similar designs. P 12×12½ (horiz) or 12½×12 (vert).

1016	25q. black and light blue	70	35
1017	35q. bright blue and red-orange	1·40	40
1018	60q. red, new blue and light green	2·00	90
1019	80q. new blue, yellow-brown and greenish yellow	2·75	1·50
1016/1019	Set of 4	6·25	2·75

Designs: Vert—35q. Ambulance and patient; 60q. Nurse and mother weighing baby. Horiz—25q. T **218**; 80q. Medical equipment.

219 Leaf Star   **220** Luna 10

1966 (10 May). Starfish. T **219** and similar vert designs. Multicoloured. P 12×12½.

1020	15q. Type **219**	55	40
1021	25q. Spiny Star	95	50
1022	35q. Brittle Star	1·60	65
1023	45q. Sea Star	2·00	75
1024	50q. Blood Star	2·30	90
1025	60q. Sea Cucumber	3·50	1·30
1026	70q. Sea Urchin	4·00	3·25
1020/1026	Set of 7	13·50	7·00

1966 (10 June). Launching of Luna 10. T **220** and similar horiz design. P 12×12½.

1027	**220**	20q. multicoloured	70	40
1028	–	30q. multicoloured	1·40	65
1029	**220**	70q. multicoloured	2·75	1·30
1030	–	80q. multicoloured	4·75	2·75
1027/1030		Set of 4	8·75	4·50

Design: 30q., 80q. Earth, Moon and trajectory of *Luna 10*.

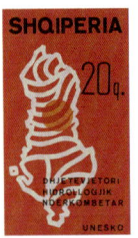 

221 Water-level Map of Albania   **222** Footballers (Uruguay, 1930)

1966 (2 July). International Hydrological Decade. T **221** and similar vert designs. P 12.

1031	20q. black, orange and red	70	40
1032	30q. black, yellow-brown, chestnut and bright green	90	65
1033	70q. black and reddish violet	2·00	1·50
1034	80q. black, yellow, orange and blue	3·50	2·50
1031/1034	Set of 4	6·50	4·50

Designs: 20q. T **221**; 30q. Water scale and fields; 70q. Turbine and electricity pylon; 80q. Hydrological decade emblem.

1966 (12 July). World Cup Football Championship (2nd series). T **222** and similar horiz designs. Inscriptions and values in black. P 12.

1035	10q. purple and yellow-orange	55	25
1036	20q. yellow-olive and light blue	70	30
1037	30q. greenish blue and orange-red	95	30
1038	35q. rose and blue	1·40	35
1039	40q. chestnut and yellow-green	1·40	40
1040	50q. yellow-green and chestnut	1·60	50
1041	55q. bright green and reddish purple	1·60	1·00
1042	60q. yellow-orange and claret	3·50	1·80
1035/1042	Set of 8	10·50	4·50

Designs: Various footballers representing World Cup winners—10q. T **222**; 20q. Italy, 1934; 30q. Italy, 1938; 35q. Uruguay, 1950; 40q. West Germany, 1954; 50q. Brazil, 1958; 55q. Brazil, 1962; 60q. Football and names of 16 finalists in 1966 Championship.

223 Tortoise

1966 (10 Aug). Reptiles. T **223** and similar horiz designs. Multicoloured. P 12½×12.

1043	10q. Type **223**	40	30
1044	15q. Grass Snake	55	30
1045	25q. Swamp Tortoise	70	35
1046	30q. Lizard	80	40
1047	35q. Salamander	1·40	55
1048	45q. Green Lizard	1·60	65
1049	50q. Slow Worm	2·00	1·00
1050	90q. Sand Viper	3·50	1·90
1043/1050	Set of 8	9·75	5·00

224 Siamese Cat

1966 (20 Sept). Cats. T **224** and similar designs. Multicoloured. P 12×12½ (vert) or 12½×12 (horiz, 25q. to 30q.).

1051	10q. Type **224**	55	30
1052	15q. Tabby	70	35
1053	25q. Kitten	1·40	40
1054	45q. Persian	2·00	65
1055	60q. Persian	3·00	1·00
1056	65q. Persian	3·50	1·30
1057	80q. Persian	4·75	1·60
1051/1057	Set of 7	14·00	5·00

225 P. Budi (writer)

1966 (5 Oct). 400th Birth Anniversary of P. Budi. P 12½×12.

1058	**225**	25q. bronze-green and flesh	1·40	65
1059		1l.75 maroon and light green	4·00	3·50

226 UNESCO Emblem

228 Hand holding Book

227 Borzoi

1966 (20 Oct). 20th Anniversary of UNESCO T **226** and similar designs. Multicoloured. P 12.

1060	5q. Type **226**	35	30
1061	15q. Tulip and open book	40	30
1062	25q. Albanian dancers	55	50
1063	1l.55 Jug and base of column	4·00	2·50
1060/1063	Set of 4	4·75	3·25

1966 (30 Oct). Dogs. T **227** and similar horiz designs. Multicoloured. P 12½×12.

1064	10q. Type **227**	70	30
1065	15q. Kuvasz	1·10	35
1066	25q. Setter	1·40	40
1067	45q. Cocker Spaniel	2·00	1·10
1068	60q. Bulldog	2·75	1·50
1069	65q. St Bernard	3·00	1·90
1070	80q. Dachshund	5·50	2·50
1064/1070	Set of 7	15·00	7·25

1966 (1 Nov). Fifth Workers' Party Congress, Tirana. T **228** and similar vert designs. Multicoloured. P 12.

1071	15q. Type **228**	35	25
1072	25q. Emblems of agriculture and industry	40	30
1073	65q. Hammer and sickle, wheat and industrial skyline	1·90	90
1074	95q. Hands holding banner on bayonet and implements	2·75	1·50
1071/1074	Set of 4	4·75	2·75

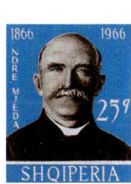

229 Ndre Mjeda (poet)

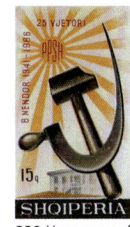

230 Hammer and Sickle

1966 (1 Nov). Birth Centenary of Ndre Mjeda. P 12½×12.

1075	**229**	25q. deep brown and bright new blue.	70	65
1076		1l.75 deep brown and bright blue-green	4·75	2·10

1966 (8 Nov). 25th Anniversary of Albanian Young Communists' Union. T **230** and similar vert designs. Multicoloured. P 12.

1077	15q. Type **230**	60	25
1078	25q. Soldier leading attack	70	35
1079	65q. Industrial worker	1·80	90
1080	95q. Agricultural and industrial vista	2·00	1·50
1077/1080	Set of 4	4·50	2·75

ALBANIA 1966

231 Young Communists and Banner

232 Golden Eagle (*Aquila chrysaëtos*)

1966 (8 Nov). 25th Anniversary of Young Communists' Union. T **231** and similar designs. Multicoloured. P 12×11½ (10q.) or 11½×12 (others).

1081	5q. Manifesto (*vert*)	40	30
1082	10q. Type **231**	70	40
1083	1l.85 Partisans and banner (*vert*)	4·25	2·40
1081/1083	*Set of 3*	4·75	2·75

1966 (20 Dec). Birds of Prey. T **232** and similar vert designs. Multicoloured. P 11½×12.

1084	10q. Type **232**	55	30
1085	15q. White-tailed Sea Eagle (*Haliaëtus albicilla*)	70	40
1086	25q. Griffon Vulture (*Gyps fulvus*)	1·40	50
1087	40q. European Sparrow Hawk (*Accipiter nisus*)	2·00	65
1088	50q. Osprey (*Pandion haliaëtus*)	2·75	90
1089	70q. Egyptian Vulture (*Neophron percnopterus*)	4·00	1·50
1090	90q. Common Kestrel (*Falco tinnunculus*)	6·00	1·90
1085/1090	*Set of 7*	11·00	4·75

233 Hake

234 Dalmatian Pelican

1967 (20 Jan). Fish. T **233** and similar horiz designs. Multicoloured. P 12.

1091	10q. Type **233**	55	30
1092	15q. Red Mullet	70	40
1093	25q. Opah	1·10	50
1094	40q. Wolffish	1·40	65
1095	65q. Lumpsucker	2·00	90
1096	80q. Swordfish	3·50	1·50
1097	1l.15 Father Lasher	5·50	1·90
1091/1097	*Set of 7*	13·50	5·50

1967 (22 Feb). Dalmatian Pelicans. T **234** and similar designs. Multicoloured. P 12.

1098	10q. Type **234**	35	30
1099	15q. Three Pelicans	40	40
1100	25q. Pelican and chicks at nest	1·90	75
1101	50q. Pelicans 'taking off' and airborne	4·00	1·00
1102	2l. Pelican 'yawning'	9·50	4·50
1098/1102	*Set of 5*	14·50	6·25

235 *Camellia williamsi*

236 Congress Emblem

1967 (10 Apr). Flowers. T **235** and similar designs. Multicoloured. P 12.

1103	5q. Type **235**	30	25
1104	10q. *Chrysanthemum indicum*	35	30
1105	15q. *Althaea rosea*	40	35
1106	25q. *Abutilon striatum*	80	40
1107	35q. *Paeonia chinensis*	1·40	50
1108	65q. *Gladiolus gandavensis*	2·75	1·00
1109	80q. *Freesia hybrida*	3·50	1·50
1110	1l.15 *Dianthus caryophyllus*	4·00	1·90
1103/1110	*Set of 8*	12·00	5·50

1967 (24 Apr). 6th Trade Unions Congress, Tirana. P 12.

1111	**236** 25q. red, sepia and light lilac	1·40	65
1112	1l.75 red, deep olive-green and grey	4·00	2·50

237 Rose

239 Fawn

238 Borsh Coast

1967 (15 May). Roses. T **237** and other vert designs showing different Roses. P 12×12½.

1113	5q. multicoloured	50	30
1114	10q. multicoloured	55	35
1115	15q. multicoloured	60	45
1116	25q. multicoloured	70	50
1117	35q. multicoloured	1·40	65
1118	65q. multicoloured	1·90	70
1119	80q. multicoloured	2·00	1·30
1120	1l.65 multicoloured	5·50	1·90
1113/1120	*Set of 8*	12·00	5·50

1967 (10 June). Albanian Riviera. T **238** and similar designs showing resorts. Multicoloured. P 12×12½ (vert) or 12½×12 (horiz).

1121	15q. Butrinti (*vert*)	60	30
1122	20q. Type **238**	70	40
1123	25q. Piqeras Village	1·10	40
1124	45q. Coastal view	1·20	45
1125	50q. Himara coast	1·40	50
1126	65q. Saranda	2·75	90
1127	80q. Dhermi	2·75	1·30
1128	1l. Sunset at sea (*vert*)	4·00	1·90
1121/1128	*Set of 8*	13·00	5·50

1967 (20 July). Roe Deer. T **239** and similar designs. Multicoloured. P 12½×12 (horiz) or 12×12½ (vert).

1129	15q. Type **239**	55	30
1130	20q. Head of buck (*vert*)	70	40
1131	25q. Head of doe (*vert*)	1·10	50
1132	30q. Doe and fawn	1·40	65
1133	35q. Doe and new-born fawn	1·70	75
1134	40q. Young buck (*vert*)	2·00	90
1135	65q. Buck and doe (*vert*)	4·00	1·30
1136	70q. Running Deer	5·50	1·90
1129/1136	*Set of 8*	15·00	6·00

240 Costumes of Malésia e Madhe Region

241 Battle Scene and Newspaper

1967 ALBANIA

(Des P. Mele and S. Kristo)

1967 (20 Aug). National Costumes. T **240** and similar designs showing costumes. Multicoloured. P 12.

1137	15q. Type **240**	55	30
1138	20q. Zadrima	60	35
1139	25q. Kukësi	70	40
1140	45q. Dardhë	1·10	65
1141	50q. Myzeqë	1·20	75
1142	65q. Tirana	1·40	90
1143	80q. Dropulli	2·40	1·30
1144	1l. Labërisë	2·75	1·50
1137/1144	Set of 8	9·75	5·50

1967 (25 Aug). 25 Years of the Albanian Popular Press. T **241** and similar vert designs. Multicoloured. P 12½×12.

1145	25q. Type **241**	70	65
1146	75q. Newspapers and printery	2·00	1·30
1147	2l. Workers with newspaper	5·50	3·25
1145/1147	Set of 3	7·50	4·75

242 University, Torch and Open Book

243 Soldiers and Flag

1967 (15 Sept). Tenth Anniversary of Tirana University. P 12½×12.

1148	**242** 25q. multicoloured	70	65
1149	1l.75 multicoloured	4·25	2·10

1967 (16 Sept). 25th Anniversary of Albanian Democratic Front. T **243** and similar horiz designs. Multicoloured. P 12.

1150	15q. Type **243**	40	30
1151	65q. Pick, rifle and flag	1·40	65
1152	1l.20 Torch and open book	3·00	1·50
1150/1152	Set of 3	4·25	2·20

244 Grey Rabbits

1967 (30 Sept). Rabbit-breeding. T **244** and similar multicoloured designs. P 12.

1153	15q. Type **244**	40	25
1154	20q. Black and white Rabbit (*vert*)	55	35
1155	25q. Brown Hare (*Lepus europaeus*)	70	45
1156	35q. Brown Rabbits	1·20	45
1157	40q. Common Rabbits (*Oryctolagus cuniculus*)	1·40	65
1158	50q. Grey Rabbit (*vert*)	3·50	75
1159	65q. Head of white Rabbit (*vert*)	4·00	90
1160	1l. White Rabbit	5·50	1·90
1153/1160	Set of 8	16·00	5·25

245 *Shkodër Wedding* (detail, Kolë Idromeno)

1967 (25 Oct). Albanian Paintings. T **245** and similar designs. P 12½×12 (*horiz*) or 12×12½ (*vert*).

1161	15q. multicoloured	60	30
1162	20q. multicoloured	70	40
1163	25q. multicoloured	1·20	55
1164	45q. multicoloured	1·30	65
1165	50q. multicoloured	1·40	90
1166	65q. multicoloured	2·50	95
1167	80q. multicoloured	2·75	1·30
1168	1l. multicoloured	5·50	1·50
1161/1168	Set of 8	14·50	6·00

Designs: Vert—20q. Head of the Prophet David (detail, 16th-century fresco); 45q. Ancient mosaic head (from Durrës); 50q. Detail, 16th-century icon; (30×51 *mm*)—1l. Our Sister (K. Idromeno). Horiz (51×30 *mm*)—15q. T **245**; 25q. *Commandos of the Hakmarrja Battalion* (S. Shijaku); 65q. *Co-operative* (farm women, Z. Shoshi); 80q. *Street in Korçë* (V. Mio).

246 Lenin and Stalin

(Des Q. Prizreni)

1967 (7 Nov). 50th Anniversary of October Revolution. T **246** and similar designs. Multicoloured. P 12.

1169	15q. Type **246**	40	30
1170	25q. Lenin with soldiers (*vert*)	95	65
1171	50q. Lenin addressing meeting (*vert*)	1·40	90
1172	1l.10 Revolutionaries	2·75	1·30
1169/1172	Set of 4	5·00	2·75

247 Common Turkey

(Des N. Prizreni)

1967 (25 Nov). Domestic Fowl. T **247** and similar designs. Multicoloured. P 12×12½ (*vert*) or 12½×12 (*horiz*).

1173	15q. Type **247**	35	30
1174	20q. Goose	40	35
1175	25q. Hen	70	40
1176	45q. Cockerel	1·40	65
1177	50q. Helmet Guineafowl	1·70	90
1178	65q. Greylag Goose (*horiz*)	2·00	90
1179	80q. Mallard (*horiz*)	3·50	1·30
1180	1l. Chicks (*horiz*)	5·25	1·50
1173/1180	Set of 8	14·00	5·75

248 First Aid

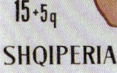
249 Arms of Skanderbeg

(Des S. Bregu and J. Talo)

1967 (1 Dec). Sixth Red Cross Congress, Tirana. T **248** and similar vert designs. Multicoloured. P 12.

1181	15q. +5q. Type **248**	1·40	65
1182	25q. +5q. Stretcher-case	2·75	1·30
1183	65q. +25q. Heart patient	8·50	4·50
1184	80q. +40q. Nurse holding child	12·00	6·25
1181/1184	Set of 4	22·00	11·50

(Des N. Prizreni)

1967 (10 Dec). 500th Death Anniversary of Castriota Skanderbeg (patriot) (First issue). T **249** and similar vert designs. Multicoloured. P 12×12½.

1185	10q. Type **249**	35	20
1186	15q. Skanderbeg	40	25
1187	25q. Helmet and sword	55	30
1188	30q. Kruja Castle	60	35
1189	35q. Petrela Castle	70	40
1190	65q. Berati Castle	1·40	50
1191	80q. Meeting of chiefs	2·40	75
1192	90q. Battle of Albulena	2·75	1·30
1185/1192	Set of 8	8·25	3·75

See also Nos. 1200/1207.

ALBANIA 1967

250 Winter Olympics Emblem

251 Skanderbeg Memorial, Tirana

(Des S. Toptani)

1967 (29 Dec). Winter Olympic Games, Grenoble. T **250** and similar vert designs. Multicoloured. P 12×12½.
1193	15q. Type **250**	25	20
1194	25q. Ice hockey	35	25
1195	30q. Figure skating	40	30
1196	50q. Skiing (slalom)	55	35
1197	80q. Skiing (downhill)	1·40	50
1198	1l. Ski jumping	3·00	1·30
1193/1198 *Set of 6*		5·25	2·50
MS1199 58×67 mm. 2l. As Type **250** but larger. Imperf		9·50	12·50

(Des S. Toptani)

1968 (17 Jan). 500th Death Anniversary of Castriota Skanderbeg (Second issue). T **251** and similar designs. Multicoloured. P 12×12½.
1200	10q. Type **251**	55	30
1201	15q. Skanderbeg portrait	70	35
1202	25q. Skanderbeg portrait (*different*)	1·20	40
1203	30q. Equestrian statue, Kruja	1·30	45
1204	35q. Skanderbeg and mountains (*horiz*)	1·40	50
1205	65q. Bust of Skanderbeg	2·75	90
1206	80q. Title page of biography	3·50	1·90
1207	90q. Skanderbeg battling with the Turks (painting) (*horiz*)	4·00	2·50
1200/1207 *Set of 8*		14·00	6·50

252 Alpine Dianthus

253 Ear of wheat and Electricity Pylon

(Des S. Qesku)

1968 (15 Feb). Flowers. T **252** and similar square designs. Multicoloured. P 12.
1208	15q. Type **252**	35	25
1209	20q. Chinese Dianthus	35	30
1210	25q. Pink Carnation	40	35
1211	50q. Red Carnation and bud	1·20	40
1212	80q. Two red Carnations	1·60	50
1213	1l.10 Yellow Carnations	2·75	1·30
1208/1213 *Set of 6*		6·00	2·75

1968 (15 Mar). Fifth Agricultural Co-operative Congress. T **253** and similar designs. Multicoloured. P 12.
1214	25q. Type **253**	70	65
1215	65q. Tractor (*horiz*)	2·00	1·30
1216	1l.10 Cow	2·75	1·90
1214/1216 *Set of 3*		5·00	3·50

254 Long-horned Goat

255 Zef Jubani

(Des N. Prizreni)

1968 (25 Mar). Goats. T **254** and similar designs. Multicoloured. P 12×12½ (vert) or 12½×12 (horiz).
1217	15q. Zane female (*vert*)	35	20
1218	20q. Kid (*vert*)	40	25
1219	25q. Long-haired Capore (*vert*)	55	30
1220	30q. Black Goat at rest	70	35
1221	40q. Kids dancing	80	40
1222	50q. Red and piebald Goats	95	50
1223	80q. Long-haired Ankara	2·75	90
1224	1l.40 Type **254**	4·00	1·90
1217/1224 *Set of 8*		9·50	4·25

1968 (30 Mar). 150th Birth Anniversary of Zef Jubani (patriot). P 12.
1225	**255** 25q. deep chocolate and yellow	70	45
1226	1l.75 indigo, black and lt violet	3·50	1·90

256 Doctor using Stethoscope

257 Servicewoman

1968 (7 Apr). 20th Anniversary of World Health Organisation. T **256** and similar designs. P 12×12½ (65q.) or 12½×12 (others).
1227	25q. claret and emerald	40	30
1228	65q. black, light greenish blue and greenish yellow	1·60	90
1229	1l.10 orange-brown and black	2·00	1·30
1227/1229 *Set of 3*		3·50	2·30

Designs: Horiz—65q. Hospital and microscope. Vert—25q. T **256**; 1l.10, Mother feeding child.

1968 (14 Apr). 25th Anniversary of Albanian Women's Union. T **257** and similar horiz designs. P 12.
1230	15q. brown-red and light salmon-red	55	30
1231	25q. bluish green and light green	70	40
1232	60q. yellow-brown and light ochre	2·00	90
1233	1l. bluish violet and light violet	3·50	1·50
1230/1233 *Set of 4*		6·00	2·75

Designs: 15q. T **257**; 25q. Teacher; 60q. Farm-girl; 1l. Factory worker.

258 Karl Marx

259 Heliopsis

(Des S. Ballauri)

1968 (5 May). 150th Birth Anniversary of Karl Marx. T **258** and similar square designs. Multicoloured. P 12.
1234	15q. Type **258**	1·00	95
1235	25q. Marx addressing students	1·50	1·40
1236	65q. *Das Kapital, Communist Manifesto* and marchers	2·75	2·50
1237	95q. Portrait of Karl Marx	5·00	4·50
1234/1237 *Set of 4*		9·25	8·50

(Des S. Qesku)

1968 (10 May). Flowers. T **259** and similar vert designs. Multicoloured. P 12×12½.
1238	15q. Type **259**	35	20
1239	20q. Red Flax	40	25
1240	25q. Orchid	55	30
1241	30q. Gloxinia	55	35
1242	40q. Orange Lily	70	40
1243	80q. Hippeastrum	2·00	1·30
1244	1l.40 Purple Magnolia	3·50	1·90
1238/1244 *Set of 7*		7·25	4·25

260 A. Frashëri and Torch   261 Shepherd (A. Kushi)

1968 (10 June). 90th Anniversary of Prizren Defence League. T **260** and similar horiz designs. P 12.

1245	25q. black and bright green	70	40
1246	40q. multicoloured	1·40	65
1247	85q. multicoloured	2·00	1·50
1245/1247	Set of 3	3·75	2·30

Designs: 25q. T **260**; 40q. League headquarters; 85q. Frashëri's manifesto and partisans.

1968 (20 June). Paintings in Tirana Gallery. T **261** and similar designs. Multicoloured. P 12½×12 (20q.) or 12×12½ (others).

1248	15q. Type **261**	25	20
1249	20q. *Tirana* (V. Mio) (*horiz*)	30	25
1250	25q. *Highlander* (G. Madhi)	35	30
1251	40q. *Refugees* (A. Buza)	40	35
1252	80q. *Partisans at Shahin Matrakut* (S. Xega)	1·10	40
1253	1l.50 *Old Man* (S. Papadhimitri)	2·75	85
1254	1l.70 *Shkodër Gate* (S. Rrota)	4·00	1·30
1248/1254	Set of 7	8·25	3·25
MS1255	90×114 mm. 2l.50, *Shkodër Costume* (Z. Colombi) (51×71 *mm*). P 12½×imperf	4·75	3·25

262 Soldier and Armoured Vehicles

1968 (10 July). 25th Anniversary of People's Army. T **262** and similar designs. P 12½.

1256	15q. olive-green, black, buff and cerise	55	35
1257	25q. lightt sepia, black, greenish blue and yellow	70	40
1258	65q. brown-purple, black, greenish blue and ultramarine	2·75	1·10
1259	95q. orange, black, drab and yellow-green	4·00	2·50
1256/1259	Set of 4	7·25	4·00

Designs: Horiz—15q. T **262**; 25q. Sailor and naval craft; 95q. Soldier and patriots. Vert—65q. Pilot and Mikoyan Gurevich MiG-17 jet fighter.

263 Common Squid (*Loligo vulgaris*)

(Des S. Qesku)

1968 (20 Aug). Marine Fauna. T **263** and similar horiz designs. Multicoloured. P 12.

1260	15q. Type **263**	40	30
1261	20q. Common Lobster (*Homarus vulgaris*)	45	40
1262	25q. Common Northern Whelk (*Buccinum undatum*)	55	50
1263	50q. Edible Crab (*Cancer pagurus*)	70	65
1264	70q. Spiny Lobster (*Palinurus vulgaris*)	1·40	1·10
1265	80q. Common Green Crab (*Carcinus maenas*)	3·00	1·30
1266	90q. Norwegian Lobster (*Nephrops norvegicus*)	3·50	1·90
1260/1266	Set of 7	9·00	5·50

264 Relay-racing

(Des S. Toptani)

1968 (23 Sept). Olympic Games, Mexico. T **264** and similar diamond-shaped designs. Multicoloured. P 12.

1267	15q. Type **264**	25	20
1268	20q. Running	30	25
1269	25q. Throwing the discus	35	30
1270	30q. Horse-jumping	40	30
1271	40q. High-jumping	45	35
1272	50q. Hurdling	55	40
1273	80q. Football	1·40	50
1274	1l.40 High-diving	2·75	1·30
1267/1274	Set of 8	5·75	3·25
MS1275	90×81 mm. 2l. Olympic Stadium (64×54 *mm*). P 12½×imperf	4·75	3·25

265 Enver Hoxha (Party Secretary)   266 Alphabet Book

(Des S. Toptani)

1968 (16 Oct). Enver Hoxha's 60th Birthday. P 12.

1276	**265** 25q. deep grey-blue	55	45
1277	35q. maroon	70	65
1278	80q. deep slate-violet	1·40	1·30
1279	1l.10 deep brown	2·00	1·40
1276/1279	Set of 4	4·25	3·50
MS1280	80½×91 mm. Type **265** 1l.50, deep slate-violet, red and gold, Imperf	£180	£225

(Des S. Toptani)

1968 (14 Nov). 60th Anniversary of Monastir Language Congress. P 12.

1281	**266** 15q. lake and slate-green	70	65
1282	85q. blackish brown and light bronze-green	4·00	2·50

267 Bohemian Waxwing (*Bombycila garrulus*)

(Des N. Prizreni)

1968 (15 Nov). Birds. Diamond-shaped designs as T **267**. Multicoloured. P 12.

1283	15q. Type **267**	35	25
1284	20q. Rose-coloured Starling (*Pastor roseus*)	40	30
1285	25q. Common Kingfishers (*Alcedo atthis ispida*)	55	35

ALBANIA 1968

1286	50q. Long-tailed Tits (*Aegithalus caodatus*)....	1·40	50
1287	80q. Wallcreeper (*Tichodroma muraria*)	2·75	1·30
1288	1l.10 Bearded Reedling (*Panurus biarmicus*)...	4·00	1·60
1283/1288 Set of 6		8·50	3·75

268 Mao Tse-tung

(Des I. Shehu)

1968 (26 Dec). Mao Tse-tung's 75th Birthday. P 12½×12.

1289	**268**	25q. black, rose-red and gold	1·40	65
1290		1l.75 black, rose-red and gold	8·75	5·75

269 Adem Reka
(dock foreman)

(Des R. Ballauri)

1969 (10 Feb). Contemporary Heroes. T **269** and similar vert designs. Multicoloured. P 12×12½.

1291	5q. Type **269**	55	45
1292	10q. Pjeter Lleshi (telegraph linesman)	70	65
1293	15q. M. Shehu and M. Kepi (fire victims)........	1·40	1·30
1294	25q. Shkurte Vata (railway worker).................	2·00	1·90
1295	65q. Agron Elezi (earthquake victim)	2·30	2·10
1296	80q. Ismet Bruca (school teacher)	2·75	2·50
1297	1l.30 Fuat Cela (blind Co-op leader)................	4·00	3·75
1291/1297 Set of 7	12·00	11·50

 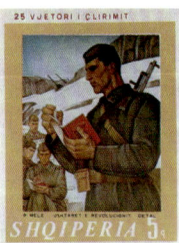

270 Meteorological Equipment

271 Student Revolutionaries
(P. Mele)

(Des N. Prizreni)

1969 (25 Feb). 20th Anniversary of Albanian Hydro-Meteorology. T **270** and similar square designs. Multicoloured. P 12.

1298	15q. Type **270**	60	40
1299	25q. 'Arrow' indicator	90	65
1300	1l.60 Met balloon and isobar map.................	4·25	2·75
1298/1300 Set of 3	5·25	3·50

1969 (20 Apr). Albanian Paintings since 1944. T **271** and similar multicoloured designs. P 12×12½ (5q.) or 12½×12 (others).

1301	5q. Type **271**	35	25
1302	25q. *Partisans, 1944* (F. Haxhiu)	40	30
1303	65q. *Steel Mill* (Ç. Ceka)	55	35
1304	80q. *Reconstruction* (V. Kilica).......................	70	40
1305	1l.10 *Harvest* (N. Jonuzi)..................................	1·40	75
1306	1l.15 *Seaside Terraces* (S. Kaceli)	1·70	1·50
1301/1306 Set of 6	4·50	3·25

MS1307 111×91 mm. 2l. *Partisans' Meeting* (N. Zajmi). Imperf	3·50	2·50

Nos. 1302/1307 are all horiz, the 65q. as T **271**, 2l. size 77×56 mm and the others 50×30 mm.

272 Self-portrait   **273** Congress Building

1969 (2 May). 450th Death Anniversary of Leonardo da Vinci. T **272** and similar drawings and paintings. P 12½×12 (40q.) or 12×12½ (others).

1308	25q. agate, pale brown and gold	40	30
1309	35q. agate, pale brown and gold	70	40
1310	40q. agate, pale brown and gold	95	50
1311	1l. multicoloured	2·75	1·30
1312	2l. agate, pale brown and gold	5·50	1·90
1308/1312 Set of 5	9·25	4·00
MS1313 65×95 mm. 2l. multicoloured. Imperf................	6·75	4·50

Designs: Vert—25q. T **272**; 35q. *Lilies*; 1l. *Portrait of Beatrice*; 2l. (No. 1312), *Portrait of a Lady*; (47×75 *mm*) 2l. (No. **MS**1313), *Mona Lisa*. Horiz—40q. Design for Helicopter.

1969 (24 May). 25th Anniversary of Permet Congress. T **273** and similar square designs. Multicoloured. P 12.

1314	25q. Type **273**	70	40
1315	2l.25 Two partisans	5·50	4·00
MS1316 95×101 mm. 1l. Albanian Arms. Imperf............	55·00	75·00

274 *Viola albanica*   **275** Plum

(Des Q. Prizreni)

1969 (30 June). Flowers. Viola Family. Vert designs as T **274**. Multicoloured. P 12×12½.

1317	5q. Type **274**	25	20
1318	10q. *Viola hortensis*	35	25
1319	15q. *Viola heterophylla*	55	30
1320	20q. *Viola hortensis* (different)	55	35
1321	25q. *Viola odorata*	70	40
1322	80q. *Viola hortensis* (different)	2·00	85
1323	1l.95 *Viola hortensis* (different)	3·50	2·30
1317/1323 Set of 7	8·00	4·25

Nos. 1318, 1320 and 1322/1323 show different versions of the same species.

(Des Q. Prizreni)

1969 (10 Aug). Fruit Trees. Vert designs as T **275** showing blossom and fruit. Multicoloured. P 12×12½.

1324	10q. Type **275**	35	20
1325	15q. Lemon	40	25
1326	25q. Pomegranate	55	30
1327	50q. Cherry	1·40	50
1328	80q. Apricot...	2·00	1·00
1329	1l.20 Apple...	3·50	1·90
1324/1329 Set of 6	7·50	3·75

1969 ALBANIA

276 Throwing the Ball　　**277** Gymnastics

(Des S. Toptani)

1969 (15 Sept). 16th European Basketball Championships, Naples. T **276** and similar multicoloured designs. P 12.

1330	10q. Type **276**		45	20
1331	15q. Trying for goal		55	25
1332	25q. Ball and net (*horiz*)		70	30
1333	80q. Scoring a goal		2·00	40
1334	2l.20 Intercepting a pass		4·00	1·60
1330/1334	Set of 5		7·00	2·50

(Des B. Dizdari)

1969 (30 Sept). National Spartakiad. Square designs as T **277**. Multicoloured. P 12.

1335	5q. Pickaxe, rifle, flag and stadium		25	15
1336	10q. Type **277**		35	20
1337	15q. Running		45	25
1338	20q. Pistol-shooting		55	30
1339	25q. Swimmer on starting block		70	40
1340	80q. Cycling		2·00	70
1341	95q. Football		2·75	1·20
1335/1341	Set of 7		6·25	3·00

278 Mao Tse-tung　　**279** Enver Hoxha

(Des I. Shehu)

1969 (1 Oct). 20th Anniversary of Chinese People's Republic. T **278** and similar multicoloured designs. P 12½×12 (85q.) or 12×12½ (others).

1342	25q. Type **278**		2·00	65
1343	85q. Steel ladle and control room (*horiz*)		6·75	2·50
1344	1l.40 Rejoicing crowd		11·50	4·50
1342/1344	Set of 3		18·00	7·00

(Des R. Ballauri)

1969 (20 Oct). 25th Anniversary of Second National Liberation Council Meeting, Berat. Vert designs as T **279**. Multicoloured. P 12×12½.

1345	25q. Type **279**		40	30
1346	80q. Star and Constitution		95	65
1347	1l.45 Freedom-fighters		2·75	1·50
1345/1347	Set of 3		3·75	2·20

280 Entry of Provisional Government, Tirana

(Des I. Shehu)

1969 (29 Nov). 25th Anniversary of Liberation. T **280** and similar horiz designs. Multicoloured. P 12½×12.

1348	25q. Type **280**		55	30
1349	30q. Oil Refinery		70	35
1350	35q. Combine-harvester		95	40
1351	45q. Hydro-electric power station		1·60	50
1352	55q. Soldier and partisans		2·30	90
1353	1l.10 People rejoicing		4·00	1·50
1348/1353	Set of 6		9·00	3·50

281 Stalin　　**282** Head of Woman

(Des S. Toptani)

1969 (21 Dec). 90th Birth Anniversary of Joseph Stalin. P 12.

1354	**281**	15q. reddish lilac	40	25
1355		25q. slate-blue	70	30
1356		1l. brown	2·30	70
1357		1l.10 chalky blue	2·75	1·30
1354/1357	Set of 4		5·50	2·30

1969 (25 Dec). Mosaics (1st series). Multicoloured designs as T **282**. P 12×12½ (vert) or 12½×12 (horiz).

1358	15q. Type **282**		35	25
1359	25q. Floor pattern (*horiz*)		40	30
1360	80q. Bird and tree (*horiz*)		1·40	50
1361	1l.10 Diamond floor pattern (*horiz*)		1·90	65
1362	1l.20 Corn in oval pattern		2·75	75
1358/1362	Set of 5		6·00	2·20

See also Nos. 1391/1396, 1564/1570 and 1657/1662.

283 Manifesto and Congress Building　　**284** '25' and Workers

(Des R. Ballauri)

1970 (21 Jan). 50th Anniversary of Lushnjë Congress. T **283** and similar vert design. P 12.

1363	25q. black, red and grey		70	45
1364	1l.25 black, greenish yellow and deep bluish green		4·00	2·50

Designs: 25q. T **283**; 1l.25, Lushjnë postmark of 1920.

(Des S. Prapaniku)

1970 (11 Feb). 25th Anniversary of Albanian Trade Unions. P 12½×12.

1365	**284**	25q. black, red, brown and grey	70	45
1366		1l.75 black, red, sepia and lavender	4·00	2·50

285 Lilium cernum　　**286** Lenin

(Des N. Prizreni)

1970 (10 March). Lilies. Multicoloured designs as T **285**. P 12½×12 (vert) or 12×12½ (horiz).

1367	5q. Type **285**		35	25
1368	15q. *Lilium candidum*		40	30

ALBANIA 1970

1369	25q. *Lilium regale*		1·40	45
1370	80q. *Lilium martagon* (horiz)		2·75	1·30
1371	1l.10 *Lilium tigrinum* (horiz)		4·00	1·50
1372	1l.15 *Lilium albanicum*		4·75	2·10
1367/1372 Set of 6			12·50	5·25

1970 (22 Apr). Birth Centenary of Lenin. Designs as T **286**, each black, silver and red. P 12.

1373	5q. Type **286**	25	20
1374	15q. Lenin making speech (horiz)	40	30
1375	25q. As worker (horiz)	70	40
1376	95q. As revolutionary (horiz)	1·60	75
1377	1l.10 Saluting	3·00	1·30
1373/1377 Set of 5		5·25	2·75

287 Frontier Guard

(Des S. Prapaniku)

1970 (25 Apr). 25th Anniversary of Frontier Force. P 12.

1378	**287**	25q. multicoloured	70	45
1379		1l.25 multicoloured	3·50	2·10

288 Jules Rimet Cup

(Des S. Toptani)

1970 (15 May). World Cup Football Championship, Mexico. T **288** and similar horiz designs. Multicoloured. P 12½×12.

1380	5q. Type **288**	20	15
1381	10q. Aztec Stadium	25	20
1382	15q. Three footballers	35	30
1383	25q. Heading goal	35	30
1384	65q. Two footballers	40	40
1385	80q. Two footballers	1·40	50
1386	2l. Two footballers	2·75	1·30
1380/1386 Set of 7		5·25	2·75

MS1387 81×74 mm. 2l. Mexican Horseman and Mount Popocatepetl. P 12×imperf. .... 4·75 4·50

Nos. 1384/1386 show different incidents. The design of No. **MS**1387 is larger, 56×45 mm.

289 New UPU Headquarters Building

(Des S. Qesku)

1970 (30 May). New UPU Headquarters Building, Berne. P 12.

1388	**289**	25q. light blue, black and new blue	40	25
1389		1l.10 flesh, black and yellow-orange	2·00	65
1390		1l.15 light blue-green, black and light emerald	2·30	1·30
1388/1390 Set of 3			4·25	2·00

290 Birds and Grapes   **291** Harvester and Dancers

(Des S. Toptani)

1970 (10 July). Mosaics (2nd series). T **290** and similar multicoloured designs. P 12×12½ (2l.25) or 12½×12 (others).

1391	5q. Type **290**	25	20
1392	10q. Waterfowl	35	25
1393	20q. Pheasant and tree-stump	55	30
1394	25q. Bird and leaves	70	35
1395	65q. Fish	1·40	50
1396	2l.25 Peacock (vert)	4·75	2·10
1391/1396 Set of 6		7·25	3·25

(Des Q. Prizreni)

1970 (28 Aug). 25th Anniversary of Agrarian Reform. T **291** and similar horiz designs. P 12×11½.

1397	15q. slate-lilac and black	55	30
1398	25q. blue and black	70	40
1399	80q. brown and black	2·00	50
1400	1l.30 orange-brown and black	2·75	1·30
1397/1400 Set of 4		5·50	2·30

Designs: 15q. T **291**; 25q. Ploughed fields and open-air conference; 80q. Cattle and newspapers; 1l.30, Combine-harvester and official visit.

292 Partisans going into Battle   **293** The Harvesters (I. Sulovari)

(Des Q. Prizreni)

1970 (3 Sept). 50th Anniversary of Battle of Vlörë. Vert designs as T **292**. P 12.

1401	15q. orange-brown, light orange and black	40	30
1402	25q. bistre-brown, light yellow and black	95	40
1403	1l.60 myrtle-green, light green and black	3·00	1·80
1401/1403 Set of 3		4·00	2·30

Designs: 15q. T **292**; 25q. Victory parade; 1l.60, Partisans.

1970 (25 Sept). 25th Anniversary of Liberation. Prize-winning Paintings. Multicoloured designs as T **293**. P 12×12½ (vert) or 12½×12 (horiz).

1404	5q. Type **293**	25	20
1405	15q. *Return of the Partisan* (D. Trebicka)	35	30
1406	25q. *The Miners* (N. Zajmi) (horiz)	35	35
1407	65q. *Instructing the Partisans* (H. Nallbani) (horiz)	40	40
1408	95q. *Making Plans* (V. Kilica) (horiz)	1·80	1·00
1409	2l. *The Machinist* (Z. Shoshi)	3·50	2·10
1404/1409 Set of 6		6·00	4·00

MS1410 67×96 mm. 2l. *The Guerrilla* (S. Shijaku) (54×75 *mm*). Imperf .... 4·75 2·50

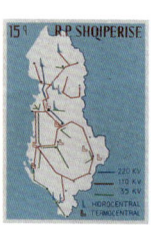 

294 Electrification Map   **295** Engels

(Des S. Toptani)

1970 (25 Oct). Completion of Rural Electrification. T **294** and similar vert designs. Multicoloured. P 12.

1411	15q. Type **294**	40	30
1412	25q. Lamp and graph	70	40
1413	80q. Erecting power lines	2·00	50
1414	1l.10 Uses of electricity	2·30	1·30
1411/1414 Set of 4		4·75	2·30

1970 ALBANIA

(Des N. Prizreni)

1970 (28 Nov). 150th Birth Anniversary of Friedrich Engels. Vert designs as T **295**. P 12×12½.
1415	25q. deep blue and bistre	70	30
1416	1l.10 maroon and bistre	1·80	75
1417	1l.15 deep olive and bistre	2·30	1·00
1415/1417 Set of 3		4·25	1·80

Designs: 25q. T **295**; 1l.10, Engels as young man; 1l.15, Engel, making speech.

295a Tractor Factory, Tirana.

1970 (4 Dec)–**71**. Industry. T **295a** and similar multicoloured designs. P 12.
1417a	10q. Type **295a** (20.1.71)	£350	£190
1417b	15q. Fertiliser factory, Fier	£350	£190
1417c	20q. Superphosphate factory, Laç (vert) (20.1.71)	£350	£190
1417d	25q. Cement factory, Elbasan (20.1.71)	£350	£190
1417e	80q. Factory, Qyteti Stalin	£350	£190
1417a/1417e Set of 5		£1600	£850

296 Beethoven's Birthplace **297** Republican Emblem

(Des S. Qesku)

1970 (16 Dec). Birth Bicentenary of Beethoven. Designs as T **296**. P 12.
1418	5q. reddish violet and gold	35	20
1419	15q. purple and silver	40	35
1420	25q. green and gold	70	40
1421	65q. bright purple and silver	1·60	1·00
1422	1l.10 deep blue and gold	3·00	1·30
1423	1l.80 black and silver	5·50	2·30
1418/1423 Set of 6		10·50	5·00

Designs: Vert—Beethoven 5q. T **296**; 15q. In silhouette; 25q. As young man; 65q. Full-face; 1l.10, Profile. Horiz—1l.80, Stage performance of *Fidelio*.

(Des S. Qesku)

1971 (11 Jan). 25th Anniversary of Republic. T **297** and similar horiz designs. P 12.
1424	15q. multicoloured	40	30
1425	25q. multicoloured	50	45
1426	80q. black, gold and bright green	1·60	1·00
1427	1l.30 black, gold and bright yellow-brown	2·30	1·50
1424/1427 Set of 4		4·25	3·00

Designs: 15q. T **297**; 25q. Proclamation; 80q. Enver Hoxha; 1l.30, Patriots.

298 Storming the Barricades **299** Conflict of Race

(Des S. Qesku)

1971 (18 Mar). Centenary of Paris Commune. Designs as T **298**. P 12.
1428	25q. blue and deep blue	70	30
1429	50q. deep yellow-green and slate-green	95	50
1430	65q. chestnut and blackish brown	1·40	65
1431	1l.10 slate-lilac and deep violet	2·40	1·30
1428/1431 Set of 4		5·00	2·50

Designs: Vert—25q. *La Marseillaise*; 50q. Women Communards. Horiz—65q. T **298**; 1l.10, Firing squad.

(Des C. Ceka)

1971 (21 Mar). Racial Equality Year. T **299** and similar horiz designs. P 12×12½.
1432	25q. black and orange-brown	40	30
1433	1l.10 black and carmine	1·40	40
1434	1l.15 black and orange-red	1·60	75
1432/1434 Set of 3		3·00	1·30

Designs: 25q. T **299**; 1l.10, Heads of three races; 1l.15, Freedom fighter.

300 Tulip **301** Postrider

(Des N. Prizreni)

1971 (25 Mar). Hybrid Tulips. T **300** and similar vert designs, showing different varieties of Tulips. P 12×12½.
1435	5q. multicoloured	25	15
1436	10q. multicoloured	35	20
1437	15q. multicoloured	45	25
1438	20q. multicoloured	55	30
1439	25q. multicoloured	70	40
1440	80q. multicoloured	2·00	50
1441	1l. multicoloured	3·50	1·00
1442	1l.45 multicoloured	5·50	2·10
1435/1442 Set of 8		12·00	4·50

1971 (15 May). 500th Birth Anniversary of Albrecht Dürer (painter and engraver). T **301** and similar designs showing Dürer's works. P 11½×12 (vert) or 12×11½ (horiz).
1443	10q. black and blackish olive	35	15
1444	15q. black and lavender	40	20
1445	25q. black and pale grey-blue	55	25
1446	45q. black and pale reddish purple	1·40	50
1447	65q. multicoloured	2·75	1·00
1448	2l.40 multicoloured	8·00	2·50
1443/1448 Set of 6		12·00	4·25
MS1449 93×90 mm. 2l.50, multicoloured. Imperf		6·75	4·50

Designs: Vert—10q. T **301**; 15q. *Three Peasants*; 25q. *Peasant Dancers*; 45q. *The Bagpiper*. Horiz—65q. *View of Kalchreut*; 2l.40, *View of Trient*. Larger—2l.50, Self-portrait.

302 Globe and Satellite (1970) **303** Mao Tse-tung

(Des N. Prizreni)

1971 (10 June). Chinese Space Achievements. T **302** and similar vert designs. Multicoloured. P 12.
1450	60q. Type **302**	1·40	65
1451	1l.20 Public Building, Tirana	2·75	1·90
1452	2l.20 Globe and satellite (1971)	5·50	3·75
1450/1452 Set of 3		8·75	5·75
MS1453 65×112 mm. 2l.50, Globe and arrow. Imperf		8·00	4·50

The date on No. 1451 refers to the passage of Chinese satellite over Tirana.

1971 (1 July). 50th Anniversary of Chinese Communist Party. T **303** and similar multicoloured designs. P 12.
1454	25q. Type **303**	90	65
1455	1l.05 Party birthplace (horiz)	2·75	2·50
1456	1l.20 Chinese celebrations (horiz)	4·00	3·25
1454/1456 Set of 3		7·00	5·75

ALBANIA 1971

304 Crested Tit (*Parus cristatus mitratus*)

(Des N. Prizreni)

1971 (15 Aug). Birds. T **304** and similar horiz designs. Multicoloured. P 12.
1457	5q. Type **304**	40	15
	a. Block of 7. Nos. 1457/1463 plus label....	21·00	
1458	10q. Serin (*Serinus canaria serinus*)	55	20
1459	15q. Linnet (*Acanthis canabina*)	80	25
1460	25q. Firecrest (wrongly inscr '*Regulus regulus*')	1·40	30
1461	45q. Rock Thrush (*Monticola saxatilis*)	2·00	40
1462	60q. Blue Tit (*Parus coeruleus*)	3·00	1·30
1463	2l.40 Chaffinch (*Fringilla coelebs*)	12·00	9·50
1457/1463 Set of 7		18·00	11·00

Nos. 1457/1463 were issued together within the sheet in *se-tenant* blocks of seven stamps and one label showing a nest.

Blocks also exist cancelled to order with the design of the 2l.40 omitted. These were prepared for sale as c-t-o 'short' sets.

305 Running

(Des S. Toptani)

1971 (15 Sept). Olympic Games, Munich (1972) (1st issue). T **305** and similar horiz designs (except No. **MS**1471). Multicoloured. P 12.
1464	5q. Type **305**	20	15
1465	10q. Hurdling	25	20
1466	15q. Canoeing	35	25
1467	25q. Gymnastics	55	30
1468	80q. Fencing	1·40	40
1469	1l.05 Football	1·80	65
1470	3l.60 Diving	5·50	1·30
1464/1470 Set of 7		9·00	3·00
MS1471 70×83 mm. 2l. Runner breasting tape (47×54 *mm*). Imperf		4·75	3·25

See also Nos. 1522/**MS**1530.

306 Workers with Banner   **307** 'XXX' and Red Flag

(Des N. Prizreni)

1971 (1 Nov). Sixth Workers' Party Congress. T **306** and similar multicoloured designs. P 12.
1472	25q. Type **306**	70	30
1473	1l.05 Congress Hall	2·00	1·60
1474	1l.20 'VI', flag, star and rifle (*vert*)	2·75	1·80
1472/1474 Set of 3		5·00	3·25

(Des N. Prizreni)

1971 (8 Nov). 30th Anniversary of Albanian Workers' Party. T **307** and similar multicoloured designs. P 12.
1475	15q. Workers and industry (*horiz*)	40	25
1476	80q. Type **307**	1·60	1·30
1477	1l.55 Enver Hoxha and flags (*horiz*)	3·50	2·10
1475/1477 Set of 3		5·00	3·25

308 Young Man (R. Kuci)   **309** Emblems and Flags

1971 (20 Nov). Albanian Paintings. T **308** and similar multicoloured designs. P 12.
1478	5q. Type **308**	20	15
1479	15q. *Building Construction* (M. Fushëkati) (*horiz*)	35	20
1480	25q. *Partisan* (D. Jukniu)	40	25
1481	80q. *Fighter Pilots* (S. Kristo) (*horiz*)	1·20	30
1482	1l.20 *Girl Messenger* (A. Sadikaj) (*horiz*)	1·60	1·00
1483	1l.55 *Medieval Warriors* (S. Kamberi) (*horiz*)	2·00	1·50
1478/1483 Set of 6		5·25	3·00
MS1484 89×70 mm. 2l. *Partisans in the Mountains* (I. Lulani). Imperf		4·75	3·25

(Des B. Dizdari)

1971 (23 Nov). 30th Anniversary of Albanian Young Communists Union. P 12.
1485	**309**	15q. multicoloured	35	15
1486		1l.35 multicoloured	2·30	1·10

310 Village Girls

(Des T. Dajci)

1971 (27 Dec). Albanian Ballet *Halili and Hajria*. T **310** and similar horiz designs showing ballet scenes. Multicoloured. P 12.
1487	5q. Type **310**	20	15
1488	10q. Parting of Halili and Hajria	25	20
1489	15q. Hajria before Sultan Suleiman	30	25
1490	50q. Hajria's marriage	80	50
1491	80q. Execution of Halili	1·40	75
1492	1l.40 Hajria killing her husband	2·75	1·50
1487/1492 Set of 6		5·25	3·00

311 Rifle-shooting (Biathlon)

(Des S. Toptani)

1972 (10 Feb). Winter Olympic Games, Sapporo, Japan. T **311** and similar horiz designs. Multicoloured. P 12.
1493	5q. Type **311**	15	10
1494	10q. Tobogganing	20	15
1495	15q. Ice hockey	25	20
1496	20q. Bobsleighing	35	25
1497	50q. Speed skating	80	65
1498	1l. Slalom skiing	1·40	1·00
1499	2l. Ski jumping	3·00	2·10
1493/1499 Set of 7		5·50	4·00
MS1500 71×91 mm. 2l.50, Figure skating. Imperf		4·75	3·25

1972 ALBANIA

312 Wild Strawberries

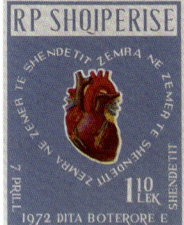
313 Human Heart

317 High Jumping

1972 (20 Mar). **Wild Forest Fruits.** T **312** and similar square designs. Multicoloured. P 12.

1501	5q. Type **312**	15	10
1502	10q. Blackberries	20	15
1503	15q. Hazelnuts	25	20
1504	20q. Walnuts	50	25
1505	25q. Strawberry-tree fruit	55	30
1506	30q. Dogwood berries	80	50
1507	2l.40 Rowanberries	5·50	1·60
1501/1507	Set of 7	7·25	2·75

(Des S. Toptani)

1972 (7 Apr). **World Health Day.** T **313** and similar vert design. Multicoloured. P 12.

1508	1l.10 Type **313**	2·30	1·50
1509	1l.20 Treatment of cardiac patient	2·40	1·60

314 Congress Delegates

315 Memorial Flame

(Des I. Shehu)

1972 (24 Apr). **7th Albanian Trade Unions Congress.** T **314** and similar vert design. Multicoloured. P 12×12½.

1510	25q. Type **314**	95	65
1511	2l.05 Congress Hall	3·75	2·10

(Des N. Prizreni)

1972 (5 May). **30th Anniversary of Martyrs' Day and Death of Kemal Stafa.** T **315** and similar designs. P 12×12½ (25q.) or 12½×12 (others).

1512	15q. multicoloured	35	15
1513	25q. pale grey, black and orange-red	55	25
1514	1l.90 black and yellow-ochre	3·50	1·40
1512/1514	Set of 3	4·00	1·60

Designs: Vert—25q. *Spirit of Defiance* (statue). Horiz—15q. T **315**; 1l.90, Kemal Stafa.

316 *Camellia japonica Kamelie*

(Des N. Prizreni)

1972 (10 May). **Camellias.** T **316** and similar vert designs, showing different varieties of flower. P 12.

1515	5q. multicoloured	20	15
1516	10q. multicoloured	25	20
1517	15q. multicoloured	35	25
1518	25q. multicoloured	55	30
1519	45q. multicoloured	80	35
1520	50q. multicoloured	1·60	50
1521	2l.50 multicoloured	6·00	2·75
1515/1521	Set of 7	8·75	4·00

(Des S. Toptani)

1972 (30 June). **Olympic Games, Munich (2nd issue).** T **317** and similar horiz designs. Multicoloured. P 12.

1522	5q. Type **317**	10	10
1523	10q. Running	15	15
1524	15q. Putting the shot	20	20
1525	20q. Cycling	35	25
1526	25q. Pole-vaulting	50	30
1527	50q. Hurdling	70	40
1528	75q. Hockey	1·40	50
1529	2l. Swimming	4·00	1·00
1522/1529	Set of 8	6·75	2·50
MS1530	59×76 mm. 2l.50, High-diving (*vert*). Imperf.	4·75	3·25

Nos. 1522/1529 were each issued in sheets of eight stamps with a central stamp-size label showing Olympic rings.

318 Articulated Bus

319 Trial of Strength

(Des N. Prizreni)

1972 (25 July). **Modern Transport.** T **318** and similar horiz designs. Multicoloured. P 12×11½.

1531	15q. Type **318**	35	15
1532	25q. Diesel railway locomotive	70	20
1533	80q. Freighter *Tirana*	95	30
1534	1l.05 Motor-car	1·40	50
1535	1l.20 Container lorry	2·75	1·00
1531/1535	Set of 5	5·50	1·90

(Des I. Shehu)

1972 (18 Aug). **First National Festival of Traditional Games.** T **319** and similar square designs. Multicoloured. P 12.

1536	5q. Type **319**	15	10
1537	10q. Pick-a-back ball game	20	15
1538	15q. Leaping game	25	20
1539	25q. Rope game	55	25
1540	90q. Leap-frog	1·80	75
1541	2l. Women's throwing game	3·50	2·10
1536/1541	Set of 6	5·75	3·25

320 Newspaper Mastheads

(Des S. Toptani)

1972 (25 Aug). **30th Anniversary of Press Day.** T **320** and similar horiz designs. P 12.

1542	15q. black and light greenish blue	25	20
1543	25q. black, myrtle-green and scarlet	40	25
1544	1l.90 black and lavender	2·50	1·70
1542/1544	Set of 3	2·75	1·90

Designs: 15q. T **320**; 25q. Printing press and partisan; 1l.90, Workers with newspaper.

ALBANIA 1972

321 Location Map and Commemorative Plaque

323 Congress Emblem

322 Partisan Conference (S. Capo)

(Des T. Dajci)

1972 (16 Sept). 30th Anniversary of Peza Conference. T **321** and similar horiz designs. Multicoloured. P 12×11½.
1545	15q. Type **321**	40	30
1546	25q. Partisans with flag	70	50
1547	1l.90 Conference Memorial	3·75	2·30
1545/1547	Set of 3	4·25	2·75

1972 (25 Sept). Albanian Paintings. T **322** and similar multicoloured designs. P 12.
1548	5q. Type **322**	15	10
1549	10q. *Head of a Woman* (I. Lulani) (*vert*)	20	15
1550	15q. *Communists* (L. Shkreli) (*vert*)	25	20
1551	20q. *Nendorit, 1941* (S. Shijaku) (*vert*)	40	25
1552	50q. *Farm Woman* (Z. Shoshi) (*vert*)	65	30
1553	1l. *Landscape* (D. Trebicka)	1·40	75
1554	2l. *Girls with Bicycles* (V. Kilica)	3·50	2·10
1548/1554	Set of 7	6·00	3·50
MS1555	55×83 mm. 2l.30, *Folk Dance* (A. Buza) (*vert*, 40×67 mm). Imperf	4·75	3·25

(Des B. Dizdari)

1972 (23 Oct). 6th Congress of Young Communists' Union. T **323** and similar vert design. P 12.
1556	25q. gold, red and silver	95	65
1557	2l.05 multicoloured	3·75	2·10

Designs: 25q. T **323**; 2l.05, Young worker and banner.

324 Lenin

325 Albanian Soldiers

(Des N. Prizreni)

1972 (7 Nov). 55th Anniversary of Russian October Revolution. T **324** and similar vert design. P 11½×12.
1558	1l.10 multicoloured	2·00	1·10
1559	1l.20 black, vermilion and rose-red	4·00	1·40

Designs: 1l.10, T **324**; 1l.10, Hammer and sickle.

(Des B. Kaceli)

1972 (29 Nov). 60th Anniversary of Independence. T **325** and similar designs. P 12×11½.
1560	15q. new blue, black and scarlet	20	15
1561	25q. black, carmine-red and lemon	40	25
1562	65q. multicoloured	95	75
1563	1l.25 black and red	3·00	1·50
1560/1563	Set of 4	4·00	2·40

Designs: Vert—25q. Ismail Qemali; 1l.25, Albanian double-headed Eagle emblem. Horiz—15q. T **325**; 65q. Proclamation of Independence, 1912.

326 Cockerel (mosaic)

327 Nicolas Copernicus

(Des F. Hasimja)

1972 (10 Dec). Ancient Mosaics from Apolloni and Butrint (3rd series). T **326** and similar multicoloured designs with silver borders. P 12½×12 (horiz) or 12×12½ (vert).
1564	5q. Type **326**	15	10
1565	10q. Bird (*vert*)	20	15
1566	15q. Partridges (*vert*)	25	20
1567	25q. Warrior's legs	45	30
1568	45q. Nude on Dolphin (*vert*)	70	40
1569	50q. Fish (*vert*)	1·10	50
1570	2l.50 Warrior's head	4·00	2·75
1564/1570	Set of 7	6·25	4·00

(Des N. Prizreni)

1973 (19 Feb). 500th Birth Anniversary of Copernicus. T **327** and similar vert designs. Multicoloured. P 12.
1571	5q. Type **327**	15	10
1572	10q. Copernicus and signature	25	15
1573	25q. Engraved portrait	35	20
1574	80q. Copernicus at desk	75	40
1575	1l.20 Copernicus and planets	2·40	1·00
1576	1l.60 Planetary diagram	4·00	1·90
1571/1576	Set of 6	7·00	3·50

328 Policeman and Industrial Scene

(Des N. Prizreni)

1973 (20 Mar). 30th Anniversary of State Security Police. T **328** and similar horiz design. P 12½×12.
1577	25q. black, new blue and pale blue	70	65
1578	1l.80 multicoloured	3·75	2·10

Designs: 25q. T **328**; 1l.80, Prisoner under escort.

329/330 Cactus Flowers

(Des S. Qesku)

1973 (25 Mar). Cacti. Various triangular designs showing different species, as in Types **329/330**. P 12.
1579	10q. multicoloured	15	10
	a. Block of 8. Nos. 1579/1586	13·50	
1580	15q. multicoloured	20	15
1581	20q. multicoloured	25	20
1582	25q. multicoloured	70	25
1583	30q. multicoloured	5·75	2·75
1584	65q. multicoloured	1·40	40
1585	80q. multicoloured	1·90	50
1586	2l. multicoloured	2·40	1·30
1579/1586	Set of 8	11·50	5·00

Nos. 1579/1586 were issued together in *se-tenant* blocks of eight within the sheet, each block containing four pairs as Types **329/330**. Blocks also exist cancelled-to-order with the 30q. replaced by a label.

331 Common Tern (*Sterna hirundo*)

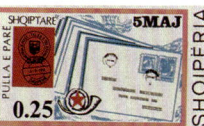

332 Postmark of 1913, and Letters

(Des N. Prizreni)

1973 (30 Apr). Sea Birds. T **331** and similar multicoloured designs. P 12½×12 (horiz) or 12×12½ (vert).

1587	5q. Type **331**	25	20
1588	15q. White-winged Black Tern (*Chlidonias leucoptera*)	40	25
1589	25q. Black-headed Gull (*Larus ridibundus*)	55	40
1590	45q. Great black-headed Gull (wrongly inscr '*Larus argentatus*')	1·40	75
1591	80q. Slender-billed Gull (*Larus genei*) (*vert*)	2·75	1·90
1592	2l.40 Sandwich Tern (*Sterna sandvicensis*)	5·50	5·00
1587/1592 Set of 6		9·75	7·75

(Des R. Ballauri)

1973 (5 May). 60th Anniversary of First Albanian Stamps. T **332** and similar horiz design. Multicoloured. P 12×11½.

1593	25q. Type **332**	1·40	65
1594	1l.80 1913 postmark, and postman	5·50	2·50

333 Albanian Woman

334 *Creation of the General Staff* (G. Madhi)

(Des B. Dizdari)

1973 (4 June). Seventh Congress of Albanian Women's Union. T **333** and similar design. P 12.

1595	25q. carmine-red and pink	70	40
1596	1l.80 black, red-orange and pale yellow	4·00	2·75

Designs: Vert—25q. T **333**. Horiz—1l.80, Albanian female workers.

1973 (10 July). 30th Anniversary of Albanian People's Army. T **334** and similar multicoloured designs, showing paintings or sculptures. P 12.

1597	25q. Type **334**	17·00	12·50
1598	40q. *August 1949* (statue, S. Haderi) (*vert*)	17·00	12·50
1599	60q. *Generation after Generation* (statue, H. Dule) (*vert*)	17·00	12·50
1600	80q. *Defend Revolutionary Victories* (M. Fushëkati)	17·00	12·50
1597/1600 Set of 4		60·00	45·00

335 *Electrification* (S. Hysa)

1973 (10 Aug). Albanian Paintings. T **335** and similar multicoloured designs. P 12.

1601	5q. Type **335**	15	10
1602	10q. *Textile Worker* (N. Nallbani) (*vert*)	20	15
1603	15q. *Gymnastics Class* (M. Fushëkati)	25	20
1604	50q. *Aviator* (F. Stamo) (*vert*)	65	40
1605	80q. *Downfall of Fascism* (A. Lakuriqi) (*vert*)	75	50
1606	1l.20 *Koci Bako* (demonstrators) (P. Mele) (*vert*)	1·40	1·00
1607	1l.30 *Peasant Girl* (Z. Shoshi) (*vert*)	2·75	2·10
1601/1607 Set of 7		5·50	4·00
MS1608 100×69 mm. 2l.05, *Battle of Tendes se Qypit* (F. Haxhiu) (88×47 *mm*). Imperf		4·75	3·25

336 *Mary Magdalene*

1973 (28 Sept). 400th Birth Anniversary of Caravaggio. T **336** and similar multicoloured designs, showing his paintings. P 12.

1609	5q. Type **336**	15	10
1610	10q. *Guitar Player* (*horiz*)	20	15
1611	15q. *Self-portrait*	25	20
	a. Black (value and bottom inscr) omitted	£100	
1612	50q. *Boy with Fruit*	65	40
1613	80q. *Basket of Fruit* (*horiz*)	1·10	1·00
1614	1l.20 *Narcissus*	1·40	1·30
1615	1l.30 *Boy peeling Apple*	2·75	2·50
	a. Black (value and bottom inscr) omitted	£150	
1609/1615 Set of 7		5·75	5·00
MS1616 80×102 mm. 2l.05, *Man in Feathered Hat*. Imperf		7·50	6·25

337 Goalkeeper with Ball

(Des S. Toptani)

1973 (15 Oct). World Cup Football Championship, Munich (1974) (1st issue). T **337** and similar horiz designs, showing goalkeepers in various poses. P 12.

1617	5q. multicoloured	15	10
1618	10q. multicoloured	20	15
1619	15q. multicoloured	30	20
1620	20q. multicoloured	35	25
1621	25q. multicoloured	45	30
1622	90q. multicoloured	1·30	40
1623	1l.20 multicoloured	1·50	75
1624	1l.25 multicoloured	2·20	1·00
1617/1624 Set of 8		5·75	2·75
MS1625 80×50 mm. 2l.05, multicoloured (Ball in net, and list of Championships). Imperf		5·00	3·50

See also Nos. 1663/**MS**1671.

338 Weightlifting

339 Ballet Scene

(Des N. Prizreni)

1973 (30 Oct). World Weightlifting Championships, Havana, Cuba. T **338** and similar designs showing various 'lifts'. P 12.

1626	5q. multicoloured	15	10
1627	10q. multicoloured	20	15
1628	25q. multicoloured	30	20
1629	90q. multicoloured	75	40
1630	1l.20 multicoloured (*horiz*)	1·20	80
1631	1l.80 multicoloured (*horiz*)	3·00	1·40
1626/1631 Set of 6		5·00	2·75

ALBANIA 1973

(Des Q. Prizreni)

1973 (5 Dec)–**74**. Albanian Life and Work. T **339** and similar multicoloured designs. P 12½×12 (vert) or 12×12½ (horiz).

1632	5q. Cement works, Kavaje (20.3.74)..................	15	10
1633	10q. Ali Kelmendi lorry factory (*horiz*) (20.3.74)...	20	15
1634	15q. Type **339**	75	20
1635	20q. Combine-harvester (*horiz*) (12.8.74)........	30	15
1636	25q. Telecommunications..................................	1·20	30
1637	35q. Skier and hotel, Dajt (*horiz*) (20.3.74)......	60	25
1638	60q. Llogora holiday village (*horiz*) (20.3.74)	1·50	50
1639	80q. Lake scene	2·50	55
1640	1l. Textile Mill (*horiz*) (12.8.74).......................	45	25
1641	1l.20 Furnacemen (*horiz*) (12.8.74).................	1·70	55
1642	2l.40 Welder and pipeline (*horiz*) (12.8.74) ...	3·50	1·80
1643	3l. Skanderbeg Statue, Tirana............................	5·75	3·00
1644	5l. Roman arches, Durrës (20.3.74)	6·50	4·00
1632/1644 Set of 13		23·00	10·50

340 Mao Tse-tung

341 Horse's Head (Géricault)

(Des S. Toptani)

1973 (26 Dec). 80th Birthday of Mao Tse-tung. T **340** and similar vert design. Multicoloured. P 12.

1645	85q. Type **340**	3·75	2·10
1646	1l.20 Mao Tse-tung at parade............................	5·00	3·50

1974 (18 Jan). 150th Death Anniversary of Jean-Louis Géricault (French painter). T **341** and similar designs inscr 'ZHERIKO'. P 12.

1647	10q. multicoloured	15	10
1648	15q. multicoloured	20	15
1649	20q. blackish brown and gold	30	20
1650	25q. black, dull lavender and gold....................	55	35
1651	1l.20 multicoloured	2·50	75
1652	2l.20 multicoloured	4·75	2·40
1647/1652 Set of 6		7·50	3·50
MS1653 90×68 mm. 2l.05, multicoloured. Imperf.................		5·00	3·50

Designs: Vert—10q. T **341**; 15q. *Male Model*; 20q. *Man and Dog*; 25q. *Head of a Negro*; 1l.20, *Self-portrait*. Horiz—2l.20, *Battle of the Giants*. (Larger)—2l.05, *Raft of the Medusa*.

342 Lenin with Crew of the 'Aurora'

(D. Trebicka)

1974 (21 Jan). 50th Death Anniversary of Lenin. T **342** and similar multicoloured paintings. P 12.

1654	25q. Type **342**	75	40
1655	60q. *Lenin* (P. Mele) (*vert*)...............................	1·50	70
1656	1l.20 *Lenin* (seated) (V. Kilica) (*vert*)..............	4·25	2·75
1654/1656 Set of 3		5·75	3·50

343 Duck

1974 (20 Feb). Ancient Mosaics from Butrint, Pogradec and Apolloni (4th series). T **343** and similar horiz designs. Multicoloured. P 12.

1657	5q. Type **343**	15	10
1658	10q. Bird and flower	20	15
1659	15q. Ornamental basket and Grapes..................	30	20
1660	25q. Duck (*different*)...	35	30
1661	40q. Donkey and Cockerel.................................	75	40
1662	2l.50 Dragon	3·75	2·10
1657/1662 Set of 6		5·00	3·00

344 Shooting at Goal

(Des Q. Prizreni)

1974 (25 Apr). World Cup Football Championship, Munich (2nd issue). T **344** and similar horiz designs, showing players in action. P 12.

1663	10q. multicoloured	15	10
1664	15q. multicoloured	20	15
1665	20q. multicoloured	30	20
1666	25q. multicoloured	35	25
1667	40q. multicoloured	60	30
1668	80q. multicoloured	1·20	55
1669	1l. multicoloured	1·50	80
1670	1l.20 multicoloured	2·50	1·50
1663/1670 Set of 8		6·00	3·50
MS1671 72×75 mm. 2l.05, multicoloured (Trophy and names of competing countries). Imperf................		5·00	3·50

345 Memorial and Arms

346 *Solanum dulcamara*

(Des Q. Prizreni)

1974 (24 May). 30th Anniversary of Permet Congress. T **345** and similar vert design. Multicoloured. P 12.

1672	25q. Type **345**	75	55
1673	1l.80 Enver Hoxha and text...............................	3·00	2·10

1974 (25 May). Useful Plants. T **346** and similar multicoloured designs. P 12×12½ (vert) or 12½×12 (horiz).

1674	10q. Type **346**	15	10
1675	15q. *Arbutus uva-ursi*	20	15
1676	20q. *Convallaria majalis*	30	20
1677	25q. *Colchicum autumnale*	60	25
1678	40q. *Borago officinalis* (*horiz*)........................	85	30
1679	80q. *Saponaria officinalis* (*horiz*)...................	1·70	55
1680	2l.20 *Gentiane lutea* (*horiz*)............................	5·00	2·20
1674/1680 Set of 7		8·00	3·50

347 Revolutionaries

(Des C. Ceka)

1974 (10 June). 50th Anniversary of 1924 Revolution. T **347** and similar design. P 12½×12 (horiz) or 12×12½ (vert).

1681	25q. black, lilac and scarlet	75	55
1682	1l.80 multicoloured	3·00	2·10

Designs: Horiz—25q. T **347**. Vert—1l.80, Prominent revolutionaries.

348 Redwing (*Turdus musicus*)

(Des N. Prizreni)

1974 (15 July). Song Birds. T **348** and similar multicoloured designs. P 12½×12 (horiz) or 12×12½ (vert).
1683	10q. Type **348**	20	15
1684	15q. European Robin (*Erithacus rubecula*)	30	20
1685	20q. Greenfinch (*Chloris chloris*)	35	25
1686	25q. Bullfinch (*Pyrrhula pyrrhula*) (vert)	60	30
1687	40q. Hawfinch (*Coccothraustes coccothraustes*) (vert)	75	35
1688	80q. Blackcap (*Sylvia atricapilla*) (vert)	2·50	85
1689	2l.20 Nightingale (*Luscina megarhyncha*) (vert)	5·75	2·10
1683/1689 *Set of 7*		9·50	3·75

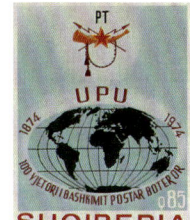

349 Globe and Post Office Emblem

(Des S. Toptani)

1974 (25 Aug). Centenary of Universal Postal Union. T **349** and similar designs. P 12×12½.
1690	85q. multicoloured	2·50	1·10
1691	1l.20 dull green, lilac and deep reddish violet	3·75	1·70
MS1692 78×78 mm. 2l.05, multicoloured. Imperf		27·00	45·00

Designs: Vert—85q. T **349**; 1l.20, UPU emblem. Square (70×70 mm)—2l.05, Text on Globe.

350 Widows (Sali Shijaku)

1974 (25 Sept). Albanian Paintings. T **350** and similar multicoloured designs. P 12½×12 (horiz) or 12×12½ (vert).
1693	10q. Type **350**	15	10
1694	15q. *Road Construction* (Danish Jukniu) (vert)	20	15
1695	20q. *Fulfilling the Plans* (Çlirim Ceka)	30	20
1696	25q. *Call to Action* (Spiro Kristo) (vert)	45	25
1697	40q. *Winter Battle* (Sabaudin Xhaferi)	60	30
1698	80q. *Three Comrades* (Çlirim Ceka) (vert)	1·50	55
1699	1l. *Step By Step, Aid the Partisans* (Guri Madhi)	2·20	1·10
1700	1l.20 *At the War Memorial* (Kleo Nini)	3·00	1·70
1693/1700 *Set of 8*		7·50	4·00
MS1701 87×78 mm. 2l.05, *Comrades* (Guri Madhi). Imperf		5·00	3·50

351 Chinese Festivities

(Des I. Shehu)

1974 (1 Oct). 25th Anniversary of Chinese People's Republic. T **351** and similar design. P 12.
1702	85q. multicoloured	4·25	2·75
1703	1l.20 black, rosine and gold	6·50	4·25

Designs: Horiz—85q. T **351**. Vert—1l.20, Mao Tse-tung.

352 Volleyball

(Des. Q. Prizreni)

1974 (9 Oct). National Spartakiad. T **352** and similar vert designs. Multicoloured. P 12×12½.
1704	10q. Type **352**	15	10
1705	15q. Hurdling	20	15
1706	20q. Hoop Exercises	30	25
1707	25q. Stadium parade	35	30
1708	40q. Weightlifting	60	35
1709	80q. Wrestling	75	40
1710	1l. Rifle drill	1·50	50
1711	1l.20 Football	2·20	55
1704/1711 *Set of 8*		5·50	2·30

353 Berat

(Des M. Quarri)

1974 (20 Oct). 30th Anniversary of Second Berat Liberation Council Meeting. T **353** and similar designs. P 12×12½ (vert) or 12½×12 (horiz).
1712	25q. carmine and black	75	40
1713	80q. greenish yellow, chocolate and black	2·20	1·00
1714	1l. reddish purple and black	4·25	2·10
1712/1714 *Set of 3*		6·50	3·25

Designs: Horiz—80q. Liberation frieze. Vert—25q. T **353**; 1l. Council members walking to meeting.

354 Security Guards patrolling Industrial Plant

(Des. Q. Prizreni)

1974 (29 Nov). 30th Anniversary of Liberation. T **354** and similar horiz designs. Multicoloured. P 12½×12.
1715	25q. Type **354**	20	15
1716	35q. Chemical Industry	30	20
1717	50q. Agriculture	40	25
1718	80q. Cultural Activities	55	30
1719	1l. Scientific Technology	1·50	55
1720	1l.20 Railway Construction	1·70	1·40
1715/1720 *Set of 6*		4·25	2·50
MS1721 81×70 mm. 2l.05, Albanians with Book (60×40 *mm*). Imperf		5·00	4·25

ALBANIA 1974

355 Head of Artemis   **356** Clasped Hands

(Des S. Toptani and F. Sulo)

1974 (25 Dec). Archaeological Discoveries. T **355** and similar vert designs. P 12×12½.

1722	10q. black, mauve and greyish silver	20	10
1723	15q. black, turquoise-green and greyish silver	30	15
1724	20q. black, stone and greyish silver	45	25
1725	25q. black, bright mauve and greyish silver	55	40
1726	40q. multicoloured	1·50	85
1727	80q. black, pale blue and greyish silver	2·20	1·70
1728	1l. black, sage-green and greyish silver	3·00	2·10
1729	1l.20 black, olive-sepia and greyish silver	4·25	2·75
1722/1729 Set of 8		11·00	7·50
MS1730 96×96 mm. 2l.05, multicoloured. Imperf.		5·00	4·25

Designs: 10q. T **355**; 15q. Statue of Zeus; 20q. Statue of Poseidon; 25q. Illyrian helmet; 40q. Greek amphora; 80q. Bust of Agrippa, 1l. Bust of Demosthenes, 1l.20, Bust of Bilia. Square (84×84 *mm*)—2l.05, Head of Artemis and Greek vase.

(Des. B. Dizdari)

1975 (11 Feb). 30th Anniversary of Albanian Trade Unions. T **356** and similar multicoloured designs. P 12.

1731	25q. Type **356**	75	35
1732	1l.80 Workers with arms raised (*horiz*)	3·00	1·70

357 *Cichorium intybus*   **358** Head of Jesus (detail, Dom Tondo)

(Des N. Prizreni)

1975 (15 Feb). Albanian Flowers. T **357** and similar square designs. Multicoloured. P 12.

1733	5q. Type **357**	15	10
1734	10q. *Sempervivum montanum*	20	15
1735	15q. *Aquilegia alpina*	25	20
1736	20q. *Anemone hortensis*	30	25
1737	25q. *Hibiscus trionum*	35	30
1738	30q. *Gentiana kochiana*	40	35
1739	35q. *Lavatera arborea*	55	40
1740	2l.70 *Iris graminea*	3·00	1·90
1733/1740 Set of 8		4·75	3·25

(Des Q. Prizreni)

1975 (20 Mar). 500th Birth Anniversary of Michelangelo. T **358** and similar vert designs. P 12×12½.

1741	5q. multicoloured	15	10
1742	10q. bistre-brown, bluish grey and gold	20	15
1743	15q. bistre-brown, bluish grey and gold	25	20
1744	20q. sepia, bluish grey and gold	30	25
1745	25q. multicoloured	35	30
1746	30q. purple-brown, bluish grey and gold	40	35
1747	1l.20 bistre, bluish grey and gold	1·10	65
1748	3l.90 multicoloured	3·00	2·00
1741/1748 Set of 8		5·25	3·50
MS1749 77×86 mm. 2l.05, multicoloured. Imperf.		5·00	3·50

Designs: As T **358**—5q. T **358**; 10q. *The Heroic Captive*; 15q. Head of Dawn; 20q. *Awakening Giant* (detail); 25q. Cumaean Sibyl (detail, Sistine chapel); 30q. Lorenzo di Medici; 1l.20, Head and shoulders of David; 3l.90, Delphic Sibyl (detail, Sistine chapel). 70×77 mm—2l.05, Head of Michelangelo.

Nos. 1742/1744 and 1746/1747 depict sculptures.

359 Horseman   **360** Frontier Guard

(Des S. Toptani)

1975 (15 Apr). Albanian Transport of the Past. T **359** and similar horiz designs. Multicoloured. P 12½×12.

1750	5q. Type **359**	15	10
1751	10q. Horse and cart	20	15
1752	15q. Ferry	25	20
1753	20q. Barque	30	25
1754	25q. Horse-drawn cab	40	30
1755	3l.35 Early motor car	3·75	1·50
1750/1755 Set of 6		4·50	2·30

(Des Q. Prizreni)

1975 (25 Apr). 30th Anniversary of Frontier Force. T **360** and similar vert design. Multicoloured. P 12.

1756	25q. Type **360**	75	35
1757	1l.80 Guards patrolling Industrial Plant	3·00	2·10

361 Patriot affixing Anti-Fascist Placard

(Des B. Dizdari)

1975 (9 May). 30th Anniversary of Victory over Fascism. T **361** and similar horiz designs. Multicoloured. P 12½×12.

1758	25q. Type **361**	45	30
1759	60q. Partisans in Battle	1·00	55
1760	1l.20 Patriot defeating Nazi soldier	2·20	1·40
1758/1760 Set of 3		3·25	2·00

362 European wigeons (*Anas penelope*)

(Des N. Prizreni)

1975 (15 June). Albanian Waterfowl. T **362** and similar diamond-shaped designs. Multicoloured. P 12.

1761	5q. Type **362**	15	10
1762	10q. Red-crested Pochards (*Netta rufina*)	20	15
1763	15q. White-fronted Geese (*Anser albifrons*)	25	20
1764	20q. Pintails (*Anas acuta*)	30	25
1765	25q. Red-breasted Mergansers (*Mergus serrator*)	35	30
1766	30q. Eiders (*Somateria mollissima*)	60	35
1767	35q. Whooper Swan (*Cignus cignus*)	85	40
1768	2l.70 Shovelers (*Spatula clypeata*)	5·00	2·50
1761/1768 Set of 8		7·00	3·75

1975 ALBANIA

363 Shygyri Kanapari (Musa Qarri)

364 Farmer with Declaration of Reform

367 Power Lines leading to Village

368 Berat

1975 (15 July). Albanian Paintings. People's Art Exhibition, Tirana. T **363** and similar multicoloured designs. P 12×12½ (vert) or 12½×12 (horiz).

1769	5q. Type **363**		10	10
1770	10q. *Sea rescue* (Agim Faja)		15	10
1771	15q. *28th November 1912* (Petrit Ceno) (horiz)		20	15
1772	20q. *Workers' Meeting* (Sali Shijaku)		25	20
1773	25q. *Shota Galica* (Ismail Lulani)		30	25
1774	30q. *Victorious Fighters* (Nestor Jonuzi)		35	30
1775	80q. *Partisan Comrades* (Vilson Halimi)		65	40
1776	2l.25 *Republic Day Celebration* (Fatmir Haxhiu) (horiz)		3·00	2·20
1769/1776	Set of 8		4·50	3·25
MS1777	68×98 mm. 2l.05, *Folk dance* (Abdurahim Buza). Imperf.		4·25	4·00

Nos. 1769/1776 were each printed in sheets of 32 stamps and four labels.

(Des M. Reci)

1975 (28 Aug). 30th Anniversary of Agrarian Reform. T **364** and similar square design. Multicoloured. P 12.

1778	15q. Type **364**	85	40
1779	2l. Agricultural scene	4·25	2·75

365 *Alcyonium palmatum*

366 Cycling

(Des D. Theodori)

1975 (25 Sept). Marine Corals. T **365** and similar vert designs. Multicoloured. P 12×12½.

1780	5q. Type **365**	10	10
1781	10q. *Paramuricea chamaeleon*	15	15
1782	20q. *Coralium rubrum*	25	25
1783	25q. *Eunicella covalim*	35	30
1784	3l.70 *Cladocora cespitosa*	7·50	2·75
1780/1784	Set of 5	7·50	3·25

(Des Q. Prizreni)

1975 (20 Oct). Olympic Games, Montreal (1976). T **366** and similar vert designs. Multicoloured. P 12½×12½.

1785	5q. Type **366**	10	10
1786	10q. Canoeing	15	15
1787	15q. Handball	20	20
1788	20q. Basketball	35	25
1789	25q. Waterpolo	50	30
1790	30q. Hockey	60	35
1791	1l.20 Pole vaulting	2·10	85
1792	2l.05 Fencing	4·25	1·60
1785/1792	Set of 8	7·50	3·50
MS1793	73×77 mm. 2l.15, Games emblem and sportsmen. Imperf.	9·25	8·75

(Des S. Toptani)

1975 (25 Oct). Fifth Anniversary of Electrification of Albanian countryside. T **367** and similar vert designs. P 12×12½.

1794	15q. multicoloured	25	15
1795	25q. deep reddish violet, rose-lilac and bright lilac	40	25
1796	80q. grey-black, turquoise-green and deep grey-green	1·50	55
1797	85q. buff, bistre-brown and brown-ochre	3·25	2·50
1794/1797	Set of 4	4·75	3·00

Designs: 15q. T **367**; 25q. High power insulators; 80q. Dam and power station; 85q. TV set, pylons and emblems of agriculture and industry.

(Des B. Dizdari)

1975 (25 Nov). AIR. Tourist Resorts. T **368** and similar horiz designs. Multicoloured. P 12.

1798	20q. Type **368**	45	40
1799	40q. Gjirokastër	60	45
1800	60q. Sarandë	1·10	55
1801	90q. Durrës	2·10	65
1802	1l.20 Krujaë	2·75	1·30
1803	2l.40 Boga	5·50	2·75
1804	4l.05 Tirana	8·50	4·00
1798/1804	Set of 7	19·00	9·00

369 Child, Rabbit and Bear planting Saplings

1975 (25 Dec). Children's Tales. T **369** and similar horiz designs. Multicoloured. P 12½×12.

1805	5q. Type **369**	10	10
1806	10q. Mother Fox and Cub	15	15
1807	15q. Ducks in School	20	20
1808	20q. Bears building	25	25
1809	25q. Animals watching television	35	30
1810	30q. Animals with log and electric light bulbs	55	35
1811	35q. Ants with spade and guitar	60	40
1812	2l.70 Boy and girl with Sheep and Dog	4·25	2·10
1805/1812	Set of 8	5·75	3·50

370 Arms and Rejoicing Crowd

371 Ice Hockey

ALBANIA 1976

(Des Q. Prizreni)

1976 (11 Jan). 30th Anniversary of Albanian People's Republic. T **370** and similar horiz design. Multicoloured. P 12.
1813	25q. Type **370**	85	40
1814	1l.90 Folk-dancers	4·75	2·30

1976 (4 Feb). Winter Olympic Games, Innsbruck. T **371** and similar vert designs. Multicoloured. P 12×12½.
1815	5q. Type **371**	10	10
1816	10q. Speed skating	15	15
1817	15q. Rifle shooting (biathlon)	20	20
1818	50q. Ski jumping	50	25
1819	1l.20 Skiing (slalom)	1·30	45
1820	2l.30 Bobsleighing	2·50	1·10
1815/1820	Set of 6	4·25	2·00
MS1821	66×80 mm. 2l.15, Figure skating (pairs)	5·00	3·00

The miniature sheet includes two vertical rows of perforations within its design.

372 Colchicum autumnale   **374** Founding the Co-operatives (Zef Shoshi)

373 Wooden Bowl and Spoon

(Des B. Marika)

1976 (10 Apr). Medicinal Plants. T **372** and similar vert designs. Multicoloured. P 12×12½.
1822	5q. Type **372**	10	10
1823	10q. Atropa belladonna	15	15
1824	15q. Gentiana lutea	20	20
1825	20q. Aesculus hippocastanum	25	25
1826	70q. Polystichum filix	85	35
1827	80q. Althaea officinalis	1·30	45
1828	2l.30 Datura stramonium	4·25	2·20
1822/1828	Set of 7	6·50	3·25

1976 (20 July). Ethnographic Studies Conference, Tirana. Albanian Artifacts. T **373** and similar multicoloured designs. P 12½×12 (horiz) or 12×12½ (vert).
1829	10q. Type **373**	15	15
1830	15q. Flask (vert)	20	20
1831	20q. Ornamental handles (vert)	25	25
1832	25q. Pistol and dagger	35	30
1833	80q. Hand-woven rug (vert)	85	45
1834	1l.20 Filigree buckle and earrings	1·70	60
1835	1l.40 Jugs with handles (vert)	2·50	1·60
1829/1835	Set of 7	5·50	3·25

1976 (8 Aug). Albanian Paintings. T **374** and similar multicoloured designs. P 12½×12 (horiz) or 12×12½ (vert).
1836	5q. Type **374**	10	10
1837	10q. Going to Work (Agim Zajmi) (vert)	15	15
1838	25q. Listening to Broadcast (Vilson Kilica)	35	30
1839	40q. Female Welder (Sabaudin Xhaferi) (vert)	50	35
1840	50q. Steel Workers (Isuf Sulovari) (vert)	85	45
1841	1l.20 1942 Revolt (Lec Shkreli) (vert)	1·40	85
1842	1l.60 Returning from Work (Agron Dine)	2·10	1·40
1836/1842	Set of 7	5·00	3·25
MS1843	93×79 mm. 2l.05, The Young Pioneer (Andon Lakuriqi)	4·25	2·75

The miniature sheet includes two horizontal rows of perforations within its design.

375 Demonstrators attacking Police   **376** Party Flag, Industry and Agriculture

1976 (28 Oct). 35th Anniversary of Anti-Fascist Demonstration led by Enver Hoxha. T **375** and similar vert design. Multicoloured. P 12×12½.
1844	25q. Type **375**	85	45
1845	1l.90 Crowd with flag	3·75	2·75

1976 (1 Nov). Seventh Workers' Party Congress. T **376** and similar vert design. Multicoloured. P 12.
1846	25q. Type **376**	85	4·75
1847	1l.20 Hand holding Party symbols, and flag	3·00	2·20

377 Communist Advance   **378** Young Communists

1976 (8 Nov). 35th Anniversary of Workers' Party. T **377** and similar vert designs. Multicoloured. P 12×12½.
1848	15q. Type **377**	25	20
1849	25q. Hands holding emblems, and revolutionary army	60	40
1850	80q. Soldiers, industrial scenes, pickaxe and rifle	1·70	60
1851	1l.20 Symbols of heavy industry and agriculture	2·30	1·60
1852	1l.70 Ballet scene and cultural symbols	3·25	2·30
1848/1852	Set of 5	7·25	4·50

1976 (23 Nov). 35th Anniversary of Young Communists' Union. T **378** and similar horiz design. Multicoloured. P 12.
1853	80q. Type **378**	2·50	1·60
1854	1l.25 Young Communists in action	4·25	3·00

379 Ballet Dancers   **380** Bashtoves Castle

1976 (15 Dec). Albanian Ballet Cuca e Maleve. T **379** and similar horiz designs showing ballet scenes. P 12.
1855	10q. multicoloured	15	45
1856	15q. multicoloured	20	60
1857	20q. multicoloured	50	1·10
1858	25q. multicoloured	65	2·20
1859	80q. multicoloured	2·00	3·25
1860	1l.20 multicoloured	2·50	4·25
1861	1l.40 multicoloured	3·25	4·75
1855/1861	Set of 7	8·25	15·00
MS1862	77×67 mm. 2l.05, multicoloured. P 12×imperf	6·50	6·25

(Des B. Zajmi)

1976 (25 Dec). Albanian Castles. T **380** and similar horiz designs. P 12.
1863	10q. black and cobalt	15	15
1864	15q. black and dull yellowish green	20	20

1977 ALBANIA

1865	20q. black and slate		25	25
1866	25q. black and light brown		40	30
1867	80q. black, rose-pink and brown-rose		1·30	60
1868	1l.20 black and dull violet-blue		1·70	95
1869	1l.40 black, brown-rose and rose-pink		2·50	1·20
1863/1869	Set of 7		5·75	3·25

Designs: 10q. T **380**; 15q. Gjirokastër; 20q. Ali Pash Tepelenë; 25q. Petrelë; 80q. Berat; 1l.20, Durrës, 1l.40, Krujë.

381 Skanderbeg's Shield and Spear

382 Ilia Oiqi

(Des Q. Prizreni)

1977 (28 Jan). Crest and Arms of Skanderbeg's Army. T **381** and similar vert designs. Multicoloured. P 12.

1870	15q. Type **381**	2·75	70
1871	80q. Helmet, sword and scabbard	9·25	4·75
1872	1l. Halberd, spear, bow and arrows	14·50	11·00
1870/1872	Set of 3	24·00	15·00

(Des Q. Prizreni)

1977 (28 Feb). Albanian Heroes. T **382** and similar horiz designs. Multicoloured. P 12×12½.

1873	5q. Type **382**	15	10
1874	10q. Ilia Dashi	20	20
1875	25q. Fran Ndue Ivanaj	65	40
1876	80q. Zeliha Allmetaj	2·00	55
1877	1l. Ylli Zaimi	2·75	95
1878	1l.90 Isuf Plloci	5·75	1·90
1873/1878	Set of 6	10·50	3·75

383 Polyvinyl-chloride Plant, Vlorë

384 Shote Galica

(Des B. Marika)

1977 (29 Mar). Sixth Five Year Plan. T **383** and similar vert designs. Multicoloured. P 12½×12.

1879	15q. Type **383**	50	40
1880	25q. Naphtha plant, Ballsh	75	60
1881	65q. Hydroelectric station, Fjerzë	2·10	1·00
1882	1l. Metallurgical complex, Elbasan	3·25	1·30
1879/1882	Set of 4	6·00	3·00

(Des B. Zajmi)

1977 (20 Apr). 50th Death Anniversary of Shote Galica (Communist partisan). T **384** and similar vert design. Multicoloured. P 12½×12.

1883	80q. deep rose-red and pink	2·10	1·10
1884	1q.25 grey-blue and pale grey-blue	3·25	1·90

Designs: 80q. T **384**; 1l.25, Shote Galica and father.

385 Crowd and Martyrs' Monument, Tirana

386 Doctor calling at Village House

(Des Z. Mati)

1977 (5 May). 35th Anniversary of Martyrs' Day. T **385** and similar vert designs. Multicoloured. P 12.

1885	25q. Type **385**	70	40
1886	80q. Clenched fist and Albanian flag	2·40	90
1887	1l.20 Bust of Qemal Stafa	4·25	1·80
1885/1887	Set of 3	6·50	2·75

(Des B. Marika)

1977 (18 June). Socialist Transformation of Villages. T **386** and similar horiz designs. Multicoloured. P 12×12½.

1888	5q. Type **386**	15	10
1889	10q. Cowherd with cattle	20	20
1890	20q. Harvesting	35	30
1891	80q. Modern village	2·10	60
1892	2l.95 Tractor and greenhouses	7·00	1·90
1888/1892	Set of 5	8·75	2·75

387 Workers outside Factory

388 Advancing Soldiers

(Des Q. Prizreni)

1977 (20 June). Eighth Trade Unions Congress. T **387** and similar horiz design. Multicoloured. P 12.

1893	25q. Type **387**	85	40
1894	1l.80 Three workers with flag	4·25	3·25

(Des Z. Mati)

1977 (10 July). All the People are Soldiers. T **388** and similar horiz designs. Multicoloured. P 12.

1895	15q. Type **388**	60	40
1896	25q. Enver Hoxha and marching soldiers	70	60
1897	80q. Soldiers and workers	2·10	1·40
1898	1l. The Armed Forces	3·50	2·30
1899	1l.90 Marching soldiers and workers	5·50	4·75
1895/1899	Set of 5	11·00	8·50

389 Two Girls with Handkerchiefs

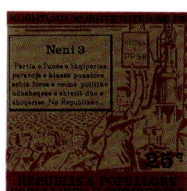

390 Armed Worker with Book

(Des N. Bakalli)

1977 (20 Aug). National Costume Dances (1st issue). T **389** and similar vert designs. Multicoloured. P 12.

1900	5q. Type **389**	15	10
1901	10q. Two male dancers	20	15
1902	15q. Man and woman in kerchief dance	25	20
1903	25q. Two male dancers (*different*)	40	30
1904	80q. Two women dancers with kerchiefs	85	45
1905	1l. 'Elbow' dance	1·40	60
1906	1l.55 Two women with kerchiefs (*different*)	2·10	1·10
1900/1906	Set of 7	4·75	2·50
MS1907	56×74 mm. 2l.05, Sabre dance. P 12×imperf	4·75	4·00

See also Nos. 1932/1936 and 1991/1995.

1977 (Oct). New Constitution. T **390** and similar square design. P 12.

1908	25q. gold, scarlet and black	85	45
1909	1l.20 gold, scarlet and black	3·25	1·60

Designs: 25q. T **390**; 1l.20, Industrial and agricultural symbols and hand with book.

391 *Beni Ecen Vet*

392 Rejoicing Crowd and Independence Memorial, Tirana

ALBANIA 1977

1977 (25 Oct). Albanian Films. T **391** and similar horiz designs. P 12½×12.
1910	10q. deep bluish green and pale brownish grey	20	15
1911	15q. multicoloured	40	35
1912	25q. pale grey-green, black and pale brownish grey	70	45
1913	80q. multicoloured	2·75	2·50
1914	1l.20 purple-brown and pale brownish grey	3·75	3·50
1915	1l.60 multicoloured	4·50	4·25
1910/1915	Set of 6	11·00	10·00

Designs: 10q. T **391**; 15q. *Rruge te Bardha*; 25q. *Rrugicat qe Kerkonin Diell*; 80q. *Ne Fillim te Veres*, 1l.20, *Lulekuqet Mbi Mure*, 1l.60, *Zonja nga Qyteti*.

(Des Q. Prizreni)

1977 (28 Nov). 65th Anniversary of Independence. T **392** and similar horiz designs. Muhicoloured. P 12½×12 (15q.) or 12×12½ (others).
1916	15q. Type **392**	25	20
1917	25q. Independence leaders marching in Tirana	60	40
1918	1f.65 Albanians dancing under National Flag	4·50	3·75
1916/1918	Set of 3	4·75	4·00

393 *Farm Workers*

394 *Pan Flute*

1977 (25 Dec). Paintings by V. Mio. T **393** and similar horiz designs. Multicoloured. P 12½×12.
1919	5q. Type **393**	15	10
1920	10q. *Landscape in the Snow*	20	15
1921	15q. *Sheep under a Walnut Tree, Springtime*	25	20
1922	25q. *Street in Korcë*	35	30
1923	80q. *Riders in the Mountains*	85	45
1924	1l. *Boats by the Seashore*	1·30	80
1925	1l.75 *Tractors Ploughing*	2·50	1·60
1919/1925	Set of 7	5·00	3·25
MS1926	67×102 mm. 2l.05, *Self-portrait*	5·75	4·75

The miniature sheet includes one horizontal row of perforations within its design.

(Des N. Bakalli)

1978 (20 Jan). Folk Music Instruments. T **394** and similar vert designs. P 12×12½.
1927	15q. dull rose, black and turquoise-green	75	40
1928	25q. greenish yellow, black and lavender	1·40	60
1929	80q. salmon, black and light blue	3·75	1·90
1930	1l.20 yellow, black and pale grey-blue	7·00	4·00
1931	1l.70 pale reddish mauve, black and bright green	15·00	8·25
1927/1931	Set of 5	25·00	13·50

Designs: 15q. T **394**; 25q. Single-string Goat's head fiddle; 80q. Trumpet; 1l.20, Drum; 1l.70, Bagpipes.

(Des N. Bakalli)

1978 (15 Feb). National Costume Dances (2nd issue). Vert designs as T **389**. Multicoloured. P 12.
1932	5q. Girl dancers with scarves	15	10
1933	25q. Male dancers	45	30
1934	80q. Kneeling dancers	1·20	60
1935	1l. Female dancers	1·40	1·10
1936	2l.30 Male dancers with linked arms	3·50	2·75
1932/1936	Set of 5	6·00	4·25

395 *Tractor Drivers* (D. Trebicka)

396 *Boy and Girl*

(Des P. Sulo)

1978 (25 Mar). Paintings of the Working Class. T **395** and similar multicoloured designs. P 12.
1937	25q. Type **395**	40	30
1938	80q. *Steeplejack* (S. Kristo)	85	40
1939	85q. *A Point in the Discussion* (S. Milori)	1·00	45
1940	90q. *Oil Rig Crew* (A. Cini) (vert)	1·20	60
1941	1l.60 *Metal Workers* (R. Karanxha)	2·10	1·40
1937/1941	Set of 5	5·00	2·75
MS1942	73×99 mm. 2l.20, *The Political Discussion* (S. Sholla)	10·00	5·50

The miniature sheet includes two horizontal rows of perforations within its design.

(Des B. Zalmi)

1978 (1 June). International Children's Day. T **396** and similar vert designs. Multicoloured. P 12.
1943	5q. Type **396**	25	15
1944	10q. Boy and girl with pickaxe and rifle	45	30
1945	25q. Children dancing	85	60
1946	1l.80 Classroom scene	5·00	4·00
1943/1946	Set of 4	6·00	4·50

397 Woman with Pickaxe and Rifle

398 Battle of Mostar Bridge

(Des Q. Prizreni)

1978 (1 June). Eighth Women's Union Congress. T **397** and similar horiz design. P 12×11½.
1947	25q. scarlet and gold	70	40
1948	1l.95 carmine-red and gold	10·50	7·00

Designs: 25q. T **397**; 1l.95, Peasant and Militia Guard with industrial installation.

(Des Q. Prizreni)

1978 (10 June). Centenary of the League of Prizren. T **398** and similar vert designs. P 12.
1949	10q. multicoloured	25	15
1950	25q. multicoloured	45	35
1951	80q. multicoloured	2·20	1·40
1952	1l.20 pale blue, black and deep violet	3·00	2·20
1953	1l.65 multicoloured	4·75	3·00
1954	2l.60 apple green, black and bronze-green	7·75	7·25
1949/1954	Set of 6	17·00	13·00
MS1955	75×69 mm. 2l.20, multicoloured. Imperf×p12	6·50	4·75

Designs: 10q. T **398**; 25q. Spirit of Skanderbeg; 80q. Albanians marching under National Flag; 1l.20, Riflemen; 1l.65, Abdyl Frasheri (founder); 2l.20, League building, crossed rifles, pen and paper; 2l.60, League Headquarters, Prizren.

399 Guerrillas with Flag

401 Man with Target Rifle

3.30L

26. 8. 1978

RICCIONE 78
(**400**)

1978 ALBANIA

(Des S. Prapanikú)

1978 (10 July). 35th Anniversary of People's Army. T **399** and similar multicoloured designs. P 12½×12 (25q.) or 12×12½ (others).
1956	5q. Type **399**		85	40
1957	25q. Men of armed forces (*horiz*)		1·70	60
1958	1l.90 Men of armed forces, civil guards and Young Pioneers		10·50	9·25
1956/1958 Set of 3			11·50	9·25

1978 (26 Aug). International Fair, Riccione. No. 1832 surch with T **400**, in blue.
1959	3l.30 on 25q. multicoloured		22·00	21·00

(Des Z. Mati)

1978 (20 Sept). 32nd National Shooting Championship. T **401** and similar designs. P 12½×12 (horiz) or 12×12½ (vert).
1960	25q. black and lemon		45	35
1961	80q. black and bright orange		1·00	80
1962	95q. black and rosine		1·40	1·00
1963	2l.40 black and carmine		3·75	3·00
1960/1963 Set of 4			6·00	4·75

Designs: Horiz—25q. T **401**; 95q. Shooting from prone position. Vert—80q. Woman with machine carbine; 2l.40, Pistol shooting.

402 Kerchief Dance

403 Enver Hoxha (after V. Kilica)

(Des N. Bakalli)

1978 (6 Oct). National Folklore Festival, Gjirokastër. T **402** and similar vert designs. Multicoloured. P 12.
1964	10q. Type **402**		20	10
1965	15q. Musicians		25	15
1966	25q. Fiddle player		40	25
1967	80q. Singers		55	40
1968	1l.20 Sabre dance		1·50	95
1969	1l.90 Girl dancers		3·25	2·30
1964/1969 Set of 6			5·50	3·75

1978 (16 Oct). Enver Hoxha's 70th Birthday. P 12×12½.
1970	**403**	75q. multicoloured	75	45
1971		1l.20 multicoloured	1·40	65
1972		2l.40 multicoloured	3·00	1·90
1970/1972 Set of 3			4·75	2·75
MS1973 68×88 mm. Type **403** 2l.20, muiticoloured			5·75	4·00

The miniature sheet includes two horizontal rows of perforations within its design.

404 Woman with Wheatsheaf

405 Pupils entering School

(Des Q. Prizreni)

1978 (15 Dec). Agriculture and Stock Raising. T **404** and similar horiz designs. Multicoloured. P 12×12½.
1974	15q. Type **404**		75	40
1975	25q. Woman with boxes of fruit		1·00	70
1976	80q. Shepherd and flock		3·75	2·75
1977	2l.60 Dairymaid and cattle		12·50	9·25
1974/1977 Set of 4			16·00	12·00

1978. T **405** and simlilar horiz designs. P 12½×12.
1978	5q. deep brown, pale grey-brown and gold		15	10
1979	10q. blue, pale blue and gold		20	15
1980	15q. reddish violet, reddish lilac and gold		35	20
1981	20q. orange-brown, pale drab and gold		45	25
1982	25q. deep carmine, pink and gold		50	30
1983	60q. olive-green, pale grey-olive and gold		2·10	55
1984	80q. greenish blue, pale blue and gold		2·75	60
1985	1l.20 deep magenta, pale mauve and gold		4·00	1·10
1986	1l.60 deep turquoise-blue, pale turquoise-blue and gold		5·25	2·30
1987	2l.40 deep green, pale green and gold		8·25	4·75
1988	3l. dull ultramarine, pale blue and gold		11·00	7·75
1978/1988 Set of 11			32·00	16·00

Designs: 5q. T **405**; 10q. Telephone, letters, telegraph wires and switchboard operators; 15q. Pouring molten iron; 20q. Dancers, musical instruments, book and artist's materials; 25q. Newspapers, radio, television and broadcasting tower; 60q. Assistant in clothes shop; 80q. Militiamen and women, tanks, ships, aircraft and radar equipment; 1l.20, Industrial complex and symbols of industry; 1l.60, Train and lorry; 2l.40, Workers hoeing fields, cattle and girl holding wheat sheaf; 3l. Microscope and nurse holding up baby.

406 Dora d'Istria

407 Stone-built Galleried House

(Des N. Bakalh)

1979 (22 Jan). 150th Birth Anniversary of Dora d'Istria (pioneer of women's rights). T **406** and similar vert design. P 12.
1989	80q. deep olive and black		2·10	1·40
1990	1l.10 deep dull purple and black		3·75	2·75

Designs: 80q. T **406**; 1l.10, Full-face portrait.

(Des N. Bakalli)

1979 (25 Feb). National Costume Dances (3rd issue). Vert designs as T **389**. Multicoloured. P 12.
1991	15q. Girl dancers with scarves		40	30
1992	25q. Male dancers		70	45
1993	80q. Girl dancers with scarves (*different*)		3·00	1·40
1994	1l.20 Male dancers with pistols		3·50	1·90
1995	1l.40 Female dancers with linked arms		4·25	2·75
1991/1995 Set of 5			10·50	6·00

(Des B. Zajmi)

1979 (20 Mar). Traditional Albanian Houses (1st series). T **407** and similar designs. Multicoloured. P 12.
1996	15q. Type **407**		25	20
1997	25q. Tower house (*vert*)		45	30
1998	80q. House with wooden galleries		1·40	55
1999	1l.20 Galleried tower house (*vert*)		2·00	90
2000	1l.40 Three-storied fortified house (*vert*)		3·00	1·60
1996/2000 Set of 5			6·50	3·25
MS2001 62×75 mm. 1l.90, Fortified tower house. P 12×imperf			10·00	6·75

See also Nos. 2116/2119.

408 Aleksandër Moissi

409 Vasil Shanto

1979 (2 Apr). Birth Centenary of Aleksandër Moissi (actor). T **408** and similar vert design showing portrait. P 12.
2002	80q. deep green, black and gold		2·10	80
2003	1l.10 orange-brown, black and gold		3·00	1·90

1979 (5 May). Anti-fascist Heroes (1st series). T **409** and similar horiz designs. P 12.
2004	**409**	15q. multicoloured	35	20
2005	–	25q. multicoloured	75	40
2006	**409**	60q. multicoloured	2·50	1·20
2007	–	90q. multicoloured	4·25	2·75
2004/2007 Set of 4			7·00	4·00

Design: 25q., 90q. Qemal Stafa.

See also Nos. 2052/2055, 2090/2093, 2126/2129, 2167/2170, 2221/2224 and 2274/2277.

ALBANIA 1979

410 Soldier, Crowd and Coat of Arms

411 Albanian Flag

(Des Q. Prizreni)

1979 (24 May). 35th Anniversary of Permet Congress. T **410** and similar horiz design. Multicoloured. P 12.
2008	25q. Soldier, factories and wheat..................	1·40	65
2009	1l.65 Type **410**	6·50	3·50

(Des N. Prizreni)

1979 (4 June). Fifth Congress of Albanian Democratic Front. P 12.
2010	**411** 25q. muilticoloured..	1·40	65
2011	1l.65 multicoloured	6·50	4·00

412 Ne Stervitje

413 Athletes round Party Flag

(Arben Basha)

1979 (15 July). Painting from Gallery of Figurative Arts. T **412** and similar horiz designs. Multicoloured. P 12.
2012	15q. Type **412**	25	20
2013	25q. *Shtigje Lufte* (Ismail Lulani)........................	40	30
2014	80q. *Agim me Fitore* (Myrteza Fushëkati)	1·40	55
2015	1l.20 *Gjithe Populli ushtare* (Muhamet Deliu)..	2·00	95
2016	1l.40 *Zjarret Ndezur Mbajme* (Jorgji Gjikopulli)..	3·00	1·40
2012/2016 Set of 5		6·25	3·00
MS2017 78×103 mm. 1l.90, *Cajme Rrethime* (Fatmir Haxhiu)		5·25	4·00

The miniature sheet includes two horizontal rows of perforations within its design.

(Des Q. Prizreni)

1979 (1 Oct). 35th Anniversary of Liberation Spartakiad. T **413** and similar vert designs. Multicoloured. P 12.
2018	15q. Type **413**	25	20
2019	25q. Rifle shooting demonstration.....................	40	30
2020	80q. Girl gymnast...	1·40	55
2021	1l.20 Footballers	2·00	1·20
2022	1l.40 High jump..	2·40	1·60
2018/2022 Set of 5		5·75	3·50

414 Founder-president

415 Congress Building

(Des Q. Prizreni)

1979 (12 Oct). Centenary of Albanian Literary Society. T **414** and similar vert designs. P 12.
2023	25q. black, light orange-brown and gold	45	30
2024	80q. black, pale ochre and gold........................	1·40	80
2025	1l.20 black, blue and gold	2·00	1·20
2026	1l.55 black, bright reddish violet and gold	2·50	1·50
2023/2026 Set of 4		5·75	3·50
MS2027 78×66 mm. 1l.90, black, buff and gold. Imperf×12		5·00	3·00

Designs: 25q. Foundation document and seal of 1880; 80q. T **414**; 1l.20, Headquarters building, 1979; 1l.55, Headquarters building, 1879; 1l.90, Four founder members, book and quill.

(Des B. Erebara)

1979 (20 Oct). 35th Anniversary of Berat Congress. T **415** and similar vert. design. Multicoloured. P 12.
2028	25q. Arms and congress document.................	1·40	1·40
2029	1l.65 Type **415**	5·75	4·75

416 Workers and Industrial Complex

417 Stalin

(Des H. Dhimo)

1979 (29 Nov). 35th Anniversary of Liberation. T **416** and similar horiz designs. Multicoloured. P 12.
2030	25q. Type **416**	45	30
2031	80q. Wheat and hand grasping hammer and pickaxe	1·40	80
2032	1l.20 Open book, star and musical instrument	1·70	1·40
2033	1l.55 Open book, compasses and gear wheel	3·00	1·60
2030/2033 Set of 4		6·00	3·75

(Des H. Dhimo)

1979 (21 Dec). Birth Centenary of Joseph Stalin. T **417** and similar horiz design. P 12.
2034	80q. indigo and scarlet......................................	2·10	1·40
2035	1l.10 indigo and bright scarlet..........................	3·00	2·75

Designs: 80q. T **417**; 1l.10, Stalin and Enver Hoxha.

418 Fireplace and Pottery, Korcë

419 Lacework

(Des Q. Prizreni)

1980 (27 Feb). Interiors (1st series). T **418** and similar horiz designs. Multicoloured. P 12.
2036	25q. Type **418**	45	30
2037	80q. Carved bed alcove and weapons, Shkodër...	1·00	95
2038	1l.20 Cooking hearth and carved chair, Mirditë..	2·10	1·40
2039	1l.35 Turkish-style chimney, dagger and embroidered jacket, Gjirokastër	3·00	2·75
2036/2039 Set of 4		6·00	4·75

See also Nos. 2075/2078.

(Des N. Majollari)

1980 (4 Mar). Handicrafts. T **419** and similar horiz. designs. Multicoloured. P 12.
2040	25q. Pipe and flask...	45	30
2041	80q. Leather handbags.......................................	1·00	95
2042	1l.20 Carved Eagle and embroidered rug	2·10	1·40
2043	1l.35 Type **419**	3·00	2·75
2040/2043 Set of 4		6·00	4·75

420 Aleksandër Xhuvani

421 Insurrectionists

1980 ALBANIA

(Des M. Fushëkati)

1980 (14 Mar). Birth Centenary of Dr. Aleksandër Xhuvani. P 12.
2044	**420**	80q. dull turquoise-blue, grey and black	3·00	2·10
2045		1l. yellow-brown, grey and black	3·75	3·50

(Des Z. Mati)

1980 (4 Apr). 70th Anniversary of Kosovo Insurrection. T **421** and similar horiz design. P 12.
2046		80q. black and scarlet-vermilion	3·00	2·00
2047		1l. black and orange-vermilion	4·25	3·50

Designs: 80q. T **421**; 1l. Battle scene.

422 *Soldiers and Workers helping Stricken Population* (D. Jukniu and I. Lulani)

423 Lenin

1980 (15 Apr). 1979 Earthquake Relief. P 12½.
2048	**422**	80q. multicoloured	3·00	2·00
2049		1l. multicoloured	4·25	3·50

(Des M. Fushëkati)

1980 (22 Apr). 110th Birth Anniversary of Lenin. P 12.
2050	**423**	80q. grey, bright carmine and rose-pink	3·00	2·00
2051		1l. multicoloured	4·25	3·50

424 Misto Mame and Ali Demi

425 *Mirela*

(Des M. Fushëkati)

1980 (5 May). Anti-fascist Heroes (2nd series). T **424** and similar horiz designs. Multicoloured. P 12.
2052		25q. Type **424**	45	30
2053		80q. Sadik Stavaleci, Vojo Kushi and Xhoxhi Martini	1·40	95
2054		1l.20 Bule Naipi and Persefoni Kokedhima	2·40	1·30
2055		1l.35 Ndoc Deda, Hydajet Lezha, Naim Gjylbegu, Ndoc Mazi and Ahmet Haxhia	2·75	2·75
2052/2055		Set of 4	6·25	4·75

(Des B. Kapexhiu)

1980 (7 June). Children's Tales. T **425** and similar horiz designs. Multicoloured. P 12.
2056		15q. Type **425**	25	20
2057		25q. *Shkarravina*	40	30
2058		80q. *Ariu Artist*	1·50	1·40
2059		2l.40 *Pika e Ujit*	5·00	4·75
2056/2059		Set of 4	6·50	6·00

426 *The Enver Hoxha Tractor Combine* (S. Shijaku and M. Fushëkati)

427 Decorated Door (Pergamen miniature)

(Des P. Sulo)

1980 (22 July). Paintings from Gallery of Figurative Arts, Tirana. T **426** and similar horiz designs. Multicoloured. P 12½.
2060		25q. Type **426**	40	30
2061		80q. *The Welder* (Harilla Dhima)	1·40	1·30
2062		1l.20 *Steel Erector* (Petro Kokushta)	2·40	2·20
2063		1l.35 *Harvest Festival* (Pandeli Lena)	2·75	2·40
2060/2063		Set of 4	6·25	5·50
MS2064		65×82 mm. 1l.80, *Communists* (Vilson Kilica) (48×71 mm)	5·75	5·50

The miniature sheet includes two horizontal rows of perforations (P 12) within its design.

1980 (27 Sept). Art of the Middle Ages. T **427** and similar vert designs, each black and gold. P 12.
2065		25q. Type **427**	40	30
2066		80q. Bird (relief)	1·00	95
2067		1l.20 Crowned Lion (relief)	2·00	1·90
2068		1l.35 Pheasant (relief)	2·20	2·10
2065/2068		Set of 4	5·00	4·75

428 Divjaka

429 Flag, Arms and Rejoicing Albanians

1980 (6 Nov). National Parks. T **428** and similar horiz designs. Multicoloured. P 12.
2069		80q. Type **428**	1·50	1·10
2070		1l.20 Lura	2·20	2·00
2071		1l.60 Thethi	3·75	3·00
2069/2071		Set of 3	6·75	5·50
MS2072		89×90 mm. 1l.80, Llogara (77×80 mm)	7·25	6·50

The miniature sheet includes two horizontal rows of perforations within its design.

(Des E. Hila)

1981 (11 Jan). 35th Anniversary of Albanian People's Republic. T **429** and similar horiz design. Multicoloured. P 12.
2073		80q. Type **429**	2·10	1·10
2074		1l. Crowd and flags outside People's Party Headquarters	3·00	1·30

(Des Q. Prizreni)

1981 (25 Feb). Interiors (2nd series). Horiz designs as T **418**. Multicoloured. P 12.
2075		25q. Sleeping mats and spirit keg, Lábara	45	30
2076		80q. Tent and milk churn, Lábara	70	55
2077		1l.20 Fireplace and covered dish, Mat	1·70	95
2078		1l.35 Interior and embroidered jacket, Dibrës	2·10	1·70
2075/2078		Set of 4	4·50	3·25

430 Wooden Cot

431 Footballers

(Des N. Marjoralli)

1981 (20 Mar). Folk Art. T **430** and similar horiz designs. Multicoloured. P 12.
2079		25q. Type **430**	45	30
2080		80q. Bucket and flask	1·00	95
2081		1l.20 Embroidered slippers	1·60	1·30
2082		1l.35 Jugs	2·00	1·70
2079/2082		Set of 4	4·50	3·75

1981 (31 Mar). World Cup Football Championship Eliminating Rounds. T **431** and similar horiz designs. Multicoloured. P 12.
2083		25q. Type **431**	1·50	65
2084		80q. Tackle	5·25	2·75
2085		1l.20 Player kicking ball	7·50	4·75
2086		1l.35 Goalkeeper saving goal	9·00	5·50
2083/2086		Set of 4	21·00	12·50

ALBANIA 1981

432 Rifleman **433** Acrobats

(Des N. Bakalli)

1981 (20 Apr). Centenary of Battle of Shtimje. T **432** and similar vert designs, each deep dull purple and Venetian red. P 12.
2087	80q. Type **432**	1·40	1·30
2088	1l. Albanian with sabre	1·70	1·60
MS2089	84×68 mm. 1l.80, Albanian with pistol. Imperf×P 12	6·50	5·50

(Des M. Fushëkati)

1981 (5 May). Anti-fascist Heroes (3rd series). Horiz designs as T **424**. Multicoloured. P 12.
2090	25q. Perlat Rexhepi and Branko Kadia	45	30
2091	80q. Xheladin Beqiri and Hajdah Dushi	1·70	80
2092	1l.20 Koçi Bako, Vasil Laçi and Mujo Ulqinaku	2·00	1·40
2093	1l.35 Mine Peza and Zoja Cure	3·50	1·60
2090/2093	Set of 4	7·00	3·75

1981 (June). Children's Circus. T **433** and similar vert designs. P 12.
2094	15q. black, light green and stone	25	20
2095	25q. black, cobalt and brownish grey	50	40
2096	80q. black, bright mauve and flesh	70	60
2097	2l.40 black, yellow-orange and greenish yellow	2·50	2·20
2094/2097	Set of 4	3·50	3·00

Designs: 15q. Monocyclists; 25q. Human pyramid; 80q. T **433**; 2l.40, Acrobats spinning from marquee pole.

434 *Rallying to the Flag, December 1911* (A. Zajmi)

(Des P. Sulo)

1981 (10 July). Paintings. T **434** and similar multicoloured designs. P 12½.
2098	25q. *Allies* (Sh. Hysa) (*horiz*)	65	30
2099	80q. *Azem Galica breaking the Ring of Turks* (A. Buza) (*horiz*)	1·30	60
2100	1l.20 Type **434**	1·70	1·40
2101	1l.35 *My Flag is my Heart* (L. Çefa)	2·50	1·70
2098/2101	Set of 4	5·50	3·50
MS2102	81×109 mm. 1l.80, *Unite under the Flag* (N. Vasia) (55×79 *mm*)	6·75	6·25

The miniature sheet includes two horizontal rows of perforations (P 12) within its design.

435 Weightlifting

(Des B. Zajmi)

1981 (30 Aug). Albanian Participation in International Sports. T **435** and similar horiz designs. Multicoloured. P 12.
2103	25q. Rifle shooting	45	30
2104	80q. Type **435**	95	60
2105	1l.20 Volleyball	1·40	1·10
2106	1l.35 Football	1·90	1·40
2103/2106	Set of 4	4·25	3·00

436 Flag and Hands holding Pickaxe and Rifle

437 Industrial and Agricultural Symbols

1981 (1 Nov). Eighth Workers' Party Congress. T **436** and similar horiz design. P 12.
2107	80q. bright scarlet, orange-brown and black	1·20	80
2108	1l. orange-vermilion and black	1·70	1·40

Designs: 80q. T **436**; 1l. Party flag, hammer and sickle.

1981 (8 Nov). 40th Anniversary of Workers' Party. T **437** and similar vert designs. Multicoloured. P 12.
2109	80q. Type **437**	70	55
2110	2l.80 Albanian flag and hand holding pickaxe and rifle	3·50	2·75
MS2111	79×98 mm. 1l.80, Enver Hoxha and book (50×68 *mm*). P 12×imperf	7·50	6·75

438 Pickaxe, Rifle and Young Communists Flag

439 F. S. Noli

1981 (23 Nov). 40th Anniversary of Young Communists' Union. T **438** and similar vert design. Multicoloured. P 12.
2112	80q. Type **438**	1·50	1·40
2113	1l. Workers' Party flag and Young Communists' emblem	3·00	2·50

(Des B. Asllani)

1982 (6 Jan). Birth Centenary of F. S. Noli. P 12.
2114	**439** 80q. olive-green and gold	2·00	95
2115	1l.10 reddish brown and gold	2·50	1·40

1982 (Feb). Traditional Albanian Houses (2nd series). Vert designs as T **407**. Multicoloured. P 12.
2116	25q. House in Bulqizë	45	30
2117	80q. House in Kosovo	2·00	1·30
2118	1l.20 House in Bicaj	3·00	1·90
2119	1l.55 House in Mat	4·00	2·40
2116/2119	Set of 4	8·50	5·25

440 Map, Globe and Bacilli **441** *Prizren Castle* (G. Madhi)

1982 (24 Mar). Centenary of Discovery of Tuberculosis Bacilli. T **440** and similar horiz design. P 12.
2120	80q. multicoloured	7·50	2·75
2121	1l.10 pale grey-brown and deep brown	10·50	4·75

Designs: 80q. T **440**; 1l.10, Robert Koch (discoverer), microscope and bacilli.

1982 (25 Apr). Paintings of Kosovo. T **441** and similar multicoloured designs. P 12½.
2122	25q. Type **441**	75	40
2123	80q. *House of the Albanian League, Prizren* (K. Buza) (*horiz*)	2·50	1·70

2124		1l.20 *Mountain Gorge, Rugovë* (K. Buza)	4·00	2·10
2125		1l.55 *Street of the Haxhi, Zekë* (G. Madhi)	5·75	2·75
2122/2125 *Set of 4*			11·50	6·25

1982 (5 May). Anti-fascist Heroes (4th series). Horiz designs as T **424**. Multicoloured. P 12.

2126	25q. Hibe Palikuqi and Liri Gero	60	35
2127	80q. Mihal Duri and Kajo Karafili	1·70	1·10
2128	1l.20 Fato Dudumi, Margarita Tutulani and Shejnaze Juka	2·50	1·60
2129	1l.55 Memo Meto and Gjok Doçi	4·00	1·90
2126/2129 *Set of 4*		8·00	4·50

442 Factories and Workers   **443** Ship in Harbour

1982 (6 June). Ninth Trade Unions Congress. T **442** and similar horiz design. Multicoloured. P 12.

2130	80q. Type **442**	4·25	2·30
2131	1l.10 Congress emblem	6·00	3·00

1982 (15 June). Children's Paintings. T **443** and similar horiz designs. Multicoloured. P 12½.

2132	15q. Type **443**	85	35
2133	80q. Forest camp	1·70	95
2134	1l.20 Houses	2·50	1·60
2135	1l.65 House and garden	5·00	2·40
2132/2135 *Set of 4*		9·00	4·75

444 Village Festival (Danish Jukniu)   **445** Voice of the People (party newspaper)

1982 (30 July). Paintings from Gallery of Figurative Arts, Tirana. T **444** and similar horiz designs. Multicoloured. P 12½.

2136	25q. Type **444**	45	30
2137	80q. *Komanit Hydro-electric Station Builders* (Ali Miruku)	1·70	1·60
2138	1l.20 *Steel Workers* (Çlirim Ceka)	2·50	1·90
2139	1l.55 *Oil Drillers* (Pandeli Lena)	3·75	2·30
2136/2139 *Set of 4*		7·50	5·50
MS2140 75×90 mm. 1l.90, *First Tapping of the Furnace* (Jorgji Gjikopulli)		7·75	5·50

The miniature sheet includes two horizontal rows of perforations (P 12) in its design.

1982 (25 Aug). 40th Anniversary of Popular Press. T **445** and similar vert design. Multicoloured. P 12.

2141	80q. Type **445**	£160	£130
2142	1l.10 Hand duplicator producing first edition of *Voice of the People*	£160	£130

446 Heroes of Peza Monument   **447** Congress Emblem

1982 (16 Sept). 40th Anniversary of Albanian Democratic Front. T **446** and similar horiz design. Multicoloured. P 12.

2143	80q. Type **446**	13·00	5·50
2144	1l.10 Peza Conference building and marchers with flag	19·00	7·75

1982 (4 Oct). Eighth Young Communists' Union Congress. P 12.

2145	**447**	80q. multicoloured	10·00	6·25
2146		1l.10 multicoloured	17·00	9·25

448 Tapesty   **449** Freedom Fighters

1982 (30 Oct). Handicrafts. T **448** and similar multicoloured designs. P 12.

2147	25q. Type **448**	80	40
2148	80q. Bags (*vert*)	1·90	1·00
2149	1l.20 Butter churns	2·75	1·40
2150	1l.55 Jug (*vert*)	4·00	2·00
2147/2150 *Set of 4*		8·50	4·25

1982 (28 Nov). 70th Anniversary of Independence. T **449** and similar horiz designs. P 12.

2151	20q. bright rose-red, vermilion and black	60	40
2152	1l.20 black, pale olive and carmine-red	3·25	1·60
2153	2l.40 reddish brown, buff and bright rose-red	5·50	3·25
2151/2153 *Set of 3*		8·50	4·75
MS2154 90×89 mm. 1l.90, multicoloured. P 12×imperf		9·25	6·25

Designs: As T **449**—20q. Ismail Qemali (patriot) and crowd around building; 1l.20, T **449**; 2l.40, Six freedom fighters. 58×55 mm—1l.90, Independence Monument, Tirana.

450 Dhërmi   **451** Male Dancers

(Des P. Sulo)

1982 (20 Dec). Coastal Views. T **450** and similar horiz designs. Multicoloured. P 12.

2155	25q. Type **450**	45	30
2156	80q. Sarandë	1·50	95
2157	1l.20 Ksamil	2·10	1·60
2158	1l.55 Lukovë	4·00	1·90
2155/2158 *Set of 4*		7·25	4·25

(Des H. Devolli)

1983 (20 Feb). Folk Dance Assemblies Abroad. T **451** and similar horiz designs. Multicoloured. P 12.

2159	25q. Type **451**	35	30
2160	80q. Male dancers and drummer	1·00	55
2161	1l.20 Musicians	1·90	1·40
2162	1l.55 Group of female dancers	2·50	1·90
2159/2162 *Set of 4*		5·25	3·75

452 Karl Marx   **453** Electricity Generation

(Des M. Fushëkati)

1983 (14 Mar). Death Centenary of Karl Marx. P 12.

2163	**452**	80q. multicoloured	3·00	1·40
2164		1l.10 multicoloured	3·75	1·90

(Des Q. Prizreni)

1983 (20 Apr). Energy Production. T **453** and similar vert design. P 12.

2165	80q. dull ultramarine and orange	2·00	1·10
2166	1l.10 mauve and turquoise-green	2·50	1·60

Designs: 80q. T **453**; 1l.10, Gas and oil production.

ALBANIA 1983

(Des M. Fushëkati)

1983 (5 May). Anti-fascist Heroes (5th series). Horiz designs as T **424**. Multicoloured. P 12.

2167	25q. Asim Zeneli and Nazmi Rushiti..............	40	30
2168	80q. Shyqyri Ishmi, Shyqyri Alimerko and Myzafer Asqeriu...................................	1·50	60
2169	1l.20 Qybra Sokoli, Qeriba Derri and Ylbere Bilibashi..	2·50	1·40
2170	1l.55 Themo Vasi and Abaz Shehu..................	3·75	1·90
2167/2170	Set of 4	7·25	3·75

454 Congress Emblem

455 Cycling

(Des Z. Mati)

1983 (1 June). Ninth Women's Union Congress. P 12½.

2171	**454** 80q. red, scarlet-vermilion and gold........	2·40	1·40
2172	1l.10 greenish blue, vermilion and gold	3·00	1·90

(Des E. Hila)

1983 (20 June). Sport and Leisure. T **455** and similar horiz designs. Multicoloured. P 12.

2173	25q. Type **455**	40	30
2174	80q. Chess	1·50	55
2175	1l.20 Gymnastics	2·50	1·40
2176	1l.55 Wrestling	3·00	1·90
2173/2176	Set of 4	6·75	3·75

456 Soldier and Militia

457 Sunny Day (Myrteza Fushëkati)

(Des P. Mele)

1983 (10 July). 40th Anniversary of People's Army. T **456** and similar vert designs. P 12.

2177	20q. gold and Indian red.........................	40	25
2178	1l.20 gold and carmine-red.............................	2·75	1·40
2179	2l.40 gold and lake-brown.............................	4·75	2·30
2177/2179	Set of 3	7·00	3·50

Designs: 20q. T **456**; 1l.20, Soldier; 2l.40, Factory guard.

(Des P. Sulo)

1983 (28 Aug). Paintings from Gallery of Figurative Arts, Tirana. T **457** and similar horiz designs. Multicoloured. P 12½.

2180	25q. Type **457**	45	30
2181	80q. *Morning Gossip* (Niko Progri)...............	1·70	95
2182	1l.20 *29th November, 1944* (Harilla Dhimo)	2·10	1·40
2183	1l.55 *Demolition* (Pandi Male)	3·00	1·70
2180/2183	Set of 4	6·50	4·00
MS2184	111×74 mm. 1l.90, *Partisan Assault* (Sali Shijaku and Myrteza Fushëkati) (99×59 *mm*). P 12×imperf	14·50	10·00

(Des N. Bakalli)

1983 (6 Oct). National Folklore Festival, Gjirokastër. Vert designs as T **402**. Multicoloured. P 12.

2185	25q. Sword dance	40	30
2186	80q. Kerchief dance	2·75	1·40
2187	1l.20 Musicians	3·00	2·00
2188	1l.55 Women dancers with garlands	5·50	3·50
2185/2188	Set of 4	10·50	6·50

458 Enver Hoxha

459 WCY Emblem and Globe

(Des V. Kilica)

1983 (16 Oct). 75th Birthday of Enver Hoxha. P 12½.

2189	**458** 80q. multicoloured	1·20	1·10
2190	1l.20 multicoloured	2·00	1·60
2191	1l.80 multicoloured	3·00	2·00
2189/2191	Set of 3	5·50	4·25
MS2192	77×98 mm. 1l.90, multicoloured (as Type **458** but with inscriptions differently arranged)	6·00	5·50

The miniature sheet includes two horizontal lines of perforations (P 12) in its design.

(Des M. Fushëkati)

1983 (10 Nov). World Communications Year. P 12.

2193	**459** 60q. multicoloured	1·00	65
2194	1l.20 blue, black and reddish orange.......	2·75	2·00

460 Combine to Triumph (J. Keraj)

461 Amphitheatre, Butrint (Buthrotum)

1983 (10 Dec). Skanderbeg Epoch in Art. T **460** and similar horiz designs. Multicoloured. P 12½.

2195	25q. Type **460**	65	30
2196	80q. *The Heroic Resistance at Krujë* (N. Bakalli)	2·20	1·40
2197	1l.20 *United we are Unconquerable by our Enemies* (N. Progri)	3·00	1·60
2198	1l.55 *Assembly at Lezhë* (B. Ahmeti)...............	4·50	2·00
2195/2198	Set of 4	9·25	4·25
MS2199	77×90 mm. *Victory over the Tuks* (G. Madhi) ...	13·00	11·50

The miniature sheet includes two horizontal lines of perforations (P 12) in its design.

(Des P. Sulo)

1983 (28 Dec). Graeco-Roman Remains in Illyria. T **461** and similar horiz designs. Multicoloured. P 12.

2200	80q. Type **461**	3·00	2·00
2201	1l.20 Colonnade, Apoloni-Çesma (Apollonium)	4·00	2·75
2202	1l.80 Vaulted gallery of amphitheatre, Dyrrah (Epidamnus)	4·50	3·25
2200/2202	Set of 3	10·50	7·25

462 Man's Head from Apoloni

463 Clock Tower, Gjirokastër

1984 ALBANIA

(Des P. Sulo)

1984 (25 Feb). Archaeological Discoveries. T **462** and similar vert designs. Multicoloured. P 12×12½.

2203	15q. Type **462**	25	20
2204	25q. Tombstone from Korçë	45	30
2205	80q. Woman's head from Apoloni	1·50	1·10
2206	1l.10 Child's head from Tren	2·20	1·60
2207	1l.20 Man's head from Dyrrah	3·00	1·90
2208	2l.20 Bronze statuette of Eros from Dyrrah	4·75	2·30
2203/2208	Set of 6	11·00	6·75

(Des Z. Mati)

1984 (30 Mar). Clock Towers. T **463** and similar vert designs. P 12.

2209	15q. slate-purple	25	20
2210	25q. deep grey-brown	45	35
2211	80q. slate-violet	1·50	95
2212	1l.10 scarlet	1·90	1·60
2213	1l.20 bronze-green	2·50	2·00
2214	2l.20 orange-brown	4·50	3·00
2209/2214	Set of 6	10·00	7·25

Designs: 15q. T **463**; 25q. Kavajë; 80q. Elbasan; 1l.10, Tirana; 1l.20, Peqin; 2l.20, Krujë.

464 Student with Microscope

465 Enver Hoxha

(Des P. Mele, Q. Prizreni and L. Kodheli)

1984 (20 Apr). 40th Anniversary of Liberation (1st issue). T **464** and similar horiz designs. Multicoloured. P 12.

2215	15q. Type **464**	25	20
2216	25q. Soldier with flag	45	30
2217	80q. Schoolchildren	1·80	1·10
2218	1l.10 Soldier, ships, aeroplanes and weapons	2·20	1·60
2219	1l.20 Workers with flag	2·75	1·90
2220	2l.20 Armed guards on patrol	4·50	2·30
2215/2220	Set of 6	11·00	6·75

See also Nos. 2255/**MS**2257.

(Des M. Fushëkati)

1984 (5 May). Anti-fascist Heroes (6th series). Horiz designs as T **424**. Multicoloured. P 12.

2221	15q. Manush Alimani, Mustafa Matohiti and Kastriot Muço	85	25
2222	25q. Zaho Koka, Reshit Çollaku and Maliq Muço	1·90	55
2223	1l.20 Lefter Talo, Tom Kola and Fuat Babani	3·50	1·90
2224	2l.20 Myslysm Shyri, Dervish Hekali and Skender Caçi	6·00	3·75
2221/2224	Set of 4	11·00	5·75

(Des Q. Prizreni)

1984 (24 May). 40th Anniversary of Permet Congress. T **465** and similar vert design. P 12.

2225	80q. reddish brown, orange-vermilion and Venetian red	4·75	3·00
2226	1l.10 black, orange-yellow and reddish lilac	5·50	4·00

Designs: 80q. T **465**; 1l.10, Resistance fighter (detail of monument).

466 Children reading Comic

467 Football in Goal

(Des Z. Mati)

1984 (1 June). Children. T **466** and similar vert designs. Multicoloured. P 12.

2227	15q. Type **466**	75	40
2228	25q. Children with toys	1·70	60
2229	60q. Children gardening and rainbow	3·25	1·60
2230	2l.80 Children flying kite bearing Albanian Arms	6·50	4·00
2227/2230	Set of 4	11·00	6·00

(Des M. Fushëkati)

1984 (12 June). European Football Championship Finals. T **467** and similar vert designs. Multicoloured. P 12.

2231	15q. Type **467**	1·40	40
2232	25q. Referee and football	1·90	55
2233	1l.20 Football and map of Europe	5·00	1·60
2234	2l.20 Football and pitch	6·00	3·00
2231/2234	Set of 4	13·00	5·00

468 *Freedom is Here* (Myrteza Fushëkati)

469 Mulberry

1984 (12 July). Paintings from Gallery of Figurative Arts, Tirana. T **468** and similar multicoloured designs. P 12½.

2235	15q. Type **468**	75	40
2236	25q. *Morning* (Zamir Mati) (vert)	1·50	80
2237	80q. *My Darling* (Agim Zajmi) (vert)	3·75	2·30
2238	2l.60 *For the Partisans* (Arben Basha)	6·25	3·50
2235/2238	Set of 4	11·00	6·25
MS2239	80×93 mm. 1l.90, *Albania* (Zamir Mati)	15·00	9·00

The miniature sheet includes two horizontal rows of perforations (P 12) within its design.

1984 (20 Aug). Flowers. T **469** and similar vert designs. Multicoloured. P 12.

2240	15q. Type **469**	4·50	1·20
2241	25q. Plantain	6·00	1·90
2242	1l.20 Hypericum	14·00	7·00
2243	2l.20 Edelweiss (*Leontopodium alpinum*)	29·00	13·00
2240/2243	Set of 4	48·00	21·00

470 Sabre Dance

(Des N. Bakalli)

1984 (21 Sept). Ausipex 84 International Stamp Exhibition, Melbourne. Sheet 72×98 mm. P 12×imperf.

MS2244	**470** 1l.90, multicoloured	6·75	6·25

471 Truck driving through Forest

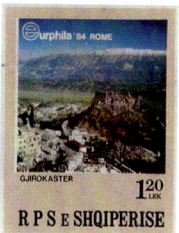
472 Gjirokastër

ALBANIA 1984

1984 (25 Sept). Forestry. T **471** and similar vert designs. Multicoloured. P 12.
2245	15q. Type **471**	1·50	95
2246	25q. Transporting logs on overhead cable....	2·30	1·60
2247	1l.20 Sawmill in forest	7·75	5·00
2248	2l.20 Lumberjack sawing down tree	11·50	6·50
2245/2248	Set of 4	21·00	12·50

1984 (13 Oct). Eurphila '84 International Stamp Exhibition, Rome. P 12½.
2249	**472**	1l.20 multicoloured	3·75	3·50

473 Football   **474** Agriculture and Industry

(Des E. Hila)

1984 (19 Oct). Fifth National Spartakiad. T **473** and similar vert designs. Multicoloured. P 12.
2250	15q. Type **473**	25	20
2251	25q. Running	70	40
2252	80q. Weightlifting	1·70	70
2253	2l.20 Pistol shooting	4·25	3·00
2250/2253	Set of 4	6·25	3·75
MS2254	70×90 mm. 1l.90, Opening ceremony	6·00	4·75

The miniature sheet includes two horizontal rows of perforations in its design.

(Des E. Laperi and S. Kristo)

1984 (29 Nov). 40th Anniversary of Liberation (2nd issue). T **474** and similar multicoloured designs. P 12.
2255	80q. Type **474**	3·50	1·60
2256	1l.10 Soldiers and flag	4·25	2·30
MS2257	68×89 mm. 1l.90, Enver Hoxha making liberation speech. P 12×imperf	7·25	5·75

475 Pot   **476** Kapo (bust)

(Des N. Baba)

1985 (25 Feb). Archaeological Discoveries in Illyria. T **475** and similar vert designs. Multicoloured. P 12×12½.
2258	15q. Type **475**	75	30
2259	80q. Terracotta head of woman	3·00	1·60
2260	1l.20 Terracotta bust of Aphrodite	3·75	1·90
2261	1l.70 Bronze statuette of Nike	6·00	3·00
2258/2261	Set of 4	12·00	6·00

(Des M. Fushëkati)

1985 (4 Mar). 70th Birthday of Hysni Kapo (politician). P 12.
2262	**476**	90q. black and rose-red	3·00	2·30
2263		1l.10 black and cobalt	3·50	3·00

477 Running   **478** Bach

(Des Q. Prizreni)

1985 (18 Mar). Olymphilex '85 Olympic Stamps Exhibition, Lausanne. T **477** and similar horiz designs. Multicoloured. P 12.
2264	25q. Type **477**	45	30
2265	60q. Weightlifting	1·20	80
2266	1l.20 Football	2·10	1·90
2267	1l.50 Pistol shooting	3·75	2·30
2264/2267	Set of 4	6·75	4·75

(Des Q. Prizreni)

1985 (31 Mar). 300th Birth Anniversary of Johann Sebastian Bach (composer). T **478** and similar vert design. P 12.
2268	80q. dull orange, reddish brown and black..	27·00	16·00
2269	1l.20 new blue, deep new blue and black	34·00	19·00

Designs: 80q. T **478**; 1l.20, Bach's birthplace, Eisenach.

479 Enver Hoxha   **480** Frontier Guards

(Des V. Kilica)

1985 (11 Apr). Enver Hoxha Commemoration. P 12½.
2270	**479**	80q. multicoloured	3·75	3·50
MS2271	67×90 mm. **479** 1l.90, multicoloured. Imperf ..			6·25	5·50

(Des S. Spahiu and B. Marika)

1985 (25 Apr). 40th Anniversary of Frontier Force. T **480** and similar horiz design. Multicoloured. P 12.
2272	25q. Type **480**	2·30	1·60
2273	80q. Frontier guard	5·50	4·75

(Des M. Fushëkati)

1985 (5 May). Anti-fascist Heroes (7th series). Horiz designs as T **424**. Multicoloured. P 12.
2274	25q. Mitro Xhani, Nimete Progonati and Kozma Nushi	1·10	80
2275	40q. Ajet Xhindoli, Mustafa Kaçaçi and Estref Caka	1·70	1·60
2276	60q. Çelo Sinani, Llambro Andoni and Meleq Gosnishti	3·00	1·90
2277	1l.20 Thodhori Mastora, Fejzi Micoli and Hysen Cino	5·00	3·75
2274/2277	Set of 4	9·75	7·25

481 Scarf on Rifle Barrel   **482** Primary School (Thoma Malo)

(Des H. Devolli and M. Fushëkati)

1985 (9 May). 40th Anniversary of VE (Victory in Europe) Day. T **481** and similar horiz design. Multicoloured. P 12.
2278	25q. Type **481**	38·00	55·00
2279	80q. Crumpled swastika and hand holding rifle butt	£100	£140

(Des N. Baba)

1985 (25 June). Paintings from Gallery of Figurative Arts, Tirana. T **482** and similar multicoloured designs. P 12½.
2280	25q. Type **482**	45	30
2281	80q. *Heroes and Mother* (Hysen Devolli) (vert)	1·90	1·60
2282	90q. *Mother writing* (Angjelin Dodmasej) (vert)	2·30	1·90
2283	1l.20 *Women off to Work* (Ksenofon Dilo)	3·00	2·30
2280/2283	Set of 4	7·00	5·50
MS2284	74×88 mm. 1l.90, *Foundry Workers* (Mikel Gurashi)	6·50	5·50

The miniature sheet includes two horizontal rows of perforations (P 12) within its design.

1985 ALBANIA

483 Scoring a Goal

484 Oranges

(Des Z. Mati)

1985 (20 July). Tenth World Basketball Championship, Spain. T **483** and similar vert designs. P 12.
2285	25q. blue and black	45	30
2286	80q. green and black	2·00	80
2287	1l.20 bluish violet and black	2·50	1·90
2288	1l.60 carmine-red and black	4·00	3·00
2285/2288 Set of 4		8·00	5·50

Designs: 25q. T **483**; 80q. Player running with ball; 1l.20, Defending goal; 1l.60, Defender capturing ball.

(Des K. Dilo)

1985 (20 Aug). Fruit Trees. T **484** and similar vert designs. Multicoloured. P 12.
2289	25q. Type **484**	75	45
2290	80q. Plums	3·75	2·30
2291	1l.20 Apples	6·25	3·00
2292	1l.60 Cherries	7·75	4·75
2289/2292 Set of 4		17·00	9·50

485 Krujë

486 War Horse Dance

(Des K. Dilo)

1985 (20 Sept). Architecture. T **485** and similar horiz designs. P 12.
2293	25q. black and Indian red	85	60
2294	80q. black, grey and red-brown	4·25	2·30
2295	1l.20 black, light brown and new blue	4·75	3·00
2296	1l.60 black, brown and Indian red	6·50	4·00
2293/2296 Set of 4		14·50	9·00

Designs: 25q. T **485**; 80q. Gjirokastër; 1l.20, Berat; 1l.60, Shkodër.

(Des N. Bakalli)

1985 (6 Oct). National Folklore Festival. Dances. T **486** and similar vert designs. P 12.
2297	25q. reddish brown, brown-red and black	85	40
2298	80q. reddish brown, brown-red and black	2·50	1·60
2299	1l.20 reddish brown, brown-red and black	3·50	1·90
2300	1l.60 reddish brown, brown-red and black	4·25	2·75
2297/2300 Set of 4		10·00	6·00
MS2301	56×82 mm. 1l.90, multicoloured. Imperf	6·50	5·50

Designs: 25q. T **486**; 80q. Pillow dance; 1l.20, Ladies' kerchief dance; 1l.60, Men's one-legged pair dance; 1l.90, Fortress dance.

487 State Arms

488 Dam across River Drin

(Des H. Devolli)

1986 (11 Jan). 40th Anniversary of Albanian People's Republic. T **487** and similar horiz design. P 12½.
2302	25q. gold, deep rose-red and black	2·30	1·60

2303	80q. multicoloured	4·75	3·00

Designs: 25q. T **487**; 80q. *Comrade Hoxha announcing the News to the People* (Vilson Kilica) and Arms.

1986 (20 Feb). Enver Hoxha Hydro-electric Power Station. T **488** and similar vert design. Multicoloured. P 12.
2304	25q. Type **488**	7·75	3·00
2305	80q. Control building	17·00	11·00

489 *Gymnospermium shqipetarum*

490 Maksim Gorky (writer)

(Des H. Agolli)

1986 (20 Mar). Flowers. T **489** and similar vert design. Multicoloured. P 12.
2306	25q. Type **489**	3·00	1·60
	a. Pair. Nos. 2306/2307	17·00	8·00
2307	1l.20 *Leucolum valentinum*	12·50	6·25

Nos. 2306/2307 were issued together in *se-tenant* pairs in booklets. They also exist imperforate from a limited printing.

1986 (20 Apr). Anniversaries. T **490** and similar designs. P 12.
2308	25q. deep chestnut	80	40
	a. Horiz strip of 4. Nos. 2308/2311	21·00	
2309	80q. dull violet	3·00	1·90
2310	1l.20 olive-green	5·50	3·00
2311	2l.40 reddish purple	11·00	7·00
2308/2311 Set of 4		18·00	11·00
MS2312	88×72 mm. 1l.90, dull violet, ultramarine and orange-yellow	7·00	6·25

Designs: As T **490**—25q. T **490** (50th death anniversary); 80q. André Ampère (physicist and mathematician, 150th death anniversary); 1l.20, James Watt (inventor, 250th birth anniversary); 2l.40, Franz Liszt (composer, death centenary). 88×72 mm—1l.90, Heads of Gorky, Ampère, Watt and Liszt.

The miniature sheet includes two vertical rows of perforations (P 12½) in its design.

Nos. 2308/2311 were issued in *se-tenant* strips of four in booklets.

(Des M. Fushëkati)

1986 (5 May). Anti-fascist Heroes (8th series). Horiz designs as T **424**. Multicoloured. P 12.
2313	25q. Ramiz Aranitasi, Inajete Dumi and Laze Nuro Ferraj	3·00	2·30
2314	80q. Dine Kalcnja, Kozma Naska, Met Hasa and Fahri Ramadani	7·25	4·00
2315	1l.20 Hiqmet Buzi, Bajram Tusha, Mumin Selami and Hajredin Bylyshi	12·00	7·75
2313/2315 Set of 3		20·00	12·50

491 Trophy on Globe

492 Tyre within Ship's Wheel, Train and Traffic Lights

(Des M. Fushëkati)

1986 (31 May). World Cup Football Championship, Mexico. T **491** and similar horiz designs. Multicoloured. P 12.
2316	25q. Type **491**	70	55
2317	1l.20 Goalkeeper's hands and ball	3·50	2·75
MS2318	97×63 mm. 1l.90, Globe-football (40×32 mm)	5·75	4·25

The miniature sheet includes horizontal and vertical rows of perforations (P 12½) enclosing the central motif, but the value of the sheet appears outside these perforations.

(Des M. Fushëkati and H. Dhimo)

1986 (10 Aug). 40th Anniversary of Transport Workers' Day. P 12.
2319	**492** 1l.20 multicoloured	19·00	11·00

ALBANIA 1986

493 Naim Frashëri (poet) **494** Congress Emblem

(Des H. Devolli)

1986 (20 Sept). Anniversaries. T **493** and similar horiz designs. Multicoloured. P 12.

2320	30q. Type **493** (140th birth anniversary)	1·10	60
2321	60q. Ndre Mjeda (poet, 120th birth anniversary)	1·90	1·60
2322	90q. Petro Nini Luarasi (journalist, 75th death anniversary)	3·00	2·30
2323	1l. Andon Zako Qajupi (poet, 120th birth anniversary)	4·00	2·40
2324	1l.20 Millosh Gjergj Nikolla (Migjeni) (revolutionary writer, 75th birth anniversary)	4·75	2·75
2325	2l.60 Urani Rumbo (women's education pioneer, 50th death anniversary)	12·50	5·00
2320/2325 Set of 6		25·00	13·00

(Des Z. Mati)

1986 (3 Nov). Ninth Workers' Party Congress, Tirana. P 12.

2326	**494**	30q. multicoloured	16·00	11·50

495 Party Stamp and Enver Hoxha's Signature **496** 'Mother Albania'

(Des H. Devolli)

1986 (8 Nov). 45th Anniversary of Workers' Party. T **495** and similar vert design. P 12.

2327	30q. rosine, gold and brownish grey	4·75	2·30
2328	1l.20 rosine, dull orange and gold	12·50	5·50

Designs: 30q. T **495**; 1l.20, Profiles of Marx, Engels, Lenin and Stalin and Tirana house where Party was founded.

(Des M. Fushëkati)

1986 (29 Nov). P 12×12½.

2329	**496**	10q. deep turquoise-blue	15	10
2330		20q. Venetian red	25	15
2331		30q. scarlet-vermilion	30	20
2332		50q. bistre-brown	30	25
2333		60q. olive-green	40	30
2334		80q. carmine-red	45	40
2335		90q. ultramarine	80	45
2336		1l.20 deep blue-green	1·60	80
2337		1l.60 purple	1·90	1·10
2338		2l.20 slate-green	3·00	1·90
2339		3l. orange-brown	4·00	3·00
2340		6l. orange-yellow	7·75	5·50
2329/2340 Set of 12			19·00	12·50

497 Marble Head of Aesculapius **498** Monument and Centenary Emblem

1987 (20 Feb). Archaeological Discoveries. T **497** and similar vert designs. Multicoloured. P 12×12½.

2341	30q. Type **497**	1·60	95
2342	80q. Terracotta figure of Aphrodite	3·00	1·60
2343	1l. Bronze figure of Pan	4·75	2·20
2344	1l.20 Limestone head of Jupiter	6·25	4·00
2341/2344 Set of 4		14·00	8·00

(Des N. Prizreni)

1987 (7 Mar). Centenary of First Albanian School, Korçë. T **498** and similar designs. P 12.

2345	30q. yellow-brown, light brown and orange-yellow	70	45
2346	80q. multicoloured	2·10	95
2347	1l.20 multicoloured	3·00	2·10
2345/2347 Set of 3		5·25	2·10

Designs: Horiz—80q. First school building; 1l.20, Woman soldier running, girl reading book and boy doing woodwork.

499 Victor Hugo (writer) **500** *Forsythia europaea*

(Des H. Devolli)

1987 (20 Apr). Anniversaries. T **499** and similar vert designs. P 12.

2348	30q. bluish violet, lavender and black	75	45
2349	80q. chestnut, yellow-ochre and black	1·80	95
2350	90q. deep slate-blue, slate-blue and black	2·75	1·80
2351	1l.30 deep yellow-green, dull yellow-green and black	3·75	3·00
2348/2351 Set of 4		8·25	5·50

Designs: 30q. T **499** (185th birth anniversary); 80p. Galileo Galilei (astronomer, 345th death anniversary); 90q. Charles Darwin (naturalist, 105th death anniversary); 1l.30, Miguel de Cervantes (writer, 440th birth anniversary).

(Des H. Agolli)

1987 (20 May). Flowers. T **500** and similar vert designs. Multicoloured. P 12.

2352	30q. Type **500**	95	55
2353	90q. *Moltkia doerfleri*	1·90	1·40
2354	2l.10 *Wulfenia baldacii*	4·25	3·75
2352/2354 Set of 3		6·50	5·25

501 Congress Emblem **502** *The Bread of Industry* (Myrteza Fushëkati)

(Des Fatmir Biba)

1987 (25 June). Tenth Trade Unions Congress, Tirana. P 12.

2355	**501**	1l.20 deep carmine, vermilion and gold	7·00	5·50

1987 (20 July). Paintings from Gallery of Figurative Arts, Tirana. T **502** and similar multicoloured designs. P 12×12½ (vert) or 12½×12 (horiz).

2356	30q. Type **502**	80	60
2357	80q. *Partisan Gift* (Skënder Kokobobo)	1·60	1·40
2358	1l. *Sowers* (Bujar Asllani) (horiz)	2·30	1·70
2359	1l.20 *At the Foundry* (Çlirim Ceka) (horiz)	3·00	2·50
2356/2359 Set of 4		7·00	5·50

1987 ALBANIA

503 Throwing the Hammer

504 Themistokli Gërmenji (revolutionary, 70th death)

1987 (29 Aug). World Light Athletics Championships, Rome. T **503** and similar horiz designs. Multicoloured. P 12½.
2360	30q. Type **503**		80	70
2361	90q. Running		2·30	1·40
2362	1l.10 Putting the shot		2·30	1·70
2360/2362	Set of 3		4·75	3·50

MS2363 85×59 mm. 1l.90, Runner, winners' podium and banner (64×24 mm). P 12½×12 .... 5·25 5·25

(Des H. Devolli)

1987 (20 Sept). Anniversaries. T **504** and similar horiz designs. P 12.
2364	30q. deep yellow-brown, bright scarlet and black		45	40
2365	80q. carmine-lake, bright scarlet and black		1·60	70
2366	90q. dull violet, rosine and black		2·00	1·40
2367	1l.30 green, scarlet and black		3·50	2·50
2364/2367	Set of 4		6·75	4·50

Designs: 30q. T **504**; 80q. Bajram Curri (organiser of Albanian League, 125th birth); 90q. Aleks Stavre Drenova (poet, 40th death); 1l.30, Gjerasim Qiriazi (educational pioneer, 126th birth).

505 Emblem

506 National Flag

(Des F. Biba)

1987 (22 Oct). Ninth Young Communists' Union Congress, Tirana. P 12.
2368	**505**	1l.20 multicoloured	8·50	6·50

(Des H. Devolli)

1987 (28 Nov). 75th Anniversary of Independence. P 12.
2369	**506**	1l.20 multicoloured	9·75	7·00

507 Post Office Emblem

508 Lord Byron (writer, bicentenary)

(Des G. Hajdori)

1987 (5 Dec). 75th Anniversary of Albanian Postal Administration. T **507** and similar vert design. Multicoloured. P 12.
2370	90q. Type **507**		9·25	6·50
2371	1l.20 National Emblem on bronze medallion		13·00	12·50

(Des H. Devolli)

1988 (10 Mar). Birth Anniversaries. T **508** and similar vert design. P 12.
2372	30q. grey-black and yellow-orange		7·00	5·50
2373	1l.20 black and mauve		28·00	22·00

Designs: 30q. T **508**; 1l.20, Eugène Delacroix (painter, 190th anniversary).

509 Oil Derrick, Tap, Houses and Wheat Ears

510 Sideritis raeseri

(Des N. Kapulli)

1988 (7 Apr). 40th Anniversary of World Health Organisation. P 12.
2374	**509**	90q. multicoloured	39·00	34·00
2375		1l.20 multicoloured	55·00	44·00

(Des A. Marika)

1988 (20 May). Flowers. T **510** and similar vert designs. Multicoloured. P 12.
2376	30q. Type **510**		14·00	8·50
	a. Booklet pane. Nos. 2376/2378 plus label		90·00	
2377	90q. Lunaria telekiana		28·00	19·00
2378	2l.10 Sanguisorba albanica		42·00	28·00
2376/2378	Set of 3		75·00	50·00

Nos. 2376/2378 were issued in horizontal se-tenant strips of three stamps and an inscribed label in booklets.

511 Flag and Woman with Book

512 Footballers

(Des N. Bakalli)

1988 (6 June). Tenth Women's Union Congress, Tirana. P 12.
2379	**511**	90q. black, bright rose-red and reddish orange	19·00	16·00

(Des M. Fushëkati)

1988 (10 June). Eighth European Football Championship, West Germany. T **512** and similar horiz designs. Multicoloured. P 12.
2380	30q. Type **512**		3·00	2·75
2381	80q. Players jumping for ball		4·25	4·00
2382	1l.20 Tackling		7·25	6·75
2380/2382	Set of 3		13·00	12·00

MS2383 78×67 mm. 1l.90, Goalkeeper saving ball. Imperf .... 17·00 16·00

513 Clasped Hands

514 Flag, Woman with Rifle and Soldier

(Des N. Prizreni)

1988 (10 June). 110th Anniversary of League of Prizren. T **513** and similar vert design. Multicoloured. P 12.
2384	30q. Type **513**		60·00	55·00
2385	1l.20 League Headquarters, Prizren		£100	95·00

(Des Q. Prizreni)

1988 (10 July). 45th Anniversary of People's Army. T **514** and similar vert design. Multicoloured. P 12.
2386	60q. Type **514**		60·00	55·00
2387	90q. Army monument, partisans and Labinot house		£100	95·00

ALBANIA 1988

515 Mihal Grameno (writer)

516 Migjeni

(Des H. Devolli)

1988 (15 Aug). T **515** and similar vert designs. Multicoloured. P 12.
2388	30q. Type **515**	22·00	20·00
2389	90q. Bajo Topulli (revolutionary)	36·00	34·00
2390	1l. Murat Toptani (sculptor and poet)	44·00	41·00
2391	1l.20 Jul Variboba (poet)	60·00	55·00
2388/2391 Set of 4		£150	£140

(Des Z. Mati)

1988 (26 Aug). 50th Death Anniversary of Millosh Nikolla (Migjeni) (writer). P 12.
2392	**516**	90q. silver and red-brown	17·00	16·00

517 Dede Skurra

518 Bride wearing Fezzes, Mirdita

(Des G. Leka)

1988 (5 Sept). Ballads. T **517** and similar square designs, each black and grey. P 12.
2393	30q. Type **517**	14·50	11·00
2394	90q. *Young Omer*	36·00	30·00
2395	1l.20 *Gjergj Elez Alia*	44·00	34·00
2393/2395 Set of 3		85·00	70·00

(Des N. Bakalli)

1988 (6 Oct). National Folklore Festival, Gjirokastër. Wedding Customs. T **518** and similar vert design. Multicoloured. P 12.
2396	30q. Type **518**	44·00	41·00
2397	1l.20 Pan Dance, Gjirokastër	£160	£120

519 Hoxha

520 Detail of Congress Document

(Des M. Fushëkati and L. Kodheli)

1988 (16 Oct). 80th Birth Anniversary of Enver Hoxha. T **519** and similar multicoloured design. P 12½.
2398	90q. Type **519**	6·50	6·00
2399	1l.20 Enver Hoxha Museum (*horiz*)	9·75	9·00

(Des Q. Prizreni)

1988 (14 Nov). 80th Anniversary of Monastir Language Congress. T **520** and similar horiz design. Multicoloured. P 12.
2400	60q. Type **520**	34·00	28·00
2401	90q. Alphabet book and Congress building	55·00	44·00

521 Steam Locomotive and Map showing 1947 Railway line

(Des T. Pustina)

1989 (28 Feb). Railway Locomotives. T **521** and similar horiz designs. Multicoloured. P 12½×12.
2402	30q. Type **521**	45	35
2403	90q. Steam locomotive and map of 1949 network	1·50	55
2404	1l.20 Diesel locomotive and 1978 network	1·70	1·10
2405	1l.80 Diesel locomotive and 1985 network	3·00	1·40
2406	2l.40 Diesel locomotive and 1988 network	6·00	2·75
2402/2406 Set of 5		11·50	5·50

522 Entrance to Two-storey Tomb

523 Mother mourning Son

(Des T. Pustina)

1989 (10 Mar). Archaeological Discoveries in Illyria. T **522** and similar square designs. P 12.
2407	30q. black, deep brown and grey-brown	45	35
2408	90q. black and dull blue-green	1·70	1·40
2409	2l.10 multicoloured	3·00	2·30
2407/2409 Set of 3		4·75	3·75

Designs: 30q. T **522**; 90q. Buckle showing battle scene; 2l.10, Earring depicting head.

(Des N. Bakalli)

1989 (5 Apr). Kostandini and Doruntina (folk tale). T **523** and similar vert designs. Multicoloured. P 12×12½.
2410	30q. Type **523**	75	40
2411	80q. Mother weeping over tomb and son rising from dead	1·50	95
2412	1l. Son and his sister on Horseback	1·50	1·40
2413	1l.20 Mother and daughter reunited	2·20	2·00
2410/2413 Set of 4		5·25	4·25

524 *Aster albanicus*

525 Johann Strauss (composer, 90th death anniversary)

1989 (10 May). Flowers. T **524** and similar vert designs. Multicoloured. P 12.
2414	30q. Type **524**	45	35
2415	90q. *Orchis papariti*	1·70	1·40
2416	2l.10 *Orchis albanica*	3·00	2·30
2414/2416 Set of 3		4·75	3·75

1989 ALBANIA

(Des N. Bakalli)

1989 (3 June). Anniversaries. T **525** and similar vert designs, each deep brown and gold. P 12.

2417	30q. Type **525**	75	40
	a. Block of 4. Nos. 2417/2420	7·75	
2418	80q. Marie Curie (physicist, 55th death anniversary)	1·50	80
2419	1l. Federico Garcia Lorca (writer, 53rd death anniversary)	2·20	1·60
2420	1l.20 Albert Einstein (physicist, 110th birth anniversary)	3·00	2·30
2417/2420 Set of 4		6·75	4·50

Nos. 3417/3420 were issued together in *se-tenant* blocks of four within the sheet.

526 State Arms, Workers' Party Flag and Crowd

527 Storming of the Bastille

(Des P. Mele)

1989 (26 June). Sixth Albanian Democratic Front Congress, Tirana. P 12.

2421	**526**	1l.20 multicoloured	12·00	6·75

1989 (7 July). Bicentenary of French Revolution. T **527** and similar horiz design. Multicoloured. P 12½.

2422	90q. Type **527**	1·00	70
2423	1l.20 Monument	1·90	1·10

528 Galley

529 Pjëter Bogdani (writer)

1989 (25 July). Ships. T **528** and similar horiz designs. P 12.

2424	30q. dull blue-green and black	75	35
2425	80q. cobalt and black	1·20	95
2426	90q. violet-blue and black	1·50	1·40
2427	1l.30 bright lilac and black	2·20	2·00
2424/2427 Set of 4		5·00	4·25

Designs: 30q. **528**; 80q. Kogge; 90q. Schooner; 1l.30, Container ship.

1989 (30 Aug). Death Anniversaries. T **529** and similar vert designs. Multicoloured. P 12.

2428	30q. Type **529** (300th anniversary)	45	35
2429	80q. Gavril Dara (writer, centenary)	1·00	55
2430	90q. Thimi Mitko (writer, centenary (1990))	1·70	1·10
2431	1l.30 Kolë Idromeno (painter, 50th anniversary)	2·50	1·40
2428/2431 Set of 4		5·00	3·00

530 Engels, Marx and Marchers

531 Gymnastics

1989 (28 Sept). 125th Anniversary of First International. T **530** and similar vert design. Multicoloured. P 12.

2432	90q. Type **530**	1·50	70
2433	1l.20 Factories, marchers and worker with pickaxe and rifle	2·20	95

(Des Z. Mati)

1989 (27 Oct). Sixth National Spartakiad. T **531** and similar vert designs. P 12½.

2434	30q. black, orange and bright scarlet	45	35
2435	80q. black, bright apple green and yellowish green	1·00	40
2436	1l. black, new blue and blue	1·20	80
2437	1l.20 black, bright purple and deep claret	1·70	1·40
2434/2437 Set of 4		4·00	2·75

Designs: 80q. Football; 1l. Cycling; 1l.20, Running.

532 Soldier

533 Chamois

(Des Z. Mati)

1989 (29 Nov). 45th Anniversary of Liberation. T **532** and similar vert designs. Multicoloured. P 12½.

2438	30q. Type **532**	75	40
	a. Booklet pane. Nos. 2438/2441	6·25	
2439	80q. Date	1·50	55
2440	1l. State Arms	1·60	95
2441	1l.20 Young couple	2·20	1·60
2438/2441 Set of 4		5·50	3·25

Nos. 2438/2441 were issued together in *se-tenant* strips of four in booklets.

(Des N. Prizreni)

1990 (15 Mar). Endangered Animals. The Chamois (*Rupicapra rupicapra*). T **533** and similar vert designs. Multicoloured. P 12.

2442	10q. Type **533**	45	35
	a. Block of 4. Nos. 2442/2445	7·50	
2443	30q. Mother and young	1·00	40
2444	80q. Chamois keeping lookout	2·75	1·40
2445	1l. Head of Chamois	3·00	1·90
2442/2445 Set of 4		6·50	3·75

Nos. 2442/2445 were issued together in *se-tenant* blocks of four within the sheet.

534 Eagle Mask

1990 (4 Apr). Masks. T **534** and similar vert designs. Multicoloured. P 12×12½.

2446	30q. Type **534**	45	35
2447	90q. Sheep	1·00	70
2448	1l.20 Goat	1·50	95
2449	1l.80 Stork	2·20	1·40
2446/2449 Set of 4		4·75	3·00

535 Caesar's Mushroom (*Amanita caesarea*)

536 Engraving Die

ALBANIA 1990

1990 (28 Apr). Fungi. T **535** and similar square designs. Multicoloured. P 12.
2450	30q. Type **535**		45	35
2451	90q. Parasol Mushroom (*Lepiota procera*)		1·00	80
2452	1l.20 Cep (*Boletus edulis*)		1·70	1·50
2453	1l.80 *Clathrus cancelatus*		2·50	2·00
2450/2453	Set of 4		5·00	4·25

1990 (6 May). 150th Anniversary of the Penny Black. T **536** and similar horiz designs. Multicoloured. P 12.
2454	90q. Type **536**		75	70
	a. Booklet pane. Nos. 2454/2456 plus label		5·50	
2455	1l.20 Mounted postal messenger		1·50	1·40
2456	1l.80 Mail coach passengers reading letters		3·00	2·00
2454/2456	Set of 3		4·75	3·75

Nos. 2454/2456 were issued in horizontal *se-tenant* strips of three stamps and a label, showing London 90 International Stamp Exhibition emblem and letters, in booklets.

537 Mascot and Flagst   **538** Young Van Gogh and Paintings

(Des N. Bakalli)

1990 (8 June). World Cup Football Championship, Italy. T **537** and similar horiz designs. Multicoloured. P 12.
2457	30q. Type **537**		45	35
2458	90q. Mascot running		1·00	95
2459	1l.20 Mascot preparing to kick ball		1·70	1·40
2457/2459	Set of 3		2·75	2·40
MS2460	80×62 mm. 3l.30, Mascot as goalkeeper. Imperf		5·00	4·75

(Des N. Vasia)

1990 (27 July). Death Centenary of Vincent van Gogh (painter). T **538** and similar horiz designs. Multicoloured. P 12.
2461	30q. Type **538**		60	35
2462	90q. Van Gogh and woman in field		1·20	1·10
2463	2l.10 Van Gogh in asylum		2·50	2·40
2461/2463	Set of 3		3·75	3·50
MS2464	88×73 mm. 2l.40, Van Gogh and *Wheatfield with Crows*. Imperf		5·75	5·50

539 Gjergj Elez Alia lying wounded

(Des N. Bakalli)

1990 (30 Aug). Gjergj Elez Alia (folk hero). T **539** and similar horiz designs. Multicoloured. P 12½×12.
2465	30q. Type **539**		45	35
2466	90q. Alia being helped onto Horse		1·00	55
2467	1l.20 Alia fighting Bajloz		1·50	1·10
2468	1l.80 Alia on Horseback and severed head of Bajloz		2·20	1·40
2465/2468	Set of 4		4·75	3·00

1990 (20 Sept). 2400th Anniversary of Berat. T **540** and similar vert designs. Multicoloured. P 12½.
2469	30q. Type **540**		35	35
	a. Block of 5. Nos. 2469/2473 plus 4 labels		5·00	
2470	90q. St Triadha's Church		45	40
2471	1l.20 River		85	80
2472	1l.80 Onufri (artist)		1·50	1·40
2473	2l.40 Nikolla		1·70	1·60
2469/2473	Set of 5		4·25	4·00

Nos. 2469/2473 were issued together in *se-tenant* blocks of five stamps and four labels in a chessboard arrangement.
Commemorative folders containing a block were also sold.

1990 (20 Oct). Illyrian Heroes. T **541** and similar vert designs, each black. P 12.
2474	30q. Type **541**		45	35
2475	90q. Teuta		75	70
2476	1l.20 Bato		1·00	95
2477	1l.80 Bardhyli		1·50	1·40
2474/2477	Set of 4		3·25	3·00

542 School and 'Globe' of Books   **543** Albanian Horsemen (Eugène Delacroix)

1990 (30 Oct). International Literacy Year. P 12.
2478	**542**	90q. multicoloured	1·00	95
2479		1l.20 multicoloured	1·50	1·40

1990 (30 Nov). Albanians in Art. T **543** and similar vert designs. Multicoloured. P 12½.
2480	30q. Type **543**		45	35
2481	1l.20 *Albanian Woman* (Camille Corot)		1·30	95
2482	1l.80 *Skanderbeg* (anon)		1·90	1·40
2480/2482	Set of 3		3·25	2·40

544 Boletini   **545** Armorial Eagle

1991 (23 Jan). 75th Death Anniversary of Isa Boletini (revolutionary). T **544** and similar vert design. Multicoloured. P 12×12½.
2483	90q. Type **544**		85	70
2484	1l.20 Boletini and flag		1·30	95

1991 (30 Jan). 800th Anniversary (1990) of Founding of Arberi State. P 12.
2485	**545**	90q. multicoloured	85	70
2486		1l.20 multicoloured	1·30	95

540 Mosque   **541** Pirroja   **546** Woman reading   **547** *Cistus albanicus*

1991 (25 Feb). 150th Birth Anniversary of Pierre Auguste Renoir (artist). T **546** and similar multicoloured designs. P 12½.

2487	30q. Type **546**	75	40
2488	90q. The Swing	1·20	80
2489	1l.20 The Boat Club (horiz)	1·70	1·40
2490	1l.80 Still life (detail) (horiz)	3·00	2·30
2487/2490	Set of 4	6·00	4·50
MS2491	94×75 mm. 3l. Portrait of Artist with Beard. Imperf	5·75	5·50

(Des A. Marika)

1991 (30 Mar). Flowers. T **547** and similar vert designs. Multicoloured. P 12.

2492	30q. Type **547**	60	55
2493	90q. Trifolium pilczii	1·20	1·10
2494	1l.80 Lilium albanicum	2·50	2·00
2492/2494	Set of 3	3·75	3·25

XIII. Republic

29 April 1991

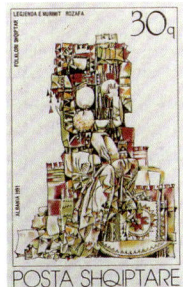
548 Rozafa breastfeeding Child

549 Mozart conducting

(Des N. Bakalli)

1991 (30 Sept). Imprisonment of Rozafa (folk tale). T **548** and similar vert designs. Multicoloured. P 12×12½.

2495	30q. Type **548**	35	25
2496	90q. The three brothers talking to old man	75	40
2497	1l.20 Building of walls around Rozafa	1·50	95
2498	1l.80 Figures symbolising water flowing between stones	2·00	1·60
2495/2498	Set of 4	4·25	3·00

(Des H. Devolli)

1991 (5 Oct). Death Bicentenary of Wolfgang Amadeus Mozart (composer). T **549** and similar multicoloured designs. P 12.

2499	90q. Type **549**	1·00	70
2500	1l.20 Mozart and score	1·60	1·10
2501	1l.80 Mozart composing	2·75	1·90
2499/2501	Set of 3	4·75	3·25
MS2502	88×69 mm. 3l. Mozart medallion and score. Imperf	8·00	7·50

550 Vitus Bering

(Des A. Kapo)

1992 (10 Jan). Explorers. T **550** and similar horiz designs. Multicoloured. P 12½.

2503	30q. Type **550**	45	35
2504	90q. Christopher Columbus and his flagship Santa Maria	1·00	40
2505	1l.80 Ferdinand Magellan and his flagship Vitoria	2·20	1·20
2503/2505	Set of 3	3·25	1·80

551 Lilienthal Biplane Glider, 1896

552 Ski Jumping

(Des N. Prizreni)

1992 (27 Jan). Aircraft. T **551** and similar horiz designs. P 12½.

2506	30q. black, dull vermilion and pale blue	45	35
2507	80q. multicoloured	75	55
2508	90q. multicoloured	1·00	80
2509	1l.20 multicoloured	1·40	95
2510	1l.80 multicoloured	1·50	1·20
2511	2l.40 black, grey and magenta	2·20	2·00
2506/2511	Set of 6	6·50	5·25

Designs: 30q. T **551**; 80q. Clément Ader's *Avion III*, 1897; 90q. Wright Brothers' Type A, 1903; 1l.20, Concorde supersonic jetliner; 1l.80, Tupolev Tu-144 jetliner (wrongly inscr '114'); 2l.40, Dornier Do-31E (wrongly inscr 'Dernier').

(Des Z. Mati)

1992 (15 Feb). Winter Olympic Games, Albertville. T **552** and similar vert designs. Multicoloured. P 12½.

2512	30q. Type **552**	45	35
2513	90q. Skiing	1·00	80
2514	1l.20 Ice skating (pairs)	1·50	1·10
2515	1l.80 Luge	2·20	1·80
2512/2515	Set of 4	4·75	3·75

553 'Europe' and Doves

1992 (31 Mar). Admission of Albania to European Security and Co-operation Conference at Foreign Ministers' Meeting, Berlin. T **553** and similar horiz design. Multicoloured. P 12½.

2516	90q. Type **553**	1·60	1·50
2517	1l.20 Members' flags and map of Europe	2·00	1·90

554 Envelopes and Emblem

555 Everlasting Flame

1992 (25 Apr). Admission of Albania to European Posts and Telecommunications Conference. T **554** and similar horiz design. Multicoloured. P 12½.

2518	90q. Type **554**	1·60	1·50
	a. Pair. Nos. 2518/2519	3·75	3·75
2519	1l.20 Emblem and tape reels	2·00	1·90

Nos. 2518/2519 were issued together in *se-tenant* pairs in sheets of ten stamps and two central labels either showing an ancient coin or inscribed 'RODOS '91'.

(Des Q. Prizreni and H. Dhimo)

1992 (5 May). National Martyrs' Day. T **555** and similar multicoloured design. P 12×12½.

2520	90q. Type **555**	75	70
2521	4l.10 Poppies (horiz)	3·75	2·75

ALBANIA 1992

 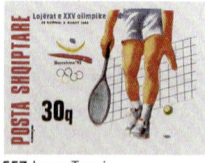

556 Pictograms   **557** Lawn Tennis

(Des B. Zajmi)

1992 (10 June). European Football Championship, Sweden. T **556** and similar horiz designs showing footballing pictograms. P 12.

2522	30q. pale yellowish green and dull yellowish green	75	40
2523	90q. Venetian red and chalky blue	1·50	95
2524	10l.80 ochre and brown-red	8·75	6·75
2522/2524	Set of 3	10·00	7·25
MS2525	90×69 mm. 5l. pink, brown-ochre and light turquoise-green. Imperf	5·00	4·75

(Des L. Sesferi)

1992 (14 June). Olympic Games, Barcelona. T **557** and similar horiz designs. Multicoloured. P 12.

2526	30q. Type **557**	60	40
2527	90q. Baseball	1·70	95
2528	1l.80 Table tennis	3·50	2·40
2526/2528	Set of 3	5·25	3·25
MS2529	89×69 mm. 5l. Torch bearer and running tracks. Imperf	5·75	5·50

558 Map and Doves   **559** Arab

(Des H. Dhimo)

1992 (5 July). European Unity. P 12.

2530	**558**	1l.20 multicoloured	1·70	1·40

(Des N. Prizreni)

1992 (10 Aug). Horses. T **559** and similar multicoloured designs. P 12.

2531	30q. Native pony (*horiz*)	45	35
2532	90q. Hungarian Nonius (*horiz*)	75	70
2533	1l.20 Type **559**	1·00	95
2534	10l.60 Haflinger	9·50	7·50
2531/2534	Set of 4	10·50	8·25

560 Map of Americas, Columbus and Ships   **561** Mother Teresa and Child

1992 (20 Aug). Europa. 500th Anniversary of Discovery of America by Columbus. T **560** and similar horiz designs. Multicoloured. P 12.

2535	60q. Type **560**	75	70
2536	3l.20 Map of Americas and Columbus meeting Amerindians	5·00	4·75
MS2537	90×70 mm. 5l. Map of Americas and Columbus. Imperf	£110	£100

1992 (4 Oct)–**95**. Mother Teresa (Agnes Gonxhe Bojaxhi) (founder of Missionaries of Charity). P 12×12½.

2538	**561**	40q. Venetian red	20	20
2539		60q. orange-brown	25	20
2540		1l. violet	30	25
2541		1l.80 slate	35	35
2542		2l. rose-carmine	40	35
2543		2l.40 light green	45	40
2544		3l.20 new blue	60	55
2545		5l. bluish violet (7.94)	45	40
2546		5l.60 purple	85	80
2547		7l.20 dull yellow-green	1·50	1·40
2548		10l. red-orange	1·70	1·60
2549		18l. orange (7.94)	1·80	1·70
2550		20l. bright purple (1994)	75	70
2551		25l. blue-green (7.94)	2·75	2·50
2552		60l. yellow-green (1995)	3·00	2·75
2538/2552	Set of 15		14·00	12·50

Numbers have been left for additions to this series.

562 Pope John Paul II   (**563**)

1993 (25 Apr). Papal Visit. P 12.

2555	**562**	16l. multicoloured	3·75	3·50

1993 (2 May). Nos. 2329/2332 and No. 2335 surch as T **563**.

2556	**496**	3l. on 10q. deep turquoise-blue	45	35
2557		6l.50 on 20q. Venetian red	1·00	95
2558		13l. on 30q. scarlet-vermilion	3·00	2·75
2559		20l. on 90q. ultramarine	4·25	4·00
2560		30l. on 50q. bistre-brown	5·75	5·50
2556/2560	Set of 4		13·00	12·00

564 Lef Nosi (first Postal Minister)   **565** Life Weighs Heavily on Man

(A. Zajmi)

1993 (5 May). 80th Anniversary of First Albanian Stamps. P 12.

2561	**564**	6l.50 bistre and olive-bistre	1·50	1·40

1993 (28 May). Europa. Contemporary Art. T **565** and similar multicoloured design. P 12.

2562	3l. Type **565**	1·50	1·40
2563	7l. *The Green Star* (E. Hila) (*horiz*)	5·75	5·50
MS2564	116×121 mm. 20l. *Gjirokastër* (B. Ahmeti). Imperf	10·00	9·50

Nos. 2562/2563 were each issued in sheetlets of five stamps and one label showing an artist's palette.

566 Running   **567** Frang Bardhi

1993 (20 June). Mediterranean Games, Agde and Roussillon (Languedoc), France. T **566** and similar horiz designs. Multicoloured. P 12.

2565	3l. Type **566**	45	35
2566	16l. Canoeing	3·00	2·75
2567	21l. Cycling	4·00	3·75
2565/2567	Set of 3	6·75	6·25
MS2568	117×84 mm. 20l. Map of Mediterranean. Imperf	5·00	4·75

1993 (20 Aug). 350th Death Anniversary of Frang Bardhi (scholar). T **567** and similar design. P 12½.
2569   6l.50 reddish brown and stone.............................. 1·70   1·60
MS2570 94×107 mm. 20l. reddish brown and gold.
    Imperf .... 5·75   5·50
    Designs: 6l.50, T **567**; 20l. Bardhi writing at desk.

568 Mascot and Flags around Stadium   **569** Gjovalin Gjadri (construction engineer)

(Des L. Mema)

1994 (17 July). World Cup Football Championship, USA. T **568** and similar vert design. Multicoloured. P 12.
2571   42l. Type **568** .... 1·70   1·60
2572   68l. Mascot kicking ball .... 2·50   2·40

(Des M. Temo. Litho Courvoisier)

1994 (31 Dec). Europa. Discoveries and Inventions. T **569** and similar vert design. P 14.
2573   50l. reddish brown, chestnut and brown...... 3·00   2·75
2574   100l. reddish brown, chestnut and brown.... 4·25   4·00
MS2575 60×80 mm. 150l. drab and reddish brown.
    Imperf .... 7·25   6·75
    Designs: 50l. T **569**; 100l. Karl Ritter von Ghega (railway engineer); 150l. Sketch of traffic project.

570 Emblem and Benz

(Des N. Luci. Litho Courvoisier)

1995 (21 Jan). 150th Birth Anniversary (1994) of Karl Benz (engineer). T **570** and similar horiz designs. Multicoloured. P 14.
2576   5l. Type **570** 35   25
2577   10l. Modern Mercedes motor car 45   40
2578   60l. First four-wheel Benz motor car, 1886.... 1·50   1·40
2579   125l. Pre-war Mercedes touring car .... 5·00   4·50
2576/2579 Set of 4 .... 6·50   6·00

571 Richard Wagner   **572** Intersections

1995 (26 Jan). Composers. T **571** and similar vert designs, each lake-brown and gold. P 12.
2580   3l. Type **571** 15   15
     a. Sheetlet of 4. Nos. 2580/2583 .... 1·90
2581   6l.50 Edvard Grieg 35   35
2582   11l. Charles Gounod 45   40
2583   20l. Pyotr Tchaikovsky 85   80
2580/2583 Set of 4 .... 1·60   1·50
    Nos. 2580/2583 were issued together in *se-tenant* sheetlets of four stamps.

(Des B. Asllani. Litho Courvoisier)

1995 (28 Jan). 50th Anniversary (1994) of Liberation. P 14.
2584   **572**   50l. black and bright scarlet .... 2·20   2·00

573 Ali Pasha   **574** Veskopoja, 1744 (left half)

(Des Q. Prizreni. Litho Courvoisier)

1995 (28 Jan). 250th Birth Anniversary (1994) of Ali Pasha of Tepelenë (Pasha of Janina, 1788–1820). T **573** and similar horiz design. P 14.
2585   **573**   60l. black, yellow and chestnut............... 2·50   2·30
MS2586 80×60 mm. 100l. lake-brown and orange (Administration building, Tepelenë). Imperf....................... 4·25   4·00

(Des B. Asllani. Litho Courvoisier)

1995 (2 Feb). 250th Anniversary (1994) of Veskopoja Academy. T **574** and similar vert design. Multicoloured. P 14.
2587   42l. Type **574** .... 1·50   1·40
     a. Horiz pair. Nos. 2587/2588 .... 4·00   3·75
2588   68l. Veskopoja, 1744 (right half) .... 2·20   2·00
    Nos. 2587/2588 were issued together in horizontal *se-tenant* pairs within the sheet, each pair forming a composite design.

575 Olympic Rings and Map

(Des L. Mema. Litho Courvoisier)

1995 (2 Feb). Centenary of International Olympic Committee. Sheet 60×80 mm. Imperf.
MS2589   **575**   80l. multicoloured .... 3·25   3·00

576 Palace of Europe, Strasbourg   **577** Hands holding Olive Branch

(Des R. Ballauri. Litho Alexandros Matsoukis, Athens, Greece)

1995 (29 June). Admission of Albania to Council of Europe. T **576** and similar horiz design. Multicoloured. P 14×13½.
2590   25l. Type **576** .... 1·50   1·40
2591   85l. State Arms and map of Europe............... 5·00   4·75

(Des T. Pustina. Litho Alexandros Matsoukis, Athens, Greece)

1995 (10 Aug). Europa. Peace and Freedom. T **577** and similar vert designs. Multicoloured. P 13½×14.
2592   50l. Type **577** .... 3·00   2·75
2593   100l. Dove flying over hands .... 5·75   5·50
MS2594 80×60 mm. 150l. Figure stretching out hands. Imperf .... 8·75   8·00

ALBANIA 1995

578 Mice sitting around Table and Stork with Fox

579 Bee on Flower

(Des N. Vasia. Litho Alexandros Matsoukis, Athens, Greece)

1995 (20 Aug). 300th Death Anniversary of Jean de La Fontaine (writer). T **578** and similar horiz designs. Multicoloured. P 14×13½.

2595	2l. Type **578**	35	25
2596	3l. Stork with Foxes around table	45	35
2597	25l. Frogs under tree	85	80
2595/2597	Set of 3	1·50	1·30
MS2598	80×60 mm. 60l. La Fontaine and animals. Imperf	3·75	3·50

(Des Z. Shoshi. Litho)

1995 (20 Aug). The Honey Bee. T **579** and similar vert designs. Multicoloured. P 12.

2599	5l. Type **579**	35	25
2600	10l. Bee and honeycomb	45	35
2601	25l. Bee on comb	2·00	1·90
2599/2601	Set of 3	2·50	2·30

580 Fridtjof Nansen

581 Flags outside UN Building, New York

(Des N. Bakalli. Litho Alexandros Matsoukis, Athens, Greece)

1995 (14 Sept). Polar Explorers. T **580** and similar vert designs. Multicoloured. P 13½×14.

2602	25l. Type **580**	1·50	1·10
	a. Block of 4. Nos. 2602/2605	6·25	
2603	25l. James Cook	1·50	1·10
2604	25l. Roald Amundsen	1·50	1·10
2605	25l. Robert Scott	1·50	1·10
2602/2605	Set of 4	5·50	4·00

Nos. 2602/2605 were issued together in *se-tenant* blocks of four stamps within the sheet, each block forming a composite design.

(Des N. Vasia. Litho Alexandros Matsoukis, Athens, Greece)

1995 (14 Sept). 50th Anniversary of United Nations Organisation. T **581** and similar horiz design. Multicoloured. P 14×13½.

2606	2l. Type **581**	40	35
2607	100l. Flags flying to right outside UN building, New York	4·00	3·75

582 Male Chorus

583 'Poet'

(Des L. Merna. Litho Alexandros Matsoukis, Athens, Greece)

1995 (17 Oct). National Folklore Festival, Berat. T **582** and similar vert design. Multicoloured. P 13½×14.

2608	5l. Type **582**	45	35
2609	50l. Female participant	2·20	2·00

(Des N. Bakalli. Litho Alexandros Matsoukis, Athens, Greece)

1995 (17 Oct). Jan Kukuzeli (11th-century poet, musician and teacher). T **583** and similar multicoloured designs showing abstract representations of Kukuzeli. P 13½×14.

2610	18l. Type **583**	80	75
2611	20l. 'Musician'	85	80
MS2612	80×80 mm. 100l. 'Teacher'. Imperf	4·25	4·00

584 Church and Preacher, Berat Krujë

585 Paul Eluard

(Des I. Zabzuni. Litho Alexandros Matsoukis, Athens, Greece)

1995 (17 Oct). 20th Anniversary of World Tourism Organisation. T **584** and similar vert designs. Multicoloured. P 13½×14.

2613	18l. Type **584**	85	80
2614	20l. Street, Shkodër	1·00	95
2615	42l. Buildings, Gjirokastër	2·50	2·30
2613/2615	Set of 3	4·00	3·75

(Des N. Bakalli. Litho Alexandros Matsoukis, Athens, Greece)

1995 (17 Oct). Poets' Birth Centenaries. T **585** and similar vert design. Multicoloured. P 13½×14.

2616	25l. Type **585**	85	80
	a. Pair. Nos. 2616/2617	3·00	3·00
2617	50l. Sergei Yessenin	2·00	1·90

Nos. 2616/2617 were issued together in *se-tenant* pairs within the sheet.

586 Louis, Film Reel and Projector

587 Elvis Presley

(Des L. Taçi. Litho Alexandros Matsoukis, Athens, Greece)

1995 (17 Nov). Centenary of Motion Pictures. Lumière Brothers (developers of cine camera). T **586** and similar vert design. Multicoloured. P 13½×14.

2618	10l. Type **586**	40	35
	a. Horiz pair. Nos. 2618/2619	3·25	3·00
2619	85l. Auguste, film reel and cinema audience	2·50	2·30

Nos. 2618/2619 were issued together in horizontal *se-tenant* pairs within the sheet.

(Des M. Temo. Litho Alexandros Matsoukis, Athens, Greece)

1995 (20 Nov). 60th Birth Anniversary of Elvis Presley (entertainer). T **587** and similar horiz design. Multicoloured. P 14×13½.

2620	3l. Type **587**	40	35
2621	60l. Presley (*different*)	2·50	2·30

588 Banknotes of 1925

589 '5', crumbling Star, Open Book and Peace Dove

(Des M. Temo. Litho Alexandros Matsoukis, Athens, Greece)
1995 (25 Nov). 70th Anniversary of Albanian National Bank. T **588** and similar vert design. Multicoloured. P 13½×14.
2622	10l. Type **588**	45	35
2623	25l. Modern banknotes	1·20	1·10

(Des E. Klefti. Litho Alexandros Matsoukis, Athens, Greece)
1995 (27 Nov). Fifth Anniversary of Democratic Movement. T **589** and similar vert design. Multicoloured. P 13½×14.
2624	5l. Type **589**	45	35
2625	50l. Woman planting tree	2·20	2·00

590 Mother Teresa   **591** Football, Union Jack, Map of Europe and Stadium

(Des L. Mema. Litho Alexandros Matsoukis, Athens, Greece)
1996 (5 May). Europa. Famous Women. Mother Teresa (founder of Missionaries of Charity). T **590** and similar vert design. P 13½×14.
2626	**590**	25l. multicoloured	1·50	1·40
2627		100l. multicoloured	5·00	4·75
MS2628	60×80 mm. 150l. Mother Teresa (*different*). Imperf		10·00	9·50

(Des E. Klefti. Litho Alexandros Matsoukis, Athens, Greece)
1996 (4 June). European Football Championship, England. T **591** and similar vert design. P 14.
2629	25l. Type **591**	1·20	1·10
2630	100l. Map of Europe, ball and player	4·75	4·25

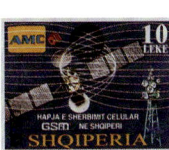

592 Satellite and Radio Mast   **593** Running

(Des A. Baboçi. Litho Alexandros Matsoukis, Athens, Greece)
1996 (1 Aug). Inauguration of Cellular Telephone Network. T **592** and similar multicoloured design. P 13×13½ (10l.) or 13½×13 (60l.).
2631	10l. Type **592**	45	35
2632	60l. User, lorry, ship and mobile telephone (*vert*)	2·50	2·30

(Des L. Mema. Litho Alexandros Matsoukis, Athens, Greece)
1996 (3 Aug). Olympic Games, Atlanta T **593** and similar vert designs. Multicoloured. P 13½×14.
2633	5l. Type **593**	40	35
2634	25l. Throwing the hammer	1·00	95
2635	60l. Long jumping	3·00	2·75
2633/2635	Set of 3	4·00	3·75
MS2636	60×80 mm. 100l. Games emblem. Imperf	3·75	3·50

594 Linked Hands   **595** Gottfried Wilhelm Leibniz (350th)

(Des A. Baboçi. Litho Alexandros Matsoukis, Athens, Greece)
1996 (5 Aug). 75th Anniversary of Albanian Red Cross. P 13½×13.
2637	**594**	50l. +10l. multicoloured	2·50	2·40

(Des M. Temo. Litho Alexandros Matsoukis, Athens, Greece)
1996 (20 Sept). Philosopher-mathematicians' Birth Anniversaries. T **595** and similar horiz design. Multicoloured. P 14½×14.
2638	10l. Type **595**	75	70
2639	85l. René Descartes (400th)	3·75	3·50

596 *The Naked Maja*   **597** Book Binding

(Des N. Bakalli. Litho Alexandros Matsoukis, Athens, Greece)
1996 (25 Sept). 250th Birth Anniversary of Francisco de Goya (artist). T **596** and similar multicoloured designs. P 14×13½.
2640	10l. Type **596**	60	55
2641	60l. *Doña Isabel Cobos de Porcel*	2·50	2·40
MS2642	80×60 mm. 100l. *Self-portrait* (24×29 *mm*). P 12½×13	3·75	3·50

(Des P. Sheqeri. Litho Alexandros Matsoukis, Athens, Greece)
1996 (5 Nov). Christian Art Exhibition. T **597** and similar vert designs. Multicoloured. P 13×14.
2643	5l. Type **597**	40	35
	a. Block of 3. Nos. 2643/2645 plus label	5·50	
2644	25l. Book clasp showing crucifixion	1·00	95
2645	85l. Book binding (*different*)	3·75	3·50
2643/2645	Set of 3	4·75	4·25

Nos. 2643/2645 were issued in *se-tenant* blocks of three stamps and one label showing a book clasp.

598 Princess   **599** State Arms, Book and Fishta

(Des M. Temo. Litho Alexandros Matsoukis, Athens, Greece)
1996 (11 Nov). 50th Anniversary of United Nations Children's Fund. Children's Paintings. T **598** and similar vert designs. P 13½×14.
2646	5l. Type **598**	35	25
2647	10l. Woman	45	35
2648	25l. Sea life	1·50	1·40
2649	50l. Harbour	2·20	2·00
2646/2649	Set of 4	4·00	3·50

(Des L. Taçi. Litho Alexandros Matsoukis, Athens, Greece)
1996 (20 Dec). 125th Birth Anniversary of Gjergj Fishta (writer and politician). T **599** and similar vert design. Multicoloured. P 13½×14.
2650	10l. Type **599**	45	35
2651	60l. Battle scene and Fishta	2·50	2·30

600 Omar Khayyam and Writing Materials   **601** Gutenberg

(Des A. Baboçi. Litho Alexandros Matsoukis, Athens, Greece)
1997 (6 Mar). 950th Birth Anniversary of Omar Khayyam (astronomer and poet). T **600** and similar vert design. Multicoloured. P 14.
2652	20l. Type **600**	75	70

ALBANIA 1997

2653		50l. Omar Khayyam and symbols of astronomy	1·70	1·60

Nos. 2652/2653 are inscribed '850' in error.

(Des L. Taçi. Litho Alexandros Matsoukis, Athens, Greece)
1997 (20 Mar). 600th Birth Anniversary of Johannes Gutenberg (printer). T **601** and similar vert designs. Multicoloured. P 14×14½.

2654		20l. Type **601**	75	70
	a.	Horiz pair. Nos. 2654/2655	3·25	3·00
2655		60l. Printing press	2·20	2·00

Nos. 2654/2655 were issued together in horizontal *se-tenant* pairs within the sheet, each pair forming a composite design.

602 Pelicans

603 Dragon

(Des L. Mema. Litho Alexandros Matsoukis, Athens, Greece)
1997 (10 Apr). The Dalmatian Pelican (*Pelecanus crispus*). T **602** and similar vert design. Multicoloured. P 14×14½.

2656		10l. Type **602**	40	35
	a.	Horiz pair. Nos. 2656/2657	3·25	3·00
2657		80l. Pelicans on shore and in flight	2·50	2·30

Nos. 2656/2657 were issued together in horizontal *se-tenant* pairs within the sheet, each pair forming a composite design.

(Des L. Taçi. Litho Alexandros Matsoukis, Athens, Greece)
1997 (5 May). Europa. Tales and Legends. *The Blue Pool*. T **603** and similar vert design. Multicoloured. P 13×14.

2658	30l. Type **603**	1·50	1·40
2659	100l. Dragon drinking from pool	5·00	4·75

604 Faik Konica

605 Male Athlete

(Des L. Boelen. Litho Alexandros Matsoukis, Athens, Greece)
1997 (25 June). 55th Death Anniversary of Faik Konica (writer and politician). P 14×14½.

2660	**604** 10l. chocolate and black	45	35
2661	25l. indigo and black	1·30	1·20
MS2662	60×80 mm. **604** 80l. blackish brown	3·75	3·50

(Des N. Vasia. Litho Alexandros Matsoukis, Athens, Greece)
1997 (17 July). Mediterranean Games, Bari. T **605** and similar vert designs. Multicoloured. P 14×14½.

2663	20l. Type **605**	75	70
2664	30l. Female athlete and rowers	1·50	1·40
MS2665	60×80 mm. 100l. Discus-thrower, javelin-thrower and runner. Imperf	3·75	3·50

606 Skanderbeg   **(607)**
1910-1997

(Des F. Kola. Litho Alexandros Matsoukis, Athens, Greece)
1997 (25 Aug). P 13.

2666	**606**	5l. scarlet and lake-brown	35	25
2667		10l. grey-olive and blackish olive	45	35
2668		20l. dull blue-green and bottle green	75	70
2669		25l. mauve and plum	85	80
2670		30l. bluish violet and deep lilac	1·00	95
2671		50l. grey and black	1·50	1·40
2672		60l. orange-brown and brown	1·70	1·60
2673		80l. light brown and brown	2·50	2·40
2674		100l. rose-carmine and brown-lake	3·25	3·00
2675		110l. blue and deep violet-blue	3·50	3·25
2666/2675 *Set of 10*			14·50	13·00

1997 (13 Sept). Mother Teresa (founder of Missionaries of Charity) Commemoration. No. 2627 optd with T **607** in silver.

2676	**590**	100l. multicoloured	5·00	4·75

608 Codex Aureus (11th-century)

609 Twin-headed Eagle (postal emblem)

(Des P. Sheqeri. Litho Alexandros Matsoukis, Athens, Greece)
1997 (15 Nov). Codices (1st series). T **608** and similar vert designs. Multicoloured. P 13×14.

2677		10l. Type **608**	40	25
	a.	Block of 3. Nos. 2677/2679 plus label	3·50	
2678		25l. *Codex Purpureus Beratinus* (7th-century) showing mountain and scribe	85	80
2679		60l. *Codex Purpureus Beratinus* showing church and scribe	1·90	1·80
2677/2679 *Set of 3*			2·75	2·50

Nos. 2677/2679 were issued together in *se-tenant* blocks of three stamps and one label depicting a church from the *Codex Aureus*. See also Nos. 2712/2714.

(Des N. Bakalli. Litho Alexandros Matsoukis, Athens, Greece)
1997 (4 Dec). 85th Anniversary of Albanian Postal Service. T **609** and similar horiz design. P 14×13½.

2680	**609**	10l. multicoloured	40	35
2681	–	30l. multicoloured	1·10	1·00

The 30l. differs from T **609** in minor parts of the design.

610 Nikete of Ramesiana

611 Man sitting at Table

(Des N. Bakalli. Litho Alexandros Matsoukis, Athens, Greece)
1998 (25 Mar). Nikete Dardani, Bishop of Ramesiana (philosopher and composer). P 14.

2682	**610**	30l. multicoloured	85	80
	a.	Horiz pair. Nos. 2682/2683	3·75	3·50
2683		100l. multicoloured	2·75	2·50

Nos. 2682/2683 were issued together in horizontal *se-tenant* pairs within the sheet. There are minor differences of design between the two values.

(Des N. Bakalli. Litho Alexandros Matsoukis, Athens, Greece)
1998 (15 Apr). Legend of Pogradeci Lake. T **611** and similar vert designs. Multicoloured. P 14×14½.

2684		30l. Type **611**	85	80
	a.	Block of 4. Nos. 2684/2687	6·25	
2685		50l. The Three Graces	1·30	1·20
2686		60l. Women drawing water	1·60	1·50

2687	80l. Man of ice	2·20	2·00
2684/2687	Set of 4	5·25	5·00

Nos. 2684/2687 were issued together in *se-tenant* blocks of four within the sheet.

612 Stylised Dancers

613 Abdyl Frashëri (founder)

(Des N. Bakalli. Litho Alexandros Matsoukis, Athens, Greece)

1998 (5 May). Europa. National Festivals. T **612** and similar vert designs. P 13×14.

2688	60l. multicoloured	3·00	2·75
2689	100l. multicoloured	3·75	3·50
MS2690	60×80 mm. 150l. multicoloured. Imperf	6·50	6·00

Designs: 60l. T **612**; 100l. Female dancer; 150l. Two dancers.

(Des L. Taçi. Litho Alexandros Matsoukis, Athens, Greece)

1998 (10 June). 120th Anniversary of League of Prizren. T **613** and similar vert designs. Multicoloured. P 13½×13.

2691	30l. Type **613**	85	80
	a. Block of 4. Nos. 2691/2694	6·25	
2692	50l. Sulejman Vokshi and partisan	1·30	1·20
2693	60l. Iljaz Pashë Dibra and crossed rifles	1·60	1·50
2694	80l. Ymer Prizreni and partisans	2·20	2·00
2691/2694	Set of 4	5·25	5·00

Nos. 2691/2694 were issued together in *se-tenant* blocks of four stamps within sheets of eight.

614 Player with Ball

615 Wrestlers in National Costume

(Des L. Mema. Litho Alexandros Matsoukis, Athens, Greece)

1998 (10 June). World Cup Football Championship, France. T **614** and similar vert designs. P 13½.

2695	60l. Type **614**	1·70	1·50
2696	100l. Player with ball (*different*)	3·00	2·75
MS2697	60×80 mm. 120l. Championship mascot. Imperf	4·00	3·50

(Des T. Pustina. Litho Alexandros Matsoukis, Athens, Greece)

1998 (5 July). European Junior Wrestling Championship. T **615** and similar horiz design. Multicoloured. P 13½.

2698	30l. Type **615**	80	70
	a. Pair. Nos. 2698/2699	2·75	2·30
2699	60l. Ancient Greek wrestlers	1·70	1·50

Nos. 2698/2699 were issued together in *se-tenant* pairs within the sheet.

616 Cabej

617 Diana, Princess of Wales

(Des M. Arapi. Litho Alexandros Matsoukis, Athens, Greece)

1998 (7 Aug). 90th Birth Anniversary of Eqerem Cabej (linguist). T **616** and similar vert design. P 14.

2700	**616**	60l. black and orange-yellow	1·60	1·40
		a. Pair. Nos. 2700/2701	4·25	3·75
2701		80l. orange-yellow, black and vermilion	2·30	2·10

Nos. 2700/2701 were issued together in *se-tenant* pairs within the sheet.

(Litho Alexandros Matsoukis, Athens, Greece)

1998 (31 Aug). Diana, Princess of Wales Commemoration. T **617** and similar vert design. Multicoloured. P 13½.

2702	60l. Type **617**	3·00	2·75
2703	100l. With Mother Teresa	4·75	4·25

618 Mother Teresa holding Child

(Des Rita Morena (60l.), M. Temo (100l.). Photo Italian Govt Ptg Wks, Rome)

1998 (5 Sept). Mother Teresa (founder of Missionaries of Charity) Commemoration. T **618** and similar multicoloured design. P 14×13½ (60l.) or 13½×14 (100l.).

2704	60l. Type **618**	2·30	2·10
2705	100l. Mother Teresa (*vert*)	4·00	3·50

Stamps of a similar design were issued by Italy.

619 Detail of Painting

(Des G. Bakalli. Litho Alexandros Matsoukis, Athens, Greece)

1998 (10 Sept). 150th Birth Anniversary of Paul Gauguin (artist). T **619** and similar multicoloured designs. P 13½.

2706	60l. Type **619**	1·60	1·40
	a. Pair. Nos. 2706/2707	4·00	3·75
2707	80l. *Women of Tahiti*	2·20	2·00
MS2708	60×80 mm. 120l. Face. Imperf	4·00	3·50

Nos. 2706/2707 were issued together in *se-tenant* pairs within the sheet.

620 Epitaph

621 Page

(Des M. Arapi. Litho Alexandros Matsoukis, Athens, Greece)

1998 (5 Oct). 625th Anniversary of Epitaph of Gllavenica (embroidery of dead Christ). T **620** and similar horiz designs. Multicoloured. P 14.

2709	30l. Type **620**	80	70
2710	80l. Close-up of upper body	2·30	2·10
MS2711	80×60 mm. 100l. Detail of epitaph (24×29 mm). P 13	3·00	2·75

(Des P. Sheqeri. Litho Alexandros Matsoukis, Athens, Greece)

1998 (15 Oct). Codices (2nd series). 11th-century Manuscripts. T **621** and similar vert designs. Multicoloured. P 13×14.

2712	30l. Type **621**	80	70
	a. Block of 3. Nos. 2712/2714 plus label	4·50	
2713	50l. Front cover of manuscript	1·20	1·10
2714	80l. Page showing mosque	2·20	2·00
2712/2714	Set of 3	3·75	3·50

Nos. 2712/2714 were issued together in *se-tenant* blocks of three stamps and one label showing the crucifixion.

ALBANIA 1998

(622)   **623** Koliqi

1998 (23 Oct). Italia '98 International Stamp Exhibition. No. **MS**2628 optd with T **622** in bright blue.
MS2715 60×80 mm. 150l. multicoloured (sold at 265l.) .... 11·50   10·50

(Des J. Martini. Litho Alexandros Matsoukis, Athens, Greece)

1998 (28 Nov). First Death Anniversary of Cardinal Mikel Koliqi (first Albanian Cardinal). T **623** and similar vert design. Multicoloured. P 14×14½.
2716	30l. Type **623**	80	70
	a. Pair. Nos. 2716/2717	3·75	3·25
2717	100l. Koliqi (different)...................	2·75	2·40

Nos. 2716/2717 were issued together in se-tenant pairs within the sheet.

624 George Washington (first President, 1789–1797)

(Des L. Taçi. Litho Alexandros Matsoukis, Athens, Greece)

1999 (15 Mar). American Anniversaries. T **624** and similar horiz designs. Multicoloured. P 14½×14.
2718	150l. Type **624** (death bicentenary)...........	4·75	4·25
	a. Block of 3. Nos. 2718/2720 plus label.......	15·00	
2719	150l. Abraham Lincoln (President 1861–1865, 190th birth anniversary)	4·75	4·25
2720	150l. Martin Luther King Jr. (civil rights campaigner, 70th birth anniversary)	4·75	4·25
2718/2720 Set of 3		13·00	11·50

Nos. 2718/2720 were issued in blocks of three stamps and one label showing the carvings at Mount Rushmore.

625 Monk Seals

(Des L. Mema. Litho Alexandros Matsoukis, Athens, Greece)

1999 (10 Apr). The Monk Seal (Monachus albiventris). T **625** and similar horiz designs. Multicoloured. P 14½×14.
2721	110l. Type **625**	3·50	3·00
	a. Sheetlet of 4. Nos. 2721/2724	18·00	
2722	110l. Two Seals (both facing left)	3·50	3·00
2723	150l. As No. 2722 but both facing right......	4·75	4·25
2724	150l. As Type **625** but Seal at back facing left and Seal at front facing right............	4·75	4·25
2721/2724 Set of 4		15·00	13·00

Nos. 2721/2724 were issued together in se-tenant sheetlets of four stamps forming a composite design.

(626)

1999 (20 Apr). 50th Anniversary of Council of Europe. No. 2590 surch with T **626**.
2725   576   150l. on 25l. multicoloured........................... 6·25   5·50

(627)   **628** Dove, Aeroplane and NATO Emblem

1999 (24 Apr). iBRA '99 International Stamp Exhibition, Nuremberg, Germany. No. 2496 surch with T **627** in black (new value) and multicoloured (emblem).
2726   150l. on 90q. multicoloured................... 5·00   4·50

(Des S. Taçi. Litho Alexandros Matsoukis, Athens, Greece)

1999 (25 Apr). 50th Anniversary of North Atlantic Treaty Organisation. T **628** and similar vert design. P 13½.
2727	**628** 10l. multicoloured..........................	1·20	1·10
2728	100l. multicoloured..........................	6·25	5·50
MS2729 69×85 mm. 250l. multicoloured. P 13		7·75	7·00

Design: 28×49 mm—250l. As T **628**, but with motifs differently arranged and without commemorative text.

629 Mickey Mouse   **630** Thethi National Park, Shkodër

(Des S.Taçi. Litho Alexandros Matsoukis, Athens, Greece)

1999 (30 Apr). Mickey Mouse (cartoon film character). T **629** and similar vert designs. Multicoloured. P 13×14.
2730	60l. Type **629**	1·90	1·50
	a. Strip of 4. Nos. 2730/2733	13·00	
2731	80l. Mickey writing letter	2·75	2·10
2732	110l. Mickey thinking................................	3·00	2·50
2733	150l. Wearing black and red jumper.................	4·75	4·25
2730/2733 Set of 4		11·00	9·25

Nos. 2730/2733 were issued together in se-tenant strips of four stamps within the sheet.

(Des S. Vllahu. Litho Alexandros Matsoukis, Athens, Greece)

1999 (1 May). Europa. Parks and Gardens. T **630** and similar horiz designs. Multicoloured. P 14×13.
2734	90l. Type **630**	4·00	3·50
2735	310l. Lura National Park, Dibra..................	10·00	9·00
MS2736 80×60 mm. 350l. Divjaka National Park, Lushnjë. Imperf...		14·00	12·50

631 Coin

(Des M. Arapi. Litho Alexandros Matsoukis, Athens, Greece)

1999 (1 June). Illyrian Coins. T **631** and similar horiz designs. Multicoloured. P 13½.
2737	10l. Type **631**	40	30
	a. Strip of 3. Nos. 2737/2739	8·00	

2738	20l. Coins from Labeateve, Bylisi and Scutari		60	40
2739	200l. Coins of King Monuni		6·75	6·25
2737/2739 Set of 3			7·00	6·25

MS2740 80×60 mm. 310l. Coin of King Gent (29×49 mm). P 13 .... 10·00 9·00

Nos. 2737/2739 were issued together in *se-tenant* strips of three stamps within the sheet.

(**632**)

1999 (2 June). Philexfrance '99 International Stamp Exhibition, Paris. No. 2512 surch with T **632** in black (new value), royal blue and scarlet-vermilion (emblem).

2741	**552**	150l. on 30q. multicoloured	5·00	4·50

633 Charlie Chaplin

634 Neil Armstrong on Moon

(Des N. Bakalli. Litho Alexandros Matsoukis, Athens, Greece)

1999 (20 June). 110th Birth Anniversary of Charlie Chaplin (film actor and director). T **633** and similar vert designs. Multicoloured. P 14×14½.

2742	30l. Type **633**	95	85
	a. Imperf×p 14½. Booklets	95	85
	ab. Booklet pane. Nos. 2742a/2744a, each×2	23·00	
2743	50l. Raising hat	1·60	1·40
	a. Imperf×p 14½. Booklets	1·60	1·40
2744	250l. Dancing	8·50	7·75
	a. Imperf×p 14½. Booklets	8·50	7·75
2742/2744 Set of 3		10·00	9·00

(Des L. Mema. Litho Alexandros Matsoukis, Athens, Greece)

1999 (25 June). 30th Anniversary of First Manned Moon Landing. T **634** and similar vert designs. Multicoloured. P 13½×14.

2745	30l. Type **634**	95	85
	a. Horiz strip of 3. Nos. 2745/2747	17·00	
2746	150l. Lunar module	5·00	4·50
2747	300l. Astronaut and American flag	10·00	9·00
2745/2747 Set of 3		14·50	13·00

MS2748 60×80 mm. 280l. Launch of *Apollo 11* (25×29 mm). P 13 .... 9·25 8·50

Nos. 2745/2747 were issued together in horizontal *se-tenant* strips of three stamps within the sheet, each strip forming a composite design.

635 Prisoner behind Bars

636 Emblem

(Des G. Tafa. Litho Alexandros Matsoukis, Athens, Greece)

1999 (6 July). The Nazi Holocaust. P 14×14½.

2749	**635**	30l. multicolored	95	85
2750		150l. black and greenish yellow	5·00	4·50

(Des L. Kakarriqi. Litho Alexandros Matsoukis, Athens, Greece)

1999 (1 Aug). 125th Anniversary of Universal Postal Union. P 14×14½.

2751	**636**	20l. multicoloured	60	55
		a. Pair. Nos. 2751/2752	2·75	2·50
2752		60l. multicoloured	2·00	1·80

Nos. 2751/2752 were issued together in *se-tenant* pairs within the sheet.

(**637**) **638** Javelin

1999 (20 Aug). China 1999 International Stamp Exhibition, Peking. No. 2497 surch with T **637** in brown (new value), vermilion and emerald (emblem).

2753	150l. on 1l.20 multicoloured	5·00	4·50

(Des E. Klefti. Litho Alexandros Matsoukis, Athens, Greece)

1999 (2 Sept). 70th Anniversary of National Athletic Championships. T **638** and similar vert designs. Multicoloured. P 14×14½.

2754	10l. Type **638**	35	30
	a. Horiz strip of 3. Nos. 2754/2756	7·75	
2755	20l. Discus	60	40
2756	200l. Running	6·50	6·00
2754/2756 Set of 3		6·75	6·00

Nos. 2754/2756 were issued together in horizontal *se-tenant* strips of three stamps within the sheet.

639 Madonna and Child

640 Bilal Golemi (veterinary surgeon)

(Litho Alexandros Matsoukis, Athens, Greece)

1999 (30 Oct). Icons by Onufri Shek (artist). T **639** and similar vert design. Multicoloured. P 14.

2757	30l. Type **639**	80	70
2758	300l. The Resurrection	9·25	8·50

Nos. 2757/2758 were ssued in sheets of four stamps, each×2.

(Des L. Taçi. Litho Alexandros Matsoukis, Athens, Greece)

1999 (28 Nov). Birth Anniversaries. T **640** and similar horiz designs. Multicoloured. P 14½×14.

2759	10l. Type **640** (centenary)	40	30
	a. Block of 4. Nos. 2759/2762	13·00	
2760	20l. Azem Galica (revolutionary) (centenary)	45	40
2761	50l. Viktor Eftimiu (writer) (centenary)	1·40	1·30
2762	300l. Lasgush Poradeci (poet) (centenary (2000))	10·00	9·00
2759/2762 Set of 4		11·00	10·00

Nos. 2759/2762 were issued together in *se-tenant* blocks of four stamps within the sheet.

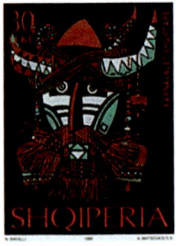 

641 Carnival Mask   **642** Bell and Flowers

(Des N. Bakalli. Litho Alexandros Matsoukis, Athens, Greece)

1999 (1 Dec). Carnivals. T **641** and similar vert design. Multicoloured. P 14.

2763	30l. Type **641**	95	85
2764	300l. Turkey mask	10·00	9·00

(Des T. Pustina and L. Kakarriqi. Litho Alexandros Matsoukis, Athens, Greece)

2000 (27 Mar). New Millennium. The Peace Bell. T **642** and similar vert design. Multicoloured. P 13½×14.

2765	40l. Type **642**	1·20	1·10
2766	90l. Bell and flowers (*different*)	3·00	2·75

643 Woman's Costume, Librazhdi   **644** Gustav Majer

(Des N. Bakalli. Litho Alexandros Matsoukis, Athens, Greece)

2000 (28 Mar). Regional Costumes (1st series). T **643** and similar vert designs. Multicoloured. P 13×14.

2767	5l. Type **643**	15	10
	a. Sheetlet of 12. Nos. 2767/2778	14·00	
2768	10l. Woman's costume, Malësia e Madhe	25	15
2769	15l. Man's costume, Malësia e Madhe	35	25
2770	20l. Man's costume, Tropojë	45	35
2771	30l. Man's costume, Dumrea	70	50
2772	35l. Man's costume, Tirane	80	70
2773	40l. Woman's costume, Tirane	1·20	1·10
2774	45l. Woman's costume, Arbëreshë	1·40	1·30
2775	50l. Man's costume, Gjirokastra	1·60	1·40
2776	55l. Woman's costume, Lunxhëri	1·70	1·50
2777	70l. Woman's costume, Çameria	2·20	2·00
2778	90l. Man's costume, Labëria	2·75	2·50
2767/2778 Set of 12		12·00	10·50

Nos. 2767/2778 were issued together in *se-tenant* sheetlets of 12 stamps.

See also Nos. 2832/2843, 2892/2903, 2943/2954, 3053/3064, 3080/3091 and 3171/3182.

(Litho Alexandros Matsoukis, Athens, Greece)

2000 (30 Mar). 150th Birth Anniversary of Gustav Majer (etymologist). P 13½×14.

2779	**644** 50l. brown-olive	1·60	1·40
	a. Pair. Nos. 2779/2780	6·00	5·50
2780	130l. brown-lake	4·00	3·75

645 Donald Duck   **646** Early Racing Car

(Des S. Taçi. Litho Alexandros Matsoukis, Athens, Greece)

2000 (6 Apr). Donald and Daisy Duck (cartoon film characters). T **645** and similar vert designs. Multicoloured. P 13×14.

2781	10l. Type **645**	45	35
	a. Vert or horiz strip of 4. Nos. 2781/2784	12·50	
2782	30l. Donald Duck	80	70
2783	90l. Daisy Duck	2·75	2·40
2784	250l. Donald Duck	7·75	7·00
2781/2784 Set of 4		10·50	9·50

Nos. 2781/2784 were issued together in vertical or horizontal *se-tenant* strips of four stamps within the sheet.

(Des L. Kakarriqi. Litho Alexandros Matsoukis, Athens, Greece)

2000 (10 Apr). Motor Racing. T **646** and similar horiz designs. Multicoloured. P 14½×14.

2785	30l. Type **646**	1·20	1·10
	a. Sheetlet of 10. Nos. 2785/2794, plus 2 labels	12·50	
2786	30l. Two-man racing car	1·20	1·10
2787	30l. Racing car with wire nose	1·20	1·10
2788	30l. Racing car with solid wheels	1·20	1·10
2789	30l. Car No. 1	1·20	1·10
2790	30l. Car No. 2	1·20	1·10
2791	30l. White Formula 1 racing car (facing left)	1·20	1·10
2792	30l. Blue Formula 1 racing car	1·20	1·10
2793	30l. Red Formula 1 racing car	1·20	1·10
2794	30l. White Formula 1 racing car (front view)	1·20	1·10
2785/2794 Set of 10		11·00	10·00

Nos. 2785/2794 were issued together in *se-tenant* sheetlets of ten stamps and two labels showing the flags of participating nations in the Formula 1 racing competition.

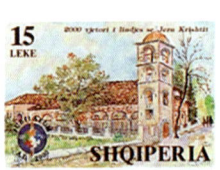 

647 Ristoz of Mborja Church, Korçë   **648** Building Europe

(Des S. Vllahu. Litho Alexandros Matsoukis, Athens, Greece)

2000 (22 Apr). Birth Bimillenary of Jesus Christ. T **647** and similar horiz designs. Multicoloured. P 14.

2795	15l. Type **647**	60	55
2796	40l. St Kolli Church, Voskopoja	1·70	1·50
2797	90l. Church of Flori and Lauri, Kosovo	4·00	3·50
2795/2797 Set of 3		5·75	5·00
MS2798 80×60 mm. 250l. Fountain of Shengjin (mosaic), Tirana (37×37 *mm*). P 13½		7·25	6·50

(Des J. P. Cousin. Litho Alexandros Matsoukis, Athens, Greece)

2000 (9 May). Europa. P 13×14.

2799	**648** 130l. multicoloured	5·50	5·00
MS2800 60×80 mm. 300l. Detail of design showing boy holding star (24×29 *mm*). P 13		13·00	12·00

649 Wolf (*Canis lupus*)   **650** Gustav Mahler (composer) (40th death anniversary)

(Des N. Bakalli. Litho Alexandros Matsoukis, Athens, Greece)

2000 (17 May). Animals. T **649** and similar horiz designs. Multicoloured. P 14½×14.

2801	10l. Type **649**	45	35
	a. Block of 4. Nos. 2801/2804	11·50	
2802	40l. Brown Bear (*Ursus arctos*)	1·10	1·00

2803	90l. Wild Boar (*Sus scrofa*)	3·00	2·75
2804	220l. Red Fox (*Vulpes vulpes*)	7·00	6·25
2801/2804	Set of 4	10·50	9·25
MS2804a	95×64 mm. Nos. 2801/2804	12·00	11·00

Nos. 2801/2804 were issued together in *se-tenant* blocks of four stamps within the sheet.

(Des N. Bakalli. Litho Alexandros Matsoukis, Athens, Greece)

2000 (30 May). WIPA 2000 International Stamp Exhibition, Vienna. P 13½×14.

2805	**650**	130l. multicoloured	4·00	3·75

651 Footballer saving Ball

652 Musicans

(Des T. Pustina. Litho Alexandros Matsoukis, Athens, Greece)

2000 (1 June). European Football Championship, Belgium and The Netherlands. T **651** and similar horiz design. Multicoloured. P 14×13½.

2806	10l. Type **651**	45	35
2807	120l. Footballer heading ball	3·50	3·25
MS2808	80×60 mm. 260l. Footballer kicking ball. Imperf	7·75	7·00

(Litho Alexandros Matsoukis, Athens, Greece)

2000 (7 June). Paintings by Picasso. T **652** and similar horiz designs. Multicoloured. P 14.

2809	30l. Type **652**	95	85
2810	40l. Abstract face	1·40	1·30
2811	250l. Two women running along beach	7·75	7·00
2809/2811	Set of 3	9·00	8·25
MS2812	60×80 mm. 400l. Painting of man (24×29 mm). P 13	12·50	11·00

653 Basketball

654 LZ-1 (first Zeppelin airship) over Lake Constance, Friedrichshafen (first flight)

(Des S. Taçi. Litho Alexandros Matsoukis, Athens, Greece)

2000 (1 July). Olympic Games, Sydney. T **653** and similar vert designs. Multicoloured. P 14×14½.

2813	10l. Type **653**	45	35
	a. Block of 4. Nos. 2813/2816	12·00	
2814	40l. Football	1·10	1·00
2815	90l. Athletics	2·30	2·10
2816	250l. Cycling	7·75	7·00
2813/2816	Set of 4	10·50	9·50

Nos. 2813/2816 were issued together in *se-tenant* blocks of four stamps within the sheet.

(Des S. Vllhu. Litho Alexandros Matsoukis, Athens, Greece)

2000 (2 July). Centenary of First Zeppelin Flight. Airship Development. T **654** and similar multicoloured designs. P 14×13.

2817	15l. Type **654**	45	35
	a. Sheetlet of 3. Nos. 2817/2819	10·50	
2818	30l. Santes-Dumont airship *Ballon No. 5* and Eiffel Tower (attempted round trip from St Cloud via Eiffel tower, 1901)	95	85
2819	300l. Beardmore airship R-34 over New York (first double crossing of Atlantic)	8·50	7·75
2817/2819	Set of 3	9·00	8·00
MS2820	80×60 mm. 300l. Ferdinand von Zeppelin and airship (24×28 mm). P 13	9·00	8·00

Nos. 2817/2819 were printed together in *se-tenant* sheetlets of three stamps.

655 Self-portrait (Picasso)

656 Yellow Gentian (*Gentiana lutea*)

(Litho Alexandros Matsoukis, Athens, Greece)

2000 (6 Oct). Espana 2000 World Stamp Exhibition, Madrid. P 14.

2821	**655**	130l. multicoloured	4·25	4·00

(Des L. Mema. Litho Alexandros Matsoukis, Athens, Greece)

2000 (10 Oct). Medicinal Plants. T **656** and similar vert design. Multicoloured. P 13½×14.

2822	50l. Type **656**	1·70	1·50
	a. Horiz pair. Nos. 2822/2823	4·25	3·75
2823	70l. Cross-leaved Gentian (*Gentiana crutiata*)	2·20	2·00

Nos. 2822/2823 were issued together in horizontal *se-tenant* pairs within the sheet.

657 Naim Frashëri (poet) and Landscape

658 Mother holding Child

(Des L. Mema. Litho Alexandros Matsoukis, Athens, Greece)

2000 (28 Nov). Personalities. T **657** and similar horiz design. Multicoloured. P 14½×14.

2824	30l. Type **657**	95	85
	a. Horiz pair. Nos. 2824/2825	3·00	2·50
2825	50l. Bajram Curri (revolutionary) and landscape	1·70	1·50

Nos. 2824/2825 were issued together in horizontal *se-tenant* pairs within the sheet, each pair forming a composite design.

(Des S. Prapaniku. Litho Alexandros Matsoukis, Athens, Greece)

2000 (14 Dec). 50th Anniversary of United Nations High Commission for Refugees. T **658** and similar vert design. Multicoloured. P 14×14½.

2826	50l. Type **658**	1·90	1·70
2827	90l. Mother breastfeeding child	2·75	2·50

659 Dede Ahmed Myftar Ahmataj

(660)

(Des I. Martini. Litho Alexandros Matsoukis, Athens, Greece)

2001 (22 Feb). Religious Leaders. T **659** and similar horiz design. Multicoloured. P 14½×14.

2828	90l. Type **659**	3·00	2·75
	a. Horiz pair. Nos. 2828/2829	6·25	5·75
2829	90l. Dede Sali Njazi	3·00	2·75

Nos. 2828/2829 were issued together in horizontal *se-tenant* pairs within sheets of four stamps.

2001 (12 Mar). For Kosovo. Nos. 2592/2593 surch as T **660** in black and red.

2830	80l. +10l. on 50l. multicoloured	7·00	6·25
2831	130l. +20l. on 100l. multicoloured	11·50	10·50

ALBANIA 2001

(Des N. Bakalli. Litho Alexandros Matsoukis, Athens, Greece)

2001 (15 Mar). Regional Costumes (2nd series). Vert designs as T **643**. Multicoloured. P 13×14.

2832	20l. Man's costume, Tropojë	80	70
	a. Sheetlet of 12. Nos. 2832/2843	9·75	
2833	20l. Woman's costume, Lumë	80	70
2834	20l. Woman's costume, Mirditë	80	70
2835	20l. Man's costume, Lumë	80	70
2836	20l. Woman's costume, Zadrime	80	70
2837	20l. Woman's costume, Shpati	80	70
2838	20l. Man's costume, Krujë	80	70
2839	20l. Woman's costume, Macukulli	80	70
2840	20l. Woman's costume, Dardhë	80	70
2841	20l. Man's costume, Lushnjë	80	70
2842	20l. Woman's costume, Dropulli	80	70
2843	20l. Woman's costume, Shmili	80	70
2832/2843 *Set of 12*		8·75	7·50

Nos. 2832/2843 were issued together in *se-tenant* sheetlets of 12 stamps.

661 Southern Magnolia (*Magnolia gandiflora*)

662 Goofy in Shorts

(Des L. Kakarriqi. Litho Alexandros Matsoukis, Athens, Greece)

2001 (30 Mar). Scented Flowers. T **661** and similar vert designs. Multicoloured. P 14×14½.

2844	10l. Type **661**	45	35
	a. Block of 4. Nos. 2844/2847	9·50	
2845	20l. Virginia Rose (*Rosa virginiana*)	80	70
2846	90l. *Dianthus barbatus*	3·00	2·75
2847	140l. Lilac (*Syringa vulgaris*)	5·00	4·50
2844/2847 *Set of 4*		8·25	7·50

Nos. 2844/2847 were issued together in *se-tenant* blocks of four within sheets of eight stamps.

(Des S. Taçi. Litho Alexandros Matsoukis, Athens, Greece)

2001 (6 Apr). Goofy (cartoon film character). T **662** and similar vert designs. Multicoloured. P 13×14.

2848	20l. Type **662**	60	55
	a. Horiz or vert strip of 4. Nos. 2848/2851	10·00	
2849	50l. Goofy in blue hat	1·60	1·40
2850	90l. Goofy in red trousers	2·75	2·50
2851	140l. Goofy in purple waistcoat	4·25	4·00
2848/2851 *Set of 4*		8·25	7·50

Nos. 2848/2851 were issued together in horizontal and vertical strips of four stamps within the sheet.

663 Vincenzo Bellini

664 Cliffs and Stream

(Des N. Bakalli. Litho Alexandros Matsoukis, Athens, Greece)

2001 (20 Apr). Composers' Anniversaries. T **663** and similar horiz design. Multicoloured. P 14×13.

2852	90l. Type **663** (birth centenary)	3·00	2·75
2853	90l. Guiseppe Verdi (death centenary)	3·00	2·75
MS2854	90×90 mm. 300l. Bellini and Verdi (75×38 mm). P 14	9·25	8·50

(Des L. Mema. Litho Alexandros Matsoukis, Athens, Greece)

2001 (29 Apr). Europa. Water Resources. T **664** and similar horiz designs. Multicoloured. P 14.

2855	40l. Type **664**	1·60	1·40
2856	110l. Waterfall	3·00	2·75
2857	200l. Lake	6·25	5·50
2855/2857 *Set of 3*		9·75	8·75
MS2858	60×80 mm. 350l. Ripples (24×78 mm). P 13	14·00	12·50

Nos. 2859/2861 are vacant.

665 Horse

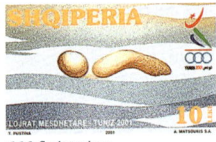
666 Swimming

(Des G. Bakalli. Litho Alexandros Matsoukis, Athens, Greece)

2001 (17 May). Domestic Animals. Two sheets containing T **665** and similar horiz designs. Multicoloured. P 14½×14.

MS2862	105×74 mm. 10l. Type **665**; 15l. Donkey; 80l. Siamese Cat; 90l. Dog	4·00	3·75
MS2863	80×60 mm. 300l. Head of Siamese Cat (49×29 *mm*)	10·00	9·00

(Des T. Pustina. Litho Alexandros Matsoukis, Athens, Greece)

2001 (1 June). Mediterranean Games, Tunis. T **666** and similar horiz designs. Multicoloured. P 14½×14.

2864	10l. Type **666**	45	35
	a. Vert strip of 3. Nos. 2864/2866	8·75	
2865	90l. Athletics	3·00	2·75
2866	140l. Cycling	5·00	4·50
2864/2866 *Set of 3*		7·50	6·75
MS2867	60×80 mm. 260l. Discus (29×24 *mm*). P 13	8·50	7·75

Nos. 2864/2866 were issued together in *se-tenant* vertical strips of three within sheets of six stamps.

667 *Eole* (first powered take-off by Clément Ader, 1890)

668 Tabakeve

(Des S. Vllahu. Litho Alexandros Matsoukis, Athens, Greece)

2001 (20 June). Aviation History. T **667** and similar horiz designs. Multicoloured. P 14×13.

2868	40l. Type **667**	1·60	1·40
	a. Sheetlet of 8. Nos. 2868/2875	13·50	
2869	40l. Blériot XI (first powered crossing of English channel by Louis Blériot, 1909)	1·60	1·40
2870	40l. *Spirit of St Louis* (first solo non-stop crossing of North Atlantic from Paris to New York by Charles Lindbergh, 1927)	1·60	1·40
2871	40l. First flight to Tirana, 1925	1·60	1·40
2872	40l. Antonov AH-10 (first flight, 1956)	1·60	1·40
2873	40l. Concorde (first flight, 1969)	1·60	1·40
2874	40l. Concorde (first commercial flight, 1970)	1·60	1·40
2875	40l. Space shuttle *Colombia* (first flight, 1981)	1·60	1·40
2868/2875 *Set of 8*		11·50	10·00

Nos. 2868/2875 were issued together in *se-tenant* sheetlets of eight stamps.

(Des S. Taçi. Litho Alexandros Matsoukis, Athens, Greece)

2001 (20 July). Old Bridges. T **668** and similar horiz designs. P 14×13½.

2876	10l. multicoloured	35	30
	a. Sheetlet of 4. Nos. 2876/2879	5·00	
2877	20l. multicoloured	45	35
2878	40l. multicoloured	1·20	1·10
2879	90l. black	2·75	2·50
2876/2879 *Set of 4*		4·25	3·75
MS2880	80×60 mm. 2l.50 multicoloured	9·00	8·00

Designs: As T **668**, 10l. T **668**; 20l. Kamares; 40l. Golikut; 90l. Mesit. 49×22 mm—2l.50 Tabakeve.

Nos. 2876/2879 were issued together in *se-tenant* sheetlets of four stamps.

669 Dimitri of Arber

670 Children encircling Globe

(Des Gj. Varfi. Litho Alexandros Matsoukis, Athens, Greece)

2001 (12 Sept). Arms (1st series). T **669** and similar vert designs. P 13.
2881	20l. Type **669**		80	70
	a. Booklet pane. No. 2881×4		3·50	
2882	45l. Balsha principality		1·50	1·30
	a. Booklet pane. No. 2882×4		6·25	
2883	50l. Muzaka family		1·60	1·40
	a. Booklet pane. No. 2883×4		6·75	
2884	90l. George Castriot (Skanderbeg)		3·00	2·75
	a. Booklet pane. No. 2884×4		12·50	
2881/2884 Set of 4			6·25	5·50

See also Nos. 2918/2921, 2965/2968, 3018/3021 and 3098/3101.

(Des Urska Golob. Litho Alexandros Matsoukis, Athens, Greece)

2001 (6 Oct). United Nations Year of Dialogue among Civilisations. Multicoloured, background colours given. P 13½×14.
2885	**670**	45l. orange-red, yellow and black	1·50	1·30
2886		50l. orange and green	1·60	1·40
2887		120l. black and red	4·00	3·50
2885/2887 Set of 3			6·50	5·50

There are minor differences in Nos. 2886/2887, with each colour forming a solid block above and below the central motif.

671 Award Ceremony (Medicins sans Frontieres, 1999 Peace Prize) and Medal

(Des M. Arapi. Litho Alexandros Matsoukis, Athens, Greece)

2001 (1 Dec). Centenary of Nobel Prizes. T **671** and similar horiz designs showing winners and Nobel medal. Multicoloured. P 14×13½.
2888	10l. Type **671**	30	20
2889	20l. Wilhelm Konrad Röntgen (1901 Physics prize)	60	55
2890	90l. Ferid Murad (1998 Medicine prize)	2·75	2·50
2891	200l. Mother Teresa (1979 Peace prize)	6·25	5·50
2888/2891 Set of 4		9·00	8·00

(Des N. Bakalli. Litho Alexandros Matsoukis, Athens, Greece)

2002 (20 Mar). Regional Costumes (3rd series). Vert designs as T **643**. Multicoloured. P 13×14.
2892	30l. Woman's costume, Gjakova	95	85
	a. Sheetlet of 12. Nos. 2892/2903	12·00	
2893	30l. Woman's costume, Prizreni	95	85
2894	30l. Man's costume, Shkodra	95	85
2895	30l. Woman's costume, Shkodra	95	85
2896	30l. Man's costume, Berati	95	85
2897	30l. Woman's costume, Berati	95	85
2898	30l. Woman's costume, Elbasani	95	85
2899	30l. Man's costume, Elbasani	95	85
2900	30l. Woman's costume, Vlora	95	85
2901	30l. Man's costume, Vlora	95	85
2902	30l. Woman's costume, Gjirokastra	95	85
2903	30l. Woman's costume, Delvina	95	85
2892/2903 Set of 12		10·50	9·25

Nos. 2892/2903 were issued together in *se-tenant* sheetlets of 12 stamps.

672 Bambi and Thumper

(Des S. Taçi. Litho Alexandros Matsoukis, Athens, Greece)

2002 (6 Apr). Bambi (cartoon film character). T **672** and similar vert designs. Multicoloured. P 13×14.
2904	20l. Type **672**	60	55
	a. Horiz or vert strip of 4. Nos. 2904/2907	9·25	
2905	50l. Bambi alone amongst flowers	1·60	1·40
2906	90l. Bambi and Thumper looking right	2·75	2·40
2907	140l. Bambi with open mouth	4·00	3·50
2904/2907 Set of 4		8·00	7·00

Nos. 2904/2907 were issued together in horizontal and vertical strips of four stamps within the sheet.

673 Fireplace   674 Acrobatic Jugglers

(Des M. Arapi. Litho Alexandros Matsoukis, Athens, Greece)

2002 (15 Apr). Traditional Fireplaces. T **673** and similar vert designs showing fireplaces. Multicoloured. P 14.
MS2908 30l. Type **673**; 40l. With columns at each side; 50l. With foliage arch; 90l. With three medallions in arch	6·25	5·50

(Des T. Pustina. Litho Alexandros Matsoukis, Athens, Greece)

2002 (1 May). Europa. Circus. T **674** and similar vert designs. Multicoloured. P 13½×13 (No. **MS**2912) or 13×14 (others).
2909	40l. Type **674**	1·20	1·10
2910	90l. Female acrobat	2·75	2·40
2911	220l. Tightrope performers	7·75	7·00
2909/2911 Set of 3		10·50	9·50
MS2912 60×80 mm. 350l. Equestrienne performer (38×38 *mm*)		14·50	13·00

675 Heading the Ball   676 Opuntia catingiola

(Des M. Arapi. Litho Alexandros Matsoukis, Athens, Greece)

2002 (6 May). Football World Championship, Japan and South Korea. T **675** and similar horiz designs. Multicoloured. P 13½.
2913	20l. Type **675**	60	55
2914	30l. Catching the ball	95	85
2915	90l. Kicking the ball from horizontal position	2·75	2·50
2916	120l. Player and ball	3·50	3·00
2913/2916 Set of 4		7·00	6·25
MS2917 80×60 mm. 360l. Emblem (50×30 *mm*). P 13		11·00	9·75

(Des Gj. Varfi. Litho Alexandros Matsoukis, Athens, Greece)

2002 (12 May). Arms (2nd series). Vert designs as T **669**. Multicoloured. P 13.
2918	20l. Gropa family	60	55
	a. Booklet pane. No. 2918×4	2·50	
2919	45l. Skurra family	1·40	1·30
	a. Booklet pane. No. 2919×4	5·75	
2920	50l. Bua family	1·60	1·40
	a. Booklet pane. No. 2920×4	6·75	
2921	90l. Topia family	3·00	2·75
	a. Booklet pane. No. 2921×4	12·50	
2918/2921 Set of 4		6·00	5·50

(Des G. Bakalli. Litho Alexandros Matsoukis, Athens, Greece)

2002 (17 May). Cacti. T **676** and similar triangular designs. Multicoloured. P 14.
MS2922 50l. Type **676**; 50l. *Neoporteria pseudoreicheana*; 50l. *Lobivia shaferi*; 50l. *Hylocereus undatus*; 50l. *Borzicactus madisoniorum*	7·75	7·00

677 Blood Group Symbols with Wings   678 Naim Kryeziu (footballer)

ALBANIA 2002

(Des S. Taçi. Litho Alexandros Matsoukis, Athens, Greece)

2002 (16 June). 50th Anniversary of Blood Bank Service. T **677** and similar vert designs. Multicoloured. P 14×14½.
2923	90l. Type **677**	3·00	2·75
2924	90l. Blood group symbols containing figures	3·00	2·75

(Des Ll. Taçi. Litho Alexandros Matsoukis, Athens, Greece)

2002 (3 July). Sports Personalities. T **678** and similar multicoloured designs. P 14.
2925	50l. Type **678**	1·60	1·40
	a. Strip of 3. Nos. 2925/2927	5·00	
2926	50l. Riza Lushta (footballer)	1·60	1·40
2927	50l. Ymer Pampuri (weightlifter)	1·60	1·40
2925/2927 Set of 3		4·25	3·75
MS2928 61×81 mm. 300l. Loro Boriçi (footballer) (vert). Imperf		9·25	8·50

Nos. 2925/2927 were issued in horizontal se-tenant strips of three stamps within the sheet.

679 Stamp, Torso and Emblem

680 Statue of Liberty

(Des A. Mandija. Litho Alexandros Matsoukis, Athens, Greece)

2002 (1 Sept). 50th Anniversary of International Federation of Stamp Dealers' Associations (IFSDA). T **679** and similar horiz design. Multicoloured. P 14×13½.
2929	50l. Type **679**	1·60	1·40
2930	100l. Part of stamp enlarged and emblem	3·00	2·75

(Des T. Pustina. Litho Alexandros Matsoukis, Athens, Greece)

2002 (11 Sept). First Anniversary of Attacks on World Trade Centre, New York. T **680** and similar multicoloured designs. P 14×13.
2931	100l. Type **680**	3·00	2·75
2932	150l. Burning towers and skyline	4·75	4·25
MS2933 61×81 mm. 350l. Statue of Liberty and World Trade Centre tower (vert)		11·00	9·75

681 Loggerhead Turtle (*Caretta caretta*)

(Des S. Vllahu. Litho Alexandros Matsoukis, Athens, Greece)

2002 (12 Sept). Fauna of Mediterranean Sea. Sheet 100×107 mm containing T **681** and similar horiz designs. Multicoloured. P 14½×14.
MS2934 50l. Type **681**; 50l. Common Dolphin (*Delphinus delphis*); 50l. Blue Shark (*Prionace glauca*); 50l. Fin Whale (*Balaenoptera physalus*); 50l. Ray (*Torpedo torpedo*); 50l. Octopus (*Octopus vulgaris*)	9·25	8·50

682 Tefta Tashko Koço

(Des H. Devolli. Litho Alexandros Matsoukis, Athens, Greece)

2002 (6 Oct). Personalities. The Stage. T **682** and similar horiz designs. Multicoloured. P 14.
2935	50l. Type **682** (singer)	1·60	1·40
	a. Block of 4. Nos. 2935/2938	6·75	
2936	50l. Naim Frashëri (actor)	1·60	1·40
2937	50l. Kristaq Antoniu (singer)	1·60	1·40
2938	50l. Panajot Kanaçi (choreographer)	1·60	1·40
2935/2938 Set of 4		5·75	5·00

Nos. 2935/2938 were issued in se-tenant blocks of four stamps within the sheet.

683 Flags

684 Satellite Dish and Outline of Stamp

(Des N. Bakalli. Litho Alexandros Matsoukis, Athens, Greece)

2002 (28 Nov). 90th Anniversary of Independence. T **683** and similar vert design. Multicoloured. P 13½×14.
2939	20l. Type **683**	60	55
2940	90l. People and Albanian flag	2·75	2·40

(Des M. Fushëkati. Litho Alexandros Matsoukis, Athens, Greece)

2002 (4 Dec). 90th Anniversary of Albanian Post and Telecommunications (1st series). T **684** and similar vert design. Multicoloured. P 13½×14.
2941	20l. Type **684**	60	55
2942	90l. Airmail envelope and telegraph machine	2·75	2·40

See also Nos. 2963/2964.

(Des N. Bakalli. Litho Alexandros Matsoukis, Athens, Greece)

2003 (1 Apr). Regional Costumes (4th series). Vert designs as T **643**. Multicoloured. P 13×14.
2943	30l. Woman's costume, Kelmendi	1·10	1·00
	a. Sheetlet of 12. Nos. 2943/2954	13·50	
2944	30l. Man's costume, Zadrime	1·10	1·00
2945	30l. Woman's costume, Zerqani	1·10	1·00
2946	30l. Man's costume, Peshkopi	1·10	1·00
2947	30l. Man's costume, Malësia e Tiranës	1·10	1·00
2948	30l. Woman's costume, Malësia e Tiranës	1·10	1·00
2949	30l. Woman's costume, Fushë Krujë	1·10	1·00
2950	30l. Man's costume, Shpati	1·10	1·00
2951	30l. Woman's costume, Myzeqe	1·10	1·00
2952	30l. Woman's costume, Labinoti	1·10	1·00
2953	30l. Man's costume, Korçë	1·10	1·00
2954	30l. Woman's costume, Labëri	1·10	1·00
2943/2954 Set of 12		12·00	11·00

Nos. 2943/2954 were issued together in se-tenant sheetlets of 12 stamps.

685 Popeye and Bluto

686 Port Palemo Castle

(Des S. Taçi. Litho Walsall)

2003 (6 Apr). Popeye (cartoon film character). T **685** and similar vert designs. Multicoloured. P 13½.
2955	40l. Type **685**	1·40	1·30
	a. Horiz or vert strip of 4. Nos. 2955/2958	11·50	
2956	50l. Popeye running	1·70	1·50
2957	80l. Popeye and Olive Oyl	2·75	2·50
2958	150l. Popeye	5·00	4·50
2955/2958 Set of 4		9·75	8·75

Nos. 2955/2958 were issued in se-tenant strips of four stamps within the sheet.

(Des M. Arapi. Litho Walsall)

2003 (15 Apr). Castles. Sheet 118×98 mm. T **686** and similar horiz designs. P 13½.
MS2959 10l. grey and black; 20l. brown-olive and black; 50l. greenish grey and black; 120l. dull mauve and black	7·00	6·25

Designs: 10l. T **686**; 20l. Petrela; 50l. Kruja; 120l. Preza.

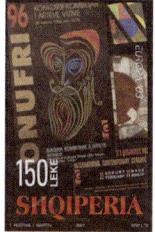 

687 Bearded Man   **688** Envelopes

(Des T. Pustina and I. Martini. Litho Walsall)

2003 (30 Apr). Europa. Poster Art. T **687** and similar vert designs. Multicoloured. P 14.
2960	150l. Type **687**	5·50	5·00
2961	200l. Eye, Apple and piano	7·00	6·25
MS2962	80×61 mm. 350l. Detail of No. 2960	12·50	11·00

(Des N. Bakalli. Litho Walsall)

2003 (5 May). 90th Anniversary of Albanian Post and Telecommunications (2nd series). T **688** and similar horiz design. Multicoloured. P 13½.
2963	50l. Type **688**	1·60	1·40
2964	1000l. Outline of stamps	37·00	34·00

(Des Gj. Varfi. Litho Walsall)

2003 (12 May). Arms (3rd series). Vert designs as T **669**. Multicoloured. P 13.
2965	10l. Ariantët family	35	20
	a. Booklet pane. No. 2965×4	1·50	
2966	20l. Jonimajt family	80	70
	a. Booklet pane. No. 2966×4	3·50	
2967	70l. Dukagjini family	2·30	2·10
	a. Booklet pane. No. 2967×4	9·50	
2968	120l. Kopili family	4·00	3·50
	a. Booklet pane. No. 2968×4	17·00	
2965/2968	Set of 4	6·75	5·75

689 Pomegranate (*Punica granatum*)   **690** Diocletian

(Des G. Bakalli. Litho Walsall)

2003 (17 May). Fruit. T **689** and similar triangular designs. Multicoloured. Self-adhesive. Die-cut perf 6½.
MS2969	50l. Type **689**; 60l. Citron (*Citrus medica*); 70l. Cantaloupe (*Cucumis melo*); 80l. Fig (*Ficus*) (inscr 'Fieus')	8·50	7·75

(Des M. Fushëkati. Litho Walsall)

2003 (20 June). Roman Emperors. T **690** and similar horiz designs. Multicoloured. P 13½.
2970	70l. Type **690**	2·30	2·10
	a. Block of 4. Nos. 2970/2973	9·50	
2971	70l. Justinian	2·30	2·10
2972	70l. Claudius II	2·30	2·10
2973	70l. Constantine	2·30	2·10
2970/2973	Set of 4	8·25	7·50

Nos. 2970/2973 were issued in se-tenant blocks of four stamps within the sheet.

691 White Stork (*Cicona cicona*)   **692** Players

(Des S. Vllahu. Litho Walsall)

2003 (20 Aug). Birds. Sheet 100×119 mm containing T **691** and similar vert designs. Multicoloured. P 14½.
MS2974	70l. Type **691**; 70l. Golden Eagle (*Aquila chrysaetos*); 70l. Eagle Owl (*Bubo bubo*); 70l. Capercaillie (*Tetrao urogallus*)	9·25	8·50

(Des N. Xharo. Litho Walsall)

2003 (2 Sept). 90th Anniversary of Albanian Football. T **692** and similar vert design. Each olive-grey, black and red. P 14½.
2975	80l. Type **692**	2·75	2·40
	a. Pair. Nos. 2975/2976	5·75	5·00
2976	80l. Group of players	2·75	2·40

Nos. 2975/2976 were issued in horizontal se-tenant pairs within the sheet, each pair forming a composite design.

693 The Luncheon (detail)   **694** Odhise Paskall

(Des S. Taçi. Litho Walsall)

2003 (20 Sept). 120th Death Anniversary of Édouard Manet (artist). T **693** and similar multicoloured designs. P 14½.
2977	40l. Type **693**	1·20	1·10
2978	100l. The Fifer	3·50	3·00
MS2979	80×60 mm. 250l. Édouard Manet (*horiz*)	7·75	7·00

(Des L. Mema. Litho Walsall)

2003 (6 Oct). Albanian Sculptors. T **694** and similar horiz designs. Multicoloured. P 13½.
2980	50l. Type **694**	1·60	1·40
	a. Block of 4. Nos. 2980/2983	6·75	
2981	50l. Llazar Nikolla	1·60	1·40
2982	50l. Janaq Paço	1·60	1·40
2983	50l. Murat Toptani	1·60	1·40
2980/2983	Set of 4	5·75	5·00

Nos. 2980/2983 were issued in se-tenant blocks of four stamps within the sheet.

695 Profile of Mother Teresa   **696** Lake, Pelicans and Pine Trees (Divjaka forest)

(Des S. Taçi. Litho)

2003 (19 Oct). Mother Teresa (humanitarian) Commemoration. T **695** and similar multicoloured designs. P 13½.
2984	40l. Type **695**	1·60	1·50
2985	250l. Mother Teresa facing front	8·00	7·25
MS2986	60×60 mm. 350l. Mother Teresa (statue) (40×40 *mm*)	11·00	10·00

(Des S. Vllahu. Litho Walsall)

2003 (20 Oct). Natural Heritage. T **696** and similar horiz designs. Multicoloured. P 13½.
2987	20l. Type **696**	65	60
2988	30l. House and Fir Trees (Hotova forest)	95	85
2989	200l. Snow-covered Fir Trees (Drenova forest)	6·50	5·75
2987/2989	Set of 3	7·25	6·50

697 Stylised Cyclist and Map of France

698 Trees, Lake and Mountain, Pushimet

(Des M. Arapi. Litho Walsall)

2003 (1 Nov). Centenary of Tour de France Cycle Race. T **697** and similar horiz design. P 14½.
2990	50l. new blue, bright scarlet and black	1·60	1·50
2991	100l. multicoloured	3·25	3·00

Designs: 50l. T **697**; 100l. Two cyclists.

2004 (23 June). Europa. Holidays. T **698** and similar vert designs. Multicoloured. Litho. P 13½.
2992	200l. Type **698**	7·25	6·50
	a. Booklet pane. Nos. 2992/2993, each×4	65·00	
2993	200l. Grassland, hills and mountains, Pushimet	7·25	6·50
MS2994	61×81 mm. 350l. Island, Pushimet	14·50	13·00

699 Goalkeeper

700 Discus Thrower (statue)

(Des I. Martini. Litho)

2004 (24 June). European Football Championship 2004, Portugal. T **699** and similar multicoloured designs. P 14.
2995	20l. Type **699**	80	75
2996	40l. Two players and goalkeeper catching ball	1·40	1·30
2997	50l. Two players	1·80	1·60
2998	200l. Players jumping for ball	7·25	6·50
2995/2998 Set of 4		10·00	9·25
MS2999	81×61 mm. 350l. Player with raised arms (38×38 mm) (circular)	13·00	11·50

(Des S. Taçi. Litho)

2004 (12 Aug). Olympic Games, Athens. T **700** and similar vert designs. Multicoloured. P 14.
3000	10l. Type **700**	40	35
3001	200l. Face (statue)	7·25	6·50
MS3002	61×81 mm. 350l. Athlete carrying Olympic torch (39×55 mm)	13·00	11·50

701 Wilhelm von Wied

702 Bugs Bunny

(Des H. Devolli. Litho)

2004 (30 Aug). Wilhem von Wied (ruler, February 6th–September 5th, 1914) Commemoration. T **701** and similar vert designs. Multicoloured. P 13½.
3003	40l. Type **701**	1·40	1·30
3004	150l. Facing left	5·00	4·75

(Des S. Taçi. Litho)

2004 (15 Sept). Bugs Bunny (cartoon character). T **702** and similar vert designs showing Bugs Bunny. Multicoloured. P 13½.
3005	40l. Type **702**	1·40	1·30
	a. Strip of 4. Nos. 3005/3008	11·50	
3006	50l. With crossed arms	1·80	1·60
3007	80l. Wearing dinner jacket	3·00	2·50
3008	150l. Facing left	5·00	4·75
3005/3008 Set of 4		10·00	9·25

Nos. 3005/3008 were issued in *se-tenant* horizontal and vertical strips of four stamps within the sheet.

703 Damaged Painting

(Des M. Arapi. Litho)

2004 (3 Oct). Mural Paintings by Nikolla Onufri, Church of Saint Mary Vllherna. T **703** and similar horiz designs. P 14.
3009	10l. Type **703**	50	45
3010	20l. Mary	80	75
3011	1000l. Saint	35·00	32·00
3009/3011 Set of 3		33·00	30·00
MS3012	80×65 mm. 400l. Crowned Christ. P 13½×14½	14·50	13·00

704 Ladybird

(Des B. Vllahu. Litho)

2004 (10 Oct). Ladybird (*Coccinella*). Sheet 120×95 mm containing T **704** and similar horiz designs showing Ladybirds. Multicoloured. P 14.
MS3013	80l.×4, Type **704**; Six-spot; With open wings; 12-spot	11·00	10·00

705 Norek Luca

706 Dushmani Principality

(Des H. Devolli. Litho)

2004 (12 Oct). Personalities. T **705** and similar horiz designs. Multicoloured. P 14.
3014	50l. Type **705** (actor) (80th birth anniversary)	1·80	1·60
	a. Block of 4. Nos. 3014/3017	7·50	
3015	50l. Jorgjia Truja (singer) (Tenth death anniversary)	1·80	1·60
3016	50l. Maria Kraja (singer) (Fifth death anniversary)	1·80	1·60
3017	50l. Zina Andri (actor) (80th birth anniversary)	1·80	1·60
3014/3017 Set of 4		6·50	5·75

Nos. 3014/3017 were issued in *se-tenant* blocks of four stamps within the sheet.

(Des Gj. Varfi. Litho)

2004 (25 Oct). Arms (4th series). T **706** and similar vert designs. Multicoloured. P 14.
3018	20l. Type **706**	80	75
	a. Booklet pane. No. 3018×4	3·50	
3019	40l. Gjuraj family	1·40	1·30
	a. Booklet pane. No. 3019×4	5·75	

3020		80l. Zaharaj family		3·00	2·50
		a. Booklet pane. No. 3020×4		12·50	
3021		150l. Spani principality		5·00	4·75
		a. Booklet pane. No. 3021×4		21·00	
3018/3021 Set of 4				9·25	8·25

707 Cactus-type Dahlia   **708** Madonna and Child (Anonim Shen Meria)

(Des G. Bakalli. Litho)

2004 (1 Nov). Dahlias. Sheet 164×77 mm containing T **707** and similar triangular designs showing dahlias. Multicoloured. P 14.
MS3022 80l.×4, Type **707**; Water Lily type; Anemone type; Dahlia .... 11·00 10·00

(Des G. Panariti (Nos. 3023/3027 and Nos. 3043/3047), A. Hasanau (Nos. 3028/3032 and Nos. 3038/3042), A. Hado (Nos. 3033/3037). Litho)

2004 (20 Nov). 50th Anniversary of National Art Gallery. T **708** and similar vert designs. Multicoloured. P 14.

3023	20l.	Type **708**	80	75
		a. Sheet of 25. Nos. 3023/3047	21·00	
3024	20l.	Saint (Mihal Anagnosti)	80	75
3025	20l.	Angel (Onufër Qiprioti)	80	75
3026	20l.	Enthroned saint holding open book (Çetiret)	80	75
3027	20l.	God and saints (Onuferi)	80	75
3028	20l.	Woman wearing scarf (Kel Kodheli)	80	75
3029	20l.	Crying woman (Vangjush Mio)	80	75
3030	20l.	Woman wearing hat (Abdurahim Buza)	80	75
3031	20l.	Semi-naked woman (Mustapha Arapi)	80	75
3032	20l.	Man with moustache (Guri Madhi)	80	75
3033	20l.	Soldier (sculpture) (Janaq Paço)	80	75
3034	20l.	Still life with grapes (Zef Kolombi)	80	75
3035	20l.	Flowers (Hasan Reci)	80	75
3036	20l.	Still life with onions (Vladimir Jani)	80	75
3037	20l.	Woman's head (sculpture) (Halim Beqiri)	80	75
3038	20l.	Men seated (Edison Gjergo)	80	75
3039	20l.	Men wearing traditional dress (Naxhi Bakalli)	80	75
3040	20l.	Family (Agron Bregu)	80	75
3041	20l.	Tree planting (Edi Hila)	80	75
3042	20l.	Holding paintbrushes (Artur Muharremi)	80	75
3043	20l.	Old man (Rembrandt)	80	75
3044	20l.	Winged Horseman (Gazmend Leka)	80	75
3045	20l.	Multicoloured circle (Damien Hirst)	80	75
3046	20l.	Corpse in cave (Edvin Rama)	80	75
3047	20l.	Viking (Ibrahim Kodra)	80	75
3023/3047 Set of 25			18·00	17·00

Nos. 3023/3047 were issued in *se-tenant* sheets of 25 stamps.

709 Bunting and NATO Emblem   **710** Two Doves

(Des X. Guga. Litho)

2004 (28 Nov). Fifth Anniversary of NATO Peacekeeping in Kosovo. T **709** and similar vert designs. Multicoloured. P 14×13½.

3048		100l. Type **709**	3·75	3·25
3049		200l. Doves and United Nations flag	7·25	6·50
MS3050		80×60 mm. 350l. Houses flying Kosovo flag	13·00	11·50

The stamp and margin of No. MS3050 form a composite design.

(Des I. Martini. Litho)

2004 (29 Nov). 60th Anniversary of Liberation. T **710** and similar horiz designs. Multicoloured. P 13½×14.

3051		50l. Type **710**	2·10	1·90
3052		200l. One Dove	7·50	6·75

(Des N. Bakalli. Litho Alexandros Matsoukis, Athens, Greece)

2004 (4 Dec). Regional Costumes (5th series). Vert designs as T **643**. Multicoloured. P 13×14.

3053		30l. Back view of woman's costume, Gramshi	1·10	1·00
		a. Sheetlet of 12. Nos. 3053/3064	13·50	
3054		30l. Front view of woman's costume, Gramshi	1·10	1·00
3055		30l. Woman's costume, Korçë	1·10	1·00
3056		30l. Man's costume, Kolonja	1·10	1·00
3057		30l. Woman's costume, Korçë (*different*)	1·10	1·00
3058		30l. Woman's costume, Librazhdi	1·10	1·00
3059		30l. Woman's costume, Përmeti	1·10	1·00
3060		30l. Woman's costume, Pogradeci	1·10	1·00
3061		30l. Man's costume, Skrapari	1·10	1·00
3062		30l. Woman's costume, Skrapari	1·10	1·00
3063		30l. Woman's costume, Tepelena	1·10	1·00
3064		30l. Woman's costume, Vlora	1·10	1·00
3053/3064 Set of 12			12·00	11·00

Nos. 3053/3064 were issued in *se-tenant* sheetlets of 12 stamps.

711 Emblem   **712** Triangular Pies

(Des T. Pustina)

2005 (1 Oct). 50th Anniversary of Europa Stamps. T **711** and similar multicoloured design. P 14.

3065		200l. Type **711**	9·00	8·50
3066		250l. Stylised figure grasping '50'	11·00	10·50
MS3067		61×81 mm. 500l. *The Circus* (Georges Seurat)	22·00	21·00

(Des X. Guga. Litho Alexandros Matsoukis, Athens)

2005 (5 Oct). Europa. Gastronomy. T **712** and similar vert design. Multicoloured. P 14.

3068		200l. Type **712**	10·00	9·50
		a. Booklet pane. Nos. 3068/3069, each×3 and MS3070	85·00	13·50
3069		200l. Stew	10·00	9·50
MS3070		60×84 mm. 350l. Sausages	17·00	16·00

713 Emblem   **714** Tom and Jerry

(Des S. Taçi. Litho Alexandros Matsoukis, Athens)

2005 (19 Oct). 50th Anniversary of United Nations Membership. P 14.
3071 **713** 40l. multicoloured .... 1·60 1·50

(Des S. Taçi. Litho Alexandros Matsoukis, Athens)

2005 (20 Oct). Tom and Jerry (cartoon characters). T **714** and similar vert designs. Multicoloured. P 13½.

3072		40l. Type **714**	1·40	1·30
		a. Strip of 4. Nos. 3072/3075	11·50	
3073		50l. Heads of Tom and Jerry	1·80	1·70
3074		80l. Jerry	2·75	2·75
3075		150l. Tom	5·00	4·75
3072/3075 Set of 4			9·75	9·50

Nos. 3072/3075 were issued in *se-tenant* horizontal and vertical strips of four stamps within the sheet.

ALBANIA 2005

715 Mountain, City and Lake

716 Starting Blocks

718 Yellow-flowered Portulaca

719 Cyclists

(Des X. Guga. Litho Alexandros Matsoukis, Athens)

2005 (21 Oct). Art. Albanian Landscapes. T **715** and similar horiz designs. Multicoloured. P 13½.

3076	10l. Type **715**	50	50
	a. Strip of 4. Nos. 3076/3079	37·00	
3077	20l. Aqueduct and castle	60	55
3078	30l. Crowd and minaret	1·20	1·10
3079	1000l. Lake and mountain fortress	34·00	32·00
3076/3079	Set of 4	33·00	31·00

Nos. 3076/3079 were issued in *se-tenant* strips of four stamps within the sheet.

(Des N. Bakalli. Litho Alexandros Matsoukis, Athens, Greece)

2005 (24 Oct). Regional Costumes (6th series). Vert designs as T **643**. Multicoloured. P 13×14.

3080	30l. Man's costume, Tirane	1·50	1·40
	a. Sheetlet of 12. Nos. 3080/3091	19·00	
3081	30l. Woman's costume, Bende Tirane	1·50	1·40
3082	30l. Back of woman's costume, Zall Dajt	1·50	1·40
3083	30l. Man's costume, Kavajë-Durrës	1·50	1·40
3084	30l. Woman's costume, Has	1·50	1·40
3085	30l. Man's costume, Mat	1·50	1·40
3086	30l. Woman's costume, Liqenas	1·50	1·40
3087	30l. Woman's costume, Klenjë	1·50	1·40
3088	30l. Woman's costume, Maleshove	1·50	1·40
3089	30l. Woman's costume, German	1·50	1·40
3090	30l. Woman's costume, Krujë	1·50	1·40
3091	30l. Man's costume, Reç	1·50	1·40
3080/3091	Set of 12	16·00	15·00

Nos. 3080/3091 were issued in *se-tenant* sheetlets of 12 stamps.

(Des I. Martini. Litho Alexandros Matsoukis, Athens)

2005 (25 Oct). Mediterranean Games, Almera. T **716** and similar multicoloured designs. P 14½×14.

3092	20l. Type **716**	1·00	95
	a. Strip of 3. Nos. 3092/3094	8·75	
3093	60l. Rings	2·50	2·40
3094	120l. Relay baton	5·00	4·75
3092/3094	Set of 3	7·75	7·25
MS3095	60×80 mm. 300l. Diver (30×50 *mm*). P 13	16·00	15·00

Nos. 3092/3094 were issued in *se-tenant* strips of three stamps within the sheet.
The stamp of No. **MS**3095 is set at an angle.

717 Globe and Emblem

(Des N. Xharo. Litho Alexandros Matsoukis, Athens)

2005 (11 Nov). Centenary of Rotary International. T **717** and similar multicoloured design. P 14.

3096	30l. Type **717**	1·30	1·20
3097	150l. Emblem (*vert*)	6·25	6·00

(Des Gj. Varfi. Litho)

2005 (14 Nov). Arms (5th series). Vert designs as T **706**. Multicoloured. P 14.

3098	10l. Bua	65	60
	a. Horiz strip of 4. Nos. 3098/3101	12·50	
	b. Booklet pane. No. 3098/×4	2·75	
3099	30l. Karl Topia	1·30	1·20
	a. Booklet pane. No. 3099/×4	5·50	
3100	100l. Dukagjini II	3·75	3·50
	a. Booklet pane. No. 3100/×4	16·00	
3101	150l. Engjej	6·25	6·00
	a. Booklet pane. No. 3101/×4	26·00	
3098/3101	Set of 4	11·00	10·00

Nos. 3098/3101 were issued in horizontal *se-tenant* strips of four stamps within the sheet.

(Des G. Bakalli. Litho Alexandros Matsoukis, Athens)

2005 (17 Nov). Portulaca. Sheet 203×60 mm containing T **718** and similar triangular designs showing portulacas. Multicoloured. P 14.

MS3102	70l.×5, Type **718**; White flowers; Red and yellow flowers; Pale pink flowers; Double dark pink flower	23·00	22·00

(Des I. Martini. Litho Alexandros Matsoukis, Athens)

2005 (20 Nov). 80th Anniversary of Cycle Race. P 13½×14.

3103	**719** 50l. multicoloured	2·40	2·30
	a. Horiz strip of 3. Nos. 3103/3105	12·00	
3104	60l. multicoloured	3·25	3·00
3105	120l. multicoloured	6·00	5·75
3103/3105	Set of 3	10·50	10·00

Nos. 3103/3105 were issued in horizontal *se-tenant* strips of three stamps within the sheet.

720 Battle Scene

(Des G. Bakalli. Litho Alexandros Matsoukis, Athens)

2005 (28 Nov). 600th Birth Anniversary of Gjergj Kastrioti (Skanderbeg). Sheet 240×82 mm containing T **720** and similar multicoloured designs. P 14.

MS3106	40l. Type **720**; 50l. Chariot and fallen Horse and rider; 60l. Archers, emblem and foot soldiers with spears; 70l. Shield bearer and archers; 80l. Soldier with raised sword and archers on rocks (30×30 *mm*) (circular); 90l. Archers firing from cliff ledge (30×30 *mm*) (circular)	19·00	18·00

The stamps and margins of No. **MS**3106 form a composite design of battle.

721 Roses growing through Helmet

722 Matia Kodheli-Marubi

(Des S. Vllahu. Litho Alexandros Matsoukis, Athens)

2005 (29 Nov). 60th Anniversary of End of World War II. T **721** and similar vert design. Multicoloured. P 14.

3107	50l. Type **721**	2·20	2·10
	a. Horiz pair. Nos. 3107/3108	12·00	11·50
3108	200l. Allied flags and statues	9·25	8·75

Nos. 3107/3108 were issued in horizontal *se-tenant* pairs within the sheet.

(Des H. Devolli. Litho Alexandros Matsoukis, Athens)

2005 (4 Dec). National Marubi Photograph Collection. T **722** and similar horiz designs. Multicoloured. P 14.

3109	10l. Type **722**	45	40
	a. Horiz strip of 4. Nos. 3109/3112	14·50	
3110	20l. Gegë Marubi	95	90
3111	70l. Pjeter Marubi (Pietro Marubbi) (photographer, artist and architect)	3·25	3·00
3112	200l. Kel Marubi (Mikel Kodheli)	9·25	8·75
3109/3112	Set of 4	12·50	11·50

Nos. 3109/3112 were issued in horizontal *se-tenant* strips of four stamps within the sheet.

(723)   **724** President George Bush

2006 (Nov–Dec). Various stamp numbers given in brackets surch in black as T **723**.

3113	40l. on 30q. multicoloured (No. 2531)	3·75	3·50
3114	40l. on 18l. multicoloured (No. 2549)	3·75	3·50
3115	40l. on 2l. multicoloured (No. 2567)	3·75	3·50
3116	40l. on 2l. multicoloured (No. 2595)	3·75	3·50
3117	40l. on 3l. multicoloured (No. 2596)	3·75	3·50
3118	40l. on 25l. multicoloured (No. 2597)	3·75	3·50
3119	40l. on 40l. multicoloured (No. 2606)	3·75	3·50
3120	40l. on 18l. multicoloured (No. 2610)	3·75	3·50
3121	40l. on 18l. multicoloured (No. 2613)	3·75	3·50
3122	40l. on 40l. multicoloured (No. 2620)	3·75	3·50
3123	40l. on 25l. multicoloured (No. 2629)	3·75	3·50
3113/3123 Set of 11		37·00	35·00

The surcharges vary in detail, depending on the size and position of the old value obliterated.

2007 (10 June). President George Bush's visit to Albania. T **724** and similar designs. Multicoloured. P 13½.

3124	20l. Type **724**	95	90
	a. Strip of 3. Nos. 3124/3126	6·50	
3125	40l. As Type **724** (suffused green)	1·90	1·80
3126	80l. As Type **724** (multicoloured)	3·50	3·25
3124/3126 Set of 3		5·75	5·25
MS3127 97×73 mm. 200l. Statue of Liberty		8·50	8·00

Nos. 3124/3126 were issued in horizontal *se-tenant* strips of three stamps within the sheet.

725 Arms of Italy and Albania   **727** Flags and Scouts

(Des B. Cami)

2007 (15 Sept). Tenth Anniversary of Italians in Albania. Granite paper. P 13½.

3128	**725** 40l. multicoloured	2·20	2·10

2007 (5 Oct). The Albanian Flag. Horiz designs showing the National Flag all slightly different. Multicoloured. P 13½×13.

3129	5l. Flag	30	25
	a. Sheet of 12. Nos. 3129/3140	£200	
3130	10l. Flag	55	55
3131	20l. Flag	1·20	1·10
3132	30l. Flag	1·80	1·60
3133	40l. Flag	2·40	2·10
3134	50l. Flag	3·00	2·75
3135	60l. Flag	3·50	3·25
3136	70l. Flag	4·00	3·75
3137	80l. Flag	4·75	4·25
3138	100l. Flag	6·00	5·25
3139	1000l. Flag	60·00	55·00
3140	2000l. Flag	£120	£110
3129/3140 Set of 12		£190	£170

Nos. 3129/3140 were printed, *se-tenant*, in sheets of 12 stamps. T **726** is unavailable.

No. 3141 is vacant.

2007 (15–17 Oct). Arms. Vert designs showing Arms. Multicoloured. P 13½×13.

3142	10l. Lança Family (17.10.07)	95	90
3143	20l. Andrea II Muzaka	1·90	1·80
3144	20l. Riki Family (17.10.07)	1·90	1·80
3145	40l. Matrënga Family	5·50	5·25
3146	60l. Kokini Family (17.10.07)	6·50	6·25
3147	80l. Lekë Dukagjini	10·00	9·75
3148	100l. Zako Family (17.10.07)	11·00	10·50
3149	150l. Konstantin Kastrioti	19·00	18·00
3142/3149 Set of 8		50·00	49·00

T **726a** is unavailable.

Nos. 3150/3152 are vacant.

(Des X. Guga)

2007 (24 Oct). Centenary of Scouting. T **727** and similar multicoloured designs. P 13½.

3153	100l. Type **727**	4·75	4·50
3154	150l. Flags and scouts (*different*)	7·50	7·00
MS3155 80×60 mm. 250l. Knot (30×25 *mm*)		12·50	12·00

728 Pink Panther   **729** Roads (Arkida)

(Des S. Taçi)

2007 (25 October). Pink Panther (cartoon character). T **728** and similar vert designs. Multicoloured. P 13×13½.

3156	40l. Type **728**	1·50	1·40
	a. Strip of 4. Nos. 3156/3159	13·00	
3157	50l. With Inspector Clouseau	2·00	1·90
3158	80l. Leaning	3·00	2·75
3159	150l. Wearing tunic	6·00	5·75
3156/3159 Set of 4		11·50	10·50

Nos. 3156/3159 were issued in horizontal *se-tenant* strips of four stamps within the sheet.

2007 (29 October). Children's Drawings. T **729** and similar multicoloured designs. P 13×13½.

3160	10l. Type **729**	70	55
	a. Strip of 4. Nos. 3160/3163	10·00	
3161	40l. Boy and flowers (Amarilda Prifti)	2·10	2·00
3162	50l. Outline of houses and viaduct (Iliaz Kasa)	2·75	2·75
3163	80l. Buildings (K. Mezini) (*horiz*)	4·25	4·00
3160/3163 Set of 4		8·75	8·25

Nos. 3160/3163 were issued in horizontal *se-tenant* strips of four stamps within the sheet, with No. 3163 laid at right angles to the other stamps, giving the appearance of a strip of four vertical stamps.

 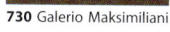 

730 Galerio Maksimiliani   **731** Sower (fresco by David Selenica)

(Des H. Dhiasa)

2007 (30 Oct). Rulers. T **730** and similar vert design. Multicoloured. P 13×13½.

3164	30l. Type **730**	1·90	1·80
	a. Pair. Nos. 3164/3165	7·75	7·25
3165	120l. Flavio Anastasi	5·50	5·25

Nos. 3164/3165 were issued in vertical *se-tenant* pairs within the sheet.

(Des R. Tasho)

2007 (31 Oct). Art. T **731** and similar vert design. Multicoloured. P 13.

3166	70l. Type **731**	3·75	3·50
3167	110l. Flowers and garlands (wall painting) (Et'hem Bey Mosque, Tirana)	7·50	7·00

ALBANIA 2007

732 Young People, Map and Stars   733 Thethi National Park (Inscr 'Parku Kombetar I Thethit')

(Des X. Guga)

2007 (31 Oct). Europa. Integration. T **732** and similar multicoloured designs. P 13×13½ (vert) or 13½×13 (horiz).
3168	200l. Type **732**	9·25	8·75
3169	200l. Young people and double-headed Eagle	9·25	8·75
MS3170	80×60 mm. 350l. Young people and flag (30×25 mm)	16·00	15·00

(Des N. Bakalli)

2007 (1 Nov). Regional Costumes (7th series). Vert designs as T **643**. Multicoloured. P 13×14.
3171	40l. Woman's costume (inscr 'German')	1·70	1·60
	a. Sheetlet of 12. Nos. 3171/3182	21·00	
3172	40l. Man's costume, Kubrin	1·70	1·60
3173	40l. Woman's costume, Gollobordë	1·70	1·60
3174	40l. Man's costume, Kerrabe Malesi	1·70	1·60
3175	40l. Woman's costume, Gur i Bardhë	1·70	1·60
3176	40l. Woman's costume, Martanesh	1·70	1·60
3177	40l. Woman's costume, Pukë	1·70	1·60
3178	40l. Woman's costume, Serice Labinot	1·70	1·60
3179	40l. Woman's costume, Shën Gjergj	1·70	1·60
3180	40l. Woman's costume, Tirane Qytet	1·70	1·60
3181	40l. Man's costume, Zalle Dajt	1·70	1·60
3182	40l. Woman's costume, Zaranike Godolesh	1·70	1·60
3171/3182	Set of 12	18·00	17·00

Nos. 3171/3182 were issued in se-tenant sheetlets of 12 stamps.

Nos. 3183/3194 are vacant.

(Des L. Mema)

2007 (5 Nov). Tourism. T **733** and similar horiz designs. Multicoloured. P 13×13½.
3195	40l. Type **733**	1·90	1·80
	a. Strip of 4. Nos. 3195/3198	11·50	
3196	50l. Luras Lake (Inscr 'Liqenet e Lures')	2·40	2·30
3197	60l. Canine's Castle (Inscr 'Kalaja Kanines')	2·75	2·75
3198	70l. Laguna Karavastase	4·00	3·75
3195/3198	Set of 4	10·00	9·50

Nos. 3195/3198 were issued in horizontal se-tenant strips of four stamps within the sheet.

734 Plane Tree   735 Pope Clement II

(Des X. Guga)

2007 (8 Nov). Natural Heritage. Elbasan Plane Trees. T **734** and similar horiz designs. Multicoloured. P 13×13½.
3199	70l. Type **734**	3·75	3·50
3200	90l. Hollow tree	4·75	4·50

(Des L. Mema)

2007 (9 Nov). P 13×13½.
3201	**735** 30l. multicoloured	1·90	1·80
	a. Pair. Nos. 3201/3202	8·75	8·25
3202	120l. multicoloured	6·50	6·25

Nos. 3201/3202 were issued in vertical se-tenant pairs within the sheet.

736 Léopold Senghor   737 Team

(Des S. Taçi)

2007 (10 Nov). Birth Centenary (2006) of Léopold Sédar Senghor (poet and first President of Senegal 1960–1980). P 13×13½.
3203	**736** 40l. multicoloured	2·75	2·75
3204	80l. multicoloured	4·75	4·50

(Des A. Skenderi)

2007 (11 Nov). 60th Anniversary of Albania as Balkan Football Champions. P 13×13½.
3205	**737** 10l. multicoloured	4·75	4·50
3206	80l. multicoloured	8·25	8·00

738 Cannon   739 Soldier wearing Gas Mask

(Des X. Guga)

2007 (12 Nov). World Heritage Site. Gjirokastra. Sheet 120×100 mm containing T **738** and similar vert designs. Multicoloured. P 13×13½.
MS3207 10l. Type **738**; 20l. Flowers in a roundel; 30l. 'Kule' (building with tall basement, a first floor for use in the cold season, and a second floor for the warm season); 60l. Bridge; 80l. Aerial view; 90l. Clock tower	16·00	15·00

(Des X. Guga)

2007 (13 Nov). Tenth Anniversary of Albania's Participation in International Military Missions. T **739** and similar vert design. Multicoloured. P 13×13½.
3208	10l. Type **739**	70	55
3209	100l. Soldiers in inflatable boat	4·75	4·50

740 Mother Teresa   741 Gaia (statue)

(Des S. Taçi)

2007 (15 Nov). Tenth Death Anniversary of Agnes Ganzhou Bojaxhiu (Mother Teresa). T **740** and similar vert design. Multicoloured. P 13×13½.
3210	**740** 60l. multicoloured	4·75	4·50
3211	130l. multicoloured	9·25	8·75
MS3212	81×61 mm. 200l. As Type **740**	37·00	36·00

(Des X. Guga)

2007 (16 Nov). Archaeology. Durrës City. T **741** and similar multicoloured designs. P 13×13½.
3213	30l. Type **741**	1·90	1·80
	a. Pair. Nos. 3213/3214	11·50	11·00
3214	120l. Gaia (close up)	9·25	8·75
MS3215	80×60 mm. 200l. Statue (detail) (horiz)	£375	£350

No. **MS**3215 was from a limited printing.
Nos. 3213/3214 were issued in vertical se-tenant pairs within the sheet.

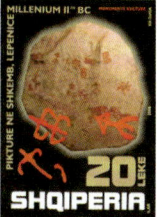 

742 Drawings   **743** Osman Kazazi

(Des X. Guga)

2007 (19 Nov). Cultural History. Tren Cave System (first occupied during Eneolithic period c. 2500–2000 BC). T **742** and similar multicoloured designs. P 13×13½ (vert) or 13½ (horiz).
3216	20l. Type **742**	95	90
3217	100l. Drawings (different)	4·75	4·50
MS3218	81×61 mm. 300l. Cave (horiz)	11·50	11·00

(Des L. Mema)

2007 (22 Nov). Personalities (1st issue). T **743** and similar horiz designs. Multicoloured. P 13×13½.
3219	10l. Type **743** (politician)	45	40
	a. Strip of 4. Nos. 3219/3222	7·25	
3220	20l. Pjetër Arbnori (politician)	65	60
3221	60l. Llazar Sotir Gusho (Lagush Poradeci) (poet)	2·20	2·10
3222	100l. Çesk Zadeja (composer)	3·75	3·50
3219/3222	Set of 4	6·25	6·00

Nos. 3219/3222 were issued in horizontal se-tenant strips of four stamps within the sheet.
See also Nos. 3223/3226.

744 Abdurrahim Buza   **745** Spheres as Player

(Des L. Mema)

2007 (22 Nov). Personalities (2nd issue). T **744** and similar vert designs. Multicoloured. P 13×13½.
3223	50l. Type **744** (artist)	1·90	1·80
	a. Strip of 4. Nos. 3223/3226	7·25	
3224	50l. Aleks Buda (historian)	1·90	1·80
3225	50l. Thimi Mitko (folklorist and nationalist)	1·90	1·80
3226	50l. Martin Camaj (writer)	1·90	1·80
3223/3226	Set of 4	6·75	6·50

Nos. 3223/3226 were issued in horizontal se-tenant strips of four stamps within the sheet.

(Des L. Mema)

2007 (26 Nov). World Cup Football Championship, Germany. T **745** and similar vert designs. Multicoloured. P 13×13½.
3227	30l. Type **745**	1·50	1·40
3228	60l. Triangles as player	4·00	3·75
3229	120l. Rectangles as player	7·75	7·25
3227/3229	Set of 3	12·00	11·00
MS3230	61×82 mm. 350l. Emblems	18·00	17·00

The stamp and margin of No. MS3230 form a composite design.

746 Ismail Kemal Bej Vlora (Ismail Qemali) (first head of state and government) and Arms   **747** Garlic

(Des L. Mema)

2007 (28 Nov). 95th Anniversary of Independence. T **746** and similar horiz design. Multicoloured. P 13×13½.
3231	50l. Type **746**	1·90	1·80
3232	110l. Ismail Qemali	4·00	3·75

(Des G. Bakalli)

2007 (3 Dec). Domestic Plants. T **747** and similar triangular designs. Multicoloured. P 14.
3233	80l. Type **747**	4·25	4·00
	a. Strip of 4. Nos. 3233/3236	18·00	
3234	80l. Onions	4·25	4·00
3235	80l. Peppers	4·25	4·00
3236	80l. Tomatoes	4·25	4·00
3233/3236	Set of 4	15·00	14·50

Nos. 3233/3236 were issued in horizontal se-tenant strips of four stamps within the sheet.

 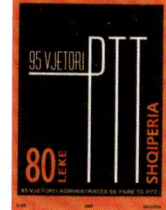

748 Blooms and Leaves   **749** Emblem

(Des A. Skenderi)

2007 (4 Dec). Wulfenia baldacci. T **748** and similar triangular design. Multicoloured. P 14.
3237	70l. Type **748**	4·75	4·50
	a. Pair. Nos. 3237/3238, plus central label	11·50	10·50
3238	100l. Flowers on single stem	6·00	5·75

Nos. 3237/3238 were issued in tête-bêche pairs within the sheet.

(Des X. Guga)

2007 (5 Dec). 95th Anniversary of National Post Office.
3239	**749**	80l. agate and vermilion	3·00	2·75
3240		90l. vermilion and black	3·25	3·25

750 New Road Surfacing   **751** Emblem and Member Flags

2007 (7 Dec). Infrastructure Improvements. Sheet 133×107 mm containing T **750** and similar horiz designs. Multicoloured. P 14.
MS3241 10l. Type **750**; 20l. Durrës port; 30l. New building, Tirana; 40l. Mother Teresa airport; 50l. Shkodra street, Hani i Hotit; 60l. Tepelenë road, Gjirokastra; 70l. Fier road, Lushnjë; 80l. Kalimash road, Morine .... 14·00   13·00

(Des B. Kafexhiu)

2008 (12 Apr). Albania in NATO. T **751** and similar horiz design. Multicoloured. P 13×13½.
3242	40l. Type **751**	1·50	1·40
	a. Pair. Nos. 3242/3243	4·00	3·75
3243	60l. Arms and emblem	2·20	2·10

Nos. 3242/3243 were issued in horizontal se-tenant pairs within the sheet.

 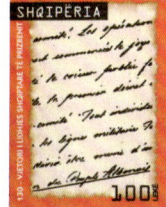

752 Map of Switzerland   **753** Script

ALBANIA 2008

(Des X. Guga)

2008 (16 June). EURO 2008 European Football Championship, Austria and Switzerland. T **752** and similar multicoloured designs. P 13×13½ (horiz) or 13½×13 (vert).

3244	50l. Type **752**	2·75	2·75
	a. Pair. Nos. 3244/3245	14·50	13·50
3245	250l. Map of Austria	11·00	10·50
MS3246	60×80 mm. 200l. Mascots (*vert*)	8·25	8·00

Nos. 3244/3245 were issued in horizontal *se-tenant* pairs within the sheet.

(Des X. Guga)

2008 (27 June). 130th Anniversary of Albanian League of Prizren. T **753** and similar vert design. P 13½×13.

3247	100l. Type **753**	3·75	3·50
	a. Pair. Nos. 3247/3248	9·50	9·00
3248	150l. Building	5·50	5·25

Nos. 3247/3248 were issued in vertical *se-tenant* pairs within the sheet.

754 Postmark   **755** John Belushi (actor)

(Des Y. Beqiri)

2008 (30 June). 95th Anniversary of Postal Service. P 13½×13.

3249	**754**	40l. multicoloured	1·50	1·40

(Des E. Faja)

2008 (9 July). Personalities of Albanian Descent. T **754** and similar horiz designs. Multicoloured. P 13×13½.

3250	5l. Type **755**	20	20
	a. Horiz strip of 4. Nos. 3250/3253	8·50	
3251	10l. Gjon Mili (photographer)	45	40
3252	20l. Koca Mi'mar Sinan Aga (Sinan) (Ottoman architect)	55	55
3253	200l. Ibrahim Kodra (artist)	7·00	6·75
3250/3253	Set of 4	7·50	7·00

Nos. 3250/3253 were issued in horizontal *se-tenant* strips of four stamps within the sheet.

756 Hand holding Quill   **757** Two Poppies

(Des B. Shijaku)

2008 (15 July). Europa. The Letter. T **756** and similar multicoloured designs. P 13½×13 (vert) or 13×13½ (horiz).

3254	100l. Type **756**	4·75	4·50
3255	150l. Hand holding quill writing Europa	6·50	6·25
MS3256	81×61 mm. 250l. Europa (*horiz*)	11·00	10·50

(Des G. Varfi)

2008 (30 July). Poppy (*Papaver rhoeas*). T **757** and similar vert design. Multicoloured. P 13½×13.

3257	50l. Type **757**	1·90	1·80
	a. Pair. Nos. 3257/3258	7·75	7·25
3258	150l. Poppy	5·50	5·25

Nos. 3257/3258 were issued in vertical *se-tenant* pairs within the sheet.

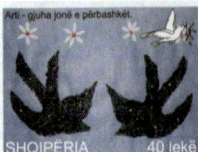

758 Swallows

2008 (1 Aug). Universal Language of Art. T **758** and similar horiz design. Multicoloured. P 13½.

3259	40l. Type **758**	1·90	1·80
	a. Pair. Nos. 3259/3260	5·25	5·00
3260	70l. Parachutists	3·25	3·00

Nos. 3259/3260 were issued in horizontal *se-tenant* pairs within the sheet.

759 Football

(Des B. Taçi)

2008 (8 Aug). Olympic Games, Beijing. T **759** and similar vert designs. Multicoloured. P 13½.

3261	20l. Type **759**	1·10	1·10
	a. Horiz strip of 4. Nos. 3261/3264	7·25	
3262	30l. Water polo	1·50	1·40
3263	40l. Athletics	1·90	1·80
3264	50l. Cycling	2·40	2·30
3261/3264	Set of 4	6·25	6·00

Nos. 3261/3264 were issued in horizontal *se-tenant* strips of four stamps within the sheet.

760 Osumi Canyons   **761** Ahmet Zogu

(Des S. Veseli)

2008 (25 Aug). Tourism. T **760** and similar vert design. Multicoloured. P 13×13½.

3265	60l. Type **760**	2·75	2·75
	a. Pair. Nos. 3265/3266	17·00	16·00
3266	250l. Komani Lake	13·00	12·50

Nos. 3265/3266 were issued in horizontal *se-tenant* pairs within the sheet.

(Des I. Martini)

2008 (1 Sept). 80th Anniversary of Coronation of King Ahmet Zogu. P 13×13½.

3267	**761**	40l. multicoloured	1·90	1·80
		a. Pair. Nos. 3267/3268	7·25	6·75
3268		100l. multicoloured	5·00	4·75

Nos. 3267/3268 were issued in horizontal *se-tenant* pairs within the sheet.

762 Azem Hajdari (politician)   **763** Ymer Prizreni

(Des Y. Beqiri)

2008 (12 Sept). Personalities. T **762** and similar vert design. Multicoloured. P 13½.
3269	40l. Type **762**	1·90	1·80
	a. Pair. Nos. 3269/3270	12·50	12·00
3270	200l. Adem Jashari (Kosovo nationalist)	10·00	9·75

Nos. 3269/3270 were issued in horizontal *se-tenant* pairs within the sheet.

2008 (20 Sept). Kosovo Nationalists. T **763** and similar vert designs. Multicoloured. P 13½.
3271	20l. Type **763**	95	90
	a. Block. Nos. 3271/3275 plus 4 labels	10·50	
3272	30l. Isa Boletini	1·50	1·40
3273	40l. Ibrahim Rugova	1·90	1·80
3274	50l. Azem Galica	2·40	2·30
3275	70l. Adem Jashari	3·25	3·25
3271/3275	Set of 5	9·00	8·75

Nos. 3271/3275 plus four labels were issued in *se-tenant* blocks of nine within the sheet, the stamps alternating with the labels giving a checkerboard effect.

764 Decius   **765** Harry Potter (Daniel Radcliffe) and Professor Dumbledore (Michael Gambon)

(Des H. Dhimo)

2008 (3 Oct). Roman Emperors of Illyrian Ancestry. T **764** and similar vert design. Multicoloured. P 13×13½.
3276	30l. Type **764**	1·50	1·40
	a. Pair. Nos. 3276/3277	12·00	11·50
3277	200l. Thrax	10·00	9·75

Nos. 3276/3277 were printed, *se-tenant* in pairs within the sheet.

(Des S. Taçi)

2008 (15 Oct). Youth Stamps. Harry Potter (character created by J. K. Rowling). T **765** and similar horiz designs showing Harry Potter and other characters. Multicoloured. P 13½.
3278	20l. Type **765**	95	90
	a. Block of 4. Nos. 3278/3281	12·50	
3279	30l. With Dobby	1·90	1·80
3280	50l. With Hermione (Emma Watson) and friends	2·75	2·75
3281	100l. With Voldemort (Ralph Fiennes)	6·50	6·25
3278/3281	Set of 4	11·00	10·50

Nos. 3278/3281 were issued in *se-tenant* blocks of four stamps within the sheet.

Nos. 3278/3281 were also available in booklet, sold for 550l.

766 Congress Buildings, Monastir, Macedonia   **767** Sinagogue, Saranda

(Des G. Varfi)

2008 (14 Nov). Centenary of Congress of Monastir (to decide on the use of Latin script for written Albanian). T **766** and similar horiz design. Multicoloured. P 13½.
3282	40l. Type **766**	2·00	1·90
	a. Pair. Nos. 3282/3283	7·25	7·00
3283	100l. Albanian script using Latin alphabet	5·00	4·75

Nos. 3282/3283 were issued in *se-tenant* blocks of four stamps within the sheet.

(Des S. Veseli)

2008 (5 Dec). Archaeological Excavations. T **767** and similar horiz designs. Multicoloured. P 13.
3284	10l. Type **767**	55	55
	a. Strip of 3. Nos. 3284/3286	8·00	
3285	50l. Orikum	3·25	3·25
3286	80l. Antigonea	4·00	3·75
3284/3286	Set of 3	7·00	6·75

Nos. 3284/3286 were printed, *se-tenant*, in horizontal strips of three stamps within the sheet.

767a Emblem   **767b** Laurel and Hardy

2009 (9 Oct). 135th Anniversary of Universal Postal Union. T **767a** and similar multicoloured designs. P 13×13½.
3286a	100l. Type **767a**	3·75	3·50
	ab. Pair. Nos. 3286a/3286b	11·50	11·00
3286b	200l. As Type **767a** (*vert*)	7·50	7·00

Nos. 3286a/3286b were printed, *se-tenant*, in pairs within the sheet.

(Des I. Martini)

2009 (16 Oct). Laurel and Hardy (Arthur Stanley Jefferson and Norvell Hardy) (comedians). T **767b** and similar multicoloured designs. P 13×13½.
3286c	100l. Type **767b**	5·50	5·25
	ca. Pair. Nos. 3286c/3286d	13·50	12·50
3286d	200l. Wearing bowler hats	7·50	7·00
MS3286e	80×60 mm. 300l. Type **767b**	11·00	10·50

768 Completed Lift   **769** Stylised Buildings

(Des Y. Beqiri)

2009 (21 Oct). Weightlifting. T **768** and similar vert designs. Multicoloured. P 13½.
3287	10l. Type **768**	55	55
	a. Block of 4. Nos. 3287/3290	13·00	
3288	60l. Jerk and lunge	2·20	2·10
3289	120l. Squatting with barbell at shoulder height	4·25	4·00
3290	150l. Squatting and grasping barbell	5·50	5·25
3287/3290	Set of 4	11·00	10·50

Nos. 3287/3290 were printed, *se-tenant*, in blocks of four stamps within the sheet.

(Des I Arapi)

2009 (30 Oct). 50th Anniversary of Court of Human Rights. P 13.
3291	**769**	200l. multicoloured	8·25	8·00

770 Flags as Map of Europe

(Des E Kaceli)

2009 (2 Nov). 60th Anniversary of Council of Europe. P 13.
3292	**770**	150l. multicoloured	6·50	6·25

ALBANIA 2009

771 Abidin Dino

(Des Y Beqiri)

2009 (11 Nov). Painters of the Diaspora. T **771** and similar horiz designs. Multicoloured. P 13.

3293	40l. Type **771**	1·30	1·20
	a. Block of 4. Nos. 3293/3296	9·75	
3294	50l. Lin Delija	1·60	1·50
3295	60l. Lika Janko	1·90	1·80
3296	150l. Artur Tashko	4·75	4·50
3293/3296	Set of 4	8·50	8·00

Nos. 3293/3296 were printed, *se-tenant*, in blocks of four stamps within the sheet.

772 Car and Traffic Controller

(Des N. Llukaçi)

2009 (16 Nov). Road Traffic Control. T **772** and similar horiz design. Multicoloured. P 13½×13.

3297	5l. Type **772**	15	15
	a. Pair. Nos. 3297/3298	33·00	32·00
3298	100l. Zebra crossing	32·00	31·00

Nos. 3297/3298 were printed, *se-tenant*, in horizontal pairs within the sheet.

773 Dove and Dragon

(Des B. Shijaku)

2009 (23 Nov). Albania–China Diplomatic Relations. P 13×13½.
| 3299 | **773** | 20l. multicoloured | 65 | 60 |

774 Choir   **775** Soldier and Arms

(Des N. Bakalli)

2009 (25 Nov). Albanian Folk Iso-Polyphony, UNESCO Oral and Intangible Cultural Heritage of Humanity (2005). T **774** and similar horiz design. Multicoloured. P 13½×13.

3300	40l. Type **775**	1·30	1·20
	a. Pair. Nos. 3300/3301	9·75	9·50
3301	250l. Musicians	8·25	8·00

Nos. 3300/3301 were printed, *se-tenant*, in horizontal pairs within the sheet.

(Des I Martini)

2009 (29 Nov). 60th Anniversary of Liberation. T **775** and similar horiz design. Multicoloured. P 13×13½.

3302	70l. Type **775**	2·20	2·10
	a. Pair. Nos. 3302/3303	9·00	8·50
3303	200l. Arms and aircraft	6·50	6·25

Nos. 3302/3303 were printed, *se-tenant*, in horizontal pairs within the sheet.

776 Mujit Dhe e Halili   **777** Mosque, Berat (1827)

(Des N. Bakalli)

2009 (5 Dec). Albanian Folklore. *Mujo and Halili* (epic poem). T **776** and similar vert design. Multicoloured. P 13×13½.

3304	30l. Type **776**	95	90
	a. Pair. Nos. 3304/3305	7·75	7·50
3305	200l. Couple on Horseback	6·50	6·25

Nos. 3304/3305 were printed, *se-tenant*, in horizontal pairs within the sheet.

(Des S. Vllahu)

2009 (9 Dec). Religious Art. T **777** and similar horiz designs. Multicoloured. P 13½×13.

3306	90l. Type **777**	3·00	2·75
	a. Horiz strip of 3. Nos. 3306/3308	10·50	
3307	100l. Fresco, Church of Mary and St Ristozit, Mborje, Korçë (1389)	3·25	3·00
3308	120l. Frescoes, Church of St Venerandes, Pllane-Lezhe Shek, 18th/19th-century	3·75	3·50
3306/3308	Set of 3	9·00	8·25

Nos. 3306/3308 were printed, *se-tenant*, in horizontal strips of three stamps within the sheet.

778 Satellite Receiver and Planets   **779** Fortress of Tirana

(Des S. Vllahu)

2009 (11 Dec). Europa. Astronomy. T **778** and similar horiz designs. Multicoloured. P 13½×13.

3309	200l. Type **778**	6·50	6·25
	a. Booklet pane. Nos. 3309/**MS**3311	16·00	15·00
3310	250l. Landing craft and vehicles on the moon	8·25	8·00
MS3311	80×60 mm. Size 30×24 mm. 350l. Satellite	11·50	11·00

(Des Y. Beqiri)

2009 (16 Dec). Archaeology. T **779** and similar vert design. Multicoloured. P 13½.

3312	30l. Type **779**	95	90
	a. Pair. Nos. 3312/3313	9·50	9·25
3313	250l. Artefacts, Tumulus of Kamenica	8·25	8·00

Nos. 3312/3313 were printed, *se-tenant*, in horizontal pairs within the sheet.

780 Rainy Beach

(Des I. Arapi)

2009 (21 Dec). National Theatre. T **780** and similar horiz designs. Multicoloured. P 13½×13.

3314	20l. Type **780**	65	60
	a. Strip of 3. Nos. 3314/3316	10·00	
3315	80l. *Pallati 176*	2·50	2·40

3316	200l. True Apology of Socrates (Apologjia e vertete e Sokratit)	6·50	6·25
3314/3316	Set of 3	8·75	8·25

Nos. 3314/3316 were printed, *se-tenant*, in horizontal strips of three stamps within the sheet.

781 Frontispiece of Book

(Des I. Martini)

2009 (28 Dec). 60th Anniversary of State Archives. T **781** and similar horiz design. Multicoloured. P 13½.

3317	40l. Type **781**	1·30	1·20
	a. Pair. Nos. 3317/3318	4·00	3·25
3318	60l. Roll of parchment	3·50	1·80

Nos. 3317/3318 were printed, *se-tenant*, in horizontal pairs within the sheet.

782 Emblems   **783** Mother Teresa

(Des G. Varfi)

2010 (12 Apr). Albania–Italy Friendship. P 13.

3319	**782** 40l. multicoloured	1·30	1·20

Stamps of a similar design were issued by Kosovo and Macedonia.

(Des Hyrije Ademi)

2010 (26 Aug). Birth Centenary of Agnes Gonxha Bojaxhiu (Mother Teresa) (founder of Missionaries of Charity). P 13.

3320	**783** 100l. multicoloured	3·25	3·00

Stamps of a similar design were issued by Kosovo and Macedonia.

784 Double-headed Eagle and European Stars   **785** Reading in Library

(Des Ministra e Integrimit (Integration Ministery))

2010 (8 Nov). Introduction of Visa-free Travel for Albanians in the EU. P 13×13½.

3321	**784** 40l. multicoloured	1·30	1·20

(Des N. Llukaçi)

2011 (18 Feb). 90th Anniversary of State Library. T **785** and similar design. Multicoloured. P 13×13½.

3322	10l. Type **785**	30	30
	a. Pair. Nos. 3322/3323	33·00	31·00
3323	100l. Using computer in library	32·00	30·00

Nos. 3322/3323 were printed, *se-tenant*, in horizontal pairs within the sheet, each pair forming a composite design.

786 Students   **787** Cockerel, Donkey and Sun

(Des E. Bulku)

2011 (20 Feb). 20th Anniversary of Student Unrest. T **786** and similar multicoloured designs. P 13.

3324	40l. Type **786**	1·30	1·20
	a. Pair. Nos. 3324/3325	3·50	3·25
3325	60l. Students protesting, rear view	1·90	1·80
MS3326	70×90 mm. 200l. Students making 'V' sign (vert)	6·75	6·50

Nos. 3324/3325 were printed, *se-tenant*, in pairs within the sheet.

(Des B. Shijaku)

2011 (25 Feb). Europa. Children's Books. T **787** and similar multicoloured designs. P 13×13½ (vert) or 13½×13 (horiz).

3327	100l. Type **787**	3·25	3·00
	a. Pair. Nos. 3327/3328	8·25	7·75
3328	150l. Girl, Pigeon and Cat	4·75	4·50
MS3329	80×60 mm. 250l. Girl with pile of books (horiz)	8·50	8·25

Nos. 3327/3328 were printed, *se-tenant*, in vertical pairs within the sheet.

788 Bull's Head   **789** Player

(Des E. Kaceli)

2011 (2 Mar). Underwater Archaeology. T **788** and similar horiz design. Multicoloured. P 13½×13.

3330	50l. Type **788**	1·60	1·50
	a. Pair. Nos. 3330/3331	10·00	9·75
3331	250l. Amphorae	8·25	8·00

Nos. 3330/3331 were printed, *se-tenant*, in horizontal pairs within the sheet.

(Des I. Martini)

2011 (10 Mar). World Cup Football Championships, South Africa. T **789** and similar vert designs. Multicoloured. P 13½×13.

3332	80l. Type **789**	2·50	2·40
	a. Pair. Nos. 3332/3333	6·50	6·25
3333	120l. Two players	3·75	3·50
MS3333a	60×80 mm. 200l. Two players (*different*)	6·75	6·50

Nos. 3332/3333 were printed, *se-tenant*, in horizontal pairs within the sheet.

790 Soldiers and Helicopter   **791** Handstamp

(Des R. Vrapi)

2011 (21 Mar). Albanian Peacekeepers. T **790** and similar horiz design. Multicoloured. P 13½×13.

3334	50l. Type **790**	1·60	1·50
	a. Pair. Nos. 3334/3335	8·25	8·00
3335	200l. Soldier, wearing beret, and tank	6·50	6·25

Nos. 3334/3335 were printed, *se-tenant*, in horizontal pairs within the sheet.

ALBANIA 2011

(Des G. Varfi)

2011 (23 Mar). 90th (2010) Anniversary of Congress of Lushnjë. T **791** and similar vert designs. Multicoloured. P 13½×13.

3336	70l. Type **791**	2·20	2·10
	a. Pair. Nos. 3336/3337	7·25	6·75
3337	150l. Building	4·75	4·50

Nos. 3336/3337 were printed, *se-tenant*, in horizontal pairs within the sheet.

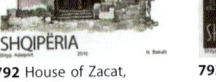

792 House of Zacat, Gjirokastër

793 Basket with Handle

(Des N. Bakalli)

2011 (31 Mar). National Day of Cultural Heritage. T **792** and similar vert designs. Multicoloured. P 13×13½.

3338	10l. Type **792**	30	30
	a. Strip of 4. Nos. 3338/3341	12·00	
3339	70l. Woven skirt from Dumre	2·20	2·10
3340	80l. Castle, Petrela	2·50	2·40
3341	120l. Lute, Shkodër	3·75	3·50
3338/3341	Set of 4	8·00	7·50

MS3341a 80×60 mm. 200l. Woman from Buzdrin, Zadrimë ... 6·75 6·50

Nos. 3338/3341 were printed, *se-tenant*, in horizontal strips of four stamps within the sheet.

(Des B. Shijaku)

2011 (6 Apr). Albanian Handicrafts. Silverwork. T **793** and similar square designs. Multicoloured. P 13.

3342	20l. Type **793**	65	60
	a. Block of 4. Nos. 3342/3345	6·75	
3343	30l. Evening bag	95	90
3344	50l. Butterfly	1·60	1·50
3345	100l. Closed cigarette case and holder	3·25	3·00
3342/3345	Set of 4	5·75	5·50

MS3346 80×60 mm. 200l. Open cigarette case and holder ... 6·75 6·50

Nos. 3342/3345 were printed, *se-tenant*, in blocks of four stamps within the sheet.

796 Tree containing Map of Europe

797 Two Boxers

(Des M. Delija)

2011 (30 July). Europa. Forests. T **796** and similar vert design. Multicoloured. P 13×13½.

3352	200l. Type **796**	6·50	6·25

MS3353 80×60 mm. 250l. As Type **796** but with colour change ... 8·50 8·25

(Des R. Vrapi)

2011 (26 Aug). Boxing. T **797** and similar horiz designs. Multicoloured. P 13½×13.

3354	50l. Type **797**	1·60	1·50
	a. Pair. Nos. 3354/3355	5·00	4·75
3355	100l. Two boxers (*different*)	3·25	3·00

MS3356 80×60 mm. 250l. Boxer wearing blue with raised fist ... 8·50 8·25

Nos. 3354/3355 were printed, *se-tenant*, in horizontal pairs within the sheet.

798 Ballot Box

799 Ismail Kadare

(Des G. Varfi)

2011 (1 Sept). 20th Anniversary of First Free Elections. P 13×13½.

3357	**798**	150l. multicoloured	4·75	4·50

(Des M. Delija)

2011 (12 Sept). 75th Birth Anniversary of Ismail Kadare. P 13.

3358	**799**	40l. multicoloured	1·30	1·20

800 Wooded Valley and River

(Des L. Kraja)

2011 (27 Sept). Tourism. Valbona River. T **800** and similar horiz design. Multicoloured. P 13.

3359	80l. Type **800**	2·50	2·40
	a. Pair. Nos. 3359/3360	6·50	6·25
3360	120l. Boulders in river	3·75	3·50

Nos. 3359/3360 were printed, *se-tenant*, in horizontal pairs within the sheet.

794 Roadway and Plan of Junction

795 House with Balcony

(Des G. Panariti)

2011 (11 Apr). Upgrade of Durrës to Kukës Road. T **794** and similar horiz designs. Multicoloured. P 13×13½.

3347	40l. Type **794**	1·30	1·20
	a. Block of 4. Nos. 3347/3350	11·50	
3348	60l. Roadworks and plan of roundabout	1·90	1·80
3349	90l. Tunnel and plan of junction	3·00	2·75
3350	150l. Viaduct and plan	4·75	4·50
3347/3350	Set of 4	9·75	9·25

Nos. 3347/3350 were printed, *se-tenant*, in blocks of four stamps within the sheet.

(Des A. Gjonaj)

2011 (14 Apr). World Heritage Sites. Berat. Sheet 165×113 mm containing T **795** and similar horiz designs. Each black and scarlet-vermilion. P 13×13½.

MS3351 Type **795**; 20l. Hillside houses facing left; 30l. Bridge; 50l. Archway and gated courtyard; 60l. Hillside houses facing right; 80l. Church in castle grounds ... 8·50 8·25

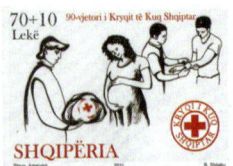

801 Worker holding Red Cross Parcel, Expectant Mother and Worker binding Injured Arm

(Des B. Shijaku)

2011 (4 Oct). 90th Anniversary of Albanian Red Cross. T **801** and similar horiz design. Each black and carmine-vermilion. P 13.
3361	70l. +10l. Type **801**		2·50	2·40
	a. Pair. Nos. 3361/3362		6·50	6·25
3362	120l. Giving and receiving aid		3·75	3·50

Nos. 3361/3362 were printed, *se-tenant*, in horizontal pairs within the sheet.

802 Pigeon wearing Helmet with Goggles and carrying Mail Bag and Globe

(Des M. Delija)

2011 (9 Oct). Stamp Day. Carrier Pigeons. T **802** and similar square design. Multicoloured. P 13.
3363	10l. Type **802**		30	30
	a. Pair. Nos. 3363/3364		33·00	31·00
3364	1000l. Globe and Pigeon (blue background)		32·00	30·00

Nos. 3363/3364 were printed, *se-tenant*, in horizontal pairs within the sheet, each pair forming a composite design.

803 Mosaic, St Michael's Basilica, Arapaj

804 Cities of the Adriatic

(Des Mikel Temo)

2011 (14 Oct). Early Christian Mosaics in Albania. T **803** and similar vert designs showing details of mosaics. Multicoloured. P 13×13½.
3365	20l. Type **803**		65	60
	a. Strip of 3. Nos. 3365/3367		6·50	
3366	60l. Church, Antigone		1·90	1·80
3367	120l. Mesaplikut Basilica		3·75	3·50
3365/3367	Set of 3		5·75	5·25

Nos. 3365/3367 were printed, *se-tenant*, in horizontal strips of three stamps within the sheet.

(Des Albanian Post)

2011 (18 Nov). Forum of Adriatic Cities. P 13.
3368	**804**	90l. multicoloured	3·00	2·75

805 Gymnospermium shqipetarum

806 Symbols of the Arts

(Des Rudina Memaga)

2011 (5 Dec). Albanian Flora. T **805** and similar vert designs. Multicoloured. P 13.
3369	30l. Type **805**		95	90
	a. Strip of 3. Nos. 3369/3371		6·75	
3370	70l. *Viola kosaninii*		2·20	2·10
3371	100l. *Aster albanicus*		3·25	3·00
3369/3371	Set of 3		5·75	5·50

Nos. 3369/3371 were printed, *se-tenant*, in horizontal strips of three stamps within the sheet.

(Des Migailed Delija)

2011 (15 Dec). 45th Anniversary of Academy of Arts. P 13.
3372	**806**	250l. multicoloured	8·25	8·00

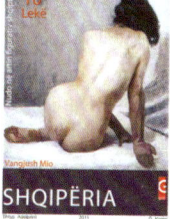

807 Nude (Vangjush Mio)

808 '20' and Dove

(Des Salim Korini)

2011 (22 Dec). Albanian Figurative Art. T **807** and similar vert designs. Multicoloured. P 13×13½.
3373	10l. Type **807**		30	30
	a. Strip of 3. Nos. 3373/3375		5·75	
3374	90l. Standing nude (Abdurrahim Buza)		1·90	1·80
3375	100l. Nude bust (sculpture) (Janaq Paço)		3·25	3·00
3373/3375	Set of 3		5·00	4·50
MS3376	90×70 mm. 250l. As No. 3375 (close up) (34×44 *mm*)		8·50	8·25

Nos. 3373/3375 were printed, *se-tenant*, in horizontal strips of three stamps within the sheet.

(Des Entela Qasemi)

2012 (22 Mar). 20th Anniversary of Democracy in Albania. P 13.
3377	**808**	100l. multicoloured	3·25	3·00

809 Towers and Castle

810 Flags of Poland and Competing Nations

(Des E. Veveçka)

2012 (21 Sept). Europa. Visit Albania. T **809** and similar horiz design. Multicoloured. P 13×13½.
3378	30l. Type **809**		95	90
	a. Pair. Nos. 3378/3379		9·50	9·25
3379	250l. Hillside towns		8·25	8·00

Nos. 3378/3379 were printed, *se-tenant*, in horizontal pairs within the sheet.

(Des S. Taçi)

2012 (28 Sept). Euro 2012 Football Championships, Poland and Ukraine. T **810** and similar square design. Multicoloured. P 13.
3380	100l. Type **810**		3·25	3·00
	a. Pair. Nos. 3380/3381		10·00	9·50
3381	200l. Flags of Ukraine and competing countries		6·50	6·25

Nos. 3380/3381 were printed, *se-tenant*, in horizontal pairs within the sheet, each pair forming a composite design.

811 Kin Dushi

812 Anniversary Emblem

(Des G. Gjikopulli)

2012 (3 Oct). 90th Birth Anniversary of Kin Dushi (writer). P 13×13½.
3382	**811**	150l. multicoloured	4·75	4·50

(Des L. Kraja)

2012 (9 Oct). 90th Anniversary of Albania in the UPU. P 13½×13.
3383 812 250l. multicoloured .... 8·25 8·00

817 Emblem

818 Ismail Qemali (First head of state) and Leaders

813 Partisans

(Des Bertrand Shijaku)

2012 (19 Oct). Centenary of Albanian General Insurrection. T **813** and similar horiz design. Multicoloured. P 13.
3384 10l. Type **813** 30 30
   a. Pair. Nos. 3384/3385 .... 33·00 31·00
3385 100l. Partisans (different) .... 32·00 30·00
Nos. 3384/3385 were printed, se-tenant, in horizontal pairs within the sheet.

(Des Zeni Ballazhi)

2012 (23 Nov). Centenary of Independence. P 13½×13.
3394 817 40l. black and scarlet .... 1·30 1·20

(Des Naji Bakalli)

2012 (28 Nov). Centenary of Proclamation of Independence. T **818** and similar vert designs. Multicoloured. P 13×13½.
3395 50l. Type **818** .... 1·60 1·50
   a. Booklet pane. Nos. 3395/3398 .... 9·25
3396 60l. Kissing National Flag and march .... 1·90 1·80
3397 70l. Flags and UN building .... 2·20 2·10
3398 100l. NATO statue and flags .... 3·25 3·00
3395/3398 Set of 4 .... 8·00 7·50

814 Rock Art

819 Early Fighters

820 Telephone, Envelopes and Wires

(Des Spiro Vllahu)

2012 (29 Oct). Rock Art in Albania. Sheet 87×136 mm containing T **814** and similar horiz designs. Multicoloured. P 13.
MS3386 20l. Type **814**; 60l. Rock art (dark green background); 150l. Rock art (pale grey green background) .... 7·50 7·25

(Des Joy Panariti)

2012 (4 Dec). Centenary of Albanian Army. T **819** and similar horiz design. Multicoloured. P 13×13½.
3399 90l. Type **819** .... 3·00 2·75
   a. Pair. Nos. 3399/3400 .... 8·00 7·50
3400 150l. Modern soldiers .... 4·75 4·50
Nos. 3399/3400 were printed, se-tenant, in horizontal pairs within the sheet.

(Des Bertrand Shijaku)

2012 (5 Dec). Centenary of Albanian Post, Telegraph and Telephones. T **820** and similar horiz design. Multicoloured. P 13×13½.
3401 80l. Type **820** .... 2·50 2·40
   a. Pair. Nos. 3401/3402 .... 9·25 9·00
   b. Booklet pane. Nos. 3401/3402, plus two labels .... 9·25
3402 200l. Handset, letter and wires .... 6·50 6·25
Nos. 3401/3402 were printed, se-tenant, in horizontal pairs within the sheet.

815 Eric Hamp (English)

816 Tropojë

(Des Naji Bakalli)

2012 (16 Nov). Albanologists. T **815** and similar horiz designs. Multicoloured. P 13.
3387 50l. Type **815** .... 1·60 1·50
   a. Strip of 3. Nos. 3387/3389 .... 6·00
3388 60l. Norbert Jokl (Austrian) .... 1·90 1·80
3389 70l. Holger Pedersen (Danish) .... 2·20 2·10
3387/3389 Set of 3 .... 5·25 4·75
Nos. 3387/3389 were printed, se-tenant, in horizontal strips of three stamps within the sheet.

(Des Naji Bakalli)

2012 (23 Nov). Dances. T **816** and similar vert designs. Multicoloured. P 13×13½.
3390 20l. Type **816** 65 60
   a. Strip of 4. Nos. 3390/3393 .... 11·00
3391 40l. Tiranë .... 1·30 1·20
3392 120l. Çamëri .... 3·75 3·50
3393 150l. Lushnjë .... 4·75 4·50
3390/3393 Set of 4 .... 9·50 8·75
Nos. 3390/3393 were printed, se-tenant, in horizontal strips of four stamps within the sheet.

821 Diver and *Posidonia oceanica*

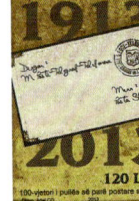
822 Early Envelope

(Des Spiro Vllahu)

2012 (14 Dec). Undersea Flora. *Posidonia oceanica*. T **821** and similar horiz design. Multicoloured. P 13×13½.
3403 10l. Type **821** 30 30
   a. Pair. Nos. 3403/3404 .... 8·75 8·50
3404 250l. *Posidonia oceanica* undersea and fibrous ball on beach .... 8·25 8·00
Nos. 3403/3404 were printed, se-tenant, in horizontal pairs within the sheet.

(Des Laert Kraja)

2013 (5 May). Centenary of First Albanian Stamp. T **822** and similar vert design. Multicoloured. P 12×14.
3405	120l. Type **822**	3·75	3·50
	a. Pair. Nos. 3405/3406	8·75	8·25
3406	150l. Reverse of envelope	4·75	4·50

Nos. 3405/3406 were printed, *se-tenant*, in horizontal pairs within the sheet.

823 Runner

824 Vedas Kokonës

(Des Gentjan Gjikopulli)

2013 (27 Aug). IAAF World Athletics Championships, Moscow. T **823** and similar vert designs. Multicoloured. P 12×14.
3407	30l. Type **823**	95	90
	a. Pair. Nos. 3407/3408	7·75	7·50
3408	200l. High jumper	6·50	6·25
MS3409	90×70 mm. 250l. Pole vaulter	8·50	8·25

Nos. 3407/3408 were printed, *se-tenant*, in horizontal pairs within the sheet.

(Des E. Bulku)

2013 (30 Aug). Birth Centenary of Vedas Kokonës (literary critic). P 13.
3410	**824** 150l. multicoloured	4·75	4·50

825 Post Van and Lorry

826 Female Police Officer

(Des L. Kraja)

2013 (4 Oct). Europa. Postal Vehicles. T **825** and similar vert designs. Multicoloured. P 13.
3411	80l. Type **825**	2·50	2·40
	a. Pair. Nos. 3411/3412	9·25	9·00
3412	200l. Ship and train	6·50	6·25
MS3413	70×50 mm. 280l. As Nos 3411/3412	9·25	9·00

Nos. 3411/3412 were printed, *se-tenant*, in horizontal pairs within the sheet, each pair forming a composite design.

No. MS3413 was issued enclosed in a folder.

(Des Gentjan Gjikopulli)

2013 (18 Oct). Centenary of Albanian Police Force. T **826** and similar vert design. Multicoloured. P 13.
3414	10l. Type **826**	30	30
	a. Pair. Nos. 3414/3415	8·75	8·50
3415	250l. Male police officer	8·25	8·00

Nos. 3414/3415 were printed, *se-tenant*, in horizontal pairs within the sheet.

827 Seilla albanica

828 Swimmers

(Des Bertrand Shijaku)

2013 (30 Oct). Albanian Flora. T **827** and similar vert designs. Multicoloured. P 13.
3416	20l. Type **827**	65	60
	a. Strip of 3. Nos. 3416/3418	8·75	
3417	90l. *Gymnospermium maloi*	3·00	2·75
3418	150l. *Tulipa albanica*	4·75	4·50
3416/3418	Set of 3	7·50	7·00

Nos. 3416/3418 were printed, *se-tenant*, in horizontal strips of three stamps within the sheet.

(Des Bertrand Shijaku)

2013 (6 Nov). Mediterranean Games, Mersin, Turkey. T **828** and similar multicoloured designs. P 13.
3419	90l. Type **828**	3·00	2·75
	a. Pair. Nos. 3419/3420	8·00	7·50
3420	150l. Athletes	4·75	4·50
MS3421	80×60 mm. 200l. Rowing (*horiz*)	6·75	6·50

Nos. 3419/3420 were printed, *se-tenant*, in horizontal pairs within the sheet.

829 Helping the Elderly

(Des Bertrand Shijaku)

2013 (15 Nov). 150th Anniversary of Red Cross. T **829** and similar horiz designs. Multicoloured. P 13.
3422	40l. Type **829**	1·30	1·20
	a. Pair. Nos. 3422/3423	6·25	6·00
3423	150l. Delivering aid	4·75	4·50
MS3424	80×60 mm. 250l. Treating accident victim	8·50	8·25

Nos. 3422/3423 were printed, *se-tenant*, in horizontal pairs within the sheet.

830 Milan Šufflay (Croatia)

(Des Naji Bakalli)

2013 (25 Nov). Albanologists. T **830** and similar horiz designs. Multicoloured. P 13.
3425	10l. Type **830**	30	30
	a. Strip of 3. Nos. 3425/3426	8·50	
3426	100l. Konstantin Jirecek (Czechoslovakia)	3·25	3·00
3427	150l. Ludwig von Thallòczy (Slovakia)	4·75	4·50
3425/3427	Set of 3	7·50	7·00

Nos. 3425/3427 were printed, *se-tenant*, in horizontal strips of three stamps within the sheet.

831 Bronze Foot (2nd/3rd-century)

832 Nikolla Naço

(Des Bertrand Shijaku)

2013 (6 Dec). New Archaeological Discoveries at Apollonia. T **831** and similar horiz designs. Multicoloured. P 13.
3428	20l. Type **831**	65	60
	a. Strip of 4. Nos. 3428/3431	11·00	
3429	90l. Bronze Horse-shaped fibula (7th/8th-century)	3·00	2·75
3430	100l. Marble bust (2nd-century)	3·25	3·00
3431	120l. Relief (2nd-century)	3·75	3·50
3428/3431	Set of 4	9·50	8·75

Nos. 3428/3431 were printed, *se-tenant*, in horizontal strips of four stamps within the sheet.

ALBANIA 2013

(Des Y. Beqiri)

2013 (18 Dec). Death Centenary of Nikolla Naço (nationalist). P 13.
3432   832   200l. multicoloured .... 6·50   6·25

833 Fuleco

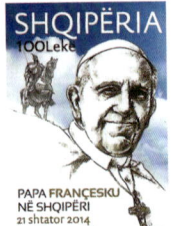
834 Pope Francis

(Des Bertrand Shijaku)

2014 (9 July). World Cup Football Championships, Brazil. T **833** and similar horiz designs showing Fuleco (championship mascot). Multicoloured. P 13.

3433	10l. Type **833**	30	30
	a. Strip of 3. Nos. 3433/3435	5·50	
3434	50l. Holding ball	1·60	1·50
3435	100l. Dribbling ball	3·25	3·00
3433/3435 Set of 3		4·75	4·25
MS3436 80×60 mm. 140l. Emblem		4·75	4·50

Nos. 3433/3435 were printed, *se-tenant*, in horizontal strips of three stamps within the sheet.

(Des Petraq Papa)

2014 (21 Sept). Pope Francis' Visit to Albania. P 13.
3437   834   100l. multicoloured .... 3·25   3·00

835 Gajdja (bagpipes)

836 The Assembly

(Des L. Kraja)

2014 (4 Oct). Europa. Musical Instruments. T **835** and similar vert designs. P 13.

3438	100l. Type **835**	3·25	3·00
	a. Pair. Nos. 3438/3439	8·25	7·75
3439	150l. Lodra (drum)	4·75	4·50
MS3440 116×67 mm. 250l. As Nos 3438/3439, plus central label		8·50	8·25

Nos. 3438/3439 were printed, *se-tenant*, in horizontal pairs within the sheet.

No. **MS**3440 was issued enclosed in a folder.

(Des Naji Bakalli)

2014 (14 Oct). 400th Anniversary of Assembly of Kuçi. T **836** and similar vert designs. Multicoloured. P 13.

3441	80l. Type **836**	2·50	2·40
	a. Pair. Nos. 3441/3442	7·50	7·25
3442	150l. Seated around Prince Andrija	4·75	4·50
MS3443 70×90 mm. 200l. Prince Andrija		6·75	6·50

Nos. 3441/3442 were printed, *se-tenant*, in horizontal pairs within the sheet.

(Des Gentjan Gjikopulli)

2014 (11 Nov). Albania–Kuwait Friendship. Sheet 108×55 mm containing T **837** and similar horiz design. Multicoloured. P 13.
MS3444   100l.×2, Type **837**; Flags of Albania and Kuwait and clasped hands .... 6·75   6·50

(Des Bertrand Shijaku)

2014 (18 Nov). 130th Birth Anniversary of Sulejman Pashë Delvinës (politician). P 13.
3445   838   150l. multicoloured .... 4·75   4·50

839 *Caretta caretta* (Loggerhead Turtle)

840 Princess Sophie of Schönburg-Waldenburg

(Des B. Shijaku)

2014 (22 Nov). Albanian Fauna. Amphibians. T **839** and similar square design. Multicoloured. P 13.

3446	80l. Type **839**	2·50	2·40
	a. Pair. Nos. 3446/3447	8·25	7·75
3447	170l. *Hyla arborea* (European Tree Frog)	5·50	5·00

Nos. 3446/3447 were printed, *se-tenant*, in horizontal pairs within the sheet.

(Des Xhoan Guga)

2014 (26 Nov). Centenary of the Monarchy. Prince Vidi (Prince William of Wied, Prince of Albania) Commemoration. Sheet 160×98 mm containing T **840** and similar vert designs. Gold and scarlet. P 13.
MS3448   60l. Type **840**; 70l. Arms; 80l. Badge; 90l. Prince Vidi .... 9·75   9·25

841 Anniversary Emblem

842 Artemis Bendis

(Des Petraq Papa)

2014 (29 Nov). 70th Anniversary of Albanian Liberation. P 13.
3449   841   40l. multicoloured .... 1·30   1·20

(Des Petraq Papa)

2014 (5 Dec). Archaeology. Artemis of Dyrrachion. T **842** and similar vert designs. Multicoloured. P 13.

3450	50l. Type **842**	1·60	1·50
	a. Strip of 4. Nos. 3450/3453	9·00	
3451	60l. Female bust	1·90	1·80
3452	70l. Female head	2·20	2·10
3453	90l. Statue of Artemis	3·00	2·75
3450/3453 Set of 4		7·75	7·25

Nos. 3450/3453 were printed, *se-tenant*, in horizontal strips of four stamps within the sheet.

837 Sabah IV Ahmad Al-Jaber Al-Sabah

838 Sulejman Pashë Delvinës

843 Flag and EU Stars

844 William Shakespeare

(Des Entela Kasemi)

2014 (8 Dec). Albanian Candidacy for Accession to EU. P 13.
3454　**843**　40l. multicoloured .... 1·30　1·20

(Des Entela Kasemi)

2014 (12 Dec). 450th Birth Anniversary of William Shakespeare. P 13.
3455　**844**　150l. multicoloured .... 4·75　4·50

845 Chair

(Des Gentjan Gjikopulli)

2014 (19 Dec). Albanian Handicrafts. Woodwork. T **845** and similar square designs. Multicoloured. P 13.
3456　40l. Type **845** .... 1·30　1·20
　　　a. Block of 4. Nos. 3456/3459 .... 7·25
3457　50l. Cradle .... 1·60　1·50
3458　60l. Shepherd's crook .... 1·90　1·80
3459　70l. Wooden spoons .... 2·20　2·10
3456/3459　Set of 4 .... 6·25　6·00
MS3460　90×70 mm. 180l. Stylised Lion, part of
　　wooden ceiling .... 6·00　5·75
　Nos. 3456/3459 were printed, *se-tenant*, in blocks of four stamps within the sheet.

846 St Mary's Church ('Kisha e
Shën Mërisë'), Himarë

(Des Laert Kraja)

2014 (24 Dec). Museum Exhibits. Frescoes ('Iconostasis in masonry'). Two sheets containing T **846** and similar horiz designs. Multicoloured. P 13.
MS3461　170×100 mm. 10l. Type **846**; 30l. Church of the Monastery of Saint Mary ('Kisha e Manastirit të Shën Mërisë), Dhërmi; 40l. Hypapante Church ('Kisha e Ipapandisë'), Dhërmi; 70l. Church of St Michael ('Kisha e Shën Mëhillit'); 90l. St George Monastery ('Manastiri i Shën Gjergjit'); 100l. Church of St Spiridon ('Kisha e Shën Spiridhonit') .... 11·00　10·50
MS3462　110×150 mm. 10l. As Type **846**; 30l. Church of the Monastery of Saint Mary ('Kisha e Manastirit të Shën Mërisë), Dhërmi; 40l. Hypapante Church ('Kisha e Ipapandisë'), Dhërmi; 70l. Church of St Michael ('Kisha e Shën Mëhillit'); 90l. St George Monastery ('Manastiri i Shën Gjergjit'); 100l. Church of St Spiridon ('Kisha e Shën Spiridhonit') .... 11·00　10·50
　No. MS3461 has white margins and No. MS3462 has illustrated margins and is cut around in an arched shape and was sold in a folder.

847 Elez Isufi　　**848** Teddy and Roll-along Horse

(Des Petraq Papa)

2014 (29 Dec). 90th Death Anniversary of Elez Isufi (nationalist and guerrilla fighter). P 13.
3463　**847**　1000l. multicoloured .... 32·00　30·00

(Des Petraq Papa)

2015 (2 Sept). Europa. Old Toys. T **848** and similar vert design. P 13×13½.
3464　130l. Type **848** .... 4·25　4·00
MS3465　80×60 mm. 250l. As Type **848** .... 8·50　8·25
MS3466　150×80 mm. 130l. As Type **848**; 250l. As stamp of MS3465 .... 12·50　12·00
　No. MS3466 has a grey background around an image as No. MS3465 and T **848**, and was issued in a folder.

849 Waterfall, Shebenik-Jabllanice National Park

(Des Artion Baboçi)

2015 (16 Sept). Tourism. National Parks. T **849** and similar horiz designs. Multicoloured. P 13.
3467　50l. Type **849** .... 1·60　1·50
　　　a. Strip of 3. Nos. 3467/3469 .... 9·75
3468　100l. Fir of Hotovë-Dangelli National Park ('Parku Kombëtar Bredhi i Hotovës-Dangëlli') .... 3·25　3·00
3469　150l. Inscr 'Parku i Dajtit' .... 4·75　4·50
3467/3469　Set of 3 .... 8·75　8·00
　Nos. 3467/3469 were printed, *se-tenant*, in horizontal strips of three stamps within the sheet.

850 *Newcastle* and Richard Trevithick

(Des Artion Baboçi)

2015 (27 Sept). 190th Anniversary of First Locomotive. T **850** and similar horiz designs. Multicoloured. P 13.
3470　50l. Type **850** .... 1·60　1·50
　　　a. Block of 4. Nos. 3470/3473 .... 10·00
3471　60l. *Salamanca* and Matthew Murray .... 1·90　1·80
3472　90l. *Rocket* and Robert Stephenson .... 3·00　2·75
3473　100l. *Locomotion* and George Stephenson .... 3·25　3·00
3470/3473　Set of 4 .... 8·75　8·25
　Nos. 3470/3473 were printed, *se-tenant*, in blocks of four stamps within the sheet.

851 Dhimitër Shuteriqi　　**852** Player and Ball

(Des Erion Kaceli)

2015 (28 Sept). National Personalities. T **851** and similar horiz designs. Each brownish black and pale olive-bistre. P 13.
3474　40l. Type **851** (writer) .... 1·30　1·20
　　　a. Block of 4. Nos. 3474/3477 .... 8·00
3475　50l. Zef Skiroi (Giuseppe Schirò) (writer) .... 1·60　1·50
3476　60l. Mahir Domi (linguist) .... 1·90　1·80
3477　100l. Gaqo Avrazi (orchestra and choir leader) .... 3·00　2·75
3474/3477　Set of 4 .... 7·00　6·50
　Nos. 3474/3477 were printed, *se-tenant*, in blocks of four stamps within the sheet.

ALBANIA 2015

(Des Erion Kaceli)

2015 (8 Oct). 85th Anniversary of Albanian Football Federation. T **852** and similar vert designs. Multicoloured. P 13.

3478	5l. Type **852**	15	15
	a. Strip of 3. Nos. 3478/3480	33·00	
3479	10l. Emblem	30	30
3480	1000l. Ball and player making overhead kick	32·00	30·00
3478/3480	Set of 3	29·00	27·00

Nos. 3478/3480 were printed, *se-tenant*, in horizontal strips of three stamps, each strip forming a composite design.

853 Joseph Nicéphore Niépce

854 Anniversary Emblem

(Des Llazar Taçi)

2015 (9 Oct). International Personalites. T **853** and similar vert designs. Multicoloured. P 13.

3481	10l. Type **853** (photographic pioneer)	30	30
	a. Strip of 4. Nos. 3481/3484	8·25	
3482	60l. Carl Ludwig Patsch (archaeologist)	1·90	1·80
3483	80l. Boris Pasternak (writer)	2·50	2·40
3484	100l. Norman Wisdom (comic actor)	3·25	3·00
3481/3484	Set of 4	7·25	6·75

Nos. 3481/3484 were printed, *se-tenant*, in horizontal strips of four stamps within the sheet.

(Des Spiro Vllahu)

2015 (24 Oct). 70th Anniversary of United Nations. P 13.

3485	**854**	180l. multicoloured	5·75	5·50

855 Jug and Vase

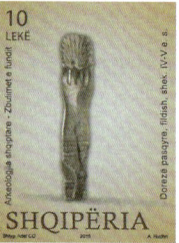
856 Ivory Mirror Handle

(Des Artion Baboçi)

2015 (6 Nov). Albanian Handicrafts. Ceramics. T **855** and similar square designs. Multicoloured. P 13.

3486	50l. Type **855**	1·60	1·50
	a. Block of 4. Nos. 3486/3489	9·75	
3487	60l. Long-necked two-handled vessel and shorter, wider vessel	1·90	1·80
3488	70l. Collection of pots and figurine	2·20	2·10
3489	120l. Jug and smaller two-handled vessel	3·75	3·50
3486/3489	Set of 4	8·50	8·00
MS3490	70×90 mm. 200l. Collection of pots and platter	6·75	6·50

Nos. 3486/3489 were printed, *se-tenant*, in blocks of four stamps within the sheet.

(Des Alban Hudhri)

2015 (18 Nov). Archaeology. Recent Discoveries. T **856** and similar vert designs. Multicoloured. P 13.

3491	10l. Type **856**	30	30
	a. Block of 4. Nos. 3491/3494	8·25	
3492	30l. Marble figure minus head	95	90
3493	60l. Dear-shaped bronze handle	1·90	1·80
3494	150l. Hermes statue	4·75	4·50
3491/3494	Set of 4	7·00	6·75

Nos. 3491/3494 were printed, *se-tenant*, in horizontal strips of four stamps within the sheet.

857 Anniversary Emblem

858 *Sabella spallanzanii*

(Des Stefan Taçi)

2015 (5 Dec). 150th Anniversary of ITU. P 13.

3495	**857**	2500l. multicoloured	80·00	75·00

(Des Petraq Papa)

2015 (23 Dec). Marine Life. T **858** and similar vert designs. Multicoloured. P 13.

3496	5l. Type **858**	15	15
	a. Pair. Nos. 3496/3497	5·25	5·00
3497	150l. *Antedon mediterranea*	4·75	4·50
MS3498	60×80 mm. 250l. *Cotylorhiza tuberculata*	8·50	8·25

Nos. 3496/3497 were printed, *se-tenant*, in horizontal pairs within the sheet.

859 Emblem and Player

860 Roller painting Contaminated Landscape Green

(Des Petraq Papa)

2016 (10 June). UEFA European Football Championship 2016, France. T **859** and similar horiz design. Multicoloured. P 13.

3499	70l. Type **859**	2·20	2·10
	a. Pair. Nos. 3499/3500	5·75	5·25
3500	100l. Player, left and emblem	3·25	3·00

Nos. 3499/3500 were printed, *se-tenant*, in horizontal pairs within the sheet, each pair forming a composite design.

(Des Doxia Sergidou)

2016 (9 July). Europa. Think Green. P 13.

3501	**860**	200l. multicoloured	6·50	6·25

861 *Tulipa kosovarica*

862 Symbols of the Exhibition

(Des S. Muraku)

2016 (27 July). Albanian Flora. T **861** and similar vert designs. Multicoloured. P 13.

3502	20l. Type **861**	65	60
	a. Strip of 3. Nos. 3502/3504	7·75	
3503	30l. *Campanula comosiformis*	95	90
3504	190l. *Solenanthus albanicus*	6·00	5·75
3502/3504	Set of 3	6·75	6·50

Nos. 3502/3504 were printed, *se-tenant*, in horizontal strips of three stamps within the sheet.

(Des Artion Baboçi)

2016 (9 Aug). Balkanphila 2016. National Stamp Exhibition. P 13.

3505	**862**	250l. multicoloured	8·25	8·00

2016 ALBANIA

863 Ndre Mjeda   **864** Emblem

(Des Gentjan Gjikopulli)

2016 (17 Aug). National Personalities. T **863** and similar vert designs. Sepia and pale olive-bistre. P 13.

3506	10l. Type **863** (priest, philologist, poet and an activist of Albanian national awakening)	30	30
	a. Strip of 3. Nos. 3506/3508	7·00	
3507	50l. Kolë Jakova (writer)	1·60	1·50
3508	150l. Jusuf Vrioni (translator, diplomat, and Albanian ambassador to UNESCO)	4·75	4·50
3506/3508	Set of 3	6·00	5·75

Nos. 3506/3508 were printed, *se-tenant*, in strips of three stamps within the sheet.

(Des Laert Kraja)

2016 (29 Aug). Albanian Membership of Human Rights Council. P 13.

3509	**864** 1000l. multicoloured	32·00	30·00

865 Books   **866** Mother Teresa's Robe

(Des Artion Baboçi)

2016 (1 Sept). Centenary of Albanian Literary Commission. P 13.

3510	**865** 60l. multicoloured	1·90	1·80

(Des Gentjan Gjikopulli)

2016 (4 Sept). Sanctification of Mother Teresa (Agnes Gonxhe Bojaxhiu). P 13½.

3511	**866** 120l. multicoloured	3·75	3·50
MS3512	60×80 mm. 120l. As Type **866**	4·00	3·75

867 Pierced Bowl   **868** Cervantes

(Des Xhoan Guga)

2016 (27 Sept). Albanian Handicrafts. Works in Stone. T **867** and similar square designs. Multicoloured. P 13.

3513	10l. Type **867**	30	30
	a. Block of 4. Nos. 3513/3516	13·50	
3514	80l. Pierced lidded pot	2·50	2·40
3515	130l. Pierced vase	4·25	4·00
3516	180l. Leaf-shaped dish	5·75	5·50
3513/3516	Set of 4	11·50	11·00
MS3517	80×60 mm. 250l. Inscised lidded pot (detail)	8·50	8·25

Nos. 3513/3516 were printed, *se-tenant*, in blocks of four stamps within the sheet.

(Des Llazar Taçi)

2016 (9 Oct). 400th Death Anniversary of Miguel de Cervantes. T **868** and similar multicoloured design. P 13½.

3518	140l. Type **868**	4·50	4·25
MS3519	80×60 mm. 200l. Don Quixote and Sancho Panza (*vert*)	6·75	6·50

869 Dritëro Agolli   **870** Themistokli Gërmenji (Chief of Police)

(Des Petraq Papa)

2016 (13 Oct). 85th Birth Anniversary of Dritëro Agolli (writer and politician). P 13½.

3520	**869** 120l. grey and olive-bistre	3·75	3·50

(Des Artion Baboçi)

2016 (10 Dec). Centenary of Korçë Region. T **870** and similar horiz design. Multicoloured. P 13½.

3521	5l. Type **870**	15	15
	a. Pair. Nos. 3521/3532	85·00	80·00
3522	2500l. Assembly	80·00	75·00

Nos. 3521/3532 were printed, *se-tenant*, in horizontal pairs within the sheet.

871 Ajuga piskoi   **872** Castle

(Des Petraq Papa)

2017 (1 Nov). Albanian Flora. T **071** and similar vert design. Multicoloured. P 13.

3523	150l. Type **871**	4·75	4·50
	a. Pair. Nos. 3523/3524	13·50	13·00
3524	250l. *Vaccinium myrtillus* (Bilberries)	8·25	8·00

Nos. 3523/3524 were printed, *se-tenant*, in horizontal pairs within the sheet.

(Des Petraq Papa)

2017 (18 Nov). Europa. Castles. T **872** and similar vert design. P 13×13½.

3525	200l. Type **872**	6·50	6·25
MS3526	80×60 mm. 250l. As Type **872**	8·50	8·25
MS3527	150×80 mm. 200l. As Type **872**; 250l. As stamp of MS3526	15·00	14·00

No. **MS**3527 has a grey background, showing stone walls, around an image as No. **MS**3526 and T **848**, and was issued in a folder.

873 Pelicans   **874** Musine Kokalari

ALBANIA 2017

(Des Artion Baboçi)

2017 (24 Nov). Tourism. National Parks. T **873** and similar horiz designs. Multicoloured. P 13½.
3528	40l. Type **873**		1·30	1·20
	a. Pair. Nos. 3528/3529		34·00	32·00
3529	100l. Flamingo and Water Buffalo ('Parku Kombëtar Divjake')		32·00	30·00

Nos. 3528/3529 were printed, *se-tenant*, in horizontal pairs within the sheet, each pair forming a composite design.

(Des Artion Baboçi)

2017 (5 Dec). National Personalities. T **874** and similar vert designs. Multicoloured. P 13.
3530	10l. Type **874** (writer and politician)		30	30
	a. Strip of 4. Nos. 3530/3533		7·00	
3531	40l. Zef Kolombi (artist)		1·30	1·20
3532	70l. Prenkë Jakova (composer)		2·20	2·10
3533	90l. Dom Nikollë Kaçorri (Prominent figure of the National Renaissance of Albania)		3·00	2·75
3530/3533 Set of 4			6·00	5·75

Nos. 3530/3533 were printed, *se-tenant*, in strips of four stamps within the sheet.

875 Ferdinand Graf von Zeppelin

(Des Llazar Taçi)

2017 (12 Dec). International Personalities. T **875** and similar horiz designs. Multicoloured. P 13½.
3534	20l. Type **875** (aviation pioneer)		65	60
	a. Strip of 3. Nos. 3534/3536		8·50	
3535	90l. Edgar Degas (artist)		3·00	2·75
3536	140l. Stefan Zweig (writer)		4·50	4·25
3534/3536 Set of 3			7·25	6·75

Nos. 3534/3536 were printed, *se-tenant*, in horizontal strips of three stamps within the sheet.

876 Swimming and Water Polo   **877** Statue of Liberty, 1950's Immigrants and Ship

(Des Bertrand Shijaku)

2017 (15 Dec). FINA World Aquatics Championships, Budapest. T **876** and similar horiz design. Multicoloured. P 13½.
3537	60l. Type **876**		1·90	1·80
	a. Pair. Nos. 3537/3538		5·25	4·75
3538	90l. Synchronised swimming and diving		3·00	2·75

Nos. 3537/3538 were printed, *se-tenant*, in horizontal pairs within the sheet.

(Des Petraq Papa)

2017 (18 Dec). International Immigration Day. T **877** and similar vert design. Multicoloured. P 13½.
3539	60l. Type **877**		1·90	1·80
	a. Pair. Nos. 3539/3540		10·50	10·00
3540	250l. Modern immigrants and ship		8·25	8·00

Nos. 3539/3540 were printed, *se-tenant*, in horizontal pairs within the sheet, each pair forming a composite design.

878 Lynx

(Des Rigels Lulo)

2017 (21 Dec). Albanian Fauna. Endangered Species. T **878** and similar horiz design. Multicoloured. P 13½.
3541	120l. Type **878**		3·75	3·50
MS3542 80×60 mm. 190l. Lynx standing			6·25	6·00

879 Glassware

(Des Xhoan Guga)

2017 (23 Dec). Albanian Handicrafts. Glassware. T **879** and similar square designs. Multicoloured. P 13.
3543	5l. Type **879**		15	15
	a. Block of 4. Nos. 3543/3546		9·00	
3544	40l. Lustre glass		1·30	1·20
3545	90l. Green jug and blue bowls		3·00	2·75
3546	130l. Curved spotted jug and wide-topped jug		4·25	4·00
3543/3546 Set of 4			7·75	7·25
MS3547 90×70 mm. 200l. Vases and drinking glasses			6·75	6·50

Nos. 3543/3546 were printed, *se-tenant*, in blocks of four stamps within the sheet.

880 Skënderbeut (S. Rrota)

2017 (27 Dec). Albanian Art. Sketches. T **880** and similar designs. P 13½.
3548	30l. grey-green and black		95	90
3549	40l. pale grey and black (*horiz*)		1·30	1·20
3550	50l. yellow-brown and black (*horiz*)		1·60	1·50
3551	80l. grey-black (*horiz*)		2·50	2·40
3552	90l. ochre and black		3·00	2·75
3553	100l. brownish grey and grey-black		3·25	3·00
3554	180l. yellow-ochre and grey-black		5·75	5·50
3555	190l. blue-grey and black		6·00	5·75
3548/3555 Set of 8			22·00	21·00

Designs: T **880**; *Kalorësi* (Z. Kolombi); Skicë studim (Study for Hell) (K. Idromeno); *Leningradi në shi* (P. Mele); *Skicë studim* (Woman's Head) (A. Kushi); *Në gjumë* (L. Blido); *Rrobaqepesja* (D. Theodhori); *Varrimi i shokut* (Z. Shoshi).

(Des Artion Baboçi)

2017 (28 Dec). European Day of Personal Data Protection. Horiz design showing symbol of protection. Multicoloured. P 13½.
3556	2500l. Lock with symbols of social media attached		80·00	75·00

T **881** is unavailable.

882 Emblem   **883** Gorica Bridge, Berat

2018 (5 May). 2018 National Year of George Kastrioti (Skanderbeg) (national hero). P 13½.
3557	**882**	250l. scarlet and black	8·25	8·00

(Des Spiro Vllahu. Litho Adel Co)

2018 (25 Oct). Europa. Bridges. T **883** and similar horiz design. P 13×13½.
3558	200l. Type **883**		6·50	6·25
MS3559	80×60 mm. 250l. Mes Bridge over Kiri river, near Shkoder		8·50	8·25
MS3560	150×80 mm. 200l. As Type **883**; 250l. As stamp of **MS**3559		15·00	14·00

No. **MS**3560 has a grey background, showing stone walls and bridge, around an image as No. **MS**3559 and as T **883**, and was issued in a folder.

884 Skanderbeg **885** Claude Debussy

(Des Laert Kraja. Litho Adel Co)

2018 (6 Nov). 550th Death Anniversary of Skanderbeg. T **884** and similar vert design. Multicoloured. P 13×13½.
3561	150l. Type **884**		4·75	4·50
3562	250l. Standing holding sword		8·25	8·00
MS3563	94×69 mm. 400l. As Type **884**; As No. 3562		13·50	12·50

(Des Sulid Kasemi. Litho Adel Co)

2018 (16 Nov). International Personalities. T **885** and similar vert design. Multicoloured. P 13.
3564	90l. Type **885**		3·00	2·75
	a. Pair. Nos. 3564/3565		9·00	8·50
3565	180l. Gustav Klimt		5·75	5·50

Nos. 3564/3565 were printed, *se-tenant*, in horizontal pairs within the sheet.

886 *Abelmoschus esculentus*

887 Printers, Printed Page and Machinery (400th anniversary of typography in Albania)

(Des Artion Baboçi. Litho Adel Co)

2018 (7 Dec). Flora. T **886** and similar vert design. Multicoloured. P 13½×13.
3566	40l. Type **886**		1·30	1·20
	a. Pair. Nos. 3566/3567		34·00	32·00
3567	100l. *Hypericum perforatum*		32·00	30·00

Nos. 3566/3567 were printed, *se-tenant*, in horizontal pairs within the sheet.

(Des Artion Baboçi. Litho Adel Co)

2018 (14 Dec). Historical Events. T **887** and similar horiz designs. Multicoloured. P 13½×13.
3568	50l. Type **887**		1·60	1·50
	a. Strip of 3. Nos. 3568/3570		10·00	
3569	120l. Woodrow Wilson (centenary of Woodrow Wilson's 14-point plan)		3·75	3·50
3570	140l. Kadri Prishtina (Hoxha Kadri) (centenary of the Kosovo National Defense Committee)		4·50	4·25
3568/3570	Set of 3		8·75	8·25

Nos. 3568/3570 were printed, *se-tenant*, in horizontal strips of three stamps within the sheet.

888 *Acipenser sturio*

(Des Rigels Lulo. Litho Adel Co)

2018 (19 Dec). Fauna. Fish. T **888** and similar horiz design. Multicoloured.
3571	5l. Type **888**		15	15
	a. Pair. Nos. 3571/3572		6·50	6·25
3572	190l. *Salmo trutta*		6·00	5·75

Nos. 3571/3572 were printed, *se-tenant*, in horizontal pairs within the sheet.

889 Thermal Springs

(Des Uljan Saraçi. Litho Adel Co)

2018 (22 Dec). Tourism. Benja Thermal Springs, Përmet. T **889** and similar vert designs. Multicoloured. P 13½.
3573	40l. Type **889**		1·30	1·20
	a. Pair. Nos. 3573/3575		85·00	80·00
3574	250l. Ottoman bridge (Ura e Kadiut)		80·00	75·00

Nos. 3573/3574 were printed, *se-tenant*, in horizontal pairs within the sheet.

890 Embroidery **891** Embroidery

892 Embroidery **893** Embroidery

894 Embroidery

(Des Stefan Taçi)

2018 (27 Dec). Albanian Handicrafts - Embroidery. P 13.
3575	**890**	40l. multicoloured	1·30	1·20
		a. Block of 4. Nos. 3575/3578	11·50	
3576	**891**	80l. multicoloured	2·50	2·40
3577	**892**	90l. multicoloured	3·00	2·75
3578	**893**	130l. multicoloured	4·25	4·00
3575/3578		Set of 4	10·00	9·25
MS3579		90×70 mm. **894** 200l. multicoloured	6·75	6·50

Nos. 3575/3578 were printed, *se-tenant*, in blocks of four stamps within the sheet.

ALBANIA 2018

895 *Erdbi liria*
(A Kostandini)

2018 (29 Dec). Albanian Art - Graphic Art. T **895** and similar multicoloured designs. P 13½.

3580	10l. Type **895**		30	30
3581	20l. *Fshatarja* (L Dhrami) *(horiz)*		65	60
3582	30l. *Portret punëtoreje* (L Dhrami)		95	90
3583	40l. *Tokë e begatë* (M Qarri)		1·30	1·20
3584	60l. *Vagonisti* (A Faja)		1·90	1·80
3585	70l. *Te korrurat* (I Shehui) *(horiz)*		2·20	2·10
3586	90l. *Vjitja* (M Qarri)		3·00	2·75
3587	100l. *Mikpritja* (P Mele) (40×40 *mm*)		3·25	3·00
3580/3587	Set of 8		12·00	11·50

STAMP BOOKLETS

The following checklist covers, in simplified form, booklets issued by Albania. It is intended that it should be used in conjunction with the main listings and details of stamps and panes listed there are not repeated.

Prices are for complete booklets

Booklet No.	Date	Contents and Cover Price	Price
SB1	20.3.86	Flowers 1 pane, No. 2306a (1l.45)	18·00
SB2	20.4.86	Anniversaries 1 pane, No. 2308a (4l.65)	22·00
SB3	20.5.88	Flowers 1 pane, No. 2376a (3l.30)	95·00
SB4	29.11.89	45th Anniversary of Liberation 1 pane, No. 2438a (3l.30)	6·50
SB5	6.5.90	150th Anniversary of the Penny Black 1 pane, No. 2454a (3l.90)	5·75
SB6	20.6.99	Charlie Chaplin (T **633**) 1 pane, No. 2742ab (60l.)	24·00
SB7	12.9.01	Arms 4 pane Nos. 2881a, 2882a, 2883a, 2884a (82l.)	30·00
SB8	12.5.02	Arms 4 panes, Nos. 2918a, 2919a, 2920a, 2921a	29·00
SB9	12.5.03	Arms 4 panes, Nos. 2965a, 2966a, 2967a, 2968a	33·00
SB10	25.10.04	Arms 4 panes, Nos. 3018a, 3019a, 3020a, 3021a	43·00
SB11	5.10.05	Europa. Gastronomy 1 pane No. 3068a	90·00
SB12	14.11.05	Arms 4 panes, Nos. 3098b, 3099a, 3100a, 3101a	55·00

GREEK OCCUPATION

100 Lepta = 1 Drachma

Italian troops invaded Greece from Albania on 29 October 1940. The Greeks counter-attacked and occupied part of southern Albania, including Koritza, until the German invasion of Greece forced them to surrender on 21 April 1941. For stamps issued in this area in 1914–1915, see under Epirus.

Stamps of Greece overprinted

ΕΛΛΗΝΙΚΗ
ΔΙΟΙΚΗϹΙϹ
(1)

1940 (10 Dec). Nos. 497, 499 to 512, 514 and 516 optd with T **1**.

1	86	5l. greenish blue and red-brown	65	1·00
		a. Opt inverted	£120	
2	–	10l. red-brown and light blue	65	1·00
3	87	20l. blue-green and black	65	1·00
		a. Opt inverted	£120	
4	88	40l. black and blue-green	65	1·00
5	–	50l. black and bistre-brown	65	1·00
6	–	80l. brown and dull violet	70	1·30
7	89	1d. green	70	1·30
		a. Opt inverted	£120	
8	–	2d. ultramarine	70	1·30
9	89	3d. red-brown	1·00	2·40
10	–	5d. scarlet	1·00	2·40
11	–	6d. olive-brown	1·30	3·00
12	90	7d. chocolate	1·30	3·00
13	89	8d. deep blue	1·30	3·00
14	–	10d. red-brown	3·00	5·50
15	91	15d. blue-green	3·50	7·25
16	92	25d. deep blue	6·00	12·00
		a. Opt inverted	£190	
17	89a	30d. brown-red	11·50	24·00
1/17	Set of 17		32·00	65·00

1940 (10 Dec). CHARITY TAX. Nos. C524/C526 optd with T **1**.

18	C **96**	10l. carmine/rose	25	1·80
19		50l. green/pale green	45	1·80
		a. Opt inverted	£100	
20		1d. blue/pale blue	1·30	3·00
18/20	Set of 3		1·80	6·00

1940 (10 Dec). POSTAGE DUE.

*(a) Nos. D453 and D455/D457 optd with T **1***

D21	D **20**	2d. vermilion	1·00	2·00
		a. Opt inverted	£110	
D22		5d. grey-blue	1·00	3·00
D23		10d. green	1·60	3·00
D24		15d. red-brown	1·40	3·00

(b) No. D458 surch and similarly optd

D25	D **20**	50l. on 25d. scarlet	65	2·75
		a. No accent (No. D458a)		
D21/D25	Set of 5		5·00	12·50

1941 (1 Mar). Greek Youth issue, Nos. 534/553, optd with T **1**, in red.

(a) POSTAGE

26		3d. blue, red and silver	1·00	1·40
27		5d. black and blue	3·75	6·50
28		10d. black and orange	5·50	9·50
29		15d. black and green	24·00	30·00
30		20d. black and lake	17·00	22·00
31		25d. black and brown	17·00	22·00
32		30d. black and purple	17·00	22·00
33		50d. black and lake	17·00	22·00
34		75d. gold, brown and blue	19·00	27·00
35		100d. blue, red and silver	23·00	30·00
		a. Opt inverted	£1300	
26/35	Set of 10		£130	£170

(b) AIR

36		2d. black and orange	1·00	1·70
		a. Opt inverted	£275	
37		4d. black and green	4·00	7·00
		a. Opt inverted	£275	
38		6d. black and lake	5·50	9·50
		a. Opt inverted	£275	
39		8d. black and blue	7·00	11·00
40		16d. black and purple	12·00	19·00
41		32d. black and orange	16·00	24·00
42		45d. black and green	17·00	24·00
43		55d. black and carmine	17·00	24·00
44		65d. black and blue	17·00	24·00
45		100d. black and purple	27·00	41·00
36/45	Set of 10		£110	£170

Nos. 36/45 were issued as postage and not air stamps.

SASENO

ITALIAN OCCUPATION

100 Centesimi = 1 Lira

Saseno (now Sazan), an Albanian island in the gulf of Valona, was occupied by Italian marines on 30 October 1914 and remained in Italian hands until 1943. Italy renounced her claims to the island by the Treaty of Paris, 10 February 1947.

1923 (Apr). Stamps of Italy, 1906–1922, (various portraits of Victor Emmanuel III), optd 'SASENO'.

1	38	10c. rose	27·00	60·00
2	37	15c. slate	27·00	60·00
3	41	20c. orange (No. 105)	27·00	60·00
4	39	25c. blue	27·00	60·00
5		30c. orange-brown	27·00	60·00
6	40	50c. mauve	27·00	60·00
7	39	60c. lake	27·00	60·00
8	34	1l. brown and green	27·00	60·00
1/8	Set of 8		£190	£425

Bulgaria

1879. 100 Centimes = 1 Franc
1881. 100 Stotinki = 1 Lev

Until 1877 Bulgaria was part of the Ottoman Empire but following a revolt and the intervention of Russia, the Treaty of Berlin, 1878, established a Principality north of the Balkan Mountains, under Turkish suzerainty, whilst in the south a semi-autonomous administration was granted to Eastern Roumelia. This was incorporated in Bulgaria in 1885.

PRINCIPALITY

Prince Alexander, 24 April 1879–4 September 1886

The dates of issue are according to local computation based on the Julian or Gregorian Calendar in use. In the 19th-century the Julian Calendar was 12 days behind the Gregorian Calendar. After 1900 the difference was 13 days. In Bulgaria the Gregorian Calendar was introduced in 1917.

1 Large Lion   **2** Large Lion

(Types **1** and **2** Des G. Ya. Kirkov of State Ptg Wks, Sofia. Eng F. Kepler. Typo Russian State Ptg Wks, St Petersburg)

1879 (1 May). Laid paper. Sheet wmk letters E Z G B (representing initials of the printing house) drawn between symmetrical curved lines, forming a lozenge-shaped pattern. P 14½×15.

1	1	5c. black and orange	£275	80·00
2		5c. black and yellow	£275	80·00
3		10c. black and green	£1200	£275
4		10c. black and deep green	£1200	£275
5		25c. black and lilac	£650	60·00
6		25c. black and purple	£650	60·00
7		50c. black and blue	£1100	£225
8	2	1f. black and red	£160	60·00

1881 (10 June). Laid paper. Wmk letters E Z G B etc. P 14½×15. Values in stotinki variously, thus:

9	1	3st. carmine and grey	49·00	9·75
10		3st. deep carmine and grey	49·00	9·75
11		5st. black and yellow	49·00	9·75
		a. Background inverted	£3750	£3250
12		5st. black and orange	49·00	9·75
13		10st. black and green	£275	30·00
14		10st. black and deep green	£275	30·00
15		15st. deep carmine and green	£300	30·00
16		15st. carmine and pale green	£300	30·00
17		25st. black and lilac	£1200	£140
18		25st. black and purple	£1200	£140
19		30st. deep blue and brown	49·00	24·00
20		30st. blue and pale brown	49·00	24·00

1882 (4 Dec). Colours changed. Laid paper. Wmk letters E Z G B etc. P 14½×15.

21	1	3st. pale orange and yellow	2·40	1·20
		a. Background inverted	£6000	£4750
22		3st. orange and yellow	2·40	1·20
23		5st. grey-green and pale green	19·00	1·80
24		5st. yellow-green and pale green	19·00	1·80
		a. Error. Rose and pale rose	£4500	£4500
25		10st. rose and pale rose	24·00	1·80
26		10st. carmine and pale rose	24·00	1·80
27		10st. scarlet and pale rose	24·00	1·80
28		15st. plum and pale mauve	24·00	1·80
29		15st. purple and pale mauve	24·00	1·80
30		25st. deep blue and pale blue	22·00	2·40
31		25st. blue and pale blue	22·00	2·40
32		30st. deep lilac and green	22·00	2·00
33		30st. purple and green	22·00	2·00
34		50st. blue and rose	22·00	2·00
35		50st. blue and flesh	22·00	2·00

See also Nos. 275/280.

(3)　　(4)　　(5)　　(6)

1884–85. Previous issues surch with Types **3** to **6** by State Ptg Wks, Sofia. (i) Typo (1.5.84) (ii) Litho (5.4.85).

(a) In black

37	1	3st. on 10st. rose and pale rose (i)	£375	£120
		a. Surch inverted	£1800	£1100
		b. Surch double	—	£2250
38		3st. on 10st. carmine and pale rose (ii)	£120	£120
39		5 on 30st. deep blue and brown (i)	£4250	£3500
40	2	50st. on 1f. black and red (ii)	£850	£550

Most of the stamps offered with '5' in black on 30st. have forged surcharges.

(b) In carmine (C.) or vermilion (V.)

41	1	5st. on 30st. deep blue and brown (i) (C.)	£225	£140
42		5st. on 30st. blue and pale brown (i) (C.)	£225	£140
		a. Surch double (Blk.+C.)	£4500	
43		5st. on 30st. blue and pale brown (ii) (V.)	£130	£120
44		15st. on 25st. deep blue and pale blue (i) (C.)	£1400	£225
		a. Surch inverted		£4500
45		15st. on 25st. blue and pale blue (ii) (V.)	£250	£160

D **7**　　A. 1884–1892　　B. Redrawn 1893

In B the background lines are wider apart and the semicircle of colour over the tablet is larger.

(Litho State Ptg Wks, Sofia)

1884 (1 Sept)–**95**. POSTAGE DUE. Lozenge perf 5 to 7½ and compound.

D46	D **7**	5st. orange	£1100	£140
		a. Yellow		
D47		25st. lake	£500	80·00
D48		50st. deep blue	85·00	55·00
		a. Blue (1895)	80·00	49·00

A　　B　　C　　D
Masculine Gender　　Feminine Gender

1885 (25 May). Wmk letters E Z G B etc. P 14½×15.

46	1	1st. slate-violet and drab (A)	43·00	14·50
47		2st. slate-green and drab (B)	43·00	11·00

1886 (13 Aug). As last, but spelling as (C) and (D).

48	1	1st. slate-violet and drab (C)	3·00	60
49		2st. slate-green and drab (D)	3·00	60

1886 (15 Aug). POSTAGE DUE. Litho. Imperf

D50	D **7**	5st. orange	£650	31·00
D51		25st. brown-lake	£950	30·00
D52		50st. deep blue	34·00	29·00
		a. Blue	30·00	27·00

Nos. D50/D52a exist on rough yellowish grey paper and on smooth whiter paper.

Value in leva, thus:

1887 (1 Jan). Wmk letters E Z G B etc. P 14½×15.

50	2	1l. black and red	85·00	11·00

BULGARIA 1887

Prince Ferdinand 1
14 August 1887–5 October 1908

(Litho State Ptg Wks, Sofia)
1887 (10 Oct). POSTAGE DUE. P 11½.
D53	D **7**	5st. orange		90·00	14·50
		a. Yellow		90·00	14·50
D54		25st. brown-lake		30·00	9·00
D55		50st. deep blue		33·00	24·00
		a. Blue		36·00	24·00

   7   **8**   **(9)**   **D 10**

(Typo Govt Ptg Works, Paris)
1889 (May)–**91**. No wmk. P 13½.
51	**7**	1st. mauve		2·40	60
52		2st. grey		3·75	1·80
53		3st. bistre-brown		1·80	60
54		5st. green		18·00	45
		a. Imperf (pair)			
55		10st. rose (5.5.89)		18·00	1·20
56		15st. orange		£110	1·20
57		25st. pale blue (1891)		18·00	1·20
58		30st. brown (1891)		21·00	1·20
59		50st. blue-green		1·20	60
60	**8**	1l. brick-red (1.8.89)		1·20	1·20
51s/60s Optd 'SPECIMEN' Set of 10				£300	

The horizontal perforation of this issue gauges slightly under 13½. See note after No. 100.

1892 (26 Jan). Surch with T **9** at Sofia.
61	**7**	15 on 30st. brown		60·00	2·40
		a. Surch inverted		£225	£200

(Typo Austrian State Ptg Wks, Vienna or State Ptg Wks, Sofia)
1892–93.
(a) P 10½
62	**7**	5st. green (1893)		£400	£300
63		10st. rose (1893)		£500	£225
64		15st. orange		55·00	2·20
65		25st. pale blue		18·00	1·80

(b) P 11
66	**7**	15st. orange		£225	22·00
67		25st. pale blue		55·00	1·80

(c) P 11½
68	**7**	5st. green (1893)		£375	22·00
69		5st. yellow-green (1893)		£250	22·00
70		10st. rose (1893)		10·00	3·00
71		15st. orange		£160	2·40
72		25st. blue		18·00	1·80

(d) Pelure paper. P 11½
73	**7**	10st. rose (1893)		12·00	2·40
		a. Imperf (pair)		£160	1·80

Early printings of the 15st. and 25st. values were made in Vienna and issued 1892. Later printings of these values and all printings of the 5st. and 10st. were made at Sofia and issued from 1893 onwards.

1892. POSTAGE DUE. Litho. P 11½×lozenge, perf.
D74	D **7**	25st. brown-lake		£600	£475

1893. POSTAGE DUE. Redrawn as B. Thick or thin paper. Litho. P 11½.
D75	D **7**	5st. orange		60·00	9·00
		a. Perf 10½		70·00	9·75
		b. Perf 11		£180	30·00
D76		25st. dull lake		30·00	9·00
		a. Perf 10½		80·00	12·00
		b. Perf 11		£180	38·00

1894 (1 Apr). POSTAGE DUE. Larger lettering. Figure of value outlined. Litho. Pelure paper. P 11½.
D77	D **10**	5st. orange		75·00	27·00

(10)   **(D 11)**   **11** Arms of Bulgaria

A   B

1895 (25 Oct). No. 49 surch with T **10**.
74		01 on 2st. slate-green and drab (R.)		1·80	60
		a. Surch inverted		13·50	11·00
		b. Pair, one without surcharge		£375	£325
		c. Surch double		£150	£150
		d. Surch on No. 47		£650	£650

1895 (18 Nov). POSTAGE DUE. Surch with T D **11**, in red.
D78	D **7**	30st. on 50st. (No. D52)		90·00	16·00
		a. Surch inverted		£350	£350
		b. Bar double		£110	£100
		c. Surch inverted and bar double		£650	£650
		d. Blue (No. D52a)		55·00	16·00
D79		30st. on 50st. (No. D55)		50·00	14·50
		a. Surch inverted		£350	£350
		b. Blue (No. D55a)		65·00	16·00

1896 (2 Feb). Baptism of Prince Boris. Litho.
(a) No wmk. Rough paper. P 13
75	**11**	1st. green		90	55
76		1st. deep green		90	50
77		15st. violet (A)		7·75	1·00
77a		25st. red		11·50	4·00

(b) Wmk Bulgarian Arms and Inscription (Principality of Bulgaria) in sheet (some stamps without wmk). Smooth paper. P 13
78	**11**	1st. blue-green		55	35
79		5st. ultramarine		55	35
80		5st. deep blue		55	35
81		15st. violet (B)		75	60
82		25st. red		9·50	4·00

D **12**   (12)   **13** Cherrywood Cannon used against the Turks

1896 (13 Mar). POSTAGE DUE. Smaller design. Litho. With or without wmk Arms in sheet. P 13×12½.
D83	D **12**	5st. orange		30·00	5·00
D84		10st. violet		18·00	4·25
D85		30st. green		14·50	3·75

No. D83 exists in two types differing in the figure of value.

1896 (30 Apr). Wmk Bulgarian Arms and Inscription (Principality of Bulgaria) in sheet (some stamps without wmk). Typo. P 13.
83	**8**	2l. rose and pale rose		5·00	3·75
		a. Perf 11½		£500	
84		3l. black and drab		7·25	8·50
		a. Perf 11½		£500	

(Typo State Pty Works, Sofia)
1896–1901. P 13.
85	**7**	1st. grey-mauve		25	25
86		1st. mauve		25	25
87		1st. dull mauve		25	25
88		2st. drab		1·60	1·40
89		3st. bistre-brown		70	70
90		5st. green		25	25
91		5st. pale green		25	25
92		5st. yellow-green		25	25
93		5st. dull green		25	25
94		10st. rose		2·00	1·40
95		10st. pale rose		2·00	1·40
96		15st. orange		1·40	70
97		15st. brown-orange		1·40	70
98		15st. red-orange		1·40	70
99		15st. yellow		1·40	70
100		25st. dull blue		1·40	70
85/100 Set of 16				13·50	9·00

The perforation in this issue is the same on all sides gauging slightly under 13, a difference which distinguishes it from the Paris printing, Nos. 51, etc. All values exist imperf.

1901. Surch as T **12**.
101	**7**	5st. on 3st. bistre-brown (No. 53) (24.5.01)		3·00	2·40
102		5st. on 3st. bistre-brown (No. 89) (24.5.01)		3·50	2·75
		a. Surch inverted		£160	£160
		b. Pair, one without surcharge		£225	£180

103		10st. on 50st. blue-green (No. 59) (24.5.01)		3·50	2·40
		a. Surch inverted		£160	£160

(Typo State Ptg Wks, Sofia)

1901 (20 Apr). 25th Anniversary of Uprising against Turkey. P 13.

104	**13**	5st. carmine		2·00	2·10
		a. '1878' for '1876'			
105		15st. green		2·00	2·10
		a. '1870' for '1876'			

14 Prince Ferdinand   **15** Prince Ferdinand

A   B

In Type A the figures '1' in the corners at top have an additional straight serif at right. In Type B this is omitted.

(Des S. Badzhov. Typo Cartographic Bureau, Russian War Department, St Petersburg)

1901 (1 Oct)–**05**. P 12½.

106	**14**	1st. greenish black and purple	40	25
		a. Imperf (pair)		£1600
107		2st. blue and slate-green	70	25
		a. Imperf (pair)		
108		3st. black and orange	70	25
109		5st. brown and emerald	2·75	35
110		10st. sepia and rose	4·00	35
111		10st. sepia and vermilion	4·00	35
112		10st. sepia and carmine-rose	4·00	35
113		15st. greenish black and lake	2·00	40
		a. Imperf (pair)		£2000
114		25st. black and blue	2·00	35
115		25st. black and deep blue	2·00	35
116		30st. black and bistre-brown	47·00	95
117		50st. brown and deep blue	2·75	40
118	**15**	1l. deep green and pale red (A)	6·00	55
		a. Redrawn (B) (1905)	£110	5·50
119		2l. black and vermilion	11·50	2·00
120		2l. black and rose	11·50	2·00
121		2l. black and carmine	11·50	2·00
122		2l. black and brick-red	11·50	2·00
123		3l. brown-lake and grey	13·50	8·00
106/123 Set of 12 (cheapest)			85·00	12·50

On 22.12.01 the Rustchuk PO overprinted current postage stamps (Nos. 109, 110, 113, 116 and 117) with a large 'T' in a circle, as shown, to convert them into postage due stamps.

D **16**   **16** Fighting at Shipka Pass   (**17**)

1901–04. POSTAGE DUE. Typo. P 11½.

D124	D **16**	5st. rose-red	1·40	75
D125		10st. green (1902)	2·40	75
D126		20st. blue (1904)	18·00	75
D127		30st. maroon	6·00	75
D128		50st. orange (1902)	16·00	15·00
D124/D128 Set of 5			39·00	16·00

(Des Kh. Tachev. Litho Hungarian State Ptg Works, Budapest)

1902 (29 Aug). 25th Anniversary of Battle of Shipka Pass. P 11½.

124	**16**	5st. carmine	4·00	1·40
125		10st. green	4·00	1·40
126		15st. blue	16·00	6·75
124/126 Set of 3			22·00	8·50

1903 (1 Oct). No. 113 surch with T **17** at Sofia.

127	**14**	10st. on 15st. greenish black and lake	75·00	2·00
		a. Surch on 10st. (No. 110)	£900	£900
		b. Surch inverted	£130	£100
		c. Surch double	£130	£100

For this surcharge in blue-black see No. 141.

18 Ferdinand I in 1887 and 1907

(Litho Hungarian State Ptg Wks, Budapest)

1907 (14 Aug). 20th Anniversary of Prince Ferdinand's Accession. P 11½.

131	**18**	5st. green	25·00	2·50
		a. Imperf (pair)	£140	
132		5st. pale green	25·00	2·50
133		5st. black-green	25·00	2·50
134		10st. brown-rose	37·00	2·50
		a. Imperf (pair)	£200	
135		10st. deep rose	37·00	2·50
136		10st. red-brown	37·00	2·50
137		25st. blue	90·00	5·00
		a. Imperf (pair)	£275	
138		25st. pale blue	90·00	5·00
		a. Background omitted		
139		25st. deep blue	90·00	5·00
131/139 Set of 9			£140	9·00

INDEPENDENT KINGDOM

Tsar Ferdinand I, 5 October 1908–3 October 1918

Prince Ferdinand proclaimed himself Tsar in 1908 and repudiated Turkish suzerainty; Bulgarian independence was recognised by Turkey in 1909.

5   **1909**   10   1

(**19**)   (**20**)   (**21**)   (**22**)

(Surch at Sofia)

1909.

*(a) Nos. 113 and 116 surch as T **19** or T **17** (No. 141) (17 June).*

140	**14**	5st. on 15st. (B.+Blk.)	3·25	2·10
		a. Surch inverted	47·00	46·00
141		10st. on 15st. (B.+Blk.)	6·75	1·40
		a. Surch inverted	47·00	46·00
142		25st. on 30st. (B.+Blk.)	£1100	£700
143		25st. on 30st. (R.)	18·00	2·75
		a. '2' omitted	£160	£160
		b. '25' double	£150	£150

*(b) Optd with T **20** (3 July (1st.)–30 Aug (5st.))*

144	**7**	1st. mauve (P 13½)	£110	90·00
145		1st. mauve (P 13)	2·20	95
		a. Opt inverted	43·00	36·00
146		1st. dull mauve (P 13)	2·20	95
		a. Opt inverted	43·00	36·00
		b. Opt double, one inverted	55·00	50·00
147		5st. green (P 13½)	£150	£150
148		5st. green (P 11½)	£160	£160
149		5st. green (P 13)	2·75	1·10
150		5st. dull green (P 13)	2·75	1·10
		a. Opt inverted	55·00	50·00

BULGARIA 1910

(c) Surch as T **21** (30 Aug (Nos. 152/154)–25 Sept (others))

151	**7**	5st. on 30st. brown (P 13½)		3·75	80
		a. Surch double		55·00	50·00
		b. Date reading '1969'		£1200	
		c. Date reading '1990'		£1100	£950
152		10st. on 15st. brown-orange (P 11½)		£900	£750
153		10st. on 15st. orange (P 13)		3·75	1·60
		a. Surch inverted		39·00	37·00
		b. Surch double		55·00	
		c. Surch triple		—	
		d. Date reading '909'		£110	95·00
154		10st. on 15st. yellow (P 13)		8·75	1·10
		a. Surch inverted		55·00	50·00
		b. Date reading '909'		£110	95·00
155		10st. on 50st. blue-green (P 13½)		55·00	50·00
		a. Date reading '1990'		£1500	
156		10st. on 50st. blue-green (P 13½) (R.)		3·75	1·60
		a. Imperf (pair)		£110	£100
		b. Date reading '909'		90·00	
		c. Date reading '1990'		£140	£140
		d. Surch on back in addition		55·00	

On Nos. 152/154 the height of the surcharge is slightly less than on Nos. 155/156.

1910 (1 Oct). Nos. 108 and 113 surch as T **22** at Sofia.

157	**14**	1st. on 3st. black and orange (B.)	9·00	2·75
158		5st. on 15st. greenish black and lake (B.)	4·25	2·00

23 King Asen Tower **24** Tsar in General's Uniform **25** Veliko Turnovo

26 Tsar Ferdinand **27** Tsar in Admiral's Uniform **28** River Isker

29 Tsar Ferdinand **30** Rila Monastery

31 Tsar and Princes (after Ya. Veshin) **32** Tsar in Coronation Robes (after A. Mitov)

33 Monastery of the Holy Trinity, Veliko Turnovo **34** Varna

(Des A. Mitov and G. Evstatiev. Eng Bradbury Wilkinson, London. Recess Govt Ptg Wks, Rome)

1911 (14 Feb). P 12.

159	**23**	1st. myrtle-green	40	20
160	**24**	2st. black and carmine	40	20
161	**25**	3st. black and lake	90	20
162	**26**	5st. black and green	2·00	20
163	**27**	10st. black and red	3·50	25
164	**28**	15st. bistre	9·00	40
165	**29**	25st. black and ultramarine	70	20
166	**30**	30st. black and blue	9·00	40
167	**31**	50st. black and ochre	47·00	70
		a. Centre inverted	—	£7500
168	**32**	1l. brown	20·00	40
169	**33**	2l. black and purple	4·50	1·60
170	**34**	3l. black and violet	24·00	8·25
159/170	Set of 12		£110	11·50

During the Balkan war of 1912–1913 stamps of this issue were obliterated in the occupied territories with the old Turkish cancellations, until these could be superseded by new Bulgarian cancellations.

For similar types see Nos. 181/184a, 229/230 and 236/237.

35 Tsar Ferdinand

ОСВОБ. ВОЙНА

1912–1913

(**36**) War of Liberation, 1912–1913

(Des S. Badzhov. Typo Austrian State Ptg Wks, Vienna)

1912 (2 Aug). Tsar's Silver Jubilee. Chalk-surfaced paper. P 12½.

171	**35**	5st. greenish grey	6·00	2·50
		a. Error. Bright green	£1200	£1100
172		10st. lake	8·75	4·50
173		25st. slate-blue	13·00	7·00
171/173	Set of 3		25·00	12·50

1913 (6 Aug). Victory over the Turks. Optd as T **36** at Sofia.

174	**23**	1st. myrtle-green (R.)	70	25
		a. 'c' for first 'o' in first word of overprint	10·50	10·50
175	**24**	2st. black and carmine (B.)	2·00	25
176	**25**	3st. black and lake (B. or Blk.)	2·40	40
177	**26**	5st. black and green (R.)	70	25
178	**27**	10st. black and red (Blk.)	70	25
179	**28**	15st. bistre (G.)	3·50	2·00
180	**29**	25st. black and ultramarine (R.)	9·50	3·50
174/180	Set of 7		18·00	6·25

The spacing of the two lines of the overprint differs for each value except the 2st. and 25st. which are the same.

D **37** (**37**) (**37**a)

(Litho State Ptg Wks, Sofia)

1915 (12 Apr). POSTAGE DUE. Thin toned paper. P 11½.

D181	D **37**	5st. dull green	75	35
D182		10st. violet	80	35
D183		20st. rose	80	35
D184		30st. orange	4·25	1·40
D185		50st. Prussian blue	1·50	80
D181/D185	Set of 5		7·25	3·00

See also Nos. D200/D204 and D239/D245.

1915 (6 July). Surch with T **37**, in red, at Sofia.

180a	**29**	10st. on 25st. black and ultramarine	1·50	35

(Recess E. Petiti, Rome)

1915 (7 Nov). Types of 1911. Re-engraved plates; colours changed.

(a) P 14.

181	**26**	5st. purple-brown and green	5·00	30
181a	**27**	10st. sepia and red-brown	35	25
182	**30**	30st. brown and olive	60	30

1916 BULGARIA

		(b) P 11½		
182a	23	1st. slate	35	25
183	28	15st. grey-olive	70	25
184	29	25st. black and deep blue	40	20
184a	32	1l. deep brown	60	35
181/184a		Set of 7	7·25	1·70

Nos. 181 to 184a differ considerably in size and details of design from stamps printed from the earlier plates and the designer's initials are omitted in Nos. 181, 181a and 184.

1916 (9 Mar). Red Cross Fund. Surch with T **37a** at Sofia.

185	7	3 on 1st. mauve (G.)	13·00	12·00
		a. Surch inverted	£160	

38
39 Bulgarian Peasant
40 Soldier and Mount Sonichka
41 Nish
42 Ohrid and Lake
43 Demir Kapija
44 Gevgeli

(Des S. Badzhov. Typo Austrian State Ptg Works, Vienna)

1917 (14 Aug)–**19**. Liberation of Macedonia. P 13×12½ (30st., 2l., 3l.) or 12½ (others).

186	38	5st. grey-green	65	55
187	39	15st. greenish grey	35	25
		a. Perf 11½	35	25
		b. Imperf (pair)	43·00	
188	40	25st. blue	35	25
189	41	30st. orange	35	25
190	42	50st. violet	1·20	90
191	43	2l. chestnut (1919)	1·20	90
192	44	3l. claret	2·00	1·80
186/192		Set of 7	5·75	4·75

A 1l. value in bluish green showing Bulgaria on the throne (vertical format) was prepared but not issued.

45 Veles
46 Bulgarian Ploughman
47 Monastery of St John, Ohrid
48 Tsar Ferdinand

(Des D. Gyudzhenov and R. Aleksiev. Typo German State Ptg Wks, Berlin)

1918–19. Liberation of Macedonia. P 13×13½ or 13½×13 (No. 194).

193	45	1st. grey	35	15
194	46	1st. grey-green (1919)	35	15
195	47	5st. green	35	15
193/195		Set of 3	95	40

1918 (1 July). 30th Anniversary of Tsar Ferdinand's Accession. Chalk-surfaced paper. P 12½×13.

196	48	1st. greenish slate	70	25
197		2st. brown	70	25
198		3st. indigo	1·50	70
199		10st. red	1·00	70
196/199		Set of 4	3·50	1·70

The 1l. indigo in this type is an essay.

Tsar (King) Boris III
3 October 1918–28 August 1943

PRINTERS The following were printed at the State Printing Works, Sofia *except where otherwise stated*.

1919 (19 June). POSTAGE DUE. Litho. Thick white paper. P 12×11½.

D200	D **37**	5st. bright green	85	20
D201		10st. dull violet	85	25
D202		20st. pale rose-red	85	25
D203		30st. red-orange	5·75	5·00
		a. Brick-red	85	25
D204		50st. deep blue	1·90	1·10
D200/D204		Set of 5 (cheapest)	4·75	1·80

49 Parliament Building
50 King Boris III

(Des S. Badzhov. Typo)

1919 (3 Oct). P 12 (1st.) or 11½ (2st.).

201	49	1st. black	35	25
		a. Imperf between (horiz strip of 3)		
202		2st. olive	35	25

(Des S. Badzhov. Typo)

1919 (3 Oct)–**21**. First Anniversary of Enthronement of King Boris III. P 11½.

203	50	3st. brown-red (1920)	25	20
		a. Venetian red	25	20
204		5st. green	25	20
		a. Emerald (1921)	25	20
205		10st. rose	25	20
		a. Scarlet (1921)	25	20
206		15st. violet	25	20
207		25st. blue	25	20
208		30st. chocolate (1920)	25	20
209		50st. yellow brown	25	20
203/209		Set of 7	1·60	1·30

All values exist on thin or thick paper, with pin roulette 12.

(51) **(52)** **(53)**

1920 (22 June). Prisoners of War Fund. Surch as T **51** (Nos. 210, 218/219), T **53** (No. 217) or T **52** (others).

210	49	1 on 2st. olive	25	20
211	50	2½ on 5st. green	25	20
212		5 on 10st. rose	25	20
213		7½ on 15st. violet	25	20
214		12½ on 25st. blue	25	20
215		15 on 30st. chocolate	25	20
216		50 on 50st. yellow-brown	25	20
217	32	50 on 1l. deep brown (No. 184a)	65	40
		a. Surch double	£110	
		b. Surch in blue	£140	
218	43	1(l.) on 2l. chestnut	65	60
		a. Surch inverted	£110	
219	44	1½(l.) on 3l. claret	1·80	1·20
210/219		Set of 10	4·25	3·25

On No. 219 the surcharge is larger.

BULGARIA 1920

These were sold at the original face-value, but only had franking value to half that amount, represented by the surcharge, the surplus being for the prisoners of war fund.

54 Vazov's Birthplace at Sopot and Cherrywood Cannon

55 The Bearfighter (character from *Under the Yoke*)

56 Ivan Vazov in 1870 and 1920

57 Vazov

58 Vazov's Houses in Plovdiv and Sofia

58a Father Paisii Khilendarski (historian)

(Des S. Badzhov and R. Aleksiev. Photo)

1920 (24 Oct). 70th Birthday of Ivan Vazov (writer). P 11½.
220	54	30st. carmine	25	20
221	55	50st. myrtle	35	25
222	56	1l. sepia	70	55
223	57	2l. brown	1·70	1·60
224	58	3l. deep violet	2·75	2·30
225	58a	5l. blue	3·50	2·50
220/225	*Set of 6*		8·25	6·75

59 Aleksandr Nevski Cathedral, Sofia

60 Monument to Alexander II, 'The Liberator', Sofia

61 Shipka Pass Monastery

62 King Boris III

63 Harvester

64 King Asen Tower

65 Rila Monastery

(Des S. Badzhov (10st.), R. Aleksiev (20st., 75st., 2l.), E. Vake (25st., 1l., 10l.), A. Mitov (50st.), G. Evstatiev (3l., 5l.). Eng and recess Bradbury Wilkinson)

1921 (23 Mar)–**23**. Types **59** to **65**, and **25** (redrawn). P 12.
226	59	10st. slate-violet (7.21)	20	20
227	60	20st. green (7.21)	20	20
228	62	25st. greenish blue (20.3.22)	20	20
229	25	50st. orange (12.21)	20	25
230		50st. deep blue (1.12.23)	8·00	4·00
231	61	75st. violet (7.21)	20	20
232		75st. deep blue (1.12.23)	35	25
233	62	1l. scarlet (25.8.21)	35	25
234		1l. deep blue (2.12.21)	70	20
235	63	2l. brown (1.6.21)	1·00	25
236	64	3l. dull purple	1·30	25
237	65	5l. blue	7·50	55
238	62	10l. maroon (25.7.21)	19·00	4·75
226/238	*Set of 13*		35·00	10·50

1921 (12 May). POSTAGE DUE. Colours changed and new values. Litho. Thick greyish paper. P 11½.
D239	D **37**	5st. yellow-green	70	70
		a. Imperf between (horiz pair)	38·00	
D240		10st. bright violet	25	15
D241		20st. pale orange	25	15
D242		50st. milky blue	25	15
D243		1l. pale blue-green	35	15
		a. Imperf between (vert pair)		
D244		2l. carmine	35	25
D245		3l. orange-brown	70	45
D239/D245	*Set of 7*		2·50	1·80

The 50st. to 3l. values were authorised for use as ordinary postage stamps in November 1923.

66 Tsar Ferdinand and Map

67 Tsar Ferdinand

68 Mount Shar

69 Bridge over Vardar, at Skopje

70 St Clement's Monastery, Ohrid

(Des B. Marinov (No. 240), R. Aleksiev (No. 241), D. Gyudzhenov (others). Typo State Ptg Wks, Berlin)

1921 (11 June). P 13×13½ or 13½×13 (Types **69**/**70**).
239	66	10st. claret	35	20
240	67	10st. claret	35	20
241	68	10st. claret	35	20
242	69	10st. mauve	35	20
243	70	20st. blue	1·00	25
239/243	*Set of 5*		2·20	95

These stamps were prepared in 1915 to commemorate the annexation of Macedonia, but were not issued until 1921. Owing to protests by Yugoslavia they were only on sale for three days and were then withdrawn. An additional 50st. value in violet, showing Bulgarian soldiers in a trench, was not placed on sale at post offices.

71 Bourchier in Bulgarian Costume

72 J. D. Bourchier

73 Rila Monastery,
Bourchier's Resting-place

(Eng and recess Bradbury Wilkinson)

1921 (30 Dec). James Bourchier (*Times* correspondent) Commemoration.
P 12.

244	71	10st. vermilion..................................	20	25
245		20st. orange....................................	20	25
246	72	30st. slate......................................	20	25
247		50st. slate-lilac................................	20	25
248		1l. purple......................................	35	25
249	73	1½l. olive-green...............................	35	45
250		2l. grey-green.................................	35	35
251		3l. grey-blue...................................	80	70
252		5l. maroon.....................................	1·50	1·50
244/252 Set of 9			3·75	3·75

10 СТОТИНКИ (**74**)   **3** ЛЕВА (**75**)   **6** ЛЕВА (**76**)

1924 (10 Nov–24 Dec). Various types surch.

(a) As T **74**

253	49	10st. on 1st. black (P 11½) (R.)..........	35	25
		a. Imperf between (horiz pair)............	47·00	
254	D 37	10st. on 20st. pale orange (No. D241)....	35	25
255		20st. on 5st. bright green (No. D200)....	37·00	41·00
		a. Imperf between (vert pair)..............	60·00	
255b		20st. on 5st. yellow-green (No. D239)....	35	25
256		20st. on 10st. dull violet (No. D201).....	8·75	8·00
		a. Imperf between (vert pair)..............	55·00	
256b		20st. on 10st. bright violet (No. D240)...	35	25
257		20st. on 30st. red-orange (No. D203)....	35	25
		a. Imperf between (vert pair)..............	55·00	

(b) As T **75** or T **76** (1l. and 6l.)

258	50	1l. on 5st. emerald (B.)....................	40	25
259	25	3l. on 50st. deep blue (R.)...............	90	35
260	62	6l. on 1l. scarlet (B.)........................	1·80	80

77   **78**

79 King Boris III   **80** King Boris III

T **80** redrawn. The shoulder does not touch the frame at left, and there are many other differences.

81 Aleksandr Nevski Cathedral, Sofia   **82** Harvesters

(Des Kh. Lozev (Nos. 261/264), G. Zhelezarov (No. 268), S. Krustev (No. 267), D. Zankov (Nos. 265/266a, 267a). Typo)

1925–28.

(a) P 13

261	77	10st. blue and scarlet/*rose* (15.6.25)	55	35
		a. Perf 11½	55	35
262		15st. orange and deep rose-red/*blue* (20.6.25)	55	35
		a. Perf 11½	55	35
		b. Error. Buff and black....................	£2000	
263		30st. buff and black (15.7.25)	55	35
		a. Perf 11½	55	35
264	78	50st. chocolate/*green* (1.6.25)	55	35
		a. Perf 11½	55	35

(b) P 11½

265	79	1l. olive-green (1.3.25)	1·30	35
266	80	1l. dull grey-olive (1926)	1·00	35
266a		1l. dull yellowish green (1928)	34·00	70
267	81	2l. deep grey-green and buff (15.7.25)	2·75	35
267a	80	2l. olive-brown (1926)	1·00	35
268	82	4l. brown-lake and greenish yellow (1.10.25)	2·75	35
		a. Imperf between (horiz pair)	17·00	
261/268 Set of 9 (excluding No. 266a)			10·00	2·75

83 Proposed Rest-home, Varna   **84** Proposed Sanatorium, Bankya

(Des G. Nikolov. Litho)

1925 (1 Sept)–29. SUNDAY DELIVERY. Litho. P 11½.

268b	83	1l. black/*green*	13·50	55
268c		1l. brown (1.5.26)	10·00	70
268d		1l. orange (1.6.27)	13·50	70
268e		1l. pink (1.5.28)	13·50	70
268f		1l. violet/*rose* (1.5.29)	13·50	70
268g	84	2l. green	2·00	70
268h		2l. violet (1.6.27)	1·40	40
268i		5l. blue	13·50	1·60
268j		5l. rose (1.6.27)	13·50	1·60
268b/268j Set of 9			85·00	7·00

For use in addition to normal postage to ensure delivery on Sundays and holidays. The funds raised from the sale of these stamps were to maintain a sanatorium for the benefit of postal, telegraph and telephone employees.

85 St Nedelya's Cathedral, Sofia, after Bomb Outrage   **86** C. Botev (poet)

(Des G. Zhelezarov. Litho)

1926 (15 Mar). P 11½.

269	85	50st. olive-black.............................	50	35

(Des Kh. Losev. Litho)

1926 (2 June). 50th Anniversary of Death of Botev. P 11½.

270	86	1l. olive-green................................	80	60
271		2l. violet-blue.................................	1·70	60
272		4l. claret..	2·40	3·00
270/272 Set of 3			4·50	3·75

87   (**88** Albatros Biplane)   **89** King Boris III

(Des Kh. Losev. Typo, centre embossed)

1926 (1 Oct)–27. P 11½.

273	87	6l. pale yellow-olive and deep blue (1927)	2·75	40
274		10l. orange-brown and blackish brown	6·75	5·25

BULGARIA 1927

1927 (1 Feb)–**35**. As T **1**, but value in stotinki, as for the issue of 1881. P 13.

(a) No wmk

275	10st. carmine and green		35	25
276	15st. black and yellow (1929)		35	25
277	30st. slate and yellow-buff		35	25
278	30st. blue and buff (1928)		35	25
279	50st. black and rose (1928)		35	25

(b) Wmk Vert Wavy Lines

280	10st. carmine and green (5.9.35)	70	25
275/280 Set of 6		2·20	1·40

1927 (7 Nov)–**28**. AIR. P 11½.

*(a) Optd as T **88** (sideways, nose at top) and additionally surch*

281	87	1l. on 6l. pale yellow-olive and deep blue (R.)		2·20	2·75
		a. Surch inverted		£500	£600

*(b) Optd wih T **88** (horiz)*

282	80	2l. olive-brown (R.) (15.4.28)	2·20	2·75
283	82	4l. brown-lake and greenish yellow (B.)	3·00	2·75
284	87	10l. orange-brown and blackish brown (G.) (15.4.28)	65·00	27·00
281/284 Set of 4			65·00	32·00

Nos. 281 and 283/284 but with the surcharge or overprint in brown, green and blue respectively were prepared but not issued.

(Des Kh. Lozev. Typo)

1928 (3 Oct)–**31**. P 12×11½.

285	89	1l. bright green	2·00	25
		a. Olive-green (1931)	2·75	25
286		2l. chocolate	2·75	25

90 Saint Clement of Ohrid   **91** Monastery of Dryanovo

(Des Ts. Lavrenov (10st., 50st., 1l.), Kh. Lozev (15st., 4l., 6l.), T. Dolapchiev (30st.), S. Velkov (5l.), D. Zankov (2l., 3l.). Typo)

1929 (12 May). 50th Anniversary of the Liberation of Bulgaria and Millenary of Tsar Simeon. T **90** (and other portraits) and T **91**. P 11½.

287	10st. deep violet	35	15
288	15st. purple	35	15
289	30st. carmine	35	15
290	50st. olive-green	45	25
291	1l. brown-red	1·40	30
292	2l. blue	1·60	30
293	3l. olive-green	3·50	1·40
294	4l. olive-brown	6·00	55
295	5l. red-brown	4·75	1·40
296	6l. greenish blue	6·00	3·00
287/296 Set of 10		22·00	7·00

Portraits: 23½×33½ mm—15st. Konstantin Miladinov (poet and folklorist); 50st. T **91**; 1l. Father Paisii Khilendarski (historian); 2l. Tsar Simeon; 4l. Vasil Levski (revolutionary); 5l. Georgi Benkovski (revolutionary); 6l. Tsar Alexander II of Russia, 'The Liberator'. 19×28½ mm—10st. T **90**; 30st. Georgi Rakovski (writer). 19×26 mm—3l. Lyuben Karavelov (journalist).

98 Convalescent Home, Varna   **99**

(Des N. Biserov. Litho)

1930–33. SUNDAY DELIVERY. P 11½.

297	98	1l. green and claret (1.6.30)	13·50	70
298		1l. yellow and green (1.9.31)	1·40	40
299		1l. bistre-brown and claret (1.6.33)	1·40	40
297/299 Set of 3			14·50	1·50

(Des N. Biserov. Typo)

1930 (12 Nov). Wedding of King Boris and Princess Giovanna of Italy. T **99** and similar horiz design. P 11½.

300	99	1l. green	35	50
301	–	2l. purple	55	55
302	99	4l. carmine	55	55
303	–	6l. deep blue	70	60
300/303 Set of 4			1·90	2·00

Design: 2l., 6l. Portraits in two medallions.
A miniature sheet containing Nos. 300/303 exists. Only 55 copies were printed and these were presented to eminent guests attending the wedding.

101 King Boris III   **102** King Boris III

(Des K. Shermaten. Typo)

1931 (3 Apr)–**37**. No wmk.

(a) Without horiz coloured frame lines at top and bottom. P 13

304	101	1l. green (12.31)	55	25
		a. Wmk Wavy Lines (7.35)	80	25
		b. Emerald (1936)	1·40	25
305		2l. carmine (9.31)	80	25
		a. Wmk Wavy Lines (7.35)	50·00	55
306		4l. orange (27.1.34)	1·00	25
307		6l. blue	90	25
		a. Wmk Wavy Lines (5.9.35)	1·30	55
308		12l. brown (4.32)	70	35

(b) With horiz coloured frame lines at top and bottom. P 12×11½ or 11½ (20l.)

308a	101	4l. orange (1936)	1·10	25
308b		6l. blue (1936)	1·80	25
308c		7l. ultramarine (7.3.37)	35	25
308d		10l. slate	27·00	3·50
308e		14l. chestnut (1.7.37)	60	70
308f	102	20l. chestnut and purple	1·70	1·40
304/308f Set of 11 (cheapest)			33·00	7·00

103 Gymnastics

104 Football   **105** The Spirit of Victory

(Des G. Nikolov (6l., 50l.), N. Biserov (others). Typo)

1931 (18 Sept). Balkan Olympic Games. Types **103/105** and similar types, dated 1931. P 11½.

309	1l. green	2·00	1·70
310	2l. brown-lake	2·75	2·40
311	4l. carmine	6·00	3·00
312	6l. blue-green	13·50	8·00
313	10l. orange-vermilion	27·00	13·50
314	12l. deep blue	90·00	41·00
315	50l. brown	90·00	95·00
309/315 Set of 7		£200	£150

Designs: 1l. T **103**; 2l. T **104**; 4l. Horse-riding (as T **104**); 6l. Fencing (as T **103**); 10l. Cycling (as T **103**); 12l. Diving (as T **105**); 50l. T **105**.
See also Nos. 326/332.

1931 BULGARIA

108 **109** Rila Monastery

(Des B. Denev. Typo)

1931 (28 Oct)–**38**. AIR. P 11½.

316	**108**	1l. green		60	40
316a		1l. maroon (27.12.38)		35	35
317		2l. maroon		60	40
317a		2l. green (27.12.38)		45	40
318		6l. light blue		80	60
318a		6l. carmine (27.12.38)		1·40	75
319		12l. carmine		1·70	60
319a		12l. light blue (27.12.38)		1·50	85
320		20l. violet		1·70	1·10
321		30l. orange		3·25	2·20
322		50l. red-brown		4·75	3·75
316/322 Set of 11				15·00	10·50

(Des N. Biserov. Typo)

1932 (9 May). AIR. P 11½.

323	**109**	18l. green		£100	55·00
324		24l. carmine		70·00	41·00
325		28l. ultramarine		41·00	34·00
323/325 Set of 3				£190	£120

These stamps were issued for use on mail carried from Sofia to Strasbourg on a flight in connection with a Philatelic Exhibition there.

D **110**   D **111**   D **112**   (**110**)

1932 (15 Aug). POSTAGE DUE Typo. P 11½.

D326	D **110**	1l. bistre		1·80	1·60
D327		2l. lake		1·80	1·60
D328		6l. maroon		4·00	1·80
D326/D328 Set of 3				8·00	3·75

1933 (5 Jan). Balkan Olympic Games. Types **103**/**105** and similar types. Colours changed, Litho. P 11½.

326		1l. blue-green	3·50	5·50
327		2l. blue	5·50	6·00
328		4l. slate-purple	8·00	7·50
329		6l. carmine	17·00	13·50
330		10l. brown	£120	90·00
331		12l. orange-vermilion	£200	£140
332		50l. claret	£550	£750
326/332 Set of 7			£800	£900

(Des N. Biserov. Typo)

1933 (10 Apr). POSTAGE DUE. P 11½.

D333	D **111**	20st. olive-brown	25	15
D334		40st. blue	25	15
D335		80st. carmine	25	15
D336	D **112**	1l. red-brown	1·40	75
D337		2l. brown-olive	1·40	1·10
D338		6l. slate-purple	70	45
D339		14l. ultramarine	1·00	75
D333/D339 Set of 7			4·75	3·25

For stamps as T D **112** but larger, see Nos. D646/D649.

1934 (27 Jan). T **101** (without frame-line) surcharged with T **110**. No wmk. P 13.

333		2 on 3l. brown-olive (B.)	10·00	1·50

111 Defending the Pass   **112** Bulgarian Veteran

(Des D. Gyudzhenov (1l.), V. Staikov (2l.), N. Biserov (3l., 7l., 14l.), N. Kozhukharov (4l.). Typo)

1934. Unveiling of Shipka Pass Memorial. Types **111**/**112** and similar vert designs. Wmk Wavy Lines.

(a) First issue
A. P 11

334A	1l. green	1·40	1·40
335A	2l. reddish orange	1·00	70
336A	3l. olive-sepia	3·50	3·50
337A	4l. carmine	2·75	1·40
338A	7l. blue	4·75	4·00
339A	14l. deep reddish purple	23·00	20·00

B. P 11½ (26 Aug)

334B	1l. green	1·40	1·40
335B	2l. reddish orange	1·00	70
336B	3l. olive-sepia	3·50	3·50
337B	4l. carmine	2·75	1·40
338B	7l. blue	4·75	4·00
339B	14l. deep reddish purple	23·00	20·00

(b) Second issue
A. P 11×10½ (2l.) or 11 (others)

340A	1l. yellowish green	1·40	1·40
341A	2l. yellow-orange	1·00	70
342A	3l. lemon	3·50	3·50
343A	4l. rose-red	2·75	1·40
344A	7l. new blue	4·75	4·00
345A	14l. ochre	23·00	20·00

B. P 11½ (21 Sept)

340B	1l. yellowish green	1·40	1·40
341B	2l. yellow-orange	1·00	70
342B	3l. lemon	3·50	3·50
343B	4l. rose-red	2·75	1·40
344B	7l. new blue	4·75	4·00
345B	14l. ochre	23·00	20·00

Designs: 1l. T **111**; 2l. Shipka Pass Memorial; 3l., 7l. Veteran standard-bearer; 4l. T **112**; 14l. Widow showing memorial to orphans.

113 Convalescent Home, Troyan   **114** Captain Georgi Mamarchev

(Des G. Nikolov. Typo)

1935 (9 Feb). SUNDAY DELIVERY. T **113** and similar horiz design. Wmk Wavy Lines. P 11½ (No. 347) or 11 (others).

346	1l. scarlet and chocolate	1·40	35
	a. Perf 11½		
347	1l. ultramarine and green	1·40	35
348	5l. ultramarine and brown-lake	4·50	1·50
346/348 Set of 3		6·50	2·00

Designs: 1l. T **113**; 5l. Convalescent Home, Bankya.

(Des K. Chokanov and D. Gyudzhenov. Typo)

1935 (5 May). Centenary of Turnovo Insurrection. T **114** and similar vert design. Wmk Wavy Lines. P 11½.

349	1l. steel blue	2·75	1·10
350	2l. brown-purple	2·75	1·60

Designs: 1l. Velcho Atanasov Dzhamdzhiyata; 2l. T **114**.

115 Aleksandr Nevski Cathedral, Sofia   **116** Girl Gymnast   **117** Janos Hunyadi

(Des N. Balkchiev (1l., 50l.), K. Penev (2l., 4l.), N. Biserov (7l.), G. Krustev (14l.). Typo)

1935 (14 June). Fifth Balkan Football Tournament. T **115** and various football types. Wmk Wavy Lines. P 11½.

351	1l. green	12·50	7·25
	a. Perf 11		
352	2l. deep blue	13·50	8·25
353	4l. rosine	16·00	10·00

BULGARIA 1935

354	7l. greenish blue		27·00	20·00
355	14l. orange		27·00	20·00
	a. Perf 11×10½			
356	50l. chocolate		£475	£400
351/356 Set of 6			£500	£425

Designs: Horiz—1l. Match in progress at Yunak Stadium, Sofia; 4l. Footballers. Vert—2l. T **115**; 7l. Herald and Balkan map; 14l. Footballers and trophy; 50l. Trophy.

(Des S. Badzhov.Typo)

1935 (10 July). Eighth Bulgarian Gymnastic Tournament. T **116** and sports types inscr '12–14 VII 1935'. Wmk Wavy Lines. P 11½.

357	1l. green	7·50	7·50
358	2l. light blue	8·00	8·00
359	4l. scarlet	8·75	8·25
360	7l. blue	11·00	13·50
361	14l. chocolate	13·50	13·50
362	50l. orange-red	£325	£275
357/362 Set of 6		£325	£300

Designs: Vert—1l. Parallel bars; 2l. Male gymnast in uniform; 4l. T **116**; 7l. Pole vault; 50l. Sports Association Emblem (athlete and Lion). Horiz—14l. Yunak Stadium, Sofia.

(Des V. Zakhariev. Typo)

1935 (4 Aug). Unveiling of Monument to Ladislas III of Poland at Varna. T **117** and designs inscr 'WARNENCZYK (A)'. Wmk Wavy Lines.

A. P 11½

363A	1l. brown-orange	4·25	2·00
364A	2l. maroon	4·25	2·40
365A	4l. vermilion	25·00	9·00
366A	7l. dull blue	4·25	3·00
367A	14l. green	4·50	2·75
363A/367A Set of 5		38·00	17·00

B. P 11

363B	1l. brown-orange	5·00	2·00
364B	2l. maroon	5·00	2·40
365B	4l. vermilion	30·00	9·00
366B	7l. dull blue	5·00	3·00
367B	14l. green	5·50	2·75
363B/367B Set of 5		45·00	17·00

Designs: Vert—1l. T **117**; 2l. King Ladislas of Hungary enthroned (22×32 *mm*); 7l. Full length portrait of King Ladislas in armour (20×31 *mm*). Horiz—4l. Varna Memorial (33×24 *mm*); 14l. Battle scene (30×25 *mm*).

Some values also exist perf compound of 10½ and 11½.

118 Dimitur

119

120

(Des N. Balkchiev (1l.), F. Filipov (2l.), K. Penev (4l., 7l.), G. Krustev (14l.). Typo)

1935 (11 Oct). 67th Death Anniversary of Khadzhi Dimitur (revolutionary). T **118** and similar designs.

A. P 11½

368A	1l. green	3·50	1·30
369A	2l. chocolate	4·75	2·30
370A	4l. carmine	13·50	6·00
371A	7l. blue	16·00	9·75
372A	14l. orange	20·00	11·00
368A/372A Set of 5		50·00	27·00

B. P 11

368B	1l. green	3·50	1·30
369B	2l. chocolate	4·75	2·30
370B	4l. carmine	13·50	6·00
371B	7l. blue	16·00	9·75
372B	14l. orange	20·00	11·00
368B/372B Set of 5		50·00	27·00

Designs: Vert—1l. Dimitur's monument at Sliven; 2l. T **118**; 7l. Revolutionary Group (dated 1868). Horiz—4l. Dimitur and Stefan Karadzha (revolutionary); 14l. Dimitur's birthplace at Sliven.

Stamps also exist perf compound of 10½ and 11½.

1936 (4 Apr)–**39**. Typo. P 13.

373	**119**	10st. vermilion (3.37)	30	20
373*a*		15st. emerald-green (23.5 36)	30	20
374	**120**	30st. maroon	30	20
374*a*		30st. chestnut (1937)	30	20
374*b*		30st. greenish blue (2.38)	30	20
375		50st. ultramarine (8.4.36)	30	20
375*a*		50st. carmine (1.38)	30	20
375*b*		50st. dark green (27.12.39)	30	20
373/375*b* Set of 8			2·20	1·40

121 Nesebur

(Des V. Zhakariev. Photo)

1936 (16 Aug). Slav Geographical and Ethnographical Congress, Sofia. T **121** and similar designs. P 11½.

376	1l. violet	4·00	2·75
377	2l. bright blue	4·00	2·75
378	7l. deep green	8·00	5·00
376/378 Set of 3		14·50	9·50

Designs: 25×34 *mm*—1l. Meteorological Bureau, Mount Musala. 23×34 *mm*—2l. Peasant girl. Horiz—7l. T **121**.

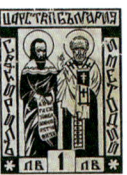
122 St Cyril and St Methodius

123 St Cyril and St Methodius

(Des I. Manev (T **122**), E. Rakarov (T **123**). Photo)

1937 (3 June). Millenary of Introduction of Cyrillic Alphabet and Slavonic Liturgy. P 11½.

379	**122**	1l. myrtle-green	65	40
380		2l. bright purple	65	40
381	**123**	4l. vermilion	70	40
382	**122**	7l. bright blue	3·75	2·50
383	**123**	14l. scarlet	3·75	2·75
379/383 Set of 5			8·50	5·75

124 Princess Marie Louise

125 King Boris III

(Des K. Khristov. Photo)

1937 (3 Oct). P 11½.

384	**124**	1l. emerald-green	65	35
385		2l. red	65	35
386		4l. vermilion	65	60
384/386 Set of 3			1·80	1·20

(Des A. Apostolov. Photo)

1937 (3 Oct–22 Nov). 19th Anniversary of Accession. P 11½.

387	**125**	2l. red	70	65

MS387*a* 76×115 mm. Type **125** 2l. (+18l.) ultramarine. Imperf. (22.11.37) .... 12·00 27·00

126 Harvesting

128 'Attar of Roses'

1938 BULGARIA

(Des B. Angelushev (10st., 15st., 50st., 7l.), A. Apostolov (30st.), A. Zhendov (1l., 3l., 4l.), V. Staikov and S. Petrov (2l., 14l.). Photo)

1938 Agricultural Products. Types **126** and **128** and similar designs. P 13.

388	**126**	10st. orange (25.10.38)	25	35
389	–	10st. red-orange (25.10.38)	25	35
390	–	15st. crimson (25.10.38)	45	35
391	–	15st. claret (25.10.38)	45	35
392	–	30st. brown (17.5.38)	35	35
393	–	30st. red-brown (25.10.38)	40	35
394	–	50st. steel-blue (17.5.38)	90	35
395	–	50st. black (17.5.38)	90	35
396	–	1l. green (25.10.38)	90	35
397	–	1l. yellow-green (25.10.38)	90	35
398	**128**	2l. carmine (22.3.38)	90	35
399	–	2l. lake (22.3.38)	90	35
400	–	3l. magenta (25.10.38)	1·80	1·40
401	–	3l. maroon (25.10.38)	1·80	1·40
402	–	4l. brown (30.5.38)	1·40	70
403	–	4l. bright purple (30.5.38)	1·40	70
404	–	7l. bluish violet (25.10.38)	2·75	1·40
405	–	7l. bright blue (25.10.38)	2·75	1·40
406	–	14l. red-brown (18.6.38)	4·50	2·50
407	–	14l. chocolate (18.6.38)	4·50	2·50
388/407 Set of 20			26·00	14·50

Designs: Vert—15st. Sunflower; 30st. Wheat; 50st. Chickens and eggs; 1l. Grapes; 3l. Strawberries; 4l. Girl carrying Grapes; 7l. Roses; 14l. Leaves of Tobacco.

129 Prince Simeon

130 Prince Simeon

(Des K. Penev (1l., 2l., 7l.), N. Biserov (4l., 14l.). Photo)

1938 (16 June). Heir Apparent's First Birthday. As Types **129** and **130** (various portraits). P 13.

408		1l. green	25	25
409		2l. carmine	25	25
410		4l. vermilion	35	35
411		7l. bright blue	1·40	80
412		14l. brown	1·40	90
408/412 Set of 5			3·25	2·30

Portraits: 1l. T **129**; 2l. As T **129** (different frame); 4l. T **130**; 7l. as T **129**; 14l. as T **130** (but slightly larger portrait in simpler frame).

131 King Boris III

132 Modern express train

(Des K. Penev. Photo)

1938 (3 Oct). 20th Anniversary of King's Accession. As T **131** (various uniforms). P 13.

413		1l. green	25	35
414		2l. lake	1·10	35
415		4l. brown	35	35
416		7l. bright blue	55	70
417		14l. magenta	55	70
413/417 Set of 5			2·50	2·20

Portraits: 1l. T **131**; 2l. Dated 3.X.1918/3.X.1938; 4l. Dated 3.X.1918/3.X.1928; 7l., 14l. Dated 3.X.1938.

(Des B. Angelushev. Photo)

1939 (26 Apr). 50th Anniversary of Bulgarian State Railways. T **132** and similar horiz designs. P 13.

418		1l. yellow-green	50	40
419		2l. red-brown	50	40
420		4l. orange	3·25	2·00
421		7l. blue	9·50	5·50
418/421 Set of 4			12·50	7·50

Designs: 1l. First Bulgarian Locomotive; 2l. T **132**. 4l. Train crossing a viaduct; 7l. King Boris as engine-driver.

133 PO Emblem
134 GPO, Sofia

(Des D. Gyudzhenov. Typo)

1939 (14 May). 60th Anniversary of Bulgarian PO. P 13.

422	**133**	1l. emerald-green	35	15
423	**134**	2l. scarlet	45	20

135 Gymnast

(**136**) ('Inundation 1939')

E **136** Bicycle Messenger

E **137** Express Delivery Van

(Des S. Badzhov. Photo)

1939 (7 July). Yunak Gymnastic Society's Rally, Sofia. T **135** and similar vert designs. P 13.

424		1l. yellowish green	50	45
425		2l. bright carmine-red	50	45
426		4l. deep orange-brown	1·00	60
427		7l. bright blue	3·25	2·00
428		14l. mauve	16·00	13·50
424/428 Set of 5			19·00	15·00

Designs: 1l. T **135**; 2l. Yunak badge; 4l. *The Discus-thrower* (statue by Miron); 7l. Rhythmic dancer; 14l. Athlete holding weight aloft.

(Des D. Uzunov (1l., 20l.), G. Apostolov (others). Photo)

1939 (6 Aug). EXPRESS LETTER. Types E **136**/E **137** and similar vert design. P 13.

E429	E **136**	5l. blue	1·80	40
E430	E **137**	6l. brown	80	40
E431	–	7l. brown	1·30	40
E432	E **137**	8l. vermilion	1·60	70
E433	E **136**	20l. carmine	2·50	1·60
E429/E433 Set of 5			7·25	3·25

Design: As T E **136**—7l. Motorcyclist and sidecar.

1939 (22 Oct). Sevlievo and Turnovo Floods Relief Fund. Surch as T **136**.

429	**39**	1l. +1l. on 15st. greenish grey (P 12½)	20	40
430	**73**	2l. +1l. on 1½l. olive-green	30	55
431		4l. +2l. on 2l. grey-green	35	60
432		7l. +4l. on 3l. grey-blue	1·10	2·00
433		14l. +7l. on 5l. maroon	1·70	2·75
429/433 Set of 5			3·25	5·75

137 Mail Plane

138 King Boris III

(Des K. Ikonomov. Photo)

1940 (15 Jan). AIR. T **137** and similar designs. P 13.

434		1l. deep blue-green	20	20
435		2l. scarlet	2·50	20
436		4l. red-orange	20	20
437		6l. blue	40	25

105

BULGARIA 1940

438		10l. sepia	70	35
439		12l. sepia	1·00	50
440		16l. bright violet	1·60	90
441		19l. bright blue	1·70	1·20
442		30l. magenta	2·50	1·70
443		45l. deep violet	6·75	4·00
444		70l. rose-carmine	5·25	4·00
445		100l. deep blue	20·00	11·00
434/445 *Set of 12*			39·00	22·00

Designs: Horiz—1l. T **137**; 6l. Loading mail at aerodrome; 12l. Aeroplanes over Sofia Palace; 16l. Mount El Tepe; 19l. Rila lakes and mountains. Vert—Aeroplane over: 2l. King Asen's Tower; 4l. Bachkovo Monastery; 45l. Aleksander Nevski Cathedral, Sofia; 70l. Shipka Pass Memorial. Vert—Aeroplane and: 10l. Mail train and express motorcycle; 30l. Swallow; 100l. Royal cypher.

(Des S. Sharankov. Typo)

1940 (10 Feb). P 13.

445*a*	**138**	1l. dull green	55	25
446		2l. scarlet	60	25

139 First Bulgarian Postage Stamp

(Des N. Biserov. Photo)

1940 (19 May). Centenary of First Adhesive Postage Stamps. T **139** and similar type, but scroll dated 1840–1940. P 13.

447		10l. olive-green	3·25	2·75
448		20l. deep blue	3·25	2·75

140 Grapes   **141** Ploughing   **142** King Boris III

(Des A. Anev. Typo)

1940 (2 Sept)–**44**. Types **140/141** and similar designs and T **142**. P 13.

(a) No wmk

449	**140**	10st. red-orange	25	20
450	–	15st. blue	25	20
451	**141**	30st. brown	25	20
452	–	50st. violet (1941)	25	20
452*a*	–	50st. bright green (1942)	25	20
453	**142**	1l. green	25	20
		a. Perf 10 (1944)	2·50	80
		b. Perf 11½ (1944)	25	20
		c. Perf 10×11½ (1944)	25	20
		d. Perf 11½×10 (1944)	50·00	55·00
454		2l. carmine-red	35	20
		a. Perf 10 (1944)	1·60	20
		b. Perf 11½ (1944)	25	20
		c. Perf 10×11½ (1944)	25	20
		d. Perf 11½×10 (1944)	46·00	41·00
455		4l. orange (7.12.41)	35	20
		a. Perf 11½ (1944)	5·25	4·75
456		6l. bright reddish violet (1944)	50	25
457		7l. blue (1944)	30	20
458		10l. blue-green (7.12.41)	50	25
449/458 *Set of 11* (*cheapest*)			3·00	2·10

(b) Wmk Wavy Lines (20.11.41)

A. Wmk vert

459A	–	50st. violet	25	20
460A	**142**	1l. green	1·20	25
461A		2l. carmine-red	25	20
462A		7l. blue	30	20
463A		10l. blue-green	50	25
459A/463A *Set of 5*			2·30	1·00

B. Wmk horiz

459B	–	50st. violet	25	20
460B	**142**	1l. green	1·20	25
461B		2l. carmine-red	25	20
462B		7l. blue	30	20
463B		10l. blue-green	50	25
459B/463B *Set of 5*			2·30	1·00

Designs: Vert—15st. Beehive. Horiz—50st. Shepherd and flock.

143 Peasant Couple and King Boris   **144** King Boris and Map of the Dobrudja

(Des B. Angelushev. Photo)

1940 (20 Sept). Recovery of the Dobrudja from Rumania. Types **143/144** and similar design incorporating miniature portrait of King Boris. P 13.

464	**143**	1l. green	20	20
465	–	2l. carmine	30	25
466	**144**	4l. brown	50	35
467		7l. blue	1·00	1·00
464/467 *Set of 4*			1·80	1·60

Design: Vert—2l. Bulgarian flags and wheatfield.

145 Bee-keeping

(Des P. Morozov and B. Angelushev. Photo)

1940–44. Agricultural Scenes. T **145** and similar designs. P 13.

468	10st. slate-purple (7.10.40)	25	20
469	10st. blue (12.5.41)	25	20
470	15st. deep blue-green (5.12.41)	25	20
471	15st. blackish olive (1.4.43)	25	20
472	30st. orange (7.12.40)	25	20
473	30st. deep green (5.12.41)	25	20
474	50st. slate-violet (5.12.41)	25	20
475	50st. red-purple (12.4.42)	25	20
476	3l. red-brown (1.4.43)	75	25
	a. Red (1944)	95	70
477	3l. blackish brown (1944)	1·90	1·40
478	5l. brown (*shades*) (1943–1944)	1·60	80
479	5l. deep blue (1944)	2·00	1·50
468/479 *Set of 12*		7·50	5·00

Designs: 10st. Threshing; 15st. Ploughing with Oxen; 30st. T **145**; 50st. Picking Apples; 3l. Shepherd; 5l. Cattle.

146 Pencho Slaveikov (poet)   **147** St Ivan Rilski

(Des D. Uzunov (1l.), S. Velkov (2l.), V. Zakhariev (3l.), K. Chokanov (4l.), V. Kotsev (7l.), G. Gerasimov (10l.). Photo)

1940 (23 Nov). National Relief. Types **146/147** and similar vert designs. P 13.

480	1l. green	20	20
481	2l. carmine	20	20
482	3l. brown	25	25
483	4l. orange	30	25
484	7l. blue	2·10	1·80
485	10l. brown	3·25	1·90
480/485 *Set of 6*		5·75	4·25

Designs: 1l. T **146**; 2l. Bishop Sofronii of Vratsa; 3l. T **147**; 4l. Marin Drinov (historian); 7l. Chernorisets Khrabur (monk); 10l. Kolo Ficheto (architect).

1940 BULGARIA

148 Johannes Gutenberg
149 Nikola Karastoyanov

(Des N. Biserov. Photo)

1940 (16 Dec). 500th Anniversary of Invention of Printing and Centenary of Bulgarian Printing. P 13.

486	**148**	1l. myrtle green	40	25
487	**149**	2l. chestnut	50	25

150 Botev
151 Arrival in Koslodui

(Des N. Tuzsuzov. Photo)

1941 (3 May). 65th Death Anniversary of Khristo Botev (poet and revolutionary). Types **150/151** and similar design. P 13.

488	**150**	1l. deep green	20	25
489	**151**	2l. scarlet	50	35
490	–	3l. brown	1·40	1·20
488/490 Set of 3			1·90	1·60

Design: Vert—3l. Botev Memorial Cross.

152 National History Museum

(Des P. Morozov (14l.), A. Mutafov (20l.), P. Kurshovski (50l.). Recess)

1941 (2 June)–**43**. Buildings in Sofia. T **152** and similar horiz designs. P 11½.

491		14l. brown (3.43)	75	60
492		20l. green (3.43)	85	65
493		50l. blue	3·75	2·40
491/493 Set of 3			4·75	3·25

Designs: 14l. T **152**; 20l. Tsaritsa Ioanna Workers' Hospital; 50l. National Bank.

P **153** Weighing Machine
P **154** Loading Motor Lorry

(Des N. Biserov. Photo)

1941 (1 July). PARCEL POST. Types P **153**/P **154** and similar designs. White chalk-surfaced paper. P 12½×13½ (vert) or 13½×12½ (horiz).

P494	P **153**	1l. deep green	20	15
P495	–	2l. rose-red	20	15
P496	P **154**	3l. bistre-brown	20	15
P497	–	4l. red-orange	20	15
P498	P **153**	5l. deep blue	20	15
P499	–	6l. purple	20	15
P500	P **153**	7l. blue	20	15
P501	P **154**	8l. deep turquoise-green	25	15
P502	–	9l. brown-olive	35	20
P503	–	10l. bright orange	55	20
P504	P **154**	20l. bluish violet	70	25
P505	–	30l. black	1·50	40
P494/P505 Set of 12			4·25	2·00

Designs: Horiz—2l., 9l., 30l. Motorcycle combination; 4l., 6l., 10l. Loading railway mail coach.

153 Thasos Island
154 Ohrid

(Des D. Gyudzhenov (1l.), B. Angelushev (2l., both), V. Zakhariev (4l.), B. Denev (7l.). Photo)

1941 (3 Oct). Reacquisition of Macedonia. Types **153/154** and similar designs. P 13.

494	1l. deep green	20	20
495	2l. orange	20	20
496	2l. carmine	20	20
497	4l. brown	20	20
498	7l. blue	95	80
494/498 Set of 5		1·60	1·40

Designs: Vert—1l. Macedonian Girl. Horiz—2l. (No. 495) T **153**; 2l. (No. 496) King Boris and map dated 1941; 4l. Poganovski Monastery; 7l. T **154**.

155 Children on Beach

(Des B. Angelushev. Photo)

1941 (15 Oct). SUNDAY DELIVERY. T **155** and similar horiz designs. P 13.

499	1l. blackish olive	20	20
500	2l. red-orange	20	25
501	5l. deep blue	1·00	40
499/501 Set of 3		1·25	75

Designs: 1l. St Konstantin Sanatorium, Varna; 2l. T **155**; 5l. Sun-bathing terrace, Bankya.

1942 (7 Jan). PARCEL POST. As Nos. P498/P505 but colours changed. Greyish ordinary paper. Photo. P 12½×13½ (vert) or 13½×12½ (horiz).

P506	P **153**	5l. bronze green	20	20
P507	–	6l. red-brown	20	20
P508	P **153**	7l. sepia	20	20
P509	P **154**	8l. dull green	20	20
P510	–	9l. blackish olive	25	20
P511	–	10l. reddish orange	25	20
P512	P **154**	20l. slate-violet	75	35
P513	–	30l. brownish black	80	40
P506/P513 Set of 8			2·50	1·80

156 Bugler at Camp
157 Folk Dancers

1942 (1 June). Work and Joy. Designs inscribed as at foot of T **156** (2l., 7l.) or of T **157** (others). Photo. P 13.

502	1l. deep blue-green	20	15
503	2l. red	30	15
504	4l. olive-black	40	20
505	7l. blue	50	30
506	14l. brown	65	40
502/506 Set of 5		1·80	1·10

Designs: Vert—1l. Guitarist and accordion player; 2l. Camp orchestra; 4l. Hoisting the flag; 14l. T **157**. Horiz—7l. T **156**.

107

BULGARIA 1942

O **158**

1942 (1 June). OFFICIAL. T O **158** (and similar type). Typo. P 13.

(a) Size 15×21 mm

O507	10st. yellow-green		20	15
O508	30st. red-orange		20	15
O509	50st. yellow-brown		20	15

(b) Size 19×23 mm

O510	1l. bright blue		20	15
O511	2l. deep green		20	15
O512	3l. mauve		20	15
O513	4l. pink		30	20
O514	5l. lake		50	25
O507/O514	Set of 8		1·80	1·20

See also Nos. O533/O534.

158 Wounded Soldier

159 Queen visiting wounded

(Des D. Gyudzhenov and V. Stoilov. Photo)

1942 (7 Sept). War Invalids. Designs inscribed as Types **158**/**159**. P 13½×12½ or 12½×13½ (vert).

507	1l. deep green		25	20
508	2l. carmine		25	20
509	4l. orange		25	20
510	7l. blue		25	20
511	14l. olive-brown		30	20
512	20l. black		70	25
507/512	Set of 6		1·80	1·10

Designs: Vert—1l. T **158**. Horiz—2l. Soldier and family; 4l. First Aid on battlefield; 7l. Widow and orphans at grave; 14l. Unknown Soldier's Memorial; 20l. T **159**.

160 Khan Kubrat (ruled 595–642)

(Des E. Rakarov. Photo)

1942–43. Historical series. T **160** and similar vert designs. P 13.

513	10st. blue-black (22.5.43)		20	20
514	15st. greenish blue (22.5.43)		20	20
515	30st. mauve (22.5.43)		20	20
516	50st. deep blue (22.5.43)		20	20
517	1l. slate-green (12.10.42)		20	20
518	2l. rose-red (12.10.42)		20	20
519	3l. brown (22.5.43)		20	20
520	4l. orange (22.5.43)		20	20
521	5l. blackish green (22.5.43)		20	20
522	7l. blue (22.5.43)		20	20
523	10l. brownish black (22.5.43)		20	20
524	14l. blackish olive (22.5.43)		40	25
525	20l. red-brown (22.5.43)		1·00	95
526	30l. black (22.5.43)		2·10	1·40
513/526	Set of 14		5·25	4·25

Designs: 10st. T **160**; 15st. Cavalry charge (Khan Asparukh, 680–701); 30st. Equestrian statue of Khan Krum (803–814); 50st. Baptism of King Boris 1 (852–889); 1l. St Naum's school; 2l. King Boris crowns his son Tsar Simeon; 3l. Golden Era of Bulgarian literature; 4l. Trial of Bogomil Vasilii; 5l. Proclamation of Second Bulgarian Empire; 7l. Ivan Asen II (1214–1281) at Trebizond; 10l. Expulsion of Evtimii, Patriarch of Turnovo; 14l. Wandering minstrels; 20l. Father Paisii Khilendarski (historian); 30l. Shipka Pass Memorial.

King Simeon II
28 August 1943–15 September 1946

161 King Boris III

162

(Des D. Gyudzhenov. Photo)

1944 (28 Feb). King Boris Mourning Issue. T **161** (and similar portraits dated 1894–1943). Frames in black. W **162**.

A. Imperf

527A	1l. olive-green		20	25
528A	2l. red-brown		25	35
529A	4l. brown		30	40
530A	5l. violet		85	1·10
531A	7l. blue		1·00	1·40
527A/531A	Set of 5		2·30	3·25

B. P 13

527B	1l. olive-green		20	25
528B	2l. red-brown		25	35
529B	4l. brown		30	40
530B	5l. violet		85	1·10
531B	7l. blue		1·00	1·40
527B/531B	Set of 5		2·30	3·25

P **163**

163 King Simeon II

всичко за фронта
(**164**)

1944 (21 Mar). PARCEL POST. Typo. Imperf.

P532	P **163**	1l. carmine	20	20
P533		3l. green	20	20
P534		5l. deep green	20	20
P535		7l. mauve	20	20
P536		10l. blue	20	20
P537		20l. brown	20	20
P538		30l. brown-purple	40	25
P539		50l. orange	75	70
P540		100l. blue	1·40	1·10
P532/P540	Set of 9		3·50	3·00

(Des A. Anev. Typo)

1944 (12 June).

A. P 13

532A	**163**	3l. red-orange	20	15

B. P 11½

532B	**163**	3l. red-orange	50	35

1944. OFFICIAL. As Nos. O510/O511, but colour and perf changed. P 10½×11½.

O533	1l. blue		1·40	60
O534	2l. vermilion		1·40	60

1945 (25 Jan). All for the Front. Parcel Post stamps. T P **163**, optd as T **164**, (No. 534 surch also). P 11½.

533	1l. carmine		20	20
534	4l. on 1l. carmine		20	20
535	7l. purple		30	20
536	20l. brown		35	20
537	30l. brown-purple		60	30
538	50l. orange		70	70
539	100l. blue (R.)		2·40	1·40
533/539	Set of 7		4·25	3·00

1945 BULGARIA

(**165** Heinkel He 111H)

(**166** Arado Ar 240 Bomber)

1945 (15 Feb). AIR.

(a) Surch as T 165. P 13

540	144	1l. green (No. 457)	20	20
541		4l. orange (No. 459)	20	20

(b) Surch as T 166. Imperf.

542	P 163	10l. on 100l. yellow (B.)	30	20
543		45l. on 100l. yellow (R.)	40	25
544		75l. on 100l. yellow (G.)	1·00	80
545		100l. yellow (V.)	1·30	1·20
540/545	Set of 6		3·00	2·50

I. Wide Crown

II. Narrow Crown

2l. and 4l. Two types of Crown

(Des I. Barov (Nos. 552, 557/560), B. Angelushev (Nos. 553, 555/556), St. Kunchev (Nos. 554, 561/562). Typo)

1945 (26 Apr)–**46**. Types **171**/**172** and similar vert designs (small Arms types). P 13.

552		30st. emerald-green (13.12.45)	25	20
553		50st. greenish blue (15.7.45)	25	20
554		1l. deep green (*shades*) (26.4.45)	25	20
555		2l. brown (I) (26.4.45)	25	20
		a. Type II (15.5.46)	25	20
556		4l. blue (I) (15.5.45)	25	20
		a. Type II (15.5.46)	25	20
557		5l. reddish violet (*shades*) (25.7 45)	25	20
558		9l. grey (20.7.45)	25	20
559		10l. turquoise-blue (4.6.45)	25	20
560		15l. brown (*shades*) (4.6.45)	25	20
561		20l. black (21.1.46)	50	20
562		20l. scarlet (21.1.46)	50	20
552/562	Set of 11		3·00	2·00

167

(Des B. Angelushev. Litho)

1945. Slav Congress.

A. Imperf (8 Mar)

546A	167	4l. vermilion	20	15
547A		10l. blue	20	15
548A		50l. claret	40	55
546A/548A	Set of 3		70	75

B. P 11½ (23 Apr)

546B	167	4l. vermilion	20	15
547B		10l. blue	20	15

173 Chain-breaker

174 VE Day

(Des B. Angelushev (Nos. 563/568), A. Zhendov (Nos. 569/570). Litho)

1945 (4 June). Liberty Loan. T **173** and similar types. Rose, laid paper. Imperf.

563		50l. orange	30	20
564		50l. brown-lake	30	20
565		100l. blue	40	25
566		100l. brown	45	25
567		150l. carmine	1·00	60
568		150l. olive-green	1·00	65
569		200l. grey-olive	1·30	1·00
570		200l. violet-blue	1·30	1·00
563/570	Set of 8		5·50	3·75
MS570*a*	Two blocks 88×123 mm. with the four values imperf (a) in brown-red and (b) in violet...... Pair		16·00	28·00

Designs: 50l. T **173**; 100l. Hand holding coin; 150l. Water-mill, 200l. Coin and symbols of industry and agriculture.

(Des G. Manolov. Typo)

1945 (1 Sept). Victory in Europe. P 13.

571	174	10l. green and brown	20	20
572		50l. green and red	65	35

1945 (Mar). Savings Campaign. Nos. 453/459 optd with slogans, Types **168**/**170**. P 13.

A. T 168

549A	143	1l. green	40	40
		a. Perf 11½	30	45
550A		2l. carmine-red (P 11½)	1·60	40
551A		4l. orange	1·00	45

B. T 169

549B	143	1l. green	30	45
550B		2l. carmine-red	1·50	45
		a. Perf 11	4·25	5·75
551B		4l. orange	1·00	45
		a. Perf 11½	5·00	8·00

C. T 170

549C	143	1l. green	30	45
		a. Perf 11½	55	45
550C		2l. carmine-red (P 11½)	1·30	45
551C		4l. orange	1·00	45
		a. Perf 11½	5·50	4·75

171

172

175

176

109

BULGARIA 1945

(Des I. Barov. Typo)

1945 (7 Sept). First Anniversary of Fatherland Front Coalition. P 13.

573	175	1l. grey-green	20	20
574		4l. deep blue	20	20
575		5l. mauve	20	20
576	176	10l. blue	20	20
577		20l. carmine	20	25
578	175	50l. green	1·00	80
579		100l. brown	1·30	1·40
573/579 Set of 7			3·00	3·00

O **177**   O **178**   O **179**

(Des I. Barov (T O **179**). Typo)

1945–50. OFFICIAL.

A. P 13 (29/30.10.45)

O581A	177	2l. turquoise-green	20	15
O582A	178	3l. orange-brown	20	15
O583A		4l. pale ultramarine	20	15
O584A	179	5l. claret (30.10.45)	20	15
O581A/O584A Set of 4			70	55

B. Imperf (1/30.10.46)

O580B	179	1l. mauve	35	15
O581B	177	2l. turquoise-green	35	15
O582B	178	3l. orange-brown	35	15
O583B		4l. pale ultramarine	35	15
O584B	179	5l. claret (30.10.45)	35	15
O580B/O584B Set of 5			1·60	70

C. P 11, 11½, 11×11½, or 11½×11 (10.10.50)

| O585c | 179 | 5l. deep brown-red | 80 | 35 |

177 Refugee Children   **178** Red Cross Train

(Des B. Angelushev. Typo)

1946 (4 Apr). Red Cross (1st Issue). Types **177/178** (and similar designs). Cross in red. P 11½.

580	177	2l. deep olive	35	15
581	–	4l. violet	35	15
582	177	10l. purple	35	15
583	–	20l. ultramarine	35	15
584	–	30l. brown	35	25
585	178	35l. grey-black	55	60
586	–	50l. purple-brown	70	60
587	178	100l. slate-brown	2·40	2·30
580/587 Set of 8			4·75	4·00

Designs: Horiz—4l., 20l. Soldier on stretcher. Vert—30l., 50l. Nurse and wounded soldier.

For 1947 issue in new colours, see Nos. 645d/645k.

179 Postal Savings Emblem   **180** Savings Bank-Note

(Des B. Angelushev, G. Manolov, A. Poplilov, N. Biserov, respectively. Typo)

1946 (12 Apr). 50th Anniversary of Savings Bank. Types **179/180** and similar designs dated 1896–1946. P 11½.

588		4l. brownish red	25	15
589		10l. deep olive	25	15
590		20l. blue	35	15
591		50l. grey-black	2·00	1·60
588/591 Set of 4			2·50	1·80

Designs: Vert—4l. T **179**; 20l. Child filling moneybox; 50l. Postal Savings Bank. Horiz—10l. T **180**.

181 Arms of Russia and Bulgaria and Spray of Oak

(Des L. Nenov. Typo)

1946 (23 May–11 July). Bulgo-Russian Congress. P 11½.

592	181	4l. claret	13·50	11·50
593		4l. orange (11.7.46)	30	25
594		20l. light blue	13·50	11·50
595		20l. green (11.7.46)	45	45
592/595 Set of 4			25·00	21·00

182 Lion Rampant

(Des St. Kunchev. Typo)

1946 (25 May). Stamp Day. Imperf.

| 596 | 182 | 20l. blue | 1·10 | 45 |

183   **184**

188   **189**   **190**

(Des I. Barov (4l., 10l., 12l., 16l., 19l.), A. Poplilov (6l.), I. Penkov (100l.), St. Kunchev (others). Typo)

1946 (15 June). AIR. Inscr 'PAR AVION'. P 13.

597	183	1l. deep dull purple	30	15
598		2l. greenish slate	30	15
599	–	4l. black	30	15
600	–	6l. greenish blue	30	15
601	184	10l. blue-green	30	15
602		12l. yellow-brown	30	35
603	–	16l. purple	30	15
		a. Imperf (pair)	£550	£425
604	184	19l. rosine	30	15
605	188	30l. orange	35	25
606	189	45l. olive-green	80	30
607		75l. reddish brown	1·20	35
608	190	100l. vermilion	2·20	60
609	–	100l. slate-green	2·20	60
597/609 Set of 13			8·25	3·00

Designs: 23×18 mm—4l. Bird carrying envelope; 18×23 mm—6l. Aeroplane and envelope; 16l. Winged envelope. 22½×18 mm—100l. Aeroplane.

1946 BULGARIA

192 Stamboliiski

193 Flags of Albania, Bulgaria, Yugoslavia and Rumania

(Des D. Gyudzhenov. Typo)

1946 (13 June). 23rd Death Anniversary of Aleksandur Stamboliiski (Prime Minister 1919–1923). P 11½.
610	**192**	100l. orange	11·00	10·50

(Des I. Barov. Typo)

1946 (6 July). Balkan Games. P 11½.
611	**193**	100l. black-brown	2·30	2·00
		a. *Tête-bêche* (pair)	5·00	4·50

194 Grenade Thrower

195 Junkers Ju 87B Stuka Dive Bombers

196 Artillery

(Des A. Poplilov (No. 613), A. and B. Tilov (No. 615), B. Angelushev (Nos. 620, 622), D. Gyudzhenov (others). Typo)

1946 (9 Aug). Military and Air Services. Types **194/195** and horiz designs as T **196**. P 11½.
612	–	2l. deep claret	25	20
613	**194**	4l. olive-grey	25	20
614	**196**	5l. Indian red	25	20
615	**195**	6l. bistre-brown	25	20
616	–	9l. magenta	25	20
617	–	10l. dull violet	25	20
618	–	20l. deep bright blue	70	25
619	–	30l. bright orange	80	35
620	–	40l. brown-olive	95	45
621	–	50l. deep green	1·10	80
622	–	60l. reddish brown	1·60	90
612/622 *Set of 11*			6·00	3·50

Designs: As T **196**—2l., 20l. Grenade thrower and machine gunner; 9l. Building pontoon-bridge; 10l., 30l. Cavalry charge; 40l. Supply column; 50l. Motor convoy; 60l. Tank.

203 St Ivan Rilski

204 Rila Monastery

(Des Ts. Lavrenov (Nos. 623, 626), I. Manev (No. 624), D. Gyudzhenov (No. 625), V. Tomov (No. 627))

1946 (26 Aug). Death Millenary of St Ivan Rilski. Types **203/204** and similar designs. P 11½.
623	**203**	1l. red-brown	25	20
624	**204**	4l. deep brown	25	20
625	–	10l. deep blue-green	35	25
626	–	20l. deep bright blue	60	30
627	–	50l. dull scarlet	2·40	1·40
623/627 *Set of 5*			3·50	2·10

Designs: Horiz—10l. Monastery entrance; 50l. Cloistered courtyard. Vert—20l. Aerial view of monastery.

PEOPLE'S REPUBLIC
15 September 1946–15 November 1990

208 'New Republic'

(Des B. Angelushev. Typo)

1946 (15 Sept). Referendum. P 11½.
628	**208**	4l. claret	25	20
629	–	20l. greenish blue	25	20
630	–	50l. bistre-brown	60	50
628/630 *Set of 3*			1·00	80

209 Assault

210 Ambuscade

(Des G. Bogdanov (T **209**), A. Poplilov (T **210**), B. Angelushev (Nos. 633, 637) and St. Kunchev (No. 636). Typo)

1946 (2 Dec). Partisan Activities. As Types **209/210** (various designs). P 11½.
631	**209**	1l. maroon	25	20
632	**210**	4l. blue-green	25	20
633	–	5l. chocolate	25	20
634	**210**	10l. scarlet	25	20
635	**209**	20l. bright blue	60	25
636	–	30l. yellow-brown	70	35
637	–	50l. black	95	80
631/637 *Set of 7*			3·00	2·00

Designs: Vert—5l., 50l. Partisan riflemen, 30l. Partisan leader.

211 Nurse and Children

212 Hungry Child

212a Partisans

(Des St. Kunchev and G. Popov (T **211**), A. Poplilov (Nos. 639/640), B. Angelushev (T **212**) and L. Nenov (No. 643). Typo)

1946 (30 Dec). Winter Relief. Types **211/212** and similar designs. P 11½.
638	**211**	1l. brown-violet	25	20
639	–	4l. vermilion	25	20
640	–	9l. brown-olive	25	20
641	**211**	10l. grey	25	20
642	**212**	20l. blue	25	20
643	–	30l. brown-red	50	25
644	**212**	40l. claret	60	45
645	**211**	50l. turquoise-green	1·10	80
638/645 *Set of 8*			3·00	2·30

Designs: Vert—4l., 9l. Child carrying gifts, 30l. Destitute mother and child.

(Des S. Sotirov. Typo)

1947 (21 Jan). Commemorating anti-fascists of 1923, 1941 and 1944. T **212a** and designs similarly inscr. P 11½.
645*a*	10l. deep brown and orange-brown	85	80
645*b*	20l. deep blue and pale blue	85	80
645*c*	70l. purple-brown and pale claret	50·00	46·00
645*a*/645*c Set of 3*		47·00	43·00

BULGARIA 1947

Designs: Horiz—10l. Group of fighters. Vert—20l. T **212a**; 70l. Soldier addressing crowd.
'BULGARIA' is in Roman characters on the 20l.

1947 (31 Jan). Red Cross (2nd Issue) As Nos. 580/587 but colours changed. Cross in red. P 11½.

645d	**177**	2l. yellow-brown	20	20
645e	–	4l. blackish olive	20	20
645f	**177**	10l. green	25	25
645g	–	20l. pale blue	60	60
645h	–	30l. yellow-green	70	70
645i	**178**	35l. grey-green	85	80
645j	–	50l. brown-red	1·20	1·20
645k	**178**	100l. blue	1·90	1·80
645d/645k Set of 8			5·25	5·25

1947 (10 Feb). POSTAGE DUE. As T D **112**, but larger (18×24 mm, instead of 16×22 mm). Typo. P 10½.

D646	1l. sepia	25	25
D647	2l. maroon	25	25
D648	8l. orange	30	25
D649	20l. blue	1·40	35
D646/D649 Set of 4		2·00	1·00

213 Olive Branch   **214** Dove of Peace

(Des A. Poplilov (T **213**), St. Kunchev (T **214**). Typo)

1947 (28 Feb). Peace. P 11½.

646	**213**	4l. olive-green	20	20
647	**214**	10l. brown-red	25	25
648	–	20l. blue	65	60
646/648 Set of 3			1·00	95

'BULGARIA' is in Roman characters on the 20l.

215 USA and Bulgaria   **216** Esperanto Emblem and Map of Bulgaria

(Des I. Manev. Typo)

1947 (31 May). AIR. Stamp Day and New York International Philatelic Exhibition. P 11½.

649	**215**	70l. +30l. brown-red	2·50	2·30

(Des I. Barov. Typo)

1947 (16 June). 30th Esperanto Congress, Sofia. P 11½.

650	**216**	20l. +10l. purple and emerald	1·30	1·20

217 GPO, Sofia   **218** National Theatre, Sofia

219 Parliament Building, Sofia   **220** President's Palace   **221** GPO, Sofia

1947–48. Government Buildings. Typo. P 13.

(a) T **217**

651	1l. blue-green (1.7.47)	25	20

(b) T **218**

652	50st. yellow-green (28.11.47)	25	20
653	2l. claret (19.8.47)	25	20
654	4l. blue (17.7.47)	25	20
655	9l. carmine (9.1.48)	75	25

(c) T **219**

656	50st. yellow-green (7.11.47)	25	20
657	2l. yellow-brown (26.9.47)	25	20
658	4l. blue (26.9.47)	25	20
659	20l. blue (9.1.48)	1·90	1·20

(d) T **220**

660	1l. emerald-green (29.12.47)	25	20

(e) T **221**

661	1l. emerald-green (29.12.47)	25	20
662	2l. brown-lake (*shades*) (9.1.48)	25	20
663	4l. blue (9.1.48)	25	20
651/663 Set of 13		4·75	3·25

222 Hydroelectric Power Station and Dam   **223** Emblem of Industry

(Des P. Vulkov (4l.), I. Manev (9l., 40l.), St. Kunchev (20l.). Typo)

1947 (6 Aug). Reconstruction. Types **222/223** and similar horiz designs. P 11½.

664	–	4l. grey-green (Type **222**)	30	20
665	–	9l. orange-brown (Miner)	40	30
666	–	20l. blue (Type **223**)	50	45
667	–	40l. brown-olive (Motor plough)	1·50	1·40
664/667 Set of 4			2·40	2·10

224 Exhibition Building   **225** Former Residence of the French Poet Lamartine

226 Rose and Grapes   **227** Aeroplane over City

(Des A. Apostolov (4l.), V. Staikov (others). Litho)

1947 (31 Aug). Plovdiv Fair.

(a) POSTAGE. P 11×11½

668	**224**	4l. scarlet	20	15
669	**225**	9l. claret	25	15
670	**226**	20l. ultramarine	50	45

(b) AIR. Imperf

671	**227**	40l. grey-green	1·90	1·70
668/671 Set of 4			2·50	2·20

228 Cycle Racing

1947 BULGARIA

229 Basketball

230 Chess

(Des Ts. Kosturkova (2l., 20l.), I. Manev (4l.),
St. Kunchev (9l.), P. Vulkov (60l.). Typo)

1947 (29 Sept). Balkan Games. As Types **228/230** and vert designs inscr '1947'. P 11½.

672	2l. rose-lilac (Type **228**)		95	50
673	4l. grey-olive (Type **229**)		1·00	60
674	9l. orange-brown (Type **230**)		1·90	70
675	20l. bright blue (Football)		2·50	80
676	60l. claret (Balkan flags)		5·75	3·75
672/676	Set of 5		11·00	5·75

231 V. E. Aprilov

232 V. E. Aprilov

(Des Ts. Kosturkova and G. Manolov. Litho)

1947–48. Death Centenary of Vasil Aprilov (educationist).

(a) P 10½
677	**231**	40l. blue (19.10.47)	1·00	60

(b) P 11½
678	**232**	4l. claret/*cream* (19.2.48)	40	20

233 Postman

234 Wireless Masts

(Des St. Penchev (40l.), D. Gyudzhenov (others). Typo)

1947 (5 Nov). Postal Employees' Relief Fund. Types **233/234** and similar vert designs. P 11½.

679		4l. +2l. brown-olive (Type **233**)	20	20
680		10l. +5l. scarlet (Lineman)	25	25
681		20l. +10l. blue (Telephonists)	40	35
682		40l. +20l. brown-purple (Type **234**)	1·90	1·70
679/682	Set of 4		2·50	2·30

235 Geno Kirov

236 *Rodina* (freighter)

(Des A. Zhendov, St. Kunchev, A. Poplilov and I. Barov. Litho)

1947 (8 Dec). Theatrical Artists Benevolent Fund. As T **235** (portraits). P 10½.

683		50st. brown	15	10
684		1l. pale blue-green	15	10
685		2l. grey-green	15	10
686		3l. blue	15	10
687		4l. scarlet	15	10
688		5l. maroon	15	10
689		9l. +5l. greenish blue	25	15
690		10l. +6l. carmine	25	25
691		15l. +7l. violet	55	35
692		20l. +15l. ultramarine	80	60
693		30l. +20l. purple	1·90	1·30
683/693	Set of 11		4·25	3·00

Designs: 50st. T **235**; 1l. Zlatina Nedeva; 2l. Ivan Popov; 3l. Atanas Kirchev; 4l. Elena Snezhina; 5l. Stoyan Buchvarov; 9l. Khristo Ganchev; 10l. Adriana Budevska; 15l. Vasil Kirkov; 20l. Sava Ognyanov; 30l. Krustyu Sarafov.

(Des P. Vulkov. Litho)

1947 (19 Dec). National Shipping Revival. P 10½.
694	**236**	50l. greenish blue/*cream*	1·30	90

237 Worker and Flag

238 Worker and Globe

(Des V. Staikov and A. Poplilov. Photo)

1948 (29 Feb). Second General Workers' Union Congress. P 11½.

(a) POSTAGE
695	**237**	4l. blue/*cream*	25	15

(b) AIR
696	**238**	60l. brown-red/*cream*	1·00	80

239

240

(Des I. Manev, B. Kotsev, V. Tomov, St. Penchev and P. Vulkov. Litho)

1948 (31 Mar). Leisure and Culture. Types **239/240** and similar vert designs. P 10½.

697		4l. carmine	25	20
698		20l. blue	50	25
699		40l. green	90	45
700		60l. chocolate	1·50	90
697/700	Set of 4		2·75	1·60

Designs: 4l. T **239**; 20l. T **240**; 40l. Workers' musical interlude; 60l. Sports girl.

241 Nikola Vaptsarov

242 Petlyakov Pe-2 Bomber over Balduin's Tower

(Des S. Sotirov, A. Poplilov, St. Kunchev and I. Barov. Litho)

1948 (18 May). Poets. T **241** and similar vert designs. P 10½.

701		4l. orange-vermilion/*cream*	25	20
702		9l. red-brown/*cream*	30	25
703		15l. claret/*cream*	40	30
704		20l. blue/*cream*	50	40
705		45l. blue-green/*cream*	1·30	1·20
701/705	Set of 5		2·50	2·10

Designs: 4l. T **241**; 9l. Peyu Yavorov; 15l. Khristo Smirnenski; 20l. Ivan Vazov; 45l. Petko Slaveikov.

BULGARIA 1948

(Des Ts. Kosturkova. Photo)
1948 (23 May). AIR. Stamp Day. P 11½.
706 **242** 50l. olive-brown/*cream* .... 2·50 2·30

243 Soldier

244 Peasants and Soldiers

(Des D. Gyudzhenov and N. Biserov. Photo)
1948 (5 July). Soviet Army Monument. As Types **243/244**. P 10½.
707		4l. orange-red/*cream*	25	20
708		10l. green/*cream*	30	25
709		20l. blue/*cream*	65	45
710		60l. olive/*cream*	1·50	1·40
707/710 Set of 4			2·40	2·10

Designs: Horiz—10l. T **244**; 20l. Soldiers of 1878 and 1944. Vert—4l. T **243**; 60l. Stalin and Spassky Tower, Kremlin.

245 Bath, Gorna Banya

246 Lion Emblem

(Des Ts. Kosturkova (2l., 20l.), G. Manolov (3l.,10l.), A. Anev (4l., 20l.), G. Zhelezarov (5l., 15l.). Typo)
1948 (20 Aug)–**49**. Designs as T **245**. P 12½.

(a) Bulgarian Mineral Baths
711	2l. claret (13.9.48) (Type **245**)	25 20
712	3l. red-orange (7.10.48) (Bankya)........	25 20
	a. Perf 11	25 20
713	4l. deep blue (20.8.48) (Sofia)	25 20
714	10l. bright purple (7.10.48) (Bankya)	50 25
715	20l. deep blue (7.10.48) (Type **245**)	1·80 30
716	20l. deep blue (5.11.48) (Sofia)	2·50 50

(b) Malyovitsa Peak
717	5l. purple-brown (29.10.48)	65 20
718	15l. olive-green (3.1.49)	1·10 20
711/718 Set of 8		6·50 1·80

(Des A. Anev and G. Manolov. Typo)
1948 (20 Aug)–**50**. P 12½.
719	**246**	50st. red-orange (5.11.48)	25	20
719a		50st. chestnut (27.9.50)	25	20
720		1l. green (20.8.48)	25	20
721		9l. black (20.8.48)	65	35
719/721 Set of 4			1·30	85

247 Dimitur Blagoev

248 Youths Marching

(Des St. Penchev (4l., 9l.), P. Vulkov (20l.), V. Tomov (60l.). Photo)
1948 (6 Sept). 25th Anniversary of September Uprising. Types **247/248** and similar designs. P 11.
722	4l. brown/*cream*	25	20
723	9l. brown-orange/*cream*	25	20
724	20l. blue/*cream*	40	35
725	60l. brown/*cream*	1·90	1·40
722/725 Set of 4		2·50	1·90

Designs: Vert—4l. T **247**; 9l. Gabril Genov. Horiz—20l. Bishop Andrei Monument; 60l. T **248**.

249 Khristo Smirnenski

250 Miner

251 Battle of Grivitsa

(Des A. Anev. Photo)
1948 (2 Oct). 50th Anniversary of Birth of Smirnenski (poet and revolutionary). P 11½.
726	**249**	4l. dark blue/*cream*	25	20
727		16l. light brown/*cream*	50	25

(Des A. Zhendov. Typo)
1948 (7 Oct). P 11×11½.
728	**250**	4l. deep blue	40	25

(Des B. Angelushev (20l.), I. Manev (others). Photo)
1948 (1 Nov). Treaty of Friendship with Rumania. T **251** and similar designs. P 11½.

(a) POSTAGE
729	20l. deep blue/*cream*	35	25

(b) AIR
730	40l. grey-black/*cream*	65	45
731	100l. mauve/*cream*	1·50	1·40
729/731 Set of 3		2·30	1·90

Designs: 20l. T **251**; 40l. Parliament buildings in Sofia and Bucharest; 100l. Projected Danube Bridge.

252 Botev's House, Kalofer

253 Botev

(Des V. Staikov (1l., 15l.), A. Apostolov (4l.), B. Angelushev (9l., 20l.), G. Atanasov (40l.), A. Poplilov (50l.). Litho)
1948 (21 Dec)–**49**. Birth Centenary of Khristo Botev (poet and revolutionary). Types **252/253** and similar designs. P 11 (1l., 15l., 50l.) or 11½ (others).
732		1l. deep green/*cream*	25	20
733		4l. purple-brown/*cream*	25	20
734		4l. purple/*cream* (2.6.49)	25	20
735		9l. violet/*cream*	25	20
736		15l. yellow-brown/*cream*	25	20
737		20l. blue/*cream*	40	20
737a		20l. deep blue/*cream* (2.6.49)	50	25
738		40l. red-brown/*cream*	90	60
739		50l. brown-olive/*cream*	1·30	80
732/739 Set of 9			4·00	2·50

Designs: Horiz—1l. T **252**; 9l. River paddle-steamer *Radetski*; 15l. Village of Kalofer; 40l. Botev's mother and verse of poem. Vert—4l. (2) T **253**; 20l. Botev in uniform; 50l. Quill, pistol and Laurel wreath.

254 Lenin

255 Road Construction

(Des G. Monolov and A. Anev. Litho)
1949 (24 Jan). 25th Death Anniversary of Lenin. T **254** and similar type inscr '1924 1949'. P 11½.
740	4l. yellow-brown/*cream*	40	25
741	20l. red-brown/*cream*	90	70

Designs: 4l. T **254**; 20l. Lenin as an orator (27×37 *mm*).

(Des D. Gyudzhenov, N. Biserov, P. Vulkov and St. Penchev. Photo)
1949 (6 Apr). National Youth Movement. Designs as T **255**. P 10½.
742	4l. brown-red/*cream*	25	20
743	5l. dark brown/*cream*	40	25

1949 BULGARIA

744		9l. blackish green/*cream*	90	60
745		10l. violet/*cream*	75	50
746		20l. dull blue/*cream*	1·50	1·20
747		40l. brown/*cream*	3·25	1·40
742/747 Set of 6			6·25	3·75

Designs: 4l. T **255**; 5l. Tunnel construction; 9l. Steam locomotive; 10l. Textile worker; 20l. Girl driving tractor; 40l. Workers in lorry.

256 Pleven Mausoleum

(Des Ts. Kosturkova. Photo)

1949 (26 June). AIR. Stamp Day. Seventh Philatelic Congress, Pleven. P 11½.

748	**256**	50l. yellow-brown	7·00	6·25

257 G. Dimitrov   **258** G. Dimitrov

(Des Ts. Kosturkova (4l.), A. Anev (20l.). Photo)

1949 (10 July). Death of Georgi Dimitrov (Prime Minister 1946–1949). P 11½.

749	**257**	4l. red-brown	40	35
750	**258**	20l. blue	1·90	70

259 Hydroelectric Power Station   **260** Symbols of Agriculture and Industry

(Des D. Gyudzhenov and N. Biserov (4l., 9l., 50l.), P. Vulkov (15l.), St. Penchev (20l.). Photo)

1949 (5 Aug). Five Year Industrial and Agricultural Plan.

(a) POSTAGE. T **259** and similar designs. P 11½ (9l., 20l.) or 11½×11 (4l., 15l.)

751	**259**	4l. blackish olive	25	20
752	–	9l. brown-red	40	30
753	–	15l. violet	65	35
754	–	20l. blue	1·90	1·00

(b) AIR. P 11×11½

755	**260**	50l. brown	5·25	2·30
751/755 Set of 5			7·50	3·75

Designs: Horiz—20l. Tractors in field. Vert—9l. Cement works; 15l. Tractors in garage.

261 Javelin and Grenade Throwing   **262** Motorcyclist and Tractor

(Des P. Vulkov (20l.), O. Bogdanova (others). Photo)

1949 (5 Sept). Physical Culture Campaign. T **261** and similar athletic designs and T **262**. P 11 (4l.), 11×11½ (9l.) or 11½ (50l.)

756	**261**	4l. brown-red	90	50
757	–	9l. deep olive	2·50	1·00
758	**262**	20l. blue	3·75	2·10
759	–	50l. claret	9·50	4·25
756/759 Set of 4			15·00	7·00

Designs: Horiz—9l. Hurdling and leaping barbed-wire. Vert—50l. Two athletes marching.

263 Globe   **264** Guardsman and Peasant   **265** Guardsman with Dog

(Des P. Vulkov. Photo)

1949 (10 Oct). AIR. 75th Anniversary of Founding of Universal Postal Union. P 11½.

760	**263**	50l. blue	3·75	2·20

(Des D. Gyudzhenov and N. Biserov (4l., 20l.), O. Bogdanova (60l.). Litho)

1949 (31 Oct). Frontier Guards. Types **264**/**265** and similar types. P 11×11½ (60l.), 11½/11 (others).

(a) POSTAGE

761	**264**	4l. orange-brown	65	60
762	–	20l. dull blue	1·90	1·50

(b) AIR

763	**265**	60l. deep olive	5·75	5·25
761/763 Set of 3			7·50	6·50

Design: Vert—20l. Guardsman on coast.

266 Georgi Dimitrov (Prime Minister 1946–1949)   **267** Unanimity   **268** Joseph Stalin

(Des P. Vulkov (4l.), I. Manev (9l.), D. Gyudzhenov and N. Biserov (20l.), St. Penchev (50l.). Litho)

1949 (13 Dec). Fatherland Front. Types **266**/**267** and similar types. P 11½.

764	**266**	4l. red-brown	40	20
765	**267**	9l. violet	1·10	70
766	–	20l. blue	1·20	80
767	–	50l. carmine	1·30	1·00
764/767 Set of 4			3·50	2·40

Designs: 20l. Man and woman with wheel-barrow and spade; 50l. Young people marching.

(Des V. Tomov. Litho)

1949 (21 Dec). Stalin's 70th Birthday. T **268** and larger type. P 11½.

768	**268**	4l. brown-orange	65	25
769	–	40l. claret	1·90	1·70

Design: (25×37 *mm*)—40l. Stalin as orator.

269 Kharalampi Stoyanov   **270** Strikers and Train

(Des V. Tomov (4l.), O. Bogdanova (20l.), A. Zhendov (60l.). Photo)

1950 (15 Feb). 30th Anniversary of Railway Strike. Types **269**/**270** and vert type inscr '1919–1949'. P 11½.

770	**269**	4l. brown	65	25

BULGARIA 1950

771	**270**	20l. blue	65	40
772	–	60l. grey-olive	1·90	1·30
770/772	Set of 3		3·00	1·80

Design: 60l. Two workers and flag.

271 Miner

272 Steam Locomotive

(Des V. Tomov (1l., 5l., 9l.), P. Vulkov (2l., 3l.), St. Penchev (4l., 10l.), O. Bogdanova (15l., 20l.). Photo)

1950 Types **271/272** and similar designs. P 11 (10l., 15l.), 11×11½ (9l., 20l.) or 13 (others).

773	**271**	1l. deep olive-green (23.2.50)	25	15
773a		1l. violet (30.4.50)	30	15
774	**272**	2l. black (23.2.50)	65	35
774a		2l. brown (18.5.50)	65	35
775	–	3l. deep blue (17.3.50)	65	15
776	–	4l. blue-green (17.3.50)	1·00	35
776a	–	4l. grey-blue (18.5.50)	4·00	1·60
777	–	5l. brown-red (17.3.50)	75	15
778	–	9l. grey (1.12.50)	50	20
779	–	10l. reddish purple (1.12.50)	50	20
780	–	15l. brown-carmine (1.12.50)	1·30	35
781	–	20l. blue (1.12.50)	1·40	40
773/781	Set of 12		11·00	4·00

Designs: Horiz—4l. Tractor; 5l., 9l. Threshing machines. Vert—3l. Ship under construction; 10l. Power station; 15l., 20l. Woman in factory.

273 Kolarov

274 Stanislas Dospevski (self-portrait)

274a *In the Field* (Khristo Stanchev)

(Des Ts. Kosturkova (4l.), A. Anev (20l.). Photo)

1950 (6 Mar). Death of Vasil Kolarov (Prime Minister 1949–1950). T **273** and similar vert design. P 11½.

| 782 | | 4l. lake-brown | 35 | 20 |
| 783 | | 20l. dull ultramarine | 1·00 | 90 |

Design: 27½×39½ mm—20l. Same portrait but different frame.

(Des P. Vulkov (4l., 20l.), O. Bogdanova (others). Photo)

1950 (15 Apr). As Types **274/274a**, painters and paintings. P 11½.

784	**274**	1l. green	75	50
785	–	4l. orange-red	2·50	80
786	–	9l. chocolate	3·75	80
787	**274a**	15l. brown	5·25	1·30
788	–	20l. deep blue	8·25	3·50
789	–	40l. red-brown	10·00	5·00
790	–	60l. brown-orange	10·50	7·25
784/790	Set of 7		37·00	17·00

Designs: Vert—4l. King Kaloyan and Desislava; 9l. Nikolai Pavlovich (self-portrait); 40l. Statue of Debelyanov (Ivan Lazarov); 60l. Peasant (Vladimir Dimitrov the Master).

275 Ivan Vazov and Birthplace, Sopot

(Des V. Tomov. Photo)

1950 (26 June). Birth Centenary of Ivan Vazov (poet). P 11½.

| 791 | **275** | 4l. olive-green | 30 | 20 |

276 Dimitrov and Birthplace, Kovachevtsi

276a G. Dimitrov

(Des L. Ivanov (4l.), V. Manski (10l.), V. Tomov (others). Photo)

1950 (2 July). First Death Anniversary of Georgi Dimitrov (statesman). As Types **276/276a** and similar designs showing Dimitrov and buildings. P 11½.

(a) POSTAGE

792		50st. brown	45	20
793		50st. green	45	20
794		1l. red-brown	65	25
795		2l. blue-grey	65	25
796		4l. purple	1·30	40
797		9l. brown-red	2·10	1·20
798		10l. carmine	3·25	1·60
799		15l. grey	3·25	1·60
800		20l. blue	5·00	3·25

(b) AIR

| 801 | | 40l. yellow-brown | 10·00 | 5·25 |
| 792/801 | Set of 10 | | 24·00 | 13·00 |

Designs: Horiz—50st. (No. 793) T **276**; 2l. Dimitrov's house, Sofia; 15l. Dimitrov signing new constitution; 20l. Portrait of Dimitrov; 40l. Mausoleum. Vert—50st. (No. 792), 1l., 4l., 9l. and 10l. Dimitrov in various poses.

277 Runners

278 Workers and Tractor

(Des V. Tomov (4l.), E. Poptoshev (9l.), L. Kuleliev (others). Photo)

1950 (21 Aug). Sports. T **277** and similar vert designs. P 10½ (9l.) or 11½ (others).

802		4l. deep green (Type **277**)	1·10	65
803		9l. red-brown (Cycling)	1·30	1·00
804		20l. deep blue (Putting the shot)	1·90	1·60
805		40l. purple (Volleyball)	3·75	3·25
802/805	Set of 4		7·25	5·75

(Des V. Tomov. Photo)

1950 (19 Sept). Second National Peace Congress. T **278** and vertical type. P 11½×10½ (4l.) or 10½×11½ (20l.).

| 806 | | 4l. brown-red | 30 | 20 |
| 807 | | 20l. ultramarine | 1·10 | 80 |

Designs: Horiz—4l. T **278**. Vert—20l. Stalin's portrait on flag and three heads.

278a

278b

279 Children on Beach

1950 (1 Oct). Typo. P 13.

807a	**278a**	2l. yellow-brown	25	20
807b		3l. carmine	25	20
807c	**278b**	5l. claret	25	20
807d		9l. turquoise-blue	25	20
807a/807d	Set of 4		90	70

Although inscribed 'OFFICIAL MAIL' the above were issued as regular postage stamps.

1950 (1 Oct). SUNDAY DELIVERY. Horiz types inscr as T **279**. Litho. P 11 (5l., 10l.) or 13 (others).

808		1l. grey-green	30	20
809	**279**	2l. brown-red	40	25
810	–	5l. orange	75	40
811	**279**	10l. blue	1·90	80
808/811	Set of 4		3·00	1·50

Designs: 1l. Sanatorium; 5l. Sun-bathing.

1950 BULGARIA

280 Molotov. Kolarov, Stalin and Dimitrov

281 Russian and Bulgarian Girls

(Des V. Tomov (4l., 50l.), V. Manski (9l.), B. Kotsev (20l.) Photo)
1950 (10 Oct). Second Anniversary of Soviet–Bulgarian Treaty of Friendship. Types **280/281** and other vert types. P 11½.

812	**280**	4l. red-brown	30	20
813	–	9l. claret	40	25
814	**281**	20l. blue	75	65
815	–	50l. blue-green	3·75	1·60
812/815	Set of 4		4·75	2·40

Designs: 9l. Spassky Tower (Moscow) and flags; 50l. Freighter and tractor.

282 Marshal Tolbukhin

283 Bulgarians Greeting Marshal

(Des V. Tomov (4l.), V. Tomov and L. Ivanov (20l.) Photo)
1950 (10 Dec). Honouring Marshal Tolbukhin. P 11½.

816	**282**	4l. magenta	45	30
817	**283**	20l. deep blue	1·90	1·00

284 A. S. Popov

285 First Bulgarian Truck

(Des Ts. Kosturkova and A. Anev. Photo)
1951 (10 Feb). 45th Death Anniversary of Aleksandr Popov (radio pioneer). P 10½.

818	**284**	4l. lake-brown	90	40
819		20l. blue	1·60	90

(Des P. Vulkov (1l.), V. Tomov (2l.), L. Ivanov and V. Manski (4l.). Photo)
1951. Various designs as T **285**. P 12½.

820		1l. violet/cream (25.4.51)	25	15
821		2l. green/cream (15.4.51)	30	15
822		4l. red-brown/cream (15.3.51)	40	15
820/822	Set of 3		85	40

Designs: 1l. First Bulgarian tractor; 2l. Fist Bulgarian steamroller; 4l. T **285**.
See also Nos. 981a/982.

286 Georgi Kirkov

287 Nacho Ivanov and Avram Stoyanov

(Des V. Tomov (4l., 9l., 15l.), A. Zhendov (others). Photo)
1951 (25 Mar). Anti-Fascist Heroes. Portrait types as Types **286/287**. P 11½.

823		1l. reddish purple	50	25
824		2l. plum	50	25
825		4l. carmine-lake	50	25
826		9l. red-brown	1·40	80
827		15l. olive-brown	3·25	1·40
828		20l. blue	3·25	2·00
829		50l. blackish olive	7·50	2·75
823/829	Set of 7		15·00	7·00

Portraits: 1l. Chankova, Adalbert Antonov-Malchika, Sasho Dimitrov and Lilyana Dimitrova; 2l. Stanke Dimitrov; 4l. T **286**; 9l. Anton Ivanov, 15l. Khristo Mikhailov; 20l. Georgi Dimitrov at Leipzig; 50l. T **287**.

288 First Bulgarian Tractor

289 Embroidery

(Des P. Vulkov (1l., 20l.), V. Tomov (2l., 40l.), L. Ivanov and V. Manski (4l.), A. Zhendov, V. Naslednikova and V. Bibina (9l.,15l.) Photo)
1951 (30 Apr). National Occupations. Designs as Types **288/289**. P 11×10½ (horiz) or 10½×11 (vert).

830		1l. yellow-brown	40	25
831		2l. violet	50	40
832		4l. red-brown	90	80
833		9l. bright violet	1·60	1·00
834		15l. reddish purple	2·75	1·60
835		20l. bright blue	5·75	2·30
836		40l. green	7·50	3·50
830/836	Set of 7		17·00	8·75

Designs: Horiz—1l. T **288**; 2l. First Bulgarian steamroller; 4l. First Bulgarian truck; 15l. Carpets; 40l. Fruit. Vert—9l. T **289**; 20l. Roses and Tobacco.

290 Turkish Attack

(Des P. Vulkov (1l.), V. Staikov (4l.), G. Gerasimov (9l.), V. Tomov (20l., 40l.). Photo)
1951 (3 May). 75th Anniversary of April Uprising. T **290** and similar horizontal types inscr '1876–1951'. P 11.

837		1l. brown/cream	90	45
838		4l. green/cream	1·00	50
839		9l. purple/cream	1·50	1·30
840		20l. blue/cream	2·30	2·00
841		40l. lake/cream	3·25	2·50
837/841	Set of 5		8·00	6·00

Designs: 1l. T **290**; 4l. Proclamation of Uprising; 9l. Cannon and cavalry; 20l. Patriots in 1876 and 1944; 40l. Georgi Benkovski and Georgi Dimitrov.

291 Dimitur Blagoev as Orator

(Des V. Staikov. Photo)
1951 (2 Aug). 60th Anniversary of First Bulgarian Social Democratic Party Congress, Buzludzha. P 10½×11.

842	**291**	1l. violet	40	25
843		4l. green	1·30	50
844		9l. reddish purple	2·10	1·60
842/844	Set of 3		3·50	2·10

BULGARIA 1951

292 Babies in Crèche   **D 293**

(Des I. Manev (1l.), P. Vulkov (9l.), V. Staikov (others). Photo)

1951 (10 Oct). Children's Day. T **292** and similar horiz designs. P 11.
845		1l. red-brown	40	25
846		4l. reddish purple	90	40
847		9l. blue-green	1·90	80
848		20l. blue	3·75	2·50
845/848	Set of 4		6·25	3·50

Designs: 1l. T **292**; 4l. Children building models; 9l. Girl and children's playground; 20l. Boy bugler and children marching.

1951 (15 Oct). POSTAGE DUE. Typo. P 10½, 11½ or compound.
D849	D **293**	1l. sepia	25	20
D850		2l. maroon	40	25
D851		8l. orange	75	65
D852		20l. blue	2·00	1·70
D849/D852	Set of 4		3·00	2·50

293 Workers   **294** Labour Medal (obverse)   **295** Labour Medal (reverse)

(Des G. Manolov. Photo)

1951 (29 Dec). Third General Workers' Union Congress. T **293** and similar vert design. P 10½ (4l.) or 11½ (1l.).
849	1l. blackish green	25	20
850	4l. brown	55	25

Designs: 1l. T **293**; 4l. Georgi Dimitrov and Vulko Chervenkov (Prime Minister).

(Des Ts. Kosturkova and G. Zhozev. Photo)

1952 (1 Feb). Order of Labour. P 13.
851	**294**	1l. carmine	25	20
852	**295**	1l. brown-lake	25	20
853	**294**	4l. green	25	20
854	**295**	4l. turquoise	25	20
855	–	9l. violet	90	25
856	**295**	9l. deep blue	90	25
851/856	Set of 6		2·50	1·20

Design: No. 855, as T **294** but value at bottom left.

Currency stabilised, 12th May, 1952

296 Vasil Kolarov Dam   **297** G. Dimitrov and Chemical Works

(Des V. Tomov. Photo)

1952. P 13 and various other perfs.
857	**296**	4st. blackish green (16.5.52)	25	20
858		12st. reddish violet (17.5.52)	40	25
859		16st. lake-brown (18.5.52)	50	30
860		44st. claret (18.5.52)	1·30	35
861		80st. blue (18.5.52)	5·25	65
857/861	Set of 5		7·00	1·60

(Des V. Tomov. Photo)

1952 (18 June). 70th Birth Anniversary of Dimitrov (statesman) T **297** and similar designs inscr '1882–1952'. P 11 (80st.) or 11½ (others).
862	16st. brown	1·10	65
863	44st. chocolate	1·90	1·30
864	80st. blue	3·25	2·00
862/864	Set of 3	5·75	3·50

Designs: Horiz—44st. Georgi Dimitrov (Prime Minister 1946–1949) and Prime Minister Vulko Chervenkov. Vert—16st. T **297**; 80st. Full-face portrait of Georgi Dimitrov.

298 Republika Power Station   **299** N. Vaptsarov

(Des V. Tomov. Photo)

1952. P 13.
866	**298**	16st. sepia (30.6.52)	75	25
867		44st. deep reddish purple (4.7.52)	2·50	40

(Des St. Penchev (16st.), S. Sotirov (44st.), A. Stamenov (80st.). Photo)

1952 (23 July). Tenth Death Anniversary of Nikola Vaptsarov (poet and revolutionary). T **299** and similar vert portraits. P 11½ (44st.) or 11 (others).
869	16st. brown-lake	1·30	90
870	44st. purple-brown	2·50	2·30
871	80st. sepia	5·00	2·50
869/871	Set of 3	8·00	5·25

Portraits: 16st. T **299**; 44st. Facing bayonets at right; 80st. Full-face.

300 Congress Delegates

(Des V. Staikov (2st.), D. Gyudzhenov (16st.), V. Tomov (44st.), P. Vulkov (80st.). Photo)

1952 (1 Sept). 40th Anniversary of First Workers' Social Democratic Youth League Congress. T **300** and similar horiz designs inscr '1912 г.'. P 11×11½.
872		2st. brown-lake	25	20
873		16st. slate-violet	50	40
874		44st. deep green	1·60	1·20
875		80st. sepia	3·25	2·50
872/875	Set of 4		5·00	3·75

Designs: 2st. T **300**; 16st. Young partisans; 44st. Factory and guards; 80st. Dimitrov addressing young workers.

301 Attack on Winter Palace, St Petersburg

(Des V. Staikov (4st.), G. Zhelezarov (8st.), V. Tomov (16st., 44st.), P. Vulkov (80st.). Photo)

1952 (6 Nov). 35th Anniversary of Russian Revolution. T **301** and similar horiz designs inscr '1917 1952'. P 11½.
876	4st. brown-lake	50	25
877	8st. deep blue-green	65	40
878	16st. deep blue	1·50	50
879	44st. sepia	1·90	65
880	80st. deep olive-brown	3·75	3·25
876/880	Set of 5	7·50	4·50

Designs: 4st. T **301**; 8st. Volga-Don canal; 16st. Dove and globe; 44st. Lenin and Stalin; 80st. Lenin, Stalin and Himlay hydroelectric station.

1952 BULGARIA

302

303 Vintagers and Grapes

304 V. Levski

(Des St. Penchev (2st.), V. Tomov (8st., 12st. and 16st.), I. Manev (others). Photo)

1952–53 National Products (Wood Carvings). Various designs as Types **302/303**. P 13.

881	–	2st. grey-brown (6.1.53)	25	20
882	–	8st. deep grey-green (6.1.53)	25	20
883	–	12st. brown (24.12.52)	50	20
884	–	16st. brown-purple (8.12.52)	1·00	20
885	302	28st. bronze-green (31.1.53)	1·40	25
886	–	44st. sepia (11.12.52)	1·90	35
887	303	80st. ultramarine (15.1.53)	2·30	45
888	–	1l. deep violet-blue (12.11.52)	5·00	80
889	–	4l. lake (27.1.53)	6·25	4·50
881/889	Set of 9		17·00	6·50

Designs: Vert—2st. Numeral in carved frame. Horiz—8st. Gift-offering to idol; 12st. Birds and Grapes; 16st. Rosegathering; 44st. Attar of Roses.

(Des B. Angelushev. Photo)

1953 (19 Feb). 80th Anniversary of Execution of Vasil Levski (revolutionary). T **304** and similar horiz design. P 11.

890		16st. brown/cream	25	20
891		44st. deep olive-brown/cream	90	40

Designs: 16st. T **304**; 44st. Levski addressing crowd.

305 Russian Army Crossing River Danube

306 Mother and Children

(Des G. Bogdanov, E. Poptoshev and I. Tabakov. Photo)

1953 (3 Mar). 75th Anniversary of Liberation from Turkey. T **305** and similar designs inscr '1878 1953'. P 11.

892		8st. deep turquoise	40	25
893		16st. brown	50	35
894		44st. deep grey-green	1·30	40
895		80st. lake-brown	3·75	2·00
896		1l. olive-black	4·50	4·00
892/896	Set of 5		9·50	6·25

Designs: Vert—16st. Battle of Shipka Pass. Horiz—8st. T **305**; 44st. Peasants welcoming Russian soldiers; 80st. Bulgarians and Russians embracing; 1l. Shipka Pass memorial and Dimitrovgrad.

(Des B. Angelushev. Photo)

1953 (9 Mar). International Women's Day. P 11.

897	306	16st. blue	40	15
898		16st. grey-green	40	15

307 Karl Marx

308 May Day Parade

(Des S. Sotirov. Photo)

1953 (30 Apr). 70th Death Anniversary of Karl Marx. T **307** and vert design inscr '1883–1953'. P 11.

899		16st. blue	45	25
900		44st. deep brown	1·10	80

Designs: 16st. T **307**; 44st. Book *Das Kapital*.

(Des A. Poplilov. Photo)

1953 (30 Apr). Labour Day. P 13.

| 901 | 308 | 16st. brown-red | 50 | 25 |

309 Stalin

310 Goce Delcev (Macedonian revolutionary)

(Des N. Petkov. Photo)

1953 (23 May). Death of Stalin. P 13.

902	309	16st. deep brown	95	40
903		16st. black	65	40

(Des V. Korenev. Photo)

1953. 50th Anniversary of Ilinden-Preobrazhenie Rising. T **310** and other designs inscr '1903–1953'. P 13.

904		16st. deep brown (8.8.53)	25	20
905		44st. deep violet (19.8.53)	1·00	65
906		1l. maroon (8.8.53)	1·40	1·00
904/906	Set of 3		2·40	1·70

Designs: Vert—16st. T **310**; 44st. Insurgents and flag facing left. Horiz—1l. Insurgents and flag facing right.

311 Soldier and Insurgents

312 Dimitur Blagoev

(Des P. Penev (16st.), V. Tomov (44st.). Photo)

1953 (18 Sept). Army Day. T **311** and similar horiz design. P 13.

907		16st. crimson	65	25
908		44st. Prussian blue	1·30	40

Designs: 16st. T **311**; 44st. Soldier, factories and combine-harvester.

(Des S. Sotirov and N. Petkov. Photo)

1953 (21 Sept). 50th Anniversary of Bulgarian Workers' Social Democratic Party. T **312** and similar vert design. P 13.

909		16st. brown (Type **312**)	65	35
910		44st. Venetian red (Dimitrov and Blagoev)	1·90	60

313 Georgi Dimitrov and Vasil Kolarov

314 Railway Viaduct

(Des B. Angelushev. Photo)

1953 (22 Sept). 30th Anniversary of September Uprising. T **313** and similar designs inscr '1923–1953'. P 13.

911		8st. greenish black	40	20
912		16st. deep red-brown	50	25
913		44st. carmine	1·60	80
911/913	Set of 3		2·30	1·10

Designs: 8st. T **313**; 16st. Insurgent and flag; 44st. Crowd of Insurgents.

(Des A. Zhendov. Photo)

1953 (17 Oct). Bulgarian–Russian Friendship. Designs as T **314**. P 13.

914		8st. blue	25	20
915		16st. blackish green	40	25
916		44st. brown-red	1·30	50
917		80st. red-orange	1·30	90
914/917	Set of 4		3·00	1·70

Designs: Horiz—8st. T **314**; 16st., Welder and industrial plant; 80st. Combine-harvester. Vert—44st. Iron foundry.

BULGARIA 1953

315 Dog Rose
(*Rosa canis*)

316 Vasil Kolarov Library

(Des B. Angelushev, St. Kunchev and I. Manev. Photo)

1953 (30 Oct)–**54**. Medicinal Flowers. T **315** and similar vert designs. P 13 (a) or 13½ (b).

918	2st. grey-blue (b)	25	20
919	4st. orange-red (a)	25	20
920	8st. deep turquoise-green (a)	25	20
	a. Perf 13½	25	20
921	12st. myrtle green (a)	25	20
922	12st. orange-red (a)	25	20
	a. Perf 13½	25	20
923	16st. violet-blue/*white* (b)	65	25
923*a*	16st. ultramarine/*cream* (a)	65	25
924	16st. lake-brown/*cream* (a)	65	25
925	20st. carmine/*cream* (a)	1·30	35
926	28st. slate-green (a)	1·00	40
927	40st. blue/*cream* (b)	90	65
	a. Perf 11	90	65
928	44st. light brown/*cream* (a)	1·90	80
	a. Perf 13½	1·90	80
929	80st. yellow-brown/*cream* (a)	2·50	1·40
930	1l. chestnut/*cream* (a)	5·00	2·50
	a. Perf 11	5·00	2·50
931	2l. deep mauve (b)	10·00	5·25
918/931	*Set of 15*	23·00	12·00
MS931*a*	161×172 mm. 12 values as above in blue-green (sold at 6l.). Imperf (18.12.53)	80·00	75·00

Designs: 2st. Deadly Nightshade (*Atropa belladonna*); 4st. Thorn-apple (*Datura stramonium*); 8st. Sage (*Salvia officinalis*); 12st. T **315**; 16st. Great Yellow Gentian (*Gentiana lutea*); 20st. Opium Poppy (*Papaver somniferum*); 28st. Peppermint (*Mentha pipenta*); 40st. Bearberry (*Uva ursi*); 44st. Coltsfoot (*Tussilago farfara*); 80st. *Primula officinalis*; 1l. Dandelion (*Taraxacum officinalis*); 2l. Foxglove (*Digitalis lanata*).

(Des St. Gospodinova. Photo)

1953 (16 Dec). 75th Anniversary of Kolarov Library, Sofia. P 13.
| 932 | **316** | 44st. brown | 75 | 45 |

317 Singer and Musician

318 Aeroplane over Mountains

(Des L. Zidarov (16st.), A. Poplilov (44st.). Photo)

1953 (26 Dec). Amateur Theatricals. T **317** and similar vert design. P 13.
| 933 | | 16st. purple-brown (Type **317**) | 40 | 20 |
| 934 | | 44st. bluish green (Folk-dancers) | 90 | 50 |

(Des S. Sotirov (8st., 20st., 80st., 4l.), V. Yonchev (12st., 16st., 1l.), V. Staikov (28st., 44st., 60st.). Photo)

1954 (12 Feb–1 Apr). AIR. T **318** and similar designs. P 13.
935	8st. deep grey-green	25	20
936	12st. lake-brown	25	20
937	16st. brown	25	20
938	20st. deep orange-red/*cream* (1.4.54)	25	20
939	28st. blue/*cream* (1.4.54)	50	25
940	44st. maroon/*cream* (1.4.54)	65	35
941	60st. red-brown/*cream* (1.4.54)	1·10	40
942	80st. blue/*cream* (1.4.54)	1·30	50
943	1l. deep bluish green/*cream* (1.4.54)	4·00	1·20
944	4l. blue	7·00	3·25
935/944	*Set of 10*	14·00	6·00

Designs: Vert—12st. Exhibition buildings, Plovdiv, 80st. Tirnovo, 4l. Partisans' Monument. Horiz—8st. T **318**; 16st. Seaside promenade, Varna; 20st. Combine-harvester in cornfield; 28st. Rila Monastery; 44st. Studena hydroelectric barrage; 60st. Dimitrovgrad; 1l. Sofia University and equestrian statue.

319 Lenin and Stalin

320 Dimitur Blagoev and Crowd

(Des St. Gospodinova, B. Angelushev, T. Bocheva-Paspaleeva and I. Khristov, respectively. Photo)

1954 (13 Mar). 30th Death Anniversary of Lenin. T **319** and similar designs inscr '1924–1954'. P 13.
945	16st. brown/*cream*	40	20
946	44st. lake/*cream*	90	35
947	80st. blue/*cream*	1·30	65
948	1l. bronze-green/*cream*	2·50	1·60
945/948	*Set of 4*	4·50	2·50

Designs: Vert—16st. T **319**; 44st. Lenin statue; 80st. Lenin-Stalin mausoleum and Kremlin; 1l. Lenin.

(Des B. Angelushev. Photo)

1954 (28 Apr). 30th Death Anniversary of Blagoev. T **320** and similar horiz design inscr '1924 1954'. P 13.
| 949 | 16st. red-brown/*cream* | 25 | 15 |
| 950 | 44st. sepia/*cream* | 1·00 | 40 |

Designs: 16st. T **320**; 44st. Blagoev writing at desk.

321 Dimitrov Speaking

322 Steam Locomotive

(Des St. Penchev and O. Bogdanova. Photo)

1954 (11 June). Fifth Death Anniversary of Dimitrov. T **321** and similar design inscr '1949 1954'. P 13.
| 951 | 44st. lake/*cream* | 65 | 40 |
| 952 | 80st. brown/*cream* | 1·30 | 90 |

Designs: Vert—44st. T **321**. Horiz—80st. Dimitrov and blast-furnace.

(Des St. Gospodinova. Photo)

1954 (30 July). Railway Workers' Day. P 13.
| 953 | **322** | 44st. deep turquoise-blue/*cream* | 2·30 | 1·00 |
| 954 | | 44st. black/*cream* | 2·30 | 1·00 |

323 Miner Operating Machinery

324 Marching Soldiers

(Des L. Zidarov. Photo)

1954 (19 Aug). Miners' Day. P 13.
| 955 | **323** | 44st. blackish green/*cream* | 65 | 25 |

(Des A. Poplilov (12st.), L. Zidarov (80st., 1l.), B. Angelushev (others). Photo)

1954 (4 Sept). Tenth Anniversary of Fatherland Front Government. T **324** and similar designs inscr' 1944–1954'. P 13.
956	12st. brown red/*cream*	25	20
957	16st. carmine-red/*cream*	30	25
958	28st. deep slate- blue/*cream*	40	30
959	44st. reddish brown/*cream*	75	40
960	80st. blue/*cream*	1·60	65
961	1l. deep green/*cream*	1·90	80
956/961	*Set of 6*	4·75	2·30

Designs: Vert—16st. Soldier and parents; 80st. Girl and boy pioneers; 1l. Dimitrov. Horiz—12st. T **324**; 28st. Industrial plant; 44st. Dimitrov and workers.

1954 BULGARIA

325 Academy Building **326** Gymnast

(Des St. Gospodinova. Photo)

1954 (27 Oct). 85th Anniversary of Academy of Sciences. P 13.
962   325   80st. black/*cream* .... 1·90   1·00

(Des V. Tomov. Photo)

1954 (21 Dec). Sports. Designs as T **326**. P 11.
963   16st. deep bluish green/*cream* .... 1·90   65
964   44st. red/*cream* .... 2·10   1·30
965   80st. chestnut/*cream* .... 4·50   2·50
966   2l. ultramarine/*cream* .... 7·00   5·25
963/966 Set of 4 .... 14·00 8·75

Designs: Vert—16st. T **326**; 44st. Wrestlers; 2l. Ski-jumper. Horiz—80st. Horse-jumper.

327 Velingrad Rest Home

(Des S. Sotirov. Photo)

1954 (28 Dec). 50th Anniversary of Trade Union Movement. T **327** and similar designs. P 13.
967   16st. myrtle green/*cream* 40   25
968   44st. Indian red/*cream* 65   40
969   80st. deep blue/*cream* .... 1·50   1·30
967/969 Set of 3 .... 2·30   1·80

Designs: Vert—44st. Foundryman. Horiz—16st. T **327**; 80st. Georgi Dimitrov, Dimitur Blagoev and Georgi Kirkov.

328 Geese   **329** Communist Party Building

(Des N. Tuzsuzov (2st. to 16st.), Zh. Zhelev (28st. to 1l.). Photo)

1955 (19 Feb)–**56**. Types **328**/**329** and simlar horiz designs. P 13½.
970   2st. myrtle green 25   15
    a.   Perf 13 25   15
971   4st. bronze green 30   20
    a.   Perf 13 30   20
972   12st. chocolate 75   35
973   16st. Indian red .... 1·30   35
    a.   Perf 13 .... 1·30   35
974   28st. ultramarine 75   40
975   44st. brown-red .... 11·50 4·50
975a   44st. bright crimson (P 11×13) (20.4.56)... 6·25   1·30
976   80st. chocolate .... 1·90   65
977   1l. myrtle green .... 2·50   1·30
970/977 Set of 9 .... 23·00 8·25

Designs: 2st. T **328**; 4st. Rooster and hens; 12st. Sow and piglets; 16st. Ewe and lambs; 28st. Telephone exchange; 44st. T **329**; 80st. Flats; 1l. Cellulose factory.

 (331)

330 Mill Girl   **332** Rejoicing Crowds

(Des B. Angelushev. Photo)

1955 (5 Mar). International Women's Day. T **330** and similar designs inscr '8. III. 1955'. P 13.
978   12st. deep brown 20   15

979   16st. deep myrtle-green 30   20
980   44st. ultramarine .... 1·40   35
981   44st. carmine-lake .... 1·40   35
978/981 Set of 4 .... 3·00   95

Designs: Horiz—12st. T **330**; 16st. Girl feeding cattle. Vert—44st. (2), Mother and baby.

1955 (8 Mar)–**57**. Stamps as Nos. 820 and 822 but colours changed and surch as T **331**.
981a   –   16st. on 1l. violet (R.) (8.4.57) 25   15
982   285   16st. on 4l. chocolate (*shades*) (B.) ..... 2·50   65
             a. Surch 11½ mm. (1956) .... 2·50   65

(Des V. Staikov Photo)

1955 (23 Apr). Labour Day. T **332** and similar vert design. P 13.
983   16st. carmine (Type **332**) 40   25
984   44st. blue (Three workers and globe)..... 90   40

333 St Cyril and St   **334** Sergei
     Methodius   Rumyantsev

(Des B. Angelushev. Photo)

1955 (21 May). 1100th Anniversary of First Bulgarian Literature. T **333** and similar horiz designs. P 13.
985   4st. blue/*cream* 25   20
986   8st. deep olive/*cream* 25   20
987   16st. black/*cream* 25   20
988   28st. brown-red/*cream* 50   40
989   44st. brown/*cream* .... 1·00   65
990   80st. carmine-red/*cream* .... 1·80   1·30
991   2l. greenish black/*cream* .... 4·50   2·75
985/991 Set of 7 .... 7·75   5·25

Designs: 4st. T **333**; 8st. Monk writing; 16st. Early printing press; 28st. Khristo Botev (poet); 44st. Ivan Vazov (poet and novelist); 80st. Dimitur Blagoev (writer and editor) and books; 2l. Dimitur Blagoev Polygraphic Complex, Sofia.

(Des St. Gospodinova. Photo)

1955 (30 June). 30th Death Anniversaries of Bulgarian Poets. T **334** and similar vert portraits inscr '1925–1955'. P 13.
992   12st. Indian red/*cream* 50   25
993   16st. orange-brown/*cream* 65   35
994   44st. slate-green/*cream* .... 1·90   1·30
992/994 Set of 3 .... 2·75   1·70

Designs: 12st. T **334**; 16st. Khristo Yasenov; 44st. Geo Milev.

335 F. Engels and Book   **336** Mother and Children

(Des St. Gospodinova and T. Bocheva. Photo)

1955 (30 July). 60th Death Anniversary of Engels. P 13.
995   335   44st. brown/*cream* .... 1·30   85

(Des B. Angelushev. Photo)

1955 (30 July). World Mothers' Congress, Lausanne. P 13.
996   336   44st. lake/*cream* .... 1·30   85

337 Youth of the   **338** Main Entrance in
     World   1892

121

BULGARIA 1955

(Des L. Zidarov. Photo)
1955 (30 July). Fifth World Youth Festival, Warsaw. P 13.
997 **337** 44st. blue/*cream* .... 1·30 85

(Des P. Dachev and C. Nikolov (16st.). Photo)
1955 (31 Aug). 16th International Fair, Plovdiv. T **338** and similar designs inscr '1955'. P 13.
998	4st. sepia/*cream*		25	20
999	16st. carmine/*cream*		30	25
1000	44st. olive-black/*cream*		65	55
1001	80st. blue/*cream*		1·50	50
998/1001 Set of 4			2·40	1·20

Designs: Vert—16st. Sculptured group; 80st. Fair poster. Horiz—4st. T **338**; 44st. Fruit.

339 Friedrich Schiller (dramatist) (150th death anniversary)

340 Industrial Plant

(Des B. Angelushev. Photo)
1955 (31 Oct). Cultural Anniversaries. Vert portraits of famous writers as T **339**. P 13.
1002	16st. reddish brown/*cream*	65	25
1003	44st. brown-red/*cream*	1·40	35
1004	60st. deep turquoise-blue/*cream*	1·80	40
1005	80st. olive-black/*cream*	2·30	80
1006	1l. purple/*cream*	4·50	2·00
1007	2l. deep olive/*cream*	5·75	4·25
1002/1007 Set of 6		15·00	7·25

Portraits: 16st. T **339**; 44st. Adam Mickiewicz (poet, death centenary); 60st. Hans Christian Andersen (150th birth anniversary); 80st. Baron de Montesquieu (philosopher, death bicentenary); 1l. Miguel de Cervantes (350th anniversary of publication of *Don Quixote*); 2l. Walt Whitman (poet) (centenary of publication of *Leaves of Grass*).

Nos. 1006/1007 were each issued with *se-tenant* labels bearing the titles of *Don Quixote* and *Leaves of Grass* respectively.

(Des Z. Zhelev (2st., 16st., 80st.), St. Gospodinova (4st., 44st.), M. Rashkov (1l.). Photo)
1955 (1 Dec). Bulgarian–Russian Friendship. Views and portraits (80st., 1l.) inscr as T **340**. P 13.
1008	2st. slate-black/*cream*	20	15
1009	4st. blue/*cream*	25	20
1010	16st. deep blue-green/*cream*	40	25
1011	44st. red-brown/*cream*	1·00	35
1012	80st. deep green/*cream*	1·50	40
1013	1l. greenish black/*cream*	1·60	90
1008/1013 Set of 6		4·50	2·00

Designs: Horiz—2st. T **340**; 4st. Dam; 16st. Danube railway bridge. Vert—44st. Monument; 80st. Ivan Michurin (botanist); 1l. Vladimir Mayakovsky (writer).

341 Emblem

342 Quinces

(Des B. Angelushev. Photo)
1956 (10 Feb). Centenary of Library Reading Rooms. T **341** and similar horiz designs inscr '1856–1956'. P 11.
1014	12st. lake/*cream*	25	20
1015	16st. deep brown/*cream*	25	25
1016	44st. slate-green/*cream*	1·50	65
1014/1016 Set of 3		1·80	1·00

Designs: 12st. T **341**; 16st. K. Pishurka writing; 44st. B. Kiro reading.

(Des V. Tomov. Photo)
1956 (14 Apr)–**57**. Fruit. T **342** and similar vert designs. P 13.
1017	4st. scarlet (Type **342**)	2·75	35
1017a	4st. bright green (Type **342**) (13.4.57)	25	15
	ab. Perf 11		
1018	8st. blue-green (Pears)	1·30	35
1018a	8st. Indian red (Pears) (13.4.57)	30	20
1019	16st. bright crimson (Apples)	2·30	40
1019a	16st. rosine (Apples) (13.4.57)	75	25
1020	44st. violet (Grapes)	2·50	80
1020a	44st. dull orange (Grapes) (13.4.57)	1·50	35
1017/1020a Set of 8		10·50	2·50

See also No. 1473.

343 Artillerymen

344 Blagoev and Birthplace at Zagorichane

(Des B. Angelushev. Photo)
1956 (28 Apr). 80th Anniversary of April Uprising. T **343** and similar horiz design inscr '1876 1956'. P 11.
1021	16st. chocolate (Type **343**)	50	40
1022	44st. deep grey-green (Cavalry charge)	70	65

(Des N. Petkov. Photo)
1956 (30 May). Birth Centenary of Dimitur Blagoev (socialist writer). P 11.
1023	**344** 44st. deep turquoise-blue	1·90	1·30

345 Cherries

346 Football

(Des B. Angelushev and St. Penchev. Photo)
1956 (29 June). Fruit. T **345** and similar vert designs. P 13.
1024	2st. carmine-lake (Type **345**)	20	15
1025	12st. blue (Plums)	25	20
1026	28st. orange-brown (Greengages)	50	35
	a. Perf 11		
1027	80st. bright carmine-red (Strawberries)	1·50	80
1024/1027 Set of 4		2·20	1·40

(Des V. Tomov and L. Zidarov, Photo)
1956 (29 Aug). Olympic Games. T **346** and similar designs inscr '1956'. P 11.
1028	4st. bright blue	75	25
1029	12st. light brown-red	90	30
1030	16st. orange-brown	1·00	35
1031	44st. deep myrtle-green	1·90	80
1032	80st. deep brown	3·25	1·70
1033	1l. crimson	4·50	2·00
1028/1033 Set of 6		11·00	4·75

Designs: Vert—4st. Gymnastics; 12st. Throwing the discus; 80st. Basketball. Horiz—16st. Pole vaulting; 44st. T **346**; 1l. Boxing.

347 Tobacco and Rose

348 Gliders

(Des D. Krustev. Photo)
1956 (1 Sept). 17th International Fair, Plovdiv. P 13.
1034	**347**	44st. carmine-red	1·90	65
1035		44st. deep green	1·90	65

(Des T. Zakhariev, A. Khadzhiev and I. R. Ivanova. Photo)
1956 (15 Oct). AIR. 30th Anniversary of Gliding Club. T **348** and similar horiz designs, inscr as in T **348**. P 13.
1036	44st. blue	50	25
1037	60st. reddish violet	65	35
1038	80st. deep turquoise-green	1·90	80
1036/1038 Set of 3		2·75	1·70

Designs: 44st. Launching glider; 60st. Glider over hangar; 80st. T **348**.

349 National Theatre

350 Wolfgang Mozart (composer, birth bicentenary)

(Des T. Zakhariev (16st.), D. Krustev (44st.). Photo)

1956 (16 Nov). Centenary of National Theatre, Sofia T **349** and similar horiz design inscr '1856 1956'. P 13.
1039		16st. red-brown	40	35
1040		44st. deep bluish-green	90	70

Designs: 16st. T **349**; 44st. Dobri Voinikov and Sava Dobroplodni (dramatists).

(Des B. Angelushev. Photo)

1956 (29 Dec). Cultural Anniversaries. T **350** and similar vert designs. P 13.
1041		16st. bronze green	40	20
1042		20st. brown	65	25
1043		40st. carmine-red	90	30
1044		44st. deep dull purple	1·00	35
1045		60st. deep slate	1·30	40
1046		80st. bistre-brown	1·90	1·20
1047		1l. bluish green	3·25	1·30
1048		2l. deep greenish blue	6·25	4·00
1041/1048	Set of 8		14·00	7·25

Designs: 16st. Benjamin Franklin (US journalist and statesman, 250th birth anniversary); 20st. Rembrandt (artist, 350th birth anniversary); 40st. T **350**; 44st. Heinrich Heine (poet, death centenary); 60st. George Bernard Shaw (dramatist, birth centenary); 80st. Fyodor Dostoevsky (novelist, 75th death anniversary); 1l. Henrik Ibsen (dramatist, 50th death anniversary); 2l. Pierre Curie (physicist, 50th death anniversary).

351 Cyclists

352 Woman with Microscope

(Des P. Rachev Photo)

1957 (6 Mar). Tour of Egypt Cycle Race. P 11.
1049	**351**	80st. chestnut	1·90	90
1050		80st. deep turquoise-blue	1·90	90

(Des B. Angelushev. Photo)

1957 (8 Mar). International Women's Day T **352** and similar designs inscr '8 MAPT 1957'. P 11.
1051		12st. blue	30	25
1052		16st. deep chestnut	40	35
1053		44st. bronze-green	75	40
1051/1053	Set of 3		1·30	90

Designs: 12st. T **352**; 16st. Women and children; 44st. Woman feeding poultry.

353 New Times

354 Lisunov Li-2 Airliner

(Des I. Zakhariev. Photo)

1957 (8 Mar). 60th Anniversary of New Times (review). P 11.
1054	**353**	16st. carmine-red	50	25

(Des St. Kunchev. Photo)

1957 (21 May). AIR. Tenth Anniversary of Bulgarian Airways. P 13.
1055	**354**	80st. blue	1·90	80

355 St Cyril and St Methodius

356 Basketball

(Des B. Angelushev. Photo)

1957 (22 May). Centenary of Canonisation of St Cyril and St Methodius (founders of Cyrillic Alphabet). P 11.
1056	**355**	44st. deep olive-green and pale buff	1·90	65

(Des St. Penchev. Photo)

1957 (20 June). Tenth European Basketball Championships. P 11.
1057	**356**	44st. deep green	3·25	90

357 Girl in National Costume

358 G. Dimitrov

(Des V. Korenev. Photo)

1957 (18 July). Sixth World Youth Festival, Moscow. P 13.
1058	**357**	44st. pale blue	1·00	40

(Des B. Angelushev. Photo)

1957 (18 July). 75th Birth Anniversary of Georgi Dimitrov (statesman). P 13.
1059	**358**	44st. carmine-red	1·90	65

359 V. Levski

360 View of Turnovo and Ludwig Zamenhof (inventor)

(Des N. Petkov. Photo)

1957 (18 July). 120th Birth Anniversary of Vasil Levski (revolutionary). P 11.
1060	**359**	44st. blackish green	1·30	40

(Des M. Velev and St. Kunchev. Photo)

1957 (27 July). 70th Anniversary of Esperanto (invented language) and 50th Anniversary of Bulgarian Esperanto Association. P 13.
1061	**360**	44st. bronze green	1·90	65

361 Soldiers in Battle

362 Woman Planting Tree

BULGARIA 1957

(Des I. Petrov and V. Barakov. Photo)
1957 (13 Aug). 80th Anniversary of Liberation from Turkey. T **361** and similar vert design inscr '1878–1958'. P 13.
1062	16st. deep bluish green	25	15
1063	44st. deep brown	1·00	35

Designs: 16st. Old and Young soldiers; 44st. T **361**.

(Des V. Staikov and V. Barakov. Photo)
1957 (16 Sept). Reafforestation Campaign. T **362** and simlar designs. P 13.
1064	2st. deep blue-green	25	15
1065	12st. deep brown	30	20
1066	16st. greenish blue	30	20
1067	44st. deep bluish green	90	40
1068	80st. green	1·50	80
1064/1068	Set of 5	3·00	1·60

Designs: Vert—2st. T **362**. Horiz—12st. Red Deer in forest; 16st. Dam and trees; 44st. Polikarpov Po-2 biplane over forest; 80st. Trees and cornfield.

363 Two Hemispheres **364** Lenin

(Des T. Zakhariev. Photo)
1957 (4 Oct). Fourth World Trade Unions Congress, Leipzig. P 13.
1069	**363**	44st. greenish blue	1·00	40

(Des B. Angelushev (60st.), V. Tomov and S. Sotirov (others). Photo)
1957 (29 Oct). 40th Anniversary of Russian Revolution. T **364** and similar vert designs inscr '1917–1957'. P 11.
1070	12st. chocolate	65	40
1071	16st. deep turquoise-blue	1·30	1·00
1072	44st. blue	3·50	1·30
1073	60st. carmine-lake	3·75	2·00
1074	80st. myrtle-green	11·00	4·50
1070/1074	Set of 5	18·00	8·25

Designs: 12st. T **364**; 16st. Cruiser *Aurora*; 44st. Dove of Peace over Europe; 60st. Revolutionaries; 80st. Oil refinery.

365 Youth and Girl   **366** Partisans

(Des D. Krustev. Photo)
1957 (28 Dec). Tenth Anniversary of National Youth Movement. P 11.
1075	**365**	16st. carmine	35	25

(Des B. Angelushev. Photo)
1957 (28 Dec). 15th Anniversary of Fatherland Front. P 11.
1076	**366**	16st. chocolate	35	25

367 Mikhail Glinka (composer, death centenary)   **368** Hotel Vasil Kolarov

(Des B. Angelushev, N. Petkov, St. Kunchev and L. Zidarov. Photo)
1957 (30 Dec). Cultural Anniversaries. T **367** and similar vert designs. P 13.
1077	12st. deep brown	75	25
1078	16st. bronze green	90	30
1079	40st. deep greenish blue	2·10	40
1080	44st. brown-lake	2·30	50
1081	60st. Indian red	2·50	1·00
1082	80st. maroon	3·75	3·50
1077/1082	Set of 6	11·00	5·25

Designs: 12st. T **367**; 16st. Jan Comenius (educationist) (300th anniversary of publication of *Didactica Opera Omnia*); 40st. Carl Linnaeus (botanist, 250th birth anniversary); 44st. William Blake (writer, birth bicentenary); 60st. Carlo Goldoni (dramatist, 250th birth anniversary); 80st. Auguste Comte (philosopher, death centenary).

(Des B. Angelushev, T. Danov, St. Kunchev and M. Velve. Photo)
1958 (20 Jan–5 July). Holiday Resorts. T **368** and similar horiz designs. P 13.
1083	4st. deep blue (5.7.58)	20	15
1084	8st. orange-brown	25	15
1085	12st. deep green	30	20
1086	16st. myrtle green	35	25
	a. Perf 11		
1087	44st. deep bluish green	65	30
1088	60st. blue	1·00	40
1089	80st. dull scarlet	1·30	50
1090	1l. purple-brown (5.7.58)	1·50	65
1083/1090	Set of 8	5·00	2·30

Designs: 4st. Skis and Pirin Mountains; 8st. Old house in Koprivshtitsa; 12st. Hostel at Velingrad; 16st. T **368**; 44st. Hotel at Momin-Prokhod; 60st. Seaside hotel and peninsula, Nesebur; 80st. Beach scene, Varna; 1l. Modern hotels, Varna.

See also No. 1552.

IMPERFORATE STAMPS. Some Bulgarian stamps issued from 1958 (No. 1091) to 1965 exist imperforate from limited printings, sometimes in different colours.

369 Brown Hare   **370** Marx and Lenin

(Des V. Korenev (2st., 80st.), V. Tomov (others). Photo)
1958 (5 Apr). Forest Animals. Designs as T **369**. P 11.
1091	2st. deep olive and light yellow-green	90	25
1092	12st. chestnut and bronze-green	1·30	40
1093	16st. brown and slate-green	1·90	50
1094	44st. yellow-brown and blue	2·30	80
1095	80st. deep brown and yellow-ochre	2·75	1·00
1096	1l. sepia and slate-blue	3·50	1·60
1091/1096	Set of 6	11·50	4·00

Designs: Vert—12st. Roe Deer. Horiz—2st. T **369**; 16st. Red Deer stag; 44st. Chamois; 80st. Brown Bear; 1l. Wild Boar.

(Des B. Angelushev. Photo)
1958 (2 June). Seventh Bulgarian Communist Party Congress. T **370** and similar horiz designs. P 11.
1097	12st. sepia	65	35
1098	16st. brown-red	1·00	40
1099	44st. deep blue	2·10	1·30
1097/1099	Set of 3	3·50	1·80

Designs: 12st. T **370**; 16st. Workers marching with banners; 44st. Lenin blast furnaces.

371 Wrestlers   **372** Chessmen and 'oval chessboard'

(Des V. Tomov. Photo)
1958 (20 June). Wrestling Championships. P 11.
1100	**371**	60st. brown-lake	2·75	2·00
1101		80st. sepia	3·25	2·50

(Des St. Kunchev. Photo)
1958 (18 July). Fifth World Students' Team Chess Championship, Sofia. P 11.
1102	**372**	80st. blue-green and pale green	15·00	13·00

1958 BULGARIA

373 Russian Pavilion

(Des P. Rachev. Photo)

1958 (14 Sept). 18th International Fair, Plovdiv. P 11.
1103	373	44st. crimson	1·30	90

374 Swimmer

(Des I. R. Ivanova (28st.), V. Tomov (others). Photo)

1958 (19 Sept). Bulgarian Students' Games. T **374** and similar designs inscr '1958'. P 11.
1104		16st. blue	40	35
1105		28st. bright orange-brown	75	40
1106		44st. bright emerald	1·10	65
1104/1106		Set of 3	2·00	1·30

Designs: Horiz—16st. T **374**. Vert—28st. Dancer; 44st. Volleyball players at net.

375 Onions   **376** Insurgent with Rifle

(Des V. Korenev (2st., 16st.), S. Georgiev (12st.), Ana and M. Velev (others). Photo)

1958 (20 Sept). Agricultural Propaganda. Vert designs as T **375**. P 13.
1107		2st. orange-brown	20	15
1108		12st. deep turquoise	25	20
1109		16st. dull yellowish green	40	30
1110		44st. deep rose-red	65	35
1111		80st. myrtle green	1·50	50
1112		1l. reddish violet	2·10	65
1107/1112		Set of 6	4·50	1·90

Designs: 2st. T **375**; 12st. Garlic; 16st. Peppers; 44st. Tomatoes, 80st. Cucumbers; 1l. Aubergines.
See also No. 1133.

(Des S. Sotirov. Photo)

1958 (23 Sept). 35th Anniversary of September Uprising. T **376** and similar vert design. P 11.
1113		16st. orange-red	65	40
1114		44st. brown-purple	1·30	90

Designs: 16st. T **376**; 44st. Insurgent helping wounded comrade.

377 Conference Emblem   **378** Exhibition Emblem

(Des D. Krustev. Photo)

1958 (24 Sept). First World Trade Unions Young Workers' Conference, Prague. P 11.
1115	377	44st. blue	1·30	90

(Des B. Angelushev. Photo)

1958 (13 Oct). Brussels International Exhibition. P 11.
1116	378	1l. blue and black	12·50	12·00

379 Sputnik over Globe   **380** Running

(Des D. Krustev. Photo)

1958 (28 Nov). AIR. International Geophysical Year. P 11.
1117	379	80st. turquoise-blue	8·75	7·75

(Des L. Zidarov (16st., 44st.), A. Poplilov (others). Photo)

1958 (29 Nov). Balkan Games. Sporting designs as T **380** inscr '1958'. P 11.
1118		16st. orange-brown/*flesh*	1·10	50
1119		44st. olive/*yellow*	1·30	80
1120		60st. blue/*blue*	2·00	90
1121		80st. emerald/*yellow-green*	2·50	1·30
1122		4l. lake/*mauve*	14·50	9·75
1118/1122		Set of 5	19·00	12·00

Designs: Horiz—44st. Throwing the javelin; 60st. High-jumping; 80st. Hurdling. Vert—16st. T **380**; 4l. Putting the shot.

381 Young Gardeners   **382** Smirnenski

(Des L. Marinov (8st., 40st.), V. Korenev (12st., 16st.), D. Krustev (44st.). Photo)

1958 (29 Nov). Fourth Dimitrov National Youth Movement Congress. T **381** and similar designs inscr '1958'. P 11.
1123		8st. bronze-green	20	15
1124		12st. brown	25	20
1125		16st. brown-purple	30	25
1126		40st. greenish blue	70	35
1127		44st. crimson	1·30	50
1123/1127		Set of 5	2·50	1·30

Designs: Horiz—12st. Farm girl with cattle; 40st. Youth with wheelbarrow. Vert—8st. T **381**; 16st. Youth with pickaxe and girl with spade; 44st. Communist Party Building.

(Des B. Angelushev. Photo)

1958 (22 Dec). 60th Birth Anniversary of Khristo Smirnenski (poet and revolutionary). P 11.
1128	382	16st. brown-red	50	25

383 First Cosmic Rocket   **384** Footballers

(Des D. Krustev. Photo)

1959 (28 Feb). AIR. Launching of First Cosmic Rocket. P 11.
1129	383	2l. yellow-brown and blue	12·50	12·00

(Des C. Nikolov. Photo)

1959 (25 Mar). Youth Football Games, Sofia. P 11.
1130	384	2l. brown/*cream*	4·50	3·25

BULGARIA 1959

385 UNESCO Headquarters, Paris **386** Skier

(Des P. Rachev. Photo)

1959 (28 Mar). Inauguration of Headquarters Building of United Nations Educational, Scientific and Cultural Organisation, Paris. P 11.
1131	**385**	2l. purple/*cream*	4·50	3·25

(Des V. Staikov. Photo)

1959 (28 Mar). 40 Years of Skiing in Bulgaria. P 11.
1132	**386**	1l. blue/*cream*	3·25	1·30

45 ст.
(387)

388 Military telegraph linesmen

1959 (1 Apr). No. 1110 surch with T **387**.
1133	45st. on 44st. deep rose-red (B.)	1·90	65

(Des St. Kunchev (60st.), G. Kovachev (1l.), A. Poplilov (2l.), M. Peikova (others). Photo)

1959 (4-16 May). 80th Anniversary of First Bulgarian Postage Stamp. Vert designs as T **388** inscr '1879–1959'. P 11.
1134	12st. yellow and deep green	35	20
1135	16st. mauve and purple	65	25
1136	60st. yellow and olive-brown	1·30	65
1137	80st. salmon and brown-red	1·40	70
1138	1l. light blue and blue	3·25	80
1139	2l. chocolate	6·25	3·25
1134/1139 Set of 6		12·00	5·25

MS1139*a* 91×121 mm. 60st. (+4l.40) orange-yellow and black (as No. 1136). Imperf (16.5.59) .... 80·00 80·00

MS1139*b* 125×125 mm. Remaining values in different colours (*sold at 5l.*). Imperf (16.5.59) .... 80·00 80·00

Designs: Horiz—16st. 19th-century mailcoach; 80st. Early postal car; 2l. Riot scene. Vert—12st. T **388**; 60st. First Bulgarian stamp of 1879; 1l. Radio tower.

389 Great Tits **390** Cotton-picking

(Des G. Kovachev (16st.), M. Peikova (45st.), V. Korenev (others). Photo)

1959 (30 June). Birds. Designs as T **389**. P 11.
1140	2st. slate-green and yellow-olive	50	25
1141	8st. bronze-green and brown-orange	90	35
1142	16st. sepia and brown	1·00	40
1143	45st. black-green and yellow-brown	2·40	1·30
1144	60st. slate-grey and blue	4·50	2·00
1145	80st. grey-brown and deep turquoise-green	6·25	3·25
1140/1145 Set of 6		14·00	6·75

Birds: Horiz—2st. T **389**; 8st. Hoopoe; 60st. Rock Partridge; 80st. European Cuckoo. Vert—16st. Great Spotted Woodpecker; 45st. Grey Partridge.

(Des L. Yotov, C. Nikolov, D. Krustev and L. Marinov. Photo)

1959–61. Five Year Plan. Designs as T **390** inscr '1959'. P 11 (2l.) or 13 (others).
1146	2st. Indian red (15.6.60)	20	15
1147	4st. yellow-brown (6.61)	20	15
1148	5st. deep green (3.7.59)	20	15
1149	10st. reddish brown (6.61)	20	20
1150	12st. reddish brown (26.9.59)	20	20
1151	15st. deep magenta (9.7.60)	25	20
1152	16st. violet (12.3.60)	30	20
1153	20st. bright orange (25.7.59)	30	25
1154	25st. blue (16.6.60)	40	30
1155	28st. emerald (25.7.59)	50	35
1156	40st. deep turquoise-blue (20.5.60)	65	40
1157	45st. chocolate (12.6.60)	65	40
1158	60st. vermilion (20.5.60)	1·30	50
1159	80st. bistre (9.6.60)	2·30	40
1160	1l. brown-lake (6.7.59)	1·30	65
	a. Perf 11		
1161	1l.25 Prussian blue (6.61)	3·75	1·30
	a. Perf 11		
1162	2l. carmine-red (22.2.60)	2·40	80
1146/1162 Set of 17		13·50	6·00

Designs: Horiz—2st. Children at play; 10st. Dairymaid milking Cow; 16st. Industrial plant; 20st. Combine-harvester; 40st. Hydroelectric barrage; 60st. Furnaceman; 1l.25, Machinist. Vert—4st. Woman doctor examining child; 5st. T **390**; 12st. Tobacco harvesting; 15st. Machinist; 25st. Power linesman; 28st. Tending Sunflowers; 45st. Miner; 80st. Fruit picker; 1l. Workers with symbols of agriculture and industry; 2l. Worker with banner.

391 Patriots **392** Piper

(Des B. Angelushev. Photo)

1959 (8 Aug). 300th Anniversary of Batak. P 11.
1163	**391**	16st. chocolate	65	30

(Des V. Tomov (16st.), L. Grozeva (1l.), V. Korenev (others). Photo)

1959 (29 Aug). Spartacist Games. Designs as T **392** inscr '1958–1959'. P 11.
1164	4st. deep olive/*cream*	20	15
1165	12st. scarlet/*yellow*	25	20
1166	16st. lake/*salmon*	40	25
1167	20st. blue/*pale blue*	65	35
1168	80st. blue-green/*pale green*	2·10	80
1169	1l. orange-brown/*orange*	2·30	1·40
1164/1169 Set of 6		5·25	2·75

Designs: Vert—4st. T **392**; 12st. Gymnasts; 1l. Urn. Horiz—16st. Girls exercising with hoops; 20st. Dancers leaping; 80st. Ballet dancers.

393 Soldiers in Lorry **394** Footballer

(Des B. Angelushev. Photo)

1959 (8 Sept). 15th Anniversary of Fatherland Front Government. T **393** and similar designs inscr '1944–1959'. P 11.
1170	12st. slate-blue and red	25	20
1171	16st. black-purple and red	25	20
1172	45st. blue and red	50	35
1173	60st. bronze-green and red	65	40
1174	80st. yellow-brown and red	1·00	50
1175	1l.25 brown and red	2·00	90
1170/1175 Set of 6		4·25	2·30

Designs: Horiz—12st. T **393**; 16st. Partisans meeting Red Army soldiers; 45st. Blast furnaces; 60st. Tanks; 80st. Combine-harvester in cornfield. Vert—1l.25, Pioneers with banner.

(Des B. Angelushev. Photo)

1959 (10 Oct). 50th Anniversary of Football in Bulgaria. P 11.
1176	**394**	1l.25 deep green/*yellow*	10·00	9·75

1959 BULGARIA

395 Tupolev Tu-104A Jetliner and Statue of Liberty

396 Globe and Letter

(Des B. Angelushev. Photo)

1959 (11 Nov). AIR. Visit of Nikita Khrushcev (Russian Prime Minister) to the United States. P 11.
1177   395   1l. pink and blue .... 5·00   4·50

(Des B. Angelushev (45st.), St. Kunchev (1l.25). Photo)

1959 (23 Nov). International Correspondence Week. T **396** and similar vert design inscr '5–11 OKT. 1959'. P 11.
1178   45st. black and green 90   35
1179   1l.25 red, black and blue .... 1·60   65
Designs: 45st. T **396**; 1l.25, Pigeon and letter.

397 Parachutist

398 N. Vaptsarov

(Des M. Popov. Photo)

1959 (3 Dec). Third Voluntary Defence Congress. P 11.
1180   397   1l.25, cream and deep bluish green .... 4·50   2·20

(Des N. Petkov and St. Kunchev. Photo)

1959 (5 Dec). 50th Birth Anniversary of Nikola Vaptsarov (poet and revolutionary). P 11.
1181   398   80st. brown and yellow-green .... 1·30   65

399 Dr. L. Zamenhof

400

(Des B. Angelushev. Photo)

1959 (14 Dec). Birth Centenary of Dr. Ludwig Zamenhof (inventor of Esperanto). P 11.
1182   399   1l.25 deep green and apple green .... 1·90   1·30

(Des St. Kunchev. Photo)

1960 (23 Feb). 50th Anniversary of State Opera. T **400** and similar vert design inscr '1908 1958'. P 11.
1183   80st. black and green (Type 399) .... 1·30   80
1184   1l.25 black and red (Lyre) .... 1·90   1·20

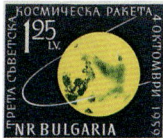
401 Trajectory of *Lunik 3* around the Moon

402 Skier

(Des B. Angelushev. Photo)

1960 (28 Mar). Flight of *Lunik 3*. P 11.
1185   401   1l.25 greenish yellow and Prussian blue ...... 9·50   7·75

(Des V. Tomov. Photo)

1960 (15 Apr). Winter Olympic Games. P 11.
1186   402   2l. brown, blue and black .... 1·90   1·60

403 Vela Blagoeva

404 Lenin

(Des B. Angelushev, N. Petkov, L. Zidarov and St. Kunchev. Photo)

1960 (26 Apr). 50th Anniversary of International Women's Day. T **403** and similar vert portrait designs inscr '1910–1960'. P 11.
1187   16st. deep chestnut and pink 25   15
1188   28st. deep yellow-olive and olive-yellow 30   20
1189   45st. blackish green and olive-green 50   25
1190   60st. Prussian blue and pale blue 65   35
1191   80st. red-brown and orange-red .... 1·00   40
1192   1l.25 olive and yellow-ochre .... 1·30   1·00
1187/1192 *Set of 6* .... 3·50   2·20
Portraits: 16st. T **403**; 28st. Anna Maimunkova; 45st. Vela Piskova; 60st. Rosa Luxemburg; 80st. Clara Zetkin; 1l.25, Nadezhda Krupskaya.

(Des B. Angelushev. Photo)

1960 (10 May). 90th Birth Anniversary of Lenin. T **404** and similar horiz design inscr '1870–1960'. P 11.
1193   16st. flesh and deep chestnut .... 2·50   1·00
1194   45st. black and rose-pink .... 4·50   2·20
Designs: 16st. T **404**; 45st. Lenin at Smolny (writing in chair).

T **405** is vacant.

406 Basketball Players

407 Moon Rocket

(Des B. Angelushev. Litho)

1960 (3 June). Seventh European Women's Basketball Championships. P 11.
1195   406   1l.25 black and yellow .... 2·50   1·30

(Des St. Goristanova. Litho)

1960 (23 June). AIR. Landing of Russian Rocket on Moon. P 11.
1196   407   1l.25 black, yellow and blue .... 9·50   7·75

408 Parachutist

409 Great Yellow Gentian (*Gentiana lutea*)

(Des M. Popov. Photo)

1960 (29 June). World Parachuting Championships, 1960. T **408** and similar design inscr '1960'. P 11.
1197   16st. deep violet-blue and lilac 65   60
1198   1l.25 claret and greenish blue .... 3·75   1·60
Designs: 16st. T **408**; 1l.25, Parachutists descending.

(Des V. Tomov, St. Goristanova and V. Purpov. Photo)

1960 (27 July). Flowers. Vert designs as T **409**. P 11.
1199   2st. yellow-orange, green and drab 30   20
1200   5st. carmine, green and yellow-green .... 1·00   25
1201   25st. orange, green and salmon .... 1·00   35

BULGARIA 1960

1202	45st. magenta, green and lilac............................		1·30	40
1203	60st. orange-red, green and buff........................		2·40	70
1204	80st. ultramarine, green and olive-grey............		2·50	2·00
1199/1204 Set of 6			7·75	3·50

Flowers: 2st. T **409**; 5st. *Tulipa rhodopea*; 25st. *Lilium jankae*; 45st. *Rhododendron ponticum*; 60st. Lady's Slipper (*Cypripedium calceolus*); 80st. *Haberlea rhodopensis*.

410 Football   **411** Racing Cyclists

(Des B. Angelushev, St. Kunchev, L. Zidarov and T. Danov. Photo)

1960 (29 Aug). Olympic Games. Horiz designs as T **410** inscr '1960'. P 11.

1205	8st. pink and brown..		25	15
1206	12st. pink and violet..		30	20
1207	16st. pink and turquoise-blue............................		40	25
1208	45st. pink and purple...		65	40
1209	80st. pink and blue...		1·40	90
1210	2l. pink and deep green......................................		1·90	1·30
1205/1210 Set of 6			4·50	3·00

Designs: 8st. T **410**; 12st. Wrestling; 16st. Weightlifting; 45st. Gymnastics; 80st. Canoeing; 2l. Running.

(Des B. Angelushev. Litho)

1960 (22 Sept). Tour of Bulgaria Cycle Race. P 11.
1211	**411**	1l. black, yellow and red............................	2·50	2·00

412 Globes

(Des I. Boyadzhiev. Photo)

1960 (12 Oct). 15th Anniversary of World Federation of Trades Unions. P 11.
1212	**412**	1l.25 cobalt and blue.................................	1·30	80

413 Popov   **414** Y. Veshin

(Des St. Kunchev. Litho)

1960 (12 Oct). Birth Centenary of Aleksandr Popov (Russian radio pioneer). P 11.
1213	**413**	90st. black and greenish blue	1·90	1·30

(Des B. Angelushev. Photo)

1960 (22 Nov). Birth Centenary of Yaroslav Veshin (painter). P 11.
1214	**414**	1l. deep olive and olive-yellow............	7·50	4·00

415 UN Headquarters. New York   **416** Boyana Church

(Des D. Krustev. Photo)

1961 (14 Jan). 15th Anniversary of United Nations Organisation. P 11.
1215	**415**	1l. cream and brown	3·25	3·00

MS1215*a* 74×57 mm. Type **415** 1l. (+1l.) rose and olive. Imperf... 15·00 14·50

(Des St. Kunchev. Photo)

1961 (28 Jan). 700th Anniversary of Boyana Murals (1959). T **416** and similar horiz designs. P 11.

1216	60st. black, emerald-green and yellow-green	1·30	50
1217	80st. blackish green, cream and orange..........	1·90	65
1218	1l.25 crimson, cream and yellow-green...........	2·50	1·30
1216/1218 Set of 3		5·25	2·20

Designs: Frescoes of—60st. T **416**; 80st. Theodor Tiron; 1l.25, Desislava.

417 Cosmic Rocket and Dogs Belka and Strelka   **419** Pleven Costume

(Des P. Rachev. Photo)

1961 (28 Jan). AIR. Russian Cosmic Rocket Flight of August, 1960. P 11.
1219	**417**	1l.25 greenish blue and red	8·75	8·50

(Des V. Korenev. Litho)

1961 (28 Jan). Provincial Costumes. Vert designs as T **419**. P 11.

1220	12st. yellow, blackish green and salmon.........	25	15
1221	16st. chocolate, buff and lilac	30	20
1222	28st. rose, black and turquoise-green	50	25
1223	45st. deep blue, vermilion and pale violet-blue..	1·00	35
1224	60st. yellow, blue and light blue........................	1·40	40
1225	80st. rose, black-green and yellow...................	1·60	90
1220/1225 Set of 6		4·50	2·00

Designs: Costumes of: 12st. Kyustendil; 16st. T **419**; 28st. Sliven; 45st. Sofia; 60st. Rhodope; 80st. Karnobat.

420 Clock Tower, Vratsa   **421** Dalmatian Pelican (*Pelecanus crispus*)

(Des B. Angelushev and St. Kunchev (16st., 45st., 60st., 80st.), M. Peikova and G. Kovachev (others). Photo)

1961 (25 Feb). Bulgarian Museums and Monuments. Designs as T **420**. Stars and figure of value in red. P 11.

1226	8st. bronze-green..	25	15
1227	12st. violet...	30	20
1228	16st. red-brown...	30	20
1229	20st. blue...	35	25
1230	28st. greenish blue..	40	30
1231	40st. red-brown...	50	35
1232	45st. olive-brown..	65	40
1233	60st. black...	90	50
1234	80st. deep yellow-olive..	1·50	60
1235	1l. deep bluish green	2·50	1·30
1226/1235 Set of 10		7·00	3·75

Designs: Vert—8st. T **420**; 12st. Clock Tower, Bansko; 20st. Agushev building, Mogilitsa (Smolensk). Horiz—28st. Oslekov House, Koprivshtitsa; 40st. Pasha's House, Melnik. 26½×26½ mm—16st. Wine jug; 45st. Lion (bas-relief); 60st. Horseman of Madara; 80st. Part of fresco, Bachkovo Monastery; 1l. Coin of Tsar Konstantin-Asen (13th-century).

(Des M. Velev (4st.), V. Tomov (80st., 2l.), V. Korenev (others). Photo)

1961 (31 Mar). Birds. Designs as T **421**. P 11.

1236	2st. greenish blue, black and salmon-red.....	30	25
1237	4st. orange, black and apple-green.................	40	30
1238	16st. orange, deep brown and light green	50	40
1239	80st. yellow, deep brown and light turquoise-green...	4·00	1·40
1240	1l. yellow, deep chocolate and light blue..	4·50	2·30
1241	2l. yellow, red-brown and light grey-blue..	5·75	2·50
1236/1241 Set of 6		14·00	6·50

Birds: 2st. Capercaillie (*Tetrao urogallus*); 4st. T **421**; 16st. Ring-necked Pheasant (*Phasianus colchicus*); 80st. Great Bustard (*Otis tarda*); 1l. Lammergeier (*Gypaetus barbatus*); 2l. Hazel Grouse (*Tetrastes bonasia*).

422 'Communications and Transport' **423** Gagarin and Rocket

(Des P. Rusinov. Photo)

1961 (1 Apr). 50th Anniversary of Transport Workers' Union. P 11.
1242 **422** 80st. bluish green and black............ 1·30 65

(Des V. Popov. Photo)

1961 (26 Apr). AIR. World's First Manned Space Flight. P 11.
1243 **423** 4l. greenish blue, black and red............ 8·75 5·75

424 Shevchenko (poet) **425** Throwing the Discus

(Des P. Rusinov. Photo)

1961 (27 Apr). Death Centenary of Taras Shevchenko (Ukrainian poet). P 11.
1244 **424** 1l. black-brown and yellow-olive............ 8·25 5·75

(Des B. Angelushev and St. Kunchev. Photo)

1961 (15 May). World Students' Games. T **425** and similar designs inscr 'FISU 1961'. P 11.
1245   4st. cobalt and black............ 25 20
1246   5st. vermilion and black............ 25 20
1247   16st. olive and black............ 40 35
1248   45st. slate-blue and black............ 65 40
1249   1l.25 yellow-brown and black............ 2·30 50
1250   2l. bright reddish violet and black............ 2·50 1·70
1245/1250 Set of 6 .... 5·75 3·00
MS1250*a* 66×66 mm. 5l. ultramarine, yellow and green (Sports Palace and inscriptions. Imperf............ 21·00 20·00
Designs: Horiz—5st. Tennis; 16st. Fencing; 45st. T **425**; 1l.25, Sports Palace, Sofia. Vert—4st. Water polo; 2l. Basketball.

426 Seahorse **427** Space Dogs

(Des V. Tomov and N. Tuzsuzov. Photo)

1961 (19 June). Black Sea Fauna. T **426** and similar designs. P 11.
1251   2st. deep sepia and green............ 25 20
1252   12st. pink and greenish blue............ 30 25
1253   16st. deep violet-blue and cobalt............ 40 35
1254   45st. brown and light blue............ 1·90 1·30
1255   1l. deep slate-blue and green............ 5·00 2·00
1256   1l.25 red-brown and light blue............ 6·25 3·25
1251/1256 Set of 6 .... 12·50 6·50
Designs: Horiz—2st. Mediterranean Monk Seals; 12st. Lung Jellyfish; 16st. Common Dolphins; 45st. T **426**; 1l. Starred Sturgeons; 1l.25, Thornback Ray.

(Des P. Rusinov (No. 1257), L. Yotov (No. 1258). Photo)

1961. AIR. Space Exploration. T **427** and another design inscr '12.11.1961'. P 11.
1257 **427** 2l. slate and brown-purple (29.6.61)... 7·50 5·75
1258 — 2l. blue, yellow and orange (28.6.61). 14·00 9·00
Design: Vert (24×41½ *mm*)—No. 1258, Venus rocket in flight.

428 Dimitur Blagoev as Orator **429** Hotel

(Des V. Staikov. Photo)

1961 (5 Aug). 70th Anniversary of First Bulgarian Social Democratic Party Congress, Buzludzha. P 11.
1259 **428** 45st. brown-red and cream............ 40 35
1260   80st. deep blue and pink............ 90 65
1261   2l. sepia and pale green............ 1·90 1·60
1259/1261 Set of 3 .... 3·00 2·30

(Des T. Danov, V. Yonchev and B. Angelushev. Photo)

1961 (25 Aug). Tourist Issue. T **429** and other vert designs. P 11.
1262   4st. cream, black and yellow-green (Type **429**)............ 20 15
1263   12st. cream, black and light blue (Hikers)............ 30 20
1264   16st. cream, black and bluish green (Tents).. 30 20
1265   1l.25 cream, black and bistre (Climber)............ 1·50 40
1262/1265 Set of 4 .... 2·10 85

430 The Golden Girl **431** Major Titov in Spacesuit

(Des V. Korenev, L. Zidarov and St. Kunchev. Photo)

1961 (10 Oct). Bulgarian Fables. T **430** and similar horiz designs. P 11.
1266   2st. black, yellow, grey and blue............ 20 15
1267   8st. grey, black and bright purple............ 25 20
1268   12st. pink and blue-green............ 40 35
1269   16st. grey, black, light blue and red............ 1·30 65
1270   45st. pink, black, grey and olive............ 2·40 1·00
1271   80st. crimson, black, grey and yellow-brown 3·25 1·30
1266/1271 Set of 6 .... 7·00 3·25
Designs: 2st. T **430**; 8st. Man and woman (*The Living Water*), 12st. Archer and Dragon (*The Golden Apple*); 16st. Horseman (*Krali Marko*; national hero); 45st. Female archer on Stag (*Samovila-Vila*: fairy); 80st. Tom Thumb and Cockerel.

(Des P. Rusinov and G. Popov. Photo)

1961 (20 Nov). AIR. Second Russian Manned Space Flight. T **431** and similar horiz design. P 11.
1272   75st. flesh, pale blue and deep olive............ 5·00 4·00
1273   1l.25 pink, pale blue and violet-blue............ 6·25 5·25
Designs: 75st. T **431**; 1l.25, *Vostok 2* in flight.

432 Caesar's Mushroom (*Amanita caesarea*) **433** Dimitur and Konstantin Miladinov (authors)

(Des M. Parpulova and St. Kunchev. Photo)

1961 (20 Dec). Fungi. T **432** and similar vert designs. Values in black. P 11.
1274   2st. red and bistre............ 20 20
1275   4st. red-brown and olive-green............ 25 20
1276   12st. red-brown and bistre............ 30 25
1277   16st. red-brown and mauve............ 30 25
1278   45st. red, yellow and orange............ 75 40
1279   80st. orange and sepia............ 1·00 80
1280   1l.25 lavender and chocolate............ 2·00 1·00
1281   2l. brown and yellow-brown............ 2·75 2·50
1274/1281 Set of 8 .... 6·75 5·00

BULGARIA 1961

Designs: 2st. T **432**; 4st. Red-staining Mushroom (*Psalliota silvatica*); 12st. Larch Bolete (*Boletus elegans*); 16st. Cep (*Boletus edulis*); 45st. Saffron Milk Cap (*Lactarius deliciosus*); 80st. Parasol Mushroom (*Lepiota procera*); 1l.25, Oyster Mushroom (*Pleurotus ostreatus*); 2l. Honey Fungus (*Armillariella mellea*).

(Des B. Angelushev. Photo)

1961 (21 Dec). Centenary of Publication of Bulgarian Popular Songs. P 11.
| 1282 | **433** | 1l.25 black and olive-green | 1·90 | 1·30 |

Currency revaluation
1 New Lev = 10 Old Leva

(434)

(435)

1962 (1 Jan). Various stamps surch as T **434** or with T **435** (No. 1288).
1283	1st. on 10st. (No. 1149)	25	20
1284	1st. on 12st. (No. 1150)	25	20
1285	2st. on 15st. (No. 1151)	25	20
1286	2st. on 16st. (No. 1152) (R.)	25	20
1287	2st. on 20st. (No. 1153)	25	20
1288	2st. on 20st. (No. 1153)	40	25
1289	3st. on 25st. (No. 1154) (R.)	30	25
	a. Surch in black	25·00	24·00
1290	3st. on 28st. (No. 1155) (R.)	30	25
1291	5st. on 44st. (No. 1087) (R.)	40	30
1292	5st. on 44st. (No. 1110) (V.)	40	30
1293	5st. on 45st. (No. 1157)	50	35
1294	10st. on 1l. (No. 1160) (P 13)	75	40
1295	20st. on 2l. (No. 1162)	1·50	90
1296	40st. on 4l. (No. 889) (V.)	3·75	2·00
1283/1296 Set of 14		8·50	5·50

436 Isker River

437 Freighter *Varna*

(Des V. Staikov. Photo)

1962 (3 Feb). AIR. Horiz designs as T **436**. P 13.
1297	1st. deep bluish green and lavender	25	20
1298	2st. deep blue and reddish purple	25	20
1299	3st. red-brown and orange-yellow	30	20
1300	10st. black-green and yellow-bistre	75	35
1301	40st. black-green, blue-green and deep olive	3·00	1·40
1297/1301 Set of 5		4·00	2·10

Designs: 1st. T **436**; 2st. Yacht at Varna; 3st. Melnik; 10st. Turnovo; 40st. Pirin Mountains.

(Des M. Velev, N. Tuzsuzov, V. Tomov and V. Popov. Photo)

1962 (1 Mar). Bulgarian Merchant Navy. T **437** and similar horiz designs. Photo. P 11.
1302	1st. turquoise-green and blue	25	20
1303	5st. light blue and green	65	25
1304	20st. violet-blue and greenish blue	1·60	65
1302/1304 Set of 3		2·30	1·00

Ships: 1st. T **437**; 5st. Tanker *Komsomols*; 20st. Liner *Georgi Dimitrov*.

438 Rila Mountains

439 Georgi Dimitrov as Typesetter

(Des V. Korenev, V. Tomov and N. Tuzsuzov. Photo)

1962 (13 Mar)–**63**. T **438** and similar horiz designs. P 13.
1305	1st. deep turquoise-green	25	20
1306	2st. greenish blue	25	20
	a. Perf 10½		
1307	6st. bright turquoise-blue	50	25
1308	8st. deep bright mauve	75	35
1309	13st. deep olive	1·50	90
1310	1l. myrtle green (6.63)	8·75	2·50
1305/1310 Set of 6		11·00	4·00

Designs: 1st. T **438**; 2st. Pirin Mountains; 6st. Fishing boats, Nesebur; 8st. Danube shipping; 13st. Viden Castle; 1l. Rhodope Mountains.

(Des M. Peikova (2st.), St. Kunchev (13st.). Photo)

1962 (19 Mar). 80th Anniversary of State Printing Office. T **439** and similar vert design inscr '1881–1961'. P 11.
| 1311 | 2st. red, black and yellow | 25 | 20 |
| 1312 | 13st. black, red-orange and yellow | 80 | 50 |

Designs: 2st. T **439**; 13st. Emblem of Printing Office.

440 Pink Roses

441 The World United against Malaria

(Des A. Tuzsuzova and N. Tuzsuzov. Litho)

1962 (28 Mar). Bulgarian Roses. T **440** and similar vert designs. P 11.
1313	1st. pink, green and violet	25	20
	a. Perf 10½		
1314	2st. carmine-red, green and orange-buff	25	20
1315	3st. carmine-red, green and pale blue	50	25
1316	4st. yellow, blue-green and green	75	35
1317	5st. pink, green and blue	1·20	40
1318	6st. carmine-red, green and turquoise-green	1·30	65
1319	8st. carmine-red, green and light yellow-green	3·25	1·30
1320	13st. yellow, green and blue	5·75	4·50
1313/1320 Set of 8		12·00	7·00

See also Nos. 1390/1392.

(Des B. Angelushev. Photo)

1962 (19 Apr). Malaria Eradication. T **441** and similar horiz design. P 11.
| 1321 | 5st. yellow, black and orange-brown | 75 | 35 |
| 1322 | 20st. yellow, green and black | 2·40 | 1·00 |

Designs: 5st. T **441**; 20st. Campaign Emblem.

442 Lenin and Front Page of *Pravda*

443 Text-book and Blackboard

(Des A. Poplilov. Photo)

1962 (5 May). 50th Anniversary of *Pravda* Newspaper. P 10.
| 1323 | **442** | 5st. indigo, rose-red and black | 2·50 | 1·60 |

(Des B. Angelushev. Photo)

1962 (21 May). Bulgarian Teachers' Congress. P 10.
| 1324 | **443** | 5st. black, yellow and blue | 65 | 35 |

444 Footballer

445 Dimitrov

(Des V. Tomov. Photo)

1962 (26 May). World Football Championship, Chile. P 11.
| 1325 | **444** | 13st. orange-brown, blue-green and black | 2·50 | 1·30 |

(Des L. Yotov. Photo)

1962 (18 June). 80th Birth Anniversary of Georgi Dimitrov (Prime Minister 1946–1949). P 11.
| 1326 | **445** | 2st. olive-green | 65 | 35 |
| 1327 | | 5st. grey-blue | 1·30 | 40 |

1962 BULGARIA

446 Bishop

(**447**)

452 Combine-harvester

453 Cover of *History of Bulgaria*

(Des St. Kunchev. Litho)

1962 (7 July). 15th Chess Olympiad, Varna. T **446** and similar vert designs inscr '1962'. P 11.

1328	1st. green, black and grey		30	20
1329	2st. bistre, black and grey		35	25
1330	3st. reddish violet, black and grey		50	30
1331	13st. brown-orange, black and grey		2·50	1·00
1332	20st. blue, black and grey		3·25	2·00
1328/1332	Set of 5		6·25	3·50

MS1332*a* 76×66 mm. 20st.+30st. scarlet and grey-green (Chess pieces). Imperf........ 16·00 15·00
 Designs (chess pieces): 1st. T **446**; 2st. Rook; 3st. Queen; 13st. Knight; 20st. Pawn.

1962 (14 July). 35th Esperanto Congress, Burgas. No. 1061 surch with T **447** in red.

1333	**360**	13st. on 44st. bronze-green	6·25	4·50

448 Festival Emblem

449 Ilyushin Il-18 Airliner

454 Andrian Nikolaev and *Vostok 3*

455 Parachutist

(Des St. Kunchev. Photo)

1962 (18 Aug). World Youth Festival, Helsinki. T **448** and similar horiz design inscr '1962'. P 11.

1334		5st. light blue, pink and blue-green	50	25
1335		13st. light blue, reddish violet and grey	1·40	40

 Designs: 5st. T **448**; 13st. Girl and emblem.

(Des D. Rusinov. Photo)

1962 (18 Aug). AIR. 15th Anniversary of TABSO Airline. P 11.

1336	**449**	13st. blue, deep ultramarine and black	1·90	65

(Des K. Mikhailov and L. Yotov. Photo)

1962 (9 Dec). AIR. First 'Team' Manned Space Flight. T **454** and similar horiz designs inscr '1962'. P 11.

1353		1st. deep olive and black	40	35
1354		2st. deep olive, blue-green and black	90	40
1355		40st. pink, greenish blue and black	5·00	2·75
1353/1355	Set of 3		5·75	3·25

 Designs: 1st. T **454**; 2st. Pavel Popovich and *Vostok 4*; 40st. *Vostok 3* and *Vostok 4* in flight.

(Des K. Mikhailov and L. Yotov. Photo)

1963 (20 Feb)–**64**. T **455** and similar designs.

A. P 10½ (20.2.63)

1356A		1st. lake-red	25	15
1357A		1st. deep orange-brown	25	15
1358A		1st. deep blue-green	25	15
1359A		1st. deep green	25	15
1360A		1st. blue	25	15
1356A/1360A	Set of 5		1·10	70

B. P 11½ (1964)

1356B		1st. lake-red	25	15
1357B		1st. deep orange-brown	25	15
1358B		1st. deep blue-green	25	15
1359B		1st. deep green	25	15
1360B		1st. blue	25	15
1356B/1360B	Set of 5		1·10	70

 Designs: Vert—No. 1356, State crest. Horiz—No. 1357, Sofia University; No. 1358, Vasil Levski Stadium, Sofia; No. 1359, The Camels (archway), Hisar; No. 1360, T **455**.

450 Apollo (*Parnassius apollo*)

451 K. E. Tsiolkovsky (scientist)

456 A. Konstantinov

457 Mars and *Mars 1* Space Probe

(Des V. Tomov (1st. to 3st.), A. Khof, V. Kantardzhieva, M. Velev and A. Balkanski (others). Photo)

1962 (13 Sept). Butterflies and Moths. T **450** and similar horiz designs. Multicoloured. P 11.

1337		1st. Type **450**	25	20
1338		2st. Eastern Festoon (*Thais cerisyi*)	30	20
1339		3st. Meleager's Blue (*Lycaena meleager*)	40	25
1340		4st. Camberwell Beauty (*Vanessa antiopa*)	50	30
1341		5st. Crimson Underwing (*Catocala dilecta*)	65	40
1342		6st. Hebe Tiger Moth (*Arctia hebe*)	1·30	50
1343		10st. Danube Clouded Yellow (*Colias balcanica*)	4·50	1·70
1344		13st. Cardinal (*Argynnis pandora*)	6·25	3·25
1337/1344	Set of 8		12·50	6·00

(Des P. Rusinov and L. Marinov. Photo)

1962 (24 Sept). AIR. 13th International Astronautics Congress. T **451** and similar horiz design inscr '1962'. P 11.

1345		5st. drab and green	6·25	2·50
1346		13st. blue and yellow	3·50	2·10

 Designs: 5st. T **451**; 13st. Moon rocket.

(Des B. Angelushev. Photo)

1963 (5 Mar). Centenary of Birth of Aleko Konstantinov (author). P 11½.

1361	**456**	5st. deep bluish green, black and red..	75	40

 No. 1361 was issued in sheets with brown *se-tenant* label portraying Bai Ganyu, hero of Konstantinov's works.

131

BULGARIA 1963

(Des L. Yotov and P. Rusinov. Photo)
1963 (5 Mar). AIR. Launching of Soviet Space Probe, *Mars 1*. T **457** and similar horiz design. P 11½.
1362	5st. rose, pale turquoise-green, black and violet-blue		1·30	65
1363	13st. light salmon, yellow, black and light blue		2·50	1·30

Designs: 5st. T **457**; 13st. Release of probe from rocket.

458 Orpheus Restaurant, Sunny Beach

459 V. Levski

(Des V. Tomov. Photo)
1963 (12 Mar–Dec). Black Sea Coast Resorts. T **458** and similar horiz designs. P 13.
1364	1st. blue (6.63)		25	20
1365	2st. vermilion (6.63)		1·30	35
1365a	2st. carmine (12.63)		9·50	40
	b. Perf 11			
1366	3st. yellow-brown (6.63)		30	25
1367	5st. purple		65	35
1368	13st. turquoise (6.63)		2·20	40
1369	20st. green (6.63)		2·50	65
1364/1369 Set of 7			15·00	2·30

Designs: Sunny Beach—1st. T **458**; 5st. The Dunes Restaurant; 2st., 3st., 13st. Various hotels; 20st. Hotel. Golden Sands.

(Des N. Petkov. Photo)
1963 (11 Apr). 90th Anniversary of Execution of Vasil Levski (revolutionary). P 10½.
1370	**459**	13st. greenish blue and pale yellow	2·50	90

460 Dimitrov, Boy and Girl

461 Eurasian Red Squirrel

(Des V. Tomov. Photo)
1963 (25 Apr). Tenth Dimitrov Communist Youth League Congress, Sofia. T **460** and similar vert design. P 11½.
1371	2st. red-brown, red and black		25	20
1372	13st. yellow-brown, turquoise and black		1·00	45

Designs: 2st. T **460**; 13st. Girl and youth holding book and hammer aloft.

(Des L. Zidarov, St. Kunchev and B. Angelushev. Litho)
1963 (30 Apr). Woodland Animals. T **461** and similar designs. Figures of value in red. P 11½.
1373	1st. brown and green/*blue-green*		25	15
1374	2st. black and green/*yellow*		30	20
1375	3st. sepia and olive/*olive-drab*		65	25
1376	5st. red-brown and ultramarine/*violet-black*		1·30	40
1377	13st. black and brown-red/*pink*		4·00	1·30
1378	20st. sepia and blue/*light blue*		4·75	2·10
1373/1378 Set of 6			10·00	4·00

Animals: Horiz—2st. East European Hedgehog; 3st. Marbled Polecat; 5st. Beech Marten; 13st. Eurasian Badger. Vert—1st. T **461**; 20st. European Otter.

462 Wrestling

463 Congress Emblem and Allegory

(Des L. Marinov and V. Popov. Photo)
1963 (31 May). 15th International Open Wrestling Championships, Sofia. T **462** and similar design. P 11½.
1379	5st. bistre and black		65	25
1380	20st. orange-brown and black		1·90	1·00

Designs: Vert—5st. T **462**. Horiz—20st. As T **462** but different hold.

(Des V. Korenev. Photo)
1963 (24 June). World Women's Congress, Moscow. P 11½.
1381	**463**	20st. light blue and black	1·90	65

464 Esperanto Star and Sofia Arms

465 Rocket, Globe and Moon

(Des St. Kunchev. Photo)
1963 (29 June). 48th World Esperanto Congress, Sofia. P 11½.
1382	**464**	13st. multicoloured	1·90	65

(Des P. Rusinov and V. Popov. Photo)
1963 (22 July). Launching of Soviet Moon Rocket *Luna 4*. T **465** and similar vert designs inscr '2.IV.1963'. P 11½.
1383	1st. pale ultramarine		25	15
1384	2st. bright purple		25	15
1385	3st. greenish blue		25	15
1383/1385 Set of 3			70	40

Designs: 1st. T **465**; 2st. Tracking equipment; 3st. *Sputniks*.

466 Valery Bykovsky in Spacesuit

(**467**)

(Des V. Tomov, N. Tuzsuzov, V. Korenev and St. Goristanova. Photo)
1963 (26 Aug). AIR. Second 'Team' Manned Space Flights. T **466** and similar horiz designs. P 11½.
1386	1st. greenish blue and lilac		25	15
1387	2st. brown and light yellow		35	20
1388	5st. red and light red		65	25
1389	20st. +10st. olive-green and light blue		3·25	1·30
1386/1389 Set of 4			4·00	1·70
MS1389a	79×68 mm. 50st. purple and red-brown (Spassky Tower and Globe). Imperf.		6·25	5·25

Designs: 1st. T **466**; 2st. Valentina Tereshkova in space suit; 5st. Globe; 20st. Bykovsky and Tereshkova.

See also Nos. 1463/1464.

1963 (31 Aug). Europa Fair, Riccione (Italy). Nos. 1314/1315 and 1318 (Roses) optd as T **467** or additionally surch.
1390	2st. carmine-red, green and orange-buff (G.)		65	25
1391	5st. on 3st. carmine-red, green and pale blue (B.)		90	40
1392	13st. on 6st. carmine-red, green and turquoise-green		2·30	65
1390/1392 Set of 3			3·50	1·20

468 Relay-racing

(Des V. Tomov. Photo)

1963 (13 Sept). Balkan Games. T **468** and similar horiz designs. Flags in red, yellow, blue, green and black. P 11½.

1393	1st. green	15	15
1394	2st. violet	20	20
1395	5st. greenish blue	25	25
1396	5st. brown-red	1·30	35
1397	13st. brown	5·00	3·75
1393/1397	Set of 5	6·25	4·25
MS1397a	74×69 mm. 50st. black and olive (as Type **468**). Imperf	8·25	8·25

Designs: 1st. T **468**; 2st. Throwing the hammer; 3st. Long jumping; 5st. High jumping; 13st. Throwing the discus. Each design includes the flags of the competing countries.

469 Slavonic Scroll

470 Insurgents

(Des B. Angelushev. Litho)

1963 (19 Sept). Fifth International Slav Congress, Sofia. P 10½.

1398	**469**	5st. vermilion, pale yellow and deep olive-green	65	30

(Des V. Korenev. Litho)

1963 (21 Sept). 40th Anniversary of September Uprising. P 11½.

1399	**470**	2st. black and vermilion	40	20

471 Aquilegia aurea

472 Khristo Smirnenski

(Des D. Rusinov. Litho)

1963 (9 Oct). Nature Protection. T **471** and similar vert floral designs. Flowers in natural colours; background colours below. P 11½ (1st.) or 10½ (others).

1400	1st. greenish blue	20	15
1401	2st. grey-olive	25	20
1402	3st. olive-yellow	30	25
1403	5st. blue	50	35
1404	6st. bright purple	65	40
1405	8st. light grey	1·30	65
1406	10st. light mauve	2·50	1·30
1407	13st. deep yellow-olive	4·50	2·30
1400/1407	Set of 8	9·25	5·00

Flowers: 1st. T **471**; 2st. Edelweiss (*Leontopodium alpinum*); 3st. *Primula deorum*; 5st. White Water Lily (*Nymphaea alba*); 6st. Tulip (*Tulipa urumovii*); 8st. *Viola delphinantha*; 10st. Alpine Clematis (*Clematis alpina*). 13st. *Anenome narcissiflora*.

(Des L. Yotov. Litho)

1963 (28 Oct). 65th Anniversary of Birth of Smirnenski (poet and revolutionary). P 10½.

1408	**472**	13st. black and lilac	1·30	50

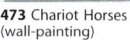
473 Chariot Horses (wall-painting)

474 Hemispheres and Centenary Emblem

(Des St. Kunchev, R. Stanoeva and A. Sertev. Litho)

1963 (28 Dec). Thracian Tombs, Kazanlik. Vert designs as T **473**. P 10½.

1409	1st. red, yellow and grey	20	15
1410	2st. reddish violet, yellow and grey	25	20
1411	3st. greenish blue, yellow and grey	30	25
1412	5st. brown, yellow and dull green	50	40
1413	13st. black, yellow and dull green	1·40	65
1414	20st. reddish purple, yellow and dull green	2·50	1·00
1409/1414	Set of 6	4·75	2·40

Designs: (wall-paintings on tombs)—1st. T **473**; 2st. Chariot race; 3st. Flautists; 5st. Tray-bearer; 13st. Funeral feast; 20st. Seated woman.

ZARSKA BULGARSKA POSTA. Labels with this inscription are bogus issues produced in Madrid in 1963–1964.

(Des B. Angelushev. Litho)

1964 (27 Jan). Red Cross Centenary. T **474** and similar horiz designs. Cross in red. P 10½.

1415	1st. olive-yellow and black	25	20
1416	2st. bright blue and black	25	20
1417	3st. slate-blue, black and grey	25	20
1418	5st. greenish blue and black	35	25
1419	13st. black and yellow-orange	1·80	70
1415/1419	Set of 5	2·50	1·40

Designs: 1st. T **474**; 2st. Blood donation; 3st. Bandaging wrist; 5st. Nurse; 13st. Henri Dunant.

475 Speed-skating

476 Head (2nd-century)

(Des R. Stanoeva, A. Sertev and D. Vlaev. Photo)

1964 (21 Feb). Winter Olympic Games, Innsbruck. Various horiz designs as T **475**. P 10½.

1420	1st. deep blue, orange-brown and light blue	25	20
1421	2st. olive-green, mauve and black	25	20
1422	3st. deep bluish green, orange-brown and black	25	20
1423	5st. multicoloured	45	25
1424	10st. red-orange, black and brownish grey	1·10	50
1425	13st. olive, red and grey	1·40	60
1420/1425	Set of 6	3·25	1·80
MS1425a	64×67 mm. 50st. red, turquoise-blue and greenish black (Girl skater). Imperf	6·75	6·75

Designs: 1st. T **475**; 2st. Figure skating; 3st. Cross-country skiing; 5st. Ski jumping. Ice hockey—10st. Goalkeeper; 13st. Players.

(Des B. Angelushev and St. Kunchev. Photo)

1964 (14 Mar). 2,500 Years of Bulgarian Art. T **476** and similar horiz designs. Borders in grey. P 10½.

1426	1st. deep bluish green and red	25	20
1427	2st. deep olive-black and red	25	20
1428	3st. bistre-brown and red	25	20
1429	5st. greenish blue and red	30	25
1430	6st. orange-brown and red	80	30
1431	8st. brown-red and red	1·20	35
1432	10st. yellow-olive and red	1·40	40
1433	13st. olive and red	1·60	1·20
1426/1433	Set of 8	5·50	2·75

Designs: 1st. T **476**; 2st. Horseman (1st to 4th-century); 3st. Jug (19th-century); 5st. Buckle (19th-century); 6st. Pot (19th-century); 8st. Angel (17th-century); 10st. Animals (8th to 10th-century); 13st. Peasant woman (20th-century).

477 The Unborn Maid

478 Turkish Lacewing (*Ascalaphus otomanus*)

(Des St. Kunchev and V. Korenev. Photo)

1964 (17 Apr). Folk Tales. T **477** and similar horiz designs. Multicoloured. P 10½.

1434	1st. Type **477**	25	20
	a. Perf 11½		

BULGARIA 1964

1435	2st. Grandfather's Glove	25	20
1436	3st. The Big Turnip	25	20
1437	5st. The Wolf and the Seven Kids	35	25
1438	8st. Cunning Peter	80	55
1439	13st. The Loaf of Corn	2·30	95
1434/1439	Set of 6	3·75	2·10

(Des M. Peikova and V. Vasileva. Photo)

1964 (16 May). Insects. T **478** and similar designs. P 11½.

1440	1st. black yellow and Venetian red	25	20
1441	2st. black, yellow-brown and deep bluish green	25	20
1442	3st. deep green, black and drab	35	25
1443	5st. violet, black and yellow-olive	1·40	40
1444	13st. yellow-brown black and bluish violet	2·75	1·40
1445	20st. orange-yellow, black and slate-blue	4·00	1·60
1440/1445	Set of 6	8·00	3·75

Insects: Vert—2st. Thread Lacewing Fly (*Nemoptera coa*); 5st. Alpine Longhorn Beetle (*Rosalia alpina*); 13st. Cockchafer (*Anisoplia austriaca*). Horiz—1st. T **478**; 3st. Cricket (*Saga natalia*); 20st. Hunting Wasp (*Scolia flavitrons*).

479 Football

(Des St. Kunchev and V. Korenev. Photo)

1964 (8 June). 50th Anniversary of Levski Physical Culture Association. Multicoloured. P 11½.

1446	2st. Type **479**	25	20
1447	13st. Handball	1·80	70
MS1447a	60×60 mm. 60st. grey-green and orange-yellow (Cup and Map of Europe). Imperf	5·75	5·50

480 Title Page and Petur Beron (author)

(Des B. Angelushev. Photo)

1964 (22 June). 140th Anniversary of First Bulgarian Primer. P 11½.

1448	**480**	20st. black and orange-brown	3·50	3·50

481 Stephenson's *Rocket*

(Des M. Peikova and V. Vasileva. Photo)

1964 (1 July). Railway Transport. T **481** and similar horiz designs. Multicoloured. P 11½.

1449	1st. Type **481**	25	20
1450	2st. Steam locomotive	25	20
1451	3st. Diesel locomotive	25	20
1452	5st. Electric locomotive	55	25
1453	8st. Steam train on bridge	1·40	40
1454	13st. Diesel train emerging from tunnel	2·00	1·50
1449/1454	Set of 6	4·25	2·40

482 Alsatian (**483**)

(Des B. Angelushev, M. Peikova and V. Vasileva. Photo)

1964 (20 Aug). Dogs. Various horiz designs as T **482**. Multicoloured. P 11½.

1455	1st. Type **482**	25	20
1456	2st. Setter	25	20
1457	3st. Poodle	55	25
1458	4st. Pomeranian	70	35
1459	5st. St Bernard	95	40
1460	6st. Fox Terrier	1·40	70
1461	10st. Pointer	5·50	2·75
1462	13st. Dachshund	6·75	4·75
1455/1462	Set of 8	14·50	8·75

1964 (22 Aug). AIR. International Cosmic Exhibition, Riccione (Italy). No. 1386 surch with T **483** and No. 1387 with similar surch in Italian.

1463	10st. on 1st. greenish blue and lilac (C.)	70	55
1464	20st. on 2st. brown and light yellow (G.)	2·00	80

484 Partisans and Flag

(Des A. Poplilov Photo)

1964 (9 Sept). 20th Anniversary of Fatherland Front Government. T **484** and similar horiz designs. Flag in red. P 11½.

1465	1st. blue and light blue	25	20
1466	2st. olive-brown and light bistre	25	20
1467	3st. lake and mauve	25	20
1468	4st. bluish violet and lavender	25	20
1469	5st. red-brown and yellow-orange	25	20
1470	6st. blue and light greenish blue	55	25
1471	8st. blue-green and light grey-green	1·10	40
1472	13st. red-brown and salmon-pink	1·40	70
1465/1472	Set of 8	3·75	2·10

Designs: 1st. T **484**; 2st. Greeting Soviet troops; 3st. Soviet Aid–arrival of goods; 4st. Industrial plant, Kremikovtsi; 5st. Combine-harvester; 6st Peace campaigners; 8st. Soldier of National Guard; 13st. Blagoev and Dimitrov. All with flag as T **484**.

(**485**) **486** Transport

1964 (13 Sept). 21st International Fair, Plovdiv. No. 1020a surch with T **485**.

1473	20st. on 44st. dull orange	2·75	95

(Des St. Kunchev. Photo)

1964 (3 Oct). First National Stamp Exhibition, Sofia. P 11½.

1474	**486**	20st. light blue	3·50	1·40

No. 1474 was issued in sheets of 12 stamps, 12 labels depicting a woman's head with inscription, and one centre label depicting a stylised bird.

487 Gymnastics **488** Vrattsata

(Des B. Angelushev. Photo)

1964 (10 Oct). Olympic Games, Tokyo T **487** and similar designs. Rings and values in red. P 11½.
1475	1st. deep green and light green	25	20
1476	2st. ultramarine and lavender	25	20
1477	3st. brown and turquoise-blue	25	20
1478	5st. violet and rose-pink	45	25
1479	13st. turquoise-blue and light blue	1·80	40
1480	20st. deep green and yellow-buff	2·00	95
1475/1480 Set of 6		4·50	2·00

MS1480a 61×67 mm. 40st.+20st. ochre, vermilion and new blue (Rings, track, etc.). Imperf. .... 6·75 6·50

Designs: 1st. T **487**; 2st. Long jump; 3st. Swimmer on starting block; 5st. Football; 13st. Volleyball; 20st. Wrestling.

(Des V. Popov, L. Marinov and P. Rusinov Photo)

1964 (26 Oct). Landscapes. T **488** and similar vert designs. P 12½×13½.
1481	1st. deep slate-green	25	20
1482	2st. light brown	25	20
1483	3st. blue	25	20
1484	4st. red-brown	35	20
1485	5st. deep bluish green	70	25
1486	6st. deep bluish violet	1·10	40
1481/1486 Set of 6		2·50	1·30

Views: 1st. T **488**; 2st. The Ritli; 3st. Maliovitsa; 4st. Broken rocks, 5st. Erkyupria; 6st. Rhodope mountain pass.

489 Paper and Cellulose Factory, Bukovtsi

490 Rila Monastery

(Des M. Peikova and V. Vasileva. Photo)

1964 (7 Dec). AIR. Industrial Buildings. T **489** and similar horiz designs. P 13.
1487	8st. greenish blue	70	20
1488	10st. bright purple	95	25
1489	13st. violet	1·10	35
1490	20st. Prussian blue	2·00	70
1491	40st. bronze-green	3·50	95
1487/1491 Set of 5		7·50	2·20

Designs: 8st. T **489**; 10st. Metal works, Plovdiv; 13st. Metallurgical works, Kremikovtsi; 20st. Petrol refinery, Burgas; 40st. Fertiliser factory, Stara-Zagora.

(Des V. Staikov. Photo)

1964 (22 Dec). Philatelic Exhibition for Franco–Bulgarian Amity. T **490** and similar design. P 11½.
1492	5st. black and drab	80	35
1493	13st. black and cobalt	2·00	80

Designs: 5st. T **490**; 13st. Nôtre-Dame, Paris (inscriptions in French).

491 500-year-old Walnut

492

(Des V. Staikov. Photo)

1964 (28 Dec). Ancient Trees. T **491** and similar vert designs. Values and inscriptions in black. P 11½.
1494	1st. Venetian red and pale cream	25	20
1495	2st. maroon and pale salmon	25	20
1496	3st. bistre-brown and pale yellow	25	20
1497	4st. grey-blue and pale blue	25	20
1498	10st. green and pale green	1·40	40
1499	13st. deep olive-green and pale yellow-green	2·00	50
1494/1499 Set of 6		4·00	1·50

Trees: 1st. T **491**; 2st. Plane (1000 years.); 3st. Plane (600 years.); 4st. Poplar (800 years.); 10st. Oak (800 years.); 13st. Fir (1200 years.).

(Des S. Markov. Photo)

1964 (30 Dec). Eighth Congress of International Union of Students, Sofia. P 11½.
1500	**492**	13st. black and pale blue	1·40 70

493 Bulgarian Veteran and Soviet Soldier (sculpture by T. Zlatarev)

494 Gold Medal

(Des L. Marinov. Photo)

1965 (15 Jan). 30 Years of Bulgarian–Russian Friendship. P 11½.
1501	**493**	2st. red and black	70 25

(Des S. Sotirov. Photo)

1965 (27 Jan). Olympic Games, Tokyo (1964). P 11½.
1502	**494**	20st. black, gold and orange-brown	2·00 95

495 Vladimir Komarov

(Des L. Yotov and P. Rusinov. Photo)

1965 (15 Feb). Flight of *Voskhod 1*. T **495** and similar designs. Multicoloured. P 11½.
1503	1st. Type **495**	25	20
1504	2st. Konstantin Feoktistov	25	20
1505	5st. Boris Yegorov	35	25
1506	13st. The three astronauts	1·60	40
1507	20st. *Voskhod 1*	2·00	70
1503/1507 Set of 5		4·00	1·60

496 Corn-cob

497 Victory against Fascism

(Des V. Tomov and M. Velev. Photo)

1965 (1 Apr). Agricultural Products. T **496** and similar vert designs. P 12½×13½.
1508	1st. orange-yellow	20	15
1509	2st. light blue-green	25	15
1510	3st. red-orange	35	15
1511	4st. yellow-olive	45	20
1512	5st. cerise	50	20
1513	10st. turquoise-blue	70	35
1514	13st. bistre	2·00	45
1508/1514 Set of 7		4·00	1·50

Designs: 1st. T **496**; 2st. Ears of wheat; 3st. Sunflowers; 4st. Sugar beet; 5st. Clover; 10st. Cotton; 13st. Tobacco.

(Des D. Rusinov and B. Dimitrov. Photo)

1965 (16 Apr). 20th Anniversary of Victory of 9 May, 1945. T **497** and similar horiz design. P 11½.
1515	5st. black, bistre and grey	25	20
1516	13st. blue, black and grey	1·10	60

Designs: 5st. T **497**; 13st. Globes on Dove (Peace).

BULGARIA 1965

498 Bullfinch (*Pyrrhula pyrrhula*)

499 Transport, Globe and Whale

(Des St. Kunchev and V. Korenev. Litho)

1965 (20 Apr). Song Birds. T **498** and similar vert designs. Multicoloured. P 11½.

1517	1st. Type **498**		25	20
1518	2st. Golden Oriole (*Oriolus oriolus*)		35	20
1519	3st. Rock Thrush (*Monticola saxatilis*)		45	20
1520	5st. Barn Swallows (*Hirundo rustica*)		95	45
1521	8st. Common Roller (*Coracias garrulus*)		1·10	75
1522	10st. Goldfinch (*Carduelis carduelis*)		3·75	1·20
1523	13st. Rose-coloured Starling (*Pastor roseus*)		4·00	2·20
1524	20st. Nightingale (*Luscinia megarhynchos*)		5·75	4·75
1517/1524 *Set of 8*			15·00	9·00

(Des St. Kunchev. Photo)

1965 (30 Apr). Fourth International Transport Conference, Sofia. P 11½.

1525	**499**	13st. silver, blue, magenta and yellow	2·00	1·50

500 ICY Emblem

501 ITU Emblem and Symbols

(Des St. Kunchev. Litho)

1965 (15 May). International Co-operation Year. P 11½.

1526	**500**	20st. red-orange, olive and black	2·00	1·00

(Des St. Kunchev. Photo)

1965 (17 May). Centenary of International Telecommunications Union. P 11½.

1527	**501**	20st. yellow, green and light blue	2·00	1·50

502 Pavel Belyaev and Aleksei Leonov

(Des S. Sotirov and V. Tomov. Litho)

1965 (20 May). Space Flight of *Voskhod 2*. T **502** and similar horiz designs inscr '18 III 1965'. P 11½.

1528	2st. deep purple, deep bluish green and light drab	70	30
1529	20st. slate-violet, black, olive-green and grey	5·50	1·90

Designs: 2st. T **502**; 20st. Leonov in space.

503 Sting Ray

504 Marx and Lenin

(Des D. Rusinov and B. Dimitrov. Litho)

1965 (10 June). Fish. T **503** and similar horiz designs. Borders in grey. P 11½.

1530	1st. gold, black and orange	20	15
1531	2st. silver, indigo and bright blue	30	15
1532	3st. gold, black and green	40	20
1533	5st. gold, black and carmine	70	30
1534	10st. silver, indigo and bright turquoise-blue	3·00	1·30
1535	13st. gold, black and Venetian red	3·75	1·70
1530/1535 *Set of 6*		7·50	3·50

Fish: 1st. T **503**; 2st. Belted Bonito; 3st. Scorpionfish; 5st. Gurnard; 10st. Horse Mackerel; 13st. Turbot.

(Des V. Tomov. Photo)

1965 (30 June). Organisation of Socialist Countries' Postal Ministers' Conference, Peking. P 10½.

1536	**504**	13st. brown and orange-red	2·75	75

505 Film and Screen

506 Quinces

(Des R. Stanoeva and A. Sertev. Photo)

1965 (30 June). Balkan Film Festival, Varna. P 10½.

1537	**505**	13st. black, silver-gilt and greenish blue	1·40	45

(Des Z. Taseva. Photo)

1965 (1 July). Fruits, etc. T **506** and similar vert designs. P 13.

1538	1st. red-orange (Type **506**)	15	15
1539	2st. yellow-olive (Grapes)	20	15
1540	3st. yellow-bistre (Pears)	35	15
1541	4st. yellow-orange (Plums)	40	20
1542	5st. carmine (Strawberries)	45	30
1543	6st. yellow-brown (Walnuts)	55	45
1538/1543 *Set of 6*		1·90	1·30

507 Ballerina

508 Dove, Emblem and Map

(Des R. Stanoeva and A. Sertev. Photo)

1965 (10 July). Ballet Competitions, Varna. P 10½.

1544	**507**	5st. black and magenta	2·75	1·50

(Des St. Kunchev. Photo)

1965 (23 July–7 Aug). Balkanphila Stamp Exhibition, Varna. T **508** and similar horiz designs. P 10½.

1545	1st. silver, ultramarine and greenish yellow	15	15
1546	2st. silver, reddish violet and greenish yellow	20	15
1547	3st. gold, blue-green and greenish yellow	40	30
1548	13st. gold, brown-red and greenish yellow	1·60	1·50
1549	20st. bistre-brown, light blue and silver (7.8.65)	2·00	1·90
1545/1549 *Set of 5*		4·00	3·50
MS1550 71×62 mm. 40st. gold and greenish blue (Type **508**). Imperf		5·50	5·00

Designs: 1st. T **508**. As T **508**—2st. Yacht emblem; 3st. Stylised fish and flowers; 13st. Stylised sun, planet and rocket. 45×25½ mm—20st. Cosmonauts Pavel Belyaev and Aleksei Leonov.

509 Escapers in Boat

(510)

1965 BULGARIA

1965 (23 July). 40th Anniversary of Political Prisoners' Escape from Bolshevik Island. P 10½.
1551   **509**   2st. black and slate 70   35

1965 (12 Aug). National Folklore Competition. No. 1084 surch with T **510**.
1552   2st. on 8st. orange-brown .... 2·75   2·75

511 Gymnast

512 Dressage

(Des M. Peikova and G. Kovachev. Photo)

1965 (14 Aug). Balkan Games. T **511** and similar vert designs. P 10½.
1553   1st. black and scarlet 25   20
1554   2st. deep purple, black and reddish purple   25   20
1555   3st. brown-purple, black and cerise 30   20
1556   5st. orange-brown, black and light red 40   30
1557   10st. deep purple, black and magenta .... 1·40   65
1558   13st. purple, black and light reddish purple.. 1·60   75
1553/1558 Set of 6 .... 3·75   2·10
Designs: 1st. T **511**; 2st. Gymnastics on bars; 3st. Weightlifting; 5st. Rally car and building; 10st. Basketball; 13st. Rally car and map.

(Des S. Sotirov. Photo)

1965 (30 Sept). Horsemanship. T **512** and similar horiz designs. P 10½.
1559   1st. plum, black and light greyish blue 25   20
1560   2st. brown-red, black and ochre 25   20
1561   3st. crimson, black and light greyish brown   25   20
1562   5st. lake-brown, deep green and sage-green 95   35
1563   10st. deep lake-brown, black and pale grey.. 4·00   1·70
1564   13st. deep purple, black, deep bluish green and orange-brown .... 4·50   2·20
1559/1564 Set of 6 .... 9·25   4·25
MS1565 80×80 mm. 40st.+20st. plum and pale bluish grey (as 13st.). Imperf .... 8·75   8·00
Designs: 1st. T **512**; 5st. Horse-racing; others, Horse-jumping (various).

513 Young Pioneers

514 Junkers Ju 52/3m over Turnovo

(Des Z. Taseva. Photo)

1965 (24 Oct). Dimitrov Septembrist Pioneers Organisation. T **513** and similar vert designs. P 10½.
1566   1st. yellow-green and turquoise-blue............ 25   20
1567   2st. mauve and bluish violet........................ 25   20
1568   3st. yellow-bistre and yellow-olive................. 25   20
1569   5st. yellow-ochre and blue............................ 40   35
1570   8st. orange and bistre-brown .... 1·40   60
1571   13st. reddish violet and crimson .... 2·00   1·00
1566/1571 Set of 6 .... 4·00   2·30
Designs: 1st. T **513**; 2st. Admitting recruit; 3st. Camp bugler; 5st. Flying model aeroplane; 8st. Girls singing; 13st. Young athlete.

(Des D. Rusinov and B. Dimitrov. Photo)

1965 (25 Nov). Bulgarian Civil Aviation. T **514** and similar horiz designs. P 10½.
1572   1st. black, grey, new blue and red 25   20
1573   2st. black, grey, reddish lilac and red 25   20
1574   3st. black, grey, light blue and red 25   20
1575   5st. black, grey, orange-yellow and red 55   35
1576   13st. black, grey, ochre and red .... 1·60   60
1577   20st. black, grey, emerald and red .... 2·75   1·00
1572/1577 Set of 6 .... 5·00   2·30
Designs: 1st. T **514**; 2st. Ilyushin Il-14M airliner over Plovdiv; 3st. Mil Mi-4 helicopter over Dimitrovgrad; 5st. Tupolev Tu-104A jetliner over Ruse; 13st. Ilyushin Il-18 airliner over Varna; 20st. Tupolev Tu-114 airliner over Sofia.

515 Women of North and South Bulgaria

516 IQSY Emblem and Earth's Radiation Zones

(Des S. Sotirov. Photo)

1965 (6 Dec). 80th Anniversary of Union of North and South Bulgaria (Eastern Roumelia). P 10½.
1578   **515**   13st. black and bright green .... 1·40   1·00

(Des St. Kunchev. Photo)

1965 (15 Dec). International Quiet Sun Year. T **516** and similar horiz designs. P 10½.
1579   1st. yellow, grey-green and bright blue 25   20
1580   2st. yellow, lake-brown, red and light purple 25   20
1581   13st. yellow, blue-green, black and greenish blue .... 1·80   60
1579/1581 Set of 3 .... 2·10   90
Designs: 1st. T **516**. IQSY emblem and—2st. Sun and solar flares; 13st. Total eclipse of the Sun.

517 Spring Greetings

518 Byala Bridge

(Des Neva and Nikola Tuzsuzov. Photo)

1966 (10 Jan). Spring. National Folklore. T **517** and similar vert designs. P 10½.
1582   1st. mauve, ultramarine and olive-grey......... 25   20
1583   2st. red, black and drab.............................. 25   20
1584   3st. violet, red and olive-grey........................ 25   20
1585   5st. red, light reddish violet and black........... 35   30
1586   8st. purple, purple-brown and light purple.... 80   35
1587   13st. mauve, black and new blue................. 1·60   45
1582/1587 Set of 6 .... 3·25   1·50
Designs: 1st. T **517**; 2st. Drummer; 3st. Birds (stylised); 5st. Folk dancer; 8st. Vase of flowers; 13st. Bagpiper.

(Des V. Korenev. Photo)

1966 (10 Feb). Ancient Monuments. T **518** and similar horiz designs. P 13.
1588   1st. turquoise-blue..................................... 25   20
1589   1st. emerald... 25   20
1590   2st. olive-green... 25   20
1591   2st. brown-purple....................................... 25   20
1592   8st. lake-brown... 80   35
1593   13st. deep blue... 1·40   60
1588/1593 Set of 6 .... 3·00   1·60
Designs: No. 1588, T **518**; No. 1589, Svilengrad Bridge; No. 1590, Fountain, Samokov; No. 1591, Ruins of Matochina Castle, Khaskovo; No. 1592, Cherven Castle, Ruse; No. 1593, Café, Bozhentsi, Gabrovo.

519 Christ (from fresco, Boyana Church)

BULGARIA 1966

(Des adapted by St. Kunchev. Litho Kultura, Budapest)

1966 (25 Feb). 2,500 Years of Culture. T **519** and similar designs. P 11½.

1594	1st. multicoloured	5·50	3·00
1595	2st. multicoloured	45	50
1596	3st. multicoloured	60	60
1597	4st. multicoloured	75	65
1598	5st. multicoloured	90	80
1599	13st. multicoloured	1·30	1·20
1600	20st. multicoloured	1·90	1·50
1594/1600	Set of 7	10·50	7·50

Designs: Horiz—2st. Destruction of the Idols (from fresco, Boyana Church); 4st. Zemen Monastery. Vert—1st. T **519**; 3st. Bachkovo Monastery; 5st. John the Baptist Church, Nesebur; 13st. Nativity (icon, Aleksandr Nevski Cathedral, Sofia); 20st. Virgin and Child (icon, Archaeological Museum, Sofia).

520 The First Gunshot at Koprivshtitsa

(Des M. Peikova and G. Kovachev. Photo)

1966 (3 Mar). 90th Anniversary of April Uprising. T **520** and similar horiz designs. Central designs in black. P 10½.

1601	1st. lake-brown and gold	25	20
1602	2st. red and gold	25	20
1603	3st. olive-green and gold	25	20
1604	5st. turquoise-blue and gold	35	30
1605	10st. bright purple and gold	90	35
1606	13st. bluish violet and gold	1·10	45
1601/1606	Set of 6	2·75	1·50

Designs: 1st. T **520**; 2st. Georgi Benkovski and Todor Kableshkov; 3st. Showing the flag at Panagyurishte; 5st. Vasil Petleshkov and Tsanko Dyustabanov; 10st. Landing of Khristo Botev's detachment at Kozlodui; 13st. Panayot Volov and Ilarion Dragostinov.

521 Luna reaching for the Moon

(Des A. Denkov. Photo)

1966 (29 Apr). Moon Landing of *Luna 9*. Sheet 70×50 mm. Imperf.

MS1607	**521** 60st. silver, black and crimson	6·75	6·25

522 WHO Building

(Des St. Kunchev. Photo)

1966 (3 May). Inauguration of World Health Organisation Headquarters, Geneva. P 10½.

1608	**522** 13st. blue and silver	1·60	75

523 Worker

(Des S. Sotirov. Photo)

1966 (9 May). Sixth Trade Unions Congress, Sofia. P 10½.

1609	**523** 20st. grey-black and pink	2·00	1·00

524 Indian Elephant **525** Boy and Girl holding Banners

(Des Z. Taseva. Litho and photo)

1966 (23 May). Sofia Zoo Animals. T **524** and similar horiz designs. Multicoloured. P 10½.

1610	1st. Type **254**	25	20
1611	2st. Tiger	25	20
1612	3st. Chimpanzee	25	20
1613	4st. Ibex	35	30
1614	5st. Polar Bear	1·40	45
1615	8st. Lion	1·60	1·50
1616	13st. American Bison	4·75	3·00
1617	20st. Eastern Grey Kangaroo	6·00	4·25
1610/1617	Set of 8	13·50	9·00

(Des Zh. Kosturkova and N. Petkov. Photo)

1966 (25 May). Third Congress of Bulgarian Sports Federation. P 10½.

1618	**525** 13st. greenish blue, red-orange and light blue	1·40	75

526 River Paddle-steamer *Radetski* and Pioneer **527** Standard-bearer Simov-Kuruto

(Des I. Kosev. Photo)

1966 (28 May). 90th Anniversary of Khristo Botev's Seizure of Paddle-steamer *Radetski*. P 10½.

1619	**526** 2st. multicoloured	35	30

(Des Ts. Kosturkova. Litho and photo)

1966 (30 May). 90th Death Anniversary of Nikola Simov-Kuruto (hero of the Uprising against Turkey). P 10½.

1620	**527** 5st. multicoloured	70	30

528 Federation Emblem **529** UNESCO Emblem

(Des V. Tomov. Photo)

1966 (6 June). Seventh International Youth Federation Assembly, Sofia. P 10½.

1621	**528** 13st. new blue and black	1·40	45

(Des I. Kosev. Photo)

1966 (8 June). 20th Anniversary of United Nations Educational, Scientific and Cultural Organisation. P 10½.

1622	**529** 20st. ochre, orange-vermilion, and black	1·60	75

530 Footballer with Ball

1966 BULGARIA

(Des Zh. Kosturkova and N. Petkov. Photo)
1966 (27 June). World Cup Football Championship, London.
(a) T **530** and similar horiz designs showing players in action. Borders in pale grey. P 10½

1623	1st. black and yellow-brown	25	20
1624	2st. black and rosine	25	20
1625	5st. black and yellow-bistre	40	30
1626	13st. black and blue	1·30	50
1627	20st. black and greenish blue	1·40	60
1623/1627 Set of 5		3·25	1·60

531 Jules Rimet Cup

(b) Sheet 60×65½ mm. T **531**. Imperf
MS1628 50st. gold, cerise and grey .... 5·50 4·25

532 Wrestling

(Des Zh. Kosturkova and N. Petkov. Photo)
1966 (29 July). Third International Wrestling Championships, Sofia. P 10½.
| 1629 | **532** | 13st. sepia, yellow-green and light brown | 1·40 | 75 |

533 Throwing the Javelin

(Des Zh. Kosturkova and N. Petkov. Photo)
1966 (10 Aug). Third Republican Spartakiad. T **533** and similar horiz design. P 10½.
| 1630 | | 2st. green, red and yellow (Type **533**) | 25 | 20 |
| 1631 | | 13st. deep bluish green, red and yellow (Running) | 1·10 | 45 |

534 Map of Balkans, Globe and UNESCO Emblem
535 Children with Construction Toy

(Des St. Kunchev. Photo)
1966 (26 Aug). International Balkan Studies Congress, Sofia. P 10½.
| 1632 | **534** | 13st. light emerald, pink and blue | 1·40 | 75 |

(Des B. Stoev and S. Anastasov. Photo)
1966 (1 Sept). Children's Day. T **535** and similar horiz designs. P 10½.
1633		1st. black, yellow-orange and carmine	20	15
1634		2st. black, red-brown and emerald	20	15
1635		3st. black, orange-yellow and ultramarine	25	20
1636		13st. black, mauve and blue	2·20	45
1633/1636 Set of 4			2·50	85

Designs: 1st. T **535**; 2st. Rabbit and Teddy Bear; 3st. Children as astronauts; 13st. Children with gardening equipment.

536 Yuri Gagarin and *Vostok 1*

(Des S. Sotirov. Photo)
1966 (29 Sept). Russian Space Exploration. T **536** and similar horiz designs. Backgrounds in deep and light grey. P 11½×11.
1637		1st. slate	20	15
1638		2st. purple	20	15
1639		3st. orange-brown	20	15
1640		5st. brown-lake	30	20
1641		8st. blue	45	30
1642		13st. greenish blue	1·60	45
1643		20st. +10st. reddish violet	2·75	85
1637/1643 Set of 7			5·25	2·00

MS1644 70x62½ mm. 30st.+10st. black, light red and light grey. Imperf .... 5·50 4·25

Designs: 1st. T **536**; 2st. German Titov and *Vostok 2*; 3st. Andrian Nikolaev, Pavel Popovich and *Vostok 3* and *Vostok 4*; 5st. Valentina Tereshkova, Valery Bykovsky and *Vostok 5* and *Vostok 6*; 8st. Vladimir Komarov, Boris Yegorov, Konstantin Feoktistov and *Voskhod 1*; 13st. Pavel Belyaev, Aleksei Leonov and *Voskhod 2*; 20st. Gagarin, Leonov and Tereshkova; 30st. Rocket and Globe.

537 St Clement (14th-century wood-carving)

538 Metodi Shatorov

(Des V. Zakhariev. Photo)
1966 (27 Oct). 1050th Death Anniversary of St Clement of Ohrid. P 11½×11.
| 1645 | **537** | 5st. bistre-brown, red and pale drab | 1·40 | 75 |

(Des M. Peikova and G. Kovachev. Photo)
1966 (8 Nov). Anti-Fascist Fighters. T **538** and similar horiz designs. Frames in gold; values in black. P 11×11½
1646		2st. bluish violet and red	20	15
1647		3st. deep olive-brown and magenta	25	15
1648		5st. deep blue and red	35	20
1649		10st. olive-brown and orange	95	35
1650		13st. brown and vermilion	1·10	45
1646/1650 Set of 5			2·50	1·00

Portraits: 2st. T **538**; 3st. Vlado Trichkov; 5st. Vulcho Ivanov; 10st. Raiko Daskalov; 13st. General Vladimir Zaimov.

539 Georgi Dimitrov (statesman)

540 Deer's-head Vessel

(Des S. Sotirov. Photo)
1966 (14 Nov). Ninth Bulgarian Communist Party Congress, Sofia. T **539** and similar vert design. P 11½×11.
| 1651 | | 2st. black and crimson | 25 | 15 |
| 1652 | | 20st. black, brown-red and pale grey | 2·40 | 60 |

Designs: 2st. T **539**; 20st. Furnaceman and steelworks.

BULGARIA 1966

(Des A. Mechkuev. Photo Kultura, Budapest)

1966 (28 Nov). The Gold Treasures of Panagyurishte. T **540** and similar horiz designs. Multicoloured. P 12×11½.

1653	1st. Type **540**	25	20
1654	2st. Amazon	35	20
1655	3st. Ram	40	20
1656	5st. Plate	50	30
1657	6st. Venus	70	35
1658	8st. Roe-buck	1·60	45
1659	10st. Amazon (*different*)	1·80	60
1660	13st. Amphora	2·00	75
1661	20st. Goat	2·75	1·50
1653/1661 Set of 9		9·25	4·00

Except for the 5st. and 13st. the designs show vessels with animal heads.

541 Bansko Hotel   **542** Christmas Tree

(Des V. Tomov. Photo)

1966 (29 Nov). Tourist Resorts. T **541** and similar horiz designs. P 11×11½.

1662	1st. blue	25	20
1663	2st. deep green	25	20
1664	2st. brown-lake	25	20
1665	20st. purple	1·60	45
1662/1665 Set of 4		2·10	95

Designs: No. 1662, T **541**; No. 1663, Belogradchik; No. 1664, Tryavna; No. 1665, Malovitsa, Rila.

(Des St. Kunchev. Photo)

1966 (12 Dec). New Year. T **542** and similar horiz design. Multicoloured. P 11×11½.

1666	2st. Type **542**	25	20
1667	13st. Moneybox	1·20	60

543 Pencho Slaveikov (poet)   **544** Dahlias (*Dahlia variabilis*)

(Des M. Peikova and G. Kovachev. Photo)

1966 (15 Dec). Cultural Celebrities. T **543** and similar vert designs. P 11×11½.

1668	1st. bistre, new blue and orange	25	20
1669	2st. brown, orange and grey	25	20
1670	3st. new blue, bistre and orange	25	20
1671	5st. light purple-brown, drab and orange	35	30
1672	8st. olive-grey, reddish purple and new blue	80	40
1673	13st. bluish violet, new blue and bright purple	95	45
1668/1673 Set of 6		2·50	1·60

Celebrities: Writers (with pen emblem)—1st. **543**; 2st. Dimcho Debelyanov (poet); 3st. Petko Todorov. Painters (with brush emblem)—5st. Dimitur Dobrovich; 8st. Ivan Murkvichka; 13st. Iliya Beshkov.

(Des St. Goristanova. Photo)

1966 (29 Dec). Flowers. T **544** and similar vert designs. Multicoloured. P 11×11½.

1674	1st. Type **544**	20	15
1675	1st. *Clematis integrifolia*	25	15
1676	2st. Poet's Narcissus (*Narcissus poeticus*)	35	15
1677	2st. Foxgloves (*Digitalis purpurea*)	40	20
1678	3st. Snowdrops (*Galanthus nivalis*)	70	30
1679	5st. Petunias (*Petunia hibrida*)	80	35
1680	13st. Tiger Lilies (*Lilium tigrinum*)	1·70	45
1681	20st. Canterbury Bells (*Campanula media*)	2·00	75
1674/1681 Set of 8		5·75	2·30

545 Ring-necked Pheasant   **546** Philately

(Des V. Korenev. Photo)

1967 (28 Jan). Hunting. T **545** and similar horiz designs. P 11½×11.

1682	1st. yellow-orange, deep red-brown and light blue	40	30
1683	2st. slate-green and pale yellow-green	45	30
1684	3st. pale buff, slate-green and light blue	55	30
1685	5st. deep sepia and pale green	1·40	75
1686	8st. yellow-brown, blackish brown and pale turquoise-green	4·00	1·50
1687	13st. brown, deep sepia and light turquoise-blue	4·75	2·20
1682/1687 Set of 6		10·50	4·75

Designs: 1st. T **545**; 2st. Chukar Partridge; 3st. Grey Partridge; 5st. Brown Hare; 8st. Roe Deer; 13st. Red Deer stag.

(Des St. Kunchev. Photo)

1967 (4 Feb). Tenth Bulgarian Philatelic Federation Congress, Sofia. P 10½.

1688	**546** 10st. yellow, black and green	3·50	2·20

547 6th-century BC Coin of Thrace   **548** Partisans listening to Radio

(Des M. Peikova and V. Vasileva. Photo)

1967 (30 Mar). Ancient Bulgarian Coins. T **547** and similar designs. Coins in silver on black background except 13st. (gold on black). Frame colours given. P 11½×11.

1689	1st. yellow-brown	20	15
1690	2st. bright purple	25	20
1691	3st. yellow-green	35	30
1692	5st. orange-brown	70	45
1693	13st. turquoise-blue	2·00	1·20
1694	20st. violet	3·50	2·20
1689/1694 Set of 6		6·25	4·00

Coins: Square—1st. T **547**; 2st. 2nd-century BC tetradrachm; 3st. 2nd-century BC Odessos (Varna) tetradrachm; 5st. 4th-century BC Macedonian coin of Philip II. Horiz (38×25 *mm*)—13st. Obverse and reverse of 4th-century BC coin of King Sevt (Thrace); 20st. Obverse and reverse of 5th-century BC coin of Apollonia (Sozopol).

(Des V. Staikov. Photo)

1967 (20 Apr). 25th Anniversary of Fatherland Front. T **548** and similar horiz design. P 11×11½.

1695	1st. multicoloured	25	20
1696	20st. multicoloured	1·90	60

Designs: 1st. T **548**; 20st. Dimitrov speaking at rally.

549 Nikola Kofardzhiev   **550** Cultural Development

(Des M. Peikova and G. Kovachev. Photo)

1967 (24 Apr). Anti-Fascist Fighters. T **549** and similar horiz designs. P 11½×11.

1697	1st. deep brown-red, black and pale blue	25	20
1698	2st. olive-green, black and pale blue	30	30

1967 BULGARIA

1699	5st. deep ochre, black and pale blue		35	35
1700	10st. deep blue, black and pale lilac		95	40
1701	13st. purple, blue and pale grey		1·40	45
1697/1701 Set of 5			3·00	1·50

Portraits: 1st. T **549**; 2st. Petko Napetov; 5st. Petko Petkov; 10st. Emil Markov; 13st. Traicho Kostov.

(Des St. Kunchev. Photo)

1967 (18 May). First Cultural Conference, Sofia. P 11½×11.

1702	**550**	13st. yellow, light emerald and gold	1·40	75

551 Angora Kitten **552** Golden Sands Resort

(Des M. Peikova and V. Vasileva. Photo)

1967 (27 May). Cats. T **551** and similar designs. Multicoloured. P 11½×11 (vert) or 11×11½ (horiz).

1703	1st. Type **551**		35	20
1704	2st. Siamese (*horiz*)		40	25
1705	3st. Abyssinian		70	30
1706	5st. European black and white		2·20	45
1707	13st. Persian (*horiz*)		2·75	1·50
1708	20st. European tabby		3·50	3·00
1703/1708 Set of 6			9·00	5·25

(Des V. Korenev. Photo)

1967 (12 June). International Tourist Year. T **552** and similar horiz designs. P 11½×11½.

1709	13st. blackish green, pale yellow, black and bright blue	70	35
1710	20st. blackish green, buff, black and turquoise-blue	1·40	60
1711	40st. blackish green, buff, black and light blue-green	3·50	1·30
1709/1711 Set of 3		5·00	2·00

Designs: 13st. T **552**; 20st. Pamporovo; 40st. Old Church, Nesebur.

553 Scene from Iliev's Opera *The Master of Boyana* **554** G. Kirkov

(Des B. Kitanov. Photo)

1967 (18 June). Third International Young Opera singers Competition, Sofia. T **553** and similar design. P 11½×11 (5st.) or 11×11½ (13st.).

1712	5st. cerise, blue and grey	35	30
1713	13st. red, deep blue, grey and light grey	1·10	60

Designs: Horiz—5st. T **553**. Vert—13st. Vocal Art (songbird on piano-key).

(Des V. Tomov. Photo)

1967 (24 June). Birth Centenary of Georgi Kirkov (patriot). P 11½×11½.

1714	**554**	2st. bistre-brown and rose-red	25	20

555 Roses and Distillery **556** DKMS Emblem

(Des Z. Taseva. Photo)

1967 (15–24 July). Economic Achievements. T **555** and similar horiz designs. Multicoloured. P 11×11½.

1715	1st. Type **555**	20	20
1716	1st. Chick and incubator	20	20
1717	2st. Cucumbers and glasshouses	25	20
1718	2st. Lamb and farm building	25	20
1719	3st. Sunflower and oil-extraction plant (24.7.67)	30	20
1720	4st. Pigs and piggery (24.7.67)	35	25
1721	5st. Hops and vines (24.7.67)	45	25
1722	6st. Grain and irrigation canals (24.7.67)	55	30
1723	8st. Grapes and Bulgar tractor (24.7.67)	60	35
1724	10st. Apples and tree	70	45
1725	13st. Honey Bees and honey	1·20	60
1726	20st. Honey Bee on flower, and hives	1·50	75
1715/1726 Set of 12	6·00	3·50

(Des St. Kunchev. Photo)

1967 (28 July). 11th Anniversary of Dimitrov Communist Youth League. P 11½×11.

1727	**556**	13st. black, red and blue	1·40	45

557 Map and Spassky Tower, Moscow Kremlin **558** Scenic 'Fish' and Rod

(Des V. Staikov. Photo)

1967 (25 Aug). 50th Anniversary of October Revolution. T **557** and similar horiz designs. P 11.

1728	1st. multicoloured	25	20
1729	2st. blackish olive and deep reddish purple	25	20
1730	3st. slate-violet and deep reddish purple	25	20
1731	5st. red and purple	25	20
1732	13st. light ultramarine and deep reddish purple	95	45
1733	20st. blue and deep reddish purple	2·00	75
1728/1733 Set of 6	3·50	1·80

Designs: 1st. T **557**; 2st. Lenin directing revolutionaries; 3st. Revolutionaries; 5st. Marx, Engels and Lenin; 13st. Soviet oil refinery; 20st. *Molniya* satellite and Moon (Soviet space research).

(Des St. Kunchev. Photo)

1967 (28 Aug). Seventh World Angling Championships, Varna. P 11.

1734	**558**	10st. bright green, gold, light blue and black	1·10	60

559 Cross-country Skiing **560** Bogdan Peak, Sredna Mountains

(Des V. Korenev and St. Goristanova. Photo)

1967 (20 Sept). Winter Olympic Games, Grenoble (1968). T **559** and similar horiz designs. P 11.

1735	1st. black, red and turquoise-blue	25	20
1736	2st. black, bistre and bright blue	25	20
1737	3st. black, light blue and brown-purple	25	20
1738	5st. black, yellow and bluish green	40	30
1739	13st. black, buff and ultramarine	2·00	60
1740	20st. +10st. black, light red, pale drab and greenish blue	3·50	1·20
1735/1740 Set of 6	6·00	2·40
MS1741 98×98 mm (diamond) 40st.+10st. black, yellow-ochre and turquoise-blue. Imperf	5·50	5·00

Designs: 1st. T **559**; 2st. Ski jumping; 3st. Biathlon; 5st. Ice hockey; 13st., 40st. Ice skating (pairs); 20st. Men's slalom.

(Des V. Zakhariev. Recess and photo)

1967 (25 Sept). Tourism. Mountain Peaks. T **560** and similar horiz designs. P 11½.

1742	1st. myrtle-green and light yellow	25	20
1743	2st. sepia and pale blue	25	20
1744	3st. deep blue and light blue	25	20
1745	5st. blackish green and light blue	35	25
1746	10st. lake-brown and light blue	60	30
1747	13st. black and light blue	70	45
1748	20st. deep blue and light reddish purple	1·40	85
1742/1748 Set of 7	3·50	2·20

Designs: Horiz—1st. T **560**; 2st. Cherni Vruh, Vitosha; 5st. Persenk, Rhodopes; 10st. Botev, Stara-Planina; 20st. Vikhren, Pirin. Vert—3st. Ruen, Osogovska Planina; 13st. Musala, Rila.

BULGARIA 1967

561 G. Rakovski

563 Railway Bridge over Yantra River

562 Yuri Gagarin, Valentina Tereshkova and Aleksei Leonov

(Des N. Petkov. Photo)

1967 (20 Oct). Death Centenary of Georgi Rakovski (newspaper editor and revolutionary). P. 11.
| 1749 | 561 | 13st. black and yellow-green | 1·40 | 75 |

(Des Zh. Kosturkova. Photo)

1967 (20 Oct). Space Exploration. T **562** and similar horiz designs. Multicoloured. P. 11.
1750		1st. Type **562**	25	20
1751		2st. John Glenn and Edward White	25	20
1752		5st. *Molniya 1*	40	30
1753		10st. *Gemini 6* and *Gemini 7*	1·40	45
1754		13st. *Luna 13*	1·50	75
1755		20st. *Gemini 10* docking with *Agena*	1·60	1·50
1750/1755	Set of 6		4·75	3·00

(Des V. Staikov. Photo)

1967 (5 Dec). Views of Turnovo (ancient capital). T **563** and similar vert views. P. 11.
1756		1st. black, drab and blue	25	20
1757		2st. multicoloured	25	20
1758		3st. multicoloured	25	20
1759		5st. black, slate and red	40	30
1760		13st. multicoloured	1·10	75
1761		20st. black, light yellow-orange and lavender	1·40	1·00
1756/1761	Set of 6		3·25	2·40

Designs: 1st. T **563**; 2st. Hadji Nikola's Inn; 3st. Houses on hillside; 5st. Town and river; 13st. House of the Monkeys; 20st. Gurko street.

564 *The Ruchenitsa* (folk-dance, from painting by Murkvichka)

(Des St. Kunchev. Photo)

1967 (8 Dec). Belgian–Bulgarian Painting and Philately Exhibition, Brussels. P. 11.
| 1762 | 564 | 20st. bronze-green and gold | 3·50 | 3·00 |

No. 1762 was issued in sheets of eight (4×2) with *se-tenant* commemorative labels in the upper and lower margins inscr in Bulgarian, Flemish and French.

565 *The Shepherd* (Zlatko Boyadzhiev)

(Des O. and V. Ionchev. Litho Kultura, Budapest)

1967 (25 Dec). Paintings in the National Gallery, Sofia. T **565** and similar designs. Multicoloured. P 12 (3st.) or 11½ (others).
1763		1st. Type **565**	25	20
1764		2st. *The Wedding* (Vladimir Dimitrov) (*vert*)	25	20
1765		3st. *The Partisans* (Ilya Petrov) (55×35 *mm*)	70	30
1766		5st. *Anastasia Penchovich* (Nikolai Pavlovich) (*vert*)	1·40	45
1767		13st. *Self-portrait* (Zakharii Zograf) (*vert*)	2·75	1·30
1768		20st. *Old Town of Plovdiv* (Tsanko Lavrenov)	3·50	1·50
1763/1768	Set of 6		8·00	3·50
MS1769	65×85 mm. 60st. *St Clement of Ohrid* (Anton Mitov)		8·00	7·25

566 Linked Satellites *Cosmos 186* and *Cosmos 188*

567 *Crossing the Danube* (Orenburgski)

(Des Zh. Kosturkova. Photo)

1967 (30 Dec). Cosmic Activities. T **566** and similar design. P. 11.
| 1770 | | 20st. multicoloured | 1·40 | 75 |
| 1771 | | 40st. multicoloured | 3·50 | 1·50 |

Designs: Vert—20st. T **566**. Horiz—40st. *Venus 4* and orbital diagram.

(Des A. Popilov. Photo)

1968 (25 Jan). 90th Anniversary of Liberation from Turkey. Paintings as T **567**. Inscr and borders in black and gold; centre colours below. P. 11.
1772		1st. blackish green	25	20
1773		2st. indigo	25	20
1774		3st. red-brown	25	20
1775		13st. chalky blue	1·60	75
1776		20st. deep turquoise	2·00	85
1772/1776	Set of 5		4·00	2·00

Designs: Vert—2st. *Flag of Samara* (Veshin); 13st. *Battle of Orlovo Gnezdo* (Popov). Horiz—1st. T **567**; 3st. *Battle of Pleven* (Orenburgski); 20st. *Greeting Russian Soldiers* (Goudienov).

568 Karl Marx

569 Gorky

(Des V. Tomov. Photo)

1968 (20 Feb). 150th Birth Anniversary of Karl Marx. P. 11.
| 1777 | 568 | 13st. brownish grey, vermilion and black | 1·40 | 45 |

(Des M. Peikova and G. Kovachev. Photo)

1968 (20 Feb). Birth Centenary of Maksim Gorky (writer). P. 11.
| 1778 | 569 | 13st. blackish green, red-orange and black | 1·40 | 45 |

570 Dancers

1968 BULGARIA

(Des D. Rusinov. Photo)

1968 (20 Mar). Ninth World Youth and Students' Festival, Sofia. T **570** and similar horiz designs. Multicoloured. P 11.

1779	2st. Type **570**		25	20
1780	5st. Running		25	20
1781	13st. 'Doves'		1·10	45
1782	20st. 'Youth' (symbolic design)		1·40	75
1783	40st. Bulgarian 5c. stamp of 1879 under magnifier, and Globe		2·30	1·70
1779/1783 Set of 5			4·75	3·00

571 *Campanula alpina*

572 *The Unknown Hero* (Ran Bosilek)

(Des V. Tomov. Photo)

1968 (25 Apr). Wild Flowers. T **571** and similar vert designs. Multicoloured. P 11.

1784	1st. Type **571**		25	20
1785	2st. Trumpet Gentian (*Gentiana acaulis*)		25	20
1786	3st. *Crocus veluchensis*		25	20
1787	5st. Siberian Iris (*Iris sibirica*)		70	30
1788	10st. Dog's-tooth Violet (*Erythronium dens-canis*)		95	35
1789	13st. Houseleek (*Sempervivum leucanthum*)		1·90	45
1790	20st. Burning Bush (*Dictamnus albus*)		2·00	75
1784/1790 Set of 7			5·75	2·20

(Des L. Zidarov. Photo)

1968 (25 Apr). Bulgarian–Danish Stamp Exhibition. Fairy Tales. T **572** and similar horiz design. Multicoloured. P 10½.

1791	13st. Type **572**		70	45
1792	20st. *The Witch and the Young Man* (Hans Andersen)		1·40	1·00

573 Memorial Temple, Shipka

574 Copper Rolling-mill, Medet

(Des St. Kunchev. Photo)

1968 (3 May). Bulgarian–West Berlin Stamp Exhibition. P 10½.

1793	**573**	13st. multicoloured	2·00	1·50

No. 1793 was issued in sheets with *se-tenant* stamp-sized label inscr in Bulgarian and German.

(Des M. Peikova and V. Vasileva. Photo)

1968 (6 May). AIR. P 13.

1794	**574**	1l. rosine	4·75	1·00

575 Lake Smolyan

576 Gymnastics

(Des St. Goristanova. Photo)

1968 (17 May–27 Sept). T **575** and similar vert designs, showing landscapes. P 13.

1795	1st. deep bluish green (17.5.68)		25	20
1796	2st. deep green (19.8.68)		25	20
1797	3st. sepia (26.8.68)		25	20
1798	8st. olive-green (27.9.68)		45	25
1799	10st. brown (13.9.68)		55	30
1800	13st. blackish olive (27.9.68)		70	35
1801	40st. greenish blue (26.8.68)		2·00	45
1802	2l. olive-brown (2.9.68)		8·00	3·00
1795/1802 Set of 8			11·00	4·50

Designs: 1st. T **575**; 2st. River Ropotamo; 3st. Lomnitza Gorge, Erma River; 8st. River Isker; 10st. Cruise ship *Die Fregatte*; 13st. Cape Kaliakra; 40st. Sozopol; 2l. Mountain road, Kamchia River.

(Des S. Sotirov. Photo)

1968 (24 June). Olympic Games, Mexico. T **576** and similar vert designs. P 10½.

1803	1st. grey-black and bright red		25	20
1804	2st. black, lake-brown and grey		25	20
1805	3st. grey-black and deep magenta		25	20
1806	10st. grey-black, olive-yellow and deep turquoise-blue		95	35
1807	13st. grey-black, pink and deep ultramarine		2·00	75
1808	20st. +10st. grey, light pink and deep blue		2·75	85
1803/1808 Set of 6			5·75	2·30
MS1809 74×76 mm. 50st.+10st. black, slate and deep turquoise-blue. Imperf			6·00	5·75

Designs: 1st. T **576**; 2st. Horse-jumping; 3st. Fencing; 10st. Boxing; 13st. Throwing the discus; 20st. Rowing; 50st. Stadium and communications satellite.

577 Dimitur on Mount Buzludzha, 1868

578 Human Rights Emblem

(Des N. Mirchev. Photo)

1968 (1 July). Centenary of Exploits of Khadzhi Dimitur and Stefan Karadzha (revolutionaries). T **577** and similar horiz design. P 10½.

1810	2st. chestnut and silver		25	20
1811	13st. blackish green and gold		1·10	60

Designs: 2st. T **577**; 13st. Dimitur and Karadzha.

(Des St. Kunchev. Photo)

1968 (8 July). Human Rights Year. P 10½.

1812	**578**	20st. gold and blue	1·60	75

579 European Black Vulture

580 Battle Scene

(Des V. Korenev. Photo)

1968 (29 July). 80th Anniversary of Sofia Zoo. T **579** and similar vert design. P 10½.

1813	1st. black, cinnamon and blue		25	30
1814	2st. black, greenish yellow and orange-brown		35	30
1815	3st. black and yellow-green		40	30
1816	5st. black, yellow and brown-lake		70	45
1817	13st. black, bistre and bluish green		4·00	2·10
1818	20st. black, light yellow-green and greenish blue		5·50	3·00
1813/1818 Set of 6			10·00	5·75

Designs: 1st. T **579**; 2st. South African Crowned Crane; 3st. Common Zebra; 5st. Leopard; 13st. Python; 20st. Crocodile.

BULGARIA 1968

(Des N. Mirchev. Photo)

1968 (22 Aug). 280th Anniversary of Chiprovtsi Rising. P 10½.
1819 **580** 13st. olive, orange-yellow, emerald and light grey .... 1·40 35

581 Caterpillar-hunter (*Calosoma sycophanta*)

582 Flying Swans

(Des M. Peikova and V. Vasileva. Photo)

1968 (26 Aug). Insects. T **581** and similar designs. P 12½×13 (vert) or 13×12½ (horiz).
1820 1st. blackish green 30 15
1821 1st. olive-brown 30 15
1822 1st. deep blue 30 15
1823 1st. chestnut 30 15
1824 1st. reddish purple 30 15
1820/1824 Set of 5 .... 1·40 70

Designs: Vert—No. 1820, T **581**; No. 1821, Stag Beetle (*Lucanus cervus*); No. 1822, *Procerus scabrosus* (Ground Beetle). Horiz—No. 1823, European Rhinoceros Beetle (*Oryctes nasicornis*); No. 1824, *Perisomena caecigena* (Moth).

(Des D. Rusinov. Photo)

1968 (12 Sept–22 Nov). Co-operation with Scandinavia. T **582** and similar horiz designs. P 10½.
1825 2st. ochre and deep green (22.11.68) .... 2·00 1·80
   a. Strip. Nos. 1825 and 1828 plus label .... 4·25 3·75
1826 5st. Prussian blue, light grey and black .... 2·00 1·80
   a. Strip. Nos. 1826/1827 plus label .... 4·25 3·75
1827 13st. reddish purple and maroon .... 2·00 1·80
1828 20st. light grey and bright violet (22.11.68) .... 2·00 1·80
1825/1828 Set of 4 .... 7·25 6·50

Designs: 2st. Wooden flask; 5st. T **582**; 13st. Rose; 20st. Viking ships. Nos. 1825 and 1828 and 1826/1827 respectively were issued together *se-tenant* with intervening double stamp-size label showing a 'bridge' of flags (inscribed in either Bulgarian or Swedish) within sheets of 20 stamps and ten labels.

583 Congress Building and Emblem

(Des St. Kunchev. Photo)

1968 (17 Sept). International Dental Congress, Varna. P 10½.
1829 **583** 20st. gold, yellow-green and red .... 1·40 45

584 Smirnenski and Verse from *Red Squadrons*

(Des G. Kovachev. Photo)

1968 (28 Sept). 70th Birth Anniversary of Khristo Smirnenski (poet). P 10½.
1830 **584** 13st. black, red-orange and gold .... 1·40 45

585 Dove with Letter

586 Dalmatian Pelican (*Pelecanus crispus*)

(Des St. Kunchev. Photo)

1968 (19 Oct). National Stamp Exhibition, Sofia and 75th Anniversary of National Philately. P 10½.
1831 **585** 20st. emerald .... 2·00 1·80

No. 1831 was issued in small sheets containing four stamps and five *se-tenant* stamp-size labels in two designs, (a) Arms, in gold and carmine; (b) magnifier and tweezers, in bright scarlet.

(Des Z. Taseva. Photo)

1968 (28 Oct). Srebirna Wildlife Reservation. Birds. T **586** and similar horiz designs. Multicoloured. P 10½.
1832 1st. Type **586** 55 30
1833 2st. Little Egret (*Egretta garzetta*) 70 35
1834 3st. Great Crested Grebe (*Podiceps cristatus*) 80 45
1835 5st. Common Tern (*Sterna hirundo*) .... 1·20 60
1836 13st. White Spoonbill (*Platalea leucorodia*) .... 3·00 2·50
1837 20st. Glossy Ibis (*Plegadis falcinellus*) .... 6·00 3·25
1832/1837 Set of 6 .... 11·00 6·75

587 Silistra Costume

588 St Arsenius (icon)

(Des N. Tuzsuzova. Litho German Bank Note Ptg Co, Leipzig)

1968 (20 Nov). Provincial Costumes. T **587** and similar vert designs. Multicoloured. P 13½.
1838 1st. Type **587** 25 20
1839 2st. Lovech 25 20
1840 3st. Yambol 25 20
1841 13st. Chirpan 90 45
1842 20st. Razgrad .... 1·40 70
1843 40st. Ikhtiman .... 3·25 1·20
1838/1843 Set of 6 .... 5·75 2·75

(Des St. Kunchev. Photo Kultura, Budapest)

1968 (25 Nov). Rila Monastery. Icons and murals. T **588** and similar multicoloured designs. P 12½×11½ (2st.) or 11½×12½ (others).
1844 1st. Type **588** 25 20
1845 2st. Carrying St Ivan Rilski's Relics (*horiz*) 25 20
1846 3st. St Michael torments the Rich Man's Soul 35 25
1847 13st. St Ivan Rilski .... 1·60 85
1848 20st. Prophet Joel .... 2·40 1·20
1849 40st. St George .... 3·75 1·90
1844/1849 Set of 6 .... 7·75 4·25
MS1850 100×74 mm. 1l. Arrival of Relics at Rila Monastery. Imperf .... 7·50 7·25

589 *Matricaria chamomilla*

590 Silkworms and Spindles

(Des St. Goristanova and V. Korenev. Photo)

1969 (2 Jan). Medicinal Plants. T **589** and similar horiz designs. Multicoloured. P 10½.
1851 1st. Type **589** 25 20
1852 1st. *Mespilus oxyacantha* 25 20
1853 2st. Lily of the Valley (*Convallaria majalis*) 25 20
1854 3st. Deadly Nightshade (*Atropa belladonna*) 35 25
1855 5st. Common Mallow (*Malva silvestris*) 40 30
1856 10st. Yellow Pheasant's-eye (*Adonis vernalis*) 95 35
1857 13st. Common Poppy (*Papaver rhoeas*) .... 1·10 45
1858 20st. Wild Thyme (*Thymus serpyllum*) .... 1·60 75
1851/1858 Set of 8 .... 4·75 2·40

(Des St .Goristanova and V. Korenev. Photo)

1969 (30 Jan). Silk Industry. T **590** and similar horiz designs. Multicoloured. P 11.
1859 1st. Type **590** 25 20
1860 2st. Worm, cocoons and pattern 25 20

1861	3st. Cocoons and spinning wheel	25	20
1862	5st. Cocoons and pattern	35	25
1863	13st. Moth, cocoon and spindles	1·10	35
1864	20st. Moth, eggs and shuttle	1·60	60
1859/1864	Set of 6	3·50	1·60

591 Death of Ivan Asen

592 Saints Cyril and Methodius (mural, Troyan Monastery)

(Des O. and V. Yonchev. Photo German Bank Note Ptg Co, Leipzig)

1969 (20 Mar). *Manasses Chronicle* (1st series). T **591** and similar vert designs. Multicoloured. P 14×13½.

1865	1st. Type **591**	25	20
1866	2st. Emperor Nicephorus invading Bulgaria	25	20
1867	3st. Khan Krum's Feast	25	20
1868	13st. Prince Sviatoslav invading Bulgaria	1·60	45
1869	20st. The Russian invasion	2·30	60
1870	40st. Jesus Christ, Tsar Ivan Alexander and Constantine Manasses	3·50	1·50
1865/1870	Set of 6	7·25	2·75

See also Nos. 1911/1916.

(Des O. and V. Yonchev. Photo German Bank Note Ptg Co, Leipzig)

1969 (23 Mar). Saints Cyril and Methodius Commemoration. P 14×13½.

| 1871 | **592** | 28st. multicoloured | 2·75 | 1·50 |

593 Galleon

594 Posthorn Emblem

(Des St. Kunchev. Photo)

1969 (31 Mar). AIR. SOFIA 1969 International Stamp Exhibition. Transport. T **593** and similar vert designs. Multicoloured. P 13½×12½.

1872	1st. Type **593**	25	20
1873	2st. Mail coach	25	20
1874	3st. Steam locomotive	25	20
1875	5st. Early motor car	35	25
1876	10st. Montgolfier balloon and Henri Giffard's steam-powered dirigible airship	55	30
1877	13st. Early flying machines	95	45
1878	20st. Modern aircraft	1·60	60
1879	40st. Rocket and planets	3·00	1·50
1872/1879	Set of 8	6·50	3·25
MS1880	57×55 mm. 1l. gold and red-orange. Imperf (Postal courier)	5·50	5·00

(Des A. Poplilov. Photo)

1969 (15 Apr). 90th Anniversary of Bulgarian Postal Services. T **594** and similar horiz designs. P 11.

1881	2st. yellow and blue-green	25	20
1882	13st. multicoloured	95	35
1883	20st. pale blue and blue	1·60	75
1881/1883	Set of 3	2·50	1·20

Designs: 2st. T **594**; 13st. Bulgarian stamps of 1879 and 1946; 20st. Post Office workers' strike, 1919.

595 ILO Emblem

596 Fox and Rabbit

(Des M. Peikova. Photo)

1969 (15 Apr). 50th Anniversary of International Labour Organisation. P 11.

| 1884 | **595** | 13st. black and light bluish green | 95 | 45 |

(Des L. Zidarov. Photo)

1969 (21 Apr). Children's Book Week. T **596** and similar horiz designs. P 11.

1885	1st. black, red-orange and emerald	25	20
1886	2st. black, light blue and orange-red	25	20
1887	13st. black, yellow-olive and light blue	1·10	45
1885/1887	Set of 3	1·40	75

Designs: 2st. Boy with Hedgehog and Squirrel; 13st. The Singing Lesson.

597 Hand with Seedling

598 St George (14th-century)

(Des V. Vasileva. Photo)

1969 (28 Apr). 10,000,000 Hectares of New Forests. P 11.

| 1888 | **597** | 2st. black, olive-green and reddish purple | 25 | 20 |

(Des St. Kunchev. Photo State Ptg Office, Budapest)

1969 (30 Apr). Religious Art. Vert designs as T **598**. Multicoloured. P 11×12.

1889	1st. Type **598**	25	20
1890	2st. The Virgin and St John Bogoslov (14th-century)	25	20
1891	3st. Archangel Michael (17th-century)	25	20
1892	5st. Three Saints (17th-century)	40	25
1893	8st. Jesus Christ (17th-century)	55	30
1894	13st. St George and St Dimitr (19th-century)	1·00	45
1895	20st. Christ, the Universal (19th-century)	1·40	60
1896	60st. The Forty Martyrs (19th-century)	1·00	2·50
1897	80st. The Transfiguration (19th-century)	5·25	3·25
1889/1897	Set of 9	12·00	7·25
MS1898	103×165 mm. 40st.×4, St Dimitr (17th-century). P 12½	13·50	13·00

599 Roman Coin

600 St George and the Dragon

(Des St. Kunchev. Photo)

1969 (25–31 May). SOFIA 1969 International Stamp Exhibition. Sofia Through the Ages. T **599** and similar vert designs. P 13×12½.

1899	1st. silver, greenish blue and gold	25	20
1900	2st. silver, bronze-green and gold	25	20
1901	3st. silver, brown-lake and gold	25	20
1902	4st. silver, reddish violet and gold	25	20

BULGARIA 1969

1903	5st. silver, purple and gold	35	25
1904	13st. silver, blue-green and gold	70	30
1905	20st. silver, ultramarine and gold	1·10	45
1906	40st. silver, carmine and gold	2·00	85
1899/1906	Set of 8	4·75	2·40
MS1907	78×72 mm. 1l. multicoloured. Imperf (31.5.69)	6·50	5·50

Designs: 1st. T **599**—2st. Roman coin showing Temple of Aesculapius; 3st. Church of St Sophia; 4st. Boyana Church; 5st. Parliament Building; 13st. National Theatre; 20st. Aleksandr Nevski Cathedral; 40st. Sofia University. 44×44 mm—1l. Arms.
See also No. **MS**2230.

(Des V. Staikov. Photo)

1969 (9 June). 38th International Philatelic Federation Congress, Sofia. P 11.

| 1908 | **600** | 40st. black, pale salmon and silver | 3·50 | 1·50 |

601 St Cyril

602 Partisans

(Des I. Kiosev. Photo)

1969 (20 June). 1,100th Death Anniversary of St Cyril. T **601** and similar vert design. P 11.

| 1909 | 2st. deep green and red/*silver* | 25 | 20 |
| 1910 | 28st. deep blue and red/*silver* | 2·30 | 85 |

Designs: 2st. T **601**; 28st. St Cyril and procession.
Nos. 1909/1910 were each issued in sheets vertically *se-tenant* with half stamp-size labels.

(Des O. and V. Yonchev. Photo German Bank Note Ptg Co, Leipzig)

1969 (5 Aug). *Manasses Chronicle* (2nd series). Designs as T **591**, but all horiz. Multicoloured. P 14.

1911	1st. Nebuchadnezzar II and Balthasar of Babylon, Cyrus and Darius of Persia	25	20
1912	2st. Cambyses, Gyges and Darius	25	20
1913	5st. Prophet David and Tsar Ivan Alexander	35	25
1914	13st. Rout of the Byzantine Army, 811	1·40	35
1915	20st. Christening of Khan Boris	2·75	45
1916	60st. Tsar Simeon's attack on Constantinople	4·00	2·50
1911/1916	Set of 6	8·00	3·50

(Des A. Poplilov. Photo)

1969 (8 Aug). 25th Anniversary of Fatherland Front Government. T **602** and similar horiz designs. P 11.

1917	1st. slate-lilac, light red and black	25	20
1918	2st. ochre, light red and black	25	20
1919	3st. bluish green, light red and black	25	20
1920	5st. brown-lake, light red and black	35	25
1921	13st. greenish blue, light red and black	95	40
1922	20st. purple-brown, emerald, light red and black	1·80	75
1917/1922	Set of 6	3·50	1·80

Designs: 1st. T **602**; 2st. Combine-harvester; 3st. Dam; 5st. Folk singers; 13st. Petroleum Refinery; 20st. Lenin, Dimitrov and flags.

603 Gymnastics

604 Construction and Soldier

(Des V. Tomov. Photo)

1969 (1 Sept). Third Republican Spartakiad. T **603** and similar horiz design. Multicoloured. P 11.

| 1923 | 2st. Type **603** | 25 | 20 |
| 1924 | 20st. Wrestling | 1·40 | 85 |

(Des V. Koronev. Photo)

1969 (5 Sept). 25th Anniversary of Army Engineers. P 13.

| 1925 | **604** | 6st. black and bright blue | 35 | 25 |

605 T. Tserkovski

606 Woman (Roman Statue)

(Des A. Poplilov. Photo)

1969 (6 Sept). Birth Centenary of Tsanko Tserkovski (poet). P 11.

| 1926 | **605** | 13st. multicoloured | 1·10 | 45 |

(Des M. Kefsizova. Photo)

1969 (22 Sept). 1,800th Anniversary of Silistra. T **606** and similar design. P 11.

| 1927 | 2st. brownish grey, ultramarine and silver | 25 | 20 |
| 1928 | 13st. drab, deep bluish green and silver | 1·50 | 60 |

Designs: Vert—2st. T **606**. Horiz—13st. Wolf (bronze).

607 Skipping-rope Exercise

608 Mann Drinov (founder)

(Des St. Goristanova and V. Korenev. Photo)

1969 (27 Sept). World Gymnastics Competition, Varna, T **607** and similar horiz designs. P 11.

1929	1st. grey, deep blue and blue-green	25	20
1930	2st. grey, chalky blue and greenish blue	25	20
1931	3st. grey, deep myrtle-green and bright emerald	25	20
1932	5st. grey, plum and vermilion	35	25
1933	13st. +5st. grey, deep violet-blue and magenta	1·60	75
1934	20st. +10st. grey, deep bluish green and deep olive-yellow	2·00	85
1929/1934	Set of 6	4·25	2·20

Designs: 1st. T **607**; 2st. Hoop exercise (pair); 3st. Hoop exercise (solo); 5st. Ball exercise (pair); 13st. Ball exercise (solo); 20st. Solo gymnast.

(Des D. Rusinov. Photo)

1969 (1 Oct). Centenary of Bulgarian Academy of Sciences. P 11.

| 1935 | **608** | 20st. black and red | 1·40 | 60 |

609 Neophit Rilski (Zakharii Zograf)

610 Pavel Banya

(Des St. Kunchev. Photo Kultura, Budapest)

1969 (3 Oct). Paintings in National Art Gallery, Sofia. T **609** and similar multicoloured designs. P 12½×11½ (horiz) or 11½×12½ (vert).

| 1936 | 1st. Type **609** | 25 | 15 |
| 1937 | 2st. *German's Mother* (Vasil Stoikov) | 35 | 20 |

1938	3st. *Worker's Family* (Nenko Balkanski) (horiz)	40	25
1939	4st. *Woman Dressing* (Ivan Nenov)	55	30
1940	5st. *Portrait of a Woman* (Nikolai Pavlovich)	70	35
1941	13st. *Krustyu Sarafov as Falstaff* (Dechko Uzunov)	1·40	45
1942	20st. *Artist's Wife* (N. Mikhailov) (horiz)	2·00	60
1943	20st. *Worker's Lunch* (Stoyan Sotirov) (horiz)	2·00	60
1944	40st. *Self-portrait* (Tseno Todorov)	2·75	95
1936/1944 Set of 9		9·50	3·50

(Des K. Gogov. Photo)

1969 (14 Oct)–**70**. Sanatoria. T **610** and similar horiz designs. P 11.

1945	2st. new blue (9.1.70)	25	20
1946	5st. bright blue	30	20
	a. Perf 12½	30	20
1947	6st. myrtle green (3.11.69)	45	25
	a. Perf 12½	45	25
	b. Perf 14×13½		
1948	20st. light emerald	1·00	45
	a. Perf 12½	1·00	45
1945/1948 Set of 4		1·80	1·00

Sanatoria: 2st. T **610**; 5st. Khisar; 6st. Kotel; 20st. Narechen Polyclinic.

611 Deep-sea Trawler

(Des M. Peikova and G. Kovachev. Photo)

1969 (30 Oct). Ocean Fisheries. T **611** and similar horiz designs, showing fish. P 11.

1949	1st. grey, blue and blackish blue	25	20
1950	1st. pale green, olive-green and black	25	20
1951	2st. pale violet, violet and black	25	20
1952	3st. light blue, violet-blue and black	25	20
1953	5st. pale mauve, mauve and black	35	30
1954	10st. pale grey, grey and black	1·80	60
1955	13st. pale flesh, salmon and black	2·75	1·00
1956	20st. light buff, ochre and black	4·00	1·90
1949/1956 Set of 8		9·00	4·25

Designs: 1st. (No. 1949), T **611**; 1st. (No. 1950), Cape Hake (*Merluccius capensis*); 2st. Scad (*Trachurus trachurus*); 3st. Pilchard (*Sardinops sagax*); 5st. Large-eyed Sea Bream (*Dentex macrophthalmus*); 10st. Chub Mackerel (*Scomber colias*); 13st. Croaker (*Otolithes macrognathus*); 20st. Big-toothed Leerfish (*Lichia vadigo*).

612 Trapeze Act   **613** V. Kubasov, Georgi Shonin and *Soyuz 6*

(Des V. Vasileva and A. Denkov. Photo)

1969 (29 Nov). Circus. Vert designs as T **612**. Multicoloured. P 11.

1957	1st. Type **612**	25	20
1958	2st. Acrobats	25	20
1959	3st. Balancing act with hoops	25	20
1960	5st. Juggler, and Bear on cycle	35	25
1961	13st. Equestrian act	95	45
1962	20st. Clowns	1·80	75
1957/1962 Set of 6		3·50	1·80

(Des S. Sotirov. Photo)

1969 (25 Dec). Space Flights of *Soyuz 6*, *Soyuz 7* and *Soyuz 8*. Vert designs as T **613**. P 11.

1963	1st. multicoloured	20	15
1964	2st. multicoloured	20	15
1965	3st. multicoloured	20	15
1966	28st. pink, new blue and chalky blue	1·80	75
1963/1966 Set of 4		2·20	1·10

Designs: 1st. T **613**; 2st. Viktor Gorbatko, Vladislav Volkov, Anatoly Filipchenko and *Soyuz 7*; 3st. Aleksei Elseev, Vladimir Shatalov and *Soyuz 8*; 28st. Three Soyuz spacecraft in orbit.

614 Khan Asparuch and Old-Bulgars crossing the Danube, 679

(Des V. Vasileva and A. Denkov. Photo)

1970 (28 Jan). History of Bulgaria (1st series). T **614** and similar horiz designs. Multicoloured. P 10½.

1967	1st. Type **614**	25	20
1968	2st. Khan Krum and defeat of Emperor Nicephorus, 811	25	20
1969	3st. Conversion of Khan Boris I to Christianity, 865	25	20
1970	5st. Tsar Simeon and Battle of Akhelo, 917	35	25
1971	8st. Tsar Samuel and defeat of Byzantines, 976	40	30
1972	10st. Tsar Kaloyan and victory over Emperor Baldwin, 1205	80	35
1973	13st. Tsar Ivan Asen II and defeat of Komnine of Epirus, 1230	1·40	45
1974	20st. Coronation of Tsar Ivailo, 1277	1·90	85
1967/1974 Set of 8		5·00	2·50

See also No. 2274/2281.

615 Bulgarian Pavilion

(Des D. Rusinov. Photo)

1970 (20 Feb). Expo 70 World's Fair, Osaka, Japan (1st issue). P 12½.

1975	**615**	20st. silver, yellow and brown	2·50	1·50

See also Nos. 2009/**MS**2013.

616 Footballers

(Des V. Vasileva and A. Denkov Litho)

1970 (4 Mar). World Football Cup, Mexico. T **616** and similar designs. P 12½.

1976	1st. multicoloured	20	15
1977	2st. multicoloured	20	15
1978	3st. multicoloured	20	15
1979	5st. multicoloured	35	20
1980	20st. multicoloured	1·80	60
1981	40st. multicoloured	3·00	85
1976/1981 Set of 6		5·25	1·90
MS1982 55×99 mm. 80st.+20st. multicoloured. Imperf		5·50	5·00

Designs: Horiz—1st. T **616**; 2st. to 40st. Various football scenes. Vert (45×69 *mm*)—80st. Football and inscription.

617 Lenin   **618** *Tephrocactus Alexanderi v. bruchi*

BULGARIA 1970

(Des A. Poplilov. Photo)

1970 (28 Mar). Birth Centenary of Lenin. Square designs as T **617**. Multicoloured. P 12½.

1983	2st. Type **617**	25	20
1984	13st. Full-face portrait	90	45
1985	20st. Lenin writing	2·10	85
1983/1985	Set of 3	3·00	1·40

(Des R. Stanoeva and A. Sertev. Photo)

1970 (30 Apr). Flowering Cacti. T **618** and similar vert designs. Multicoloured. P 12½.

1986	1st. Type **618**	25	20
1987	2st. *Opuntia drummondii*	25	20
1988	3st. *Hatiora cilindrica*	25	20
1989	5st. *Gymnocalycium vatteri*	35	25
1990	8st. *Heliantho cereus grandiflorus*	70	45
1991	10st. *Neochilenia andreaeana*	2·75	85
1992	13st. *Peireskia vargasii v. longispina*	3·25	1·50
1993	20st. *Neobesseya rosiflora*	3·75	1·60
1986/1993	Set of 8	10·50	4·75

622 Rose, and Woman with Baskets of Produce

(Des V. Tomov. Photo)

1970 (20 June). Expo 70 World's Fair, Osaka, Japan (2nd issue). T **622** and horiz designs. Multicoloured. P 12½.

2009	1st. Type **622**	25	20
2010	2st. Three dancers	25	20
2011	3st. Girl in National Costume	25	20
2012	28st. Dancing couples	2·40	1·00
2009/2012	Set of 4	2·75	1·40
MS2013	75×90 mm. 40st. Bulgarian pavilion. Imperf	2·50	2·30

619 Rose   **620** Union Badge

(Des V. Tomov and Zh. Tishev. Litho German Bank Note Ptg Co, Leipzig)

1970 (5 June). Bulgarian Roses. Vert designs as T **619** showing different varieties. P 13½.

1994	1st. multicoloured	25	20
1995	2st. multicoloured	35	20
1996	3st. multicoloured	40	20
1997	4st. multicoloured	60	25
1998	5st. multicoloured	70	30
1999	13st. multicoloured	1·40	60
2000	20st. multicoloured	2·75	1·30
2001	28st. multicoloured	4·75	2·10
1994/2001	Set of 8	10·00	4·75

(Des M. Peikova and G. Kovachev. Photo)

1970 (8 June). 70th Anniversary of Agricultural Union. P 12½.

2002	**620** 20st. black, gold and red-orange	1·90	60

623 UN Emblem

(Des D. Rusinov. Photo)

1970 (14 July). 25th Anniversary of United Nations. P 12½.

2014	**623** 20st. gold, turquoise-blue and greenish blue	1·40	75

624 I. Vasov   **625** Edelweiss Sanatorium, Borovets

(Des M. Peikova and G. Kovachev. Photo)

1970 (15 July). 120th Birth Anniversary of Ivan Vasov (writer). P 12½.

2015	**624** 13st. chalky blue	1·30	45

(Des St. Goristanova and V. Korenev. Photo)

1970 (30 July–9 Dec). Health Resorts. T **625** and similar horiz designs. P 13.

2016	1st. bluish green (2.10.70)	25	20
2017	2st. deep olive (5.8.70)	25	20
2018	4st. bright blue (26.10.70)	25	20
2019	8st. greenish blue (9.12.70)	70	30
2020	10st. turquoise-blue	95	35
2016/2020	Set of 5	2·20	1·10

Designs: 1st. T **625**; 2st. Panorama Hotel, Pamporovo; 4st. Yachts, Albena; 8st. Harbour scene, Rusalka; 10st. Shtastlivetsa Hotel, Mount Vitosha.

621 Gold Bowl

(Des M. Peikova. Photo)

1970 (15 June). Gold Treasures of Thrace. T **621** and similar square designs. P 12½.

2003	1st. black, blue and gold	25	20
2004	2st. black, lilac and gold	25	20
2005	3st. black, red and gold	25	20
2006	5st. black, green and gold	40	30
2007	13st. black, orange and gold	1·90	75
2008	20st. black, violet and gold	2·30	1·50
2003/2008	Set of 6	4·75	2·75

Designs: 1st. T **621**; 2st. Three small bowls; 3st. Plain lid; 5st. Pear-shaped ornaments; 13st. Large lid with pattern; 20st. Vase.

626 Hungarian Retriever   **627** Fireman with Hose

(Des V. Tomov and Zh. Tishev. Photo)

1970 (10 Aug). Dogs. T **626** and similar multicoloured designs. P 12½.

2021	1st. Type **626**	25	20
2022	2st. Retriever (*vert*)	35	20
2023	3st. Great Dane (*vert*)	40	20
2024	4st. Boxer (*vert*)	55	25
2025	5st. Cocker Spaniel (*vert*)	70	40
2026	13st. Dobermann Pinscher (*vert*)	1·80	1·00
2027	20st. Scottish Terrier (*vert*)	4·00	1·50
2028	28st. Russian Hound	4·50	1·90
2021/2028	Set of 8	11·50	5·00

1970 BULGARIA

(Des St. Goristanova and V. Korenev. Photo)
1970 (3 Sept). Fire Protection. T **627** and similar horiz design. P 12½.
2029	1st. grey, yellow and black	35	20
2030	3st. vermilion, grey and black	40	30

Designs: 1st. T **627**; 3st. Fire-engine.

628 Congress Emblem

629 Two Male Players

(Des St. Kunchev. Photo)
1970 (14 Sept). Seventh World Sociological Congress, Varna. P 12½.
2031	**628**	13st. multicoloured	1·10	35

(Des Zh. Kosturkova. Photo)
1970 (20–22 Sept). World Volleyball Championships. T **629** and similar vert designs. P 12½.
2032	2st. greenish blue, black and chocolate	25	20
2033	2st. pale orange, black and blue (22.9.70)	25	20
2034	20st. yellow, black and blue-green	1·70	85
2035	20st. bright green, yellow, black and greenish blue (22.9.70)	1·70	85
2032/2035 Set of 4		3·50	1·90

Designs: 2st. (No. 2032), T **629**; 2st. (No. 2033), Two female players; 20st. (No. 2034), Male player; 20st. (No. 2035), Female player.

630 Cyclists

632 Beethoven

631 Enrico Caruso and Scene from *Il Pagliacci*

(Des V. Korenev. Photo)
1970 (30 Sept). 20th Round-Bulgaria Cycle Race. P 12½.
2036	**630**	20st. mauve, olive-yellow and myrtle-green	1·40	75

(Des V. Tomov. Photo German Bank Note Ptg Co, Leipzig)
1970 (15 Oct). Opera Singers. T **631** and similar horiz designs. Multicoloured. P 14.
2037	1st. Type **631**	25	20
2038	2st. Khristina Morfova and *The Bartered Bride*	25	20
2039	3st. Petur Raichev and *Tosca*	25	20
2040	10st. Tsvetana Tabakova and *The Flying Dutchman*	55	35
2041	13st. Katya Popova and *The Masters*	70	45
2042	20st. Fyodor Chaliapin and *Boris Godunov*	2·75	1·70
2037/2042 Set of 6		4·25	2·75

(Des A. Poplilov. Photo)
1970 (15 Oct). Birth Bicentenary of Ludwig von Beethoven (composer). P 12½.
2043	**632**	28st. steel blue and reddish purple	3·75	3·00

633 Ivan Asen II Coin

(Des D. Rusinov. Photo)
1970 (2 Nov). Bulgarian Coins of the 14th-century. T **633** and similar horiz designs. Multicoloured. P 12½.
2044	1st. Type **633**	25	20
2045	2st. Theodor Svetoslav	25	20
2046	3st. Mikhail Shishman	25	20
2047	13st. Ivan Alexander and Mikhail Asen	60	35
2048	20st. Ivan Sratsimir	1·70	60
2049	28st. Ivan Shishman (initials)	2·30	85
2044/2049 Set of 6		4·75	2·20

634 Luna 16

635 Engels

(Des A. Denkov. Photo)
1970 (14 Nov). Moon Mission of *Luna 16*. Sheet 51×70 mm. Imperf.
MS2050	**634**	1l. red, silver and deep ultramarine	9·50	8·75

(Des A. Poplilov. Photo)
1970 (28 Nov). 150th Birth Anniversary of Friedrich Engels. P 12½.
2051	**635**	13st. yellow-brown, blackish brown and vermilion	1·40	75

636 Snow Crystal

637 *Lunokhod 1* on Moon

(Des St. Kunchev. Photo)
1970 (15 Dec). New Year. P 12½×13.
2052	**636**	2st. multicoloured	25	20

(Des A. Denkov. Photo)
1970 (18 Dec). Moon Mission of *Lunokhod 1*. Sheet 60×72 mm. Imperf.
MS2053	**637**	80st. silver, black, purple and light blue	8·00	7·25

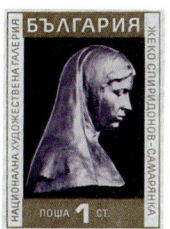

638 *Girl's Head* (Zheko Spiridonov)

639 Birds and Flowers

(Des St. Kunchev. Photo)

1970 (28 Dec). Modern Bulgarian Sculpture. T **638** and similar vert designs. P 12½.

2054	1st. violet and gold	25	20
2055	2st. bronze-green and gold	25	20
2056	3st. brown-lake and gold	25	20
2057	13st. slate-green and gold	95	35
2058	20st. brown-red and gold	1·60	60
2059	28st. bistre-brown and gold	2·00	85
2054/2059 Set of 6		4·75	2·20
MS2060 61×72 mm. 1l. chestnut and gold. Imperf.		5·00	4·75

Sculptures: 1st. T **638**. As T **638**—2st. *Third Class* (Ivan Funev); 3st. *Elin Pelin* (Marko Markov); 13st. *Nina* (Andrei Nikolov); 20st. *Kneeling Woman* (Yavorov monument, Ivan Lazarov); 28st. *Engineer* (Ivan Funev). 36½×41 mm—1l. *Refugees* (Sekul Krumov).

(Des St. Kunchev. Photo)

1971 (25 Jan). Spring. T **639** and similar horiz designs showing birds and flowers. P 12½×13.

2061	1st. multicoloured	20	15
2062	2st. multicoloured	20	15
2063	3st. multicoloured	20	15
2064	5st. multicoloured	25	20
2065	13st. multicoloured	70	30
2066	20st. multicoloured	1·50	60
2061/2066 Set of 6		2·75	1·40

640 *Khan Asparuch crossing Danube* (Boris Angelushev)

(Des M. Peikova. Photo German Bank Note Ptg Co, Leipzig)

1971 (6 Mar). Bulgarian History. Paintings. T **640** and similar horiz designs. Multicoloured. Photo. P 13½×14.

2067	2st. Type **640**	25	20
2068	3st. *Ivailo in Turnovo* (Ilya Petrov)	25	20
2069	5st. *Cavalry Charge, Benkovski* (P. Morozov)	70	30
2070	8st. *General Gurko entering Sofia, 1878* (D. Gyudzhenov)	1·40	45
2071	28st. *Greeting Red Army* (Stefan Venev)	5·25	2·50
2067/2071 Set of 5		7·00	3·25
MS2072 137×131 mm. Nos. 2067/2070		2·50	2·20

See also No. **MS**2228.

641 Running

(Des Zh. Kosturkova. Photo)

1971 (13 Mar). Second European Indoor Track and Field Championships. T **641** and similar horiz design. Multicoloured. P 12½×13.

2073	2st. Type **641**	25	20
2074	20st. Putting the shot	2·40	75

642 School Building

(Des Z. Taseva. Photo)

1971 (16 Mar). Foundation of first Bulgarian Secondary School, Bolgrad, 1858. T **642** and similar horiz design. P 12½.

2075	2st. green, yellow-brown and silver	25	20
2076	20st. violet, yellow-brown and silver	1·70	60

Designs: 2st. T **642**; 20st. Dimitur Mutev, Prince Bogoridi and Sava Radulov (founders).

643 Communards

(Des St. Goristanova and V. Korenev. Photo)

1971 (18 Mar). Centenary of Paris Commune. P 12½×13.

2077	**643**	20st. black and claret	1·20	75

644 Georgi Dimitrov challenging Hermann Goering (photomontage, J. Hartfield)

646 G. Rakovski

(Des D. Rusinov. Photo)

1971 (11 Apr). 20th Anniversary of 'Fédération Internationale des Résistants'. P 12½.

2078	**644**	2st. multicoloured	25	20
2079		13st. multicoloured	1·80	75

645 Gagarin and Space Scenes

(Des D. Rusinov. Photo)

1971 (12 Apr). Tenth Anniversary of First Manned Space Flight. Sheet 80×53 mm. Imperf.

MS2080	**645**	40st.+20st. multicoloured	5·50	5·00

(Des A. Poplilov. Photo)

1971 (14 Apr). 150th Birth Anniversary of Georgi Rakovski (politician and revolutionary). Photo. P 12½.

2081	**646**	13st. blackish brown, pale cream and light olive-green	1·00	35

647 Worker and Banner (People's Progress)

648 Pipkov and Music

(Des A. Denkov. Photo)

1971 (20 Apr). Tenth Bulgarian Communist Party Congress. T **647** and similar multicoloured designs. P 12½.

2082	1st. Type **647**	25	20
2083	2st. Symbols of Technical Progress (*horiz*)	25	20
2084	13st. Men clasping hands (Bulgarian-Soviet Friendship)	1·60	60
2082/2084 Set of 3		1·90	90

(Des K. Kotseva and V. Dokev. Photo)

1971 (20 May). Birth Centenary of Panaiot Pipkov (composer). P 12½.
2085   **648**   13st. black, bright green and silver .... 1·20   75

649 Three Races

650 Mammoth

(Des V. Korenev. Photo)

1971 (20 May). Racial Equality Year. P 12½.
2086   **649**   13st. multicoloured .... 1·20   75

(Des A. Denkov. Photo)

1971 (29 May). Prehistoric Animals. Multicoloured designs as T **650**. P 12½.
2087   1st. Type **650** 25   20
2088   2st. Bear (vert) 25   20
2089   3st. Hipparion 25   20
2090   13st. Mastodon .... 2·75   85
2091   20st. Dinotherium (vert) .... 4·00   2·20
2092   28st. Sabre-toothed Tiger .... 4·75   3·00
2087/2092 Set of 6 .... 11·00   6·00

651 Façade of Ancient Building   **652** Weights Emblem on Map of Europe

(Des K. Gogov. Photo)

1971 (10 June). Ancient Buildings of Koprivshtitsa. T **651** and similar horiz designs showing different façades. P 12½.
2093   1st. myrtle-green, red-brown and light yellow-green 20   15
2094   2st. red-brown, myrtle-green and buff 20   15
2095   6st. violet, brown-lake and blue 55   30
2096   13st. carmine-red, blue and yellow-orange... 1·40   60
2093/2096 Set of 4 .... 2·10   1·10

(Des S. Nenov. Photo)

1971 (19 June). 30th European Weightlifting Championships, Sofia. T **652** and similar vert design. Multicoloured. P 12½.
2097   2st. Type **652** 25   20
2098   13st. Figures XXX supporting weights........... 1·80   60

653 Frontier Guard and Dog

654 Tweezers, Magnifying Glass and 'Stamp'

(Des V. Tomov. Photo)

1971 (26 June). 25th Anniversary of Frontier Guards. Photo. P 12½.
2099   **653**   2st. olive-green, green and pale blue-green.. 25   20

(Des V. Korenev. Photo)

1971 (10 July). Ninth Congress of Bulgarian Philatelic Federation. P 12½.
2100   **654**   20st. +10st. olive-brown, black and orange-red.................................. 2·40   1·00

655 Congress Meeting (sculpture)

(Des L. Marinov. Photo)

1971 (31 July). 80th Anniversary of Bulgarian Social Democratic Party, Buzludzha. P 12½.
2101   **655**   2st. emerald, cream and carmine-red... 25   20

656 Mother (Ivan Nenov)
657 Factory, Botevgrad

(Des V. and O. Ionchev. Photo German Bank Note Ptg Co, Leipzig)

1971 (2 Aug). Paintings from the National Art Gallery (1st series). T **656** and similar vert designs. Multicoloured. P 14×13½.
2102   1st. Type **656** 25   20
2103   2st. Lazarova (Stefan Ivanov)............. 25   20
2104   3st. Portrait of Yu. Kh. (Kiril Tsonev) ... 40   30
2105   13st. Portrait of a Lady (Dechko Uzunov)......... 1·40   45
2106   20st. Young Woman from Kalotina (Vladimir Dimitrov)................................. 2·00   1·00
2107   40st. Goryanin (Stoyan Venev).......... 2·75   1·70
2102/2107 Set of 6 .... 6·25   3·50
See also Nos. 2145/2150.

(Des M. Peikova. Photo)

1971 (25 Aug). Industrial Buildings. T **657** and similar designs. P 13.
2108   1st. bright violet 20   15
2109   2st. bright orange-red..................... 20   15
2110   10st. blackish violet 40   25
2111   13st. cerise 75   30
2112   40st. chocolate .... 2·30   60
2108/2112 Set of 5 .... 3·50   1·30
Designs: Vert—2st. Petro-chemical plant, Pleven. Horiz—10st. Chemical works, Vratsa; 13st. Maritsa-Istok plant, Dimitrovgrad; 40st. Electronics factory, Sofia.

658 Free-style Wrestling

659 Posthorn Emblem

(Des St. Goristanova and V. Korenev. Photo)

1971 (27 Aug). European Wrestling Championships. T **658** and similar horiz design. P 12½.
2113   2st. black, turquoise-blue and bright emerald 20   15
2114   13st. black, turquoise-blue and bright vermilion..................................... 1·30   60
Designs: 2st. T **658**; 13st. Greco-Roman wrestling.

BULGARIA 1971

(Des St. Kunchev. Photo)

1971 (15 Sept). Eighth Organisation of Socialist Countries' Postal Administrations Congress. P 12½.
2115 659 20st. gold and emerald................. 1·40 75

660 Entwined Ribbons

661 'New Republic' Statue

(Des D. Rusinov. Photo)

1971 (20 Sept). Seventh European Biochemical Congress, Varna. P 12½.
2116 660 13st. rosine, purple-brown and black..... 1·40 75

(Des St. Kunchev. Photo)

1971 (20 Sept). 25th Anniversary of People's Republic. T **661** and similar vert design. P 13×12½.
2117 2st. scarlet, yellow and gold.................... 20 15
2118 13st. dull green, vermilion and gold............. 1·30 60
Designs: 2st. T **661**; 13st. Bulgarian flag.

662 Cross-country Skiing

663 Brigade Members

(Des St. Goristanova and V. Korenev. Photo)

1971 (25 Sept). Winter Olympic Games, Sapporo, Japan. T **662** and similar horiz designs. Multicoloured. P 12½.
2119 1st. Type **662**................................... 25 20
2120 2st. Downhill skiing............................. 25 20
2121 3st. Ski jumping................................. 25 20
2122 4st. Figure skating.............................. 25 20
2123 13st. Ice hockey................................. 1·40 85
2124 28st. Slalom skiing.............................. 2·40 1·50
2119/2124 Set of 6................................... 4·25 2·75
MS2125 60×70 mm. 1l. Olympic flame and stadium. Imperf.. 5·50 3·75

(Des V. Tomov. Photo)

1971 (13 Oct). 25th Anniversary of Youth Brigades Movement. P 13.
2126 663 2st. deep violet-blue........................ 25 20

664 UNESCO Emblem and Wreath

665 The Footballer

(Des I. Kosev. Photo)

1971 (4 Nov). 25th Anniversary of United Nations Educational, Scientific and Cultural Organisation. P 12½.
2127 664 20st. multicoloured.......................... 1·40 75

(Des St. Kunchev. Photo State Printing Works, Budapest)

1971 (10 Nov). 75th Birth Anniversary of Kiril Tsonev (painter). T **665** and similar multicoloured designs, showing his paintings. P 12×11½ (2st., 20st.) or 11½×12 (others).
2128 1st. Type **665**................................... 25 20
2129 2st. *Landscape* (*horiz*)......................... 25 20
2130 3st. Self-portrait................................ 30 25
2131 13st. *Lilies*.................................... 1·40 45
2132 20st. *Woodland Scene* (*horiz*).................. 2·00 85
2133 40st. *Portrait of a Young Woman*................ 2·75 1·00
2128/2133 Set of 6................................... 6·25 2·75

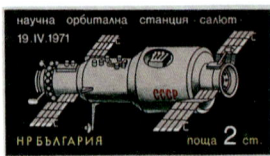
666 Salyut Space-station

(Des A. Denkov. Photo)

1971 (20 Dec). Russian Space Programme. *Soyuz 11* Mission. T **666** and similar horiz designs. Multicoloured. P 12½.
2134 2st. Type **666**................................... 25 20
2135 13st. *Soyuz 11*.................................. 60 40
2136 40st. Docking of Salyut and *Soyuz 11*............ 3·00 1·00
2134/2136 Set of 3................................... 3·50 1·40
MS2137 70×74 mm. 80st. Cosmonauts G. Dobrovolsky, Vladislav Volkov and V. Patsaev (victims of *Soyuz 11* disaster). Imperf.................................. 4·00 3·75

667 *Vikhren* (ore carrier)

(Des M. Peikova. Photo)

1972 (8 Jan). Construction of One Million Tons of Shipping in Bulgaria. P 12½.
2138 667 18st. lilac, magenta and black............... 1·90 75

668 Goce Delçev

670 Bulgarian Worker

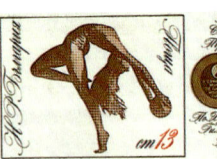
669 Gymnast with Ball

(Des G. Nedyalkov. Photo)

1972 (21 Jan). Birth Centenaries of Macedonian Revolutionaries. T **668** and similar horiz portraits. P 12½.
2139 2st. black and orange-red........................ 20 15
2140 5st. black and yellow-green...................... 25 20
2141 13st. black and olive-yellow..................... 95 40
2139/2141 Set of 3................................... 1·30 70
Designs: 2st. T **668**; 5st. Jan Sandanski; 13st. Dame Gruev (centenary in 1971).

(Des I. Kiosev. Photo)

1972 (10 Feb). Fifth World Gymnastics Championships, Havana, Cuba. T **669** and similar horiz designs. Multicoloured. P 12½.
2142 13st. Type **669**.................................. 1·40 45
2143 18st. Gymnast with hoop.......................... 2·00 85
MS2144 61×74 mm. 70st. Team with hoops. Imperf.... 6·00 5·75

1972 BULGARIA

(Des O. and V. Ionchev. Photo German Bank Note Ptg Co, Leipzig)

1972 (20 Feb). Paintings from the National Gallery (2nd series). Horiz designs similar to T **656**. Multicoloured. P 13½×14.

2145	1st. *Melnik* (Petur Mladenov)	25	20
2146	2st. *Ploughman* (Pencho Georgiev)	25	20
2147	3st. *By the Death-bed* (Aleksandur Zhendov)	35	25
2148	13st. *Family* (Vladimir Dimitrov)	1·60	45
2149	20st. *Family* (Nenko Balkanski)	2·00	60
2150	40st. *Father Paisii* (Koyu Denchev)	2·40	75
2145/2150 Set of 6		6·25	2·20

(Des T. Momchilov. Photo)

1972 (7 Mar). Seventh Bulgarian Trade Unions Congress. P 12½.

2151	**670**	13st. multicoloured	95	30

671 Singing Harvesters   **672** Heart and Tree Emblem

(Des I. Kosev. Photo State Ptg Wks, Budapest)

1972 (29 Mar). 90th Birth Anniversary of Vladimir Dimitrov, the Master (painter). T **671** and similar multicoloured designs. P 12×11½ (3st., 13st.) or 11½×12 (others).

2152		1st. Type **671**	25	20
2153		2st. *Farm Worker*	25	20
2154		3st. *Women Cultivators* (horiz)	30	20
2155		13st. *Peasant Girl* (horiz)	70	30
2156		20st. *My Mother*	2·00	1·20
2157		40st. *Self-portrait*	2·75	1·70
2152/2157 Set of 6			5·75	3·50

(Des A. Stareishinski. Photo)

1972 (30 Apr). World Heart Month. P 12½.

2158	**672**	13st. multicoloured	2·00	1·00

673 St Mark's Cathedral   **675** Lamp of Learning and Quotation

674 Dimitrov at Typesetting Desk

(Des St. Kunchev. Photo)

1972 (6 May). UNESCO Save Venice Campaign. T **673** and similar vert design. P 13×12½.

2159		2st. pale turquoise-blue, turquoise-green and bronze-green	35	30
2160		13st. pale turquoise-green, slate-violet and Venetian red	1·60	75

Designs: 2st. T **673**; 13st. Palace of the Doge.

(Des I. Kiosev. Photo)

1972 (8 May). 90th Birth Anniversary of Georgi Dimitrov (statesman) (1st issue). T **674** and similar horiz designs. Multicoloured. P 12½.

2161		1st. Type **674**	25	20
2162		2st. September Uprising of 1923	25	20
2163		3st. Dimitrov at Leipzig Trial	25	20
2164		5st. Dimitrov addressing workers	30	25
2165		13st. Dimitrov with Bulgarian crowd	50	45
2166		18st. Addressing young people	70	60
2167		28st. Dimitrov with children	1·40	85
2168		40st. Dimitrov's mausoleum	2·40	1·30
2169		80st. Portrait head (olive-green and gold centre)	6·50	3·00
2161/2169 Set of 9			11·50	6·25
MS2170 87×84 mm. As No. 2169, but centre in brown-red and gold. Imperf			8·75	8·00

For 80st. imperforate and with different coloured centre see No. 2173.
See also No. 2173.

(Des A. Stareishinski. Photo)

1972 (12 May). 250th Birth Anniversary of Father Paisii Khilendarski (historian). T **675** and similar vert design. P 12½.

2171		2st. sepia, blue-green and gold	25	20
2172		13st. sepia, blue-green and gold	1·60	60

Designs: 2st. T **675**; 13st. Paisii writing.

(Des I. Kosev. Photo)

1972 (18 June). 90th Birth Anniversary of Georgi Dimitrov (statesman) (2nd issue). As No. 2169, but centre in red and gold. Imperf.

2173		80st. multicoloured	13·50	13·00

676 Canoeing

(Des A. Denkov and St. Kunchev. Photo)

1972 (25 June). Olympic Games, Munich. T **676** and similar horiz designs. Multicoloured. P 12½.

2174		1st. Type **676**	25	20
2175		2st. Gymnastics	25	20
2176		3st. Swimming	25	20
2177		13st. Volleyball	70	45
2178		18st. Hurdling	1·40	60
2179		40st. Wrestling	2·40	1·10
2174/2179 Set of 6			4·75	2·50
MS2180 64×60 mm. 80st. Running track and sports. Imperf			5·50	5·00

677 Angel Kunchev   **678** Golden Sands

(Des I. Kosev. Photo)

1972 (30 June). Death Centenary of Angel Kunchev (patriot). P 12½.

2181	**677**	2st. maroon, gold and purple	25	20

(Des V. Vasileva. Photo)

1972 (16 Sept). Hotels at Black Sea Resorts. T **678** and similar vert designs. Multicoloured. P 12½.

2182		1st. Type **678**	25	20
2183		2st. Druzhba	25	20
2184		3st. Sunny Beach	25	20
2185		13st. Primorsko	95	30
2186		28st. Rusalka	1·80	60
2187		40st. Albena	2·00	70
2182/2187 Set of 6			5·00	2·00

BULGARIA 1972

679 Canoeing (Bronze Medal)
680 Subi Dimitrov

(Des St. Kunchev and A. Stareishinski. Photo)

1972 (28 Sept). Bulgarian Medal Winners, Olympic Games, Munich. T **679** and similar horiz designs. Multicoloured. P 12½.

2188	1st. Type **679**	25	20
2189	2st. Long-jumping (Silver Medal)	25	20
2190	3st. Boxing (Gold Medal)	25	20
2191	18st. Wrestling (Gold Medal)	1·80	60
2192	40st. Weightlifting (Gold Medal)	2·40	1·20
2188/2192	Set of 5	4·50	2·20

See also No. 2206.

(Des M. Peikova and G. Kovachev. Photo)

1972 (30 Oct). Resistance Heroes. T **680** and similar vert portraits. Multicoloured. P 13.

2193	1st. Type **680**	25	20
2194	2st. Tsvyatko Radoinov	25	20
2195	3st. Iordan Lyutibrodski	25	20
2196	5st. Mito Ganev	40	25
2197	13st. Nedelcho Nikolov	1·40	45
2193/2197	Set of 5	2·30	1·20

681 Commemorative Text
682 *Lilium rhodopaeum*

(Des St. Kunchev. Photo)

1972 (3 Nov). 50th Anniversary of USSR. P 12½×13½.

2198	**681** 13st. red, yellow and gold	1·10	45

(Des V. Vasileva. Photo)

1972 (25 Nov). Protected Flowers. T **682** and similar vert designs. Multicoloured. P 12½.

2199	1st. Type **682**	25	20
2200	2st. Marsh Gentian (*Gentiana pneumonanthe*)	25	20
2201	3st. Sea Lily (*Pancratium maritimum*)	25	20
2202	4st. Globe Flower (*Trollius europaeus*)	35	25
2203	18st. *Primula frondosa*	1·40	60
2204	23st. Pale Pasqueflower (*Pulsatilla vernalis*)	2·00	1·20
2205	40st. *Fritillaria stribrnyi*	2·75	1·50
2199/2205	Set of 7	6·50	3·75

СВЕТОВЕН ПЪРВЕНЕЦ
(**683**)
684 Dobri Chintulov

1972 (27 Nov). Bulgaria, World Weightlifting Champions. No. 2192 optd with T **683**, in red.

2206	40st. multicoloured	3·00	1·50

(Des K. Kunev and M. Rashkov. Photo)

1972 (28 Nov). 150th Birth Anniversary of Dobri Chintulov (poet). P 12½.

2207	**684** 2st. multicoloured	50	30

685 Forehead Ornament (19th-century)
686 Divers with Cameras

(Des I. Kiosev. Recess German Bank Note Ptg Co, Leipzig)

1972 (27 Dec). Antique Jewellery. T **685** and similar horiz designs. P 14×13½.

2208	1st. black and red-brown	25	20
2209	2st. black and blue-green	25	20
2210	3st. black and greenish blue	25	20
2211	8st. black and brown-red	70	30
2212	23st. black and chestnut	1·80	75
2213	40st. black and violet	2·75	1·70
2208/2213	Set of 6	5·50	3·00

Designs: 1st. T **685**; 2st. Belt-buckle (19th-century); 3st. Amulet (18th-century); 8st. Pendant (18th-century); 23st. Earrings (14th-century); 40st. Necklace (18th-century).

(Des A. Denkov, K. Kunev and A. Stareishinski. Photo)

1973 (24 Jan). Underwater Research in Black Sea. T **686** and similar designs. P 12½.

2214	1st. black, yellow and light blue	25	20
2215	2st. black, yellow and new blue	25	20
2216	18st. black, yellow-orange and greenish blue	1·40	85
2217	40st. black, yellow-orange and bright blue	2·75	1·00
2214/2217	Set of 4	4·25	2·00
MS2218	118×98 mm. 20st.×4. Designs as Nos 2214/2217, but background colours changed. Imperf (sold at 1l.)	10·00	9·50

Designs: Horiz—1st. T **686**; 2st. Divers with *Shelf 1* (underwater research vessel). Vert—18st. Diver with diving bell *NIV 100*; 40st. Lifting balloon.

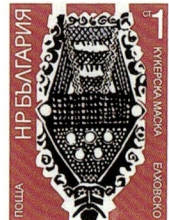

687 The Hanging of Vasil Levski (Boris Angelushev)
688 Elhovo Mask

(Des St. Kunchev. Photo)

1973 (19 Feb). Death Centenary of Vasil Levski (patriot). T **687** and similar vert design. P 13×12½.

2219	2st. deep bluish green and claret	25	20
2220	20st. brown, pale cream and light grey-green	2·40	1·00

Designs: 2st. T **687**; 20st. *Vasil Levski* (Georgi Danchov).

(Des V. Vasileva. Photo)

1973 (26 Feb). Kukeris Carnival Masks. T **688** and similar vert designs. Multicoloured. P 12½.

2221	1st. Type **688**	25	20
2222	2st. Breznik	25	20
2223	3st. Khisar	25	20
2224	13st. Radomir	95	45
2225	20st. Karnobat	1·40	85
2226	40st. Pernik	6·00	5·50
2221/2226	Set of 6	8·25	6·75

689 Copernicus
690 Vietnamese Girl

(Des K. Kunev and P. Rashkov. Photo)

1973 (21 Mar). 500th Birth Anniversary of Nicolas Copernicus. P 12½.
| 2227 | **689** | 28st. brown-purple, black and buff | 3·00 | 2·20 |

1973 (3 Apr). Visit Bulgaria by Air. No. **MS**2072 surch with various airline emblems and new sheet value.
| MS2228 | 137×131 mm. Nos. 2067/2070 surch with new sheet value of 1l. | 30·00 | 30·00 |

Although originally issued on 3 April it is understood that most of the sheets were not distributed until much later.

(Des A. Stareishinski. Photo)

1973 (16 Apr). Vietnam Peace Treaty. P 12½.
| 2229 | **690** | 18st. multicoloured | 1·00 | 75 |

1973 (4 May). IBRA 73 Stamp Exhibition, Munich. No. **MS**1907 optd with 'IBRA' and Olympic symbols, in green.
| MS2230 | 78×72 mm. 1l. multicoloured | 70·00 | 65·00 |

This sheet also exists with the overprint in grey from a limited printing.

691 Common Poppy (*Papaver rhoeas*)   **692** Botev (after T. Todorov)

(Des L. Chekhlarov. Photo)

1973 (15 May). Wild Flowers. T **691** and similar vert designs. Multicoloured. P 13.
2231		1st. Type **691**	25	20
2232		2st. Ox-eye Daisy (*Leucanthemum vulgare*)	25	20
2233		3st. Peony (*Paeonia peregrina*)	25	20
2234		13st. Cornflower (*Centaurea cyanus*)	95	45
2235		18st. Corn Cockle (*Agrostemma githago*)	8·25	6·00
2236		28st. Meadow Buttercup (*Ranunculus acer*)	2·75	1·60
2231/2236	Set of 6		11·50	7·75

(Des St. Kunchev. Photo)

1973 (2 June). 125th Birth Anniversary of Khristo Botev (poet and revolutionary). P 13.
| 2237 | **692** | 2st. brown, stone and metallic grey-green | 25 | 20 |
| 2238 | | 18st. bronze green, pale sage green and bronze | 1·80 | 1·50 |

693 Asen Khalachev and Insurgents

(Des M. Peikova and G. Kovachev. Photo)

1973 (6 June). 50th Anniversary of June Uprising at Pleven. T **693** and similar horiz design. P 13.
| 2239 | | 1st. black, vermilion and gold | 20 | 15 |
| 2240 | | 2st. black, yellow-orange and gold | 20 | 15 |

Designs: 1st. T **693**; 2st. *Wounded Worker* (illustration by Boris Angelushev to the poem *September* by Geo Milev).

694 Stamboliiski (from sculpture by A. Nikolov)

(Des I. Kosev. Photo)

1973 (14 June). 50th Death Anniversary of Aleksandur Stamboliiski (Prime Minister 1919–1923). P 12½.
| 2241 | **694** | 18st. deep brown and orange | 70 | 75 |
| 2242 | | 18st. bright orange | 7·00 | 5·75 |

695 Muskrat   **696** Turnovo

(Des M. Peikova and G. Kovachev. Photo)

1973 (29 June). Bulgarian Fauna. T **695** and similar multicoloured designs. P 13×12½ (3st., 12st.) or 12½×13 (others).
2243		1st. Type **695**	25	20
2244		2st. Racoon-dog	25	20
2245		3st. Mouflon (*vert*)	25	20
2246		12st. Fallow Deer (*vert*)	95	45
2247		18st. European Bison	2·40	1·50
2248		40st. Elk	8·50	5·75
2243/2248	Set of 6		11·50	7·50

(Des V. Vasileva. Photo)

1973 (30 July). AIR. Views of Bulgarian Cities. T **696** and similar vert designs. Multicoloured. P 13.
2249		2st. Type **696**	25	20
2250		13st. Rusalka	95	35
2251		20st. Plovdiv	4·75	4·25
2252		28st. Sofia	1·40	1·20
2249/2252	Set of 4		6·50	5·50

697 *Insurgents on the March* (Boris Angelushev)   **698** Congress Emblen

(Des St. Kunchev. Photo)

1973 (20 Aug). 50th Anniversary of September Uprising. T **697** and similar designs. P 12½.
2253		2st. multicoloured	25	20
2254		5st. bluish violet, pale pink and lake	35	25
2255		13st. multicoloured	95	45
2256		18st. blackish olive, pale cream and lake	1·90	1·40
2253/2256	Set of 4		3·00	2·10

Designs: Horiz—2st. T **697**; 5st. *Armed Train* (Boris Angelushev); 18st. Georgi Dimitrov and Vasil Kolarov. Vert—13st. Patriotic poster by N. Mirchev.

(Des S. Kamenov. Photo)

1973 (27 Aug). Eighth World Trade Union Congress, Varna. P 12½.
| 2257 | **698** | 2st. multicoloured | 25 | 20 |

699 Sun Emblem and Olympic Rings   **700** Prince Kaloyan

(Des St. Kunchev and A. Stareishinski. Photo)

1973 (29 Aug). Olympic Congress, Varna. T **699** and similar multicoloured designs. P 13.
| 2258 | | 13st. Type **699** | 2·75 | 85 |

BULGARIA 1973

2259	28st. Lion emblem of Bulgarian Olympic Committee		3·50	2·20
MS2260	61×77 mm. 80st. Footballers (40×25 *mm*)		6·75	5·75

No. **MS**2260 has a new blue frame to both the stamp and the sheet. The sheet also exists imperforate, and imperforate with this frame colour changed to reddish purple, both from limited printings.

(Des St. Kunchev. Photo German Bank Note Ptg Co, Leipzig)

1973 (24 Sept). Frescoes from Boyana Church. T **700** and similar square portraits. Multicoloured. P 13.

2261	1st. Type **700**		25	20
2262	2st. Desislava		25	20
2263	3st. Saint		30	20
2264	5st. St Eustratius		70	35
2265	10st. Tsar Constantine Asen		1·20	75
2266	13st. Deacon Laurentius		1·40	85
2267	18st. Virgin Mary		1·90	1·20
2268	20st. St Ephraim		2·20	1·50
2269	28st. Jesus Christ		6·75	2·20
2261/2269 Set of 9			13·50	6·75
MS2270	56×76 mm. 80st. Scribes. Imperf		9·50	9·25

701 Smirnenski and Cavalry Charge

(Des A. Stareishinski. Photo)

1973 (29 Sept). 75th Birth Anniversary and 50th Death Anniversary of Khristo Smirnenski (poet). P 12½.

2271	**701**	1st. greenish blue, red and gold	25	20
2272		2st. ultramarine, red and gold	50	25

702 Human Rights Emblem

704 Finn Class Yacht

703 Tsar Todor Svetoslav and Byzantine Embassy, 1307

(Des St. Kunchev. Photo)

1973 (10 Oct). 25th Anniversary of Declaration of Human Rights. P 12½.

2273	**702**	13st. gold, red and ultramarine	90	75

(Des P. Kulekov. Photo)

1973 (23 Oct). History of Bulgaria (2nd series). T **703** and similar horiz designs. Multicoloured. P 13½.

2274	1st. Type **703**	25	20
2275	2st. Tsar Mikhail Shishman in battle against the Byzantines, 1328	25	20
2276	3st. Battle of Rosokastro, 1332, and Tsar Ivan Aleksandr	25	20
2277	4st. Defence of Turnovo, 1393, and Patriarch Evtimii	25	20
2278	5st. Tsar Ivan Shishman's attack on the Turks	35	25
2279	13st. Momchil attacks Turkish ships at Umur, 1344	80	35
2280	18st. Meeting of Tsar Ivan Sratsimir and King Sigismund of Hungary's Crusaders, 1396	1·20	45

2281	28st. Embassy of Empress Anne of Savoy meets Boyars Balik, Teodor and Dobrotitsa		3·00	2·20
2274/2281 Set of 8			5·75	3·75

(Des A. Stareishinski. Litho German Bank Note Ptg Co, Leipzig)

1973 (29 Oct). Sailing. T **704** and similar vert designs, showing various yachts and dinghies. Multicoloured. P 13.

2282	1st. Type **704**	25	20
2283	2st. Flying Dutchman class	25	20
2284	3st. Soling class	25	20
2285	13st. Tempest class	95	45
2286	20st. 470 class	1·40	85
2287	40st. Tornado class	5·50	5·00
2282/2287 Set of 6		7·75	6·25

Nos. 2282/2287 also exist imperforate from a limited printing with different coloured backgrounds.

705 Balchik (Bencho Obreshkov)

(Des St. Kunchev. Litho State Security Ptg Works, Moscow)

1973 (10 Nov). 25th Anniversary of Bulgarian National Gallery, and 150th Birth Anniversary of Stanislav Dospevski (artist) (No. **MS**2294). T **705** and similar multicoloured designs, showing paintings. P 12.

2288	1st. Type **705**	25	20
2289	2st. *Mother and Child* (Stoyan Venev)	25	20
2290	3st. *Rest* (Tsenko Boyadzhiev)	25	20
2291	13st. *Vase with Flowers* (Sirak Skitnik) (*vert*)	1·10	35
2292	18st. *Mary Kuneva* (Iliya Petrov) (*vert*)	1·40	45
2293	40st. *Winter in Plovdiv* (Zlatyu Boyadzhiev) (*vert*)	5·50	5·00
2288/2293 Set of 6		8·00	5·75
MS2294	100×95 mm. 50st. *Domnika Lambreva* (S. Dospevski) (*vert*); 50st. *Self-portrait* (S. Dospevski) (*vert*)	8·00	5·75

706 Footballers and Emblem

707 Old Testament Scene (wood carving)

(Des St. Kunchev. Photo)

1973 (12 Dec). World Cup Football Championship, Munich (1974). Sheet 62×94 mm. P 13.

MS2295	**706**	28st. multicoloured (*sold at* 1l.)	8·00	7·75

A restricted issue of No. **MS**2295 overprinted with 'ARGENTINA 78' etc. appeared in 1978.

(Des K. Kunev and P. Rashkov. Photo)

1974 (15 Jan). Wood Carvings from Rozhen Monastery. T **707** and similar vert designs. P 13.

2296	1st. brown, cream and brown-lake	25	20
	a. Horiz strip of 3. Nos. 2296/2298	80	
2297	2st. brown, cream and brown-lake	25	20
2298	3st. brown, cream and brown-lake	25	20
2299	5st. blackish olive, cream and green	40	25
	a. Horiz pair. Nos. 2299/2300	1·00	60
2300	8st. blackish olive, cream and green	55	30
2301	13st. olive-brown, cream and chestnut	80	45
	a. Horiz pair. Nos. 2301/2302	2·50	1·40
2302	28st. olive-brown, cream and chestnut	1·60	85
2296/2302 Set of 7		3·75	2·20

Designs: 1st., 2st., 3st. Passover Table; 5st., 8st. Abraham and the Angel; 13st., 28st. The Expulsion from Eden.
Nos. 2296/2298, 2299/2300 and 2301/2302 respectively were issued together *se-tenant* within their sheets, forming three composite designs.

708 Lenin (N. Mirchev)

(Des M. Peikova and G. Kovachev. Litho State Ptg Works, Moscow)

1974 (28 Jan). 50th Death Anniversary of Lenin. T **708** and similar horiz design. Multicoloured. P 12.
2303	2st. Type **708**	25	20
2304	18st. *Lenin with Workers* (V. Serov)	1·40	85

709 *Blagoev addressing Meeting* (G. Kovachev)

(Des M. Peikova and G. Kovachev. Litho State Ptg Works, Moscow)

1974 (28 Jan). 50th Death Anniversary of Dimitur Blagoev (founder of Bulgarian Social Democratic Party). P 12.
2305	**709**	2st. multicoloured	25	20

710 Sheep   **711** Social Economic Integration Emblem

(Des V. Vasileva. Photo)

1974 (1 Feb). Domestic Animals. T **710** and similar horiz designs. P 13.
2306	1st. purple-brown, buff and bright green	25	20
2307	2st. dull purple, slate-violet and carmine-red	25	20
2308	3st. brown, pink and deep emerald	25	20
2309	5st. brown, buff and deep turquoise-blue	35	25
2310	13st. black, violet-blue and orange-brown	1·60	45
2311	20st. red-brown, pink and ultramarine	3·75	2·50
2306/2311	Set of 6	5·75	3·50

Designs: 1st. T **710**; 2st. Goat; 3st. Pig; 5st. Cow; 13st. Buffalo; 20st. Horse.

(Des A. Mechkuev. Photo)

1974 (11 Feb). 25th Anniversary of the Council for Mutual Economic Aid. P 13.
2312	**711**	13st. multicoloured	1·10	75

712 Footballers   **713** Folk-singers

(Des V. Vasileva and A. Stareishinski. Photo)

1974 (25 Mar). World Cup Football Championship, Munich. T **712** and similar horiz designs, showing footballers. P 13½×13.
2313	1st. multicoloured	25	20
2314	2st. multicoloured	25	20
2315	3st. multicoloured	25	20
2316	13st. multicoloured	80	35
2317	28st. multicoloured	1·40	75
2318	40st. multicoloured	3·25	2·20
2313/2318	Set of 6	5·50	3·50
MS2319	66×78 mm. 1l. multicoloured (55×30 *mm*)	5·50	4·25

No. **MS**2319 also exists imperforate from a restricted printing.

(Des A. Stareishinski. Photo)

1974 (25 Apr). Festival of Amateur Arts and Fourth Republican Sports Day. T **713** and similar vert designs. Multicoloured. P 13.
2320	1st. Type **713**	25	20
2321	2st. Folk-dancers	25	20
2322	3st. Piper and drummer	25	20
2323	5st. Wrestling	30	25
2324	13st. Athletics	1·60	1·50
2325	18st. Gymnastics	1·10	75
2320/2325	Set of 6	3·50	2·75

714 Cosmic Research (Penko Bambov)   **715** Motor cars

(Des St. Kunchev. Photo German Bank Note Ptg Co, Leipzig)

1974 (20 May). Mladost '74 Youth Stamp Exhibition, Sofia. T **714** and similar square designs. Multicoloured. P 13.
2326	1st. Type **714**	25	20
2327	2st. Salt Production (Mariana Bliznakova)	25	20
2328	3st. Fire-dancer (Detelina Lalova)	25	20
2329	28st. Friendship (Vanya Boyanova)	3·75	3·25
2326/2329	Set of 4	4·00	3·50
MS2330	70×70 mm. 60st. Spring (Vladimir Kunchev) (40×40 *mm*)	4·75	4·25

A further miniature sheet, face value 80st. showing a Horseman, was issued on 23 May in a restricted printing.

(Des St. Kunchev. Photo)

1974 (25 May). World Automobile Federation's Spring Congress, Sofia. P 13.
2331	**715**	13st. multicoloured	95	60

716 Period Architecture

(Des St. Kunchev. Photo)

1974 (20 June). United Nations Educational, Scientific and Cultural Organisation's Executive Council's 94th Session, Varna. P 13.
2332	**716**	18st. multicoloured	95	60

717 Chinese Aster   **718** 19th-Century Postboy

BULGARIA 1974

(Des M. Yoich. Photo)

1974 (22 June). Bulgarian Flowers. T **717** and similar horiz designs. Multicoloured. P 13.

2333	1st. Type **717**	25	20
2334	2st. Mallow	25	20
2335	3st. Columbine	25	20
2336	18st. Tulip	1·40	35
2337	20st. Marigold	1·60	45
2338	28st. Pansy	3·75	2·50
2333/2338	*Set of 6*	6·75	3·50
MS2339	80×60 mm. 80st. Gaillarde (44×33 *mm*)	4·75	4·25

(Des K. Kunev and P. Rashkov. Photo)

1974 (5 Aug). Centenary of the Universal Postal Union. T **718** and similar horiz designs. P 13½×13.

2340	2st. violet and pale yellow-orange	25	20
2341	18st. dull yellowish green and pale yellow-orange	1·40	60
MS2342	80×58 mm. 28st. pale turquoise-blue and pale yellow-orange (*sold at* 80st.)	4·00	3·50

Designs: 2st. T **718**; 18st. 19th-century mail coach; 28st. UPU emblem.

No. **MS**2342 also exists imperforate from a restricted printing.

719 Young Pioneer and Komsomol Girl

720 Communist Soldiers with Flag

(Des M. Konstantinova. Photo)

1974 (12 Aug). 30th Anniversary of Dimitrov Septembrist Pioneers Organisation. T **719** and similar vert designs. Multicoloured. P 13.

2343	1st. Type **719**	25	20
2344	2st. Pioneer with Doves	25	20
MS2345	60×84 mm. 60st. Emblem with portrait of Dimitrov (34×44 *mm*)	3·50	3·00

(Des P. Rashkov. Photo)

1974 (29 Aug). 30th Anniversary of Fatherland Front Government. T **720** and similar vert designs. Multicoloured. P 13.

2346	1st. Type **720**	25	20
2347	2st. Soviet Liberators	25	20
2348	5st. Industrialisation	30	25
2349	13st. Modern Agriculture	80	35
2350	18st. Science and Technology	1·50	85
2346/2350	*Set of 5*	2·75	1·70

721 Stockholm and Emblems

722 Gymnast on Beam

(Des St. Kunchev. Photo)

1974 (18 Sept). Stockholmia '74 International Stamp Exhibition. Sheet 65×72 mm. P 13.

MS2351	**721** 40st. bright blue, emerald and bistre-yellow	7·50	7·50

(Des L. Chekhlarov. Photo)

1974 (19 Oct). 18th World Gymnastics Championships, Varna. T **722** and similar vert design. Multicoloured. P 13.

2352	2st. Type **722**	25	20
2353	13st. Gymnast on horse	95	75

723 Doves on Script

724 Envelope with Arrow pointing to Postal Code

(Des St. Kunchev. Photo)

1974 (29 Oct). European Security and Co-operation Conference. Sheet 97×117 mm containing T **723** and similar vert designs. P 13×13½.

MS2354 13st. chrome-yellow, blue and chestnut (Type **723**); 13st. blue, mauve and chestnut (Map of Europe and script); 13st. emerald, light blue and chestnut (Leaves on script); 13st. multicoloured (Commemorative text) (*sold at* 60st.) .... 3·50 3·50

No. **MS**2354 also exists imperforate from a restricted printing.

A restricted issue of No. **MS**2354 with each stamp overprinted 'EUROPA' appeared in 1979.

(Des K. Kunev. Photo)

1974 (20 Nov). Introduction of the Postal Coding System (1975). P 13.

2355	**724**	2st. yellowish green, yellow and black	25	20

725 Sourovachka (twig decorated with coloured ribbons)

726 Icon of St Theodor Stratilat

(Des St. Kunchev. Photo)

1974 (5 Dec). New Year. P 13.

2356	**725**	2st. multicoloured	25	20

(Des M. Peikova and G. Kovachev. Photo)

1974 (28 Dec). Bulgarian History. T **726** and similar vert designs. P 13.

2357	1st. multicoloured	25	20
2358	2st. bluish grey, mauve and black	25	20
2359	3st. grey, pale greenish blue and black	25	20
2360	5st. grey, slate-lilac and black	30	25
2361	8st. black, gold and vermilion	35	30
2362	13st. grey, bright green and black	70	35
2363	18st. black, gold and vermilion	1·10	45
2364	28st. grey, bright blue and black	2·75	1·50
2357/2364	*Set of 8*	5·25	3·00

Designs: 1st. T **726**; 2st. Bronze medallion; 3st. Carved capital; 5st. Silver bowl of Sivin Jupan: 8st. Clay goblet; 13st. Lioness (torso); 18st. Gold tray; 28st. Double-headed Eagle.

727 Apricot

728 Peasant with Flag

(Des L. Chekhlarov. Photo)

1975 (3 Feb). Fruit Tree Blossoms. T **727** and similar vert designs. Multicoloured. P 13.

2365	1st. Type **727**	25	20

1975 BULGARIA

2366	2st. Apple	25	20
2367	3st. Cherry	25	20
2368	19st. Pear	95	30
2369	28st. Peach	2·30	75
2365/2369	Set of 5	3·50	1·50

(Des St. Kunchev and A. Stareishinski. Photo)

1975 (20 Feb). 75th Anniversary of Bulgarian People's Agrarian Union. Sheet 104×95 mm containing T **728** and similar vert designs. P 13.
MS2370 2st. reddish brown, bright orange and yellowish green; 5st. yellow-brown, bright orange and yellowish green; 13st. sepia, bright-orange and yellowish green; 18st. chestnut, bright orange and yellowish green .... 2·00 1·80
Designs: 2st. T **728**; 5st. Rebels keeping watch during 1923 September Uprising; 13st. Dancing; 18st. Woman harvesting fruit.

729 Spanish 6c. Stamp of 1850 and Espana Emblem

730 Star and Arrow

(Des St. Kunchev. Photo)

1975 (24 Feb). Espana 1975 International Stamp Exhibition, Madrid. Sheet 68×100 mm. P 13.
MS2371 **729** 40st. multicoloured .... 8·00 7·75

(Des P. Petrov. Photo)

1975 (20 Mar). 30th Anniversary of Victory in Europe Day. T **730** and similar vert designs. P 13.
2372	2st. rosine, black and gold	25	20
2373	13st. greenish blue, black and gold	1·10	45

Designs: 2st. T **730**; 13st. Peace Dove and broken sword.

731 Weights and Measures

732 Tree and Open Book

(Des P. Petrov. Photo)

1975 (21 Mar). Centenary of the Metre Convention. P 13×13½.
| 2374 | **731** | 13st. black, deep mauve and silver | 40 | 30 |

(Des P. Petrov. Photo)

1975 (25 Mar). 50th Anniversary of the Bulgarian Forestry School. P 13.
| 2375 | **732** | 2st. multicoloured | 25 | 20 |

733 Michelangelo

734 Festival Emblem

(Des A. Stareishinski. Photo)

1975 (28–31 Mar). 500th Birth Anniversary of Michelangelo. T **733** and similar designs. P 13.
2376	2st. brown-purple and deep grey-blue	25	20
2377	13st. chalky blue and deep mauve	80	45
2378	18st. sepia and deep green	1·60	85
2376/2378	Set of 3	2·40	1·40
MS2379 70×84 mm. **733** 2st. yellow-olive and red (sold at 60st.) (31.3.75)		2·75	2·50

Designs: Vert—2st. T **733**. Horiz (sculptures from Giuliano de Medici's tomb)—13st. *Night*; 18st. *Day*.

(Des St. Kunchev. Photo)

1975 (15 May). Festival of Humour and Satire, Gabrovo. P 13.
| 2380 | **734** | 2st. multicoloured | 25 | 20 |

735 Woman's Head and Emblem

736 Vasil and Sava Kokareshkov

(Des St. Kunchev. Photo)

1975 (20 May). International Women's Year. P 13.
| 2381 | **735** | 13st. multicoloured | 70 | 30 |

(Des G. Nedyalkov. Photo)

1975 (30 May). Young Martyrs to Fascism. T **736** and similar horiz designs. P 13½×13.
2382	1st. black, turquoise-green and gold	20	15
2383	2st. black, deep magenta and gold	20	15
2384	5st. black, rose-carmine and gold	25	20
2385	13st. black, bright blue and gold	80	55
2382/2385	Set of 4	1·30	95

Designs: 1st. T **736**; 2st. Mitko Palauzov and Ivan Vasilev; 5st. Nikola Nakev and Stefcho Kraichev; 13st. Ivanka Pashkulova and Detelina Mincheva.

737 Mother feeding Child (Jean Millet)

738 Gabrovo Costume

(Des St. Kunchev. Recess and photo State Ptg Wks, Moscow)

1975 (6 June). World Graphic Exhibition, Sofia. Celebrated Drawings and Engravings. T **737** and similar multicoloured designs. P 11½×12 (40st.) or 12×11½ (others).
2386	1st. Type **737**	25	20
2387	2st. *Mourning a dead Daughter* (Goya)	25	20
2388	3st. *The Reunion* (Iliya Beshkov)	25	20
2389	13st. *Seated Nude* (Auguste Renoir)	70	30
2390	20st. *Man in a Fur Hat* (Rembrandt)	95	75
2391	40st. *The Dream* (Honoré Daumier) (*horiz*)	2·75	1·60
2386/2391	Set of 6	4·75	3·00
MS2392 80×95 mm. 1l. *Temptation* (Albrecht Dürer) (37×53 mm)		5·00	4·25

(Des V. Vasileva. Photo)

1975 (30 June). Women's Regional Costumes. T **738** and similar vert designs. Multicoloured. P 13.
2393	2st. Type **738**	25	20
2394	3st. Trun costume	25	20
2395	5st. Vidin costume	30	25
2396	13st. Goce Delcev costume	1·00	50
2397	18st. Ruse costume	2·10	85
2393/2397	Set of 5	3·50	1·80

BULGARIA 1975

739 Bird (manuscript illumination)   **740** Ivan Vazov

(Des K. Kunev. Litho State Ptg Wks, Moscow)

1975 (8 July). Original Bulgarian Manuscripts. Decorated Lettering. T **739** and similar square designs. Multicoloured. P 11.

2398	1st. Type **739**	25	20
2399	2st. Head	25	20
2400	3st. Abstract design	25	20
2401	8st. Pointing finger	45	30
2402	13st. Imaginary creature	85	45
2403	18st. Abstract design	1·90	60
2398/2403 Set of 6		3·50	1·80

(Des G. Nedyalkov. Photo)

1975 (9 July). 125th Birth Anniversary of Ivan Vazov (writer). T **740** and similar vert design. Multicoloured. P 13.

2404	2st. Type **740**	25	20
2405	13st. Vazov seated	80	30

741 Soyuz and Aleksei Leonov   **742** Ryukyu Sailing Boat, Map and Emblems

(Des St. Kunchev and A. Stareishinski. Photo)

1975 (15 July). Apollo–Soyuz Space Link. T **741** and similar horiz designs. P 13.

2406	13st. bright blue, pale brownish grey and deep rose-red	70	35
2407	18st. bluish violet, pale brownish grey and deep rose-red	1·20	45
2408	28st. dull ultramarine, pale brownish grey and deep rose-red	2·50	85
2406/2408 Set of 3		4·00	1·50
MS2409 76×84 mm. 1l. deep ultramarine, pale, brownish grey and deep rose-red		5·50	4·25

Designs: 13st. T **741**; 18st. Apollo and Thomas Stafford; 28st. The Link-up; 1l. Apollo and Soyuz after docking procedure.

(Des St. Kunchev. Photo)

1975 (5 Aug). International Exposition, Okinawa. P 13.

2410	**742** 13st. multicoloured	70	30

743 St Cyril and St Methodius   **744** Footballer

(Des St. Kunchev. Photo)

1975 (21 Aug). Balkanphila V. Stamp Exhibition, Sofia. T **743** and similar designs. P 13.

2411	2st. blackish brown, stone and red	25	20
2412	13st. blackish brown, stone and deep green	80	35
MS2413 90×86 mm. 50st. sepia, orange-brown and reddish orange		2·75	2·50

Designs: Vert—2st. T **743**; 13st. St Constantine and St Helene; Horiz—50st. Sophia Church, Sofia (53×43 *mm*).

(Des Kh. Khristov. Photo)

1975 (21 Sept). 8th Inter-Toto (Football Pools) Congress, Varna. P 13.

2414	**744** 2st. multicoloured	25	20

745 Death's-head Hawk Moth (*Acherontia atropos*)   **746** UN Emblem

(Des A. Stareishinski. Photo)

1975 (23 Oct). Hawk Moths. T **745** and similar horiz designs. Multicoloured. P 13.

2415	1st. Type **745**	25	20
2416	2st. Oleander Hawk Moth (*Daphnis nerii*)	25	20
2417	3st. Eyed Hawk Moth (*Smerinthus ocellata*)	25	20
2418	10st. Mediterranean Hawk Moth (*Deilephila nicea*)	80	30
2419	13st. Elephant Hawk Moth (*Choerocampa elpenor*)	1·40	60
2420	18st. Broad-bordered Bee Hawk Moth (*Macroglossum fuciformis*)	2·50	1·00
2415/2420 Set of 6		5·00	2·30

(Des B. Ikonomov. Photo)

1975 (24 Oct). 30th Anniversary of the United Nations Organisation. P 13.

2421	**746** 13st. deep carmine, stone and black	70	30

747 Map of Europe on Peace Dove   **748** D. Khristov

(Des St. Kunchev. Photo)

1975 (29 Oct). European Security and Co-operation Conference, Helsinki. P 13.

2422	**747** 18st. rose-lilac, ultramarine and greenish yellow	1·10	95

The stamp was issued in sheets of five, with four *se-tenant* labels.

(Des A. Stareishinski. Photo)

1975 (11 Nov). Birth Centenary of Dobri Khristov (composer). P 13.

2423	**748** 5st. red-brown, greenish yellow and emerald	25	20

749 Constantine's Rebellion against the Turks

(Des B. Stoev. Photo)

1975 (27 Nov). Bulgarian History. T **749** and similar horiz designs. Multicoloured. P 13.

2424	1st. Type **749**	25	20
2425	2st. Vladislav III's campaign	25	20
2426	3st. Battle of Turnovo	25	20
2427	10st. Battle of Chiprovtsi	40	30
2428	13st. 17th-century partisans	1·10	45
2429	18st. Return of banished peasants	1·50	75
2424/2429 Set of 6		3·50	1·90

1975 **BULGARIA**

750 First Aid

(Des N. Kovachev. Photo)

1975 (5 Dec). 90th Anniversary of the Bulgarian Red Cross. T **750** and similar horiz design. P 13×13½.
2430	2st. Venetian red, black and scarlet		20	15
2431	13st. deep turquoise-green, black and scarlet		95	30

Designs: 2st. T **750**; 13st. Peace and International Co-operation.

751 Ethnographical Museum, Plovdiv

(Des St. Kunchev. Photo)

1975 (17 Dec). European Architectural Heritage Year. P 13.
2432	**751**	80st. purple-brown, chrome-yellow and bronze-green	3·00	3·00

The stamp was issued in sheets of three, with three *se-tenant* labels.

752 Christmas Lanterns   **753** Egyptian Galley

(Des St. Kunchev. Photo)

1975 (22 Dec). Christmas and New Year. T **752** and similar horiz design. Multicoloured. P 13.
2433	2st. Type **752**		25	15
2434	13st. Stylised Peace Dove		70	45

(Des St. Kunchev. Photo German Bank Note Ptg Co, Leipzig)

1975 (25 Dec). Historic Ships (1st series). T **753** and similar square designs. Multicoloured. P 13.
2435	1st. Type **753**		20	15
2436	2st. Phoenician galley		20	15
2437	3st. Greek trireme		20	15
2438	5st. Roman galley		25	20
2439	13st. *Mora* (Norman ship), 1066		80	45
2440	18st. Venetian galley		1·60	75
2435/2440 Set of 6			3·00	1·70

See also Nos. 2597/2602, 2864/2869, 3286/3291 and 3372/3377.

754 Modern Articulated Tramcar

(Des I. Bogdanov. Photo)

1976 (12 Jan). 75th Anniversary of the Sofia Tramways. T **754** and similar horiz design. Multicoloured. P 13½×13.
2441	2st. Type **754**		25	20
2442	13st. Early 20th-century tramcar		1·20	45

755 Skiing

(Des A. Stareishinski. Photo)

1976 (30 Jan). Winter Olympic Games, Innsbruck. T **755** and similar multicoloured designs. P 13.
2443	1st. Type **755**		25	20
2444	2st. Cross-country skiing (*vert*)		25	20
2445	3st. Ski jumping		25	20
2446	13st. Biathlon (*vert*)		65	40
2447	18st. Ice hockey (*vert*)		70	45
2448	23st. Speed skating (*vert*)		2·30	75
2443/2448 Set of 6			4·00	2·00
MS2449 70×80 mm. 80st. Ice skating (pairs) (30×55 mm)			4·50	3·75

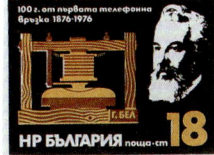

756 Stylised Bird   **757** Alexander Graham Bell and early Telephone

(Des A. Stareishinski. Photo)

1976 (1 Mar). 11th Bulgarian Communist Party Congress. T **756** and similar vert designs. Multicoloured. P 13.
2450	2st. Type **756**		20	15
2451	5st. '1956–1976, Fulfilment of the Five Year Plans'		25	20
2452	13st. Hammer and Sickle		70	35
2450/2452 Set of 3			1·00	65
MS2453 55×65 mm. 50st. Georgi Dimitrov (Prime Minister and Party secretary-general, 1945–1949) (33×43 mm)			2·50	2·20

(Des N. Kovachev. Photo)

1976 (10 Mar). Telephone Centenary. P 13.
2454	**757**	18st. brown-ochre, yellow-brown and deep purple-brown	95	45

758 Mute Swan (*Cygnus olor*)

(Des L. Chekhlarov. Photo State Ptg Works, Moscow)

1976 (27 Mar). Water-fowl. T **758** and similar horiz designs. Multicoloured. P 11½×12.
2455	1st. Type **758**		25	20
2456	2st. Ruddy Shelduck (*Tadorna ferruginea*)		30	25
2457	3st. Common Shelduck (*Tadorna tadorna*)		35	30
2458	5st. Garganey (*Anas querquedula*)		1·50	45
2459	13st. Mallard (*Anas platyrhynchas*)		2·00	1·20
2460	18st. Red-crested Pochard (*Netta rufina*)		5·50	3·75
2455/2460 Set of 6			9·00	5·50

759 Guerrillas' Briefing   **760** Kozlodui Atomic Energy Centre

BULGARIA 1976

(Des B. Stoev. Photo)

1976 (5 Apr). Centenary of April Uprising (1st issue). T **759** and similar horiz designs. Multicoloured. P 13.

2461	1st. Type **759**	15	15
2462	2st. Peasants briefing	15	15
2463	5st. Krishina, Horse and guard	25	20
2464	13st. Rebels with cannon	80	45
2461/2464 Set of 4		1·20	85

See also Nos. 2529/**MS**2534.

(Des J. Minchev. Photo)

1976 (7 Apr). Five Year Plan. Modern Industrial Installations. T **760** and similar vert designs. P 13.

2465	5st. dull blue-green	35	20
2466	8st. lake	40	30
2467	10st. myrtle green	70	35
2468	13st. bluish violet	90	40
2469	20st. emerald	1·10	45
2465/2469 Set of 5		3·00	1·50

Designs: 5st. T **760**; 8st. Bobovdol plant; 10st. Sviloza chemical works; 13st. Devnya chemical works; 20st. Sestrimo dam.

761 Guard with Patrol-dog **762** Worker with Spade

(Des P. Ferdzhanov. Photo)

1976 (15 May). 30th Anniversary of Frontier Guards. T **761** and similar horiz design. Multicoloured. P 13.

2470	2st. Type **761**	25	20
2471	13st. Mounted guards	70	35

(Des P. Ferdzhanov. Photo)

1976 (20 May). 30th Anniversary of Youth Brigades Movement. P 13.
2472   **762**   2st. multicoloured   25   20

763 Botev **764** Martyrs of First Congress (relief)

(Des St. Kunchev and A. Stareishinski. Photo)

1976 (25 May). Death Centenary of Khristo Botev (poet). P 13.
2473   **763**   13st. bronze green and ochre   95   45

No. 2473 was issued with *se-tenant* label bearing a quotation from Botev's poetry.

(Des P. Petrov. Photo)

1976 (28 May). 85th Anniversary of First Bulgarian Social Democratic Party Congress, Buzludzha. T **764** and similar vert design. Multicoloured. P 13.

2474	2st. Type **764**	20	15
2475	5st. Modern memorial, Buzludzha Peak	25	20

765 Dimitur Blagoev **766** Thematic Stamps

(Des P. Petrov. Photo)

1976 (28 May). 120th Birth Anniversary of Dimitur Blagoev (founder of Bulgarian Social Democratic Party). P 13.
2476   **765**   13st. blue-black, dull vermilion and gold   95   45

(Des St. Kunchev. Photo)

1976 (5 June). 12th Bulgarian Philatelic Federation Congress. Sheet 73×103 mm. P 13.
MS2477   **766**   50st. multicoloured   4·50   3·75

767 Children Playing

(Des N. Stoyanov. Photo)

1976 (15 June). Child Welfare. T **767** and similar horiz designs, showing children at play. P 13.

2478	1st. multicoloured	20	15
2479	2st. multicoloured	25	20
2480	5st. multicoloured	30	10
2481	23st. multicoloured	1·40	75
2478/2481 Set of 4		1·90	1·30

Designs: 1st. T **767**; 2st. Girls with pram and boy on rocking horse; 5st. Playing ball; 23st. Dancing.

768 Wrestling **769** Belt Buckle, Vidin

(Des A. Stareishinski. Photo)

1976 (25 June). Olympic Games, Montreal. T **768** and similar multicoloured designs. P 13.

2482	1st. Type **768**	20	15
2483	2st. Boxing (*vert*)	25	20
2484	3st. Weightlifting (*vert*)	30	25
2485	13st. Canoeing (*vert*)	70	35
2486	18st. Gymnastics (*vert*)	95	45
2487	28st. Diving (*vert*)	1·50	75
2488	40st. Athletics (*vert*)	2·00	1·50
2482/2488 Set of 7		5·25	3·25
MS2489 70×80 mm. 1l. Weightlifting (*vert*)		4·00	3·50

(Des St. Kunchev. Photo)

1976 (30 July). Thracian Art (8th/4th-centuries BC). T **769** and similar vert designs. Multicoloured. P 13.

2490	1st. Type **769**	20	15
2491	2st. Brooch, Durzhanitsa	20	15
2492	3st. Mirror handle, Chukarka	25	20
2493	5st. Helmet cheek guard, Gurlo	35	15
2494	13st. Gold decoration, Orizovo	70	30
2495	18st. Decorated horse-harness, Brezovo	95	35
2496	20st. Greave, Mogilanska Mogila	1·20	45
2497	28st. Pendant, Bukovtsi	1·40	75
2490/2497 Set of 8		4·75	2·30

770 Partisans at Night (Petrov)

(Des K. Kunev. Photo German Bank Note Ptg Co, Leipzig)

1976 (11 Aug). Paintings by Iliya Petrov and Tsanko Lavrenov from the National Gallery. T **770** and similar multicoloured designs. P 14.
2498   2st. Type **770**   25   20

2499	5st. *Kurshum-Khan* (Lavrenov)............................		30	25
2500	13st. *Seated Woman* (Petrov) (*vert*).................		70	35
2501	18st. *Boy seated in Chair* (Petrov) (*vert*)..........		1·40	45
2502	28st. *Old Plovdiv* (Lavrenov) (*vert*)..................		1·60	60
2498/2502 Set of 5			3·75	1·70
MS2503 60×82 mm. 80st. *Self-portrait* (Petrov) (*vert*)...			3·50	3·25

771 Weightlifting   772 Fish on Line

(Des St. Kunchev. Photo)

1976 (6 Sept). Gold Medal Winners, Montreal Olympic Games. Sheet 98×116 mm, containing vert designs as T **771**, each with medal in brown-red and gold. P 13.

MS2504 25st. yellow (Type **771**); 25st. new blue (Rowing); 25st. emerald (Running); 25st. scarlet (Wrestling).. 4·00   3·75

(Des P. Petrov. Photo)

1976 (21 Sept). World Sports Fishing Congress, Varna. P 13.

2505   **772**   5st. multicoloured.. 40   35

773 The Pianist   774 St Theodor

(Des Y. Petrov. Photo)

1976 (30 Sept). 75th Birth Anniversary of A. Zhendov (caricaturist). P 13×13½.

2506	2st. bottle green, pale cinnamon and blue-green..	15	15
2507	5st. deep violet, pale lilac and bright violet....	35	20
2508	13st. black, rose and deep claret......................	70	35
2506/2508 Set of 3		1·10	65

Designs: 2st. T **773**; 5st. *Trick or Treat*; 13st. *The Leader*.

(Des St. Kunchev. Litho State Ptg Works, Moscow)

1976 (4 Oct). Zemen Monastery. Frescoes. T **774** and similar vert designs. Multicoloured. P 12×12½.

2509	2st. Type **774**	20	15
2510	3st. St Paul the Apostle...................................	25	20
2511	5st. St Joachim..	40	25
2512	13st. Prophet Melchisadek................................	80	30
2513	19st. St Porphyrius...	1·10	35
2514	28st. Queen Doya..	1·40	45
2509/2514 Set of 6		3·75	1·50
MS2515 60×76 mm. 1l. *Holy Communion*		4·00	3·75

775 Legal Document   776 Horse Chestnut (*Aesculus hippocastanum*)

(Des S. Kamenov. Photo)

1976 (5 Oct). 25th Anniversary of State Archives. P 13.

2516   **775**   5st. black, lake-brown and new blue ...   40   35

(Des V. Vasileva. Photo)

1976 (14 Oct). Plants. T **776** and similar vert designs. Multicoloured. P 13.

2517	1st. Type **776**	20	15
2518	2st. Shrubby Cinquefoil (*Potentilla fruticosa*)	25	20
2519	5st. Holly (*Ilex aquifolium*)..............................	35	25
2520	8st. Yew (*Taxus baccata*).................................	40	35
2521	13st. *Daphne pontica*.......................................	70	45
2522	23st. Judas Tree (*Cercis siliquastrum*)	1·80	1·50
2517/2522 Set of 6		3·25	2·50

777 Cloud over Sun   778 Dimitur Polyanov

(Des A. Stareishinski. Photo)

1976 (10 Nov). Protection of the Environment. T **777** and similar horiz design. Multicoloured. P 13.

2523	2st. Cloud over tree.......................................	25	20
2524	18st. Type **777**	95	45

(Des N. Kovachev. Photo)

1976 (19 Nov). Birth Centenary of Dimitur Polyanov (poet). P 13.

2525   **778**   2st. deep reddish lilac and pale orange   25   20

 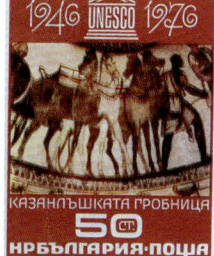

779 Congress Emblem   780 Warrior with Horses (vase painting)

(Des Y. Petrov. Photo)

1976 (28 Nov). 33rd Bulgarian People's Agrarian Union Congress. T **779** and similar vert design. Multicoloured. P 13.

2526	2st. Type **779**	25	20
2527	13st. Flags..	80	30

(Des St. Kunchev. Photo)

1976 (3 Dec). 30th Anniversary of United Nations Educational, Scientific and Cultural Organisation. Sheet 71×81 mm. P 13.

MS2528   **780**   50st. multicoloured..   3·50   3·25

781 Khristo Botev (Zlatyu Boyadzhiev)   782 Tobacco Workers

(Des V. Vasileva. Photo German Bank Note Ptg Co, Leipzig)

1976 (8 Dec). Centenary of April Uprising (2nd issue). T **781** and similar square designs. Multicoloured. P 13.

2529	1st. Type **781**	20	15
2530	2st. *Partisan carrying Cherrywood Cannon* (Iliya Petrov)	25	20

BULGARIA 1976

2531	3st. *Necklace of Immortality* (Dechko Uznunov)		30	25
2532	13st. *April 1876* (Georgi Popov)		55	35
2533	18st. *Partisans* (Stoyan Venev)		1·00	45
2529/2533 Set of 5			2·00	1·30
MS2534 45×82 mm. 60st. *The Oath* (Svetlin Rusev). Imperf			2·75	2·75

(Des St. Kunchev. Photo)

1976 (16 Dec). 70th Birth Anniversary of Veselin Staikov (artist). T **782** and similar horiz designs. Multicoloured. P 13.

2535	1st. Type **782**	15	15
2536	2st. *Melnik*	20	15
2537	13st. *Boat Builders*	70	40
2535/2537 Set of 3		95	65

783 Snowflake

784 Zakhari Stoyanov

(Des St. Kunchev. Photo)

1976 (20 Dec). New Year. P 13.
| 2538 | **783** | 2st. multicoloured | 30 | 15 |

(Des St. Kunchev. Photo)

1976 (30 Dec). 125th Birth Anniversary of Zakhari Stoyanov (writer). P 13.
| 2539 | **784** | 2st. reddish brown, brown-red and gold | 30 | 15 |

785 Bronze Coin of Septimus Severus

(Des Kh. Khristov. Photo)

1977 (28 Jan). Coins Struck in Serdica. T **785** and similar horiz designs. Multicoloured. P 14.

2540	1st. Type **785**	20	15
2541	2st. Bronze coin of Caracalla	25	20
2542	13st. Bronze coin of Caracalla (*different*)	40	40
2543	18st. Bronze coin of Caracalla (*different*)	85	45
2544	23st. Copper coin of Diocletian	1·40	75
2540/2544 Set of 5		2·75	1·80

786 Championships Emblem

787 Congress Emblem

(Des S. Kamenov. Photo)

1977 (14 Feb). World Ski-Orienteering Championships. P 13.
| 2545 | **786** | 13st. pale blue, orange-vermilion and ultramarine | 85 | 40 |

(Des S. Kamenov. Photo)

1977 (24 Feb). Fifth Congress of Bulgarian Tourist Associations. P 13.
| 2546 | **787** | 2st. multicoloured | 30 | 15 |

788 Symphyandra wanneri

789 V. Kolarov

(Des L. Chekhlarov. Photo)

1977 (2 Mar). Mountain Flowers. T **788** and similar vert designs. Multicoloured. P 13.

2547	1st. Type **788**	20	15
2548	2st. *Petcovia orphanidea*	25	20
2549	3st. *Campanula lanata*	30	20
2550	13st. *Campanula scutellata*	85	45
2551	43st. Nettle-leaved Bellflower (*Campanula trachelium*)	2·75	1·50
2547/2551 Set of 5		4·00	2·30

(Des N. Kovachev. Photo)

1977 (21 Mar). Birth Centenary of Vasil Kolarov (Prime Minister 1949–1950). P 13.
| 2552 | **789** | 2st. pale grey, black and new blue | 25 | 20 |

790 Congress Emblem

791 Joint

(Des S. Kamenov. Photo)

1977 (25 Mar). Eighth Bulgarian Trade Unions Congress. P 13.
| 2553 | **790** | 2st. multicoloured | 25 | 20 |

(Des L. Chekhlarov. Photo)

1977 (31 Mar). World Rheumatism Year. P 13.
| 2554 | **791** | 23st. multicoloured | 1·40 | 75 |

792 Wrestling

(Des V. Vasileva. Photo)

1977 (15 Apr). World University Games, Sofia (1st issue). T **792** and similar horiz designs. Multicoloured. P 13.

2555	2st. Type **792**	25	20
2556	13st. Running	70	40
2557	23st. Handball	1·30	60
2558	43st. Gymnastics	2·10	1·20
2555/2558 Set of 4		4·00	2·20

See also No. **MS**2591.

793 Ivan Vazov National Theatre

794 Congress Emblem

1977 BULGARIA

(Des Yu. Minchev. Photo)

1977 (30 Apr). Buildings in Sofia. T **793** and similar horiz designs. P 13.

2559	12st. brown-red/*pale grey-brown*	55	30
2560	13st. chestnut/*pale grey-brown*	70	40
2561	23st. deep turquoise-blue/*pale grey-brown*	1·10	45
2562	30st. deep green/*pale grey-brown*	1·70	60
2563	80st. violet/*pale grey-brown*	2·75	1·70
2564	1l. red-brown/*pale grey-brown*	3·75	2·10
2559/2564	Set of 6	9·50	5·00

Designs: 12st. T **793**; 13st. Party Building; 23st. People's Army Building; 30st. Clement of Ohrid University; 80st. National Art Gallery; 1l. National Assembly Building.

(Des B. Yonov. Photo)

1977 (9 May). 13th Dimitrov Communist Youth League Congress. P 13.

2565	**794**	2st. bright scarlet, bright green and gold	25	20

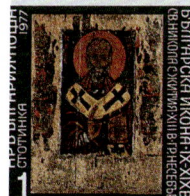

795 St Nicholas, Nesebur

(Des St. Kunchev. Photo German Bank Note Ptg Co, Leipzig)

1977 (10 May). Bulgarian Icons. T **795** and similar square designs. Multicoloured. P 13.

2566	1st. Type **795**	20	15
2567	2st. Old Testament Trinity, Sofia	25	20
2568	3st. The Royal Gates, Veliko Turnovo	30	25
2569	5st. Deisis, Nesebur	40	30
2570	13st. St Nicholas, Elena	70	40
2571	23st. The Presentation of the Blessed Virgin, Rila Monastery	1·10	45
2572	35st. The Virgin Mary with Infant, Varna	1·70	1·10
2573	40st. St Demetrius on Horseback, Provadiya	3·75	1·50
2566/2573	Set of 8	7·50	4·00
MS2574	100×99 mm. 1l. The 12 Festival Days, Rila Monastery. Imperf	5·75	4·50

796 Wolf (*Canis lupus*)

(Des A. Stareiskinski. Litho State Ptg Wks, Moscow)

1977 (16 May). Wild Animals. T **796** and similar horiz designs. Multicoloured. P 12.

2575	1st. Type **796**	20	15
2576	2st. Red Fox (*Vulpes vulpes*)	25	20
2577	10st. Weasel (*Mustela nivalis*)	70	40
2578	13st. Wild Cat (*Felis silvestris*)	1·00	75
2579	23st. Golden Jackal (*Canis aureus*)	2·75	1·50
2575/2579	Set of 5	4·50	2·75

797 Congress Emblem

798 Crafty Peter riding a Donkey (drawing by Iliya Beshkov)

(Des D. Tasev. Photo)

1977 (17 May). Third Bulgarian Culture Congress. P 13.

2580	**797**	13st. multicoloured	70	45

(Des St. Kunchev. Photo)

1977 (19 May). 11th Festival of Humour and Satire, Gabrovo. P 13.

2581	**798**	2st. multicoloured	25	20

799 Congress Emblem

800 Newspaper Masthead

(Des S. Kamenov. Photo)

1977 (26 May). 8th Congress of the Popular Front, Sofia. P 13.

2582	**799**	2st. multicoloured	25	20

(Des P. Petrov. Photo)

1977 (3 June). Centenary of Bulgarian Daily Press. P 13.

2583	**800**	2st. multicoloured	25	20

801 St Cyril

802 Conference Emblem

(Des B. Yonov. Photo)

1977 (7 June). 1150th Birth Anniversary of St Cyril. Sheet 106×87 mm. P 13.

MS2584	**801**	1l. multicoloured	5·00	4·50

(Des St. Kunchev. Photo)

1977 (7 June). International Writers Conference, Sofia. P 13.

2585	**802**	23st. new blue, light blue and pale yellow-green	2·10	1·50

Printed in sheets of eight stamps and four different labels.

803 Map of Europe

804 Basketball

(Des St. Kunchev. Photo)

1977 (10 June). 21st Congress of European Organisation for Quality Control, Varna. P 13.

2586	**803**	23st. multicoloured	1·40	60

(Des B. Ikonomov. Photo)

1977 (15 June). Women's European Basketball Championships. P 13.

2587	**804**	23st. multicoloured	1·40	75

BULGARIA 1977

805 Weightlifter

806 Georgi Dimitrov

(Des S. Nenov. Photo)

1977 (15 June). World Junior Weightlifting Championships, Sofia. P 13.
2588   805   13st. multicoloured 70   40

(Des St. Kunchev. Photo)

1977 (17 June). 95th Birth Anniversary of Georgi Dimitrov (statesman). P 13.
2589   806   13st. purple-brown and orange-vermilion .... 1·00   45

807 Tail Section of Tupolev Tu-154 Jetliner

808 Games Emblem

(Des St. Kunchev. Photo)

1977 (29 June). 30th Anniversary of Balkanair (Bulgarian Airline). P 13.
2590   807   35st. multicoloured .... 1·40   75

Issued in sheets of six stamps and three labels bearing Balkanair's emblem.

(Des St. Kunchev. Photo)

1977 (10 Aug). World University Games, Sofia (2nd issue). Sheet 84×76 mm. P 13.
MS2591   808   1l. multicoloured .... 4·25   3·75

809 TV Towers, Berlin and Sofia

810 Elin Pelin, *alias* Dimitur Stoyanov (writer)

(Des P. Petrov. Photo)

1977 (12 Aug). Sozphilex '77 Stamp Exhibition, East Berlin. P 13.
2592   809   25st. new blue and royal blue .... 1·40   75

(Des St. Kunchev and A. Stareishinski. Photo)

1977 (26 Aug). Writers and Painters. T **810** and similar vert designs. P 13.
2593   2st. reddish brown and gold 25   20
2594   5st. deep olive and gold 35   30
2595   13st. reddish purple and gold 55   40
2596   23st. ultramarine and gold .... 1·70   75
2593/2596 Set of 4 .... 2·50   1·50

Designs: 2st. T **810**; 5st. Peyu Yavorov (poet); 13st. Boris Angelushev (painter and illustrator); 23st. Tseno Todorov (painter).

Nos. 2593/2596 were each issued in sheets of eight stamps and eight labels depicting an illustration.

(Des St. Kunchev. Photo German Bank Note Ptg Co, Leipzig)

1977 (29 Aug). Historic Ships (2nd series). Square designs as T **753**. Multicoloured. P 13.
2597   1st. Hansa kogge 20   15
2598   2st. Caravelle *Santa Maria* 25   20
2599   3st. Drake's ship *Golden Hind* 30   25
2600   12st. Carrack *Santa Catherina* 50   40
2601   13st. Galleon *Corona* 55   45
2602   43st. Mediterranean galley .... 2·75   90
2597/2602 Set of 6 .... 4·00   2·10

811 Women Canoeists

(Des N. Kovachev. Photo)

1977 (1 Sept). World Canoe Championships, Sofia. T **811** and similar horiz design. P 13.
2603   2st. new blue and olive-yellow 25   20
2604   23st. ultramarine and turquoise-green .... 1·40   60

Designs: 2st. T **811**; 23st. Men canoeists.

812 Balloon over Plovdiv

813 Presidents Zhivkov and Brezhnev

(Des S. Kamenov. Photo)

1977 (3 Sept). AIR. 85th Anniversary of Panair International Aviation Exhibition, Plovdiv. P 13.
2605   812   25st. red-orange, yellow and reddish brown .... 1·40   75

(Des Kh. Khristov. Photo)

1977 (7 Sept). Soviet Bulgarian Friendship. P 13.
2606   813   18st. purple-brown, bright scarlet and gold 85   75

Issued in sheets of three stamps and three labels arranged chessboard fashion. Price is for stamp with label.

814 Conference Building

815 Newspaper Mastheads

(Des Kh. Khristov. Photo)

1977 (12 Sept). 64th International Parliamentary Conference, Sofia. P 13.
2607   814   23st. yellowish green, salmon-pink and rose-red ..... 1·40   60

(Des St. Kunchev. Photo)

1977 (12 Sept). 50th Anniversary of Official Newspaper *Rabotnichesko Delo* (Workers' Press). P 13.
2608   815   2st. bright rose-red, yellow-green and grey 25   20

816 *The Union of Earth and Water*

817 Cossack with Bulgarian Child (Angelushev)

(Des St. Kunchev. Litho State Ptg Wks, Moscow)

1977 (23 Sept). 400th Birth Anniversary of Rubens. T **816** and similar vert designs. Multicoloured. P 11½.
2609	13st. Type **816**	85	40
2610	23st. *Venus and Adonis* (detail)	1·70	1·50
2611	40st. *Amorous Shepherd* (detail)	3·50	2·40
2609/2611	Set of 3	5·50	3·75
MS2612	71×87 mm. 1l. *Portrait of a Chambermaid*	5·50	4·50

(Des L. Chekhlarov. Photo)

1977 (30 Sept). Centenary of Liberation from Turkey (1978) (1st issue). Posters. T **817** and similar vert designs. P 13.
2613	2st. multicoloured	25	20
2614	13st. green, dull ultramarine and carmine-vermilion	70	40
2615	23st. royal blue, red and green	1·30	55
2616	25st. multicoloured	1·40	60
2613/2616	Set of 4	3·25	1·60

Designs: 2st. T **817**; 13st. Bugler (Chekhlarov); 23st. Mars (god of war) and Russian soldiers (Petrov); 25st. Flag of Russian Imperial Army (Iliev). See also No. **MS**2636.

818 Albena, Black Sea

819 Dr. Nikolai Pirogov (Russian surgeon)

(Des L. Chekhlarov. Photo)

1977 (5 Oct). Tourism. T **818** and similar horiz design. P 13.
2617	35st. greenish blue, deep blue-green and reddish brown	1·60	75
	a. Pair. Nos. 2617/2618	3·75	1·70
2618	43st. pale yellow, deep green and royal blue	1·80	85

Designs: 35st. T **818**; 43st. Rila Monastery.
Nos. 2617/2618 were issued in sheets containing four of each design plus one centre label.

(Des N. Kovachev. Photo)

1977 (14 Oct). Centenary of Dr. Pirogov's Visit to Bulgaria. P 13.
2619	**819** 13st. brown, brown-ochre and olive-green	70	40

820 Space-walking

821 Soviet Emblems and Decree (D. Ivanov)

(Des T. Aleksieva and Zh. Aleksiev. Photo)

1977 (14 Oct). AIR. 20th Anniversary of First Artificial Satellite. T **820** and similar horiz designs. Multicoloured. P 13.
2620	12st. Type **820**	70	40
2621	25st. Space probe over Mars	1·40	60
2622	35st. Space probe *Venus 4* over Venus	2·10	75
2620/2622	Set of 3	3·75	1·60

(Des St. Kunchev. Photo)

1977 (21 Oct). 60th Anniversary of Russian Revolution. T **821** and similar vert designs showing posters. P 13.
2623	2st. bright rose-red, black and stone	25	20
2624	13st. dull vermilion and deep purple	85	45
2625	23st. dull vermilion and reddish violet	1·50	60
2623/2625	Set of 3	2·30	1·10

Designs: 2st. T **821**; 13st. Lenin (Kh. Belchev); 23st. '1977' as flame (St. Kunchev).

822 Diesel Train on Bridge

823 Petko Slaveikov

(Des B. Yonov. Photo)

1977 (9 Nov). 50th Anniversary of Transport, Bridges and Highways Organisation. P 13.
2626	**822** 13st. pale yellow, sage green and emerald	1·10	75

(Des St. Kunchev and A. Stareishinski. Photo)

1977 (15 Nov). Birth Anniversary of Petko Slaveikov (poet). P 13.
2627	**823** 8st. chocolate and gold	40	40

Issued in sheets of eight stamps and eight labels.

824 Decorative Initials of New Year Greeting

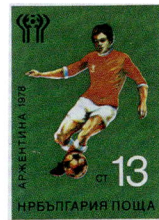

825 Footballer

(Des St. Kunchev. Photo)

1977 (1 Dec). New Year. T **824** and similar horiz design. Multicoloured. P 13.
2628	2st. Type **824**	25	20
2629	13st. Fireworks	70	40

(Des S. Nenov. Photo)

1978 (30 Jan). World Cup Football Championship, Argentina. T **825** and similar vert designs. Multicoloured. P 13.
2630	13st. Type **825**	70	45
2631	23st. Shooting the ball	2·10	1·20
MS2632	77×61 mm. 50st. Struggle for ball	3·50	3·00

826 Baba Vida Fortress, Vidin

827 Television Mast, Moscow

BULGARIA 1978

(Des St. Kunchev. Photo)

1978 (9 Feb). AIR. The Danube European River. T **826** and similar horiz design. Multicoloured. P 13.
2633	25st. Type **826**	1·30	1·10
2634	35st. Friendship Bridge	1·80	1·50

Issued in sheets containing five stamps of each value plus two labels, one showing a map of the Danube, the other a hydrofoil and fish.

(Des R. Serteva and A. Sertev. Photo)

1978 (1 Mar). 20th Anniversary of Organisation of Socialist Countries' Postal Administrations (OSS). P 13.
2635	**827**	13st. multicoloured	70 40

828 Shipka Monument

829 Red Cross in Laurel Wreath

(Des St. Kunchev. Photo)

1978 (3 Mar). Centenary of Liberation from Turkey (2nd issue). Sheet 55×73 mm. P 13.
MS2636	**828**	50st. multicoloured	2·10 1·80

(Des S. Nenov. Photo)

1978 (15 Mar). AIR. Centenary of Bulgarian Red Cross. P 13.
2637	**829**	25st. bright scarlet, brown-ochre and blue	1·40 75

830 'XXX' formed from Bulgarian and Russian National Colours

831 Leo Tolstoy (Russian writer)

(Des S. Kamenov. Photo)

1978 (18 Mar). 30th Anniversary of Bulgarian–Soviet Friendship. P 13.
2638	**830**	2st. multicoloured	25 20

(Des A. Stareishinski. Photo)

1978 (28 Mar). Famous Personalities. T **831** and similar vert designs. P 13.
2639		2st. olive-green and yellow	30 20
2640		5st. reddish brown and olive-bistre	35 30
2641		13st. deep bluish green and dull mauve	55 40
2642		23st. red-brown and brownish grey	65 40
2643		25st. blackish brown and sage green	70 45
2644		35st. violet and pale blue	2·10 75
2639/2644	Set of 6		4·25 2·30

Designs: 2st. T **831**; 5st. Fyodor Dostoevsky (Russian writer); 13st. Ivan Turgenev (Russian writer); 23st. Vassily Vereshchagin (Russian artist); 25st. Giuseppe Garibaldi (Italian patriot); 35st. Victor Hugo (French writer).

832 Nikolai Roerich (artist)

833 Bulgarian Flag and Red Star

(Des St. Kunchev. Photo)

1978 (5 Apr). Nikolai Roerich Exhibition, Sofia. P 13.
2645	**832**	8st. stone, grey-green and deep carmine	70 40

(Des B. Yonov. Photo)

1978 (18 Apr). Communist Party National Conference, Sofia. P 13.
2646	**833**	2st. multicoloured	25 20

834 Goddess

835 Spirit of Nature

(Des V. Vasileva. Photo)

1978 (26 Apr). Philaserdica 79 International Stamp Exhibition (1st issue). Ancient Ceramics. T **834** and similar horiz designs. Multicoloured. P 13.
2647		2st. Type **834**	25 20
2648		5st. Mask with beard	35 30
2649		13st. Decorated vase	70 40
2650		23st. Vase with scallop design	1·10 90
2651		35st. Head of Silenus	1·70 1·50
2652		53st. Cockerel	6·00 2·30
2647/2652	Set of 6		9·00 5·00

See also Nos. 2674/**MS**2679a, 2714/2719, 2721/2725, **MS**2752, 2753 and 2754.

(Des St. Kunchev. Photo)

1978 (29 Apr). Birth Centenary of Andrei Nikolov (sculptor). P 13.
2653	**835**	13st. grey-blue, mauve and reddish violet	70 40

836 Heart and Arrows

(Des Kh. Khristov. Photo)

1978 (12 May). World Hypertension Month. P 13.
2654	**836**	23st. orange-red, yellow-orange and brownish-grey	1·40 60

837 Kor Karoli and Map of Route

(Des St. Kunchev. Photo)

1978 (19 May). Georgi Georgiev's World Voyage. P 13.
2655	**837**	23st. new blue, magenta and emerald	2·75 1·20

838 Doves

(Des B. Yonov. Photo)

1978 (31 May). 11th World Youth and Students' Festival, Havana. P 13.
2656	**838**	13st. multicoloured	70 40

1978 BULGARIA

839 *Portrait of a Young Man* (Dürer)

840 *Fritillaria stribrnyi*

(Des St. Kunchev. Photo German Bank Note Ptg Co, Leipzig)

1978 (19 June). Paintings. T **839** and similar square designs. Multicoloured. P 13.

2657	13st. Type **839**	40	30
2658	23st. *Bathsheba at the Fountain* (Rubens)	70	40
2659	25st. *Signor de Moret* (Hans Holbein the Younger)	85	45
2660	35st. *Self Portrait with Saskia* (Rembrandt)	1·10	60
2661	43st. *Lady in Mourning* (Tintoretto)	1·40	75
2662	60st. *Old Man with a Beard* (Rembrandt)	1·80	1·10
2663	80st. *Man in Armour* (Van Dyck)	4·25	2·50
2657/2663	Set of 7	9·50	5·50

(Des T. Aleksieva and Zh. Aleksiev. Photo)

1978 (27 June). Flowers. T **840** and similar vert designs. Multicoloured. P 13.

2664	1st. Type **840**	20	15
2665	2st. *Fritillaria drenovskyi*	25	20
2666	3st. *Lilium rhodopaeum*	30	25
2667	13st. *Tulipa urumoffi*	70	40
2668	23st. *Lilium jankae*	85	45
2669	43st. *Tulipa rhodopaea*	2·75	1·50
2664/2669	Set of 6	4·50	2·75

841 Varna

(Des T. Momchilov. Photo)

1978 (13 July). 63rd Esperanto Congress, Varna. P 13.

2670	841	13st. orange, carmine and dull yellowish-green	1·10	60

842 Delçev

843 Freedom Fighters

(Des B. Stoev. Photo)

1978 (1 Aug). 75th Death Anniversary of Goce Delçev (Macedonian revolutionary). P 13.

2671	**842**	13st. multicoloured	85	40

(Des B. Stoev. Photo)

1978 (1 Aug). 75th Anniversary of Ilinden-Preobrazhenie Rising. P 13.

2672	**843**	5st. black and rose-red	40	30

844 *The Sleeping Venus* (Giorgione)

(Des St. Kunchev. Photo German Bank Note Ptg Co, Leipzig)

1978 (17 Aug). World Masters of Art. Sheet 71×71 mm. Imperf.

MS2673	**844**	1l. multicoloured	3·25	3·00

845 *Market* (Naiden Petkov)

846 Black Woodpecker (*Drycopus martius*)

(Des K. Kunev. Litho State Ptg Wks, Moscow)

1978 (28 Aug). Philaserdica 79 International Stamp Exhibition (2nd issue). Paintings of Sofia. T **845** and similar horiz designs. Multicoloured. P 12.

2674	2st. Type **845**	20	15
2675	5st. *View of Sofia* (Emil Stoichev)	30	30
2676	13st. *View of Sofia* (Boris Ivanov)	40	40
2677	23st. *Tolbukhin Boulevard* (Nikola Tanev)	1·00	45
2678	35st. *National Theatre* (Nikola Petrov)	1·20	60
2679	53st. *Market* (Anton Mitov)	1·40	1·50
2674/2679	Set of 6	4·00	3·00
MS2679a	186×106 mm. Nos. 2674/2679	9·00	8·75

(Des L. Chekhlarov. Photo)

1978 (1 Sept). Woodpeckers. T **846** and similar vert designs. Multicoloured. P 13.

2680	1st. Type **846**	20	15
2681	2st. Syrian Woodpecker (*Dendrocopos syriacus*)	25	20
2682	3st. Three-toed Woodpecker (*Picoides tridactylus*)	30	25
2683	13st. Middle spotted Woodpecker (*Dendrocopos medius*)	1·40	75
2684	23st. Lesser spotted Woodpecker (*Dendrocopos minor*)	2·10	1·10
2685	43st. Green Woodpecker (*Picus viridis*)	5·50	3·25
2680/2685	Set of 6	8·75	5·25

847 Ivan Vazov National Theatre, Sofia

848 Elka 55 Computer

BULGARIA 1978

(Des T. Aleksieva and Zh. Aleksiev. Recess and photo Postal Ptg Wks, Prague)

1978 (1 Sept). Praga 78 and Philaserdica 79 International Stamp Exhibitions. Sheet 153×110 mm, containing T **847** and similar horiz designs. Multicoloured. P 11½×11.
MS2686 (a) 40st. Type **847**; (b) 40st. Festival Hall, Sofia; (c) 40st. Charles Bridge, Prague; (d) 40st. Belvedere Palace, Prague.. 4·25   4·00

(Des B. Yotov. Photo)

1978 (3 Sept). Plovdiv International Fair. Fluorescent overprint of Philaserdica 79 emblems. P 13.
2687 **848** 2st. multicoloured........................ 25   20

849 *September 1923* (Boris Angelushev)   **850** *Khristo Danov*

(Des P. Petrov. Photo)

1978 (5 Sept). 55th Anniversary of September Uprising. P 13.
2688 **849** 2st. scarlet vermilion and brown-lake.. 25   20

(Des A. Stareishinski. Photo)

1978 (18 Sept). 150th Birth Anniversary of Khristo Danov (first Bulgarian publisher). P 13.
2689 **850** 2st. pale orange and lake....................... 70   45
Issued in sheets of ten stamps and ten labels depicting printing press. Price is for stamp plus label.

851 *The People of Vladaya* (Todor Panaiotov)   **852** *Hands supporting Rainbow*

(Des St. Kunchev. Photo)

1978 (20 Sept). 60th Anniversary of Vladaya Mutiny. P 13.
2690 **851** 2st. pale lilac, reddish brown and light crimson 25   20

(Des V. Kitanov. Photo)

1978 (3 Oct). International Anti-Apartheid Year. P 13.
2691 **852** 13st. multicoloured 70   40

853 *Pipeline and Flags*   **854** *Acrobats*

(Des V. Kitanov. Photo)

1978 (3 Oct). Inauguration of Orenburg–USSR Natural Gas Pipeline. P 13.
2692 **853** 13st. multicoloured 70   40

(Des K. Gogov. Photo)

1978 (4 Oct). Third World Sports Acrobatics Championships, Sofia. P 13.
2693 **854** 13st. multicoloured 70   40

855 *Salvador Allende*   **856** *Human Rights Emblem*

(Des St. Kunchev. Photo)

1978 (11 Oct). 70th Birth Anniversary of Salvador Allende (Chilean politician). P 13.
2694 **855** 13st. deep brown and vermilion............... 70   40

(Des St. Kunchev. Photo)

1978 (18 Oct). 30th Anniversary of Declaration of Human Rights.
2695 **856** 23st. greenish yellow, vermilion and deep ultramarine .... 1·40   75

857 *Levski and Matei Mitkaloto* (Kalina Taseva)   **858** *Tourist Home, Plovdiv*

(Des N. Kovachev. Litho State Ptg Wks, Moscow)

1978 (25 Oct). History of Bulgaria. Paintings. T **857** and similar designs. Multicoloured. P 12.
2696   1st. Type **857** 20   15
2697   2st. *Give Strength to my Arm* (Zlatyu Boyadzhiev).. 25   20
2698   3st. *Rumena Voevoda* (Nikola Mirchev) (horiz)... 30   25
2699   13st. *Kolyu Ficheto* (Elza Goeva).................... 70   40
2700   23st. *A Family of the National Revival Period* (Naiden Petkov) .... 1·50   90
2696/2700 Set of 5 .... 2·75 1·70

(Des St. Kunchev. Photo)

1978 (1 Nov). European Architectural Heritage. T **858** and similar vert design. Multicoloured. P 13.
2701   43st. Type **858** .... 1·50   75
          a. Pair. Nos. 2701/2702 .... 3·50 1·80
2702   43st. Tower of the Prince, Rila Monastery....... 1·70   90
Nos. 2701/2702 were issued in small sheets containing three of No. 2701, two of No. 2702 and one label bearing a decorative motif.

859 *Geroi Plevny* and Route Map   **860** *Mosaic Bird* (Santa Sofia Church)

(Des V. Petrov. Photo)

1978 (1 Nov). Opening of Varna–Ilichovsk Ferry Service. P 13.
2703 **859** 13st. bright violet-blue, dull scarlet and yellow-green 70   40
Stamps of a similar design were issued by Russia.

(Des St. Kunchev. Photo)

1978 (20 Nov). Bulgaria 78 National Stamp Exhibition, Sofia. P 13.
2704 **860** 5st. multicoloured 55   45
Issued in sheets of eight stamps and eight labels bearing the exhibition emblem.

1978 BULGARIA

861 Monument to St Clement of Ohrid (university patron) (Lyubomir Dalchev)

862 Nikola Karastoyanov

(Des A. Sertev. Photo)
1978 (8 Dec). 90th Anniversary of Sofia University. P 13.
2705   861   2st. slate-lilac, black and yellow-olive ..   25   20

(Des K. Kunev and V. Konovalov. Photo)
1978 (12 Dec). 200th Birth Anniversary of Nikola Karastoyanov (first Bulgarian printer). P 13.
2706   862   2st. brown, pale stone and chestnut....   55   40
Issued in sheets of eight stamps and eight labels depicting a printing press. Price is for stamp with label.

863 Initial from 13th-century Bible Manuscript

864 Ballet Dancers

(Des Kh. Khristov. Photo)
1978 (15 Dec). Centenary of Cyril and Methodius People's Library. T **863** and similar vert designs. Multicoloured. P 13½ (23st.) or 13 (others).
2707   2st. Type **863**   25   20
2708   13st. Monk writing (from a 1567 manuscript)..........................   70   40
2709   23st. Decorated page from 16th-century manuscript Bible.....................   1·30   60
2707/2709 Set of 3 ....   2·00   1·10
MS2710 63×94 mm. 80st. Seated saint with attendant (from 13th-century manuscript Bible).......   2·75   2·50

(Des A. Sertev and R. Stanoeva. Photo)
1978 (22 Dec). 50th Anniversary of Bulgarian Ballet. P 13.
2711   864   13st. bronze-green, magenta and lavender.....................................   70   40

865 Tree of Birds

866 1961 Communist Congress Stamp

(Des St. Kunchev. Photo)
1978 (22 Dec). New Year. T **865** and similar horiz design. Multicoloured. P 13.
2712   2st. Type **865**   20   20
2713   13st. Posthorn   40   30

(Des St. Kunchev. Photo)
1978 (30 Dec). Philaserdica 79 International Stamp Exhibition (3rd issue) and Bulgarian Stamp Centenary (1st issue). T **866** and similar designs dated '1978'. P 13.
2714   2st. scarlet and yellowish green.................   20   20
2715   13st. claret and ultramarine   35   30
2716   23st. bronze-green and bright magenta   40   40
2717   35st. deep brownish grey and new blue ....   1·40   60
2718   53st. deep dull green and rosine ....   2·10   90
2714/2718 Set of 5 ....   4·00   2·20
MS2719 62×87 mm. 1l. black, orange-yellow and bluish green ....   2·75   2·50
Designs: Horiz—2st. 1901 Cherrywood Cannon Stamp; 13st. 1946 New Republic Stamp; 23st. 1957 Canonisation of St Cyril and St Methodius stamp; 1l. First Bulgarian stamp. Vert—35st. T **866**; 53st. 1962 Dimitrov stamp.
No. **MS**2719 also exists imperf from a restricted printing.
See also Nos. 2721/2725 and **MS**2755.

867 Council Building, Moscow and Flags

(Des A. Mechnev. Photo)
1979 (25 Jan). 30th Anniversary of Council of Mutual Economic Aid. P 13.
2720   867   13st. multicoloured...........................   70   40

(Des St. Kunchev. Photo)
1979 (30 Jan). Philaserdica 79 International Stamp Exhibition (4th issue) and Bulgarian Stamp Centenary (2nd issue). As Nos. 2714/2718, but inscr '1979' and colours changed. P 13.
2721   2st. scarlet and greenish blue.........................   25   20
2722   13st. claret and bright yellowish green..............   70   40
2723   23st. deep green, pale yellow and Indian red...   85   45
2724   35st. deep brownish grey and deep brown-red..   1·40   60
2725   53st. brown-olive and bright violet ....   1·80   90
2721/2725 Set of 5 ....   4·50   2·30

868 National Bank

868a

(Des S. Nenov. Photo)
1979 (13 Feb). Centenary of Bulgarian National Bank. P 13.
2726   868   2st. grey, deep grey and orange-yellow   25   20

1979 (26 Feb). Coil stamps. T **868a** and similar vert design. Photo. P 14.
2726a   2st. dull ultramarine...................................   20   20
2726b   5st. deep carmine   35   25
Designs: 2st. T **868a**; 5st. Similar to T **868a** but with different pattern.
Nos. 2726a/2726b have every fifth stamp numbered on the back.

869 Stamboliiski

870 Child's Head as Flower

(Des A. Stareishinski. Photo)
1979 (28 Feb). Birth Centenary of Aleksandur Stamboliiski (Prime Minister 1919–1923).
2727   869   2st. bistre-brown and yellow-orange....   25   20

BULGARIA 1979

(Des. V. Kantardzhieva. Photo)
1979 (8 Mar). International Year of the Child. P 13.
2728 870 23st. multicoloured .... 1·40 60

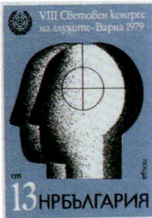
871 Profiles

872 '75' and Emblem

1979 (20 Mar). Eighth World Congress for the Deaf, Varna. Photo. P 13.
2729 871 13st. blackish green and cobalt 70 40

1979 (20 Mar). 75th Anniversary of Bulgarian Trade Unions. Photo. P 13.
2730 872 2st. deep green and pale orange........... 25 20

873 Soviet War Memorial

874 Rocket

(Des Kh. Khristo. Photo)
1979 (2 Apr). Centenary of Sofia as Capital of Bulgaria. Sheet 106×105 mm containing T **873** and similar vert designs. Multicoloured. P 13.
MS2731 2st. Type **873**; 5st. Mother and child (sculpture); 13st., 23st., 25st. Bas-relief from Monument to the Liberators of 1876, plus label....... 2·75 2·50
The 13st., 23st. and 25st. values form a composite design.

(Des St. Kunchev. Photo)
1979 (11 Apr–14 May). Soviet–Bulgarian Space Flight. T **874** and similar designs. Multicoloured. P 13.
2732 2st. Georgi Ivanov (*horiz*) (14.5.79) 25 20
2733 12st. Type **874** 55 40
2734 13st. Nikolai Rukavishnikov and Ivanov (*horiz*) (14.5.79) .... 1·10 45
2735 25st. Link-up with Salyut space station (*horiz*) .... 1·40 55
2736 35st. Capsule descending by parachute.......... 1·70 60
2732/2736 Set of 5 .... 4·50 2·00
MS2737 67×86 mm. 1l. Globe and orbiting space craft (*horiz*).. 3·50 3·25
No. **MS**2737 also exists imperforate from a restricted printing.

875 Carrier Pigeon and Tupolev Tu-154 Jetliner over Hemispheres

876 Running

(Des St. Kunchev. Photo)
1979 (8 May). Centenary of Bulgarian Post and Telegraph Services. T **875** and similar horiz design. Multicoloured. P 13.
2738 2st. Type **875** 25 20
2739 5st. Old and new telephones........................ 35 25
2740 13st. Morse apparatus and teleprinter 70 40
2741 23st. Old radio transmitter and aerials............ 1·00 45
2742 35st. TV tower and satellite............................ 1·40 60
2738/2742 Set of 5 .... 3·25 1·70
MS2743 64×69 mm. 50st. Ground receiving station (38×28 mm).. 3·50 3·25
No. **MS**2743 also exists imperf from a restricted printing.

1979 (15 May). Olympic Games, Moscow (1980) (1st issue). Athletics. T **876** and similar multicoloured designs. Photo. P 13.
2744 2st. Type **876** 25 20
2745 13st. Pole vault (*horiz*) 70 60
2746 25st. Discus... 1·40 1·10
2747 35st. Hurdles (*horiz*) .... 2·10 1·50
2748 43st. High jump (*horiz*) .... 2·75 1·80
2749 1l. Long jump .... 4·25 3·00
2744/2749 Set of 6 .... 10·50 7·50
MS2750 90×65 mm. 2l. Shot put............................ 10·50 10·00
See also Nos. 2773/**MS**2779, 2803/**MS**2809, 2816/**MS**2822, 2834/**MS**2840 and 2851/**MS**2857.

877 Thracian Gold Leaf Collar

878 First Bulgarian Stamp and 1975 European Security Conference Stamp

(Des St. Kunchev. Photo)
1979 (16 May). 48th International Philatelic Federation Congress, Sofia. Sheet 77×86 mm. P 13.
MS2751 877 1l. multicoloured .... 5·50 5·25

(Des St. Kunchev. Photo)
1979 (18 May). Philaserdica 79 International Stamp Exhibition, Sofia (5th issue). Sheet 63×61 mm. P 13.
MS2752 878 1l. multicoloured .... 9·75 9·50

879 Hotel Vitosha-New Otani

880 Good Morning, Little Brother (illus by Kukuliev of folktale)

(Des St. Kunchev. Photo)
1979 (20 May). Philaserdica 79 International Stamp Exhibition, Sofia (6th issue), and Bulgaria Day. P 13.
2753 879 2st. pink and ultramarine 25 20

(Des V. Korenev. Photo)
1979 (23 May). Philaserdica 79 International Stamp Exhibition, Sofia (7th issue), and Bulgarian–Russian Friendship. P 13.
2754 880 2st. multicoloured 25 20

881 First Bulgarian Stamp

882 Man on Donkey (Boris Angelushev)

(Des St. Kunchev. Photo)

1979 (23 May). Centenary of First Bulgarian Stamp (3rd issue). Sheet 91×121 mm. P 13.
MS2755 881 5l. black, orange-yellow and carmine vermilion .... 65·00 65·00

(Des St. Kunchev. Photo)

1979 (23 May). Festival of Humour and Satire, Gabrovo. P 13½.
2756 882 2st. multicoloured 25 20

887 House of Journalists, Varna

888 Children of Different Races

883 Four Women

884 Clocktower, Byala Cherkva

(Recess and litho German Bank Note Ptg Co, Leipzig)

1979 (31 May). 450th Death Anniversary of Albrecht Dürer (artist). T **883** and similar multicoloured designs. P 14×13½.
2757	13st. Type **883**	55	40
2758	23st. *Three Peasants talking*	85	45
2759	25st. *The Cook and his Wife*	1·10	60
2760	35st. *Portrait of Eobanus Hessus*	1·70	90
2757/2760 Set of 4		3·75	2·10
MS2761 80×81 mm. 80st. *Rhinoceros* (horiz). Imperf		2·75	2·50

(Des St. Kunchev. Photo State Ptg Wks, Moscow)

1979 (5 June). AIR. Clocktowers (1st series). T **884** and similar vert designs. Multicoloured. P 12×12½.
2762	13st. Type **884**	35	30
2763	23st. Botevgrad	65	45
2764	25st. Pazardzhik	70	60
2765	35st. Gabrovo	1·00	90
2766	53st. Tryavna	2·10	1·50
2762/2766 Set of 5		4·25	3·50

See also Nos. 2891/2895.

(Des V. Kantardzhieva. Photo)

1979 (17 July). 20th Anniversary of House of Journalists (holiday home), Varna. P 13.
2771 887 8st. yellow-orange, black and bright blue 40 30

1979 (17 July). Banners for Peace Children's Meeting, Sofia. Photo. P 13.
2772 888 2st. multicoloured 25 20

889 Parallel Bars

890 Virgin and Child (Nesebur)

1979 (31 July). Olympic Games, Moscow (1980) (2nd issue). Gymnastics. T **889** and similar multicoloured designs. Photo. P 13.
2773	2st. Type **889**	25	20
2774	13st. Horse exercise (*horiz*)	40	30
2775	25st. Rings exercise	80	40
2776	35st. Beam exercise	1·40	55
2777	43st. Uneven bars	1·60	1·50
2778	1l. Floor exercise	4·25	3·00
2773/2778 Set of 6		7·75	5·25
MS2779 65×88 mm. 2l. Horizontal bar		11·00	10·50

(Des St. Kunchev. Photo State Ptg Wks, Moscow)

1979 (7 Aug). Icons of the Virgin and Child. T **890** and similar square designs. Multicoloured. P 12.
2780	13st. Type **890**	35	30
2781	23st. Nesebur (*different*)	70	45
2782	35st. Sozopol	1·10	60
2783	43st. Sozopol (*different*)	1·30	90
2784	53st. Samokov	2·10	1·50
2780/2784 Set of 5		5·00	3·50

885 Petko Todorov (birth centenary)

886 Congress Emblem

1979 (26 June). Bulgarian Writers. T **885** and similar vert designs. Photo. P 13.
2767	2st. agate, orange-brown and bistre-yellow	35	30
2768	2st. grey-green and greenish yellow	35	30
2769	2st. crimson and orange-yellow	35	30
2767/2769 Set of 3		95	80

Designs: No. 2767, T **885**; No. 2768, Dimitur Dimov (70th birth anniversary); No. 2769, Stefan Kostov (birth centenary).

Nos. 2767/2769 were each issued *se-tenant* with label depicting the title page of one of the author's works.

1979 (8 July). 18th Congress of International Theatrical Institute, Sofia. Photo. P 13.
2770 886 13st. cobalt, blue and black 55 40

891 Anton Bezenshek

892 Mountaineer

(Des I. Kiosev. Photo)

1979 (9 Aug). Centenary of Bulgarian Stenography. P 13.
2785 891 2st. pale yellow and deep greenish grey 25 20

(Des L. Chekhlarov. Photo)

1979 (28 Aug). 50th Anniversary of Bulgarian Alpine Club. P 13.
2786 892 2st. multicoloured 25 20

BULGARIA 1979

893 Commemorative Inscription

894 Rocket and Flowers

(Des D. Rusinov. Photo)

1979 (31 Aug). Centenary of Bulgarian Public Health Services. P 13×13½.
2787	**893**	2st. black, silver and deep green	30	25

No. 2787 was issued *se-tenant* with half stamp-size labels depicting Dr. Mollov.

(Des D. Tasev. Photo)

1979 (4 Sept). 35th Anniversary of Fatherland Front Government. T **894** and similar vert designs. Multicoloured. P 13.
2788		2st. Type **894**	25	20
2789		5st. Russian and Bulgarian flags	35	30
2790		13st. '35' in National Colours	55	40
2788/2790	*Set of 3*		1·00	80

895 IZOT-0250 Computer

(Des V. Popov. Photo)

1979 (8 Sept). 35th Plovdiv Fair. P 13.
2791	**895**	2st. multicoloured	25	20

896 Games Emblem

897 Footballer

(Des St. Kunchev. Photo)

1979 (20 Sept). World University Games, Mexico. P 13.
2792	**896**	5st. indian red, pale orange-yellow and deep grey-blue	35	25

(Des K. Gogov. Photo)

1979 (2 Oct). 50th Anniversary of DFS Lokomotiv Football Team. P 13.
2793	**897**	2st. orange-vermilion and black	25	20

898 Lyuben Karavelov

899 Cross-country Skiing

(Des I. Bogdanov. Photo)

1979 (4 Oct). Death Centenary of Lyuben Karavelov (newspaper editor and President of Bulgarian Revolutionary Committee). P 13.
2794	**898**	2st. grey-olive and new blue	25	20

(Des A. Stareishinski. Photo)

1979 (25 Oct). Winter Olympics, Lake Placid (1980). T **899** and similar vert designs. P 13.
2795		2st. bright crimson, violet and black	25	20
2796		13st. red-orange, violet-blue and black	55	40
2797		23st. deep turquoise-green, dull blue and black	1·00	45
2798		43st. bluish violet, greenish blue and black	2·50	75
2795/2798	*Set of 4*		3·75	1·60
MS2799	68×77 mm. 1l. blue-green, light greenish blue and black. Imperf		3·25	3·00

Designs: 2st. T **899**; 13st. Speed skating; 23st. Skiing; 43st. Luge; 1l. Skiing (*different*).

The miniature sheet as No. **MS**2799 but also depicting satellites on the margin comes from a limited printing.

900 Woman from Thrace

901 Canoeing (Canadian pairs)

(Des St. Kunchev. Photo German Bank Note Ptg Co, Leipzig)

1979 (31 Oct). 80th Birth Anniversary of Dechko Uzunov (artist). T **900** and similar vert designs. Multicoloured. P 14×13½.
2800		12st. *Figure in Red*	55	30
2801		13st. Type **900**	55	30
2802		23st. *Composition II*	1·70	90
2800/2802	*Set of 3*		2·50	1·40

A miniature sheet for the 1982 World Cup Football Championship, containing Nos. 1981 and 2316, was issued 28 November 1979 in a limited printing.

1979 (30 Nov). Olympic Games, Moscow (1980) (3rd issue). Water Sports. T **901** and similar multicoloured designs. Photo. P 13.
2803		2st. Type **901**	25	20
2804		13st. Swimming (freestyle)	70	
2805		25st. Swimming (backstroke) (*horiz*)	1·50	1·10
2806		35st. Kayak (*horiz*)	1·90	1·50
2807		43st. Diving	2·50	1·80
2808		1l. Springboard diving	4·25	3·00
2803/2808	*Set of 6*		10·00	6·75
MS2809	64×88 mm. 2l. Water polo		11·00	10·50

902 Nikola Vaptsarov

903 *Dawn in Plovdiv* (Ioan Leviev)

1979 (7 Dec). 70th Birth Anniversary of Nikola Vaptsarov (writer). Photo. P 13.
2810	**902**	2st. rose and lake	30	25

No. 2810 was issued *se-tenant* with a label depicting one of Vaptsarov's works.

1979 (10 Dec). History of Bulgaria. Paintings. T **903** and similar horiz designs. Multicoloured. Litho. P 12×12½ (35st.) or 12½×12 (others).
2811		2st. *The First Socialists* (Boyan Petrov)	25	20
2812		13st. *Dimitur Blagoev as Editor of 'Rabotnik'* (Dimitur Gyudzhenov)	55	40
2813		25st. *Workers' Party March* (Stoyan Sotirov)	1·10	60
2814		35st. Type **903**	1·70	1·20
2811/2814	*Set of 4*		3·25	2·20

1979 BULGARIA

904 Doves in Girl's Hair

(Des St. Kunchev. Photo)

1979 (14 Dec). New Year. P 13.
2815 **904** 13st. multicoloured............................ 55 40

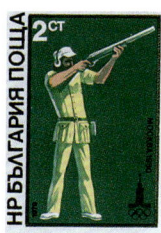

905 Shooting

During 1980 miniature sheets were issued for the European Security and Co-operation Conference, Madrid (two sheets, one at 50st., one containing 13st.×6), the World Cup Football Championship, Spain (50st.) and for Nature Protection and 49th FIP Congress, Essen (containing 5st., 13st., 25st., 35st. and 43st.). Supplies and distribution of these sheets were restricted, and it is understood they were not available at face value.

(Des A. Stareishinski. Photo)

1980 (22 Jan). 50th Anniversary of International Puppet Theatre Organisation (UNIMA) (1979). P 13.
2829 **908** 2st. multicoloured............................ 25 20

909 Thracian Rider (3rd-century votive tablet)   **910** Meeting of Lenin and Dimitrov (Aleksandur Poplilov)

(Des N. Kovachev. Photo)

1980 (29 Jan). Centenary of National Archaeological Museum, Sofia. T **909** and similar vert design. P 13.
2830   2st. bistre-brown, copper and purple-brown............................ 25 20
2831   13st. bistre-brown, gold and bottle-green............................ 55 40
Designs: 2st. T **909**; 13st. Grave stele of Deines (5th/6th-century).

(Des N. Kovachev. Litho State Ptg Wks, Moscow)

1980 (28 Mar). 110th Birth Anniversary of Lenin. P 12.
2832 **910** 13st. multicoloured............................ 55 40

1979 (22 Dec). Olympic Games, Moscow (1980) (4th issue). T **905** and similar multicoloured designs. Photo. P 13.
2816   2st. Type **905**............................ 25 20
2817   13st. Judo (*horiz*)............................ 70 40
2818   25st. Wrestling (*horiz*)............................ 1·50 1·20
2819   35st. Archery............................ 1·90 1·50
2820   43st. Fencing (*horiz*)............................ 2·50 1·70
2821   1l. Fencing (*different*)............................ 4·25 3·00
2816/2821 Set of 6............................ 10·00 7·25
MS2822 65×89 mm. 2l. Boxing............................ 11·00 10·50

906 Procession with Relics of Saints

(Des St. Kunchev. Photo German Bank Note Ptg Co, Leipzig)

1979 (25 Dec). Frescoes of Saints Cyril and Methodius in St Clement's Basilica, Rome. T **906** and similar square designs. Multicoloured. P 13.
2823   2st. Type **906**............................ 25 20
2824   13st. Cyril and Methodius received by Pope Adrian II............................ 55 40
2825   23st. Burial of Cyril the Philosopher............................ 85 45
2826   25st. St Cyril............................ 1·10 60
2827   35st. St Methodius............................ 1·70 90
2823/2827 Set of 5............................ 4·00 2·30

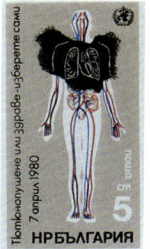 

911 Diagram of Blood Circulation with Lungs obscured by Smoke   **912** Basketball

(Des V. Kantardzhieva. Photo)

1980 (7 Apr). World Health Day. Anti-smoking Campaign. P 13.
2833 **911** 5st. multicoloured............................ 35 25

1980 (10 Apr). Olympic Games, Moscow (5th issue). T **912** and similar vert designs. Multicoloured. Photo. P 13.
2834   2st. Type **912**............................ 25 20
2835   13st. Football............................ 65 40
2836   25st. Hockey............................ 1·60 1·10
2837   35st. Cycling............................ 1·80 1·50
2838   43st. Handball............................ 2·75 1·80
2839   1l. Volleyball............................ 4·25 3·00
2834/2839 Set of 6............................ 10·00 7·25
MS2840 66×90 mm. 2st. Weightlifting............................ 12·00 11·50

907 Television Screen showing Emblem   **908** Puppet of Krali Marko (national hero)

(Des N. Kovachev. Photo)

1979 (29 Dec). 25th Anniversary of Bulgarian Television. P 13½.
2828 **907** 5st. new blue and deep ultramarine.... 55 45
No. 2828 was issued with *se-tenant* half stamp-size label depicting Sofia television tower.

913 Emblem, Cosmonauts and Space Station

175

BULGARIA 1980

(Des St. Kunchev. Litho State Ptg Wks, Moscow)

1980 (22 Apr). Intercosmos Space Programme. Sheet 111×102 mm. P 12.
MS2841 913 50st. multicoloured............................... 2·75 2·50

Stamps of a similar design were issued by Czechoslovakia, Germany, Poland and Russia.

914 Peno Penev

915 Penny Black

(Des St. Kunchev. Photo)

1980 (22 Apr). 50th Birth Anniversary of Peno Penev (poet). P 13½.
2842 914 5st. agate, orange-red and blue-green 40 35

No. 2842 was issued with *se-tenant* half stamp-size label bearing extract from poem.

1980 (24 Apr). London 1980 International Stamp Exhibition. Photo. P 13.
2843 915 25st. agate and brown red...................... 1·70 1·50

Issued in sheets of six stamps and three labels depicting Sir Rowland Hill.

A further limited printing of the sheetlet was issued with additional marginal inscription, each sheetlet being numbered; this was re-issued in 1982 with the stamps and marginal inscription overprinted for 19th UPU Congress, Hamburg, the sheetlet surcharged 2l. and renumbered.

916 Dimitur Khr. Chorbadzhyski Chudomir (self-portrait)

917 Nikolai Gyaurov

(Des Zh. Kosturkova. Photo)

1980 (29 Apr). 90th Birth Anniversary of Dimitur Khr. Chorbadzhyski Chudomir (artist). T **916** and similar horiz design. P 13.
2844 5st. pink, bistre-brown and deep turquoise-blue.................................. 35 25
2845 13st. black, pale blue and deep blue-green.. 55 40

Designs: 5st. T **916**; 13st. *Our People*.

(Des A. Stareishinski. Photo)

1980 (30 Apr). 50th Birth Anniversary of Nikolai Gyaurov (opera singer). P 13.
2846 917 5st. orange-yellow, orange-brown and bright green.................................. 40 30

No. 2846 was issued with *se-tenant* stamp-size label depicting scene from *Boris Godunov*.

918 Soviet Soldiers raising Flag on Berlin Reichstag

919 Open Book and Sun

(Des P. Petrov. Photo)

1980 (6 May). 35th Anniversary of Victory in Europe Day. T **918** and similar vert design. P 13.
2847 5st. gold, purple-brown and black................. 35 25
2848 13st. gold, purple-brown and black................. 55 40

Designs: 5st. T **918**; 13st. Soviet Army Memorial, Berlin-Treptow.

(Des B. Yonov. Photo)

1980 (12 May). 75th Anniversary of Bulgarian Teachers' Union. P 13.
2849 919 5st. deep reddish purple and orange-yellow 35 25

920 Stars representing Member Countries

921 Greek Girl with Olympic Flame

(Des K. Gogov. Photo)

1980 (14 May). 25th Anniversary of Warsaw Pact. P 13.
2850 920 13st. multicoloured............................ 55 40

(Des A. Stareishinski. Photo)

1980 (10 June). Olympic Games, Moscow (6th issue). T **921** and similar vert designs. Multicoloured. P 13.
2851 2st. Type **921** 25 20
2852 13st. Spartacus monument, Sandanski 55 55
2853 25st. Liberation monument, Sofia (detail)....... 1·60 1·20
2854 35st. Liberation monument, Plovdiv................ 2·00 1·40
2855 43st. Liberation monument, Shipka Pass......... 2·75 1·80
2856 1l. Liberation monument, Ruse..................... 4·25 3·00
2851/2856 Set of 6 .... 10·50 7·25
MS2857 66×92 mm. 2l. Athlete with Olympic flame, Moscow .... 11·00 10·50

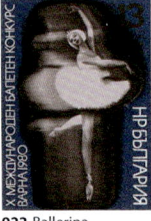
922 Ballerina

923 Europa Hotel, Sofia

(Des R. Stanoeva and A. Sertev. Photo)

1980 (1 July). Tenth International Ballet Competition, Varna. P 13.
2858 922 13st. multicoloured............................ 55 40

(Des Kh. Khristov. Photo)

1980 (11 July). Hotels. T **923** and similar multicoloured designs. P 13.
2859 23st. Type **923** 85 45
2860 23st. Bulgaria Hotel, Burgas (*vert*)................ 85 45
2861 23st. Plovdiv Hotel, Plovdiv............................. 85 45
2862 23st. Riga Hotel, Ruse (*vert*) 85 45
2863 23st. Varna Hotel, Druzhba............................ 85 45
2859/2863 Set of 5 .... 3·75 2·00

(Des St. Kunchev. Photo German Bank Note Ptg Co, Leipzig)

1980 (14 July). Historic Ships (3rd series). Square designs as T **753**. Multicoloured. P 13.
2864 5st. Hansa kogge *Jesus of Lübeck* 35 25
2865 8st. Roman galley 40 30
2866 13st. *Eagle* (galleon) 55 40
2867 23st. *Mayflower* 85 45
2868 35st. Maltese galleon .... 1·50 60
2869 53st. *Royal Louis* (galleon) .... 2·20 1·50
2864/2869 Set of 6 .... 5·25 3·25

1980 BULGARIA

924 Parachute Descent
925 Clown and Children

(Des L. Chekhlarov. Photo)

1980 (6 Aug). 15th World Parachute Championships, Kazanluk. T **924** and similar vert design. Multicoloured. P 13.
2870	13st. Type **924**	55	40
2871	25st. Parachutist in free fall	1·10	45

(Des V. Kantardzhieva. Litho)

1980 (1 Sept). First Anniversary of Banners for Peace Children's Meeting. T **925** and similar multicoloured designs. P 12.
2872	3st. Type **925**	30	25
2873	5st. Cosmonauts in Spaceship (vert)	35	25
2874	8st. Picnic	40	30
2875	13st. Children with Ices	55	40
2876	25st. Children with Cat (vert)	70	45
2877	35st. Crowd	1·10	60
2878	43st. *Banners for Peace* monument (vert)	2·20	90
2872/2878	Set of 7	5·00	2·75

926 Assembly Emblem
927 Iordan Iovkov

(Des Y. Petrov. Photo)

1980 (4 Sept). Assembly of People's Parliament for Peace, Sofia. P 13.
2879	**926** 25st. multicoloured	85	60

(Des T. Aleksieva. Photo)

1980 (19 Sept). Birth Centenary of Iordan Iovkov (writer). P 13½.
2880	**927** 5st. multicoloured	40	40

No. 2880 was issued with *se-tenant* half stamp-size label depicting drawing by T. Panaiotov of scene from Iovkov's work *Over the Wire*.

 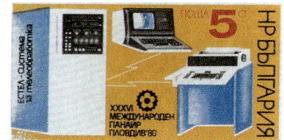

928 Yakovlev Yak-24 Helicopter, Missile Launcher and Tank
929 Computer

(Des K. Gogov. Photo)

1980 (23 Sept). Bulgarian Armed Forces. T **928** and similar vert designs. Multicoloured. P 13.
2881	3st. Type **928**	30	25
2882	5st. Mikoyan Gurevich MiG-21 jet fighter, radar antennae and missile transporter	35	25
2883	8st. Mil Mi-24 helicopter, missile boat and *Ropucha* (landing ship)	40	30
2881/2883	Set of 3	95	70

(Des R. Stanoeva and A. Sertev. Photo)

1980 (24 Sept). 36th Plovdiv Fair. P 13.
2884	**929** 5st. multicoloured	35	25

930 Virgin and Child with St Anne
931 *Parodia saint-pieana*

(Des A. Stareishinski. Photo)

1980 (10 Oct). Paintings by Leonardo da Vinci. T **930** and similar square designs. Multicoloured. P 13.
2885	5st. Type **930**	35	25
2886	8st. Angel (detail *The Annunciation*)	40	30
2887	13st. Virgin (detail *The Annunciation*)	55	40
2888	25st. Adoration of the Kings (detail)	1·00	60
2889	35st. Woman with Ermine	1·70	75
2885/2889	Set of 5	3·50	2·10
MS2890	57×80 mm. 50st. Mona Lisa. Imperf	2·10	2·00

(Des St. Kunchev. Litho State Ptg Wks, Moscow)

1980 (22 Oct). AIR. Clocktowers (2nd series). Vert designs as T **884**. Multicoloured. P 12×12½.
2891	13st. Byala	55	40
2892	23st. Razgrad	70	45
2893	25st. Karnobat	85	60
2894	35st. Sevlievo	1·30	75
2895	53st. Berkovitsa	2·40	1·20
2891/2895	Set of 5	5·25	3·00

(Des M. Konstantinova. Photo)

1980 (4 Nov). Cacti. T **931** and similar vert designs. Multicoloured. P 13.
2896	5st. Type **931**	35	25
2897	13st. *Echinopsis bridgesii*	55	40
2898	25st. *Echinocereus purpureus*	1·10	60
2899	35st. *Opuntia bispinosa*	1·70	1·20
2900	53st. *Mamillopsis senilis*	3·25	1·50
2896/2900	Set of 5	6·25	3·50

932 UN Building and Bulgarian Arms

(Des St. Kunchev. Photo)

1980 (25 Nov). 25th Anniversary of United Nations Membership. Sheet 64×86 mm. P 13.
MS2901	**932** 60st. multicoloured	5·00	4·75

933 Przewalski's Horse

(Des V. Korenev and St. Goristanova. Litho State Ptg Wks, Moscow)

1980 (27 Nov). Horses. T **933** and similar horiz designs. Multicoloured. P 12½×12.
2902	3st. Type **933**	30	25

177

BULGARIA 1980

2903	5st. Tarpan	35	25
2904	13st. Arabian	85	75
2905	23st. Anglo-Arabian	2·10	1·50
2906	35st. Draught Horse	4·25	3·75
2902/2906	Set of 5	7·00	5·75

934 Vasil Stoin

(Des E. Klincharov. Photo)

1980 (5 Dec). Birth Centenary of Vasil Stoin (collector of folk songs). P 13.
2907	**934**	5st. reddish violet, yellow-ochre and gold	35	25

935 Armorial Lion   **936** Red Star

(Des St. Kunchev. Photo)

1980 (8 Dec). New Year. 1300th Anniversary of Bulgarian State. T **935** and similar horiz design. Multicoloured. P 13.
2908		5st. Type **935**	35	25
2909		13st. Dish and dates '681/1981'	55	40

(Des St. Kunchev. Photo)

1980 (26 Dec). 12th Bulgarian Communist Party Congress (1st issue). P 13.
2910	**936**	5st. orange-yellow and rosine	35	25

See also Nos. 2920/MS2923.

> During 1981 miniature sheets were issued for Olympic Games medal winners (50st.), World Cup Football Championship, Spain (50st.), 125th Anniversary of Danube Commission (two sheets, one containing 25st.×2, the other 35st.×8) and the European Security and Co-operation Conference, Madrid (35st.×2). Supplies and distribution of these sheets were restricted, and it is understood they were not available at face value.

937 Cross-country Skier   **938** Midland Hawthorn (*Crataegus oxyacantha*)

(Des Kh. Aleksiev. Photo)

1981 (15 Jan). World Ski-racing Championship, Velingrad. P 13.
2911	**937**	43st. red-orange, bright blue and black	1·70	90

(Des V. Kantardzhieva. Photo)

1981 (22 Jan). Useful Plants. T **938** and similar vert designs. Multicoloured. P 13.
2912		3st. Type **938**	30	25
2913		5st. Perforate St John's Wort (*Hypericum perforatum*)	35	25
2914		13st. Elder (*Sambucus nigra*)	55	40
2915		25st. Dewberry (*Rubus caesius*)	1·20	45
2916		35st. Lime (*Tilia argentea*)	1·50	75
2917		43st. Dog Rose (*Rosa canina*)	2·20	1·50
2912/2917	Set of 6		5·50	3·25

939 Skier   **940** Nuclear Traces

(Des Kh. Aleksiev. Photo)

1981 (27 Feb). Alpine Skiing World Championships, Borovets. P 13.
2918	**939**	43st. yellow, black and blue	1·70	90

(Des K. Gogov. Photo)

1981 (10 Mar). 25th Anniversary of Nuclear Research Institute, Dubna, USSR. P 13.
2919	**940**	13st. black and silver	55	40

941 'XII' formed by Flag   **942** Palace of Culture

(Des P. Petrov. Photo)

1981 (12 Mar). 12th Bulgarian Communist Party Congress (2nd issue). T **941** and similar horiz designs. P 13×13½.
2920		5st. multicoloured	35	25
2921		13st. rosine, brownish black and deep ultramarine	55	40
2922		23st. rosine, brownish black and deep ultramarine	1·00	75
2920/2922	Set of 3		1·70	1·30
MS2923	68×86 mm. 50st. multicoloured		2·10	2·00

Designs: 5st. T **941**; 13st. Stars; 23st. Computer tape; 50st. Georgi Dimitrov and Dimitur Blagoev.

Nos. 2920/2922 were each issued with *se-tenant* half stamp-size inscribed label.

(Des St. Kunchev. Photo)

1981 (13 Mar). Opening of Palace of Culture, Sofia. P 13.
2924	**942**	5st. deep olive, light green and vermilion	35	25

943 Self-portrait   **944** Squacco Heron (*Ardeola ralloides*)

(Des K. Gogov. Litho State Ptg Wks, Moscow)

1981 (23 Mar). 170th Birth Anniversary (1980) of Zakharii Zograf (artist). T **943** and similar multicoloured designs. P 12×12½. (vert) or 12½×12 (horiz).
2925		5st. Type **943**	35	25
2926		13st. *Portrait of Khristiania Zografska*	55	40
2927		23st. The Transfiguration (icon from Preobrazhenie Monastery)	1·10	45
2928		25st. *Doomsday* (detail) (*horiz*)	1·30	75
2929		35st. *Doomsday* (different detail) (*horiz*)	1·90	1·50
2925/2929	Set of 5		4·75	3·00

1981 BULGARIA

(Des L. Chekhlarov. Litho State Ptg Wks, Moscow)

1981 (7 Apr). Birds. T **944** and similar vert designs. Multicoloured. P 12.

2930	5st. Type **944**	35	25
2931	8st. Eurasian Bittern (*Botaurus stellaris*)	55	30
2932	13st. Cattle Egret (*Ardeola ibis*)	1·00	45
2933	25st. Great Egret (*Casmerodius albus*)	2·10	90
2934	53st. Black Stork (*Ciconia nigra*)	3·75	2·00
2930/2934	Set of 5	7·00	3·50

945 Liner *Georgi Dimitrov*

(Des Kh. Khristov. Photo)

1981 (15 Apr). Centenary of Bulgarian Shipbuilding. T **945** and similar horiz designs. Multicoloured. P 13.

2935	35st. Type **945**	1·40	45
2936	43st. Freighter *Petimata ot RMS*	1·90	70
2937	53st. Tanker *Khan Asparukh*	2·50	85
2935/2937	Set of 3	5·25	1·80

946 Hofburg Palace, Vienna **947** 'XXXIV'

(Des St. Kunchev. Photo)

1981 (15 May). WIPA 1981 International Stamp Exhibition, Vienna. P 13.

2938	**946**	35st. crimson, vermilion and deep green	1·40	90

(Des Y. Petrov. Photo)

1981 (18 May). 34th Bulgarian People's Agrarian Union Congress. T **947** and similar horiz designs. P 13½.

2939	5st. multicoloured	35	25
2940	8st. yellow-orange, black and ultramarine	40	30
2941	13st. multicoloured	70	40
2939/2941	Set of 3	1·30	85

Designs: 5st. T **947**; 8st. Flags; 13st. Bulgarian Communist Party and Agrarian Union flags.

948 Wild Cat **949** *Crafty Peter* (sculpture, Georgi Chapkanov)

(Des A. Stareishinski. Photo)

1981 (27 May). International Hunting Exhibition, Plovdiv. T **948** and similar horiz designs. P 13½.

2942	5st. stone, black and chestnut	35	25
2943	13st. black, chestnut and pale olive-sepia	55	40
2944	23st. orange-brown, black and pale orange	1·40	60
2945	25st. black, chestnut and dull purple	1·70	75
2946	35st. orange-brown, black and grey-brown	2·20	90
2947	53st. brown-ochre, black and dull green	3·50	1·50
2942/2947	Set of 6	8·75	4·00

MS2948 78×103 mm. 1l. brown-ochre, black and dull yellow-green (52×42 *mm*). P 13 .... 4·25 4·00

Designs: 5st. T **948**; 13st. Wild Boar; 23st. Mouflon; 25st. Chamois; 35st. Roebuck; 53st. Fallow Deer; 1l. Red Deer.

Nos. 2942/2947 were each issued with *se-tenant* half stamp-size label depicting an ornamental hunting gun.

(Des St. Kunchev. Photo)

1981 (28 May). Festival of Humour and Satire, Gabrovo. P 13.

2949	**949**	5st. multicoloured	35	25

950 Bulgarian Arms and UNESCO Emblem **951** Deutsche Flugzeugwerke DFWCV Biplane

(Des St. Kunchev. Photo)

1981 (11 June). 25th Anniversary of United Nations Educational, Scientific and Cultural Organisation Membership. P 13.

2950	**950**	13st. multicoloured	55	40

(Des Zh. Aleksiev. Litho State Ptg Wks, Moscow)

1981 (24 June). AIR. Aircraft. T **951** and similar horiz designs. Multicoloured. P 12½×12.

2951	5st. Type **951**	35	25
2952	12st. LAS-7 monoplane	40	40
2953	25st. LAS-8 monoplane	1·00	55
2954	35st. DAR-1 biplane	1·40	75
2955	45st. DAR-3 biplane	1·60	1·00
2956	55st. DAR-9 biplane	2·00	1·40
2951/2956	Set of 6	6·00	4·00

952 'Eye' **953** Veliko Turnovo Hotel

(Des N. Kovachev. Photo)

1981 (9 July). Centenary of State Statistical Office. P 13.

2957	**952**	5st. multicoloured	35	25

(Des Kh. Khristov. Photo)

1981 (13 July). Hotels. P 13.

2958	**953**	23st. multicoloured	85	45

954 Flying Figure

(Des R. Stanoeva and A. Sertev. Photo)

1981 (16 July). 90th Anniversary of First Bulgarian Social Democratic Party Congress, Buzludzha. T **954** and similar horiz designs showing sculptures by Velichko Minekov. P 13.

2959	5st. light blue, black and apple green	35	25
2960	13st. cinnamon, black and reddish orange	55	40

Designs: 5st. T **954**; 13st. *Advancing Female*.

955 Animal-shaped Dish

BULGARIA 1981

(Des St. Kunchev. Photo German Bank
Note Ptg Co, Leipzig)

1981 (21 July). Golden Treasure of Old Saint Nicholas. T **955** and similar square designs. Multicoloured. P 13.

2961	5st. Type **955**	35	25
2962	13st. Jug with decorated neck............................	55	40
2963	23st. Jug with loop pattern................................	75	60
2964	25st. Jug with bird pattern................................	90	75
2965	35st. Decorated vase...	1·10	1·10
2966	53st. Decorated dish...	2·40	1·80
2961/2966	Set of 6	5·50	4·50

956 Badge and Map of Bulgaria

(Des K. Gogov. Photo)

1981 (28 July). 35th Anniversary of Frontier Guards. P 13.
2967   **956**   5st. multicoloured..   35   25

957 Saints Cyril and Methodius (9th-century)

(Des I. Kosev. Photo)

1981 (10 Aug). 1300th Anniversary of Bulgarian State. T **957** and similar horiz designs. P 13.

2968	5st. deep dull green and greyish green........	35	25
2969	5st. blackish brown and yellow........................	35	25
2970	8st. violet and deep lilac....................................	40	30
2971	12st. mauve and reddish purple.......................	55	35
2972	13st. dull slate-purple and agate......................	55	35
2973	13st. dull yellowish green and black................	55	35
2974	16st. emerald and myrtle green........................	70	40
2975	23st. black and light blue...................................	1·00	45
2976	25st. bottle green and turquoise-green...........	1·10	60
2977	35st. brown and ochre..	1·50	75
2978	41st. deep rose-red and rose-pink....................	1·80	90
2979	43st. deep carmine and rose.............................	1·80	90
2980	53st. chocolate and light brown.......................	2·00	1·00
2981	55st. myrtle green and pale blue-green..........	2·10	1·10
2968/2981	Set of 14	13·50	7·25

MS2982 Two sheets, each 83×74 mm. (a) 50st. olive-grey and blackish olive; (b) 1l. grey-brown, brownish black and light brown..................................... 6·25 6·00

Designs:— 5st. (No. 2968), Madara Horsemen (8th-century); 5st. (No. 2969) T **597**; 8st. Plan of Round Church at Veliki Preslav (10th-century); 12st. Four Evangelists of Ivan Aleksandr (1356); 13st. (No. 2972), Column of Ivan Asen II (13th-century); 13st. (No. 2973), *Manasses Chronicle* (14th-century); 16st. Rising of April 1876; 23st. Arrival of Russian liberation troops, 1877; 25st. Foundation ceremony of Bulgarian Social Democratic Party, 1891; 35st. Rising of September 1923; 41st. Formation of Fatherland Front Government, 9 September 1944; 43st. Bulgarian Communist Party Congress, 1948; 50st. Bas-relief of Lion at Stara Zagora (10th-century); 53st. Tenth Communist Party Congress, 1971; 55st. Kremikovtsi metallurgical combine; 1l. Leonid Brezhnev and Todor Yovkov.

958 Volleyball Players

959 *Pegasus* (bronze sculpture)

1981 (16 Sept). European Volleyball Championships. Photo. P 13.
2983   **958**   13st. bright crimson, deep ultramarine
                and black...   55   40

1981 (2 Oct). Day of the Word. Photo. P 13.
2984   **959**   5st. pale yellow and dull olive...................   35   25

960 Loaf of Bread

961 Mask

1981 (16 Oct). World Food Day. Photo. P 13.
2985   **960**   13st. black, orange-brown and myrtle
                green...   55   40

(Des L. Chekhlarov. Photo)

1981 (30 Oct). Centenary of Bulgarian Professional Theatre. P 13.
2986   **961**   5st. multicoloured..   35   25

962 Examples of Bulgarian Art

963 Footballer

(Des St. Kunchev. Photo)

1981 (21 Nov). Cultural Heritage Day. P 13.
2987   **962**   13st. yellow-green and brown-red...........   55   40
See also No. **MS**2993.

(Des Kh. Aleksiev. Photo)

1981 (25 Nov). World Cup Football Championship, Spain (1982). T **963** and similar vert designs. Multicoloured. P 13.

2988	5st. Type **963**	35	25
2989	13st. Player heading ball	40	40
2990	43st. Goalkeeper catching ball	1·20	90
2991	53st. Player kicking ball...................................	1·50	1·40
2988/2991	Set of 4	3·00	2·75

964 Dove encircled by Barbed Wire

965 *Mother* (Lilyana Ruseva)

(Des P. Rashkov. Photo)

1981 (2 Dec). Anti-apartheid Campaign. P 13.
2992   **964**   5st. black, deep carmine and orange-
                yellow...   35   25

1981 (11 Dec). 13th Bulgarian Philatelic Federation Congress. Sheet 51×72 mm containing design as T **962** but inscr 'XIII KONGRES NA SBF SOFIYA' at foot. P 13.
MS2993 60st. blue and bright crimson.............................. 12·00 11·50

1981 BULGARIA

(Des V. Kantardzhieva. Litho German Bank Note Ptg Co, Leipzig)

1981 (16 Dec). 35th Anniversary of United Nations Children's Fund (UNICEF). T **965** and similar vert designs. Multicoloured. P 14.

2994	53st. Type **965**	2·10	75
2995	53st. *Bulgarian Madonna* (Vasil Stoilov)	2·10	75
2996	53st. *Village Madonna* (Ivan Milev)	2·10	75
2997	53st. *Mother* (Vladimir Dimitrov)	2·10	75
2994/2997	Set of 4	7·50	2·75

966 8th-century Ceramic from Pliska

(Des St. Kunchev. Photo)

1981 (22 Dec). New Year. T **966** and similar horiz design. Multicoloured. P 13.

2998	5st. Armorial Lion	35	25
2999	13st. Type **966**	55	40

> During 1982 sets were issued for World Cup Football Championship, Spain (5st., 13st., 30st., **MS**2×50st.), Tenth Anniversary of First European Security and Co-operation Conference (5st., 13st., 25st., 30st., **MS**1l.), World Cup Results (5st., 13st., 30st., **MS**2×50st.) and Tenth Anniversary (1983) of European Security and Co-operation Conference, Helsinki (5st., 13st., 25st., 30st., **MS**1l.). Supplies and distribution of these stamps were restricted and it is understood they were not available at face value.

967 Bagpipes   **968** Book

(Des L. Chekhlarov. Photo)

1982 (14 Jan). Musical Instruments. T **967** and similar vert designs. Multicoloured. P 13.

3000	13st. Type **967**	30	30
3001	25st. Single and double flutes	70	35
3002	30st. Rebec	85	40
3003	35st. Flute and pipe	95	45
3004	44st. Mandolin	1·60	60
3000/3004	Set of 5	4·00	1·90

1982 (20 Jan). 125th Anniversary of Public Libraries. Photo. P 13.

| 3005 | **968** | 5st. dull green and deep green | 35 | 25 |

969 Sofia Plains

1982 (10 Feb). Birth Centenary of Nikola Petrov (artist). T **969** and similar square designs. Multicoloured. Litho. P 12½.

3006	5st. Type **969**	35	25
3007	13st. *Girl embroidering*	55	40
3008	30st. *Fields of Peshtera*	1·50	75
3006/3008	Set of 3	2·20	1·30

970 Woman's Head and Dove   **971** Peasant Woman

1982 (8 Mar). International Decade of Women. Sheet 66×76 mm. Photo. P 13.

| MS3009 | **970** | 1l. multicoloured | 3·50 | 3·25 |

1982 (25 Mar). Birth Centenary of Vladimir Dimitrov (artist). T **971** and similar multicoloured designs. Litho. P 14.

3010	5st. Figures in a landscape (*horiz*)	35	25
3011	8st. Town and harbour (*horiz*)	40	30
3012	13st. Town scene (*horiz*)	55	35
3013	25st. Reapers	70	40
3014	30st. Woman and child	85	55
3015	35st. Type **971**	1·40	60
3010/3015	Set of 6	3·75	2·20
MS3016	65×58 mm. 50st. Self-portrait (*horiz*)	2·10	2·00

972 Georgi Dimitrov   **973** Summer Snowflake (*Leucojum aestivum*)

(Des T. Momchilov. Photo)

1982 (5 Apr). Ninth Bulgarian Trade Unions Congress, Sofia. T **972** and similar horiz design. P 13½.

3017	5st. cinnamon, chocolate and lake-brown	40	30
3018	5st. chestnut and deep new blue	40	30

Designs: No. 3017, T **972**; No. 3018, Palace of Culture, Sofia.
Nos. 3017/3018 were each issued with *se-tenant* half stamp-size label showing congress emblem and text.

(Des V. Kitanov. Photo)

1982 (10 Apr). Flowers. T **973** and similar vert designs. Multicoloured. P 13.

3019	3st. Type **973**	30	25
3020	5st. Chicory (*Cichorium intybus*)	35	25
3021	8st. Rosebay Willowherb (*Chamaenerium angustifolium*)	40	30
3022	13st. Solomon's Seal (*Polygonatum officinale*)	55	40
3023	25st. Sweet Violet (*Viola odorata*)	1·20	45
3024	35st. *Ficaria verna*	1·90	75
3019/3024	Set of 6	4·25	2·20

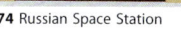

974 Russian Space Station   **975** Georgi Dimitrov

BULGARIA 1982

1982 (12 Apr). 25th Anniversary of First Soviet Artificial Satellite. Photo. P 13½.
3025 **974** 13st. multicoloured 70 45
No. 3025 was issued with *se-tenant* half stamp-size label depicting K. Tsiolkovski (space pioneer).

(Des K. Gogov. Photo)

1982 (7 May). Sozphilex '82 Stamp Exhibition, Veliko Tirnovo. Sheet 61×82 mm. P 13.
MS3026 **975** 50st. vermilion and black .... 5·00 4·75

976 Dimitrov and Congress Emblem

978 Abstract with Birds

977 First French and Bulgarian Stamps

(Des St. Chakarov. Photo)

1982 (25 May). 14th Dimitrov Communist Youth League Congress, Sofia. P 13.
3027 **976** 5st. multicoloured 35 25

(Des P. Petrov. Photo)

1982 (28 May). Philexfrance 82 International Stamp Exhibition, Paris. P 13½×13.
3028 **977** 42st. multicoloured .... 1·40 75

(Des St. Kunchev. Litho)

1982 (8 June). Alafrangi Frescoes from 19th-century Houses. T **978** and similar vert designs showing flower and bird patterns. P 11½.
3029 5st. multicoloured 35 25
3030 13st. multicoloured 55 40
3031 25st. multicoloured 70 45
3032 30st. multicoloured 85 60
3033 42st. multicoloured .... 1·40 75
3034 60st. multicoloured .... 2·30 90
3029/3034 Set of 6 .... 5·50 3·00

979 Georgi Dimitrov   980 Georgi Dimitrov

(Des A. Stareishinski. Photo)

1982 (15 June). Birth Centenary of Georgi Dimitrov (statesman). Sheet 76×52 mm. P 13.
MS3035 **979** 50st. multicoloured .... 2·10 2·00

1982 (21 June). Ninth Fatherland Front Congress, Sofia. Photo. P 13.
3036 **980** 5st. multicoloured 35 25

981 Aeroplane

982 Atomic Bomb Mushroom-cloud

(Des P. Feredzhanov. Photo)

1982 (29 June). 35th Anniversary of Balkanair (state airline). P 13.
3037 **981** 42st. deep new blue, light green and vermilion .... 1·40 90
No. 3037 was issued with *se-tenant* label bearing airline emblem and inscription.

(Des N. Nikolov. Photo)

1982 (15 July). Nuclear Disarmament Campaign. P 13.
3038 **982** 13st. multicoloured 55 40

983 Lyudmila Zhivkova

984 Emblem

(Des St. Kunchev. Photo)

1982 (26 July–4 Aug). 40th Birth Anniversary of Lyudmila Zhivkova (founder of Banners for Peace Children's Meetings). P 13.
3039 **983** 5st. multicoloured (4.8.82) 35 25
3040   13st. multicoloured (4.8.82) 55 40
MS3041 62×67 mm. Type **983** 1l. multicoloured .... 2·75 2·50

(Des I. Bogdanov. Photo)

1982 (27 July). Tenth Anniversary of United Nations Environment Programme. P 13.
3042 **984** 13st. emerald and deep new blue 55 40

985 Wave Pattern

(Des D. Tasev. Photo)

1982 (27 July). Fifth Bulgarian Painters' Association Congress. P 13½.
3043 **985** 5st. multicoloured 40 30
No. 3043 was issued with *se-tenant* half stamp-size inscribed label.

986 Child Musicians

(Des St. Kunchev and A. Stareishinski. Litho German Bank Note Ptg Co, Leipzig)

1982 (10 Aug). Second Banners for Peace Children's Meeting (1st issue). T **986** and similar horiz designs showing children's paintings. Multicoloured. P 14.
3044 3st. Type **986** 30 25
3045 5st. Children skating 35 25

3046	8st. Adults, children and flowers		40	30
3047	13st. Children with flags		55	40
3044/3047	Set of 4		1·40	1·10
MS3048	70×110 mm. 50st. Children in 'Sun' balloon (vert). Perf or imperf		2·75	2·50

See also Nos. 3057/**MS**3063.

987 Moscow Park Hotel, Sofia

988 Cruiser *Aurora* and Satellite

(Des Kh. Khristov. Photo)

1982 (20 Oct). Hotels. T **987** and similar vert design. Multicoloured. P 13.

3049	32st. Type 987	1·30	60
3050	32st. Black Sea Hotel, Varna	1·30	60

(Des K. Gogov. Photo)

1982 (4 Nov). 65th Anniversary of Russian October Revolution. P 13.

3051	**988**	13st. bright scarlet and violet-blue	55	40

989 Hammer and Sickle

990 The Piano

(Des K. Gogov. Photo)

1982 (9 Dec). 60th Anniversary of USSR. P 13.

3052	**989**	13st. bright scarlet, gold and bluish violet	55	40

(Des T. Vardzhiev. Litho State Ptg Wks, Budapest)

1982 (23 Dec). Birth Centenary of Pablo Picasso (artist). T **990** and similar vert designs. Multicoloured. P 11½×12½.

3053	13st. Type 990	55	40
3054	30st. *Portrait of Jacqueline*	70	55
3055	42st. *Maternity*	1·90	1·20
3053/3055	Set of 3	2·75	1·90
MS3056	61×79 mm. 1l. *Self-portrait*	3·75	3·50

991 Boy and Girl

(Des St. Kunchev and A. Stareishinski. Litho German Bank Note Ptg Co, Leipzig)

1982 (28 Dec). Second Banners for Peace Children's Meeting (2nd issue). T **991** and similar multicoloured designs. P 14.

3057	3st. Type 991	30	25
3058	5st. Market place	35	25
3059	8st. Children in fancy dress (vert)	40	30
3060	13st. Chickens (vert)	55	40
3061	25st. Interlocking heads	1·10	45
3062	30st. Lion	1·30	60
3057/3062	Set of 6	3·50	2·00
MS3063	70×109 mm. 50st. Boy and girl in garden (vert). Perf or imperf	2·75	2·50

992 Lions

993 Broadcasting Tower

(Des St. Kunchev. Photo)

1982 (28 Dec). New Year. T **992** and similar horiz design. Multicoloured. P 13.

3064	5st. Type 992	35	25
3065	13st. Decorated letters	55	40

(Des V. Kantardzhieva. Photo)

1982 (29 Dec). 60th Anniversary of Avram Stoyanov Broadcasting Institute. P 13.

3066	**993**	5st. ultramarine	35	25

994 Dr. Robert Koch

995 Simón Bolívar (bicentenary)

(Des T. Tonchev. Photo)

1982 (30 Dec). Centenary of Discovery of Tubercule Bacillus. P 13.

3067	**994**	25st. yellow and olive-green	1·00	45

(Des T. Vardzhiev. Photo)

1982 (30 Dec). Birth Anniversaries. T **995** and similar vert design. P 13.

3068	30st. pale yellow-olive and olive-grey	1·10	60
3069	30st. pale yellow and yellow-brown	1·10	60

Designs: No. 3068, T **995**; No. 3069, Rabindranath Tagore (philosopher, 120th Anniversary).

> During 1983 sets were issued for European Security and Co-operation Conference, Budapest (5st., 13st., 25st., 30st., **MS**1l.), Olympic Games, Los Angeles (5st., 13st., 30st., 42st., **MS**2×50st.), Winter Olympic Games, Sarajevo (horiz designs, 5st., 13st., 30st., 42st., **MS**1l.) and European Security and Co-operation Conference, Madrid (5st., 13st., 30st., 42st., **MS**1l.). Supplies and distribution of these stamps were restricted, and it is understood they were not available at face value.

996 Vasil Levski

(Des I. Bogdanov. Photo)

1983 (10 Feb). 110th Death Anniversary of Vasil Levski (revolutionary). P 13×13½.

3070	**996**	5st. yellow-brown and blackish green	35	25

997 Skier

(Des A. Stareishinski. Photo)

1983 (15 Feb). Universiade '83 University Games, Sofia. P 13.

3071	**997**	30st. multicoloured	1·10	60

BULGARIA 1983

998 Pike (*Esox lucius*)

999 Karl Marx

(Des A. Stareishinski. Photo)

1983 (24 Mar). Freshwater Fish. T **998** and similar horiz designs. Multicoloured. P 13½×13.

3072		3st. Type **998**	30	25
3073		5st. Sturgeon (*Huso huso*)	35	25
3074		13st. Chub (*Leuciscus cephalus*)	55	40
3075		25st. Perch (*Lucioperca lucioperca*)	1·10	45
3076		30st. Catfish (*Silurus glanis*)	1·30	60
3077		42st. Trout (*Salmo trutta fario*)	2·75	1·20
3072/3077	Set of 6		5·75	2·75

(Des I. Kiosev. Photo)

1983 (5 Apr). Death Centenary of Karl Marx. P 13×13½.

3078	**999**	13st. bright scarlet, deep purple and lemon	55	40

1000 Hašek and Illustrations from *The Good Soldier Schweik*

1001 Martin Luther

(Des I. Kiosev. Photo)

1983 (20 Apr). Birth Centenary of Jaroslav Hašek (Czech writer). P 13.

3079	**1000**	13st. reddish brown, pale brownish grey and deep olive	55	40

(Des I. Kiosev. Photo)

1983 (10 May). 500th Birth Anniversary of Martin Luther (Protestant reformer). P 13½×13.

3080	**1001**	13st. pale bluish grey, blackish brown and chestnut	85	45

1002 People forming Initials

(Des P. Petrov. Photo)

1983 (13 May). 55th Anniversary of Young Workers' Union. P 13½×13.

3081	**1002**	5st. vermilion, black and salmon	35	25

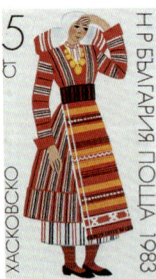
1003 Khaskovo Costume

1004 Old Man feeding Chicken

(Des V. Vasileva. Litho)

1983 (17 May). Costumes. T **1003** and similar vert designs. Multicoloured. P 14.

3082		5st. Type **1003**	35	25
3083		8st. Pernik	40	30
3084		13st. Burgas	55	40
3085		25st. Tolbukhin	1·10	45
3086		30st. Blagoevgrad	1·30	60
3087		42st. Topolovgrad	2·75	95
3082/3087	Set of 6		5·75	2·75

1983 (20 May). Sixth International Festival of Humour and Satire, Gabrovo. P 13.

3088	**1004**	5st. multicoloured	35	25

1005 Smirnenski

1006 Emblem

(Des P. Petrov. Photo)

1983 (25 May). 85th Birth Anniversary of Khristo Smirnenski (poet). P 13.

3089	**1005**	5st. orange-red, sepia and olive-yellow	35	25

(Des V. Kitanov. Photo)

1983 (27 May). 17th International Geodesy Federation Congress. P 13.

3090	**1006**	30st. bright green, deep ultramarine and orange-yellow	1·00	60

1007 Stylised Houses

1008 Chessmen on Map of Europe

(Des Kh. Khristov. Photo)

1983 (6 June). Interarch '83 World Architecture Biennale, Sofia. P 13.

3091	**1007**	30st. multicoloured	1·10	60

(Des Maglena Konstantinova. Photo)

1983 (20 June). Eighth European Chess Team Championship, Plovdiv. P 13.

3092	**1008**	13st. multicoloured	55	40

1009 Brazilian and Bulgarian Football Stamps

1010 Valentina Tereshkova

(Des S. Gruev. Photo)

1983 (24 June). Brasiliana 83 International Stamp Exhibition, Rio de Janeiro. Sheet 73×103 mm. P 13.

MS3093	**1009**	1l. slate-green, reddish brown and gold	3·50	3·25

(Des Tekla Aleksieva. Photo)

1983 (28 June). AIR. 20th Anniversary of First Woman in Space. Sheet 121×75 mm containing T **1010** and similar vert design, each deep ultramarine and chestnut. P 13.

MS3094		50st. Type **1010**; 50st. Svetlana Savitskaya, 1982 cosmonaut	4·25	4·00

1983 BULGARIA

1011 Television Mast, Tolbukhin

1012 Lenin addressing Congress

(Des L. Chekhlarov. Photo)

1983 (20 July). AIR. World Communications Year. T **1011** and similar vert designs. P 13.

3095	5st. pale blue and lake		35	25
	a. Strip of 3. Nos. 3095/3097		1·90	
3096	13st. pale magenta and lake		55	40
3097	30st. bright lemon and lake		85	45
3095/3097 Set of 3			1·60	1·00

Designs: 5st. T **1011**; 13st. Postwoman; 30st. Radio tower, Mount Botev.

Nos. 3095/3097 were issued together in *se-tenant* strips of three within the sheet.

(Des P. Petrov. Photo)

1983 (29 July). 80th Anniversary of Second Russian Social Democratic Workers' Party Congress. P 13.

3098	**1012**	5st. plum, deep reddish purple and gold	35	25

1013 Pistol and Dagger on Book

1014 Crystals and Hammers within Gearwheel

(Des T. Vardzhiev. Photo)

1983 (29 July). 80th Anniversary of Ilinden-Preobrazhenie Rising. P 13.

3099	**1013**	5st. greenish yellow and blackish green	35	25

(Des St. Kunchev. Photo)

1983 (10 Aug). 30th Anniversary of Mining and Geology Institute, Sofia. P 13.

3100	**1014**	5st. olive-grey, blackish purple and dull blue	35	25

1015 Georgi Dimitrov and Revolution Scenes

(Des I. Kiosev. Photo)

1983 (18 Aug). 60th Anniversary of September Uprising. T **1015** and similar horiz design. Multicoloured. P 13½×13.

3101	5st. Type **1015**	35	25
3102	13st. Wreath and revolution scenes	55	40

1016 Animated Drawings

1017 Angora

(Des K. Gogov. Photo)

1983 (15 Sept). Third Animated Film Festival, Varna. P 14×13½.

3103	**1016**	5st. multicoloured	35	25

(Des V. Kitanov. Photo)

1983 (26 Sept). Cats. T **1017** and similar multicoloured designs. P 13.

3104		5st. Type **1017**	35	25
3105		13st. Siamese	70	40
3106		20st. Abyssinian (*vert*)	1·00	45
3107		25st. European	1·30	80
3108		30st. Persian (*vert*)	1·60	1·00
3109		42st. Khmer	2·50	1·50
3104/3109 Set of 6			6·75	4·00

1018 Trevithick's Locomotive, 1803

1019 Liberation Monument, Plovdiv

(Des St. Kunchev. Photo)

1983 (20 Oct). Locomotives (1st series). T **1018** and similar horiz designs. Multicoloured. P 13.

3110	5st. Type **1018**	35	25
3111	13st. Blenkinsop's rack locomotive *Prince Royal*, 1810	70	40
3112	42st. Hedley's *Puffing Billy*, 1812	2·75	1·40
3113	60st. *Der Adler* (first German locomotive), 1835	3·75	2·00
3110/3113 Set of 4		6·75	3·75

See also Nos. 3159/3163.

(Des Veni Kantardzhieva. Photo)

1983 (4 Nov). 90th Anniversary of Bulgarian Philatelic Federation and Fourth National Stamp Exhibition, Plovdiv. Sheet 65×79 mm. P 13.

MS3114	**1019**	50st. grey, royal blue and scarlet-vermilion	2·10	2·00

1020 Mask and Laurel as Lyre

1021 Ioan Kukuzel

(Des Ralitsa Stanoeva. Photo)

1983 (2 Dec). 75th Anniversary of National Opera, Sofia. P 13×13½.

3115	**1020**	5st. brown-lake, black and gold	35	25

(Des I. Kiosev. Photo)

1983 (5 Dec). Bulgarian Composers. T **1021** and similar vert designs. P 13×13½.

3116	5st. pale yellow, chocolate and grey-olive	30	25

185

BULGARIA 1983

3117	8st. pale yellow, chocolate and dull vermilion	35	25
3118	13st. pale yellow, chocolate and bottle green	40	40
3119	20st. pale yellow, chocolate and royal blue	55	45
3120	25st. pale yellow, chocolate and brownish grey	70	55
3121	30st. pale yellow, chocolate and red-brown	85	60
3116/3121	Set of 6	2·75	2·30

Designs: 5st. T **1021**; 8st. Georgi Atanasov; 13st. Petko Stainov; 20st. Veselin Stoyanov; 25st. Lyubomir Pipkov; 30st. Pancho Vladigerov.

Nos. 3116/3121 were each issued with *se-tenant* label depicting the score of one of the composer's works.

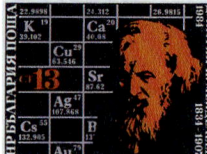
1026 Mendeleev and Formulae

1027 *General Vl. Zaimov* (bulk carrier)

(Des I. Kiosev. Photo)

1984 (14 Mar). 150th Birth Anniversary of Dmitry Mendeleev (chemist). P 13.
| 3134 | **1026** | 13st. multicoloured | 55 | 40 |

(Des M. Peikova. Photo)

1984 (21 Mar). Ships. T **1027** and similar horiz designs. Multicoloured. P 13½×14.
3135		5st. Type **1027**	35	25
3136		13st. *Mesta* (tanker)	55	40
3137		25st. *Veleka* (tanker)	95	45
3138		32st. *Geroite na Odesa* (ferry)	1·10	60
3139		42st. *Rozhen* (bulk carrier)	1·90	75
3135/3139		Set of 5	4·25	2·20

1022 Snowflake

1023 Angelo Donni

(Des St. Kunchev. Photo)

1983 (10 Dec). New Year. P 13.
| 3122 | **1022** | 5st. bright emerald, blue and gold | 35 | 25 |

(Des St. Kunchev. Photo German Bank Note Ptg Co, Leipzig)

1983 (22 Dec). 500th Birth Anniversary of Raphael (artist) (1st issue). T **1023** and similar vert designs. Multicoloured. P 14.
3123		5st. Type **1023**	35	25
3124		13st. *Portrait of a Cardinal*	55	40
3125		30st. *Baldassare Castiglioni*	70	60
3126		42st. *Woman with a Veil*	1·40	75
3123/3126		Set of 4	2·75	1·80
MS3127		59×98 mm. 1l. *Sistine Madonna*	3·00	2·75

See also Nos. 3204/**MS**3208.

1028 World Cup Stamps

1029 Pigeon with Letter over Globe

(Des Ralitsa Stanoeva. Photo)

1984 (18 Apr). España 84 International Stamp Exhibition, Madrid. Sheet 89×110 mm. P 13.
| **MS**3140 | **1028** | 2l. multicoloured | 10·50 | 10·00 |

(Des Maglena Konstantinova. Photo)

1984 (24 Apr). Mladost '84 Youth Stamp Exhibition, Pleven (1st issue). P 13.
| 3141 | **1029** | 5st. multicoloured | 35 | 25 |

See also Nos. 3171/3172 and **MS**3176.

1024 Eurasian Common Shrew (*Sorex araneus*)

1025 Karavelov

(Des B. Kitanov. Photo)

1983 (30 Dec). Protected Mammals. T **1024** and similar horiz designs. Multicoloured. P 13.
3128		12st. Type **1024**	70	45
3129		13st. Greater Horseshoe Bat (*Rhinolophus ferrum equinum*)	1·00	65
3130		20st. Common Long-eared Bat (*Plecotus auritus*)	1·50	80
3131		30st. Forest Dormouse (*Dryomys nitedula*)	2·40	1·00
3132		42st. Fat Dormouse (*Glis glis*)	4·50	1·50
3128/3132		Set of 5	9·00	4·00

> During 1984 sets were issued for European Confidence and Security-building Measures and Disarmament Conference, Stockholm (5st., 13st., 30st., 42st., **MS**1l.) and Winter Olympic Games, Sarajevo (vert designs, 5st., 13st., 30st., 42st., **MS**1l.). Supplies and distribution of these stamps were restricted and it is understood that they were not available at face value.

(Des I. Bogdanov. Photo)

1984 (31 Jan). 150th Birth Anniversary of Lyuben Karavelov (poet). P 13×13½.
| 3133 | **1025** | 5st. deep violet-blue, olive-bistre and reddish brown | 35 | 25 |

1030 Wild Cherries (*Prunus avium*)

1031 *Vitosha Conference* (K. Buyukliiski and P. Petrov)

(Des L. Chekhlarov. Photo)

1984 (5 May). Fruit. T **1030** and similar vert designs. Multicoloured. P 13.
3142		5st. Type **1030**	35	25
3143		8st. Wild Strawberries (*Fragaria vesca*)	40	35
3144		13st. Dewberries (*Rubus caesius*)	55	40
3145		20st. Raspberries (*Rubus idaeus*)	85	45
3146		42st. Medlars (*Mespilus germanica*)	2·20	60
3142/3146		Set of 5	4·00	1·80

(Des D. Karapantev. Photo)

1984 (17 May). 60th Anniversary of Bulgarian Communist Party Conference, Vitosha. P 13½×13.
| 3147 | **1031** | 5st. blackish purple, pale cinnamon and rosine | 35 | 25 |

1984 BULGARIA

1032 Security Conference 1980 13st. Stamp

(Des St. Kunchev. Photo)

1984 (22 May). Fifth International Stamp Fair, Essen. Sheet 94×147 mm containing T **1032** and similar horiz design. Multicoloured. P 13.
MS3148 1l.50 Type **1032**; 1l.50 Security Conference 1981 35st. stamp... 11·00 10·50

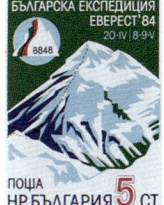

1033 Athlete and Doves   **1034** Mount Everest

(Des A. Stareishinski. Photo)

1984 (23 May). Sixth Republican Spartakiad. P 13.
3149   **1033**   13st. multicoloured........................ 55 40

(Des Kh. Khristov. Photo)

1984 (31 May). Bulgarian Expedition to Mount Everest. P 13.
3150   **1034**   5st. multicoloured.......................... 35 25

1035 Kogge

(Des Tekla Aleksieva. Photo)

1984 (11 June). Universal Postal Union Congress Philatelic Salon, Hamburg. Sheet 100×107 mm. P 13.
MS3151   **1035**   3l. multicoloured........................ 9·75 9·50

1036 Drummer   **1037** Seal

(Des A. Stareishinski. Photo)

1984 (12 June). Sixth Amateur Performers Festival. P 13.
3152   **1036**   5st. multicoloured.......................... 35 25

(Des T. Momchilov. Photo)

1984 (27 June). 50 Years of Bulgarian–USSR Diplomatic Relations. P 13.
3153   **1037**   13st. multicoloured........................ 55 40

1038 Rock Dove   **1039** Production Quality
(*Columba livia*)   Emblem

(Des B. Kitanov. Litho German Bank Note Ptg Co, Leipzig)

1984 (6 July). Pigeons and Doves. T **1038** and similar horiz designs. Multicoloured. P 14.
3154   5st. Type **1038**.................................. 35   25
3155   13st. Stock Dove (*Columba oenas*)........ 55   40
3156   20st. Wood Pigeon (*Columba palumbus*)..... 85   45
3157   30st. Turtle Dove (*Streptopelia turtur*)..... 1·40   60
3158   42st. Domestic Pigeon (*Columba* var. *domestica*)................................... 1·80   75
3154/3158 Set of 5 .... 4·50 2·20

(Des B. Kitanov. Photo)

1984 (31 July). Locomotives (2nd series). Horiz designs as T **1018**. Multicoloured. P 13.
3159   13st. *Best Friend*, Charleston, USA, 1830........ 55   40
3160   25st. *Saxonia*, Dresden, 1836.................. 1·00   45
3161   30st. *Lafayette*, USA, 1837..................... 1·30   60
3162   42st. *Borsig*, Germany, 1841................... 1·80   75
3163   60st. *Philadelphia*, USA, 1843................. 2·75 1·20
3159/3163 Set of 5 .... 6·75 3·00

(Des P. Petrov. Photo)

1984 (8 Aug). 40th Anniversary of Fatherland Front Government. T **1039** and similar vert designs. P 13.
3164   5st. vermilion, deep emerald and yellowish green... 35   25
3165   20st. orange-vermilion and bright violet........ 85   45
3166   30st. orange-vermilion and deep new blue..... 1·30   60
3164/3166 Set of 3 .... 2·30 1·20
Designs: 5st. T **1039**; 20st. Monument to Soviet Army, Sofia; 30st. Figure nine and star.

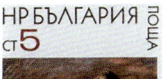

1040 Boy with   **1041** Mausoleum of
Harmonica   Russian Soldiers

(Des K. Kunev. Photo German Bank Note Ptg Co, Leipzig)

1984 (7 Sept). Paintings by Nenko Balkanski. T **1040** and similar multicoloured designs. P 14.
3167   5st. Type **1040**.................................. 35   25
3168   30st. *Window in Paris*............................ 1·30   60
3169   42st. *Portrait of Two Women* (horiz)........ 2·00   75
3167/3169 Set of 3 .... 3·25 1·40
MS3170 65×110 mm. 1l. *Self-portrait*................. 3·50 3·25

1984 (20 Sept). Mladost '84 Youth Stamp Exhibition, Pleven (2nd issue). T **1041** and similar vert design. Photo. P 13.
3171   5st. multicoloured.................................. 35   25
3172   13st. black, deep green and orange-red...... 55   40
Designs: 5st. T **1041**; 13st. Panorama building.

1042 Pioneers saluting   **1043** Vaptsarov (after D. Nikolov)

187

BULGARIA 1984

(Des Tekla Aleksieva. Photo)
1984 (21 Sept). 40th Anniversary of Dimitrov Septembrist Pioneers Organisation. P 13.
3173 **1042** 5st. multicoloured 35 25

1984 (2 Oct). 75th Birth Anniversary of Nikola I. Vaptsarov (poet). Photo. P 13.
3174 **1043** 5st. yellow-ochre and brown-lake 35 25

1044 Goalkeeper saving goal

1045 Profiles

(Des D. Tasev. Photo)
1984 (3 Oct). 75th Anniversary of Bulgarian Football. P 13.
3175 **1044** 42st. multicoloured .... 1·40 75

1984 (5 Oct). Mladost '84 Youth Stamp Exhibition, Pleven (3rd issue). Sheet 50×76 mm. Photo. P 13.
MS3176 **1045** 50st. multicoloured .... 2·10 2·00

1046 Devil's Bridge, River Arda

(Des Kh. Aleksiev. Photo)
1984 (5 Oct). Bridges. T **1046** and similar horiz designs. Multicoloured. P 13½×13.
3177   5st. Type **1046**... 35 25
3178   13st. Kolo Ficheto Bridge, Byala 85 60
3179   30st. Asparukhov Bridge, Varna .... 1·30 1·20
3180   42st. Bebresh Bridge, Botevgrad .... 2·75 2·10
3177/3180 Set of 4 .... 4·75 3·75

Nos. 3177/3180 were each issued in sheetlets of six stamps.
A miniature sheet, 1l. depicting Friendship Bridge, Ruse, exists but supply and distribution were limited.

1047 Olympic Emblem

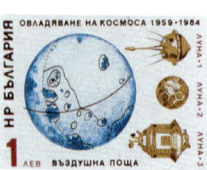
1048 Moon and *Luna 1*, *Luna 2* and *Luna 3*

(Des Kh. Khristov. Photo)
1984 (24 Oct). 90th Anniversary of International Olympic Committee. P 13.
3181 **1047** 13st. multicoloured 55 40

(Des Tekla Aleksieva. Photo)
1984 (24 Oct). 25th Anniversary of First Moon Rocket. Sheet 79×57 mm. P 13.
MS3182 **1048** 1l. multicoloured .... 4·25 4·00

1049 Dalmatian Pelican with Chicks

1050 Anton Ivanov

(Des A. Stareishinski. Photo)
1984 (2 Nov). Wildlife Protection. Dalmatian Pelican (*Pelecanus crispus*). T **1049** and similar vert designs. P 13.
3183   5st. multicoloured 70 45
3184   13st. lavender, black and orange-brown .... 1·40 60
3185   20st. multicoloured .... 2·10 1·50
3186   32st. multicoloured .... 5·00 2·30
3183/3186 Set of 4 .... 8·25 4·25

Designs: 5st. T **1049**; 13st. Two Pelicans; 20st. Pelican on water; 32st. Pelican in flight.

(Des I. Bogdanov. Photo)
1984 (2 Nov). Birth Centenary of Anton Ivanov (revolutionary). P 13.
3187 **1050** 5st. pale yellow, lake-brown and scarlet-vermilion 35 25

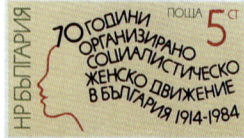
1051 Girl's Profile with Text as Hair

(Des Ralitsa Stanoeva. Photo)
1984 (9 Nov). 70th Anniversary of Bulgarian Women's Socialist Movement. P 13.
3188 **1051** 5st. multicoloured 35 25

1052 Snezhanka Television Tower

1053 Birds and Posthorns

(Des Kh. Khristov. Photo)
1984 (23 Nov). Television Towers. T **1052** and similar vert design. P 13.
3189   5st. deep ultramarine, deep grey-green and bright mauve 35 25
3190   1l. deep brown, bright mauve and olive-bistre .... 3·00 1·50

Designs: 5st. T **1052**; 1l. Orelek television tower.

(Des St. Kunchev. Photo)
1984 (5 Dec). New Year. T **1053** and similar horiz design. Multicoloured. P 13.
3191   5st. Type **1053**... 35 25
3192   13st. Decorative pattern 55 40

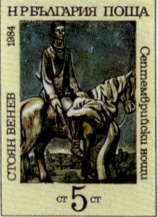
1054 September Nights

1055 Peacock (*Inachis io*)

(Des V. Vasileva. Litho)
1984 (10 Dec). 80th Birth Anniversary of Stoyan Venev (artist). T **1054** and similar vert designs. Multicoloured. P 13.
3193   5st. Type **1054**... 35 25
3194   30st. *Man with Three Orders*........................ 1·10 60
3195   42st. *The Hero*... 1·90 75
3193/3195 Set of 3 .... 3·00 1·40

(Des L. Chekhlarov. Litho)
1984 (14 Dec). Butterflies. T **1055** and similar horiz designs. Multicoloured. P 11½.
3196   13st. Type **1055**....................................... 55 40
3197   25st. Swallowtail (*Papilio machaon*) .... 1·00 45
3198   30st. Great Banded Grayling (*Brintesia circe*).. 1·30 60

3199	42st. Orange-tip (*Anthocharis cardamines*)......		1·80	75
3200	60st. Red Admiral (*Vanessa atalanta*)		2·75	1·10
3196/3200 Set of 5			6·75	3·00
MS3201 75×60 mm. 1l. Poplar Admiral (*Limenitis populi*)..			3·50	3·25

1056 Augusto Sandino
1057 Tupolev Tu-154 Jetliner

(Des G. Nikolov. Photo)

1984 (18 Dec). 50th Death Anniversary of Augusto Sandino (Nicaraguan revolutionary). P 13×13½.

3202	**1056**	13st. black, scarlet-vermilion and lemon...	55	40

(Des Tekla Aleksieva. Photo)

1984 (21 Dec). 40th Anniversary of International Civil Aviation Organisation. P 13½×13.

3203	**1057**	42st. multicoloured..	1·40	75

1058 The Three Graces (detail)
1060 Eastern Hog-nosed Skunk (*Conepatus leuconotus*)

1059 Sofia

1984 (28 Dec). 500th Birth Anniversary (1983) of Raphael (artist) (2nd issue). T **1058** and similar vert designs. Multicoloured. Litho. P 14.

3204		5st. Type **1058**..	35	25
3205		13st. *Cupid and the Three Graces* (detail)........	40	40
3206		30st. *Original Sin* (detail)................................	1·00	55
3207		42st. *La Fornarina*..	2·00	70
3204/3207 Set of 4			3·50	1·70
MS3208 106×95 mm. 1l. *Galatea* (detail)..........................			3·25	3·00

Nos. 3204/3207 were each issued in separate sheetlets of six stamps and also together in *se-tenant* sheetlets of four.

(Des D. Tasev. Photo)

1984 (29 Dec). Maiden Voyage of Danube Cruise Ship *Sofia*. P 13.

3209	**1059**	13st. deep blue, new blue and lemon	55	40

A miniature sheet for Tenth Anniversary of European Security and Co-operation Conference, Helsinki, containing 3×50st., was issued in 1985 in a limited quantity.

(Des A. Stareishinski. Photo)

1985 (17 Jan). Mammals. T **1060** and similar horiz designs. P 13.

3210		13st. black, grey-blue and yellow-orange.......	40	40
3211		25st. black, light brown and yellowish green	1·00	45
3212		30st. black, brown and lemon	1·10	55
3213		42st. multicoloured..	1·70	75
3214		60st. multicoloured..	2·50	1·20
3210/3214 Set of 5			6·00	3·00

Designs: 13st. T **1060**; 25st. Banded Linsang (*Prionodon linsang*); 30st. Zorilla (*Ictonix striatus*); 42st. Banded Palm Civet (*Hemigalus derbyanus*); 60st. Broad-striped Galidia (*Galidictis fasciata*).

1061 Nikolai Liliev

(Des D. Nikolov. Photo)

1985 (25 Jan). Birth Centenary of Nikolai Liliev (poet). P 13.

3215	**1061**	30st. buff, deep yellow-brown and gold	1·00	60

1062 Tsvyatko Radoinov
1063 Asen Zlatarov

(Des D. Nikolov. Photo)

1985 (29 Jan). 90th Birth Anniversary of Tsvyatko Radoinov (resistance fighter). P 13.

3216	**1062**	5st. reddish brown and scarlet-vermilion...	35	25

(Des T. Vardzhiev. Photo)

1985 (14 Feb). Birth Centenary of Asen Zlatarov (biochemist). P 13.

3217	**1063**	5st. brown-purple, pale yellow and green..	35	25

1064 Research Ship *Akademik*
1065 Lenin Monument, Sofia

(Des Tekla Aleksieva. Photo)

1985 (1 Mar). 13th General Assembly and 25th Anniversary of Intergovernmental Oceanographic Commission. Sheet 90×60 mm. P 13.

MS3218	**1064**	80st. multicoloured......................................	2·75	2·50

(Des S. Gruev. Photo)

1985 (12 Mar). 115th Birth Anniversary of Lenin. Sheet 55×87 mm. P 13.

MS3219	**1065**	50st. multicoloured......................................	1·70	1·60

1066 Olive Branch and Sword Blade
1067 Bach

(Des R. Kolev. Photo)

1985 (19 Mar). 30th Anniversary of Warsaw Pact. P 13.

3220	**1066**	13st. multicoloured.......................................	40	30

BULGARIA 1985

(Des A. Stareishinski. Photo)

1985 (25 Mar). Composers. T **1067** and similar vert designs. P 13.
3221	42st. deep steel blue and orange-vermilion..		2·00	90
3222	42st. bluish violet and light green		2·00	90
3223	42st. stone, lake-brown and bright orange....		2·00	90
3224	42st. stone, reddish brown and orange-red...		2·00	90
3225	42st. stone, bottle green and new blue		2·00	90
3226	42st. stone, deep reddish purple and yellowish green		2·00	90
3221/3226 Set of 6			11·00	4·75

Designs: No. 3221, T **1067**; No. 3222, Mozart; No. 3223, Tchaikovsky; No. 3224, Modest Petrovich Musorgsky; No. 3225, Giuseppe Verdi; No. 3226, Filip Kutev.

1068 Girl with Birds   1069 Saint Methodius

(Des St. Kunchev. Litho German Bank Note Ptg Co, Leipzig)

1985 (26 Mar). Third Banners for Peace Children's Meeting, Sofia. T **1068** and similar multicoloured designs showing children's paintings. P 14.
3227	5st. Type **1068**...	30	25
3228	8st. Children painting	35	25
3229	13st. Girl among flowers	40	30
3230	20st. Children at market stall......................	70	40
3231	25st. Circle of children.................................	85	45
3232	30st. Nurse..	1·00	60
3227/3232 Set of 6		3·25	2·00
MS3233 70×110 mm. 50st. Children dancing (*vert*). Perf or imperf.......................................		2·75	2·50

Nos. 3227/3232 were issued both in separate sheets and together in *se-tenant* sheetlets of six.

(Des S. Gruev. Photo)

1985 (6 Apr). 1100th Death Anniversary of Saint Methodius. P 13.
3234	**1069**	13st. multicoloured	1·00	45

1070 Soldiers and Nazi Flags   1071 Woman carrying Child and Man on Donkey

(Des D. Nikolov. Photo)

1985 (30 Apr). 40th Anniversary of VE (Victory in Europe) Day. T **1070** and similar horiz designs. Multicoloured. P 13½.
3235	5st. Type **1070**...	30	25
3236	13st. 11th Infantry parade, Sofia.....................	40	30
3237	30st. Soviet soldier with orphan	1·10	45
3235/3237 Set of 3		1·60	90
MS3238 90×123 mm. 50st. Soldier raising Soviet flag.		2·10	2·00

Nos. 3235/3237 were each issued with *se-tenant* half stamp-size label depicting an Order.

Nos. 3235/3237 were issued both in separate sheets and together in *se-tenant* sheetlets of six stamps and six labels (*Price for sheetlet*: £4.25 un).

(Des S. Dukov. Photo)

1985 (30 Apr). Seventh International Festival of Humour and Satire, Gabrovo. P 13½.
3239	**1071**	13st. black, lemon and dull vermilion .	55	40

No. 3239 was issued with *se-tenant* half stamp-size label bearing festival emblem.

1072 Profiles and Flowers

(Des I. Bogdanov. Photo)

1985 (21 May). International Youth Year. P 13.
3240	**1072**	13st. multicoloured	40	30

1073 Ivan Vazov   1074 Monument to Unknown Soldier and City Arms

(Des P. Petrov. Photo)

1985 (30 May). 135th Birth Anniversary of Ivan Vazov (poet). P 13½.
3241	**1073**	5st. blackish brown and stone	35	25

No. 3241 was issued with *se-tenant* half stamp-size label depicting Vazov's birthplace, Vazovgrad.

(Des K. Gogov. Photo)

1985 (1 June). Millenary of Khaskovo. P 13.
3242	**1074**	5st. multicoloured	30	25

1075 Festival Emblem   1076 Indira Gandhi

(Des D. Tashev. Photo)

1985 (25 June). 12th World Youth and Students' Festival, Moscow. P 13.
3243	**1075**	13st. multicoloured	40	30

(Des D. Nikolov. Photo)

1985 (26 June). Indira Gandhi (Indian Prime Minister) Commemoration. P 13.
3244	**1076**	30st. deep brown, reddish orange and lemon	1·00	45

1077 Vasil E. Aprilov (founder)   1078 Congress Emblem

1985 BULGARIA

(Des I. Bogdanov. Photo)

1985 (30 June). 150th Anniversary of New Bulgarian School, Gabrovo. P 13.

| 3245 | **1077** | 5st. dull violet-blue, maroon and olive-green.. | 30 | 25 |

(Des Kh. Khristov. Photo)

1985 (30 June). 36th International Shorthand and Typing Federation Congress (Intersteno), Sofia. P 13.

| 3246 | **1078** | 13st. multicoloured..................................... | 40 | 30 |

1079 Aleksandr Nevski Cathedral, Sofia

1080 State Arms and UN Flag

(Des R. Kolev. Photo)

1985 (9 July). Sixth General Assembly of World Tourism Organisation, Sofia. P 13.

| 3247 | **1079** | 42st. green, royal blue and yellow-orange... | 1·40 | 75 |

(Des St. Kunchev. Photo)

1985 (16 July). 40th Anniversary of United Nations Organisation (No. 3248) and 30th Anniversary of Bulgaria's Membership (No. 3249). T **1080** and similar horiz design. Multicoloured. P 13.

| 3248 | | 13st. Doves around UN emblem........................ | 40 | 30 |
| 3249 | | 13st. Type **1080**... | 40 | 30 |

1081 Rosa Trakijka

1082 Peace Dove

(Des I. Bogdanov. Litho National Ptg Wks, Havana)

1985 (20 July). Roses. T **1081** and similar vert designs. Multicoloured. P 13.

3250		5st. *Rosa damascena*	30	25
3251		13st. Type **1081**..	40	30
3252		20st. Radiman..	70	40
3253		30st. Marista..	85	45
3254		42st. Valentina...	1·40	60
3255		60st. Maria	2·10	75
3250/3255 Set of 6			5·25	2·50

Nos. 3250/3255 were issued both in separate sheets and together in *se-tenant* sheetlets of six (*Price of sheetlet*: £6·25 *un*).

(Des St. Kunchev. Photo)

1985 (1 Aug). Tenth Anniversary of European Security and Co-operation Conference, Helsinki. P 13.

| 3256 | **1082** | 13st. multicoloured..................................... | 40 | 30 |

1083 Water Polo

1084 Edelweiss

(Des Kh. Aleksiev. Litho National Ptg Wks, Havana)

1985 (2 Aug). European Swimming Championships, Sofia. T **1083** and similar multicoloured designs. P 12½.

3257		5st. Butterfly stroke (*horiz*)	30	25
3258		13st. Type **1083**..	40	30
3259		42st. Diving	1·70	75
3260		60st. Synchronised swimming (*horiz*)................	2·50	90
		a. Inscr and face value inverted	9·00	9·00
3257/3260 Set of 4			4·50	2·00

On No. 3260/3260a the swimmer's head is at the foot of the stamp.

(Des L. Chekhlarov. Photo)

1985 (15 Aug). 90th Anniversary of Bulgarian Tourist Organisation. P 13.

| 3261 | **1084** | 5st. multicoloured.. | 30 | 25 |

1085 State Arms

1086 Footballers

(Des S. Gruev. Photo)

1985 (29 Aug). Centenary of Union of E. Roumelia and Bulgaria. P 14×13½.

| 3262 | **1085** | 5st. black, reddish orange and deep yellow-green .... | 30 | 25 |

(Des D. Tashev. Photo)

1985 (29 Aug). World Cup Football Championship, Mexico (1986) (1st issue). T **1086** and similar designs showing footballers. P 13.

3263		5st. multicoloured	30	25
3264		13st. multicoloured	40	30
3265		30st. multicoloured	1·00	60
3266		42st. multicoloured	2·10	70
3263/3266 Set of 4			3·50	1·70
MS3267 54×76 mm. 1l. multicoloured (*horiz*)................			3·50	3·25

See also Nos. 3346/**MS**3352.

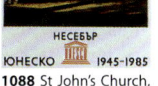
1087 Computer Picture of Boy

(Des L. Chekhlarov. Photo)

1985 (24 Sept). International Young Inventors' Exhibition, Plovdiv. T **1087** and similar horiz designs. Multicoloured. P 13.

3268		5st. Type **1087**...	30	25
3269		13st. Computer picture of youth	40	30
3270		30st. Computer picture of cosmonaut...............	1·10	45
3268/3270 Set of 3			1·60	90

1088 St John's Church, Nesebur   1089 Lyudmila Zhivkova Palace of Culture

(Des K. Kunev. Litho National Ptg Wks, Havana)

1985 (25 Sept). 40th Anniversary of United Nations Educational, Scientific and Cultural Organisation. T **1088** and similar multicoloured designs. P 12½.

| 3271 | | 5st. Type **1088**... | 30 | 25 |
| 3272 | | 13st. Rila Monastery .... | 40 | 30 |

BULGARIA 1985

3273	35st. Soldier (fresco, Ivanovo Rock Church) ...	1·40	60
3274	42st. Archangel Gabriel (fresco, Boyana Church)...	1·70	75
3275	60st. Thracian woman (fresco, Kazanlak tomb)	2·75	95
3271/3275	Set of 5	6·00	2·50
MS3276	100×83 mm. 1l. Madara Horseman (*horiz*). Imperf	2·75	2·50

(Des K. Kunev. Litho National Ptg Wks, Havana)

1985 (8 Oct). 23rd United Nations Educational, Scientific and Cultural Organisation General Session, Sofia. Sheet 62×95 mm. P. 13.

MS3277	**1089**	1l. multicoloured...............................	2·75	2·50

1090 Colosseum, Rome

1091 Gladiolus

(Des St. Kunchev. Photo)

1985 (15 Oct). Italia '85 International Stamp Exhibition, Rome. P 13½.

3278	**1090**	42st. multicoloured..........................	1·40	75

No. 3278 was issued with *se-tenant* half stamp-size label showing the exhibition emblem.

(Des G. Gadelev. Photo)

1985 (22 Oct)–86. Flowers. T **1091** and similar vert designs. P 13×13½.

3279	5st. rose-red and rosine..............................	30	25
3280	5st. royal blue and grey-blue.......................	30	25
3281	5st. bright reddish violet and dull violet	30	25
3282	8st. light new blue and new blue (29.7.86) .	35	25
3283	8st. reddish orange and brown-red (29.7.86)	35	25
3284	32st. yellow-orange and ochre (29.7.86)........	1·00	45
3279/3284	Set of 6	2·30	1·50

Designs: No. 3279, T **1091**; No. 3280, Garden Iris (*Iris germanica*); No. 3281, Dwarf Morning Glory (*Convolvulus tricolor*); No. 3282, Morning Glory (*Ipomoea tricolor*); No. 3283, Anenome coronaria; No. 3284, Golden-rayed Lily (*Lilium auratum*).

1092 St Methodius

1093 Cologne Cathedral

(Des St. Kunchev. Photo)

1985 (22 Oct). Cultural Congress of European Security and Co-operation Conference, Budapest. Sheet 105×93 mm containing T **1092** and similar vert designs. Multicoloured. P 13.

MS3285	50st. St Cyril; 50st. Map of Europe (imperf×p 13); 50st. Type **1092**	5·50 5·25

No. **MS**3285 also exists imperforate from a limited printing.

(Des St. Kunchev. Photo German Bank Note Ptg Co, Leipzig)

1985 (28 Oct). Historic Ships (4th series). 17th-century Ships. Square designs as T 753. Multicoloured. P 13.

3286	5st. Dutch fly...	30	25
3287	12st. *Sovereign of the Seas* (English galleon)..	40	30
3288	20st. Mediterranean polacca.....................	70	40
3289	25st. *Prince Royal* (English warship)	85	45
3290	42st. Xebec...	1·50	90
3291	60st. English warship.................................	2·50	1·10
3286/3291	Set of 6	5·75	3·00

(Des P. Petrov. Photo)

1985 (4 Nov). Philatelia '85 International Stamp Exhibition, Cologne. Sheet 109×56 mm containing T **1093** and similar vert design, each black, bright new blue and scarlet. Imperf.

MS3292 30st. Type **1093**; 30st. Aleksandr Nevski Cathedral, Sofia...	2·10 2·00

1094 Bacho Kiro

1095 Hands, Sword and Bible

(Des T. Vardzhiev. Photo)

1985 (6 Nov). Revolutionaries. T **1094** and similar vert design. P 13.

3293	5st. ochre, deep bistre-brown and deep violet-blue..	30	25
3294	5st. sage green, maroon and deep bistre-brown	30	25

Designs: No. 3293, T **1094**; No. 3294, Georgi S. Rakovski.

(Des T. Vardzhiev. Photo)

1985 (6 Nov). 150th Anniversary of Turnovo Uprising. P 13.

3295	**1095**	13st. grey-brown, deep blue and brown-purple..	40	30

1096 *1185 Revolution* (G. Bogdanov)

1097 Emblem

(Des Kh. Khristov. Photo (1l.), litho (others))

1985 (15 Nov). 800th Anniversary of Liberation from Byzantine Empire. T **1096** and similar horiz designs. Multicoloured. P 13.

3296	5st. Type **1096**..	30	25
3297	13st. *1185 Revolution* (Al. Terziev)	55	30
3298	30st. *Battle of Klakotnitsa, 1230* (B. Grigorov and M. Ganovski)...........................	70	45
3299	42st. *Veliko Turnovo* (Ts. Lavrenov)	2·10	75
3296/3299	Set of 4	3·25	1·60
MS3300	74×80 mm. 1l. Church of St Dimitrius, Veliko Turnovo (38×28 *mm*). Imperf...............................	2·75	2·50

(Des P. Petrov. Photo)

1985 (29 Nov). Balkanfila '85 Stamp Exhibition, Vratsa. Sheet 55×80 mm. P 13.

MS3301	**1097**	40st. greenish blue, black and deep greenish blue..	1·40	1·30

1098 Emblem and Globe

1099 Popov

(Des St. Kunchev. Photo)

1985 (2 Dec). International Development Programme for Posts and Telecommunications. P 13.

3302	**1098**	13st. multicoloured...........................	40	30

(Des A. Stareishinski. Photo)

1985 (11 Dec). 70th Birth Anniversary of Anton Popov (revolutionary). P 13.

3303	**1099**	5st. brown-lake..............................	30	25

1985 **BULGARIA**

1100 Doves around Snowflake

(Des St. Kunchev. Photo)

1985 (11 Dec). New Year. T **1100** and similar horiz design. Multicoloured. P 13.
3304		5st. Type **1100**..	30	25
3305		13st. Circle of stylised Doves.................................	40	30

1101 Pointer and Chukar Partridge

(Des A. Stareishinski. Litho National Ptg Wks, Havana)

1985 (27 Dec). Hunting Dogs. T **1101** and similar horiz designs. Multicoloured. P 13×12½.
3306		5st. Type **1101**..	30	25
3307		8st. Irish Setter and European Pochard	35	25
3308		13st. English Setter and Mallard.........................	40	30
3309		20st. Cocker Spaniel and Woodcock.................	55	40
3310		25st. German Pointer and Rabbit	85	45
3311		30st. Bulgarian Bloodhound and Boar.............	1·10	50
3312		42st. Dachshund and Fox...	2·20	75
3306/3312	Set of 7		5·25	2·50

1102 Person in Wheelchair and Runners
1103 Georgi Dimitrov (statesman)

(Des K. Gogov. Photo)

1985 (30 Dec). International Year of Disabled Persons (1984). P 13.
3313	**1102**	5st. multicoloured	30	25

(Des K. Gogov. Photo)

1985 (30 Dec). 50th Anniversary of Seventh Communist International Congress, Moscow. P 13.
3314	**1103**	13st. brown-lake..	50	30

1104 Emblem within '40'
1105 Blagoev

(Des D. Tasev. Photo)

1986 (21 Jan). 40th Anniversary of United Nations Children's Fund. P 13.
3315	**1104**	13st. bright new blue, gold and black	50	30

(Des A. Stareishinski. Photo)

1986 (28 Jan). 130th Birth Anniversary of Dimitur Blagoev (founder of Bulgarian Social Democratic Party). P 13.
3316	**1105**	5st. maroon and orange-red	30	25

1106 Hands and Dove within Laurel Wreath

(Des K. Gogov. Photo)

1986 (31 Jan). International Peace Year. P 13½×13.
3317	**1106**	5st. multicoloured	30	25

1107 *Dactylorhiza romana*

(Des L. Chekhlarov. Litho National Ptg Wks, Havana)

1986 (12 Feb). Orchids. T **1107** and similar horiz designs. Multicoloured. P 13×12½.
3318		5st. Type **1107**	30	25
3319		13st. *Epipactis palustris*	40	30
3320		30st. *Ophrys cornuta*	55	45
3321		32st. *Limodorum abortivum*	70	55
3322		42st. *Cypripedium calceolus*	1·10	60
3323		60st. *Orchis papilionacea*	2·10	70
3318/3323	Set of 6		4·75	2·50

Nos. 3318/3323 were issued both in individual sheets and together in *se-tenant* sheetlets (*Price for sheetlet*: £5·50 un).

Nos. 3318/3323 exist imperforate from a limited printing.

 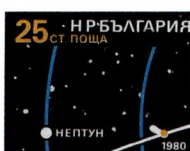

1108 Angora Rabbit
1110 Neptune and Comet Position, 1980

1109 Front Page and Ivan Bogorov

(Des A. Stareishinski. Litho State Ptg Wks, Moscow)

1986 (24 Feb). Rabbits. T **1108** and similar horiz designs. P 12½×12.
3324		5st. greenish slate, black and chestnut..........	30	25
3325		25st. bright carmine-red and black	85	40
3326		30st. olive-sepia, yellow and black.....................	1·00	45
3327		32st. dull orange and black....................................	1·10	55
3328		42st. dull vermilion and black...............................	1·40	60
3329		60st. new blue and black...	2·50	85
3324/3329	Set of 6		6·50	2·75

Designs: 5st. French Grey; 25st. T **1108**; 30st. English Lop-eared; 32st. Belgian; 42st. English Spotted; 60st. Dutch black and white Rabbit.

Nos. 3324/3329 exist imperforate from a limited printing.

(Des I. Bogdanov. Photo)

1986 (28 Feb). 140th Anniversary of *Bulgarian Eagle*. P 13.
3330	**1109**	5st. multicoloured	30	25

BULGARIA 1986

(Des K. Gogov. Photo)

1986 (7 Mar). Appearance of Halley's Comet. Sheet 120×114 mm containing T **1110** and similar horiz designs, each blackish violet, new blue and yellow. P 13½×13.

MS3331	25st. Type **1110**; 25st. Sun, Earth, Mars, Saturn and comet positions, 1985 and 1910–1986; 25st. Uranus and comet positions, 1960, 1926, 1948 and 1970; 25st. Jupiter and comet position, 1911	2·75	2·50

No. **MS**3331 exists imperforate from a limited printing.

 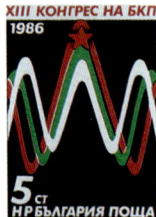

1111 Bashev   **1112** Wave Pattern

(Des A. Stareishinski. Photo)

1986 (12 Mar). 50th Birth Anniversary (1985) of Vladimir Bashev (poet). P 13×13½.

3332	**1111**	5st. royal blue and new blue	30	25

(Des P. Petrov. Photo)

1986 (17 Mar). 13th Bulgarian Communist Party Congress. T **1112** and similar vert designs. P 13.

3333	5st. deep blue, emerald and rosine	30	25
3334	8st. deep new blue and scarlet-vermilion	35	25
3335	13st. deep new blue, scarlet-vermilion and light new blue	40	30
3333/3335	Set of 3	95	70
MS3336	60×77 mm. 50st. multicoloured. Imperf	1·40	1·30

Designs: 5st. T **1112**; 8st. Printed circuit as tail of shooting star; 13st. Computer picture of man; 50st. Steel construction tower.

1113 Vostok 1

(Des K. Gogov. Photo)

1986 (28 Mar). 25th Anniversary of First Man in Space. Sheet 105×100 mm containing T **1113** and similar horiz design, each blackish blue and turquoise-blue. P 13½×13.

MS3337	50st. Type **1113**; 50st. Yuri Gagarin	2·75	2·50

No. **MS**3337 exists imperforate from a limited printing.

1114 Monument, Panagyurishte   **1115** Gymnast

(Des D. Karapantev. Photo)

1986 (30 Mar). 110th Anniversary of April Uprising. T **1114** and similar vert design. P 13.

3338	5st. black, stone and deep emerald	30	25
3339	13st. black, stone and bright scarlet	40	30

Designs: 5st. T **1114**; 13st. Statue of Khristo Botev, Vratsa.

(Des Kh. Aleksiev. Photo)

1986 (12 May). 75th Anniversary of Levski-Spartak Sports Club. Sheet 81×65 mm. Imperf.

MS3340	**1115**	50st. multicoloured	1·40	1·30

1116 Stylised Ear of Wheat   **1117** Transport Systems

(Des B. Ikonomov and O. Funev. Photo)

1986 (19 May). 35th Bulgarian People's Agrarian Union Congress. T **1116** and similar vert designs. P 13.

3341	5st. gold, reddish orange and black	30	25
3342	8st. gold, new blue and black	35	25
3343	13st. multicoloured	40	30
3341/3343	Set of 3	95	70

Designs: 5st. T **1116**; 8st. Stylised ear of Wheat on globe; 13st. Flags.

(Des St. Kunchev. Photo)

1986 (27 May). Socialist Countries' Transport Ministers Conference. P 13.

3344	**1117**	13st. multicoloured	40	30

1118 Emblem   **1119** Player with Ball

(Des O. Khristov. Photo)

1986 (28 May). 17th International Book Fair, Sofia. P 13.

3345	**1118**	13st. olive-grey, bright scarlet and black	40	30

(Des S. Krustev. Photo)

1986 (30 May). World Cup Football Championship, Mexico (2nd issue). T **1119** and similar multicoloured designs. P 13½.

3346	5st. Type **1119**	30	25
3347	13st. Player tackling (horiz)	40	30
3348	20st. Player heading ball (horiz)	55	40
3349	30st. Player kicking ball (horiz)	90	50
3350	42st. Goalkeeper (horiz)	1·30	55
3351	60st. Player with trophy	2·40	70
3346/3351	Set of 6	5·25	2·40
MS3352	95×75 mm. 1l. Azteca Stadium (42×31 mm). P 13	2·75	2·50

Nos. 3346/3351 were each issued with *se-tenant* half stamp-size label depicting a landmark in Mexico.

Nos. 3346/**MS**3352 exist imperforate from limited printing. Nos. 3346/3351 both in separate sheets and together in *se-tenant* sheetlets of six stamps and six labels.

1120 Square Brooch

(Des Kh. Khristov. Litho German Bank Note Ptg Co, Leipzig)

1986 (7 July). Treasures of Preslav. T **1120** and similar multicoloured designs. P 13½×13.

3353	5st. Type **1120**	30	25
3354	13st. Pendant (vert)	40	30
3355	20st. Wheel-shaped pendant	55	40
3356	30st. Breast plate decorated with birds and chalice	90	45
3357	42st. Pear-shaped pendant (vert)	1·20	60
3358	60st. Enamelled Cockerel on gold base	1·40	75
3353/3358	Set of 6	4·25	2·50

1121 Fencers with Sabres

(Des A. Sertev. Photo)

1986 (25 July). World Fencing Championships, Sofia. T **1121** and similar horiz designs. Multicoloured. P 13.
3359	5st. Type **1121**		30	25
3360	13st. Fencers		40	30
3361	25st. Fencers with rapiers		85	45
3359/3361	Set of 3		1·40	90

1122 Stockholm Town Hall

1123 White Stork (*Ciconia ciconia*)

(Des St. Kunchev. Photo)

1986 (25 Aug). Stockholmia 86 International Stamp Exhibition. P 13.
3362 **1122** 42st. deep brown, Venetian red and carmine-lake .... 1·00 90

No. 3362 was issued in sheetlets of three stamps and three labels depicting various Viking stone carvings.

(Des A. Stareishinski. Litho German Bank Note Ptg Co, Leipzig)

1986 (29 Aug). Nature Protection. Sheet 138×90 mm containing T **1123** and similar vert designs. Multicoloured. P 14.
MS3363 30c. Type **1123**; 30c. Yellow Water Lily (*Nuphar lutea*); 30c. Fire Salamander (*Salamandra salamandra*); 30c. White Water Lily (*Nymphaea alba*)............ 5·50 5·25

The miniature sheet contains the four stamps arranged around a central label depicting the oldest Oak tree in Bulgaria at Granit village, Stara Zagora.

No. **MS**3363 also exists imperforate from a limited printing.

1124 Arms and Parliament Building, Sofia

(Des St. Kunchev. Photo)

1986 (15 Sept). 40th Anniversary of People's Republic. P 13.
3364 **1124** 5st. bright turquoise-green, scarlet-vermilion and bright green 30 25

1125 Posthorn

1126 All Pull Together

(Des St. Kunchev. Photo)

1986 (24 Sept). 15th Organisation of Socialist Countries' Postal Administrations Session, Sofia. P 13.
3365 **1125** 13st. multicoloured 40 30

(Des Kh. Khristov. Photo)

1986 (3 Oct). 40th Anniversary of Voluntary Brigades. P 13.
3366 **1126** 5st. multicoloured 30 25

1127 Dove and Book as Pen Nib

1128 Wrestlers

(Des Veni Kantardzhieva. Photo)

1986 (13 Oct). Tenth International Journalists Association Congress, Sofia. P 13.
3367 **1127** 13st. greenish-blue and deep blue....... 40 30

(Des Kh. Aleksiev. Photo)

1986 (Oct). 75th Anniversary of Levski-Spartak Sports Club. P 13.
3368 **1128** 5st. multicoloured 30 25

1129 Saints Cyril and Methodius with Disciples (fresco)

1130 Old and Modern Telephones

(Des K. Kunev. Photo)

1986 (28 Oct). 1100th Anniversary of Arrival in Bulgaria of Pupils of Saints Cyril and Methodius. P 13½.
3369 **1129** 13st. reddish brown and buff................. 50 40

No. 3369 was issued with *se-tenant* half stamp-size inscribed label.

(Des S. Krustev. Photo)

1986 (5 Nov). Centenary of Telephone in Bulgaria. P 13.
3370 **1130** 5st. multicoloured 30 25

1131 Weightlifter

(Des L. Chekhlarov. Photo)

1986 (6 Nov). World Weightlifting Championships, Sofia. P 13.
3371 **1131** 13st. multicoloured 40 30

(Des St. Kunchev. Photo German Bank Note Ptg Co, Leipzig)

1986 (20 Nov). Historic Ships (5th series). 18th-century ships. Square designs as T **753**. Multicoloured. P 13.
3372		5st. *King of Prussia*	30	25
3373		13st. *Indiaman*	40	30
3374		25st. *Xebek*	65	40
3375		30st. *Sv. Pavel*	70	45
3376		32st. Top-sail schooner	90	55
3377		42st. *Victory*	1·60	1·10
3372/3377	Set of 6		4·00	2·75

1132 Hofburg Conference Centre, Vienna (*Illustration reduced, actual size 109×86 mm*)

1133 Silver Jug decorated with seated Woman

BULGARIA 1986

(Des St. Kunchev. Photo)

1986 (27 Nov). European Security and Co-operation Conference Review Meeting, Vienna. Sheet 109×86 mm containing T **1132** and similar vert designs. P 13.
MS3378 50st. brown-olive, bright orange and bright green (Hofberg Vienna); 50st. dull yellowish green, bright orange and new blue (imperf×p 13) (Vienna Town Hall); 50st. multicoloured (United Nations Centre, Vienna).. 5·50 5·25

No. **MS**3378 also exists imperforate from a limited printing.

(Des St. Gruev. Photo)

1986 (5 Dec). 14th Congress of Bulgarian Philatelic Federation and 60th Anniversary of International Philatelic Federation. T **1133** and similar vert design showing repoussé work found at Rogozen. P 13.
3379   10st. slate-black, black and bright turquoise-blue... 35 25
       a. Block of 2. Nos. 3379/3380 plus 2 labels... 75 55
3380   10st. slate-green, black and scarlet-vermilion... 35 25

Designs: No. 3379, T **1133**; No. 3380, Silver jug decorated with Sphinx.

Nos. 3379/3380 were printed in alternate horizontal rows within the same sheet, No. 3379 with *se-tenant* label showing the Congress emblem and No. 3380 with *se-tenant* label showing the FIP anniversary emblem.

Nos. 3379/3380 also exist imperforate from a limited printing.

1134 Doves between Pine Branches

1135 Earphones as '60' on Globe

(Des St. Kunchev. Photo)

1986 (9 Dec). New Year. T **1134** and similar horiz design. P 13.
3381   5st. carmine-vermilion, yellowish green and new blue... 30 25
3382   13st. bright magenta, new blue and violet.... 40 30

Designs: 5st. T **1134**; 13st. Fireworks and snowflakes.

(Des V. Kitanov. Photo)

1986 (10 Dec). 60th Anniversary of Bulgarian Amateur Radio. P 13.
3383   **1135**   13st. multicoloured.................................. 40 30

1136 *The Walnut Tree* (Danail Dechev)

(Des B. Mavrodinov. Litho German Bank Note Ptg Co, Leipzig)

1986 (10 Dec). 90th Anniversary of Sofia Art Academy. Modern Paintings. Sheet 146×102 mm containing T **1136** and similar horiz designs. Multicoloured. P 14.
MS3384 25st. Type **1136**; 25st. *Resistance Fighters and Soldiers* (Iliya Beshkov); 30st. *Melnik* (Veselin Staikov); 30st. *The Olive Grove* (Kiril Tsonev)................. 4·25 4·00

1137 General Augusto Sandino and Flag

(Des St. Kunchev. Photo)

1986 (16 Dec). 25th Anniversary of Sandinista National Liberation Front of Nicaragua. P 13.
3385   **1137**   13st. multicoloured.................................. 40 30

1138 Dimitur and Konstantin Miladinov (authors)

1139 Pencho Slaveikov (poet)

(Des T. Vardzhiev. Photo)

1986 (17 Dec). 125th Anniversary of Publication of Bulgarian Popular Songs. P 13.
3386   **1138**   10st. deep blue, buff and brown-red... 35 25

(Des I. Bogdanov (Nos. 3387/3389), T. Vardzhiev (No. 3390). Photo)

1986 (17 Dec). Writers' Birth Anniversary. T **1139** and similar vert designs. Multicoloured. P 13.
3387   5st. Type **1139** (125th Anniversary)................ 30 25
3388   5st. Stoyan Mikhailovski (130th Anniversary)... 30 25
3389   8st. Nikola Atanasov (dramatist) (centenary)... 35 25
3390   8st. Ran Bosilek (children's author) (centenary)... 35 25
3387/3390 Set of 4 .... 1·20 90

1140 Raiko Daskalov

1141 *Girl with Fruit*

(Des T. Vardzhiev. Photo)

1986 (22 Dec). Birth Centenary of Raiko Daskalov (politician). P 13.
3391   **1140**   5st. purple-brown................................... 30 25

(Des St. Kunchev. Litho German Bank Note Ptg Co, Leipzig)

1986 (23 Dec). 500th Birth Anniversary of Titian (painter). T **1141** and similar vert designs. Multicoloured. P 14.
3392   5st. Type **1141**.. 30 25
3393   13st. *Flora*.. 40 30
3394   20st. *Lucretia and Tarquin*........................... 55 40
3395   30st. *Caiphas and Mary Magdalene* (detail)..... 70 40
3396   32st. *Toilette of Venus* (detail)....................... 85 45
3397   42st. *Self-portrait*... 1·50 60
3392/3397 Set of 6 .... 3·75 2·20
MS3398 105×75 mm. 1l. *Danae* (32×54 mm) .... 4·25 3·75

Nos. 3392/3397 were issued both in separate sheets and also together in *se-tenant* sheetlets (*Price of sheetlet*: £5 *un*).

1142 Fiat, 1905

(Des E. Stankev. Litho North Korean Stamp Ptg Wks, Pyongyang)

1986 (30 Dec). Racing Cars. T **1142** and similar horiz designs. P 13½.
3399   5st. deep brown, rosine and black................. 30 25
3400   10st. brown-red, vermilion and black 35 25
3401   25st. yellowish green, rosine and black......... 70 45

1987 BULGARIA

3402	32st. deep brown, rosine and black		85	55
3403	40st. bright violet, vermilion and black		1·10	60
3404	42st. deep grey, black and scarlet-vermilion		1·50	70
3399/3404	Set of 6		4·25	2·50

Designs: 5st. T **1142**; 10st. Bugatti, 1928; 25st. Mercedes, 1936; 32st. Ferrari, 1952; 40st. Lotus, 1985; 42st. Maclaren, 1986.

1143 Steam Locomotive

(Des Maglena Konstantinova. Litho North Korean Stamp Ptg Wks, Pyongyang)

1987 (19 Jan). 120th Anniversary of Ruse–Vama Railway. P 13½.
3405 **1143** 5st. multicoloured 30 25

1144 Debelyanov   **1145** Lazarus Ludwig Zamenhof (inventor)

(Des D. Nikolov. Photo)

1987 (20 Jan). Birth Centenary of Dimcho Debelyanov (poet). P 13.
3406 **1144** 5st. deep bright blue, greenish yellow and greenish blue 30 25

(Des D. Karapantev. Photo)

1987 (12 Feb). Centenary of Esperanto (invented language). P 13.
3407 **1145** 13st. deep violet-blue, greenish yellow and emerald 40 30

1146 The Blusher (*Amanita rubescens*)   **1147** Worker

(Des L. Chekhlarov. Litho North Korean Stamp Ptg Wks, Pyongyang)

1987 (26 Feb). Edible Fungi. T **1146** and similar vert designs. Multicoloured. P 11½.

3408	5st. Type **1146**	30	25
3409	20st. Royal Boletus (*Boletus regius*)	40	40
3410	30st. Red-capped Scaber Stalk (*Leccinum aurantiacum*)	55	45
3411	32st. Shaggy Ink Cap (*Coprinus comatus*)	70	55
3412	40st. Bare-toothed Russula (*Russula vesca*)	1·00	60
3413	60st. Chanterelle (*Cantharellus cibarius*)	1·10	75
3408/3413	Set of 6	3·75	2·75

Nos. 3408/3413 were issued both in separate sheets and also together in *se-tenant* sheetlets (*Price of sheetlet: £5 un*)

(Des S. Krustev. Photo)

1987 (25 Mar). Tenth Trade Unions Congress, Sofia. P 13.
3414 **1147** 5st. blue-violet and carmine-vermilion 30 25

1148 Silver-gilt Plate with Design of Hercules and Auge

1149 Ludmila Zhivkova Festival Complex, Varna

(Des T. Vardzhiev. Photo German Bank Note Ptg Co, Leipzig)

1987 (31 Mar). Treasure of Rogozen. T **1148** and similar square designs. Multicoloured. P 13.

3415	5st. Type **1148**	30	25
3416	8st. Siver-gilt jug with design of Lioness attacking Stag	35	30
3417	20st. Silver-gilt plate with quatrefoil design	40	40
3418	30st. Silver-gilt jug with design of Horse rider	55	45
3419	32st. Silver-gilt pot with Palm design	70	55
3420	42st. Silver jug with chariot and Horses design	85	60
3415/3420	Set of 6	2·75	2·30

(Des Kh. Khristov. Photo)

1987 (7 Apr). Modern Architecture. Sheet 107×100 mm containing T **1149** and similar horiz designs. Multicoloured. P 13½×13.
MS3421 30st. Type **1149**; 30st. Ministry of Foreign Affairs building, Sofia; 30st. Interpred building, Sofia; 30st. Hotel, Sandanski .... 2·75 2·50

No. **MS**3421 also exists imperforate from a limited printing.

1150 Wrestlers   **1151** Totem Pole

(Des St. Gruev. Photo)

1987 (22 Apr). 30th European Freestyle Wrestling Championships, Turnovo. T **1150** and similar vert design. P 13.

3422	5st. deep lilac, rose-carmine and violet	30	25
3423	13st. deep turquoise-blue, rose-carmine and blue	40	30

Designs: 5st. T **1150**; 13st. Wrestlers (*different*).

(Des St. Kunchev. Photo)

1987 (24 Apr). Capex'87 International Stamp Exhibition, Toronto. P 13.
3424 **1151** 42st. multicoloured .... 1·10 60

(Des D. Tasev. Photo)

1987 (11 May). Tenth Fatherland Front Congress. P 13.
3425 **1152** 5st. emerald, orange-vermilion and deep ultramarine 30 25

(Des Kh. Aleksiev. Photo)

1987 (13 May). 15th Dimitrov Communist Youth League Congress. P 13.
3426 **1153** 5st. brown-purple, emerald and bright scarlet 30 25

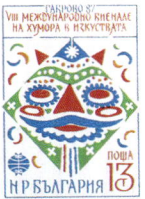 

1152 'X' and Flags   **1153** Georgi Dimitrov and Profiles

1154 Mask   **1155** Mastheads

197

BULGARIA 1987

(Des I. Bogdanov. Photo)

1987 (15 May). Eighth International Festival of Humour and Satire, Gabrovo. P 13×13½.

3427	**1154**	13st. multicoloured	40	30

(Des P. Petrov. Photo)

1987 (28 May). 60th Anniversary of *Rabotnichesko Delo* (newspaper). P 13.

3428	**1155**	5st. bright crimson and black	30	25

1156 Mariya Gigova
1157 Man breaking Chains around Globe and Kolarov

(Des A. Stareishinski. Photo)

1987 (29 May–5 Aug). 13th World Rhythmic Gymnastics Championships, Varna. T **1156** and similar vert designs. P 13.

3429		5st. deep ultramarine and yellow-ochre (5.8.87)	30	25
		a. Perf 13×13½		
3430		8st. bright crimson and yellow-ochre (5.8.87)	35	25
		a. Perf 13×13½		
3431		13st. turquoise-blue and stone (5.8.87)	40	30
		a. Perf 13×13½		
3432		25st. carmine-lake and yellow-ochre (5.8.87)	70	45
3433		30st. new blue and greenish yellow (5.8.87)	85	55
		a. Perf 13×13½		
3434		42st. deep magenta and yellow-ochre (5.8.87)	1·10	60
		a. Perf 13×13½		
3429/3434 *Set of 6*			3·25	2·20
MS3435 78×87 mm 1l. reddish violet and yellow-ochre. P 13×13½			2·75	4·00

Designs: 5st. T **1156**; 8st. Iliana Raeva; 13st. Aneliya Ralenkova; 25st. Dilyana Georgieva; 30st. Liliya Ignatova; 42st. Bianka Panova; 1l. Neshka Robeva.

(Des D. Nikolov. Photo)

1987 (3 June). 110th Birth Anniversary of Vasil Kolarov (Prime Minister 1949–1950). P 13.

3436	**1157**	5st. multicoloured	30	25

1158 Stela Blagoeva
1159 Levski

(Des P. Petrov. Photo)

1987 (4 June). Birth Centenary of Stela Blagoeva. P 13.

3437	**1158**	5st. deep reddish brown and rose-pink	30	25

(Des T. Varadzhiev. Photo)

1987 (19 June). 150th Birth Anniversary of Vasil Levski (revolutionary). T **1159** and similar horiz design. P 13.

3438		5st. lake-brown and bronze green	30	25
3439		13st. bronze green and chestnut	40	30

Designs: 5st. T **1159**; 13st. Levski and Bulgarian Revolutionary Central Committee emblem.

1160 Roe Deer (*Capreolus capreolus*)
1161 Barbed Wire as Dove

(Des K. Gogov. Litho Cuban National Ptg Wks, Havana)

1987 (23 June). Stags. T **1160** and similar multicoloured designs. P 13.

3440		5st. Type **1160**	30	25
3441		10st. Elk (*Alces alces*) (horiz)	35	25
3442		32st. Fallow Deer (*Dama dama*)	85	40
3443		40st. Sika Deer (*Cervus nippon*)	1·00	45
3444		42st. Red Deer (*Cervus elaphus*) (horiz)	1·10	60
3445		60st. Reindeer (*Rangifer tarandus*)	1·50	75
3440/3445 *Set of 6*			4·50	2·40
MS3445a 145×131 mm. Nos. 3340/3345. Imperf			5·00	4·75

(Des S. Krustev. Photo)

1987 (8 July). International Namibia Day. P 13.

3446	**1161**	13st. black, scarlet-vermilion and bright yellow-orange	40	30

1162 Kirkov
1163 *Phacelia tanacetifolia*

(Des A. Stareishinski. Photo)

1987 (17 July). 120th Birth Anniversary of Georgi Kirkov (pseudonym: Maistora) (politician). P 13×13½.

3447	**1162**	5st. brown-lake and dull brown-rose	30	25

(Des Ralitsa Stanoeva. Litho Cuban National Ptg Wks, Havana)

1987 (29 July). Flowers. T **1163** and similar vert designs. Multicoloured. Litho. P 13.

3448		5st. Type **1163**	30	25
3449		10st. Sunflower (*Helianthus annuus*)	35	25
3450		30st. False Acacia (*Robinia pseudoacacia*)	70	45
3451		32st. Dutch Lavender (*Lavandula vera*)	75	55
3452		42st. Small-leaved Lime (*Tilia parvifolia*)	1·00	60
3453		60st. *Onobrychis sativa*	1·40	75
3448/3453 *Set of 6*			4·00	2·50

Nos. 3448/3453 were issued both in separate sheets of 40 stamps and together in *se-tenant* sheetlets of six stamps (*Price of sheetlet*: £4·25 un).

1164 Mil Mi-8 Helicopter, Tupolev Tu-154 Jetliner and Antonov An-12 Transport

1987 (25 Aug). 40th Anniversary of Balkanair. Photo. P 13.

3454	**1164**	25st. multicoloured	70	45

1987 BULGARIA

1165 1879 5c. Stamp

1166 Copenhagen Town Hall

(Des St. Kunchev. Photo)

1987 (3 Sept). Bulgaria '89 International Stamp Exhibition, Sofia (1st issue). P 13.
3455 1165 13st. multicoloured 40 30
See also Nos. 3569, 3579/3582 and 3602/3605.

(Des Kh. Khristov. Photo)

1987 (8 Sept). Hafnia '87 International Stamp Exhibition, Copenhagen. P 13.
3456 1166 42st. multicoloured .... 1·00 75
No. 3456 was issued in sheetlets of three stamps and three inscribed labels.

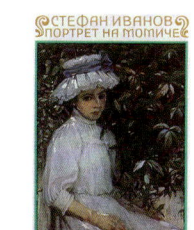

1167 Portrait of Girl (Stefan Ivanov)

1168 Battle Scene

(Des St. Kunchev. Litho German Bank Note Ptg Co, Leipzig)

1987 (15 Sept). Paintings in Sofia National Gallery. T **1167** and similar vert designs. Multicoloured. P 14.
3457 5st. Type **1167** 30 25
3458 8st. Woman carrying Grapes (Bencho Obreshkov) 35 25
3459 20st. Portrait of a Woman wearing a Straw Hat (David Perez) 50 35
3460 25st. Women listening to Marimba (Kiril Tsonev) 55 40
3461 32st. Boy with Harmonica (Nenko Balkanski).. 85 45
3462 60st. Rumyana (Vasil Stoilov) .... 1·50 60
3457/3462 Set of 6 .... 3·75 2·10

1987 (15 Sept). 75th Anniversary of Balkan War. Photo. P 13½×13.
3463 1168 5st. black, stone and orange-red 30 25

1169 Emblem

1171 Winter Wren (Troglodytes troglodytes)

1170 Mastheads

1987 (15 Sept). 30th Anniversary of International Atomic Energy Agency. Photo. P 13½×13.
3464 1169 13st. new blue, light green and bright scarlet 40 30

(Des I. Bogdanov. Photo)

1987 (24 Sept). 95th Anniversary of *Rabotnik*, 90th Anniversary of *Rabotnicheski Vestnik* and 60th Anniversary of *Rabotnichesko Delo* (newspapers). P 13.
3465 1170 5st. deep rose-red, deep Prussian blue and gold........................... 30 25

(Des I. Bogdanov. Litho North Korean Stamp Ptg Wks, Pyongyang)

1987 (12 Oct). Birds. T **1171** and similar vert designs. Multicoloured. P 12.
3466 5st. Type **1171** 30 25
3467 13st. Yellowhammer (*Emberiza citrinella*)......... 40 30
3468 20st. European Nuthatch (*Sitta europaea*)....... 55 40
3469 30st. Blackbird (*Turdus merula*) 85 45
3470 42st. Hawfinch (*Coccothraustes coccothraustes*) .... 1·30 60
3471 60st. Dipper (*Cinclus cinclus*) .... 1·80 75
3466/3471 Set of 6 .... 4·75 2·50
Nos. 3466/3471 were issued both in separate sheets and together in *se-tenant* sheetlets (Price of sheetlet: £5 un).

1172 Vega Automatic Space Station

(Des St. Gruev. Photo)

1987 (16 Oct–24 Dec). 30th Anniversary of Soviet Space Exploration. Sheet 98×98 mm containing T **1172** and similar horiz design. P 13½×13.
MS3472 50st. deep violet-blue, reddish orange and blackish purple (Type **1172**); 50st. deep violet-blue, blue and blackish purple (Soyuz spacecraft docking with *Mir* space station)........................ 3·50 3·25
No. **MS**3472 exists imperforate from a limited printing.
The spaceship in the bottom margin of No. **MS**3472 is inscribed '1961 BOCTOK' and was issued in December. In the initial printing issued in October the inscription read '1964 BOCTOK1'; only a very small quantity was issued, perforated and imperforate.

1173 Lenin and Revolutionary

1174 Biathlon

(Des A. Stareishinski. Litho)

1987 (22 Oct). 70th Anniversary of Russian Revolution. T **1173** and similar horiz design. P 13.
3473 5st. brown-purple and orange-red 30 25
3474 13st. deep ultramarine and orange-red 40 30
Designs: 5st. T **1173**; 13st. Lenin and cosmonaut.

(Des Kh. Aleksiev. Litho German Bank Note Ptg Co, Leipzig)

1987 (27 Oct). Winter Olympic Games, Calgary. T **1174** and similar vert designs. Multicoloured. P 13×13½.
3475 5st. Type **1174** 30 25
3476 13st. Slalom 40 30
3477 30st. Figure skating (women's).................... 70 45
3478 42st. Four-man bobsleigh .... 1·10 75
3475/3478 Set of 4 .... 2·30 1·60
MS3479 65×87 mm. 1l. Ice hockey........................ 2·75 2·50
No. **MS**3479 also exists imperforate from a limited printing.

BULGARIA 1987

1175 Socfilex Emblem within Folk-design Ornament

1176 Helsinki Conference Centre

(Des St. Kunchev. Photo)

1987 (25 Dec). New Year. T **1175** and similar horiz design. Mutlicoloured. P 13.
3480		5st. Type **1175**...	30	25
3481		13st. Emblem within flower ornament.............	40	30

(Des St. Kunchev. Photo)

1987 (30 Dec). European Security and Co-operation Conference Review Meeting, Vienna. Sheet 140×100 mm containing T **1176** and similar vert designs. P 13.
MS3482 50st. lavender, red-brown and bright Indian red (Type **1176**); 50st. multicoloured (Map of Europe) (imperf×P 13); 50st. multicoloured (Vienna Conference Centre)	6·25	6·00

No. **MS**3482 also exists imperforate from a limited printing.

1177 Kabakchiev

1178 *Scilla bythynica*

(Des Tekla Aleksieva. Photo)

1988 (20 Jan). 110th Birth Anniversary of Khristo Kabakchiev (Communist Party official). P 13×13½.
3483	**1177**	5st. multicoloured	30	25

(Des B. Kitanov. Litho North Korean Stamp Ptg Wks, Pyongyang)

1988 (25 Jan). Marsh Flowers. T **1178** and similar vert designs. Multicoloured. P 12.
3484		5st. Type **1178**...	30	25
3485		10st. *Geum rhodopaeum*	35	25
3486		13st. *Caltha polypetala*	40	30
3487		25st. Fringed Water Lily (*Nymphoides peltata*)	55	40
3488		30st. *Cortusa matthioli*	70	45
3489		42st. Water Soldier (*Stratiotes aloides*)	85	60
3484/3489 Set of 6			2·75	2·00

Nos. 3484/3489 were issued both in separate sheets and together in *se-tenant* sheetlets (Price of sheetlet: £3·50 *un*).

1179 Commander on Horseback

1180 Emblem

(Des S. Krustev. Photo)

1988 (15 Feb). 110th Anniversary of Liberation from Turkey. T **1179** and similar horiz design. Multicoloured. P 13.
3490		5st. Type **1179**...	30	25
3491		13st. Soldiers..	40	30

(Des P. Petrunov. Photo)

1988 (22 Mar). Public Sector Workers' Eighth International Congress, Sofia. P 13.
3492	**1180**	13st. multicoloured	40	30

1181 *Yantra*, 1888

(Des Maglena Konstantinova. Litho North Korean Stamp Ptg Wks, Pyongyang)

1988 (25 Mar). Centenary of State Railways. Locomotives. T **1181** and similar horiz designs. Multicoloured. P 11.
3493		5st. Type **1181**..	30	25
3494		13st. *Khristo Botev*, 1905	40	30
3495		25st. Steam locomotive No. 807, 1918.............	70	40
3496		32st. Steam locomotive, 1943	85	45
3497		42st. Diesel locomotive, 1964	1·10	60
3498		60st. Electric locomotive, 1979	1·80	75
3493/3498 Set of 6			4·75	2·50

Nos. 3493/3498 were issued both in individual sheets and together in *se-tenant* sheetlets (Price of sheetlet: £5 *un*).

1182 Ivan Nedyalkov (Shablin)

1183 Traikov

(Des A. Stareishinski. Photo)

1988 (31 Mar). Post Office Anti-fascist Heroes. T **1182** and similar horiz designs. P 13½×13.
3499		5st. pale cinnamon and lake-brown	30	25
3500		8st. bluish grey and royal blue........................	35	25
3501		10st. sage green and olive-green	35	25
3502		13st. pink and carmine-lake............................	40	30
3499/3502 Set of 4			1·30	95

Designs: 5st. T **1182**; 8st. Delcho Spasov; 10st. Nikola Ganchev (Gudzho); 13st. Ganka Rasheva (Boika).

(Des E. Stankev. Litho)

1988 (8 Apr). 90th Birth Anniversary of Georgi Traikov (politician). P 13×13½.
3503	**1183**	5st. bright orange and reddish brown	30	25

1184 Red Cross, Red Crescent and Globe

1185 Girl

(Des D. Tasev. Photo)

1988 (26 Apr). 125th Anniversary of International Red Cross. P 13.
3504	**1184**	13st. multicoloured	40	30

(Des St. Kunchev. Litho German Bank Note Ptg Co, Leipzig)

1988 (28 Apr). Fourth Banners for Peace Children's Meeting, Sofia. T **1185** and similar multicoloured designs showing children's paintings. P 14.
3505		5st. Type **1185**..	30	25
3506		8st. Artist at work...	35	25
3507		13st. Circus (*horiz*)...	40	30
3508		20st. Kite flying (*horiz*)	55	35
3509		32st. Accordion player	70	40
3510		42st. Cosmonaut	85	45
3505/3510 Set of 6			2·75	1·80

MS3511 86×90 mm. 50st. Emblem within film frame (Youth Film Festival) (*horiz*) .... 1·40   1·30
No. **MS**3511 also exists imperforate from a limited printing.

1186 Marx

1187 Herring Gull (*Larus argentatus*)

1191 1856 Handstamp of Russian Duchy of Finland

1192 Player taking Corner Kick

1988 (7 June). Finlandia '88 International Stamp Exhibition, Helsinki. Litho. P 13.
3528   **1191**   30st. blue and vermilion 75   60
No. 3528 was issued in sheetlets of three stamps and three labels bearing the Exhibition emblems of Finlandia '88 and Bulgaria '89 exhibitions.
An imperforate sheetlet with additional marginal inscriptions was issued in March 1989 in a limited printing.

(Des A. Stareishinski. Litho)

1988 (5 May). 170th Birth Anniversary of Karl Marx. P 13.
3512   **1186**   13st. vermilion, black and greenish yellow 40   30

1988 (6 May). Birds. T **1187** and similar vert designs. Multicoloured. Litho. P 13×13½.
3513   5st. Type **1187** 30   25
3514   5st. White Stork (*Ciconia ciconia*) 30   25
3515   8st. Grey Heron (*Ardea cinerea*) 40   30
3516   8st. Carrion Crow (*Corvus corone*) 40   30
3517   10st. Northern Goshawk (*Accipiter gentilis*)... 70   45
3518   42st. Eagle Owl (*Bubo bubo*) .... 2·10   60
3513/3518 Set of 6 .... 3·75   1·90

(Des I. Bogdanov. Litho)

1988 (10 June). Eighth European Football Championship, West Germany. T **1192** and similar multicoloured designs. P 13.
3529   5st. Type **1192** 20   15
3530   13st. Goalkeeper and player 35   25
3531   30st. Referee and player 85   45
3532   42st. Player with trophy .... 1·20   60
3529/3532 Set of 4 .... 2·30   1·30
MS3533 90×69 mm. 1l. Stadium (*horiz*) .... 3·00   2·75
No. **MS**3533 also exists imperforate from a limited printing.

1188 African Elephant (*Loxodonta africana*)

1189 Soyuz TM Spacecraft, Flags and Globe

1193 Portrait of Child

1194 Valentina Tereshkova

(Des K. Kunev. Litho German Bank Note Ptg Co, Leipzig)

1988 (14 June). Second Death Anniversary of Dechko Uzunov (painter). T **1193** and similar vert designs. Multicoloured. P 13×13½.
3534   5st. Type **1193** 20   15
3535   13st. Portrait of Mariya Vasileva 35   25
3536   30st. Self-portrait 85   45
3534/3536 Set of 3 .... 1·30   75

(Des A. Stareishinski. Photo)

1988 (16 June). 25th Anniversary of First Woman in Space. Sheet 87×56 mm. P 13½×13.
MS3537   **1194**   1l. pink and royal blue .... 3·00   2·75
No. **MS**3537 also exists imperforate from a limited printing.

(Des L. Chekhlarov. Litho Cuban National Ptg Wks, Havana)

1988 (20 May). Centenary of Sofia Zoo. T **1188** and similar horiz designs. Multicoloured. P 13.
3519   5st. Type **1188** 20   15
3520   13st. White Rhinoceros (*Ceratotherium simum*) 35   25
3521   25st. Hunting Dog (*Lycaon pictus*) 75   30
3522   30st. Eastern White Pelican (*Pelecanus onocrotalus*) 85   40
3523   32st. Abyssinian Ground Hornbill (*Bucorvus abissinicus*) .... 1·00   50
3524   42st. Snowy Owl (*Nyctea scandiaca*) .... 1·30   80
3519/3524 Set of 6 .... 4·00   2·20
Nos. 3519/3524 were issued both in separate sheets and also together in *se-tenant* sheetlets (Price of sheetlet: £4·25 un).

(Des D. Tasev. Photo)

1988 (7 June). Second Soviet–Bulgarian Space Flight. T **1189** and similar vert design. Multicoloured. P 13.
3525   5st. Type **1189** 20   15
3526   13st. Rocket on globe 35   25

1190 Young Inventor

(Des St. Kunchev. Litho)

1988 (7 June). International Young Inventors' Exhibition, Plovdiv. P 13½×13.
3527   **1190**   13st. multicoloured 35   25

1195 St John

1196 High Jumping

1988 (27 June). Icons from Kurdzhali. T **1195** and similar vert design. Multicoloured. Litho. P 13×13½.
3538   5st. Type **1195** 20   15
3539   8st. St George and Dragon 25   20

BULGARIA 1988

1988 (25 July). Olympic Games, Seoul. T **1196** and similar vert designs. Multicoloured. Litho. P 13.

3540	5st. Type **1196**..	20	15
3541	13st. Weightlifting	35	25
3542	30st. Wrestling	75	35
3543	42st. Gymnastics	1·20	45
3540/3543	*Set of 4*	2·30	1·10
MS3544	115×75 mm. 1l. Volleyball	3·00	2·75

No. **MS**3544 also exists imperforate from a limited printing.

1197 Dimitur and Karadzha

1198 Magazines

1988 (25 July). 120th Death Anniversary of Khadzhi Dimitur and Stefan Karadzha (revolutionaries). P 13.

3545	**1197**	5st. deep green, black and chestnut .	20	15

1988 (26 July). 30th Anniversary of *Problems of Peace and Socialism* (magazine). P 13.

3546	**1198**	13st. multicoloured	35	25

1199 The Dead Tree (Roland Udo)

1200 University Building

(Litho German Bank Note Ptg Co, Leipzig)

1988 (27 July). Paintings in Lyudmila Zhivkova Art Gallery. T **1199** and similar vert designs. Multicoloured. P 14.

3547	30st. Type **1199**...	75	45
3548	30st. *Algiers Harbour* (Albert Marque)	75	45
3549	30st. *Portrait of Hermine David* (Jule Pasquin) ...	75	45
3550	30st. *Madonna and Child with Two Saints* (Giovanni Rosso) ...	75	45
3547/3550	*Set of 4*	2·75	1·60

(Des D. Karapantev. Litho)

1988 (22 Aug). Centenary of St Clement of Ohrid University, Sofia. P 13.

3551	**1200**	5st. black, greenish yellow and yellowish green	20	15

1201 Czechoslovakia 1918 Stamp Design

1202 Korea 1884 5m. Stamp

(Des St. Kunchev. Litho)

1988 (22 Aug). Praga '88 International Stamp Exhibition, Prague. P 13.

3552	**1201**	25st. rosine and bright royal blue	60	45

No. 3552 was issued in sheetlets of three stamps and three labels bearing the emblems of Praga '88 and Bulgaria '89 exhibitions.

An imperforate sheetlet with additional marginal inscriptions was issued in March 1989 in a limited printing.

(Des St. Kunchev. Litho)

1988 (1 Sept). Olymphilex '88 Olympic Stamps Exhibition, Seoul. P 13.

3553	**1202**	62st. carmine-vermilion and emerald ..	1·70	1·50

No. 3553 was issued in sheetlets of three stamps and three labels bearing the emblems of Olymphilex '88 and Bulgaria '89 exhibitions.

1203 Anniversary Emblem

1204 Parliament Building, Sofia, and Map

(Des G. Dobroslavov. Litho)

1988 (15 Sept). 25th Anniversary of Kremikovtsi Steel Mills. P 13.

3554	**1203**	5st. deep blue-violet, rosine and cobalt	20	15

(Des St. Kunchev. Litho)

1988 (16 Sept). 80th Interparliamentary Conference, Sofia. P 13.

3555	**1204**	13st. blue and carmine-vermilion	35	25

1205 Chalice, Glinena

(Des L. Chekhlarov. Litho)

1988 (20 Sept). Kurdzhali Culture. T **1205** and similar multicoloured design. P 13.

3556	5st. Type **1205**...	20	15
3557	8st. Part of ruined fortifications, Perperikon (*vert*)	25	20

1206 Soldiers

1207 Brown Bear (*Ursus arctos*)

(Des D. Ushtavaliiski. Litho)

1988 (23 Sept). 300th Anniversary of Chiprovtsi Rising. P 13.

3558	**1206**	5st. multicoloured	20	15

(Des V. Tsenov. Litho Cuban National Ptg Wks, Havana)

1988 (26 Sept). Bears. T **1207** and similar horiz designs. Multicoloured. P 12½.

3559	5st. Type **1207**...	20	15
3560	8st. Polar Bear (*Thalassarctos maritimus*)	25	20
3561	13st. Sloth Bear (*Melursus ursinus*)	35	25
3562	20st. Sun Bear (*Helarctos malayanus*)	60	30
3563	32st. Asiatic Black Bear (*Selenarctos thibetanus*)	85	45
3564	42st. Spectacled Bear (*Tremarctos ornatus*)	1·50	60
3559/3564	*Set of 6*	3·50	1·75

Nos. 3559/3564 were issued both in separate sheets and together in *se-tenant* sheetlets of six (*Price of sheetlet*: £3·75 *un*).

1208 Emblem

(Des A. Stareishinski. Litho)

1988 (17 Oct). 80th Council of Mutual Economic Aid Transport Commission Meeting, Sofia. P 13½×13.

3565	**1208**	13st. bright crimson and black	35	25

1988 BULGARIA

1209 Emblem

1210 Amphitheatre, Plovdiv

(Des Kh. Khristov. Litho)
1988 (29 Oct). World Ecoforum. P 13.
3566 **1209** 20st. multicoloured 60 35

(Des Kh. Khristov. Litho)
1988 (2 Nov). Plovdiv '88 National Stamp Exhibition. P 13.
3567 **1210** 5st. pale lemon, deep brown and rosine 20 15

An imperforate sheetlet containing six examples of No. 3567 and with marginal inscriptions was issued in March 1989 in a limited printing.

1211 Transmission Towers

1212 1879 5c. Stamp

(Des Kh. Khristov. Litho)
1988 (17 Nov). 25th Anniversary of Radio and Television. P 13.
3568 **1211** 5st. bronze green, ultramarine and brown-ochre 20 15

(Des St. Kunchev. Litho)
1988 (22 Nov). Bulgaria '89 International Stamp Exhibition (2nd issue). P 13.
3569 **1212** 42st. yellow-orange, black and deep mauve 85 75

No. 3569 was issued with *se-tenant* label showing the exhibition emblem.
An imperforate sheetlet containing three stamps and three labels and with marginal inscriptions was issued in March 1989 in a limited printing.

1213 *Ruse* (river boat)

(Des Kh. Khristov. Litho)
1988 (25 Nov). 40th Anniversary of Danube Commission. Sheet 104×124 mm containing T **1213** and similar horiz design. Multicoloured. P 13½×13.
MS3570 1l. Type **1213**; 1l. *Al. Stamboliiski* (river cruiser) .... 5·75 5·50

No. **MS**3570 also exists imperforate from a limited printing.

1214 Children and Cars

1215 Rila Hotel, Borovets

(Des D. Tasev. Litho)
1988 (28 Nov). Road Safety Campaign. P 13½×13.
3571 **1214** 5st. multicoloured 20 15

(Des Tekla Aleksieva. Litho)
1988 (19 Dec). Hotels. T **1215** and similar horiz designs. Multicoloured. P 13.
3572 5st. Type **1215** 20 15
3573 8st. Pirin Hotel, Bansko 25 20
3574 13st. Shtastlivetsa Hotel, Vitosha 35 25
3575 30st. Perelik Hotel, Pamporovo 75 45
3572/3575 Set of 4 .... 1·40 95

1216 Tree Decoration

1217 Space Shuttle *Buran*

(Des St. Kunchev. Litho)
1988 (20 Dec). New Year. T **1216** and similar vert design. Multicoloured. P 13.
3576 5st. Type **1216** 20 15
3577 13st. Bulgaria '89 emblem, tree and decorations 35 25

(Des Emiliya Stankeva. Litho)
1988 (28 Dec). Energiya–*Buran* Space Flight. Sheet 102×67 mm. P 13½×13.
MS3578 **1217** 1l. deep dull blue .... 3·00 2·75

No. **MS**3578 also exists imperforate from a limited printing.

1218 Mail Coach

1988 (29 Dec). Bulgaria '89 International Stamp Exhibition, Sofia (3rd issue). Mail Transport. T **1218** and similar horiz designs. Multicoloured. Litho. P 13½×13.
3579 25st. Type **1218** 75 45
3580 25st. Paddle-steamer 75 45
3581 25st. Lorry 75 45
3582 25st. Biplane 75 45
3579/3582 Set of 4 .... 2·75 1·60

Five imperforate sheetlets, four each containing four examples of one design and the fifth containing all four designs, were issued in March 1989 in a limited printing.

1219 India 1947 1½a. Independence Stamp

1220 France 1850 10c. Ceres Stamp

(Des St. Kunchev. Litho)
1989 (14 Jan). India '89 International Stamp Exhibition, New Delhi. P 13.
3583 **1219** 62st. olive-green and red-orange .... 1·50 1·20

No. 3583 was issued in sheetlets of three stamps and three labels bearing the emblems of India '89 and Bulgaria '89 exhibitions.
An imperforate sheetlet was issued in May 1989 in a limited printing.

(Des St. Kunchev. Litho)
1989 (23 Jan). Philexfrance '89 International Stamp Exhibition, Paris. P 13.
3584 **1220** 42st. ochre and ultramarine 85 75

No. 3584 was issued in sheetlets of three stamps and three labels bearing the emblems of Philexfrance '89 and Bulgaria '89 exhibitions.
An imperforate sheetlet was issued in May 1989 in a limited printing.

BULGARIA 1989

1221 Slalom   **1222** Don Quixote (sculpture, House of Humour and Satire)

(Des Kh. Aleksiev. Litho)

1989 (30 Jan). Sofia '89 University Winter Games, Sofia. Sheet 84×142 mm containing T **1221** and similar vert designs. Multicoloured. Imperf.
MS3585 25st. Type **1221**; 25st. Ice hockey; 25st. Biathlon; 25st. Speed skating .... 3·00   2·75

No. **MS**3585 has simulated perforations. The sheet also exists without this simulation from a limited printing.

(Des I. Bogdanov. Litho)

1989 (7 Feb). International Festival of Humour and Satire, Gabrovo. P 13½×13.
3586   **1222**   13st. multicoloured 45   25

1223 Ramonda serbica   **1224** Common Noctule Bat (*Nyctalus noctula*)

(Des B. Kitanov. Litho)

1989 (22 Feb). Flowers. T **1223** and similar vert designs. Multicoloured. P 13×13½.
3587   5st. Type **1223**.. 20   15
3588   10st. *Paeonia maskula* 30   20
3589   25st. *Viola perinensis* 60   35
3590   30st. *Dracunculus vulgaris*................................. 75   45
3591   42st. *Tulipa splendens* .... 1·20   60
3592   60st. *Rindera umbellata* .... 1·50   75
3587/3592 Set of 6 .... 4·00   2·30

Nos. 3587/3592 were issued both in separate sheets and together in *se-tenant* sheetlets of six (*Price of sheetlet*: £4·25 *un*).

(Des G. Drummond. Litho)

1989 (27 Feb). Bats. T **1224** and similar horiz designs. Multicoloured. P 13.
3593   5st. Type **1224**.. 30   20
3594   13st. Greater Horseshoe Bat (*Rhinolophus ferrumequinum*)... 45   35
3595   30st. Large Mouse-eared Bat (*Myotis myotis*).... 1·50   60
3596   42st. Particoloured Frosted Bat (*Vespertilio murinus*)... 2·20   1·70
3593/3596 Set of 4 .... 4·00   2·50

Nos. 3593/3596 were issued both in separate sheets and together in *se-tenant* sheetlets of four (*Price of sheetlet*: £5·75 *un*).

1225 Stamboliiski   **1226** Launch of *Soyuz 33*

(Des Milena Ioich and P. Rashkov. Litho)

1989 (1 Mar). 110th Birth Anniversary of Aleksandur Stamboliiski (Prime Minister 1919–1923). P 13.
3597   **1225**   5st. black and orange................................ 20   15

1989 (10 Apr). Tenth Anniversary of Soviet–Bulgarian Space Flight. Sheet 130×90 mm containing T **1226** and similar vert design. Multicoloured. P 13.
MS3598 50st. Type **1226**; 50st. Cosmonauts Nicolai Rukavishnikov and Georgi Ivanov .... 3·00   2·75

No. **MS**3598 also exists imperforate from a limited printing.

1227 Young Inventor

(Des Kh. Aleksiev. Litho)

1989 (20 Apr). International Young Inventors' Exhibition, Plovdiv. P 13½×13.
3599   **1227**   5st. multicoloured 20   15

1228 Stanke Dimitrov-Marek (Party activist)   **1229** John the Baptist (Toma Vishanov)

(Des Milena Ioich and P. Rashkov. Litho)

1989 (28 Apr). Birth Centenaries. T **1228** and similar design. P 13.
3600   5st. bright carmine-red and black 20   15
3601   5st. bright rose-red and black 20   15

Designs: Vert—No. 3600, T **1228**. Horiz—No. 3601, Petko Yenev (revolutionary).

(Des Tekla Aleksieva and Zh. Aleksiev. Litho)

1989 (28 Apr). Bulgaria '89 International Stamp Exhibition, Sofia (4th issue). Icons. T **1229** and similar vert designs. Multicoloured. P 13×13½.
3602   30st. Type **1229**... 75   45
3603   30st. *St Dimitur* (Ivan Terziev) 75   45
3604   30st. *Archangel Michael* (Dimitur Molerov) 75   45
3605   30st. *Madonna and Child* (Toma Vishanov)..... 75   45
3602/3605 Set of 4 .... 2·75   1·60

Five imperforate sheetlets, four containing four examples of one design and the fifth containing all four designs, were issued in May 1989 in a limited printing.

1230 Fax Machine and Woman reading Letter   **1231** Nike in Quadriga (relief)

(Des Tekla Aleksieva and Zh. Aleksiev. Litho)

1989 (5 May). 110th Anniversary of Bulgarian Post and Telegraph Services. T **1230** and similar vert designs. Multicoloured. P 13×13½.

3606	5st. Type **1230**...	20	15
3607	8st. Telex machine and old telegraph machine	25	20
3608	35st. Modern and old telephones	85	60
3609	42st. Dish aerial and old radio	1·20	75
3606/3609	Set of 4	2·30	1·50

Three imperforate sheetlets, each containing six examples of one design (Nos. 3606, 3607 or 3608), were issued in a limited printing.

(Des Tekla Aleksieva and Zh. Aleksiev. Litho)

1989 (22 May). 58th International Philatelic Federation Congress, Sofia. Sheet 87×120 mm. P 13.

MS3610	**1231**	1l. multicoloured...	3·00	2·75

No. **MS**3610 also exists imperforate from a limited printing.

1232 A. P. Aleksandrov, A. Ya. Solovov and V. P. Savinikh

1233 Party Programme

(Des I. Bogdanov. Litho)

1989 (7 June). AIR. Soyuz TM5 Soviet–Bulgarian Space Flight. P 13½×13.

3611	**1232**	13st. multicoloured	45	30

(Des S. Krustev. Litho)

1989 (15 June). 70th Anniversary of First Bulgarian Communist Party Congress, Sofia. P 13×13½.

3612	**1233**	5st. black, vermilion and brown-lake..........	30	20

1234 Sofronii Vrachanski (250th Anniversary)

1235 Birds

(Des T. Vardzhiev. Litho)

1989 (15 June). Writers' Birth Anniversaries. T **1234** and similar vert designs. P 13.

3613	5st. pale green, bistre-brown and black........	30	20
3614	5st. pale olive-green, bistre and black	30	20

Designs: No. 3613, T **1234**; No. 3614, Iliya Bluskov (150th Anniversary).

(Des V. Konovalov and K. Kunev (30st., 42st.). Litho)

1989 (26 June). Bicentenary of French Revolution. T **1235** and similar horiz designs. Each black, bright scarlet and deep ultramarine. P 13.

3615	13st. Type **1235**...	45	30
3616	30st. Jean-Paul Marat	75	35
3617	42st. Maximilien Robespierre	1·00	45
3615/3617	Set of 3	2·00	1·00

1236 Gymnastics

1237 Aprilov

(Des D. Tasev. Litho)

1989 (30 June). Seventh Friendly Armies Summer Spartakiad. T **1236** and similar horiz designs. Multicoloured. P 13.

3618	5st. Type **1236**...	30	20
3619	13st. Show-jumping..	45	30
3620	30st. Long jumping...	75	45
3621	42st. Shooting	1·00	60
3618/3621	Set of 4	2·30	1·40

(Des T. Vardzhiev. Litho)

1989 (1 Aug). Birth Bicentenary of Vasil Aprilov (educationist). P 13.

3622	**1237**	8st. azure, deep violet-blue and black..	35	25

1238 Zagorchinov

1239 Woman in Kayak

(Des T. Vardzhiev. Litho)

1989 (5 Aug). Birth Centenary of Stoyan Zagorchinov (writer). P 13.

3623	**1238**	10st. deep turquoise, pale grey-brown and black...	35	25

(Des D. Tashev. Litho)

1989 (11 Aug). Canoeing and Kayak Championships, Plovdiv. T **1239** and similar vert designs. Multicoloured. P 13.

3624	**1239**	13st. Type **1239**	45	30
3625		30st. Man in kayak	1·00	45

1240 Felix Nadar taking Photograph from his Balloon *Le Géant* (1863) and Airship *Graf Zeppelin* over Aleksandr Nevski Cathedral, Sofia

(Des Kh. Aleksiev. Litho)

1989 (29 Aug). 150th Anniversary of Photography. P 13½×13.

3626	**1240**	42st. black, stone and lemon	1·50	60

1241 Lammergeier and Lynx

1242 Soldiers

(Des I. Bogdanov. Litho)

1989 (29 Aug). Centenary of Natural History Museum. P 13.

3627	**1241**	13st. multicoloured	45	35

(Des D. Nikolov. Litho)

1989 (30 Aug). 45th Anniversary of Fatherland Front Government. T **1242** and similar vert designs. Multicoloured. P 13.

3628	5st. Type **1242**...	30	20
3629	8st. Welcoming officers....................................	35	25
3630	13st. Crowd of youths......................................	45	30
3628/3630	Set of 3	1·00	70

BULGARIA 1989

1243 Lyubomir Dardzhikov

1244 Yasenov

1249 Tiger and Balloon of Flags

1250 Boy on Skateboard

(Des A. Stareishinski. Litho)

1989 (22 Sept). 48th Death Anniversaries of Post Office War Heroes. T **1243** and similar vert designs. Multicoloured. P 13.
3631	5st. Type **1243**...	30	20
3632	8st. Ivan Bankov Dobrev	35	25
3633	13st. Nestor Antonov	45	30
3631/3633	Set of 3	1·00	70

(Des T. Vardzhiev. Litho)

1989 (25 Sept). Birth Centenary of Khristo Yasenov (writer). P 13.
3634	**1244**	8st. grey-brown, red-brown and black...	35	25

1245 Lorry leaving Weighbridge

1246 Nehru

(Des M. Chankov. Litho)

1989 (25 Sept). 21st Transport Congress, Sofia. P 13.
3635	**1245**	42st. new blue and royal blue	1·50	85

(Des Tekla Aleksieva and Zh. Aleksiev. Litho)

1989 (10 Oct). Birth Centenary of Jawaharlal Nehru (Indian statesman). P 13.
3636	**1246**	13st. stone, brown and black	45	30

1247 Cranes flying

1248 Javelin Sand Boa (*Eryx jaculus turcicus*)

(Des Tekla Aleksieva and Zh. Aleksiev. Litho)

1989 (12 Oct). Ecology Congress of European Security and Co-operation Conference, Sofia. Sheet 130×85 mm containing T **1247** and similar vert design. Multicoloured. P 13.
MS3637 50st. Type **1247**; 1l. Cranes flying (*different*)...	5·75 5·50

No. **MS**3637 also exists imperforate from a limited printing.

(Des L. Cheklarov. Litho)

1989 (20 Oct). Snakes. T **1248** and similar horiz designs. Multicoloured. P 13.
3638	5st. Type **1248**...	30	20
3639	10st. Aesculapian Snake (*Elaphe longissima*)..	35	25
3640	25st. Leopard Snake (*Elaphe situla*)	75	45
3641	30st. Four-lined Rat Snake (*Elaphe quatuorlineata*)	85	60
3642	42st. Cat Snake (*Telescopus fallax*)	1·30	75
3643	60st. Whip Snake (*Coluber rubriceps*)................	1·70	85
3638/3643	Set of 6	4·75	2·75

Nos. 3638/3643 were issued both in separate sheets and together in *se-tenant* sheetlets (*Price of sheetlet*: £5 un).

(Des I. Konstantinov. Litho)

1989 (4 Nov). Young Inventors' Exhibition, Plovdiv. P 13.
3644	**1249**	13st. multicoloured	45	30

(Des D. Tasev. Litho)

1989 (10 Nov). Children's Games. Sheet 100×120 mm containing T **1250** and similar vert designs. Multicoloured. P 13×13½.
MS3645 30st.+15st. Type **1250**; 30st.+15st. Girl with ball and doll; 30st.+15st. Girl jumping over ropes; 30st.+15st. Boy with toy train..............................	5·00 4·75

No. **MS**3645 also exists imperforate from a limited printing.

1251 Goalkeeper saving Ball

1252 Gliders

(Des G. Gadelev. Litho)

1989 (1 Dec). World Cup Football Championship, Italy (1990) (1st issue). T **1251** and similar vert designs. Multicoloured. P 13.
3646	5st. Type **1251**...	30	20
3647	13st. Player tackling..	45	30
3648	30st. Player heading ball	75	45
3649	42st. Player kicking ball	1·70	75
3646/3649	Set of 4	3·00	1·50
MS3650 109×54 mm. 50st. Player tackling; 50st. Players...		3·00	2·75

No. **MS**3650 also exists imperforate from a limited printing. See also Nos. 3675/**MS**3679.

(Des E. Stankev. Litho)

1989 (8 Dec). 82nd International Airsports Federation General Conference, Varna. Aerial Sports. T **1252** and similar horiz designs. Multicoloured. P 13.
3651	5st. Type **1252**...	30	20
3652	13st. Hang gliding..	45	30
3653	30st. Parachutist landing	1·00	50
3654	42st. Free falling parachutist............................	1·20	60
3651/3654	Set of 4	2·75	1·40

1253 Children on Road Crossing

1254 Santa Claus's Sleigh

(Des Ralitsa Stanoeva. Litho)

1989 (12 Dec). Road Safety. P 13.
3655	**1253**	5st. multicoloured	30	20

(Des St. Kunchev. Litho)

1989 (25 Dec). New Year. T **1254** and similar vert design. Multicoloured. P 13.
3656	5st. Type **1254**...	30	20
3657	13st. Snowman	45	30

1989 BULGARIA

1255 European Shorthair
1256 Christopher Columbus and Santa Maria

(Des D. Karapantev. Litho)

1989 (26 Dec). Cats. T **1255** and similar designs. P 13×13½ (vert) or 13½×13 (horiz).

3658	5st. black and bistre-yellow	30	20
3659	5st. black and light grey	30	20
3660	8st. black and yellow	35	25
3661	10st. black and orange-brown	35	25
3662	10st. black and cobalt	35	25
3663	13st. black and rose-red	45	30
3658/3663 Set of 6		1·90	1·30

Designs: Horiz—No. 3659, Persian; No. 3660, European Shorthair (different); No. 3662, Persian (different). Vert—No. 3658, T **1255**, No. 3661, Persian (different); No. 3663, Siamese.

(Des A. Stareishinski. Litho)

1990 (17 Jan). Navigators and their Ships. T **1256** and similar horiz designs. Multicoloured. P 13.

3664	5st. Type **1256**	30	20
3665	8st. Vasco da Gama and *São Gabriel*	35	25
3666	13st. Ferdinand Magellan and *Vitoria*	45	30
3667	32st. Francis Drake and *Golden Hind*	85	60
3668	42st. Henry Hudson and *Discovery*	1·30	75
3669	60st. James Cook and HMS *Endeavour*	1·70	85
3664/3669 Set of 6		4·50	2·75

Nos. 3664/3669 were issued both in separate sheets and together in *se-tenant* sheetlets of six stamps (*Price of sheetlet: £5·25 un*).

1257 Banner
1258 Portrait of Madeleine Rono (Maurice Brianchon)

(Des P. Petrunov. Litho)

1990 (23 Feb). Centenary of Esperanto (invented language) in Bulgaria. P 13.
3670 **1257** 10st. stone, emerald and black............ 35 25

(Des St. Kunchev. Litho)

1990 (23 Mar). Paintings. T **1258** and similar vert designs. Multicoloured. P 14.

3671	30st. Type **1258**	1·00	60
3672	30st. *Still Life* (Suzanne Valadon)	1·00	60
3673	30st. *Portrait of a Woman* (Moise Kisling)	1·00	60
3674	30st. *Portrait of a Woman* (Giovanni Boltraffio)	1·00	60
3671/3674 Set of 4		3·50	2·20

1259 Players
1260 Bavaria 1849 1k. Stamp

(Des S. Krustev. Litho)

1990 (26 Mar). World Cup Football Championship, Italy (2nd issue). T **1259** and similar horiz designs showing various match scenes. P 13.

3675	5st. multicoloured	30	20
3676	13st. multicoloured	45	30
3677	30st. multicoloured	85	45
3678	42st. multicoloured	1·50	60
3675/3678 Set of 4		2·75	1·40
MS3679 80×125 mm. 2×50st. multicoloured		3·75	3·50

No. **MS**3679 exists imperforate from a limited printing.

(Des St. Kunchev. Litho)

1990 (6 Apr). Essen '90 International Stamp Fair. P 13.
3680 **1260** 42st. black and red............ 1·20 1·00

No. 3680 was issued in sheetlets of three stamps and three different labels.

1261 Penny Black
1262 '100' and Rainbow

(Des St. Kunchev. Litho)

1990 (10 Apr). Stamp World London '90 International Stamp Exhibition. Sheet 90×140 mm containing T **1261** and similar horiz design. P 13.
MS3681 50st. black and deep new blue (Type **1261**); 50st. black and bright scarlet (Sir Rowland Hill (instigator of postage stamps)).................. 3·00 2·75

(Des D. Tasev. Litho)

1990 (17 Apr). Centenary of Co-operative Farming. P 13.
3682 **1262** 5st. multicoloured................ 30 20

1263 Elderly Couple at Rest
1264 Map

(Des D. Nikolov. Litho)

1990 (24 Apr). Birth Centenary of Dimitur Chorbadzhyski Chudomir (artist). P 13.
3683 **1263** 5st. multicoloured................ 30 20

(Des Kh. Khristov. Litho)

1990 (1 May). Centenary of Labour Day. P 13×13½.
3684 **1264** 10st. multicoloured................ 35 25

1265 Emblem

(Des A. Stareishinski. Litho)

1990 (13 May). 125th Anniversary of International Telecommunications Union. P 13½×13.
3685 **1265** 20st. bright blue, bright scarlet and black.................. 75 45

BULGARIA 1990

1266 Belgium 1849 10c. Epaulettes Stamp

1267 Lamartine and his House

(Des St. Kunchev. Litho)

1990 (23 May). Belgica '90 International Stamp Exhibition, Brussels. P 13.
| 3686 | **1266** | 30st. olive-brown and emerald | 85 | 75 |

No. 3686 was issued in sheetlets of three stamps and three different labels.

(Des Maglena Konstantinova. Litho)

1990 (15 June). Birth Bicentenary of Alphonse de Lamartine (poet). P 13½×13.
| 3687 | **1267** | 20st. multicoloured | 75 | 45 |

1268 Brontosaurus

(Des I. Bogdanov. Litho Cuban National Ptg Wks, Havana)

1990 (19 June). Prehistoric Animals. T **1268** and similar horiz designs. Multicoloured. P 12½.
3688	5st. Type **1268**	30	20
3689	8st. Stegosaurus	35	25
3690	13st. Edaphosaurus	45	30
3691	25st. Rhamphorhynchus	85	60
3692	32st. Protoceratops	1·20	75
3693	42st. Triceratops	1·70	85
3688/3693	Set of 6	4·25	2·75

Nos. 3688/3693 were issued both in individual sheets and together in se-tenant sheetlets (Price of sheetlet: £5 un).

1269 Swimming

(Des E. Stankev. Litho)

1990 (13 July). Olympic Games, Barcelona (1992) (1st issue). T **1269** and similar horiz designs. Multicoloured. P 13½×13.
3694	5st. Type **1269**	30	20
3695	13st. Handball	45	30
3696	30st. Hurdling	85	60
3697	42st. Cycling	1·50	70
3694/3697	Set of 4	2·75	1·60

MS3698 77×117 mm. 50st. Tennis player serving; 50st. Tennis player waiting to receive ball ... 3·75 3·50

No. **MS**3698 also exists imperforate from a limited printing. See also Nos. 3840/**MS**3844.

1270 Southern Festoon (*Zerynthia polyxena*)

1272 Iosif I

1271 Airbus Industrie A310 Jetliner

(Des T. Vardzhiev. Litho Cuban National Ptg Wks, Havana)

1990 (8 Aug). Butterflies and Moths. T **1270** and similar vert designs. Multicoloured. P 13.
3699	5st. Type **1270**	30	20
3700	10st. Jersey Tiger Moth (*Panaxia quadripunctaria*)	35	25
3701	20st. Willow-herb Hawk Moth (*Proserpinus proserpina*)	60	45
3702	30st. Striped Hawk Moth (*Hyles lineata*)	85	60
3703	42st. *Thecla betulae*	1·00	85
3704	60st. Cynthia's Fritillary (*Euphydryas cynthia*)	1·70	1·20
3699/3704	Set of 6	4·25	3·25

Nos. 3699/3704 were issued both in separate sheets and together in se-tenant sheetlets of six stamps (Price of sheetlet: £5 un).

(Des D. Tasev. Litho)

1990 (30 Aug). Aircraft T **1271** and similar horiz designs. Multicoloured. P 13½×13.
3705	5st. Type **1271** (wrongly inscr 'A300')	30	20
3706	10st. Tupolev Tu-204 jetliner	35	25
3707	25st. Concorde supersonic jetliner	60	45
3708	30st. Douglas DC-9 jetliner	75	60
3709	42st. Ilyushin Il-86 jetliner	1·00	75
3710	60st. Boeing 747-300/400 jetliner	1·70	1·20
3705/3710	Set of 6	4·25	3·00

Nos. 3705/3710 were issued both in separate sheets and together in se-tenant sheetlets of six stamps (Price of sheetlet: £5 un).

(Des Ralitsa Stanoeva. Litho)

1990 (27 Sept). 150th Birth Anniversary of Exarch Iosif I. P 13.
| 3711 | **1272** | 5st. bright mauve, black and green | 30 | 20 |

1273 Road and UN Emblem within Triangles

1274 Putting the Shot

(Des St. Kunchev. Litho)

1990 (9 Oct). International Road Safety Year. P 13.
| 3712 | **1273** | 5st. multicoloured | 30 | 20 |

(Des Kh. Aleksiev. Litho)

1990 (16 Oct). Olymphilex '90 Olympic Stamps Exhibition, Varna. T **1274** and similar vert designs. Multicoloured. P 13×13½.
3713	5st. Type **1274**	30	20
3714	13st. Throwing the discus	45	30
3715	42st. Throwing the hammer	1·00	75
3716	60st. Throwing the javelin	1·50	1·20
3713/3716	Set of 4	3·00	2·20

Nos. 3713/3716 also exist in se-tenant, imperforate sheetlets of four stamps from a limited printing.

1275 Sputnik (first artificial satellite, 1957)

(Des I. Bogdanov. Litho)

1990 (22 Oct). Space Research. T **1275** and similar multicoloured designs. P 13½×13.
| 3717 | 5st. Type **1275** | 30 | 20 |
| 3718 | 8st. Vostok and Yuri Gagarin (first manned flight, 1961) | 35 | 25 |

3719	10st. Aleksei Leonov spacewalking from *Voskhod 2* (first spacewalk, 1965)		35	25
3720	20st. Soyuz–Apollo link, 1975		60	45
3721	42st. Space shuttle *Columbia*, 1981		1·50	75
3722	60st. Space probe *Galileo*		1·70	1·20
3717/3722 Set of 6			4·25	2·75
MS3723 90×71 mm. 1l. Neil Armstrong from *Apollo 11* on lunar surface (first manned moon landing, 1969) (28×53 mm). P 13×13½			3·00	2·75

No. **MS**3723 also exists imperforate from a limited printing.

REPUBLIC
15 November 1990

1276 St Clement of Ohrid   **1277** Tree

(Des A. Popilov. Litho)

1990 (29 Nov). 1150th Birth Anniversary of St Clement of Ohrid, Bishop of Velitsa. P 13.

3724	**1276**	5st. chestnut, black and deep green	30	20

(Des L. Chekhlarov. Litho)

1990 (25 Dec). Christmas. T **1277** and similar vert design. Multicoloured. P 13.

3725		5st. Type **1277**	30	20
3726		20st. Father Christmas	60	35

1278 Skaters

(Des S. Nenov. Litho)

1991 (18 Jan). European Figure Skating Championships, Sofia. P 13½×13.

3727	**1278**	15st. multicoloured	45	35

1279 Chicken

(Des T. Vardzhiev. Litho)

1991 (11 Feb)–**92**. Farm Animals. T **1279** and similar horiz designs. Chalk-surfaced paper. P 13½ (95st.) or 14×13½ (others).

3728	20st. olive-sepia and black (21.8.91)	20	15
3729	25st. deep violet-blue and black (21.8.91)	30	20
3730	30st. red-brown and black	35	25
3731	40st. purple-brown and black (21.8.91)	45	30
3732	62st. deep bluish green and black	65	45
3733	86st. lake and black (21.8.91)	80	50
3734	95st. deep mauve and black (5.5.92)	95	60
3735	1l. sepia and black (21.8.91)	1·00	75
3736	2l. deep dull green and black	2·20	1·50
3737	5l. blue-violet and black	3·75	2·20
3738	10l. deep violet-blue and black (22.2.91)	6·50	3·00
	a. Ordinary paper.		
3728/3738 Set of 11		15·00	9·00

Designs: 20st. Sheep; 25st. Goose; 30st. T **1279**; 40st. Horse; 62st., 95st. Billy Goat; 86st. Sow; 1l. Donkey; 2l. Bull; 5l. Common Turkey; 10l. Cow.

No. 3738a is on whiter paper with creamier gum.

Nos. 3739/3745 are vacant.

 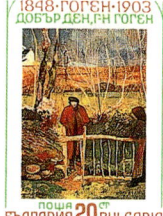

1280 Death Cap (*Amanita phalloides*)   **1281** *Good Day* (Paul Gauguin)

(Des A. Stareishinski. Litho Cuban National Ptg Wks, Havana)

1991 (19 Mar). Fungi. T **1280** and similar vert designs. Multicoloured. P 12½×13.

3746		5st. Type **1280**	20	15
3747		10st. *Amanita verna*	30	20
3748		20st. Panther Cap (*Amanita pantherina*)	35	30
3749		32st. Fly Agaric (*Amanita muscaria*)	45	35
3750		42st. Beefsteak Morel (*Gyromitra esculenta*)	60	45
3751		60st. Satan's Mushroom (*Boletus satanas*)	1·50	75
3746/3751 Set of 6			3·00	2·00

Nos. 3746/3751 were issued both in separate sheets and together in *se-tenant* sheetlets of six stamps (*Price of sheetlet*: £3·75 un).

(Des St. Kunchev. Litho)

1991 (1 Apr). Paintings. T **1281** and similar vert designs. Multicoloured. P 13.

3752		20st. Type **1281**	30	20
3753		43st. *Madame Dobini* (Edgar Degas)	50	30
3754		62st. *Peasant Woman* (Camille Pissarro)	75	45
3755		67st. *Woman with Black hair* (Edouard Manet)	80	65
3756		80st. *Blue Vase* (Paul Cézanne)	1·00	90
3757		2l. *Madame Samari* (Pierre Auguste Renoir)	2·50	1·60
3752/3757 Set of 6			5·25	3·75
MS3758 65×90 mm. 3l. *Self-portrait* (Vincent van Gogh)			3·75	3·50

1282 Map   **1284** *Meteosat* Weather Satellite

1283 Postman on Bicycle, Envelopes and Paper

(Des St. Kunchev. Litho)

1991 (11 Apr). 700th Anniversary of Swiss Confederation. P 13.

3759	**1282**	62st. vermilion and bright reddish violet	85	60

(Des M. Chankov. Litho)

1991 (7 May). 100 Years of Philatelic Publications in Bulgaria. P 13.

3760	**1283**	30st. multicoloured	45	35

BULGARIA 1991

(Des S. Krustev. Litho)

1991 (10 May). Europa. Europe in Space. T **1284** and similar vert design. Multicoloured. P 13×13½.

3761	43st. Type **1284**	1·50	75
3762	62st. Ariane rocket	2·20	1·00

1285 Przewalski's Horse

(Des Kh. Aleksiev. Litho Cuban National Ptg Wks, Havana)

1991 (21 May). Horses. T **1285** and similar horiz designs. Multicoloured. P 13×12½.

3763	5st. Type **1285**	30	20
3764	10st. Tarpan	35	25
3765	25st. Black Arab	40	30
3766	35st. White Arab	45	35
3767	42st. Shetland Pony	60	45
3768	60st. Draught Horse	1·50	75
3763/3768	Set of 6	3·25	2·10

Nos. 3763/3768 were issued both in separate sheets and together in *se-tenant* sheetlets of six stamps (*Price of sheetlet*: £3·75 *un*).

1286 Expo '91

(Des Konstantina Konstantinova. Litho)

1991 (6 June). Expo '91 Exhibition, Plovdiv. P 13½×13.

3769	**1286**	30st. multicoloured	45	35

1287 Mozart

(Des Maglena Konstantinova. Litho)

1991 (2 July). Death Bicentenary of Wolfgang Amadeus Mozart (composer). P 13.

3770	**1287**	62st. multicoloured	85	60

1288 Astronaut and Rear of Space Shuttle *Columbia*

(Des M. Chankov. Litho)

1991 (23 July). Space Shuttles. T **1288** and similar multicoloured designs. P 13.

3771	12st. Type **1288**	30	20
3772	32st. Satellite and *Challenger*	45	35
3773	50st. *Discovery* and satellite	60	35
3774	86st. Satellite and *Atlantis* (vert)	75	45
3775	1l.50 Launch of *Buran* (vert)	1·80	60
3776	2l. Satellite and *Atlantis* (different) (vert)	2·20	75
3771/3776	Set of 6	5·50	2·40
MS3777	86×74 mm. 3l. Earth, *Atlantis* and Moon	3·75	3·50

No. **MS**3777 also exists imperforate from a limited printing.

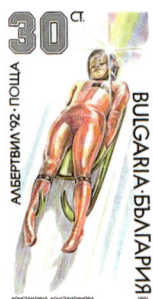

1289 Luge

1290 Sheraton Hotel Balkan, Sofia

(Des Konstantina Konstantinova. Litho)

1991 (7 Aug). Winter Olympic Games, Albertville (1992). T **1289** and similar vert designs. Multicoloured. P 13×13½.

3778	30st. Type **1289**	45	35
3779	43st. Skiing	60	45
3780	67st. Ski jumping	85	60
3781	2l. Biathlon	3·00	1·70
3778/3781	Set of 4	4·50	2·75
MS3782	128×86 mm. 3l. Two-man bobsleigh	3·75	3·50

No. **MS**3782 also exists imperforate from a limited printing.

(Des E. Stankev. Litho)

1991 (6 Sept). P 13.

3783	**1290**	62st. multicoloured	75	60

No. 3783 was issued both in large sheets and in sheetlets of three stamps and three labels showing world map (*Price of sheetlet*: £2·40 *un*).

1291 Japanese Chin   **1292** Arms

(Des Kh. Aleksiev. Litho)

1991 (11 Oct). Dogs. T **1291** and similar vert designs. Multicoloured. P 13×13½.

3784	30st. Type **1291**	35	25
3785	43st. Chihuahua	45	30
3786	62st. Miniature Pinscher	60	35
3787	80st. Yorkshire Terrier	75	45
3788	1l. Mexican Hairless	1·00	75
3789	3l. Pug	3·00	1·50
3784/3789	Set of 6	5·50	3·25

Nos. 3784/3789 were issued both in separate sheets and together in *se-tenant* sheetlets of six stamps (*Price of sheetlet*: £6·50 *un*).

(Des St. Kunchev. Litho)

1991 (21 Oct). Philatelia '91 Stamp Fair, Cologne. P 13.

3790	**1292**	86st. multicoloured	85	75

No. 3790 was issued in sheetlets of three stamps and three different labels.

1293 Brandenburg Gate

1294 Japan 1871 48mon Dragon Stamp

(Des Kh, Khristov. Litho)

1991 (23 Oct). Bicentenary of Brandenburg Gate, Berlin. Sheet 90×70 mm. P 13.

MS3791	**1293**	4l. bottle green and cobalt	3·75	3·50

No. **MS**3791 also exists imperforate from a limited printing.

1991 BULGARIA

(Des St. Kunchev. Litho)
1991 (11 Nov). Phila Nippon '91 International Stamp Exhibition, Tokyo. P 13.
3792 **1294** 62st. black, brown and bright turquoise-blue............ 75 60
No. 3792 was issued in sheetlets of three stamps and three labels each bearing the exhibition emblem and a different motif.

1295 Early Steam Locomotive and Tender

(Des Veni Kantardzhieva. Litho)
1991 (30 Nov). 125th Anniversary of the Railway in Bulgaria. T **1295** and similar horiz design. Multicoloured. P 13.
3793 30st. Type **1295**............................ 45 35
3794 30st. Early passenger carriage............ 45 35

1296 Ball ascending to Basket   **1297** Christ carrying the Cross

(Des Veni Kantardzhieva and Mariya Dimitrova. Litho)
1991 (6 Dec). Centenary of Basketball. T **1296** and similar horiz designs. Multicoloured. P 13½×13.
3795 43st. Type **1296**.................................. 45 30
3796 62st. Ball level with basket mouth............ 60 35
3797 90st. Ball entering basket.................... 75 45
3798 1l. Ball in basket................................ 85 60
3795/3798 Set of 4 .... 2·40 1·50

(Des St. Kunchev. Litho)
1991 (13 Dec). 450th Birth Anniversary of El Greco (painter). T **1297** and similar vert designs. Multicoloured. P 13.
3799 43st. Type **1297**.................................. 35 20
3800 50st. *Holy Family with St Anna*............ 45 25
3801 60st. *St John of the Cross and St John the Evangelist*.. 60 30
3802 62st. *St Andrew and St Francis*............ 75 35
3803 1l. *Holy Family with Magdalene*............ 85 40
3804 2l. *Cardinal Fernando Niño de Guevara*... 1·50 60
3799/3804 Set of 6 .... 4·00 1·90
MS3805 68×86 mm. 3l. Detail of *Holy Family with St Anna* (different) (39×50 mm). P 13........... 2·50 2·00

1298 Snowman, Moon, Candle, Bell and Heart

(Des L. Chekhlarov. Litho)
1991 (18 Dec). Christmas. T **1298** and similar horiz design. Multicoloured. P 13.
3806 30st. Type **1298**.................................. 45 30
3807 62st. Star, clover, Angel, house and Christmas tree.................................... 60 45

1299 Small Pasqueflower (*Pulsatilla pratensis*)

(Des Maglena Konstantinova. Litho)
1991 (20 Dec). Medicinal Plants. T **1299** and similar horiz designs. Multicoloured. P 13.
3808 30st. (+15st.) Pale Pasqueflower (*Pulsatilla vernalis*).. 30 25
3809 40st. Type **1299**.................................. 30 25
3810 55st. *Pulsatilla halleri*........................ 35 30
3811 60st. *Aquilegia nigricans*..................... 45 35
3812 1l. Sea Buckthorn (*Hippophae rhamnoides*) 75 45
3813 2l. Blackcurrant (*Ribes nigrum*)............ 1·50 60
3808/3813 Set of 8 .... 3·25 2·00
No. 3808 includes a *se-tenant* premium-carrying label for 15st. inscribed 'ACTION 2000. For Environment Protection', price is for stamp and label.
Nos. 3808/3813 were issued both in separate sheets and together in *se-tenant* sheetlets of six stamps without the label but with the 15st. premium included in the purchase price (*Price of sheetlet*: £3·75 un).

1300 Greenland Seals (*Phogophoca graenlandica*)

(Des E. Stankev. Litho)
1991 (24 Dec). Marine Mammals. T **1300** and similar horiz designs. Multicoloured. P 13.
3814 30st. Type **1300**.................................. 20 15
3815 43st. Killer Whales (*Orcinus orca*)........... 30 20
3816 62st. Walruses (*Odobenus rosmarus*)....... 35 30
3817 68st. Bottle-nosed Dolphins (*Tursiops truncatus*).. 45 35
3818 1l. Mediterranean Monk Seals (*Monachus monachus*).. 75 45
3819 2l. Common Porpoises (*Phocaena phocaena*).. 1·50 60
3814/3819 Set of 6 .... 3·25 1·80
Nos. 3814/3819 were issued both in separate sheets and together in *se-tenant* sheetlets of six stamps (*Price of sheetlet*: £3·75 un).

1301 Synagogue

(Des St. Kunchev. Litho)
1992 (5 Mar). 500th Anniversary of Jewish Settlement in Bulgaria. P 13.
3820 **1301** 1l. multicoloured........................... 75 45

1302 Rossini, *The Barber of Seville* and Figaro

BULGARIA 1992

(Des T. Vardzhiev. Litho)
1992 (11 Mar). Birth Bicentenary of Gioacchino Rossini (composer). P 13.
3821 **1302** 50st. multicoloured.......................... 45 30

1303 Plan of Fair

(Des G. Stareishinski. Litho)
1992 (25 Mar). Centenary of Plovdiv Fair. P 13.
3822 **1303** 1l. black and stone........................ 75 45

1304 Volvo 740

(Des K. Krustev (Nos. 3823, 3827), I. Panaiotov (No. 3824), Kh. Stoyanov (others). Litho)
1992 (26 Mar). Motor Cars. T **1304** and similar horiz designs. Multicoloured. P 13½×13.
3823 30st. Type **1304**............................... 30 15
3824 45st. Ford Escort.............................. 35 30
3825 50st. Fiat Croma.............................. 45 35
3826 50st. Mercedes Benz 600.................. 45 35
3827 1l. Peugeot 605............................... 1·00 45
3828 2l. BMW 316................................... 1·70 60
3823/3828 Set of 6................................... 3·75 2·00

1305 Amerigo Vespucci

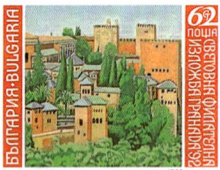
1306 Granada

(Des E. Stankev. Litho)
1992 (22 Apr). Explorers. T **1305** and similar vert designs. Multicoloured. P 13.
3829 50st. Type **1305**............................... 45 35
3830 50st. Francisco de Orellana............... 45 35
3831 1l. Ferdinand Magellan..................... 85 45
3832 1l. Jiménez de Quesada................... 85 45
3833 2l. Sir Francis Drake........................ 1·50 50
3834 3l. Pedro de Valdivia....................... 2·20 75
3829/3834 Set of 6................................... 5·75 2·50
MS3835 121×83 mm. 4l. Christopher Columbus........... 3·75 3·00

(Des St. Kunchev. Litho)
1992 (23 Apr). Granada '92 International Stamp Exhibition. P 13.
3836 **1306** 62st. multicoloured.................. 60 45
 No. 3836 was issued in sheetlets of three stamps and three labels bearing the exhibition emblem and different motifs.

1307 *Santa Maria*

(Des St. Gruev. Litho)
1992 (24 Apr). Europa. 500th Anniversary of Discovery of America by Columbus. T **1307** and similar horiz design. Multicoloured. P 13.
3837 1l. Type **1307**................................. 2·20 75
  a. Horiz pair. Nos. 3837/3838............. 6·25 1·70
3838 2l. Christopher Columbus................ 3·75 95
 Nos. 3837/3838 were issued together in horizontal *se-tenant* pairs within the sheet, each pair forming a composite design.

1308 House

(Des D. Tasev. Litho)
1992 (12 June). SOS Children's Village. P 13.
3839 **1308** 1l. multicoloured........................ 85 45

1309 Long Jumping

(Des Kh. Aleksiev. Litho)
1992 (15 July). Olympic Games, Barcelona (2nd issue). T **1309** and similar multicoloured designs. P 13.
3840 50st. Type **1309**............................... 45 30
3841 50st. Swimming............................... 45 30
3842 1l. High jumping.............................. 75 45
3843 3l. Gymnastics................................ 2·30 75
3840/3843 Set of 4................................... 3·50 1·60
MS3844 52×75 mm. 4l. Olympic Torch (*vert*)........... 3·00 2·50

1310 1902 Laurin and Klement Motorcycle

(Des A. Radevski. Litho)
1992 (30 July). Motorcycles. T **1310** and similar horiz designs. Multicoloured. P 13.
3845 30st. Type **1310**............................... 35 15
3846 50st. 1928 Puch 200 Luxus................ 45 30
3847 50st. 1931 Norton CS 1..................... 45 30
3848 70st. 1950 Harley-Davidson............... 60 35
3849 1l. 1986 Gilera SP 01........................ 85 45
3850 2l. 1990 BMW K 1............................ 1·70 60
3845/3850 Set of 6................................... 4·00 1·90

1311 Genoa

1312 Grasshopper

(Des St. Kunchev. Litho)
1992 (18 Sept). Genova '92 International Thematic Stamp Exhibition. P 13.
3851 **1311** 1l. multicoloured........................ 85 45

(Des T. Vardzhiev. Litho)

1992 (25 Sept)–**93**. Insects. T **1312** and similar horiz designs. Multicoloured. P 13½×14.

3852	1l. Four-spotted Libellula (15.12.93).............		20	15
3853	2l. *Raphidia notata* (15.12.93).......................		45	35
3854	3l. Type **1312** (30.11.92)...............................		1·20	45
3855	4l. Stag Beetle (15.12.93)...............................		1·50	60
3856	5l. Fire Bug (15.12.93)....................................		1·70	75
3857	7l. Ant...		3·00	1·50
3858	20l. Wasp..		7·25	2·20
3859	50l. Praying Mantis (30.11.92)......................		17·00	3·25
3852/3859 *Set of 8*			29·00	8·25

Nos. 3860/3861 are vacant.

1313 Silhouette of Head on Town Plan

1314 Oak (*Quercus mestensis*)

(Des M. Chankov. Litho)

1992 (30 Sept). 50th Anniversary of Institute of Architecture and Building. P 13.

3862	**1313**	1l. deep rose-red and black	85	45

(Des Konstantina Konstantinova. Litho)

1992 (16 Oct). Trees. T **1314** and similar vert designs. Multicoloured. P 13.

3863	50st. Type **1314**...		45	20
3864	50st. Horse Chestnut (*Aesculus hippocastanum*)..		45	20
3865	1l. Oak (*Quercus thracica*)		85	35
3866	1l. Macedonian Pine (*Pinus peuce*)...............		85	35
3867	2l. Maple (*Acer heldreichii*)		1·70	45
3868	3l. Pear (*Pyrus bulgarica*)		2·20	60
3863/3868 *Set of 6*			5·75	1·90

1315 Embroidered Flower

(Des V. Paskalev. Litho)

1992 (23 Oct). Centenary of Folk Museum, Sofia. P 13.

3869	**1315**	1l. multicoloured	85	45

1316 *Bulgaria* (freighter)

(Des L. Chekhlarov. Litho)

1992 (30 Oct). Centenary of National Shipping Fleet. T **1316** and similar horiz designs. Multicoloured. P 13.

3870	30st. Type **1316**...		30	15
3871	50st. *Kastor* (tanker)..................................		45	20
3872	1l. *Geroite na Sebastopol* (ferry)..................		85	35
3873	2l. *Aleko Konstantinov* (tanker)...................		1·50	45
3874	2l. *Bulgaria* (tanker)		1·50	45
3875	3l. *Varna* (container ship)............................		2·30	85
3870/3875 *Set of 6*			6·25	2·20

1317 Council Emblem

(Des St. Gruev and D. Dosev. Litho)

1992 (6 Nov). Admission to Council of Europe. P 13.

3876	**1317**	7l. multicoloured	5·50	3·25

1318 Family exercising on Beach

1319 Father Christmas (Ani Bacheva)

(Des Konstantina Konstantinova. Litho)

1992 (17 Nov). Fourth World Sport for All Congress, Varna. Sheet 58×75 mm. P 13.

MS3877	**1318**	4l. multicoloured.............................	3·00	2·75

(Des V. Paskalev. Litho)

1992 (1 Dec). Christmas. T **1319** and similar horiz designs showing children's drawings. Multicoloured. P 13½×13.

3878	1l. Type **1319**..		75	45
3879	7l. Madonna and Child (Georgi Petkov)......		4·75	1·90

1320 Leopard (*Panthera pardus*)

(Des Olga Paskaleva. Litho)

1992 (18 Dec). Big Cats. T **1320** and similar vert designs. Multicolourcd. P 13.

3880	50st. Type **1320**...		45	20
3881	50st. Cheetah (*Acinonyx jubatus*)................		45	20
3882	1l. Jaguar (*Panthera onca*)		85	45
3883	2l. Puma (*Felis concolor*)		1·70	75
3884	2l. Tiger (*Panthera tigris*)		1·70	75
3885	3l. Lion (*Panthera leo*).................................		2·20	85
3880/3885 *Set of 6*			6·50	3·00

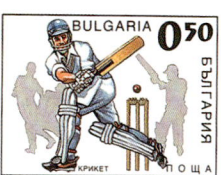
1321 Cricket

(Des S. Krustev. Litho)

1992 (18 Dec). Sport. T **1321** and similar horiz designs. Multicoloured. P 13.

3886	50st. Type **1321**...		45	20
3887	50st. Baseball...		45	20
3888	1l. Pony and trap racing		85	45
3889	1l. Polo..		85	45
3890	2l. Hockey...		1·70	75
3891	3l. American football		2·20	85
3886/3891 *Set of 6*			5·75	2·50

BULGARIA 1992

1322 Tengmalm's Owl (*Aegolius funereus*)

1323 *Khan Kubrat* (Dimitur Gyudzhenov)

(Des Kh. Aleksiev. Litho)

1992 (23 Dec). Owls. T **1322** and similar multicoloured designs. P 13.
3892		30st. Type **1322**..................................	30	15
3893		50st. Tawny Owl (*Strix aluco*) (horiz)	45	20
3894		1l. Long-eared Owl (*Asio otus*)	85	45
3895		2l. Short-eared Owl (*Asio flammeus*)	1·70	75
3896		2l. Scops Owl (*Otus scops*) (horiz)	1·70	75
3897		3l. Barn Owl (*Tyto alba*)	2·50	85
3892/3897		Set of 6	6·75	2·75

(Des D. Karapantev. Litho)

1992 (28 Dec). Historical Paintings. T **1323** and similar multicoloured designs. P 13.
3898		50st. Type **1323**................................	45	20
3899		1l. *Khan Asparukh* (Nikolai Pavlovich)...........	85	45
3900		2l. *Khan Tervel at Tsarigrad* (Dimitur Panchev)...............................	1·50	75
3901		3l. *Prince Boris* (Nikolai Pavlovich)	2·30	1·20
3898/3901		Set of 4	4·50	2·30
MS3902		75×90 mm. 4l. *The Warrior* (Mito Ganovski) (vert)	3·00	2·75

1324 Sculpted Head

1325 Shooting

(Des St. Kunchev. Litho)

1993 (1 Jan). Centenary of National Archaeological Museum, Sofia. P 13½×13½.
3903	**1324**	1l. multicoloured	85	45

(Des E. Stankev. Litho)

1993 (5 Feb). Borovets '93 Biathlon Championship. T **1325** and similar vert design. Multicoloured. P 13½×13½.
3904		1l. Type **1325**..............................	85	45
3905		7l. Cross-country skiing	5·75	2·50

1326 Rilski

1327 *Morning* (sculpture, Georgi Chapkunov)

(Des I. Kosev. Litho)

1993 (22 Apr). Birth Bicentenary of Neofit Rilski (compiler of Bulgarian grammar and dictionary). P 13½×13.
3906	**1326**	1l. bistre and Indian red	85	45

(Des St. Kunchev. Litho)

1993 (29 Apr). Europa. Contemporary Art. T **1327** and similar vert design. Multicoloured. P 13½×13.
3907		3l. Type **1327**..............................	2·20	75
3908		8l. *Composition* (D. Buyukliiski)............	3·75	2·20

1328 Goldfish

1329 Apple (*Malus domestica*)

(Des L. Chekhlarov. Litho)

1993 (29 June). Fish. T **1328** and similar horiz designs. Multicoloured. P 13.
3909		1l. Type **1328**..............................	45	20
3910		2l. Yucatan Sailfish (*Molliensia velifera*)	60	30
3911		3l. Two-striped Killifish (*Aphyosemion bivittatum*)..................................	85	35
3912		3l. Angelfish (*Pterophyllum eimekei*)	85	35
3913		4l. Discus (*Symphysodon discus*)	1·30	45
3914		8l. Pearl Gourami (*Trichogaster leeri*).........	2·75	85
3909/3914		Set of 6	6·00	2·30

(Des Konstantina Konstantinova. Litho)

1993 (8 July). Fruits. T **1329** and similar vert designs. Multicoloured. P 13½×13½.
3915		1l. Type **1329**..............................	45	20
3916		2l. Peach (*Persica vulgaris*)	60	30
3917		2l. Pear (*Pyrus sativa*)	60	30
3918		3l. Quince (*Cydonia oblonga*)	85	35
3919		5l. Pomegranate (*Punica granatum*)	1·70	45
3920		7l. Fig (*Ficus carica*)	2·50	75
3915/3920		Set of 6	6·00	2·10

1330 Monteverdi

1331 High Jumping

(Des I. Kosev. Litho)

1993 (20 July). 350th Death Anniversary of Claudio Monteverdi (composer). P 13½×13.
3921	**1330**	1l. bronze green, yellow and orange-red............................	45	20

(Des S. Kasurov. Litho)

1993 (20 July). International Games for the Deaf, Sofia. T **1331** and similar horiz designs. Multicoloured. P 13.
3922		1l. Type **1331**..............................	45	20
3923		2l. Swimming	60	30
3924		3l. Cycling	85	35
3925		4l. Tennis	1·50	45
3922/3925		Set of 4	3·00	1·20
MS3926		86×75 mm. 5l. Football....................	1·50	1·40

1332 Baptism (from *Manasses Chronicle*)

1333 Prince Alexander

(Des V. Paskalev (T **1332**), T. Vardzhiev (Boris I), St. Gruev (Simeon I), K. Gogov (Cavalry). Litho)

1993 (16 Sept). 1100th Anniversary of Preslav and Introduction of Cyrillic Script. Sheet 113×110 mm containing T **1332** and similar horiz designs. Multicoloured. P 13½.
MS3927	5l. Type **1332**; 5l. Prince Boris I (after Dimitur Gyudzhenov); 5l. Tsar Simeon I (after Dimitur Gyudzhenov); 5l. Cavalry charge (from *Manasses Chronicle*)	5·75 5·50

1993 (23 Sept). Death Centenary of Prince Alexander I. P 13×13½.
3928 **1333** 3l. multicoloured 85 35

1334 Tchaikovsky

1335 Crossbow

(Des L. Metodiev. Litho.)
1993 (30 Sept). Death Centenary of Pyotr Tchaikovsky (composer). P 13½×13.
3929 **1334** 3l. multicoloured 85 35

(Des Konstantina Konstantinova. Litho.)
1993 (22 Oct). Weapons. T **1335** and similar vert designs. Multicoloured. P 13½×14.
3930 1l. Type **1335** 45 20
3931 2l. 18th-century flintlock pistol 60 30
3932 3l. Revolver 85 35
3933 3l. Luger pistol 85 35
3934 5l. Mauser rifle .... 1·60 45
3935 7l. Kalashnikov assault rifle .... 2·30 85
3930/3935 Set of 6 .... 6·00 2·30

1336 Newton

1337 '100' on Stamps and Globe

(Des St. Gruev. Litho.)
1993 (29 Oct). 350th Birth Anniversary of Sir Isaac Newton (mathematician). P 13½×13.
3936 **1336** 1l. multicoloured 45 20

(Des Kh. Aleksiev. Litho.)
1993 (16 Nov). Centenary of Bulgarian Philately. P 13½×13.
3937 **1337** 1l. multicoloured 45 20

1338 'Ecology' in Cyrillic Script

1339 Mallard (*Anas platyrhynchos*)

(Des T. Likho. Litho.)
1993 (17 Nov). Ecology. T **1338** and similar horiz design. Multicoloured. P 13½×13.
3938 1l. Type **1338** 45 20
3939 7l. 'Ecology' in English .... 2·30 75

(Des R. Iliev. Litho.)
1993 (25 Nov). Hunting. T **1339** and similar horiz designs. Multicoloured. P 13½×13.
3940 1l. Type **1339** 45 20
3941 1l. Ring-necked Pheasant (*Phasianus colchicus*) 45 20
3942 2l. Red Fox (*Vulpes vulpes*) 60 30
3943 3l. Roe Deer (*Capreolus capreolus*) 75 45
3944 6l. European Brown Hare (*Lepus europaeus*) .... 1·50 60
3945 8l. Wild Boar (*Sus scrofa*) .... 2·20 85
3940/3945 Set of 6 .... 5·25 2·30

1340 Taurus, Gemini and Cancer

1341 Sofia Costume

(Des N. Gogova. Litho.)
1993 (1 Dec). Christmas. T **1340** and similar horiz designs showing signs of the zodiac. Multicoloured. P 13½×13.
3946 1l. Type **1340** 30 15
       a. Vert pair. Nos. 3946/3947 .... 65 35
3947 1l. Leo, Virgo and Libra 30 15
3948 7l. Aquarius, Pisces and Aries .... 1·70 60
       a. Vert pair. Nos. 3948/3949 .... 3·75 1·30
3949 7l. Scorpio, Sagittarius and Capricorn ..... 1·70 60
3946/3949 Set of 4 .... 3·50 1·40

Nos. 3946/3947 and 3948/3949 respectively were issued together in vertical *se-tenant* pairs within their sheets. When placed together the four stamps form a composite design.

(Des Tekla Aleksieva. Litho.)
1993 (16 Dec). Costumes. T **1341** and similar vert designs. Multicoloured. P 13½×14.
3950 1l. Type **1341** 30 15
3951 1l. Plovdiv 30 15
3952 2l. Belograd 45 30
3953 3l. Oryakhovo 60 45
3954 3l. Shumen 60 45
3955 8l. Kurdzhali .... 1·70 75
3950/3955 Set of 6 .... 3·50 2·00

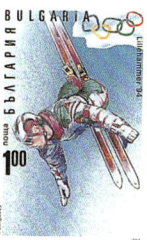
1342 Freestyle Skiing

1343 Self-portrait and *Tsar Simeon*

(Des T. Vardzhiev. Litho.)
1994 (8 Feb). Winter Olympic Games, Lillehammer, Norway. T **1342** and similar vert designs. Multicoloured. P 13.
3956 1l. Type **1342** 30 15
3957 2l. Speed skating 45 30
3958 3l. Two-man luge 75 35
3959 4l. Ice hockey .... 1·00 45
3956/3959 Set of 4 .... 2·30 1·10
MS3960 59×90 mm. 5l. Speed skiing .... 1·20 1·10

(Des I. Kosev. Litho.)
1994 (16 Feb). Death Centenary of Nikolai Pavlovich (artist). P 13½×13.
3961 **1343** 3l. multicoloured 75 45

1344 Plesiosaurus

(Des Konstantina Konstantinova. Litho.)
1994 (27 Apr). Prehistoric Animals. T **1344** and similar horiz designs. Multicoloured. P 13.
3962 2l. Type **1344** 45 30
3963 3l. Archaeopteryx 75 45
3964 3l. Iguanodon 75 45
3965 4l. Edmontonia .... 1·00 60

BULGARIA 1994

3966	5l. Styracosaurus	1·20	75
3967	7l. Tyrannosaurus	1·70	85
3962/3967	Set of 6	5·25	3·00

1345 Players (Chile, 1962) **1346** Photoelectric Analysis (Georgi Nadzhakov)

(Des T. Likho. Litho)

1994 (28 Apr). World Cup Football Championship, USA. T **1345** and similar multicoloured designs. P 13.

3968	3l. Type **1345**	75	45
3969	6l. Players (England, 1966)	1·50	60
3970	7l. Goalkeeper making save (Mexico, 1970)	1·60	75
3971	9l. Player kicking (West Germany, 1974)	2·00	85
3968/3971	Set of 4	5·25	2·40
MS3972	90×123 mm. 5l. Player punching air (Mexico, 1986) (vert); 5l. Player tackling (USA, 1994)	3·00	2·75

See also No. **MS**3996.

(Des Konstantina Konstantinova. Litho)

1994 (29 Apr). Europa. Discoveries. T **1346** and similar horiz design. Multicoloured. P 14×13½.

3973	3l. Type **1346**	1·50	75
3974	15l. Cardiogram and heart (Professor Ivan Mitev)	5·00	2·20

1347 Khristov **1348** Sleeping Hamster

(Des P. Vulchev. Litho)

1994 (18 May). 80th Birth Anniversary of Boris Khristov (actor). P 13.

3975	**1347**	3l. multicoloured	75	45

(Des G. Vásárhelyi. Litho)

1994 (23 Sept). The Common Hamster (*Cricetus cricetus*). T **1348** and similar vert designs. Multicoloured. P 13.

3976	3l. Type **1348**	60	45
3977	7l. Hamster looking out of burrow	1·30	75
3978	10l. Hamster sitting up in grass	2·20	1·00
3979	15l. Hamster approaching berry	3·25	1·60
3976/3979	Set of 4	6·50	3·50

1349 Space Shuttle, Satellite and Dish Aerial **1350** Baron Pierre de Coubertin (founder of modern games)

(Des T. Vardzhiev. Litho)

1994 (4 Nov). North Atlantic Co-operation Council (North Atlantic Treaty Organisation and Warsaw Pact members). P 13.

3980	**1349**	3l. multicoloured	75	45

(Des K. Ivanov. Litho)

1994 (7 Nov). Centenary of International Olympic Committee. P 13×13½.

3981	**1350**	3l. multicoloured	75	45

1351 Christ Pantocrator **1352** Vechernik

(Des V. Aleksandrov and M. Enev. Litho)

1994 (24 Nov). Icons. T **1351** and similar vert designs. Multicoloured. P 13×13½.

3982	2l. Type **1351**	45	20
3983	3l. Raising of Lazarus	75	35
3984	5l. Passion of Christ	85	45
3985	7l. Archangel Michael	1·50	60
3986	8l. Sts Cyril and Methodius	1·70	75
3987	15l. Madonna Enthroned	3·75	85
3982/3987	Set of 6	8·00	3·00

(Des K. Karamfilov. Litho)

1994 (1 Dec). Christmas. Breads. T **1352** and similar vert design. Multicoloured. P 13×13½.

3988	3l. Type **1352**	75	45
3989	15l. Bogovitsa	3·75	1·90

1353 Golden Showers (**1354**)

(Des A. Yaneva. Litho)

1994 (12 Dec). Roses. T **1353** and similar horiz designs. Multicoloured. P 13.

3990	2l. Type **1353**	45	20
3991	3l. Caen Peace Monument	75	35
3992	5l. Thérèse of Lisieux	1·20	45
3993	7l. Zambra 93	1·70	60
3994	10l. Gustave Courbet	2·50	75
3995	15l. Honoré de Balzac	3·75	85
3990/3995	Set of 6	9·25	4·00

1994 (15 Dec). Bulgaria's Fourth Place in World Cup Football Championship. No. **MS**3972 optd with T **1354** in the margin.

MS3996 90×123 mm. 5l. multicoloured; 5l. multicoloured .... 26·00 25·00

1994 BULGARIA

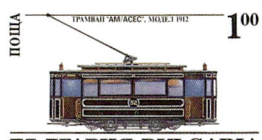

1355 AM/ASES, 1912

(Des O. Gochev. Litho)

1994 (29 Dec). Trams. T **1355** and similar horiz designs. Multicoloured. P 13.
3997	1l. Type **1355**	20	15
3998	2l. AM/ASES, 1928	45	30
3999	3l. MAN/AEG, 1931	75	35
4000	5l. DTO, 1942	1·20	45
4001	8l. Republika, 1951	2·20	85
4002	10l. Kosmonavt articulated tramcar, 1961	2·50	1·00
3997/4002	Set of 6	6·50	2·75

1356 Petleshkov and Flag

1357 Daisy growing through Cracked Helmet

(Des K. Ivanov. Litho)

1995 (27 Feb). 150th Birth Anniversary of Vasil Petleshkov (leader of 1876 April uprising). P 13½×13.
4003	**1356**	3l. multicoloured	75	40

(Des Ya. Vasev. Litho)

1995 (3 May). Europa. Peace and Freedom. T **1357** and similar vert design. Multicoloured. P 13.
4004	3l. Type **1357**	1·50	75
4005	15l. Dove with Olive branch on rifle barrel	5·25	2·30

1358 Player

(Des T. Likho. Litho)

1995 (25 May). Centenary of Volleyball. Sheet 92×75 mm containing T **1358** and similar multicoloured design. P 13.
MS4006 10l. Type **1358**; 15l. Player hitting ball (vert).. 5·25 5·00

1359 Sea Lily (*Pancratium maritimum*)

1360 Emperor Penguin (*Aptenodytes forsteri*)

(Des Krasimira Despotova. Litho)

1995 (23 June). European Nature Conservation Year. Sheet 70×99 mm containing T **1359** and similar horiz design. Multicoloured. P 13.
MS4007 10l. Type **1359**; 15l. Imperial Eagle (*Aquila heliaca*) .... 6·75 6·50

(Des E. Ivanov and T. Likho. Litho)

1995 (29 June). Antarctic Animals. T **1360** and similar multicoloured designs. P 13.
4008	1l. Shrimp (*Euphausia superba*) (horiz)	30	15
4009	2l. Icefish (*Chaenocephalus*) (horiz)	45	30
4010	3l. Sperm Whale (*Physeter catodon*) (horiz)	60	40
4011	5l. Weddell's Seal (*Leptonychotes weddelli*) (horiz)	1·10	45
4012	8l. Arctic Skua (*Stercorarius skua*) (horiz)	1·80	90
4013	10l. Type **1360**	2·30	1·10
4008/4013	Set of 6	6·00	3·00

1361 Stambolov

(Des P. Vulchev. Litho)

1995 (6 July). Death Centenary of Stefan Stambolov (politician). P 13.
4014	**1361**	3l. multicoloured	75	45

1362 Pole Vaulting

1363 Pea (*Pisum sativum*)

(Des E. Stankev. Litho)

1995 (17 July). Olympic Games, Atlanta (1996) (1st issue). T **1362** and similar horiz designs. Multicoloured. P 13.
4015	3l. Type **1362**	60	40
4016	7l. High jumping	1·50	75
4017	10l. Long jumping	2·30	1·10
4018	15l. Triple jumping	3·25	1·50
4015/4018	Set of 4	7·00	3·50

See also Nos. 4083/**MS**4087.

(Des Tekla Aleksieva. Litho)

1995 (31 July). Food Plants. T **1363** and similar vert designs. Multicoloured. P 13.
4019	2l. Type **1363**	45	30
4020	3l. Chickpea (*Cicer arietinum*)	60	40
4021	3l. Soya Bean (*Glicine max*)	60	40
4022	4l. Spinach (*Spinacia oleracea*)	90	45
4023	5l. Peanut (*Arachis hypogaea*)	1·10	60
4024	15l. Lentil (*Lens esculenta*)	3·00	1·50
4019/4024	Set of 6	6·00	3·25

1364 '100'

1365 Ivan Nikolov-Zograf

BULGARIA 1995

(Des Konstantina Konstantinova. Litho)
1995 (21 Aug). Centenary of Organised Tourism. P 13.
4025	**1364**	3l. multicoloured	75	45

(Des St. Kunchev. Litho)
1995 (4 Sept). Birth Centenary of Vasil Zakhariev (painter). T **1365** and similar vert designs. P 13.
4026	2l. multicoloured	45	30
4027	3l. multicoloured	60	40
4028	5l. black, grey-brown and yellow-green......	1·10	45
4029	10l. multicoloured	2·30	1·10
4026/4029 Set of 4		4·00	2·00

Designs: 2l. T **1365**; 3l. *Rila Monastery*; 5l. *Self-portrait*; 10l. *Raspberry Collectors*.

1366 'Dove-Hands' holding Globe

(Des I. Klimentov. Litho)
1995 (12 Sept). 50th Anniversary of United Nations Organisation. P 13.
4030	**1366**	3l. multicoloured	75	45

1367 Polikarpov Po-2 Biplane   1368 Charlie Chaplin and Mickey Mouse

(Des S. Iliev and G. Todorov. Litho)
1995 (26 Sept). Aircraft. T **1367** and similar horiz designs. Multicoloured. P 13.
4031	3l. Type **1367**..	60	40
4032	5l. Lisunov Li-2 airliner.............................	1·10	45
4033	7l. Junkers Ju 52.....................................	1·50	75
4034	10l. Focke Wulf Fw 58	2·30	1·10
4031/4034 Set of 4		5·00	2·40

(Des Ikonomov. Litho)
1995 (16 Oct). Centenary of Motion Pictures. T **1368** and similar vert designs. Multicoloured. P 13.
4035	2l. Type **1368**..	45	30
4036	3l. Marilyn Monroe and Marlene Dietrich ..	60	40
4037	5l. Nikolai Cherkasov and Humphrey Bogart..	90	45
4038	8l. Sophia Loren and Liza Minelli................	1·80	60
4039	10l. Gérard Philipe and Toshiro Mifune.........	2·30	75
4040	15l. Katya Paskaleva and Nevena Kokanova	3·00	1·10
4035/4040 Set of 6		8·25	3·25

1369 Agate   1370 Mary and Joseph

(Des Ts. Ostoich. Litho)
1995 (20 Nov). Minerals. T **1369** and similar horiz designs. Multicoloured. P 13½×13.
4041	1l. Type **1369**..	30	15
4042	2l. Sphalerite...	45	30
4043	5l. Calcite..	1·10	40
4044	7l. Quartz..	1·50	45
4045	8l. Pyromorphite..	1·80	60
4046	10l. Almandine..	2·40	75
4041/4046 Set of 6		6·75	2·40

(Des K. Borisova. Litho)
1995 (8 Dec). Christmas. T **1370** and similar horiz design. Multicoloured. P 13½×13.
4047	3l. Type **1370**..	75	45
4048	15l. Three wise men approaching stable......	3·00	1·50

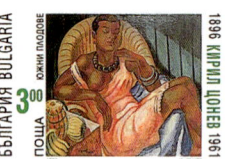

1371 Polynesian Woman with Fruit

(Des K. Kunev. Litho)
1996 (25 Jan). Birth Centenary of Kiril Tsonev (painter). P 13.
4049	**1371**	3l. multicoloured	75	45

1372 Luther (after Lucas Cranach the elder)   1373 Preobrazhenie

(Des K. Gogov. Litho)
1996 (5 Feb). 450th Death Anniversary of Martin Luther (Protestant reformer). P 13.
4050	**1372**	3l. multicoloured	75	45

(Des Tekla Aleksieva and Zh. Aleksiev. Litho)
1996 (28 Feb). Monasteries. T **1373** and similar horiz designs. P 14×13½.
4051	3l. blue-green...	25	15
4052	5l. carmine..	45	30
4053	10l. deep ultramarine..................................	60	45
4054	20l. yellow-orange......................................	1·50	60
4055	25l. chestnut..	1·80	90
4056	40l. bright purple..	3·00	1·50
4051/4056 Set of 6		6·75	3·50

Designs: 3l. T **1373**; 5l. *Arapov*; 10l. *Dryanovo*; 20l. *Bachkov*; 25l. *Troyan*; 40l. *Zograf*.

Nos. 4057/4062 are vacant.

1374 Bulgarian National Bank   1375 Yew (*Taxus baccata*)

(Des St. Kunchev. Litho)
1996 (15 Apr). Fifth Anniversary of European Reconstruction and Development Bank. T **1374** and similar vert design. P 13.
4063	7l. dull green, vermilion and deep ultramarine..	75	45
4064	30l. deep ultramarine, vermilion and bright purple...	3·00	1·10

Designs: 7l. T **1374**; 30l. *Palace of Culture, Sofia*.

(Des Konstantina Konstantinova. Litho)
1996 (23 Apr). Conifers. T **1375** and similar horiz designs. Multicoloured. P 13½×13.
4065	5l. Type **1375**..	45	15
4066	8l. Silver Fir (*Abies alba*)............................	60	30
4067	10l. Norway Spruce (*Picea abies*)................	75	40
4068	20l. Scots Pine (*Pinus silvestris*)..................	1·50	45
4069	25l. *Pinus heldreichii*..................................	1·80	60
4070	40l. Juniper (*Juniperus excelsa*)..................	3·00	1·50
4065/4070 Set of 6		7·25	3·00

1996 BULGARIA

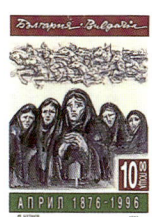

1376 Battle Scene and Mourning Women

1377 Modern Officer's Parade Uniform

(Des I. Bogdanov. Litho)

1996 (1 May). 120th Anniversaries. T **1376** and similar multicoloured design. P 13×13½ (10l.) or 13½×13 (40l.).
4071	10l. Type **1376** (April uprising)		75	45
4072	40l. Khristo Botev and script (poet, death anniversary) (*horiz*)		3·00	1·80

(Des A. Vuchkov. Litho)

1996 (6 May). Military Uniforms. T **1377** and similar vert designs. Multicoloured. P 13.
4073	5l. Type **1377**		1·40	45
4074	8l. Second World War combat uniform		40	30
4075	10l. Balkan War uniform		60	40
4076	20l. Guard officer's ceremonial uniform		1·20	60
4077	25l. Serbo–Bulgarian War officer's uniform		1·50	75
4078	40l. Russo–Turkish War soldier's uniform		2·30	1·40
4073/4078 Set of 6			6·75	3·50

1378 Monument

1379 Elisaveta Bagryana (poet)

(Des Ts. Ostoich. Litho)

1996 (13 May). 50th Anniversary of the Republic. P 13×13½.
4079	**1378**	10l. multicoloured	75	45

(Des P. Vulchev. Litho)

1996 (29 May). Europa. Famous Women. T **1379** and similar horiz design. Multicoloured. P 13.
4080	10l. Type **1379**		3·00	1·50
4081	40l. Katya Popova (opera singer)		3·75	2·30

1380 Player

1381 Nikola Stanchev (wrestling, Melbourne 1956)

(Des S. Despodov. Litho)

1996 (4 June). European Football Championship, England. Sheet 71×86 mm containing T **1380** and similar vert design. Multicoloured. P 13.
MS4082 10l. Type **1380**; 15l. Player (*different*)			3·00	2·75

(Des E. Stankev. Litho)

1996 (4 July). Olympic Games, Atlanta (2nd issue). Bulgarian Medal Winners. T **1381** and similar vert designs. Multicoloured. P 13.
4083	5l. Type **1381**		30	15
4084	8l. Boris Georgiev (boxing, Helsinki 1952)		60	30
4085	10l. Ivanka Khristova (putting the shot, Montreal 1976)		90	45
4086	25l. Z. Iordanova and S. Otsetova (double sculls, Montreal 1976)		2·00	75
4083/4086 Set of 4			3·50	1·50
MS4087 89×68 mm. 15l. Olympic stadium, Athens 1896			2·30	2·10

1382 The Letter (detail)

1383 Water Flea (*Gammarus arduus*)

(Des A. Sertev. Litho)

1996 (9 July). 250th Birth Anniversary of Francisco Goya (painter). T **1382** and similar multicoloured designs. P 13.
4088	5l. Detail of fresco		30	15
4089	8l. Type **1382**		75	40
4090	26l. 3rd of May 1808 in Madrid (detail)		2·00	90
4091	40l. Neighbours on a Balcony (detail)		3·00	1·50
4088/4091 Set of 4			5·50	2·75
MS4092 99×73 mm. 10l. Clothed Maja (50×26 mm); 15l. Naked Maja (50×26 mm). P 13½×13			2·30	2·10

(Des T. Vardzhiev. Litho)

1996 (30 July). Aquatic Life. T **1383** and similar horiz designs. Multicoloured. P 13½×13.
4093	5l. Type **1383**		3·75	1·50
4094	10l. Common Water Louse (*Asellus aquaticus*)		45	25
4095	12l. European River Crayfish (*Astacus astacus*)		55	25
4096	25l. Prawn (*Palaemon serratus*)		60	30
4097	30l. *Cumella limicola*		70	40
4098	40l. Mediterranean Shore Crab (*Carcinus mediterraneus*)		75	45
4093/4098 Set of 6			6·00	2·75

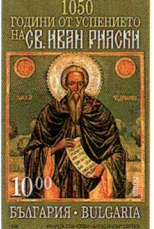 

1384 St Ivan

1385 Tryavna

(Des Ralitsa Stanoeva and A. Sertev. Litho)

1996 (3 Sept). 1050th Death Anniversary of Ivan Rilski (founder of Rila Monastery). Sheet 56×87 mm. P 13.
MS4099	**1384**	10l. multicoloured	1·50	1·40

(Des Maya Buyukliiska. Litho)

1996 (12 Sept). Houses. T **1385** and similar horiz designs. P 14×13½.
4100	10l. bistre-brown and stone		45	25
4101	15l. bright crimson and chrome yellow		60	45
4102	30l. deep green and olive-yellow		1·20	60
4103	50l. bright violet and bright mauve		2·10	1·10
4104	60l. blue-green and bright apple green		2·75	1·50
4105	100l. ultramarine and turquoise-blue		4·25	2·30
4100/4105 Set of 6			10·00	5·50

Designs: 10l. T **1385**; 15l. Nesebur; 30l. Tryavna (*different*); 50l. Koprivshtitsa; 60l. Plovdiv; 100l. Koprivshtitsa (*different*).

1386 Philadelphia, 1836

1387 Anniversary Emblem and Academy

219

BULGARIA 1996

(Des L. Chekhlarov. Litho)

1996 (24 Sept). Steam Locomotives. T **1386** and similar horiz designs. Multicoloured. P 13.

4106	5l. Type **1386**	45	30
4107	10l. *Jenny Lind*, 1847	75	40
4108	12l. *Liverpool*, 1848	90	45
4109	26l. *Anglet*, 1876	2·00	90
4106/4109	Set of 4	3·75	1·80

(Des P. Vulchev. Litho)

1996 (14 Oct). Centenary of National Arts Academy. P 13.

4110	**1387**	15l. black and orange-yellow	1·20	45

1388 Sword and Miniature from *Chronicle of Ivan Skilitsa*

(Des St. Gruev. Litho)

1996 (21 Oct). 1100th Anniversary of Tsar Simeon's Victory over the Turks. T **1388** and similar horiz design. Multicoloured. P 13.

4111	10l. Type **1388**	75	45
	a. Horiz pair. Nos. 4111/4112	4·00	2·10
4112	40l. Dagger and right-hand detail of miniature	3·00	1·50

Nos. 4111/4112 were issued together in horizontal *se-tenant* pairs within the sheet, each pair forming a composite design.

1389 Fish and Diver (Dilyana Lokmadzhieva)

1390 Christmas Tree

(Des M. Kolchev. Litho)

1996 (18 Nov). 50th Anniversary of United Nations Children's Fund. Children's Paintings. T **1389** and similar horiz designs. Multicoloured. P 13.

4113	7l. Type **1389**	60	45
4114	15l. Circus (Velislava Dimitrova)	1·20	60
4115	20l. Man and artist's pallet (Miglena Nikolova)	1·70	75
4116	60l. Family meal (Darena Dencheva)	4·75	2·40
4113/4116	Set of 4	7·50	3·75

(Des Maiya Cholakova. Litho)

1996 (26 Nov). Christmas. T **1390** and similar vert design. Multicoloured. P 13×13½.

4117	15l. Type **1390**	1·10	45
4118	60l. Star over basilica and Christmas tree	4·50	2·30

1391 *Zograf Monastery*

1392 Pointer

(Des S. Kasurov. Litho)

1996 (11 Dec). Birth Centenary of Tsanko Lavrenov (painter). P 13.

4119	**1391**	15l. multicoloured	1·10	45

(Des V. Paunov. Litho)

1997 (25 Feb). Puppies. T **1392** and similar horiz designs. Multicoloured. P 13.

4120	5l. Type **1392**	40	30
4121	7l. Chow Chow	45	35
4122	25l. Carakachan Dog	1·50	75
4123	50l. Basset Hound	3·00	1·50
4120/4123	Set of 4	4·75	2·50

1393 Bell

1394 Man drinking

(Des Krasimira Despotova. Litho)

1997 (10 Mar). 150th Birth Anniversary of Alexander Graham Bell (telephone pioneer). P 13.

4124	**1393**	30l. multicoloured	1·50	75

(Des K. Kunev. Litho)

1997 (20 Mar). Birth Centenary of Ivan Milev (painter). T **1394** and similar vert designs showing murals from Kazaluk. Multicoloured. P 13.

4125	5l. Type **1394**	45	30
4126	15l. Woman praying	60	35
4127	30l. Reaper	75	60
4128	60l. Mother and child	2·30	1·20
4125/4128	Set of 4	3·75	2·20

1395 Lady March (symbol of spring)

1396 Konstantin Kisimov in Character

(Des Tekla Aleksieva. Litho)

1997 (14 Apr). Europa. Tales and Legends. T **1395** and similar vert design. Multicoloured. P 13×13½.

4129	120l. Type **1395**	3·75	1·50
4130	600l. St George (National Symbol)	3·00	1·50

(Des I. Bogdanov. Litho)

1997 (16 Apr). Birth Centenary of Konstantin Kisimov (actor). P 13.

4131	**1396**	120l. multicoloured	45	40

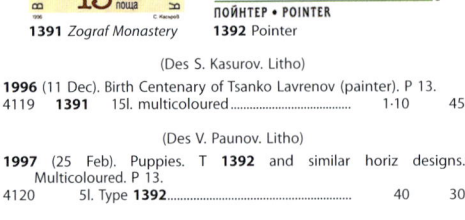

1397 Heinrich von Stephan

1398 Old Town, Nesebur

(Des M. Kolchev. Litho)

1997 (21 Apr). Death Centenary of Heinrich von Stephan (founder of Universal Postal Union). P 13.

4132	**1397**	60l. multicoloured	45	40

(Des Maya Buyukliiska. Litho)

1997 (2 May). Historic Sights. T **1398** and similar vert designs. P 13½×14.

4133	80l. reddish brown and black	25	15
4134	200l. bright violet and black	40	25

4135	300l. yellow and black		45	40
4136	500l. dull yellowish green and black		75	45
4137	600l. yellow and black		1·10	60
4138	1000l. orange and black		1·80	1·10
4133/4138	Set of 6		4·25	2·75

Designs: 80l. T **1398**; 200l. Sculpture, Ivanovské Church; 300l. Christ (detail of icon), Boyana Church; 500l. Horseman (stone relief), Madara; 600l. Figure of woman (carving from sarcophagus), Sveshary; 1000l. Tomb decoration, Kazanlak.

1399 Gaetano Donizetti   **1400** *Trifolium rubens*

(Des P. Bulchev. Litho)

1997 (29 May). Composers' Anniversaries. T **1399** and similar horiz designs. Multicoloured. P 13½×13.

4139	120l. Type **1399** (birth bicentenary)		60	45
	a. Sheetlet of 4. Nos. 4139/4142		2·50	
4140	120l. Franz Schubert (birth bicentenary)		60	45
4141	120l. Felix Mendelssohn-Bartholdy (150th death anniversary)		60	45
4142	120l. Johannes Brahms (death centenary)		60	45
4139/4142	Set of 4		2·20	1·60

Nos. 4139/4142 were issued together in *se-tenant* sheetlets of four stamps.

(Des Mladena Elezova. Litho)

1997 (24 June). Flowers in *The Red Book*. T **1400** and similar horiz designs. Multicoloured. P 13.

4143	80l. Type **1400**		30	15
4144	100l. *Tulipa hageri*		40	25
4145	120l. *Inula spiraeifolia*		45	30
4146	200l. Thin-leafed Peony (*Paeonia tenuifolia*)		1·10	45
4143/4146	Set of 4		2·00	1·00

1401 Anniversary Emblem   **1402** Evlogii Georgiev

(Des S. Iliev and G. Todorov. Litho)

1997 (29 June). 50th Anniversary of Civil Aviation. P 13.

4147	**1401**	120l. multicoloured	45	40

(Des A. Sertev. Litho)

1997 (3 July). Death Centenary of Evlogii Georgiev. P 13.

4148	**1402**	120l. multicoloured	45	40

1403 Show Jumping and Running   **1404** St Basil's Cathedral

(Des T. Vardzhiev. Litho)

1997 (25 July). World Modern Pentathlon Championship, Sofia. T **1403** and similar horiz designs. Multicoloured. P 13.

4149	60l. Type **1403**	40	15
4150	80l. Fencing and swimming	45	30
4151	100l. Running and fencing	60	40
4152	120l. Shooting and swimming	75	45
4153	200l. Show jumping and shooting	90	60
4149/4153	Set of 5	2·75	1·70

(Des Konstantina Konstantinova. Litho)

1997 (30 July). 850th Anniversary of Moscow and Moskva 97 International Stamp Exhibition. Sheet 87×96 mm. P 13.

MS4154	**1404**	120l. multicoloured	1·60	1·50

No. **MS**4154 also contains a label which forms a composite design with the stamp.

1405 D 2500 M Boat Engine   **1406** Goddess with Mural Crown

(Des O. Gochev. Litho)

1997 (8 Sept). Centenary of Diesel Engine. T **1405** and similar horiz designs. Multicoloured. P 13½×13.

4155	80l. Type **1405**	45	25
4156	100l. D 2900 T tractor engine	60	40
4157	120l. D 3900 A truck engine	75	45
4158	200l. D 2500 K fork-lift truck engine	1·20	60
4155/4158	Set of 4	2·75	1·50

(Des T. Vardzhiev. Litho)

1997 (2 Oct). 43rd General Assembly of Atlantic Club, Sofia. T **1406** and similar horiz designs. P 13.

4159	120l. magenta, new blue and bright ultramarine	60	45
	a. Sheetlet of 4. Nos. 4159/4162	2·50	
4160	120l. emerald, new blue and bright ultramarine	60	45
4161	120l. bistre-brown, new blue and bright ultramarine	60	45
4162	120l. bright violet, new blue and bright ultramarine	60	45
4159/4162	Set of 4	2·20	1·60

Designs: No. 4159, T **1406**; No. 4160, Eagle on globe; No. 4161, Venue; No. 4162, Venue (*different*).

Nos. 4159/4162 were issued together in *se-tenant* sheetlets of four stamps.

1407 Cervantes and Don Quixote with Sancho Panza

(Des S. Deslodov. Litho)

1997 (15 Oct). 450th Birth Anniversary of Miguel de Cervantes (writer). P 13.

4163	**1407**	120l. multicoloured	75	45

1408 Asen Raztsvetnikov

(Des P. Petrunov. Litho)

1997 (5 Nov). Birth Centenary of Asen Raztsvetnikov (writer and translator). P 13.

4164	**1408**	120l. multicoloured	75	45

BULGARIA 1997

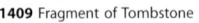

1409 Fragment of Tombstone

1410 Star and Houses forming Christmas Tree

(Des K. Gogov. Litho)

1997 (18 Nov). Millenary of Coronation of Tsar Samuel. T **1409** and similar horiz design. Multicoloured. P 13½×13.

4165	120l. Type **1409**...	75	45
	a. Horiz pair. Nos. 4165/4166................	3·75	2·00
4166	600l. Tsar Samuel and knights in battle..........	2·75	1·40

Nos. 4165/4166 were issued together in horizontal *se-tenant* pairs within the sheet.

(Des I. Ugrinova. Litho)

1997 (8 Dec). Christmas. T **1410** and similar vert design. Multicoloured. P 13×13½.

4167	120l. Type **1410**...	60	40
4168	600l. Stable with Christmas tree roof...............	2·75	1·50

1411 Speed Skating

(Des E. Stankev. Litho)

1997 (17 Dec). Winter Olympic Games, Nagano, Japan (1998). T **1411** and similar horiz designs. Multicoloured. P 13½×13.

4169	60l. Type **1411**...	30	25
4170	80l. Skiing..	40	30
4171	120l. Shooting (biathlon).................................	45	40
4172	600l. Ice skating..	3·50	2·30
4169/4172	Set of 4...	4·25	3·00

See also No. 4189.

1412 Radiometric System R-400

(Des St. Gruev. Litho)

1997 (22 Dec). 25th Anniversary of Bulgarian Space Experiments. Sheet 87×68 mm. P 13.

| MS4173 | **1412** | 120l. multicoloured........................... | 1·50 | 1·40 |

1413 State Arms

1414 Khristo Botev (after B. Petrov)

(Des K. Gogov. Litho)

1997 (22 Dec). P 13½×13.

| 4174 | **1413** | 120l. multicoloured........................... | 45 | 30 |

(Des B. Mavrodinov. Litho)

1998 (6 Jan). 150th Birth and 120th Death (1996) Anniversary of Khristo Botev (poet and revolutionary). P 13.

| 4175 | **1414** | 120l. multicoloured........................... | 45 | 30 |

1415 Bertolt Brecht

1416 Arrows

(Des S. Deslodov. Litho)

1998 (10 Feb). Birth Centenary of Bertolt Brecht (playwright).

| 4176 | **1415** | 120l. multicoloured........................... | 45 | 30 |

(Des P. Petrunov. Litho)

1998 (13 Feb). Centenary of Bulgarian Telegraph Agency. P 13.

| 4177 | **1416** | 120l. multicoloured........................... | 45 | 30 |

1417 Swallow at Window

1418 Tsar Alexander II

(Des B. Kitanov. Litho)

1998 (24 Feb). 120th Birth Anniversary of Aleksandur Bozhinov (children's illustrator). T **1417** and similar horiz designs. P 13½×13.

4178	120l. Type **1417**...	45	30
	a. Sheetlet of 4. Nos. 4178/4181................	1·90	
4179	120l. Blackbird with backpack on branch.......	45	30
4180	120l. Father Frost and children......................	45	30
4181	120l. Maiden Rositsa in field holding hands up to rain...	45	30
4178/4181	Set of 4...	1·60	1·10

Nos. 4178/4181 were issued together in *se-tenant* sheetlets of four stamps.

(Des N. Pekarev. Litho)

1998 (27 Feb). 120th Anniversary of Liberation from Turkey. T **1418** and similar vert design. Multicoloured. P 13.

4182	120l. Type **1418**...	45	30
	a. Pair. Nos. 4182/4183................................	3·00	1·40
4183	600l. Independence monument, Ruse.............	2·30	1·00

Nos. 4182/4183 were issued together in *se-tenant* pairs within the sheet.

1419 Christ ascending and Hare pulling Cart of Eggs

1420 Torch Bearer

(Des V. Vulkanov. Litho)

1998 (27 Mar). Easter. P 13×13½.

| 4184 | **1419** | 120l. multicoloured........................... | 45 | 30 |

(Des Maya Buyukliiska. Litho)

1998 (30 Mar). 75th Anniversary of Bulgarian Olympic Committee. P 13.

| 4185 | **1420** | 120l. multicoloured........................... | 45 | 30 |

1998 BULGARIA

1421 Map of Participating Countries

(Des S. Krustev. Litho)

1998 (24 Apr). Phare International Programme for Telecommunications and Post. P 13.
4186   **1421**   120l. multicoloured   45   30

1422 Girls in Folk Costumes   (**1423**)

(Des M. Konstantinova. Litho)

1998 (27 Apr). Europa. National Festivals. T **1422** and similar horiz design. Multicoloured. P 13.
4187   120l. Type **1422** ....   1·50   75
4188   60l. Boys wearing dance masks ....   3·75   3·00

1998 (29 Apr). Winning of Gold Medal in 15km Biathlon by Ekaterina Dafovska at Winter Olympic Games, Nagano. No. 4171 optd with T **1423**.
4189   **1423**   120l. multicoloured ....   5·25   4·50

1424 Dante and Virgil in Hell   **1425** Footballer and Club Badge

(Des A. Sertev. Litho)

1998 (30 Apr). Birth Bicentenary of Eugène Delacroix (artist). P 13½×13.
4190   **1424**   120l. multicoloured   45   30

(Des Ts. Ostoich. Litho)

1998 (15 May). 50th Anniversary of TsSKA Football Club. P 13.
4191   **1425**   120l. multicoloured   45   30

1426 European Tabby   **1427** Oh, You are Jealous!

(Des Konstantina Konstantinova. Litho)

1998 (28 May). Cats. T **1426** and similar vert designs. Multicoloured. P 13×13½.
4192   60l. Type **1426**   25   15
4193   80l. Siamese   40   25
4194   120l. Exotic Shorthair   45   30
4195   600l. Birman ....   2·40   1·20
4192/4195   Set of 4 ....   3·25   1·70

(Des R. Kolev. Litho)

1998 (4 June). 150th Birth Anniversary of Paul Gauguin (artist). P 13.
4196   **1427**   120l. multicoloured   45   30

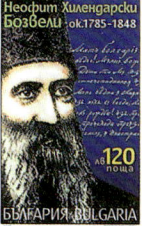 

1428 Neofit Khilendarski-Bozveli   **1429** Tackling

(Des Ralitsa Stanoeva. Litho)

1998 (4 June). 150th Death Anniversary of Neofit Khilendarski-Bozveli (priest and writer). P 13.
4197   **1428**   120l. multicoloured   45   30

(Des O. Gochev. Litho)

1998 (10 June). World Cup Football Championship, France. T **1429** and similar horiz designs. Multicoloured. P 13½×13.
4198   60l. Type **1429**   25   15
4199   80l. Players competing for ball   40   25
4200   120l. Players and ball   45   30
4201   600l. Goalkeeper ....   2·40   1·20
4198/4201   Set of 4 ....   3·25   1·70
MS4202   68×91 mm. 120l. Lion, ball and Eiffel Tower...   1·50   1·40

1430 A. Aleksandrov   **1431** Vasco da Gama

(Des P. Petrunov. Litho)

1998 (17 June). Tenth Anniversary of Second Soviet–Bulgarian Space Flight. P 13.
4203   **1430**   120l. multicoloured   60   40

(Des Ya. Gyuzelev. Litho)

1998 (23 June). Expo '98 World's Fair, Lisbon. 500th Anniversary of Vasco da Gama's Voyage to India. T **1431** and similar horiz design. Multicoloured. P 13.
4204   600l. Type **1431** ....   2·50   75
             a. Sheetlet. Nos. 4204/4205 plus two
                labels ....   5·25   1·60
4205   600l. *São Gabriel* (Vasco da Gama's ship) ...   2·75   80
Nos. 4204/4205 were issued together in sheetlets of two stamps and two labels, forming a composite design.

1432 Focke Wulf FW 61, 1937

(Des E. Stankev. Litho)

1998 (7 July). Helicopters. T **1432** and similar horiz designs. Multicoloured. P 13.
4206   80l. Type **1432**   40   25
4207   100l. Sikorsky R-4, 1943   50   30
4208   120l. Mil Mi-V12, 1970   65   40
4209   200l. McDonnell-Douglas MD-900, 1995 ...   95   50
4206/4209   Set of 4 ....   2·30   1·30

1433 Mediterranean Monk Seal (*Monachus monachus*)

BULGARIA 1998

(Des Krasimira Despotova. Litho)
1998 (14 July). International Year of the Ocean. Sheet 67×88 mm. P 13.
MS4210 1433   120l. multicoloured.................... 5·50 5·25

1434 Dimitur Talev   **1435** Aleksandur Malinov (Prime Minister, 1931)

(Des S. Daskalov. Litho)
1998 (14 Sept). Birth Centenary of Dimitur Talev (writer). P 13.
4211 1434 180l. multicoloured.................. 80 50

(Des Kh. Zhablyanov. Litho)
1998 (22 Sept). 90th Anniversary of Independence. P 13.
4212 1435 180l. black, slate-blue and lemon.......... 80 50

1436 *Limenitis redukta* and *Ligularia sibirica*   **1437** Khristo Smirnenski

(Des Z. Stoyanov. Litho)
1998 (24 Sept). Butterflies and Flowers. T **1436** and similar vert designs. Multicoloured. P 13.
4213   60l. Type **1436**.............................. 25 15
4214   180l. Painted Lady (*Vanessa cardui*) and *Anthemis macrantha*.................. 80 40
4215   200l. Red Admiral (*Vanessa atalanta*) and *Trachelium jacquinii*.............. 95 50
4216   600l. *Anthocharis gruneri* and *Geranium tuberosum*.......................... 2·50 1·40
4213/4216 Set of 4.. 4·00 2·20

(Des Kh. Zhablyanov. Litho)
1998 (29 Sept). Birth Centenary of Khristo Smirnenski (writer). P 13.
4217 1437 180l. multicoloured.................. 80 50

1438 Silhouette of Man   **1439** Giordano Bruno

(Des Ya. Vasev. Litho)
1998 (26 Oct). 50th Anniversary of Universal Declaration of Human Rights. P 13.
4218 1438 180l. multicoloured.................. 80 50

(Des T. Ushev. Litho)
1998 (26 Oct). 450th Birth Anniversary of Giordano Bruno (scholar). P 13.
4219 1439 180l. multicoloured.................. 80 50

1440 Man diving through Heart (I Love You)   **1441** Madonna and Child

(Des B. Dimovski. Litho)
1998 (1 Nov). Greetings Stamps. T **1440** and similar multicoloured designs. P 13.
4220   180l. Type **1440**.. 80 50
4221   180l. Making wine (holiday) (*vert*)........... 80 50
4222   180l. Man in chalice (birthday) (*vert*)....... 80 50
4223   180l. Waiter serving wine (name day) (*vert*)... 80 50
4220/4223 Set of 4.. 3·00 1·80
See also No. 4862.

(Des M. Tsvetkova and Maria Aimitrova. Litho)
1998 (2 Dec). Christmas. P 13½×13.
4224 1441 180l. multicoloured.................. 80 50

1442 Ivan Geshov   **1443** National Assembly Building, Sofia

(Des St. Kunchev and L. Metodiev. Litho)
1999 (8 Feb). 150th Birth Anniversary of Ivan Evstratiev Geshov (politician). P 13.
4225 1442 180l. multicoloured.................. 80 50

(Des G. Yankov (No. 4226), S. Krustev (No. 4227), N. Tsachev (No. 4228), N. Pekarev (No. 4229), O. Gochev (No. 4230), Ya. Zhablyanov (No. 4231). Litho)
1999 (10 Feb). 120th Anniversary of Third Bulgarian State. T **1443** and similar horiz designs. Multicoloured. P 13.
4226   180l. Type **1443**.. 80 50
             a. Sheetlet of 6. Nos. 4226/4231............... 5·00
4227   180l. Council of Ministers.......................... 80 50
4228   180l. Statue of Justice (Supreme Court of Appeal).. 80 50
4229   180l. Coins (National Bank)........................ 80 50
4230   180l. Army... 80 50
4231   180l. Lion emblem of Sofia and lamp post.... 80 50
4226/4231 Set of 6.. 4·25 2·75
Nos. 4226/4231 were issued together in *se-tenant* sheetlets of six stamps.

1444 Georgi Karakashev (stage designer) and Set of *Kismet*   **1445** Rainbow Lory (*Trichoglossus haematodus*)

(Des T. Ushev (180l.), L. Metodiev (200l.), Ya. Gyuzelev (300l.), G. Atanasov (600l.). Litho)
1999 (12 Mar). Birth Centenaries. T **1444** and similar horiz designs. Multicoloured. P 13.
4232   180l. Type **1444**.. 80 30
4233   200l. Bencho Obreshkov (artist) and *Lodki*.... 90 40
4234   300l. Score and Asen Naidenov (conductor of Sofia Opera)............................... 1·20 50
4235   600l. Pancho Vladigerov (composer) and score of *Vardar*................................ 2·75 1·10
4232/4235 Set of 4.. 5·00 2·10

1999 BULGARIA

(Des E. Stankev. Litho)

1999 (15 Mar). Bulgaria '99 European Stamp Exhibition. Parrots. Sheet 100×110 mm containing T **1445** and similar vert designs. Multicoloured. P 13½×13.

| MS4236 | 600l. Type **1445**; 600l. Eastern Rosella (*Platycercus eximius*); 600l. Budgerigar (*Melopsittacus undulates*) 600l. Green-winged Macaw (*Ara chloroptera*) | 17·00 | 16·00 |

1446 Sun and Emblem

(Des T. Likho. Litho)

1999 (29 Mar). 50th Anniversary of North Atlantic Treaty Organisation. P 13.

| 4237 | **1446** | 180l. multicoloured | 80 | 40 |

1447 Decorated Eggs   **1448** Duck and Ropotamo Reserve

(Des Maglena Konstantinova. Litho)

1999 (1 Apr). Easter. P 13½×13.

| 4238 | **1447** | 180l. multicoloured | 80 | 40 |

(Des Mladena Elezova. Litho)

1999 (13 Apr). Europa. Parks and Gardens. T **1448** and similar horiz design. Multicoloured. P 13.

| 4239 | 180l. Type **1448** | 1·40 | 1·10 |
| 4240 | 600l. Central Balkan National Park | 3·50 | 3·00 |

1449 Albrecht Dürer (self-portrait) and Nuremberg

(Des R. Kolev. Litho)

1999 (15 Apr). iBRA '99 International Stamp Exhibition, Nuremberg, Germany. P 13.

| 4241 | **1449** | 600l. multicoloured | 3·25 | 1·30 |

No. 4241 was issued in sheetlets of three stamps and three labels showing Bavaria 1849 1k. stamp and different engravings of a town.

1450 Anniversary Emblem

(Des S. Daskalov. Litho)

1999 (5 May). 50th Anniversary of Council of Europe. P 13.

| 4242 | **1450** | 180l. multicoloured | 2·00 | 80 |

1451 Honoré de Balzac (novelist)

(Des V. and Marina Kitanov. Litho)

1999 (18 May). Birth Anniversaries. T **1451** and similar horiz designs. Multicoloured. P 13.

4243	180l. Type **1451** (bicentenary)	80	25
4244	200l. Johann Wolfgang von Goethe (poet and playwright) (250th anniversary)	1·40	50
4245	300l. Aleksandr Pushkin (poet) (bicentenary)	1·60	65
4246	600l. Diego de Silva Velázquez (painter) (400th anniversary)	3·00	1·10
4243/4246	Set of 4	6·00	2·30

 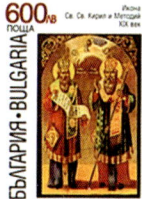

1452 Penny Farthing   **1453** Sts Cyril and Methodius

(Des Kh. Zhablyanov. Litho)

1999 (1 June). Bicycles. T **1452** and similar horiz designs. Multicoloured. P 13.

4247	180l. Type **1452**	80	20
4248	200l. Road racing bicycles	1·00	25
4249	300l. Track racing bicycles	1·60	50
4250	600l. Mountain bike	3·00	80
4247/4250	Set of 4	5·75	1·60

(Des Ivelina Velinova. Litho)

1999 (15 June). Bulgaria '99 European Stamp Exhibition, Sofia (1st issue). 19th-century Icons of Sts Cyril and Methodius. Sheet 100×110 mm containing T **1453** and similar vert designs. Multicoloured. P 13½×13½.

| MS4251 | 600l. Type **1453**; 600l. St Cyril with scroll and staff and St Methodius; 600l. Sts Cyril and Methodius with scrolls; 600l. St Cyril with crucifix, St Methodius and Christ | 17·00 | 16·00 |

See also Nos. **MS**4265 and **MS**4272.

Currency Reform

1000 (old) lev = 1 (new) lev

1454 Sopot Monastery Fountain   **1455** *Oxytropis urumovii*

(Des P. Petrunov. Litho)

1999 (5 July)–**2003**. Fountains. T **1454** and similar vert designs.

(a) P 13½×14.

4252	1st. light brown	20	15
4253	8st. deep blue-green and black (22.11.99)	20	15
4254	10st. deep brown	60	25
4255	18st. new blue	80	30
4256	20st. bright blue (3.8.99)	80	30
4257	60st. lake-brown and black (22.11.99)	2·40	80
4252/4257	Set of 6	4·50	1·80

(b) Perf 12½ (with one diamond-shaped hole on each vert side)

4258	1st. light brown (11.02)	20	15
4259	8st. deep blue-green and black (3.03)	20	15
4260	10st. deep brown (11.02)	60	25
4261	18st. new blue (11.02)	80	30
4262	20st. bright blue (11.02)	80	30
4263	60st. lake-brown and black (3.03)	2·40	1·60
4258/4263	Set of 6	4·50	2·50

Designs: 1st. T **1454**; 8st. Peacock Fountain, Karlovo; 10st. Peev Fountain, Kopivshtitsa; 18st. Sandanski Fountain; 20st. Eagle Owl Fountain, Karlovo; 60st. Fountain, Sokolski Monastery.

No. 4264 is vacant.

BULGARIA 1999

(Des Krasimira Despotova. Litho)

1999 (20 July). Bulgaria '99 European Stamp Exhibition, Sofia (2nd issue). Flowers in Pirin National Park. Sheet 109×100 mm containing T **1455** and similar horiz designs. Multicoloured. P 13½×13.

MS4265 60st. Type **1455**; 60st. Bellflower (*Campanula transsilvanica*); 60st. Iris (*Iris reichenbachii*); 60st. Spotted Gentian (*Gentiana punctata*)........................ 24·00 22·00

1456 Cracked Green Russula (*Russula virenscens*)

1457 Diagram of Path of Eclipse

(Des Konstantina Konstantinova. Litho)

1999 (27 July). Fungi. T **1456** and similar horiz designs. Multicoloured. P 13½×13.

4266	10st. Type **1456**........................	60	15
	a. Sheetlet of 4. Nos. 4266/4269	6·00	
4267	18st. Field Mushroom (*Agaricus campestris*)...	80	25
4268	20st. *Hygrophorus russula*	1·20	50
4269	60st. Wood Blewit (*Lepista nuda*)	3·25	65
4266/4269 *Set of 4*...		5·25	1·40

Nos. 4266/4269 were issued together in *se-tenant* sheetlets of four stamps.

(Des E. Ivanov and T. Likho. Litho)

1999 (10 Aug). Solar Eclipse (11 Aug 1999). Sheet 90×90 mm. P 13.

MS4270 **1457** 20st. multicoloured.......................... 3·00 2·75

1458 Four-leaved Clover

1459 1884 25st. Postage Due Stamp

(Des Ralitza Karapanteva. Litho)

1999 (23 Sept). Centenary of Organised Peasant Movement. P 13.

| 4271 | **1458** | 18st. multicoloured................................ | 60 | 30 |

(Des O. Gochev. Litho)

1999 (5 Oct). Bulgaria '99 European Stamp Exhibition, Sofia (3rd issue). 125th Anniversary of Universal Postal Union. Sheet 110×102 mm containing T **1459** and similar vert designs. Multicoloured. P 13×13½.

MS4272 60st. Type **1459**; 60st. Dove and hand with letter; 60st. Globe and left half of messenger; 60st. Right half of messenger with letter and globe .... 17·00 16·00

The stamps form a composite design of the Bulgarian Lion.

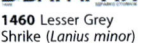

1460 Lesser Grey Shrike (*Lanius minor*)

1461 Greek Tortoise (*Testudo graeca*)

(Des Z. Stoyanov. Litho)

1999 (6 Oct). Song Birds and their Eggs. T **1460** and similar vert designs. Multicoloured. P 13.

4273	8st. Type **1460**........................	50	15
4274	18st. Mistle Thrush (*Turdus viscivorus*)..............	80	25
4275	20st. Dunnock (*Prunella modularis*)	1·00	40
4276	60st. Ortolan Bunting (*Emberiza hortulana*) ...	2·75	95
4273/4276 *Set of 4*...		4·50	1·60

(Des P. Petrunov. Litho)

1999 (8 Oct). Reptiles. T **1461** and similar horiz designs. Multicoloured. P 13.

4277	10st. Type **1461**........................	60	15
4278	18st. Swamp Turtle (*Emys orbicularis*)..............	80	25
4279	30st. Hermann's Tortoise (*Testudo hermanni*) .	1·40	65
4280	60st. Caspian Turtle (*Mauremys caspica*)	2·75	1·10
4277/4280 *Set of 4*...		5·00	1·90

1462 Boxing (16 medals)

(Des G. Gadelev. Litho)

1999 (10 Oct). Bulgarian Olympic Medal Winning Sports. T **1462** and similar horiz designs. Multicoloured. P 13.

4281	10st. Type **1462**........................	60	15
4282	20st. High jumping (17 medals).......................	1·00	30
4283	30st. Weightlifting (31 medals).......................	1·40	50
4284	60st. Wrestling (60 medals)............................	2·75	95
4281/4284 *Set of 4*...		5·25	1·70

1463 Police Light and Emblem

1464 Jug

(Des M. Chankov. Litho)

1999 (8 Nov). Tenth European Police Conference. P 13.

| 4285 | **1463** | 18st. multicoloured................................ | 60 | 30 |

(Des Maiya Cholakova. Litho)

1999 (15 Nov)–**2002**. Gold Artefacts from Panagyurishte. T **1464** and similar vert designs.

A. P 13½×14

4286A	2st. yellow-brown and deep green	20	15
4287A	3st. yellow-brown and deep turquoise-green ...	20	15
4288A	5st. yellow-brown and deep ultramarine.........	20	15
4289A	30st. yellow-brown and reddish violet..........	1·00	50
4290A	1l. yellow-brown and deep rose-red	3·50	1·60
4286A/4290A *Set of 5*..		4·50	2·30

B. Perf 12½ (with one diamond-shaped hole on each vert side)

4286B	2st. yellow-brown and deep green (11.02)..	20	15
4287B	3st. yellow-brown and deep turquoise-green (11.02)................................	20	15
4288B	5st. yellow-brown and deep ultramarine (11.02)................................	20	15
4289B	30st. yellow-brown and reddish violet (11.02)	1·00	50
4290B	1l. yellow-brown and deep rose-red (2.02)	3·50	1·60
4286B/4290B *Set of 5*..		4·50	2·30

Designs: 2st. T **1464**; 3st. Human figures around top of drinking horn; 5st. Bottom of Chamois-shaped drinking horn; 30st. Decorated handle and spout; 1l. Head-shaped jug.

1465 Virgin and Child

1466 Scout beside Fire

1999 BULGARIA

(Des K. Andreev. Litho)

1999 (22 Nov). Christmas. Religious Icons. T **1465** and similar vert design. Multicoloured. P 13.

4291	18st. Type **1465**..		60	40
4292	60st. Jesus Christ...		2·50	95

(Des Tekla Aleksieva. Litho)

1999 (6 Dec). Scouts. T **1466** and similar horiz designs. Multicoloured. P 13.

4293	10st. Type **1466**..		60	25
4294	18st. Scout helping child...................................		80	30
4295	30st. Scout saluting...		1·20	50
4296	60st. Girl and boy scouts...................................		2·40	95
4293/4296 Set of 4...			4·50	1·80

1467 Emblem   **1468** Emblem and Flag

(Des T. Likho. Litho)

1999 (21 Dec). Expo 2005 World's Fair, Aichi, Japan. P 13.

4297	**1467**	18st. multicoloured............................	80	30

(Des S. Daskalov. Litho)

2000 (15 Feb). Bulgarian Membership of European Union. P 13.

4298	**1468**	18st. multicoloured............................	2·00	1·10

1469 White Stork (*Ciconia ciconia*)   **1470** Peter Beron and Scientific Instruments

(Des V. Paunov. Litho)

2000 (22 Mar). Endangered Species. Sheet 80×60 mm. P 13.

MS4299	**1469**	60st. multicoloured............................	4·00	3·75

(Des S. Petrunov (No. 4300), I. Karaleev (No. 4301) and A. Atanasov (No. 4302). Litho)

2000 (30 Mar). Birth Anniversaries. T **1470** and similar horiz designs. Multicoloured. P 13.

4300		10st. Type **1470** (scientist, bicentenary)..........	60	25
4301		20st. Zakhari Stoyanov (writer, 150th anniversary)..	1·00	40
4302		50st. Kolyo Ficheto (architect, bicentenary).....	2·00	80
4300/4302 Set of 3...			3·25	1·30

1471 Madonna and Child with Circuit Board   **1472** Judo

(Des R. Kolev. Litho)

2000 (26 Apr). Europa. T **1471** and similar horiz designs. Multicoloured. P 13.

4303		18st. Type **1471**...	2·00	80
4304		60st. Madonna and Child (Leonardo da Vinci) with circuit board......................	4·00	3·25

(Des B. Filchev. Litho)

2000 (28 Apr). Olympic Games, Sydney. T **1472** and similar horiz designs. Multicoloured. P 13.

4305		10st. Type **1472**..	40	15
4306		18st. Tennis...	60	25
4307		20st. Pistol shooting...	80	30
4308		60st. Long jump..	2·40	95
4305/4308 Set of 4...			3·75	1·50

1473 Puss in Boots (Charles Perrault)   **1474** Friends (detail) (Assen Vasiliev)

(Des Al. Aleksov. Litho)

2000 (23 May). Children's Fairytales. T **1473** and similar horiz designs. Multicoloured. P 13½×13.

4309		18st. Type **1473**...	70	50
		a. Sheetlet of 3. Nos. 4309/4311 plus 3 labels..	2·20	
4310		18st. Little Red Riding Hood (Brothers Grimm)...	70	50
4311		18st. Thumbelina (Hans Christian Andersen)..	70	50
4309/4311 Set of 3...			1·90	1·40

Nos. 4309/4311 were issued together in *se-tenant* sheetlets of three stamps and three labels.

(Des M. Kolchev. Litho)

2000 (23 May). Artists' Birth Centenaries. T **1474** and similar horiz designs. Multicoloured. P 13.

4312		18st. Type **1474**..	70	40
4313		18st. All Soul's Day (detail) (Pencho Georgiev)...	70	40
4314		18st. Veliko Turnovo (detail) (Ivan Khristov)....	70	40
4315		18st. At the Fountain (sculpture) (detail) (Ivan Funev)...	70	40
4312/4315 Set of 4...			2·50	1·40

1475 Roman Mosaic (detail), Stara Zagora

(Des G. Yankov. Litho)

2000 (31 May). EXPO 2000, World's Fair, Hanover, Germany. P 13.

4316	**1475**	60st. multicoloured............................	2·75	1·10

No. 4316 was issued with a *se-tenant* label.

1476 Johannes Gutenberg (inventor of printing press) and Printed Characters   **1477** La Jaune (Lebaudy-Juillot airship) and Eiffel Tower, 1903

(Des I. Bogdanov. Litho)

2000 (20 June). Anniversaries. T **1476** and similar horiz designs. Multicoloured. P 13.

4317		10st. Type **1476** (600th birth anniversary)......	40	15
4318		18st. Johann Sebastian Bach (composer, 250th death anniversary).....................	60	25
4319		20st. Guy de Maupassant (writer, 150th birth anniversary)................................	1·00	40

BULGARIA 2000

4320	60st. Antoine de Saint-Exupéry (writer and aviator, birth centenary)		3·00	80
4317/4320	Set of 4		4·50	1·40

(Des Kh. Aleksiev. Litho)

2000 (3 July). Centenary of First Zeppelin Flight. Airship Development. T **1477** and similar vert designs. Multicoloured. P 13.

4321	10st. Type **1477**	40	15
4322	18st. LZ-13 *Hansa* (Zeppelin airship) over Cologne	60	25
4323	20st. N-1 *Norge* over Rome	1·00	40
4324	60st. *Graf Zeppelin* over Sofia	3·00	90
4321/4324	Set of 4	4·50	1·50

1478 Ivan Vazov and Text

(Des L. Metodiev. Litho)

2000 (9 July). 150th Birth Anniversary of Ivan Vazov (writer). P 13.

4325	**1478**	18st. multicoloured	80	40

1479 Letter 'e' with Hands   **1480** St Atanasii Church, Startsevo

(Des V. Kitanov. Litho)

2000 (19 July). 25th Anniversary of Organisation for Security and Co-operation in Europe Helsinki Final Act (establishing governing principles). Sheet 68×92 mm containing T **1479** and other similar horiz design. Multicoloured. P 13.

MS4326	20st. Type **1479**; 20st. Three 'e's	4·00	3·25

(Des I. Gazdov. Litho)

2000 (1 Sept)–02. Churches. T **1480** and similar horiz designs. P 14×13½.

4327	22st. black and new blue	80	15
	a. Perf 12½ (with one diamond-shaped hole on each vert side) (11.02)	80	65
4328	24st. black and bright mauve	1·00	25
	a. Perf 12½ (with one diamond-shaped hole on each vert side) (11.02)	1·00	80
4329	50st. black and yellow	2·00	50
	a. Perf 12½ (with one diamond-shaped hole on each vert side) (11.02)	2·00	1·60
4330	65st. black and bright green	2·50	80
	a. Perf 12½ (with one diamond-shaped hole on each vert side) (11.02)	2·50	2·10
4331	300st. black and pale orange	8·00	3·25
4332	500st. black and rose	14·00	5·50
4327/4332	Set of 6	25·00	9·50

Designs: 22st. T **1480**; 24st. St Clement of Ohrid, Sofia; 50st. Mary of the Ascension, Sofia; 65st. St Nedelya, Nedelino; 3l. Mary of the Ascension, Sofia, (*different*); 5l. Mary of the Ascension, Pamporovo.

1481 Ibex (*Capra ibex*)   **1482** Field Gladiolus (*Gladiolus segetum*)

(Des T. Vardzhiev. Litho)

2000 (25 Sept). Animals. T **1481** and similar horiz designs. Multicoloured. P 13.

4333	10st. Type **1481**	60	25
4334	22st. Argali (*Ovis ammon*)	80	30
4335	30st. European Bison (*Bison bonasus*)	1·20	50
4336	65st. Yak (*Bos grunniens*)	2·75	65
4333/4336	Set of 4	4·75	1·50

(Des Z. Stoyanov. Litho)

2000 (17 Oct). Spring Flowers. T **1482** and similar vert designs. Multicoloured. P 13×13½.

4337	10st. Type **1482**	60	25
4338	22st. Liverwort (*Hepatica nobilis*)	80	30
4339	30st. Pheasant's Eye (*Adonis vernalis*)	1·20	50
4340	65st. Peacock Anemone (*Anemone pavonina*)	2·75	65
4337/4340	Set of 4	4·75	1·50

1483 Crowd and Emblem   **1484** Order of Gallantry, 1880

(Des P. Petrunov. Litho)

2000 (3 Nov). 50th Anniversary of European Convention on Human Rights. P 13½×13.

4341	**1483**	65st. multicoloured	4·00	1·60

(Des St. Kunchev and A. Apostolov. Litho)

2000 (28 Nov). Medals. T **1484** and similar vert designs. Multicoloured. P 13.

4342	12st. Type **1484**	60	25
4343	22st. Order of St Aleksandur, 1882	1·00	40
4344	30st. Order of Merit, 1891	1·20	50
4345	65st. Order of Cyril and Methodius, 1909	3·00	65
4342/4345	Set of 4	5·25	1·60

1485 Prince Boris-Mihail   **1486** Seal

(Des K. Andreev. Litho)

2000 (28 Nov). Bimillenary of Christianity. Sheet 105×83 mm containing T **1485** and similar horiz designs. Multicoloured. P 13½×13.

4346	22st. Type **1485**	1·00	40
	a. Sheetlet of 4. Nos. 4346/4349	7·75	
4347	22st. St Sofroni Vrachanski	1·00	40
4348	65st. Mary and Child (detail)	2·75	65
4349	65st. Antim I	2·75	65
4346/4349	Set of 4	6·75	1·90

(Des P. Rashkov. Litho)

2000 (8 Dec). 120th Anniversary of Supreme Audit Office. P 13×13½.

4350	**1486**	22st. multicoloured	1·00	40

1487 Microchip, Planets and *The Proportions of Man* (Leonardo da Vinci)

(Des B. Filichev. Litho)

2001 (8 Jan). New Millennium. Paper with fluorescent fibres. P 13.

4351	**1487**	22st. multicoloured	1·00	40

1488 Tram

1489 Muscat Grapes and Evsinograd Palace

(Des B. Benev. Litho)

2001 (12 Jan). Centenary of the Electrification of Bulgarian Transport. T **1488** and similar horiz design. Multicoloured. P 13.

4352	22st. Type **1488**	1·00	40
	a. Pair. Nos. 4352/4353	4·25	1·20
4353	65st. Train carriages	3·00	65

Nos. 4352/4353 each×2 were issued together in *se-tenant* sheetlets of four stamps.

(Des S. Daskaov. Litho)

2001 (7 Feb). Viticulture. T **1489** and similar vert designs. Multicoloured. Paper with fluorescent fibres. P 13.

4354	12st. Type **1489**	60	25
4355	22st. Gumza grapes and Baba Vida Fortress	1·00	40
4356	30st. Shiroka Melnishka Loza grapes and Melnik Winery	1·20	50
4357	65st. Mavrud grapes and Asenova Krepost Fortress	3·00	65
4354/4357	Set of 4	5·25	1·60

1490 '@' and Microcircuits

(Des K. Andreev. Litho)

2001 (1 Mar). Information Technology. Sheet 82×95 mm containing T **1490** and similar horiz design. Multicoloured. Paper with fluorescent fibres. P 13.

MS4358 Type **1490**; 65st. John Atanasoff (computer pioneer) and ABC .... 40·00 38·00

1491 Southern Europe and Emblem

1492 Eagle and Lakes, Rila

(Des T. Vardzhiev. Litho)

2001 (4 Apr). Tenth Anniversary of the Atlantic Club of Bulgaria. Sheet 87×67 mm. Paper with fluorescent fibres. P 13.

MS4359 **1491** 65st. multicoloured .... 8·00 7·25

(Des A. Apostolov. Litho)

2001 (18 Apr). Europa. Water Resources. T **1492** and similar vert design. Multicoloured. Paper with fluorescent fibres. P 13.

4360	22st. Type **1492**	2·00	1·60
4361	65st. Cave and waterfall, Rhodope	33·00	30·00

1493 Building, Bridge and Todor Kableschkov

(Des Maiya Cholakova. Litho)

2001 (1 May). 125th Anniversary of the April Uprising and 150th Birth Anniversary of Todor Kableschkov (revolutionary leader). Paper with fluorescent fibres. P 13.

| 4362 | **1493** | 22st. multicoloured .... | 1·00 | 40 |

1494 Juvenile Egyptian Vulture in Flight

(Des S. Dechev. Litho)

2001 (21 May). Endangered Species. Egyptian Vulture (*Neophron perconpterus*). T **1494** and similar horiz designs. Multicoloured. Paper with fluorescent fibres. P 13.

4363	12st. Type **1494**	60	25
4364	22st. Juvenile landing	1·00	40
4365	30st. Adult and chick	1·20	50
4366	65st. Adult and eggs	2·75	80
4363/4366	Set of 4	5·00	1·80

1495 Georgi (Gundy) Asparuchov (footballer)

1496 Rainbow and People

(Des L. Metodiev. Litho)

2001 (29 June). Sportsmen. T **1495** and similar horiz designs. Multicoloured. Paper with fluorescent fibres. P 13.

4367	22st. Type **1495**	1·00	45
	a. Sheetlet of 3. Nos. 4367/4369 plus 3 labels	5·25	
4368	30st. Dancho (Dan) Kolev (wrestler)	1·20	55
4369	65st. General Krum Lekarski (equestrian)	2·75	1·20
4367/4369	Set of 3	4·50	2·00

Nos. 4367/4369 were issued together in *se-tenant* sheetlets of three stamps plus three labels, the stamps arranged in a checkerboard fashion with a label showing each sportsman at left (No. 4368) or right (others).

(Des N. Pekarev. Litho)

2001 (11 July). 50th Anniversary United Nations High Commissioner for Refugees. Paper with fluorescent fibres. P 13.

| 4370 | **1496** | 65st. multicoloured .... | 2·75 | 95 |

1497 Alexander Zhendov

1498 Court Seal

(Des I. Bogdanov. Litho)

2001 (24 July). Artists' Birth Centenaries. T **1497** and similar horiz design. Multicoloured. Paper with fluorescent fibres. P 13.

4371	22st. Type **1497**	1·00	40
4372	65st. Ilya Beshkov	3·00	1·90

(Des N. Tachev. Litho)

2001 (3 Oct). Tenth Anniversary of Constitutional Court. Paper with fluorescent fibres. P 14×13.

| 4373 | **1498** | 25st. multicoloured .... | 1·00 | 40 |

BULGARIA 2001

1499 Flags

1500 Children encircling Globe

(Des T. Vardzhiev. Litho)

2001 (5 Oct). North Atlantic Treaty Organisation Summit, Sofia. Sheet 116×111 mm containing T **1499** and similar horiz designs. Paper with fluorescent fibres. P 13½×13.
MS4374 12st. Type **1499**; 24st. Streamer of flags; 25st. Flags in upper right semi-circle; 65st. Flags in upper left semi-circle .... 10·00 9·50

(Des M. Doncheva. Litho)

2001 (9 Oct). United Nations Year of Dialogue among Civilisations. Paper with fluorescent fibres. P 13.
4375 **1500** 65st. multicoloured .... 2·50 95

1501 Black Sea Turbot (*Scopthalmus maeoticus*)

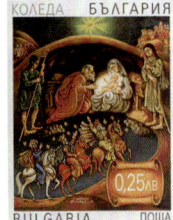

1502 The Nativity

(Des Krasimira Despotova. Litho)

2001 (31 Oct). International Day for the Protection of the Black Sea. Sheet 73×91 mm. Paper with fluorescent fibres. P 13.
MS4376 **1501** 65st. multicoloured .... 3·50 3·00

(Des V. Vulkanov. Litho)

2001 (19 Nov). Christmas. Paper with fluorescent fibres. P 13.
4377 **1502** 25st. multicoloured .... 1·00 60

1503 Cape Shabla Lighthouse

1504 Icon

(Des B. Kitanov. Litho)

2001 (19 Nov)–03. Lighthouses. T **1503** and similar horiz design. Paper with fluorescent fibres. P 14.
4378 25st. scarlet-vermilion and dark green .... 1·00 60
    a. Perf 12½ (with one diamond-shaped hole on each vert side) (3.03) .... 1·00 60
4379 32st. deep blue and chrome-yellow .... 1·20 70
    a. Perf 12½ (with one diamond-shaped hole on each vert side) (2.03) .... 1·20 70
Designs: 25st. T **1503**; 32st. Kaliakra Cape lighthouse.
See also No. MS4881.

(Des M. Enev. Litho)

2001 (27 Nov). Zographu Monastery, Mount Athos. Sheet 85×105 mm containing T **1504** and similar horiz design. Multicoloured. Paper with fluorescent fibres. P 13.
MS4380 65st. Type **1504**; 25st. Monastery Buildings ... 5·00 4·25

1505 Father Christmas (from film by Al. Zahariev)

2001 (12 Dec). Bulgarian Animation. Paper with fluorescent fibres. Litho. P 13½×13.
4381 **1505** 25c. multicoloured .... 1·20 70
No. 4381 was issued in sheetlets of three stamps and three labels.

1506 Vincenzo Bellini

(Des S. Dechev. Litho)

2001 (17 Dec). Birth Bicentenary of Vincenzo Bellini (composer). Paper with fluorescent fibres. P 13.
4382 **1506** 25st. multicoloured .... 1·20 70

1507 Crowd and Ancient Calendar

(Des P. Vulchev. Litho)

2001 (21 Dec). Founders of Bulgarian State (1st Series). T **1507** and similar horiz designs. Multicoloured. Paper with fluorescent fibres. P 13.
4383 10st. Type **1507**.. 60 35
4384 25st. Khans, Kubrat and Asparuh...................... 1·20 70
4385 30st. Khans, Krum and Omurtag....................... 1·40 85
4386 65st. King Boris and Tsar Simeon..................... 3·00 1·80
4383/4386 Set of 4.. 5·50 3·25
See also Nos. 4424/4427, 4456/4459, 4511/4514, 4559/4562 and 4610/4613.

1508 '€' Symbol and Stars

(Des V. Kitanov. Litho)

2002 (3 Jan). The Euro (European currency). Paper with fluorescent fibres. P 14×13.
4387 **1508** 65l. multicoloured .... 3·00 1·80

1509 Matches

(Des T. Likho. Litho)

2002 (21 Jan). 50th Anniversary of United Nations Disarmament Commission. Paper with fluorescent fibres. P 13×14.
4388 **1509** 25f. multicoloured .... 1·20 70

2002 BULGARIA

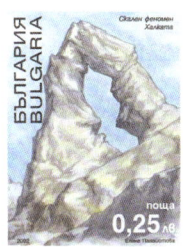
1510 Limestone Arch

1511 Figure Skater

(Des Elena Panatsomova. Litho)

2002 (29 Jan). BALKANMAX '02 International Stamp Exhibition. Sheet 95×87 mm containing T **1510** and similar vert design. Multicoloured. Paper with fluorescent fibres. P 13.
MS4389 25f. Type **1510**; 65f. Long-legged Buzzard
(*Buteo rufinus*) .... 43·00   42·00

(Des N. Atanasov. Litho)

2002 (5 Feb). Winter Olympic Games, Salt Lake City. T **1511** and similar horiz design. Multicoloured. Paper with fluorescent fibres. P 13.
4390   25f. Type **1511** .... 1·20   70
4391   65f. Speed skater .... 3·00   1·80

1512 Station Building and Bearded Penguins

1513 Performing Elephant

(Des T. Vardzhiev. Litho)

2002 (20 Mar). Tenth National Antarctic Expedition. P 13½×13.
4392   **1512**   25f. multicoloured .... 1·20   70
No. 4392 was issued in sheetlets of three stamps plus three labels, the stamps arranged checkerboard fashion.

(Des E. Stankev. Litho)

2002 (22 Mar). Europa. Circus. T **1513** and similar horiz design. Multicoloured. Paper with fluorescent fibres. P 13.
4393   25f. Type **1513** .... 1·20   70
4394   65f. Clown .... 3·00   1·80
See also Nos. 4863 and **MS**4920*a*.

1514 Veselin Stojano

1515 *Illustrated Landscape* (Vasil Barakov)

(Des A. Atanasov. Litho)

2002 (27 Mar). Birth Centenaries. T **1514** and similar horiz design. Multicoloured. paper with fluorescent fibres. P 13.
4395   25f. Type **1514** (composer) .... 1·20   70
4396   65f. Angel Karaliechev (writer) .... 1·40   85

(Des D. Trendafilov. Litho)

2002 (17 Apr). Art. T **1515** and similar multicoloured designs. Paper with fluorescent fibres. P 13.
4397   10st. Type **1515** 60   35
4398   25st. Book illustration from *Under the Yoke* (novel by Ivan Vazov) (Boris Angulshev) (*horiz*) .... 1·20   70
4399   65st. *The Balcony and Canary* (Ivan Nenov) .... 3·00   1·80
4397/4399 Set of 3 .... 4·25   2·50

1516 Stefan Kanchev

1517 Melon (*Cucumis melo*)

(Des D. Tassev. Litho)

2002 (26 Apr). First Death Anniversaries of Stamp Designers. T **1516** and similar horiz design. Multicoloured. P 13.
4400   25c. Type **1516** .... 1·20   70
4401   65c. Alex Popilov .... 3·00   1·80

(Des S. Dechev. Litho)

2002 (8 May). Fruits. T **1517** and similar horiz designs. Multicoloured. Paper with fluorescent fibres. P 13.
4402   10st. Type **1517** 60   35
4403   25st. Watermelon (*Citrullus lanatus*) .... 1·20   70
4404   27st. Pumpkin (*Cucurbita pepo*) .... 1·30   80
4405   65st. Calabash (*Lagenaria siceraria*) .... 3·00   1·80
4402/4405 Set of 4 .... 5·50   3·25

1518 Cock Bird

1519 Pope John Paul II and Monument to Cyril and Methodius

(Des Z. Stoyanov. Litho)

2002 (10 May). Poultry. T **1518** and similar multicoloured designs. Paper with fluorescent fibres. P 13.
4406   10st. Type **1518** 60   35
4407   20st. Leghorn pair (*horiz*) .... 1·00   60
4408   25st. Two cocks fighting (*horiz*) .... 1·20   70
4409   65st. Plymouth Rock pair (inscr 'Plimouth Rock') .... 3·00   1·80
4406/4409 Set of 4 .... 5·25   3·00

(Des Z. Stoyanov. Litho)

2002 (24 May). Pope John Paul II's Visit to Bulgaria. Paper with fluorescent fibres. P 13.
4410   **1519**   65st. multicoloured .... 3·00   1·80

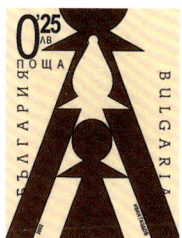
1520 Chess Pieces

1521 Flag and Stars

(Des I. Gazdov. Litho)

2002 (27 May). Chess. Sheet 91×71 mm containing T **1520** and similar vert design. Paper with fluorescent fibres. P 13.
MS4411 25c. chocolate, pale cinnamon and black (Type **1520**); 65c. multicoloured (Hand holding pawn) .... 4·00   3·50

(Des S. Daskalov. Litho)

2002 (29 May). Tenth Anniversary of Bulgaria's Admission to Council of Europe. Paper with fluorescent fibres. P 13.
4412   **1521**   25st. multicoloured .... 1·20   70

BULGARIA 2002

1522 Rabbit

1523 *Marie-Luisa* (First ocean-going liner)

1528 Exhibition Emblem

(Des A. Appostolov. Litho)

2002 (12 Aug)–08. Woodcarvings by Peter Kuschlev. T **1522** and similar vert designs. Paper with fluorescent fibres.

A. P 14

4413A	6st. light brown and black		30	20
	a. Ordinary paper. Imperf×p13 (3.08)			
4414A	12st. dull orange and black		60	35
	a. Ordinary paper. Imperf×p13 (3.08)			
4415A	36st. yellow-olive and black		1·60	95
	a. Ordinary paper. Imperf×p13 (3.08)			
4416A	44st. brown-rose and black		2·00	1·20
	a. Ordinary paper. Imperf×p13 (3.08)			
4413A/4416A	Set of 4		4·00	2·40

B. Perf 12½ (with one diamond-shaped hole on each vert side) (11.02)

4413B	6st. light brown and black		30	20
4414B	12st. dull orange and black		60	35
4415B	36st. yellow-olive and black		1·60	95
4416B	44st. brown-rose and black		2·00	1·20
4413B/4416B	Set of 4		4·00	2·40

Designs: 6st. T **1522**; 12st. Deer; 36st. Bird; 44st. Boar.

(Des Maglena Konstantinova. Litho)

2002 (18 Oct). Merchant Ships. T **1523** and similar horiz designs. Multicoloured. Paper with fluorescent fibres. P 13.

4417	12st. Type **1523**		60	35
4418	36st. *Persenk* (cargo ship)		1·60	95
4419	49st. *Kaliakra* (sail training ship)		2·40	1·40
4420	65st. *Sofia* (container ship)		3·00	1·80
4417/4420	Set of 4		6·75	4·00

1524 Father Christmas and Sun

1525 Flag and NATO Emblem

(Des Bagryana Tasseva. Litho)

2002 (20 Nov). Christmas. Paper with fluorescent fibres. P 13½×13.

4421	**1524**	36st. multicoloured	1·60	95

(Des Ivellina Velinova. Litho)

2002 (21 Nov). Bulgaria's Participation in NATO Conference, Prague. Sheet 85×65 mm. Paper with fluorescent fibres. P 13.

MS4422	**1525**	65st. multicoloured	6·00	5·50

1526 Paper Bird

1527 Tsar Samuil

(Des R. Kolev. Litho)

2002 (22 Nov). 30th Anniversary of Security and Co-operation in Europe Conference. Sheet 85×60 mm. Paper with fluorescent fibres. P 13.

MS4423	**1526**	65st. multicoloured	5·00	4·25

(Des Dea Vulcheva. Litho)

2002 (6 Dec). Founders of Bulgarian State (2nd series). T **1527** and similar horiz designs. Multicoloured. Paper with fluorescent fibres. P 13.

4424	18st. Type **1527**		80	50
4425	36st. Tsars Peter II and Assen		1·60	95
4426	49st. Tsar Kaloyan		2·00	1·20
4427	65st. Tsar Ivan Assen II		2·75	1·70
4424/4427	Set of 4		6·50	4·00

(Des B. Ionov. Litho)

2003 (10 Jan). Europalia Cultural Exhibition, Belgium. P 13.

4428	**1528**	65l. multicoloured	3·00	1·80

1529 Rose Pickers (Stoyan Sotirov)

1530 Space Construction surrounding Earth

(Des K. Gogov. Litho)

2003 (28 Jan). Artists' Birth Centenaries. T **1529** and similar horiz designs. Multicoloured. P 13.

4429	18l. Type **1529**		80	50
4430	36l. *The Blind Fiddler* (Illya Petrov)		1·60	95
4431	65l. *Swineherd* (Zlatyo Boyadjiev)		2·75	1·70
4429/4431	Set of 3		4·75	2·75

(Des K. Andreev. Litho)

2003 (7 Feb). Space Exploration. Sheet 104×85 mm. Fluorescent security markings. P 13.

MS4432	**1530**	65l. multicoloured	4·00	3·50

1531 Statue of Russian and Bulgarian Soldiers

1532 Exarch Stefan I, Menorah Candlestick and Dimitar Peshev

(Des P. Rashkov. Litho)

2003 (28 Feb). 125th Anniversary of Bulgarian State. P 13.

4433	**1531**	36l. multicoloured	1·60	95

(Des T. Vardzhiev. Litho)

2003 (10 Mar). 60th Anniversary of Rescue of Bulgarian Jews. P 13.

4434	**1532**	36l. multicoloured	1·60	95

1533 Silhouettes of Birds and Woman

(Des I. Gazdov. Litho)

2003 (17 Mar). Europa. Poster Art. T **1533** and similar horiz design. Multicoloured. P 13.

4435	36l. Type **1533**		1·60	95
	a. Pair. Nos. 4435/4436		4·50	3·00
4436	65l. Chicken, legs and farm animals		2·75	1·70

Nos. 4435/4436 were issued in vertical *se-tenant* pairs within the sheet.

1534 Vase with Fifteen Sunflowers   **1535** Pterodactylus

(Des N. Mladenov. Litho)

2003 (19 Mar). 150th Birth Anniversary of Vincent van Gogh (artist). Sheet 70×90 mm. P 13.
MS4437 **1534** 65l. multicoloured .... 3·00 2·75

(Des Z. Stoyanov. Litho)

2003 (24 Apr). Dinosaurs. T **1535** and similar horiz designs. Multicoloured. P 13.
4438	30st. Type **1535**.................................	1·20	70
	a. Horiz strip of 4. Nos. 4438/4441...............	7·50	
4439	36st. Gorgosaurus................................	1·20	70
4440	49st. Mesosaurus.................................	2·20	1·30
4441	65st. Monoclonius................................	2·75	1·70
4438/4441	Set of 4...	6·50	4·00

Nos. 4438/4441 were issued in horizontal se-tenant strips of four stamps within the sheet.

1536 Nymphoides peltata

(Des B. Kitanov. Litho)

2003 (15 May). Water Plants (1st issue). T **1536** and similar horiz designs. Multicoloured. P 13.
4442 **1536** 36st. multicoloured .... 1·60 95

See also Nos. 4447/4450.

1537 Honey Bee (*Apis mellifera*)   **1538** *Butomus umbellatus*

(Des H. Kourouch. Litho)

2003 (17 June). Bees. T **1537** and similar horiz designs. Multicoloured. P 13.
4443	20st. Type **1537**................................	80	50
4444	30st. *Anthidium manicatum*..................	1·20	70
4445	36st. Bumble Bee (*Bombus subteraneus*)	1·60	95
4446	65st. Blue Carpenter Bee (*Xylocopa violacea*)	2·75	1·70
4443/4446	Set of 4...	5·75	3·50

(Des Elena Panaiotova. Litho)

2003 (25 July). Water Plants (2nd issue). T **1538** and similar vert designs. Multicoloured. P 13.
4447	20st. Type **1538**................................	80	50
4448	36st. *Sagirraria sagittifolia*...................	1·60	95
4449	50st. *Menyanthes trifoliata*...................	2·20	1·30
4450	65st. *Iris pseudoacorus*........................	2·75	1·70
4447/4450	Set of 4...	6·50	4·00

1539 Gotze Delchev

(Des I. Bogdanov. Litho)

2003 (1 Aug). Death Centenary of Gotze Delchev (revolutionary). Centenary of Macedonian Uprising. P 13.
4451 **1539** 36st. multicoloured .... 1·60 95

1540 Mountains

(Des L. Methodiev. Litho)

2003 (19 Sept). International Year of Mountains. P 13.
4452 **1540** 65st. multicoloured .... 3·00 1·80

No. 4452 was issued in sheetlets of three stamps and three stamp-size labels showing rivers.

1541 Bulgarian and USA Flags as Bowtie   **1542** John Atanasoff

(Des T. Licho. Litho)

2003 (19 Sept). Centenary of Bulgaria–USA Diplomatic Relations. P 13.
4453 **1541** 65st. multicoloured .... 2·75 1·70

(Des H. Aleksiev. Litho)

2003 (3 Oct). Birth Centenary of John Atanasoff (computer pioneer). P 13.
4454 **1542** 65st. multicoloured .... 3·00 1·80

No. 4454 was issued with se-tenant stamp-size label.

1543 Pawn and Buildings   **1544** Tsar Ivan Alexander

(Des E. Stankev. Litho)

2003 (10 Oct). European Chess Championship, Plovdiv. P 13.
4455 **1543** 65st. multicoloured .... 2·75 1·70

(Des P. Vulcheva. Litho)

2003 (18 Oct–23 Dec). Founders of Bulgarian State (3rd series). T **1544** and similar horiz designs. Multicoloured. P 13.
4456	30st. Type **1544** (23.12)......................	1·20	70
4457	45st. Despot Dobrotitsa (23.12)...............	1·80	1·10
4458	65st. Tsar Ivan Shishman.......................	2·75	1·70
4459	89st. Tsar Ivan Sratsimir (23.12)..............	3·25	1·90
4456/4459	Set of 4...	8·00	4·75

BULGARIA 2003

1545 Taekwondo

1546 Father Christmas

(Des S. Nenov. Litho)

2003 (27 Oct). 80th Anniversary of National Olympic Committee. T **1545** and similar vert designs. Multicoloured. P 13.
4460	20st. Type **1545**..	80	50
4461	36st. Mountain biking.....................................	1·60	95
4462	50st. Softball..	2·20	1·30
4463	65st. Canoe slalom...	2·75	1·70
4460/4463 Set of 4		6·50	4·00

(Des D. Trendafilov. Litho)

2003 (24 Nov). Christmas. P 13.
4464	**1546**	65st. multicoloured...........................	2·75	1·70

1547 Carriage and Man wearing Top Hat

(Des D. Tasev. Litho)

2003 (28 Nov). Carriages. T **1547** and similar horiz designs. Multicoloured. P 13.
4465	30st. Type **1547**..	1·20	70
4466	36st. Closed carriage with woman passenger...	1·60	95
4467	50st. State coach, woman and Dog................	2·20	1·30
4468	65st. Couple and large carriage....................	2·75	1·70
4465/4468 Set of 4		7·00	4·25

1548 FIFA Centenary Emblem

1549 Eye, Square, Compass and Statue

(Des M. Yaranov. Litho)

2003 (12 Dec). Centenary of FIFA (Fédération Internationale de Football Association). T **1548** and similar multicoloured designs. P 13.
4469	20st. Type **1548**..	80	50
4470	25st. Early players..	1·00	60
4471	36st. Early players and rules.........................	1·60	95
4472	50st. FIFA fair play trophy (*vert*).................	2·20	1·30
4473	65st. FIFA world player trophy (*vert*)..........	2·75	1·70
4469/4473 Set of 5		7·50	4·50

(Des E. Ivanov and L. Pavlov. Litho)

2003 (22 Dec). Tenth Anniversary of Re-establishment of Masonic Activity in Bulgaria. P 13.
4474	**1549**	80st. multicoloured...........................	3·25	1·90

1550 *Noctua tertia*

(Des S. Detchev. Litho)

2004 (15 Jan–Oct). Moths. T **1550** and similar horiz designs. Multicoloured. Paper with fluorescent fibres.

A. Perf 12½ (with one diamond-shaped hole on each vert side)
4475A	40st. Type **1550**..	1·60	95
4476A	45st. *Rethera komarovi*................................	1·80	1·10
4477A	55st. *Symtomis marjana*..............................	2·20	1·30
4478A	80st. *Arctia caja*...	3·25	1·90
4475A/4478A Set of 4		8·00	4·75

B. Without gum. P 14×13½ (Oct 2004)
4475B	40st. Type **1550**..	1·60	95
4476B	45st. *Rethera komarovi*................................	1·80	1·10
4477B	55st. *Symtomis marjana*..............................	2·20	1·30
4478B	80st. *Arctia caja*...	3·25	1·90
4475B/4478B Set of 4		8·00	4·75

Nos. 4475B/4478B were issued without gum. The issue was limited to approximately 3000.
See also No. **MS**4839.

1551 Mask

1552 OSCE Emblem and Bridge

(Des L. Vesselinov. Litho)

2004 (23 Jan). SERVA, International Masquerade Festival, Pernik. P 13.
4479	**1551**	80st. multicoloured...........................	3·50	2·00

No. 4479 was issued in *se-tenant* sheetlets of three stamps and three stamp-size labels showing bells.
See also No. 4865.

(Des St. Gruev. Litho)

2004 (30 Jan). Bulgaria, Chair of Organisation for Security and Co-operation in Europe. P 13.
4480	**1552**	80st. multicoloured...........................	3·25	1·90

1553 Theatre Façade

1554 Atanas Dalchev

(Des S. Despodov. Litho)

2004 (19 Feb). Centenary of Ivan Vazov National Theatre, Sofia. P 13.
4481	**1553**	45st. multicoloured...........................	2·00	1·20

No. 4481 was issued with a *se-tenant* stamp size label showing an early play bill.

(Des S. Petrunov. Litho)

2004 (25 Mar). Birth Centenaries. T **1554** and similar horiz design. Multicoloured. P 13.
4482	45st. Type **1554** (poet)..................................	1·80	1·10
4483	80st. Lubomir Pipkov (composer).................	3·25	1·90

1555 NATO Emblem and National Colours

1556 Georgi Ivanov

(Des T. Vardjiev. Litho)

2004 (2 Apr). Accession to Full Membership of NATO. P 13.
4484	**1555**	80st. multicoloured...........................	3·25	1·90

(Des B. Benev. Litho)

2004 (15 Apr). 25th Anniversary of First Bulgarian in Space. Sheet 84×68 mm. P 13.
MS4485	**1556**	80st. multicoloured...........................	4·00	3·50

2004 BULGARIA

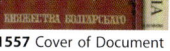
1557 Cover of Document

1558 Globe surmounted by Mortar Board

(Des Ivelina Velinova. Litho)

2004 (16 Apr). 125th Anniversary of Turnovska Constitution and Restoration of Bulgarian State. Sheet 86×67 mm. P 13.
MS4486 **1557** 45st. multicoloured .... 12·00 11·00

(Des M. Todorov. Litho)

2004 (3 May). Bulgarian Dream (graduate assistance) Programme. P 13.
4487 **1558** 45st. multicoloured .... 1·80 1·10

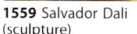
1559 Salvador Dali (sculpture)

1560 Luben Dimitrov (sculptor) and Boris Ivanov (cinema director)

(Des P. Trendafilov. Litho)

2004 (12 May). Birth Centenary of Salvador Dali (artist). Sheet 85×65 mm. P 13.
MS4488 **1559** 80st. multicoloured .... 6·00 5·50

(Des A. Attanassov. Litho)

2004 (21 May). Birth Centenaries. T **1560** and similar horiz design. Multicoloured. P 13.
4489   45st. Type **1560** .... 2·00 1·40
4490   80st. Vassil Stoilov and Stoyan Venev
        (artists) .... 3·25 2·20

1561 Mountains and Skiers

(Des Elaena Panayotova. Litho)

2004 (27 May). Europa. Holidays. T **1561** and similar horiz design. Multicoloured. P 13.
4491   45st. Type **1561** .... 2·00 1·40
4492   80st. Beach scene .... 3·25 2·20

1562 Christo Stoychkov

(Des R. Toshev. Litho)

2004 (2 June). Bulgarian Footballers. T **1562** and similar horiz designs. Multicoloured. P 13.
4493   45st. Type **1562** .... 2·00 1·40
        a. Block of 4. Nos. 4493/4496 .... 8·25

4494   45st. Georgi Asparuchov .... 2·00 1·40
4495   45st. Krassimir Balakov .... 2·00 1·40
4496   45st. Nikola Kotkov .... 2·00 1·40
4493/4496 Set of 4 .... 7·25 5·00
Nos. 4493/4496 were issued in se-tenant blocks of four stamps within the sheet.

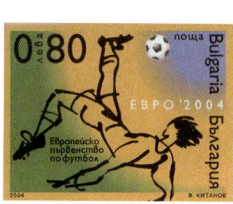
1563 Footballer and Ball

1564 Seal

(Des V. Kitanov. Litho)

2004 (11 June). European Football Championship 2004, Portugal. Sheet 85×67 mm. P 13.
MS4497 **1563** 80st. multicoloured .... 3·50 2·75

(Des C. Alexiev. Litho)

2004 (23 June). 125th Anniversary of Bulgaria–Austria Diplomatic Relations. P 13.
4498 **1564** 80st. multicoloured .... 3·25 2·20

1565 Lion (statue), Flag and Document

(Des S. Krustev. Litho)

2004 (26 June). 125th Anniversary of Ministry of Interior. P 13.
4499 **1565** 45st. multicoloured .... 2·00 1·40

1566 de Dion Button Post Car (1905)

1567 Red Kite (*Milvus milvus*)

(Des Natalia Kuruch. Litho)

2004 (16 July). 125th Anniversary of Postal Service. Sheet 93×80 mm. P 13.
MS4500 **1566** 45st. multicoloured .... 12·00 11·00
No. **MS**4500 contains a se-tenant stamp size label, which with the stamp forms a composite design.

(Des Krassimira Despotova. Litho)

2004 (28 July). Endangered Species. Preservation of the Black Sea. Sheet 86×86 mm containing T **1567** and similar horiz design. Multicoloured. P 13.
MS4501 45st. Type **1567**; 80st. *Blennius ocellaris* .... 6·00 5·50

1568 Runner holding Torch and Olympic Flame (Berlin, 1936)

BULGARIA 2004

(Des I. Gazdov. Litho)

2004 (5 Aug). Olympic Games, Athens 2004. T **1568** and similar horiz designs showing runner and Olympic flame. Multicoloured. P 13.

4502	10st. Type **1568**	60	40
4503	20st. Munich, 1972	80	55
4504	45st. Moscow, 1980	2·00	1·40
4505	80st. Athens, 2004	3·25	2·20
4502/4505	Set of 4	6·00	4·00

1569 *Krum* (steamer)

(Des E. Stankev. Litho)

2004 (6 Aug). 125th Anniversary of Bulgarian Navy. T **1569** and similar horiz designs. Multicoloured. P 13.

4506	10st. Type **1569**	60	40
4507	25st. *Druski* (torpedo boat)	1·00	70
4508	45st. *Christo Botev* (mine-sweeper)	2·00	1·40
4509	80st. *Smeli* (frigate)	3·25	2·20
4506/4509	Set of 4	6·25	4·25

1570 Square and Compass

(Des I. Bogdanov. Litho)

2004 (20 Sept). 125th Anniversary of Bulgarian Masonic Movement. P 13.

4510	**1570**	45st. multicoloured	10·00	9·00

1571 Patriarch Ephtimius Turnovski

(Des P. Vulcheva. Litho)

2004 (15 Nov). Founders of Bulgarian State (4th series). T **1571** and similar horiz designs. Multicoloured. P 13.

4511	10st. Type **1571**	60	40
4512	20st. Kniaz Fruzhin and Kniaz Constantine	1·00	70
4513	45st. Georgi Peyachevich and Peter Partchevich	2·00	1·40
4514	80st. Piessii Hilendarski	3·50	2·50
4511/4514	Set of 4	6·50	4·50

1572 *Polyporus squamosus*

(Des S. Dechev. Litho)

2004 (17 Nov). Fungi. Sheet 125×93 mm containing T **1572** and similar horiz designs. Multicoloured. P 13.
MS4515 10st. Type **1572**; 20st. *Fomes fomentarius*; 45st. *Piptoporus betulinus*; 80st. *Laetiporus sulphureus* ... 7·00 6·25

1573 Two Sturgeon

(Des Z. Stoyanov. Litho)

2004 (18 Nov). Sturgeon (*Huso huso*). T **1573** and similar horiz designs showing Sturgeon. Multicoloured. P 13.

4516	80st. Type **1573**	3·50	2·50
	a. Horiz strip of 4. Nos. 4516/4519	14·50	
4517	80st. From below	3·50	2·50
4518	80st. Looking down	3·50	2·50
4519	80st. Eating	3·50	2·50
4516/4519	Set of 4	12·50	9·00

Nos. 4516/4519 were issued in horizontal *se-tenant* strips of four stamps within the sheet.

1574 Father Christmas

(Des D. Tassev. Litho)

2004 (24 Nov). Christmas. P 13.

4520	**1574**	45st. multicoloured	2·00	1·40

1575 Hands

(Des T. Varjiev. Litho)

2004 (6 Dec). 12th Organisation for Security and Co-operation in Europe (OSCE) Council, Sofia. Sheet 84×67 mm. P 13.
MS4521 **1575** 80st. multicoloured ... 4·00 3·50

1576 Geo Milev   **1577** Emblem

(Des D. Trendafilov. Litho)

2005 (17 Jan). Birth Centenary of Georghi Milev Kassabov (Geo Milev) (writer and revolutionary). P 13½.

4522	**1576**	45st. multicoloured	2·00	1·40

(Des V. Attanassov. Litho)

2005 (23 Feb). Centenary of Rotary International (charitable organisation). P 13.

4523	**1577**	80st. multicoloured	3·25	2·20

2005 BULGARIA

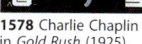
1578 Charlie Chaplin in *Gold Rush* (1925)

1579 The Monument (lithograph) (Nickolai Pavlovitch)

(Des C. Alexiev. Litho)

2005 (25 Feb). History of Cinema. Sheet 88×118 mm containing T **1578** and similar vert designs. Multicoloured. P 13½.
MS4524 10st. Type **1578**; 20st. Scene from *Battleship Potemkin* (Bronenoset Potemkin) (1925); 45st. Marlene Dietrich in *Blue Angel* (Der Baue Engel) (1930); 80st. Vassil Ghendov in *Bulgarian is a Gallant Man* (first Bulgarian film) .... 7·00 6·25

(Des S. Daskalov. Litho)

2005 (11 Mar). 135th Anniversary of Exarchate (independent Bulgarian ecclesiastical organisation). Sheet 68×88 mm. P 13.
MS4525 **1579** 45st. multicoloured .... 3·00 2·75

1580 European Stars and Bulgarian Flag

1581 Panayot Hitov and Philip Totyo

(Des L. Vesselinov. Litho)

2005 (16 Mar). Volunteers for Europe (educational campaign). P 13½.
4526 **1580** 80st. multicoloured .... 3·25 2·20

(Des R. Toshev. Litho)

2005 (21 Mar). 175th Birth Anniversary of Panayot Hitov and Philip Totyo (revolutionaries). P 13½.
4527 **1581** 45st. multicoloured .... 2·00 1·40

1582 Robert Peary

(Des T. Alexieva. Litho)

2005 (23 Mar). Polar Explorers. Sheet 64×95 mm containing T **1582** and similar horiz design. Multicoloured. P 13½.
MS4528 45st. Type **1582** (American) (North Pole, 1909); 80st. Roald Amundsen (Norwegian) (South Pole, 1911) .... 5·50 5·00

1583 Peugeot (1936)

1584 Hans Christian Andersen

(Des D. Tassev. Litho)

2005 (20 Apr). Fire Engines. Sheet 136×77 mm containing T **1583** and similar horiz design. Multicoloured. P 13½.
MS4529 10st. Type **1583**; 20st. Mercedes (1935); 45st. Magirus (1934); 80st. Renault (1925) .... 7·00 6·25

(Des I. Gazdov. Litho)

2005 (20 May). Birth Bicentenary of Hans Christian Andersen (writer). Sheet 87×78 mm. P 13½.
MS4530 **1584** 80st. multicoloured .... 3·50 3·00

1585 Hand holding Scroll

(Des C. Gogov. Litho)

2005 (24 May). Cyrillic Alphabet. Sheet 88×59 mm. P 13½.
MS4531 **1585** 80st. multicoloured .... 3·50 3·00

1586 Electric Locomotive 46

(Des Krassimira Despotova. Litho)

2005 (26 May). Railways. T **1586** and similar horiz design. Multicoloured. P 13½.
4532   45st. Type **1586**........................ 2·00 1·40
         a. Pair. Nos. 4532/4533 .... 5·50 3·75
4533   80st. Modern locomotive DMV 10 .... 3·25 2·20
Nos. 4532/4533 were issued in horizontal and vertical *se-tenant* pairs within the sheet.

1587 *Radetski* (revolutionary ship) (Georgi Dimov)

2005 (27 May). Children's Painting. P 13½.
4534   **1587** 45st. multicoloured .... 2·00 1·40

1588 Blinis

1589 Stylised Figures

(Des T. Vardjiev. Litho)

2005 (28 May). Europa. Gastronomy. T **1588** and similar horiz design. Multicoloured. P 13½.
4535   45st. Type **1588**........................ 2·00 1·40
         a. Horiz pair. Nos. 4535/4536 .... 5·50 3·75
         b. Booklet pane. Nos. 4535/4536, each×2. 11·50
4536   80st. Bread, Kebab and Tomatoes .... 3·25 2·20
Nos. 4535/4536 were issued in horizontal *se-tenant* pairs within sheets of ten stamps.

BULGARIA 2005

(Des Svetlin Belezdrov. Litho)

2005 (28 May). 50th Anniversary of Europa CEPT Postage Stamps. T **1589** and similar vert design. P 13½.
4537	45st. reddish violet, bright green and black..	2·00	1·40
4538	80st. new blue, magenta and black	3·25	2·20

Designs: 45st. T **1589**; 80st. Square of figures.

1590 *Cordulegaster bidentata*

1591 Elias Canetti

(Des E. Stankev. Litho)

2005 (29 June). Dragonflies. T **1590** and similar multicoloured designs. P 13×13½ (vert) or 13½×13 (horiz).
4539	10st. Type **1590**...	65	45
4540	20st. *Erythromma najas* (horiz)	85	60
4541	45st. *Sympetrum pedemontanum* (horiz)	1·90	1·40
4542	80st. *Brachytron pratense*	3·50	2·75
4539/4542	Set of 4...	6·25	4·75

(Des Ivelina Velinova. Litho)

2005 (25 July). Birth Centenary of Elias Canetti (writer). P 13.
4543	**1591**	80st. multicoloured	3·50	2·75

1592 *Synema globosum*

1593 Flag as Tree Bark

(Des S. Dechev. Litho)

2005 (29 July). Spiders. T **1592** and similar vert designs. Multicoloured. P 13×13½.
4544	10st. Type **1592**...	65	45
4545	20st. *Argiope bruennichi*	85	60
4546	45st. *Eresus cinnaberinus*	1·90	1·40
4547	80st. *Araneus diadematus*	3·50	2·75
4544/4547	Set of 4...	6·25	4·75

(Des T. Licho. Litho)

2005 (26 Aug). 110th Anniversary of Organised Tourism. P 13½×13.
4548	**1593**	45st. multicoloured	2·00	1·70

1594 Map

1595 Girl wearing Traditional Costume, Sofia

(Des I. Bogdanov. Litho)

2005 (6 Sept). 120th Anniversary of Unification of Bulgaria. P 13½×13½.
4549	**1594**	45st. multicoloured	2·00	1·70

(Des Anna Tuzsuzova. Litho)

2005 (5 Oct). Women's Traditional Costumes. T **1595** and similar vert designs. Multicoloured. P 13½×13.
4550	20st. Type **1595**...	85	70
4551	25st. Pleven	1·10	90
4552	45st. Sliven	1·90	1·60
4553	80st. Stara Zagora	3·50	3·00
4550/4553	Set of 4...	6·50	5·50

1596 Stamen Grigoroff (discoverer)

1597 Chess Board and Antoaneta Steffanova (Women's World Chess Champion)

(Des Natalya Kuruch. Litho)

2005 (31 Oct). Centenary of Discovery of *Lactobacillus bulgaricus Grigoroff* (yoghurt bacilli) (1st issue). Sheet 94×81 mm. P 13½×13.
MS4554 **1596** 80st. multicoloured .... 3·25 2·75

See also No. **MS**4557.

(Des B. Benev. Litho)

2005 (10 Nov). Chess. P 13×13½.
4555	**1597**	80st. multicoloured	2·50	2·10

1598 Virgin and Child

1599 Stamen Grigoroff (discoverer)

(Des L. Metodiev. Litho)

2005 (30 Nov). Christmas. P 13×13½.
4556	**1598**	45st. multicoloured	2·10	1·80

(Des Natalya Kuruch. Litho)

2005 (2 Dec). Centenary of Discovery of *Lactobacillus bulgaricus Grigoroff* (yoghurt bacilli) (2nd issue). Sheet 94×81 mm. Imperf.
MS4557 **1599** 80st. multicoloured .... 32·00 26·00

The design of No. **MS**4557 is as T **1596** with the addition of an Owl in the top right corner. The sheets include a perforated number. No. **MS**4557 was issued in limited quantities.

1600 Stylised Couple

(Des T. Licho. Litho)

2005 (14 Dec). 50th Anniversary of Membership of United Nations. Sheet 86×88 mm. P 13.
MS4558 **1600** 80st. multicoloured .... 3·25 2·75

1601 Patriarchs Illarion Makariopolski and Antim I

1602 *Rosa pendulina*

(Des P. Vulcheva. Litho)

2005 (20 Dec). Founders of Bulgarian State (5th series). T **1601** and similar horiz designs. P 13.

4559	10st. chocolate and dull green		40	35
4560	20st. brown and dull green		85	70
4561	45st. deep claret and dull green		1·70	1·40
4562	80st. brown-purple and dull green		3·25	2·75
4559/4562	Set of 4		5·50	4·75

Designs: 10st. T **1601**; 20st. Georgi Rakovski and Vassil Levski; 45st. Luben Karavelov and Christo Botev; 80st. Panayot Volov and Pavel Bobekov.

(Des D. Damyanov. Litho)

2006 (23 Jan). Roses. T **1602** and similar vert designs. Multicoloured. P 13 (with large indented perf on each horiz side).

4563	54st. Type **1602**		1·70	90
4564	1l.50 *Rosa gallica*		4·50	2·75
4565	2l. *Rosa spinosissima*		6·25	3·50
4566	10l. *Rosa arvensis*		29·00	21·00
4563/4566	Set of 4		37·00	25·00

1603 Wolfgang Amadeus Mozart

1604 Ellin Pellin (writer)

(Des A. Appostolov. Litho)

2006 (27 Jan). 250th Birth Anniversary of Wolfgang Amadeus Mozart. P 13.

4567	**1603**	1l. multicoloured	11·00	9·25

No. 4567 has a *se-tenant* stamp size label inscribed for the anniversary attached at right.

(Des L. Methodiev. Litho)

2006 (31 Jan). 115th Anniversary of National Philatelic Press. Bulgarian Philatelists. T **1604** and similar horiz designs. Multicoloured. P 13.

4568	35st. Type **1604**		1·30	1·10
4569	55st. Lazar Dobritch (circus artiste)		1·90	1·60
4570	60st. Boris Christov (opera singer)		2·10	1·80
4571	1l. Bogomil Nonev (writer)		3·50	3·00
4568/4571	Set of 4		8·00	6·75

Nos. 4568/4571 were each issued with a *se-tenant* stamp size label showing a stamp attached at right.

1605 Snowboarder

1606 Sextant

(Des C. Alexiev. Litho)

2006 (10 Feb). Winter Olympic Games, Turin. Sheet 86×118 mm containing T **1605** and similar vert design. Multicoloured. P 13.

MS4572	55st. Type **1605**; 1l. Ice dancers		5·75	4·75

(Des T. Vardjiev. Litho)

2006 (28 Feb). Tenth Anniversary of Bulgarian Antarctic Cartography. Sheet 86×69 mm. P 13.

MS4573	**1606**	1l. multicoloured	4·50	3·75

1607 Ship (15th-century manuscript)

(Des T. Licho. Litho)

2006 (14 Mar). 610th Anniversary of Battle at Nikopol. P 13.

4574	**1607**	1l.50 multicoloured	5·25	4·50

1608 *Martes martes*

1609 Stylised Figure and Stars

(Des S. Dechev. Litho)

2006 (28 Mar). Ecology. Sheet 86×118 mm containing T **1608** and similar horiz design. Multicoloured. P 13.

MS4575	55st. Type **1608**; 1l.50 *Ursus arctos*		7·25	6·25

The stamps of No. **MS**4575 overlap and share a central area containing a leaf enclosed in a heart.

(Des S. Balazdrov. Litho)

2006 (25 Apr). Europa. Integration. T **1609** and similar horiz design. Multicoloured. P 13 (with large indented hole on each horiz side).

4576	55st. Type **1609**		2·10	1·80
4577	1l. Star as flower		4·50	3·75

Nos. 4576/4577 were each issued with a *se-tenant* stamp size label attached at right.

1610 Emblem

1611 Mastheads

(Des T. Vardjiev. Litho)

2006 (27 Apr). Meeting of NATO Foreign Ministers, Sofia. Sheet 87×70 mm. P 13.

MS4578	**1610**	1l.50 multicoloured	4·75	4·00

(Des L. Vesselinov. Litho)

2006 (28 Apr). 70th Anniversary of *Trud* Newspaper. P 13.

4579	**1611**	55st. multicoloured	3·25	2·75

1612 Vesselin Topalov

1613 Building Façade

(Des B. Benev. Litho)

2006 (4 May). Vesselin Topalov. World Chess Champion. Sheet 87×71 mm. P 13.

MS4580	**1612**	1l.50 multicoloured	4·50	3·75

No. **MS**4580 also exist imperforate.

BULGARIA 2006

(Des R. Kolev. Litho)

2006 (5 May). 25th Anniversary of National Palace of Culture. P 13.
| 4581 | **1613** | 55st. multicoloured | 2·30 | 1·90 |

No. 4581 was issued with a *se-tenant* stamp size label.

1614 *Circus aeruginosus*

(Des L. Chehlarov. Litho)

2006 (9 May). Raptors. T **1614** and similar horiz designs. Multicoloured. P 13.
4582	10st. Type **1614**	40	35
4583	35st. *Circus cyaneus*	1·30	1·10
4584	55st. *Circus macrourus*	1·90	1·60
4585	1l. *Circus pygargus*	3·25	2·75
4582/4585	Set of 4	6·25	5·25

1615 Building Façade, Ship and Sailor

(Des Magdalena Konstantinova. Litho)

2006 (20 May). 125th Anniversary of Nikola Vaptsarov Naval Academy, Varna. P 13.
| 4586 | **1615** | 55st. multicoloured | 2·10 | 1·80 |

1616 Players

(Des S. Petrunov. Litho)

2006 (9 June). World Cup Football Championship, Germany. Sheet 87×87 mm. P 13.
| MS4587 | **1616** | 1l. multicoloured | 3·50 | 3·00 |

1617 Emblem **1618** Gena Dimitrova

(Des V. Kitanov. Litho)

2006 (29 June). 50th Anniversary of Bulgaria in UNESCO. P 13.
| 4588 | **1617** | 1l. multicoloured | 2·75 | 2·30 |

(Des V. Kitanov. Litho)

2006 (18 July). 65th Birth Anniversary and First Death Anniversary of Gena Dimitrova (opera singer). P 13.
| 4589 | **1618** | 1l. multicoloured | 3·75 | 3·25 |

1619 *Saponaria stranjensis* **1620** Rover Maestro

(Des Z. Stoyanov. Litho)

2006 (28 July). Flora. T **1619** and similar vert designs. Multicoloured. P 13.
4590	10st. Type **1619**	40	35
	a. Strip of 4. Nos. 4590/4593	7·00	
4591	35st. *Trachystemon orientalis*	1·30	1·10
4592	55st. *Hypericum calycinum*	1·90	1·60
4593	1l. *Rhododendron ponticum*	3·25	2·75
4590/4593	Set of 4	6·25	5·25

Nos. 4590/4593 were issued in horizontal *se-tenant* strips of four stamps within the sheet.

(Des I. Gazdov. Litho)

2006 (29 Sept). Bulgaria Automobile Industry. T **1620** and similar vert designs. Multicoloured. P 13.
4594	10st. Type **1620**	40	35
4595	35st. Moskovitch	1·30	1·10
4596	55st. Bulgaralpine	1·90	1·60
4597	1l. Bulgarrnault	3·50	3·00
4594/4597	Set of 4	6·50	5·50

1621 *Return of the Prodigal Son* **1622** *All Soul's Day* (Ivan Murkvitchka)

(Des St. Gruev. Litho)

2006 (25 Oct). 400th Birth Anniversary of Rembrandt Harmenszoon van Rijn. Sheet 65×84 mm. P 13.
| MS4598 | **1621** | 1l. multicoloured | 4·00 | 3·25 |

(Des D. Trendaffilov. Litho)

2006 (27 Oct). Art Anniversaries. T **1622** and similar vert designs. Multicoloured. P 13.
4599	10st. Type **1622** (150th birth anniversary)	40	35
4600	35st. *Sozopol–Houses* (Vesselin Statkov) (birth centenary)	1·30	1·10
4601	55st. *Sofia in Winter* (Nikola Petrov) (90th death anniversary)	1·90	1·60
4602	1l. *T. Popova* (John Popov) (birth centenary)	3·25	2·75
4599/4602	Set of 4	6·25	5·25

1623 Competitors **1624** Post Van

(Des S. Nenov. Litho)

2006 (3 Nov). World Sambo Championship, Sofia. P 13.
| 4603 | **1623** | 55st. multicoloured | 2·50 | 2·10 |

(Des Ivelina Velinova. Litho)
2006 (17 Nov). Post Europ. Sheet 85×75 mm. P 13.
MS4604 **1624** 1l. multicoloured.. 22·00 18·00
No. MS4604 was issued with a *se-tenant* label.

1625 Angel

(Des Deya Vulcheva. Litho)
2006 (24 Nov). Christmas. P 13.
4605 **1625** 55st. multicoloured.. 2·50 2·10

1626 Ballot Box and Flags

(Des S. Târlea (No. 4606) or S. Balezdrov (No. 4607). Litho)
2006 (29 Nov). Bulgaria and Romania's Membership of European Union. T **1626** and similar horiz design. Multicoloured. P 13.
4606 55st. Type **1626**.. 2·10 1·80
4607 1l.50 'EU'... 5·25 4·50
MS4608 97×87 mm. Nos. 4606/4607........................ 8·00 6·50
Stamps of a similar design were issued by Romania.

1627 Peter Dimkov

1628 Generals Danail Nikolaev and Racho Petrov

(Des V. Attanassov. Litho)
2006 (20 Dec). 120th Birth Anniversary of Peter Dimkov (naturopath). P 13.
4609 **1627** 55st. multicoloured.. 2·50 2·10

(Des P. Vulcheva. Litho)
2006 (21 Dec). Founders of Bulgarian State (6th series). T **1628** and similar horiz designs. Multicoloured.
4610 10st. Type **1628**.. 40 35
4611 35st. Petko Karavelov and Marin Drinov .... 1·30 1·10
4612 55st. Konstantin Stoylov and Stephan Stambolov.. 1·90 1·60
4613 1l. Prince Albert I of Bulgaria............................ 3·25 2·75
4610/4613 Set of 4... 6·25 5·25

1629 Aircraft and Terminal Building

(Des D. Damyanov. Litho)
2006 (27 Dec). New Airport Terminal, Sofia. Sheet 87×72 mm. P 13.
MS4614 **1629** 55st. multicoloured.. 3·25 2·75

No. MS4615 and T **1630** have been left for Membership of EU, issued on 31 January 2007, not yet received.

1631 Emilian Stanev

1632 Flags as Stars

(Des A. Apostolov. Litho)
2007 (28 Feb). Birth Centenary of Nikola Stoyanov Stanev (Emilian Stanev) (writer). P 13.
4616 **1631** 55st. multicoloured.. 2·00 1·70
No. 4616 was issued with a *se-tenant* stamp size label.

(Des P. Alexandrov. Litho)
2007 (23 Mar). 50th Anniversary of Treaty of Rome. P 13.
4617 **1632** 1l. multicoloured.. 3·75 3·25

1633 Ivan Dimov

(Des L. Metodiev. Litho)
2007 (27 Mar). Theatre Personalities. T **1633** and similar horiz designs. Multicoloured. P 13.
4618 10st. Type **1633**.. 40 35
4619 55st. Sava Ognyanov.. 1·90 1·60
4620 1l. Krustyo Sarfov... 3·75 3·25
4618/4620 Set of 3... 5·50 6·75

1634 Sputnik

(Des K. Andreev. Litho)
2007 (25 Apr). 50th Anniversary of First Manmade Satellite. Sheet 87×56 mm. P 13.
MS4621 **1634** 1l. multicoloured.. 3·25 2·75

1635 Campfire

1636 DAR-3 Garvan II (1937)

(Des E. Stankev. Litho)
2007 (26 Apr). Europa. Centenary of Scouting. T **1635** and similar horiz designs. Multicoloured.
(a) Sheet stamps. P 13 (with one large indented hole on each horiz side)
4622 55st. Type **1635**.. 2·10 1·80
4623 1l.50 Route finding... 5·25 4·50
(b) Booklet stamps. Size 31×23 mm. P 13
4624 55st. As Type **1635**.. 2·10 1·80
4625 1l. As No. 4623... 5·25 4·50

(Des E. Stankev. Litho)
2007 (27 Apr). Military Aircraft. T **1636** and similar horiz designs. Multicoloured. P 13.
4626 10st. Type **1636**.. 40 35
4627 35st. DAR-9 Siniger (1939)................................ 1·30 1·10
4628 55st. Kaproni Bulgarski KB-6 Papagal (1939) . 1·70 1·40

BULGARIA 2007

4629	1l. Kaproni Bulgarski KB-11A Fanzan	3·75	3·25
4626/4629	Set of 4	6·50	5·50

1637 Boris I

1637a Basilica and Saint Cyril

(Des S. Krustev. Litho)

2007 (2 May). 1100th Death Anniversary of Knyaz (Prince) Boris I (Michael). P 13.

4630	**1637**	55st. multicoloured	2·30	1·90

(Des Iliya Gruev. Litho)

2007 (21 May). 150th Anniversary of Excavation of San Clement Basilica, Rome. P 13.

4630a	**1637a**	1l. multicoloured	3·25	2·75

1638 Dimcho Debelyanov

1639 St Spass Monastery, Lozenski

(Des Christo Alekiev. Litho)

2007 (23 May). Birth Anniversaries. T **1638** and similar vert designs. Multicoloured. P 13.

4631	10st. Type **1638** (poet) (120th)	40	35
4632	35st. Nenko Balkanski (artist) (centenary)	1·30	1·10
4633	55st. Vera Lukova (artist) (centenary)	1·70	1·40
4634	1l. Theodor Trayanov (poet) (125th)	3·75	3·25
4631/4634	Set of 4	6·50	5·50

(Des Anatoliy Stankulov. Litho)

2007 (30 May). Monasteries. T **1639** and similar vert designs. Multicoloured. P 13 (with large indented hole on each horiz side).

4635	63st. Type **1639**	2·10	1·80
4636	75st. St Mina, Obradovski	2·50	2·10
4637	1l.20 St George the Victor, Kremikovski	3·75	3·25
4638	2l.20 Three Saints, Chepinski	7·25	6·25
4635/4638	Set of 4	14·00	12·00

1640 Symbols of Transport

(Des Teodor Liho. Litho)

2007 (30 May). International Transport Forum, Sofia. P 13.

4639	**1640**	1l. multicoloured	3·75	3·25

1641 Presidents of Bulgaria and Azerbaijan

1642 Onosma thracica

(Des Dimitar Tassev. Litho)

2007 (1 June). 15th Anniversary of Bulgaria–Azerbaijan Diplomatic Relations. Sheet 86×64 mm. P 13.

MS4640	**1641**	1l. multicoloured	4·00	3·25

(Des Dimitar Tassev. Litho)

2007 (6 July). Flora. T **1642** and similar vert designs. Multicoloured. P 13 (with large indented holr on each horiz side).

4641	10st. Type **1642**	40	35
4642	45st. Astracantha aitosensis	1·50	1·20
4643	55st. Veronica krumovii	1·90	1·60
4644	1l. Verbascum adrianopolitanum	3·25	2·75
4641/4644	Set of 4	6·25	5·25

1643 Vassal Levski

1644 Sailor

(Des Cyril Gogov. Litho)

2007 (18 July). 170th Birth Anniversary of Vassal Levski (revolutionary leader). P 13.

4645	**1643**	55st. multicoloured	2·30	1·90

(Des Stephan Nenov. Litho)

2007 (21 July). Junior World Sailing Championship, Olympian Class 470, Burgas. P 13.

4646	**1644**	1l. multicoloured	3·75	3·25

1645 Lieutenant Colonel Pavel Kalitin (painting) and *Battle at Stara Zagora* (Nikola Kozhuharov)

(Des Natalya Kuroch. Litho)

2007 (31 July). 130th Anniversary of Battle at Stara Zagora. P 13.

4647	**1645**	55st. multicoloured	2·30	1·90

1646 Players

(Des Razvigor Kolev. Litho)

2007 (5 Sept). Rugby. 50th (2005) Anniversary of Locomotiv Rugby Club, Sofia. World Rugby Championship 2007, France. P 13.

4648	**1646**	55st. multicoloured	2·30	1·90

1647 *Lutra lutra* (Otter)

(Des Stephan Gruev. Litho)

2007 (10 Sept). Ecology. 15th Anniversary of Ropotamo Reserve. Sheet 85×85 mm containing T **1647** and similar horiz design. Multicoloured. P 13.
MS4649 55st. Type **1647**; 1l. *Haliaeetus albicilla*
(White-tailed Eagle)... 5·75   4·75
The stamps and margins of No. **MS**4649 form a composite design.

1648 *Alcedo atthis* (Kingfisher)   **1649** Emblem

(Des Zdravko Stoyanov. Litho)

2007 (11 Sept). Endangered Species. Birds. Sheet 97×130 mm containing T **1648** and similar horiz design. Multicoloured. P 13.
MS4650 10st. Type **1648**; 35st. *Tichodroma muraria* (Wallcreeper); 55st. *Bombycilla garrulous* (Waxwing); 1l. *Phoenicopterus ruber* (Flamingo).......... 7·25   6·25

(Des Valentin Attanassov. Litho)

2007 (21 Sept). Tenth Anniversary Grand Lodge of the Ancient Freemasons. P 13.
4651   **1649**   55st. multicoloured........................... 2·30   1·90

1650 Centre Building

(Des Deya Vulcheva. Litho)

2007 (9 Oct). Inauguration of Exchange and Sorting Centre, Sofia. Sheet 87×63 mm. P 13.
MS4652   **1650**   55st. multicoloured................. 2·50   2·10

1651 Ivan Hadjiski   **1652** Woman holding Offerings

(Des Dimitar Trendaffilov. Litho)

2007 (12 Oct). Birth Centenary of Ivan Hadjiski (social psychologist). P 13.
4653   **1651**   55st. multicoloured........................... 2·30   1·90

(Des Rumen Statkov. Litho)

2007 (27 Nov). Christmas. P 13.
4654   **1652**   55st. multicoloured........................... 2·30   1·90

1653 Rumyana Neykova (European 2000m. skiff rowing champion)   **1654** '100' and Soldier

(Des Razvigor Kolev. Litho)

2007 (19 Dec). Women Sports Personalities. T **1653** and similar horiz designs. Multicoloured. P 13.
4655   10st. Type **1653**.. 40   35
4656   35st. Stanka Zlateva (World freestyle
         wrestling champion)................................. 1·30   1·10
4657   1l. Stefka Kostadinova (World record high
         jump (30.8.1987))..................................... 3·25   2·75
4655/4657 Set of 3.. 4·50   3·75

(Des Svetlin Belezdrov. Litho)

2007 (20 Dec). Centenary of Military Reconnaissance. P 13.
4658   **1654**   55st. multicoloured........................... 2·30   1·90

1655 Hristo Botev

(Des Ivan Bogdanov. Litho)

2008 (6 Jan). 150th Birth Anniversary of Hristo Botev (poet and revolutionary). P 13.
4659   **1655**   55st. multicoloured........................... 2·30   1·90

 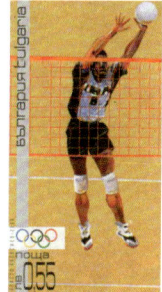

1656 Polar Bear   **1657** Volleyball Player

(Des Todor Vardjiev. Litho)

2008 (10 Jan). International Polar Year. 20th Anniversary of Bulgarian Antarctic Expedition. Sheet 115×85 mm containing T **1656** and similar horiz design. Multicoloured. P 13.
MS4660 55st. Type **1656**; 1l. Skua stealing Penguin
chick, plus 2 labels... 5·75   4·75
The stamps, labels and margins of No. **MS**4660 form a composite design.

(Des Christo Alexiev)

2008 (25 Feb). Olympic Games, Beijing. Sheet 88×109 mm containing T **1657** and similar vert design. Multicoloured. P 13.
MS4661 55st. Type **1657**; 1l. Two players............. 5·75   4·75
The stamps of No. **MS**4661 form a composite design of a volleyball match.

BULGARIA 2008

1658 Arms of Bulgaria

1659 Envelope as Postman

(Des Atanass Atanassov)

2008 (29 Feb). 130th Anniversary of San Stefano Peace Treaty (treaty between Russia and the Ottoman Empire at the end of the Russo–Turkish War (setting up an autonomous self-governing tributary principality of Bulgaria)). P 13.
4662   1658   55st. multicoloured .... 2·30   1·60

(Des Stoyan Dechev)

2008 (22 Apr). Europa. The Letter. T 1659 and similar horiz designs. Multicoloured (background colour given). P 13.
4663   55st. Type 1659 .... 2·30   1·60
4664   55st. As Type 1659 (purple) .... 2·30   1·60
    a. Booklet pane. No. 4664×4 .... 9·50
4665   1l. Envelope as Pigeon (bright blue) .... 4·25   3·50
4666   1l. As No. 4665 (yellow) .... 4·25   3·50
    a. Booklet pane. No. 4666×4 .... 18·00
4663/4666 Set of 4 .... 12·00   9·25

Nos. 4663 and 4665, respectively, were issued in blocks of four stamps within sheets of eight, the two blocks laid *tête-bêche* to each other and separated by a gutter of two stamp labels. The booklet panes Nos. 4664a and 4666a have the stamps arranged with first stamp in the top row upright and the second stamp upside down and the first stamp in bottom row upside down and the second stamp upright. Giving two *tête-bêche* pairs.

See also No. 4989.

1660 Captain Dimiter Spissarevski

(Des Lyidmil Metodiev)

2008 (25 Apr). History of Military Aviation. Pilots' Birth Anniversaries. T 1660 and similar horiz design. Multicoloured. P 13.
4667   55st. Type 1660 (90th birth anniversary) .... 1·90   1·60
    a. Pair. Nos. 4667/4668 .... 6·25   5·00
4668   1l. General Stoyan Stoyanov (95th birth anniversary) .... 4·00   3·25

Nos. 4667/4668 were issued in horizontal *se-tenant* pairs within the sheet, each pair forming a composite design.

1661 Women from the Rhodopes (Boris Kotsev)

(Des Ivelina Velinova)

2008 (7 May). Artists' Birth Centenaries. T 1661 and similar horiz designs. Multicoloured. P 13.
4669   10st. Type 1661 40   35
4670   35st. Nude (Eliezer Alsheh) .... 1·50   1·20
4671   55st. Nude (Vera Nedova) .... 2·10   1·80
4672   1l. Maritsa (Assen Peykov) .... 4·25   3·50
4669/4672 Set of 4 .... 7·50   6·25

1662 Club Members

(Des Anatoli Stankulov)

2008 (7 May). 60th Anniversary of CSKA Central Sports Club. Sheet 90×58 mm. P 13½.
MS4673   1662   55st. multicoloured .... 2·50   2·10

1663 White-headed Marmoset (*Callithrix geoffroyi*)

1664 Alexander Alexandrov

(Des Lyudmil Chehlarov)

2008 (14 May). 120th Anniversary of Zoological Gardens, Sofia. Two sheets containing T 1663 and similar vert designs. Multicoloured. P 13.
MS4674a 126×130 mm 10st. Type 1663; 20st. Hippopotamus (*Hippopotamus amphibius*); 35st. Bactrian Camel (*Camelus bactrianus*); 55st. Meerkat (*Suricata suricatta*); 60st. Blue-and-yellow Macaw (*Ara ararauna*); 1l. Eurasian Lynx (*Lynx lynx*) .... 10·50   8·75
MS4674b 66×85 mm 55st. Meerkat (*Suricata suricatta*). Imperf .... 55·00   44·00

(Des Rumen Stakov)

2008 (9 June). 20th Anniversary of Alexander Alexandrov's Flight in Orbital Space Station *MIR*. Sheet 85×61 mm. P 13.
MS4675   1664   1l. multicoloured .... 4·25   3·50

1665 BMW R12 Single Carb, 1935

(Des Nenko Atanassov)

2008 (16 June). 70th Anniversary of Union of Bulgarian Philatelists. P 13.
4676   1665   60st. multicoloured .... 2·50   2·10
MS4677 106×92 mm. 60st. As Type 1665. Imperf .... 55·00   44·00

No. MS4677 is from a limited printing.

1666 *Canis aureus* (Golden Jackal)   1667

(Des Zdravko Stoyanov)

2008 (21 July). Strandja Nature Park. Sheet 104×79 mm containing T 1666 and similar multicoloured design. P 13.
MS4678 60st. Type 1666; 11.50 *Aquila pomarina* (Lesser Spotted Eagle) (*vert*) .... 8·00   6·50
The stamps and margins of No. MS4678 form a composite design.

244

2008 BULGARIA

(Des Nikolay Mladenov)

2008 (30 July). 20th Anniversary of Bulgaria–European Economic Community. P 13.

| 4679 | **1667** | 1l. black and olive-yellow | 4·00 | 3·25 |

1668 Wagons Lits (sleeeping car)

(Des Stephan Gruev)

2008 (11 Sept). 120th Anniversary of Orient Express. T **1668** and similar horiz design. Multicoloured. P 13.

4680		60st. Type **1668**	2·10	1·80
		a. Pair. Nos. 4680/4681	7·50	6·50
4681		1l.50 Steg Wien locomotive No. 5	5·25	4·50

Nos. 4680/4681 were issued in horizontal *se-tenant* pairs within the sheet.

The stamps also show the Arms of cities enroute and the emblems of the Orient Express (60st.) or the Bulgarian State Railways (1l.50).

1669 Nikola and Dimitar Petkov

(Des Svetlin Balezdrov)

2008 (18 Sept). Birth Anniversaries of Dimitar Petkov (Prime Minister 1906–1907) (150th) and Nikola Petkov (politician, son of Dimitar Petkov and leader of Bulgarian Agrarian National Union) (115th). P 13.

| 4682 | **1669** | 60st. multicoloured | 2·50 | 2·10 |

1670 Tsar Ferdinand

1671 Arms of the Templars

(Des Simeon Krustev)

2008 (22 Sept). Centenary of Proclamation of Independence. Sheet 48×87 mm. P 13.

| MS4683 | **1670** | 60st. multicoloured | 2·75 | 2·30 |

(Des Valetin Atanasov)

2008 (30 Sept). 700th Anniversary (2007) of Disbanding of Knights Templar (Order of the Temple) by King Philip IV of France. P 13.

| 4684 | **1671** | 1l. multicoloured | 3·50 | 3·00 |

1672 Race Car (2008)

(Des Emilyan Stankev)

2008 (16 Oct). Ferrari Cars. T **1672** and similar horiz designs. Multicoloured. P 13.

4685		60st. Type **1672**	2·10	1·80
		a. Pair. Nos. 4685/4686		
4686		1l. Race car (1952)	3·50	3·00
MS4687	94×56 mm. 60st. As No. 4685. Imperf		42·00	35·00

Nos. 4685/4686 were issued in horizontal *se-tenant* pairs within the sheet.

No. **MS**4687 is from a limited printing.

1673 Arms

(Des Theodor Licho)

2008 (24 Oct). 130th Anniversary of Bulgarian Red Cross Societies. P 13.

| 4688 | **1673** | 60st. multicoloured | 2·50 | 2·10 |

1674 Virgin Mary, Rila Monastery (12th-century)

(Des Natalia Kuruch. Litho)

2008 (21 Nov). Bulgarian Icons. T **1674** and similar vert designs. Multicoloured. P 13.

4689		50st. Type **1674**	1·70	1·40
		a. Strip of 3. Nos. 4689/4691	7·25	
4690		60st. Virgin and Child, Troyan Monastery (18th-century)	2·10	1·80
4691		1l. Virgin and Child, Bachkovo Monastery (14th-century)	3·25	2·75
4689/4691 Set of 3			6·25	5·25
MS4691a	112×73 mm. 60st. As No. 4690. Imperf		42·00	35·00

Nos. 4689/4691 were issued in *se-tenant* strips of three stamps within the sheet.

No. **MS**4691a is from a limited printing.

1675 Virgin and Child

1676 Saint Clement of Ohrid (St Kliment Ohridski)

(Des Ivan Gazdov. Litho)

2008 (21 Nov). Christmas. P 13.

| 4692 | **1675** | 60st. multicoloured | 2·50 | 2·10 |

(Des Damyan Damyanov. Litho)

2008 (25 Nov). 120th Anniversary of Sofia University, St Kliment Ohridski. P 13.

| 4693 | **1676** | 60st. multicoloured | 2·50 | 2·10 |

BULGARIA 2008

1677 Andranik Ozanyan (Armenian general in Balkan Wars of Independence)

2008 (10 Dec). Nationalist Liberation Movements of Bulgaria and Armenia. T **1677** and similar horiz design. Multicoloured. P 13.
4694	60st. Type **1677**............................		2·10	1·80
	a. Pair. Nos. 4694/4695..................		7·25	6·25
4695	1l.50 Peyo Yavorov (Bulgarian poet and revolutionary)..................		5·00	4·25

Nos. 4694/4695 were issued in *se-tenant* pairs within the sheet.
Stamps of a similar design were issued by Armenia.

1678 Emblem

(Des Nenko Attanassov. Litho)

2009 (23 Jan). Bulgaria 2009. European Philatelic Exhibition. P 13.
4696	**1678**	60st. multicoloured............................	2·50	2·30

1679 Abraham Lincoln

(Des Plamen Valtschev. Litho)

2009 (6 Feb). Birth Bicentenaries. T **1679** and similar horiz designs. Each pale sage-green, pale brown-olive and brown-olive. P 13.
4697	10st. Type **1679** (President of USA)...........		40	40
4698	50st. Nikolai Gogol (writer)............................		1·70	1·50
4699	60st. Charles Darwin (naturalist)...................		2·10	1·90
4700	1l. Edgar Allan Poe (writer)............................		3·25	3·00
4697/4700	Set of 4...		6·75	6·00
MS4701	55×105 mm. 60st. Charles Darwin (*different*). Imperf...........		32·00	29·00

No. **MS**4701 is from a limited printing.

1680 *Scolopax rusticola* (Eurasian Woodcock)   **1681** Amethyst

(Des Simeon Krustev. Litho)

2009 (2 Mar). Ecology. Balkan Mountains. T **1680** and similar horiz design. Multicoloured. P 13.
4702	60st. Type **1680**............................		2·50	2·30
	a. Pair. Nos. 4702/4703..................		6·50	6·00
4703	1l. *Monticola saxatilis* (Rufous-tailed Rock Thrush)...........		3·75	3·50
MS4704	106×85 mm. 1l.60 As Nos. 4702/4703. Imperf...........		6·25	5·75

Nos. 4702/4703 were printed, *se-tenant*, in pairs within the sheet, each pair forming a composite design.
Stamps of a similar design were issued by Serbia.

(Des Adrian Bekyarov. Litho)

2009 (24 Mar). 120th Anniversary of National Natural Science Museum. P 13.
4705	**1681**	60st. multicoloured............................	2·50	2·30
MS4706	87×61 mm. 60st. As Type **1681**. Imperf...........		42·00	38·00

No. **MS**4706 is printed with the European Philatelic Exhibition emblem in the margin.
No. **MS**4706 is from a limited printing.

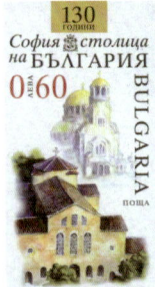 

1682 Hagia Sofia Church and St Alexander Nevsky Cathedral   **1683** Penguins and Narwhal

(Des Ludmil Vesselinov. Litho)

2009 (25 Mar). 130th Anniversary of Sofia as Capital of Bulgaria. P 13.
4707	**1682**	60st. multicoloured............................	2·50	2·30

(Des Maglena Konstantinova. Litho)

2009 (27 Mar). Preserve Polar Regions and Glaciers. Sheet 127×63 mm containing T **1683** and similar horiz design. Multicoloured. P 13.
MS4708	60st. Type **1683**; 1l.50 Polar Bear, Elephant Seal and White-tailed Eagle.................	8·00	7·25

1684 Flags as '60'   **1685** Bicycle

(Des Todor Vardjiev. Litho)

2009 (30 Mar). 60th Anniversary of NATO (No. 4709). Fifth Anniversary of Bulgaria's Membership of NATO (No. 4710). T **1684** and similar horiz design. Multicoloured. P 13.
4709	60st. Type **1684**............................		1·90	1·70
	a. Pair. Nos. 4709/4710..................		7·00	6·25
4710	1l.50 Bulgarian flag as '5'............................		4·75	4·25

Nos. 4709/4710 were printed, *se-tenant*, in sheets of two pairs of stamps separated by two stamp size labels

(Des Stoyan Dechev. Litho)

2009 (31 Mar). Bicycles. T **1685** and similar vert designs. Multicoloured. P 13.
4711	10st. Type **1685**............................		40	40
	a. Horiz strip of 4. Nos. 4711/4714.........		7·50	
4712	50st. Purple cycle............................		1·70	1·50
4713	60st. Penny-farthing cycles............................		1·90	1·70
4714	1l. Early pedal-less cycle............................		3·25	2·75
4711/4714	Set of 4...		6·50	5·75
MS4715	130×71 mm. 60st. As No. 4714. Imperf...........		42·00	38·00

Nos. 4711/4714 were printed, *se-tenant*, in horizontal strips of four stamps within the sheet, each strip forming a composite design.
No. **MS**4717 is from a limited printing.

1686 Georgi Ivanov

(Des Ivan Bogdanov. Litho)
2009 (9 Apr). 30th Anniversary of Space Flight of First Bulgarian Cosmonaut. Sheet 93×93 mm. P 13.
MS4716 **1686** 60st. multicoloured.................................. 2·75 2·50

1687 *Arms (1879)*

(Des Stephan Gruev)
2009 (15 Apr). 130th Anniversary of Restoration of State. Sheet 105×84 mm containing T **1687** and similar horiz design. Multicoloured. P 13.
MS4717 60st. Type **1687**; 1l. Arms (1997) .... 5·75 5·25

1688 *Rathbunia alamosensis*   **1689** *Spiral Galaxy IC 342*

(Des Zdravko Stoyanov)
2009 (24 Apr). Cacti. T **1688** and similar vert designs. Multicoloured. P 13.
4718	10st. Type **1688**..	40	40
	a. Strip of 4. Nos. 4718/4721	8·75	
4719	50st. Mammillaria pseudoperbella	1·70	1·50
4720	60st. Obregonia degeneri	1·90	1·70
4721	1l.50 Inscr 'Astrophytum mayas'	4·50	4·25
4718/4721 Set of 4		7·75	7·00
MS4722 71×108 mm. 60st. As No. 4720. Imperf		42·00	38·00

No. 4718/4721 were printed, *se-tenant*, in horizontal strips of four stamps within the sheet.
No. **MS**4722 is printed with the European Philatelic Exhibition emblem in the margin.
No. **MS**4722 is from a limited printing.

(Des Rossen Toshev)
2009 (28 Apr). Europa. Astronomy. T **1689** and similar vert designs. Multicoloured.
(a) Sheet stamps. P 13 (with one diamond shaped hole on each vert side)
4723	60st. Type **1689**..	2·10	1·90
4724	1l.50 Andromeda Galaxy (M 31).......................	5·25	4·75
MS4725 112×90 mm. Size 29×39 mm. 60st.×2, As No. 4723×2; 1l.50×2, As No. 4724×2		15·00	14·00

(b) Booklet stamps. P 13
4726	60st. As Type **1689**	2·10	1·90
	a. Booklet pane. Nos. 4726×3 and 4727....	13·00	
	b. Booklet pane. Nos. 4726 and 4727×3....	22·00	
4727	1l.50 As No. 4724 (Andromeda Galaxy (M 31))...	5·25	4·75

Nos. 4723/4724 have pale lilac borders and diamond shaped holes in each vertical side, whereas Nos. 4726/4727 have white borders and are perforated all round.

1690 *Members Flags surrounding Euro*

(Des Cyril Gogov)
2009 (20 May). Tenth Anniversary of Euro Currency. P 13.
4728 **1690** 1l. multicoloured........................... 3·25 3·00

1691 *Landscape* (Vassil Ivanov) (birth centenary)

(Des Villiam Kitanov)
2009 (27 May). Artists' Anniversaries. T **1691** and similar horiz designs. Multicoloured. P 13.
4729	10st. Type **1691**..	40	40
4730	50st. *Three Vases* (Georgi Kolarov) (birth centenary)...	1·50	1·30
4731	60st. *The Black Sea* (Alexander Mutaffov) (130th birth anniversary)................................	1·90	1·70
4732	1l. *Cast Shadows* (Konstantine Sturkelov) (120th birth anniversary)................................	3·25	3·00
4729/4732 Set of 4...		6·25	5·75

1692 *Fan*   **1693** *Bubo bubo (Eurasian Eagle Owl)*

(Des Ludmil Metodiev)
2009 (28 May). 80th Anniversary of Locomotive Sofia Sports Club. P 13.
4733 **1692** 60st. multicoloured............................. 2·50 2·30

(Des Christo Alexiev)
2009 (30 May). Owls. T **1693** and similar vert designs. Multicoloured. P 13.
4734	10st. Type **1693**..	40	40
	a. Horiz strip of 4. Nos. 4734/4737...............	9·50	
4735	50st. *Athene noctua* (Little Owl)......................	1·50	1·30
4736	60st. *Strix uralensis* (Ural Owl)........................	2·10	1·90
4737	1l.50 *Glaucidium passerinum* (Eurasian Pygmy Owl)..	5·25	4·75
4734/4737 Set of 4...		8·25	7·50

Nos. 4734/4737 were printed, *se-tenant*, in strips or blocks of four stamps within sheets of eight.

1694 *Motorcycle and Rider*   **1695** *Petko Voivoda*

(Des Nikolai Mladenov)
2009 (16 June). SuperMoto European Championship. Sheet 96×85 mm. P 13.
MS4738 **1694** 60st. multicoloured.......................... 2·75 2·50

BULGARIA 2009

(Des Appostol Appostolov)

2009 (17 June). 165th Birth Anniversary of Petko Voivoda (nationalist). P 13.
4739 **1695** 60st. multicoloured .... 2·50 2·30

1696 Todor Burmov (first Minister for Internal Affairs)

(Des Lyudmil Vesselinov)

2009 (26 June). 130th Anniversary of Ministry of Internal Affairs. P 13.
4740 **1696** 60st. multicoloured .... 2·50 2·30

1697 Airmail Envelope

(Des Svetlin Balezdrov)

2009 (29 June). 130th Anniversary of Bulgarian Communications. Sheet 97×117 mm containing T **1697** and similar horiz design. Multicoloured. P 13.
MS4741 60st. Type **1697**; 1l. Telephone .... 5·75 5·25

1698 Neil Armstrong and Lunar Module

(Des Natalia Kuruch. Litho)

2009 (20 July). 40th Anniversary of First Moon Landing. Sheet 101×84 mm. P 13.
MS4742 **1698** 60st. multicoloured .... 2·50 2·30
       a. Overprinted for Bulgaria 2009. Imperf .... 42·00 38·00

1699 Symbols of Science

(Des Nikolai Tsachev)

2009 (9 Oct). 140th of National Academy of Science. P 13.
4743 **1699** 60st. multicoloured .... 2·50 2·30

1700 Flags as Pen and Ink

1701 Flags and Rose

(Des Ivelina Velinova)

2009 (15 Oct). 130th Anniversary of Bulgaria–Italy Diplomatic Relations. Sheet 101×71 mm. P 13½.
MS4744 **1700** 1l. multicoloured .... 4·25 3·75
Stamps of a similar design were issued by Italy.

(Des Theodor Licho)

2009 (1 Nov). 130th Anniversary of First Bulgarian Diplomatic Relations. Sheet 113×113 mm. P 13½.
MS4745 **1701** 1l. multicoloured .... 3·25 2·75

1702 Anniversary Cake enclosed in TV Screen

(Des Georgi Yankov)

2009 (14 Nov). 50th Anniversary of National Television. P 13½.
4746 **1702** 60st. multicoloured .... 2·50 2·30

1703 Fokker E. III Monoplane and Marko Parvanov (Bulgarian gunner)

(Des Ivan Gazdov)

2009 (18 Nov). History of Bulgarian Military Aviation. T **1703** and similar horiz design. Multicoloured. P 13.
4747 60st. Type **1703** .... 1·90 1·70
      a. Pair. Nos. 4747/4748 .... 5·25 5·00
4748 1l. Assen Jordanoff (aircraft designer) and Jordanov-1 ... 3·25 3·00
Nos. 4747/4748 were printed, *se-tenant*, in horizontal pairs within the sheet, each pair forming a composite design.

1704 Virgin and Child

(Des Damyan Damyanov)

2009 (7 Dec). Christmas. P 13.
4749 **1704** 60st. multicoloured .... 2·50 2·30

1705 Nikola Vaptsarov

(Des Attanass Attanassov)

2009 (20 Nov). Birth Centenary of Nikola Vaptsarov (poet, communist and revolutionary). P 13.
4750 **1705** 60st. multicoloured .... 2·50 2·30

2010 BULGARIA

1706 Dimitar Milandinov

1707 Headset and Microphone

(Des Simeon Krustev)

2010 (7 Jan). Birth Bicentenary of Dimitar Milandinov (poet and folklorist). P 13.
4751 1706 60st. multicoloured .... 2·50 2·30

(Des Stoyan Dechev)

2010 (25 Jan). 75th Anniversary of Bulgarian National Radio. P 13.
4752 1707 60st. multicoloured .... 2·50 2·30

1708 Luge

(Des Oleg Gochev)

2010 (5 Feb). Winter Olympic Games, Vancouver. Sheet 98×90 mm containing T 1708 and similar horiz design. Multicoloured. P 13.
MS4753 60st. Type 1708; 1l. Snowboarder .... 5·75 5·25

1709 Frederic Chopin

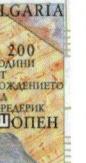
1710 *Paeonia suffruticosa* var. *rockii*

(Des Appostol Appostolov)

2010 (1 Mar). Birth Bicentenary of Frederic Chopin (composer). P 13.
4754 1709 1l. multicoloured .... 3·25 3·25
No. 4754 was printed, *se-tenant*, with a stamp size label within sheets of two stamps and two labels.

(Des Zdravko Stoyanov)

2010 (23 Mar). Peonies. Sheet 80×86 mm containing T 1710 and similar vert design. Multicoloured. P 13.
MS4755 60st×2, Type 1710; *Paeonia officinalis* 'Rubra Plena' .... 4·50 4·00

1711 General Georgi Vazov (1860–1934)

(Des Rosen Toshev)

2010 (26 Mar). 150th Birth Anniversaries of Bulgarian Commanders. Sheet 113×102 mm containing T 1711 and similar horiz designs. Multicoloured. P 13.
MS4756 60st.×5, Type 1711; General Ivan Fichev (1860–1931); General Stilian Kovachev (1860–1939); Colonel Vladimir Serafimov (1860–1934); General Dimitar Geshev (1860–1922) .... 10·00 9·00
No. MS4756 also contains a stamp size label showing the Order of Bravery.

1712 Chess Pieces

1713 House and Hedgehog

(Des Georgi Yankov)

2010 (22 Apr). World Chess Championship Match 2010 between Viswanathan Anand (winner) and Veselin Topalov. Sheet 69×85 mm. P 13.
MS4757 1712 1l. ochre, black and light grey .... 3·75 3·50

(Des Maglena Konstantinova)

2010 (23 Apr). Europa. Children's Books. T 1713 and similar vert designs. Multicoloured.
    (a) *Sheet stamps.* P 13×13½
4758   60st. Type 1713 .... 2·10 1·90
    a. Pair. Nos. 4758/4759 .... 8·25 7·50
4759   1l.50 Hare and fairy carrying lantern .... 2·75 2·50
MS4760 106×85 mm. 60st. As Type 1713; 1l.50 As No. 4759. P 13 .... 6·75 6·00
    (b) *Booklet stamps.* P 13½
4761   60st. As Type 1713 (29×39 *mm*) .... 2·10 1·90
    a. Booklet pane. Nos. 4761/4762, plus label .... 9·00
4762   1l.50 As No. 4759 .... 2·75 2·50
Nos. 4758/4759 were printed, *se-tenant*, in pairs within the sheet.
The stamps of the booklet pane No. 4761a are separated by an illustrated stamp size label.
The stamps of No. MS4760 have no white borders and, with the margins form a composite design.

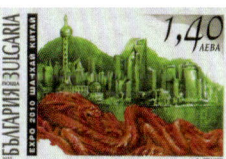
1714 Dragon and Shanghai Skyline

1714a Flag

(Des Maglena Konstantinova)

2010 (23 Apr). Expo 2010, Shanghai. Sheet 113×74 mm. P 13.
MS4763 1714 1l.40 multicoloured .... 17·00 16·00

(Des Teodor Liho)

2010 (4 May). Centenary of Bulgaria–Spain Diplomatic Relations. P 13½×13.
4764 1714a 1l. multicoloured .... 3·25 3·00

1715 Bird, Mouse and Whale

(Des Viliam Kitanov)

2010 (21 May). International Year of Biodiversity. Sheet 78×60 mm. P 13.
MS4765 1715 1l.50 multicoloured .... 5·75 5·25

BULGARIA 2010

1716 Emanuil Manolov

1716a Bulgarian Shepherd Dog

(Des Apostol Apostolov)

2010 (8 June). Composers Anniversaries. T **1716** and similar horiz design. Multicoloured. P 13.

4766	1l. Type **1716** (150th birth anniversary)	3·25	3·00
4767	1l. Robert Schumann (birth bicentenary)	3·25	3·00

Nos. 4766/4767 were each printed, *se-tenant*, with an illustrated stamp size label at right in sheets of two stamps plus two labels.

(Des Viktor Paunov)

2010 (9 June). Balkan Dogs. Sheet 86×77 mm. Imperf.

MS4767a	**1716a**	60st. multicoloured	42·00	38·00

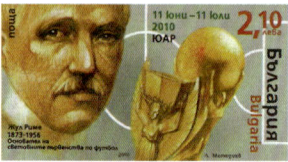
1717 Jules Rimet and Trophies

(Des Lyudmil Metodiev)

2010 (10 June). World Cup Football Championships, South Africa. Sheet 79×55 mm. P 13.

MS4768	**1717**	2l.10 multicoloured	7·25	6·75

1718 St Procopius

1719 *Manoeuvres* (1899)

(Des Natalia Kuruch)

2010 (16 June). Death Bicentenary of St Procopius of Varna. P 13.

4769	**1718**	60st. multicoloured	2·50	2·30

(Des Boris Kitanov)

2010 (23 July). 150th Birth Anniversary of Yaroslav Veshin (Czech artist). P 13½×13.

4770	1l. Type **1719**	3·25	2·75
	a. Strip of 2. Nos. 4770/4771, plus label	6·75	5·75
4771	1l. *Return from Market* (1898)	3·25	2·75

No. 4770/4771 were printed, *se-tenant*, in vertical strips of two stamps surrounding a central stamp size illustrated label.

1720 *Summer and Autumn* (Les Saisons) (1900)

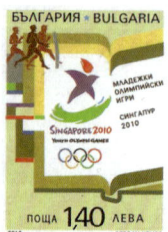
1721 Athletes, Emblem and Book

(Des Nikolay Mladenov)

2010 (23 July). 150th Birth Anniversary of Alphonse (Alfons) Maria Mucha (Czech artist). Sheet 116×108 mm containing T **1720** and similar vert designs. Multicoloured. P 13.

MS4772	1l.×2 Type **1720**; *Winter and Spring* (Les Saisons (1900))	6·75	6·25

(Des Stefan Nenov)

2010 (30 July). Youth Olympic Games, Singapore 2010. P 13.

4773	**1721**	1l.40 multicoloured	5·75	5·25

1722 Entwined Tree Trunks

1723 Magirus Feuerwehrwerke Fire-fighting Appliance

(Des Christina Borissova)

2010 (3 Sept). 125th Anniversary of Bulgaria's Reunification. P 13.

4774	**1722**	60st. multicoloured	2·50	2·30

2010 (21 Oct). History of Fire Fighting Precautions in the Balkans. Sheet 102×71 mm. Imperf.

MS4775	**1723**	65st. multicoloured	32·00	29·00

1724 Giant Panda (*Ailuropoda melanoleuca*)

1725 Jak-23

(Eng Christo Aleksiev)

2010 (28 Oct). Pandas. Sheet 95×126 mm containing T **1724** and similar vert designs. Multicoloured. P 13.

MS4776 10st. Type **1724**; 60st. Giant Panda seated; 1l. Red Panda (*Ailurus fulgens*); 1l.50 Red Panda, head and shoulders .... 11·00 10·00

(Des Todor Vardjiev)

2010 (12 Nov). 60th Anniversary of Military Jet Aviation. T **1725** and similar horiz designs. Multicoloured. P 13.

4777	50st. Type **1725**	1·50	1·30
4778	65st. Mikoyan-Gurevich type MiG-15	2·10	1·90
4779	1l. Mikoyan MiG-29	3·75	3·50
4777/4779	Set of 3	6·50	6·00

1726 Santa wearing Spectacles

1727 Female Figures from Thracian Tomb of Svestari

(Des Svetlin Balezdrov)

2010 (19 Nov). Christmas. P 13.

4780	**1726**	65st. multicoloured	2·50	2·30

(Des Ivan Gazdov)

2010 (24 Nov). Regions. Northeastern Region. Sheet 85×113 mm containing T **1727** and similar vert designs. Multicoloured. P 13.
MS4781 10st. Type **1727**; 50st. Balchik Palace; 65st. Srebarna Nature Reserve; 1l. Pobiti Kamani rock formations.. 8·00 7·25

1728 Self-Portrait

1729 San Cristobal Cathedral, Havana

(Des Valeri Alexandrov)

2010 (26 Nov). Birth Bicentenary of Zahari Hristovich Dimitrov (Zahari Zograf) (artist). Sheet 61×70 mm. P 13.
MS4782 **1728** 1l.50 multicoloured................................. 5·25 4·75

(Des Tzvetan Iliev)

2010 (10 Dec). 50th Anniversary of Bulgaria–Cuba Diplomatic Relations. T **1729** and similar horiz design. Multicoloured. P 13.
4783 65c. Type **1729**.. 2·10 1·90
 a. Pair. Nos. 4783/4784................................. 7·50 7·00
4784 1l.40 St Alexander Nevsky Cathedral, Sofia.... 5·25 4·75
Nos. 4783/4784 were printed, *se-tenant*, in horizontal pairs within the sheet.
Stamps of a similar design were issued by Cuba.

1730 Griffon Vulture

1731 *Hydrurga leptonyx* (Leopard Seal)

(Des Emilian Stankev)

2010 (22 Dec). Balkanfila 2010 International Stamp Exhibition, Plovdiv. Balkan Vulture Preservation. Griffon Vulture (*Gyps fulvus*). Sheet 88×78 mm. Imperf.
MS4785 **1730** 65st. multicoloured................................. 32·00 29·00

(Des Stoyan Dechev)

2011 (7 Jan). Antarctica. P 13 (with one diamond shaped hole on each vert side).
4786 **1731** 58st. black and scarlet-vermilion........... 2·10 1·90
No. 4786 was printed both in large sheets, and in sheets of two stamps and two stamp-size labels.
See also No. **MS**4858*a*.

1732 Princess Clementine and Soldiers

1733 Vanga

(Des Simeon Krastev)

2011 (24 Jan). 125th Anniversary of 9th Plovdiv Infantry Regiment. P 13.
4787 **1732** 65st. multicoloured................................. 2·75 2·50
No. 4787 was printed with a *se-tenant* stamp size label at foot.

(Des Ivan Bogdanov)

2011 (31 Jan). Birth Centenary of Vangelia Pandeva Dimitrova (Vanga) (blind mystic, healer and herbalist). P 13.
4788 **1733** 65st. multicoloured................................. 2·50 2·30

1734 Space and Haricot Bean

(Des Georgi Yankov)

2011 (1 Apr). Day of Humour and Joke (April Fool's Day). 35th Anniversary of Discovery of Planet Gabrovo (named after Bulgarian town). P 13×13½.
4789 **1734** 65st. multicoloured................................. 2·75 2·50
No. 4789 has a *se-tenant* stamp size label attached at right which, with the stamp forms a composite design of planets and space.

1735 Politicians

1736 Yuri Gagarin

(Des Tsvetan Iliev)

2011 (11 Apr). 20th Anniversary of Atlantic Club of Bulgaria. Sheet 87×78 mm. P 13.
MS4790 **1735** 1l. multicoloured....................................... 3·25 2·75

(Des Zdravko Stoyanov)

2011 (12 Apr). 50th Anniversary of First Manned Space Flight. 50th Anniversary of Launching of First Space Probe to Venus. Sheet 83×103 mm containing T **1736** and similar vert design. Multicoloured. P 13.
MS4791 65st. Type **1736**; 1l.50 *Venera 1*........................... 8·00 7·25

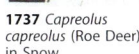
1737 *Capreolus capreolus* (Roe Deer) in Snow

1738 Emperor Galerius

(Des Victor Paunov)

2011 (28 Apr). Europa. Forests. T **1737** and similar vert design. Multicoloured. P 13.
4792 65st. Type **1737**.. 2·50 2·30
4793 1l.50 *Scolopax rusticola* (Woodcock)............ 6·00 5·25
MS4794 106×85 mm. As Nos. 4792/4793....................... 9·00 8·00

(Des Plamen Valchev)

2011 (30 Apr). 1700th Anniversary of Serdica Edict of Religious Tolerance, issued by Roman Emperor Galerius. Sheet 102×65 mm. P 13.
MS4795 **1738** 65st. multicoloured................................. 2·75 2·50

BULGARIA 2011

1739 Emblem

1740 Rabbit as Newspaper Boy

(Des Todor Vardjiev)
2011 (2 May). 20th Anniversary of Commission on Protection of Competition. P 13.
4796 **1739** 65st. multicoloured .... 2·50 2·30

(Des Natalia Kuruch)
2011 (27 May). 120th Anniversary of Philatelic Press. Sheet 91×81 mm. Imperf.
MS4797 **1740** 65st. multicoloured............................. 32·00 30·00
See also No. 4864.

1741 Bear and Woodpecker

1742 *Sander, Esox lucius, Hucho hucho* and *Aspius aspius*

(Des Ivan Gazdov)
2011 (10 June). Regions. North Central Bulgaria. Sheet 85×113 mm containing T **1741** and similar vert designs. Multicoloured. P 13×13½.
MS4798 65st Type **1741**; 65st. Coin and church; 1l. Castle; 1l. Woman knitting and textiles.......................... 11·00 10·00

(Des Stefan Gruev)
2011 (29 June). Museum of the Danube Fishing, Tutrakan. Sheet 157×84 mm containing T **1742** and similar horiz designs. Multicoloured. P 13.
MS4799 65st. Type **1742**; 65st. *Abramis brama, Barbus barbus, Ctenopharyngodon idella, Cyprinus carpio* and *Carassius carassius*; 1l. *Huso huso* and *Acipenser ruthenus*; 1l. *Siurus glanis* and *Loto lota*...... 11·00 10·00

1743 Mounted Soldiers

(Des Iliya Gruev)
2011 (26 July). 1200th Anniversary of Khan Krum Victory at Varbitsa Pass. P 13½×13.
4800 **1743** 65st. multicoloured .... 2·50 2·30

1744 *Rhodophyllus sinuatus*

(Des Todor Vardjiev)
2011 (29 July). Poisonous Fungi. Sheet 125×93 mm containing T **1744** and similar horiz designs. Multicoloured. P 13.
MS4801 65st. Type **1744**; 65st. *Inocybe patouillardii*; 1l. *Russula emetica*; 1l. *Omphalotus olearius*.................. 11·00 10·00

1745 Tall Ship

1746 Fridtjof Nansen

(Des Viliam Kitanov)
2011 (25 Aug). Tall Ships Regatta, 2011. Sheet 90×66 mm. P 13.
MS4802 **1745** 1l. multicoloured............................. 3·75 3·50

(Des Dimitar Trendafilov)
2011 (10 Oct). 150th Birth Anniversary of Fridtjof Wedel-Jarlsberg Nansen (explorer, humanitarian and winner of 1922 Nobel Peace Prize). Sheet 103×77 mm. P 13×13½.
MS4803 **1746** 1l. multicoloured............................. 3·75 3·50

1747 Franz Liszt

1748 William Gladstone

(Des Damyan Damyanov)
2011 (21 Oct). Birth Bicentenary of Franz Liszt. P 13.
4804 **1747** 1l. multicoloured .... 3·25 2·75
No. 4804 was issued in sheetlets of two stamps and two labels (showing hands on piano keys).

(Des Kiril Gogov)
2011 (27 Oct). 145th Anniversary of First Railway in Bulgaria. Sheet 112×82 mm containing T **1748** and similar horiz designs. Multicoloured. P 13½.
MS4805 65st. Type **1748**; 1l. Early carriage; 1l.50 Early steam locomotive.. 11·00 10·00
No. **MS**4085 was issued with a stamp-size label showing a map of the railway.

1749 Laika

1750 Can-AM Renegade 800

(Des Krasimira Despotova)
2011 (28 Oct). Dogs in Space. Sheet 98×98 mm containing T **1749** and similar horiz designs. Multicoloured. P 13½.
MS4806 65st. Type **1749**; 65st. Belka and Streka; 1l. Chernushka; 1l. Zvezdochka................................. 12·00 11·00

(Des Lyudmil Veselinov)

2011 (29 Oct). Peter Tsenkov and Todor Hristov, First Bulgarians to compete in Dakar Rally. P 13.
4807   **1750**   1l.50 multicoloured ....   5·25   4·75

No. 4807 was printed in sheetlets of two stamps and two stamp-size labels.

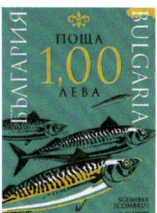 

1751 *Scomber scombrus* (Atlantic Mackerel)   **1752** Yosif Tsankov

(Des Nikolay Mladenov)

2011 (31 Oct). International Black Sea Action Day. Sheet 137×87 mm containing T **1751** and similar vert design. Multicoloured. P 13½.
MS4808 1l.×2 Type **1751**; *Mytilus galloprovincialis* (Blue Mussel) .... 7·25   6·75

(Des Lyudmil Metodiev)

2011 (7 Nov). Birth Centenary of Yosif Tsankov (composer). P 13½×13.
4809   **1752**   65st. multicoloured ....   2·50   2·30

No. 4809 was printed, *se-tenant*, with a stamp size illustrated label at left.

1753 '65' as Snowman   **1754** '120', Medical Bag and Building

(Des Yana Levieva)

2011 (17 Nov). Christmas. P 13½.
4810   **1753**   65st. multicoloured ....   2·50   2·30

(Des Nenko Atanasov)

2011 (1 Dec). 120th Anniversary of Military Medical Academy, Sofia. P 13.
4811   **1754**   65st. multicoloured ....   2·50   2·30

1755 Garden Flowers   **1756** Cross

(Des Maya Cholakova)

2012 (16 Mar). Garden Flowers. T **1755** and similar multicoloured design. P 13 (with one large indented hole on each horiz side (65st.) or each vert side (1l.)).
4812   65st. Type **1755** ....   2·10   1·90
4813   1l. Flowers (*different*) (*vert*) ....   3·25   2·75

(Des Teodor Liho)

2012 (22 Mar). 700th Anniversary of disbanding of Order of the Temple (Knights Templar) by Pope Clement V. P 13½×13.
4814   **1756**   65st. black and scarlet-vermilion ....   2·50   2·30

1757 Anton Mitov   **1758** Baldwin Tower, Tsarevets Fortress

(Des Rosen Toshev)

2012 (28 Mar). Personalities. T **1757** and similar horiz designs. Multicoloured. P 13×13½.
4815   65st. Type **1757** (artist) (150th birth anniversary) ....   2·10   1·90
4816   65st. Dimcho Debelyanov (writer) (125th birth anniversary) ....   2·10   1·90
4817   1l. Petya Dubarova (writer) (50th birth anniversary) ....   3·25   2·75
4818   1l. Yana Yazova (writer) (birth centenary) ...   3·25   2·75
4815/4818 Set of 4 ....   9·75   8·50

(Des Krasimira Despotova)

2012 (4 Apr). Europa. Visit Bulgaria. T **1758** and similar vert design. Multicoloured.

(a) Sheet stamps. P 13 (with one large indented hole on each vert side)
4819   65st. Type **1758** ....   2·50   2·30
4820   1l.50 Patriarchal Cathedral, Tsarevets ....   6·00   5·25
MS4821 85×126 mm. Nos. 4819/4820 ....   9·00   8·00

(b) Booklet stamps. P 13×imperf (one horiz side)
4821*a*   65st. As Type **1758** ....   2·50   2·30
         b. Booklet pane. No. 4821*a*×4 ....   10·50
4821*c*   1l.50 As No. 4820 ....   6·00   5·25
         d. Booklet pane. No. 4821*c*×4 ....   25·00

Nos. 4821*a*/4821*c*, respectively, each×4 plus two stamp-size labels, were printed in booklets of eight stamps and four labels.

The booklet panes have straight edges, giving stamps with either top or bottom imperforate.

1759 Gentoo Penguins (*Pygoscelis papua*) and Bulgarian Flag

(Des Stefan Gruev)

2012 (7 Apr). 20th Bulgarian Antarctic Expedition. T **1759** and similar horiz design. P 13½×13.
4822   1l.40 Type **1759** ....   5·25   4·75
MS4823 100×87 mm. 65st. Hut, flag, Gentoo Penguin and chick ....   29·00   27·00

No. 4822 was printed in sheets of two stamps and two stamp size labels.

No. MS4823 is from a limited printing.

1760 *Titanic* at Night   **1761** Albatros D. II Aircraft

(Des Hristo Aleksiev)

2012 (10 Apr). Centenary of the loss of the *Titanic*. Sheet 100×50 mm. P 13½.
MS4824   **1760**   1l.40 multicoloured ....   4·50   4·00

BULGARIA 2012

(Des Georgi Yankov)

2012 (12 Apr). Centenary of Bulgarian Aviation in Balkan War. The Battle of Edirne. P 13½.
4825 1761 65st. multicoloured .... 3·25   2·75

1762 Parashkev Hadjiev

(Des Lyudmil Metodiev)

2012 (27 Apr). Birth Centenary of Parashkev Hadjiev (composer). P 13½.
4826 1762 65st. multicoloured .... 2·50   2·30

No. 4826 was printed, *se-tenant*, with a stamp size label, the whole forming a composite design.

1763 Anniversary Emblem   1764 9th-century Stone Lion

(Des Viliam Kitanov)

2012 (7 May). 20th Anniversary of Bulgaria's Membership of Council of Europe. P 13.
4827 1763 1l. multicoloured .... 3·25   2·75

(Des Ilya Gruev)

2012 (16 May). Archaeology. P 13.
4828 1764 65st. multicoloured .... 2·50   2·30

1765 Truck

(Des Tatyana Uzunova)

2012 (30 May). 50th Anniversary of AEBTRI (Association of Bulgarian Enterprises for International Road Transport and Roads). Sheet 100×71 mm. P 13.
MS4829 1765 2l.10 multicoloured .... 7·25   6·75

1766 Football

(Des Svetlin Belezdrov)

2012 (8 June). Euro 2012. European Football Championships, Poland and Ukraine. Sheet 100×102 mm. P 13½.
MS4830 1766 1l. multicoloured .... 3·50   3·25

1767 *Silybum marianum*   1768 Paisius of Hilendar

(Des Stoyan Dechev)

2012 (14 June). Flora. Prickly Plants. T **1767** and similar horiz designs. Multicoloured. P 13.
4831 65st. Type **1767** .... 2·10   1·90
   a. Sheetlet of 4. Nos. 4831/4834 .... 11·00
4832 65st. *Carduus acanthoides* .... 2·10   1·90
4833 1l. *Centaurea solstitialis* .... 3·25   2·75
4834 1l. *Dipsacus laciniatus* .... 3·25   2·75
4831/4834 Set of 4 .... 9·75   8·25

Nos. 4831/4834 were printed, *se-tenant*, in vertical sheetlets of four stamps, with the values alternating.

(Des Apostol Apostolov)

2012 (22 June). 250th Anniversary of *Istoriya Slavyanobolgarskaya* (Slavonic–Bulgarian history) by Paisius of Hilendar. P 13.
4835 1768 65st. multicoloured .... 2·50   2·30

1769 Rogozen Treasure   1770 Gymnast

(Des Ivan Gazdov)

2012 (12 July). Regions. North-western Bulgaria. Sheet 85×113 mm containing T **1769** and similar vert designs. Multicoloured. P 13×13½.
MS4836 65st Type **1769**; 65st. Cave paintings in Magura Cave; 1l. Meschite Tower; 1l. Baba Vida Fortress .... 11·00   10·00

(Des Ralitsa Nikolova)

2012 (16 July). Olympic Games, London. Sheet 82×67 mm. P 13½×13.
MS4837 1770 1l.50 multicoloured .... 5·75   5·25

1771 Vasil Levski

(Des Atanas Atanasov)

2012 (18 July). 175th Birth Anniversary of Vasil Levski (revolutionary). P 13½×13.
4838 1771 65st. multicoloured .... 2·50   2·30

(Des Stoyan Dechev)

2012 (17 Aug). Moths. Australia 2013 and Thailand 2013 International Stamp Exhibition. Sheet 98×66 mm containing horiz designs as T **1550**. Multicoloured. P 13 (with one diamond-shaped hole on each vert side).
MS4839 40st. As Type **1550**; 45st. *Rethera komoarovi* (As No. 4476); 55st. *Symtomis marjana* (As No. 4477); 80st. *Arctia caja* (As No. 4478) .... 75·00   65·00

The stamps of No. **MS**4839 are as Nos. 4475/4478 of 2004.
No. **MS**4839 is from a limited printing.

1772 *Impression: Rising Sun* (Claude Monet) and Claude Debussy   1773 Fair Emblem

(Des Deya Valcheva)

2012 (22 Aug). Impressionism. 150th Birth Anniversary of Claude Debussy. P 13.
4840 **1772** 1l. multicoloured .... 3·25 3·00
No. 4840 was printed, *se-tenant*, with a stamp-size label at left, in sheetlets of four stamps, the stamp and label forming a composite design of the painting.

(Des Tatyana Uzunova)

2012 (24 Sept). 120th Anniversary of Plovdiv International Fair. P 13.
4841 **1773** 65st. multicoloured .... 2·50 2·30

1774 Ivan Stoyanovich   **1775** Monument of Liberty, Rousse

(Des Ivan Bogdanov)

2012 (25 Sept). 150th Birth Anniversary of Ivan Petrov Stoyanovich (revolutionary and statesman). P 13.
4842 **1774** 65st. multicoloured .... 2·50 2·30

(Des Nikolay Mladenov)

2012 (10 Oct). 150th Birth Anniversary of Arnoldo Zocchi (Italian sculptor). P 13.
4843 **1775** 1l. blue .... 3·25 2·75

1776 *Primula deorum*   **1777** First Railway Mail Van and *Rousse-Mid 19th-century* (by Felix Kaniz)

(Des Viktor Paunov)

2012 (18 Oct). Ecology. Parangalitsa Reserve. Sheet 96×83 mm containing T **1776** and similar vert design. Multicoloured. P 13.
MS4844 65st. Type **1776**; 1l.50 *Felis silvestris silvestris* (European Wildcat) .... 7·25 6·75

(Des Maglena Konstantinova)

2012 (22 Oct). Transport. Railway Post Wagons. Sheet 169×95 mm containing T **1777** and similar horiz designs. Multicoloured. P 13.
MS4845 65st. Type **1777**; 65st. Mail van (1888–1904) and 19th-century postcard showing views of Sofia; 1l. First Bulgarian State Railways mail van (1895–1930) and postcard showing folk costumes; 1l. First Bulgarian State Railways three axle mail van and 20th-century railway map .... 11·00 10·00

1778 Eurocopter AS532 Cougar Helicopter

(Des Ralitsa Nikolova)

2012 (27 Oct). Military Helicopters. Sheet 87×67 mm. Imperf.
MS4846 **1778** 65st. multicoloured .... 29·00 27·00
No. **MS**48446 is from a limited printing.

1779 Andalusian

(Des Emilyan Stankev)

2012 (28 Oct). Horses. T **1779** and similar horiz designs showing Horses. Multicoloured. P 13.
4847 65st. Type **1779** .... 2·30 2·10
  a. Pair. Nos. 4847 and 4849 .... 5·50 5·00
4848 65st. Irish Cob (Gypsy Vanner) .... 2·30 2·10
  a. Pair. Nos. 4848 and 4850 .... 5·50 5·00
4849 1l. Arab .... 3·25 3·00
4850 1l. Haflinger Pony .... 3·25 3·00
4847/4850 Set of 4 .... 10·00 9·25
Nos. 4847 and 4849, each×2, and Nos. 4848 and 4850, each×2, respectively, were each printed in sheets of four stamps and two stamp-size labels.

1780 Centenary Emblem

(Des Damyan Damyanov)

2012 (30 Oct). Centenary of Ministry of Railways, Posts and Telegraphs. P 13.
4851 **1780** 65st. multicoloured .... 2·50 2·30

1781 Sword Hilt, Lion and Seal   **1782** Stylised Tree

(Des Maya Cholakova)

2012 (7 Nov). Centenary of Discovery of Khan Kubrat's Grave and Funerary Hoard (founder of Old Great Bulgaria). P 13.
4852 **1781** 1l. multicoloured .... 3·25 3·00

(Des Ivelina Velinova)

2012 (20 Nov). Christmas. P 13.
4853 **1782** 65st. multicoloured .... 2·50 2·30

 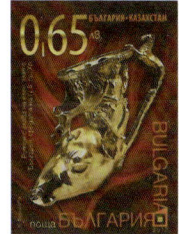

1783 Valley of the Roses (perfume industry) (Vasilena Vasileva)   **1784** Thracian Gold Rhyton (4th-century BC) (Bulgaria)

(Des Martin Rusev)

2012 (28 Nov). International Year of Chemistry. Winning Entry (12–14 years) in Global Design a Stamp Competition, Chemistry as a Cultural Enterprise. P 13.
4854 **1783** 65st. multicoloured .... 2·50 2·30

BULGARIA 2012

(Des Kristina Borisova)

2012 (12 Dec). 20th Anniversary of Bulgaria–Kazakhstan Diplomatic Relations. T **1784** and similar vert design. Multicoloured. P 13.
4855		65st. Type **1784**	2·10	1·90
	a.	Pair. Nos. 4855/4856		
4856		1l.40 Two gold Deer linked by Bird	4·25	3·75

Stamps of a similar design were issued by Kazakhstan.

1785 Planets in Orbit

(Des Todor Vardjiev)

2012 (21 Dec). Grand Parade of the Planets 2012. Sheet 102×63 mm. P 13.
MS4857	**1785**	1l. multicoloured	3·50	3·25

1786 Emblem

(Des Maya Staykova)

2013 (4 Jan). Tourism. P 13.
4858	**1786**	1l. multicoloured	3·25	3·00

1786a Antarctica (*Illustration reduced, actual size* 99×66 *mm*)

(Des Stoyan Dechev)

2013 (4 Feb). 25th Anniversary of Bulgarian Antarctic Base. Sheet 99×66 mm design as T **1786a** containing two designs as T **1731**. P 13 (with one diamond shaped hole on each vert side).
MS4858a		58st.×2 As Type **1731**×2	75·00	65·00

No. **MS**4858a is from a limited printing (2100).

1787 Anniversary Emblem   **1788** General Skobelev mounted on a Horse (N. D. Dmitriev-Orenburgski) (detail)

(Des Viliam Kitanov)

2012 (28 Feb). 130th Anniversary of Bulgarian Maritime Administration. P 13½×13.
4859	**1787**	65st. multicoloured	2·75	2·50

No. 4859 was printed, *se-tenant*, with a stamp-size label inscribed for the anniversary at left.

(Des Christina Borissova)

2013 (5 Mar). 135th Anniversary of End of Russo–Turkish War. Sheet 70×87 mm. P 13×13½.
MS4860	**1788**	1l.40 multicoloured	5·25	4·75

A stamp of a similar design was issued by Russia.

1789 Anniversary Emblem   **1790** Bells (as label of No. 4479)

(Des Nikolay Mladenov)

2013 (10 Mar). 70th Anniversary of Saving Bulgarian Jews. P 13×13½.
4861	**1789**	1l.40 emerald, scarlet-vermilion and black	5·75	5·25

No. 4861 was printed in sheets of two stamps and two stamp-size labels.

(Des B. Dimovski, Emilyan Stankev, Stoyan Detchev, Natalia Kuruch and Lyudmil Veselinov)

2013 (29 Mar). Greetings Stamps. T **1790** and similar multicoloured designs. P 13 (with one large indented hole on each vert side) (vert stamps) or (with one large indented hole on each horiz side) (horiz stamp).
4862		65st. As No. 4221 (making wine)	3·00	2·75
4863		65st. As No. 4394 (clown) (*horiz*)	3·00	2·75
4864		65st. As T **1740** (Rabbit as newspaper boy)	3·00	2·75
4865		1l. Type **1790**	4·25	3·75
4862/4865		*Set of* 4	12·00	11·00

1791 Team Members, 1925

(Des Lyudmil Veselinov)

2013 (29 Mar). Centenary of Cherno More Football Club. P 13½×13.
4866	**1791**	65st. multicoloured	3·00	2·75

1792 Winning Team Members, 1943

(Des Lyudmil Veselinov)

2013 (5 Apr). Centenary of Slavia Football Club. P 13½×13.
4867	**1792**	65st. multicoloured	3·00	2·75

1793 Valentina Tereshkova (USSR)   **1794** Battle Scene

2013 BULGARIA

(Des Rosen Toshev)

2013 (12 Apr). 50th Anniversary of First Woman in Space. Sheet 81×67 mm. Imperf.
MS4868 **1793** 65st. multicoloured.................... 32·00 29·00

(Des Tatyana Uzunova)

2013 (10 Apr). Centenary of End of First Balkan War. Sheet 120×105 mm containing T **1794** and similar horiz designs. Multicoloured. P 13½.
MS4869 65st. Type **1794**; 65st. Triumphal arch; 1l. Surrender of Edirne Fortress; 1l. Tsar Ferdinand on Horseback.................... 14·50 13·50

1794a FC CSKA and FC Barcelona at Nou Camp Stadium in 1959

1795 Citroën Jumper 2.2 HDI

(Des Lyudmil Veselinov)

2013 (23 Apr). 65th Anniversary of CSKA Football Club. P 13½×13.
4869a **1794a** 65st. multicoloured.................... 3·00 2·75

(Des Emilyan Stankev)

2013 (24 Apr). Europa. Postal Transport. T **1795** and similar vert design. Multicoloured. P 13.
(a) Sheet stamps and miniature sheet. P 13
4870   65st. Type **1795**.................... 3·00 2·75
4871   1l.50 Citroën Berlingo 1.6 HDI.................... 6·25 5·75
MS4872 74×87 mm. As Nos. 4870/4871.................... 10·00 9·00
(b) Booklet stamps. P 13×imperf.
4872a 65st. As Type **1795**, background colour changed.................... 3·00 2·75
       aa. Booklet pane. No. 4872a×4.................... 12·50
4872b 1l.50 As No. 4871, background colour changed.................... 6·25 5·75
       ba. Booklet pane. No. 4872b×4.................... 26·00

The booklet panes Nos. 4872aa and 4872ba, respectively, have straight vertical edges giving stamps with either left or right edges imperforate depending on position.

1796 Steam Locomotive and Railway Act of 1885 (fragment)

(Des Valentin Shtinkov)

2013 (14 May). 125th Anniversary of Bulgarian State Railways. Sheet 137×61 mm. P 13.
MS4873 **1796** 1l.40 multicoloured.................... 6·25 5·75

No. **MS**4873 was issued with a stamp-size label showing a speeding train.

1797 Richard Wagner

(Des Lyudmil Metodiev)

2013 (22 May). Birth Bicentenary of Richard Wagner. P 13.
4874   **1797** 1l. multicoloured.................... 4·25 3·75

No. 4874 was printed in sheets of 20 stamps and 20 stamp-size labels, each stamp and label forming a composite design.

1798 Western Capercaillie (*Tetrao urogallus*) **1799** Davy Lamp

(Des Maglena Konstantinova)

2013 (22 May). Ecology. Mantaritsa Reserve. Sheet 102×104 mm. P 13.
MS4875 **1798** 1l.50 multicoloured.................... 6·75 6·25

(Des Georgi Yankov)

2013 (28 May). 60th Anniversary of St Ivan of Rila Mining and Geology University. P 13.
4876   **1799** 65st. multicoloured.................... 2·75 2·50

1800 Children

(Des Momchil Kolchev)

2013 (30 May). SOS Children's Villages. P 13.
4877   **1800** 65st. multicoloured.................... 2·50 2·30

1801 Soyuz–TM–5

(Des Damyan Damyanov)

2013 (30 May). 25th Anniversary of Alexander Alexandrov's Space Flight. Sheet 86×87 mm. P 13.
MS4878 **1801** 1l.50 multicoloured.................... 6·75 6·25

1802 Saints Cyril and Methodius, Jesus Christ and Angels

1803 Fortified Building, Kovachevitsa Village

(Des Kristina Borisova)

2013 (12 June). 1150th Anniversary of Arrival of Saints Cyril and Methodius to Great Moravia. Sheet 96×123 mm. P 13.
MS4879 **1802** 3l.20 multicoloured.................... 13·00 12·00

A stamp of a similar design was issued by Czech Republic, Slovakia and Vatican City.

BULGARIA 2013

(Des Ivan Gazdov)

2013 (17 June). Regions. South-western Bulgaria. Sheet 85×115 mm containing T **1803** and similar vert designs. Multicoloured. P 13×13½.
MS4880 65st. Type **1803**; 65st. Fox and Black Woodpecker, Skakavitsa Reserve; 1l. Fresco, Zemen Monastery; 1l. Vasil Levski and St Petka of the Saddlers Church .... 13·00 12·00

(Des Viliam Kitanov)

2013 (16 Aug). Sofia 2013. International Philatelic Salon. Lighthouses. Sheet 96×66 mm containing horiz designs as T **1503**. P 13 (with one diamond-shaped hole on each vert side).
MS4881 25st. red and green; 32st. blue and yellow..... 75·00 65·00
Designs: 25st. As T **1503** (Cape Shabla lighthouse); 32st. As No. 4379 (Kaliakra Cape lighthouse).
No. MS4881 is from a limited printing (2100).

1804 Tsar Boris III

(Des Rosen Toshev)

2013 (30 Aug). 70th Death Anniversary of Tsar Boris III. Sheet 86×79 mm. P 13½×13.
MS4882   **1804**   1l.50 multicoloured...........................   5·75   5·25

1805 Flags of Bulgaria and USA as Stars

(Des Teodor Liho)

2013 (12 Sept). 110th Anniversary of Bulgaria–USA Diplomatic Relations. P 13½×13.
4883   **1805**   1l.40 multicoloured...........................   5·25   4·75

1806 Early Team Members

(Des Lyudmil Veselinov)

2013 (25 Oct). Centenary of Botev Plovdiv Football Club. P 13½×13.
4884   **1806**   65st. multicoloured...........................   2·30   2·10

An imperforate miniature sheet as No. MS4860 was issued for the 135th Anniversary of Russo–Turkish War on 25 October 2013.

No. 4885 and T **4807** are vacant.

1808 *Cymbidium iridioides*

(Des Todor Vardjiev)

2013 (26 Oct). Flora. Orchids. Sheet 128×98 mm containing T **1808** and similar horiz designs. Multicoloured. P 13.
MS4886 65st. Type **1808**; 65st. *Dendrobium fimbriatum*; 1l. *Epidendrum radicans*; 1l. *Dendrobium nobile*.. 12·00 11·50

1809 Siamese Kitten   **1810** Emblem

(Des Hristo Aleksiev)

2013 (26 Oct). Kittens. T **1809** and similar multicoloured designs showing kittens. P 13.
4887   65st. Type **1809**.. 2·50 2·30
   a. Pair. Nos. 4887 and 4889........................ 6·50 6·00
4888   65st. Scottish Fold (*horiz*)................................ 2·50 2·30
   a. Pair. Nos. 4888 and 4890........................ 6·50 6·00
4889   1l. Birman.. 3·75 3·50
4890   1l. Somali (*horiz*).. 3·75 3·50
4887/4890 Set of 4.. 11·00 10·50
Nos. 4887 and 4889, and Nos. 4888 and 4890, respectively, were printed, *se-tenant*, in horizontal and vertical pairs within sheets.

(Des Stefan Gruev)

2013 (27 Oct). 25th Anniversary of Green Balkans Society. Sheet 87×103 mm. P 13×13½.
MS4891   **1810**   1l. multicoloured...........................   4·00   3·50

1811 Koldari Carollers

(Des Nenko Atanasov)

2013 (22 Nov). Christmas. P 13.
4892   **1811**   65s. multicoloured...........................   2·50   2·30

1812 Serdika City Underground Station

(Des Stoyan Dechev)

2013 (22 Nov). Sofia Metropolitan Railway. Sheet 242×58 mm containing T **1812** and similar horiz designs. Multicoloured. P 13.
MS4893 65s. Type **1812**; 1l. Luvov Most Station; 1l.50 Overground railway .... 12·50 11·50
No. MS4893 also contains a stamp size label, which, with the stamps and margins, form a composite design.
No. MS4893 was issued in a folder.

1813 Griffon

(Des Iliya Gruev)

2013 (18 Dec). Cultural and Historical Heritage. T **1813** and similar horiz design. Multicoloured. P 13 (with one enlarged hole on each horiz side).
4894   1l. Type **1813**.. 3·75 3·50
4895   1l. Galloping Horse (detail) and rhyton......... 3·75 3·50

2014 BULGARIA

1814 Ski Jump

(Des Damyan Damyanov)

2014 (31 Jan). Winter Olympic Games, Sochi. Sheet 80×80 mm. P 13½×13.
MS4896 1814 1l.40 multicoloured............................ 5·75 5·25

1815 *Boletus pinophilus* (Pine Bolete)

(Des Stoyan Dechev)

2014 (10 Feb). Fungi. T **1815** and similar horiz designs. Multicoloured. P 13 (with one large indented hole on each vert side).
4897 10st. Type **1815**.. 40 40
4898 20st. *Coprinus picaceus* (Magpie Inkcap)..... 85 75
4899 50st. *Amanita citrina* (False Death Cap)........ 1·90 1·70
4900 1l. *Russula virescens* (Quilted Green Russula).. 3·75 3·50
4897/4900 Set of 4.. 6·25 5·75
See also Nos. **MS**4903 and **MS**4904.

1816 Team Members

(Des Lyudmil Veselinov)

2014 (21 Feb). Centenary (2013) of Levski Football Club. P 13½×13.
4901 **1816** 65st. multicoloured.......................... 2·50 2·30
No. 4901 is known with '2013' and '2014' imprint dates, price is the same for both.

1817 Galileo Galilei

(Des Rosen Toshev)

2014 (21 Feb). 450th Birth Anniversary of Galileo Galilei (astronomer). P 13½×13.
4902 **1817** 1l. multicoloured............................... 3·75 3·50

(Des Stoyan Dechev)

2014 (28 Feb). ESSEN 2014 International Stamp Exhibition, Germany. Sheets 96×66 mm containing horiz designs as T **1815**. Multicoloured. P 14×13½.
MS4903 25st. *Boletus pinophilus* (As Type **1815**); 32st. *Amanita citrina* (As No. 4899) .... 42·00 38·00
MS4904 20st. *Coprinus picaceus* (As No. 4898); 1l. *Russula virescens* (As No. 4900) .... 42·00 38·00
Nos. **MS**4903/**MS**4904 are from limited printings (3000).

1818 Table as Sea with National Flags as Boat Sails

(Des Nenko Atanasov)

2014 (7 Mar). 135th Anniversary of Bulgaria–Romania Diplomatic Relations. P 13.
4905 **1818** 80st. multicoloured......................... 3·25 2·75
A stamp of a similar design was issued by Romania.

1819 Galloping Horse Treading on a Flying Swallow

(Des Emilian Stankev)

2014 (14 Mar). 65th Anniversary of Bulgaria–China Diplomatic Relations. Sheet 86×84 mm. P 13.
MS4906 1819 2l.10 multicoloured........................ 8·50 7·50

1820 Saint Sophronius

(Des Lyudmil Metodiev)

2014 (17 Mar). 275th Birth Anniversary of Saint Sophronius (Stoyko Vladislavov) of Vratsa (leading figure in early Bulgarian National Revival). P 13.
4907 **1820** 65st. multicoloured......................... 2·50 2·30

1821 Cover of First Bulgarian Constitution 1879

(Des Ivelina Velinova)

2014 (3 Apr). 135th Anniversary of Bulgarian Parliament. T **1821** and similar horiz designs. Multicoloured. P 13½×13.
MS4908 162×87 mm. 10st. Type **1821**; 20st. Exarch Antim I, the first chairman of the National Assembly; 30st. Diary and the bell of the first National Assembly; 65st. Present Bulgarian Constitution and parliamentary bell.................. 5·25 4·75
MS4909 102×73 mm. 1l. Exarch Antim I..................... 4·00 3·50

1822 William Shakespeare (450th birth anniversary)

(Des Atanass Atanassov)

2014 (5 Apr). Personalities. Sheet 128×97 mm containing T **1822** and similar horiz designs. Multicoloured. P 13.
MS4910 65st. Taras Shevenko (writer) (birth bicentenary); 1l. Type **1822**; 65st. Richard Strauss (composer) (150th birth anniversary); 1l. Mikhail Lermontov (writer) (birth bicentenary)................. 13·00 12·00

259

BULGARIA 2014

1823 Masonic Symbols

(Des William Kitanov)

2014 (15 Apr). Centenary of Zaria Masonic Lodge. P 13½×13.
4911   1823   65st. multicoloured .... 2·50   2·30

1824 *Kaliakra*

(Des Valentin Shtinkov)

2014 (17 Apr). 30th Anniversary of Sail Training Vessel, *Kaliakra*. P 13½×13.
4912   1824   65st. multicoloured .... 2·75   2·50
No. 4912 was printed in sheets of two stamps and two stamp size labels.

1825 Drummer   **1826** Elm Tree, Sliven

(Des Maglena Konstantinova)

2014 (29 Apr). Europa. Musical Instruments. T **1825** and similar vert design. Multicoloured. P 13 (No. **MS**4915) or 13 (with one indented hole) (others).
4913   65st. Type **1825** .... 2·50   2·30
4914   1l.50 Shepherd playing flute .... 6·00   5·25
MS4915 126×86 mm. 2l.15 Nos. 4913/4914 ...... 9·00   8·00

(Des Todor Angeliev)

2014 (12 May). Ecology. Elm Tree, Sliven, European Tree of the Year 2014. Sheet 86×100 mm. P 13½×13.
MS4916 1826   1l. multicoloured .... 4·25   3·75

1827 Stephan Parushev
(first postmaster)

(Des Apostol Apostolov)

2014 (14 May). 135th Anniversary of Bulgarian Post. Sheet 59×50 mm. P 13.
MS4917 1827   1l. multicoloured .... 4·25   3·75

1828 Poppies and Kozloduy Plant

(Des Tahsin Ahmed)

2014 (20 May). 40th Anniversary of Kozloduy Nuclear Power Plant. P 13½×13.
4918   1828   65st. multicoloured .... 2·50   2·30

1829 Player

(Des Hristo Aleksiev)

2014 (12 June). World Cup Football Championships, Brazil. Sheet 85×55 mm. P 13½×13.
MS4919 1829   2l.10 multicoloured .... 8·00   7·25

1830 Symbols of Journalism

(Des Todor Vardjiev)

2014 (17 June). 175th Anniversary of Bulgarian Journalism. P 13½×13.
4920   1830   65st. multicoloured .... 2·50   2·30

(Des Emilian Stankev)

2014 (7 July). Bulgarian Circus Art. Sheet 129×99 mm containing two horiz designs as T **1513**. Multicoloured. P 13.
MS4920*a* 65st.×2 Clown (As No. 4394) .... 40·00   36·00

1831 Flags

(Des Khanija Betredinova and Todor Vardjiev)

2014 (7 July). 135th Anniversary of Bulgaria–Russia Diplomatic Relations. P 13.
4921   1831   1l.40 multicoloured .... 5·00   4·50
A stamp of a similar design was issued by Russia.

1832 Guards and Prince (Knyaz)   **1833** Peter Deunov
Alexander of Battenburg

(Des Simeon Krastev)

2014 (10 July). 135th Anniversary of Bulgarian National Guards Unit. P 13.
4922   1832   65st. multicoloured .... 2·50   2·30

(Des Apostol Apostolov.)

2014 (11 July). 150th Birth Anniversary of Master Peter Deunov (philosopher and spiritual teacher). Sheet 132×81 mm. P 13.
MS4923 1833   1l.50 multicoloured .... 5·75   5·25

2014 BULGARIA

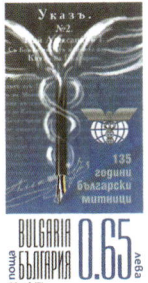
1834 Pen creating Emblem

1835 Berlin Electrical Tram, 1900

(Des Kristina Borisova)

2014 (6 Aug). 135th Anniversary of Bulgarian Customs Department. P 13×13½.
| 4924 | 1834 | 65st. multicoloured | 2·50 | 2·30 |

(Des Krasimira Despotova)

2014 (21 Oct). History of the Electric Tramway. 125th Anniversary of Federation of European Philatelic Associations. T **1835** and similar horiz designs. Multicoloured. P 13.
4925		30st. Type **1835**	1·30	1·10
4926		65st. Glasgow Electrical Tram, 1930	2·50	2·30
4927		80st. Melbourne Electrical Tram, 1945	3·00	2·75
4928		1l. Sofia Electrical Tram, 2014	3·75	3·50
4925/4928	Set of 4		9·50	9·00
MS4929	125×94 mm 30st. As Type **1835**; 65st. As No. 4926; 80st. As No. 4927; 1l. As No. 4928		11·00	10·00

1836 *Bombycilla garrulus* (Bohemian Waxwing)

1837 Ferdinand Magellan

(Des Stefan Gruev)

2014 (25 Oct). Birds. International Stamp Exhibition BULCOLLECTO 2014, Plovdiv. T **1836** and similar horiz designs. Multicoloured. P 13.
4930		30st. Type **1836**	1·10	95
4931		50st. *Erythropygia galactotes* (Rufous tailed Scrub Robin)	1·70	1·50
4932		1l. *Melanocorypha yeltoniensis* (Black Lark)	3·25	2·75
4933		1l.50 *Hippolais icterina* (Icterine Warbler)	4·75	4·25
4930/4933	Set of 4		9·75	8·50
MS4934	127×87 mm 30st. As Type **1836**; 50st. As No. 4931; 1l. As No. 4932; 1l.50 As No. 4933		11·00	10·00

(Des Emilian Stankev)

2014 (25 Oct). International Philatelic Exhibition Bulgaria–Portugal. Great Navigators. Ferdinand Magellan. Sheet 70×85 mm. P 13.
| MS4935 | **1837** | 65st. multicoloured | 34·00 | 30·00 |

1838 Early Coin from Perperikon Archaeological Complex

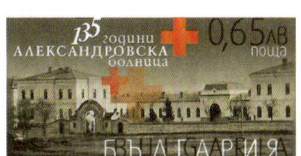
1839 Early University Campus

(Des Ivan Gazdov)

2014 (25 Oct). Regions. South Central Bulgaria. Sheet 85×115 mm containing T **1838** and similar vert designs. Multicoloured. P 13×13½.
| MS4936 | 65st. Type **1838**; 65st. House of Plovdiv Ethnographic Museum; 1l. National Astronomical Observatory, Rozhen; 1l. Chamois, Biosphere Nature Reserve, Kupena | 13·00 | 12·00 |

(Des Teodor Lihov)

2014 (30 Oct). 135th Anniversary of Alexandrovska University Hospital. P 13½×13.
| 4937 | 1839 | 65st. multicoloured | 2·50 | 2·30 |

1840 King Wladislaw III of Poland and Hungary

1841 Flags and Emblems

(Des Maya Cholakova)

2014 (10 Nov). 570th Anniversary of Battle of Varna. Sheet 108×78 mm. P 13.
| MS4938 | 1840 | 1l.50 multicoloured | 6·25 | 5·75 |

(Des Iliya Gruev)

2014 (11 Nov). 20th Anniversary of Bulgaria–Sovereign Military Order of Malta Diplomatic Relations. P 13.
| 4939 | 1841 | 1l.50 multicoloured | 6·00 | 5·25 |

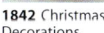
1842 Christmas Decorations

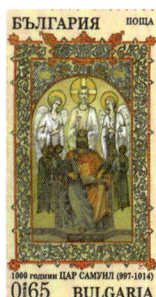
1843 Tsar Samuel of Bulgaria

(Des Ralitsa Nikolova)

2014 (20 Nov). Christmas. P 13×13½.
| 4940 | 1842 | 65st. multicoloured | 2·50 | 2·30 |

(Des Tatyana Uzunova)

2014 (25 Nov). Millenary of Battle of Belasitsa. Sheet 79×102 mm. P 13×13½.
| MS4941 | 1843 | 65st. multicoloured | 2·75 | 2·50 |

1844 Stylised Church Entrance

1845 Nikolai Rainov, 1889–1954

261

BULGARIA 2014

(Des Maya Staikova)

2014 (5 Dec). Centenary of Russian Church Saint Nicholas the Miracle-Maker, Sofia. P 13.
4942 **1844** 65st. multicoloured .... 2·50 2·30

(Des Plamen Valchev)

2014 (6 Dec). 125th Birth Anniversaries of Bulgarian Painters. T **1845** and similar horiz designs showing portraits of the artists. Multicoloured. P 13½×13.
4943	30st. Konstantin Shtarkelov 1889–1961	1·30	1·10
4944	65st. Type **1845**	2·50	2·30
4945	80st. Mihail Kats, 1889–1964	3·00	2·75
4946	1l. Ivan Lazarov, 1889–1952	3·75	3·50
4943/4946	*Set of 4*	9·50	8·50

1846 Petar Uvaliev

(Des Todor Angeliev)

2015 (12 Jan). Birth Centenary of Petar Hristov Uvaliev (film producer, writer, director and broadcaster). P 13.
4947 **1846** 65st. multicoloured .... 2·50 2·30

1847 '100' and Stylised Camera

(Des Georgi Yankov)

2015 (13 Jan). Centenary of Bulgarian Cinema. P 13½×13.
4948 **1847** 65st. multicoloured .... 2·50 2·30

1848 Clock with Zodiac Display

(Des Ivelina Velinova)

2015 (20 Feb). Antique Timepieces. T **1848** and similar horiz designs showing timepieces. Multicoloured. P 13 (with one diamond-shaped hole on each vert side).
4949	5st. Type **1848**..	20	20
4950	30st. Rococo clock..	1·10	95
4951	80st. Pocket watch..	3·00	2·75
4949/4951	*Set of 3*...	3·75	3·50

See also No. MS5057.

1849 Apollo–Soyuz in Space

1850 Salute

(Des Emiliyan Stankev)

2015 (20 Feb). 40th Anniversary of Apollo–Soyuz Test Project. Sheet 87×72 mm. P 13.
MS4952 **1849** 65st. multicoloured .... 2·75 2·50

(Des Luba Tomova)

2015 (27 Mar). Centenary of Bulgarian Union of Disabled Veterans and War Victims. P 13.
4953 **1850** 65st. multicoloured .... 2·50 2·30

1851 Soldier on Rocking Horse   **1852** Dachshund

(Des Ralitsa Nikolova)

2015 (20 Apr). Europa. Old Toys. T **1851** and similar vert design. Multicoloured. P 13 (No. **MS**4956) or 13 (with one indented hole) (others).
| 4954 | 65st. Type **1851**.. | 2·10 | 1·90 |
| 4955 | 1l.50 Doll... | 4·50 | 4·25 |

MS4956 108×86 mm. 65st. As Type **1851**; 1l.50 As No. 4955... 9·00 8·00

(Des Viktor Paunov)

2015 (28 Apr). Thematic Philatelic Exhibition. Pets. Sheet 86×70 mm. Imperf.
MS4957 **1852** 65st. multicoloured............... 34·00 30·00
No. **MS**4957 is from a limited printing.

1853 Forest Trees and Leaves

(Des Tahsin Ahmed)

2015 (7 May). Ecology. Forestry in Bulgaria. Sheet 85×64 mm. P 13½×13.
MS4958 **1853** 1l. multicoloured...................... 3·50 3·25

1854 Red Cross and Building

(Des Teodor Liho)

2015 (14 May). Red Cross. 70th Anniversary of Plovdiv Medical University. P 13½×13.
4959 **1854** 65st. multicoloured .... 2·50 2·30

1855 Telegraph Transmitter and Keyboard

(Des Iliya Gruev)

2015 (18 May). 150th Anniversary of ITU (International Telecommunication Union). P 13½×13.
4960 **1855** 1l. multicoloured......................... 3·25 3·00

1856 Marek Football Club Team

(Des Lyudmil Veselinov)

2015 (25 May). Centenary of Marek Football Club. P 13½×13.
4961　**1856**　65st. multicoloured .... 2·50　2·30

1857 Wrestlers

(Des Lyudmil Veselinov)

2015 (29 May). European Games, Baku, Azerbaijan. Sheet 96×96 mm. P 13½×13.
MS4962　**1857**　1l.40 multicoloured .... 5·75　5·25

1858 Red Cross Emblem, Ribbons and Hospital Façade

(Des Teodor Liho)

2015 (17 June). 65th Anniversary of Sofia Oncology Hospital. P 13½×13.
4963　**1858**　65st. multicoloured .... 2·50　2·30

1859 Traditional Wedding　　**1860** Baby, Building and Princess Mare Louise (founder)

(Des Stoyan Dechev)

2015 (6 Aug). Folk Art. T **1859** and similar horiz designs. Multicoloured. P 13½×13.
4964　　50st. Type **1859** .... 2·10　1·90
　　　a. Sheet of 3. Nos. 4964/4966 plus 3 labels .... 8·50
4965　　65st. Singers and musicians .... 2·50　2·30
4966　　1l. Women .... 3·75　3·50
4964/4966 Set of 3 .... 7·50　7·00
MS4966a 161×116mm. Nos. 4964/4966 .... 8·75　8·00
　Nos. 4964/4966 were each printed in sheets of 40 stamps, and together, in sheets of three stamps and three stamp-size labels.

(Des Teodor Liho)

2015 (6 Aug). Red Cross. 111th Anniversary of Maichin Dom, University Obstetrics and Gynecology Hospital, Sofia. P 13½×13.
4967　**1860**　65st. multicoloured .... 2·50　2·30

1861 Stefan Kanchev　　**1862** St Anastasia Island

(Des Todor Vardjiev)

2015 (6 Aug). Birth Centenary of Stefan Kanchev (artist and stamp designer). Sheet 100×73 mm. P 13.
MS4968　**1861**　1l.50 multicoloured .... 5·75　5·25

(Des Ivan Gazdov)

2015 (15 Aug). Regions. South-eastern Bulgaria. Sheet 85×115 mm containing T **1862** and similar vert designs. Multicoloured. P 13×13½.
MS4969 65st. Type **1862**; 65st. Torso, Kabyle Archaeological Reserve; 1l. Woman performing Nestinarstvo (fire ritual); 1l. Grapes and wine glass (wine making) .... 13·00　12·00

1863 Symbols of Science and Education　　**1864** Alphonse de Lamartine

(Des Yana Aneva, Daniela Draganova, Boyana Pavlova, Velichka Yordanova and Angelina Konzova)

2015 (16 Sept). Greetings Stamps. T **1863** and similar multicoloured designs. P 13 (with one large indented hole on each horiz side) (horiz stamps) or (with one large indented hole on each vert side) (vert stamp).
4970　　65st. Type **1863** .... 2·50　2·30
4971　　65st. White Swallow (Hope and Prosperity) 2·50　2·30
4972　　65st. Family on Ferris Wheel (vert) .... 2·50　2·30
4973　　1l. Trophy (Sport) .... 3·75　3·50
4974　　1l. Bird and ribbon (Baba Marta (first day of spring)) .... 3·75　3·50
4970/4974 Set of 5 .... 13·50　12·50

(Des Simeon Krastev)

2015 (21 Oct). 225th Birth Anniversary of Alphonse de Lamartine (writer, poet and politician). P 13×13½.
4975　**1864**　1l.50 multicoloured .... 5·25　4·75

1865 Roald Amundsen, 1872–1928

(Des Tekla Aleksieva)

2015 (23 Oct). Polar Explorers. Sheet 65×95 mm containing T **1865** and similar horiz design. Multicoloured. P 13.
MS4976 30st. Type **1865**; 40st. Robert Peary, 1856–1920 .... 34·00　30·00
　No. **MS**4976 is from a limited printing.

1866 Mother and Cubs   **1867** *Viola rhodopaea*

(Des Rosen Toshev)

2015 (23 Oct). Endangered Species. Eurasian Wolf (*Canis lupus lupus*). T **1866** and similar horiz designs. Multicoloured. P 13.
4977		65st. Type **1866**...	2·50	2·30
		a. Block or strip of 4. Nos. 4977/4980........	22·00	
4978		80st. Wolf, crouching......................................	3·00	2·75
4979		1l.40 Wolf, facing left....................................	5·00	4·50
4980		3l. Group of Wolves..	10·50	9·50
4977/4980 Set of 4..			19·00	17·00
MS4981 117×97 mm. Nos. 4977/4980			22·00	20·00

Nos. 4977/4980 were printed, both in sheets, and together, *se-tenant*, in blocks of four stamps.

(Des Stefan Gruev)

2015 (6 Nov). Mountain Flowers. Veliko Turnovo 2015 National Philatelic Exhibition. Sheet 145×83 mm containing T **1867** and similar vert designs. Multicoloured. P 13×13½.
MS4982 10st. Type **1867**; 50st. *Veronica kellererii*; 65st. *Papaver degenii*; 1l. *Colchicum borisii* .... 9·00   8·00

1868 Peter and Assen   **1869** Locomotive, 1891

(Des Cyrill Gogov)

2015 (8 Nov). 830th Anniversary of Peter and Assen's Uprising and Restoration of the Bulgarian State. Sheet 52×60 mm. P 13.
MS4983 **1868** 1l.50 multicoloured..................... 5·75   5·25

(Des Maglena Konstantinova)

2015 (18 Nov). Transport. Old Railway Stations and Locomotives. Sheet 125×95 mm containing T **1869** and similar horiz designs. Multicoloured. P 13.
MS4984 65st. Type **1869**; 1l. Locomotive, 1897; 1l.50 Locomotive, 1887; 2l. Locomotive, 1890...................... 19·00   18·00

The stamps of No. **MS**4984 share a common background design of 19th-century railway stations.

1870 Emblem   **1871** Symbols of Christmas

(Des Phillip Boyadjiev)

2015 (1 Dec). Technology+Innovation Network, Science and Technology Park. P 13.
4985 **1870** 1l. indigo, apple-green and chrome-yellow .... 3·75   3·50

(Des Nikolay Tsachev)

2015 (2 Dec). Christmas. P 13×13½.
4986 **1871** 1l. multicoloured.............................. 3·75   3·50

1872 4th-century Roman Theatre

(Des Tatyana Uzunova)

2015 (21 Dec). Plovdiv. European Capital of Culture 2019. Sheet 87×73 mm. P 13½×13.
MS4987 **1872** 1l. multicoloured............................. 4·00   3·50

1873 Emil Dimitrov

2015 (23 Dec). 75th Birth Anniversary of Emil Dimitrov (singer). P 13.
4988 **1873** 65st. multicoloured.......................... 2·50   2·30

1874 Envelope as Postman (as T **1659**)

(Des Stoyan Dechev)

2015 (23 Dec). Postcrossing (people from many countries sending each other traditional postcards). P 13.
4989 **1874** 1l. multicoloured................................ 4·25   3·75

1875 Mask

(Des Lyudmil Veselinov)

2016 (28 Jan). 25th International Festival of Masquerade Games, Surova. UNESCO List of Intangible Cultural Heritage of Humanity. Sheet 101×71 mm. P 13½×13.
MS4990 **1875** 1l.50 multicoloured..................... 5·75   5·25

An imperforate miniature sheet containing a single 65st. stamp showing Seuthes III and coins was printed in limited numbers and released on 28 February 2016.

1876 Asen Stareyshinski and Posters

(Des Nenko Atanasov. Litho)

2016 (30 Mar). 80th Birth Anniversary of Asen Stareyshinski (artist). P 13.
4991 **1876** 65st. multicoloured.......................... 2·50   2·30

1877 Roller painting Contaminated Landscape Green

(Des Doxia Sergidou (Nos. 4992 and 4995) or Viliam Kitanov (others).)

2016 (26 Apr). Europa. Think Green. T **1877** and similar horiz design. Multicoloured.

(a) Sheet stamps and miniature sheet. P 13 (with one diamond-shaped hole on each horiz side.)

4992	1l. Type **1877**...............................	3·25	3·00
4993	2l. Leaf and brush painting industrial smog green.....................	7·25	6·50
MS4994	71×103 mm. As Nos. 4992/4993.......	11·00	10·00

(b) Booklet stamps. P 13×imperf.

4995	1l. As Type **1877**.........................	3·25	3·00
	a. Booklet pane. No. 4995×4	13·50	
4996	2l. As No. 4993.............................	6·75	6·25
	a. Booklet pane. No. 4996×4	28·00	

Post Europ decided that member countries should issue a joint stamp, 'Think Green', to that end a design-a-stamp competition was held which was won by Doxia Sergidou of Cyprus.

The booklet panes Nos. 4995a and 4996a, respectively, each have one straight horizontal and one vertical edge, giving stamps with either left or right vertical and either upper or lower edges imperforate depending on position.

1878 Pencho Slaveykov

(Des Todor Angeliev)

2016 (27 Apr). 150th Birth Anniversary of Pencho Petkov Slaveykov (poet). P 13.

4997	**1878**	65st. multicoloured.........................	2·50	2·30

1879 Ham riding Mercury-Redstone 2, 31 January 1961

(Des Tahcin Ahmed. Litho)

2016 (28 Apr). Space 2016. Year of the Monkey. 55th Anniversary of Ham's Space Flight (first hominid in space). Sheet 86×74 mm. P 13.

MS4998	**1879**	2l. multicoloured..........................	8·00	7·25

No. **MS**4998 was also available, in limited numbers, imperforate, with the emblem of New York Stamp Show 2016 displayed in the margin.

1880 St George's Church

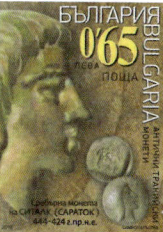

1881 Tsar Sitalces (Sitalk) and Coins

(Des Svetlin Balezdrov)

2016 (5 May). 180th Anniversary of St George's Church, Kavarna. P 13 (with one diamond-shaped hole on each vert side).

4999	**1880**	65st. multicoloured.........................	2·50	2·30

(Des Simeon Krastev)

2016 (10 May). Antique Thracian Coins. T **1881** and similar vert designs. Multicoloured. P 13.

5000	65st. Type **1881**...........................	2·50	2·30
5001	1l. Tsar Metok and coins................	3·75	3·50
5002	1l.50 Hebrizelm and coins.............	5·25	4·75
5003	2l. Kotis I and coins......................	7·25	6·75
5000/5003	Set of 4...	17·00	16·00
MS5004	162×1293 mm. As Nos. 5000/5003....	19·00	18·00

Nos. 5000/5003, respectively, were each issued with a stamp-size label, the whole forming a composite design.

1882 Old Man

(Des Plamen Valchev)

2016 (12 May). Birth Centenary of Alexander Poplilov (artist and stamp designer). P 13½×13.

5005	**1882**	65st. multicoloured.........................	2·50	2·30

1883 Team Members

(Des Ventsislav Yordanov)

2016 (15 May). Centenary of FC Beroe, Stara Zagora. P 13.

5006	**1883**	65st. multicoloured.........................	2·50	2·30

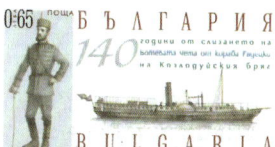

1884 Hristo Botev and *Radetsky*

(Des Atanas Atanasov)

2016 (18 May). 140th Anniversary of Hristo Botev's Disembarkation from Steam Ship *Radetsky* in Uprising against Ottoman Occupation. P 13.

5007	**1884**	65st. multicoloured.........................	2·50	2·30

1885 Ships

(Des Valentin Shtinkov)

2016 (26 May). 150th Anniversary of Ruse Port. P 13½×13.

5008	**1885**	1l. multicoloured............................	3·75	3·50

1886 Chess Pieces

(Des Ivan Gazdov)

2016 (12 July). Chess. Sheet 83×93 mm. P 13×13½.
MS5009 **1886** 3l. multicoloured............................. 9·00 8·75

1887 Stork migrating, Israeli and Bulgarian Flags

(Des Tuvia Kurtz, Miri Nistor, Lalo Nikolov)

2016 (13 Sept). Fauna: Bird Migration. White Stork. P 13.
5010 **1887** 2l.20 multicoloured............................. 6·25 5·75
A stamp of a similar design was issued by Israel.

1888 Exarch Anthim I

(Des Ludmil Metodiev)

2016 (15 Sept). Birth Bicentenary of Exarch Anthim I (educationalist and clergyman). P 13½×13.
5011 **1888** 65st. multicoloured............................. 2·50 2·30

1889 Tsarevgrad Tarnov

(Des Tetyana Uzunova)

2016 (22 Sept). Trapezitsa Architectural Museum Reserve, Veliko Tyrnovo (restored with the support of the Heydar Aliyev Foundation). Sheet 86×75 mm. P 13.
MS5012 **1889** 1l.50 multicoloured............................. 5·75 5·25
A stamp of a similar design was issued by Azerbaijan.

1890 Griffon Vulture, Vulchi Dol Reserve

(Des Dilyana Attanassova-Elshishka)

2016 (7 Oct). Wiki loves Earth Wikimedia Commons International Photographic Competition 2016. P 13.
5013 **1890** 2l. multicoloured............................. 7·25 6·75

1891 Bugler and Score

(Des Tetyana Uzunova)

2016 (7 Oct). Centenary of *Great is our Soldier* (march of 23rd Shipka Infantry Regiment, World War I) (Official Anthem of Bulgarian Army since 2001). Sheet 79×108 mm. P 13.
MS5014 **1891** 2l. multicoloured............................. 8·00 7·25

1892 Laying Eggs   **1892a** British Blue Cat

(Des Denitsa Peneva)

2016 (21 Oct). Endangered Species. Spur-thighed Tortoise (*Testudo graeca*). T **1892** and similar horiz designs. Multicoloured. P 13.
5015   65st. Type **1892**............................. 2·10 1·90
5016   80st. Eggs hatching............................. 3·25 2·75
5017   1l.40 Tortoise facing left............................. 5·25 4·75
5018   3l.10 Two Tortoises............................. 10·50 9·50
5015/5018 Set of 4............................. 19·00 17·00
MS5019 106×87 mm. As Nos. 5015/5018............................. 22·00 20·00

(Des Rosen Toshev)

2016 (22 Oct). International Collectors Fair. Bulcollecto 2016. Supercat of Bulgaria (British Shorthair Cat). Sheet 92×102 mm. Imperf.
MS5019*a* **1892a** 65st. multicoloured............................. 34·00 30·00
No. **MS**5019*a* is from a limited printing.

1893 BMW R 1200GS

(Des Emiliyan Stankev)

2016 (22 Oct). Transport. Adventure Motorcycles. T **1893** and similar horiz designs. Multicoloured. P 13½×13.
5020   65st. Type **1893**............................. 2·10 1·90
5021   1l.50 Suzuki V-Strom 1000............................. 5·25 4·75
5022   2l. Honda VFR800X Crossrunner............................. 7·25 6·75
5023   3l. Ducati Multistrada 1200S............................. 10·50 9·50
5020/5023 Set of 4............................. 23·00 21·00
MS5024 158×83 mm. As Nos. 5020/5023............................. 26·00 24·00
An imperforate miniature sheet, containing a single 65st. stamp, as T **1893** was also released.

1894 Inflatable Landing Craft   **1895** Cat as Fireplace

(Des Ivelina Velinova)

2016 (14 Nov). 25th Anniversary of Bulgarian Antarctic Expedition. P 13.
5025   1894   65st. multicoloured .... 2·50   2·30

(Des Nikolay Mladenov)

2016 (16 Nov). Christmas. P 13×13½.
5026   1895   1l. multicoloured .... 3·75   3·50

1896 Louis-Emil Eyer (Swiss-Bulgarian sportsman) and Flags

1897 *Self-portrait*

(Des Lyiba Tomova)

2016 (16 Nov). Centenary of Bulgaria–Switzerland Diplomatic Relations. P 13.
5027   1896   1l. multicoloured .... 3·75   3·50

(Des Deya Valchena)

2016 (17 Nov). Birth Bicentenary of Dimitar Dobrovitch (artist). Sheet 140×78 mm containing T 1897 and similar vert design. Multicoloured. P 13×13½.
MS5028   65st. Type 1897; 2l. *The Spinner* .... 10·00   9·00
No. MS5028 also contains two stamp-sized labels.

1898 Konstantin Velichkov (founder)

(Des Todor Vardjiev)

2016 (22 Nov). 120th Anniversary of National Academy of Arts P 13.
5029   1898   65st. multicoloured .... 2·50   2·30

1899 Vassil Yonchev, Typefaces and Books

1900 Georgi Bonchev

(Des Alexandra Gogova)

2016 (22 Nov). Birth Centenary of Vasil Yonchev (painter and book illustrator). P 13.
5030   1899   65st. multicoloured .... 2·50   2·30

(Des Soyan Dechev)

2016 (7 Dec). 150th Birth Anniversary of Georgi Bonchev (academician). P 13½×13½.
5031   1900   65st. multicoloured .... 2·50   2·30

1901 National Palace of Culture

(Des Lyudmil Vesselinov)

2016 (9 Dec). 35th Anniversary of National Palace of Culture. P 13½×13.
5032   1901   1l.50 multicoloured .... 5·75   5·25
No. 5032 was printed, *se-tenant*, with a stamp-size label attached at right, showing exhibits.

1902 Vladimir Stoychev

1903 Rooster

(Des Iliya Gruev)

2017 (24 Feb). 125th Birth Anniversary of Vladimir Stoychev (general and diplomat). Sheet 81×61 mm. P 13.
MS5033   1902   2l. multicoloured .... 8·00   7·25

(Des Apostol Apostolov)

2017 (28 Feb). Chinese New Year. Year of the Rooster. Sheet 80×85 mm. Imperf.
MS5034   1903   65st. multicoloured .... 34·00   30·00
No. MS5034 is from a limited printing.

1904 Aircraft

(Des Svetlin Balezdrov)

2017 (22 Mar). 70th Anniversary of Bulgarian Aviation. P 13½×13.
5035   1904   65st. multicoloured .... 2·75   2·50
No. 5035 also contains a perforated stamp-size label showing aircraft's shadow.

1905 Emblem

(Des Emilio Borata)

2017 (4 Apr). Centenary of Rotary International. P 13½×13.
5036   1905   2l. multicoloured .... 7·25   6·75

1906 Young Couple

(Des Georgi Yankov)

2017 (7 Apr). Varna. European Youth Capital 2017. P 13½×13.
5037   1906   1l. multicoloured .... 3·75   3·50

1907 Mosaic

(Des Nenko Atanasov)

2017 (11 Apr). Plovdiv. European Capital of Culture 2019. Antique Mosaics. Sheet 121×80 mm containing T **1907** and similar horiz design. Multicoloured. P 13.
MS5038 1l. Type **1907**; 1l.50 Mosaic showing Crane.... 10·00   9·00
 No. **MS**5038 also contains two stamp-size labels showing mosaics.

1908 Ella Fitzgerald

(Des Rosen Toshev)

2017 (28 Apr). Birth Centenary of Ella Fitzgerald (singer). Sheet 95×95 mm. P 13.
MS5039   **1908**   2l. multicoloured........................ 8·00   7·25
 No. **MS**5039 is also available imperforate from a limited printing.

1909 Eurocopter AS 565 MB Panther

(Des Valentin Shtinkov)

2017 (29 Apr). Centenary of Bulgarian Naval Aviation. P 13.
5040   **1909**   65st. multicoloured........................ 2·50   2·30

1910 Euxinograd   **1911** Toscanini

(Des Emilian Stankev)

2017 (4 May). Europa. Castles. T **1910** and similar horiz design. Multicoloured.

 (a) Sheet stamps. P 13 (with one large indented hole on each horiz side)
5041   65st. Type **1910**.................................... 3·25   2·75
5042   2l.10 Patriarchal Cathedral, Tsarevets .... 7·25   6·75
MS5043 85×106 mm. Nos. 5041/5042 .... 11·00 10·00

 (b) Booklet stamps. P 13×imperf (one horiz side)
5043a   65st. As Type **1910** .... 3·25   2·75
   aa. Booklet pane. No. 5043a/5043b,
       each×4 .... 43·00
5043b   2l.10 As No. 5042 .... 7·25   6·75
 Nos. 5041 and 5042, respectively, were printed both in sheets, and, each×4, in booklets of eight stamps.
 The booklet panes have straight edges, giving stamps with either top or bottom imperforate.

(Des Atanas Atanasov)

2017 (4 May). 150th Birth Anniversary of Arturo Toscanini (composer). P 13.
5044   **1911**   1l. multicoloured........................ 4·00   3·50
 No. 5044 was printed, *se-tenant*, with a stamp-size label, showing Toscanini's signature and baton, at left.

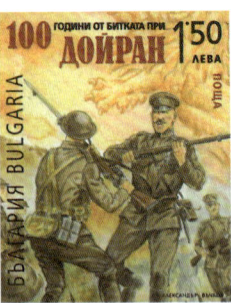

1912 Soldiers

(Des Alexander Vachkov)

2017 (9 May). Centenary of Battle of Doiran. Sheet 58×82 mm. P 13×13½.
MS5045   **1912**   1l.50 multicoloured................ 5·75   5·25

1913 *Delphinus delphis ponticus* (Black Sea Dolphin)

(Des Natalia Kohal and Kapka Kaneva. Litho)

2017 (22 May). Flora and Fauna of the Black Sea. Sheet 87×95 mm containing T **1913** and similar horiz design. Multicoloured. P 13.
MS5046 65st. Type **1913**; 2l. *Barnea candida* .... 11·00 10·00

1914 Grigor Vachkov   **1915** Embroidered Rose

(Des Rada Miladinova. Litho)

2017 (26 May). 85th Birth Anniversary of Grigor Vachkov (actor). P 13½×13.
5047   **1914**   65st. multicoloured........................ 2·50   2·30

(Des Margarita Doncheva. Litho)

2017 (2 June). Rose Festival, Kazanlak. P 13×13½.
5048   **1915**   65st. multicoloured........................ 2·50   2·30

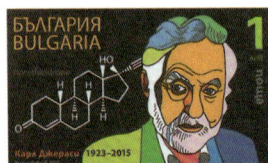

1916 Carl Djerassi

(Des Georgi Pavlov. Litho)

2017 (8 June). Carl Djerassi (chemist and writer) Commemoration. P 13.

| 5049 | **1916** | 1l. multicoloured | 3·75 | 3·50 |

1917 Simeon Saxe-Coburg-Gotha

1918 Ahtopol

(Des Lyudmil Metodiev. Litho)

2017 (16 June). 80th Birth Anniversary of Simeon Saxe-Coburg-Gotha (King Simeon II 1943–1946, Prime Minister 2001–2005). P 13.

| 5050 | **1917** | 1l.50 multicoloured | 5·75 | 5·25 |

No. 5050 was issued with a *se-tenant* stamp-size label.

(Des Todor Vardjiev. Litho)

2017 (22 June). Lighthouses of the Bulgarian Black Sea Coast. T **1918** and similar vert designs. Multicoloured. P 13.

5051		65st. Type **1918**	2·50	2·30
5052		1l. Cape Shabla	3·75	3·50
5053		1l.50 Burgas East Mole	5·25	4·75
5054		2l. Cape Galata	7·25	6·75
5051/5054		Set of 4	17·00	16·00
MS5055		93×125 mm. 65st. As Type **1918**; 1l. As No. 5052; 1l.50 As No. 5053; 2l. As No. 5054	19·00	18·00

1919 Ivan Aivazovsky and *The Ninth Wave* (detail)

1920 Rayna Knyaginya

(Des Nikolai Tsavhev. Litho)

2017 (26 July). Birth Bicentenary of Ivan Aivazovsky (artist). P 13.

| 5056 | **1919** | 1l. multicoloured | 3·75 | 3·50 |

(Des Ivelina Velinova. Litho)

2017 (27 July). Bandung 2017. World Philatelic Exhibition. Sheet 72×72 mm containing horiz designs T **1848**. Multicoloured. P 13×imperf.

MS5057 5st.×2 Clock with Zodiac Display (As Type **1848**)×2; 30st.×2 Rocco clock (As No. 4950)×2 .... 25·00 23·00

The stamps of No. **MS**5057 are imperforate between the designs. No. **MS**5057 is from a limited printing.

(Des Simeon Krustev. Litho)

2017 (28 July). Death Centenary of Rayna Popgeogieva Futekova (Rayna Knyaginya) (teacher and revolutionary). P 13.

| 5058 | **1920** | 1l. multicoloured | 3·75 | 3·50 |

1921 Rayko Raychev

(Des Damyan Damyanov. Litho)

2017 (8 Aug). Birth Centenary of Rayko Raychev (pathologist). P 13.

| 5059 | **1921** | 65st. multicoloured | 2·50 | 2·30 |

1922 Emblem

(Des Tetyana Uzunova. Litho)

2017 (28 Aug). International Year of Sustainable Tourism for Development. Sheet 98×71 mm. P 13.

MS5060 **1922** 2l.10 multicoloured .... 8·00 7·25

1923 Symbols of Airport

(Des Emilio Borata. Litho)

2017 (13 Sept). 80th Anniversary of Sofia Airport. P 13.

| 5061 | **1923** | 65st. multicoloured | 2·50 | 2·30 |

1924 Symbols of Space Exploration

1925 Dimitar Trendafilov

(Des Christo Alexiev. Litho)

2017 (9 Oct). 60th Anniversary of Bulgarian Astronautical Society. Sheet 48×80 mm. P 13.

MS5062 **1924** 65st. multicoloured .... 2·75 2·50

(Des Nenko Attanassov. Litho)

2017 (11 Oct). 80th Birth Anniversary of Dimitar Trendafilov (graphic artist and calligrapher). P 13.

| 5063 | **1925** | 65st. multicoloured | 2·75 | 2·50 |

No. 5063 was printed, *se-tenant*, with a stamp-size label at right showing calligraphy.

1926 Pelé scoring his first Goal for Brazil and Trophy (*Illustration reduced, actual size 96×31 mm*)

(Des Velichka Yordanova. Litho)

2017 (20 Oct). Brasilia 2017 World Philatelic Exhibition. Sheet 96×85mm. P 13×imperf.

MS5064 **1926** 1l. multicoloured, plus 2 labels .... 22·00 20·00

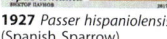
1927 *Passer hispaniolensis* (Spanish Sparrow)

1928 Roller Skates

BULGARIA 2017

(Des Victor Paunov. Litho)

2017 (21 Oct). International Stamp Exhibition BULCOLLECTO 2017, Plovdiv. Birds, Sparrows. T **1927** and similar vert designs. Multicoloured. P 13.

5065		65st. Type **1927**	2·50	2·30
5066		1l. *Passer montanus* (Eurasian Tree Sparrow)	3·75	3·50
5067		1l.50 *Passer domesticus* (House Sparrow)	5·25	4·75
5068		2l. *Petronia petronia* (Rock Sparrow)	7·25	6·75
5065/5068	Set of 4		17·00	16·00
MS5069 97×117 mm As Nos. 5065/5068			24·00	21·00

No. **MS**5069 was available with two marginal inscriptions, one for the exhibition, the other inscribed Fauna.

(Des Stoyan Dechev. Litho)

2017 (21 Oct). Transport. Alternative City Transport. T **1928** and similar horiz designs. Multicoloured. P 13½×13.

5070		65st. Type **1928**	2·50	2·30
5071		1l.40 Segway	4·50	4·25
5072		1l.50 Trainers and hoverboard	5·00	4·50
5073		2l. Scooter	6·75	6·00
5070/5073	Set of 4		17·00	15·00
MS5074 158×83 mm. As Nos. 5070/5073			22·00	20·00

1929 Emblem **1930** Emblem

(Des Todor Angeliev. Litho)

2017 (1 Nov). First Bulgarian Presidency of Council of the European Union. P 13.
5075 **1929** 1l. multicoloured .... 3·25 3·00

(Des Phillip Boyadjiev. Litho)

2017 (2 Nov). 20th Anniversary of Communication Regulation Commission. P 13.
5076 **1930** 65st. new blue, black and vermilion .... 2·50 2·30

1931 Stained Glass Window **1932** J. Palencia

(Des Nikolay Mladenov. Litho)

2017 (16 Nov). Christmas. P 13×13½.
5077 **1931** 1l. multicoloured .... 3·25 3·00

(Des Ventsislav Yordanov. Litho)

2017 (28 Nov). 65th Death Anniversary of Julio Palencia (used his position to save Jews during WWII). P 13.
5078 **1932** 1l.50 multicoloured .... 5·25 4·75

1933 Zeppelin L59

(Des Emiliyan Stankev. Litho)

2017 (14 Dec). Centenary of First Zeppelin Flight. Sheet 101×101 mm. P 13½×13.
MS5079 **1933** 65s. multicoloured .... 55·00 48·00

1934 Boys eating Grapes and Melon

(Des Kapka Kaneva. Litho)

2017 (14 Dec). 400th Birth Anniversary of Bartolomé Esteban Murillo (artist). P 13.
5080 **1934** 1l. multicoloured .... 3·25 3·00

1935 Dan Kolov

(Des Ivan Gazdov. Litho)

2017 (19 Dec). 125th Birth Anniversary of Dan Kolov (Doncho Kolev Danev) (wrestler). P 13.
5081 **1935** 65st. multicoloured .... 2·50 2·30

1936 Emblem and St Sofia (statue)

(Des Valentin Stinkov)

2018 (20 Feb). Sofia. European Capital of Sport. P 13.
5082 **1936** 1l.50 multicoloured .... 4·75 4·25

No. 5082 was printed with a stamp-size label showing stylised athletes at left.

1937 Stylised Dog

(Des Ralitsa Nikolova. Litho)

2018 (23 Feb). Chinese New Year. Year of the Dog. Sheet 85×83 mm.
MS5083 **1937** 65st. multicoloured .... 22·00 19·00

No. **MS**5083 was available in two formats, one on white paper with gum, the second on granite paper with no gum and with perforated number in the margin.

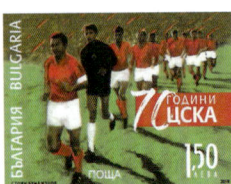

1938 Players

2018 BULGARIA

(Des Stoyan Bundjulov)

2018 (7 Mar). Centenary of CSKA Sofia. Sheet 86×66 mm. P 13.
MS5084 **1938** 1l.50 multicoloured................................ 5·00   4·50

No. MS5084 was available in two formats, one on white paper with gum, the second on granite paper with no gum and with perforated number in the margin.

1939 Eduard Ivanovich von Totleben   **1940** Templars

(Des Christina Borissova)

2018 (20 Mar). 140th Anniversary of Russo–Turkish War of Liberation. Sheet 168×96 mm containing T **1939** and similar vert design. P 13.
MS5085 1l. Type **1939**; 1l.80 General Nikolai
Grigorevich Stoletov .... 9·25   8·00

(Des Yasen Guzelev)

2018 (17 Apr). 900th Anniversary of Order of Knights Templars (Poor Fellow-Soldiers of Christ and of the Temple of Solomon). Sheet 92×63 mm. P 13×13½.
MS5086 **1940** 2l.50 multicoloured................................ 8·25   7·25

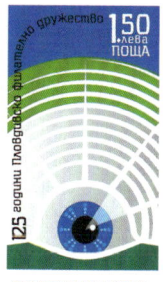 

1941 Emblem   **1942** Covered Bridge, Lovech

(Des Petar Chuchuligov)

2018 (20 Apr). 125th Anniversary of Plovdiv Philatelic Society (beginning of organised philatelic movement in Bulgaria). Sheet 70×86 mm. P 13×13½.
MS5087 **1941** 1l.50 multicoloured................................ 5·00   4·50

(Des Maya Cholakova)

2018 (25 Apr). Europa. Bridges. T **1942** and similar horiz design. Multicoloured. P 13½.
5088 95st. multicoloured.. 3·00   2·75
  a. Pair. Nos. 5088 and 5089............................... 9·50   9·25
5088b 95st. sepia, orange-brown and black................ 3·00   2·75
  c. Booklet pane. No. 5088b×4............................ 12·00
5089 2l. multicoloured.. 6·50   5·50
5089a 2l. sepia, emerald and black............................ 6·50   5·50
  b. Booklet pane. No. 5089a×4........................... 26·00
5088/5089a Set of 4 .... 17·00   15·00
MS5090 85×126 mm. 2l.95 As Nos. 5088 and 5089...... 9·75   8·50
Designs: 95st. (No. 5088) T **1942**; 95st. (No. 5088c) As T **1942**; 2l. (No. 5089) Kadin Most Bridge, Nevestono; 2l. (No. 5089b) As No. 5089.

Nos. 5088/5089 were printed, se-tenant, in vertical pairs within blocks of four stamps in sheets of eight stamps and two stamp-size labels.

Nos. 5088b and 5089a, respectively, each×4, were also printed in booklets of eight stamps.

1943 Georgi Asparuho   **1944** Emblem

(Des Emilian Stankev)

2018 (4 May). 75th Birth Anniversary of Georgi Asparuhov (footballer). Sheet 90×116 mm. P 13½×13.
MS5091 **1943** 2l. multicoloured................................. 6·75   5·75

(Des Parashkev Feredjanov)

2018 (16 May). Bulgarian Presidency of Council of the European Union. P 13×13½.
5092 **1944** 1l.50 multicoloured................................ 4·75   4·25

 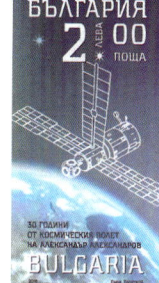

1945 Christ using Compass   **1946** Mir Space Station

(Des Atanas Atanasov)

2018 (19 May). 25th Anniversary of United Grand Lodge of Bulgaria. P 13×13½.
5093 **1945** 65st. multicoloured............................... 2·10   1·80
MS5094 85×126 mm. 2l.50 As Type **1945**................... 8·25   7·25

(Des Emil Hristov)

2018 (5 June). 30th Anniversary of Alexander Alexandrov's Space Flight on Mir Manned Orbital Station. Sheet 101×101 mm. P 13×13½.
MS5095 **1946** 2l. multicoloured................................ 6·75   5·75

1947 Player and Ball

(Des Plamen Valchev)

2018 (14 June). World Cup Football Championships, Russia. T **1947** and similar horiz design. Multicoloured. P 13.
5096 1l. Type **1947**.. 3·25   2·75
5097 2l. Football in orbit.. 6·50   5·50
MS5098 132×57 mm. 3l. As Nos. 5096/5097............... 9·75   8·75

A miniature sheet containing a single 65st. stamp commemorating the 80th Anniversary of Bulgaria Philatelists was printed in limited numbers and released on 20 July 2018.

1948 Soldiers

BULGARIA 2018

(Des Alexander Vachkov)

2018 (20 July). 140th Anniversary of the Bulgarian Army. Sheet 75×55 mm. P 13½×13.

MS5099 **1948** 1l.50 multicoloured................................. 5·00 4·50

1949 Mounted Soldiers

(Des Nenko Atanasov)

2018 (15 Aug). 1300th Anniversary of Khan Tervel's Victory over the Arab Army. Sheet 95×80 mm. P 13½×13.

MS5100 **1949** 2l. multicoloured...................................... 6·75 5·75

1950 Modern Locomotive

(Des Maglena Konstantinova)

2018 (26 Sept). 130th Anniversary of Bulgarian State Railways. T **1950** and similar horiz designs. Multicoloured. P 13.

5101	65st. Type **1950**...		2·10	1·80
5102	1l.20 Steam locomotive.................................		3·75	3·25
5103	1l.50 Steam locomotive and passengers in Edwardian dress		4·75	4·25
5104	2l. Carriages and passengers		6·50	5·50
5101/5104	Set of 4		15·00	13·50
MS5105	127×96 mm. 5l.35 As Nos. 5101/5104..............		18·00	16·00

1951 Cranes and Lifting Gear

(Des Tahsin Ahmed)

2018 (18 Oct). 180th Anniversary of the Port of Lom. P 13.

5106 **1951** 95st. multicoloured .... 3·00 2·75

1952 *Bos primigenius* (Aurochs)

(Des Deya Valcheva)

2018 (19 Oct). Fauna. Extinct Species. T **1952** and similar horiz design. Multicoloured. P 13½×13.

5107	65st. Type **1952**..		2·10	1·80
5108	1l.20 *Hydrodamalis gigas* (Steller's Sea Cow)..		3·75	3·25
5109	1l.50 *Thylacinus cynocephalus* (Tasmanian Wolf)...		4·75	4·25
5110	2l. *Pinguinus impennis* (Great Auk)................		6·50	5·50
5107/5110	Set of 4		15·00	13·50
MS5111	101×71 mm. 65st As Type **1952**......................		2·20	1·90
MS5112	136×87 mm. 5l.35 As Nos. 5107/5110..............		18·00	16·00

1953 Thomas Mayne Reid (American novelist)

1954 St Constantine and St Helena's Icon and Bare Feet

(Des Svetlin Balezdrov)

2018 (19 Oct). Artists' Birth Anniversaries. Sheet 108×87 mm containing T **1953** and similar horiz designs. Multicoloured. P 13×13½ (with one diamond-shaped hole on each horiz side).

MS5113 65st. Type **1953** (bicentenary); 65st. Charles-François Gounod (French composer) (bicentenary); 1l.50 Jacopo Tintoretto (Italian painter) (500th anniversary); 1l.50 Ingmar Bergman (Swedish director, writer and producer) (centenary)................. 14·50 12·50

(Des Margarita Doncheva)

2018 (20 Oct). Nestinarstvo. Barefoot Dance on Embers holding St Constantine and St Helena's Icon. Sheet 85×81 mm. P 13×13½.

MS5114 **1954** 2l. multicoloured...................................... 6·75 5·75

1955 Boris III

1956 Candle

(Des Todor Vardjiev)

2018 (20 Nov). Centenary of the Accession of Boris III to the Throne Tsar of the Bulgarians. Sheet 70×51 mm. P 13½×13.

MS5115 **1955** 2l. multicoloured...................................... 6·75 5·75

(Des Nikolay Mladenov)

2018 (28 Nov). Christmas. P 13.

5116 **1956** 1l.50 multicoloured................................... 4·75 4·25

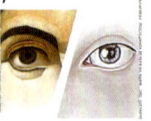
1957 Eyes

1958 Saints Cyril and Methodius monument and Library

(Des Ilia Gruev)

2018 (5 Dec). 70th Anniversary of National Art Gallery. P 13×13½.

5117 **1957** 1l.50 multicoloured .... 4·75 4·25

(Des Stoyan Dechev)

2018 (5 Dec). 140th Anniversary of Saints Cyril and Methodius National Library. P 13.

5118 **1958** 1l.50 multicoloured .... 4·75 4·25

No. 5118 has a stamp-size label showing Michail Bubotinov (founder), attached at right.

1959 University Building
1960 Symbols of Space Exploration

(Des Jaklina Simova)

2018 (8 Dec). 130th Anniversary of St Kliment Ohridski University, Sofia. P 13.
5119 **1959** 85st. multicoloured .... 2·75 2·40
No. 5119 has a stamp-size label, showing Evlogy and Hristo Georgiev (financiers of University building), attached at left.

Two sheets, one in a folder, each containing a 1l. stamp, celebrating the birth centenary of Nelson Mandela, were put on sale 12 December 2018, from a limited printing.

(Des Viliam Kitanov)

2018 (21 Dec). P 13.
5120 **1960** 1l. multicoloured .... 4·75 4·25

STAMP BOOKLETS

The following checklist covers, in simplified form, booklets issued by Spain. It is intended that it should be used in conjunction with the main listings and details of stamps and panes listed there are not repeated.

Prices are for complete booklets

Booklet No.	Date	Contents and Cover Price	Price
SB1	28.5.05	Europa. Gastronomy No. 4535b×2	12·00
SB2	22.4.08	Europa. The Letter Nos. 4664a and 4666a	30·00
SB3	28.4.09	Europa. Astronomy Nos. 4726a/4726b	24·00
SB4	23.4.10	Europa. Children's Books No. 4761a	11·00
SB5	4.4.12	Europa. Visit Bulgaria Nos. 4821ab and 4821cd	35·00
SB6	24.4.13	Europa. Postal Transport Nos. 4872aa and 4872ba	40·00
SB7	26.4.16	Europa. Think Green Nos. 4995a and 4996a	45·00
SB8	4.5.17	Europa. Castles No. 5043aa	45·00

Eastern Roumelia and South Bulgaria

40 Paras = 1 Piastre

A. EASTERN ROUMELIA

The Congress of Berlin, 1878, decided that Eastern Roumelia, south of the Balkan Mountains, should become semi-autonomous, and remain in the Turkish Empire.

(1) (2) 3

1880. Stamps of Turkey, handstamped with T **1**, in blue.
(a) Issue of Jan 1876
1   ½ pre. on 20pa. green (No. 78) .... 80·00 65·00
(b) T 9
2   20pa. plum and green .... £100 80·00
3   2pi. black and flesh £170 £120
4   5pi. rose and pale blue £500 £600
The 10pa. was prepared but not issued (*Price £70 un*).

1880. T **9** of Turkey handstamped with T **1** and further handstamped with T **2** (both in blue), in Philippopolis.
5   10pa. black and mauve £140 £110
The 10pa. overprinted with T **2** only was prepared but not issued (*Price £65 un*).

(Typo Constantinople)
1881. P 13½.
6   **3**   5pa. black and olive-green .... 23·00 1·60
7   10pa. black and blue-green .... 90·00 1·60
         a. Error. 10pa. black and carmine £750
8   20pa. black and carmine .... 2·00   1·40
9   1pi. black and pale blue .... 6·75   5·25
         b. Black and lilac-blue £375
10   5pi. red and grey-blue .... 65·00 £100
6/10 Set of 5 .... £160 £100
6s/10s H/S 'Obrasetz' (in Cyrillic) Set of 5 .... £600
The error consisting of No. 9 *se-tenant* with a 1pi. stamp of Turkey, formerly No. 9a, is listed under Turkey No. 93a.
Stamps of the above series perf 11½, *tête-bêche* pairs and imperforate stamps are from unissued remainder stocks.

1884. Colours changed. P 11½.
11 **3**   5pa. deep lilac and pale lilac .... 9·75   65
         a. Perf 13½ .... 1·30   4·50
12   10pa. bright green and pale green 40   65
         a. Perf 13½ .... 36·00 21·00

The following were prepared but not issued. *Prices un*.

	Perf 11½	Perf 13½	Perf 11½×13
20pa. Rose	65	25.00	†
1pi. blue	1.30	£170	65.00
5pi. brown	£475	£550	†

B. SOUTH BULGARIA

Following a revolt in favour of union with Bulgaria in Philippopolis (Plovdiv), the chief town of East Roumelia, the following stamps were issued by the new régime, the name being changed to South Bulgaria.

The dates of issue are according to the Julian Calendar then in use. In the 19th-century the Julian Calendar was 12 days behind the Gregorian Calendar.

(4) (5)

EASTERN ROUMELIA AND SOUTH BULGARIA 1885

T 4. Lion with four toes on each leg. Height from end of claw on left leg to top of crown, 14 mm.
T 5. Lion with three toes on each leg. Height of Lion 15 to 16 mm.

> There are many dangerous forgeries of these overprints, and collectors are warned to purchase only from responsible firms.

1885 (10 Sept). T **3** optd.

A. With T **4**
(i) Stamps of 1881. P 13½
(a) In dull blue or blue

13	5pa. black and olive-green	£400	£450
14	10pa. black and blue-green	£1100	£1000
15	20pa. black and carmine	£400	
16	1pi. black and blue	55·00	£110
17	5pi. red and grey-blue	£1100	

(b) In black

18	1pi. black and blue	44·00	95·00

(ii) Stamps of 1884. P 11½
(a) In dull blue or blue

19	5pa. deep lilac and pale lilac	41·00	£100
20	10pa. bright green and pale green	48·00	90·00
21	20pa. rose and pale rose	£350	£475

(b) In black

22	10pa. bright green and pale green (P 13½)	85·00	£140
23	20pa. rose and pale rose	65·00	£100

B. With T **5**
(i) Stamps of 1881. P 13½
(a) In dull blue or blue

24	20pa. black and carmine	£400	
25	1pi. black and blue	95·00	£120
26	5pi. red and grey-blue	£1000	

(b) In black

27	1pi. black and blue	80·00	£100
28	5pi. red and grey-blue	£800	

(ii) Stamps of 1884. P 11½
(a) In dull blue or blue

29	5pa. deep lilac and pale lilac	27·00	65·00
	a. Perf 13½	£100	£120
30	10pa. bright green and pale green	48·00	90·00
31	20pa. rose and pale rose	£325	£475

(b) In black

32	5pa. deep lilac and pale lilac	70·00	80·00
	a. Perf 13½	47·00	80·00
33	10pa. bright green and pale green	80·00	
34	20pa. rose and pale rose	65·00	80·00

Many of the above are found with inverted or double overprint.

(6)   (7)

Inscription= 'South Bulgaria'

T 6. Circular 'O' at top.
T 7. Oval 'O' at top.

1885 (11 Sept). T **3** optd.

A. With T **6**
(i) Stamps of 1881. P 13½

35	5pa. black and olive-green	£325	
36	10pa. black and blue-green	£375	
37	20pa. black and carmine	£160	£200
38	1pi. black and blue	£100	£130
39	5pi. red and grey-blue	£2500	

(ii) Stamps of 1884. P 11½

40	5pa. deep lilac and pale lilac	£275	£325
	a. Perf 13½	29·00	43·00
41	10pa. bright green and pale green	34·00	42·00
42	20pa. rose and pale rose	34·00	60·00

B. With T **7**
(i) Stamps of 1881. P 13½

43	5pa. black and olive-green	£375	£325
44	10pa. black and blue-green	£275	£325
45	20pa. black and carmine	£100	£120
46	1pi. black and blue	£140	£180
47	5pi. red and grey-blue	£2500	

(ii) Stamps of 1884. P 11½

48	5pa. deep lilac and pale lilac	£275	£350
	a. Perf 13½	34·00	55·00
49	10pa. bright green and pale green	65·00	80·00
50	20pa. rose and pale rose	34·00	33·00

Many of the above are known with inverted or double overprint.

Some of these stamps are known with red overprints, and with double overprints, one of each type, or in different colours, but these are extremely rare.

Bulgarian stamps were used in South Bulgaria from 1 October 1885.

BULGARIAN OCCUPATION OF ROMANIA

DOBRUJA DISTRICT, 1916–17

100 Stotinki = 1 Leva

(1)

1916–17. Stamps of Bulgaria of 1915, optd with T **1**. P 11½ (1st., 25st.) or 14 (others).

1	**23**	1st. slate (R.)	25	25
2	**26**	5st. purple-brown and green (R.)	4·75	3·00
3	**27**	10st. sepia and red-brown (B.)	45	35
4	**29**	25st. black and deep blue (B.)	45	35

Many errors of lettering in this overprint are known, also double and inverted overprints.

Epirus

100 Lepta = 1 Drachma

A. PROVISIONAL GOVERNMENT

At the end of 1913, after the Powers had decided that Epirus was to be included in Albania, the population, who were largely Greek, set up a Provisional Government and declared their autonomy.

1

1914 (10 Feb). Issued at Chimara. Handstamped. Seal in blue, value in second colour. Imperf. No gum.

1	**1**	1l. black and blue	£375	£225
2		5l. blue and red	£375	£225
3		10l. red and black	£375	£225
4		25l. blue and red	£375	£225
1/4 Set of 4			£1400	£800

The majority of stamps on the market are forgeries.

1914 (2 Mar). Issued at Argyrocastro. Stamps of Turkey variously surch 'ΑΥΤΟΝΟΜΟΣ ΗΠΕΙΡΟΣ' and value vertically reading up or down. (Types of Turkey are illustrated at beginning of Albania.)

*(a) On issue of 1908, T **25**. P 12*

5		1d. on 2½pi. black-brown (R.)	10·00	10·00
		a. Perf 13½		
6		2d. on 2½pi. black-brown (R.)	12·50	12·50
		a. Perf 13½		
7		5d. on 25pi. myrtle green	80·00	80·00
8		5d. on 50pi. brown	£150	£150

*(b) On issue of 1908, T **25** optd with T **26**. P 12*

9		40l. on 2pi. black (R.)	95·00	95·00
10		80l. on 2pi. black (R.)	95·00	95·00

*(c) On issue of 1909–1911, T **28**. P 12*

11		5l. on 10pa. green (R.)	2·50	2·50
12		10l. on 20pa. rose-carmine ('10' italic)	2·50	2·50
		a. Larger surch with '10' upright	2·50	2·50
13		20l. on 1pi. bright blue (R.)	2·50	2·50
14		25l. on 1pi. bright blue (R.)	2·50	2·50
15		30l. on 2pa. olive-green	2·50	2·50
16		40l. on 2pi. blue-black (R.)	2·50	2·50
17		50l. on 2pa. olive-green	2·75	2·75
18		80l. on 2pi. blue-black (R.)	3·00	3·00
19		1d. on 5pi. slate-purple	10·00	10·00
20		2d. on 5pi. slate-purple	12·50	12·50
21		5d. on 10pi. dull red	65·00	65·00
22		5d. on 50pi. brown	£150	£150

Surcharges on other stamps are trials.
Dangerous forgeries exist.

The following stamps were printed together in sheets: Nos. 5 and 6; 5a and 6a; 9 and 10; 12 and 12a; 13 and 14; 15 and 17; 16 and 18; 19 and 20. *Se-tenant* pairs may therefore be found.

2　　3　　ΕΛΛΗΝΙΚΗ
　　　　　　1914
　　　　　　ΧΕΙΜΑΡΡΑ
　　　　　　(4)

(Litho Aspiotis, Corfu)

1914. Zigzag roulette 14.

*(a) T **2** (inscr 'Epirus') (5.3.14)*

23	**2**	10l. carmine-red	65	65
24		25l. blue	70	70

*(b) T **3** (Inscr 'ΑΥΤΟΝΟΜΟΣ ΗΠΕΙΡΟΣ') (26.3.14)*

25	**3**	1l. orange	65	65
26		5l. green	65	65
27		50l. brown	80	80
28		1d. violet	2·10	2·10
29		2d. grey-black	18·00	18·00
30		5d. olive-green	23·00	23·00
23/30 Set of 8			42·00	42·00

1914 (24 Aug). Issued at Chimara. Types of Greece (2l. and 3l. engraved, others litho) optd with T **4**, with or without Greek initials 'S.S.' (=S Spiromilos) in manuscript in black.

31	**29**	1l. green	28·00	28·00
32	**30**	2l. carmine	28·00	28·00
33	**29**	3l. vermilion	31·00	31·00
34	**31**	5l. green	31·00	31·00
35	**29**	10l. carmine	31·00	31·00
36	**30**	20l. grey-lilac	65·00	65·00
37		25l. ultramarine	£100	£100
38	**31**	50l. indigo-purple	£130	£130
31/38 Set of 8			£400	£400

Dangerous forgeries exist.

 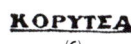

5　　　ΚΟΡΥΤΣΑ
　　　　(6)

(Litho Aspiotis, Corfu)

1914 (28 Aug). Zigzag roulette 14.

39	**5**	1l. brown and blue	90	1·80
40		5l. yellow-green and blue	90	1·80
41		10l. rose and blue	90	1·80
42		25l. indigo and blue	90	1·80
43		50l. violet and blue	90	2·30
44		1d. carmine and blue	6·25	10·00
45		2d. yellow and blue	1·90	5·00
46		5d. deep green and blue	12·50	14·00
39/46 Set of 8			23·00	35·00

1914 (25 Sept). Issued at Koritza. Nos. 42/43 optd with T **6** in blue.

47	**5**	25l. indigo and blue	6·25	6·25
48		50l. violet and blue	19·00	19·00

7 King Constantine I of Greece

(Litho Papachrysantu, Athens)

1914 (25 Oct). Issued at Chimara. P 11½.

49	**7**	1l. yellow-green	£130	70·00
50		2l. orange-brown	65·00	50·00
51		5l. grey-blue	£130	50·00
52		10l. orange-brown	65·00	50·00
53		20l. carmine	65·00	50·00
54		25l. grey-blue	£130	70·00
55		50l. yellow-green	£130	75·00
56		1d. carmine	£130	75·00
57		2d. yellow-green	£190	£100
58		5d. orange-brown	£325	£225
49/58 Set of 10			£1200	£750

The stamps in the same colours were printed together in the sheet and it is possible to find stamps of different values *se-tenant*, but unused stamps are very scarce.

A　　　　　　　　B

1l., 2l., 3l., 5l., 10l., 25l., 30l., 40l. and 50l. values in design A and 1d., 2d., 3d., 5d., 10d. and 25d. values as design B (with different centres showing ancient coins) were privately produced, probably in early 1914, and are believed to have been printed in France. Following the seizure by Epirots of Moschopolis (Voskopojë) in June 1914 the commander of the local forces was persuaded to issue the stamps.

The majority of known covers are dated October or November 1914, are addressed to various stamp dealers and contained offers or shipments of the stamps. There is little evidence that the stamps were actually available to the general public for postal purposes. After the occupation of Epirus by Greek troops the remaining stock was sent to Athens where it was destroyed in 1931. (*Price for set of 15: £44 un; £120 c.t.o.*).

All values are known imperforate. Some values exist in different colours or with inverted centres. All except the 10d. and 25d. values can be found with a two-line overprint.

Various other purported issues of Epirus are considered to be bogus.

83	**31**	30l. carmine-red	9·50	9·50
84	**30**	40l. deep blue	11·00	11·00
85	**31**	50l. brown-purple	16·00	16·00

The 'I omitted' error occurs on position 28 and the 'No point after B' on position 52 of the sheet of 100.

In June 1916 Northern Epirus was taken over by Italian troops and after the war it was incorporated in Albania. For issues for this area made in 1940–1941, see under Albania (Greek Occupation).

B. NORTHERN EPIRUS

GREEK OCCUPATION

In December 1914 the Powers agreed to a provisional occupation of Epirus by Greek troops. This was the same area as that which had declared its autonomy but it was now known as Northern Epirus.

"Β. ΗΠΕΙΡΟΣ"
(**8**) (=Northern Epirus)

1914 (8 Dec)–**15**. Types of Greece optd with T **8** horizontally.

59	**35**	1l. brown	1·30	1·30
		a. Opt inverted	30·00	24·00
		b. Opt double	30·00	24·00
		c. Opt double, one inverted	31·00	25·00
60	**36**	2l. scarlet	1·90	1·90
		a. Opt inverted	30·00	24·00
		b. Opt double	30·00	24·00
		bc. Opt double, one inverted	35·00	28·00
		c. *Carmine* (1915)	3·25	3·25
		ca. Opt double	30·00	24·00
61		3l. orange	1·30	1·30
		a. Opt inverted	24·00	19·00
		b. Opt double	24·00	19·00
62	**35**	5l. green	1·90	1·90
		a. Opt inverted	41·00	33·00
63		10l. rose-red	3·25	3·25
		a. Opt inverted	60·00	47·00
64		20l. bright violet	10·50	10·50
		a. Opt inverted	60·00	47·00
65	**36**	25l. pale blue	3·75	3·75
		a. Opt inverted		
		b. Opt double		
66	**35**	30l. green	15·00	16·00
67	**36**	40l. indigo	19·00	21·00
68	**35**	50l. deep blue	21·00	24·00
69	**36**	1d. dull purple	£110	£110
		a. Opt inverted	£375	
		b. Opt double	£450	

Nos. 59/62 optd in red were not issued.

1915. Stamps of Greece, 1911–1913, optd with T **8** sideways (reading downwards on 5d., upwards on other values).

(a) Engraved

70	**29**	3l. vermilion	9·50	9·50
71	**31**	30l. carmine-red	65·00	65·00
72	**32**	1d. ultramarine	65·00	65·00
73		2d. vermilion	90·00	90·00
74		3d. carmine	£110	£110
75		5d. grey-blue		
		a. Opt double	£850	

(b) Lithographed

76	**29**	1l. green	1·30	1·30
		a. 'I' omitted	23·00	
77	**30**	2l. carmine	1·30	1·30
		a. 'I' omitted	23·00	
		b. No point after 'B'	23·00	
78	**29**	3l. vermilion	6·50	6·50
		a. No point after 'B'	38·00	
		b. Pair, one with opt omitted		
79	**31**	5l. green	1·30	1·30
		a. 'I' omitted	25·00	
		b. No point after 'B'	25·00	
		c. Opt double	28·00	
80	**29**	10l. carmine	2·50	2·50
81	**30**	20l. purple-grey	3·50	3·50
82		25l. blue	3·75	3·75
		a. No point after 'B'	35·00	

Greece

1861. 100 Lepta = 1 Drachma
2002. 100 cents = 1 Euro

KINGDOM

King Otho
6 February 1833–23 October 1862

King Otho was deposed, and a Provisional Government ruled Greece until Prince William of Denmark was chosen as King George I of the Hellenes.

The dates of issue are according to local computation on the Julian or Gregorian Calendar in use. In the 19th-century the Julian Calendar was 12 days behind the Gregorian Calendar. After 1900 the difference was 13 days. In Greece the Gregorian Calendar was introduced on 16 February 1923 which became 1 March.

Unoverprinted Greek stamps were used in Greek Post Offices in the Turkish Empire until their closure in 1881. Until 1863 the numbered cancellations noted in brackets were used, after that date town cancellations were also used: Constantinople (No. 95), Smyrna (No. 96), Alexandria (No. 97), Salonika (No. 98), Ioannina (No. 99), Galatz (No. 100), Ibraila (No. 101), Bucharest (No. 102), Larissa (No. 103), Preveza (No. 104), Arta (No. 105) and Volos (No. 135). There were also post offices in Crete at Canea (open Mar–Nov 1881, No. 162), Rethymnon (open 1881–1885, No. 163) and Iraklion (open 1881–1882, No. 164). Larissa, Arta and Volos became domestic post offices in 1881 after the cession of Thessaly to Greece.

PRICES. The prices for early Greek stamps are for fine specimens, with original gum if unused. Inferior specimens, both unused and used, are worth much less.

1 Hermes

Paris print

(Eng A. Barre. Electrotypes. Ptd first by E. Meyer, Paris, later at Athens)
1861 (1 Oct). T **1**. Paris print. Imperf. On cream paper unless otherwise stated.

		(i) Without figures at back		
1		1l. chocolate	£650	£600
		a. Red-brown	£850	£650
2		2l. olive-bistre	75·00	85·00
		a. Brown-buff/buff	75·00	85·00
3		5l. emerald/greenish	£850	£170
4		20l. blue/bluish	£1000	£120
		a. Deep blue/bluish	£1200	£275
		b. Pelure paper	£1600	£550
5		40l. mauve/blue	£350	£160
6		80l. carmine	£275	£160
		(ii) With large figures 8 mm high at back		
7		10l. red-orange/blue	£850	£600
		a. '0' of '10' inverted	—	£2000
		b. '1' of '10' inverted	—	£2750
		c. '10' inverted		
		d. Without '10' at back		

The figures on the back are outlined more thickly on the right-hand outer edge with the '0' also on the left inner curve. Inverted numerals can be identified by the thicker outer edge being wrongly on the left side. Only two examples of No. 7c are known.

The Paris-printed stamps have the shading on cheek and neck of Mercury made up of fine lines and dots. In those printed in Athens the lines are unbroken and thicker.

Trial impressions of Paris exist in many different shades, of which some are indistinguishable from those of the issued stamps. These are often found with false gum which is thin and smooth, differing greatly from that on the issued stamps, which is generally thick, often brownish, and always 'crackly'. Stamps with false gum are worth about the same as those without gum. The variety No. 7d comes from proof sheets. There is an essay of the 10l. in orange-red/*blue*, which is also without figures at the back.

Athens print

(I)   (II)

1861 (Nov)–**62**. First Athens print. On cream paper *unless otherwise stated.*

	A. Coarse print		
	(i) Without figures at back		
9A	2l. grey-brown (*shades*)/*straw*	90·00	£120
	a. Deep bistre-brown/*cream*	£100	£120
	c. Brown/*straw*	£6000	—
10A	20l. deep blue/*bluish* (*shades*) (quadrillé background)	—	£14000
	a. Ultramarine/*bluish* (*shades*)	—	£15000
	b. Ultramarine/*bluish* (thin paper)	—	£17000
	B. Fine print		
8B	1l. deep chocolate	£950	£1000
	a. Pale chocolate	£550	£550
	b. Yellowish chocolate	£350	£400
9B	2l. grey-brown (*shades*)/*straw*		
	a. Deep bistre-brown/*cream*	47·00	65·00
	b. Dull yellow-brown/*cream*	60·00	75·00
	(ii) With figures 6 mm high at back Figure at back of 5l., Type I		
11A	5l. green (*shades*)/*greenish*	£300	£160
	a. Yellow-green to olive-green/*greenish*	£300	£160
	b. Blue-green/*greenish*	£325	£130
	c. Emerald-green/*greenish*	£375	£180
	d. Double '5' at back	—	£3250
12A	10l. yellow-orange/*bluish*	£850	£170
	a. Ochre/*bluish green*	£1600	£225
	b. Vermilion/*bluish green*	£2000	£350
	d. '1' of '10' at back inverted	—	£1900
	e. '0' of '10' at back inverted	—	£1900
13A	20l. deep blue/*bluish*	£7500	£500
	a. Indigo-blue/*bluish*	£9000	£600
	b. Pale Prussian blue/*bluish*	£6000	£275
	c. Deep dull chalky blue/*bluish*	£8500	£450
	d. '0' of '20' at back inverted	—	£1700
	e. '20' at back double	—	£2500
14A	40l. mauve/*bluish*	£7500	£550
	a. Dull mauve/*bluish*	£7500	£550
	B. Fine print		
11B	5l. green (*shades*)/*greenish*	£250	£120
	a. Yellow-green to olive-green/*greenish*	£250	£120
	b. Blue-green/*greenish*	£325	£160
	c. Emerald-green/*greenish*	£325	£160
	d. Double '5' at back		
12B	10l. yellow-orange/*bluish*	£600	£120
	b. Vermilion/*bluish green*	£850	£180
	c. Red-orange/*bluish*	£1100	£250
	d. '1' of '10' at back inverted	—	£1800
	e. '0' of '10' at back inverted	—	
13B	20l. deep blue/*bluish*	£3500	£170
	d. '0' of '20' at back inverted		
	e. '20' at back double	—	

GREECE 1862

14B	40l. mauve/*bluish*	£4000	£425
	a. Dull mauve/*bluish*	£4000	£425
15B	80l. rose	£1300	£180
	a. Carmine	£1300	£180
	b. Deep carmine-red	£1300	£180

All values of the First Athens issue frequently present a cloudy whitish contour outlining various parts of the Hermes head, usually on one of the sides.

The 20l. without figures on the back (the earliest known printing in Athens), is known only with the postmarks '1', '13' and '44', whereas the Paris print in deep blue (No. 4a) is only known with the postmark '9'.

The following characteristics are also helpful for distinguishing these printings from subsequent ones:

(a) These stamps, with the exception of the 80l., were printed with the 'hard' method of printing (like the Paris and 1870 issues). They do not, therefore, present any reliefs of the white parts of the Hermes head.

(b) The control numbers on the back are very delicate, sometimes presenting a peculiar dotting appearance.

The 5l., 10l., 20l. and 40l. values in both the coarse and fine prints sometimes show a yellow wash on the surface of the paper, either on the front or more rarely on the back, and exceptionally on both sides of the stamp. Stamps with the wash on the front are worth about twice the value of the normals, both unused and used. With the wash on the back they are worth about three times normal and with it on both sides, about four times.

The 80l. stamp is of a very fine print and has thin and delicately designed red-orange figures on the back. All the later 80l. prints have carmine figures. This stamp was printed with the newly adopted 'soft' method of printing when a piece of cloth, known as a 'blanket' was used on the printing screen. This caused an accentuated relief on the white parts of the stamps. A faint vertical lining of the background is often visible.

See first note below No. 7 on how to identify inverted figures at back.

1862–67. Second Athens print. Printings made at Athens before the plates were cleaned in 1867. On cream paper *unless otherwise stated*. With figures at back except on the 1l. and 2l.

Figure at back of 5l., Type II

16	1l. chocolate-brown (*solid background*)	46·00	46·00
	a. Chocolate-brown (*vert line background*)	65·00	65·00
	b. Chocolate-brown (*horiz line background*)	65·00	65·00
	c. Olive-brown	70·00	70·00
	d. Chocolate brown (*smudgy print*)	46·00	46·00
	e. Red-brown (*smudgy print*)	£120	£120
	f. Purple-brown (*coarse print*)	£120	£120
	g. Deep purple-brown (*coarse print*)	£120	£120
17	2l. yellow-bistre	13·00	23·00
	a. Pale yellow-bistre	13·00	23·00
	b. Dull bistre (*smooth print*)	70·00	85·00
18	5l. yellowish green/*greenish*	£325	85·00
	a. Bluish green/*greenish*	£325	46·00
	b. Yellow-green/*greenish* (*coarse print*)	£225	20·00
	c. '5' at back double	—	£2250
19	10l. yellowish orange/*bluish*	£600	75·00
	a. Pale orange-yellow/*bluish*	£325	46·00
	b. Orange/*blue*	£500	85·00
	ba. '10' on face instead of at back (on 19b)	—	£19000
	c. Red-orange/*blue*	£500	21·00
	d. '01' instead of '10'	£7500	£150
20	20l. blue/*bluish*	£300	17·00
	a. Pale blue/*bluish* (*very fine print*)	£300	17·00
	b. Deep bright blue/*bluish* (*very fine print*)	£425	41·00
	c. Dull greenish blue/*bluish*	£300	17·00
	d. Cobalt/*bluish* (*coarse print*)	£1300	29·00
	e. Blue/*greenish*	£1600	29·00
	f. Indigo-blue/*bluish*	£3250	£100
	g. '80' at back (on 20a)	—	£2250
	h. Double '20' at back	—	£1200
21	40l. mauve/*blue*	£425	29·00
	a. Bright mauve/*blue*	£425	29·00
	b. Rose-mauve/*lilac*	£1200	23·00
	c. Double figures at back	—	£1700
22	80l. carmine	95·00	55·00
	a. Deep carmine	70·00	20·00
	b. Rose-carmine	70·00	18·00
	c. '8' at back inverted	—	£450

Most of these stamps vary more or less in shade. Nos. 16c and 17a are exceedingly fine prints. In this group the numerals at back are thin and delicate as compared with those on later issues.

King George I

31 October 1863–18 March 1913

1867–69. Printings made in Athens after the plates were cleaned. On cream paper *unless otherwise stated*. With figures at back except the 1l. and 2l.

23	1l. reddish brown	55·00	65·00
	a. Deep red-brown	55·00	60·00
	b. Fawn	90·00	90·00
24	2l. yellowish bistre	29·00	40·00
25	5l. bright green/*greenish*	£5000	£120
	a. Yellow-green/*greenish*	£5000	£120
26	10l. orange-vermilion/*bluish*	£1400	33·00
	a. '10' at back inverted	—	£1800
27	20l. pale bright blue/*bluish*	£1000	20·00
	a. Double '20' at back	—	£1300
	b. Double print		
28	40l. rosy mauve/*blue*	£300	30·00
	a. Dull rosy mauve/*blue*	£300	30·00
	b. '20' at back corrected to '40'	£2750	£2500
29	80l. carmine-rose	£180	£200

The stamps of this period show none of the blots and specks of colour which distinguish the later printings of the preceding set. No. 23a has rather short lines of shading on the cheek.

1870. Special printing made in Athens under the supervision of German workmen. Very fine impressions.

30	1l. fawn	£140	£225
	a. Deep fawn	£160	£250
31	20l. pale blue/*bluish*	£1600	23·00
	a. Bright blue/*bluish*	£1900	29·00
	b. '02' at back		£1000
	c. Inverted '20' at back		£1100

The 1l. has short lines of shading on the cheek and clear spandrels. The 20l. has short dotted lines of shading on cheek, resembling the Paris print, and very pale spandrels.

1870–71. Later printings from the cleaned plates. On cream paper *unless otherwise stated*. With figures at back except the 1 and 2l.

32	1l. dull brown	£300	£300
	a. Red-brown	£300	£300
33	2l. pale yellow-bistre/*deep cream*	18·00	40·00
34	5l. yellow-green/*greenish*	£6000	£100
35	10l. pale red-orange/*greenish*	£1200	49·00
36	20l. dull blue/*bluish*	£1200	17·00
	a. Deep dull blue/*bluish*	£1400	23·00
	b. '02' at back	—	£450
	c. '20' at back double	—	£1000
37	40l. pale salmon/*greenish*	£700	75·00
	a. Lilac-rose (*solferino*)/*greenish*	—	£98000
38	80l. carmine-rose	£180	£200
	a. Deep carmine-red	£180	£200
	b. '80' at back inverted	—	£3000
	c. '8' for '80' at back	—	£1400

The 5l. is on thin transparent paper without any pronounced mesh, and must not be confused with No. 40a. The 10l. has coarse orange, instead of vermilion, figures. The 40l. was printed in a fugitive colour and is found in reddish salmon, salmon and, in the worst cases, a dirty yellow; the prices quoted are for stamps of good colour. No. 37a, of which only a few examples are known, was used only at Piraeus, from 12–14 July 1871; in colour it is the exact shade of the numerals at the back of the pale salmon stamps. The 80l. (Nos. 38 and 38a) are believed to have been printed in 1869, but were only used during this period; they are characterised by their pale and delicate spandrels. The stamps of this set have thick, coarse figures at back.

1872–75. Thin transparent paper. With figures at the back except on the 1l. and 2l.

39	1l. grey-brown/*buff*	40·00	60·00
	a. Deep reddish brown/*buff*	65·00	85·00
	b. Red-brown/*buff*	65·00	85·00
	c. Grey-brown/*straw*	46·00	65·00
39d	2l. brownish bistre	£300	£350
40	5l. green/*greenish*	£500	23·00
	a. Sage-green/*greenish*	£1400	60·00
	b. Deep bright green/*greenish*	£600	35·00
	c. Emerald-green/*greenish*	£1400	60·00
	d. '5' at back double		£160
41	10l. red-orange/*pale greenish*	£800	29·00
	a. Without numerals at back	£7000	£1700
	b. '10' at back inverted		£1600
	c. '0' for '10' at back		£400
	d. Orange-vermilion/*lavender*	£6000	£110
	da. '0' for '10' at back (on 41d)	—	£425
42	20l. deep bright blue/*bluish*	£1000	23·00
	aa. '20' at back inverted		
	a. Deep indigo-blue/*bluish*	£1800	48·00
	b. Pale bright blue/*bluish*	£1400	41·00
	c. Grey-blue/*bluish*	£1200	35·00
	d. Deep blue/*blue*	£1000	23·00
43	40l. dull rosy mauve/*blue*	£750	70·00
	a. Deep bright purple/*blue*		£850
	b. Rosy mauve/*blue*	£600	55·00
	ba. Red-lilac, figures at back bistre		£225
	c. Double '40' at back		£1100
	d. Bistre/*blue*	35·00	50·00
	e. Bistre-brown/*blue*	35·00	50·00
	f. Pale dull olive-green/*blue*		£300
44	80l. carmine-rose	£160	£180

The paper of this series varies from medium to very thin, and, except on the 1l., shows a pronounced mesh when looked through in a strong light.

1875–80. On cream paper (except No. 48a). With figures at back except on the 1l. and 2l.

45	1l. red-brown	35·00	46·00
	a. Black-brown	60·00	70·00
	b. Dark red-brown	35·00	46·00
	c. Pale red-brown	35·00	46·00
	d. Grey-brown	60·00	70·00
	e. Double print		
46	2l. bistre	23·00	23·00
	a. Stone	23·00	23·00
47	5l. yellow-green	£160	23·00
	a. Deep yellow-green	£225	35·00
	b. Emerald-green	£1200	£110
	c. Clear bright green	£450	50·00
48	10l. orange	£180	17·00
	aa. On yellow, no figures at back		
	a. Orange/yellow	£325	35·00
	b. Orange-vermilion	£180	17·00
	ba. Orange-vermilion double print		£1600
	c. '00' at back	£900	£110
	d. '1' instead of '10' at back		£200
	e. '0' for '10' at back		£170
	f. '01' instead of '10' at back		£400
	g. Double '10' at back		£600
49	20l. Prussian blue	£2500	60·00
	a. Deep blue	£225	17·00
	b. Royal blue	£400	46·00
	c. Ultramarine	£130	17·00
	d. Double '20' at back	—	£700
	e. '02' at back	—	£350
	f. '20' at back inverted	—	£7000
	g. '2' of '20' at back inverted	—	£2000
50	40l. rose-buff	23·00	70·00
	a. Pale buff	23·00	70·00

The impressions in this issue are generally coarse, though the first printings of the 5l., 10l. and 20l. (Nos. 47, 48 and 49), which are on highly surfaced paper, are very good prints. No. 47c is always a remarkably fine clear print. No. 48aa, of which very few specimens exist, is only known with postmark of Smyrna dated 1877.

1876. Without figures at back.

(i) Paris print

51	30l. olive-brown/*cream*	£225	46·00
	a. Brown/*cream*	£375	£100
52	60l. deep green/*green*	29·00	85·00

(ii) Athens print

53	30l. grey-brown/*cream*	60·00	9·25
	a. Grey-brown/*buff*	60·00	9·25
	b. Dark red-brown/*cream*	60·00	9·25
54	60l. deep green/*buff*	£475	50·00

1881–87. Without figures at back.

(i) On cream paper. Imperf

55	5l. yellow-green	17·00	2·30
	a. Green	37·00	10·50
	b. Pale yellow-green	60·00	29·00
56	10l. orange	17·00	2·30
	a. Yellow-orange	19·00	4·50
	b. Bright orange-vermilion	£4250	55·00
	c. Orange-red	£4250	55·00
57	20l. ultramarine	£325	£130
58	20l. carmine-lake	£225	10·50
59	20l. bright rosine	4·00	4·00
	a. Pale rosine	5·25	4·00
60	30l. ultramarine	£160	11·00
	a. Deep ultramarine	£170	11·00
	b. Dull ultramarine	£160	11·00
61	40l. mauve	55·00	11·50
	a. Deep mauve	65·00	29·00

(ii) On thin buff paper. Imperf (1882)

62	1l. red-brown	£100	70·00
63	5l. deep bright green	85·00	50·00
64	10l. orange	£140	90·00

(iii) On cream paper. P 11½ (1881)

65	1l. red-brown	27·00	9·50
66	2l. bistre	38·00	21·00

(iv) On cream paper. Pin perf 15–15½ (1887)

67	1l. grey-brown (No. 45d)	30·00	37·00
	a. Red-brown (No. 45)	30·00	37·00
68	2l. bistre (No. 46)	30·00	37·00
	a. Pale yellow-bistre (No. 33)	30·00	37·00
69	5l. pale yellow-green (No. 55b)	27·00	31·00
70	10l. yellow-orange (No. 56a)	33·00	39·00
71	20l. rosine (No. 59)	27·00	31·00
72	40l. mauve (No. 61)	£100	85·00
	a. Deep mauve (No. 61a)	£100	85·00
45ds, 46s, 55as, 56s, 59s, 61s Optd 'SPECIMEN' Set of 6			£600

The other values formerly listed with the 11½ perforation are now omitted as they were not issued to the public. They were perforated at the head post office in Athens on request, entirely for philatelic purposes, and at a time when the stamps of the first type had been superseded for some years.

The pin perforations were the work of the Postmaster of Corfu, who in 1887, perforated all his remaining stock of obsolete stamps and issued them in the ordinary way. They are found with the postmark 'KERKYRA' in a circle with date in the centre.

The rouletted stamps formerly listed were entirely unofficial.

D **2** Small letters above numeral   D **3** Larger letters above numeral

(Litho Austrian State Ptg Wks, Vienna)

1875 (1 Mar). POSTAGE DUE. T D **2**. Centres in black.

A. Perf 10–11

D73A	1l. green	2·00	2·30
D74A	2l. green	2·50	2·30
D75A	5l. green	2·50	2·30
D76A	10l. green	2·50	1·50
D77A	20l. green	£110	44·00
D78A	40l. green	20·00	20·00
D79A	60l. green	80·00	40·00
D80A	70l. green	20·00	20·00
D81A	80l. green	23·00	23·00
D82A	90l. green	20·00	20·00
D83A	1d. green	20·00	20·00
	g. Centre inverted	£600	
	h. Broad 'M'	£100	£100
D84A	2d. green	29·00	29·00
	g. Centre inverted		£300

B. Perf 10–11×12½–13

D73B	1l. green	2·00	3·50
D74B	2l. green	£120	65·00
D75B	5l. green	4·75	2·75
D76B	10l. green	7·00	3·50
D77B	20l. green	80·00	48·00
D78B	40l. green	35·00	26·00
D79B	60l. green	80·00	41·00
D80B	70l. green	18·00	20·00
D81B	80l. green	23·00	32·00
D82B	90l. green	23·00	35·00
D83B	1d. green	23·00	35·00
	g. Centre inverted	—	
	h. Broad 'M'	£350	£350
D84B	2d. green	40·00	40·00
	g. Centre inverted		

C. Perf 12½–13

D73C	1l. green	2·20	2·50
D74C	2l. green	2·50	3·50
D75C	5l. green	17·00	17·00
D76C	10l. green	60·00	37·00
D77C	20l. green	80·00	48·00
D78C	40l. green	80·00	28·00
D79C	60l. green	80·00	40·00
D80C	70l. green	41·00	41·00
D81C	80l. green	25·00	25·00
D82C	90l. green	40·00	40·00
D83C	1d. green	40·00	40·00
	h. Broad 'M'	£325	£325
D84C	2d. green	40·00	40·00

D. Perf 8½–9½

D73D	1l. green	3·75	5·50
D74D	2l. green	3·25	5·00
D75D	5l. green	8·00	5·25
D76D	10l. green	17·00	6·00
D77D	20l. green	60·00	65·00
D78D	40l. green	35·00	23·00
D79D	60l. green	80·00	80·00
D80D	70l. green	23·00	23·00
D81D	80l. green	41·00	41·00
D82D	90l. green	35·00	35·00
D83D	1d. green	35·00	35·00
	h. Broad 'M'	£350	£350
D84D	2d. green	40·00	40·00

E. Perf 8½–9½×10–11

D73E	1l. green		
D74E	2l. green	28·00	28·00
D75E	5l. green	21·00	22·00
D76E	10l. green	20·00	12·50
D77E	20l. green	80·00	46·00
D78E	40l. green	30·00	23·00
D79E	60l. green	80·00	40·00
D80E	70l. green	18·00	16·00
D81E	80l. green	£120	40·00

GREECE 1876

D82E	9ol. green		40·00	48·00
D83E	1d. green		40·00	48·00
	h. Broad 'M'			
D84E	2d. green		£225	£225

F. Perf 8½–9½×12½–13

D74F	2l. green		£170	£170
D75F	5l. green		£170	£170
D77F	20l. green		£180	£180

The imperforate varieties are now regarded as of doubtful status with the possible exception of the 40l. and 1d.
The variety on the 1d. shows a broad, short 'M' in 'DPAXMH'.
In this issue there is a wide range of shades of green.

(Litho Austrian State Ptg Wks, Vienna)

1876 (June). POSTAGE DUE. T D **3**. Centres in black.

(a) Perf 12–13

D85	1l. yellow-green		1·40	1·40
	a. Green		1·40	1·40
D86	2l. yellow-green		1·40	1·40
	a. Green		1·40	1·40
D87	5l. grey-green			
	a. Green			
D88	10l. yellow-green		1·80	1·40
	a. Blue-green		1·80	1·40
	b. Green		2·30	1·40
D89	20l. yellow-green		3·00	3·00
	a. Blue-green		3·00	3·00
	b. Green		3·00	3·00
D90	40l. green		90·00	85·00
D91	60l. blue-green		10·50	10·50
D92	70l. green			£300
D93	80l. green		£200	
D94	100l. green		15·00	15·00
D95	200l. green		17·00	16·00

(b) Perf 10½ (x), 10½–11 (y) or 11 (z)

D96	1l. yellow-green (x)		£250	£250
	a. Green (y)		£250	£250
D97	2l. yellow-green (x)		£250	£250
	a. Green (y)		£250	£250
D98	5l. grey-green (z)		£425	£375
	a. Green (y)		2·30	1·70
D99	10l. green (y)		80·00	46·00
	a. Perf 10½–11×12–13. Yellow-green		3·00	2·30
D100	20l. green (y)		80·00	75·00
D101	40l. green (y)		46·00	43·00
	a. Grey-green (x)		40·00	17·00
D102	60l. grey-green (x)		46·00	23·00
	a. Green (y)		35·00	29·00
D103	70l. green (y)		35·00	29·00
D104	80l. green (y)		25·00	21·00
D105	90l. green (y)		35·00	29·00
D106	100l. green (y)		35·00	29·00
D107	200l. green (y)			

(c) Perf 11½

D108	1l. yellow-green		9·25	9·25
D109	2l. yellow-green		9·25	9·25
D110	5l. grey-green			
D111	40l. grey-green		£100	£100
D112	60l. grey-green		48·00	

(d) Perf 9–9½

D113	20l. green		21·00	29·00
D114	60l. green		35·00	29·00
D115	70l. green		41·00	41·00
D116	80l. green		48·00	48·00
D74s/D76s, D78s, D80s/D84s, D85s, D89s, D91s, D94s, D95s *Optd* 'SPECIMEN' Set of 14			£400	

2 Hermes

(Des H. Hendrickx. Eng A. Doms. Electrotypes. Ptd first at the Belgian Stamp Printing Works, Malines; later at Athens)

1886–88. Belgian print.

(a) Imperf

73	2	1l. pale brown (2.88)	3·25	2·50
74		2l. pale ochre (8.88)	8·75	£180
75		5l. bright green (2.88)	11·50	2·75
76		10l. yellow-orange (2.88)	18·00	2·50
77		20l. carmine (2.88)	27·00	2·40
78		25l. dull blue (4.86)	£150	2·50
79		40l. bright mauve (2.88)	£100	27·00
80		50l. grey-green (4.86)	8·25	3·50
81		1d. grey (4.86)	£120	4·00

(b) P 11½

81a	2	1l. pale brown	5·75	5·75
82		40l. bright mauve	£160	£160
83		50l. grey-green	17·00	6·25
84		1d. grey	£170	6·50
78s, 80s, 81s *Optd* 'SPECIMEN' Set of 3				

The Belgian-printed stamps may be distinguished from those of Athens by the impression being smoother and finer, and by the paper being more highly surfaced.
The stamps perforated 13½ and most of the lower values with the 11½ perforation are now omitted as they were never officially issued. They were perforated, by the official machines, to the order of private individuals for philatelic purposes. See note following No. 72.

1889–95. Athens print.

(a) Imperf

85	2	1l. brown	2·30	1·20
		a. Black-brown	5·75	2·30
		b. Yellow-brown	29·00	7·00
86		2l. stone	1·20	1·40
		a. Pale bistre	3·50	3·50
		b. Pale ochre	1·30	1·40
87		5l. yellow-green	9·25	2·00
		a. Bright green	25·00	5·25
		b. Green	4·75	1·40
		c. Emerald	70·00	10·50
88		10l. orange-yellow	90·00	3·50
		a. Orange	50·00	3·50
		b. Red-orange	40·00	2·30
89		20l. carmine	3·50	2·30
		a. Aniline rose	£200	11·50
		b. Scarlet	65·00	1·20
		c. Rose-pink	80·00	3·50
		d. Pink	4·50	2·30
90		25l. dull blue	£160	5·75
		a. Deep blue	£130	5·75
		b. Ultramarine	£120	5·75
		c. Bright blue	£120	8·00
		d. Pale blue	70·00	1·20
91		25l. purple (1893)	3·50	1·20
		a. Pale purple	17·00	3·50
92		40l. purple (1891)	£130	23·00
93		40l. blue (1893)	8·00	2·30
94		1d. grey (1895)	£400	7·00

(b) P 13½

95	2	1l. yellow-brown	70·00	£450
		a. Black-brown	23·00	29·00
96		2l. stone	1·20	9·25
		a. Pale ochre		
97		10l. orange-yellow		£300
		a. Red-orange		£300
98		20l. carmine-rose	70·00	29·00
		a. Scarlet	60·00	23·00
99		40l. purple	£100	40·00

Other values, perf 13½, were not issued.

(c) P 11½

100	2	1l. brown	2·30	1·20
		a. Black-brown	5·75	2·30
		b. Yellow-brown	90·00	90·00
101		2l. stone	1·20	1·20
		a. Pale ochre	2·30	2·30
102		5l. yellow-green	11·50	1·20
		a. Bright green	46·00	3·50
		b. Green	9·25	1·20
		c. Emerald	£170	23·00
		d. Pale green	70·00	17·00
103		10l. orange-yellow	£140	4·50
		a. Red-orange	40·00	2·30
		b. Orange	50·00	3·50
104		20l. carmine-rose	£120	5·75
		a. Carmine	80·00	2·30
		b. Scarlet	46·00	1·20
		c. Pink	£120	1·20
105		25l. dull blue	£225	46·00
		a. Deep blue	£225	46·00
		b. Ultramarine	£140	17·00
		c. Bright blue	£100	9·25
		d. Pale blue	90·00	2·30
106		25l. purple	17·00	3·50
		a. Pale purple	11·50	2·30
107		40l. purple	£130	35·00
108		40l. blue	14·00	3·50
109		1d. grey	£500	9·25

Pairs of all values, imperf between, are frequently found. They are worth about 50% above the price for two normal singles.
The early printings of some values are to be found with a watermark, 'ΧΑΡΤΗΣ ΔΗΜΟΣΙΑΣ ΥΠΗΡΕΣΙΑΣ' (paper for the Public Services), across the middle and bottom of the sheet, in double-lined capitals about 36 mm. high. In the middle of each pane (i.e. six times in each sheet) appear the letters 'E.X.' about 14 mm. high.

All values may be found perforated 8½–9¼ by the postmaster at Astakos and with a rough pin-perforation by the postmaster at Amphissa. Normally stamps with the official 11½ perforation were issued only in Athens and neighbourhood, the provinces being supplied with imperf stamps.

3 Wrestlers

4 Discus-thrower

5 Vase depicting Pallas Athene

6 Quadriga or Chariot-driving

7 Acropolis and Stadium

8 'Hermes', after the statue by Praxiteles

9 'Victory', after the statue by Pæonius

(Des Professor Gillieron. Eng E. Mouchon. Typo French Govt Ptg Wks, Paris)

1896 (25 Mar). First International Olympic Games. P 13½×14 (Types **5**, **8/9**) or 14×13½ (others).

110	**3**	1l. ochre	4·00	2·75
111		2l. pink	3·50	2·75
		a. Without engraver's name at foot	32·00	22·00
112	**4**	5l. mauve	14·50	4·75
113		10l. slate	14·50	6·00
114	**5**	20l. red-brown	29·00	6·50
115	**6**	25l. red	35·00	8·50
116	**5**	40l. pale violet	17·00	9·50
117	**6**	60l. grey-black	46·00	24·00
118	**7**	1d. blue	£120	28·00
119	**8**	2d. bistre	£325	95·00
		a. Imperf between (pair)		
120	**9**	5d. green	£600	£550
121	–	10d. brown	£700	£600
110/121	Set of 12		£1700	£1200

Design: As T **6**—10d. Parthenon.

ΛΕΠΤΑ
20
(**11**)

ΔΡΑΧΜΗ
1
(**12**)

1900 (Sept). Surch as T **11** or T **12** (dr. values).
I. T **2**. Athens print of 1889–1895
(a) Imperf

122	**2**	20l. on 25l. blue	3·50	1·20
		a. Deep blue	46·00	46·00
		b. Ultramarine	90·00	60·00
123		1d. on 40l. purple	17·00	7·00
124		2d. on 40l. purple	£500	

(b) P 11½

125	**2**	20l. on 25l. blue	3·50	1·20
		a. Deep blue	75·00	75·00
		b. Ultramarine	90·00	90·00
		c. Perf 13½	£120	£120
126		1d. on 40l. purple	23·00	11·50
		a. Perf 13½	70·00	60·00
127		2d. on 40l. purple	£275	
		a. Perf 13½	11·50	14·00

II. T **2**. *Belgian print*

128	**2**	2d. on 40l. bright mauve (Imperf)	£325	
129		2d. on 40l. bright mauve (P 11½)	£350	

Pairs imperf between are frequently found in these provisionals and are worth about 50% more than the price of two normal stamps.

III. T **1**. *Athens print.*
(a) Imperf

130	**1**	30l. on 40l. deep mauve (No. 61a)	7·00	7·00
		a. Mauve (No. 61)	17·00	17·00
		b. 'A' for 'Λ' in 'ΛΕΠΤΑ'	£140	£140
131		40l. on 2l. pale yellow-bistre/*deep cream* (No. 33)	9·25	9·25
		a. 'A' for 'Λ' in 'ΛΕΠΤΑ'	£170	£170
132		50l. on 40l. rose-buff (No. 50)	7·00	7·00
		a. 'A' for 'Λ' in 'ΛΕΠΤΑ'	£140	£140
133		3d. on 10l. orange/*cream* (No. 56)	60·00	60·00
		a. Yellow-orange/*cream* (No. 56a)	60·00	£650
134		5d. on 40l. dull rosy mauve/*blue* (No. 28a)	£150	£170
		a. Rosy mauve/*blue* (No. 28)	£170	£200
		b. Rosy mauve/*blue* (thin paper) (No. 43b)	£550	
		c. '20' at back corrected to '40'	£2000	

(b) P 11½

135	**1**	30l. on 40l. deep mauve	11·50	11·50
		a. Mauve	20·00	20·00
		b. 'A' for 'Λ' in 'ΛΕΠΤΑ'	£170	£200
136		40l. on 2l. stone	17·00	17·00
		a. 'A' for 'Λ' in 'ΛΕΠΤΑ'	£200	£200
137		50l. on 40l. rosy buff	11·50	11·50
		a. 'A' for 'Λ' in 'ΛΕΠΤΑ'	£225	£225
138		3d. on 10l. orange	65·00	65·00
		a. Yellow-orange	65·00	65·00
139		5d. on 40l. dull rosy mauve/*blue*	£170	£190
		a. Rosy mauve/*blue*	£190	£225
		b. Rosy mauve/*blue* (thin paper)	£600	
		c. '20' at back corrected to '40'	£2000	

In the 30l., 40l. and 50l. there are two types of surcharge: (1) Narrow figure '0' as illustrated (97 times in sheet of 150); (2) Wider '0' (53 times).

Nos. 130b, 131a, 132a, 135b, 136a, 137a occur in positions 35 and 50, in conjunction with narrow '0'. This error with wide '0' is a forgery.

On Nos. 130/139 the distance between the word and figures of the surcharge varies within the sheet between 1½ and 4 mm.

Pairs imperf between. The note after No. 129 also applies here.

A M
ΛΕΠΤΑ
25
(**13**)

A M
ΔΡΑΧΜΗ
1
(**14**) 'A M' = 'Axia Metallike' (see note after No. 182)

1900 (Oct)–**01** (Jan). Surch as T **13** or T **14**.
I. On T **2**, *Belgian print, in black*
(a) Imperf

140	**2**	25l. on 40l. bright mauve	5·75	11·50
141		50l. on 25l. dull blue	29·00	29·00

(b) P 11½

142	**2**	25l. on 40l. bright mauve	11·50	17·00
143		50l. on 25l. dull blue	60·00	70·00

II. On T **1**, *Athens print, in black*
(a) Imperf

144	**1**	1d. on 40l. bistre/*blue* (thin paper)	£120	£170
145		2d. on 5l. green/*cream*	17·00	29·00

(b) P 11½

146	**1**	1d. on 40l. bistre/*blue* (thin paper)	£160	£180
147		2d. on 5l. green/*cream*	23·00	40·00

Pairs, imperf between. The note after No. 129 also applies here.

(Dec 1900–Jan 1901)
III. On Olympic Games issue of 1896, in red.

148		5l. on 1d. blue	23·00	35·00
		a. Surcharge double	£300	
149		25l. on 40l. pale violet	£120	90·00
		a. With 50l. surch in black in addition	£475	£475
150		50l. on 2d. bistre	£100	80·00

GREECE 1901

151	1d. on 5d. green		£375	£250
	a. 'Δ' for 'Λ' in 'ΔΡΑΧΜΗ'		£950	£700
152	2d. on 10d. brown		80·00	£130
	a. 'Δ' for 'Λ' in 'ΔΡΑΧΜΑΙ'		£450	£350
148/152	Set of 5		£650	£550

The note below No. 139c regarding the two types of '0' also applies to Nos. 149a and 150.

15

16

DIFFERENCES BETWEEN THE DIES

1l. I. Reticulated shading in rectangular ornaments below words 'ΛΕΠΤΟΝ' faint. II. Shading stands out clearly.
2l. I. The curved line below 'ΛΕΠΤΑ' at left is doubled by a thinner line starting below the 'Ε'. II. The thin line starts to the left of the 'Λ'.
3l. I. Reticulated shading in rectangular ornament below words 'ΛΕΠΤΑ' clear. II. Shading faint.
5l. I. Outer vertical margin of panels containing 'ΕΛΛΑΣ' hardly shaded at all. II. Bold horizontal shading.
20l. I. Single thick line below 'ΛΕΠΤΑ' at left. II. Two thinner lines below 'ΛΕΠΤΑ'.
40l. I. Curved line below 'ΛΕΠΤΑ' at left doubled below 'ΛΕ'. II. Curved line doubled throughout.
50l. I. Vertical line outlining right forearm of Hermes at left doubled near elbow; vertical lines of shading at each end of bands containing 'ΛΕΠΤΑ' clear and bold. II. Line on arm single throughout. Shading in bands faint.

(Printed by Perkins Bacon. 1l. to 1d. recess; 2d. to 5d. litho)

1901 (1 July)–**02**. W **18** (sideways on the 1d. thin paper). P 13½ (lepta values) or 12½ (others).

17 Hermes, after the 'Mercury' of Giovanni da Bologna

18

1l. I

1l. II

I. Thick paper

153	15	1l. brown (I)	1·00	35
		a. Imperf (pair)	30·00	
154		2l. grey (I)	1·00	35
155		3l. orange (I)	1·00	60
156	16	5l. green (I)	1·00	35
		a. Imperf (pair)	41·00	
157		10l. rose-carmine	3·50	45
158	15	20l. mauve (I)	7·50	35
159	16	25l. blue	9·25	45
160	15	30l. violet	20·00	2·00
		a. Imperf (pair)	£350	
161		40l. dark brown (I)	50·00	5·75
		b. Die II	46·00	3·75
		b. Dies I and II in pair	£200	46·00
162		50l. brown-lake (I)	35·00	3·50
163	17	1d. black	60·00	2·30
164		2d. bronze	14·00	10·50
165		3d. silver	16·00	14·50
		a. Imperf (pair)	£1800	
166		5d. gold	18·00	14·50

2l. I — 2l. II

3l. I — 3l. II

5l. I — 5l. II

II. Thin paper
A. Die I

167A	15	1l. brown	70	25
		a. Perf 11½	£150	
		b. Imperf (pair)	21·00	
168A		2l. grey	80	25
		a. Imperf (pair)	29·00	
169A		3l. yellow-orange	90	35
		a. Imperf (pair)	29·00	
170A	16	5l. green	80	35
		a. Imperf (pair)	21·00	
		b. Yellow-green	80	35
171A		10l. carmine (shades)	1·20	35
		a. Aniline red	1·20	35
		b. Imperf (pair)	32·00	
172A	15	20l. mauve	2·10	35
		a. Imperf (pair)	29·00	
173A	16	25l. blue	2·10	35
		a. Imperf (pair)	29·00	
174A	15	30l. purple	21·00	4·50
			00	£375
175A		40l. black-brown	3·00	2·10
		a. Dies I and II in pair	14·00	
		b. Dark red-brown	21·00	1·20
		ba. Dies I and II in pair	85·00	
176A		50l. brown-lake	21·00	1·20
177A	17	1d. black (P 14×12½)	70·00	46·00
		a. Perf 12½	75·00	60·00
		b. Perf 14	70·00	55·00
		c. Perf 14×imperf (pair)	£600	—
		d. Imperf (pair)	£600	—

20l. I — 20l. II

40l. I — 40l. II

II. Thin paper
B. Die II

167B	15	1l. brown	80	35
		a. Perf 11½	£225	
		b. Imperf (pair)	21·00	—
		c. Dark red-brown	80	35
168B		2l. grey	90	35
		a. Imperf (pair)	25·00	—
169B		3l. yellow-orange	1·20	35
		a. Imperf (pair)	25·00	—
170B	16	5l. green		
172B	15	20l. mauve	1·70	35
		a. Imperf (pair)	25·00	
175B		40l. black-brown	1·70	35
		a. Dark red-brown	16·00	80
176B		50l. brown-lake	21·00	4·50
		a. Imperf (pair)	£120	

50l. I — 50l. II

There was only one plate for the 40l. on which the first four vertical rows were Die I and the other six Die II. This is the only value which contained both dies on the same sheet. Unlike all the others the second die of the 5 lepta is actually the original one retouched. The 10l. die was also retouched for later plates, but the difference is too slight for inclusion in this catalogue.

Though we have included all the known imperforate varieties, it appears doubtful whether all of them were actually issued in that state. On the other hand some are only known used.

19 Head of Hermes

D **20**

(Recess Perkins Bacon & Co.)

1902 (1 Jan). P 13½.
178	**19**	5l. orange	2·50	1·20
		a. Imperf (pair)	£120	
179		25l. emerald-green	37·00	2·50
180		50l. bright blue	37·00	2·50
		a. Imperf (pair)	£950	
181		1d. scarlet	37·00	11·00
182		2d. chestnut	70·00	49·00
178/182	Set of 5		£170	60·00

The letters 'AM' stand for 'Axia Metallike'='metal (i.e. gold) value'. The stamps were intended for use on foreign parcels and had to be paid for at the 'gold' rate.

The remainders of this issue were used as Postage Due stamps for a short time in 1913.

(Printed by Perkins Bacon & Co. 1l. to 1d. recess; 2d. to 5d. litho)

1902 (Mar). POSTAGE DUE. W **18**. P 13½.
D183	D **20**	1l. brown	60	40
D184		2l. grey	60	40
		a. Imperf (pair)	75·00	
D185		3l. orange	60	40
		a. Imperf (pair)	75·00	
D186		5l. green	60	40
		a. Imperf (pair)	75·00	
D187		10l. scarlet	60	40
D188		20l. pale purple	60	40
D189		25l. blue	11·50	5·75
		a. Imperf (pair)	£130	
D190		30l. deep purple	70	40
		a. Imperf (pair)	95·00	
D191		40l. black-brown	85	55
D192		50l. brown-lake	70	45
		a. Imperf (pair)	£130	
D193		1d. black	1·70	90
		a. Imperf (pair)	£130	
D194		2d. bronze	2·50	3·50
D195		3d. silver	4·00	8·00
D196		5d. gold	6·25	24·00
D183/D196	Set of 14		29·00	41·00

The 3l. in purple is a colour trial.

See also Nos. D252/D264, D269/D283, D451/D458, D480/D481 and D595/D598.

20 Athlete throwing Discus

21 Jumper

22 Victory

23 Atlas offering the Apples of Hesperides to Hercules

24 Struggle between Hercules and Antaeus

25 Wrestlers

26 'Daemon' or God of the Games

27 Race, Ancient Greeks

28 Offerings for the Olympic Games

(Recess Perkins Bacon & Co.)

1906 (25 Mar). Second Olympic Games Issue, Athens. W **18**. P 13½–14.
183	**20**	1l. brown	60	35
		a. Imperf (pair)	£425	
184		2l. grey	65	35
		a. Imperf (pair)	£425	
185	**21**	3l. orange	75	35
		a. Imperf (pair)	£425	
186		5l. green	1·30	60
		a. Imperf (pair)	£180	
187	**22**	10l. carmine-red	3·50	60
		a. Imperf (pair)	£425	
188	**23**	20l. purple	5·75	60
		a. Imperf (pair)	£900	
189	**24**	25l. ultramarine	6·00	70
		a. Imperf (pair)	£900	
190	**25**	30l. deep purple	7·00	4·50
		a. Double impression	£1300	
191	**26**	40l. sepia	7·00	4·50
192	**23**	50l. brown-lake	16·00	5·25
193	**27**	1d. grey-black	85·00	22·00
		a. Imperf (pair)	£1500	
194		2d. rose	£140	47·00
195		3d. yellow-olive	£180	£150
196	**28**	5d. slate-blue	£225	£160
183/196	Set of 14		£600	£350

29 Head of Hermes

30 Iris

31 Hermes

32 Hermes and Arcas

33 Head of Hermes

(Eng T. Macdonald. Aspiotis)

1911–23. Zigzag roulette 13–13½.

(a) Recess (1911–1921)
197	**29**	1l. green (*shades*)	70	40
		a. Imperf (pair)	£130	£130

GREECE 1912

198	30	2l. carmine	70	35
199	29	3l. vermilion	1·00	35
		a. Imperf (pair)	£350	£350
200	31	5l. green	2·40	40
		a. Yellow-green	2·40	40
		b. Imperf (pair)	44·00	44·00
201	29	10l. carmine	12·50	40
		a. Imperf (pair)	75·00	75·00
202	30	20l. lilac	3·75	1·20
		a. Imperf (pair)	£325	£325
203		25l. bright ultramarine	18·00	1·00
		a. Prussian blue	£225	£130
		b. Rouletted in black	£300	£250
		c. Imperf (pair)	£450	£450
204	31	30l. carmine-red	4·25	2·00
205	30	40l. deep blue	14·50	7·00
		a. Imperf (pair)	£500	
206	31	50l. deep purple	19·00	4·00
		a. Imperf (pair)	£500	

Design (1d. to 10d.), 20×26½ mm.

207	32	1d. ultramarine	27·00	1·20
		a. Imperf (pair)	£500	
208		2d. vermilion	36·00	1·60
		a. Imperf (pair)	£500	
209		3d. carmine	36·00	1·80
		a. Imperf (pair)	£500	
		b. Design 20¼×25¼ mm. (1921)	£160	95·00
210		5d. grey-blue	39·00	6·50
		a. Imperf (pair)	£350	
		b. Design 20¼×25¼ mm. (1921)	£325	35·00
211		10d. deep blue	£400	£130
		a. Imperf (pair)	£2250	
		b. Design 20¼×25¼ mm. (1921)	85·00	60·00
212	33	25d. deep blue	80·00	47·00
		a. Imperf (pair)	£3500	

(b) Litho (Jan 1913–1923)

213	29	1l. green (shades)	30	25
		a. No stop after 'ΕΛΛΑΣ'	95·00	90·00
		b. Imperf (pair)	£100	
214	30	2l. carmine	30	25
		a. Imperf (pair)	£140	
215	29	3l. vermilion	30	25
		a. Imperf (pair)	£200	
216	31	5l. green	30	25
		a. Imperf (pair)	70·00	
217	29	10l. carmine	30	25
		a. Imperf (pair)	90·00	
218	30	15l. dull blue (3.18)	60	35
219		20l. purple-grey	65	35
		a. Imperf (pair)	£110	
220		25l. ultramarine	7·00	75
		a. Blue	70	25
		b. Imperf (pair)	£275	
		c. Double impression		
221	31	30l. carmine-red (4.14)	90	35
		a. Imperf (pair)	£200	
222	30	40l. deep blue (1.14)	3·00	70
		a. Imperf (pair)	£275	
223	31	50l. brown-purple (shades) (1.14)	5·75	30
		a. Imperf (pair)	£375	
		b. Imperf between (pair)		
224		80l. brown-purple (6.23)	8·00	1·50
		a. Imperf (pair)	£130	
225	32	1d. ultramarine (10.19)	9·25	60
		a. Imperf (pair)	£140	
226		2d. vermilion (10.19)	9·25	70
		a. Imperf (pair)	£160	
227		3d. carmine (10.20)	15·00	80
		a. Imperf (pair)	£400	
228		5d. pale grey-blue (6.22)	20·00	85
		a. Imperf (pair)	£475	
		b. Imperf between (pair)	£475	
229		10d. deep grey-blue (1922)	20·00	1·20
230	33	25d. slate-blue (5.22)	21·00	2·50

The 25l., 40l. and 1d. were also printed, during 1926, by a Vienna firm. The size and the rouletting of stamps of this printing vary slightly from the usual.

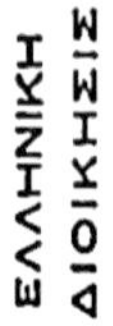

(**34** 'Greek Administration') (*reading up*)

VARIETIES

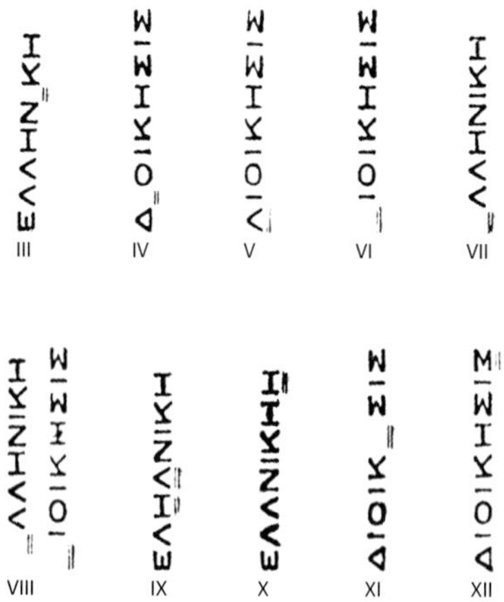

III   IV   V   VI   VII

VIII   IX   X   XI   XII

1912 (Oct)–**13**. Optd with T **34**. For use in the territories acquired as a result of the Balkan Wars.

A. Optd in black
X. Reading up
*(i) On stamp of 1901. T **15***

231X		20l. mauve (No. 172B)	4·50	3·75
		b. Opt double	55·00	55·00
		e. Variety V	20·00	20·00

*(ii) On stamps of 1911, recess. Types **29/33***

232AX		1l. green	1·10	1·10
		ab. Opt double	34·00	
		ac. Variety III	16·00	16·00
		ad. Variety IV	16·00	16·00
		ae. Variety V	16·00	16·00
233AX		2l. carmine	1·10	1·10
		ab. Opt double	31·00	28·00
		ac. Variety III	12·50	12·50
		ad. Variety IV	12·50	12·50
		ae. Variety V	12·50	12·50
		af. Variety VI	12·50	12·50
		ag. Variety VII	12·50	12·50
		ah. Variety VIII	12·50	12·50
234AX		3l. vermilion	1·10	1·10
		ab. Opt double	25·00	25·00
		ac. Variety III	12·50	12·50
		ad. Variety IV	16·00	16·00
		ae. Variety V	16·00	16·00
		af. Variety VI	12·50	12·50
		ag. Variety VII	12·50	12·50
		ah. Variety VIII	12·50	12·50
235AX		5l. green	1·30	1·30
		ab. Opt double	16·00	16·00
		ac. Variety III	12·50	12·50
		ad. Variety IV	12·50	12·50
		ae. Variety V	12·50	12·50
		af. Variety VI	12·50	12·50
		ag. Variety VII	12·50	12·50
		ah. Variety VIII	12·50	12·50
236AX		10l. carmine	2·20	2·20
		ab. Opt double	16·00	16·00
		ac. Variety III	12·50	12·50
		ad. Variety IV	12·50	12·50
		ae. Variety V	12·50	12·50
237AX		20l. lilac	3·25	2·50
		aa. Imperf (pair)	£1500	—
		ab. Opt double	28·00	28·00
		ac. Variety III	16·00	16·00
		ad. Variety IV	16·00	16·00
238AX		25l. bright ultramarine	3·25	3·25
		ab. Opt double	31·00	28·00
		ac. Variety III	12·50	12·50
		ad. Variety IV	19·00	19·00
		ae. Variety V	19·00	19·00
239AX		30l. carmine-red	3·75	3·25
		ab. Opt double	44·00	38·00
		ac. Variety III	16·00	16·00
		ad. Variety IV	22·00	22·00
		ae. Variety V	16·00	16·00
240AX		40l. deep blue	6·25	5·00
		ab. Opt double	44·00	38·00
		ac. Variety III	31·00	31·00
		ad. Variety IV	38·00	38·00
		ae. Variety V	38·00	38·00

1912 GREECE

241AX	50l. deep purple		7·00	6·25
	ab. Opt double		55·00	44·00
	ac. Variety III		44·00	38·00
	ad. Variety IV		47·00	41·00
	ae. Variety V		50·00	50·00
242AX	1d. ultramarine		16·00	3·50
	ab. Opt double		£130	£130
	ac. Variety III		44·00	38·00
	ad. Variety IV		47·00	41·00
	ae. Variety V		50·00	50·00
243AX	2d. vermilion		70·00	38·00
	ab. Opt double		£160	£160
	ac. Variety III		£400	£400
	ad. Variety IV		£400	£400
	ae. Variety V		£1200	£1100
	ai. Variety IX		£1200	£1100
	aj. Variety X		£1200	£1100
	ak. Variety XI		£1800	£1600
244AX	3d. carmine		£150	£150
	ac. Variety III		£400	£375
	ad. Variety IV		£400	£375
245AX	5d. grey-blue		31·00	38·00
	ab. Opt double		60·00	60·00
	ac. Variety III		£150	£150
	ad. Variety IV		£150	£150
	ai. Variety IX		£950	£950
	aj. Variety X		£950	£950
	ak. Variety XI			—
246AX	10d. deep blue		£375	£375
	ab. Opt double		£1400	£1400
	ac. Variety III		£1800	£1600
	ad. Variety IV		£1800	£1600
247AX	25d. deep blue (opt horiz)		£375	£375
	al. Variety XII		£1900	£1800

(iii) On stamps of 1911, litho. Types **29/31**

248AX	1l. green		75	75
	aa. On No. 213a		£130	
	ab. Opt double		31·00	
	af. Variety VI		12·50	12·50
	ag. Variety VII		12·50	12·50
	ah. Variety VIII		12·50	12·50
249AX	5l. green		1·00	1·00
	ab. Opt double		12·50	10·00
	ae. Variety V		12·50	12·50
	af. Variety VI		12·50	12·50
	ag. Variety VII		12·50	12·50
	ah. Variety VIII		12·50	12·50
250AX	10l. carmine		2·50	2·50
	ab. Opt double		12·50	12·50
	ae. Variety V		12·50	12·50
251AX	25l. ultramarine		6·25	5·00
	b. Opt double		31·00	28·00
	e. Variety V		25·00	25·00

Y. Reading down
(i) On stamp of 1901. T **15**

231Y	20l. mauve (No. 172B)		10·00	8·75

(ii) On stamps of 1911, recess. Types **29/33**

232AY	1l. green		31·00	31·00
	ab. Opt double		15·00	
	ad. Variety IV			
	ae. Variety V			
233AY	2l. carmine		2·50	2·50
	ab. Opt double		95·00	95·00
	ac. Variety III		£1300	
	ad. Variety IV			
	ae. Variety V		£650	
	af. Variety VI		7·50	7·50
	ag. Variety VII		7·50	7·50
	ah. Variety VIII		7·50	7·50
234AY	3l. vermilion		1·90	1·90
	ac. Variety III		£1300	
	ad. Variety IV			
	ae. Variety V			
	af. Variety VI		7·50	7·50
	ag. Variety VII		7·50	7·50
	ah. Variety VIII		7·50	7·50
235AY	5l. green		2·50	2·50
	ab. Opt double		£160	£160
	ac. Variety III			
	ad. Variety IV			
	ae. Variety V			
	af. Variety VI		19·00	19·00
	ag. Variety VII		19·00	19·00
	ah. Variety VIII		19·00	19·00
236AY	10l. carmine		£190	£190
	ac. Variety III			
	ad. Variety IV			
	ae. Variety V			
237AY	20l. lilac		9·50	8·75
	ab. Opt double		£250	£250
	ac. Variety III		£100	£100
	ad. Variety IV		£100	£100
238AY	25l. bright ultramarine		£130	£130
	ac. Variety III			
	ad. Variety IV			
	ae. Variety V			
239AY	30l. carmine-red		£500	£500
	ac. Variety III			
	ad. Variety IV			
	ae. Variety V			
240AY	40l. deep blue		£275	£225
	ac. Variety III			
	ad. Variety IV			
	ae. Variety V			
241AY	50l. deep purple		£500	£450
	ab. Opt double		£950	£950
	ac. Variety III		£2500	£2500
	ad. Variety IV			
	ae. Variety V			
242AY	1d. ultramarine		£100	£100
	ac. Variety III		£1100	£1100
	ad. Variety IV			
	ae. Variety V			
243AY	2d. vermilion		£190	£180
	ac. Variety III			
	ad. Variety IV			
	ae. Variety V			
	ai. Variety IX			—
	aj. Variety X			—
	ak. Variety XI			—
244AY	3d. carmine		£130	£130
	ac. Variety III			
	ad. Variety IV			—
245AY	5d. grey-blue		£700	£650
	ac. Variety III			
	ad. Variety IV			
247AY	25d. deep blue (opt horiz)		£375	£375
	al. Variety XII		£1900	£1800

(iii) On stamps of 1911, litho. Types **29/31**

248AY	1l. green		3·75	3·75
	ab. Opt double		75·00	75·00
	af. Variety VI		£225	£225
	ag. Variety VII		£225	£225
	ah. Variety VIII		£225	£225
249AY	5l. green		1·30	1·30
	ab. Opt double		£160	£160
	ae. Variety V			
	af. Variety VI		12·50	12·50
	ag. Variety VII		12·50	12·50
	ah. Variety VIII		12·50	12·50
250AY	10l. carmine		2·50	3·25
	ae. Variety V			
	af. Variety VI		19·00	19·00
	ag. Variety VII		19·00	19·00
	ah. Variety VIII		19·00	19·00
251AY	25l. ultramarine		80·00	80·00
	ab. Opt double		65·00	38·00
	ae. Variety V			

B. Optd in red, reading up. On stamps of 1911
(i) Recess

232B	29	1l. green	65	65
		bc. Variety III	9·50	9·50
233B	30	2l. carmine	15·00	15·00
		bb. Opt double	44·00	44·00
234B	29	3l. vermilion	12·50	12·50
235B	31	5l. green	65	65
		bc. Variety III	9·50	9·50
237B	30	20l. lilac	19·00	4·50
		bb. Opt double	£130	£130
		bc. Variety III	25·00	25·00
238B		25l. bright ultramarine	90·00	80·00
239B	31	30l. carmine-red	£100	£100
		bb. Opt double	£250	£250
240B	30	40l. deep blue	3·25	5·00
		bc. Variety III	31·00	31·00
241B	31	50l. deep purple	3·75	3·75
		bc. Variety III	31·00	31·00
242B	32	1d. ultramarine	19·00	19·00
		bc. Variety III	44·00	44·00
243B		2d. vermilion	£100	£130
		bb. Opt double	£120	£120
		bc. Variety III	£450	£450
		bj. Variety X		
		bk. Variety XI		
244B		3d. carmine	38·00	38·00
		bc. Variety III	£190	£190
245B		5d. grey-blue	£375	£300
		bb. Opt double		

GREECE 1912

		bc. Variety III		
		bj. Variety X		
		bk. Variety XI		
246B		10d. deep blue	55·00	80·00
		bc. Variety III	£450	£450
247B	**33**	25d. deep blue	£700	£750
		ba. Opt double (reading up)	£1600	£1600
		c. Opt reading down		
		d. Opt horiz	90·00	£200

(ii) Litho

248B	**29**	1l. green	11·50	11·50
		ba. On No. 213a	£275	£275
		c. Opt reading down	£1000	
		ca. On No. 213a, reading down		
249B	**31**	5l. green	65	65
		bc. Variety III	9·50	9·50
250B	**29**	10l. carmine	95·00	£100
251B	**30**	25l. ultramarine	2·50	2·50
		bc. Variety III	19·00	19·00
		c. Opt reading down	£325	
		cc. Variety III		

1912 (Dec). POSTAGE DUE. Nos. D183/D196 optd with T **34**.

(a) In black, reading up

D252A	D **20**	1l. brown	75	75
		aa. Opt double	19·00	
		ab. Variety III	12·50	12·50
		b. Opt reading down	12·50	12·50
		c. Opt double, one reading up, one down	25·00	
D253A		2l. grey	75	75
		aa. Opt double	19·00	
		ab. Variety III	12·50	12·50
		b. Opt reading down	12·50	12·50
		c. Opt double, one reading up, one down	25·00	
D254A		3l. orange	40	40
		aa. Opt double	19·00	
		ab. Variety III	12·50	12·50
D255A		5l. green	40	40
		aa. Opt double	19·00	19·00
		ab. Variety III	19·00	19·00
D256A		10l. scarlet	1·60	1·60
		aa. Opt double	21·00	21·00
		ab. Variety III	19·00	19·00
D257A		20l. pale purple	1·60	1·60
		ab. Variety III	25·00	25·00
D258A		30l. deep purple	5·00	5·00
		ab. Variety III	28·00	28·00
D259A		40l. black-brown	10·00	10·00
		aa. Opt double	£110	
		ab. Variety III	50·00	50·00
D260A		50l. brown-lake	14·00	14·00
		ab. Variety III	65·00	65·00
D261A		1d. black	44·00	44·00
D262A		2d. bronze		
		b. Opt reading down	31·00	31·00
D263A		3d. silver		
		b. Opt reading down	£100	£100
D264A		5d. gold		
		b. Opt reading down	£160	£190

(b) In red, reading up

D252D	D **20**	1l. brown	1·00	1·00
		db. Variety III	15·00	15·00
D253D		2l. grey	1·00	1·00
		da. Opt double	50·00	50·00
		db. Variety III	19·00	19·00
D255D		5l. green	1·00	1·00
		db. Variety III	19·00	19·00
D256D		10l. scarlet		
D257D		20l. pale purple	1·00	1·00
		db. Variety III	21·00	21·00
D258D		30l. deep purple	7·00	7·00
		db. Variety III	95·00	95·00
		e. Opt reading down	40·00	40·00
		eb. Variety III	£130	£130
D259D		40l. black-brown	1·00	1·00
		db. Variety III	25·00	25·00
D260D		50l. brown-lake	1·00	1·00
		db. Variety III	25·00	25·00
D261D		1d. black	12·50	12·50
D262D		2d. bronze	16·00	16·00
D263D		3d. silver	28·00	28·00
D264D		5d. gold	44·00	44·00

(c) In carmine, reading down

D253F	D **20**	2l. grey	5·00	5·00
		fb. Variety IV	18·00	18·00
		fc. Variety VI	18·00	18·00
		fd. Variety VII	18·00	18·00
		fe. Variety VIII	18·00	18·00
		g. Opt reading up	5·00	7·50
		gc. Variety VI	65·00	65·00
		gd. Variety VII	65·00	65·00
		ge. Variety VIII	65·00	65·00
D254F		3l. orange	10·00	10·00
		fb. Variety IV	23·00	23·00
		fc. Variety VI	23·00	23·00
		fd. Variety VII	23·00	23·00
		fe. Variety VIII	23·00	23·00
		g. Opt reading up	90·00	£110
		gc. Variety VI	£550	£550
		gd. Variety VII	£550	£550
		ge. Variety VIII	£550	£550
D255F		5l. green	10·00	10·00
		fb. Variety IV	18·00	18·00
		fc. Variety VI	18·00	18·00
		fd. Variety VII	18·00	18·00
		fe. Variety VIII	18·00	18·00
D256F		10l. scarlet	10·00	10·00
		fb. Variety IV	18·00	18·00
		fc. Variety VI	18·00	18·00
		fd. Variety VII	18·00	18·00
		fe. Variety VIII	18·00	18·00
D261F		1d. black	40·00	40·00
		fa. Opt double	£250	£250
		g. Opt reading up	50·00	55·00
D262F		2d. bronze	80·00	80·00
		g. Opt reading up	£190	£180
D263F		3d. silver	£300	£300
D264F		5d. gold	£650	£650

A minor variety with large 'E' in 'ΕΛΛΗΝΙΚΗ' is found in all values.

King Constantine I

18 March 1913–12 June 1917

35 Vision of Constantine over Athens and Salamis

36 Victorious Eagle over Mount Olympus

(Litho Aspiotis)

1913 (16 Apr)–**15**. Victory stamps, used only in newly acquired territories in Macedonia, Epirus and the Aegean Islands.

A. Zigzag roulette 13–13½.

252A	**35**	1l. brown	65	65
253A	**36**	2l. scarlet	65	65
		a. Carmine (1915)	1·60	1·60
254A		3l. orange	65	65
255A	**35**	5l. green	1·50	90
256A		10l. rose-red	11·50	65
257A		20l. bright violet	31·00	6·25
258A	**36**	25l. pale blue	3·75	1·30
		a. Prussian blue		
259A	**35**	30l. green	£100	3·75
260A	**36**	40l. indigo	18·00	6·25
261A	**35**	50l. deep blue	6·25	3·75
262A	**36**	1d. dull purple	31·00	6·25
263A	**35**	2d. grey-brown	70·00	10·00
		a. Yellow-brown	—	
264A	**36**	3d. grey-blue	£275	50·00
265A	**35**	5d. drab	£275	60·00
266A	**36**	10d. rose-carmine	£325	£450
267A	**35**	25d. grey-black	£325	£450
252A/267A		Set of 16	£1300	£950

B. Imperf (pairs)

252B	**35**	1l. brown	£750	
253B	**36**	2l. scarlet	£750	
		a. Carmine (1915)		
254B		3l. orange	£700	
255B	**35**	5l. green	£225	
256B		10l. rose-red	£275	
257B		20l. bright violet	£2500	
258B	**36**	25l. pale blue	£2750	
259B	**35**	30l. green	£2750	
260B	**36**	40l. indigo	£2750	
264B		3d. grey-blue	£4250	

Dangerous forgeries exist of the 10d. and 25d.

The Mount Athos opt (see after D283a) was also applied to Nos. 252/267 which were surcharged in addition. These stamps were not issued.

1913 GREECE

37 Hoisting the Greek Flag at Suda Bay, 1 May 1913

(Recess Bradbury Wilkinson & Co.)

1913 (15 Nov). Union of Crete with Greece. P 14½.

268	37	25l. black and blue		14·00	6·25
		a. Imperf (pair)		£1400	£1900

This stamp was used only in Crete.

(Litho Aspiotis)

1913 (Dec)–**26**. POSTAGE DUE. Lithographed. Zigzag roulette.

D269	D **20**	1l. green		25	25
D270		2l. carmine		25	25
D271		3l. vermilion		25	25
D272		5l. green		25	25
		a. 'o' for 'p' in word at foot		5·00	5·00
		b. Imperf (pair)		£225	£500
		c. Double impression		75·00	
		d. Imperf between (pair)		£190	
D273		10l. carmine		40	40
D274		20l. slate-grey		40	40
D275		25l. ultramarine		40	40
D276		30l. scarlet		40	40
D277		40l. slate-blue		40	40
D278		50l. brown		40	40
		a. 'o' for 'p' in word at foot		75·00	75·00
D279		80l. brown-purple (10.5.24)		65	65
D280		1d. ultramarine		£110	85·00
		a. Blue		23·00	23·00
D281		2d. vermilion		23·00	1·30
D282		3d. carmine		12·50	3·75
D283		5d. pale blue		50·00	19·00
		a. Slate-blue (3.26)		12·50	6·25

The 5l., 10l., 20l., 1d., 2d. and 3d. values exist in a re-drawn type in which there is no accent shown on the first 'O' of 'GPAMMATOSHMON'.

In 1916 No. D186 and all values except the 80l. and the 3d. and 5d. were overprinted in Greek 'I(era) Koinotis Ag(iou) Orous', for the Mount Athos Monastery district, but were never issued.

During 1922–1923 several values of the unoverprinted stamps were used as ordinary postage stamps during a shortage of the latter. At the same period some Mount Athos stamps were used up as postage due stamps, without being noticed; D186, D273 and D275 are known used (*Price £225 each*).

See also Nos. C521/C522.

COMPULSORY CHARITY TAX STAMPS. These were for compulsory additional use at certain periods of the year for various funds. They are given C numbers. They were all lithographed by Aspiotis (later Aspioti-Elka) of Corfu, *unless otherwise stated*.

C **38** Dying Soldier, Widow and Child

(Des Matheopoulo)

1914 (31 Mar)–**15**. Zigzag roulette 13½.

C269	C **38**	2l. scarlet vermilion		75	50
		a. *Carmine* (1915)		75	50
		ab. Imperf (pair)		£225	
C270		5l. blue		90	65
		a. Imperf (pair)		£550	

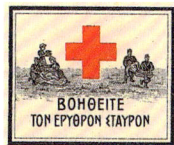

C **39** Red Cross, Nurses, Wounded and Bearers

1915 (Sept). Red Cross. Zigzag roulette 13½.

C271	C **39**	(5l.) Red and blue		24·00	2·75
		a. Imperf (pair)		£190	

C **40** Greek Women's Patriotic League Badge

(**38**) 'E.T.' = Greek Post

1915 (Sept). Greek Women's Patriotic League. P 11½.

C272	C **40**	(5l.) Red and blue		1·90	1·60
		a. Imperf (pair)		55·00	

Nos. C271/C272 were not for compulsory use on certain days. They were supplied by the charity bodies to certain postal officials who were allowed to retain 10% of the amount sold over the counter and the balance was paid by the GPO to the charities.

See also Nos. C344/C347.

On 29 September 1916, Eleftherios Venizelos, who had broken with King Constantine because of the sympathy of the king for the Central Powers, set up a Provisional Government, favourable to the Allies, first in Crete, and on 9 October at Salonika. Nos. 269/285 were used in southern and central Greece, which were under Royalist control.

1916 (1 Nov). Royalist issue. Optd with T **38**.

(a) Lithographed

269	**29**	1l. green (R.)		40	25
		a. Opt double, one inverted		31·00	20·00
270	**30**	2l. rose-red		40	40
		a. Opt inverted		44·00	31·00
271	**29**	3l. vermilion		50	40
		a. Opt inverted		70·00	50·00
272	**31**	5l. green (R.)		65	65
		a. Opt inverted		65·00	44·00
		b. Opt double		70·00	50·00
		c. Opt double, one inverted		70·00	50·00
273	**29**	10l. carmine		1·30	40
		a. Opt inverted		65·00	44·00
274	**30**	20l. purple-grey (R.)		1·90	40
		a. Opt inverted		£130	80·00
275		25l. blue (R.)		1·90	40
		a. Opt inverted		33·00	23·00
276	**31**	30l. carmine-red		2·50	1·30
		a. Opt inverted		31·00	20·00
277	**30**	40l. slate-blue (R.)		19·00	6·25
278	**31**	50l. purple-brown (R.)		65·00	3·00

(b) Engraved

279	**29**	3l. vermilion		75	65
		a. Opt inverted		70·00	50·00
280	**31**	30l. carmine-red		2·50	1·50
281	**32**	1d. ultramarine (R.)		70·00	5·50
		a. Rouletted in black		£550	
282		2d. vermilion		34·00	5·00
283		3d. carmine		20·00	3·75
284		5d. grey blue		90·00	15·00
285		10d. deep blue (R.)		31·00	25·00
		a. Opt inverted		£550	£425

Nos. 286/296 were used in northern Greece and the Greek islands, which were under the control of the Venizelist Provisional Government.

39 Iris

(Litho Perkins Bacon & Co.)

1917 (5 Feb). Venizelist issue. Sheet wmk 'SPECIAL POSTAGE PAPER LONDON'.

A. P 14

286A	**39**	1l. green		40	40
287A		5l. yellow-green		40	40
288A		10l. rose-carmine		90	40
289A		25l. light blue		90	40
290A		50l. grey-purple		7·50	2·75

GREECE 1917

291A	1d. ultramarine		5·00	1·30
292A	2d. dull vermilion		6·25	2·00
293A	3d. claret		25·00	5·00
294A	5d. slate-blue		10·00	6·25
295A	10d. deep blue		90·00	25·00
296A	25d. slate		£150	£180

B. Imperf (pairs)

286B	**39**	1l. green	19·00
287B		5l. yellow-green	19·00
288B		10l. rose-carmine	19·00
289B		25l. light blue	31·00
290B		50l. grey-purple	45·00
291B		1d. ultramarine	45·00
292B		2d. dull vermilion	45·00
293B		3d. claret	90·00
294B		5d. slate-blue	90·00
295B		10d. deep blue	£180
296B		25d. slate	£300

A 4d., in grey-brown, was only used fiscally (*Price* £7·50 *un*.). No. 296B imperf pair (*Price* £21·00 *un*.).

K. Π.
λεπτοῦ
1
(C **41**) (Thick 'K. Π.')

K. Π.
λεπτοῦ
1
(C **42**) (Taller, thinner 'K. Π')

The letters 'K. Π.' stand for 'Kolnonike Pronea' or 'Social Providence'. This represented an extra tax, part of the proceeds of which went to those who had suffered from the war blockade.

The following minor varieties exist:
  No stop after 'K' (all values).
  No stop after 'Π' (all values).
  Stop raised after 'Π' (all values).
  Stop before 'Π' (Nos. C303/C309).
  Comma after 'K' (Nos. C303/C305).
  Comma after 'Π' (Nos. C303/C305).
These are worth three to four times the prices for the normal stamps.

1917 (Apr).

*(a) Surch as T C **41**. Thin paper. Die II (C297/C300).*

C297	**15**	1l. on 1l. brown	1·40	5·75
		a. '—' on 'ü'	4·50	15·00
		b. Surch double, one inverted	12·00	
		c. *Brown* surch	17·00	34·00
C298		1l. on 3l. orange	20	75
		a. '—' over 'ü'	4·50	3·75
		b. 'λεπτο'	6·25	8·75
		c. 'λεπτ'		
		d. ''λεποῦ'		
		e. 'λεπτρῦ'		
		f. 'λεπτοῦ'		
C299		5l. on 1l. brown	1·90	2·50
		a. Surch inverted	23·00	
		b. Surch double	15·00	
		c. Surch double, one inverted	15·00	
C300		5l. on 20l. mauve	40	2·20
		a. Surch inverted	25·00	
		b. Surch double	19·00	
		c. Surch double, one inverted	19·00	
		d. Die I	1·60	2·50
C301		10l. on 30l. purple	95	3·25
		a. Surch double	22·00	
		c. Surch double, one inverted	22·00	
		d. Thick paper	65	2·50
C302		30l. on 30l. purple	1·10	2·75
		a. Surch inverted	25·00	
		b. Surch double	28·00	
		c. Surch double, one inverted	31·00	
		d. Thick paper	1·10	3·75
		da. Surch treble, one inverted	44·00	

*(b) Surch as T C **42***

*(i) On Types **15** and **17***

C303	**15**	1l. on 3l. orange (thin paper, Die II)	35	75
		a. 'K. M.' in top line	19·00	25·00
		b. Surch inverted	8·75	
		c. Surch double	8·75	
		d. Surch double, one inverted	19·00	
		e. Thin paper, Die I	4·00	
		ea. 'K. M.' in top line	34·00	
C304		5l. on 40l. deep brown (thick paper, Die I)	65	1·50
		a. Thick paper, Die II	65	1·90
		ab. Dies I and II in pair	14·00	50·00
		b. Thin paper, Die I	65	1·90

		ba. Thin paper, Die II	50	1·50
		bb. Dies I and II in pair	13·50	
		bc. Surch double	16·00	
		c. *Deep red-brown* (I)	3·50	6·25
		ca. Die II	2·50	3·75
		cb. Dies I and II in pair	25·00	
C305		5l. on 50l. lake (II)	45	1·90
		a. Surch inverted	19·00	
		b. Surch double, one inverted	50·00	
C306	**17**	5l. on 1d. black (thick paper)	3·25	8·75
		a. Thin paper. Perf 12×14	1·20	4·00
		ab. Perf 14	2·50	7·50
		ac. Imperf (pair)		
		ad. Surch inverted	33·00	
		ae. Surch double	25·00	

No. C306 with red surcharge is an essay.

*(ii) On Types **35/36**.*

C307	**36**	5l. on 25l. pale blue	25	65
		a. Surch inverted	12·50	
		b. Surch double	12·00	
		c. Surch double, one inverted	12·00	
C308		5l. on 40l. dull blue	25	40
		a. Surch inverted	16·00	
		b. Surch double	12·00	
		c. Surch double, one inverted	12·00	
C309	**35**	5l. on 50l. deep blue	25	45
		a. Surch inverted	16·00	
		b. Surch double	12·00	
		c. Surch double, one inverted	12·00	

Similar surcharges on Nos. 183 and 185 were unauthorized.

C **43**

K. Π.
λεπτοῦ
1
(C **44**)

K. Π.
5 λεπι. 5
(C **45**)

K.Π.
10 ΛΕΠΤΑ 10
(C **46**)

K. Π.
5 Λεπτὰ 5
(C **47**)

1917. Social Providence Fund. Fiscal stamps, T C **43**, surch. Zigzag roulette 13.

*(a) As T C **44**, in brownish red*

C310	1l. on 10l. blue	1·30	2·50
C311	1l. on 80l. blue	1·30	2·50
C312	5l. on 60l. blue	10·00	12·50
C313	5l. on 80l. blue	5·00	3·75
	a. Surch inverted	—	90·00
C314	10l. on 70l. blue	44·00	75·00
C315	10l. on 90l. blue	28·00	65·00
C316	20l. on 20l. blue	£9500	£8000
C317	20l. on 30l. blue	12·50	12·50
C318	20l. on 40l. blue	34·00	38·00
C319	20l. on 50l. blue	15·00	19·00
C320	20l. on 60l. blue	£650	
C321	20l. on 80l. blue	£150	
C322	20l. on 90l. blue	9·50	14·00
	a. Surch inverted		£110

As last, P 11½ vertically through centre of stamps

C323	5l. on 10l. blue	28·00	44·00
C324	5l. on 60l. blue	14·50	24·00
C325	5l. on 80l. blue	18·00	31·00
C326	10l. on 70l. blue	14·50	31·00
C327	10l. on 90l. blue	41·00	65·00

*(b) As T C **45**, in red-brown (Br.) or black*

C328	1l. on 50l. purple (Blk.)	1·40	2·50
C329	5l. on 10l. blue (Br.)	1·40	2·50
	a. Surch inverted		

1918 GREECE

	b. '5' at left inverted		£140	
C330	5l. on 10l. purple (Br.)		1.40	2.50
C331	10l. on 50l. purple (Br.)		12.00	21.00
C332	10l. on 50l. purple (Blk.)		55.00	
C333	20l. on 2d. blue (Blk.)		16.00	31.00
	a. '30' for '20' at right		95.00	

(c) As T C 46, in black, but thin double lines through old value (Corfu issue)

C334	1l. on 10l. blue		2.20	2.75
C335	5l. on 50l. blue		80.00	£130
C336	10l. on 50l. blue		£950	£1000
C337	20l. on 50l. blue		£18000	

(d) As T C 46, in black (bar through old value)

C338	10l. on 50l. blue		18.00	15.00
C339	20l. on 50l. blue		42.00	35.00
C340	30l. on 50l. blue		28.00	25.00

(e) As T C 47, in black

C341	5l. on 10l. purple and red		15.00	20.00
	a. 'K' with serifs		23.00	33.00

T C 43 with surcharges higher than 30l. are fiscal stamps.

King Alexander
12 June 1917–25 October 1920

 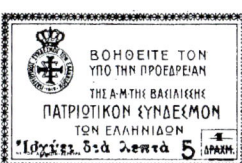

C 48 Wounded Soldier   C 49

1918 (June). Red Cross. Zigzag roulette 13½.

C342	C 48	5l. scarlet, blue and yellow	12.50	1.90

1918. No. C342 optd 'Π.Π.' (= P.I.P. initials of the Patriotic Charity League).

C343	C 48	5l. scarlet, blue and yellow	17.00	1.90
		a. Opt double	£250	

King Constantine 1 (restored)
20 December 1920–27 September 1922

1922. Greek Women's Patriotic League. Surch in red as in T C **49**. P 11½.

C344	C 49	5l. on 10l. red and blue	£450	19.00
C345		5l. on 20l. red and blue	£140	95.00
C346		5l. on 50l. red and blue	£450	£350
C347		5l. on 1d. red and blue	12.50	90.00

Nos. C344/C347 were not issued without surcharge. Dangerous forgeries exist of Nos. C344/C346.

Examples of the 10l., 20l. and 50l. without surcharge were never issued (*Price* 65p. *each*).

King George II
27 September 1922–25 March 1924

ΕΠΑΝΑΣΤΑΣΙΣ
1922
ΛΕΠΤΑ 10

(**46** 'Revolution, 1922')

1923 (8 May). Revolution of 1922. Various stamps of Greece and Crete, optd or surch as T **46**.

I. On stamps of Greece
*(a) Types **35** and **36***

340		5l. on 3l. orange	65	65
341		10l. on 20l. bright violet	3.25	3.25
342		10l. on 25l. pale blue	1.90	1.90
343		10l. on 30l. green	1.90	1.90
		a. Imperf (pair)	£800	
344		10l. on 40l. indigo	2.75	2.75
345		50l. on 50l. deep blue	90	90
346		2d. on 2d. grey-brown	£120	£120
347		3d. on 3d. grey-blue	8.75	8.75
		a. Imperf (pair)	£1000	
348		5d. on 5d. drab	9.50	9.50
349		10d. on 1d. dull purple	22.00	22.00
350		10d. on 10d. rose-carmine	£1600	

*(b) T **39***

351		5l. on 10l. rose-carmine	55	55
352		50l. on 50l. grey-purple	65	65
353		1d. on 1d. ultramarine	65	65
354		2d. on 2d. dull vermilion	80	80
355		3d. on 3d. claret	3.75	3.75
356		5d. on 5d. slate-blue	5.00	4.50
357		25d. on 25d. slate	50.00	50.00

II. On stamps of Crete
(a) Pictorials of 1900

358		5l. on 1l. chocolate (No. 1)	55.00	
359		10l. on 10l. scarlet (No. 3)	55	55
360		10l. on 25l. blue (No. 5B)	£200	
361		10l. on 25l. blue (No. 15)	65	65
362		50l. on 50l. deep lilac (No. 16)	80	1.30
363		50l. on 50l. ultramarine (No. 14)	16.00	22.00
364		50l. on 1d. indigo-violet (No. 17)	7.25	7.50
365		50l. on 5d. black and green (No. 19)	65.00	

(b) Pictorials of 1905

366		10l. on 20l. blue-green	£250	£275
367		10l. on 25l. ultramarine	60	60
		a. Surch double	85.00	
368		50l. on 50l. brown	65	65
369		50l. on 1d. sepia and carmine	5.75	8.00
370		3d. on 3d. black and orange	28.00	31.00
371		5d. on 5d. black and olive-green	19.00	25.00

No. 366 is found with forged overprint, used.

(c) Stamps of 1907–1908.

372		10l. on 10l. dull carmine*	65	65
373		10l. on 25l. black and blue (No. 30)	2.75	3.25
374		50l. on 5d. black and green (No. 31)	7.50	8.75

*No. 372 is on Crete No. 36 but without opt T **22**.

*(d) Stamps with overprint Types **22**, **28** or **30**.*

375		5l. on 1l. chocolate (No. 58)	65	65
376		5l. on 5l. green (No. 60)	65	65
377		10l. on 10l. dull carmine (No. 61)	65	65
378		10l. on 20l. blue-green (No. 62)	65	65
379		10l. on 25l. ultramarine (No. 63)	65	65
380		50l. on 50l. brown (No. 39)	£1900	
381		50l. on 50l. brown (No. 64)	95	95
382		50l. on 1d. sepia and carmine (No. 65)	9.00	12.50
383		3d. on 3d. black and orange (No. 56)	38.00	55.00
384		3d. on 3d. black and orange (No. 66)	25.00	33.00
385		5d. on 5d. black and olive-green (No. 67)	£450	£500

*(e) Postage Due stamps, T D **8***

386		5l. on 5l. red	65	65
387		5l. on 10l. red	65	65
388		10l. on 20l. red	24.00	25.00
389		50l. on 40l. red	70	1.30
390		50l. on 50l. red	70	1.30
391		50l. on 1d. red	90	1.60
392		50l. on 1d. red (No. D18)	19.00	23.00
393		2d. on 2d. red	1.60	2.50

*(f) Postage Due stamps with overprint T **22***

394		5l. on 5l. red	7.50	11.50
395		5l. on 10l. red	2.50	3.25
		a. Cretan opt inverted (No. D46a)		
396		10l. on 20l. red	£100	£110

*(g) Postage Due stamps with overprint T **30***

397		5l. on 5l. red	55	55
398		5l. on 10l. red	55	55
399		10l. on 20l. red	70	70
400		50l. on 50l. red	90	1.10
401		50l. on 1d. red	8.25	9.00
402		2d. on 2d. red	14.50	15.00

340s/349s, 351s/357s, 359s, 361s/364s, 366s/371s, 372s/374s, 375s/379s, 381s/385s, 386s/393s, 394s/396s, 397s/402s Optd 'SPECIMEN set of 58 .... £950

The Postage Due stamps with overprint T **46** were sold as ordinary postage stamps.

Nos. 350, 358, 360, 365 and 380 were not issued.

FIRST REPUBLIC
25 March 1924–25 November 1935

47 Lord Byron   **48** Byron at Missolonghi

GREECE 1924

(Recess Bradbury Wilkinson)
1924 (16 Apr). Byron Centenary. P 12.
403	**47**	80l. indigo	80	40
404	**48**	2d. black and violet	3·25	1·10

C **50** Wounded Soldier and Family

49 Grave of Marco Botzaris

1924 (12 June)–**26**. Red Cross Fund.
(a) P 13½×12½ (Aspiotis)
C405	C **50**	10l. scarlet, blue and yellow	2·20	1·30

(b) P 11½ (M. Erginos, Athens) (1926)
C406	C **50**	10l. scarlet, blue and yellow	65	65
		a. Imperf (pair)	44·00	

(Litho Aspiotis)
1926 (24 Apr). Centenary of Fall of Missolonghi. Zigzag roulette.
405	**49**	25l. mauve	1·80	65

50 Fortress

(Des A. Gavallas. Litho in Milan)
1926 (21 Oct). AIR. Aeroespresso Co. issue. T **50** and similar horiz designs, each showing a Savoia Marchetti S-55C flying boat. Multicoloured. P 11½.
406		2d. Type **50**	3·25	4·50
		a. Imperf between (pair)	£1100	
407		3d. Acropolis	41·00	15·00
408		5d. Map of Greece and Mediterranean	3·25	2·50
409		10d. Colonnade	38·00	15·00
406/409 *Set of 4*			75·00	33·00

Nos. 406 and 408 were issued both in sheets of 15 and of 25. No. 407 was issued both in sheets of 15 stamps and one blank label and in sheets of 25.

51 Corinth Canal

52 Dodecanese Costume

53 Temple of Theseus, Athens

54 Acropolis

I

II

I

II

I

II

(Original dies and plates eng by T. Macdonald, London. Re-engraved dies of 1933–1935 and No. 419e by De La Rue. Recess Aspiotis; 1d. later by Perkins Bacon; 3d. and 15d. later in Poland)

1927 (1 Apr)–**35**. Types **51** to **54** and similar types. P 12½, 13 and compound (Aspiotis); 13¾ (P.B.); 11½, 11½×11, 11½×12¾ and 12¾×11½ (Polish).
410		5l. deep green	20	15
		a. Imperf between (pair)	£250	£225
411		10l. scarlet	50	20
		a. Imperf between (pair)	£250	£225
412		20l. violet (to purple)	50	15
		a. Imperf between (pair)	£275	£250
413		25l. blue-green	90	25
		a. Imperf between (pair)	£275	£250
414		40l. blue-green	90	25
415		50l. violet (to purple)	1·90	25
		a. Imperf between (pair)	£275	£250
		b. Re-engraved (1933)	5·00	1·40
416		80l. black and indigo	1·50	40
		a. Imperf (pair)	£1600	
417		1d. brown and blue (*shades*) (I)	1·80	30
		a. Imperf (pair)	£275	£300
		b. Centre inverted	—	£23000
		c. Centre double	£500	£550
		d. Frame double	£500	£550
		e. Perkins Bacon ptg. P 13½ (II) (24.12.31)	19·00	85
		f. Aspiotis (re-engraved) (1933)	3·75	1·30
418		2d. black and blue-green	18·00	40
		a. Imperf (pair)	£1600	£2500
		b. Re-engraved. Black and deep green (1933)	3·75	45
419		3d. black and purple	16·00	40
		a. Centre double	£500	£550
		b. Centre inverted	—	£23000
		c. Imperf (pair)	£1800	£2750
		d. Polish ptg (1934)	6·25	50
419e		4d. brown (1.11.35)	28·00	1·60
420		5d. black and orange	28·00	1·60
		a. Imperf (pair)	£1600	£2750
		b. Centre inverted	—	£13000
421		10d. black and claret (I)	75·00	9·50
		a. Re-engraved (II) (1935)	85·00	2·30
422		15d. black and yellow-green	£130	18·00
		a. Polish ptg (1934)	£200	28·00
423		25d. black and green (I)	£160	18·00
		a. Re-engraved (II) (1935)	85·00	23·00
410/423 *Set of 15 (cheapest)*			£325	40·00

Designs: Vert (18×25 *mm*)—5l. T **51**; 10l. T **52**; 20l. Macedonian costume; 25l. Monastery of Simon Peter, Athos; 40l. White Tower, Salonika; 50l. and 80l. Corinth Canal. Horiz (25×18 *mm*)—1d. T **53**; 2d. Acropolis; 3d. Cruiser *Averoff*; 4d. Mistra Cathedral (32×22 *mm*)— 5d. and 15d. Academy of Sciences, Athens: 10d. Temple of Theseus, Athens; 25d. T **54**.

Printings. 50l. In the 1927 printing the white markings forming the bow of the ship appear as a faint cross. In the 1933 redrawing there is a white mark to left of the vertical line of the bows only.

1d. Illustrations I and II show the difference in the figures of value in the 1927 and Perkins Bacon printings. In the 1933 redrawing the figures are similar to I, but the left-hand '1' has very little serif to the left of the base, giving it a lop-sided appearance. The lines slanting down to the right from the peak of the roof are much more clearly defined in the Perkins Bacon and 1933 types than in the 1927 issue.

2d. In the 1927 issue the heavy shading of the ground in the foreground extends to below the trees to the right of the left-hand group of buildings at the foot of the hill. In the 1933 issue the heavy shading does not extend to the left much beyond the right-hand group of buildings.

Generally speaking, the shading and details of the 50l., 1d. and 2d. of 1933 are much clearer than those of 1927.

Polish printings. Apart from the difference of perf, the lines of shading, etc, in the Polish printings are much sharper than in the Aspiotis printing.

10d. and 25d. Illustrations I and II show the differences between the figures of value in the 1927 and 1935 printings. In the re-engraved issue of 1935 the details of the design are much sharper.

A 1l. brown in T **52** was prepared but not issued, most of the stock being destroyed. (*Price un.*, £450).

See also Nos. C523 and C591/C592.

1927 GREECE

55 General Favier and Acropolis

56 Navarino Bay and Pylos

57 Battle of Navarino   **58** Sir Edward Codrington

(Recess Bradbury Wilkinson)
1927 (1 Aug). Centenary of Liberation of Athens from the Turks. P 12.
424	**55**	1d. scarlet	65	45
425		3d. slate-blue	5·00	80
426		6d. green	26·00	17·00
424/426	Set of 3		28·00	16·00

(Litho Aspiotis)
1927 (20 Oct)–**28**. Centenary of Battle of Navarino. P 13½×12½ (Nos. 427/428) or 12½×13 (others).
427	**56**	1d.50 dull grey-green	3·75	60
		aa. Imperf (pair)	£375	£550
		a. Imperf between (pair)	£650	
428	**57**	4d. dull blue	16·00	2·10
		a. Imperf (pair)	—	£3750
429	**58**	5d. grey and brown ('Sir Codrington') (1st ptg)	9·50	5·75
		a. Black and brown (2nd ptg)	16·00	8·25
430		5d. black and brown ('Sir Edward Codrington')	60·00	16·00
431	–	5d. black and ultramarine (de Rigny)	55·00	13·00
432	–	5d. black and carmine (Van der Heyden)	31·00	12·00
427/432	Set of 6		£160	45·00

Small quantities of the 1d.50 and 5d. (No. 429) were issued at Navarino on 20 Oct 1927. The other values appeared on 17 March 1928.

59 Righas Ferreo   **60** Patriarch Gregory V   **61** Greece in 1830 and 1930

62 Declaration of Independence   **63** Sortie from Missolonghi

(Recess Perkins Bacon (P) or Bradbury Wilkinson (B))
1930 (1 Apr). Centenary of Independence. Various portraits (except 4d., 25d. and 50d.) and Types **61** to **63** all dated 1830–1930. Perkins Bacon values, P 13½; Bradbury Wilkinson, P 12.
433		10l. brown (P)	20	15
		a. Imperf between (pair)	£225	
434		20l. black (B)	20	25
435		40l. blue-green (B)	30	25
436		50l. vermilion (P)	35	40
437		50l. blue (B)	35	40
438		1d. carmine (P)	45	40
439		1d. brown-orange (B)	45	40
440		1d.50 light blue (P)	65	30
		a. Imperf (pair)	£300	
441		1d.50 scarlet (B)	65	30
442		2d. red-orange (P)	65	40
443		3d. purple-brown (B)	2·20	85
444		4d. deep blue (P)	6·25	1·20
445		5d. violet (P)	2·50	2·00
446		10d. black (P)	12·50	8·50
447		15d. yellow-green (P)	22·00	15·00
448		20d. bluish slate (P)	41·00	19·00
449		25d. slate-grey (B)	38·00	27·00
450		50d. brown-lake (B)	75·00	75·00
433/450	Set of 18		£180	£140

Designs: (P 20×29 *mm*. B 21½×30 *mm*)—10l. T **59**; 20l. T **60**; 40l. A. Ypsilanti, 50l. (No. 436) Lascarina Bouboulina; (No. 437) Ath. Diakos; 1d. (No. 438) Th. Kolokotronis; (No. 439) C. Kanaris, 1d.50, (No. 440) Karaiskakis; (No. 441) M. Botzaris; 2d. A. Miaoulis; 3d. L. Kondouriotis; 5d. Count Capodistria; 10d. P. Mavromikhalis; 15d. Solomos; 20d. Korais; 4d. T **61**; 25d. T **62**; 50d. T **63**.

(Litho Aspiotis)
1930 (5 Nov). POSTAGE DUE. P 13½×12½–13½.
D451	D **20**	50l. brown	30	50
D452		1d. pale blue	30	50
D453		2d. vermilion	30	50
D454		3d. carmine-red	38·00	38·00
D455		5d. slate-blue	30	50
D456		10d. green	30	1·90
D457		15d. red-brown	40	2·30
D458		25d. vermilion	90	2·75
		a. No accent on last 'e' of word in lowest tablet	31·00	65·00
D451/D458	Set of 8		37·00	42·00

See also Nos. D480/D481 and D595/D598.

64 Monastery of Arkadi, Crete and Abbot Gabriel

(Recess Bradbury Wilkinson)
1930 (8 Nov). Defence of Arkadi Monastery against the Turks. P 12.
451	**64**	8d. violet	44·00	1·60

The monastery was blown up by the Abbot on 8 November 1866.

(**65**)   **66** Airship *Graf Zeppelin* and Acropolis

1932 (24 Apr–7 Aug). Surch as T **65** in red.
452	–	1d.50 on 5d. black and ultramarine (No. 431)	3·75	25
453	–	1d.50 on 5d. black and carmine (No. 432)	3·75	25
		a. Surcharge double	£130	
454	**55**	2d. on 3d. slate-blue (7.8.32)	3·75	45
455	**58**	2d. on 5d. black and brown (No. 429*a*) (7.8.32)	7·50	25
456		2d. on 5d. black and brown (No. 430) (7.8.32)	15·00	25
457	**55**	4d. on 6d. green	5·00	1·30
452/457	Set of 6		35·00	2·50

GREECE 1933

(Des A. Gavallas. Litho Aspioti-Elka)

1933 (2 May). AIR. Aeroespresso Co. issue. P 13×12½.

458	**66**	30d. carmine-red	38·00	28·00
459		100d. dull blue	£100	70·00
460		120d. brown	£100	70·00
458/460 Set of 3			£200	£150

67 Swinging the Propeller   **68** 'Flight'

69 Italy–Greece–Rhodes–Turkey Air Routes   **70** Hermes and Marina Fiat MF.5 Flying Boat

(Recess Bradbury Wilkinson)

1933 (10 Oct). AIR. Aeroespresso Co. issue. Types **67** to **70** and other designs all inscr 'ΕΝΑΕΡ ΤΑΧΥΑΡ' etc. P 12.

461		50l. orange and green	50	65
462		1d. red-orange and deep blue	70	75
463		3d. chestnut and purple	1·30	1·30
464		5d. blue and orange	14·00	10·00
465		10d. black and scarlet	1·90	2·75
466		20d. green and black	24·00	15·00
467		50d. indigo and brown	80·00	95·00
461/467 Set of 7			£110	£110

Designs: Horiz—50l. T **67**; 1d. Temple of Neptune, Corinth; 3d. Marina Fiat MF.5 flying boat over Hermoupolis; 10d. T **69**. Vert—5d. T **68**; 20d. T **70**; 50d. Woman and Marina Fiat MF.5 flying boat. The 1d. is known used, bisected.

> **PRINTERS.** In the following postage stamps, *unless otherwise stated,* the recess-printed stamps as well as those printed by recess and litho combined, were executed by De La Rue & Co., in conjunction with Aspiotis, Corfu (later Aspioti-Elka); the lithographed issues were made by Aspioti-Elka. From the beginning of 1953 both lithographed and engraved issues were printed by Aspioti-Elka, *unless otherwise stated.*

71 Greece   **73** Junkers G.24 Aeroplane and Acropolis

1933 (2 Nov). AIR. Government issue. Recess. Perfs as shown.

468	**71**	50l. green (P 13×13½)	65	75
469		1d. claret (P 13×12½)	1·60	90
470	–	2d. bright violet (P 13×13½)	1·70	1·70
471	**73**	5d. bright blue (P 12½×13)	12·50	7·50
		a. Imperf (pair)	£1000	
472	–	10d. carmine (P 13×13½)	22·00	12·50
473	**71**	25d. deep blue (P 13×13½)	65·00	31·00
474	**73**	50d. brown (P 13½×13)	95·00	80·00
		a. Imperf (pair)	£1500	
468/474 Set of 7			£180	£120

Design: As T **71**—2d., 10d. Ikarian Island.

74 Admiral Kondouriotis and cruiser *Averoff*   **75** 'Greece'

76 Statue (Youth of Marathon)   C **77** St Demetrius

1933. Recess. P 13½×13 (50d.) or 13×13½ (others).

475	**74**	50d. grey-blue and black (16.12.33)	95·00	4·50
476	**75**	75d. purple-lake and black (2.11.33)	£225	£225
		a. Imperf (pair)	£1600	
477	**76**	100d. grey-green and brown (16.12.33)	£950	39·00
475/477 Set of 3			£1100	£250

(Litho Kontogony, Athens)

1934 (22 Sept). Salonika International Exhibition Fund. P 11½.

C478	C **77**	20l. red-brown	40	25
		a. Imperf between (pair)	12·50	
		b. Imperf (pair)	12·50	

See also No. C573.

78 Athens Stadium, Entrance

(Des L. Sowiński. Eng Wl. Vacek. Recess, in Poland)

1934 (10 Dec). P 11½.

479	**78**	8d. blue	£140	2·75
		a. Perf 13×11½	£140	2·75

C **78** Allegory of Health

1934 (28 Dec). Postal Staff Anti-tuberculosis Fund. P 13½ (50l.) or 13½×13 (others).

C480	C **78**	10l. orange and blue-green	25	25
C481		20l. orange and blue	45	40
C482		50l. orange and green	4·00	4·75
C480/C482 Set of 3			4·25	4·75

(Recess Aspiotis)

1935 (1 Nov). POSTAGE DUE. P 12½×13.

D480	D **20**	50d. orange	50	6·25
D481		100d. blue-green	50	6·25

1935 GREECE

79 Sun Chariot

80 Hermes

(Des M. Biskinis. Recess)

1935–39. AIR. Mythological designs as Types **79/80**. P 13×12½, 12½×13 or 13½×13 (5d.).

(a) Grey-white paper. Size 34×23½ or 23½×34 mm. (10.11.1935)

480		1d. scarlet	2·50	1·40
481		2d. grey-blue	2·50	1·80
482		5d. mauve	31·00	12·50
483		7d. ultramarine	47·00	15·00
484		10d. brown	6·25	5·50
485		25d. rose-carmine	7·50	10·00
486		30d. green	2·50	3·75
487		50d. mauve	10·00	14·50
488		100d. brown	3·25	9·25
480/488		Set of 9	£100	65·00

(b) White paper. Size 34¼×24 or 24×34¼ mm. (1937–1939)

488a		1d. scarlet	40	40
488b		2d. grey-blue	40	40
488c		5d. mauve	40	50
488d		7d. ultramarine	40	50
488e		10d. orange-red (1.3.39)	5·00	7·75
488a/488e		Set of 5	6·00	8·50

Designs: Horiz—1d. T **79**; 2d. Iris; 30d. Triptolemus; 100d. Phrixus and Helle. Vert—5d. Daedalus and Icarus: 7d. Minerva; 10d. T **80**; 25d. Zeus and Ganymede; 50d. Bellerophon on Pegasus.

King George II (restored)
25 November 1935–1 April 1947

(81)

(82)

A plebiscite held on 3 November 1935 resulted in a vote for the restoration of the monarchy.

1935 (24 Nov). Restoration of Greek Monarchy. Surch as T **81** or T **82**.

489	**81**	50l. on 40l. (No. D277) (Br.)	45	40
490		3d. on 3d. (No. D282) (B.)	1·60	1·50
491		3d. on 3d. (No. D454) (B.)	5·00	2·20
492	**82**	5d. on 100d. (No. 477) (Br.)	3·25	2·20
493		15d. on 75d. (No. 476) (B.)	12·50	8·00
489/493		Set of 5	21·00	13·00

1935 (13 Dec)–**39**. As Nos. C480/C482, but inscr 'ΕΛΛΑΣ' at top. P 13×13½, 13 (No. C494) or 12½ (No. C497).

C494	C **78**	10l. orange and blue-green (1935)	40	75
C495		20l. orange and blue (1935)	65	1·30
C496		50l. orange and green (1935)	1·60	2·50
C497		50l. orange and brown (2.12.39)	60	55
C494/C497		Set of 4	3·00	4·50

83 King Constantine

84

(Portrait, recess; frame, litho)

1936 (18 Nov). Re-interment of King Constantine and Queen Sophia. W **84**. P 12½×13½.

494	**83**	3d. brown and black	70	40
495		8d. blue and black	1·60	1·90

ΠΡΟΝΟΙΑ
(C **85**)

85 Pallas Athene (Minerva)

1937 (20 Jan–June). Nos. D273 and 415b optd as T C **85**.

C498		10l. carmine (B.)	1·30	35
		a. Opt inverted	42·00	
C499		50l. violet (R.)	1·40	40
		a. Opt inverted (16.2.37)	65	45
C500		50l. violet (G.) (16.6.37)	65	35
C498/C500		Set of 3	3·50	1·40

No. C498 exists in the two types mentioned in the first footnote after No. D283a.

No. C498a occurs on the original type with accent.

On one or two sheets of No. C499 the overprint was accidentally inverted and these stamps were sold at post offices before the mistake was discovered. To prevent speculation the Postal Authorities deliberately printed a supply with inverted overprint and put them on sale at the chief post offices.

(Recess Bradbury Wilkinson)

1937 (17 Apr). Centenary of Athens University. P 12.

496	**85**	3d. orange-brown	65	55

86 Bull-leaping

87 Zeus and Thunderbolt

88 Amphictyonic Coin

89 King George II

89a Statue of King Constantine

90 St Paul on Mount Areopagus

GREECE 1937

91 Leo III (the Isaurian) destroying the Saracens

92 'Glory' of Psara

1937–38. As Types **86/92** (various designs). Nos. 497/502 and 514, litho; Nos. 503/513 and 515/516, recess.

(a) W **84**. P 13½×12½ *(horiz)*; 12½×13½ *(vert)* or 13×12 (T **89**).

497	86	5l. greenish blue and red-brown (1.11.37)	15	20
498	–	10l. red-brown and light blue (inscr 'TYPIN' etc) (1.11.37)	15	20
499	87	20l. blue-green and black (1.11.37)	15	20
500	88	40l. black and blue-green (1.11.37)	15	20
501	–	50l. black and bistre-brown (1.11.37)	15	20
502	–	80l. brown and dull violet (1.11.37)	15	20
503	89	1d. green (24.1.37)	20	20
504	–	2d. ultramarine (1.11.37)	20	25
505	89	3d. red-brown (24.1.37)	25	20
506	–	5d. scarlet (1.11.37)	20	25
507	–	6d. olive-brown (1.11.37)	20	30
508	90	7d. chocolate (1.11.37)	1·50	2·10
509	89	8d. deep blue (24.1.37)	1·50	75
510	–	10d. red-brown (1.11.37)	20	30
511	91	15d. blue-green (1.11.37)	25	40
512	92	25d. deep blue (1.11.37)	20	40
513	89	100d. lake (24.1.37)	17·00	16·00

As No. 498, but correctly inscr 'TIPYN', etc, instead of 'TYPIN', etc.

514	–	10l. red-brown and light blue (1938)	35	55

(b) No wmk. P 12½×13½

515	**89a**	1d.50 green (9.10.38)	50	35
516	–	30d. brown-red (9.10.38)	3·75	5·25
497/516 Set of 20			24·00	26·00

Designs: Vert—10l. (Nos. 498, 514) Court lady of Tiryns; 80l. Venus of Milo. Horiz—50l. Chairing Diagoras of Rhodes; 2d. Battle of Salamis; 5d. Panathenaic chariot; 6d. Alexander the Great at Battle of Issus; 10d. Temple of St Demetrius, Salonika.

For other values in T **92**, but smaller, see Nos. 609/616.
See also Nos. 605/608, C619/C620, C698, C699 and C706.

93 Prince Paul and Princess Frederika Louise

94 Arms of Greece, Rumania, Turkey and Yugoslavia

1938. Royal Wedding. Recess. W **84**. P 13½×12½.

517	93	1d. green (8.2.38)	20	30
518		3d. red-brown (9.1.38)	50	30
519		8d. blue (24.1.38)	1·20	1·60
517/519 Set of 3			1·70	2·00

1938 (8 Feb). Balkan Entente. Litho. P 12½.

520	94	6d. blue	10·50	2·75

Stamps of a similar design were issued by Rumania, Turkey and Yugoslavia.

(C **95**)   (**95**)   C **96** Queens Olga and Sophia

1938. Nos. D272 and D274 surch with T C **95**.

C521	D **20**	50l. on 5l. green (B.) (1.6.38)	10·00	1·60
		a. Imperf between (vert pair)	£110	
		b. 'o' for 'p' in word at foot	50·00	50·00
C522		50l. on 20l. slate-grey (B.) (18.7.38)	4·50	1·30

Nos. C521/C522 exist in the two types mentioned in the first footnote after D283*a*.

1938–39. AIR. Nos. D278 and D451 optd with T **95** (Junkers G.24 aeroplane).

521	D **20**	50l. brown (R.) (8.8.38)	20	40
		a. 'o' for 'p' in word at foot	12·50	25·00
522		50l. brown (R.) (26.6.39)	20	40

For other values, see Nos. 554/560.

1938 (13 Sept). No. 412 surch as T C **95**, but size 15×17 mm.

C523		50l. on 20l. (V.)	80	1·00

1939 (1 Feb). P 13½×12.

C524	C **96**	10l. carmine/*rose*	15	20
C525		50l. green/*pale green*	20	25
C526		1d. blue/*pale blue*	30	40
C524/C526 Set of 3			60	75

See also Nos. C554, C642 and C643.

96 Arms of Ionian Islands

97 Corfu Bay and Citadel

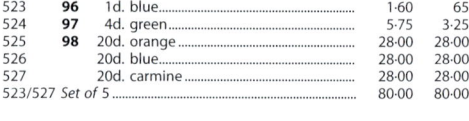

98 King George I of Greece and Queen Victoria

1939 (21 May). 75th Anniversary of Cession of Ionian Islands. Recess. P 12½ (1d.) or 13½×12½ (others).

523	**96**	1d. red	1·60	65
524	**97**	4d. green	5·75	3·25
525	**98**	20d. orange	28·00	28·00
526		20d. blue	28·00	28·00
527		20d. carmine	28·00	28·00
523/527 Set of 5			80·00	80·00

99 Javelin-thrower

100 Arms of Greece, Rumania, Turkey and Yugoslavia

1939 (1 Oct). Tenth Pan-Balkan Games, Athens. Vert designs as T **99**. Litho. P 12½×13½.

528		50l. myrtle/*green* (Runner)	35	40
529		3d. carmine/*pink* (Type **99**)	1·40	50
530		6d. red-brown/*pale orange* (Discus-thrower)	6·00	3·50
531		8d. blue/*grey* (Jumper)	6·00	4·50
528/531 Set of 4			12·50	8·00

1940 (27 May). Balkan Entente. Litho. W **84**. P 13×12½.

532	**100**	6d. pale blue	16·00	2·50
533		8d. bluish slate	14·00	3·25

Stamps of a similar design were issued by Rumania, Turkey and Yugoslavia.

101 Greek Youth Badge

1940 GREECE

102 Youths on Parade   **103** Meteora Monasteries, Thessaly

1940 (3 Aug). Fourth Anniversary of Greek Youth Organisation. Designs as Types **101/103**. Litho. W **84**. Nos. 534 and 543, perf 13½×12½; others perf 12½.

(a) POSTAGE

534		3d. blue, red and silver	1·30	1·30
535		5d. black and blue	8·25	6·50
536		10d. black and orange	11·00	12·50
537		15d. black and green	70·00	70·00
538		20d. black and lake	55·00	43·00
539		25d. black and blue	55·00	50·00
540		30d. black and purple	55·00	50·00
541		50d. black and blue	95·00	60·00
542		75d. gold, brown and blue	95·00	65·00
543		100d. blue, red and silver	£140	£110
534/543 Set of 10			£550	£425

(b) AIR

544		2d. black and orange	2·50	95
545		4d. black and green	16·00	4·50
546		6d. black and lake	16·00	7·50
547		8d. black and blue	41·00	12·50
548		16d. black and purple	50·00	26·00
549		32d. black and orange	80·00	65·00
550		45d. black and green	£110	75·00
551		55d. black and carmine	95·00	75·00
552		65d. black and blue	£100	75·00
553		100d. black and purple	£110	80·00
544/553 Set of 10			£550	£375

Designs: Postage. Horiz As T **101**—3d., 100d. Greek Youth badge. Vert—5d. Boy, and 10d. girl members; 15d. Javelin-thrower; 20d. T **102**; 50d. Youths on parade; 25d. Standard-bearer and buglers; 30d. Three youths in uniform; 75d. Coat of Arms.
Air. (Vert. Landscapes with aeroplanes above)—2d. T **103**; 4d. Simon Peter Monastery, Mount Athos; 6d., 16d. Isle of Santorin (Thira); 8d. Pantanassa Church, Mistra; 32d. Ponticonissi, Corfu; 45d. The Acropolis; 55d. The Erechtheum; 65d. The Temple of Nike, Athens; 100d. The Temple of Zeus.

1940 (1 Dec). Postal Staff Anti-Tuberculosis Fund. No. C525 optd with T C **104**.

C554	C **96**	50l. green/*pale green* (R.)	30	40
		a. Opt inverted	34·00	

1941 (15 Mar–1 July). AIR. Postage Due stamps surch or optd only, as in T **104**, in red.

(a) Rouletted. Litho

554	D **20**	1d. on 2d. pale red (No. D281) (1.7.41)	20	40
		a. Surch inverted	44·00	
		b. Surch double	16·00	
555		5d. slate-blue (No. D283a)	£150	£225

(b) Perf. Litho

556	D **20**	1d. on 2d. vermilion (No. D453)	20	40
		a. Surch inverted	36·00	
557		5d. grey-blue (No. D455)	20	40
		a. Opt double	36·00	
		b. Vert pair, one without opt	£190	
		c. Opt inverted	45·00	
558		10d. green (No. D456) (1.7.41)	25	40
		a. Opt inverted	18·00	
		b. Imperf (pair)	£375	
559		25d. scarlet (No. D458) (1.7.41)	80	3·50
		a. No accent (No. D458a)	31·00	75·00
		b. Opt inverted	£140	

(c) Perf. Recess

560	D **20**	50d. orange (No. D480) (1.7.41)	1·30	3·75
555/560 Set of 7			£140	£200

For red aeroplane overprint on 50l. brown, see Nos. 521/522.

GERMAN AND ITALIAN OCCUPATION

April 1941–October 1944

The Axis invasion began on 6 April 1941 and was completed by the capture of Crete on 31 May 1941.

Κ.Π.
λεπτῶν
50
(C **105**)

50
═══
(C **106**)

1941 (1 Nov). Social Funds. No. 410 surch with T C **105**.

C561	**51**	50l. on 5l. deep green (R.)	30	45
		a. Surch inverted	31·00	

1941 (15 Nov). Postal Staff Anti-Tuberculosis Fund. Surch as T C **106**.

C562	C **78**	50 on 10l. (No. C480)	95	10·00
C563		50 on 10l. (No. C494)	30	25
		a. Surch inverted	44·00	

50
(D **105**)   **105** 'Boreas'   **ΔΡ. 1**
(C **107**)

1942 (1 Jan). POSTAGE DUE. No. D276 surch with T D **105**.

D564	D **20**	50 on 30l. scarlet	4·50	15·00

1942 (15 Aug)–**43**. AIR. Winds (symbolic designs). T **105** and similar horiz designs. Litho. W **84**. P 12½.

(a) First issue (15.8.42)

561		2d. emerald and pale green	20	65
		a. No wmk	16·00	
562		5d. orange-red and pale orange	20	65
		a. Imperf (pair)	£250	
563		10d. red-brown and orange-brown	25	65
564		20d. dull ultramarine and pale blue	55	1·30
565		25d. red-orange and pale orange	30	1·30
566		50d. grey-black and bluish grey	1·60	2·50
		a. Double impression	90·00	
561/566 Set of 6			2·75	6·25

(b) Second issue (15.9.43)

567		10d. carmine-red and salmon	25	40
		a. Imperf (pair)	75·00	
568		25d. deep bluish green and pale grey	25	40
		a. Imperf (pair)	75·00	
569		50d. violet-blue and dull violet-blue	25	40
		a. Imperf (pair)	75·00	
570		100d. slate-black and bluish grey	25	40
		a. Imperf (pair)	75·00	
571		200d. claret and brown-rose	25	40
		a. Imperf (pair)	75·00	
572		400d. slate-green and violet-blue	25	40
		a. Imperf (pair)	75·00	
567/572 Set of 6			1·40	2·20

Designs: 2d., 100d. T **105** (North wind); 5d. 'Notos' (South); 10d. 'Apiliotis' (East); 20d. 'Lips' (South-west); 25d. 'Zephyr' (West); 50d. 'Kekias' (North-east); 200d. 'Evros' (South-east); 400d. 'Skiron' (North-west).
See also Nos. 594f/594j and 600/604.

1942 (1 Sept). Sample Fair, Salonika. No. C478 surch with T C **107**.

C573	C **77**	1d. on 20l. red-brown (G.)	30	15
		a. Surch double	22·00	

106 Windmills on Mykonos Island   **107** Houses on Hydra Island

GREECE 1942

108 Edessa

No. 574b

1942 (1 Sept)–**44**. Designs as Types **106**/**108**. Litho. W **84**. P 12½.
573	2d. reddish brown		15	25
574	5d. blue-green (1.12.42)		15	25
	a. Imperf (pair)			
	b. Square 'O' for Greek 'P'		6·25	13·00
575	10d. pale blue		15	25
	a. Imperf (pair)		95·00	
576	15d. bright purple		15	25
	a. Imperf (pair)		95·00	
577	25d. brown-orange		15	25
	a. Imperf (pair)		65·00	
	b. Double impression		14·00	38·00
578	50d. blue		15	25
	a. Imperf (pair)		65·00	
579	75d. carmine (1.12.42)		15	25
580	100d. black (1.12.42)		15	25
581	200d. ultramarine (1.12.42)		15	25
	a. Without printer's imprint		6·25	12·50
582	500d. olive-brown (15.3.44)		15	25
	a. Imperf (pair)		65·00	
583	1,000d. red-brown (15.3.44)		20	25
	a. Imperf (pair)		80·00	
	b. Double impression		19·00	65·00
584	2,000d. blue (15.3.44)		20	25
	a. Imperf (pair)		80·00	
	b. Double impression		19·00	65·00
585	5,000d. scarlet (1.7.44)		20	25
	a. Imperf (pair)		80·00	
586	15,000d. bright purple (1.7.44)		20	25
	a. Imperf (pair)		80·00	
587	25,000d. green (1.7.44)		20	25
	a. Imperf (pair)		80·00	
588	500,000d. blue (15.9.44)		30	50
	a. Imperf (pair)		80·00	
589	2,000,000d. turquoise-green (15.9.44)		30	1·50
590	5,000,000d. lake (15.9.44)		30	1·50
573/590 Set of 18			3·00	6·50

Designs: (31×21 *mm*)—2d., 2,000,000d. T **106**; 5d., 5,000,000d. Burzi Fortress, Nauplion; 10d., 500,000d. Katokhi on Aspropotamos River; 15d. Heraklion, Crete; 25d. T **107**; 50d. Meteora Monastery; 75d. T **108**; 100d., 200d. Monastery on Mount Athos; 500d., 5,000d. Konitza Bridge; 1,000d., 15,000d. Ekatontapiliani Church, Paros; 2,000d., 25,000d. Kerkyra (Corfu) Island.

The error No. 574b occurs on position 15 in part of the printing.
See also Nos. C599, 594a/594e, C600, 595/599 and C605.

(C **109**)   110 Child

1942 (1 Dec)–**43**. Postal Staff Anti-Tuberculosis Fund. Nos. 410 and 413 surch as T C **109**.
C591	51	10d. on 5l. deep green (R.) (1.12.42)	25	30
		a. Surch inverted	38·00	
C592	–	10d. on 25l. blue-green (R.)	25	30
		a. Surch inverted	38·00	

1943 (1 Oct). Children's Welfare Fund. T **110** and similar designs. Litho. W **84**. P 12×13½.
592	25d. +25d. green	25	45
	a. Imperf (pair)	50·00	
593	100d. +50d. bright purple	25	45
	a. Imperf (pair)	50·00	
594	200d. +100d. brown	25	50
	a. Imperf (pair)	65·00	
592/594 Set of 3		70	1·30

Designs: 25d. T **110**; 100d. Mother and Child; 200d. Madonna and Child.

1943 (11 Oct). POSTAGE DUE. Litho. W **84**. P 12½.
D595	D **20**	10d. orange-red	25	3·50
D596		25d. blue	25	3·50
D597		100d. sepia	25	3·50
D598		200d. reddish violet	25	3·50
D595/D598 Set of 4			90	12·50

(C **111**)

111

1944 (15 Mar). Postal Staff Anti-Tuberculosis Fund. No. 580 optd with T C **111**.
C599	100d. black (R.)	25	30
	a. Opt. double	12·50	
	b. Opt. inverted	6·25	

1944 (11 June). Fund for Victims of Piraeus Air Raid. Nos. 576/580 and 567/571 surch with T **111**, in blue.

(a) POSTAGE
594a	100,000d. on 15d. bright purple	80	1·40
594b	100,000d. on 25d. brown-orange	80	1·40
594c	100,000d. on 50d. blue	80	1·40
594d	100,000d. on 75d. carmine	80	1·40
594e	100,000d. on 100d. black	80	1·40

(b) AIR
594f	100,000d. on 10d. carmine	80	1·40
594g	100,000d. on 25d. blue-green	80	1·40
594h	100,000d. on 50d. ultramarine	80	1·40
594i	100,000d. on 100d. blue-black	80	1·40
594j	100,000d. on 200d. claret	80	1·40
594a/594j Set of 10		7·25	12·50

(C **112**)   (112)

1944 (1 July). Postal Staff Anti-Tuberculosis Fund. No. 579 surch with T C **112**.
C600	5,000d. on 75d. carmine (B.)	25	50

1944 (20 July). Children's Convalescent Camp Fund. Surch as T **112**, in blue.

(a) POSTAGE. Nos. 573/577
595	50,000 +450,000d. on 2d.	80	1·20
596	50,000 +450,000d. on 5d.	80	1·20
597	50,000 +450,000d. on 10d.	80	1·20
598	50,000 +450,000d. on 15d.	80	1·20
599	50,000 +450,000d. on 25d.	80	1·20
	a. Surch inverted	39·00	

(b) AIR. Nos. 567/571
600	50,000 +450,000d. on 10d.	80	1·20
	a. Surch inverted	23·00	
601	50,000 +450,000d. on 25d.	80	1·20
	a. Surch inverted	23·00	
602	50,000 +450,000d. on 50d.	80	1·20
	a. Surch inverted	23·00	
603	50,000 +450,000d. on 100d.	80	1·20
	a. Surch inverted	23·00	
604	50,000 +450,000d. on 200d.	80	1·20
	a. Surch inverted	23·00	
595/604 Set of 10		7·25	11·00

(C **113**)

1944 (1 Aug). Postal Staff Anti-Tuberculosis Fund. No. 573 surch with T C **113**.
C605	**106**	25,000d. on 2d. reddish brown (B.)	40	80
		a. Surch double	26·00	
		b. Additional surch on back	90·00	

INDEPENDENCE REGAINED

October 1944

ΔΡΑΧΜΑΙ ΝΕΑΙ

(**113** Trans. 'New drachmas')

1944 (11 Nov)–45. Nos. 501, 504 and 506/507, optd with T **113**, in blue.

605		50l. black and bistre-brown	25	30
	a.	Opt double	25·00	
606		2d. ultramarine	25	30
607		5d. scarlet	25	30
	a.	Opt inverted	31·00	
608		6d. olive-brown (15.5.45)	25	30
605/608 Set of 4			90	1·10

REGENCY

30 December 1944–27 September 1946

1945 (1 Mar–10 Aug). As T **92**, but reduced to 22½×33 mm. Litho. W **84**. P 12½×13½.

609	**92**	1d. purple	20	25
610		3d. claret	20	25
	a.	Imperf (pair)	70·00	
611		5d. ultramarine	20	25
	a.	Imperf (pair)	70·00	
612		10d. chocolate	25	25
	a.	Imperf (pair)	70·00	
613		20d. violet	45	30
	a.	Imperf (pair)	70·00	
614		50d. blue-green (10.8.45)	80	65
615		100d. greenish blue (10.8.45)	8·25	12·00
	a.	Imperf (pair)	70·00	
616		200d. blackish green (10.8.45)	6·25	3·00
	a.	Imperf (pair)	80·00	
609/616 Set of 8			15·00	15·00

114 'OXI'=No!   **115** President Roosevelt   (**116**)

1945 (28 Oct). Resistance to Italian Ultimatum. Litho. P 12½×13½.

617	**114**	20d. orange-red	30	30
	a.	Imperf (pair)	95·00	
618		40d. blue	30	40
	a.	Imperf (pair)	95·00	

1945 (8 Nov). Postal Staff Anti-Tuberculosis Fund. No. 500 surch as T C **113**.

C619	**88**	1d. on 40l. black and blue-green (B.)	20	20
	a.	Surch double	19·00	
C620		2d. on 40l. black and blue-green (R.)	20	20
	a.	Surch inverted	26·00	

1945 (21 Dec). Roosevelt Mourning issue. Borders in black. Litho. P 12½×13½.

619	**115**	30d. brown-purple	30	25
	a.	Centre inverted	75·00	
	b.	Imperf (pair)	50·00	
620		60d. blue-grey	30	25
	a.	Centre inverted	75·00	
	b.	Imperf (pair)	50·00	
621		200d. slate-violet	40	25
	a.	Imperf (pair)	75·00	
	b.	Centre inverted	50·00	
619/621 Set of 3			90	70

1946 (10 Feb)–**47**. Variously surch as T **116**.

622		10d. on 10d. (No. 567) (6.3.46)	45	30
	a.	Surch inverted	£180	
623		10d. on 2000d. (No. 584) (R.) (20.7.46)	45	30
624		20d. on 50d. (No. 569) (R.) (6.3.46)	45	30
	a.	Surch inverted	£225	
625		20d. on 500d. (No. 582) (R.) (5.47)	45	30
	a.	Surch double	£130	
626		20d. on 1000d. (No. 583) (8.7.46)	45	30
627		30d. on 5d. (No. 574) (R.) (5.47)	45	30
	a.	On No. 574b	£150	90·00
628		50d. on 50d. (No. 578) (R.) (22.9.47)	45	30
629		50d. on 25,000d. (No. 587) (R.) (6.3.46)	65	30
630		100d. on 10d. (No. 575) (R.) (21.12.47)	2·20	30
631		100d. on 2,000,000d. (No. 589) (R.) 6.3.46)	1·40	30
632		130d. on 20l. (No. 499) (R.) (10.2.46)	1·30	40
633		250d. on 20l. (No. 499) (R.) (8.7.46)	1·40	40
	a.	Surch double	£140	
634		300d. on 80l. (No. 502) (10.2.46)	1·30	50
	a.	Surch in red-brown	25·00	25·00
635		450d. on 75d. (No. 579) (21.12.47)	2·75	55
636		500d. on 5,000,000d. (No. 590) (6.3.46)	5·00	90
		Surch inverted	£150	
637		1000d. on 500,000d. (No. 588) (R.) (6.3.46)	21·00	2·20
	a.	Surch double		
638		2000d. on 5000d. (No. 585) (28.3.46)	70·00	7·00
639		5000d. on 15,000d. (No. 586) (28.3.46)	£275	49·00
	a.	Surch in blue	£325	£350
622/639 Set of 18 (cheapest)			£350	60·00

All the above are postage stamps despite the fact that some air stamps were used for surcharging.

A 150d. on 20l. is fraudulent.

(C **117**)   **117** E. Venizelos

1946. Postal Staff Anti-Tuberculosis Fund. Surch as T C **117**, in red.

C640	**86**	20d. on 5l. (No. 497) (20.7.46)	1·90	75
C641	**88**	20d. on 40l. (No. 500) (11.3.46)	75	25

1946 (25 Mar). Tenth Death Anniversary of Venizelos (statesman). Litho. W **84**. P 12½×13½.

640	**117**	130d. sage-green	65	40
641		300d. red-brown	65	40

1946 (20 Sept). Social Funds. No. C526 surch as T C **117** in red.

C642	C **96**	50d. on 1d. blue/pale blue	90	30
	a.	Violet oupt	21·00	2·50

King George II (restored)
27 September 1946–1 April 1947

A plebiscite held on 1 September 1946 resulted in a vote for the return of the King of Greece.

1-9-1946

(**118**)

1946 (28 Sept). Restoration of Monarchy. Surch as T **118**, in shades of blue.

642	**89**	50d. on 1d. green	90	30
643		250d. on 3d. red-brown	1·90	30
	a.	Surch inverted	55·00	
644		600d. on 8d. deep blue	16·00	1·90
	a.	Additional surch on back (inverted)	£200	
	b.	Surch in red	£300	
645		3000d. on 100d. lake	34·00	1·90
642/645 Set of 4			48·00	4·00

119 Women carrying Munitions, Pindos Mountains   **120** Torpedoing of Cruiser *Helle*

1946 (28 Oct)–**47**. First Victory Issue. As Types **119**/**120** (war episodes). Recess. P 12½.

646		50d. green (1.5.47)	50	30
647		100d. ultramarine (1.5.47)	75	30

GREECE 1946

648		250d. yellow-green	1·10	30
649		500d. red-brown (1.5.47)	1·60	40
650		600d. chocolate (1.5.47)	1·90	1·00
651		1000d. violet (1.5.47)	8·75	50
652		2000d. ultramarine (1.5.47)	44·00	3·25
653		5000d. carmine (1.5.47)	55·00	2·50
		a. Imperf (pair)	£2000	
646/653 Set of 8			£100	7·75

Designs: Horiz—50d. Convoy; 250d. T **119**; 500d. Column of infantry; 1000d. Supermarine Spitfire Mk IIB fighter aeroplane and pilot; 2000d. Torpedo-boat *Hyacinth* towing submarine *Perla*. Vert—100d. T **120**; 600d. Badge, Alpine troops and outlined map of Italy; 5000d. Monument at El Alamein.

See also No. 682.

121 Panayiotis Tsaldaris

(**122**)

1946 (15 Nov). Tenth Death Anniversary of P. Tsaldaris (statesman). Litho. P 12×13½.

654	**121**	250d. red-brown and salmon	7·50	1·40
		a. Imperf (pair)	£140	
655		600d. deep blue and pale blue	7·50	1·90
		a. Imperf (pair)	£140	

King Paul I
1 April 1947–6 March 1964

1947 (Apr). King George II Mourning Issue. Surch as T **122**.

656	**89**	50d. on 1d. green (15.4.47)	1·60	30
		a. Surch double	£100	
657		250d. on 3d. red-brown (6.4.47)	2·75	30
		a. Surch double	£100	
		b. Pair, one without surch	£130	
658		600d. on 8d. deep blue (15.4.47)	8·25	1·10
		a. Surch double	£110	
656/658 Set of 3			11·50	1·50

(C **123**)

124 Castelrosso Fortress

125 Dodecanese Vase

126 Apollo (T K 1 of Dodecanese Is)

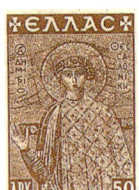
C **127** St Demetrius

1947 (20 Apr). Postal Staff Anti-Tuberculosis Fund. Surch with T C **123** in red.

C659	C **96**	50d. on 50l. (No. C525)	90·00	
C660		50d. on 50l. (No. C554)	5·25	65
C661	C **96**	50d. on 50l. green/*pale green*	1·30	40
		a. Surch double		
		a. Surch inverted		

1947 (20 Nov)–**51**. Restoration of Dodecanese Islands to Greece. Types **124/126** and similar designs. Litho. W **84**. P 13½×12 (horiz) or 12×13½ (vert).

659	**124**	20d. ultramarine	65	20
		a. Imperf (pair)	£425	
660	**125**	30d. flesh and brown-black	65	20
		a. Imperf (pair)	£400	
661	–	50d. blue	75	20
662	–	100d. deep olive and pale olive	55	20
		a. Imperf (pair)	£425	
663	–	200d. brown-orange (5.11.50)	1·90	20
664	–	250d. grey	1·50	20
		a. Imperf (pair)	£425	
665	–	300d. yellow-orange (15.9.50)	2·10	20
666	–	400d. light blue (5.11.50)	2·75	20
667	**126**	450d. blue (12.1.48)	3·50	20
668	–	450d. blue and pale blue (1.7.48)	2·75	20
		a. Imperf (pair)	£425	
669	**126**	500d. vermilion	2·50	20
670	–	600d. brown-purple	3·50	30
		a. Imperf (pair)	£450	
671	–	700d. magenta (20.8.50)	4·75	25
		a. Imperf (pair)	£450	
672	–	700d. turquoise-green (10.4.51)	38·00	25
		a. Imperf (pair)	£450	
673	–	800d. green and violet (5.11.50)	6·00	30
674	–	1000d. brown-olive	3·75	40
		a. Imperf (pair)	£375	
675	**126**	1300d. carmine (15.9.50)	31·00	30
676	**124**	1500d. orange-brown (1.12.50)	£160	80
677	**125**	1600d. greenish blue and ultramarine (5.9.50)	11·50	30
678		2000d. salmon and brown (5.4.50)	90·00	55
		a. Imperf (pair)	£225	
679	–	2600d. green (5.9.50)	19·00	1·40
680	–	5000d. violet (5.4.50)	90·00	90
681	–	10,000d. ultramarine (5.4.50)	£150	1·10
659/681 Set of 23			£575	8·75

Designs: Horiz—100d., 400d. St John's Convent, Patmos. Vert—50d., 300d. Woman in National Costume; 200d., 250d. Emmanuel Xanthos; 600d., 700d. (2), 5000d. Statue of Hippocrates; 450d. (No. 668), 800d. Casos Island and 19th-century frigate; 1000d., 2600d., 10000d. Colossus of Rhodes.

1948 (25 Jan). Church Restoration Fund. P 12×13½.

C682	C **127**	50d. yellow-brown	40	30

128 Battle of Crete

129 Column of Women and Children

(Recess Bradbury Wilkinson, London)

1948 (15 Sept). Second Victory Issue. W **84**. P 13×13½.

682	**128**	1000d. blue-green	9·50	75

1949 (1 Feb). Abduction of Greek Children to neighbouring countries. T **129** and similar types. Litho. W **84**. P 13½×12 (horiz) or 12×13½ (vert).

683		450d. violet and mauve	10·50	1·10
684		1000d. brown and sepia	19·00	75
685		1800d. lake and buff	14·00	75
683/685 Set of 3			39·00	2·30

Designs: Horiz—450d. T **129**. Vert—1000d. Captive children and map of Greece; 1800d. Hand menacing woman and child.

1950 (1 Mar). Postal Staff Anti-tuberculosis Fund. Surch as T C **117** (21½ mm) sideways (reading upwards) in blue.

C686		50d. on 10l. (No. 498)	3·00	65
		a. Surch reading down	45·00	38·00
C687		50d. on 10l. (No. 514)	1·80	40
		a. Surch reading down	45·00	38·00

130 Map and Flags

131 Youth of Marathon

1950 (28 Apr). Battle of Crete. Recess. W **84**. P 13½×13.
686	**130**	1000d. blue	24·00	65
		a. Imperf (pair)	£2250	

1950 (21 May). 75th Anniversary of Universal Postal Union. Recess. W **84**. P 13×13½.
687	**131**	1000d. green/*buff*	3·25	65
		a. Imperf (pair)	£1700	

132 To the Unknown God

133 St Paul

134 St Paul

135 'Industry'

(Des Jean Kefalinos. Recess.)

1951 (15 June). 19th centenary of St Paul's Travels in Greece. Types **132/134** and similar type inscr '51–1951'. P 13½×12½ (700d. and 1600d.), 12½×13½ (others).
688	**132**	700d. bright purple	4·50	65
689	**133**	1600d. greenish blue	25·00	3·75
690	**134**	2600d. yellow-brown	34·00	5·75
691	–	10,000d. brown-lake	£275	£110
688/691 Set of 4			£300	£110

Design: Vert—as T **134**: 10,000d. St Paul preaching to Athenians.

1951 (20 Sept). Reconstruction Issue. T **135** and similar vert designs. Recess. W **84**. P 13×13½.
692		700d. orange	5·00	40
693		800d. blue-green	9·50	45
694		1300d. turquoise	15·00	45
695		1600d. olive-green	42·00	50
696		2600d. grey-violet	£120	2·75
697		5000d. purple	£140	60
692/697 Set of 6			£300	4·75

Designs: 700d. T **135**; 800d. Fish and trident ('Fishing'); 1300d. Workmen and column ('Reconstruction'), 1600d. Ceres and tractors ('Agriculture'); 2600d. Women and loom ('Home Crafts'); 5000d. Map and stars ('Electrification').

(C **136**) (C **137**)

1951. Postal Staff Welfare Funds. No. 497 surch with T C **136**, in red.
C698	86	50d. on 5l. greenish blue and red-brown	4·00	50

1951 (20 Oct). Postal Staff Anti-Tuberculosis Fund. No. 505 surch with T C **137**.
C699	89	50d. on 3d. red-brown	1·90	25

136 Blessing before Battle

137 King Paul

138 'Spirit of Greece'

(Des Professor Ghalanis. Recess.)

1952 (29 Aug). AIR. Anti-Communist Campaign. T **136** and similar designs. W **84**. P 12½×13½.
698		1000d. deep blue	1·60	40
699		1700d. deep bluish green	10·50	1·60
700		2700d. brown	23·00	4·00
701		7000d. deep green	70·00	18·00
698/701 Set of 4			95·00	22·00

Designs: 1000d. T **136**; 1700d. 'Victory' over mountains; 2700d. Infantry attack; 7000d. 'Victory' and soldiers.

(Des Professor Ghalanis. Recess.)

1952 (14 Dec). 50th Birthday of King Paul. Recess. W **84**. P 13×12½.
702	**137**	200d. deep emerald	2·20	40
703		1000d. carmine-red	7·50	45
704	**138**	1400d. pale blue	29·00	2·30
705	**137**	10,000d. reddish purple	85·00	14·50
702/705 Set of 4			£110	16·00

ΠΡΟΣΘΕΤΟΝ
ΔΡ. 100

(C **139**)

1952 (15 Dec). State Welfare Fund. No. 509 surch with T C **139**, in red.
C706	89	100d. on 8d. deep blue	2·20	30

PRINTERS. From 1953 to 1983 all stamps (litho or recess) were printed by Aspioti-Elka, *unless otherwise stated.*

139 Oranges

C **140** Argostoli, Cephalonia

1953 (1 July). National Products. T **139** and similar allegorical designs. Recess. W **84**. P 13×14 (vert) or 14×13 (horiz).
706		500d. orange and carmine-red	2·30	30
707		700d. yellow-ochre and deep brown	2·75	30
		a. Imperf (pair)	£750	
708		1000d. dull green and deep blue	5·50	30
		a. Imperf (pair)	£750	
709		1300d. yellow-brown and maroon	10·00	40
710		2000d. pale blue-green and deep brown	31·00	50
		a. Imperf (pair)	£750	
711		2600d. olive-bistre and slate-lilac	41·00	1·70
712		5000d. apple-green and deep brown	55·00	90
706/712 Set of 7			£130	4·00

Designs: Vert—700d. Tobacco (Tobacco plant); 1300d. Wine (wineglass and vase); 2000d. Figs (basket of Figs); 2600d. Dried Fruit (Grapes and Currant bread); 5000d. Grapes (male figure holding Grapes). Horiz—500d. T **139**; 1000d. Olive oil (Pallas Athene and Olive branch).

(Litho Government Mint)

1953 (15 Nov). Ionian Island Earthquake Fund. T C **140** and similar vert design. W **84**. P 12½.
C713		300d. indigo and grey-green	3·75	25
C714		500d. deep brown and buff	4·25	1·10

Designs: 300d. Church of Faneromeni, Zante; 500d. T **140**.

GREECE 1954

140 Bust of Pericles   **141** Alexander the Great   **142** Hunting Wild Boar

1954 (15 Jan). Ancient Greek Art. Designs showing sculptures, etc, as Types **140**/**142**. Litho. W **84**. P 13×12½ (large vert designs) or 13 (others).

713	**140**	100d. chestnut	65	25
714	–	200d. black	65	25
715	–	300d. blue-violet	1·40	25
716	–	500d. green	2·10	25
717	–	600d. rose	2·30	25
718	**141**	1000d. black and deep blue	3·25	25
719	–	1200d. olive-green	3·25	25
720	–	2000d. orange-brown	14·00	30
721	**142**	2400d. greenish blue	14·00	55
		a. Double impression	£225	
722	–	2500d. deep bluish green	21·00	40
723	–	4000d. claret	41·00	55
724	–	20,000d. reddish purple	£300	1·70
713/724 Set of 12			£375	4·75

Designs: As T **140**—200d. Mycenaean Ox-head vase; 1200d. Head of charioteer of Delphi; 2000d. Vase of Dipylon; 2500d. Man carrying calf; 20,000d. Two pitcher-bearers. As T **141**—300d. Bust of Homer; 500d. Zeus of Istiaea; 600d. Youth's head; 4000d. Dish depicting voyage of Dionysus.

See also Nos. 733a/741.

143 Athlete Bearing Torch   **144** Extracts from *Hansard* (Parliamentary Debates)

(Des A. Tassos. Recess)

1954 (15 May). AIR. Fifth Anniversary of North Atlantic Treaty Organisation. T **143** and similar vert designs. W **84**. P 13×13½.

725		1200d. orange	7·00	55
726		2400d. deep green	60·00	4·50
727		4000d. deep blue	£100	5·25
725/727 Set of 3			£150	9·25

Designs: 1200d. T **143**; 2400d. Amphictyonic coin; 4000d. Pallas Athene.

Currency revalued: 1000 old drachmai=one new drachma

(Litho State Bank)

1954 (22–24 Sept). Enosis (Union of Cyprus with Greece). W **84**. P 12½.

728	**144**	1d.20 black and pale yellow (24.9.54)	5·00	60
729	–	2d. black and salmon	27·00	5·00
730	–	2d. black and light blue	27·00	5·00
731	–	2d.40 black and lavender	27·00	3·75
732	–	2d.50 black and pink	27·00	3·75
733	–	4d. black and pale yellow-green	80·00	5·50
728/733 Set of 6			£170	21·00

On No. 728 the text of the report is in Greek, on Nos. 730 and 731 in French, and in English on the others.

I   II

Two types of 2d.50:
  Type I. Ten dots at upper righthand corner.
  Type II. Only nine dots at corner.

1955–60. As Nos. 713/724 but colours changed and new values.

733a	**140**	10l. light emerald (12.1.59)	70	20
734	–	20l. deep bluish green (10.7.55)	65	25
734a	–	20l. bright reddish purple (29.12.58)	80	20
735	**140**	30l. yellow-brown (10.7.55)	1·00	25
736	–	50l. lake (14.4.55)	1·60	30
736a	–	50l. turquoise-green (12.1.59)	1·40	20
736b	–	70l. red-orange (2.1.59)	65	20
737	–	1d. turquoise-green (10.7.55)	2·75	25
737a	–	1d. red-brown (27.12.58)	3·50	20
737b	–	1d.50 light blue (3.1.59)	31·00	30
738	**141**	2d. black and bistre-brown (10.7.55)	16·00	25
738a		2d.50 black and deep magenta (I) (14.3.59)	28·00	30
		ab. Type II	33·00	1·00
739	**142**	3d. orange-red (10.7.55)	12·50	30
739a	–	3d. cobalt (1.9.60)	4·00	45
740	–	3d.50 rose-carmine (10.7.55)	25·00	80
741	–	4d. bright blue (10.7.55)	£110	50
733a/741 Set of 16			£225	5·75

Designs: As T **140**—20l. (2) Mycenaean Ox-head vase; 70l. Head of charioteer of Delphi; 1d.50, Two pitcher bearers; 3d. (No. 739a), Man carrying calf. As T **141**—50l. (2) Zeus of Istiaea; 1d. (2) Youth's head; 3d.50, Bust of Homer; 4d. Dish depicting voyage of Dionysus.

No. 738ab occurs in five positions on the sheet, printed from one particular plate.

145 Samian Coin depicting Pythagoras   **146** Rotary Emblem and Globe

1955 (20 Aug). Pythagorean Congress. T **145** and similar designs. Litho. W **84**. P 13½×12 (6d.) or 12×13½ (others).

742	**145**	2d. green	6·00	50
743	–	3d.50 black	18·00	3·50
744	**145**	5d. reddish purple	80·00	2·50
745	–	6d. blue	65·00	43·00
742/745 Set of 4			£150	45·00

Designs: Vert—3d.50, Representation of Pythagorean theorem. Horiz—6d. Map of Samos.

1956 (15 May). 50th Anniversary of Rotary International. Litho. W **84**. P 12×13½.

746	**146**	2d. ultramarine	24·00	90

147 King George I   C **148** Zeus (Macedonian Coin of Philip II)   **148** Dionysios Solomos

(Des A. Tassos. Eng H. Woyty-Wimmer (1d.50, 3d., 10d.), D.L.R. (others). Recess Aspioti-Elka)

1956 (21 May). Royal Family. T **147** and similar portraits. W **84**. P 12½×13½ (vert) or 13½×12½ (horiz).

747	10l. deep slate-violet	25	15
748	20l. deep reddish purple	25	15
749	30l. sepia	25	15
750	50l. red-brown	65	15
751	70l. ultramarine	1·00	30
752	1d. light blue	1·30	30
753	1d.50 slate-blue	5·00	30
754	2d. black	6·25	30
755	3d. deep brown	4·75	25
756	3d.50 chestnut	17·00	40
757	4d. deep dull green	17·00	40
758	5d. carmine	13·00	40
759	7d.50 ultramarine	13·00	2·40
760	10d. deep blue	75·00	1·10
747/760 Set of 14		£140	6·00

300

Portraits: Horiz—10l. King Alexander; 5d. King Paul and Queen Frederika; 10d. King and Queen and Crown Prince Constantine. Vert—20l. Crown Prince Constantine; 30l. T **147**; 50l. Queen Olga; 70l. King Otto; 1d. Queen Amalia; 1d.50, King Constantine; 2d. King Paul; 3d. King George II; 3d.50, Queen Sophia; 4d. Queen Frederika; 7d.50, King Paul.
See also Nos. 764/777.

(Litho Perivolaraki-Lykogianni and Aspioti-Elka, Athens)

1956 (6–26 Sept). Macedonian Cultural Fund. T C **148** and similar vert portrait. W **84**. P 13½.

C761	50l. crimson	2·50	80
	a. Imperf (pair)	£500	
C762	1d. blue (Aristotle) (26.9.56)	8·50	1·80

This was the last of the Compulsory Charity Tax stamps.

(Des A. Tassos. Litho)

1957 (26 Mar). Death Centenary of D. Solomos (national poet). T **148** and similar horiz designs. W **84**. P 12×13½ (3d.50) or 13½×12 (others).

761	2d. buff and lake-brown	7·50	50
762	3d.50 greenish grey and blue	7·50	3·00
763	5d. bistre and deep bluish green	13·00	12·50
761/763 Set of 3		25·00	14·50

Designs: 2d. D. Solomos and K. Mantzaros (composer); 3d.50, T **148**; 5d. Zante landscape and D. Solomos.

1957 (15 Nov). As Nos. 747/760 but colours changed.

764	10l. claret	30	30
765	20l. orange	30	30
766	30l. black	30	30
767	50l. deep grey-green	50	30
768	70l. reddish purple	1·30	70
769	1d. deep rose-red	1·70	30
770	1d.50 yellow-green	3·25	30
771	2d. carmine-red	6·50	30
772	3d. deep blue	7·75	30
773	3d.50 slate-purple	14·50	30
774	4d. red-brown	16·00	30
775	5d. deep grey-blue	15·00	30
776	7d.50 orange-yellow	3·75	1·90
777	10d. deep emerald	95·00	1·10
764/777 Set of 14		£150	6·25

149 *Argo* (5th-century, BC)

150 The Piraeus (Port of Athens)

(Des A. Tassos. Litho)

1958 (30 Jan). Greek Merchant Marine Commemoration. T **149** and similar horiz ship designs. W **84**. P 13½×12½.

778	50l. red, black, grey and dull blue	50	20
779	1d. ochre, black, pale blue and bright blue	55	30
	a. Black (portholes) omitted	£325	
780	1d.50 red, black, light blue and blue	2·20	1·30
781	2d. brown, black, pale blue and deep violet-blue	65	40
782	3d.50 black, red, light blue and blue	3·25	1·70
	a. Double impression of black	£250	
783	5d. red, black, light blue and blue-green	16·00	14·00
778/783 Set of 6		21·00	16·00

Designs: 50l. *Michael Carras* (tanker); 1d. *Queen Frederika* (liner); 1d.50, Full-rigged sailing ship of 1821; 2d. Byzantine galley; 3d.50, 6th-century BC galley; 5d. T **149**.

(Des A. Tassos. Litho)

1958 (1 July). AIR. Greek Ports. Various horiz designs as T **150**. W **84**. P 13½×13.

784	10d. brown-red, blue, black and pale grey	25·00	25
785	15d. brown-red, slate-blue, black and grey-drab	2·75	40
786	20d. ultramarine, black, brown-red and dull turquoise-blue	25·00	25
787	25d. brown-red, black, ultramarine and slate-grey	3·50	75
788	30d. brown-red, black, slate-blue and turquoise-green	2·40	80
789	50d. ultramarine, black and brown	9·25	90
790	100d. bright blue, black and yellow-brown	70·00	4·00
784/790 Set of 7		£120	6·75

Designs: Ports of: 10d. T **150**; 15d. Salonika; 20d. Patras; 25d. Hermoupolis (Syra); 30d. Volos (Thessaly); 50d. Kavalla; 100d. Heraklion (Crete).

151 Narcissus and Flower

152 Jupiter's Head and Eagle (Olympia 4th-century BC coin)

(Des A. Tassos. Litho)

1958 (15 Sept). International Congress for Protection of Nature, Athens. T **151** and various mythological and floral vert designs. W **84**. P 13×13½ (20l. to 70l.), 13×12½ (1d.) or 12½×13½ (others).

791	20l. multicoloured	30	20
792	30l. multicoloured	30	20
793	50l. multicoloured	35	20
794	70l. multicoloured	40	30
795	1d. multicoloured	50	40
796	2d. multicoloured	90	65
797	3d.50 multicoloured	80	55
	a. Imperf (pair)	£650	
798	5d. multicoloured	7·50	8·25
791/798 Set of 8		10·00	9·75

Designs: 20l. T **151**; 30l. Daphne and Apollo; 50l. Venus and Adonis (Venus and Hibiscus); 70l. Pan and the Nymph (Pan and Pine cones). 21½×26 mm—1d. Crocus. 22×32 mm—2d. Iris; 3d.50, Tulip; 5d. Cyclamen.

(Des A. Tassos. Litho Perivolaraki-Lykogianni)

1959 (24 Mar). Ancient Greek coins. Designs as T **152** showing both sides of each coin. W **84**. P 14×14½ (1d., 4d.50, 6d., 8d.50) or 14½×14 (others).

799	10l. grey-green, black and red-brown	50	20
800	20l. grey, black and blue	50	20
801	50l. grey, black and purple	60	20
802	70l. grey, black and ultramarine	90	30
803	1d. grey, black and carmine	2·30	20
804	1d.50 grey, black and yellow-brown	3·25	20
805	2d.50 drab, black and cerise	4·00	20
806	4d.50 grey, black and deep bluish green	10·50	60
807	6d. pale blue, black and olive	37·00	30
808	8d.50 drab, black and carmine-red	11·50	2·20
799/808 Set of 10		65·00	4·25

Designs: Horiz Coins showing—10l. T **152**; 20l. Athene's head and Owl (Athens 5th-century BC); 50l. Nymph Arethusa and chariot (Syracuse 5th-century BC); 70l. Hercules and Jupiter (Alexander the Great 4th-century BC); 1d.50, Griffin and squares (Abdera, Thrace 5th-century BC); 2d.50, Apollo and lyre (Chalcidice, Macedonia 4th-century BC). Vert—1d. Helios and Rose (Rhodes 4th-century BC); 4d.50, Apollo and labyrinth (Crete 3rd-century BC); 6d. Venus and Apollo (Paphos, Cyprus 4th-century BC); 8d.50, Ram's heads and incised squares (Delphi 5th-century BC).
See also Nos. 909/917.

153 Amphitheatre, Delphi

154 'Victory' and Greek soldiers through the ages

(Des A. Tassos. Litho)

1959 (20 June). Ancient Greek Theatre. Designs as T **153**. W **84**. P 13½×13 (3d.50, 4d.50) or 13×13½ (others).

809	20l. orange-brown, black, light brown and light blue	45	20
810	50l. red-brown, sepia and light olive-drab	45	25
811	1d. brown, yellow-brown, grey and green	50	30
812	2d.50 brown and light blue	1·00	60
813	3d.50 brown, green and red	20·00	19·00
814	4d.50 orange-brown and black	2·30	1·30
815	6d. orange-brown, grey and black	3·00	1·60
809/815 Set of 7		25·00	21·00

GREECE 1959

Designs: Vert—20l. Ancient theatre audience (after a Pharsala, Thessaly, vase of 580 BC); 50l. Clay mask of 3rd-century BC; 1d. Flute, drum and lyre; 2d.50, Actor (3rd-century statuette); 6d. Performance of a satirical play (after a mixing bowl of 410 BC). Horiz—3d.50, T **153**, 4d.50, Performance of Euripides' *Andromeda* (after vase of 4th-century BC).

1959 (29 Aug). Tenth Anniversary of Greek Anti-Communist Victory. Litho. W **84**. P 13×13½.

816	**154**	2d.50 light blue, blue, black and red-brown	7·50	65

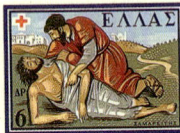

155 The Good Samaritan

156 Imre Nagy (former Prime Minister of Hungary)

(Des A. Tassos. Litho)

1959 (21 Sept). Red Cross Commemoration. Designs as T **155**. Cross in red. W **84**. P 13½×12½ (20l., 3d., 6d.) or 12½×13½ (others).

817		20l. multicoloured	30	20
818		50l. deep olive-grey, red, blue and deep blue	40	30
819		70l. black, red-brown, yellow-brown and blue	55	50
820		2d.50 black, orange-brown, grey-brown and red-brown	1·00	70
821		3d. multicoloured	12·50	14·00
822		4d.50 black, orange-brown and red-brown	2·30	1·70
823		6d. multicoloured	2·50	1·50
817/823		Set of 7	18·00	17·00

Designs: Horiz—20l. Hippocrates Tree, Cos; 6d. T **155**. Vert—50l. Bust of Aesculapius; 70l. St Basil (after mosaic in Hosios Loukas Monastery, Boeotia); 2d.50, Achilles and Patroclus (from vase of 6th-century BC); 3d. (32×47½ *mm*) Red Cross, globe, infirm people and nurses; 4d.50, J. H. Dunant.

1959 (8 Dec). Third Anniversary of Hungarian Revolt. Litho. W **84**. P 13×13½.

824	**156**	4d.50 sepia, light orange-brown and brown-red	2·30	2·75
825		6d. black, light blue and ultramarine	2·30	2·75

157 Kostes Palamas

158 Brig in Storm

(Des A. Tassos. Litho)

1960 (25 Jan). Birth Centenary of Palamas (poet). W **84**. P 12½×13½.

826	**157**	2d.50 magenta, pale mauve, grey and deep maroon	9·25	80

(Des A. Tassos. Litho)

1960 (7 Apr). World Refugee Year. T **158** and similar horiz design. W **84**. P 13½×13.

827		2d.50 multicoloured	80	35
828		4d.50 multicoloured	2·40	1·40

Designs: 2d.50, T **158**; 4d.50, Ship in calm waters.

159 Scout emulating St George

160 Sprinting

(Des A. Tassos. Litho)

1960 (23 Apr). 50th Anniversary of Greek Boy Scout Movement. Designs as T **159**. W **84**. P 13×13½ (20l., 30l., 40l., 2d.50) or 13½×13 (others).

829		20l. multicoloured	30	25
830		30l. multicoloured	30	25
831		40l. multicoloured	30	25
832		50l. multicoloured	30	25
833		70l. multicoloured	40	30
834		1d. multicoloured	90	40
835		2d.50 multicoloured	2·50	1·20
836		6d. multicoloured	4·00	2·75
829/836		Set of 8	8·00	5·00

Designs: Vert—20l. T **159**; 30l. Ephebi Oath and Scout Promise; 40l. Scouts in fire rescue work; 2d.50, Crown Prince Constantine in uniform of Chief Greek Scout. Horiz—50l. Scouts planting tree; 70l. Scouts with map; 1d. Scouts on beach; 6d. Greek Scout flag and medal.

(Des A. Tassos. Litho)

1960 (12 Aug). Olympic Games. Designs as T **160**. W **84**. P 13×13½ (20l., 70l., 2d.50, 5d.) or 13½×13 (others).

837		20l. red-brown, black and blue	30	25
838		50l. red-brown, brown and black	40	30
839		70l. red-brown, black, light green and bronze-green	40	30
840		80l. red-brown, black, grey and drab	40	30
		a. Imperf (pair)	£900	
841		1d. red-brown, black, buff and blue	55	40
842		1d.50 red-brown, black, orange and deep brown	65	50
843		2d.50 red-brown, black, ultramarine and light blue	1·60	75
844		4d.50 red-brown, black, ultramarine, yellow and brown	1·90	1·20
		a. Double impression of black	£750	£900
845		5d. red-brown, black, green and turquoise	4·00	1·80
846		6d. red-brown, black, brown and violet-blue	4·00	1·80
847		12d.50 black, buff, grey, brown-red and brown	24·00	21·00
837/847		Set of 11	34·00	26·00

Designs: Vert—20l. Official holding plaque; 70l. Athlete taking oath; 2d.50, Discus-throwing; 5d. Javelin-throwing. Horiz—50l. Olympic flame; 80l. Cutting Olive branches; 1d. Entrance of judges; 1d.50, Long-jumping; 4d.50, T **160**; 6d. Crowning the victor; 12d.50, Quadriga or chariot-driving.

161 Conference Emblem

162 Crown Prince Constantine and *Nirefs*

(Des P. Rahikainen. Litho)

1960 (19 Sept). First Anniversary of European Postal and Telecommunications Conference. W **84**. P 13½×12½.

848	**161**	4d.50 ultramarine	12·50	3·25

(Des A. Tassos. Litho)

1961 (18 Jan). Victory of Crown Prince in Dragon Class Yacht-races. Olympic Games. W **84**. P 13½×13.

849	**162**	2d.50 multicoloured	1·40	65

163 Kastoria

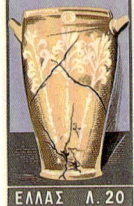

164 Lilies Vase of Knossos

(Des A. Tassos. Recess)

1961 (15 Feb). Tourist Publicity. T **163** and similar designs. W **84**. P 13½×12.

850		10l. indigo	30	20
851		20l. plum	30	20
852		50l. blue	30	20
853		70l. deep purple	35	20

854	80l. ultramarine		70	30
855	1d. red-brown		90	20
856	1d.50 emerald		1·60	20
857	2d.50 carmine-red		4·50	20
858	3d.50 reddish violet		2·20	65
859	4d. deep green		15·00	20
860	4d.50 deep blue		1·90	20
861	5d. lake		15·00	20
862	6d. myrtle-green		3·75	20
863	7d.50 black		95	30
864	8d. deep ultramarine		8·25	30
865	8d.50 orange-red		9·25	70
866	12d.50 sepia		3·25	1·40
850/866 Set of 17			60·00	5·25

Designs: Horiz—10l. T **163**; 20l. The Meteora Monasteries; 50l. Hydra; 70l. Acropolis, Athens; 80l. Mykonos; 1d. Salonika; 1d.50, Olympia; 2d.50, Knossos; 3d.50, Rhodes; 4d. Epidavros; 4d.50, Sounion; 5d. Temple of Zeus, Athens; 7d.50, Yannina; 12d.50, Delos. Vert—6d. Delphi; 8d. Mount Athos; 8d.50, Santorini.

(Des A. Tassos. Litho)

1961 (30 June). Minoan Art. T **164** and similar designs. W **84**. P 13×13½ (20l., 1d.50, 4d.50) or 13½×13 (others).

867	20l. multicoloured		60	20
868	50l. multicoloured		60	20
869	1d. multicoloured		80	25
870	1d.50 multicoloured		1·90	25
871	2d.50 multicoloured		9·25	25
872	4d.50 multicoloured		3·75	2·75
873	6d. multicoloured		17·00	1·90
874	10d. multicoloured		17·00	11·50
867/874 Set of 8			46·00	16·00

Designs: Vert—20l. T **164**; 1d.50, Knossos rhyton-bearer; 4d.50, Part of Hagia Trias sarcophagus. Horiz—50l. Partridge and Fig-pecker (Knossos frieze); 1d. Kamares fruit dish; 2d.50, Ladies of Knossos Palace (painting); 6d. Knossos dancer (painting); 10d. Kamares prochus and pithos with spout.

165 Reactor Building   **166** Doves

(Des A. Tassos. Litho)

1961 (31 July). Inauguration of Democritus Nuclear Research Centre, Aghia Paraskevi. T **165** and similar horiz design. W **84**. P 13½×13.

875	2d.50 deep magenta and mauve		95	45
876	4d.50 deep blue and light grey-blue		1·90	1·10

Designs: 2d.50, T **165**; 4d.50, Democritus and atomic symbol.

(Des T. Kurpershoek. Litho)

1961 (18 Sept). Europa. W **84**. P 13½×12.

877	**166**	2d.50 red and pink	65	65
		a. Pink underprint omitted	15·00	21·00
878		4d.50 ultramarine and pale blue	65	65

 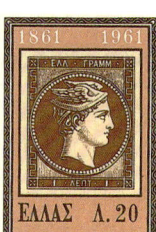

167 Emperor Nicephorus Phocas   **168** Hermes 1l. stamp of 1861

(Des A. Tassos. Litho)

1961 (22 Sept). Millenary of Liberation of Crete from the Saracens. W **84**. P 13½×12½.

879	**167**	2d.50 multicoloured	1·30	70

1961 (20 Dec). Centenary of First Greek Postage Stamps. T **168** and similar vert designs showing Hermes stamps of 1861. Multicoloured. Litho. W **84**. P 13×13½.

880	20l. Type **168**		30	20
881	50l. 2l.		30	20
882	1d.50 5l.		40	25
883	2d.50 10l.		40	25
884	4d.50 20l.		85	40
885	6d. 40l.		1·30	70
886	10d. 80l.		3·25	2·75
880/886 Set of 7			6·00	4·25

169 Ptolemais Steam Plant   **170** Zappion Building

(Des A. Tassos. Litho)

1962 (14 Apr). Electrification Project. T **169** and similar designs. Multicoloured. W **84**. P 13×13½ (20l., 50l.), or 13½×13 (others).

887	20l. Tauropos Dam (*vert*)		30	20
888	50l. Ladhon River hydroelectric plant (*vert*)		35	20
889	1d. Type **169**		40	20
890	1d.50 Louros River Dam		45	30
891	2d.50 Aliverion steam plant		1·60	30
892	4d.50 Salonika hydroelectric sub-station		1·80	1·40
893	6d. Agra River power station		5·50	4·50
887/893 Set of 7			9·25	6·50

(Des A. Tassos. Litho)

1962 (3 May). North Atlantic Treaty Organisation Ministers' Conference, Athens. T **170** and similar designs. W **84**. P 13½×12½ (2d.50), 13½×14 (6d.) or 12½×13½ (others).

894	2d.50 sepia, green, red and light blue		45	25
895	3d. sepia, brown and buff		45	25
896	4d.50 black and blue		70	50
897	6d. black and brown-red		70	50
894/897 Set of 4			2·10	1·40

Designs: Horiz—2d.50, T **170**. Vert—3d. Ancient Greek warrior with shield; 4d.50, Soldier kneeling (after Marathon tomb); 6d. (21×37 *mm*) Soldier (statue in Temple of Aphea, Aegina).

171 Europa Tree   **172** Protection

(Des L. Weyer. Litho)

1962 (17 Sept). Europa. W **84**. P 13½×12½.

898	**171**	2d.50 red and black	1·30	45
899		4d.50 bright blue and black	3·50	1·40

1962 (30 Oct). Greek Farmers' Social Insurance Scheme. Litho. W **84** (sideways). P 13×13½.

900	**172**	1d.50 black, yellow-brown and carmine	60	25
901		2d.50 black, yellow-brown and emerald-green	85	25

173 Demeter, Goddess of Corn   **174** Kings of the Greek Dynasty

(Des A. Tassos. Litho)

1963 (25 Apr). Freedom from Hunger. T **173** and similar vert design. Multicoloured. W **84**. P 12½×13½.

902	2d.50 Type **173**		55	20
903	4d.50 Wheat ears and Globe		1·30	70

(Des A. Tassos. Recess)

1963 (29 June). Centenary of Greek Royal Dynasty. W **84**. P 13½×13.

904	**174**	50l. carmine	35	20
905		1d.50 deep green	90	25

906		2d.50 red-brown	1·70	20
907		4d.50 ultramarine	3·50	1·20
908		6d. violet	4·50	60
904/908 Set of 5			9·75	2·20

1963 (5 July). As Nos. 799/808 (Ancient Greek coins), but colours changed and new values.

909	50l. drab, black and deep violet-blue (No. 801)		30	20
910	80l. drab, black and bright purple (No. 802)		35	20
911	1d. grey, black and green (No. 803)		45	20
912	1d.50 drab, black and cerise (No. 804)		1·70	20
913	3d. drab, black and olive (No. 799)		1·10	20
914	3d.50 grey, black and red (No. 800)		1·10	45
915	4d.50 grey, black and red-brown (No. 806)		1·10	30
916	6d. grey, black and blue-green (No. 807)		1·10	20
917	8d.50 grey, black and blue (No. 808)		2·50	1·50
909/917 Set of 9			8·75	2·75

 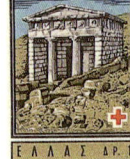

175 Athens at Dawn (after watercolour by Lord Baden-Powell) 176 Delphi

(Des A. Tassos. Litho)

1963 (1 Aug). 11th World Scout Jamboree, Marathon. T **175** and similar designs. W **84** (sideways on vert format). P 13½×13 (horiz) or 13×13½ (others).

918	1d. salmon, blue, olive, light brown and pale blue		40	30
919	1d.50 yellow-orange, black and deep blue		40	30
920	2d.50 flesh, black, bistre, blue, lake and grey		1·80	30
921	3d. black, cinnamon and deep green		1·10	75
922	4d.50 yellow-brown, brown, black, blue and light blue		1·90	1·00
918/922 Set of 5			5·00	2·40

Designs: Vert—1d.50, Jamboree badge; 2d.50, Crown Prince Constantine, Chief Scout of Greece; 4d.50, Scout bugling with Atlantic Trumpet Triton. Horiz—1d. T **175**; 3d. A. Lefkadites (founder of Greek Scout Movement) and Lord Baden-Powell.

(Des A. Tassos. Litho)

1963 (16 Sept). Red Cross Centenary. T **176** and similar vert designs. Multicoloured. W **84**. P 12½×13½.

923	1d. Type **176**		75	40
924	2d. Centenary emblem		35	20
925	2d.50 Queen Olga		40	20
926	4d.50 Henri Dunant		1·40	1·00
923/926 Set of 4			2·50	1·60

177 Co-operation 178 Great Lavra Church

(Des A. Holm. Litho)

1963 (16 Sept). Europa. W **84**. P 13½×12½.

927	**177**	2d.50 deep green	5·00	65
928		4d.50 bright purple	9·50	3·75

(Des A. Tassos. Litho)

1963 (5 Dec). Millenary of Mount Athos Monastic Community. T **178** and similar designs. W **84**. Multicoloured. P 13½×13 (1d., 6d.) or 13×13½ (others).

929	30l. Vatopediou Monastery		40	20
930	80l. Dionysion Monastery		40	20
931	1d. Protaton Church, Karyae		50	20
932	2d. Stavronikita Monastery		1·90	20
933	2d.50 Cover of Nicephorus Phocas Gospel, Great Lavra Church		4·00	20
934	3d.50 St Athanasius the Athonite (fresco)		1·80	1·20
935	4d.50 11th-century papyrus, Iviron Monastery		1·60	60
936	6d. Type **178**		1·80	55

929/936 Set of 8	11·00	3·00

The 1d. and 6d. are horiz, the rest vert.

King Constantine II

6 March 1964–1 June 1973

179 King Paul 180 Gold Coin

(Des A. Tassos. Litho)

1964 (6 May). Death of Paul I. W **84**. P 12×13½.

937	**179**	30l. brown	30	20
938		50l. bright violet	30	20
939		1d. bronze-green	1·30	20
940		1d.50 red-orange	55	20
941		2d. blue	1·10	20
942		2d.50 deep dull purple	1·10	20
943		3d.50 brown-purple	1·40	30
944		4d. ultramarine	2·50	30
945		4d.50 indigo	2·75	1·10
946		6d. cerise	4·50	65
937/946 Set of 10			14·00	3·25

(Des A. Tassos. Litho)

1964 (10 June). Byzantine Art Exhibition, Athens. T **180** and similar vert. designs. Multicoloured. W **84**. P 12×13½.

947		1d. Type **180**	30	20
		a. Imperf (pair)	£300	
948		1d.50 Two Saints	30	25
		a. Imperf (pair)	£300	
949		2d. Archangel Michael	30	25
		a. Imperf (pair)	£300	
950		2d.50 Young Lady	45	25
		a. Imperf (pair)	£300	
951		4d.50 Angel	1·60	90
		a. Imperf (pair)	£300	
947/951 Set of 5			2·75	1·70

Design origins: 1d. reign of Emperor Basil II (976–1025); 1d.50, from Harbaville's 10th-century ivory triptych (Louvre); 2d. 14th-century Constantinople icon (Byzantine Museum, Athens); 2d.50, from 14th-century fresco *The Birth of the Holy Virgin* by Panselinos (Protaton Church, Mount Athos); 4d.50, from 11th-century mosaic (Daphne Church, Athens).

181 Trident of Paxi 182 Child

(Des A. Tassos. Litho)

1964 (20 July). Centenary of Union of Ionian Islands with Greece. T **181** and similar horiz designs inscr '1864–1964'. W **84**. P 13½×12.

952	20l. greenish grey, deep greenish grey and dull blue-green		30	20
953	30l. multicoloured		30	20
954	1d. deep brown, light brown and red-brown		30	20
955	2d. multicoloured		30	20
956	2d.50 dull green, blackish olive and deep dull green		55	20
957	4d.50 multicoloured		1·40	95
958	6d. multicoloured		1·30	50
952/958 Set of 7			4·00	2·20

Designs: 20l. T **181**; 30l. Venus of Cythera; 1d. Ulysses of Ithaca; 2d. St George of Levkas; 2d.50, Zakynthos of Zante; 4d.50, Cephalus of Cephalonia; 6d. War galley emblem of Corfu.

(Des A. Tassos. Litho)

1964 (10 Sept). 50th Anniversary of National Institution of Social Welfare (PIKPA). W **84**. P 13½×12.

959	**182**	2d.50 multicoloured	1·30	50

1964 GREECE

183 Europa Flower

184 King Constantine II and Queen Anne-Marie

(Des G. Bétemps. Litho)

1964 (14 Sept). Europa. W **84**. P 13×13½.
960	**183**	2d.50 brown-red and light emerald	3·75	95
961		4d.50 brown and light drab	6·25	1·60

(Des A. Tassos. Recess)

1964 (18 Sept). Royal Wedding. W **84**. P 13½×14.
962	**184**	1d.50 deep green	40	20
963		2d.50 carmine	35	20
964		4d.50 ultramarine	80	45
962/964	*Set of 3*		1·40	75

185 Peleus and Atalanta (amphora)

186 *Christ stripping off His garments*

187 Aesculapius Theatre, Epidauros

(Des A. Tassos. Litho)

1964 (24 Oct). Olympic Games, Tokyo. T **185** and similar designs. Multicoloured. W **84**. P 12½×13½ (vert) or 13½×12½ (horiz).
965		10l. Type **185**	30	20
966		1d. Running (bowl)	30	20
967		2d. Jumping (pot)	30	20
968		2d.50 Throwing the discus	55	20
969		4d.50 Chariot-racing (sculpture)	90	40
970		6d. Boxing (vase)	50	30
971		10d. Apollo (part of frieze, Zeus Temple, Olympia)	1·10	50
965/971	*Set of 7*		3·50	1·80

The 1d., 2d., 4d.50 and 6d. are horiz.

(Des A. Tassos. Litho)

1965 (6 Mar). 350th Death Anniversary of El Greco (painter). T **186** and similar designs. Multicoloured. W **84**. P 13½×12 (1d.50) or 12×13½ (others).
972		50l. Type **186**	30	20
973		1d. *Angels' Concert*	30	20
974		1d.50 El Greco's signature (*horiz*)	30	20
975		2d.50 Self-portrait	30	20
976		4d.50 *Storm-lashed Toledo*	70	50
972/976	*Set of 5*		1·70	1·20

1965 (30 Apr). Greek Artistic Festivals. T **187** and similar vert design. Multicoloured. Litho. W **84**. P 12×13½.
977		1d.50 Type **187**	45	40
978		4d.50 Herod Atticus Theatre, Athens	80	45

188 ITU Emblem and Symbols

189 New Member making Affirmation (after Tsokos)

1965 (30 Apr). Centenary of International Telecommunications Union. Litho. W **84**. P 13½×12.
979	**188**	2d.50 red, deep blue and bluish grey	75	25

(Des A. Tassos. Litho)
1965 (31 May). 150th Anniversary of Philiki Hetaeria (Friends' Society). T **189** and similar horiz design. Multicoloured. W **84**. P 13½×12½.
980		1d.50 Type **189**	30	20
981		4d.50 Society flag	70	35

190 AHEPA Emblem

191 Venizelos as Revolutionary

(Des A. Tassos. Litho)

1965 (30 June). American Hellenic Educational Progressive Association (AHEPA) Congress, Athens. W **84** (sideways). P 13½×12.
982	**190**	6d. black, yellow-olive and light blue..	75	45

(Des and eng A. Tassos. Recess)

1965 (30 June). Birth Centenary of E. Venizelos (statesman). T **191** and similar vert designs. W **84**. P 12×13½.
983		1d.50 bronze-green	40	30
984		2d. deep blue	65	55
985		2d.50 brown	35	30
983/985	*Set of 3*		1·30	1·00

Designs: 1d.50, T **191**; 2d. Venizelos signing Treaty of Sèvres (1920); 2d.50, Venizelos.

192 Games' Flag

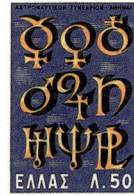
193 Symbols of the Planets

(Des A. Tassos. Litho)

1965 (11 Sept). Balkan Games, Athens. T **192** and similar designs. Multicoloured. W **84**. P 13×13½ (2d.) or 13½×13 (others).
986		1d. Type **192**	30	30
987		2d. Victor's medal (*vert*)	30	30
988		6d. Karaiskakis Stadium, Athens	50	35
986/988	*Set of 3*		1·00	85

(Des A. Tassos. Litho)

1965 (11 Sept). International Astronautic Conference, Athens. T **193** and similar vert designs Multicoloured. W **84**. P 12×13½.
989		50l. Type **193**	30	30
990		2d.50 Astronaut in space	30	30
991		6d. Rocket and spaceship	50	35
989/991	*Set of 3*		1·00	85

194 Europa Sprig

195 Hipparchus (astronomer) and Astrolabe

(Des H. Karlsson. Litho)

1965 (21 Oct). Europa. W **84**. P 13½×12½.
992	**194**	2d.50 deep blue, black and pale slate-violet	2·20	55
993		4d.50 green, black and yellow-olive	2·75	85

(Des A. Tassos. Litho)

1965 (21 Oct). Opening of Evghenides Planetarium, Athens. W **84**. P 13½×12½.
994	**195**	2d.50 black, crimson and turquise-green	75	30

GREECE 1965

196 Carpenter Ants

197 St Andrew's Church, Patras

198 T. Brysakes

(Des A. Tassos. Litho)

1965 (30 Nov). 50th Anniversary of PO Savings Bank. T **196** and similar vert design. Multicoloured. P 12½×13½.
995	10l. Type **196**	30	20
996	2d.50 Savings Bank and book	55	30

(Des A. Tassos. Litho)

1965 (30 Nov). Restoration of St Andrew's Head to Greece. T **197** and similar vert design. Multicoloured. P 12½×13½.
997	1d. Type **197**	25	20
998	5d. St Andrew, after 11th-century mosaic, Hosios Loukas Monastery, Boeotia	45	30

(Des A. Tassos. Litho)

1966 (28 Feb). Modern Greek Painters. Vert portraits as T **198**. Multicoloured. W **84**. P 12×13½.
999	80l. Type **198**	30	20
1000	1d. N. Lytras	30	20
1001	2d.50 C. Volonakes	30	20
1002	4d. N. Gyses	40	30
1003	5d. G. Jacobides	40	30
999/1003 Set of 5		1·50	1·10

199 Greek 25d. Banknote of 1867

200 Geannares (revolutionary leader)

(Des A. Tassos. Recess)

1966 (30 Mar). 125th Anniversary of Greek National Bank. T **199** and similar designs. W **84**. P 12½×13½.
1004	1d.50 bronze-green	30	20
1005	2d.50 brown	25	20
1006	4d. royal blue	35	20
1007	6d. black	65	35
1004/1007 Set of 4		1·40	85

Designs: Vert (23×33½ mm)—1d.50, J.-G. Eynard; 2d.50, G. Stavros (founders). Horiz (As T **199**)—4d. National Bank headquarters, Athens; 6d. T **199**.

(Des A. Tassos. Litho)

1966 (18 Apr). Centenary of Cretan Revolt. T **200** and similar designs. Multicoloured. W **84**. P 12×13½ (2d.) or 13½×12 (others).
1008	2d. Type **200**	30	20
1009	2d.50 Explosion of gun-powder machine, Arkadi Monastery (horiz)	30	20
1010	4d.50 Map of Crete (horiz)	45	35
1008/1010 Set of 3		95	70

201 Movement of Water (Decade of World Hydrology)

202 Tragedian's Mask of 4th-century BC

(Des A. Tassos. Litho)

1966 (18 Apr). United Nations Events. T **201** and similar designs. W **84**. P 13½×12 (5d.) or 12×13½ (others).
1011	1d. grey-blue, orange-brown and black	30	20
1012	3d. multicoloured	30	20
1013	5d. black, new blue and brown-red	45	35
1011/1013 Set of 3		95	70

Designs: Vert—1d. T **201**; 3d. United Nations Educational, Scientific and Cultural Organisation emblem (20th anniversary). Horiz—5d. World Health Organisation building (inauguration of headquarters, Geneva).

(Des A. Tassos. Litho)

1966 (26 May). 2,500th Anniversary of Greek Theatre. T **202** and similar designs. W **84**. P 12×13½ (vert) or 13½×12 (horiz).
1014	1d. yellow-green, black, blue and grey	25	20
1015	1d.50 black, red and orange-brown	25	20
1016	2d.50 black, green and pale yellow-green	30	20
1017	4d.50 red, flesh, black and reddish lilac	60	35
1014/1017 Set of 4		1·30	85

Designs: Horiz—1d.50, Dionysus in a Thespian ship-chariot (vase painting, 500–480 BC); 2d.50, Theatre of Dionysus, Athens. Vert—1d. T **202**; 4d.50, Dionysus dancing (after vase painting by Kleophrades, circa 500 BC).

203 Boeing 707 Jetliner crossing Atlantic Ocean

204 Tending Plants

(Des A. Tassos. Litho)

1966 (26 May). Inauguration of Greek Airways' Transatlantic Flights. W **84**. P 13½×13.
1018	**203** 6d. deep blue, new blue and light blue	70	45

(Des A. Tassos. Litho)

1966 (19 Sept). Greek Tobacco. T **204** and similar vert design. Multicoloured. W **84**. P 12×13½.
1019	1d. Type **204**	40	30
1020	5d. Sorting leaf	80	50

205 Europa Ship

206 Horseman (embroidery)

(Des G. and J. Bender. Litho)

1966 (19 Sept). Europa. W **84**. P 12×13½.
1021	**205** 1d.50 olive-black, yellow-olive and light yellow-olive	1·40	45
1022	4d.50 deep red-brown, light red-brown and pale red-brown	3·50	80

(Des A. Tassos. Litho)

1966 (21 Nov). Greek Popular Art. T **206** and similar designs. Multicoloured. W **84**. P 12×13½ (vert) or 13½×12 (horiz).
1023	10l. Knitting-needle boxes	30	20
1024	30l. Type **206**	30	20
1025	50l. Cretan lyre	30	20
1026	1d. Massa (Musical instrument)	30	20
1027	1d.50 Cross and Angels (bas-relief after Melios)	30	20
1028	2d. Sts Constantine and Helen (icon)	1·60	20
1029	2d.50 Carved altar-screen, St Nicholas' Church, Galaxidion	30	20
1030	3d. 19th-century ship of Skyros (embroidery)	40	20
1031	4d. Psiki (wedding procession) (embroidery)	1·30	20
1032	4d.50 Distaff	55	30
1033	5d. Earrings and necklace	1·10	20
1034	20d. Detail of handwoven cloth	3·25	70
1023/1034 Set of 12		9·00	2·75

The 10l., 50l., 1d., 2d. 2d.50, 4d.50 and 5d. designs are vertical.

1966 GREECE

207 Princess Alexia

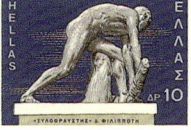
208 Woodcutter (after D. Filippotes)

(Des A. Tassos. Recess)

1966 (19 Dec). Princess Alexia's First Birthday (July 10th, 1966). T **207** and similar vert designs. W **84**. P 13½×14.
1035	2d. green	35	20
1036	2d.50 chocolate	45	20
1037	3d.50 ultramarine	75	35
1035/1037	Set of 3	1·40	70

Portraits: 2d. T **207**; 2d.50, Royal Family; 3d.50, Queen Anne-Marie with Princess Alexia.

(Des A. Tassos. Litho)

1967 (28 Feb). Greek Sculpture. T **208** and similar designs. Multicoloured. W **84**. P 12×13½ (vert) or 13½×12 (horiz).
1038	20l. Night (I. Cossos)	25	20
1039	50l. Penelope (L. Drossos)	25	20
1040	80l. Shepherd (G. Phitalis)	25	20
1041	2d. Woman's Torso (K. Demetriades)	40	20
1042	2d.50 Kolokotronis (L. Sochos)	30	20
1043	3d. Girl Sleeping (I. Halepas)	1·10	40
1044	10d. Type **208**	70	30
1038/1044	Set of 7	3·00	1·50

The 20l. to 2d.50 are vert designs.

209 Olympic Rings (Olympic Day)

210 Cogwheels

(Des A. Tassos. Litho)

1967 (6 Apr). Sports Events. T **209** and similar multicoloured designs. W **84**. P 12×13½ (5d.) or 13½×12 (others).
1045	1d. Type **209**	30	20
1046	1d.50 Marathon Cup, first Olympics (1896)	30	20
1047	2d.50 Hurdling	50	20
1048	5d. The Discus-thrower, after C. Demietriades	75	55
1049	6d. Ancient Olympic stadium	1·40	40
1045/1049	Set of 5	3·00	1·40

The 2d.50 commemorates the European Athletics Cup, 1967; the 5d. (vert), the European Highest Award Championships, 1968; and the 6d. the Inauguration of International Academy buildings, Olympia.

(Des O. Bonnevalle. Litho)

1967 (2 May). Europa. W **84**. P 12×13½.
1050	**210** 2d.50 brown, light brown, black and pale brown	1·90	40
1051	4d.50 bronze-green, light green, black and pale green	4·75	1·60

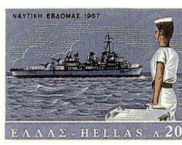
211 Lonchi (destroyer) and Sailor

212 The Plaka, Athens

(Des A. Tassos. Litho)

1967 (26 June). Nautical Week. T **211** and similar designs. W **84**. P 12×13½ (1d.) or 13½×12 (others).
1052	20l. multicoloured	35	20
1053	1d. multicoloured	35	20
1054	2d.50 multicoloured	35	20
1055	3d. multicoloured	95	65
1056	6d. multicoloured	70	45
1052/1056	Set of 5	2·40	1·50

Designs: Vert—1d. Eugene Eugenides (cadet ship). Horiz—20l. T **211**; 2d.50, Merchant Marine Academy, Aspropyrgos, Attica; 3d. Averoff (cruiser) and Naval School, Poros; 6d. Australis (liner) and figurehead.

(Des A. Tassos. Litho)

1967 (26 June). International Tourist Year. T **212** and similar designs. W **84**. P 12×13½ (6d.) or 13½×12 (others).
1057	2d.50 multicoloured	30	20
1058	4d.50 multicoloured	1·10	45
1059	6d. multicoloured	95	20
1057/1059	Set of 3	2·10	75

Designs: Horiz—2d.50, Island of Skopelos; 4d.50, Apollo's Temple, Bassai, Peloponnese. Vert—6d. T **212**.

213 Soldier and Phoenix

214 Industrial Skyline

(Design suggested by A. Skylitses, Mayor of Piraeus. Litho)

1967 (30 Aug). National Revolution of 21 April (1967). W **84**. P 12×13½.
1060	**213** 2d.50 multicoloured	30	20
1061	3d. multicoloured	30	20
1062	4d.50 multicoloured	75	55
1060/1062	Set of 3	1·20	85

1967 (29 Nov). First Convention of UN Industrial Development Organisation, Athens. Litho. W **84**. P 13½×14.
| 1063 | **214** 4d.50 ultramarine, black and light blue | 75 | 50 |

215 Seaside Scene (A. Pelaletos)

216 Throwing the Javelin

(Des by schoolchildren (names in brackets). Litho)

1967 (20 Dec). Children's Drawings. T **215** and similar horiz designs. Multicoloured. W **84**. P 13½×12½.
1064	20l. Type **215**	30	20
1065	1d.50 Steamer and Island (L. Tsirikas)	30	20
1066	3d.50 Country Cottage (K. Ambeliotis)	70	65
1067	6d. The Church on the Hill (N. Frangos)	55	25
1064/1067	Set of 4	1·70	1·20

(Des G. Velissarides (50l., 1d., 6d.), SEGAS Bureau (others). Litho)

1968 (28 Feb). Sports Events, 1968. T **216** and similar designs. W **84**. P 12½.
1068	50l. multicoloured	30	20
1069	1d. multicoloured	30	20
1070	1d.50 multicoloured	30	20
1071	2d.50 multicoloured	45	20
1072	4d. multicoloured	65	35
1073	4d.50 multicoloured	1·50	70
1074	6d. multicoloured	70	30
1068/1074	Set of 7	3·75	1·90

Designs: Horiz—50l. T **216**; 1d. Long-jumping; 4d. Olympic rings (Olympic Day). Vert—1d.50, Apollo's Head, Temple of Zeus; 2d.50, Olympic scene on Attic vase; 4d.50, Throwing the Discus, sculpture by Demetriades (European Athletic Championships, 1969); 6d. Long-distance running.

The 50l., 1d. and 6d. publicise the Balkan Games and the 1d.50 and 2d.50 the Olympic Academy Meeting.

GREECE 1968

217 FIA and ELPA Emblems

218 Europa Key

222 GAPA Emblem

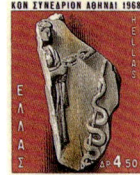
223 Hand of Aesculapius (fragment of bas relief; from Asclepios Temple, Athens)

(Des Greek Auto & Touring Club (ELPA). Litho)

1968 (29 Mar). General Assembly of International Automobile Federation (FIA), Athens. W **84**. P 13½×14.

1075	**217**	5d. blue and orange-brown	1·30	50

(Des H. Schwarzenbach. Litho)

1968 (29 Mar). Europa. W **84**. P 13½×12.

1076	**218**	2d.50 bistre, brown, black and brown-red	2·00	50
1077		4d.50 bistre, brown, black and bluish-violet	3·25	1·40

219 Athene defeats Alkyoneus (from frieze, Altar of Zeus, Pergamos)

1968 (27 Apr). Hellenic Fight for Civilisation Exhibition, Athens. T **219** and similar multicoloured designs. Litho. W **84**. P 13½×13 (10l., 1d.50), 13½×14 (20l., 50l., 2d.50) or 13×13½ (3d., 4d.50, 6d.).

1078		10l. Type **219**	30	20
1079		20l. Athene attired for battle (bronze from Piraeus)	30	20
1080		50l. Alexander the Great (from sarcophagus of Alexander of Sidon)	30	20
1081		1d.50 Emperors Constantine and Justinian making offerings to the Holy Mother (Byzantine mosaic)	40	30
1082		2d.50 Emperor Constantine Paleologos (lithograph by D. Tsokos)	40	20
1083		3d. *Greece in Missolonghi* (painting by Delacroix)	40	30
1084		4d.50 *Evzone* (Greek soldier, painting by G. B. Scott)	65	55
1085		6d. *Victory of Samothrace* (statue)	70	45
1078/1085 *Set of 8*			3·00	2·20

The 1d.50 is horiz as T **219**, the 20l., 50l., and 2d.50 are 24×37 mm, and the remainder 28×40 mm.

(Des G. Velissarides. Litho)

1968 (11 July). Regional Congress of Greek-American Progressive Association (GAPA). W **84**. P 14×13½.

1089	**222**	6d. multicoloured	1·20	70

(Des by Congress committee. Litho)

1968 (8 Sept). Fifth European Cardiological Congress, Athens. W **84**. P 13½×14.

1090	**223**	4d.50 black, orange-yellow and brown-lake	2·20	1·20

224 Panathenaic Stadium

225 PZL P.24 1 ramming Savoia Marchetti S. M.79-11 Sparviero Bomber

(Des P. Gravalos. Litho)

1968 (25 Sept). Olympic Games, Mexico. T **224** and similar multicoloured designs. W **84**. P 13×14 (10d.) or 14×13½ (others).

1091		2d.50 Type **224**	55	25
1092		5d. Ancient Olympia	1·10	30
1093		10d. One of Pindar's odes	2·40	1·10
1091/1093 *Set of 3*			3·75	1·50

The 10d. is vert (28×40 *mm*).

(Des G. Velissarides (2d.50), P. Gravalos (others). Litho)

1968 (8 Nov). Royal Hellenic Air Force. T **225** and similar multicoloured designs. W **84**. P 13½×14 (8d.) or 14×13½ (others).

1094		2d.50 Type **225**	40	20
1095		3d.50 Mediterranean flight in Breguet 19 bomber, 1928	55	20
1096		8d. Farman HF.111 biplane and Lockheed F-104G Super Starfighter (*vert*)	1·40	90
1094/1096 *Set of 3*			2·10	1·20

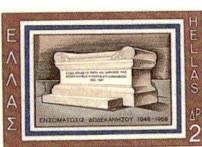
220 The Unknown Priest and Teacher (Rhodes monument)

221 Congress Emblem

226 Goddess Hygeia

227 St Zeno, the Letter-carrier

(Des G. Velissarides (2d.), P. Gravalos (5d.). Litho)

1968 (11 July). 20th Anniversary of Dodecanese Union with Greece. T **220** and similar multicoloured design. W **84**. P 14×13½ (2d.) or 13½×14 (5d.).

1086		2d. Type **220**	70	20
1087		5d. Greek flag on map (*vert*)	1·70	90

(Des P. Gravalos. Litho)

1968 (11 July). 19th Biennial Congress of Greek Orthodox Archdiocese of North and South America. W **84**. P 13½×14.

1088	**221**	6d. multicoloured	1·20	70

(Des G. Velissarides. Litho)

1968 (8 Nov). 20th Anniversary of World Health Organisation. W **84**. P 13½×14.

1097	**226**	5d. multicoloured	1·50	70

(Des P. Gravalos. Litho)

1969 (10 Feb). Greek Post Office Festival. W **84**. P 13½×14.

1098	**227**	2d.50 multicoloured	95	50

1969 GREECE

228 Workers Festival Parade (detail from Minoan vase)

229 Yacht Harbour, Vouliagmeni

(Des G. Velissarides (1d.50), P. Gravalos (10d.). Litho)

1969 (10 Feb). 50th Anniversary of International Labour Organisation. T **228** and similar horiz design. Multicoloured. W **84**. P 13½×12½.
1099	1d.50 Hephaestus and Cyclops (detail from ancient bas-relief)............................	50	20
1100	10d. Type **228**......................................	1·50	90

(Des P. Gravalos (1d.), G. Velissarides (others). Litho)

1969 (12 Mar). Tourism. T **229** and similar multicoloured designs. W **84**. P 13×13½ (5d.) or 13½×13 (others).
1101	1d. Type **229**..	40	20
1102	5d. *Chorus of Elders* (Ancient drama) (*vert*)..	1·50	95
1103	6d. View of Astypalia................................	65	30
1101/1103	Set of 3	2·30	1·30

230 Ancient Coin of Kamarina

231 Colonnade

(Des G. Velissarides (2d.50), P. Gravalos (4d.50). Litho)

1969 (4 Apr). 20th Anniversary of North Atlantic Treaty Organisation. T **230** and similar multicoloured design. W **84**. P 12½×13½ (2d.50) or 13½×12½ (4d.50).
1104	2d.50 Type **230**	50	25
1105	4d.50 Going into Battle (from Corinthian vase) (*horiz*)............................	1·40	1·10

(Des L. Gasbarra and G. Belli. Litho)

1969 (5 May). Europa. W **84**. P 13½×12.
1106	**231** 2d.50 multicoloured	5·00	45
1107	4d.50 multicoloured	8·75	1·70

232 Gold Medal

233 19th-century Brig and Steamship (I. Poulakas)

(Des G. Velissarides (20l.), P. Gravalos (others). Litho)

1969 (5 May). Ninth European Athletic Championships, Athens. T **232** and similar multicoloured designs. W **84**. P 12×13½ (vert) or 13½×12 (horiz).
1108	20l. Type **232**..	30	20
1109	3d. Pole-vaulting, and ancient pentathlon contest....................................	40	30
1110	5d. Relay-racing, and Olympic race *c* 525 BC (*horiz*)............................	55	30
1111	8d. Throwing the discus, modern and *c* 480 BC.....................................	2·10	1·10
1108/1111	Set of 4	3·00	1·70

(Des L. Montesantou (2d., 4d.50), P. Gravalos (others). Litho)

1969 (28 June). Navy Week and Merchant Marine Year. T **233** and similar multicoloured designs. W **84**. P 12×13½ (80l.), 13½×12½ (2d., 4d.50) or 13½×12½ (others).
1112	80l. Type **233**..	30	20
1113	2d. *Olympic Garland* (tanker) (*horiz*)............	30	20
1114	2d.50 *Themistocles* and *Karteria*, War of Independence, 1821 (anon) (41×29 *mm*)	40	20
1115	4d.50 *Velos* (modern destroyer) (*horiz*)............	1·50	45
1116	6d. The Battle of Salamis (K. Volonakis) (41×29 *mm*)..	2·10	1·00
1112/1116	Set of 5	4·25	1·80

234 Raising the Flag on Mount Grammos

(Des P. Gravalos, from Army photograph. Litho)

1969 (31 Aug). 20th Anniversary of Communists' Defeat on Mounts Grammos and Vitsi. W **84**. P 12½×13½.
1117	**234** 2d.50 multicoloured	1·30	50

235 Athena Promachos

236 Demetrius Karatasios (statue by G. Demetriades)

(Des P. Gravalos. Litho)

1969 (12 Oct). 25th Anniversary of the Liberation. T **235** and similar vert designs. Multicoloured. W **84**. P 13½×14 (5d.) or 12½×13½ (others).
1118	4d. Type **235**..	40	20
1119	5d. 'Resistance' (21×37 *mm*)................	2·10	95
1120	6d. Map of Eastern Mediterranean theatre.	70	20
1118/1120	Set of 3	3·00	1·20

(Des G. Velissarides (1d.50, 2d.50), P. Gravalos (others). Litho)

1969 (12 Nov). Heroes of Macedonia's Fight for Freedom. T **236** and similar vert designs. Multicoloured. W **84**. P 12×13½.
1121	1d.50 Type **236**......................................	25	20
1122	2d.50 Emmanuel Pappas (statue by N. Perantinos)............................	25	20
1123	3d.50 Pavlos Melas (from painting by P. Mathiopoulos)....................	30	30
1124	4d.50 Capetan Kolas................................	1·10	1·00
1121/1124	Set of 4	1·70	1·50

237 Dolphin Mosaic, Delos. (110 BC)

238 Overwhelming the Cretan Bull (sculpture)

(Des G. Velissarides (1d.50, 5d.), P. Gravalos (others) Litho)

1970 (16 Jan). Greek Mosaics. T **237** and similar multicoloured designs. W **84**. P 13½×12½ (1d.), 12½×13½ (6d.) or 12×13½ (others).
1125	20l. Angel of the Annunciation, Daphne (11th-century) (*vert*)........................	30	20
1126	1d. Type **237**..	30	20
1127	1d.50 The Holy Ghost, Hosios Loukas Monastery (11th-century) (*vert*)...............	35	30
1128	2d. Hunter, Pella (4th-century BC) (*vert*).......	55	20

GREECE 1970

1129	5d. Bird, St George's Church, Salonika (5th-century) (vert)		70	50
1130	6d. Christ, Nea Moni Church, Khios (5th-century) (vert)		1·70	1·10
1125/1130 Set of 6			3·50	2·30

Nos. 1125 and 1127/1129 are smaller, 23×34 mm.

(Des G. Velissarides (1d., 1d.50, 2d.), P. Gravalos (others). Litho)

1970 (16 Mar). The Labours of Hercules. T **238** and similar designs. W **84**. P 13½×12 (horiz) or 12×13½ (vert).

1131	20l. multicoloured	30	20
1132	30l. multicoloured	30	20
1133	1d. black, pale blue and slate-blue	50	20
1134	1d.50 agate, sage-green and yellow-ochre	50	20
1135	2d. multicoloured	3·25	20
1136	2d.50 sepia, dull scarlet and buff	50	20
1137	3d. multicoloured	3·25	20
1138	4d.50 multicoloured	65	30
1139	5d. multicoloured	65	20
1140	6d. multicoloured	65	20
1141	20d. multicoloured	2·75	90
1131/1141 Set of 11		12·00	2·75

Designs: Horiz—20l. T **238**; 30l. Hercules and Cerberus (from decorated pitcher); 1d.50, The Lernean Hydra (from stamnos); 2d. Hercules and Geryon (from amphora); 4d.50, Combat with the River-god Achelous (from pitcher); 5d. Overwhelming the Nemean Lion (from amphora); 6d. The Stymphalian Birds (from vase); 20d. Wrestling with Antaeus (from bowl). Vert—1d. Golden Apples of the Hesperides (sculpture); 2d.50, The Erymanthine Boar (from amphora); 3d. The Centaur Nessus (from vase).

239 Flaming Sun

240 Satellite and Dish Aerial

(Des P. Gravalos (3d.), L. le Brocquy (others). Litho)

1970 (21 Apr). Europa. T **239** and similar design. W **84**. P 12×13½ (3d.) or 13½×12 (others).

1142	**239**	2d.50 orange-yellow and cerise	3·75	80
1143	–	3d. deep blue and new blue	3·75	80
1144	**239**	4d.50 orange-yellow and ultramarine	12·00	2·75
1142/1144 Set of 3			18·00	4·00

Design: Vert—3d. 'Owl' and CEPT emblem.

(Des G. Velissarides. Litho)

1970 (21 Apr). Satellite Earth Telecommunications Station, Thermopylae. W **84**. P 13½×12.

1145	**240**	2d.50 multicoloured	65	30
1146		4d.50 multicoloured	1·70	1·30

241 Saints Cyril and Methodius with Emperor Michael III (from 12th-century wall-painting)

242 Cephalonian Fir

(Des G. Velissarides (5d.), P. Gravalos (others). Litho)

1970 (17 May). Saints Cyril and Methodius Commemoration. T **241** and similar vert designs. Multicoloured. W **84**. P 13½×14 (50l.), 12½×13½ (5d.) or 12×13½ (others).

1147	50l. Saints Demetrius, Cyril and Methodius (mosaic) (21×37 mm)	30	20
1148	2d. St Cyril (Russian miniature) (25×32 mm)	1·10	75
	a. Horiz pair. Nos. 1148 and 1150	2·30	1·60
1149	5d. Type **241**	65	20
1150	10d. St Methodius (Russian miniature) (25×32 mm)	1·10	75
1147/1150 Set of 4		2·75	1·70

Nos. 1148 and 1150 were issued together in horizontal se-tenant pairs within the sheet, each pair forming a composite design.

(Des G. Velissarides (2d.50), P. Gravalos (others). Litho)

1970 (1 June). Nature Conservation Year. T **242** and similar multicoloured designs. W **84**. P 12×13½ (2d.50), 13½×12½ (6d.) or 12½×13½ (others).

1151	80l. Type **242**	50	50
1152	2d.50 Jankaea heldreichii (plant)	1·90	40
1153	6d. Rock Partridge (horiz)	3·00	55
1154	8d. Wild Goat	4·00	3·00
1151/1154 Set of 4		8·50	4·00

No. 1152 is smaller, 23×34 mm.

243 Cultural Links

244 New UPU Headquarters Building, Berne (Opening)

(Des G. Velissarides. Litho)

1970 (1 Aug). American-Hellenic Educational Progressive Association Congress, Athens. W **84**. P 13½×12½.

1155	**243**	6d. multicoloured	1·70	50

(Des G. Velissarides (50l., 4d.50), P. Gravalos (others). Litho)

1970 (7 Oct). Anniversaries. T **244** and similar multicoloured designs. W **84**. P 13½×12 (50l.), 12½×13½ (3d.50, 4d.) or 12½×13½ (others).

1156	50l. Type **244**	30	20
1157	2d.50 Emblem (International Education Year) (vert)	65	20
1158	3d.50 Mahatma Gandhi (birth centenary) (vert)	35	30
1159	4d. '25' (25th anniversary of United Nations) (vert)	1·30	20
1160	4d.50 Beethoven (birth bicentenary) (vert)	2·75	1·60
1156/1160 Set of 5		4·75	2·30

Nos. 1157 and 1160 are larger, 28½×41 mm.

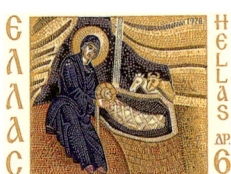
245 The Nativity

(Des G. Velissarides (2d.), P. Gravalos (others). Litho)

1970 (5 Dec). Christmas. Scenes from The Mosaic of the Nativity, Hosios Loukas Monastery. T **245** and similar multicoloured designs. W **84**. P 13½×12½ (6d.) or 12½×13½ (others).

1161	2d. The Shepherds (vert)	40	25
1162	4d.50 The Magi (vert)	60	40
1163	6d. Type **245**	1·50	95
1161/1163 Set of 3		2·30	1·40

246 Death of Bishop of Salona in Battle, Alamana (lithograph)

(Des G. Velissarides (50l., 2d.), P. Gravalos (others). Litho)

1971 (8 Feb). 150th Anniversary of War of Independence (1st Issue). The Church. T **246** and similar multicoloured designs. W **84**. P 13×13½ (50l., 2d.) or 12×13½ (others).

1164	50l. Warriors taking the oath (medal) (vert)	30	20
1165	2d. Patriarch Gregory V (statue by Phitalis) (vert)	35	20
1166	4d. Type **246**	40	30
1167	10d. Bishop Germanos blessing the Standard (Vryzakis)	1·90	1·30
1164/1167 Set of 4		2·75	1·80

See also Nos. 1168/1173, 1178/1180, 1181/1186 and 1187/1189.

(Des G. Velissarides (6d.), P. Gravalos (others). Litho)

1971 (15 Mar). 150th Anniversary of War of Independence (2nd Issue). The War at Sea. Horiz designs dated as T **246**. Multicoloured. W **84**. P 13½×12½ (3d., 6d.) or 13½×13 (others).

1168	20l. *Leonidas* (warship) (37×24 *mm*)	25	20
1169	1d. *Pericles* (warship) (37×24 *mm*)	35	20
1170	1d.50 *Terpsichore* (warship) (from painting by Roux) (37×24 *mm*)	35	20
1171	2d.50 *Karteria* (warship) (from painting by Hastings) (37×24 *mm*)	35	20
1172	3d. *Battle of Samos* (contemporary painting) (40×28 *mm*)	1·00	45
1173	6d. *Turkish Frigate ablaze, Battle of Yeronda* (Michalis) (40×28 *mm*)	2·30	1·10
1168/1173 Set of 6		4·25	2·10

247 Spyridon Louis winning Marathon, Athens 1896

(Des P. Gravalos (3d.), G. Velissarides (8d.). Litho)

1971 (10 Apr). 75th Anniversary of Olympic Games Revival. T **247** and similar multicoloured design. W **84**. P 13½×13 (3d.) or 13×13½ (8d.).

1174	3d. Type **247**	95	30
1175	8d. P. de Coubertin and Memorial, Olympia (*vert*)	2·50	1·40

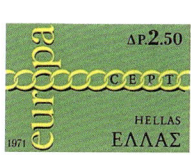 

248 Europa Chain   **249** Kaltetsi Monastery and Seal of Peloponnesian Senate

(Des H. Haflidason. Litho)

1971 (18 May). Europa. W **84**. P 13½×12.

1176	**248**	2d.50 yellow, emerald and black	3·75	50
1177		5d. yellow, orange and black	11·50	2·30

(Des P. Gravalos (15d.), G. Velissarides (others). Litho)

1971 (21 June). 150th Anniversary of War of Independence (3rd Issue). Teaching the People. Multicoloured designs dated as T **246**. W **84**. P 12×13½.

1178	50l. Eugenius Voulgaris	35	20
1179	2d.50 Dr. Adamantios Korais	35	20
1180	15d. *The Secret School* (N. Ghyzis)	2·10	1·30
1178/1180 Set of 3		2·50	1·50

Sizes: 50l., 2d.50, 23×34 mm. 15d. as T **246**.

(Des G. Velissarides (1d., 9d.), P. Gravalos (others). Litho)

1971 (21 Sept). 150th Anniversary of War of Independence (4th Issue). The War on Land. Multicoloured designs dated as T **246**. W **84**. P 12×13½ (6d.50, 9d.), 13½×12½ (2d.) or 12½×13½ (others).

1181	50l. Battle of Corinth (Krazeisen)	35	20
1182	1d. *Sacrifice of Kapsalis* (Vryzakis)	35	20
1183	2d. *Suliot Women in Battle* (Deneuville)	40	20
1184	5d. *Battle of Athens* (Zographos)	50	25
1185	6d.50 Battle of Maniaki (lithograph)	75	25
1186	9d. *Death of Markos Botsaris at Karpenisi* (Vryzakis)	1·70	1·20
1181/1186 Set of 6		3·75	2·10

Sizes: 50l., 1d., 5d. 25×50 mm. 2d. 40×25 mm. 6d.50, 9d. as T **246**.

(Des G. Velissarides (20d.), P. Gravalos (others). Litho)

1971 (19 Oct). 150th Anniversary of War of Independence (5th Issue). Government. T **249** and similar horiz designs. W **84**. P 13½×12½.

1187	2d. black, light green and yellow-brown	45	20
1188	2d.50 black, light blue and blue	45	20
1189	20d. black, light olive-yellow and sepia	3·00	2·00
1187/1189 Set of 3		3·50	2·20

Designs: 2d. T **249**; 2d.50, National Assembly Memorial, Epidavros, and Seal of Provincial Administration; 20d. Signature and seal of John Capodistria, first President of Greece.

250 Hosios Loukas Monastery, Boeotia   **251** Cretan Costume

(Des P. Gravalos. Litho)

1972 (17 Jan). Greek Monasteries and Churches. T **250** and similar horiz designs. Multicoloured. W **84**. P 14×13½.

1190	50l. Type **250**	25	20
1191	1d. Daphni Church, Attica	25	20
1192	2d. Monastery of St John the Divine, Patmos	30	20
1193	2d.50 Panaghia Koumbelidiki Church, Kastoria	30	20
1194	4d.50 Panaghia ton Chalkeon, Salonika	45	30
1195	6d.50 Panaghia Paregoritissa Church, Arta	45	30
1196	8d.50 St Paul's Monastery, Mount Athos	2·10	1·80
1190/1196 Set of 7		3·75	3·00

(Des G. Velissarides (2d., 3d. and 4d.50), P. Gravalos (others). Litho)

1972 (1 Mar). Greek Regional Costumes (1st series). Exhibits from Benaki Museum. T **251** and similar vert designs inscr '1972'. Multicoloured. W **84**. P 12×13½.

1197	50l. Type **251**	30	20
1198	1d. Pindus bride	30	20
1199	2d. Warrior-chief, Missolonghi	30	20
1200	2d.50 Sarakatsan woman, Attica	30	20
	a. '1972' omitted	12·50	6·25
1201	3d. Nisiros woman	35	20
1202	4d.50 Megara woman	40	20
1203	6d.50 Trikeri woman	45	20
1204	10d. Pylaia woman, Macedonia	4·50	1·60
1197/1204 Set of 8		6·25	2·75

No. 1200a occurs on R1/5 on sheets from the end of the printing. See also Nos. 1232/1248 and 1282/1296.

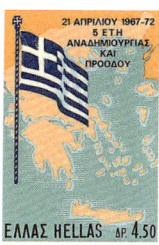 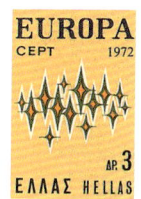

252 Flag and Map   **253** Communications

(Des G. Velissarides (2d.50) and P. Gravalos (others). Litho)

1972 (21 Apr). Fifth Anniversary of 1967 Revolution. T **252** and similar multicoloured designs. W **84**. P 13×13½.

1205	2d.50 Commemorative medal (*horiz*)	30	20
1206	4d.50 Type **252**	50	30
1207	5d. Facets of modern development	65	45
1205/1207 Set of 3		1·30	85

(Des P. Huovinen. Litho)

1972 (2 May). Europa. W **84**. P 12½×13½.

1208	**253**	3d. multicoloured	1·60	45
1209		4d.50 multicoloured	4·00	1·80

254 Acropolis, Athens   **255** Gaia delivering Erecthonius to Athene

(Des P. Gravalos. Litho)

1972 (26 May). 20th Anniversary of Acropolis Motor Rally. T **254** and similar horiz design. Multicoloured. W **84**. P 13½×12½.

1210	4d.50 Type **254**	1·10	75
1211	5d. Emblem and map	1·10	75

GREECE 1972

(Des I. Svoronos. Litho)

1972 (26 June). Greek Mythology. Museum Pieces (1st series). T **255** and similar horiz designs. W **84**. P 14×13½.

1212	1d.50 black and yellow-olive..................	35	20
	a. Horiz strip of 4. Nos. 1212/1215.............	2·10	
1213	2d. black and Prussian blue......................	35	30
1214	2d.50 black and orange-brown.................	35	30
1215	5d. black and deep brown........................	1·00	55
1212/1215 Set of 4		1·80	1·20

Designs: 1d.50, T **255**; 2d. Uranus (altar-piece); 2d.50, The Gods repulsing the Giants; 5d. Zeus.

Nos. 1212/1215 were issued together in horizontal *se-tenant* strips of four within the sheet of 40 stamps. The three low values were also each issued in separate sheets of 50 stamps (*Price per horiz pair of one value*: £41 un, £41 used).

See also Nos. 1252/1255 and 1271/1274.

256 Young Athlete (statue)   **257** Young Stamp Collector

(Des P. Gravalos. Litho)

1972 (28 July). Olympic Games, Munich. Ancient Olympics. T **256** and similar multicoloured designs. W **84**. P 13½×14 (vert) or 14×13½ (horiz).

1216	50l. Type **256**	30	20
1217	1d.50 Wrestlers (bas-relief) (*horiz*).......	30	20
1218	3d.50 Female athlete (statuette)............	65	35
1219	4d.50 Ball game (bas-relief) (*horiz*).......	80	45
1220	10d. Runners (amphora) (*horiz*)............	2·40	1·10
1216/1220 Set of 5		4·00	2·10

(Des P. Gravalos. Litho)

1972 (15 Nov). Stamp Day. W **84**. P 13×13½.
| 1221 | **257** | 2d.50 multicoloured....................... | 30 | 25 |

258 The Birth of Christ   **259** University Buildings

(Des G. Velissarides. Litho)

1972 (15 Nov). Christmas. T **258** and similar vert design. Multicoloured. W **84**. P 13½×14.

1222	2d.50 Pilgrimage of the Magi.................	35	30
	a. Horiz pair. Nos. 1222/1223.................	75	65
1223	4d.50 Type **258**	35	30

Nos. 1222/1223 were issued together in horizontal *se-tenant* pairs within the sheet, each pair forming a composite design.

(Des V. Constantinea. Litho)

1973 (30 Mar). Centenary of National Polytechnic University, Athens. W **84**. P 13½×13.
| 1224 | **259** | 2d.50 multicoloured....................... | 45 | 25 |

260 Spring (wall fresco)

(Des P. Gravalos. Litho)

1973 (30 Mar). Archaeological Discoveries, Island of Thera. T **260** and similar multicoloured designs. W **84**. P 13×13½ (vert) or 13½×13 (horiz).

1225	10l. Type **260**	25	20
1226	20l. Barley (jug)...............................	25	20
1227	30l. Blue Apes (fresco) (*horiz*)............	25	20
1228	1d.50 Bird (jug)................................	30	25
1229	2d.50 Swallows (detail, Spring fresco) (*horiz*)..	30	25
1230	5d. Wild Goats (fresco) (*horiz*)...........	30	25
1231	6d.50 Wrestlers (detail, fresco) (*horiz*)	1·20	1·10
1225/1231 Set of 7		2·50	2·20

(Des G. Velissarides (10l., 20l., 1d.50, 3d.50 and 8d.50) and P. Gravalos (others). Litho)

1973 (18 Apr). Greek Regional Costumes (2nd series). Vert designs similar to T **251** but inscr '1973'. Multicoloured. W **84**. P 12½×13½.

1232	10l. Peloponnese................................	20	20
1233	20l. Central Greece.............................	20	20
1234	30l. Locris (Livanates).........................	20	20
1235	50l. Skyros (male)..............................	20	20
1236	1d. Spetsai.......................................	20	20
1237	1d.50 Almyros...................................	20	20
1238	2d.50 Macedonia (Roumlouki)..............	20	20
1239	3d.50 Salamis....................................	30	20
1240	4d.50 Epirus (Souli)............................	30	20
1241	5d. Lefkas (Santa Maura).....................	40	20
1242	6d.50 Skyros (female).........................	40	20
1243	8d.50 Corinth....................................	70	30
1244	10d. Corfu (Garitsa)............................	70	20
1245	15d. Epirus.......................................	80	20
1246	20d. Thessaly (Karagouniko).................	2·00	20
1247	30d. Macedonia (Episkopi)...................	2·75	20
1248	50d. Thrace (Makra Gefyra)..................	6·25	4·25
1232/1248 Set of 17		14·50	6·75

261 Europa Posthorn

(Des L. F. Anisdahl. Litho)

1973 (2 May). Europa. W **84**. P 13½×12½.

1249	**261**	2d.50 blue and new blue..................	80	30
1250		3d. rosine, orange and lake............	1·40	35
1251		4d.50 buff, bronze-green and grey-green	3·50	1·20
1249/1251 Set of 3			5·25	1·70

SECOND REPUBLIC

1 June 1973

262 Olympus (from photograph by Boissonnas)   **263** Dr. G. Papanicolaou

(Des P. Gravalos. Litho)

1973 (25 June). Greek Mythology (2nd series). T **262** and similar horiz designs. W **84**. P 14×13½.

1252	1d. black and grey.............................	45	30
	a. Horiz strip of 4. Nos. 1252/1255........	2·50	
1253	2d. multicoloured..............................	45	30
1254	2d.50 black, grey and buff...................	45	30
1255	4d.50 multicoloured...........................	1·00	70
1252/1255 Set of 4		2·10	1·40

Designs: 1d. T **262**; 2d. Zeus in combat with Typhoeus (amphora); 2d.50, Zeus at Battle of Giants (altar relief); 4d.50, The Punishment of Atlas and Prometheus (vase).

Nos. 1252/1255 were issued together in horizontal *se-tenant* strips of four within the sheet of 40.

1973 GREECE

(Des V. Constantinea. Litho)

1973 (10 Aug). Honouring Dr. George Papanicolaou (cancer specialist). W **84**. P 13×13½.

1256	263	2d.50 multicoloured	35	25
1257		6d.50 multicoloured	50	35

264 Our Lady of the Annunciation **265** Triptolemus in a Chariot (vase)

(Des V. Constantinea. Litho)

1973 (10 Aug). 150th Anniversary of Discovery of Miraculous Icon of Our Lady of the Annunciation, Tinos. W **84**. P 13×13½.

1258	264	2d.50 multicoloured	55	40

(Des V. Constantinea. Litho)

1973 (22 Oct). European Transport Ministers' Conference, Athens. W **84**. P 13×13½.

1259	265	4d.50 multicoloured	60	45

266 Child examining Stamp   **267** G. Averof

(Des V. Constantinea. Litho)

1973 (15 Nov). Stamp Day. W **84**. P 13½×13.

1260	266	2d.50 multicoloured	35	25

(Des and eng Aspioti-Elka. Recess)

1973 (15 Nov). National Benefactors (1st series). T **267** and similar vert portraits. W **84**. P 13×13½.

1261		1d.50 purple-brown	30	25
1262		2d. carmine	30	25
1263		2d.50 green	30	25
1264		4d. reddish lilac	35	25
1265		6d.50 black	75	40
1261/1265 Set of 5			1·80	1·30

Portraits: 1d.50, T **267**; 2d. A. Arsakis; 2d.50, C. Zappas; 4d. A. Syngros; 6d.50, I. Varvakis.

See also Nos. 1315/1318.

 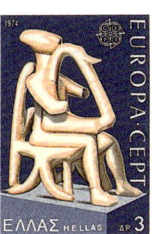

268 Lord Byron in Suliot Costume (Thomas Phillips)   **269** Harpist of Keros

(Des P. Gravalos and V. Constantinea. Litho)

1974 (4 Apr). 150th Death Anniversary of Lord Byron. T **268** and similar vert design. Multicoloured. W **84**. P 13×13½.

1266		2d.50 Type **268**	35	25
1267		4d.50 Byron taking the Oath at the Grave of Markos Botsaris (lithograph)	35	25

(Des P. Gravalos and V. Constantinea. Litho)

1974 (10 May). Europa. Ancient Greek Sculptures. T **269** and similar vert designs. Multicoloured. W **84**. P 13×13½.

1268		3d. Type **269**	90	25
1269		4d.50 Athenian Maiden	1·20	35
1270		6d.50 Charioteer of Delphi (bronze)	3·50	1·20
1268/1270 Set of 3			5·00	1·60

270 Theocracy of Zeus (vase)   **271** UPU Emblem within Mycenaean Vase Design

(Des P. Gravalos and V. Constantinea. Litho)

1974 (25 June). Greek Mythology (3rd series). T **270** and similar designs. W **84**. P 13×13½ (vert) or 13½×13 (horiz).

1271		1d.50 black and yellow-orange	30	25
1272		2d. blackish brown, Venetian red and yellow-orange	35	25
1273		2d.50 black, red-brown and yellow-orange	35	25
1274		10d. blackish brown, brown-red and yellow-orange	65	45
1271/1274 Set of 4			1·50	1·10

Designs: Horiz—2d. Athena's Birth (vase); 2d.50, Artemis, Apollo and Lito (vase). Vert—1d.50, T **270**; 10d. Hermes (vase).

(Des P. Gravalos and V. Constantinea. Litho)

1974 (14 Sept). Centenary of Universal Postal Union. T **271** and similar multicoloured designs. W **84**. P 12×13½ (vert) or 13½×12 (horiz).

1275		2d. Type **271**	30	25
1276		4d.50 Hermes (horiz)	30	25
1277		6d.50 Woman reading letter	45	35
1275/1277 Set of 3			95	75

 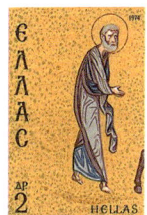

272 Crete 1d. Stamp, 1905   **273** Joseph

(Des P. Gravalos and V. Constantinea. Litho)

1974 (15 Nov). Stamp Day. W **84**. P 13½×13.

1278	272	2d.50 black, carmine-red and blackish lilac	30	25

(Des P. Gravalos and V. Constantinea. Litho)

1974 (15 Nov). Christmas. T **273** and similar vert designs. Multicoloured. W **84**. P 13½×14.

1279		2d. Type **273**	30	25
		a. Horiz strip of 3. Nos. 1279/1281	95	
1280		4d.50 Virgin and Child on Donkey	30	25
1281		8d.50 Jacob	30	25
1279/1281 Set of 3			80	70

Nos. 1279/1281 were issued together in horizontal *se-tenant* strips of three stamps within the sheet, each strip forming a composite design.

(Des P. Gravalos and V. Constantinea. Litho)

1974 (5 Dec). Greek Regional Costumes (3rd series). Vert designs similar to T **251** but inscr '1974'. Multicoloured. W **84**. P 12×13½.

1282		20l. Megara costume	25	25
1283		30l. Salamis costume	25	25
1284		50l. Edipsos costume	25	25
1285		1d. Kymi costume	25	25
1286		1d.50 Sterea Hellas costume	25	25
1287		2d. Desfina costume	25	25

GREECE 1975

1288	3d. Epirus costume		25	25
1289	3d.50 Naousa costume		25	25
1290	4d. Hasia costume		25	25
1291	4d.50 Thasos costume		25	25
1292	5d. Skopelos costume		25	25
1293	6d.50 Epirus costume		25	25
1294	10d. Pelion costume		45	25
1295	25d. Kerkyra costume		1·00	25
1296	30d. Boeotia (Tanagra) costume		3·25	1·80
1282/1296 Set of 15			7·00	4·75

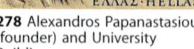

278 Alexandros Papanastasiou (founder) and University Buildings **279** Greek 100d. Stamp, 1933

(Des P. Gravalos and V. Constantinea. Litho)

1975 (29 Sept). 50th Anniversary of Thessaloniki University. T **278** and similar horiz designs. W **84**. P 13½×13.

1311	1d.50 sepia and pale olive-sepia	35	25
1312	4d. multicoloured	35	25
1313	11d. multicoloured	50	35
1311/1313 Set of 3		1·10	75

Designs: 1d.50, T **278**; 4d. Original University building; 11d. Plan of University city.

(Des P. Gravalos and V. Constantinea. Litho)

1975 (15 Nov). Stamp Day. W **84**. P 13½×13½.

1314	**279** 11d. brown, cream and bronze-green	60	45

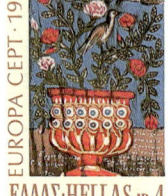

274 Secret Assembly, Vostitsa **275** Roses in Vase

(Des P. Gravalos and V. Constantinea. Litho)

1975 (24 Mar). 150th Death Anniversary of Grigorios Dikeos-Papaflessas (soldier). T **274** and similar designs. W **84**. P 13½×12 (horiz) or 12×13½ (vert).

1297	4d. brownish black, brown and stone	25	25
1298	7d. multicoloured	35	25
1299	11d. multicoloured	45	40
1297/1299 Set of 3		95	80

Designs: Vert—7d. Papaflessas in uniform. Horiz—4d. T **274**; 11d. Aghioi Apostoli (Chapel), Kalamata.

(Des P. Gravalos and V. Constantinea. Litho)

1975 (10 May). Europa. T **275** and similar vert designs. Multicoloured. W **84**. P 13×13½.

1300	4d. Type **275**	80	40
1301	7d. Erotokritos and Aretussa	1·50	70
1302	11d. Girl and sheep	4·50	1·60
1300/1302 Set of 3		6·00	2·40

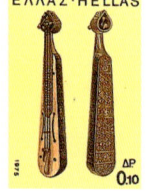

280 Evangelos Zappas and Zappeion Building **281** Pontos Lyre

(Des P. Gravalos and V. Constantinea. Litho)

1975 (15 Nov). National Benefactors (2nd series). T **280** and similar horiz designs. W **84**. P 13½×13.

1315	1d. black, olive-grey and deep green	35	25
1316	4d. black, deep grey and red-brown	35	25
1317	6d. black, brown-grey and orange	40	25
1318	11d. black, brownish grey and Venetian red	50	40
1315/1318 Set of 4		1·40	1·00

Designs: 1d. T **280**; 4d. Georgios Rizaris and Rizarios Ecclesiastical School; 6d. Michael Tositsas and Metsovion Technical University; 11d. Nicolaos Zosimas and Zosimea Academy.

(Des P. Gravalos and V. Constantinea. Litho)

1975 (15 Dec). Musical Instruments. T **281** and similar multicoloured designs. W **84**. P 12×13½ (vert) or 13½×12 (horiz).

1319	10l. Type **281**	25	25
1320	20l. Musicians (Byzantine mural)	25	25
1321	1d. Cretan lyre	25	25
1322	1d.50 Tambourine	25	25
1323	4d. Cithern-player (from amphora) (horiz)	25	25
1324	6d. Bagpipes	25	25
1325	7d. Lute	25	25
1326	10d. Barrel-organ	25	25
1327	11d. Pipes and zournades	40	25
1328	20d. Praising God (Byzantine mural) (horiz)	50	25
1329	25d. Drums	70	25
1330	30d. Kanonaki (horiz)	2·30	1·40
1319/1330 Set of 12		5·25	3·75

276 Mansion, Kastoria **277** Neolithic Goddess (sculpture)

(Des P. Gravalos and V. Constantinea. Litho)

1975 (26 June). National Architecture. T **276** and similar horiz designs. W **84**. P 13½×12½.

1303	10l. black and new blue	25	25
1304	40l. black and red	35	25
1305	4d. black and bistre	35	25
1306	6d. black and ultramarine	35	25
1307	11d. black and red-orange	45	35
1303/1307 Set of 5		1·60	1·20

Designs: 10l. T **276**; 40l. House, Arnea, Halkidiki; 4d. House, Veria; 6d. Mansion, Siatista; 11d. Mansion, Ambelakia, Thessaly.

(Des P. Gravalos and V. Constantinea. Litho)

1975 (29 Sept). International Women's Year. T **277** and similar vert designs. W **84**. P 13×13½.

1308	1d.50 agate, deep mauve and mauve	35	25
1309	8d.50 black, maroon and ochre	35	25
1310	11d. black, deep slate-blue and light greenish blue	50	35
1308/1310 Set of 3		1·10	75

Designs: 1d.50, T **277**; 8d.50, Confrontation between Antigone and Creon; 11d. Women Looking to the Future.

282 Early Telephone and Globe

(Des P. Gravalos and V. Constantinea. Litho)

1976 (23 Mar). Telephone Centenary. T **282** and similar horiz design. Multicoloured. W **84**. P 13½×12.

1331	7d. Type **282**	45	30
	a. Horiz pair. Nos. 1331/1332	95	65

1332 11d. Modern telephone and globe................. 45 30
Nos. 1331/1332 were issued together in horizontal *se-tenant* pairs within the sheet, each pair forming a composite design.

283 Battle of Missolonghi

(Des P. Gravalos and V. Constantinea. Litho)

1976 (23 Mar). 150th Anniversary of Battle of Missolonghi. W **84**. P 13½×13.
1333 **283** 4d. multicoloured............................. 30 25

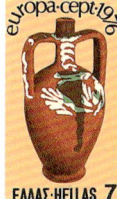 

284 Florina Jug **285** Lion attacking Bull

(Des P. Gravalos and V. Constantinea. Litho)

1976 (10 May). Europa. T **284** and similar vert designs. Multicoloured. W **84**. P 12½×12 (8d.50) or 13×13½ (others).
1334 7d. Type **284** 75 35
1335 8d.50 Plate with bird design (25×30 *mm*)........ 75 35
1336 11d. Egina pitcher .... 2·75 1·10
1334/1336 *Set of 3* .... 3·75 1·60

(Des P. Gravalos and V. Constantinea. Litho)

1976 (10 May). Ancient Sealing-stones. T **285** and similar multicoloured designs. W **84**. P 13×13½ (8d.50), 13½×13 (11d.) or 12½×12 (others).
1337 2d. Type **285** 30 25
1338 4d.50 Water Birds 30 25
1339 7d. Wounded Bull 30 25
1340 8d.50 Head of Silenus (27×40 *mm*)......... 30 25
1341 11d. Cow feeding Calf (40×27 *mm*)......... 50 30
1337/1341 *Set of 5* .... 1·50 1·20

286 Long-jumping **287** Lemnos

(Des P. Gravalos and V. Constantinea. Litho)

1976 (25 June). Olympic Games, Montreal. T **286** and similar horiz designs. Multicoloured. W **84**. P 12×13½ (11d.) or 13½×13 (others).
1342 50l. Type **286** 30 25
1343 2d. Hand-ball 30 25
1344 3d.50 Wrestling 30 25
1345 4d. Swimming 45 25
1346 11d. Athens and Montreal stadiums (52×37 *mm*) 45 30
1347 25d. The Olympic flame .... 1·60 1·10
1342/1347 *Set of 6* .... 3·00 2·20

(Des P. Gravalos and V. Constantinea. Litho)

1976 (26 July). Tourist Publicity. T **287** and similar horiz designs. Multicoloured. W **84**. P 13×13½ (30d.) or 13½×13 (others).
1348 30d. Type **287** 70 25
1349 50d. Lesbos .... 1·40 25
1350 75d. Chios .... 1·70 25
1351 100d. Samos .... 3·25 2·00
1348/1351 *Set of 4* .... 6·25 2·50

288 The Magi speaking to the Jews **289** Lascaris Book of Grammar, 1476

(Des P. Gravalos and V. Constantinea. Litho)

1976 (8 Dec). Christmas. T **288** and similar vert design, showing illustrations from manuscripts at Esfigmenou Monastery. Multicoloured. W **84**. P 13×13½.
1352 4d. Type **288** 35 25
1353 7d. Adoration of the Magi 45 35

(Des P. Gravalos and V. Constantinea. Litho)

1976 (8 Dec). 500th Anniversary of First Book printed in Greek. W **84**. P 13×13.
1354 **289** 4d. multicoloured............................. 30 25

290 Heinrich Schliemann **291** Patients visiting Aesculapius (relief)

(Des P. Gravalos and V. Constantinea. Litho)

1976 (8 Dec). Centenary of Schliemann's Excavation of the Royal Graves, Mycenae. T **290** and similar multicoloured designs. W **84**. P 13½×13 (4d., 7d.) or 13×13½ (others).
1355 2d. Type **290** 35 25
1356 4d. Gold bracelet (*horiz*) 35 25
1357 5d. Silver and gold brooch................. 35 25
1358 7d. Gold diadem (*horiz*) 50 25
1359 11d. Gold mask .... 1·00 65
1355/1359 *Set of 5* .... 2·30 1·50

(Des P. Gravalos and V. Constantinea. Litho)

1977 (15 Mar). International Rheumatism Year. T **291** and similar vert designs. W **84**. P 12×13½ (50l., 20d.) or 12½×12 (others).
1360 50l. black, stone and brown-red......... 30 25
1361 1d. black, yellow-orange and red........ 30 25
1362 1d.50 black, stone and brown-red........ 30 25
1363 2d. black, yellow-orange and red........ 30 25
1364 20d. black, stone and brown-red........ 50 30
1360/1364 *Set of 5* .... 1·50 1·20
Designs: 22×27 mm—1d. Ancient clinic; 1d.50, Aesculapius curing a young man (relief); 2d. Hercules and nurse. 23×34 mm—50l. T **291**; 20d. Cured patient offering model of leg (relief).

292 Fortresses of Mani **293** Emblem and Transport

(Des P. Gravalos and V. Constantinea. Litho)

1977 (16 May). Europa. T **292** and similar multicoloured designs. P 13×14 (7d.) or 14×13 (others).
1365 5d. Type **292** .... 1·50 25
1366 7d. Santorin (*vert*)............................. 1·50 35
1367 15d. Lassithi Plain, Crete.................... 4·00 1·20
1365/1367 *Set of 3* .... 6·25 1·60

GREECE 1977

(Des P. Gravalos and V. Constantinea. Litho)

1977 (16 May). 45th European Conference of Ministers of Transport. P 14×13.

| 1368 | **293** | 7d. multicoloured | 30 | 25 |

294 Alexandria Lighthouse (Roman coin)

(Des P. Gravalos and V. Constantinea. Litho)

1977 (23 July). The Civilising Influence of Alexander the Great. T **294** and similar horiz designs. Multicoloured. P 13½×13.

1369	50l. Type **294**	35	25
1370	1d. Placing the Works of Homer in Achilles' Tomb (fresco, Raphael)	35	25
1371	1d.50 Descending to sea bed in special ship (Flemish miniature)	35	25
1372	3d. In search of water of life (Hindu plate)	45	25
1373	7d. Alexander the Great on Horseback (Coptic carpet)	45	25
1374	11d. Listening to oracle (Byzantine manuscript)	55	25
1375	30d. Death of Alexander the Great (Persian miniature)	95	50
1369/1375	Set of 7	3·00	1·80

295 Wreath in Front of University

296 Archbishop Makarios

(Des. G. Varlamos (4d.), P. Gravalos and V. Constantinea (7d.), L. Orfanos (20d.). Litho)

1977 (23 July). Restoration of Democracy. T **295** and similar designs. P 13½×12 (4d.), 12×12½ (7d.) or 12½×12 (20d.).

1376	4d. blue, pale brown-olive and black	35	25
1377	7d. multicoloured	45	25
1378	20d. multicoloured	60	40
1376/1378	Set of 3	1·30	80

Designs: 4d. T **295**. 26×22 mm—7d. Demonstrators in front of University. 22×26 mm—20d. Flags, University and hand with Olive branch.

1977 (10 Sept). Archbishop Makarios Commemoration. T **296** and similar horiz design. Litho. P 13×13½ (4d.) or 13½×13 (7d.).

| 1379 | 4d. black and brownish grey | 35 | 25 |
| 1380 | 7d. black, sepia and pale stone | 35 | 35 |

Designs: 4d. T **296**; 7d. Makarios and map of Cyprus.

297 Melas Building, Athens (former post office)

1977 (22 Sept). 19th-century Hellenic Architecture. T **297** and similar horiz designs. Litho. P 13½×13.

1381	50l. black, stone and Venetian red	30	25
1382	1d. black, stone and turquoise-green	30	25
1383	1d.50 black, stone and light blue	30	25
1384	2d. black, stone and pale yellow-olive	35	25
1385	5d. black, stone and bistre-yellow	35	25
1386	50d. black, stone and salmon	85	50
1381/1386	Set of 6	2·20	1·60

Designs: 50l. T **297**; 1d. Institution for the Blind, Thessalonika; 1d.50, Town Hall of Hermoupolis, Syros; 2d. Branch Office of National Bank, Piraeus; 5d. Ilissia (Palace of Duchess of Plakentia), Athens; 50d. Municipal Theatre, Patras.

298 Battle of Navarino

299 Parthenon and Industrial Complex

(Des P. Gravalos and V. Constantinea. Litho)

1977 (20 Oct). 150th Anniversary of Battle of Navarino. T **298** and similar horiz design. P 13½×13.

| 1387 | 4d. pale yellow, black and brown | 30 | 25 |
| 1388 | 7d. multicoloured | 35 | 25 |

Designs: 4d. T **298**; 7d. Admirals Van der Heyden, Sir Edward Codrington and Comte de Rigny.

(Des P. Gravalos and V. Constantinea (Nos. 1390/1392). Litho)

1977 (20 Oct). Environmental Protection. T **299** and similar multicoloured designs. P 14×13½ (4d., 7d.) or 13½×14 (others).

1389	3d. Type **299**	35	25
1390	4d. Birds and fish (*horiz*)	35	25
1391	7d. Living and dead trees (*horiz*)	35	25
1392	30d. Head of Erechtheum Caryatid and chimneys	80	60
1389/1392	Set of 4	1·70	1·20

300 Map of Greece and Ships

301 The Port of Kalamata (C. Parthenis)

(Des L. Orfanos (5d.), P. Gravalos and V. Constantinea (others). Litho)

1977 (15 Dec). Greeks Abroad. T **300** and similar horiz designs. Multicoloured. P 13½×12.

1393	4d. Type **300**	30	25
1394	5d. Globe and Greek flag	30	25
1395	7d. Globe and Swallows	30	25
1396	11d. Envelope with flags	30	25
1397	13d. Map of the World	55	40
1393/1397	Set of 5	1·60	1·30

(Des P. Gravalos and V. Constantinea. Litho)

1977 (15 Dec). Greek Paintings. T **301** and similar multicoloured designs. P 13×13½ (2d.50, 11d.) or 13½×13 others).

1398	1d.50 Type **301**	35	25
1399	2d.50 *Arsanas* (S. Papaloucas) (*vert*)	35	25
1400	4d. *Santorin* (C. Maleas)	35	25
1401	7d. *The Engagement* (N. Gyzis)	35	25
1402	11d. *The Straw Hat* (N. Lytras) (*vert*)	35	25
1403	15d. *Spring* (G. Iacovidis)	50	35
1398/1403	Set of 6	2·00	1·40

302 *Ebenus cretica*

303 Horse Postman and Pre-stamp Cancel

(Des P. Gravalos and V. Constantinea, from paintings by N. Goulandris. Litho)

1978 (30 Mar). Greek Flora. T **302** and similar vert designs. Multicoloured. P 13×13½.

1404	1d.50 Type **302**	30	25
1405	2d.50 *Fritillaria rhodokanakis*	30	25
1406	3d. *Campanula oreadum*	30	25
1407	4d. *Lilium heldreichii*	30	25

1978 GREECE

1408	7d. *Viola delphinantha*		35	25
1409	25d. *Paeonia rhodia*		60	45
1404/1409	Set of 6		1·90	1·50

(Des P. Gravalos and V. Constantinea. Litho)

1978 (15 May–25 Sept). 150th Anniversary of Postal Service. T **303** and similar horiz designs. Multicoloured. P 13½×12.

1410	4d. Type **303**	30	25
1411	5d. *Maximilianos* (passenger steamer) and Greek Hermes stamp	30	25
1412	7d. Mail train and 1896 Olympic Games stamp	35	25
1413	30d. Postmen on motorcycles and 1972 'Stamp Day' commemorative	85	65
1410/1413	Set of 4	1·60	1·30
MS1414	101×92 mm. Nos. 1410/1413 (sold at 60d.) (25.9.78)	2·00	1·60

304 Lighting the Olympic Flame

305 St Sophia, Salonika

(Des P. Gravalos and V. Constantinea. Litho)

1978 (15 May). 80th International Olympic Committee Session, Athens. T **304** and similar vert design. Multicoloured. P 13½×14.

1415	7d. Type **304**	1·20	50
1416	13d. Start of 100 m. race	1·90	1·20

(Des P. Gravalos and V. Constantinea. Litho)

1978 (15 May). Europa. T **305** and similar vert design. Multicoloured. P 14×13½ (4d.) or 13½×14 (7d.).

1417	4d. Type **305**	1·60	45
1418	7d. Lysicrates' Monument, Athens	3·00	1·00

306 Bust of Aristotle

307 Rotary Emblem (50th Anniversary)

(Des P. Gravalos and V. Constantinea. Litho)

1978 (10 July). 2300th Death Anniversary of Aristotle. T **306** and similar vert designs. Multicoloured. P 13×14 (20d.) or 13×13½ (others).

1419	2d. Type **306**	35	25
1420	4d. *The School of Athens* (Raphael, detail)	35	25
1421	7d. Map of Chalkidiki and statue plinth	45	30
1422	20d. Aristotle the Wise (Byzantine fresco) (21×37 *mm*)	70	50
1419/1422	Set of 4	1·70	1·20

(Des P. Gravalos and V. Constantinea. Litho)

1978 (21 Sept). Anniversaries and Events. T **307** and similar multicoloured designs. P 12½.

1423	1d. Type **307**	30	25
1424	1d.50 Surgery (11th Greek Surgery Congress) (*vert*)	30	25
1425	2d.50 Ugo Foscolo (poet, birth bicentenary)	30	25
1426	5d. Bronze head (25th anniversary of European Convention on Human Rights)	30	25
1427	7d. Hand with reins (Conference of Ministers of Culture of Council of Europe countries) (*vert*)	40	30
1428	13d. *Wright Flyer I* and Daedalus and Icarus (75th anniversary of first powered flight) (*vert*)	70	60
1423/1428	Set of 6	2·10	1·70

308 The Poor Woman with Five Children

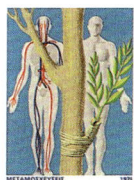

309 Grafted Plant and Circulation Diagram

(Des C. Kourabas. Litho)

1978 (6 Nov). *The Twelve Months* (Greek fairy tale). T **308** and similar horiz designs. Multicoloured. P 14×13.

1429	2d. Type **308**	30	25
1430	3d. The poor woman and the twelve months	30	25
1431	4d. The poor woman and the gold coins	30	25
1432	20d. The poor woman with her children and the rich woman with the Snakes	50	35
1429/1432	Set of 4	1·30	1·00

(Des P. Gravalos and V. Constantinea. Litho)

1978 (6 Nov). Transplants. T **309** and similar vert design. Multicoloured. P 12×13½.

1433	4d. Type **309**	35	25
1434	10d. *The Miracle of Sts Cosmas and Damian* (Alonso de Sedano)	45	25

310 Virgin and Child

311 First Academy, Nauplion, and Cadet

(Des P. Gravalos and V. Constantinea. Litho)

1978 (15 Dec). Christmas. Icons from Stavronikita Monastery, Mount Athos. T **310** and similar vert design. Multicoloured. P 13×13½.

1435	4d. Type **310**	30	25
1436	7d. The Baptism of Christ	35	25

(Des P. Gravalos and V. Constantinea. Litho)

1978 (15 Dec). 150th Anniversary of Military Academy. T **311** and similar multicoloured designs. P 12×13½ (2d.) or 13½×12 (others).

1437	1d.50 Type **311**	30	25
1438	2d. Academy Coat of Arms (*vert*)	30	25
1439	10d. Modern Academy, Athens, and cadet	45	35
1437/1439	Set of 3	95	75

312 Destroyer

313 Map of Greece

(Des P. Gravalos and V. Constantinea. Litho)

1978 (15 Dec). Greek Naval Ships. T **312** and similar horiz designs. Multicoloured. P 13½×12.

1440	50l. Type **312**	30	25
1441	1d. *Andromeda* (motor torpedo-boat)	30	25
1442	2d.50 *Papanicolis* (submarine)	30	25
1443	4d. *Psara* (cruiser)	30	25
1444	5d. *Madonna of Hydra* (armed sailing caique)	35	25
1445	7d. Byzantine dromon	35	25
1446	50d. Athenian trireme	90	55
1440/1446	Set of 7	2·50	1·80

(Des P. Gravalos and V. Constantinea. Litho)

1978 (28 Dec). The Greek State. P 14×13½.

1447	**313**	7d. multicoloured	30	25
1448		11d. multicoloured	35	25

GREECE 1979

1449	13d. multicoloured		45	35
1447/1449	Set of 3		1·00	75

314 Kitsos Tsavellas

315 Figurine found at Amoraos

(Des P. Gravalos and V. Constantinea. Litho)

1979 (12 Mar). The Struggle of the Souliots. T **314** and similar designs. P 12½×13½ (1d.50, 20d.) or 13½×12½ (others).

1450	1d.50 cinnamon, black and brown		30	25
1451	3d. multicoloured		30	25
1452	10d. multicoloured		35	25
1453	20d. pale ochre, black and brown		40	35
1450/1453	Set of 4		1·20	1·00

Designs: Horiz—3d. Souli Castle; 10d. Fighting Souliots. Vert—1d.50, T **314**; 20d. the dance of Zalongo.

(Des P. Gravalos and V. Constantinea. Litho)

1979 (26 Apr). Art of the Aegean. P 13×14.

1454	**315**	20d. multicoloured	65	50

316 Cretan Postmen

317 Nicolas Skoufas

(Des P. Gravalos and V. Constantinea. Litho)

1979 (12 May). Europa. T **316** and similar vert design. Multicoloured. P 13×14.

1455	4d. Type **316**		1·30	30
	a. Horiz pair. Nos. 1455/1456		2·75	90
1456	7d. Mounted postman		1·30	55

Nos. 1455/1456 were issued together in horizontal *se-tenant* pairs within the sheet, each pair forming a composite design.

(Des P. Gravalos and V. Constantinea. Litho)

1979 (12 May). Anniversaries and Events. T **317** and similar multicoloured designs. P 14×13 (2d., 4d.) or 13×14 (others).

1457	1d.50 Type **317** (founder of Friendly Society, birth bicentenary)		30	25
1458	2d. Locomotives (75th anniversary of railway) (*horiz*)		30	25
1459	3d. Basketball (European Basketball Championship)		30	25
1460	4d. Fossil Moonfish *Mene psarianos* (seventh International Congress of Mediterranean Neogene) (*horiz*)		30	25
1461	10d. Greek church (Balkan Tourist Year)		30	25
1462	20d. Victory of Paeonius and flags (50th anniversary of Balkan Sports)		60	50
1457/1462	Set of 6		1·90	1·60

318 Flags of Member States forming Ear of Wheat

319 Girl with Dove (classic statue)

(Des P. Gravalos and V. Constantinea. Litho)

1979 (28 May). Signing of Treaty of Accession of Greece to European Community. T **318** and similar horiz design. Multicoloured. P 13×13½ (7d.) or 13½×13 (30d.).

1463	7d. Type **318**		40	35
1464	30d. European Parliament		65	60

(Des P. Gravalos and V. Constantinea. Litho)

1979 (27 June). International Year of the Child. T **319** and similar vert designs. Multicoloured. P 13×13½.

1465	5d. Type **319**		40	35
1466	8d. Girl with Doves		40	35
1467	20d. Mother and Children (Iacovides, detail)		45	40
1465/1467	Set of 3		1·10	1·00

320 Head of Philip of Macedonia

321 Purple Heron (*Ardea purpurea*)

(Des P. Gravalos and V. Constantinea. Litho)

1979 (15 Sept). Archaeological Discoveries from Vergina. T **320** and similar designs. Multicoloured. P 14×13 (14d.) or 13×14 (others).

1468	6d. Type **320**		40	35
1469	8d. Gold wreath		40	35
1470	10d. Copper vessel		40	35
1471	14d. Golden casket (*horiz*)		45	25
1472	18d. Silver ewer		45	25
1473	20d. Detail of decoration of golden quiver		45	30
1474	30d. Iron cuirass		95	65
1468/1474	Set of 7		3·25	2·30

(Des N. Goulandris. Litho)

1979 (15 Oct). Endangered Birds. T **321** and similar designs. Multicoloured. P 12½×13½ (vert) or 13½×12½ (horiz).

1475	6d. Type **321**		30	25
1476	8d. Audouin's Gull (*Larus audouini*)		30	25
1477	10d. Eleonora's Falcon (*Falco eleonorae*) (*horiz*)		30	25
1478	14d. Common Kingfisher (*Alcedo athis*) (*horiz*)		30	25
1479	20d. Eastern White Pelican (*Pelecanus onocrotalus*)		45	25
1480	25d. White-tailed Sea Eagle (*Haliaetus albicila*)		1·50	95
1475/1480	Set of 6		2·75	2·00

322 Agricultural Bank of Greece (50th Anniversary)

323 Parnassos

(Des P. Gravalos and V. Constantinea. Litho)

1979 (24 Nov). Anniversaries and Events. T **322** and similar designs. P 13½×14 (vert) or 14×13½ (horiz).

1481	3d. black, olive-yellow and deep olive		25	25
1482	4d. multicoloured		25	25
1483	6d. multicoloured		30	25
1484	8d. multicoloured		30	25
1485	10d. multicoloured		30	25
1486	12d. multicoloured		30	25
1487	14d. multicoloured		35	25
1488	18d. multicoloured		50	40
1489	25d. multicoloured		95	70
1481/1489	Set of 9		3·25	2·50

Designs and events: Vert—4d. Cosmas the Aetolian (death bicentenary); 6d. Basil the Great (1600th death anniversary); 8d. Magnifying glass and map of Balkan countries (Balkanfila '79 stamp exhibition); 12d. Aristotelis Valaoritis (poet, death centenary); 14d. Golfer (World Golfing Championship); 18d. Bust of Hippocrates (International Hippocratic Foundation, Kos). Horiz—3d. T **322**; 10d. Ionic column and map of Balkans (Balkanfila '79 stamp exhibition); 25d. Parliamentary meeting (104th anniversary of Greek parliament).

(Des P. Gravalos and V. Constantinea. Litho)

1979 (15 Dec). Landscapes. T **323** and similar designs. Multicoloured. P 12½×13½ (vert) or 13½×12½ (horiz).

1490	50l. Type **323**		35	25
1491	1d. Tempi (horiz)		35	25
1492	2d. Milos		35	25
1493	4d. Vikos Gorge		35	25
1494	5d. Missolonghi (horiz)		35	25
1495	6d. Louros Aqueduct		35	25
1496	7d. Samothrace		35	25
1497	8d. Sithonia, Chalkidike (horiz)		35	25
1498	10d. Samaria Gorge		35	25
1499	12d. Sifnos		35	25
1500	14d. Kymi (horiz)		45	25
1501	18d. Ios		45	25
1502	20d. Thassos		55	25
1503	30d. Paros (horiz)		95	25
1504	50d. Cephalonia		1·90	75
1490/1504 Set of 15			7·00	3·75

324 Gate of Galerius   **325** Aegosthena Castle

(Des P. Gravalos and V. Constantinea. Litho)

1980 (15 Mar). First Hellenic Nephrology Congress, Thessalonika. P 13½×12½.

1505	**324**	8d. azure, black and brown-red	40	25

(Des P. Gravalos and V. Constantinea. Litho)

1980 (15 Mar). Castles, Caves and Bridges. T **325** and similar multicoloured designs. P 12½×13½ (vert) or 13½×12½ (horiz).

1506	4d. Type **325**		30	25
1507	6d. Byzantine castle, Thessalonika (horiz)		30	25
1508	8d. Perama cave, Ioannina		30	25
1509	10d. Dyros cave, Mani		30	25
1510	14d. Arta bridge (horiz)		45	25
1511	20d. Kalogiros bridge, Epirus (horiz)		50	25
1506/1511 Set of 6			1·90	1·40

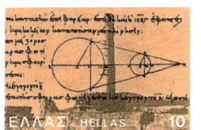 

326 Aristarchus's Theorem and Temple of Hera   **327** George Seferis (writer)

(Des P. Gravalos and V. Constantinea. Litho)

1980 (5 May). 2300th Birth Anniversary of Aristarchus of Samos (astronomer). T **326** and similar horiz design. P 13½×12½.

1512	10d. salmon, black and deep grey-brown		50	40
1513	20d. multicoloured		80	55

Designs: 10d. T **326**; 20d. Heliocentric system.

(Des P. Gravalos and V. Constantinea. Litho)

1980 (5 May). Europa. T **327** and similar horiz design. P 13½×12½.

1514	8d. bistre-brown, pale greenish blue and black		1·60	40
1515	14d. light brown, black and cream		2·40	75

Designs: 8d. T **327**; 14d. Maria Callas (opera singer).

328 Open Book   **329** Fire-fighting

(Des P. Gravalos and V. Constantinea. Litho)

1980 (5 May). Energy Conservation. T **328** and similar vert design. Multicoloured. P 13½×12½ (8d.) or 12½×13½ (20d.).

1516	8d. Type **328**		45	25
1517	20d. Lightbulb as a candle		55	40

(Des P. Gravalos and V. Constantinea. Litho)

1980 (14 July). Anniversaries and Events. T **329** and similar multicoloured designs. P 12½.

1518	4d. Type **329** (50th anniversary of fire brigade)		30	25
1519	6d. St Demetrius (mosaic) (1700th birth anniversary) (vert)		30	25
1520	8d. Revolutionaries (75th anniversary of Theriso revolution)		30	25
1521	10d. Ancient vase and Olive branch (World Olive Oil Year) (vert)		30	25
1522	14d. International press emblem (15th International Journalists Federation congress) (vert)		30	25
1523	20d. Constantinos Ikonomos (cleric and scholar, birth bicentenary) (vert)		60	50
1518/1523 Set of 6			1·90	1·60

330 Olympia and Coin of Elia   **331** Asbestos

(Des P. Gravalos and V. Constantinea. Litho)

1980 (11 Aug). Olympic Games, Moscow. T **330** and similar horiz designs showing Greek stadia. Multicoloured. P 13½×13.

1524	8d. Type **330**		35	25
1525	14d. Delphi and Delphic coin		65	45
1526	18d. Epidaurus and coin of Olympia		35	25
1527	20d. Rhodes and coin of Kos		45	25
1528	50d. Panathenaic stadium and First Olympic Games medal		1·60	75
1524/1528 Set of 5			3·00	1·80

(Des P. Gravalos and V. Constantinea. Litho)

1980 (22 Sept). Minerals. T **331** and similar multicoloured designs. P 12½×13½ (vert) or 13½×12½ (horiz).

1529	6d. Type **331**		30	25
1530	8d. Gypsum (vert)		30	25
1531	10d. Copper		30	25
1532	14d. Barite (vert)		60	35
1533	18d. Chromite		30	25
1534	20d. Mixed sulphides (vert)		45	25
1535	30d. Bauxite (vert)		65	45
1529/1535 Set of 7			2·50	1·80

332 Dassault Mirage III Jet Fighter   **333** Left Detail of Poulakis's Painting

(Des P. Gravalos and V. Constantinea. Litho)

1980 (31 Oct). Anniversaries and Events. T **332** and similar multicoloured designs. P 12½.

1536	6d. Breakdown truck (20th anniversary of Automobile and Touring Club of Greece road assistance service) (horiz)		30	25
1537	8d. Type **332** (50th anniversary of Air Force)		30	25
1538	12d. Piper PA-18 Super Cub light aeroplane outside hangar (50th anniversary of Thessalonika Flying Club) (horiz)		35	25
1539	20d. Harbour scene (50th anniversary of Piraeus Port Organisation)		55	45
1540	25d. Association for Macedonian Studies headquarters (40th anniversary)		70	55
1536/1540 Set of 5			2·00	1·60

(Des P. Gravalos and V. Constantinea. Litho)

1980 (10 Dec). Christmas. T **333** and similar vert designs showing details from *He is Happy Thanks to You* by T. Poulakis (in St John's Monastery, Patmos). Multicoloured. P 13½×14.

1541	6d. Type **333**		35	30
	a. Horiz strip of 3. Nos. 1541/1543		1·30	
1542	14d. Virgin and Child (centre)		40	30
1543	20d. Right detail		45	35
1541/1543 Set of 3			1·10	85

GREECE 1981

Nos. 1541/1543 were issued together in horizontal *se-tenant* strips of three within sheets of 12 stamps, each strip forming a composite design.

334 Fresh and Canned Vegetables

335 Kira Maria (Alexandrian folk dance)

(Des P. Gravalos and V. Constantinea. Litho)
1981 (16 Mar). Exports. T **334** and similar vert designs. Multicoloured. P 12½.

1544	9d. Type **334**	30	25
1545	17d. Fruit	30	25
1546	20d. Cotton	35	25
1547	25d. Marble	60	35
1544/1547 Set of 4		1·40	1·00

(Des P. Gravalos and V. Constantinea. Litho)
1981 (4 May). Europa. T **335** and similar horiz design. Multicoloured. P 13½×12½.

1548	12d. Type **335**	1·00	25
1549	17d. Sousta (Cretan dance)	2·00	75

336 Olympic Stadium, Kalogreza

337 Human Figure showing kidneys

(Des P. Gravalos and V. Constantinea. Litho)
1981 (4 May). European Athletics Championships, Athens (1982) (1st issue). T **336** and similar horiz design. P 14×13½.

1550	12d. grey-blue, black and new blue	45	25
1551	17d. multicoloured	65	45

Designs: 12d. T **336**; 17d. Athletes converging on Greece.
See also Nos. 1586/1588.

(Des P. Gravalos and V. Constantinea. Litho)
1981 (22 May). Anniversaries and Events. T **337** and similar designs. P 13½×14 (vert) or 14×13½ (horiz).

1552	2d. multicoloured	30	25
1553	3d. multicoloured	30	25
1554	6d. multicoloured	30	25
1555	9d. yellow-ochre, black and red-brown	30	25
1556	12d. multicoloured	35	25
1557	21d. multicoloured	60	50
1558	40d. rosine, bright ultramarine and dull ultramarine	1·00	85
1552/1558 Set of 7		2·75	2·30

Designs and events: Vert—2d. T **337** (eighth World Nephrology Conference, Athens); 3d. Potez 25 biplane, glider, parachutist, model glider and emblem (50th anniversary of Greek National Air Club); 6d. Meteora Monasteries, Thessaly, and Konitsa Bridge, Epirus (International Historical Symposium, Volos, and centenary of incorporation of Thessaly and Epirus into Greece); 12d. Oil rig (first Greek oil production); 40d. Heart (15th World Cardiovascular Surgery Conference, Athens). Horiz—9d. Bowl with 'eye' decoration (50th anniversary of Greek Ophthalmological Society); 21d. Globes, plant and coin (foundation in Athens of World Association for International Relations).

(Des P. Gravalos and V. Constantinea. Litho)
1981 (30 June). Shells, Fish and Butterflies. T **338** and similar horiz designs. Multicoloured. P 14×13½.

1559	4d. Type **338**	35	25
1560	5d. Painted Comber (Fish)	35	25
1561	12d. Mediterranean Parrotfish	35	25
1562	15d. Dentex (Fish)	35	25
1563	17d. Apollo (*Parnassius apollo*) (Butterfly)	70	60
1564	50d. Pale Clouded Yellow (*Colias hyale*) (Butterfly)	1·60	1·20
1559/1564 Set of 6		3·25	2·50

(Des P. Gravalos and V. Constantinea. Litho)
1981 (30 Sept). Bell Towers and Altar Screens. T **339** and similar multicoloured designs. P 12½×13½ (vert) or 13½×12½ (horiz).

1565	4d. Type **339**	35	25
1566	6d. Altar gate, St Paraskevi Church, Metsovo	35	25
1567	9d. Altar gate, Pelion (*horiz*)	35	25
1568	12d. Bell tower, Saints Constantine and Helen Church, Halkiades, Epirus	35	25
1569	17d. Altar screen, St Nicholas Church, Velvendos (*horiz*)	35	25
1570	30d. Icon of St Jacob and stand, Alexandroupolis Church Museum	50	35
1571	40d. Upper section of altar gate, St Nicholas Church, Makrinitsa	95	85
1565/1571 Set of 7		3·00	2·20

340 Town Scene

341 Old Parliament Building (museum)

(Des P. Gravalos and V. Constantinea. Litho)
1981 (20 Nov). Anniversaries and Events. T **340** and similar multicoloured designs. P 13½×14 (vert) or 14×13½ (horiz).

1572	3d. Type **340** (Council of Europe Urban Renaissance campaign)	35	25
1573	9d. St Simeon, Archbishop of Thessalonika (miniature) (Canonisation in Greek Orthodox Church) (*vert*)	35	25
1574	12d. Child Jesus (detail of Byzantine icon) (Breastfeeding campaign) (*vert*)	50	30
1575	17d. Gina Bachauer (pianist, Fifth death anniversary) (*vert*)	60	40
1576	21d. Constantine Broumidis (artist, 175th birth anniversary) (*vert*)	65	40
1577	50d. 'Phoenix' banknotes, 1831 (150th anniversary of first Greek banknotes)	1·20	90
1572/1577 Set of 6		3·25	2·30

(Des A. Tassos (21d.), P. Gravalos and V. Constantinea (others). Litho)
1982 (15 Mar). Anniversaries and Events. T **341** and similar multicoloured designs. P 12½×13½ (vert) or 13½×12½ (horiz).

1578	2d. Type **341** (centenary of Historical and Ethnological Society)	35	25
1579	9d. Angelos Sikelianos (poet, 31st death anniversary) (*vert*)	35	25
1580	15d. Harilaos Tricoupis (politician, 150th birth anniversary) (*vert*)	35	25
1581	21d. Mermaid (History of Aegean Islands exhibition) (*vert*)	55	50
1582	30d. Airbus Industrie A300 jetliner and emblem (25th anniversary of Olympic Airways)	85	65
1583	50d. Skull of Petralona man and Petralona cave (Third European Congress of Anthropology, Petralona) (*vert*)	1·30	95
1578/1583 Set of 6		3·50	2·50

338 Variable Scallops

339 Aegean Island Bell Tower

342 Flight from Missolonghi

343 Pole Vaulter and Wreath

(Des P. Gravalos and V. Constantinea. Litho)

1982 (10 May). Europa. T **342** and similar vert design. Multicoloured. P 13½×14.
1584	21d. Bust of Miltiades and shield (Battle of Marathon)	4·50	80
1585	30d. Type **342**	7·50	1·80

(Des P. Gravalos and V. Constantinea. Litho)

1982 (10 May). European Athletic Championships, Athens (2nd issue). T **343** and similar multicoloured designs. P 13½×14 (25d.) or 14×13½ (others).
1586	21d. Type **343**	40	25
1587	25d. Women runners (*vert*)	55	25
1588	40d. Athletes at start of race, shot putter, high jumper and hurdler	1·20	90
1586/1588	Set of 3	1·90	1·30

344 Lectionary Heading

345 Karaiskakis's Camp in Piraeus (detail, von Krazeisen)

(Des P. Gravalos and V. Constantinea. Litho)

1982 (28 June). Byzantine Book Illustrations. T **344** and similar multicoloured designs. P 12½×13½ (vert) or 13½×12½ (horiz).
1589	4d. Type **344**	35	25
1590	6d. Initial letter E (*vert*)	35	25
1591	12d. Initial letter T (*vert*)	45	25
1592	15d. Canon-table of Gospel readings (*vert*)	45	25
1593	80d. Heading of zoology book	1·80	1·10
1589/1593	Set of 5	3·00	1·90

(Des V. Constantinea (12d.), P. Gravalos (50d.). Litho)

1982 (20 Sept). Birth Bicentenary of Georges Karaiskakis (revolutionary leader). T **345** and similar vert design. P 13×14.
1594	12d. pale yellow-olive, black and ultramarine	55	25
1595	50d. multicoloured	1·30	85

Designs: 12d. T **345**; 50d. Karaiskakis meditating.

346 Cypriot Disappearances Demonstration

347 Demonstration in Athens, 25 March 1942 (P. Zachariou)

(Des V. Constantinea (15d.), P. Gravalos (75d.). Litho)

1982 (20 Sept). Amnesty International Year of Disappearances. T **346** and similar vert design. Multicoloured. P 13½×14.
1596	15d. Type **346**	50	25
1597	75d. Victims, barbed wire and candle	1·90	1·50

(Des P. Gravalos. Litho)

1982 (8 Nov). National Resistance, 1941–1944. T **347** and similar multicoloured designs. P 12½.
1598	1d. Type **347**	35	25
1599	2d. *Kalavryta's Sacrifice* (S. Vasiliou)	35	25
1600	5d. *Resistance in Thrace* (A. Tassos) (*vert*)	35	25
1601	9d. *The Onset of the Struggle in Crete* (P. Gravalos) (*vert*)	45	25
1602	12d. Resistance fighters (*vert*)	45	25
1603	21d. *Gorgopotamos* (A. Tassos) (*vert*)	60	25
1604	30d. *Kaisariani, Athens* (G. Sikeliotis)	80	35
1605	50d. *Struggle in Northern Greece* (V. Katraki)	1·80	1·10

1598/1605	Set of 8	4·75	2·75
MS1606	Two sheets (a) 90×81 mm. Nos. 1598/1599 and 1604/1605; (b) 81×90 mm. Nos. 1600/1603	7·25	5·00

348 Mary and Jesus

349 Figurehead from Tsamados's *Ares* (brig)

(Des V. Constantinea and P. Gravalos. Litho)

1982 (6 Dec). Christmas. T **348** and similar horiz design showing early Christian bas reliefs. Multicoloured. P 13½×12½.
1607	9d. Type **348**	35	25
1608	21d. Jesus in manger	55	35

Nos. 1607/1608 were printed together in *se-tenant* pairs within the sheet.

(Des P. Gravalos. Litho)

1983 (14 Mar). 25th Anniversary of International Maritime Organisation. Ships' Figureheads. T **349** and similar multicoloured designs. P 14×13½ (horiz) or 13½×14 (vert).
1609	11d. Type **349**	35	25
1610	15d. Miaoulis's *Ares* (full-rigged ship) (*vert*)	35	25
1611	18d. Topsail schooner from Sphakia (*vert*)	60	25
1612	25d. Bouboulina's *Spetses* (full-rigged ship) (*vert*)	70	35
1613	40d. Babas's *Epameinondas* (brig) (*vert*)	1·10	55
1614	50d. *Carteria* (steamer)	2·00	1·20
1609/1614	Set of 6	4·50	2·50

350 Letter and Map of Greece showing Postcode Districts

351 Archimedes

(Des V. Constantinea (15d.), P. Gravalos (25d.). Litho)

1983 (14 Mar). Inauguration of Postcode. T **350** and similar vert design. Multicoloured. P 12½.
1615	15d. Type **350**	35	25
1616	25d. Hermes' head within posthorn	80	50

(Des V. Constantinea (25d.), P. Gravalos (80d.). Litho)

1983 (28 Apr). Europa. T **351** and similar horiz design. Multicoloured. P 12½×13½ (25d.) or 13×14 (80d.).
1617	25d. Acropolis, Athens (49×34 *mm*)	3·50	85
1618	80d. Type **351**	7·75	2·50

352 Rowing

353 Marinos Antypas (farmers' leader)

(Des V. Constantinea (50d., 80d.), P. Gravalos (others). Litho)

1983 (28 Apr). Sports. T **352** and similar multicoloured designs. P 14×13½ (horiz) or 13½×14 (vert).
1619	15d. Type **352**	35	25
1620	18d. Water skiing (*vert*)	50	25
1621	27d. Windsurfing (*vert*)	1·20	80
1622	50d. Ski lift (*vert*)	1·00	65
1623	80d. Skiing	3·00	1·90
1619/1623	Set of 5	5·50	3·50

GREECE 1983

(Des V. Constantinea (20d., 32d.), A. Tassos (27d.), G. Varlamos (40d.),P. Gravalos (others). Litho

1983 (11 July). Personalities. T **353** and similar vert designs. P 13½×14.

1624	6d. multicoloured	35	25
1625	9d. multicoloured	35	25
1626	15d. multicoloured	35	25
1627	20d. multicoloured	45	25
1628	27d. multicoloured	55	25
1629	32d. multicoloured	85	40
1630	40d. pale yellow, deep chocolate and black	1·00	40
1631	50d. multicoloured	1·50	85
1624/1631 Set of 8		4·75	2·50

Designs: 6d. T **353**; 9d. Nicholas Plastiras (soldier and statesman); 15d. George Papandreou (statesman); 20d. Constantin Cavafy (poet); 27d. Nikos Kazantzakis (writer); 32d. Manolis Calomiris (composer); 40d. George Papanicolaou (medical researcher); 50d. Despina Achladioti, 'Matron of Rho' (patriot).

 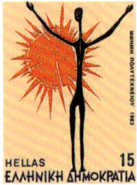

354 Democritus   **355** Poster by V. Katraki

(Des P. Gravalos. Litho Alexandros Matsoukis, Athens)

1983 (26 Sept). First International Democritus Congress, Xanthe. P 13½×13.

1632	**354** 50d. multicoloured	1·40	70

(Des P. Gravalos (30d.). Litho Alexandros Matsoukis, Athens)

1983 (17 Nov). Tenth Anniversary of Polytechnic School Uprising. T **355** and similar vert design. Multicoloured. P 13½×13.

1633	15d. Type **355**	35	25
1634	30d. Students leaving Polytechnic	70	40

356 Deification of Homer   **357** Horse's Head, Chariot of Selene

(Des V. Constantinea. Litho Alexandros Matsoukis, Athens)

1983 (19 Dec). Homeric Odes. T **356** and similar multicoloured designs. P 13×13½ (vert) or 13½×13 (horiz).

1635	2d. olive-sepia and deep brown	35	25
1636	3d. reddish brown, pale orange and orange	35	25
1637	4d. pale yellow, orange-brown and deep reddish brown	35	25
1638	5d. multicoloured	35	25
1639	6d. yellow-orange and deep reddish brown	35	25
1640	10d. pale orange, reddish brown and orange	35	25
1641	14d. orange, pale orange and reddish brown	35	25
1642	15d. pale orange, orange and deep reddish brown	45	25
1643	20d. bistre, greenish black and deep reddish brown	45	25
1644	27d. deep reddish brown, pale orange and orange	50	30
1645	30d. reddish brown, pale orange and orange	65	25
1646	32d. orange, deep reddish brown and pale orange	85	30
1647	50d. reddish brown, pale orange and orange	1·10	25
1648	75d. reddish brown, pale orange and brown-red	1·80	45
1649	100d. olive-sepia, sage green and deep brown	3·50	1·00
1635/1649 Set of 15		10·50	4·25

Designs: Horiz—3d. Abduction of Helen by Paris (pot); 4d. Wooden Horse; 5d. Achilles throwing dice with Ajax (jar); 14d. Battle between Ajax and Hector (dish); 15d. Priam requesting body of Hector (pot); 27d. Ulysses escaping from Polyphemus's cave; 32d. Ulysses and Sirens; 50d. Ulysses slaying suitors; 75d. Heroes of Iliad (cup). Vert—2d. T **356**; 6d. Achilles; 10d. Hector receiving arms from his parents (vase); 20d. Blinding of Polyphemus; 30d. Ulysses meeting Nausica; 100d. Homer (bust).

(Des V. Constantinea. Litho Alexandros Matsoukis, Athens)

1984 (15 Mar). Parthenon Marbles. T **357** and similar horiz designs. Multicoloured. P 14½×14.

1650	14d. Type **357**	85	25
1651	15d. Dionysus	60	25
1652	20d. Hestia, Dione and Aphrodite	95	45
1653	27d. Ilissus	1·30	45
1654	32d. Lapith and Centaur	2·50	1·30
1650/1654 Set of 5		5·50	2·40
MS1655 105×81 mm. 15d. Horseman (left); 21d. Horseman (right); 27d. Heroes (left); 32d. Heroes (right). P 13×13½		11·00	9·00

358 Bridge   **359** Ancient Stadium, Olympia

(Des J. Larrivière. Litho Alexandros Matsoukis, Athens)

1984 (30 Apr). Europa. 25th Anniversary of European Post and Telecommunications Conference. P 14½×14.

1656	**358** 15d. multicoloured	1·40	45
	a. Pair. Nos. 1656/1657	5·00	2·30
1657	25d. multicoloured	3·25	1·70

Nos. 1656/1657 were issued both in separate sheets and together in sheets containing 20 se-tenant pairs. They were also issued in booklets containing two se-tenant pairs.

(Des P. Gravalos. Litho Alexandros Matsoukis, Athens)

1984 (30 Apr). Olympic Games, Los Angeles. T **359** and similar vert designs. Multicoloured. P 14×14½.

1658	14d. Type **359**	45	30
	a. Strip of 5. Nos. 1658/1662	7·00	
1659	15d. Athletes preparing for training	50	35
1660	20d. Flute player, discus thrower and long jumper	80	45
1661	32d. Athletes training	1·30	85
1662	80d. K. Vikelas and Panathenaic Stadium	3·75	2·00
1658/1662 Set of 5		6·00	3·50

Nos. 1658/1662 were issued both in separate sheets and together in sheets containing four se-tenant strips and in booklets containing one se-tenant strip.

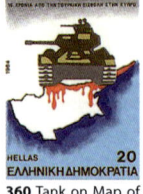 

360 Tank on Map of Cyprus   **361** Pelion Train

(Des P. Gravalos. Litho Alexandros Matsoukis, Athens)

1984 (10 July). Tenth Anniversary of Turkish Invasion of Cyprus. T **360** and similar horiz design. Multicoloured. P 13½×13 (20d.) or 13×13½ (32d.).

1663	20d. Type **360**	70	25
1664	32d. Hand grasping barbed wire and map of Cyprus	1·10	80

(Des P. Gravalos. Litho Alexandros Matsoukis, Athens)

1984 (20 July). Railway Centenary. T **361** and similar multicoloured designs. P 13×13½ (horiz) or 13½×13 (vert).

1665	15d. Type **361**	1·30	45
1666	20d. Steam goods train on Papadia Bridge (vert)	3·00	1·60
1667	30d. Piraeus-Peloponnese steam train	1·40	80
1668	50d. Cogwheel railway, Kalavryta (vert)	3·50	1·70
1665/1668 Set of 4		8·25	4·00

1984 GREECE

362 Athens 5th-century BC Silver Coin on Plan of City

363 '10' enclosing Arms

(Des M. Amarantos (15d.), P.-E. Mela (100d.). Litho Alexandros Matsoukis, Athens)

1984 (12 Oct). 150th Anniversary of Athens as Capital. T **362** and similar horiz design. Multicoloured. P 13½×13 (15d.) or 13×13½ (100d.).
1669	15d. Type **362**		80	30
1670	100d. Symbols of ancient Athens and skyline of modern Athens		2·75	1·50

(Des P. Gravalos. Litho Alexandros Matsoukis, Athens)

1984 (12 Oct). Tenth Anniversary of Revolution. P 13×13½.
1671	**363**	95d. multicoloured	2·50	90

364 Annunciation

365 Running

(Des V. Constantinea. Litho Alexandros Matsoukis, Athens)

1984 (6 Dec). Christmas. T **364** and similar vert designs showing scenes from Hagion Panton icon by Athanasios Touritas. Multicoloured. P 13½×13.
1672	14d. Type **364**	95	60
	a. Block of 4. Nos. 1672/1675	5·00	
1673	20d. Nativity	1·10	75
1674	25d. Presentation in Temple	1·10	75
1675	32d. Baptism of Christ	1·50	1·10
1672/1675 Set of 4		4·25	3·00

Nos. 1672/1675 were issued together in *se-tenant* blocks of four within sheets of 16 or 40 stamps. A booklet containing one *se-tenant* block was also issued.

(Des P. Gravalos. Litho Alexandros Matsoukis, Athens)

1985 (1 Mar). 16th European Indoor Athletics Championships, New Phaleron. T **365** and similar horiz designs. Multicoloured. P 13½×13½.
1676	12d. Type **365**	35	30
1677	15d. Putting the shot	50	25
1678	20d. Sports stadium (37×24 *mm*)	75	30
1679	25d. Hurdling	1·00	35
1680	80d. High jumping	2·00	1·20
1676/1680 Set of 5		4·25	2·20

366 Catacomb Niche

(Des P. Gravalos. Litho Alexandros Matsoukis, Athens)

1985 (29 Apr). Catacombs of Melos. T **366** and similar horiz designs. Multicoloured. P 14½×14.
1681	15d. Type **366**	45	25
1682	20d. Martyrs' altar and niches, central passageway	60	35
1683	100d. Niches	2·40	1·60
1681/1683 Set of 3		3·00	2·00

367 Apollo and Marsyas

(Des P. Gravalos. Litho Alexandros Matsoukis, Athens)

1985 (29 Apr). Europa. T **367** and similar horiz design. Multicoloured. P 14×14½.
1684	27d. Type **367**	1·20	95
	a. Pair. Nos. 1684/1685	4·00	2·75
1685	80d. Nikos Skalkotas and Dimitris Mitropoulos (composers)	2·50	1·50

Nos. 1684/1685 were issued both in separate sheets and together in sheets containing ten *se-tenant* pairs. They were also issued in booklets.

368 Coin (315 BC) and Salonika (relief)

369 Urn on Map of Cyprus

(Des P. Gravalos. Litho Alexandros Matsoukis, Athens)

1985 (24 June). 2300th Anniversary of Salonika. T **368** and similar horiz designs. Multicoloured. P 14×14½ (5d., 95d.) or 14½×14 (others).
1686	1d. Type **368**	35	25
1687	5d. Saints Demetrius and Methodius (mosaics) (49×34 *mm*)	70	35
1688	15d. Galerius's Arch (detail) (Roman period)	55	25
1689	20d. Salonika's eastern walls (Byzantine period)	70	25
1690	32d. Upper City, Salonika	70	25
1691	50d. Greek army liberating Salonika, 1912	1·20	25
1692	80d. Soldier's legs and Salonika (German occupation 1941–1944)	2·30	60
1693	95d. Contemporary views of Salonika (60th anniversaries of Aristotelian University and International Trade Fair) (49×34 *mm*)	4·25	2·20
1686/1693 Set of 8		9·75	4·00

(Des P. Gravalos. Litho Alexandros Matsoukis, Athens)

1985 (24 June). 25th Anniversary of Republic of Cyprus. P 13×13½.
1694	**369**	32d. multicoloured	1·20	70

370 Democracy crowning the City (relief)

371 Children of different Races

(Des P. Gravalos. Litho Alexandros Matsoukis, Athens)

1985 (7 Oct). Athens, Cultural Capital of Europe. T **370** and similar designs. P 13½×13 (vert) or 13×13½ (horiz).
1695	15d. multicoloured	45	25
1696	20d. black, light grey and turquoise-blue	45	30
1697	32d. multicoloured	1·00	35
1698	80d. multicoloured	3·00	1·60
1695/1698 Set of 4		4·50	2·30

Designs: Horiz—20d. Tritons and Dolphins (mosaic floor, Roman Baths, Hieratis); 80d. Capodistrian University, Athens. Vert—15d. T **370**; 32d. Angel (fresco, Pentelis Cave).

GREECE 1985

(Des P. Gravalos. Litho Alexandros Matsoukis, Athens)

1985 (7 Oct). International Youth Year (1st issue) (15d., 25d.) and 40th Anniversary of United Nations Organisation (27d., 100d.). T **371** and similar vert designs. Multicoloured. P 14.

1699	15d. Type **371**	35	25
1700	25d. Doves and youths	60	30
1701	27d. Interior of UN General Assembly	1·10	45
1702	100d. UN building, New York, and UN emblem	2·40	1·80
1699/1702	Set of 4	4·00	2·40

372 Girl with Flower Crown

(Des P. Gravalos. Litho Aspioti-Elka)

1985 (22 Nov). International Youth Year (2nd issue). Piraeus '85 Stamp Exhibition. Sheet 87×62 mm. P 14×13.

MS1703 **372** 100d. multicoloured .... 3·50 3·25

373 Folk Dance **374** Hestia

(Des P. Gravalos. Litho Aspioti-Elka)

1985 (9 Dec). Pontic Culture. T **373** and similar multicoloured designs. P 12½×13½ (27d.) or 13½×12½ (others).

1704	12d. Type **373**	45	30
1705	15d. Monastery of Our Lady of Soumela	45	30
1706	27d. Women's costumes (vert)	85	45
1707	32d. Trapezus High School	90	45
1708	80d. Sinope Castle	1·90	1·40
1704/1708	Set of 5	4·00	2·50

(Des P. Gravalos. Litho Alexandros Matsoukis, Athens)

1986 (17 Feb). Gods of Olympus. T **374** and similar horiz designs.

A. P 13

1709A	5d. salmon, black and olive-sepia	35	25
1710A	18d. salmon, black and olive-sepia	35	25
1711A	27d. salmon, black and blue	60	30
1712A	32d. salmon, black and carmine-red	80	35
1713A	35d. salmon, black and dull reddish brown	90	45
1714A	40d. salmon, black and carmine-red	1·00	45
1715A	50d. salmon, black and greenish grey	1·40	45
1716A	110d. salmon, black and dull reddish brown	2·00	45
1717A	150d. salmon, black and greenish grey	3·25	45
1718A	200d. salmon, black and blue	5·00	50
1719A	300d. salmon, black and deep violet-blue	8·00	1·40
1720A	500d. salmon, black and deep violet-blue	18·00	4·50
1709A/1720A	Set of 12	37·00	8·75

B. P 13×imperf

1709B	5d. salmon, black and olive-sepia	45	25
1710B	18d. salmon, black and olive-sepia	45	25
1711B	27d. salmon, black and blue	85	25
1712B	32d. salmon, black and carmine-red	1·00	25
1713B	35d. salmon, black and dull reddish brown	1·00	25
1714B	40d. salmon, black and carmine-red	1·00	25
1715B	50d. salmon, black and greenish grey	1·30	25
1716B	110d. salmon, black and dull reddish brown	2·75	35
1717B	150d. salmon, black and greenish grey	6·00	35
1718B	200d. salmon, black and blue	6·25	35
1719B	300d. salmon, black and deep violet-blue	9·75	35
1720B	500d. salmon, black and deep violet-blue	21·00	5·75
1709B/1720B	Set of 12	47·00	8·00

Designs: 5d. T **374**; 18d. Hermes: 27d. Aphrodite; 32d. Ares; 35d. Athene; 40d. Hephaestus; 50d. Artemis; 110d. Apollo; 150d. Demeter; 200d. Poseidon; 300d. Hera; 500d. Zeus.

Nos. 1709A/1720A were each issued in sheets of 50; Nos. 1709B/1720B were each issued in strips of five within packets of 100 stamps.

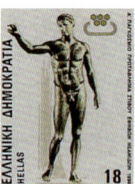  

375 Ephebos of Antikythera **376** Fastening Seat Belt **377** Intelpost

(Des P. Gravalos. Litho Aspioti-Elka)

1986 (3 Mar). Sports Events and Anniversaries. T **375** and similar designs. P 12½.

1721	18d. olive-green, black and light grey	65	30
1722	27d. yellow, black and orange-red	1·90	65
1723	32d. multicoloured	2·50	1·20
1724	35d. olive-green, black and pale bistre	3·00	1·50
1725	40d. multicoloured	2·30	95
1726	50d. multicoloured	2·30	55
1727	110d. multicoloured	9·25	2·75
1721/1727	Set of 7	20·00	7·00

Designs: Vert—18d. T **375** (First World Junior Athletics Championships); 32d. Footballers (Pan-European Junior Football Finals); 35d. Wrestlers (sculpture) (Pan-European Freestyle and Greco-Roman Wrestling Championships); 50d. Cyclists (Sixth International Round Europe Cycling Meet. Horiz—27d. *Diadoumenos* (sculpture by Polycleitus) (First World Junior Athletics Championships); 40d. Volleyball players (Men's World Volleyball Championships); 110d. *Victory* (unadopted design by Nikephoros Lytras for first Olympic Games commemoratives, 1896) (90th anniversary of modern Olympic Games).

(Des P. Gravalos. Litho Aspioti-Elka)

1986 (3 Mar). European Road Safety Year. T **376** and similar vert designs. Multicoloured. P 12½×13½.

1728	18d. Type **376**	55	25
1729	27d. Motorcyclist in traffic	1·50	1·00
1730	110d. Child strapped in back seat of car and speed limit signs	3·50	2·00
1728/1730	Set of 3	5·00	3·00

(Des Post Office Advertising Dept. Litho Aspioti-Elka)

1986 (23 Apr). New Postal Services. T **377** and similar horiz design. Multicoloured. P 13½×14 (18d.) or 14×13½ (110d.).

1731	18d. Type **377**	60	30
1732	110d. 'Express Mail' banner around globe	2·50	2·20

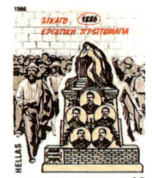

378 Sapling between Hands and burning Forest **379** Victims' Memorial and Workers

(Des V. Constantinea. Litho Aspioti-Elka)

1986 (23 Apr). Europa. T **378** and similar horiz design.

A. Sheet stamps. P 14×13½

1733A	35d. yellowish green, black and dull orange	5·50	3·25
	a. Pair. Nos. 1733A/1734A	13·50	7·75
1734A	110d. ultramarine, black and yellowish green	7·50	4·25

B. Booklet stamps. Imperf×p 13½

1733B	35d. yellowish green, black and dull orange	11·00	6·25
	a. Booklet pane. Nos. 1733B/1734B each×2	55·00	
1734B	110d. ultramarine, black and yellowish green	14·00	9·25

Designs: 35d. T **378**; 110d. Prespa Lake.

Nos. 1733A/1734A were issued together in *se-tenant* pairs within the sheet.

(Des V. Constantinea. Litho Aspioti-Elka)

1986 (23 Apr). Centenary of Chicago May Day Strike. P 12½.

1735	**379**	40d. multicoloured	1·30	75

380 Swearing-in of Venizelos Government

1986 GREECE

(Des V. Constantinea. Litho Aspioti-Elka)

1986 (30 June). 50th Death Anniversary of Eleftherios Venizelos (politician) (18d.) and Sixth International Crete Conference, Hania (110d.). T **380** and similar horiz design. Multicoloured. P 14×12½.

1736	18d. Type **380**		60	35
1737	110d. Hania harbour		2·50	1·70

381 Dove and Sun   **382** Madonna and Child

(Des S. Karachristos (18d.), P. Gravalos (35d.), P.-C. Sotiriou (110d.). Litho Aspioti-Elka)

1986 (6 Oct). International Peace Year. T **381** and similar multicoloured designs. P 12½.

1738	18d. Type **381**		45	30
1739	35d. Dove holding Olive branch with flags as leaves		95	70
1740	110d. Dove with Olive branch flying out of globe (*horiz*)		2·40	1·70
1738/1740	Set of 3		3·50	2·40

(Des V. Constantinea. Litho Aspioti-Elka)

1986 (1 Dec). Christmas. T **382** and similar vert designs showing icons. Multicoloured. P 12½ (46d.) or 13½×14 (others).

1741	22d. Type **382**		45	25
1742	46d. Adoration of the Magi (24×32 *mm*)		1·30	80
1743	130d. Christ enthroned with St John the Evangelist		3·25	1·50
1741/1743	Set of 3		4·50	2·30

Nos. 1741 and 1743 depict the centre and one side panel of a triptych.

383 The Fox and the Grapes   **384** *Composition* (Achilleas Apergis)

(Des P. Gravalos. Litho M. A. Moatsos, Athens)

1987 (5 Mar). Aesop's Fables. T **383** and similar horiz designs. Multicoloured.

A. P 12½×13

1744A	2d. Type **383**		45	25
1745A	5d. *The North Wind and the Sun*		45	25
1746A	10d. *The Stag at the Spring and the Lion*		65	30
1747A	22d. *Zeus and the Snake*		1·30	25
1748A	32d. *The Crow and the Fox*		2·00	45
1749A	40d. *The Woodcutter and Hermes*		3·00	95
1750A	46d. *The Ass in a Lion's Skin and the Fox*		4·25	1·10
1751A	130d. *The Hare and the Tortoise*		8·75	1·90
1744A/1751A	Set of 8		19·00	5·00

B. P 13½×imperf

1744B	2d. Type **383**		50	25
1745B	5d. *The North Wind and the Sun*		60	25
1746B	10d. *The Stag at the Spring and the Lion*		1·20	25
1747B	22d. *Zeus and the Snake*		3·00	25
1748B	32d. *The Crow and the Fox*		4·00	35
1749B	40d. *The Woodcutter and Hermes*		5·00	35
1750B	46d. *The Ass in a Lion's Skin and the Fox*		8·25	40
1751B	130d. *The Hare and the Tortoise*		38·00	1·50
1744B/1751B	Set of 8		55·00	3·25

Nos. 1744A/1751A were each issued in sheets of 50 and Nos. 1744B/1751B each in strips of five within packets of 100 stamps.

(Des P. Gravalos. Litho Aspioti-Elka, Athens)

1987 (4 May). Europa. Sculptures. T **384** and similar horiz design. Multicoloured.

A. Sheet stamps. P 12½

1752A	40d. Type **384**		5·25	3·00
	a. Pair. Nos. 1752A/1753A		12·50	7·00
1753A	130d. *Delphic Light* (Gerasimos Sklavos)		6·75	3·75

B. Booklet stamps. Imperf×p 12½

1752B	40d. As Type **384**		5·25	2·75
	a. Booklet pane. Nos. 1752B/1753B each×2		24·00	
1753B	130d. *Delphic Light* (Gerasimos Sklavos)		6·75	3·75

385 Player shooting Goal and Indoor Court   **386** Banner and Students

(Des T. Katsoulidis (No. **MS**1757), V. Constantinea (others). Litho Aspioti-Elka, Athens)

1987 (4 May–June). 25th European Men's Basketball Championship, Athens. T **385** and similar multicoloured designs. P 12½ (25d.) or 13½×14 (others).

1754	22d. Type **385**		1·10	75
1755	25d. Emblem and spectators (32×24 *mm*)		60	30
1756	130d. Players		3·25	1·90
1754/1756	Set of 3		4·50	2·75
MS1757	113×63 mm. 40d. Players; 60d. Players around goal; 100d. Player shooting goal (each 28×40 *mm*). P 13×14 (3.6.87)		11·50	9·25

(Des P. Gravalos. Litho Aspioti-Elka, Athens)

1987 (4 May). 150th Anniversaries of Athens University (3d., 23d.) and National Metsovio Polytechnic Institute (others). T **386** and similar multicoloured designs. P 14×13½ (horiz) or 13½×14 (vert).

1758	3d. Type **386**		45	25
1759	23d. Medal and Owl		60	25
1760	40d. Building façade, measuring instruments and computer terminal (*vert*)		1·00	70
1761	60d. Students outside building (*vert*)		1·70	1·30
1758/1761	Set of 4		3·50	2·30

 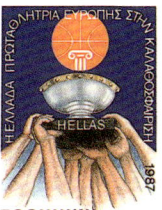

387 Ionic and Corinthian Capitals, Temple of Apollo, Phigaleia-Bassae   **388** Hands holding Cup Aloft

(Des V. Constantinea. Litho Aspioti-Elka, Athens)

1987 (1 July). Classical Architecture Capitals. T **387** and similar horiz designs. Multicoloured. P 13½×12½.

1762	2d. Type **387**		30	25
1763	26d. Doric capital, Parthenon		65	35
1764	40d. Ionic capital, The Erechtheum		95	55
1765	60d. Corinthian capital, The Tholos, Epidaurus		2·50	1·70
1762/1765	Set of 4		4·00	2·50

(Des P. Gravalos. Litho M. A. Moatsos, Athens)

1987 (1 Oct). Greek Victory in European Basketball Championship. P 13×14.

1766	**388**	40d. multicoloured	1·60	1·30

389 Diploma Engraving (Yiannis Kephalinos)   **390** Angel and Christmas Tree (left half)

GREECE 1987

(Des P. Gravalos. Litho M. A. Moatsos, Athens)

1987 (1 Oct). 150th Anniversary of Fine Arts High School (No. 1767) and 60th Anniversary of Panteios Political Science High School (No. 1768). T **389** and similar multicoloured design. P 12½×13½ (26d.) or 13½×12½ (60d.).

1767	26d. Type **389**	60	25
1768	60d. School campus (*horiz*)	1·60	1·20

(Des P. Gravalos. Litho M. A. Moatsos, Athens)

1987 (2 Dec). Christmas. T **390** and similar vert design. P 13×12½.

1769	26d. Type **390**	90	55
	a. Horiz pair. Nos. 1769/1770	1·90	1·20
	b. Booklet pane. Nos. 1769/1770, each×2	9·25	
1770	26d. Angel and Christmas Tree (right half)	90	55

Nos. 1769/1770 were issued together in horizontal *se-tenant* pairs within the sheet, each pair forming a composite design.

391 Eleni Papadaki in *Hecuba* (Euripides) and Philippi Amphitheatre

392 *Codonellina* sp. (polyzoan)

(Des V. Constantinea. Litho M. A. Moatsos, Athens)

1987 (2 Dec). Greek Theatre. T **391** and similar horiz designs. Multicoloured. P 14×13½.

1771	2d. Type **391**	45	25
1772	4d. Christopher Nezer in *The Wasps* (Aristophanes) and Dodona amphitheatre	45	25
1773	7d. Emilios Veakis in *Oedipus Rex* (Sophocles) and Delphi amphitheatre	50	25
1774	26d. Marika Kotopouli in *The Shepherdess's Love* (Dimitris Koromilas)	75	40
1775	40d. Katina Paxinou in *Abraham's Sacrifice* (Vitzentzos Comaros)	1·20	45
1776	50d. Kyveli in *Countess Valeraina's Secret* (Gregory Xenopoulos)	1·30	45
1777	60d. Karolos Koun and stage set	2·30	1·20
1778	100d. Dimitris Rontiris teaching National Theatre dancers an ancient dance	3·50	90
1771/1778	Set of 8	9·50	3·75

(Des V. Constantinea. Litho M. A. Moatsos, Athens)

1988 (2 Mar). Marine Life. T **392** and similar horiz designs. Multicoloured.

A. P 13½×12½

1779A	30d. Type **392**	1·60	60
1780A	40d. *Diaperoecia major* (polyzoan (clump-forming animals)) and Rainbow Wrasse	1·90	70
1781A	50d. *Artemia* (marine animal)	2·40	80
1782A	60d. *Posidonia oceanica* (plant) and Marmora Sea Bream	5·50	2·30
1783A	100d. *Padina pavonica* (plant)	8·75	2·30
1779A/1783A	Set of 5	18·00	6·00

B. Imperf×p 12½

1779B	30d. Type **392**	7·25	50
1780B	40d. *Diaperoecia major* (polyzoan (clump-forming animals)) and Rainbow Wrasse	7·50	55
1781B	50d. *Artemia* (marine animal)	9·75	55
1782B	60d. *Posidonia oceanica* (plant) and Marmora Sea Bream	17·00	2·20
1783B	100d. *Padina pavonica* (plant)	24·00	1·40
1779B/1783B	Set of 5	60·00	4·75

Nos. 1779A/1783A were each issued in sheets of 50 and Nos. 1779B/1783B each in strips of five within packets of 100 stamps.

393 Ancient Olympia

394 Satellite and Fax Machine

(Des Lee Hea Ok (170d.), T. Katsoulidis (others). Litho M. A. Moatsos, Athens)

1988 (6 May). Olympic Games, Seoul. T **393** and similar horiz designs. Multicoloured.

A. P 13½×12½

1784A	4d. Type **393**	85	40
	c. Horiz strip of 5. Nos. 1784A/1788A	27·00	—
1785A	20d. Ancient athletes in Gymnasium	2·20	60
1786A	30d. Modern Olympics centenary emblem	4·00	1·30
1787A	60d. Ancient athletes training	7·00	4·25
1788A	170d. Runner with Olympic flame	12·00	4·00
1784A/1788A	Set of 5	23·00	9·50

B. Imperf×p 12½

1784B	4d. Type **393**	1·20	30
	c. Horiz strip of 5. Nos. 1784B/1788B	36·00	
1785B	20d. Ancient athletes in Gymnasium	1·90	50
1786B	30d. Modern Olympics centenary emblem	6·25	1·60
1787B	60d. Ancient athletes training	9·25	3·75
1788B	170d. Runner with Olympic flame	16·00	4·25
1784B/1788B	Set of 5	31·00	9·25

Nos. 1784A/1788A were issued together in horizontal *se-tenant* strips of five within sheets of 20 stamps.

Nos. 1784B/1788B were issued together in *se-tenant* strips of five in booklets and separately in post office packets of 100; the set price for Nos. 1784B/1788B is for a set of singles.

Stamps of a similar design were issued by South Korea.

(Des P. Gravalos. Litho M. A. Moatsos, Athens)

1988 (6 May). Europa. Transport and Communications. T **394** and similar vert design. Multicoloured.

A. P 12½

1789A	60d. Type **394**	8·25	3·25
	a. Pair. Nos. 1789A/1790A	23·00	8·25
1790A	150d. Modern express and commuter trains	13·50	4·75

B. Imperf×p 14

1789B	60d. Type **394**	8·75	3·50
	a. Pair. Nos. 1789B/1790B	24·00	9·00
	b. Booklet pane. No. 1789B c×2	49·00	
1790B	150d. Modern express and commuter trains	14·50	5·25

Nos. 1789A/1790A were issued together in *se-tenant* pairs within sheets of 16 stamps.

Nos. 1789B/1790B were issued together in *se-tenant* pairs in booklets and separately in post office packets of 100 stamps.

395 Kataraktis Falls

396 Emblem

(Des S.-P. Metaxas. Litho M. A. Moatsos, Athens)

1988 (4 July). European Campaign for Rural Areas. Waterfalls. T **395** and similar vert designs. Multicoloured.

A. P 12½×13½

1791A	10d. Type **395**	4·25	60
1792A	60d. Edessa waterfalls	12·50	4·00
1793A	100d. River Edessaios cascades	16·00	2·75
1791A/1793A	Set of 3	29·00	6·50

B. Imperf×p 14

1791B	10d. Type **395**	9·75	1·40
1792B	60d. Edessa waterfalls	24·00	2·20
1793B	100d. River Edessaios cascades	37·00	6·25
1791B/1793B	Set of 3	65·00	8·75

Nos. 1791A/1793A were each issued in sheets of 50 stamps. Nos. 1791B/1793B each in strips of five within packets of 100 stamps.

(Des P. Gravalos. Litho M. A. Moatsos, Athens)

1988 (4 July). 20th European Postal Workers Trade Unions Congress.

A. P 12½

1794A	**396**	60d. multicoloured	15·00	3·75

B. Imperf×p 14

1794B	**396**	60d. multicoloured	29·00	1·80

No. 1794A was issued in sheets of 50 stamps.
No. 1974B in strips of five within packets of 100 stamps.

397 Mytilene Harbour, Lesbos (painting by Theophilos)

398 Eleftherios Venizelos, Map and Flag

1988 GREECE

(Des P. Gravalos. Litho Alexandros Matsoukis, Athens)

1988 (7 Oct). Prefecture Capitals (1st series). T **397** and similar multicoloured designs.

A. P 13

1795A	2d. Type **397**	30	25
	a. Booklet pane. Nos. 1795A×4, 1798A×4, 1801A×4 and 1802A×4	6·25	—
1796A	3d. Alexandroupolis lighthouse, Evros (*vert*)	30	25
1797A	4d. St Nicholas's bell-tower, Kozani (*vert*)	30	25
1798A	5d. Workmen's centre, Hermoupolis, Cyclades (*vert*)	30	25
1799A	7d. Sparta Town Hall, Lakonia	30	25
1800A	8d. Pegasus, Leukas	45	25
1801A	10d. Castle of the Knights, Rhodes, Dodecanese (*vert*)	45	25
1802A	20d. Acropolis, Athens (*vert*)	45	25
1803A	25d. Aqueduct, Kavala	60	25
1804A	30d. Castle and statue of Athanasios Diakos, Lamia, Phthiotis (*vert*)	65	25
1805A	50d. Preveza Cathedral bell-tower and clock (*vert*)	1·30	25
1806A	60d. Esplanade, Corfu	1·80	90
1807A	70d. Aghios Nikolaos, Lassithi	2·40	50
1808A	100d. Six Springheads, Polygyros, Khalkidiki	4·25	65
1809A	200d. Church of Paul the Apostle, Corinth, Corinthia	9·00	95
1795A/1809A	Set of 15	21·00	5·25

B. P 13×imperf (horiz) or imperf×p 13 (vert)

1795B	2d. Type **397**	35	25
1796B	3d. Alexandroupolis lighthouse, Evros (*vert*)	35	25
1797B	4d. St Nicholas's bell-tower, Kozani (*vert*)	45	25
1798B	5d. Workmen's centre, Hermoupolis, Cyclades (*vert*)	45	25
1799B	7d. Sparta Town Hall, Lakonia	45	25
1800B	8d. Pegasus, Leukas	55	25
1801B	10d. Castle of the Knights, Rhodes, Dodecanese (*vert*)	55	25
1802B	20d. Acropolis, Athens (*vert*)	55	25
1803B	25d. Aqueduct, Kavala	55	25
1804B	30d. Castle and statue of Athanasios Diakos, Lamia, Phthiotis (*vert*)	65	25
1805B	50d. Preveza Cathedral bell-tower and clock (*vert*)	1·60	25
1806B	60d. Esplanade, Corfu	2·20	30
1807B	70d. Aghios Nikolaos, Lassithi	3·50	35
1808B	100d. Six Springheads, Polygyros, Khalkidiki	6·25	40
1809B	200d. Church of Paul the Apostle, Corinth, Corinthia	7·75	80
1795B/1809B	Set of 15	24·00	4·25

Nos. 1795A/1809A were each issued in sheets of 50 stamps.

Nos. 1795B/1809B each in strips of five within packets of 100 stamps.

The outer edges of the booklet pane are imperforate, giving stamps with one side imperforate.

See also Nos. 1848/1862, 1911/1922 and 1955/1964.

(Des P. Gravalos. Litho M. A. Moatsos, Athens)

1988 (7 Oct). 75th Anniversaries of Union of Crete and Greece (30d.) and Liberation of Epirus and Macedonia (70d.). T **398** and similar horiz design. Multicoloured.

A. P 12½

1810A	30d. Type **398**	1·50	50
1811A	70d. Flags, map and 'Liberty'	2·75	1·50

B. P 14×imperf

1810B	30d. Type **398**	6·75	70
1811B	70d. Flags, map and 'Liberty'	9·75	1·80

Nos. 1810A/1811A were each issued in sheets of 50 stamps.

Nos. 1810B/1811B each in strips of five within packets of 100 stamps.

399 *Adoration of the Magi* (El Greco)

400 Map of EEC and Castle of the Knights, Rhodes

401 Ancient Olympia and High Jumper

(Des V. Constantinea. Litho M. A. Moatsos, Athens)

1988 (2 Dec). Christmas. T **399** and similar multicoloured design. P 12½.

1812	30d. Type **399**	1·70	70
	a. Booklet pane. No. 1812×10	18·00	

1813	70d. *The Annunciation* (Kostas Parthenis) (*horiz*)	2·75	1·50
	a. Imperf×p 14	11·00	2·20

The outer edges of the booklet pane are imperforate, giving stamps with one side imperforate.

No. 1813a was issued in strips of five within packets of 100 stamps.

(Des P. Gravalos. Litho M. A. Moatsos, Athens)

1988 (2 Dec). European Economic Community Meeting of Heads of State, Rhodes. T **400** and similar vert design. Multicoloured.

A. P 12½

1814A	60d. Type **400**	3·50	2·50
1815A	100d. Members' flags and coin	5·25	2·30

B. P 14×imperf

1814B	60d. Type **400**	6·50	2·50
1815B	100d. Members' flags and coin	10·00	2·50

Nos. 1814A/1815A were each issued in sheets of 50 stamps.

Nos. 1814B/1815B each in strips of five within packets of 100 stamps.

(Des P. Gravalos (170d.), T. Patraskidis (others). Litho M. A. Moatsos, Athens)

1989 (17 Mar). Centenary (1996) of Modern Olympic Games (1st issue). T **401** and similar vert designs. Multicoloured.

A. P 13½×14

1816A	30d. Type **401**	95	50
	a. Strip of 4. Nos. 1816A/1819A	12·00	
1817A	60d. Wrestlers and Delphi	2·20	1·50
1818A	70d. Acropolis, Athens, and swimmers	2·75	2·00
1819A	170d. Stadium and Golden Olympics emblem	5·75	2·30
1816A/1819A	Set of 4	10·50	5·50

B. Imperf×p 13½

1816B	30d. Type **401**	1·10	55
	a. Strip of 4. Nos. 1816B/1819B	12·50	
1817B	60d. Wrestlers and Delphi	2·20	1·40
1818B	70d. Acropolis, Athens, and swimmers	3·25	1·70
1819B	170d. Stadium and Golden Olympics emblem	5·50	1·50
1816B/1819B	Set of 4	11·00	4·75

Nos. 1816A/1819A were issued together in *se-tenant* strips of four within sheets of 16 stamps.

Nos. 1816B/1189B were issued together in *se-tenant* strips in booklets and separately in post office packets of 100; the set price for Nos. 1816B/1819B is for a set of singles.

See also Nos. 1863/1867, **MS**1995 and 1998/2001.

402 Flags

403 Whistling Bird

(Des P. Gravalos. Litho M. A. Moatsos, Athens)

1989 (22 May). International Anniversaries. T **402** and similar horiz designs. Multicoloured.

A. P 14×13½

1820A	30d. Type **402** (fifth anniversary of Six-nation Initiative for Peace and Disarmament)	1·40	70
1821A	50d. Flag and 'Liberty' (bicentenary of French Revolution)	1·70	90
1822A	60d. Flag and ballot box (third direct European Parliament elections)	3·75	2·00
1823A	70d. Coins (centenary of Interparliamentary Union)	4·50	2·00
1824A	200d. Flag (40th anniversary of Council of Europe)	9·00	2·40
1820A/1824A	Set of 5	18·00	7·25

B. P 13½×imperf

1820B	30d. Type **402** (fifth anniversary of Six-nation Initiative for Peace and Disarmament)	3·50	60
1821B	50d. Flag and 'Liberty' (bicentenary of French Revolution)	13·00	3·75
1822B	60d. Flag and ballot box (third direct European Parliament elections)	19·00	4·50
1823B	70d. Coins (centenary of Interparliamentary Union)	19·00	4·50
1824B	200d. Flag (40th anniversary of Council of Europe)	21·00	6·00
1820B/1824B	Set of 5	70·00	17·00

Nos. 1820A/1804A were each issued in sheets of 50 stamps.

Nos. 1820B/1824B each in strips of five within packets of 100 stamps.

GREECE 1989

(Des D. Mytaras. Litho M. A. Moatsos, Athens)

1989 (22 May). Europa. Children's Toys. T **403** and similar vert design. Multicoloured.

A. P 12½×13½

1825A	60d. Type **403**	5·50	2·00
	a. Pair. Nos. 1825A/1826A	14·00	4·75
1826A	170d. Butterfly	7·75	2·50

B. Imperf×p 13½

1825B	60d. Type **403**	5·50	3·00
	a. Pair. Nos. 1825B/1826B	13·00	6·25
	b. Booklet pane. No. 1825Bc×2	27·00	
1826B	170d. Butterfly	7·00	3·00

Nos. 1825A/1826A were issued together in *se-tenant* pairs within sheets of 16 stamps.

Nos. 1825B/1826B were issued together in booklets and separately in strips of five within post office packets of 100 stamps.

404 Magnifying Glass and Bird

405 Dog Roses

(Des V. Constantinea. Litho M. A. Moatsos, Athens)

1989 (25 Sept). Balkanfila XII International Stamp Exhibition, Salonika. T **404** and similar horiz designs. Multicoloured. P 13½×12½.

1827	60d. Type **404**	1·40	70
1828	70d. Eye looking through magnifying glass	1·50	1·00
MS1829	86×61 mm. 200d. Stamp collectors (42×30 mm). P 14×13	5·75	5·50

(Des V. Constantinea. Litho M. A. Moatsos, Athens)

1989 (8 Dec). Wild Flowers. T **405** and similar horiz designs. Multicoloured. P 13½×12½.

1830	8d. Type **405**	45	30
1831	10d. Common Myrtle	45	30
1832	20d. Common Poppies	60	35
1833	30d. Anemones	80	40
1834	60d. Dandelions and Chicory	1·30	60
1835	70d. Mallow	1·80	65
1836	200d. Thistles	4·00	2·50
1830/1836	Set of 7	8·50	4·50

406 Brown Bear (*Ursus arctos*)

407 Gregoris Lambrakis

(Des V. Constantinea. Litho M. A. Moatsos, Athens)

1990 (16 Mar). Endangered Animals. T **406** and similar horiz designs. Multicoloured. P 13½×12½.

1837	40d. Type **406**	1·10	35
1838	70d. Loggerhead Turtle (*Caretta caretta*)	1·90	70
1839	90d. Mediterranean Monk Seal (*Monachus monachus*)	3·00	90
1840	100d. Lynx (*Lynx lynx*)	4·25	1·80
1837/1840	Set of 4	9·25	3·50

(Des V. Constantinea. Litho M. A. Moatsos, Athens)

1990 (11 May). Politicians' Death Anniversaries. T **407** and similar vert design. Multicoloured. P 12½×13½.

1841	40d. Type **407** (27th anniversary)	95	65
1842	40d. Pavlos Bakoyiannis (first anniversary)	95	65

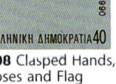
408 Clasped Hands, Roses and Flag

409 Old Central Post Office Interior

(Des P. Gravalos (70d.), Y. Papadakis (others). Litho M. A. Moatsos, Athens)

1990 (11 May). National Reconciliation. T **408** and similar vert designs. Multicoloured. P 12½×13½.

1843	40d. Type **408**	80	25
1844	70d. Dove with banner	1·40	65
1845	100d. Map and hands holding Roses	2·10	1·80
1843/1845	Set of 3	3·75	2·40

(Des P. Gravalos. Litho M. A. Moatsos, Athens)

1990 (11 May). Europa. Post Office Buildings. T **409** and similar horiz designs.

A. Sheet stamps. P 13½×12½

1846A	70d. Type **409**	5·50	2·20
	a. Pair. Nos. 1846A/1847A	14·00	5·00
1847A	210d. Exterior of modern post office	7·75	2·50

B. Booklet stamps. Imperf×p 12½

1846B	70d. As Type **409**	5·50	2·20
	a. Booklet pane. Nos. 1846B/1847B each×2	29·00	
1847B	210d. Exterior of modern post office	8·25	5·00

Nos. 1846A/1847A were issued together in *se-tenant* pairs within sheets of 16 stamps.

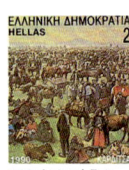
410 Animal Fair (D. Gioldassi) (Karditsa)

411 Yachting

(Des P. Gravalos. Litho M. A. Moatsos, Athens)

1990 (20 June). Prefecture Capitals (2nd series). T **410** and similar multicoloured designs.

A. P 13×12½ (vert) or 12½×13 (horiz)

1848A	2d. Type **410**	45	25
1849A	5d. Fort, Trikala (*horiz*)	45	25
1850A	8d. Street, Veroia (Imathia)	45	25
1851A	10d. Monument to Fallen Heroes, Missolonghi (Aetolia) (*horiz*)	45	25
1852A	15d. Harbour, Chios (*horiz*)	50	30
1853A	20d. Street, Tripolis (Arcadia) (*horiz*)	50	30
1854A	25d. City and Town Hall (woodcut, A. Tasou) (Volos, Magnesia) (*horiz*)	90	45
1855A	40d. Town Hall, Kalamata (Messenia) (*horiz*)	1·10	45
1856A	50d. Market, Pyrgos (Elia) (*horiz*)	1·30	45
1857A	70d. Lake and island, Yiannina (*horiz*)	1·50	55
1858A	80d. Harbour sculpture, Rethymnon	2·10	65
1859A	90d. Argostoli (*Cephalonia*) (*horiz*)	2·40	65
1860A	100d. Citadel and islet, Nauplion (*Argolis*) (*horiz*)	2·50	70
1861A	200d. Lighthouse, Patras (*Akhaia*)	6·00	75
1862A	250d. Street, Florina (*horiz*)	8·50	1·10
1848A/1862A	Set of 15	26·00	6·50

B. Imperf×p 13½ (vert) or P 13½×imperf (horiz)

1848B	2d. Type **410**	30	25
1849B	5d. Fort, Trikala (*horiz*)	30	25
1850B	8d. Street, Veroia (Imathia)	30	25
1851B	10d. Monument to Fallen Heroes, Missolonghi (Aetolia) (*horiz*)	45	25
1852B	15d. Harbour, Chios (*horiz*)	45	25
1853B	20d. Street, Tripolis (Arcadia) (*horiz*)	55	25
1854B	25d. City and Town Hall (woodcut, A. Tasou) (Volos, Magnesia) (*horiz*)	80	50
1855B	40d. Town Hall, Kalamata (Messenia) (*horiz*)	80	50
1856B	50d. Market, Pyrgos (Elia) (*horiz*)	95	50
1857B	70d. Lake and island, Yiannina (*horiz*)	1·00	70
1858B	80d. Harbour sculpture, Rethymnon	1·80	55
1859B	90d. Argostoli (*Cephalonia*) (*horiz*)	1·90	70
1860B	100d. Citadel and islet, Nauplion (*Argolis*) (*horiz*)	1·90	55
1861B	200d. Lighthouse, Patras (*Akhaia*)	4·50	60
1862B	250d. Street, Florina (*horiz*)	7·25	60
1848B/1862B	Set of 15	21·00	6·00

Nos. 1848A/1862A were each issued in sheets of 50 stamps.

Nos. 1848B/1862B each in strips of five within packets of 100 stamps.

(Des P. Gravalos. Litho M. A. Moatsos, Athens)

1990 (13 July). Centenary (1996) of Modern Olympic Games (2nd issue). T **411** and similar vert designs. Multicoloured. P 12½×13½.

1863	20d. Type **411**	75	35
	a. Strip of 5. Nos. 1863/1867	12·50	

1864	50d. Wrestling	1·10	45
1865	80d. Running	1·60	1·30
1866	100d. Handball	2·30	1·20
1867	250d. Football	6·25	2·10
1863/1867	Set of 5	11·00	4·75

Nos. 1863/1867 were issued both in separate sheets of 50 and together in *se-tenant* strips of five within sheets of 20 stamps.

412 Schliemann and Lion Gate, Mycenae

413 Woman knitting (lithograph, Vasso Katraki)

(Des E. Jünger. Litho M. A. Moatsos, Athens)

1990 (11 Oct). Death Centenary of Heinrich Schliemann (archaeologist). P 14×13½.
1868   **412**   80d. multicoloured .... 10·50   5·25

(Des P. Gravalos. Litho M. A. Moatsos, Athens)

1990 (11 Oct). 50th Anniversary of Greek–Italian War. T **413** and similar vert designs. Multicoloured. P 12½.

1869	50d. Type **413**	1·00	50
1870	80d. *Virgin Mary protecting Army* (lithograph, George Gounaropoulou)	1·50	1·10
1871	100d. *Women's War Work* (lithograph, Kosta Grammatopoulou)	2·10	1·40
1869/1871	Set of 3	4·25	2·75

414 Hermes

(Des P. Gravalos. Litho M. A. Moatsos, Athens)

1990 (14 Dec). Stamp Day. Sheet 87×62 mm. P 14×13.
MS1872   **414**   300d. multicoloured .... 19·00   16·00

415 Calliope, Euterpe and Erato

(Des P. Gravalos. Litho M. A. Moatsos, Athens)

1991 (11 Mar). The Nine Muses. T **415** and similar horiz designs. Multicoloured. P 12½.

1873	50d. Type **415**	1·10	50
1874	80d. Terpsichore, Polyhymnia and Melpomene	2·20	1·10
1875	250d. Thalia, Clio and Urania	4·75	2·10
1873/1875	Set of 3	7·25	3·25

416 Battle Scene (Ioannis Anousakis)

(Des I. Mylonas (300d.). Litho M. A. Moatsos, Athens)

1991 (20 May). 50th Anniversary of Battle of Crete. T **416** and other horiz design. Multicoloured. P 12½×14 (60d.) or 12½ (300d.).

1876	60d. Type **416**	2·75	75
1877	300d. Map and flags of allied nations (32×24 mm)	6·25	2·75

417 Icarus pushing Satellite   418 Swimming

(Des P. Gravalos. Litho M. A. Moatsos, Athens)

1991 (20 May). Europa. Europe in Space. T **417** and similar horiz design. Multicoloured.

A. Sheet stamps. P 12½

1878A	80d. Type **417**	5·00	3·00
	a. Pair. Nos. 1878A/1879A	14·50	8·25
1879A	300d. Chariot of the Sun	8·75	5·00

B. Booklet stamps. Imperf×p12½

1878B	80d. As Type **417**	5·25	3·25
	a. Booklet pane. Nos. 1878B/1879B each×2	30·00	
1879B	300d. Chariot of the Sun	9·25	5·75

Nos. 1878A/1879A were issued together in *se-tenant* pairs within the feet.

(Des P. Gravalos. Litho M. A. Moatsos, Athens)

1891 (25 June). 11th Mediterranean Games, Athens. T **418** and similar vert designs. Multicoloured. P 13½×14.

1880	10d. Type **418**	55	35
1881	60d. Basketball	95	45
1882	90d. Gymnastics	1·70	50
1883	130d. Weightlifting	2·75	80
1884	300d. Throwing the hammer	5·75	3·00
1880/1884	Set of 5	10·50	4·50

419 Pillar of Democracy   420 Europa and Zeus as Bull (from Attic vase)

(Des P. Gravalos. Litho M. A. Moatsos, Athens)

1991 (20 Sept). 2500th Anniversary of Birth of Democracy. P 13½×14.
1885   **419**   100d. black, stone and bright blue .... 2·75   1·10

(Des V. Constantinea. Litho M. A. Moatsos, Athens)

1991 (20 Sept). Greek Presidency of European Postal and Telecommunications Conference. Sheet 81×62 mm. P 14×13.
MS1886   **420**   300d. multicoloured .... 28·00   27·00

421 President Konstantinos Karamanlis signing Treaty of Athens

422 Emblem and Speed Skaters

(Des P. Gravalos. Litho M. A. Moatsos, Athens)

1991 (9 Dec). Tenth Anniversary of Greek Admission to European Community. T **421** and similar vert design. Multicoloured. P 13×14.

1887	50d. Type **421**	1·10	45
1888	80d. Map of Europe and President Karamanlis	1·80	80

(Des T. Katsoulidis. Litho M. A. Moatsos, Athens)

1991 (9 Dec). Winter Olympic Games, Albertville. T **422** and similar vert design. Multicoloured. P 12½×13½.
1889   80d. Type **422** .... 2·30   1·30

GREECE 1992

		a. Pair. Nos. 1889/1890	8·00	3·50
1890		300d. Slalom skier	5·50	1·90

Nos. 1889/1890 were issued together in *se-tenant* pairs within the sheet.

423 Throwing the Javelin

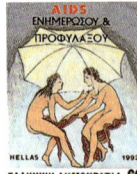
424 Couple beneath Umbrella

(Des A. Rouhier (90d.), K. Michotas (340d.), P. Gravalos (others). Litho M. A. Moatsos, Athens)

1992 (3 Apr). Olympic Games, Barcelona. T **423** and similar multicoloured designs. P 14×13½ (90d., 340d.) or 12½ (others).

1891	10d. Type **423**	90	40
1892	60d. Show jumping	1·80	60
1893	90d. Runner (37×24 *mm*)	2·75	1·20
1894	120d. Gymnastics	4·50	1·10
1895	340d. Runners' heads forming Olympic rings (37×24 *mm*)	8·75	2·75
1891/1895 *Set of 5*	17·00	5·50

(Des V. Constantinea. Litho M. A. Moatsos, Athens)

1992 (22 May). Health. T **424** and similar vert designs. Multicoloured. P 12½.

1896	60d. Type **424** (anti-AIDS campaign)	80	35
1897	80d. Doctor examining child (First European Gastroenterology Week)	1·70	60
1898	90d. Crab killing flower on healthy plant (anti-cancer campaign)	1·80	70
1899	120d. Hephaestus's forge (from 6th-century BC urn) (European Year of Social Security, Hygiene and Health in the Workplace)	2·50	1·30
1900	280d. Alexandros Onassis Cardiosurgical Centre, Athens	7·50	2·75
1896/1900 *Set of 5*	13·00	5·25

425 *Santa Maria*, Map and Columbus

(Des P. Gravalos. Litho M. A. Moatsos, Athens)

1992 (22 May). Europa. 500th Anniversary of Discovery of America by Columbus. T **425** and similar horiz design. Multicoloured.

A. Sheet stamps. P 13½×12½

1901A	90d. Type **425**	4·25	2·40
	a. Pair. Nos. 1901A/1902A	14·00	6·50
1902A	340d. Chios in late 15th-century	9·00	3·75

B. Booklet stamps. Imperf×p 12½

1901B	90d. As Type **425**	5·25	2·75
	a. Booklet pane. Nos. 1901B/1901B each×2	33·00	
1902B	340d. Chios in late 15th-century	10·50	5·75

Nos. 1901A/1902A were issued together in *se-tenant* pairs within the sheet.

426 Proetus, Bellerophon and Pegasus

427 Head of Hercules in Lion Skin (relief)

(Des K. Michotas. Litho M. A. Moatsos, Athens)

1992 (8 June). European Transport Ministers' Conference, Athens. Sheet 85×59 mm. P 14×13.

MS1903	**426**	300d. multicoloured	16·00	15·00

(Des P. Gravalos (10d., 80d., 340d.), V. Constantinea (60d., 90d., 120d.). Litho M. A. Moatsos, Athens)

1992 (17 July). Macedonia. T **427** and similar multicoloured designs. P 12½.

1904	10d. Type **427**	60	25
1905	20d. Map of Macedonia and bust of Aristotle (*horiz*)	80	25
1906	60d. Alexander the Great at Battle of Issus (mural) (*horiz*)	1·20	25
1907	80d. Tomb of Philip II at Vergina and Manolis Andronikos (archaeologist)	2·10	55
1908	90d. Deer hunt (mosaic, Pella)	3·00	55
1909	120d. Macedonian coin	4·25	1·50
1910	340d. 4th-century church at Philippi and Apostle Paul	13·50	4·00
1904/1910 *Set of 7*	23·00	6·50

428 Piraeus

429 Column, Map, Flags and European Community Emblem

(Des P. Gravalos. Litho Alexandros Matsoukis, Athens)

1992 (12 Oct). Prefecture Capitals (3rd series). T **428** and similar multicoloured designs.

A. P 13

1911A	10d. Type **428**	30	25
1912A	20d. Amphissa (Phocis)	35	25
1913A	30d. The Heraion, Samos	45	30
1914A	40d. Canea	65	30
1915A	50d. Zakynthos	70	30
1916A	60d. Karpenisi (Evrytania)	85	45
1917A	70d. Cave, Kilkis (*vert*)	1·00	45
1918A	80d. Door of Town Hall, Xanthi (*vert*)	1·60	60
1919A	90d. Macedonian Struggle Museum, Thessaloniki	2·20	65
1920A	120d. Tsanakleous School, Komotini (Rhodope)	4·25	1·10
1921A	340d. Spring, Drama	7·25	2·30
1922A	400d. Pinios Bridge, Larissa	9·50	3·50
1911A/1922A *Set of 12*	26·00	9·50

B. P 10½×imperf (horiz) or imperf×p 10½ (vert)

1911B	10d. Type **428**	35	25
1912B	20d. Amphissa (Phocis)	35	25
1913B	30d. The Heraion, Samos	45	25
1914B	40d. Canea	60	25
1915B	50d. Zakynthos	75	30
1916B	60d. Karpenisi (Evrytania)	85	30
1917B	70d. Cave, Kilkis (*vert*)	1·00	30
1918B	80d. Door of Town Hall, Xanthi (*vert*)	2·50	40
1919B	90d. Macedonian Struggle Museum, Thessaloniki	3·00	40
1920B	120d. Tsanakleous School, Komotini (Rhodope)	4·25	65
1921B	340d. Spring, Drama	8·00	1·50
1922B	400d. Pinios Bridge, Larissa	10·50	2·50
1911B/1922B *Set of 12*	29·00	6·50

Nos. 1911A/1922A were each issued in sheets of 50 stamps.
Nos. 1911B/1922B each in strips of five within packets of 100 stamps.

(Des V. Constantinea. Litho M. A. Moatsos, Athens)

1992 (12 Oct). European Single Market. P 14×13.

1923	**429**	90d. multicoloured	2·00	1·30

430 Headstone (4th-century BC)

431 Georgakis Olympios at Sekkou Monastery, 1821

1993 GREECE

(Des V. Constantinea. Litho M. A. Moatsos, Athens)

1993 (26 Feb). 2400th Anniversary of Rhodes. T **430** and similar vert designs. Multicoloured. P 13×14.

1924	60d. Type **430**	1·40	55
1925	90d. Aphrodite bathing (statue)	2·40	1·20
1926	120d. St Irene (from St Catherine's church)	1·90	1·10
1927	250d. St Paul's Gate, Naillac Mole	7·50	3·00
1924/1927	Set of 4	12·00	5·25

(Des V. Constantinea and K. Michotas. Litho M. A. Moatsos, Athens)

1993 (25 May). Historical Events. T **431** and similar multicoloured designs. P 13×14 (vert) or 14×13 (horiz).

1928	10d. Type **431** (War of Independence)	60	25
1929	30d. Theodore Kolokotronis (War of Independence)	80	30
1930	60d. Pavlos Melas (military hero)	1·20	45
1931	90d. *Glory crowns the Casualties* (Balkan Wars, 1912–1913)	3·00	1·00
1932	120d. Soldiers of Sacred Company, El Alamein, 1942 (*horiz*)	4·75	1·50
1933	150d. Sacred Company on Aegean Island, 1943–1945 (*horiz*)	5·25	2·00
1934	200d. Victims' Monument, Kalavryta (destruction of village, 1943)	10·50	3·25
1928/1934	Set of 7	23·00	8·00

432 *The Benefits of Transportation* (Konstantinus Parthenis) (left half)

433 Athens Concert Hall

(Des K. Michotas. Litho M. A. Moatsos, Athens)

1993 (25 May). Europa. Contemporary Art. T **432** and similar vert design. Multicoloured.

A. Sheet stamps. P 13×14

1935A	90d. Type **432**	3·50	1·80
	a. Horiz pair. Nos. 1935A/1936A	14·00	8·25
1936A	350d. *The Benefits of Transportation* (right half)	9·75	6·25

B. Booklet stamps. Imperf×p13½

1935B	90d. As Type **432**	4·00	2·30
	a. Booklet pane. Nos. 1935B/1936B each×2	29·00	
1936B	350d. *The Benefits of Transportation* (right half)	10·00	6·50

Nos. 1935A/1936A were issued together in *se-tenant* pairs within the sheet, each pair forming a composite design.

(Des V. Constantinea (30d., 200d.), K. Michotas (others). Litho Alexandros Matsoukis, Athens)

1993 (4 Oct). Modern Athens. T **433** and similar horiz designs. Multicoloured. P 14.

1937	30d. Type **433**	2·00	35
1938	60d. Iliou Melathron (former house of Heinrich Schliemann (archaeologist), now Numismatic Museum)	2·30	45
1939	90d. National Library	2·30	85
1940	200d. Athens Eye Hospital	8·50	2·75
1937/1940	Set of 4	13·50	4·00

434 Presidency Emblem and Map

(Des V. Constantinea. Litho Alexandros Matsoukis, Athens)

1993 (20 Dec). Greek Presidency (1994) of European Union (1st issue). Sheet 84×60 mm. P 14.

MS1941	**434** 400d. multicoloured	9·25	8·75

See also Nos. 1953/1954.

435 Hermes leading Selene's Chariot (Boeotian vase)

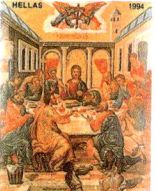

436 Last Supper (icon by Michael Damaskinou, St Catherine's Church, Heraklion, Crete)

(Des V. Constantinea. Litho Alexandros Matsoukis, Athens)

1994 (7 Mar). Second Pan-European Transport Conference. P 13×13½.

1942	**435** 200d. multicoloured	4·50	2·20

(Des V. Constantinea. Litho Alexandros Matsoukis, Athens)

1994 (8 Apr). Easter. T **436** and similar multicoloured designs. P 14.

1943	30d. Type **436**	70	25
1944	60d. Crucifixion (detail of wall painting, Great Meteoron)	1·00	25
1945	90d. Burial of Christ (icon, Church of the Presentation of the Lord, Patmos) (*horiz*)	1·40	55
1946	150d. Resurrection (detail, illuminated manuscript from Mount Athos) (*horiz*)	3·75	1·50
1943/1946	Set of 4	6·25	2·30

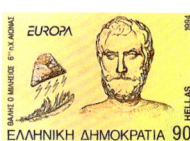

437 Thales of Miletus (philosopher)

438 Demetrios Vikelas (first president) (after G. Roilos)

(Des K. Michotas. Litho Alexandros Matsoukis, Athens)

1994 (9 May). Europa. Discoveries. T **437** and similar horiz design. Multicoloured.

A. Sheet stamps. P 14

1947A	90d. Type **437**	3·50	1·90
	a. Pair. Nos. 1947A/1948A	13·00	6·50
1948A	350d. Konstantinos Karatheodoris (mathematician) and equations	8·75	4·25

B. Booklet stamps. Imperf×p 14

1947B	90d. As Type **437**	3·50	2·10
	a. Booklet pane. Nos. 1947B/1948B each×2	26·00	
1948B	350d. Konstantinos Karatheodoris (mathematician) and equations	8·75	4·25

Nos. 1947A/1948A were issued together in *se-tenant* pairs within the sheet.

(Des M. Angelopoulos and V. Constantinea (120d.), P. Gravalos (400d.), V. Constantinea (others). Litho Alexandros Matsoukis, Athens)

1994 (6 June). Sports Events and Anniversary. T **438** and similar multicoloured designs. P 14.

1949	60d. Type **438** (centenary of International Olympic Committee)	1·40	35
1950	90d. Modern footballer and ancient relief (World Cup Football Championship, USA) (*horiz*)	1·50	90
1951	120d. Ball, net and Laurel (World Volleyball Championship, Piraeus and Salonika)	4·50	1·10
1949/1951	Set of 3	6·75	2·10
MS1952	68×70 mm. 400d. Modern footballers, Statue of Liberty and ancient relief (World Cup) (41×51 mm)	9·25	8·75

439 'Greece' driving EU Chariot

440 Parigoritissas Byzantine Church, Arta

(Des K. Michotas. Litho Alexandros Matsoukis, Athens)

1994 (21 June). Greek Presidency of European Union (2nd issue). T **439** and similar horiz design. Multicoloured. P 13×13½.
1953	90d. Type **439**		2·10	1·00
1954	120d. Doric columns and EU flag		2·75	1·30

(Des K. Michotas. Litho Alexandros Matsoukis, Athens)

1994 (5 Oct). Prefecture Capitals (4th series). T **440** and similar multicoloured designs.

A. P 13
1955A	10d. Tsalopoulou mansion house, Katerini (Pieria) (*vert*)	35	25
1956A	20d. Type **440**	35	25
1957A	30d. Bridge and tower, Levadia (Boeotia) (*vert*)	55	35
1958A	40d. Koumbelidikis church, Kastoria	60	35
1959A	50d. Outdoor theatre, Grevena	75	35
1960A	60d. Waterfall, Edessa (Pella)	85	35
1961A	80d. Red House, Chalkida (Euboea)	1·50	50
1962A	90d. Government House, Serres	1·90	60
1963A	120d. Town Hall, Heraklion	2·10	85
1964A	150d. Church of Our Lady of the Annunciation, Igoumenitsa (Thesprotia) (*vert*)	3·50	1·10
1955A/1964A	*Set of* 10	11·00	4·50

B. Imperf×p 10½ (*vert*) *or 10½×imperf* (*horiz*)
1955B	10d. Tsalopoulou mansion house, Katerini (Pieria) (*vert*)	35	25
1956B	20d. Type **440**	35	25
1957B	30d. Bridge and tower, Levadia (Boeotia) (*vert*)	50	25
1958B	40d. Koumbelidikis church, Kastoria	60	25
1959B	50d. Outdoor theatre, Grevena	85	30
1960B	60d. Waterfall, Edessa (Pella)	1·00	30
1961B	80d. Red House, Chalkida (Euboea)	1·50	35
1962B	90d. Government House, Serres	3·00	45
1963B	120d. Town Hall, Heraklion	3·25	85
1964B	150d. Church of Our Lady of the Annunciation, Igoumenitsa (Thesprotia) (*vert*)	4·25	1·20
1955B/1964B	*Set of* 10	14·00	4·00

Nos. 1955A/1964A were each issued in sheets of 50 stamps. Nos. 1955B/1964B each in strips of five within packets of 100 stamps.

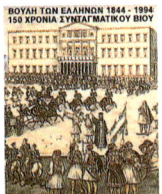
441 *Declaration of Constitution* (detail, Karl Haupt)

442 Mercouri and Demonstrators (fighter for Democracy)

(Des V. Constantinea. Litho Alexandros Matsoukis, Athens)

1994 (21 Nov). 150th Anniversary of Constitution. T **441** and similar multicoloured designs. P 13×14 (60d.) or 14×13 (others).
1965	60d. Type **441**	85	35
1966	150d. Ioannis Makrygiannis, Andreas Metaxas and Dimitrios Kallergis (from *Neos Aristophanes* (magazine)) (*horiz*)	1·90	75
1967	200d. *The Night of 3rd September, 1843* (anon) (*horiz*)	4·75	1·20
1968	340d. Article 107 of 1844 Constitution and Parliament Seal (*horiz*)	8·50	2·20
1965/1968	*Set of* 4	14·50	4·00

(Des K. Michotas (60d.), V. Constantinea (others). Litho Alexandros Matsoukis, Athens)

1995 (7 Mar). Melina Mercouri (actress and Minister of Culture) Commemoration. T **442** and similar multicoloured designs. P 13×14 (340d.) or 14×13 (others).
1969	60d. Type **442**	1·10	35
1970	90d. Mercouri and Acropolis (politician)	1·20	60
1971	100d. Mercouri in three roles (actress)	4·75	1·40
1972	340d. Mercouri with flowers (*vert*)	10·50	3·00
1969/1972	*Set of* 4	16·00	4·75

443 Prisoners behind Barbed Wire

444 Emblem

(Des K. Michotas. Litho Alexandros Matsoukis, Athens)

1995 (3 May). Europa. Peace and Freedom. T **443** and similar horiz design. Multicoloured.

A. Sheet stamps. P 14
1973A	90d. Type **443**	3·25	2·40
	a. Horiz pair. Nos. 1973A/1974A	12·50	7·25
1974A	340d. Doves flying from crushed barbed wire	8·50	4·50

B. Booklet stamps. Imperf×p13½
1973B	90d. As Type **443**	3·50	2·40
	a. Booklet pane. Nos. 1973B/1974B each×2	26·00	
1974B	340d. Doves flying from crushed barbed wire	8·75	5·00

Nos. 1973A/1974A were issued together in *se-tenant* pairs within the sheet, each pair forming a composite design.

(Des D. Mitaras (10d., 300d.), M. Vardopoulou (others). Litho Alexandros Matsoukis, Athens)

1995 (21 June). Anniversaries and Events. T **444** and similar multicoloured designs. P 13×13½ (horiz) or 13½×13 (vert).
1975	10d. Type **444** (fifth World Junior Basketball Championship)	90	25
1976	70d. Agriculture University, Athens (75th anniversary) (*horiz*)	1·60	30
1977	90d. Delphi (50th anniversary of United Nations Organisation)	1·90	45
1978	100d. Greek flag and returning soldier (50th anniversary of end of Second World War)	2·30	55
1979	120d. *Peace* (statue by Kifisodotos) (50th anniversary of United Nations Organisation)	2·30	1·10
1980	150d. Dolphins (European Nature Conservation Year) (*horiz*)	3·50	95
1981	200d. Old telephone and modern key-pad (centenary of telephone in Greece)	6·00	1·30
1982	300d. Owl sitting on ball (29th European Basketball Championship)	12·00	3·00
1975/1982	*Set of* 8	27·00	7·00

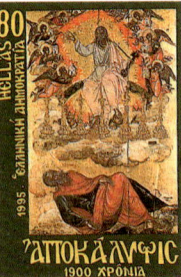
445 The First Vision of the Apocalypse (icon, Thomas Bathas)

446 Goddess Athene with Argonauts

(Des M. Vardopoulou. Litho Alexandros Matsoukis, Athens)

1995 (18 Sept). 1900th Anniversary of the Apocalypse of St John. T **445** and similar multicoloured designs. P 14.
1983	80d. Type **445**	3·25	50
1984	110d. St John dictating to Prochoros in front of the Cave of the Apocalypse (miniature from the Four Gospels, Codex 81 of library of Patmos Monastery)	3·50	1·20
1985	300d. Trumpet of the First Angel (gilded Gospel cover) (*horiz*)	8·25	2·40
1983/1985	*Set of* 3	13·50	3·75

(Des V. Constantinea. Litho Alexandros Matsoukis, Athens)

1995 (6 Nov). Jason and the Argonauts. T **446** and similar horiz designs. Multicoloured. P 13×13½.
1986	80d. Type **446**	1·20	50
1987	120d. Phineas (blind seer), god Hermes and the Voreadae pursuing Harpies	2·00	95
1988	150d. Medea, Nike and Jason taming Bull	2·75	85

1989	200d. Jason and Medea killing Snake and taking the Golden Fleece		4·50	1·30
1990	300d. Jason presenting Golden Fleece to Pelias		7·75	2·50
1986/1990	Set of 5		16·00	5·50

447 Psyttaleia

448 1l. Stamp

(Des G. Papageorgiou. Litho Alexandros Matsoukis, Athens)

1995 (18 Dec). Lighthouses. T **447** and similar vert designs. Multicoloured. P 14.

1991	80d. Type **447**	1·60	60
1992	120d. Sapientza	2·75	95
1993	150d. Kastri, Othonoi	4·25	2·50
1994	500d. Zourva, Hydra	11·00	3·75
1991/1994	Set of 4	18·00	7·00

(Des M. Vardopoulou. Litho Alexandros Matsoukis, Athens)

1996 (25 Mar). Centenary of Modern Olympic Games (3rd issue). Reproduction of Olympic Games issue of 1896. Three sheets, each 88×88 mm, containing designs as T **448**. Inscriptions in brown, backgrounds flesh; colour of reproduction listed below. P 13½×13 (vert) or 13×13½ (horiz).

MS1995 3 sheets. (a) 80d. ochre (Type **448**); 120d. pink (2l.); 150d. purple-brown (5l.); 650d. brown-olive (10d.). (b) 80d. Venetian red (25l.); 120d. blue-black (60l.); 150d. Prussian blue (1d.); 650d. reddish brown (10d.). (c) 80d. orange-brown (20l.); 120d. grey-lilac (40l.); 150l. bistre-brown (2d.); 650d. deep grey-green (5d.) .... 70·00 65·00

No. **MS**1995 was issued in a presentation folder.

449 Sappho (poet)

450 Running

(Des M. Vardopoulou. Litho Alexandros Matsoukis, Athens)

1996 (4 May). Europa. Famous Women. T **449** and similar vert design.

A. Sheet stamps. P 14

1996A	120d. multicoloured	4·00	2·50
	a. Pair. Nos. 1996A/1997A	18·00	10·50
1997A	430d. orange-brown, black and ultramarine	12·50	7·50

B. Booklet stamps. Imperf×p14

1996B	120d. multicoloured	4·25	3·00
	a. Booklet pane. Nos. 1996B/1997B each×2	37·00	
1997B	430d. orange-brown, black and ultramarine	13·50	8·00

Designs: 120d. T **449**; 430d. Amalia Fleming.

Nos. 1996A/1997A were issued together in *se-tenant* pairs within the sheet.

(Des M. Vardopoulou. Litho Alexandros Matsoukis, Athens)

1996 (4 June). Centenary of Modern Olympic Games (4th issue). T **450** and similar multicoloured designs. P 13½.

1998	10d. Type **450**	2·30	45
1999	80d. Throwing the discus	2·40	85
2000	120d. Weightlifting	4·25	1·30
2001	200d. Wrestling (*horiz*)	7·50	3·25
1998/2001	Set of 4	15·00	5·25

451 Hippocrates

452 Mytilene

(Des K. Michotas. Litho Alexandros Matsoukis, Athens)

1996 (8 July). First International Medical Olympiad, Athens. T **451** and similar vert design. P 13½×13.

2002	80d. orange-brown, flesh and black	3·50	1·60
2003	120d. olive-brown, turquoise-green and black	4·75	2·50

Designs: 80d. T **451**; 120d. Galen.

(Des K. Michotas. Litho Alexandros Matsoukis, Athens)

1996 (7 Oct). Castles (1st series). T **452** and similar horiz designs. Multicoloured.

A. P 13×13½

2004A	10d. Type **452**	35	25
2005A	20d. Lindos	45	25
2006A	30d. Rethymnon	55	25
2007A	70d. Assos Cephalonia	80	55
2008A	80d. Castle of the Serbs	1·30	75
2009A	120d. Monemvasia	2·10	1·10
2010A	200d. Didimotihon	4·25	1·50
2011A	430d. Vonitsas	9·25	3·50
2012A	1000d. Nikopolis	19·00	9·25
2004A/2012A	Set of 9	34·00	16·00

B. Imperf×p 13½

2004B	10d. Type **452**	35	25
2005B	20d. Lindos	45	25
2006B	30d. Rethymnon	55	25
2007B	70d. Assos Cephalonia	80	35
2008B	80d. Castle of the Serbs	1·30	60
2009B	120d. Monemvasia	2·10	75
2010B	200d. Didimotihon	4·25	90
2011B	430d. Vonitsas	9·50	2·10
2012B	1000d. Nikopolis	19·00	6·75
2004B/2012B	Set of 9	34·00	11·00

Nos. 2004A/2012A were each issued in sheets of 50 stamps.
Nos. 2004B/2012B each in strips of five within packets of 100 stamps.

See also Nos. 2069/2078.

453 Puppets

(Des V. Constantinea. Litho Alexandros Matsoukis, Athens)

1996 (15 Nov). Shadow Puppets. T **453** and similar horiz designs. Multicoloured. P 14.

2013	80d. Type **453**	1·60	85
2014	100d. Men courting woman	1·60	1·10
2015	120d. Soldiers	3·50	1·20
2016	200d. Men fighting Dragon	5·75	1·90
2013/2016	Set of 4	11·00	4·50

454 Inscription on Wine Jug (720 BC)

455 Papandreou, Cap, Degree and Books

(Des K. Michotas. Litho Alexandros Matsoukis, Athens)

1996 (18 Dec). The Greek Language. T **454** and similar horiz designs. Multicoloured. P 13×13½.

2017	80d. Type **454**	1·20	85
2018	120d. Homer's *Iliad* (papyrus scroll, 436–445)	2·10	1·10
2019	150d. Psalm (6th-century)	3·00	1·50
2020	350d. Dionysios Solomos (writer) and verse of poem (1824)	10·50	3·75
2017/2020	Set of 4	15·00	6·50

(Des T. Toumbas. Litho Alexandros Matsoukis, Athens)

1997 (12 Feb). Andreas Papandreou (Prime Minister, 1981–1989 and 1993–1996) Commemoration. T **455** and similar horiz designs. Multicoloured. P 13×13½.

2021	80d. Type **455** (Doctorate in Economics, Harvard University, 1943)	1·60	60
2022	120d. Return from exile, 1974, and smoking pipe	2·10	85
2023	150d. Parliament building and Papandreou	3·50	1·30

GREECE 1997

2024	500d. State flag, Dove and Papandreou wearing glasses		7·75	4·00
2021/2024	Set of 4		13·50	6·00

456 St Dimitrios (patron saint) (fresco, Aghios Nikolaos Orphanos Church)

457 Trikomo

(Des K. Michotas. Litho Alexandros Matsoukis, Athens)

1997 (26 Mar). Thessaloniki, Cultural Capital of Europe. T **456** and similar multicoloured designs. P 13½.

2025	80d. Type **456**	1·20	50
2026	100d. Hippocratic Hospital (*horiz*)	2·30	85
2027	120d. Marble statue pedestal (2nd-century) and circular relief of woman's head	2·50	1·20
2028	150d. Mosaic (detail) in cupola of Rotunda	3·50	1·50
2029	300d. 14th-century chalice (*horiz*)	10·00	3·50
2025/2029	Set of 5	18·00	6·75

(Des M. Vardopoulou. Litho Alexandros Matsoukis, Athens)

1997 (24 Apr). Macedonian Bridges. T **457** and similar horiz designs. Multicoloured. P 14.

2030	80d. Type **457**	1·40	60
2031	120d. Portitsa	1·90	85
2032	150d. Ziakas	3·50	1·30
2033	350d. Kastro	8·25	2·75
2030/2033	Set of 4	13·50	5·00

458 Prometheus the Fire-stealer

459 Running

(Des M. Vardopoulou. Litho Alexandros Matsoukis, Athens)

1997 (19 May). Europa. Tales and Legends. T **458** and similar horiz design. Multicoloured.

A. Sheet stamps. P 14

2034A	120d. Type **458**	3·25	1·90
	a. Pair. Nos. 2034A/2035A	12·00	7·25
2035A	430d. Knights (Digenis Akritas)	8·00	5·00

B. Booklet stamps. Imperf×p 13½

2034B	120d. multicoloured	3·50	2·40
	a. Booklet pane. Nos. 2034B/2035B each×2	25·00	
2035B	430d. Knights (Digenis Akritas)	8·25	4·75

Nos. 2034A/2035A were issued together in *se-tenant* pairs within the sheet.

(Des P. Gravalos. Litho Alexandros Matsoukis, Athens)

1997 (11 July). Sixth World Athletics Championships, Athens. T **459** and similar horiz designs. Multicoloured. P 13½×13½.

2036	20d. Type **459**	55	40
2037	100d. Nike (statue)	1·60	75
2038	140d. High jumping	2·75	1·20
2039	170d. Hurdling	3·50	1·80
2040	500d. Stadium, Athens	10·50	3·75
2036/2040	Set of 5	17·00	7·00

460 Alexandros Panagoulis (resistance leader)

461 Vassilis Avlonitis

(Des M. Vardopoulou. Litho Alexandros Matsoukis, Athens)

1997 (31 Oct). Anniversaries. T **460** and similar multicoloured designs. Multicoloured. P 13×13½ (horiz) or 13½×13 (vert).

2041	20d. Type **460** (20th death anniversary (1996))	60	55
2042	30d. Grigorios Xenopoulos (writer, 130th birth anniversary)	65	55
2043	40d. Odysseaó Elytió (poet, first death anniversary) (*horiz*)	80	55
2044	50d. Panayiotis Kanellopoulos (Prime Minister, 1945 and 1967, tenth death anniversary (1996))	1·50	55
2045	100d. Harilaos Trikoupis (Prime Minister 1881–1885, death centenary (1996)) (*horiz*)	3·25	1·30
2046	170d. Maria Callas (opera singer, 20th death anniversary) (*horiz*)	4·75	2·00
2047	200d. Rigas Velestinlis-Feraios (revolutionary writer, death bicentenary (1998))	6·25	2·30
2041/2047	Set of 7	16·00	7·00

(Des M. Vardopoulou. Litho Alexandros Matsoukis, Athens)

1997 (17 Dec). Greek Actors. T **461** and similar horiz designs. Multicoloured. P 13×13½.

2048	20d. Type **461**	60	45
2049	30d. Vassilis Argyropoulos	70	45
2050	50d. Georgia Vassileiadou	85	55
2051	70d. Lambros Constantaras	1·00	60
2052	100d. Vassilis Logothetidis	2·00	1·50
2053	140d. Dionysis Papagiannopoulos	2·50	2·20
2054	170d. Nikos Stavrides	3·75	2·50
2055	200d. Mimis Fotopoulos	8·25	5·75
2048/2055	Set of 8	18·00	12·50

462 'Greece', Greek Flag and Colossus of Rhodes

463 Aghia Sofia Hospital, Athens

(Des K. Michotas. Litho Alexandros Matsoukis, Athens)

1998 (27 Feb). 50th Anniv of Incorporation of Dodecanese Islands into Greece. T **462** and similar vert designs. Multicoloured. P 13½×13.

2056	100d. German commander signing surrender to British and Greek military authorities at Simi, 1945	1·60	1·50
2057	140d. Type **462**	2·75	2·00
2058	170d. Greek and British military representatives as transfer ceremony, Rhodes, 1947	4·00	2·50
2059	500d. Raising Greek flag, Kasos, 1947	9·00	5·75
2056/2059	Set of 4	16·00	10·50

1998 (30 Apr). Anniversaries and Events. T **463** and similar multicoloured designs. Litho. P 13×13½ (horiz) or 13½×13 (vert).

2060	20d. Type **463** (centenary of Aghia Sofia Children's Hospital)	40	30
2061	100d. St Xenophon's Monastery (millenary) (*vert*)	1·40	1·30
2062	140d. Woman in traditional costume (Fourth International Thracian Congress, Nea Orestiada) (*vert*)	1·80	1·90
2063	150d. Parthenon and congress emblem (International Cardiography Research Congress, Rhodes)	2·10	1·90
2064	170d. Sculpture of man and young boy (Cardiography Congress) (*vert*)	3·75	2·50
2065	500d. Emblem (50th anniversary of Council of Europe) (*vert*)	10·00	8·75
2060/2065	Set of 6	18·00	15·00

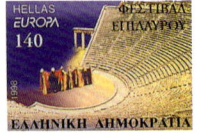

464 Ancient Theatre, Epidavros

(Litho Alexandros Matsoukis, Athens)
1998 (29 May). Europa. National Festivals. T **464** and similar horiz design.

A. Sheet stamps. Imperf×p 14

2066A	140d. Type **464**		3·00	2·20
	a. Pair. Nos. 2066A/2067A		12·50	9·00
2067A	500d. Festival in Herod Atticus Theatre, Athens		8·75	6·50

B. Booklet stamps. Imperf×p 13½

2066B	140d. As Type **464**		3·25	2·75
	a. Booklet pane. Nos. 2066B/2067B each×2		27·00	
2067B	500d. Festival in Herod Atticus Theatre, Athens		9·50	7·75

465 Players

1998 (15 June). World Basketball Championship, Athens. Sheet 70×68 mm containing T **465**. Litho. P 14×14½.
MS2068 **465** 300d. multicoloured.................................... 7·25 6·00

466 Ierapetra, Crete

1998 (15 July). Castles (2nd series). T **466** and similar multicoloured designs. Litho.

A. P 13x13½

2069A	30d. Type **466**		40	30
2070A	50d. Corfu		45	35
2071A	70d. Limnos		60	40
2072A	100d. Argolis		75	50
2073A	150d. Iraklion, Crete		1·10	65
2074A	170d. Naupaktos (*vert*)		1·90	1·30
2075A	200d. Ioannina (*vert*)		3·00	1·50
2076A	400d. Platamona		6·75	2·50
2077A	550d. Karitainas (*vert*)		9·00	3·75
2078A	600d. Fragkokastello, Crete		9·75	4·25
2069A/2078A	Set of 10		30·00	14·00

B. Imperf×p 13½

2069B	30d. As Type **466**		40	30
2070B	50d. Corfu		45	35
2071B	70d. Limnos		60	40
2072B	100d. Argolis		75	50
2073B	150d. Iraklion, Crete		1·10	65
2074B	170d. Naupaktos (*vert*)		1·90	1·30
2075B	200d. Ioannina (*vert*)		3·00	1·50
2076B	400d. Platamona		6·75	2·50
2077B	550d. Karitainas (*vert*)		9·00	3·75
2078B	600d. Fragkokastello, Crete		9·75	4·25
2069B/2078B	Set of 10		30·00	14·00

The stamps perforated on all four sides were each issued in sheets of 50 stamps; those perforated on two sides only were each issued in strips of five within packets of 100 stamps.

467 Church of St George of the Greeks (18th-century copperplate)

(Des M. Vardopoulou. Litho Alexandros Matsoukis, Athens)
1998 (26 Oct). 500th Anniversary of Greek Orthodox Community in Venice. T **467** and similar multicoloured designs. P 14.

2079	30d. Type **467**		40	30
2080	40d. Christ Pantocrator (icon) (*vert*)		75	55
2081	140d. Illuminated script of hymn *Epi Soi hairei* by Georgios Klontzas (*vert*)		2·30	1·50
2082	230d. St George of the Greeks (illuminated manuscript, 1640)		5·25	2·75
2079/2082	Set of 4		7·75	4·50

468 Homer (poet)   **469** Ancient Trireme and Circulation of Mediterranean Sea Currents

(Des I. Gourzis. Litho Alexandros Matsoukis, Athens)
1998 (18 Dec). Ancient Greek Writers. T **468** and similar vert designs. P 13½×13.

2083	20d. lake-brown and gold		40	30
2084	100d. purple-brown and gold		2·30	1·90
2085	140d. brown-red and gold		3·00	2·40
2086	200d. black and gold		4·00	3·50
2087	250d. deep brown and gold		5·25	4·50
2083/2087	Set of 5		13·50	11·50

Designs: No. 2083, T **468**; No. 2084, Sophocles (poet); No. 2085, Thucydides (historian); No. 2086, Plato (philosopher); No. 2087, Demosthenes (orator).

(Des M. Vardopoulou. Litho Alexandros Matsoukis, Athens)
1999 (19 Feb). International Year of the Ocean. T **469** and similar horiz designs. Multicoloured. P 13×13½.

2088	40d. Type **469**		40	30
2089	100d. Galleon (detail of icon Thou art Great, O Lord by I. Kornaros)		1·40	1·30
2090	200d. *Aigaio* (oceanographic vessel), astrolabe and seismic sounding of seabed		2·75	2·50
2091	500d. Apollo on ship (3rd-century BC silver tetradrachmon coin of Antigonus Dosonos)		6·25	5·00
2088/2091	Set of 4		9·75	8·25

470 Konstantinos Karamanlis   **471** Mount Olympus and Flowers

1999 (19 Apr). First Death Anniversary of Konstantinos Karamanlis (Prime Minister 1955–1963 and 1974; President 1980–1985 and 1990–1995). T **470** and similar multicoloured designs. P 14.

2092	100d. Type **470**		1·10	1·00
2093	170d. Karamanlis and jubilant crowd, 1974		1·80	1·50
2094	200d. Karamanlis and Council of Europe emblem, 1979		3·50	1·90
2095	500d. Karamanlis and Greek flag (*vert*)		5·25	4·50
2092/2095	Set of 4		10·50	8·00

(Des M. Vardopoulou. Litho Alexandros Matsoukis, Athens)
1999 (26 May). Europa. Parks and Gardens. T **471** and similar horiz design. Multicoloured.

A. Sheet stamps. P 14

2096A	170d. Type **471**		2·40	1·90
	a. Horiz pair. Nos. 2096A/2097A		10·50	8·00
2097A	550d. Letter, script and pen		7·50	6·00

B. Booklet stamps. Imperf×p 13

2096B	170d. As Type **471**		2·75	2·00
	a. Booklet pane. Nos. 2096B/2097B each×2		22·00	
2097B	550d. Letter, script and pen		7·75	6·00

Nos. 2096A/2097A were issued together in *se-tenant* pairs within the sheet, each pair forming a composite design.

472 Ancient Greek and Japanese Noh Theatre Masks

473 Temple of Hylates Apollo, Kourion

(Des M. Vardopoulou. Litho Alexandros Matsoukis, Athens)

1999 (28 June). Centenary of Diplomatic Relations between Greece and Japan. P 14.

| 2098 | **472** | 120d. multicoloured | 1·50 | 1·30 |

Stamps of a similar design were issued by Japan.

(Des A. Ladommatos. Litho Alexandros Matsoukis, Athens)

1999 (28 June). 4000 Years of Greek Culture. T **473** and similar vert designs. Multicoloured. P 13½×13.

2099	120d. Type **473**	1·20	1·00
	a. Block of 4. Nos. 2099/2102	5·00	
2100	120d. Mycenaean pot depicting warriors (Athens)	1·20	1·00
2101	120d. Mycenaean amphora depicting Horse (Nicosia)	1·20	1·00
2102	120d. Temple of Apollo, Delphi	1·20	1·00
2099/2102 Set of 4		4·25	3·50

Nos. 2099/2102 were issued together in *se-tenant* blocks of four stamps within the sheet, each block having a composite design of a rosette at the centre.

Stamps of a similar design were issued by Cyprus.

474 Trains

(Des M. Vardopoulou. Litho Alexandros Matsoukis, Athens)

1999 (8 Nov). Fifth Anniversary of Community Support Programme. T **474** and similar horiz designs. Multicoloured. P 13×13½.

2103	20d. Type **474** (modernisation of railways)	30	25
2104	120d. Bridge over River Antirrio	1·20	1·00
2105	140d. Compact disc, delivery lorries and conveyor belt (modernisation of Post Office)	1·50	1·30
2106	250d. Athens underground train	2·30	1·90
2107	500d. Control tower, Eleftherios Venizelos airport, Athens	5·25	4·50
2103/2107 Set of 5		9·50	8·00

475 Helicopter and Commandos in Inflatable Boat

(Des K. Michotas. Litho Alexandros Matsoukis, Athens)

1999 (13 Dec). Armed Forces. T **475** and similar horiz designs. Multicoloured. P 13½.

2108	20d. Type **475**	30	25
2109	30d. Missile corvette	40	30
2110	40d. Two F-16 aircraft	45	40
2111	50d. CL-215 aircraft dispersing water on forest fire	60	50
2112	70d. Destroyer	75	65
2113	120d. Forces distributing aid in Bosnia	1·50	1·30
2114	170d. Dassault Mirage 2000 jet fighter above Aegean	2·30	1·90
2115	250d. Helicopters, tanks and soldiers on joint exercise	3·00	2·50
2116	600d. Submarine *Okeanos*	6·00	5·00
2108/2116 Set of 9		14·00	11·50

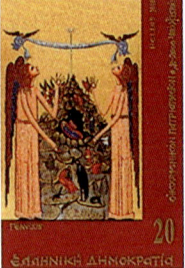 

476 Birth of Christ

477 Building Europe

(Des I. Mitrakas. Litho Alexandros Matsoukis, Athens)

2000 (1 Jan). Birth Bimillenary of Jesus Christ. Icons. T **476** and similar multicoloured designs. P 14×14½ (170d.), 13½ (200d.), 13½×14 (500d.) or 14½×14 (others).

2117	20d. Type **476**	30	25
2118	50d. Discussion between men of different denominations	75	65
2119	120d. Angels praising God	1·20	1·00
2120	170d. Epiphany (*horiz*)	2·30	1·90
2121	200d. Communion (35×35 *mm*)	2·75	2·30
2122	500d. Heavenly beings above priests and worshippers (27×57 *mm*)	5·25	4·50
2117/2122 Set of 6		11·50	9·50

(Des J.-P. Cousin. Litho Alexandros Matsoukis, Athens)

2000 (9 May). Europa. P 13½×13.

2123	**477**	170d. multicoloured	4·50	3·75
		a. Imperf×13. Booklets	4·50	3·75
		ab. Booklet pane. No. 2123a×4	19·00	

478 *Ilissos* (steamship)

479 Rainbow over Village (Spyros Dalakos)

(Des G. Papageorgiou. Litho Alexandros Matsoukis, Athens)

2000 (26 June). Ships. T **478** and similar horiz designs. Multicoloured. P 14½×14.

2124	10d. Type **478**	40	30
2125	120d. *Adrias* (destroyer)	1·10	90
2126	170d. *Ia II* (steamship)	2·30	1·90
2127	400d. *Vas Olga* (destroyer)	6·00	5·00
2124/2127 Set of 4		8·75	7·25

(Des M. Vardopoulou. Litho Alexandros Matsoukis, Athens)

2000 (26 June). Stampin the Future. Winning Entries in Children's International Painting Competition. T **479** and similar horiz designs. Multicoloured. P 14½×14.

2128	130d. Type **479**	1·10	90
2129	180d. Robots (Moshovaki-Chaiger Ornella)	1·50	1·30
2130	200d. Cars and house (Zisis Zariotis)	2·75	2·30
2131	620d. Children astride rocket (Athina Limioudi)	6·75	5·75
2128/2131 Set of 4		11·00	9·25

480 Torch and Flag

481 Emblem and Olympic Rings

(Des Lynda Warner. Litho Alexandros Matsoukis, Athens)

2000 (15 Sept). Olympic Games, Sydney. T **480** and similar vert design. Multicoloured. P 13½.

| 2132 | 200d. Type **480** | 2·30 | 1·90 |
| 2133 | 650d. Torch, flag and Sydney Opera House | 6·75 | 5·75 |

Stamps of a similar design were issued by Australia.

(Litho Alexandros Matsoukis, Athens)

2000 (7 Nov). Olympic Games 2004, Athens (1st issue). T **481** and similar vert designs all showing the Olympic Rings and emblem. P 14×14½.

2134	10d. multicoloured	30	25
2135	50d. multicoloured	75	65
2136	130d. multicoloured	1·10	90
2137	180d. multicoloured	2·30	1·90
2138	200d. multicoloured	3·00	2·50
2139	650d. multicoloured	6·00	5·00
2134/2139 Set of 6		12·00	10·00

The backgrounds of Nos. 2134/2139 show progressively, an enlarged portion of the emblem from the second to the eighth pair of leaves.

See also Nos. **MS**2169, 2191/**MS**2196, 2207/2210, **MS**2211, 2216/2221, **MS**2222, 2234/2238, **MS**2239, 2246/2251, 2252/**MS**2258, 2259/2263, 2264/**MS**2270, **MS**2271, **MS**2272, 2275/**MS**2279, **MS**2285 and 2286/**MS**2288.

482 Crete 1901 1d. Stamp

483 Orpheus Christ (sculpture)

(Des M. Vardopoulou. Litho Alexandros Matsoukis, Athens)

2000 (18 Dec). Centenary of First Crete Stamp. Sheet 104×73 mm containing T **482** and similar vert design. Multicoloured. P 14×14½.
MS2140 200d. Type **482**; 650d. Crete 1901 6d. stamp .... 23·00 21·00

(Des I. Papadakis. Litho Alexandros Matsoukis, Athens)

2000 (18 Dec). Birth Bimillenary of Jesus Christ. T **483** and similar multicoloured designs. P 14×14½ (vert) or 14½×14 (horiz).

2141	20d. Type **483**	15	15
2142	30d. The Good Shepherd (sculpture)	30	25
2143	40d. Christ Pantocrator (mosaic, Holy Monastery of Sina)	45	40
2144	100d. Anapeson in the Protato of Mount Athos (fresco, Manuel Panselinos) (horiz)	75	65
2145	130d. Christ (icon)	1·10	90
2146	150d. Christ (icon)	1·20	1·00
2147	180d. Christ Pantocrator (Encaustic icon)	1·50	1·30
2148	1000d. Christ Pantocrator (Byzantine coin) (horiz)	11·50	9·50
2141/2148 Set of 8		15·00	12·50

484 Mother and Child holding Money Box

485 Dried Earth

(Des M. Vardopoulou. Litho Alexandros Matsoukis, Athens)

2001 (15 May). Anniversaries and Events. T **484** and similar multicoloured designs. P 13½×14 (vert) or 14×13½ (horiz).

2149	20d. Type **484** (centenary of Post Office Savings Bank)	30	25
2150	130d. Euro currency and emblem (centenary of Post Office Savings Bank) (horiz)	1·50	1·30
2151	140d. Refugees (50th anniversary of United Nations High Commission for Refugees) (horiz)	2·00	1·60
2152	180d. Emblem and crowd (75th anniversary of Thessalonika International Trade Fair)	2·30	1·90
2153	200d. University façade (75th anniversary of Aristotle University, Thessalonika) (horiz)	2·50	2·10
2154	500d. Academy building (75th anniversary of Academy of Athens) (horiz)	5·25	4·50
2155	700d. Ioannis Zigdis (politician, third death anniversary)	9·00	7·50
2149/2155 Set of 7		21·00	17·00

(Des M. Vardopoulou. Litho Alexandros Matsoukis, Athens)

2001 (15 May). Europa. Water Resources. T **485** and similar horiz design. Multicoloured.

A. Sheet stamps. P 14½×14

2156A	180d. Type **485**	2·30	1·90
	a. Horiz Pair. Nos. 2156A/2157A	11·00	9·25
2157A	650d. Pool of water and droplet	8·25	7·00

B. Booklet stamps. Imperf×p 13½

2156B	180d. As Type **485**	3·00	2·50
	a. Booklet pane. Nos. 2156B/2157B each×2	25·00	
2157B	650d. Pool of water and droplet	9·00	7·50

Nos. 2156A/2157A were issued together in horizontal *se-tenant* pairs within the sheet.

486 Little Egret

(Des M. Vardopoulou. Litho Alexandros Matsoukis, Athens)

2001 (27 June). Flora and Fauna. T **486** and similar multicoloured designs. P 13½×14 (140d., 150d.) or 14×13½ (others).

2158	20d. Type **486**	15	15
2159	50d. White Storks	45	40
2160	100d. Bearded Vulture	90	75
2161	140d. Orchid (vert)	1·20	1·00
2162	150d. Dalmatian Pelican (vert)	1·40	1·10
2163	200d. Lily, Plastina Lake, Karditsa	1·80	1·50
2164	700d. Egyptian Vulture	6·25	5·25
2165	850d. Black Vulture	13·50	11·50
2158/2165 Set of 8		23·00	19·00

487 Emblem

488 The Annunciation (13th-century minature) (detail)

(Des K. Michotas. Litho Alexandros Matsoukis, Athens)

2001 (8 Sept). New Name of Hellenic Post. P 13.

2166	**487** 140d. deep new blue and yellow	1·50	1·30
	a. Sheetlet of 10 plus 10 labels. Nos. 2166/2167	39·00	
2167	200d. deep new blue	2·30	1·90

Nos. 2166/2167 were issued in horizontal pairs together with *se-tenant* half stamp-size labels within sheets of ten stamps and ten labels.

Sheets could also be Personalised by the addition of a portrait photograph in place of the logo on the labels for the cost of 3,400d. per sheetlet available only from ELTA Post Office Pavilion, Thessaloniki International Trade Fair.

(Des K. Michotas. Litho Alexandros Matsoukis, Athens)

2001 (5 Dec). 1700th Anniversary of Christianity in Armenia. Sheet 63×85 mm. P 13.
MS2168 **488** 850d. multicoloured .... 12·00 10·00

489 Figures of Swimmers from Amphora

490 Kamakaki, Salamina

(Des G. Varlamos. Litho Alexandros Matsoukis, Athens)

2001 (5 Dec). Olympic Games 2004, Athens (2nd issue). Sheet 80×70 mm. P 14.
MS2169 **489** 1200d. multicoloured .... 15·00 12·50

GREECE 2002

New Currency
2002 100 cents = 1 euro

(Des M. Vardopoulou. Litho Alexandros Matsoukis, Athens)

2002 (2 Jan). Traditional Dances. T **490** and similar horiz designs. Multicoloured.

A. P 13×13½ (horiz) or 13½×13 (vert).

2170A	2c. Type **490**	15	10
2171A	3c. Prikia (bride's dowry)	20	15
2172A	5c. Zagorissios, Epirus (*vert*)	25	25
2173A	10c. Balos, Aegean Islands	35	30
2174A	15c. Synkathistos, Thrace	40	35
2175A	20c. Tsakonikos, Peloponnese (*vert*)	55	45
2176A	30c. Pyrrichios (Sera) (Pontian Greek)	70	60
2177A	35c. Fourles, Kythnos (*vert*)	80	70
2178A	40c. Apokriatos, Skyros	95	80
2179A	45c. Kotsari (Pontian Greek)	1·10	90
2180A	50c. Pentozalis, Crete (*vert*)	1·20	1·00
2181A	55c. Karagouna, Thessaly	1·40	1·20
2182A	60c. Hassapiko, Smyrneikos	1·50	1·30
2183A	65c. Zalistos, Naoussa	1·80	1·50
2184A	85c. Pogonissios, Epirus	2·30	2·00
2185A	€1 Kalamtianos, Peloponnese	2·75	2·30
2186A	€2 Maleviziotis, Crete	5·50	4·50
2187A	€2.15 Tsamikos, Roumeli	5·75	5·00
2188A	€2.60 Zeibekikos (*vert*)	7·00	6·00
2189A	€3 Nyfiatikos, Corfou	8·00	7·00
2190A	€4 Paschaliatikos	11·00	9·25
2170A/2190A *Set of 21*		48·00	41·00

B. Imperf×p 13½

2170B	2c. Type **490**	15	10
2171B	3c. Prikia (bride's dowry)	20	15
2172B	5c. Zagorissios, Epirus (*vert*)	25	25
2173B	10c. Balos, Aegean Islands	35	30
2174B	15c. Synkathistos, Thrace	40	35
2175B	20c. Tsakonikos, Peloponnese (*vert*)	55	45
2176B	30c. Pyrrichios (Sera) (Pontian Greek)	70	60
2177B	35c. Fourles, Kythnos (*vert*)	80	70
2178B	40c. Apokriatos, Skyros	95	80
2179B	45c. Kotsari (Pontian Greek)	1·10	90
2180B	50c. Pentozalis, Crete (*vert*)	1·20	1·00
2181B	55c. Karagouna, Thessaly	1·40	1·20
2182B	60c. Hassapiko, Smyrneikos	1·50	1·30
2183B	65c. Zalistos, Naoussa	1·80	1·50
2184B	85c. Pogonissios, Epirus	2·30	2·00
2185B	€1 Kalamtianos, Peloponnese	2·75	2·30
2186B	€2 Maleviziotis, Crete	5·50	4·50
2187B	€2.15 Tsamikos, Roumeli	5·75	5·00
2188B	€2.60 Zeibekikos (*vert*)	7·00	6·00
2189B	€3 Nyfiatikos, Corfou	8·00	7·00
2190B	€4 Paschaliatikos	11·00	9·25
2170B/2190B *Set of 21*		48·00	41·00

The stamps perforated on all four sides were each issued in sheets of 25 stamps; those perforated on two sides only were each issued in strips of five within books of 100 stamps.

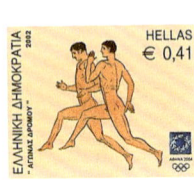

491 Runners (vase painting) **492** Performing Elephant

(Des P. Gravalos (No. **MS**2196), G. Varlamos (others). Litho Alexandros Matsoukis, Athens)

2002 (15 Mar). Olympic Games 2004, Athens (3rd issue). T **491** and similar horiz designs. Multicoloured. P 13½×14 (Nos. 2192, 2194) or 14×13½ (others).

2191	41c. Type **491**	1·40	1·20
2192	59c. Charioteer (8th-century bronze statuette) (*vert*)	2·00	1·70
2193	80c. Javelin thrower (vase painting)	2·30	2·00
2194	€2.05 Doryphoros (Spear Bearer) (statue, Polycleitos) (*vert*)	5·50	4·50
2195	€2.35 Weightlifter (vase painting)	6·75	5·75
2191/2195 *Set of 5*		16·00	13·50
MS2196 121×80 mm. €5 Crypt of the ancient Olympic stadium, Olympia (49×29 *mm*). P 13		18·00	17·00

(Des D. Mytaras. Litho Alexandros Matsoukis, Athens)

2002 (9 May). Europa. Circus. T **492** and similar vert design. Multicoloured.

A. Sheet stamps. P 13½×14

2197A	60c. Type **492**	2·40	2·30
	a. Horiz pair. Nos. 2197A/2198A	12·00	11·00
2198A	€2.60 Equestrian acrobat	9·00	8·00

Nos. 2197/2198 were issued together in *se-tenant* pairs within the sheet.

B. Booklet stamps. Imperf×p 13½

2197B	60c. As Type **492**	2·40	2·30
	a. Booklet pane. Nos. 2197B/2198B each×2	30·00	
2198B	€2.60 Equestrian acrobat	9·00	8·00

Nos. 2197A/2198A were issued together in *se-tenant* pairs within the sheet.

493 Navy Scout

(Des M. Vardopoulou. Litho Alexandros Matsoukis, Athens)

2002 (26 June). Scouts. T **493** and similar horiz designs. Multicoloured. P 13×13½.

2199	45c. Type **493**	1·20	1·00
2200	60c. Scout and World Conference emblem	1·60	1·40
2201	70c. Air scout and Cub scouts planting tree	1·90	1·60
2202	€2.15 Scouts, mountains and map	6·00	5·25
2199/2202 *Set of 4*		9·75	8·25

494 Fragment of 5th-century BC Tablet, Acropolis, Athens
495 Man wearing Olive Wreath holding Two Ears of Corn

(Des P. Katsoulidis. Litho Alexandros Matsoukis, Athens)

2002 (23 Sept). The Greek Language. T **494** and similar multicoloured designs. P 13½.

2203	45c. Type **494**	1·20	1·00
2204	60c. 13th-century BC Linear B script tablet	1·60	1·40
2205	90c. Manuscript and General Makrygiannis (writer)	2·75	2·30
2206	€2.15 Manuscript and page from 11th-century Byzantine manuscript, Mount Athos	6·00	5·00
2203/2206 *Set of 4*		10·50	8·75

(Des A. Fassianos. Litho Alexandros Matsoukis, Athens)

2002 (30 Oct). Olympic Games 2004, Athens (4th issue). T **495** and similar vert designs. Multicoloured. P 13½.

2207	45c. Type **495**	1·20	1·00
	a. Sheetlet of 8. Nos. 2207/2210, each×2	17·00	
2208	60c. Man wearing wreath and chewing ear of Corn	1·60	1·40
2209	€2.15 Man beside column wearing wreath and chewing ear of Corn	5·75	5·00
2210	€2.60 Man beside tilted column holding wreath	7·00	6·00
2207/2210 *Set of 4*		14·00	12·00

Nos. 2207/2210 were issued separately in sheets of 25 stamps and together in *se-tenant* sheetlets of eight (2×4).

496 Façade

(Des M. Vardopoulou. Litho Alexandros Matsoukis, Athens)

2002 (30 Oct). Olympic Games 2004, Athens (5th issue). Early Stadia. Sheet 120×75 mm. P 13.

MS2211 **496** €6 multicoloured		19·00	16·00

2002 GREECE

497 Chrysostomos Papadopoulos (1923–1938)

498 Discus

(Des Katerina Papadimitropoulou. Litho Alexandros Matsoukis, Athens)

2002 (10 Dec). Archbishops of Athens. T **497** and similar horiz designs. Multicoloured. P 13×13½.
2212	10c. Type **497**	30	25
2213	45c. Chrysanthos Philippides (1938–1941)	1·40	1·20
2214	€2.15 Damaskinos Papandreou (1941–1949)	6·75	5·75
2215	€2.60 Seraphem Tikas (1974–1998)	11·00	9·25
2212/2215 Set of 4		18·00	15·00

(Des K. Tsoklis. Litho Alexandros Matsoukis, Athens)

2003 (11 Feb). Olympic Games 2004, Athens (6th issue). T **498** and similar vert designs. Multicoloured. P 14.
2216	2c. Type **498**	15	10
2217	5c. Shot put	20	15
2218	47c. Javelin	1·40	1·20
2219	65c. High jump	1·80	1·50
2220	€2.17 Hurdles	6·00	5·00
2221	€2.85 Dumbbells	7·75	6·50
2216/2221 Set of 6		16·00	13·00

499 Athena (Girl Mascot)   **500** Globe

(Litho Alexandros Matsoukis, Athens)

2003 (11 Feb). Olympic Games 2004, Athens (7th issue). Sheet 128×82 mm containing T **499** and similar horiz design. Multicoloured. P 13×13½.
MS2222 €2.50 Type **499**; €2.85 Phevos (boy mascot) .. 19·00 16·00

(Des M. Vardopoulou (No. **MS**2223(b)), Katerina Papadimitropoulou (Nos. **MS**2223(a), **MS**2223(d), **MS**2223(e), **MS**2223(h)/**MS**2223(l)); Pin Communication (No. **MS**2223(f)) or A. Fassianos (Nos. **MS**2223(c), **MS**2223(g)). Litho Alexandros Matsoukis, Athens)

2003 (18 Mar). Greetings Stamps. Sheet 123×124 containing T **500** and similar square designs. Multicoloured. P 14.
MS2223 47c. (a) Type **500** (corporate); 47c. (b) 2004 Olympic emblem (sponsor); 47c. (c) Man wearing wreath (Greece); 47c. (d) Roses (wedding); 47c. (e) Grid and skyline (corporate); 47c. (f) Stylised train (children); 47c. (g) Couple (social occasion); 65c. (h) Statue head (Greece); 65c. (i) Acropolis (Greece) ...... 21·00 18·00

Nos. **MS**2223(a)/**MS**2223(i) were each available individually printed on gummed A4 sheets of 15 stamps and 15 labels, which could be personalised by the addition of a photograph or company logo, from the Central Philatelic Office, at double face value.

501 Swallow and European Stars   **502** Stylised Figure

(Des P. Xenikopdakis (47c.), M. Papadimitriou (65c.), M. Vardopoulou (€2.85), E. Apostolou (47c., 65c., €2.17). Litho Alexandros Matsoukis, Athens)

2003 (16 Apr). Greek Presidency of the European Union. T **501** and similar square designs. Multicoloured. P 14.
2224	47c. Type **501**	1·40	1·20
2225	65c. White Tower, Thessaloniki formed from letters	2·00	1·70
2226	€2.17 Swallows (fresco, Thera)	6·00	5·25
2227	€2.85 Stars and flags of member countries as jigsaw puzzle	8·75	7·50
2224/2227 Set of 4		16·00	14·00

(Des I. Moralis. Litho Alexandros Matsoukis, Athens)

2003 (8 May). Europa. Poster Art. T **502** and similar vert design. Multicoloured.

A. Sheet stamps. P 13½
2228A	65c. Type **502**	2·75	2·30
	a. Horiz pair. Nos. 2228A/2229A	11·50	9·50
2229A	€2.85 House with flag pole and veranda	8·00	7·00

Nos. 2228/2229 were issued in *se-tenant* pairs within the sheet.

B. Booklet stamps. Imperf×p 13½
2228B	65c. As Type **502**	2·75	2·30
	a. Booklet pane. Nos. 2228B/2229B each×2	23·00	
2229B	€2.85 House with flag pole and veranda	8·00	7·00

Nos. 2228A/2229A were issued together in *se-tenant* pairs within the sheet.

503 Apple floating in Space and Trees   **504** High Jump

(Des D. Nalbadis. Litho Alexandros Matsoukis, Athens)

2003 (5 June). Environmental Protection. T **503** and similar vert designs. Multicoloured. P 13½.
2230	15c. Type **503**	40	35
2231	47c. Apple floating in water	1·40	1·20
2232	65c. Wreath above waves	1·90	1·60
2233	€2.85 Planet above Apple tree	7·75	6·75
2230/2233 Set of 4		10·50	9·00

(Des Mina Valyraki. Litho Alexandros Matsoukis, Athens)

2003 (9 Sept). Olympic Games 2004, Athens (8th issue). T **504** and similar multicoloured designs. P 13½.
2234	5c. Type **504**	15	10
2235	47c. Wrestlers	1·40	1·20
2236	65c. Runners	1·80	1·50
2237	80c. Cyclists (*vert*)	2·20	1·80
2238	€4 Windsurfer (*vert*)	11·00	9·25
2234/2238 Set of 5		15·00	12·50
MS2238a 120×155 mm. Nos. 2234/2238		19·00	17·00

505 Athena (Girl Mascot)

(Litho Alexandros Matsoukis, Athens)

2003 (9 Sept). Olympic Games 2004, Athens (9th issue). Sheet 128×80 mm containing T **505** and similar horiz design. Multicoloured. P 13×13½.
MS2239 €2.50 Type **505**; €2.85 Phevos (boy mascot) .. 23·00 20·00

506 Stair Maker

(M. Vardopoulou. Litho Alexandros Matsoukis, Athens)

2003 (17 Oct). Traditional Trades and Crafts. T **506** and similar horiz designs. Multicoloured. P 13½.
2240	3c. Type **506**	15	10
2241	10c. Shoemaker	25	25
2242	50c. Smith	1·40	1·20
2243	€1 Typesetter	2·75	2·30

GREECE 2003

2244	€1.40 Sponge diver	3·75	3·25
2245	€4 Hand weaver	11·00	9·25
2240/2245	Set of 6	17·00	14·50
MS2245a	115×149 mm. Nos. 2240/2245	30·00	28·00

507 Weightlifting

508 Volos

(Des A. Fassianos. Litho Alexandros Matsoukis, Athens)

2003 (28 Nov). Olympic Games 2004, Athens (10th issue). Athletes. T **507** and similar vert designs. Multicoloured. P 13½.

2246	20c. Type **507**	65	55
2247	30c. Throwing javelin	95	85
2248	40c. Charioteers	1·30	1·10
2249	47c. Soldier carrying spear and shield	1·60	1·40
2250	€2 Running	6·50	5·50
2251	€2.85 Throwing discus	9·00	8·00
2246/2251	Set of 6	18·00	16·00
MS2251	120×150 mm. Nos. 2246/2251	33·00	31·00

(Des T. Katsouldis. Litho Alexandros Matsoukis, Athens)

2004 (15 Jan). Olympic Games 2004, Athens (11th issue). Cities. T **508** and similar horiz designs. Multicoloured. P 13×13½.

2252	1c. Type **508**	15	15
2253	2c. Patra	15	15
2254	5c. Herakleio, Crete	15	15
2255	47c. Athens	1·60	1·40
2256	€1.40 Thessalonika	4·50	4·00
2257	€4 Athens	13·00	11·00
2252/2257	Set of 6	18·00	15·00
MS2258	120×135 mm. Nos. 2252/2257	29·00	27·00

509 Spiros Louis

510 Swimming

(Des Myrsini Vardopoulou. Litho and embossed)

2004 (15 Jan). Olympic Games 2004, Athens (12th issue). Greek Olympic Champions. T **509** and similar horiz designs. Multicoloured. P 13×13½.

2259	3c. Type **509** (marathon, 1896)	15	15
2260	10c. Aristides Konstantinides (cycling, 1896)	30	30
2261	€2 Ioannis Fokianos (modern Olympic pioneer)	6·50	5·50
2262	€2.17 Ioannis Mitropoulos (gymnast, 1896)	7·00	6·25
2263	€3.60 Konstantinos Tsiklitiras (long jump, 1912)	12·00	10·50
2259/2263	Set of 5	23·00	20·00

(Des Myrsini Vardopoulou. Litho and embossed)

2004 (24 Mar). Olympic Games 2004, Athens (13th issue). Sport Disciplines. T **510** and similar multicoloured designs.

2264	5c. Type **510**	15	15
2265	10c. Hands applying Rosin	30	30
2266	20c. Canoeing	65	55
2267	47c. Relay race	1·60	1·40
2268	€2 Gymnastics floor exercise (vert)	6·50	5·75
2269	€5 Gymnastics ring exercise (vert)	16·00	14·50
2264/2269	Set of 6	23·00	20·00
MS2270	162×140 mm. Nos. 2264/2269	32·00	31·00

511 Woman holding Torch

512 Dove and Olympic Rings

(Des G. Stathopoulos. Litho Alexandros Matsoukis, Athens)

2004 (4 May). Olympic Games 2004, Athens (14th issue). Greetings Stamps. Sheet 90×75 mm containing T **511** and similar square design. Multicoloured. P 14.

MS2271	47c. Type **511**; €2.50 Woman and buildings	14·50	13·50

No. MS2271 (T **511**) was also available printed on gummed A4 sheets of 15 stamps and 15 labels, which could be personalised by the addition of a photograph or company logo, from the Central Philatelic Office, for €15.

(Des AlterVision. Litho Alexandros Matsoukis, Athens)

2004 (4 May). Olympic Games 2004, Athens (15th issue). Sheet 128×81 mm containing T **512** and similar horiz design. Multicoloured. P 14.

MS2272	47c. Type **512**; €2.50 Dove and children	14·50	13·50

513 Yacht

514 Obverse and Reverse of 3 Drachma Coin (480–450 BC)

(Des D. Mytaras. Litho Alexandros Matsoukis, Athens)

2004 (4 May). Europa. Holidays. T **513** and similar vert design. Multicoloured.

A. Sheet stamps. P 14

2273A	65c. Type **513**	3·25	2·75
	a. Horiz Pair. Nos. 2273A/2274A	13·50	12·00
2274A	€2.85 Hot air balloon	9·50	8·50

Nos. 2273/2274 were issued in horizontal se-tenant pairs within the sheet.

B. Booklet stamps. Imperf×p 13½

2273B	65c. As Type **513**	3·75	3·25
	a. Booklet pane. Nos. 2273B/2274B each×2	30·00	
2274B	€2.85 Hot air balloon	10·50	9·50

Nos. 2273A/2274A were issued together in horizontal se-tenant pairs within the sheet.

(Des M. Vardopoulou. Litho Alexandros Matsoukis, Athens)

2004 (15 June). Olympic Games 2004, Athens (16th issue). Ancient Coins. T **514** and similar horiz designs. Multicoloured. P 13½.

2275	47c. Type **514**	1·60	1·40
2276	65c. Philip of Macedonia gold stater	2·10	1·80
2277	€2 Obverse and reverse of 2 drachma coin (460 BC)	6·50	5·50
2278	€2.17 Obverse and reverse of 4 drachma coin	7·00	6·50
2275/2278	Set of 4	15·00	13·50
MS2279	140×120 mm. Nos. 2275/2278	24·00	22·00

515 Championship Trophy

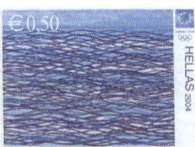
516 Sea

(Des M. Vardopoulou and A. Lygka. Litho Alexandros Matsoukis, Athens)

2004 (16 July). Greece, European Football Champions, 2004 T **515** and similar horiz designs. Multicoloured. P 13×13½.

2280	47c. Type **515**	1·60	1·40
2281	65c. Team members	2·10	1·80
2282	€1 Team members with raised arms	3·25	2·75
2283	€2.88 Outstretched hands and trophy	9·25	8·00
2280/2283	Set of 4	14·50	12·50
MS2284	160×135 mm. Nos. 2280/2283	22·00	20·00

No. 2280 was also available printed on gummed A4 sheets of 15 stamps and 15 labels, which could be personalised by the addition of a photograph or company logo, from the Central Philatelic Office, for €15.

(Des M. Vardopoulou. Litho Alexandros Matsoukis, Athens)

2004 (23 July). Olympic Games 2004, Athens (17th issue). Modern Art. Three sheets containing T **516** and similar multicoloured designs. P 13×13½ (horiz) or 13½×13 (vert).

MS2285 (a) 120×80 mm. 50c. Type **516**; €2.50 Rainbow. (b) 120×80 mm. €1 Multicoloured paint brush and glass; €2 Roller making Greek flag. (c) 135×163 mm. As Nos. MS2285(a)/MS2285(b) .... 55·00 50·00

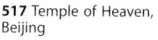

517 Temple of Heaven, Beijing

518 Athena and Phevos holding Athens 2004 Emblem

(Des M. Vardopoulou. Litho Alexandros Matsoukis, Athens)

2004 (13 Aug). Olympic Games 2004, Athens (18th issue). Athens 2004–Beijing 2008. T **517** and similar square designs. Multicoloured. P 14.

2286	50c. Type **517**	1·60	1·40
2287	65c. Parthenon, Athens	2·10	1·80
MS2288	90×120 mm. Nos. 2286/2287	25·00	22·00

(Des Eleni Apostolou. Litho Alexandros Matsoukis, Athens)

2004 (13 Aug). Olymphilex 2004, International Olympic Stamp and Memorabilia Exhibition. Sheet 81×70 mm. P 13½.

MS2289	**518** €6 multicoloured	26·00	24·00

519 Thomas Bimis and Nikos Siranidis

520 Horse Riders

2004 (17 Aug–Sept). Greek Olympic Medal Winners. T **519** and similar square designs. Multicoloured. Litho. P 13.

2290	65c. Type **519** (gold) (synchronised diving)	2·50	2·20
	a. Digital print (17.8.04)	46·00	1·40
	b. Sheetlet of 16. Nos. 2290; 2292/2306	40·00	
2292	65c. Ilias Iliadis (gold) (judo)	2·50	2·20
	a. Digital print (18.8.04)	2·50	2·20
2293	65c. Emilia Tsoulfa and Sofia Bekatorou (gold) (women's sailing)	2·50	2·20
	a. Digital print (22.8.04)	2·50	2·20
2294	65c. Pyrros Dimas (bronze) (weight lifting)	2·50	2·20
	a. Digital print (22.8.04)	2·50	2·20
2295	65c. Dimosthenis Tabacos (gold) (gymnastics)	2·50	2·20
	a. Digital print (23.8.04)	2·50	2·20
2296	65c. Anastasia Kelesidou (silver) (discus)	2·50	2·20
	a. Digital print (23.8.04)	2·50	2·20
2297	65c. Vasilis Polymeros and Nikos Skiathitis (bronze) (rowing)	2·50	2·20
	a. Digital print (23.8.04)	2·50	2·20
2298	65c. Athanasia Tzoumeleka (gold) (20km. walk)	2·50	2·20
	a. Digital print (24.8.04)	2·50	2·20
2299	65c. Chrysopigi Devezi (silver) (triple jump)	2·50	2·20
	a. Digital print (24.8.04)	2·50	2·20
2300	65c. Fani Chalkia (gold) (400m. hurdles)	2·50	2·20
	a. Digital print (26.8.04)	2·50	2·20
2301	65c. Nikos Kaklamanakis (silver) (sailing)	2·50	2·20
	a. Digital print (26.8.04)	2·50	2·20
2302	65c. Artiom Kiourgian (bronze) (Greco-roman wrestling)	2·50	2·20
	a. Digital print (26.8.04)	2·50	2·20
2303	65c. Women's water polo team (silver)	2·50	2·20
	a. Digital print (27.8.04)	2·50	2·20
2304	65c. Mirela Maniani (bronze) (women's javelin) (9.04)	2·50	2·20
	a. Digital print (28.8.04)	2·50	2·20
2305	65c. Elisavet Mystakidou (silver) (women's Taekwondo) (9.04)	2·50	2·20
	a. Digital print (29.8.04)	2·50	2·20
2306	65c. Alexandros Nikolaidis (silver) (men's Taekwondo) (9.04)	2·50	2·20
	a. Digital print (30.8.04)	2·50	2·20
2290/2306 Set of 16		36·00	32·00
2290a/2306a Set of 16		36·00	32·00

Nos. 2290a/2306a were printed digitally in sheetlets of ten stamps at the main post office where the event shown was held, each sheet inscribed in bottom right hand corner with an emblem of the relevant city. The stamps were then printed in litho, also in sheetlets of ten stamps, a few days later.

Nos. 2290; 2292/2306, respectively, were issued individually in sheetlets of ten and together in sheetlets of 16 stamps.

No. 2291 was left for a stamp that was later withdrawn from circulation when the athlete, Leonidas Sampanis, was stripped of his medal after failing a drug test.

(Des A. Fassianos. Litho Alexandros Matsoukis, Athens)

2004 (22 Sept). Paralympics. T **520** and similar vert designs. Multicoloured. P 13½.

2307	20c. Type **520**	65	55
2308	49c. Disabled runner	1·60	1·40
2309	€2 Wheelchair basket ball players	6·50	5·50
2310	€2.24 Wheelchair archer	7·25	6·50
2307/2310 Set of 4		14·50	12·50

521 Santorini

(Des Myrsini Vardopoulou. Litho)

2004 (27 Dec). Tourism. Greek Islands. T **521** and similar horiz designs. Multicoloured. P 14.

2311	2c. Type **521**	15	15
2312	3c. Karpathos	15	15
2313	5c. Crete-Vai	15	15
2314	10c. Mykonos	30	30
2315	49c. Chania	1·60	1·40
2316	50c. Kastelorizo	1·60	1·40
2317	€1 Astypalaia	3·25	2·75
2318	€2 Serifos	6·50	5·50
2319	€2.24 Milos	7·25	6·25
2320	€4 Skiathos	13·00	11·00
2311/2320 Set of 10		31·00	26·00

Nos. 2311/2320, respectively, were issued in sheets of 25 stamps. The stamps were also available in packs of 100 stamps from Central Post Offices and the Central Philatelic Office. It is reported that these stamps exist perf 13×imperf.

522 Necklace (730 BC)

523 Formula Diagram and 'E=mc^2' (75th anniversary of State Laboratory)

(Des Myrsini Vardopoulou. Litho Alexandros Matsoukis, Athens)

2005 (25 Feb). Jewellery. T **522** and similar multicoloured designs. P 14×13½ (horiz) or 13½×14 (vert).

2321	1c. Type **522**	15	15
2322	15c. Snake-shaped bracelet (2nd/3rd-century BC) (vert)	50	40
2323	30c. Necklace with Bulls head pendant (5th-century)	95	85
2324	49c. Central part of crown (2nd-century)	1·60	1·40
2325	$4 Earring (8th-century BC) (vert)	13·00	11·00
2321/2325 Set of 5		14·50	12·50

(Des Anthoula Lygka. Litho Alexandros Matsoukis, Athens)

2005 (5 Apr). Anniversaries and Events. T **523** and similar multicoloured designs. P 14×13½ (horiz) or 13½×14 (vert).

2326	1c. Type **523**	15	15
2327	4c. Sugar cubes and stop sign (41st European Association for Diabetes Meeting) (horiz)	15	15
2328	5c. Electrocardiogram chart and heart (54th European Society for Cardiovascular Surgery Congress) (horiz)	15	15

2329	40c. I. Kondilakis (first president) (90th anniversary of ESIA (journalists' union of Athens)		1·30	1·10
2330	49c. Emblem (2005-Year of Economic Competitiveness)		1·60	1·40
2331	€1.40 Woman examining breast (25th anniversary of Senologic Hellenic Society)		4·50	4·00
2332	€3.50 Angel (painting, Alekos Kontopoylos) (birth centenary) (*horiz*)		11·50	10·00
2326/2332 Set of 7			17·00	15·00

2350	49c. Flowers		1·90	1·70
2351	49c. Figures		1·90	1·70
2352	65c. Church		3·00	2·50
2345/2352 Set of 8			14·50	13·00

Nos. 2345/2352, respectively, were each available printed on gummed A4 sheets of stamps and labels which could be personalised by the addition of a photograph or company logo, from the Central Philatelic Office.

Nos. 2345/2347 in sheets of ten stamps and labels priced €10, Nos. 2348/2351 in sheets of 15 stamps and labels priced €15 and No. 2352 in sheets of ten stamps and ten labels priced €13.

524 *Gladiolus illyricus*   **525** Agiorgitiko Peloponnese

528 Rocket and Mountaineers (Fokion Dimitriadis)   **529** Two Players, Referee and Ball

(Des Myrsini Vardopoulou. Litho Alexandros Matsoukis, Athens)

2005 (5 Apr). Flowers. T **524** and similar vert designs. P 13½×14.

2333	20c. Type **524**	65	55
2334	40c. *Crocus sieberi*	1·30	1·10
2335	49c. *Narcissus tazetta*	1·60	1·40
2336	€1.40 *Rhododendron luteum*	4·50	4·00
2337	€3 *Tulipa boetica*	9·50	8·50
2333/2337 Set of 5		16·00	14·00

(Des C. Garoufalis. Litho Alexandros Matsoukis, Athens)

2005 (19 May). Wine. T **525** and similar horiz designs showing grape varieties. Multicoloured. P 14.

2338	20c. Type **525**	65	55
2339	49c. White Grapes on cloth (Assyrtiko Santorini)	1·60	1·40
2340	65c. Black Grapes and coin (Xinomavro Macedonia)	2·10	1·80
2341	€2.24 White Grapes and barrel (Robola Kefalonia)	7·25	6·25
2342	€2.40 Black Grapes (Moschofilero Peloponnese)	7·75	6·75
2338/2342 Set of 5		17·00	15·00

(Litho Alexandros Matsoukis, Athens)

2005 (16 Sept). Caricatures. T **528** and similar vert designs. Multicoloured. P 14.

2353	15c. Type **528**	50	45
2354	20c. Woman and man (Archelaus)	70	60
2355	30c. Stick figure (Themos Annios)	1·00	95
2356	50c. Man tying woman's shoe (Dimitris Galanis)	1·70	1·60
2357	65c. Chef icing globe with atomic rocket (Kostas Mitropoulis)	2·20	2·00
2358	€4 Stylised couple (vase painting) (Asteas)	13·50	12·50
2353/2358 Set of 6		18·00	16·00

Self-adhesive designs as Nos. 2353/2358 were also issued in premium stamp booklets sold at €9.90.

(Des Myrsini Vardopoulou. Litho Alexandros Matsoukis, Athens)

2005 (7 Oct). Greece, European Basketball Champions, 2005 (Eurobasket 2005, Belgrade). T **529** and similar horiz designs. Multicoloured. P 14.

2359	30c. Type **529**	1·00	95
2360	50c. Trophy	1·70	1·60
2361	65c. Team members	2·20	2·00
2362	€3.65 Holding trophy aloft	12·00	11·00
2359/2362 Set of 4		15·00	14·00
MS2363 165×138 mm. Nos. 2359/2362		17·00	16·00

526 Dakos   **527** Blackboard

530 Mini Cooper   **531** Ethnikos Sports Club Emblem

(Des Myrsini Vardopoulou. Litho Alexandros Matsoukis, Athens)

2005 (19 May). Europa. Gastronomy. T **526** and similar horiz design.

A. Sheet stamps. P 14½×14

2343A	65c. Type **526**	2·40	2·10
	a. Horiz pair. Nos. 2343A/2344A	11·50	10·00
2344A	€2.35 Rusk, Tomato, herbs, oil and Feta Cheese	8·75	7·75

B. Booklet stamps. Imperf×p 13½

2343B	65c. As Type **526**	2·40	2·10
	a. Booklet pane. Nos. 2343B/2344B each×2	23·00	
2344B	€2.35 Rusk, Tomato, herbs, oil and Feta Cheese	8·75	7·75

Nos. 2343A/2344A were issued in horizontal *se-tenant* pairs within the sheet, each pair forming a composite design.

(Des Anthoula Lygka (Nos. 2346/2347) or Eleni Apostolou (No. 2348/2353). Litho Alexandros Matsoukis, Athens)

2005 (15 July). Greetings Stamps. T **527** and similar square designs. Multicoloured. P 14.

2345	49c. Type **527**	1·90	1·70
2346	49c. Envelopes	1·90	1·70
2347	49c. Girl reading	1·90	1·70
2348	49c. Globe and stamp	1·90	1·70
2349	49c. Grid	1·90	1·70

(Des Anthoula Lygka. Litho Alexandros Matsoukis, Athens)

2005 (11 Nov). Cars. T **530** and similar horiz designs. Multicoloured. P 14.

2364	1c. Type **530**	15	15
2365	30c. Fiat 500	1·00	95
2366	50c. Citroen 2CV	1·70	1·60
2367	€2.25 Volkswagen Beetle	7·75	7·00
2368	€2.85 Ford Model T	9·75	9·00
2364/2368 Set of 5		18·00	17·00

Booklet pane Nos. 2364a was issued with 14 pages of text in premium stamp booklets.

(Litho Alexandros Matsoukis, Athens)

2005 (30 Nov). Sports Clubs. T **531** and similar square designs. Multicoloured. P 14.

2369	30c. Type **531**	1·00	95
2370	50c. Panionios Football Club	1·70	1·60
2371	50c. Iraklis Football Club	1·70	1·60
2372	50c. Panathinakos Football Club	1·70	1·60
2373	65c. PAOK Football Club	2·20	2·00

2374	65c. Panellinios Sports Club	2·20	2·00
2375	€4 Omilos Ereton Athletics Club	13·50	12·50
2369/2375	Set of 7	22·00	20·00

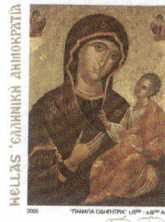

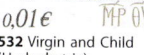
532 Virgin and Child (Hodeghetria)

533 Building Façade

(Des Myrsini Vardopoulou. Litho Alexandros Matsoukis, Athens)

2005 (20 Dec). Christmas. T **532** and similar vert designs showing icons. Multicoloured. P 14.

2376	1c. Type **532**	25	25
2377	20c. Kardiotissa	70	60
2378	70c. Glykophiloussa	2·50	2·30
2379	€3.20 Virgin, Child and symbols of the Passion	11·00	10·00
2376/2379	Set of 4	13·00	12·00

(Des Myrsini Vardopoulou. Litho Alexandros Matsoukis, Athens)

2006 (10 Jan). 50th Anniversary of Europa Stamps. Sheet 105×81 mm containing T **533** and similar horiz design. P 14.

| MS2380 | €1.50 Type **533**; €2.50 As No. 1617 | 20·00 | 19·00 |

534 Ancient Drama (Dionisis Fotopoulos)

535 Kouros of Anavissos (National Archaeological Museum)

(Des Myrsini Vardopoulou. Litho Alexandros Matsoukis, Athens)

2006 (28 Feb). Patras. European Capital of Culture 2006. T **534** and similar multicoloured designs. P 13×13½ (horiz) or 13½×13 (vert).

2381	1c. Type **534**	15	15
2382	15c. *Travelling* (Dimitris Milionis)	50	45
2383	20c. *Child and Art* (Rania Kapeliari)	85	80
2384	50c. *Carnival* (Charis Pressas)	1·70	1·60
	a. Size 30×30 mm. Perf 14	2·50	2·40
2385	65c. Patras–2006 emblem (*vert*)	3·00	2·75
	a. Size 30×30 mm. Perf 14	3·25	3·00
2386	€2.25 *Poetry and Music* (Kelly Mendrinou)	8·50	7·75
2387	€2.30 Icon (*vert*)	10·00	9·25
2381/2387	Set of 7	22·00	20·00

(Des Myrsini Vardopoulou. Litho Alexandros Matsoukis, Athens)

2006 (7 Apr). Museum Exhibits. T **535** and similar multicoloured designs. P 14.

2388	5c. Type **535**	15	15
2389	20c. Marble seated figure (Museum of Cycladic Art, Athens)	70	60
2390	50c. Spiral (29×30 mm)	1·70	1·60
2391	65c. Parthenon pediment (Acropolis Museum) (*horiz*)	2·50	2·30
2392	€1.40 Antinopolis (painting) (Benaki Museum, Athens)	6·00	5·50
2393	€2.25 *Concert of the Angels* (Domenicos Theotokopoulos) (National Art Gallery) (*horiz*)	9·25	8·50
2388/2393	Set of 6	18·00	17·00

536 As T **21**

537 Moon and Multicoloured Twisted Strands

(Des Anthi Lygka. Litho Alexandros Matsoukis, Athens)

2006 (7 Apr). Centenary of Intercalated Olympic Games, Athens. T **536** and similar horiz designs showing 1906 stamps Second Olympic Games Issue, Athens. Multicoloured. P 14.

| MS2394 | Two sheets, each 105×81 mm. (a) 20c. Type **536**; 30c. As Type **25**; 50c. As Type **22**; €2. As Type **26**. (b) 50c. As Type **23**; 65c. As Type **27**; 85c. As Type **28**; €1. As Type **24** | 24·00 | 22·00 |

(Des Myrsini Vardopoulou. Litho Alexandros Matsoukis, Athens)

2006 (15 May). Europa. Integration. T **537** and similar vert design.

A. Sheet stamps. P 14½×14

2395A	65c. Type **537**	3·50	3·00
	a. Horiz pair. Nos. 2395A/2396A	17·00	14·50
2396A	€3 Green twisted strands and sun	12·00	11·00

B. Booklet stamps. Imperf×p 13½

2395B	65c. As Type **537**	3·50	3·00
	a. Booklet pane. Nos. 2395B/2396B each×2	32·00	
2396B	€3 Green twisted strands and sun	12·00	11·00

Nos. 2395A/2396A were issued in horizontal *se-tenant* pairs within the sheet.

538 Book and Archive Building (90th anniversary of state archives)

539 Lesvos

(Des Eleni Apostolou (Nos. 2397/2399 and 2401/2402) or Myrsini Vardopoulou (No. 2400). Litho Alexandros Matsoukis, Athens)

2006 (15 May). Anniversaries and Events. T **538** and similar square designs. Multicoloured. P 14.

2397	15c. Type **538**	45	40
2398	20c. European stars (25th anniversary of membership of EU)	70	60
2399	50c. Circle of squares (Eurovision Song Contest, Athens)	1·70	1·60
2400	65c. Olive tree (2006 Year of Olive Oil and Olives)	2·50	2·30
2401	€1.40 Tinia (god)	6·00	5·50
2402	€3 Council chamber (Greece's participation in UN Security Council 2005–2006)	9·25	8·50
2397/2402	Set of 6	19·00	17·00

Nos. 2400 was available printed on gummed A4 sheets of ten stamps and ten labels which could be personalised by the addition of a photograph or company logo, priced €13, from the Central Philatelic Office.

(Des Myrsini Vardopoulou. Litho)

2006 (16 June). Tourism. Greek Islands. T **539** and similar horiz designs. Multicoloured.

A. P 14

2403A	1c. Type **539**	15	15
2404A	3c. Hydra	15	15
2405A	10c. Sifnos	15	15
2406A	20c. Lefkada	35	30
2407A	40c. Samothrace	1·70	1·60
2408A	50c. Syros	2·75	2·40
2409A	65c. Rhodes	1·70	1·60
2410A	85c. Cephalonia	3·50	3·00
2411A	€2.25 Corfu	9·25	8·50
2412A	€5 Naxos	19·00	17·00
2403A/2412A	Set of 10	33·00	32·00

GREECE 2006

B. Imperf×p 13½

2403B	1c. Type **539**	15	15
2404B	3c. Hydra	15	15
2405B	10c. Sifnos	15	15
2406B	20c. Lefkada	35	30
2407B	40c. Samothrace	1·70	1·60
2408B	50c. Syros	2·75	2·40
2409B	65c. Rhodes	1·70	1·60
2410B	85c. Cephalonia	3·50	3·00
2411B	€2.25 Corfu	9·25	8·50
2412B	€5 Naxos	19·00	17·00
2403B/2412B	*Set of 10*	33·00	32·00

The stamps perforated on all four sides were issued in sheets of 25 stamps, those perforated on two sides only, were only available in packs of 100 stamps from Central Post Offices and the Central Philatelic Office.

No. 2408A, sold at €10, and No. 2409A, sold at €13, were also available printed on gummed A4 sheets of ten stamps and ten labels which could be personalised by the addition of a photograph or company logo.

Nos. 2408B/2409B were issued with a *se-tenant* stamp size label which could be personalised with the addition of a photograph or a logo.

540 *Olympias* (trireme)

(Des Myrsini Vardopoulou. Litho)

2006 (14 Sept). Ancient Technology. T **540** and similar multicoloured designs. P 14.

2413	3c. Type **540**	15	15
2414	5c. 1st-century odometer (Heron of Alexandria)	15	15
2415	50c. 3rd-century piston water pump (Ktesibius) (*vert*)	1·70	1·60
2416	65c. The Antikythera mechanism, 80 BC (*vert*)	2·20	2·00
2417	€3.80 1st-century automatic temple gates (Heron of Alexandria) (*vert*)	13·00	12·00
2413/2417	*Set of 5*	15·00	14·50

541 Team members (left)   **542** Apollon Kalamarias

(Des Myrsini Vardopoulou. Litho Alexandros Matsoukis, Athens)

2006 (16 Oct). Greece World Basketball Championship Silver Medallists. Sheet 105×81 mm containing T **541** and similar horiz designs. Multicoloured. P 14.

MS2418	50c. Medal; €2 Type **541**; €3 Team members (right)	20·00	19·00

The stamps and margins of No. **MS**2418 form a composite design.

(Des Eleni Apostolou. Litho Alexandros Matsoukis, Athens)

2007 (12 Mar). Sports Clubs. T **542** and similar square designs. Multicoloured. P 14.

2419	2c. Type **542**	15	15
2420	3c. Atromitos Athinon	15	15
2421	52c. Aris Thessalonikis	1·70	1·60
2422	€2.27 Ethnikos Peiraio	7·75	7·00
2423	€3.20 Apollon Smirnis	11·00	10·00
2419/2423	*Set of 5*	19·00	17·00

543 Bleuette (doll, 1905)   **544** Faces

(Des Myrsini Vardopoulou. Litho Alexandros Matsoukis, Athens)

2006 (22 Dec). Children's Toys. T **543** and similar multicoloured designs. P 14.

2424	5c. Type **543**	15	15
2425	15c. Wooden aircraft (1940–1945)	45	40
2426	30c. Paper Mâché head dolls (1925–1930)	1·00	95
2427	40c. Wheeled Horses and Cat (1920–1990)	1·40	1·20
2428	52c. Clockwork Cat, wheeled Duck and dominoes (1930–1960)	1·90	1·70
2429	72c. Parachutist (*c.* 1950) (*vert*)	2·50	2·30
2430	€2.27 Aeroplane carousel (*c.* 1950) (*vert*)	9·50	8·75
2431	€4 Puppet show of the Resistance (1941–1945) (*vert*)	13·50	12·50
2424/2431	*Set of 8*	27·00	25·00

(Des Eleni Apostolou. Litho Alexandros Matsoukis, Athens)

2007 (12 Mar). Greetings Stamps. T **544** and similar square designs. Multicoloured. P 14.

2432	52c. Type **544**	1·90	1·70
2433	52c. Crescents	1·90	1·70
2434	52c. Artemis	1·90	1·70
2435	52c. Earth from space	1·90	1·70
2436	52c. Globe	1·90	1·70
2437	65c. Parthenon	2·20	2·00
2438	65c. Kore Phrasikleia	2·20	2·00
2432/2438	*Set of 7*	12·50	11·50
MS2439	118×122 mm. Nos. 2432/2438	18·00	16·00

Nos. 2432/2436 were available printed on gummed A4 sheets of ten or 15 stamps and ten or 15 labels which could be personalised by the addition of a photograph or company logo, priced €10 or €15.

Nos. 2437/2438 were available only in sheets of ten stamps and ten labels.

All sheets could be purchased from the Central Philatelic Office.

545 Costis Palamas (poet and critic) (engraving by Giannis Gourzis)   **546** Scorpio

(Des Myrsini Vardopoulou. Litho Alexandros Matsoukis, Athens)

2007 (25 Apr). Anniversaries and Events. T **545** and similar square designs. Multicoloured. P 14.

2440	2c. Type **545**	15	15
2441	10c. Poseidon and head with gold mask (Year of Greece in China) (*horiz*)	35	30
2442	20c. Emblem (First Symposium of Seven Wise Men in Cardiovascular Surgery, Athens and Delphi)	70	60
2443	52c. Figures with arms raised (Second UNI Postal Global Union World Conference, Athens) (*horiz*)	1·70	1·60
2444	65c. Rainbow and stars (50th anniversary of Treaty of Rome)	2·50	2·30
2445	85c. Georgios Kotzias (30th death anniversary)	3·50	3·00
2446	€1 Rigas Velestinlis (revolutionary) (engraving by Giannis Gourzis) (250th birth anniversary)	4·00	3·50
2447	€2.27 Light bulb as air balloon (2007 year of innovation)	8·75	8·00
2448	€3 Blind justice (125th anniversary of Legal Council of State) (*horiz*)	12·00	11·00
2440/2448	*Set of 9*	30·00	27·00

(Des Maria Zissimopoulou and Eleni Apostolou. Litho Alexandros Matsoukis, Athens)

2007 (25 May). Western Zodiac. T **546** and similar multicoloured designs. P 14.

2449	2c. Type **546**	15	15
2450	3c. Cancer	15	15
2451	5c. Capricorn	15	15
2452	10c. Taurus	35	30
2453	20c. Sagittarius (*vert*)	70	60
2454	40c. Leo (*vert*)	1·40	1·20
2455	52c. Virgo (*vert*)	1·90	1·70
2456	65c. Aries	2·20	2·00
2457	85c. Aquarius	3·00	2·75
2458	€1 Libra	3·50	3·00

2459	€2.27 Pisces		7·75	7·25
2460	€2.80 Gemini		9·50	8·75
2449/2460	Set of 12		28·00	25·00

547 Emblem and Part of Dove

(Des Myrsini Vardopoulou. Litho Alexandros Matsoukis, Athens)

2007 (25 May). Europa. Centenary of Scouting. T **547** and similar horiz designs. Multicoloured.

A. Sheet stamps. P 14½×14

2461A	65c. Type **547**	2·50	2·30
	a. Horiz pair. Nos. 2461A/2462A	17·00	14·50
2462A	€3.15 Part of Dove and scouts	13·00	11·50

B. Booklet stamps. Imperf×p 14

2461B	65c. As Type **547**	2·50	2·30
	a. Booklet pane. Nos. 2461B/2462B each×2	32·00	
2461B	€3.15 Part of Dove and scouts	13·00	11·50

Nos. 2461A/2462A were issued in horizontal *se-tenant* pairs within the sheet, each pair forming a composite design.

548 Asclepius (statue)
(Ampuria Museum, Spain)

(Des Myrsini Vardopoulou. Litho Alexandros Matsoukis, Athens)

2007 (28 June). Asclepius (demigod of medicine). Sheet 120×76 mm containing T **548** and similar vert design. Multicoloured. P 14.

MS2463	€2.50×2, Type **548**; Asclepius (head) (National Archaeological Museum)	17·00	16·00

549 Basilica of San Clemente, Rome   **550** Ergotelis Sports Club

(Litho Alexandros Matsoukis, Athens)

2007 (28 Sept). Anniversaries and Events. T **549** and similar multicoloured designs. P 14.

2464	2c. Type **549** (150th anniversary of excavation and discovery of St Cyril's grave)	15	15
2465	3c. Emblem (50th anniversary of University of Macedonia)	15	15
2466	€4 Konstantinos Tsatsos (politician and writer) (president 1975–1980) (50th death anniversary) (*vert*)	13·50	12·50
2464/2466	Set of 3	12·50	11·50

(Des Myrsini Vardopoulou (54c.) or Eleni Apostolou (others). Litho Alexandros Matsoukis, Athens)

2007 (2 Nov). Sports Clubs. T **550** and similar square designs. P 14.

2467	2c. Type **550**	15	15
2468	4c. OFI Football Club	15	15
2469	54c. Olympiacos Club of Fans of Piraeus (umbrella organisation)	1·90	1·70
2470	€2.29 Doxa Dramas Sports Club	8·00	7·25
2471	€5 Mytilini Nautical Club	17·00	16·00
2467/2471	Set of 5	24·00	23·00

551 Aphrodite (Greek)   **552** Chios

(Des Myrsini Vardopoulou. Litho Giesecke & Devrient Matsoukis, Athens)

2007 (14 Dec). Statues. T **551** and similar vert design. Multicoloured. P 14×13½.

2472	54c. Type **551**	1·90	1·70
2473	€2.40 Anahit (Armenian)	8·25	7·50

Stamps of the same design were issued by Armenia.

2008 (27 Feb). Islands. T **552** and similar horiz designs. Multicoloured. P 14½×14.

2474	2c. Type **552**	15	15
2475	5c. Amorgos	15	15
2476	10c. Nissiros	35	30
2477	20c. Paxi	70	65
2478	40c. Leros	1·40	1·30
2479	54c. Kalymnos	1·90	1·80
2480	67c. Kos	2·40	2·20
2481	€1 Simi	3·50	3·25
2482	€2.29 Zakynthos	7·75	7·25
2483	€4 Inousses	13·50	13·00
2474/2483	Set of 10	29·00	27·00

Nos. 2484/2493 have been left for coil stamps not yet received.

553 Discus Thrower   **554** Heart

(Des Alekos Fassianos and Anthi Lygka)

2008 (14 Mar). Olympic Games, Beijing. T **553** and similar multicoloured designs. P 13½×13 (vert) or 13×13½ (horiz).

2494	3c. Type **553**	15	15
2495	35c. Lighting Olympic flame	1·20	1·10
2496	67c. Cyclist (*horiz*)	2·40	2·20
2497	67c. Torch relay	2·40	2·20
2494/2497	Set of 4	5·50	5·00

(Des Anthi Lygka)

2008 (21 Apr). Personal Stamps. T **554** and similar square designs. Multicoloured. P 13.

2498	54c. Type **554**	1·90	1·80
2499	54c. Kites	1·90	1·80
2500	54c. Digital symbols	1·90	1·80
2501	54c. Letter	1·90	1·80
2502	67c. Flag	2·40	2·20
2503	67c. Pillar and capitol	2·40	2·20
2498/2503	Set of 6	11·00	10·50
MS2504	120×122 mm. Nos. 2498/2503	12·00	11·00

555 Ink bottle, Pen and Letters   **556** Emblem

(Des Anthi Lygka)

2008 (26 May). Europa. The Letter. T **555** and similar horiz design. Multicoloured.

A. Sheet stamps. P 14×14½

2505A	67c. Type **555**	2·50	2·40

GREECE 2008

	a. Horiz Pair. Nos. 2505A/2506A	17·00	15·00
2506A	€3.17 Letter, script and pen	13·00	12·00

B. Booklet stamps. Imperf×p 14

2505B	67c. As Type 555	2·50	2·40
	a. Booklet pane. Nos. 2505B/2506B each×2	32·00	
2506B	€3.17 Letter, script and pen	13·00	12·00

Nos. 2505A/2506A were issued in horizontal *se-tenant* pairs within the sheet, each pair forming a composite design.

(Des Anthi Lygka)

2008 (20 June). Anniversaries and Events. T **556** and similar vert designs. Multicoloured. P 13½×14.

2507	3c. Type **556** (180th anniversary of Hellenic Post)	15	15
2508	5c. Symbols of Greece (180th anniversary of Hellenic Post)	15	15
2509	10c. Ioannis Kapodistrias (180th anniversary of his election as first head of state of newly-liberated Greece)	35	30
2510	57c. Dimitris Rodopoulos (M. Karagatsis) (writer) (birth centenary)	2·00	1·90
2511	70c. Fish (International Year of Planet Earth)	2·40	2·20
2512	€1.85 '50' (50th anniversary of National Hellenic Reseach Foundation)	6·00	5·50
2513	€3 Emblem (centenary of National Council of Women)	10·00	9·50
2507/2513 Set of 7		19·00	18·00

557 Feta Cheese

558 Diagoras Rhodos Sports Club

(Des Apostolos Chatzaras)

2008 (19 Sept). Traditional Products. T **557** and similar vert designs. Multicoloured. P 13½×14 (vert) or 14×13½ (horiz).

2514	3c. Type **557**	15	15
2515	5c. Mastic gum from Chios	15	15
2516	20c. Olive oil (*horiz*)	70	65
2517	57c. Ouzo spirit	2·00	1·90
2518	€1 Pistachio Nuts from Aigina	3·50	3·25
2519	€4 Honey	13·50	13·00
2514/2519 Set of 6		18·00	17·00

(Des Eleni Apostolou)

2008 (20 Oct). Sports Clubs. T **558** and similar square designs. Multicoloured. P 13½×14.

2520	40c. Type **558**	1·40	1·30
2521	57c. AEK Football Club	2·00	1·80
2522	70c. Asteras Tripolis Football Club	2·40	2·20
2523	€2 Panserraikos Football Club	6·75	6·50
2524	€3 Keriraikos Sports Club	10·00	9·50
2520/2524 Set of 5		20·00	19·00

559 Alexander the Great and the Mermaid

560 Manos Katrakis

(Des Giorgos Stathopoulos)

2008 (16 Dec). Fairy Tales. T **559** and similar horiz designs. Multicoloured. P 14.

2525	10c. Type **559**	35	30
2526	57c. *Little Red Riding Hood*	2·00	1·90
2527	€1 *The Fairies*	3·50	3·25
2528	€1.85 *The Girl and the Matches*	6·25	6·00
2529	€3 *Arion and the Lyre*	10·00	9·50
2525/2529 Set of 5		20·00	19·00

(Des Kostas Spyriounis. Litho Giesecke & Devrient Matsoukis)

2009 (9 Feb). Actors. T **560** and similar horiz designs. Multicoloured. P 14.

2530	1c. Type **560**	15	15
2531	20c. Dinos Iliopoulos	35	30
2532	35c. Elli Lambeti	1·20	1·10
2533	40c. Alekos Alexandrakis	1·40	1·30
2534	50c. Aliki Vougiouklaki	1·70	1·60
2535	57c. Tzeni Karezi	2·00	1·90
2536	€1 Dimitris Horn	3·50	3·25
2537	€2.42 Nikos Kourkoulos	8·25	7·75
2538	€3.50 Thanos Kotsopoulos	12·00	11·00
2530/2538 Set of 9		27·00	26·00
MS2539 153×148 mm. Nos. 2530/2538 (sold at €9.04)		31·00	29·00

561 Sivitanidios School

562 Pulsar (model)

(Des Anthi Liga (5c., 10c., 20c., 57c. and €3), Alekos Fasianos (50c.) or Giorgos Stamatopoulos (70c.). Litho Giesecke & Devrient Matsoukis)

2009 (30 Mar). Anniversaries and Events. T **561** and similar multicoloured designs. P 14.

2540	5c. Type **561** (80th anniversary)	15	15
2541	10c. Emblem (70th anniversary of University of Piraeus) (*vert*)	45	40
2542	20c. Exhibits (180th anniversary of National Archaeological Museum)	60	55
2543	50c. Dove carrying envelope (Greek presidency of UPU Postal Operations Council)	1·70	1·60
2544	57c. Braille (birth bicentenary of Louis Braille (inventor of Braille writing for the blind))	2·00	1·90
2545	70c. '€' (tenth anniversary of Euro)	2·40	2·20
2546	€2.42 Lord Byron (engraving) (Philhellenism and International Solidarity Day) (*vert*)	8·25	7·75
2547	€3 Buildings (National Real Estate Registry)	10·00	9·50
2540/2547 Set of 8		23·00	22·00
MS2548 80×121 mm. €1×2, Polar ice; Water (Preserve Polar Regions and Glaciers) (30×30 *mm*) (circular)		8·50	8·00

(Des Eleni Apostolou Litho Giesecke & Devrient Matsoukis)

2009 (11 May). Europa. Astronomy. T **562** and similar horiz design. Multicoloured.

(a) Sheet stamps. P 14

2549	70c. Type **562**	2·50	2·40
	a. Horiz pair. Nos. 2549/2550	17·00	15·00
2550	€3.20 Aristarchos telescope	13·00	12·00

(b) Booklet stamps. Imperf×p 14

2551	70c. As Type **562**	2·50	2·40
	a. Booklet pane. Nos. 2551/2552, each×2	32·00	
2552	€3.20 As No. 2550	13·00	12·00

Nos. 2549/2550 were printed, *se-tenant*, in pairs within the sheet, each pair forming a composite design.

No. 2551/2552, each×2, were printed, *se-tenant*, in pairs in booklets of four stamps.

563 Acropolis

564 Lighthouse, Didmi Islet, Gaidouronisi

(Des Dimitrios Koukos. Litho Giesecke & Devrient Matsoukis)

2009 (20 June). Greek Monuments of World Cultural Heritage. T **563** and similar horiz design. Multicoloured. P 14.

2553	57c. Type **563**	2·00	1·90
2554	57c. Meteora	2·00	1·90
2555	70c. Delphi	2·40	2·20
2556	70c. Mycenae	2·40	2·20
2557	€2 Mystras	6·75	6·50
2558	€3 Delos	10·00	9·50
2553/2558 Set of 6		23·00	22·00
MS2559 146×136 mm. Nos. 2553/2558		26·00	24·00

Nos. 2553/2556 were also issued in individual sheets of ten stamps and ten labels.

(Des Dimitrios Koukos. Litho Giesecke & Devrient Matsoukis)

2009 (21 Aug). Lighthouses. T **564** and similar multicoloured designs. P 14.

2560	1c. Type **564**	20	15
2561	57c. Tourlitis, Andros	2·00	1·90
2562	70c. Chania	2·50	2·40
2563	€1 Korakas, Paros (*horiz*)	4·25	4·00
2564	€4.20 Strongyli, Kastellorizo (*horiz*)	14·50	13·50
2560/2564 Set of 5		21·00	20·00
MS2565 150×133 mm. Nos. 2560/2564 (*sold at €6.48*)		24·00	22·00

565 Theseus and The Minotaur

566 Adult and Child's Hands

2009 (21 Aug). Myths and Legends. T **565** and similar multicoloured designs. P 14.

2566	1c. Type **565**	20	15
2567	5c. Heracles and Triton	45	30
2568	57c. Odysseus and the Sirens	2·00	1·90
2569	70c. Talas and the Dioskouroi	2·40	2·20
2570	€5 Bellerophon riding Pegasus	17·00	16·00
2566/2570 Set of 5		20·00	18·00

2009 (7 Dec). Rights of the Child. T **566** and similar multicoloured designs. P 14.

2571	20c. Type **566**	50	50
2572	58c. Small girl leaning against wall (*horiz*)	2·00	1·90
2573	72c. Adults and children's hands linked in circle (*horiz*)	2·50	2·40
2574	€1 Silhouette of child at window	3·50	3·25
2575	€4 Child's profile against dark background	13·50	13·00
2571/2575 Set of 5		20·00	19·00

567 2009 European Basketball Championship Gold Medal (men's under-20 team)

568 *Stuffed Head* (Giannis Gaitis)

2009 (15 Dec). Basketball. Three sheets, each 105×81 mm containing T **567** and similar horiz designs showing medals won by Greek athletes in 2009. Multicoloured. P 14.

MS2576 €2 Type **567**		7·25	6·75
MS2577 €2 World Championship silver medal (men's under-19 team)		7·25	6·75
MS2578 €2 European Championship bronze medal (men's team)		7·25	6·75

(Des Eleni Apostolou)

2010 (11 Feb). Modern Greek Art. T **568** and similar vert designs. Multicoloured. P 14.

2579	1c. Type **568**	20	15
2580	5c. *Orpheus, Hermes and Eurydice* (Nikos Engonopoulos)	35	25
2581	50c. *Erotic* (Yannis Moralis)	1·70	1·60
2582	58c. *Sailor at Table* (Yannis Tsarouchis)	2·75	2·50
2583	€2.43 *Wattle Fences* (Nikos Hadjikyriakos-Ghika)	8·25	7·75
2584	€3 *The Drawing* (Diamantis Diamantopoulos)	10·00	9·50
2579/2584 Set of 6		21·00	20·00
MS2585 148×135 mm. €6.57 As Nos. 2579/2584		24·00	22·00

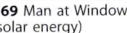

569 Man at Window (solar energy)

570 Book as Air Balloon, Boy and Staircase

(Des Alekos Fasianos and Myrsini Vardopoulou)

2010 (26 Apr). Renewable Energy Development. T **569** and similar multicoloured designs. P 14.

2586	1c. Type **569**	20	15
2587	40c. Waterfall, turbine and Goat (hydropower)	1·40	1·30
2588	58c. Wind turbine and woman with wind tossed hair (wind power) (*horiz*)	2·00	1·90
2589	72c. Man holding ear of Corn and bicycle (self-sufficiency)	2·50	2·40
2590	€2.43 Yacht (wave power)	8·25	7·75
2591	€2.50 Plants (bio energy)	8·50	8·00
2586/2591 Set of 6		21·00	19·00

(Des Myrsini Vardopoulou)

2010 (4 Apr). Europa. Children's Books.

(a) Sheet stamps. P 14½×14

2592	72c. Type **570**	3·50	3·25
	a. Pair. Nos. 2592/2593	15·00	14·50
2593	€3.22 Staircase as bookmark, book as house and girl	11·00	10·50

(b) Booklet stamps. Imperf×p 14

2593a	72c. As Type **570**	3·50	3·25
	aa. Booklet pane. Nos. 2593a/2593b, eachx2	30·00	
2593b	€3.22 As No. 2593	11·00	10·50

Nos. 2592/2593 were printed, *se-tenant* pairs, in horizontal pairs within the sheet, each pair forming a composite design.

Nos. 2593a/2593b, eachx2, were issued in booklets of four stamps.

571 Peplos Kore   **572** Athenian and Persian Warriors

(Des Dimitrios Koukos)

2010 (21 June). New Acropolis Museum. T **571** and similar multicoloured designs. P 14×13½.

2594	5c. Type **571**	20	15
2595	58c. Parthenon Gallery	2·00	1·90
2596	72c. Parthenon frieze (*detail*)	2·50	2·40
2597	€1 Entrance to museum building	3·50	3·25
2598	€4 Dog (statue)	13·50	13·00
2594/2598 Set of 5		19·00	19·00
MS2599 136×147 mm. €6.35 As Nos. 2594/2598		22·00	21·00

(Des Myrsini Vardopopoulou. Litho and die-stamped gold foil)

2010 (23 July). 2500th Anniversary of Battle of Marathon. T **572** and similar horiz designs. P 14.

2600	50c. bronze, black and gold	1·70	1·60
2601	58c. multicoloured	2·00	1·90
2602	72c. deep lilac, gold and black	2·50	2·40
2603	€3 multicoloured	10·00	9·50
2600/2603 Set of 4		14·50	14·00

Designs: 50c. T **572**; 58c. Phalanx of soldiers; 72c. Two warriors (*different*); €3 Bronze helmet.

573 Vasilis Tsitsanis (songwriter and bouzouki player)

574 Limnos

GREECE 2010

(Des Eleni Apostolou)

2010 (16 Sept). Greek Popular Music. T **573** and similar horiz designs. Multicoloured. P 14.

2604	10c. Type **573**	20	15
2605	20c. Giorgos Zampetas (bouzouki musician)	35	30
2606	58c. Stylianos (Stelios) Kazantzidis (singer)	2·00	1·90
2607	72c. Grigoris Bithikotsis (folk singer and songwriter)	2·50	2·40
2608	€1 Vicky Moscholiou (singer)	3·50	3·25
2609	€4.80 Sotiria Bellou (singer and performer of rebetiko style music)	16·00	16·00
2604/2609 Set of 6		22·00	22·00
MS2610 135×147 mm. €7.40 As Nos. 2604/2609		26·00	24·00

(Des Mysini Vardopoulou (58c.) or Eleni Apostolou (others))

2010 (14 Oct). Islands. T **574** and similar multicoloured designs.

(a) Sheet stamps. P 14

2611	2c. Type **574**	20	15
2612	5c. Paros	25	20
2613	20c. Ithaki	50	50
2614	40c. Tinos	1·40	1·30
2615	50c. Skyros	1·70	1·60
2616	(58c.) Paper boat and green square (29×29 mm)	2·00	1·90
2617	(72c.) Stairway and red circle (29×29 mm)	2·50	2·40
2618	€1 Evia–Chalkida	3·50	3·25
2619	€2 Samos	6·75	6·50
2620	€4 Kassos	13·50	13·00
2611/2620 Set of 10		29·00	28·00

(b) Coil Stamps. Imperf×p 14

2621	2c. As Type **574**	20	15
2622	5c. As No. 2612	25	20
2623	20c. As No. 2613	50	50
2624	40c. As No. 2614	1·40	1·30
2625	50c. As No. 2615	1·70	1·60
2626	(58c.) As No. 2616	2·00	1·90
2627	(72c.) As No. 2617	2·50	2·40
2628	€1 As No. 2618	3·50	3·25
2629	€2 As No. 2019	6·75	6·50
2630	€4 As No. 2620	13·50	13·00
2621/2630 Set of 10		29·00	28·00

Nos. 2616 and 2626 were for use on inland mail.
Nos. 2617 and 2627 were for use on overseas mail.

575 Municipal Theatre, Piraeus

(Des Christos Papanikolaou and Myrsini Vardopoulou)

2010 (15 Nov). Architecture. T **575** and similar horiz designs. Multicoloured. P 14.

2631	20c. Type **575**	70	65
2632	58c. Benaki Museum	2·00	1·90
2633	€2.43 National Theatre	8·25	7·75
2634	€2.50 National Gallery, Nafplio	8·50	8·00
2631/2634 Set of 4		18·00	16·00

576 Doves, Stars and Holly

(Des Giorgos Stathopoulos and Eleni Apostolou)

2010 (10 Dec). Christmas. T **576** and similar horiz designs. Multicoloured.

(a) Sheet stamps. Ordinary gum. P 14

2635	50c. Type **576**	1·70	1·60
2636	58c. Angel blowing horn	2·00	1·90
2637	€1 Sailing ship	3·50	3·25
2638	€3.50 Decorated tree, Holly and two birds	12·00	11·00
2635/2638 Set of 4		17·00	16·00

(b) Self-adhesive. Die-cut perf 14

MS2639 100×150 mm. 50c. As Type **576**; 58c. As No. 2636; €1 As No. 2637; €3.50 As No. 2638 .... 19·00 18·00

577 Aigaion V (coloured wood engraving)
578 Clasped Arms (European Year of Volunteering)

(Des Myrsini Vardopoulou. Litho and die-stamped bright scarlet foil)

2011 (20 Jan). Greek Engravers of 20th-century. T **577** and similar designs. P 14.

2640	3c. multicoloured	20	15
2641	30c. black and bright scarlet (*horiz*)	1·00	95
2642	60c. black, scarlet-vermilion and bright scarlet	2·00	1·90
2643	€1 black and bright scarlet (*horiz*)	3·50	3·25
2644	€4 black and bright scarlet	13·50	13·00
2640/2644 Set of 5		18·00	17·00

Designs: 3c. T **577**; 30c. *To Pagoni* (Peacock) (wood engraving); 60c. *Maria* (woman) (wood engraving); €1 *Plastikes Rimes* (still life) (wood engraving); €4 *Mikros Kavalaris* (Horseman) (stone engraving).

(Des Anthoula Lygka)

2011 (23 Feb). Anniversaries. T **578** and similar designs. P 14.

2645	3c. multicoloured	20	15
2646	10c. multicoloured (*vert*)	45	25
2647	20c. black and crimson (*vert*)	70	65
2648	60c. multicoloured (*vert*)	2·00	1·90
2649	€1.50 multicoloured	5·50	5·25
2650	€3 black and bright yellow-green (*vert*)	11·00	10·50
2645/2650 Set of 6		18·00	17·00

Designs: 3c. T **578**; 10c. Pediment, frieze and Ionic column (85th anniversary of Academy of Athens); 20c. Alexandros Papadiamantis (writer) (death centenary); 60c. Aircraft over Crete (70th anniversary of Battle of Crete); €1.50 Globe and OECD emblem (50th anniversary of Organisation for Economic Co-operation and Development (OECD)); €3 Spyridon-Filiskos Samaras (composer) (150th birth anniversary).

579 Stylised Figures (volunteer programme)
580 Ship, 15th-century BC

(Des Eleni Apostolou)

2011 (18 Mar). Special Olympics, Athens. T **579** and similar multicoloured designs. P 14.

2651	2c. Type **579**	20	15
2652	4c. Figure and buildings (Athens host city)	25	20
2653	60c. Games emblem (*vert*)	2·00	1·90
2654	75c. Apollon, games mascot (*vert*)	2·50	2·40
2655	€4.20 Emblems and games colours as band at foot of stamp	14·50	13·50
2651/2655 Set of 5		18·00	16·00
MS2656 175×100 mm. 60c. As No. 2653, plus stamp size label		3·50	3·25

A booklet containing 24 pages each with a single example of No. 2653 plus a different stamp size label illustrating the disciplines and four pages of text and illustrations was on sale for €18.

(Des Anthoula Lygka)

2011 (18 Apr). Greek Ships. T **580** and similar multicoloured designs. P 14.

2657	2c. Type **580**	20	15
2658	20c. Hellenic Polyreme, 4th/2nd-century BC (*horiz*)	55	50
2659	60c. Triakontoros, 15th/4th-century BC (*horiz*)	2·00	1·90
2660	75c. Hellenic Trireme, 7th/4th-century BC (*horiz*)	2·50	2·40

2661		€2.47 Macedonian Hexareme, 4th/3rd-century BC (*horiz*)	8·25	7·75
2662		€2.50 Byzantine Dromon, 5th/11th-century AD	8·50	8·00
2657/2662		Set of 6	20·00	19·00
MS2663		175×117 mm. €6.53 As Nos. 2657/2662	23·00	22·00

581 Heron, Deer and Wasp
582 Stylised Waves

(Des Militiades Petalas and Eleni Apostolou. Litho and foil die-stamped)

2011 (17 May). Europa. Forests. T **581** and similar vert design. Multicoloured.

(a) Sheet stamps. P 14

2664		75c. Type **581**	2·50	2·40
	a.	Pair. Nos. 2664/2665	17·00	15·00
2665		€3.25 Tree boles and leaves	13·00	12·00

(b) Booklet stamps. Imperf×p 14

2666		75c. As Type **581**	2·50	2·40
	a.	Booklet pane. Nos. 2666/2667, each×2	32·00	
2667		€3.25 Tree boles and leaves	13·00	12·00

Nos. 2664/2665 were printed, *se-tenant*, in horizontal pairs within the sheet, each pair forming a composite design.

Nos. 2666/2667, each×2, were issued in booklets of four stamps.

(Des Myrsini Vardopoulou)

2011 (22 June). Tourism. Visit Greece Campaign. T **582** and similar horiz designs. Multicoloured.

(a) Sheet stamps. Ordinary gum. P 14

2668		1c. Type **582**	20	15
2669		3c. Mask	25	20
2670		60c. Paper boat	2·00	1·90
2671		75c. Stylised column capitals	2·50	2·40
2672		€4 Cliff-top houses	13·50	13·00
2668/2672		Set of 5	17·00	16·00

(b) Booklet stamp. Self-adhesive. Die-cut perf 11½

2673		75c. Stylised column capitals	2·50	2·40

583 School Book Cover from 1954
584 Hermes (As T **1**)

2011 (5 Sept). Primary School Reading Books. T **583** and similar vert designs show covers of school books. Multicoloured.

(a) Ordinary gum. P 14½×14

2674		2c. Type **583**	20	15
2675		20c. Children seated on picnic rug reading	50	45
2676		60c. Older girl helping younger boy to read	2·00	1·90
2677		75c. Children working in garden	2·50	2·40
2678		€1 Children picking flowers	3·50	3·25
2679		€3.50 Boys marching under banner	12·00	11·00
2674/2679		Set of 6	19·00	17·00
MS2680		145×155 mm. €6.07 As Nos. 2674/2679	21·00	20·00

(b) Size 30×31 mm. Personal stamp. P 14

2681		60c. As No. 2676	3·50	3·25

(c) Booklet stamp. Self-adhesive. Die-cut perf 13½

2682		60c. As No. 2676	2·00	1·90

No. 2681 was issued in sheets of ten stamps and ten labels, which could be personalised by the addition of a logo of photograph (*sold for €10*).

(Recess)

2011 (1 Oct). 150th Anniversary of First Greek Stamp. P 13½×14.

2683	**584**	15c. chocolate, deep green and sage green	50	50
2684	**584**	50c. dull orange, bright carmine and magenta	1·70	1·60
2685	**584**	60c. deep green, vermilion and dull rose	2·00	1·90
2686	**584**	75c. dull orange, indigo and new blue	2·50	2·40
2687	**584**	€1 deep dull blue, brown and dull orange	3·50	3·25
2688	**584**	€2 deep magenta, dull orange and yellow-brown	6·75	6·50
2689	**584**	€5 orange-vermilion, myrtle-green and dull green	17·00	16·00
2683/2689		Set of 7	31·00	29·00
MS2689*a*		70×90 mm. €5 As No. 2689	18·00	17·00

585 Vassilis Diamantopoulos
586 Medal and Flag (Greek Women's Water Polo Team)

2011 (22 Nov). Actors. T **585** and similar horiz designs. Multicoloured. P 14×13½.

2690		1c. Type **585**	20	15
2691		5c. Rena Vlachopoulou	30	25
2692		50c. Orestis Makris	1·70	1·60
2693		60c. Thanasis Veggos	2·00	1·90
2694		€2.47 Mary Aroni	8·25	7·75
2695		€2.50 Sapfo Notara	8·50	8·00
2690/2695		Set of 6	19·00	18·00
MS2696		135×147 mm. €6.13 As Nos. 2690/2695	22·00	21·00

2011 (15 Dec). Greek Gold Medal Winners, World Swimming Championships, Shanghai. Two sheets, each 90×70 mm containing T **586** and similar horiz design. Multicoloured. P 14×13½.

MS2697		€3 Type **586**	10·50	10·00
MS2698		€3 Spyros Gianniotis	10·50	10·00

587 *Palinurus elephas*
588 *Hippocampus guttulatus*

(Des Anthoula Lygka)

2012 (21 Feb). Riches of Greek Seas. Marine Fauna. T **587** and similar horiz designs. Multicoloured.

(a) Sheet stamps. P 14½×14

2699		2c. Type **587**	20	15
2700		3c. *Octopus vulgaris*	25	20
2701		5c. *Anemonia viridis*	30	25
2702		20c. *Caretta caretta*	50	50
2703		35c. *Epinephelus marginatus*	70	65
2704		50c. *Dentex dentex*	1·40	1·30
2705		(60c.) *Hippocampus guttulatus*	1·90	1·80
2706		€1 *Aurelia aurita*	3·50	3·25
2707		(€2.47) *Dasyatis pastinaca*	8·50	8·00
2708		€3 *Charcharias taurus*	10·00	9·50
2699/2708		Set of 10	25·00	23·00

(b) Coil Stamps. Imperf×p 14

2709		2c. As Type **587**	20	15
2710		3c. As No. 2700	25	20
2711		5c. As No. 2701	30	25
2712		20c. As No. 2702	50	50
2713		35c. As No. 2703	70	65
2714		50c. As No. 2704	1·40	1·30
2715		(60c.) As No. 2705	1·90	1·80
2716		€1 As No. 2706	3·50	3·25
2717		(€2.47) As No. 2707	8·50	8·00
2718		€3 As No. 2708	10·00	9·50
2709/2718		Set of 10	25·00	23·00

2012 (21 Feb). Personal Stamp. P 14.

2719	**588**	(60c.) multicoloured	3·50	3·25

No. 2719 was printed with a *se-tenant* label which could be personalised with a photograph or logo.

GREECE 2012

589 Football

(Des Anthoula Lygka)

2012 (21 Feb). Children's Games of the Old Neighbourhood. T **589** and similar multicoloured designs.

(a) Ordinary gum. P 14½×14 (horiz) or 14×14½ (vert)
2720	2c. Type **589**	20	15
2721	10c. Scooter (*vert*)	30	25
2722	35c. Skipping rope	1·20	1·10
2723	(60c) Marbles (*vert*)	2·00	1·90
2724	€2 Spinning tops	6·75	6·50
2725	€3 Hop scotch	10·00	9·50
2720/2725	Set of 6	18·00	17·00

(b) Booklet stamp. Self-adhesive. Die-cut perf 13½
2726	(60c) As No. 2723	2·00	1·90

(c) Miniature Sheet. Self-adhesive. Die-cut perf 13½
MS2727	€6.07 As Nos. 2720/2725	21·00	20·00

590 Sun and Island

(Litho and foil die-stamped)

2012 (10 May). Europa. Visit Greece. T **590** and similar horiz design. Multicoloured.

(a) Sheet stamps. P 14×13½
2728	75c. Type **590**	3·00	2·75
	a. Pair. Nos. 2728/2729	17·00	16·00
2729	€3.25 Sun setting over island	12·50	12·00

(b) Booklet stamps. Imperf×p 13
2730	75c. As Type **590**	3·00	2·75
	a. Booklet pane. Nos. 2730/2731×2	32·00	
2731	€3.25 As No. 2729	12·50	11·50

Nos. 2728/2729 were printed, *se-tenant*, in horizontal pairs within the sheet, each pair forming a composite design.

Nos. 2730/2731, each×2, were issued in booklets of four stamps.

591 Rock Climbing, Tzoumerka, Epirus

592 Emblem

(Des Myrsini Vardopoulou)

2012 (25 June). Tourism. Visit Greece Campaign. T **591** and similar horiz designs. Multicoloured.

(a) Sheet stamps. Ordinary gum. P 14
2732	1c. Type **591**	20	15
2733	10c. Rope bridge over Evinos River	30	25
2734	62c. Couple hiking, Samaria Gorge	2·20	2·10
2735	78c. Canoeing, Acheron River, Epirus	2·75	2·50
2736	€2 Hiking in valley, Rodori, Thrace	6·75	6·50
2737	€2.50 Hiking in fields, Xanthi, Thrace	8·50	8·00
2732/2737	Set of 6	19·00	18·00

(b) Booklet stamps. Self-adhesive. Die-cut perf 12×11½
2738	62c. As No. 2734	2·20	2·10
2739	78c. As No. 2735	2·75	2·50

(Des Myrsini Vardopoulou)

2012 (2 July). Olympic Games, London 2012. T **592** and similar vert design. Multicoloured. P 14.
2740	78c. Type **592**	2·75	2·50
2741	€1.70 Athletes	5·75	5·50

593 Dimitris Chondrokoukis (High Jump)

594 Brig *Paron*, 1821

(Des Eleni Apostolou)

2012 (15 July). Greek Olympic Gold Medal Winners. Two sheets, each 90×70 mm containing T **593** and similar horiz design. Multicoloured. P 14½×13½.
MS2742	€2.50 Type **593**	9·00	8·50
MS2743	€2.50 Vlassis Maras (Gymnastics)	9·00	8·50

(Des Anthoula Lygka)

2012 (12 Sept). Greek Ships. T **594** and similar vert designs. Multicoloured. P 14.
2744	1c. Type **594**	20	15
2745	15c. Galliot, 17th-century	35	30
2746	62c. Corvette, 18th-century	2·50	2·40
2747	78c. *Ionian*, Cretan Galley, 16th-century	3·00	3·00
2748	€2 Sakoleva, 19th-century	6·75	6·50
2749	€2.50 *Latinadiko* in Shipyard, 18th-century	8·50	8·00
2744/2749	Set of 6	19·00	18·00
MS2750	175×117 mm. €6.06 As Nos. 2744/2749	23·00	22·00

595 Battle of Deskati   **596** Bauble and Triangle

2012 (26 Oct). Centenary of Liberation of Thessaloniki. T **595** and similar horiz designs. Multicoloured. P 13½ (No. 2752) or 14 (others).
2751	40c. Type **595**	1·40	1·30
2752	62c. Greek Army entering Thessaloniki (50×26 mm)	2·20	2·10
2753	85c. Armoured Cruiser *G. Averof*	3·00	2·75
2754	€2.50 Battle of Sarantaporos	8·50	8·00
2751/2754	Set of 4	13·50	13·00

2012 (12 Dec). Christmas. T **596** and similar vert designs. Multicoloured.

(a) Sheet stamps. Ordinary gum. P 14
2755	10c. Type **596**	30	25
2756	62c. Tree-shaped bauble	2·20	2·10
2757	78c. Stocking-shaped bauble	2·75	2·50
2758	€3 Parcel	10·00	9·50
2755/2758	Set of 4	14·00	13·00

(b) Booklet stamp. Self-adhesive. Die-cut perf 13½
2759	62c. As No. 2756	2·20	2·10
2760	78c. As No. 2757	2·75	2·50

597 Women of Epirus in Struggle

598 Symbols

2013 GREECE

(Des Anthoula Lygka)

2013 (21 Feb). National Historical Events. Centenary of Liberation of Ioannina. Paintings by Kenan Messare. T **597** and similar horiz designs. Multicoloured. P 14.

2761	3c. Type **597**	20	15
2762	55c. *Campaign*	1·80	1·70
2763	62c. *Shell Blast*	2·10	2·00
2761/2763	Set of 3	3·75	3·50

(Des Konstantinos Staikos and Eleni Apostolou)

2013 (28 Mar). 2400th Anniversary of Plato's Academy. Sheet 90×70 mm containing T **598** and similar vert design. Multicoloured. P 13½.

MS2764 €1 Type **598**; €2 'N' .... 10·00 9·50

599 *Taxidi sta Kithira* (Voyage to Cythera, 1984)

600 Post Van

(Des Theano Venieri. Litho and foil die-stamped)

2013 (22 Apr). Greek Cinema. T **599** and similar vert designs. Multicoloured. P 14.

2765	20c. Type **599**	65	60
2766	30c. *Elektra* (Electra, 1962)	95	90
2767	62c. *O Thiassos* (The Travelling Players, 1975)	2·10	2·00
2768	€2.80 *O Drakos* (The Ogre of Athens, 1956)	9·00	8·50
2765/2768	Set of 4	11·50	11·00

(Des Anthoula Lygka)

2013 (9 May). Europa. Postal Transport. T **600** and similar horiz design. Multicoloured.

(a) Sheet stamps. P 14×13½

2769	78c. Type **600**	2·75	2·50
	a. Pair. Nos. 2769/2770	15·00	14·00
2770	€3.28 Post bicycle	11·50	11·00

(b) Booklet stamps. Imperf×p 13

2771	78c. As Type **600**	2·75	2·50
	a. Booklet pane. Nos. 2771/2772×2	30·00	
2772	€3.28 As No. 2770	11·50	11·00

Nos. 2769/2770 were printed, *se-tenant*, in horizontal pairs within the sheet, each pair forming a composite design.
Nos. 2771/2772, each×2, were issued in booklets of four stamps.

601 Yachts

602 Mount Olympus

(Des Marina Lasithiotaki)

2013 (4 June). Tourism. Visit Greece Campaign. Sailing. T **601** and similar horiz designs. Multicoloured. P 13½×13.

(a) Sheet stamps. Ordinary gum. P 14

2773	5c. Type **601**	35	30
2774	30c. Three yachts in line	95	90
2775	47c. Two yachts tacking	1·60	1·50
2776	(62c.) Yacht in full sail	2·10	2·00
2777	(78c.) Three yachts	2·50	2·40
2778	€3 Yacht with yellow sail	9·50	9·00
2773/2778	Set of 6	15·00	14·50
MS2778a	100×150 mm. Nos. 2773/2775	3·50	3·25
MS2778b	100×150 mm. Nos. 2776/2778	15·00	14·50

(b) Booklet stamps. Self-adhesive. Die-cut perf 13

2779	(62c.) As No. 2776	2·10	2·00
2780	(78c.) As No. 2777	2·50	2·40

2013 (19 July). Centenary of First Ascent of Summit of Mount Olympus. T **602** and similar square designs showing Mount Olympus. Multicoloured. P 14.

2781	5c. Type **602**	20	15
2782	10c. Sun behind	35	30
2783	A (78c.) Bare peak and snow at foot	2·20	2·10
2784	€3.50 Snow-covered peaks	11·00	10·50
2781/2784	Set of 4	12·50	12·00

603 Andrew N. Liveris

604 Earth

2013 (16 Sept). Personalities. Winners of IFG (International Foundation for Greece) Award. T **603** and similar multicoloured designs. Multicoloured. P 14½×14 (horiz) or 14×14½ (others).

2785	5c. Type **603**	20	15
2786	10c. Aristides Patrinos	35	30
2787	20c. Jim Giannopoulo	45	40
2788	72c. Stavros Niarchos (*horiz*)	2·00	1·80
2789	80c. Vangelis	2·40	2·20
2790	€3 Nikos Aliagas	9·00	8·50
2785/2790	Set of 6	13·00	12·00

2013 (3 Oct). The Four Elements. T **604** and similar vert designs. Multicoloured. P 13½.

2791	5c. Type **604**	20	15
2792	47c. Water	1·50	1·40
2793	€1 Air	3·00	2·75
2794	€2.50 Fire	7·50	7·00
2791/2794	Set of 4	11·00	10·00
MS2795	100×150 mm. €4.02 As Nos. 2791/2794	13·00	12·00

605 Liberation

606 Post Box and PC Leads

2013 (3 Oct). Centenary of Liberation of Ioannina. P 14.

2796	**605** €2.40 multicoloured	7·25	6·75

(Litho Enschedé)

2013 (2 Dec). From Physical to Digital Post. Multicoloured.

(a) Sheet stamps. P 13½

2797	1c. Type **606**	20	15
2798	10c. 'POST' with fingerprint and memory stick	35	30
2799	72c. Quick Response Code	2·30	2·10
2800	€2.62 Memory stick as key	8·00	7·50
2797/2800	Set of 4	9·75	9·00

(b) Booklet stamps. Self-adhesive. Die-cut perf 14

2801	72c. As No. 2799	2·30	2·10

No. 2801 was printed in booklets of ten stamps. The stamps are peeled from the booklet cover and cannot therefore be collected as panes.

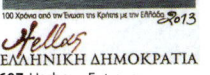
607 Harbour Entrance

608 Sky, Mountains and Decorated Panel

2013 (2 Dec). Centenary of Crete–Greece Union. T **607** and similar square design. Multicoloured. P 14.

2802	72c. Type **607**	2·30	2·10
2803	€1 Early map of Crete	3·00	2·75

(Litho Enschedé)

2014 (15 Jan). Greek Presidency of European Union. T **608** and similar square designs. Multicoloured. P 14.

2804	3c. Type **608**	20	15
2805	72c. Aegean Sea Odes	2·30	2·10
2806	€2 Stylised yacht (part of EU Greek Presidency emblem)	6·75	6·25
2807	€2.15 Fresco fragment, Iklaina of Messina c. 1400–1300 BC	7·00	6·50
2804/2807	Set of 4	14·50	13·50
MS2808	120×80 mm. 3c. As Type **608**; €2.15 As No. 2807	8·00	7·25
MS2809	120×80 mm. 72c. As No. 2805; €2 As No. 2806	9·50	8·75

609 Corinth Canal

610 *Carduelis chloris* (Greenfinch)

(Litho Enschedé)

2014 (20 Mar). Anniversaries. T **609** and similar multicoloured designs. P 14.

2810	5c. Type **609** (120th anniversary)	20	15
2811	38c. Bicentenary of Filiki Eteria (Society of Friends formed to overthrow Ottoman rule and establish an independent Greek state) (*vert*)	1·20	1·10
2812	72c. 150th Anniversary of Union of Ionian Islands with Greece (*vert*)	2·50	2·40
2813	90c. Thessaloniki. European Youth Capital 2014 (*vert*)	3·00	2·75
2814	€1.50 50th Anniversary of University of Ioannina	4·75	4·50
2815	€1.95 300th Birth Anniversary of St Cosmas of Aeotolia	6·75	6·25
2810/2815	Set of 6	17·00	15·00

2014 (20 Mar). Songbirds. T **610** and similar square designs. Multicoloured.

(a) Sheet stamps. Ordinary gum. P 14

2816	72c. Type **610**	2·50	2·40
2817	72c. *Luscinia megarhynchos* (Nightingale)	2·50	2·40
2818	€1 *Carduelis cannabina* (Linnet)	3·25	3·00
2819	€1.62 *Carduelis spinus* (Siskin)	5·50	5·00
2820	€2.62 *Carduelis carduelis* (Goldfinch)	8·75	8·00
2816/2820	Set of 5	20·00	19·00

(b) Booklet stamps. Ordinary gum. P 14

2821	72c. As Type **610**	2·50	2·40
2822	72c. As No. 2817	2·50	2·40
2823	€1 As No. 2818	3·25	3·00
2824	€1.62 As No. 2819	5·50	5·00
2825	€2.62 As No. 2820	8·75	8·00
2821/2825	Set of 5	20·00	19·00

(c) Booklet stamp. Self-adhesive. Die-cut perf 12×11½

2826	72c. As Type **610**	2·50	2·40
2827	72c. As No. 2817	2·50	2·40

Nos. 2821/2825 were printed in booklets of five panes, each with a single example, interleaved with 18 pages of text and illustrations and sold for €12.

No. 2826/2827, respectively, were each printed in booklets of ten stamps. The stamps are peeled from the booklet cover and cannot therefore be collected as panes.

610a Emblem

611 Eggs (April)

(Des Theano Venieri)

2014 (12 Apr). Thessaloniki. European Youth Capital 2014. T **610a** and similar multicoloured design. Multicoloured.

(a) Sheet stamp. Ordinary gum. P 14

2827a	90c. Type **610a**	3·00	2·75

(b) Booklet stamps. Size 28×40 mm. Self-adhesive. Die-cut perf 12×11½

2827b	90c. As Type **610a**	3·00	2·75

Nos. 2827a/2827b are as No. 2813

No. 2827a was issued in sheets of ten stamps and ten labels.

(Des Eleni Apostolou)

2014 (24 Apr). The 12 Months in Folk Art. T **611** and similar multicoloured designs.

(a) Coil Stamps. Ordinary gum. Imperf×14 (horiz) or 14×imperf (vert).

2828	2c. Type **611**	20	15
2829	20c. Wooden tools (July) (*vert*)	75	70
2830	40c. Elves using crosscut saw (December)	1·40	1·30
2831	50c. Pomegranates (January)	1·70	1·50
2832	72c. Swallows and ribbons (March)	2·50	2·40
2833	80c. Melons and beach (August)	2·75	2·50
2834	85c. Woven straw (June) (*vert*)	2·75	2·75
2835	90c. Goddess, candle and seeds (November)	3·00	2·75
2836	€1 Grapes (September)	3·50	3·25
2837	€2.62 Floral wreath (May)	9·00	8·50
2838	€3 Mask (February)	9·75	9·00
2839	€3.10 Ploughing (October)	10·50	9·75
2828/2839	Set of 12	43·00	40·00

(b) Booklet stamps. Self-adhesive. Die-cut perf 14

2840	72c. As No. 2832	2·50	2·40
2841	80c. As No. 2833	2·75	2·50

No. 2840/2841 respectively, were each printed in booklets of ten stamps. The stamps are peeled from the booklet cover and cannot therefore be collected as panes.

612 Cretan Lyra

(Des Myrsini Vardopoulou)

2014 (19 May). Europa. Musical Instruments. T **612** and similar horiz design. Multicoloured.

(a) Sheet stamps. P 14

2842	90c. Type **612**	3·00	2·75
	a. Pair. Nos. 2842/2843	15·00	14·50
2843	€3.40 Early muscian	11·50	11·00

(b) Booklet stamps. Imperf×p 14

2844	90c. As Type **612**	3·00	2·75
	a. Booklet pane. Nos. 2844/2845, each×2.	30·00	
2845	€3.40 As No. 2843	11·50	11·00

Nos. 2842/2843 were printed, *se-tenant*, in horizontal pairs within the sheet, each pair forming a composite design.

Nos. 2844/2845, each×2, were issued in booklets of four stamps.

613 Bicycle and Cyclists

(Des Mariana Lasithiotaki)

2014 (12 June). Ecologocal Transportation. The Bicycle. T **613** and similar square designs. Multicoloured.

(a) Sheet stamps. P 14

2846	72c. Type **613**	2·50	2·40
2847	72c. Child's training cycle	2·50	2·40
2848	80c. Woman's cycle	2·75	2·50
2849	€2 Folding cycle and train	7·25	6·75
2846/2849	Set of 4	13·50	12·50

(b) Booklet stamps. Self-adhesive. Die-cut perf 14

2850	72c. As Type **613**	2·50	2·40
2851	80c. As No. 2848	2·75	2·50

No. 2850/2851, respectively, were each printed in booklets of ten stamps. The stamps are peeled from the booklet cover and cannot therefore be collected as panes.

614 Competition Mascot

615 Mediterranean

(Des Myrsini Vardopoulou)

2014 (12 June). World Cup Football Championshisp, Brazil. T **614** and similar vert design. Multicoloured. P 14.

2852	90c. Type **614**		3·00	2·75
	a. Pair. Nos. 2852/2853		7·75	7·25
2853	€1.30 Player		4·50	4·25
MS2854	86×80 mm. 90c. As Type **614**		3·25	3·00
MS2855	86×80 mm. €1.13 As No. 2853		5·00	4·50

(Des Helen Apostollou. Litho Enschedé)

2014 (9 July). EUROMED. Euromed 2014 Postal Conference. Booklet Stamp. Imperf×14.

2856	**615**	€3 multicoloured	10·00	9·50
		a. Booklet pane. No. 2856×2	21·00	

No. 2856 was printed in booklets of two stamps.

616 Santorini

617 *Entombment of Christ* (detail)

2014 (8 Aug). Tourism. Visit Greece Campaign. T **616** and similar square designs. Multicoloured.

(a) Sheet stamps. Ordinary gum. P 14

2857	(80c.) Type **616**	4·50	4·25
2858	(80c.) Statues of Deer, harbour of Rhodes city, Rhodes island	4·50	4·25
2859	(80c.) Boat	4·50	4·25
2857/2859	Set of 3	12·00	11·50

(b) Booklet stamps. Size 40×40 mm. Self-adhesive. Die-cut perf 14

2860	(80c.) As Type **616**	2·75	2·50
2861	(80c.) As No. 2858	2·75	2·50
2862	(80c.) As No. 2859	2·75	2·50
2860/2862	Set of 3	7·50	6·75

Nos. 2857/2859 were each issued in sheets of ten stamps and ten labels.

(Des Myrsini Vardopoulou. Litho and gold foil die-stamped Enschedé)

2014 (10 Sept). 400th Death Anniversary of El Greco (Domenikos Theotokopoulos). Sheet 85×90 mm containing T **617** and similar vert design. Multicoloured. P 13½.

MS2863 €1 Type **617**; €1.50 Christ (detail from *Entombment of Christ*) .... 9·00 8·50

The stamps and margins of No. MS2863 form a composite design of the painting.

618 Kóstas Várnalis

(Litho Enschedé)

2014 (23 Oct). Contemporary Greek Writers. Multicoloured. P 13½×14.
2864 10c. Type **618** 35 30

2865	40c. Didó Sotiríou		1·40	1·30
2866	€2 Antonis Samarakis		7·00	6·50
2867	€2.10 Stratis Tsirkas		7·25	6·75
2864/2867	Set of 4		14·50	13·50

619 Tree of Presents

620 Misko (pasta company) (1928)

(Litho Giesecke and Devrient Matsoukis SA)

2014 (12 Dec). Christmas for Children. Booklet Stamps. T **619** and similar multicoloured designs. Multicoloured. Self-adhesive. Die-cut perf 14.

2868	72c. Type **619**	2·50	2·40
2869	72c. Elf and toys (42×42 *mm*)	2·50	2·40
2870	90c. Reindeer and toys	3·25	3·00
2871	90c. Sack of toys (42×42 *mm*)	3·25	3·00
2868/2871	Set of 4	10·50	9·75

(Litho Enschedé)

2014 (18 Dec). Memorable Advertisements. T **620** and similar vert design. Multicoloured.

(a) Sheet stamps. Ordinary gum. P 14×13½

2872	72c. Type **620**	2·50	2·40
2873	72c. Papadopoulos biscuits	2·50	2·40

(b) Booklet stamps. Self-adhesive. Die-cut perf 11½×12

2873a	72c. As Type **620**	2·50	2·40
2874	72c. As No. 2873	2·50	2·40

621 Pavlos Palaeologos (writer) and Dimitris Psathas (satirist)

(Litho and gold foil die-stamped)

2015 (21 Jan). Centenary of ESIEA. Journalists Union of Athens Daily Newspapers. T **621** and similar horiz designs. Multicoloured. P 13½×14.

2875	1c. Type **621**	20	15
2876	20c. Ioannis Iakovos Meyer (editor of *Greek Chronicles*) and Vlasis Gavrielides (journalist)	75	70
2877	50c. Maria Rezan and Nikos Karantinos (journalists)	1·70	1·50
2878	72c. Emilios Hourmouzios and Marios Ploritis (journalists, theatre critics and playwrights)	2·40	2·20
2879	€2.62 Emblems	9·00	8·50
2875/2879	Set of 5	12·50	11·50

622 Agios Nikolaos, Methana

2015 (26 Feb). Thermal Springs of Greece. T **622** and similar horiz designs. Multicoloured. P 14.

2880	5c. Type **622**	20	15
2881	10c. Loutraki Perachora	35	30
2882	23c. Ikaria	75	70
2883	72c. Thermae Sylla Spa and Wellness Hotel, Edipsos	2·40	2·20
2884	90c. Loutraki Aridaia	3·00	2·75

2885	€2 Vouliagmeni Lake		6·75	6·25
2880/2885	Set of 6		12·00	11·00

623 Bavarian 40-45, 1951

2015 (30 Mar). Railways of Greece. Steam Locomotives. T **623** and similar horiz designs. Multicoloured.

(a) Sheet stamps. Ordinary gum. P 14×13½
2886	20c. Type 623	75	70
2887	72c. Austrian La901-940, 1925–1927	2·50	2·40
2888	80c. American G401-420, 1915	2·75	2·50
2889	€2.50 French Z501-517, 1890–1901	9·00	8·50
2886/2889	Set of 4	13·50	12·50

(b) Booklet stamps. Self-adhesive. Die-cut perf 13½×12½
2890	72c. As No. 2887	2·50	2·40
2891	80c. As No. 2888	2·75	2·50

624 Dimitros Opropoulos and Spyros Moustaklis

(Litho and gold foil die-stamped)

2015 (21 Apr). Figures of Resistance Against the Greek Military Junta. T **624** and similar horiz designs. Multicoloured. P 13½×14.
2892	72c. Type 624	2·50	2·40
2893	72c. Nikiforos Mandilaras and Panagiotis Elis	2·50	2·40
2894	72c. Sakis Karagiorgas and Kostas Georgakis	2·50	2·40
2895	90c. Giorgos Tsarouhas and Giannis Halkidis	3·25	3·00
2892/2895	Set of 4	9·75	9·25

625 Spinning Top

(Litho)

2015 (11 May). Europa. Old Toys. T **625** and similar horiz design. Multicoloured.

(a) Sheet stamps. P 14
2896	90c. Type 625	3·00	2·75
	a. Pair. Nos. 2896/2897	15·00	14·50
2897	€3.40 Catapult and car	11·50	11·00

(b) Booklet stamps. Imperf×p 14
2898	90c. As Type 625	3·00	2·75
	a. Booklet pane. Nos. 2898/2899	15·00	
2899	€3.40 As No. 2897	11·50	11·00

Nos. 2896/2897 were printed, *se-tenant*, in horizontal pairs within the sheet, each pair forming a composite design.
Nos. 2898/2899, were issued in booklets of two stamps.

626 Ships

627 Owl wearing Mortarboard

(Des Myrsini Vardropoulou. Litho Enschedé)

2015 (20 May). Anniversaries. European Maritime Day. Piraeus 2015 (No. 2902) or European Sea Ports Organisation (ESPO) Congress 2015 (others). T **626** and similar horiz designs. Multicoloured. P 13½×14.
2900	72c. Type 626	2·50	2·40
2901	80c. Ship and mooring	2·75	2·50
2902	80c. Stylised yachtsman	2·75	2·50
2900/2902	Set of 3	7·25	6·75

(Des Anthoula Lyga. Litho Enschedé)

2015 (11 June). Personalised Stamps. Three sheets, each 100×100 mm, containing T **627** and similar square designs. Multicoloured. P 14×13½.
MS2903	Type 627; 72c. Sun and birds; 72c. Rainbow, envelopes and aircraft; 90c. Handshake	11·50	10·50
MS2904	Bride and groom riding bicycles; 72c. Pram; 72c. Birds kissing enclosed in heart; 90c. Balloons carrying baby in sling	11·50	10·50
MS2905	Flag; 72c. Birds from illustrated missal; 90c. Ionic capital; 90c. Early Greek stylised Horses	12·00	11·00

628 Fishing Boat

629 Diver

(Des Anthoula Lyga. Litho Enschedé)

2015 (9 July). EUROMED. Boats of the Mediterranean.

(a) Sheet stamps. P 14
2906	628	€3 multicoloured	10·00	9·50

(b) Booklet stamps. Imperf×p 14
2906a	€3 As Type 628	10·00	9·50
	aa. Booklet pane. No. 2906a×2	21·00	

No. 2906a was printed in booklets of two stamps.

(Des Helen Apostolou. Litho)

2015 (20 July). Tourism. Visit Greece Campaign. Diving. T **629** and similar horiz designs. Multicoloured.

(a) Sheet stamps. Ordinary gum. P 14
2907	10c. Type 629	35	30
2908	50c. Diver and pot	1·80	1·70
2909	80c. Diver and elongated Sea Sponges	2·75	2·50
2910	80c. Diver and Byzantine wreck	2·75	2·50
2911	€1.62 Diver and sarcophagus, Sapientza	5·50	5·25
2912	€2 Diver and Fan Coral	7·00	6·50
2907/2912	Set of 6	18·00	17·00

(b) Booklet stamp. Self-adhesive. Die-cut perf 13
2913	80c. As No. 2909	2·75	2·50
2914	80c. As No. 2910	2·75	2·50

630 Volcano, Milos

631 Portrait of Thomas Flangini (oil painting, 17th-century)

(Des Myrsini Vardopoulou. Litho Enschedé)

2015 (5 Sept). Volcanoes of Greece. T **630** and similar horiz designs showing volcanoes. Multicoloured. P 13½×14.
2915	1c. Type 630	20	15
2916	20c. Nisyros	60	55
2917	€1 Santorini	3·25	3·00
2918	€2 Nisyros *(different)*	7·00	6·50
2915/2918	Set of 4	10·00	9·25

(Des Theano Venieri. Litho and foil die-stamped Enschedé)

2015 (9 Oct). 350th Anniversary of Flangini College. T **631** and similar vert designs. Multicoloured. P 14×13½.
2919	3c. Type 631	20	15
2920	72c. Panagia (engraving, late 18th-century)	2·40	2·20

2921	€1.50 Flangini College (detail of engraving by Domenico Lovisa, 18th-century)		5·25	5·00
2922	€2 Emblem of Hellenic Institute of Byzantine and Post-Byzantine Studies in Venice		7·00	6·50
2919/2922 Set of 4			13·50	12·50

632 Ant and Moneybox

(Des Myrsini Vardopoulou. Litho and foil die-stamped Giesecke & Devrient Matsoukis SA)

2015 (30 Oct). 115th Anniversary of Greek Postal Savings Bank. Sheet 68×90 mm.
MS2923 **632** €1 multicoloured .... 3·50 3·25

633 Exhibition Emblem   **634** Chinese Junk and Greek Trireme

(Des Myrsini Vardopoulou. Litho Giesecke & Devrient Matsoukis SA)

2015 (4 Nov). Anniversaries. 70th Anniversary of United Nations (No. 2926) or NOTOS 2015 International Philatelic Exhibition (others). T **633** and similar multicoloured designs. Multicoloured. P 13½×14.

2924	72c. Type **633**	2·40	2·20
2925	90c. Origami Dove	3·25	3·00
2926	€1 '70' (vert)	3·50	3·25
2924/2926 Set of 3		8·25	7·50
MS2927 78×90 mm. €1.62 As Nos. 2924/2925		5·75	5·25

(Des Myrsini Vardopoulou. Litho Giesecke & Devrient Matsoukis SA)

2015 (4 Nov). International Year of Maritime Co-operation between Greece and China. Sheet 68×90 mm. P 14.
MS2928 **634** €3 multicoloured .... 10·50 9·75

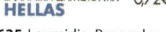

635 Loumidis–Papagalos   **636** Thessaloniki and Haifa (symbols of Greece and Israel)

(Des Anthoula Lyga. Litho (and foil die-stamped (No. 2929)) Giesecke & Devrient Matsoukis SA)

2015 (14 Dec). Company Trademarks. T **635** and similar vert designs. Multicoloured. P 14.

2929	72c. Type **635**	2·40	2·20
2930	72c. Sun Spices	2·40	2·20
2931	72c. Attiki Honey	2·40	2·20
2932	72c. Pitsos Household Appliances	2·40	2·20
2933	90c. Hatzopoulos Packing Company (85th anniversary)	3·25	3·00
2929/2933 Set of 5		11·50	10·50

(Des Eleni Apostolou. Litho Giesecke & Devrient Matsoukis SA)

2016 (9 Feb). 25th Anniversary of Greece–Israel Diplomatic Relations. P 14.

2934	**636** 90c. multicoloured	3·00	2·75
MS2935 68×90 mm. 90c. As Type **636**		3·25	3·00

Stamps of a similar design were issued by Israel.

637 Kostas Maragoudakis

(Des Theano Venieri. Litho Veridos Matsoukis SA)

2016 (23 Feb). 75th Anniversary of National Liberation Front (EAM). T **637** and similar horiz designs. Multicoloured. P 14½×14.

2936	20c. Type **637**	75	70
2937	50c. Apostolos Santas (Lakis)	1·80	1·70
2938	€1 Manolis Glezos	3·50	3·25
2939	€2 Vardis Vardinogiannis	7·00	6·50
2940	€2.10 Stelios Zamanos	7·25	6·75
2936/2940 Set of 5		18·00	17·00

638 Central Bank (E. Troump)   **639** Emblem

(Des Myrsini Vardopoulou. Litho, embossed and gold foil die-stamped Veridos Matsoukis SA)

2016 (30 Mar). 175th Anniversary of National Bank. T **638** and similar horiz designs. Multicoloured. P 14.

2941	5c. Type **638**	20	15
2942	10c. Ludwig Square (J. Rabe)	35	30
2943	50c. The First Governors (G. Iakovidis)	1·70	1·50
2944	€2.62 Karatzas Building, 2002	9·00	8·50
2941/2944 Set of 4		10·00	9·50

(Des Eleni Apostolou. Litho Veridos Matsoukis SA)

2016 (18 Apr). 2016. Year of Greece in Russia. T **639** and similar vert designs. Multicoloured. P 13½.

2945	80c. Type **639**	2·75	2·50
2946	80c. Coil (symbol of civilisation)	2·75	2·50
2947	80c. Ionic pillar capital and onion domes (tourism)	2·75	2·50
2948	90c. 'www.elrv2016.gr' (communication)	3·25	3·00
2945/2948 Set of 4		10·50	9·50
MS2949 156×116 mm. €3.30 As Nos. 2945/2948		11·50	11·00

640 Sotiris Paraskevaides

(Des Myrsini Vardopoulou. Litho Veridos Matsoukis SA)

2016 (21 Apr). Greek Labour Movement. T **640** and similar horiz designs. Multicoloured. P 14.

2950	5c. Type **640**	25	20
2951	50c. Tasos Tuscon	1·70	1·50
2952	€1 Napoleon Soukatzidis	3·50	3·25
2953	€2 Kostas Theos	7·00	6·50
2950/2953 Set of 4		11·00	10·50

641 Roller painting Contaminated Landscape Green   **642** Aristotle

(Des Doxia Sergidou (Nos. 2954 and 2956) or Mirsini Vardopoulou (others). Litho Veridos Matsoukis SA)

2016 (11 May). Europa. Think Green. T **641** and similar horiz design. Multicoloured.

(a) Sheet stamps. P 14

2954	90c. Type **641**	3·00	2·75
	a. Pair. Nos. 2954/2955	15·00	14·50
2955	€3.40 Green tree and hills	11·50	11·00

(b) Booklet stamps. Imperf×p 14

2956	90c. As Type **641**	3·00	2·75
	a. Booklet pane. Nos. 2956/2957, each×2	30·00	
2957	€3.40 As No. 2955	11·50	11·00

Post Europ decided that member countries should issue a joint stamp, 'Think Green', to that end a design-a-stamp competition was held which was won by Doxia Sergidou of Cyprus.

Nos. 2954/2955 were printed, *se-tenant*, in horizontal pairs within the sheet.

Nos. 2956/2957, each×2, were issued in booklets of four stamps.

(Des Iannis Gourzis. Litho Veridos Matsoukis SA)

2016 (23 May). 2400th Birth Anniversary of Aristotle.

(a) Ordinary gum. P 14

2958	72c. Type **642**	2·40	2·20
2959	80c. Aristotle and Alexander	2·75	2·50
2960	€1 Aristotle and Plato	3·50	3·25
2958/2960	Set of 3	7·75	7·25
MS2961	64×74 mm. As No. 2958	2·50	2·40
MS2962	64×74 mm. As No. 2959	3·00	2·75
MS2963	64×74 mm. As No. 2960	3·75	3·50

(b) Booklet stamps. Self-adhesive. Die-cut perf 14

2964	72c. As Type **642**	2·40	2·20
2965	80c. As No. 2959	2·75	2·50

Nos. 2964/2965, respectively, were each issued in booklets of ten stamps.

643 Bartholomew I

(Des Anthoula Linga. Veridos Matsoukis SA)

2016 (10 June). Anniversaries. 25th Anniversary of Ecumenical Patriarch Bartholomew. Sheet 81×90 mm containing T **643** and similar vert design. Multicoloured. P 14.

MS2966 Type **643**; €1 Seal .... 6·75 6·25

644 Emblem

(Des Anthoula Linga. Veridos Matsoukis SA)

2016 (16 June). The Holy and Great Council of the Orthodox Church. Sheet 81×91 mm. P 14.

MS2967 **644** multicoloured .... 3·25 3·00

645 Sotiris Petroulas   **646** Gymnast

(Des Anthoula Linga. Veridos Matsoukis SA)

2016 (8 July). Members of the Lambrakis Youth Movement. T **645** and similar horiz designs. Multicoloured. P 14.

2968	20c. Type **645**	75	70
2969	72c. Andreas Lentakis	2·40	2·20
2970	80c. Mikis Theodorakis	2·75	2·50
2971	€2 Christos Rekleitis	7·00	6·50
2968/2971	Set of 4	11·50	10·50

(Des Myrsini Vardopoulou)

2016 (8 July). Olympic Games, Rio 2016. T **646** and similar vert design. Multicoloured. P 14.

2972	80c. Type **646**	2·75	2·75
2973	90c. Runner	3·25	3·00

647 Fish   **648** Rita Wilson

(Des Myrsini Vardopoulos. Veridos Matsoukis SA)

2016 (8 July). EUROMED. Fish of the Mediterranean. P 14.

2974 **647** €3 multicoloured .... 10·00 9·50

(Des Anthoula Linga. Veridos Matsoukis SA)

2016 (1 Sept). Personalities. Greek Personalities living Abroad. T **648** and similar vert designs. Multicoloured. P 14×14½.

2975	72c. Type **648**	2·40	2·20
2976	80c. Costas Gavras	2·75	2·50
2977	90c. John Katsimatidis	3·25	3·25
2978	€1 George Stefanopoulos	3·50	3·25
2979	€1.20 Peter Diamandis	4·25	4·00
2975/2979	Set of 5	14·50	13·50

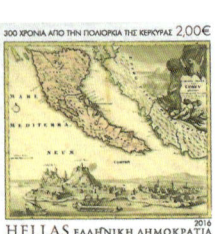 

649 Map   **650** Early Marathon Runner

(Des Myrsini Vardopoulos.)

2016 (20 Oct). 300th Anniversary of the Siege of Corfu. P 14.

2980 **649** €2 multicoloured .... 7·00 6·50

2016 GREECE

(Des Myrsini Vardopoulos. Veridos Matsoukis SA)

2016 (10 Nov). 120th Anniversary of First Marathon of the Modern Olympics. Sheet 76×96 mm containing T **650** and similar vert design. Multicoloured. P 14.

MS2981	90c. Type **650**; €2.10 Modern runner	10·50	9·75

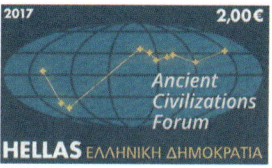

655 Emblem

(Des Stratos Efthimiou and Anthoula Lygka)

2017 (24 Apr). Ancient Civilisations Forum. Athens 2017. Sheet 110×80 mm. P 14.

MS3009	**655**	€2 multicoloured	7·25	6·75

651 Early TV exploding into Modern Flat Screen TV
652 *Cistus creticus*

(Des Myrsini Vardopoulos. Veridos Matsoukis SA)

2016 (24 Nov). 50th Anniversary of ERT (state television). P 14.

2982	**651**	€1.50 multicoloured	5·00	4·75

656 Emblem

(Des Anthoula Lygka. Litho and foil die-stamped Veridos Matsoukis SA)

2017 (11 May). 80th Anniversary of the Apostoliki Diakonia of the Church of Greece. T **656** and similar multicoloured design. P 14.

3010	72c. Type **656**	2·50	2·40
MS3011	70×90 mm. €2 Saint Helen (*vert*)	7·25	6·75

(Des Anthoula Linga. Veridos Matsoukis SA)

2016 (14 Dec). Flora. Flowering Herbs of Greece. T **652** and similar vert designs. Multicoloured. P 14.

2983	20c. Type **652**	75	70
2984	40c. *Origanum dictamus*	1·40	1·30
2985	50c. *Hypericum empetrifolium*	1·80	1·70
2986	72c. *Sideritis clandestina*	2·50	2·40
2987	€1 *Origanum vulgare*	3·50	3·25
2988	€2.62 *Salvia fruticosa*	9·00	8·50
2983/2988	Set of 6	17·00	16·00

653 The Kiss
654 Art

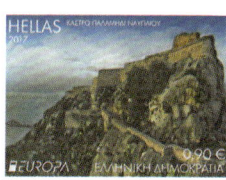 

657 Castle of Palamidi, Nafplio
658 Conifer oozing Resin and Ancient Trees

(Des Myrsini Vardopoulou. Veridos Matsoukis SA)

2017 (15 Mar). 150th Anniversary of National Archaeological Museum. T **653** and similar multicoloured designs.

(a) Ordinary gum. P 14

2989	10c. Type **653**	35	30
2990	50c. Odysseus of Antikythera (*vert*)	1·70	1·50
2991	72c. Diadoumenos (*vert*)	2·50	2·40
2992	90c. Poseidon of Livadostra (*vert*)	3·25	3·00
2993	€1.50 Athenian Youth (fresco) (*vert*)	5·00	4·75
2994	€2 The Mycenaean Lady (fresco)	7·00	6·50
2989/2994	Set of 6	18·00	17·00
MS2995	90×70 mm. 10c. As Type **653**	45	40
MS2996	70×90 mm. 50c. As No. 2990	1·80	1·70
MS2997	70×90 mm. 72c. As No. 2991	2·75	2·50
MS2998	70×90 mm. 90c. As No. 2992	3·25	3·00
MS2999	70×90 mm. €1.50 As No. 2993	5·25	5·00
MS3000	90×70 mm. €2 As No. 2994	7·25	6·75

(b) Booklet stamp. Self-adhesive. Die-cut perf 14

3001	72c. As No. 2991	2·50	2·40

No. 3001 was issued in booklets of ten stamps.

(Des Myrsini Vardopoulou. Veridos Matsoukis SA)

2017 (18 May). Europa. Castles. T **657** and similar horiz design. Multicoloured.

(a) Sheet stamps. P 14

3012	90c. Type **657**	3·00	2·75
	a. Horiz pair. Nos. 3012/3013	15·00	14·50
3013	€3.40 Castle of Methoni	11·50	11·00

(b) Booklet stamps. Imperf×p 13

3014	90c. As Type **657**	3·00	2·75
	a. Booklet pane. Nos. 3014/3015	15·00	
3015	€3.40 As No. 3013	11·50	11·00

Nos. 3012/3013 were printed, *se-tenant*, in horizontal pairs within the sheet, each pair forming a composite design.

Nos. 3014/3015 were issued in booklets of two stamps.

(Des Myrsini Vardopoulos. Veridos Matsoukis SA)

2017 (27 June). EUROMED. Trees of the Mediterranean. P 14.

3016	**658**	€2.62 multicoloured	9·00	8·50
MS3017	70×90 mm. €2.62 As Type **658**		9·25	8·75

(Des Anthoula Lyga. Veridos Matsoukis SA)

2017 (7 Apr). Personalised Stamps. T **654** and similar square designs. Multicoloured.

(a) Ordinary gum. P 14

3002	72c. Type **654**	2·50	2·40
3003	72c. Music	2·50	2·40
3004	72c. Literature	2·50	2·40
3005	72c. Athletics	2·50	2·40
3006	80c. Tourism	2·75	2·50
3007	90c. Winery	3·25	3·00
3002/3007	Set of 6	14·50	13·50

(b) Booklet stamp. Self-adhesive. Die-cut perf 14

3008	80c. As No. 3006	2·75	2·50

No. 3008 was issued in booklets of ten stamps.

659 Chilon of Sparta
660 Chinese Costume

GREECE 2017

(Des Theano Venieri and Iannis Gourzis.
Veridos Matsoukis SA)

2017 (27 July). The Seven Wise Men of Greek Antiquity. T **659** and similar vert designs. Multicoloured. P 14.

3018	5c. Type **659**		20	15
3019	10c. Cleobulus of Lindos		40	35
3020	20c. Periander of Corinth		75	70
3021	50c. Pittacus of Mytilene		1·70	1·50
3022	80c. Solon of Athens		2·75	2·50
3023	€1 Thales of Miletus		3·50	3·25
3024	€2 Bias of Priene		7·00	6·50
3018/3024	Set of 7		14·50	13·50

(Des Myrsini Vardopoulou. Veridos Matsoukis SA)

2017 (8 Sept). Year of Cultural Exchange and Cultural Co-operation between Greece and China. T **660** and similar designs. P 14.

3025	50c. multicoloured	1·80	1·70
3026	90c. emerald, myrtle-green and black (*horiz*)	3·25	3·00
3027	€2 multicoloured	7·00	6·50
3025/3027	Set of 3	11·00	10·00
MS3028	105×70 mm. 90c. emerald, myrtle-green and black (*horiz*)	3·50	3·25
MS3029	105×70 mm.€2.50 multicoloured	9·00	8·50

Designs: 50c. T **660**; 90c. Olive branch and Bamboo (emblem); €2 Greek costume; No. **MS**3028 As No. 3026; No. **MS**3029 As Nos. 3025 and 3027.

661 Memorial to the Fallen in the Battle of Power Station

662 Alexandros Argyropoulos

(Des Theano Venieri. Veridos Matsoukis SA)

2017 (11 Oct). World War II. The Battle of the Athens-Piraeus Electric Company's Plant, Keratsini. P 14.

3030	50c. multicoloured	1·80	1·70
3031	€1 black (*horiz*)	3·50	3·25
MS3032	70×105 mm. 50c. multicoloured	2·00	1·80
MS3033	105×70 mm.€1 black (*horiz*)	3·75	3·50

Designs: 50c. T **661**; €1 Engraving of the battle by Thomas Molos; No. **MS**3031 As T **661**; No. **MS**3032 As No. 3030.

(Des Marina Lasithiotaki. Veridos Matsoukis SA)

2017 (16 Nov). Figures from Greek Philately. T **662** and similar vert designs. Multicoloured. P 14.

3034	5c. Type **662**		20	15
3035	20c. Charilis Binos		75	70
3036	72c. Moses Konstantinis		2·50	2·40
3037	90c. Georgios Papastephano		3·25	3·00
3038	€1.50 Stephanos Makrymichalos		5·00	4·75
3039	€2.50 Nikolaos Atzaritis		8·75	8·00
3034/3039	Set of 6		18·00	17·00

663 Artemis

664 Penguin

(Des Theano Venieri. Veridos Matsoukis SA)

2017 (24 Nov). The Sanctuary of Artemis Amarynthia. P 14.

3040	**663**	€1 multicoloured	3·50	3·25
MS3041	70×90 mm. €1 As Type **663**		3·75	3·50

(Des Anthoula Lygka)

2017 (5 Dec). Christmas. T **664** and similar vert designs. Multicoloured.

(a) Sheet stamps. Ordinary gum. P 14

3042	72c. Type **664**	2·50	2·40
	a. Strip of 4. Nos. 3042/3045	11·00	
3043	72c. Deer	2·50	2·40
3044	72c. Squirrel	2·50	2·40
3045	90c. Bear	3·25	3·00
3042/3045	Set of 4	9·75	9·25

(b) Booklet stamps. Self-adhesive. Die-cut 14

3046	72c. As No. 3043	2·50	2·40
3047	90c. As No. 3045	3·25	3·00

Nos. 3042/3045 were printed, *se-tenant*, in horizontal strips of four stamps, each strip forming a composite design.
Nos. 3046/3047, respectively, were each printed in booklets of ten stamps.

665 MTPY Building

666 Myrtis

(Des Marina Lasithiotaki. Veridos Matsoukis SA)

2017 (8 Dec). 150th Anniversary of the Civil Servants Joint Stock Fund (MTPY). T **665** and similar vert designs. Multicoloured. P 14.

3048	72c. Type **665**	2·50	2·40
3049	€2.50 Dimitrios N. Levidis (founder of MTPY)	8·75	8·00

(Des Anthoula Linga. Veridos Matsoukis SA)

2018 (15 Feb). Classical Antiquity. Myrtis (reconstruction of young girl's head from skeletal remains). Sheet 70×90 mm. P 14.

MS3050 **666**	€1.50 multicoloured	5·75	5·25

667 Symbols of Gender

(Des Myrsini Vardopoulou. Litho and varnish (90c.) or litho (other) Veridos Matsoukis SA)

2018 (8 Mar). International Women's Day. T **667** and similar design. Multicoloured. P 14.

3051	72c. Type **667**	2·50	2·40
3052	90c. Woman's profile and Rose (*vert*)	3·25	3·00

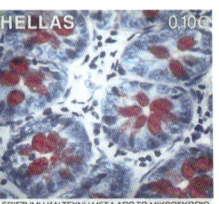

668 Flowers

(Des Marina Lasithiotaki. Veridos Matsoukis SA)

2018 (19 Mar). Science reveals Art through the Microscope. T **668** and similar square designs. Multicoloured. P 14.

3053	10c. Type **668**	40	35
3054	20c. Butterfly	75	70
3055	72c. Heart	2·50	2·40
3056	€1 Wreath	3·50	3·25
3057	€2 Deer	7·00	6·50
3053/3057	Set of 5	12·50	12·00

2018 GREECE

669 AEK Emblem   670 Ioánnis Fokás

(Des Anthoula Lygka. Veridos Matsoukis SA)

2018 (30 Mar). Basketball. 50th Anniversary of AEK Winning the FIBA European Cup Winners' Cup. T **669** and similar horiz design. Multicoloured. P 14.
3058	72c. Type **669**	2·50	2·40
3059	90c. Panathenaic Stadium	3·25	3·00
MS3060	110×75 mm. 72c. As Type **669**	2·75	2·50
MS3061	110×75 mm. 90c. As No. 3059	3·50	3·25

(Des Marina Lasithiotaki. Veridos Matsoukis SA)

2018 (24 Apr). Ioánnis Fokás (Juan de Fuca) (first Seafarer in Southwest Canada) Commemoration. Sheet 90×70 mm. P 14.
MS3062	**670** €2.50 multicoloured	9·00	8·50

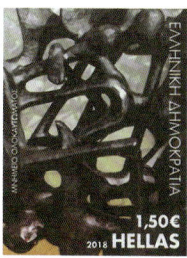 

671 Holocaust Monument   672 Bee

(Des Eleni Apostolou. Veridos Matsoukis SA)

2018 (16 May). The Holocaust of Greek Jews. Three sheets containing T **671** and similar multicoloured designs. P 14.
MS3063	70×85 mm. €1.50 Type **671**	5·75	5·25
MS3064	85×70 mm. €1.50 Monasteriotes' Synagogue (horiz)	5·75	5·25
MS3065	85×70 mm. €1.50 Holocaust Museum in Thessaloniki (horiz)	5·75	5·25

(Des Anthoula Lyngka. Veridos Matsoukis SA)(horiz)

2018 (20 May). World Bee Day. *Apes mellifera*. T **672** and similar horiz designs. Multicoloured. P 14.
3066	50c. Type **672**	1·80	1·70
3067	72c. On honeycomb	2·50	2·40
3068	80c. Two Bees	2·75	2·50
3069	€2 Collecting pollen	7·00	6·50
3066/3069	Set of 4	12·50	12·00
MS3070	90×70 mm. 50c. As Type **672**	2·00	1·80
MS3071	90×70 mm. 72c. As No. 3067	2·75	2·50
MS3072	90×70 mm. 80c. As No. 3068	3·00	2·75
MS3073	90×70 mm. €2 As No. 3069	7·25	6·75

673 Anniversary Emblem   674 Rio Antirrio Bridge

(Des Theanos Venieri. Veridos Matsoukis SA)

2018 (21 May). Centenary of the General Confederation of Greek Workers. Sheet 90×80 mm containing T **673** and similar square design. Multicoloured. P 14.
MS3074	€1×2, Type **673**; Members of the Confederation	7·25	6·75

(Des Myrsini Vardopoulou. Giesecke & Devrient Matsoukis SA)

2018 (24 May). Europa. Bridges. T **674** and similar horiz design. Multicoloured.

(a) Sheet stamps. P 14
3075	90c. Type **674**	3·00	2·75
	a. Pair. Nos. 3075/3076	15·00	14·50
3076	€3.40 Plaka Bridge	11·50	11·00

(b) Booklet stamps. Imperf×p 13
3077	90c. As Type **674**	3·00	2·75
	a. Booklet pane. Nos. 3077/3078	15·00	
3078	€3.40 As No. 3076	11·50	11·00

Nos. 3075/3076 were printed, *se-tenant*, in horizontal pairs within the sheet.

Nos. 3077/3078 were issued in booklets of two stamps.

675 Hellenic Army Academy Emblem   676 Nikolaos Psaroudakis

(Des Theano Venieri. Giesecke & Devrient Matsoukis SA)

2018 (15 June). 190th Anniversary of the Hellenic Army Academy. T **675** and similar multicoloured designs. P 14.
3079	72c. Type **675**	2·50	2·40
3080	80c. Ioánnis Kapodístrias awards a decoration to a cadet	2·75	2·50
3081	€1 Lowering the Flag (horiz)	3·50	3·25
3082	€2.62 Cadet	9·00	8·50
3079/3082	Set of 4	16·00	15·00

(Des Theano Venieri. Litho and gold foil die-stamped (90c.) or litho (others) Giesecke & Devrient Matsoukis SA)

2018 (19 June). Anniversaries. T **676** and similar vert designs. Multicoloured. P 14.
3083	72c. Type **676** (founder of the Christian Democracy newspaper and movement) (birth centenary)	2·50	2·40
3084	80c. Mathematical symbols (centenary of Hellenic mathematical society)	2·75	2·50
3085	90c. Emblem (25th anniversary of Inter-Parliamentary Assembly on Orthodoxy) (32×42 mm)	3·00	2·75
3083/3085	Set of 4	7·50	7·00

677 Mansion, Pelion   678 Erotokritos and Aretousa

(Des Myrsini Vardopoulos. Veridos Matsoukis SA)

2018 (20 July). EUROMED. Houses of the Mediterranean. T **677** and similar vert designs. P 14.

(a) Sheet stamps. P 13½×14
3086	72c. Type **677**	2·50	2·40
3087	72c. Tower, Mani	2·50	2·40
3088	80c. A Cycladic house	2·75	2·50
3089	90c. Dodecanese house	3·00	2·75
3086/3089	Set of 4	9·75	9·00

(b) Booklet stamps. Imperf×p 14
3090	72c. As Type **677**	2·50	2·40
	a. Booklet pane. Nos. 3090/3093	11·00	

3091	72c. As No. 3087		2·50	2·40
3092	80c. As No. 3088		2·75	2·50
3093	90c. As No. 3089		3·00	2·75
3090/3093 Set of 4			9·75	9·00

(c) Miniature sheets. 100×80 mm. P 14

MS3094 As Type **677**		2·75	2·50
MS3095 As No. 3087		2·75	2·50
MS3096 As No. 3088		3·00	2·75
MS3097 As No. 3089		3·25	3·00

Nos. 3090/3093 were printed in booklets of four stamps.

(Des Anthoula Lygka. Veridos Matsoukis SA)

2018 (25 July). Centenary of Museum of Modern Greek Culture. Two sheets 70×85 mm containing T **678** and similar vert design. Multicoloured. P 14.

MS3098 Type **678**		3·75	3·50
MS3099 Alexander the Great		3·75	3·50

679 Emblem

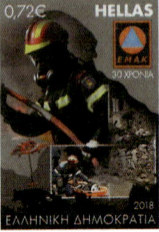
680 Firefighter

(Litho and foil die-stamped)

2018 (25 Aug). 125th Anniversary of Corinth Canal. Booklet Stamp. Self-adhesive. Die-cut perf 14.

3100	**679**	(72c.) multicoloured	2·50	2·40

No. 3100 was issued in booklets of ten stamps.
The stamps are peeled from the booklet cover.

(Des Theano Venieri. Giesecke & Devrient Matsoukis SA)

2018 (5 Sept). Anniversaries. T **680** and similar multicoloured designs. P 14.

3101	72c.	Type **380** (30th anniversary of Special Disaster Response Unit (EMAK))	2·50	2·40
3102	80c.	Emblem (83rd Thessaloniki International Trade Fair) (*horiz*)	2·75	2·50
3103	€1	Building (50␣anniversary of Orthodox Academy of Crete (OAC)) (*horiz*)	3·50	3·25
3101/3103 Set of 3			8·00	7·25

681 Il Duce (*Duce Narrates* by Stamatis Polenakis)

(Litho and foil die-stamped)

2018 (27 Sept). 11th Syros International Animation Festival and Fair (Anima Syros 11). Booklet Stamps. T **681** and similar horiz designs. Multicoloured. Self-adhesive. Die-cut wavy edge (interrupted).

3104	80c.	Type **681**	2·75	2·50
3105	80c.	Pandora and Plato (*The Strawberry Birds* by Nikos Vergitsis and Giorgos Nikoloulias)	2·75	2·50
3106	80c.	Granny (*My Stuffed Granny* by Effie Pappa)	2·75	2·50
3107	80c.	Family (by Aliki Theofilopoulos)	2·75	2·50
3108	80c.	Festival emblem	2·75	2·50
3104/3108 Set of 5			12·50	11·50

Nos. 3104/3108, each×2, were issued in booklets of ten stamps.
The stamps are peeled from the booklet cover.

682 Socrates

683 'POSTES HELLENIQUES'

(Litho and foil die-stamped)

2018 (1 Oct). Centenary of Greece–Ethiopia Diplomatic Relations. *Socrates' Life*, play by the National Ethiopian Theatre at the Odeon of Herodes Atticus, Athens. Booklet Stamps. T **682** and similar horiz designs. Multicoloured. Self-adhesive. Die-cut perf 13.

3109	(72c.)	Type **682**	2·50	2·40
3110	(72c.)	Flags of Greece and Ethiopia	2·50	2·40
3111	(72c.)	Head of Socrates containing stars ('Ethiopia Socrates in the Heroic')	2·50	2·40
3109/3111 Set of 3			6·75	6·50

Nos. 3109/3110, each×4, and No. 3111×2, were issued in booklets of ten stamps.
The stamps are peeled from the booklet cover.

(Des Myrsini Vardopoulou. Veridos Matsoukis SA)

2018 (9 Oct). 190th Anniversary of Hellenic Post. T **683** and similar vert designs. Multicoloured. P 14.

3112	10c.	Type **683**	40	35
3113	50c.	Early brown metal wall-mounted post box	1·80	1·70
3114	72c.	Modern yellow 'ΕΛΤΑ' post box	2·50	2·40
3115	€2.62	Early post box with peaked roof	9·00	8·50
3112/3115 Set of 4			12·50	11·50

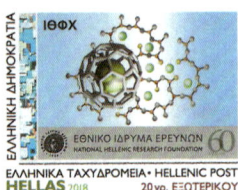
684 Cell Structures

(Litho and foil die-stamped)

2018 (10 Oct). 60th Anniversary of National Hellenic Research Foundation (EIE). Booklets Stamps. T **684** and similar horiz designs. Multicoloured. Self-adhesive. Die-cut perf 13.

3116	(72c.)	Type **684**	2·50	2·40
3117	(72c.)	Research equipment	2·50	2·40
3118	(72c.)	'EKT'	2·50	2·40
3119	(72c.)	Institute building	2·50	2·40
3120	(72c.)	Anniversary emblem	2·50	2·40
3121	(72c.)	Research equipment detail	2·50	2·40
3122	(72c.)	Nerve tangles	2·50	2·40
3123	(72c.)	Book shelves	2·50	2·40
3124	(72c.)	Library	2·50	2·40
3116/3124 Set of 9			20·00	19·00

Nos. 3116/3123 and No. 3124×2, were printed in booklets of ten stamps.
No. 3124 was also printed in booklets of ten stamps.
In both booklets the stamps were peeled from the booklet cover.

685 Symbols of Union

686 Father Christmas

2018 GREECE / Machine Labels

(Litho and holography)

2018 (16 Nov). 70th Anniversary of Union of the Dodecanese with Greece. Booklet Stamp. Multicoloured. Self-adhesive. Die-cut perf 13.

| 3125 | **685** | (72c.) multicoloured | 2·40 | 2·50 |

No. 3125 was printed in booklets of ten stamps.

(Des Anthoula Lygka. Litho Veridos Matsoukis SA)

2018 (23 Nov). Christmas. T **686** and similar multicoloured designs.

(a) Sheet stamps. Ordinary gum. Size 34×44 mm. P14

3126	72c. Type **686**	2·50	2·40
3127	72c. Girl writing Christmas letter	2·50	2·40
3128	80c. Posting letter	2·75	2·50
3129	90c. Opening present	3·00	2·75

(b) Sheet stamps. Ordinary gum. Size 29×29 mm. P 14

| 3130 | 72c. As Type **686** | 2·50 | 2·40 |

(c) Booklet stamps. Self-adhesive. Die-cut 14

| 3131 | 72c. As Type **686** | 2·50 | 2·40 |
| 3132 | 80c. As No. 3127 | 2·75 | 2·50 |

687 Telecommunications Satellite

(Des Myrsini Vardopoulou. Litho Veridos Matsoukis SA)

2018 (30 Nov). Hellenic Space Agency. Sheet 90×70 mm. P 14.

| MS3133 | **687** | €2.50 multicoloured | 8·75 | 8·25 |

(Litho Veridos Matsoukis SA)

2018 (7 Dec). 190th Anniversary of Greece-Russia Diplomatic Relations. Booklet Stamps. Two vert designs showing symbols of Russia and Greece. Multicoloured. Self-adhesive. Die-cut perf 14.

| 3134 | (72c.) Ioánnis Antónios | 2·50 | 2·40 |
| 3135 | (72c.) Greek and Russian flags | 2·50 | 2·40 |

T **688** is unavailable.

689 Residential Guard

(Des Kostas I. Spyriounis. Litho and gold foil die-stamped Veridos Matsoukis SA)

2018 (12 Dec). 180th Anniversary of the Presidential Guard. T **689** and similar multicoloured designs. P 14.

3136	5c. Type **689**	20	15
3137	10c. Guards marching (*horiz*)	40	35
3138	20c. Group of guards (*horiz*)	75	70
3139	€1 Guard facing left in silhouette	3·50	3·25
3140	€2 Guard against national flag	7·00	6·50
3136/3140	Set of 5	10·50	9·75

MACHINE LABELS

All Greek Frama labels were printed in red.

A

1984 (26 Mar). T **A** in red. Number in the bottom frame indicates issuing machine. Face values 1 to 999d. in 1d. steps.

26.3.84 Nos. 2/3 and 6/9
28.6.84 Nos. 1, 4/5 and 10

Machine Number 001 Rhodes airport (withdrawn November 1987)
002 Athens East Airport (withdrawn 26.1.88)
003 Thessaloniki Central PO (withdrawn 28.1.88)
004 Heraklion Airport (withdrawn November 1987)
005 Corfu Airport (withdrawn November 1987)
006 Piraeus Central PO (withdrawn November 1987)
007 Syntagma Square PO, Athens (withdrawn January 1988)
008 Athens Sorting Centre (withdrawn May 1986)
009 Athens Central PO (withdrawn December 1987)
010 Athens Railway Station (withdrawn November 1987)

B

1991 (29 Apr). T **B** in red. Number in the bottom frame indicates issuing machine. Face values 5 to 1000d. in 5d. steps.

23.3.92 01 Kypseli PO, Athens
29.4.91 02 Athens East Airport
26.10.91 03 Thessaloniki Central P.O
23.3.92 04 Ampelokipi PO, Athens
23.3.92 05 Pagrali PO, Athens
26.10.01 06 Piraeus Central P
29.4.91 07 Syntagma Square PO, Athens
23.3.92 08 Athens East Airport
29.4.91 09 Eolou PO, Athens
23.3.92 10 Acropolis PO, Athens

Commemorative labels with special designs were available from machines at the following exhibitions:

22 Nov–1 Dec 1985 Piraeus '85
6–15 June 1986 Philatelic Literature Exhibition, Athens
25 Oct–2 Nov 1986 Heraklion '86
7–15 Nov 1987 Heraklion '87
27 Nov–6 Dec 1987 Athens '87
27 Mar–3 Apr 1988 Ioannina '88
4–11 Nov 1988 Maxhellas '88, Athens
15–23 June 1991 Hellas-Cyprus '91, Heraklion
26 Oct–3 Nov 1991 Mytilini '91
20–27 May 1992 Philatelic '92, Athens
23–31 Oct 1993 Rhodes '93
5–9 Nov 1994 Panhellenic '94, Kifisia
22–28 Nov 1995 Athens Piraeus '95
25 Mar–6 Apr 1996 Centenary of the Modern Olympic Games

A **1** Greek Galleon

1998 (13 July). Multicoloured designs as T A **1**. Number in right hand frame indicates issuing machine. Face values 5 to 1000d. in 5d. steps.

Fixed values: 13.7.98 100d., 130d., 140d., 170d. 100d., 140d., 170d., 400d., 450d.
1.9.98 100d., 160d., 170d., 200d.
2.2.00 0d., 120d., 170d., 200d., 500d., 600d.

2002 (2 Jan). Multicoloured designs as T A **1** but face values in Euros. Numbers in right-hand frame indicates issuing machine. Face values 1c. to €5 in 1c. steps.

Fixed values: 2.2.02 41c., 53c., 59c., 88c. (as Type A **1**)
11.3.02 45c., 55c., 60c., 65c.
24.5.03 47c., 60c., 65c., 67c.

2004 (May). Olympics Games, Athens. Multicoloured designs showing the Parthenon. Face values 1c.. to €1.99 in 1c. steps.

Fixed values: 5.04 62c., 78c., 85c., 1.20 (Parthenon)

GREECE / Machine Labels / Stamp Booklets

A **3** Temple

2007 Multicoloured designs as T A **3** showing a temple. Face values 1c. to €1.99 in 1c. steps.
Fixed values: 2007 62c., 78c., 85c., €1.20 (Type A **3**)

A **4** Ink Pen and Letter

2011 (Nov). Multicoloured designs as T A **4**. Face values 1c. to €1.99 in 1c. steps.
Fixed values: 11.11 52c., 78c., 85c., €1.20 (Type A **4**)

STAMP BOOKLETS

The following checklist covers, in simplified form, booklets issued by Greece. It is intended that it should be used in conjunction with the main listings and details of stamps and panes listed there are not repeated.

From 1976 for several years sachets of stamps were available from vending machines. Stamps to the value of 10 or 20d. were torn from normal sheets in stock at the post offices and folded inside cardboard covers. These are not included in the list below.

Also excluded from this list are the Post Office packets containing 100 stamps in strips of five issued from 1986 onwards.

Prices are for complete booklets

Booklet No.	Date	Contents and Cover Price	Price
SB1	1930	Centenary of Independence 1 pane, No. 433×10; 1 pane, No. 434×10; 1 pane, No. 436×10; 1 pane, No. 440×10 (23d.)	—
SB2	1930	Centenary of Independence 1 pane, No. 433×10; 1 pane, No. 434×10; 1 pane, No. 437×10; 1 pane, No. 440×10 (23d.)	—
SB3	1930	Centenary of Independence 1 pane, No. 433×10; 1 pane, No. 434×10; 1 pane, No. 437×10; 1 pane, No. 441×10 (23d.)	—
SB4	30.8.67	Greek Popular Art 2 panes, No. 1026×4; 2 panes, No. 1027×4; 1 pane, No. 1029×4 (30d.)	£275
SB5	30.8.67	Greek Popular Art 1 pane, No. 1026×4; 4 panes, No. 1027×4; 1 pane, No. 1029×4; 1 pane, No. 1030×4 (50d.)	£350
SB6	2.1.84	Homeric Odes 1 pane, No. 1642×10 (150d.)	25·00
SB7	30.4.84	Europa 1 pane, No. 1656a×2 (84d.)	10·50
SB8	30.4.84	Olympic Games 1 pane, Nos. 1658/1662 (161d.)	7·25
SB9	10.7.84	Tenth Anniversary of Turkish Invasion of Greece 1 pane, No. 1663×2; 1 pane, No. 1664×2 (104d.)	7·75
SB10	6.12.84	Christmas 1 pane, No. 1672a (91d.)	5·25
SB11	29.4.85	Europa 1 pane, Nos. 1684×2 and 1685 (134d.)	5·25
SB12	23.4.86	Europa 1 pane, No. 1733Ba (290d.)	60·00
SB13	4.5.87	Europa 1 pane, No. 1752Ba (340d.)	25·00
SB14	4.5.87	Athens University 1 pane, No. 1759×10 (230d.)	10·00
SB15	2.12.87	Christmas 1 pane, No. 1769a×5 (260d.)	9·50
SB16	6.5.88	Olympic Games, Seoul 1 pane, No. 1784Bc (284d.)	37·00
SB17	6.5.88	Europa 1 pane, No. 1789Bd (420d.)	50·00
SB18	7.10.88	Prefecture Capitals 1 pane, No. 1795Ac (152d.)	6·50
SB19	2.12.88	Christmas (T **399**) 1 pane, No. 1812a (300d.)	19·00
SB20	17.3.89	Centenary of Modern Olympics 1 pane, No. 1816Bc (330d.)	13·00
SB21	22.5.89	Europa 1 pane, No. 1825Bd (460d.)	28·00
SB22	11.5.90	Europa 1 pane, No. 1846Ba (560d.)	30·00
SB23	20.5.91	Europa 1 pane, No. 1878Ba (760d.)	31·00
SB24	22.5.92	Europa 1 pane, No. 1901Ba (860d.)	34·00
SB25	25.5.93	Europa 1 pane, No. 1935Ba (880d.)	30·00
SB26	9.5.94	Europa 1 pane, No. 1947Ba (880d.)	27·00
SB27	3.5.95	Europa 1 pane, No. 1973Ba (860d.)	27·00
SB28	22.4.96	Europa 1 pane, No. 1996Ba (1100d.)	38·00
SB29	19.5.97	Europa 1 pane, No. 2034Ba (1100d.)	26·00
SB30	29.5.98	Europa 1 pane, No. 2066Ba (1280d.)	28·00
SB31	24.5.99	Europa 1 pane, No. 2095Ba (1440d.)	23·00
SB32	9.5.00	Europa 1 pane, No. 2123ab (680d.)	20·00
SB33	15.5.01	Europa 1 pane, No. 2156Ba (1660d.)	26·00
SB34	9.5.02	Europa 1 pane, No. 2197Ba (€6.40)	31·00
SB35	8.5.03	Europa 1 pane, No. 2228Ba (€7)	24·00
SB35a	4.5.04	Europa. Holidays 1 pane, No. 2273Ba (€7)	24·00
SB36	19.5.05	Europa. Gastronomy. 1 pane, No. 2343Ba (€6)	24·00
SB37	15.5.06	Europa. Integration. 1 pane, No. 2395Ba (€7.30)	33·00
SB38	25.5.07	Europa. Centenary of Scouting. 1 pane, No. 2461Ba (€7.60)	33·00
SB39	26.5.08	Europa. The Letter 1 pane, No. 2505Ba (€7.68)	33·00
SB40	26.5.10	Europa. Children's Books No. 2593aaa (€7.88)	31·00
SB41	17.5.11	Europa. Forests No. 2666a (€8)	33·00
SB42	22.6.11	Tourism No. 2673×10 (€7.50)	26·00
SB43	18.4.12	Children's Games No. 2726×10 (€6)	21·00
SB44	10.5.12	Europa. Visit Greece 1 pane. No. 2730a (€8)	33·00
SB45	25.6.12	Tourism No. 2738×10 (€6.20)	23·00
SB46	25.6.12	Tourism No. 2739×10 (€7.80)	29·00
SB47	12.12.12	Christmas No. 2759×10 (€6.20)	23·00
SB48	12.12.12	Christmas No. 2760×10 (€7.80)	29·00
SB49	9.5.13	Europa. Postal Transport 1 pane. No. 2771a (€8.12)	31·00
SB50	4.6.13	Tourism. Sailing No. 2779×10 (€6.20)	22·00
SB51	4.6.13	Tourism. Sailing No. 2780×10 (€7.80)	26·00
SB52	2.12.13	From Physical to Digital Post. Self-adhesive No. 2801×10 (€7.20)	24·00
SB53	20.3.14	Songbirds. Self-adhesive No. 2826×10 (€7.20)	26·00
SB54	20.3.14	Songbirds. Self-adhesive No. 2827×10 (€7.20)	26·00
SB55	20.3.14	Songbirds 5 panes. Nos. 2821/2825, plus 18 pages of text (€12)	42·00
SB55a	12.4.14	Thessaloniki. European Youth Capital 2014. Self-adhesive No. 2827b×10 (€9)	
SB56	24.4.14	The 12 Months in Folk Art. Self-adhesive No. 2840×10 (€7.20)	26·00
SB57	24.4.14	The 12 Months in Folk Art. Self-adhesive No. 2841×10 (€8)	29·00
SB58	19.5.14	Europa. Musical Instruments No. 2844a (€8.30)	31·00
SB59	12.6.14	Ecological Transport. Self-adhesive No. 2850×10 (€7.20)	26·00

SB60	12.6.14	Ecological Transport. Self-adhesive No. 2851×10 (€8)	29·00
SB61	7.7.14	Euromed. Self-adhesive No. 2856a (€6)	22·00
SB62	8.8.14	Tourism. Self-adhesive No. 2860×10 (€8)	29·00
SB63	8.8.14	Tourism. Self-adhesive No. 2861×10 (€8)	29·00
SB64	8.8.14	Tourism. Self-adhesive No. 2862×10 (€8)	29·00
SB65	12.12.14	Christmas Nos. 2868/2869, each×5 (€7.20)	26·00
SB66	12.12.14	Christmas Nos. 2870/2871, each×5 (€9)	34·00
SB67	18.12.14	Memorable Advertisements. Self-adhesive Nos. 2873a/2874, each×5 (€7.20)	26·00
SB68	30.3.15	Railways of Greece. Self-adhesive No. 2890×10 (€7.20)	26·00
SB69	30.3.15	Railways of Greece. Self-adhesive No. 2891×10 (€8)	29·00
SB70	11.5.15	Europa. Old Toys No. 2898a, each×2 (€8.60)	16·00
SB71	9.7.15	Euromed No. 2906a×2 (€6)	16·00
SB72	20.7.15	Tourism. Self-adhesive Nos. 2913/2914, each×5 (€8)	29·00
SB73	11.5.16	Europa. Think Green No. 2956a, each×2 (€8.60)	65·00
SB74	23.5.16	2400th Birth Anniversary of Aristotle. Self-adhesive No. 2964×10 (€7.20)	24·00
SB75	23.5.16	2400th Birth Anniversary of Aristotle. Self-adhesive No. 2965×10 (€8)	29·00
SB76	15.3.15	150th Anniversary of Archaeological Museum. Self-adhesive No. 3001×10 (€7.20)	26·00
SB77	7.4.17	Personalised Stamps. Self-adhesive No. 3008×10 (€8)	29·00
SB78	18.5.17	Europa. Castles No. 3014a (€4.30)	16·00
SB79	5.12.17	Christmas. Self-adhesive No. 3046×10 (€7.20)	26·00
SB80	5.12.17	Christmas. Self-adhesive No. 3047×10 (€9)	34·00
SB81	24.5.18	Europa. Bridges No. 3077a, each×2 (€8.60)	31·00
SB82	20.7.18	Euromed No. 3090a (€3.14)	11·50
SB83	25.8.18	125th Anniversary of Corinth Canal. Self-adhesive No. 3100×10 (€7.20)	26·00
SB84	27.9.18	11th Syros International Animation Festival and Fair. Self-adhesive Nos. 3104/3108, each×5 (€8)	30·00
SB85	1.10.18	Centenary of Greece-Ethiopia Diplomatic Relations Nos. 3109/3110, each×4, and No. 3111×2 (€7.20)	26·00
SB86	10.10.18	60th Anniversary of National Hellenic Research Foundation Nos. 3116/3123 and No. 3124×2 (€7.20)	26·00
SB87	10.10.18	60th Anniversary of National Hellenic Research Foundation No. 3124×10 (€7.20)	26·00
SB88	16.11.18	70th Anniversary of Union of the Dodecanese with Greece. Self-adhesive No. 3125×10 (€7.20)	26·00
SB89	23.11.18	Christmas. Self-adhesive No. 3131×10 (€7.20)	26·00
SB90	23.11.18	Christmas. Self-adhesive No. 3132×10 (€8)	30·00
SB91	7.12.18	190th Anniversary of Greece-Russia Diplomatice Relations. Self-adhesive No. 3134×10 (€7.20)	26·00
SB92	7.12.18	190th Anniversary of Greece-Russia Diplomatice Relations. Self-adhesive No. 3135×10 (€7.20)	26·00

BALKAN WAR ISSUES

100 Lepta = 1 Drachma

All except Kavalla were united to Greece by the Treaty of London, 30 May 1913.

IKARIA

(Icaria, Nicaria)

A. FREE STATE

This island declared its independence from Turkey, as a free state, at the end of July 1912.

1 Hermes, from an old Coin

(Litho Grundmann & Co., Athens)

1912 (8 Oct). P 11½.

1	**1**	2l. orange	2·50	3·50
2		5l. green	2·50	3·50
3		10l. rose	2·50	3·50
4		25l. blue	2·50	3·50
5		50l. deep lilac	3·75	5·00
6		1d. brown	5·00	11·50
7		2d. carmine	6·25	17·00
8		5d. grey	8·75	30·00
1/8 *Set of* 8			30·00	70·00

B. GREEK OCCUPATION

The island was occupied by Greek troops on 4 (17) November 1912 and at first used the Greek stamps overprinted 'E??HNIKH ?IOKHSIS' Greece T **34**.

ΕΛΛΗΝΙΚΗ
ΔΙΟΙΚΗΣΙΣ

(**2** 'Greek Administration')

1913. Stamps of Greece, 1911–1913, handstamped with T **2**.

		(a) Engraved		
9	**30**	2l. carmine	75·00	50·00
10	**29**	3l. vermilion	75·00	50·00
		(b) Lithographed		
11	**29**	1l. green	75·00	50·00
12		3l. vermilion	75·00	50·00
13	**31**	5l. green	75·00	50·00
14	**29**	10l. carmine	75·00	50·00
9/14 *Set of* 6			£400	£275

KAVALLA

Kavalla was taken by the Greeks in June 1913.

ΕΛΛΗΝΙΚΗ
ΛΙΟΙΚΗΣΙΣ

(**1** Trans 'Greek Administration')

1913 (1 July). Stamps of Bulgaria of 1911 surch as T **1**, in red (vert on Nos. 3, 6 and 9/11).

1	**23**	5l. on 1st. myrtle-green	38·00	38·00

GREECE / BALKAN WAR ISSUES

2	27	10l. on 10st. black and red	£700	£600
3	28	10l. on 15st. bistre	£110	80·00
4	29	10l. on 25st. black and ultramarine	65·00	50·00
5	24	15l. on 2st. black and carmine	£110	80·00
6	25	20l. on 3st. black and lake	£110	80·00
7	26	25l. on 5st. black and green	31·00	19·00
8	27	50l. on 10st. black and red	65·00	41·00
		a. Surch in blue	31·00	31·00
9	28	1d. on 15st. bistre	£375	£325
10	30	1d. on 30st. black and blue	£150	£150
11	31	1d. on 50st. black and ochre	£225	£225

Extensive forgeries of the above exist.

For French Post Offices in Kavalla (Cavalle), see under French Post Offices in the Turkish Empire in French colonies or Central Asia of this catalogue.

KHIOS
(Chios)

Khios was occupied by Greek forces on 11 (24) November 1912.

1913 (May). T **30** (litho) of Greece, opt 'Ε*Δ'.

1		25l. ultramarine (R.)	90·00	£100
		a. Greek 'L' for 'D' in opt	£325	£275
		b. Opt inverted	£325	£325

The overprint was made because of the absence of the overprint 'ΕΛΛΗΝΙΚΗ ΔΙΟΙΚΗΣΙΣ', Greece (T **34**) on a supply of 25l. stamps sent to Khios.

LESVOS
(Lesbos)

This island was formerly called Mytilene, from the name of the chief town. It was occupied by Greek forces on 8 (21) November 1912.

Types of Turkey are illustrated at beginning of Albania.

(**1** 'Greek Possession Mytilene')

1912 (9 Nov). Stamps of Turkey, optd with T **1**, in black, reading up or down.

1	28	2pa. olive-green	3·50	3·50
2		5pa. brown-ochre	3·50	3·50
3		10pa. green (Pl. II)	3·50	3·50
4		20pa. rose-carmine (Pl. II)	3·50	3·50
5		1pi. ultramarine (Pl. II)	7·00	7·00
6		2pi. blue-black	34·00	34·00
7	25	2½pi. brown	17·00	17·00
8	28	5pi. slate-purple	38·00	38·00
9		10pi. dull red	£170	£170
		a. Opt in blue	£170	£170

1912. Stamps of Turkey with opt T **26** in red, optd with T **1**, in black, reading up or down.

10	28	10pa. green (Pl. II)	11·50	11·50
10a		20pa. rose-carmine	11·50	11·50
		b. Opt in blue	75·00	75·00
10c		1pi. ultramarine	11·50	11·50
11	25	2pi. black	80·00	80·00

ΛΕΠΤΑ 25 **ΔΡΑΧΜΗ** **ΔΙΔΡΑΧΜΟΝ**
(2) (3) (4)

1912 (Nov). Stamps as above surch with values in Greek, as Types **2/4**, in blue (Nos. 12/13) or black (others).

12	28	25l. on 2pa. olive-green. (No. 1)	15·00	15·00
13		50l. on 20pa. rose-carmine (No. 4)	15·00	15·00
14		1d. on 20pa. rose-carmine (No. 10b)	65·00	65·00
15		2d. on 1pi. ultramarine (No. 5)	38·00	38·00

1912. Postage Due stamp of Turkey, 1908, optd with T **1** for postal use.

16	25	1pi. black/*crimson*	85·00	85·00

There are large numbers of forgeries of these provisionals, nearly all with forged postmarks.

LIMNOS
(Lemnos)

Limnos was occupied by Greek marines on 7 (20) October 1912.

ΛΗΜΝΟΣ
(1)

VARIETIES OF OVERPRINT

I. 'ΔΗΜΝΟΣ'
II. 'ΛΗΜΝΟΞ'

Variety I occurs in position 95, variety II in position 69.

1912–13. Stamps of Greece optd with T **1**.

(a) On stamp of 1901

1	15	20l. mauve	7·00	5·25
		a. Variety I	7·50	7·50

(b) On stamps of 1911, engraved

2	29	1l. green	75	75
		a. Variety I	5·00	5·00
		b. Variety II	7·50	7·50
		c. Opt double	19·00	
		d. Opt inverted	19·00	
3	30	2l. carmine	90	90
		a. Variety I	5·00	5·00
		b. Variety II	7·50	7·50
		c. Opt double	19·00	
		d. Opt inverted	19·00	
		g. Opt in red	3·75	3·75
4	29	3l. vermilion	90	90
		a. Variety I	5·00	5·00
		b. Variety II	7·50	7·50
		c. Opt double	19·00	
		d. Opt inverted	19·00	
		g. Opt in red	3·75	3·75
5	31	5l. green	90	90
		a. Variety I	5·00	5·00
		b. Variety II	7·50	7·50
		c. Opt double	21·00	
6	29	10l. carmine	1·30	1·30
		a. Variety I	7·50	7·50
		b. Variety II	12·50	12·50
		c. Opt double	21·00	
		d. Opt inverted	21·00	
7	30	20l. lilac	1·90	1·90
		a. Variety I	7·50	7·50
		b. Variety II	12·50	12·50
		c. Opt double	31·00	
		d. Opt inverted	19·00	
		g. Opt in red	15·00	15·00
8		25l. ultramarine	2·30	2·30
		b. Variety II	12·50	12·50
		c. Opt double	31·00	
9	31	30l. carmine-red	3·75	3·75
		a. Variety I	10·00	10·00
		b. Variety II	15·00	15·00
		d. Opt inverted	65·00	
		g. Opt in red	7·50	7·50
10	30	40l. deep blue	5·75	5·75
		a. Variety I	10·00	10·00
		b. Variety II	19·00	19·00
		g. Opt in red	2·50	2·50
		ga. Variety I	28·00	28·00
11	31	50l. deep purple	5·75	5·75
		b. Variety II	19·00	19·00
		g. Opt in red	2·50	2·50
		ga. Variety I		
12	32	1d. ultramarine	7·50	7·50
		b. Variety II	20·00	20·00
		c. Opt double	70·00	
		g. Opt in red	3·75	3·75
		ga. Variety I	28·00	28·00
13		2d. vermilion	25·00	25·00
		b. Variety II	£150	£150
		g. Opt in red	£375	£350
14		3d. carmine (No. 209)	28·00	28·00
		b. Variety II	£150	£150
		g. Opt in red	19·00	19·00
		ga. Variety I	95·00	95·00
15		5d. grey-blue (No. 210)	33·00	33·00
		b. Variety II		
		c. Opt double	95·00	
		g. Opt in red	75·00	75·00
		ga. Variety I	£225	£225
16		10d. deep blue (No. 211)	£100	£100
		b. Variety II	£750	£750
		g. Opt in red	£150	£130
		ga. Variety I	£550	£550
17	33	25d. deep blue (No. 212)	£190	£190
		g. Opt in red	£225	£190

(c) On stamps of 1913, lithographed

18	29	1l. green	75	75
		a. Variety I	5·00	5·00
		c. Opt double	19·00	

GREECE / BALKAN WAR ISSUES

		e. On No. 213a	£300	£300
		g. Opt in red	2·50	2·50
		ga. On No. 213a	£450	£325
19	31	5l. green	90	90
		a. Variety I	8·75	8·75
		g. Opt in red		
		ga. Variety I		
20	29	10l. carmine	90	90
		a. Variety I	7·50	7·50
		c. Opt double	21·00	
		d. Opt inverted	£150	
		e.	5·00	5·00
21	30	25l. ultramarine	3·75	3·75
		a. Variety I	7·50	7·50
		g. Opt in red		
		ga. Variety I		

*(d) On No. 248 (with opt T **34**)*

| 22 | 29 | 1l. green | 31·00 | 31·00 |

SAMOS

From 1832 to 1912 an independent principality under Turkish suzerainty with British, French and Russian protection. For stamps of French Post Office in Vathy, the capital, used between 1893 and 1914, see French Post Offices in the Turkish Empire in French Colonies or Central Asia of this catalogue.

Between 1878 and 1911 various local issues were prepared but their use was forbidden by the Turkish authorities and it is doubtful if many were postally used.

A. PROVISIONAL GOVERNMENT

Following a revolt in September 1912, and the withdrawal of the Turkish garrison, a provisional government under Themistocles Sophoulos declared for union with Greece on 11 (24) November 1912. The dates of issue are expressed first in the Julian calendar and then in the Gregorian calendar.

1 Map of Samos   **2** Hermes

(Handstruck. Govt. Building, Vathy)

1912 (14–27 Nov). Imperf.

1	1	5l. dull green	31·00	11·50
		a. Tête-bêche (pair)	£650	£500
2		10l. red	25·00	11·50
		a. Tête-bêche (pair)	£650	£500
3		25l. blue	65·00	23·00
		a. Tête-bêche (pair)	£3500	£2250
		b. Error. Dull green	£700	£650

Nos. 1/3 in other colours are colour trials.

(Litho. G. Stangel & Co., Athens)

1912 (29 Nov–12 Dec).

(A) P 11½

4A	2	1l. grey	2·50	1·90
5A		5l. yellow-green	2·50	1·90
6A		10l. carmine	3·75	2·30
7A		25l. pale blue	10·00	2·50
8A		50l. brown-purple	23·00	7·50

(B) Imperf (singles)

4B	2	1l. grey	50·00	38·00
5B		5l. yellow-green	50·00	38·00
6B		10l. carmine	50·00	38·00
7B		25l. pale blue	50·00	38·00
8B		50l. brown-purple	50·00	38·00

ΕΛΛΑΣ
(3)

4 Scene of Turkish Repulse, 1824

1912 (22 Dec–4 Jan). T **2** redrawn, optd with T **3** in Athens.

9		1l. grey	1·30	1·30
		a. Imperf (pair)	£130	50·00
10		5l. green	1·30	1·30
		a. Imperf (pair)	£130	50·00
11		10l. rose-pink	1·30	1·30
		a. Imperf (pair)	£130	50·00
12		25l. deep blue	2·50	1·90
		a. Imperf (pair)	£130	50·00
13		50l. chocolate	12·50	8·75
		a. Imperf (pair)	£130	50·00
14		1d. orange	19·00	16·00

Nos. 6 and 11 were officially used bisected as 5l. stamps.

(Des Ramphos. Litho G. Travlos, Samos)

1913 (Jan). Turkish Evacuation Commemoration. Signed T.S., in black ink (25d.) or red ink (others). P 12.

15	4	1d. brown	25·00	12·50
		a. Imperf (pair)	£325	
16		2d. blue	25·00	12·50
		a. Imperf (pair)	£325	
17		5d. olive-green	50·00	23·00
		a. Imperf (pair)	£500	
18		10d. yellow-green	£160	£160
		a. Imperf (pair)	£2000	
		b. Imperf between (pair)	£1600	
19		25d. red	£140	£160
		a. Imperf (pair)	£2000	
		b. Imperf between (pair)	£1600	

The initials are those of the local President, Themistocles Sophoulis. Stamps may be found without them. Nos. 15/17 were issued on 4/17 Jan. and Nos. 18/19 on 24 Jan./6 Feb. Forgeries exist.

B. GREEK ADMINISTRATION

Samos was united to Greece by the Treaty of London on 30 May 1913.

ΕΛΛΑΣ
(5)

1914 (1–14 Feb). Nos. 4/8 optd at Vathy with T **5**.

20	2	1l. grey	10·00	7·50
21		5l. yellow-green	10·00	7·50
22		10l. carmine	10·00	7·50
		a. Opt double		
23		25l. pale blue	14·50	14·00
24		50l. chocolate	11·00	10·00
		a. Opt double	£150	

The Provisional Government was dissolved at the end of 1914, after which the stamps of Greece were placed on sale. The following stamps were authorised by the Greek Governor, with the agreement of the Ministry of Finance in Athens.

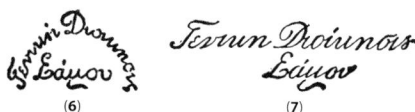

(6)   (7)

1915 (17–30 Jan). Vathy Hospital Fund.

*(a) Nos. 9/14 optd with T **6**, No. 26 additionally surch 'ΛΕΠΤΟΝ'*

25		1l. grey (R.)	23·00	28·00
		a. Black opt	£225	£225
26		1l. on 1d. orange (R.)	25·00	29·00
		a. Surch inverted	£375	£375
		b. Surch double	£375	£375
27		5l. green	2·50	3·25
		a. Opt double	£250	£250
		b. Red opt	£190	£190
28		10l. rose-pink	2·50	3·25
		a. Opt inverted	£170	£170
		b. Red opt	£190	£190
29		25l. deep blue	2·50	3·25
		a. Red opt	£190	£190
30		50l. chocolate	2·50	3·25
		a. Red opt	£190	£190
31		1d. orange (R.)	3·75	3·75
		a. Opt inverted	£250	£250
		b. Black opt	£225	£225
		ba. Black opt double	£250	£250

*(b) Nos. 15/19 optd with T **7***

32	4	1d. brown (R.)	31·00	25·00
33		2d. blue (R.)	38·00	38·00
		a. Opt double		
34		5d. olive-green (R.)	31·00	25·00
35		10d. yellow-green	£100	75·00
		a. Opt inverted	£1600	£1600
36		25d. red	£950	£800

Nos. 25/36 are also embossed with a cross within a circular pattern and inscription, with or without initials.

Nos. 30/34 were also used on Icaria.

BRITISH FIELD OFFICE IN SALONICA

These overprints were originally prepared for use by a civilian post office to be set up on Mount Athos, Northern Greece. When the project was abandoned they were placed on sale at the Army Field Office in Salonica.

Levant
(S 1)

1916 (end Feb–9 Mar). Stamps of Great Britain, optd with T S **1** by Army Printing Office, Salonica.

S1	105	½d. green	70·00	£325
		a. Opt double	£4500	£5000
		b. Vert pair, one without opt	£2250	£3000
S2	104	1d. scarlet	70·00	£325
		a. Opt double	£3000	£3500
S3	106	2d. reddish orange (Die I)	£200	£475
S4		3d. bluish violet	£160	£475
S5		4d. grey-green	£190	£475
S6	107	6d. reddish purple (chalk-surfaced paper)	£110	£400
		a. Vert pair, one without opt	£2250	£3250
S7	108	9d. agate	£400	£750
		a. Opt double	£17000	£12000
S8		1s. bistre-brown	£350	£650
S1/S8 Set of 8			£1400	£3500

There are numerous forgeries of this overprint.

All values can be found with an additional albino overprint, inverted on the gummed side. These are worth a 25% premium.

ITALIAN OCCUPATION OF CORFU

31 August–27 September 1923

As a sequel to the murder on Greek soil of Italian officers on a Greco-Albanian Boundary Commission, Italian warships bombarded Corfu and troops occupied the town on 31 August 1923.

100 Centesimi = 1 Lira
100 Lepta = 1 Drachma

CORFÙ (1)   CORFU Lepta 60 (2)

1923 (20 Sept). Stamps of Italy (various portraits of Victor Emmanuel III) optd with T **1**.

1	37	5c. green	9·50	10·00
2	38	10c. rose	9·50	10·00
3	37	15c. slate	9·50	10·00
4	41	20c. orange (No. 105)	9·50	10·00
5	39	30c. orange-brown	9·50	10·00
6	40	50c. mauve	9·50	10·00
7	39	60c. blue	9·50	10·00
8	34	1l. brown and green	9·50	10·00
1/8 Set of 8			70·00	70·00

1923 (24 Sept). Stamps of Italy surch as T **2**.

9	38	25l. on 10c. rose	£110	50·00
10	39	60l. on 25c. blue	16·00	
11		70l. on 30c. orange-brown	16·00	
12	40	1d.20l. on 50c. mauve	50·00	47·00
13	34	2d.40l.. on 1l. brown and green	50·00	47·00
14		4d.75l. on 2l. myrtle and orange	16·00	

Nos. 10, 11 and 14 were not sent to Corfu as the island was evacuated by Italian troops on 27 September, before they could arrive.

ITALIAN OCCUPATION OF CORFU AND PAXOS

1941–1943

Issues made during the occupation of the Ionian Islands by Italian troops.

100 Lepta = 1 Drachma

CORFU (1)

1941 (5 June). Stamps of Greece optd with T **1**.
(a) On Postage issue of 1937–1938. Nos. 497/516

1	86	5l. greenish blue and red-brown	7·50	4·75
2	–	10l. red-brown and light blue (No. 498)	3·25	3·25
3	–	10l. red-brown and light blue (No. 514)	£1400	£950

4	–	20l. blue-green and black	3·25	3·25
5	–	40l. black and blue-green	3·50	3·75
6	–	50l. black and bistre-brown	3·25	3·25
7	–	80l. brown and dull violet	3·50	5·75
8	89	1d. green	16·00	16·00
9	89a	1d.50 green	12·50	12·50
10	–	2d. ultramarine	9·75	7·00
11	89	3d. red-brown	16·00	16·00
12	–	5d. scarlet	9·75	8·25
13	–	6d. olive-brown	9·75	9·50
14	90	7d. chocolate	14·00	9·50
15	89	8d. deep blue	31·00	28·00
16	–	10d. red-brown	£700	£275
17	91	15d. blue-green	36·00	30·00
18	92	25d. deep blue	26·00	30·00
19	89a	30d. brown-red	£130	£120
20	89	100d. lake	£425	£275
1/20 Set of 20			£2500	£1600

No. 2 is inscr 'TYPIN' and No. 3 is corrected to 'TIPYN'.

(b) On Air stamps, Nos. 521/522 and 480/488

21	D 20	50l. brown (rouletted)	95·00	34·00
22		50l. brown (perf)	14·50	11·00
23	79	1d. scarlet	£1000	£350
24	–	2d. grey-blue	16·00	7·50
		a. Opt double		
25	–	5d. mauve	21·00	14·00
26	–	7d. ultramarine	21·00	14·00
27	80	10d. brown	£1300	£550
28	–	10d. orange-red	85·00	55·00
29	–	25d. rose-carmine	£140	70·00
30	–	30d. green	£160	95·00
31	–	50d. mauve	£150	90·00
32	–	100d. brown	£1600	£900

(c) On Charity Tax Stamps, Nos. C524/C526

33	C 96	10l. carmine/rose	3·50	6·25
34		50l. green/pale green	3·75	6·25
35		1d. blue/pale blue	47·00	39·00

(d) On Postage Due stamps, Nos. D273, D275, D279, D452/D453, D455/D458 and D480/D481

D36	D 20	10l. carmine	5·00	5·00
D37		25l. ultramarine	6·25	5·000
D38		80l. brown-purple	£1600	£450
D39		1d. pale blue	£2250	£1000
D40		2d. vermilion	12·00	12·50
D41		5d. slate-blue	30·00	31·00
D42		10d. green	25·00	25·00
D43		15d. red-brown	30·00	25·00
D44		25d. vermilion	30·00	25·00
D45		50d. orange	30·00	25·00
D46		100d. blue-green	£900	£600

These issues were superseded by the general issues made for the Italian Occupation of the Ionian Islands.

ITALIAN OCCUPATION OF CEPHALONIA AND ITHACA

1941–1943

Issues made during the occupation of the Ionian Islands by Italian troops.

100 Lepta = 1 Drachma

ITALIA
Occupazione Militare
Italiana isole
Cefalonia e Itaca
(1)

PRICES. Prices are for unsevered pairs except where overprint was applied to single stamps. Single stamps from severed pairs are worth 1/3 unused and ½ used prices.

1941 (20 May–Aug). Stamps of Greece optd with T **1** across a pair of stamps, sideways (reading downwards) on horizontal designs and horizontally on vertical designs.
(a) On Postage issue of 1937–1938. Nos. 497 etc

1	86	5l. blue and red-brown	33·00	33·00
		a. Reading upwards	36·00	36·00
2	–	10l. red-brown and light blue (No. 514)	33·00	33·00
		a. On No. 498	£130	£120
3	87	20l. green and black	33·00	33·00

GREECE / ITALIAN OCCUPATION ISSUES / GERMAN OCCUPATION OF ZANTE

4	88	40l. black and green	33·00	33·00
		a. Reading upwards	36·00	36·00
5	–	50l. black and bistre-brown	33·00	33·00
		a. Reading upwards	36·00	36·00
6	–	80l. brown and violet	50·00	50·00
7	89	1d. green	£350	£250
8	89a	1d.50 green	£225	£130
9	–	2d. ultramarine	36·00	42·00
		a. Reading upwards	60·00	55·00
10	–	5d. scarlet	£130	55·00
		a. Reading upwards	£160	£110
11	–	6d. olive-brown	£130	55·00
		a. Reading upwards	£160	£110
12	90	7d. chocolate	£130	55·00
		a. Reading upwards	£160	£110
13	89	8d. deep blue	£300	£150
14	–	10d. red-brown	£130	60·00
		a. Reading upwards	£160	£110
15	91	15d. blue-green	£250	£100
		a. Reading upwards	£250	£170
16	92	25d. deep blue	£300	£160
17	89a	30d. brown-red	£1300	£700
	(b) On Air stamps. Nos. 521, 488a/488d and 485/488			
18	D 20	50l. brown	£110	£2250
		a. On No. 521a	£120	£110
19	79	1d. scarlet	£170	£160
		a. On No. 480	£100	95·00
20	–	2d. grey-blue	85·00	90·00
		a. Reading upwards	£2500	£1500
		b. Horiz opt on horiz pair	£1700	£1200
		c. Horiz opt on single stamp	80·00	65·00
		d. On No. 481	£100	£100
21	–	5d. mauve	£850	£850
		a. Reading down on single stamp	£850	£850
		b. Reading up on single stamp	£225	£200
22	–	7d. ultramarine	£160	£120
		a. On No. 483	£650	£500
23	–	25d. rose-carmine	£550	£600
24	–	30d. green	£750	£650
		a. Reading upwards	£1400	£1200
		b. Horiz opt on single stamp	£3000	£3500
25	–	50d. mauve	£1600	£1800
26	–	100d. brown	£2000	£2500
		a. Reading upwards		
	(c) On Charity Tax stamps			
27		10l. carmine (No. C498)	39·00	48·00
28		10l. carmine/*rose* (No. C524)	48·00	42·00
		a. Horiz opt on horiz pair	£190	£190
		b. Horiz opt on single stamp	£1100	£1300
29		50l. green/*pale green* (No. C525)	39·00	33·00
		a. Reading upwards	48·00	43·00
		b. Horiz opt on horiz pair	48·00	48·00
		c. Horiz opt on single stamp	£350	£350
30		50l. green/*pale green* (No. C554)	£1000	£1100
		a. Reading upwards	£1000	£1100
31		1d. blue/*pale blue* (No. C526)	£100	85·00
		a. Reading upwards	£130	£110

Nos. 1 to 31a. A wrong fount 'C' exists in all values optd in pairs.

Contemporary stamps were also overprinted similarly with a handstamp but the word 'isole' is spelt 'isola'. There was another type of overprint issued in Ithaca arranged in four lines: 'occupazione/ (or Occupazione) Militare Italiana/Isole/Cefalonia e Itaca'. All these are rare and outside the scope of this catalogue.

These issues were superseded by the general issues made for the Italian Occupation of the Ionian Islands.

ITALIAN OCCUPATION OF THE IONIAN ISLANDS

1941–1943

The Ionian Islands consist of Corfu (Kerkira), Paxos (Paxoi) Santa Maura (Levkas), Ithaca (Ithaki), Cephalonia (Kefalinia) and Zante (Zakinthos).

After the armistice between the Greek forces on the mainland of Greece and those of the Axis powers on 23 April 1941, Italian troops occupied the islands.

100 Centesimi = 1 Lira

ISOLE JONIE

(1)

1941 (1 Sept). Stamps of Italy optd with T **1**.

(a) On Postage stamps of 1929–1942, Nos. 239 etc

1	98	5c. brown (R.) (Romulus, Remus and Wolf)	1·10	3·50
2	100	10c. sepia (R.) (Augustus the Great)	1·10	3·50
3	99	20c. carmine (Julius Caesar)	1·10	3·50
4	102	25c. green (Victor Emmanuel III)	1·10	3·50
5	103	30c. brown (R.) (Victor Emmanuel III)	1·10	3·50
6		50c. bright violet (R.)	1·10	3·50
7	102	75c. carmine	1·10	3·50
8		1l.25 blue (R.)	1·10	3·50
	(b) On Air stamp of 1930, No. 271			
9	110	50c. sepia (Pegasus)	1·50	4·75
	(c) On Postage Due stamps of 1934, Nos. D396 etc. (Arms)			
D10	D **141**	10c. blue	2·75	6·50
D11		20c. carmine	2·75	6·50
D12		30c. orange-vermilion	2·75	6·50
D13	D **142**	1l. orange	2·75	6·50

Stamps as above further optd or surch 'BOLLO' are fiscals.

On the island of Cerigo (Kithyra), which is off the south coast of Greece, stamps of Greece without overprint continued to be used during the occupation.

The following overprints on Greek stamps are bogus: 'CERIGO/Occupazione Militare/Italiana'; 'ISOLA ITALIANA DI/PAXO/ANNO XIXo'; 'ITALIA/SANTA MAURA'.

GERMAN OCCUPATION OF ZANTE

1943–1944

In September 1943, after the armistice between the Kingdom of Italy and the Allies, German troops took over control of the Ionian Islands from Italian forces.

The following issue was made by the local administration.

100 Centesimi = 1 Lira = 8 Drachma

(1)

1943 (22 Oct). Stamps of Italian Occupation of Ionian Islands (optd 'ISOLE JONIE') further handstamped with T **1** in black.

(a) POSTAGE. Types 102 and 103

1		25c. green	50·00	80·00
		a. Optd with Type **1** in red	80·00	£120
2		50c. bright violet	50·00	80·00
		a. Optd with Type **1** in red	80·00	£120
	(b) AIR. T 110			
3		50c. sepia	65·00	£120
		a. Optd with Type **1** in red	£325	£500

The 10c. value exists with handstamp in black and in red but was not issued.

Inverted handstamps exist.

In 1941 whilst under Italian military occupation contemporary Greek stamps were handstamped 'OCCUPAZIONE/MILITARE DI/ZANTE/1–5–XIX'. These are rare and outside the scope of this catalogue.

Castelrosso

A. FRENCH OCCUPATION

100 Centimes = 1 Franc = 4 Piastres

This island off the South coast of Asia Minor was occupied by the French Navy on 27 December 1915 and at first used French Post Offices in the Levant stamps with special cancellations. It is now called Kastellorizon.

B. N. F.
CASTELLORIZO

(F **1**) 'B.N.F.'=Base Navale Française

1920 (19 June). Stamps of 1902–1920 of French Post Offices in the Turkish Empire (inscr 'LEVANT') optd with T F **1**. (sideways reading down on Nos. F10/F13).

F1	11	1c. grey	65·00	65·00
F2		2c. claret	65·00	65·00
F3		3c. orange-red	65·00	65·00
F4		5c. yellow-green	75·00	75·00
F5	14	10c. carmine	90·00	90·00
F6		15c. pale red	£120	£120
F7		20c. purple-brown	£130	£130
F8		1pi. on 25c. blue	£110	£110
F9		30c. deep lilac	£130	£130
F10	13	40c. red and pale blue	£225	£225
F11		2pi. on 50c. brown and lavender	£225	£225
F12		4pi. on 1f. lake and yellow-green	£275	£275
F13		20pi. on 5f. deep blue and buff	£800	£800
F1/F13 Set of 13			£2250	£2250

Nos. F1/F9 were overprinted in blocks of 25 and Nos. F10/F13 in blocks of ten. All values exist with 'S' instead of 'Z' in 'CASTELLORIZO' (positions 8 and 18 in setting of 25, once in setting of 10) (Price: twice the normal); and with no stop after 'N' (Price: 2½ times the normal). Nos. F1/F9 also exist with 'CASTELLORIZO' inverted (position 4) (Price: 2½ times the normal).

Double and inverted overprints also exist.

O. N. F.
Castellorizo
(F **2**)   (F **3**)

'ONF'=Occupation Navale Française
'OF'=Occupation Française

1920 (June–July). Optd with T F **2**.

(a) Stamps of French Post Offices in the Turkish Empire (inscr 'LEVANT') (July)

F14	11	1c. grey	33·00	34·00
F15		2c. claret	33·00	34·00
F16		3c. orange-red	38·00	40·00
F17		5c. yellow-green (R.)	35·00	35·00
F18	14	10c. carmine	39·00	39·00
F19		15c. pale red	55·00	55·00
F20		20c. purple-brown	85·00	85·00
F21		1pi. on 25c. blue (R.)	80·00	75·00
F22		30c. deep lilac (R.)	80·00	75·00
F23	13	40c. red and pale blue	80·00	75·00
F24		2pi. on 50c. brown and lavender	80·00	85·00
F25		4pi. on 1f. lake and yellow-green	95·00	95·00
F26		20pi. on 5f. deep blue and buff	£425	£425
F14/F26 Set of 13			£1000	£1000

An 8pi. on 2f. was prepared but not issued.

Nos. F14/F22 exist with the errors 'CASETLLORIZO' and 'ASTELLORIZO'; also without dot over 'i' and broken 'F'.

(b) Nos. 358 and 363 (Sower) of France (June)

F27	18	10c. red	46·00	37·00
F28		25c. blue	46·00	37·00

The above exist with overprint inverted and also without dot over 'i' and broken 'F'.

The 5c., 15c., 20c., 30c., 40c. and 50c. and 1f. and 5f. of the 1916–1919 issue of France also exist with this overprint but are only known unused and it is doubtful if they were issued.

1920 (July). Stamps of France optd with T F **3**.

F29	18	5c. blue-green (No. 357)	£190	£190
F30		10c. red (No. 358)	£190	£190
F31		20c. brown-lake (No. 337)	£190	£190
F32		25c. blue (No. 364)	£190	£190
F33	13	50c. cinnamon and lavender (No. 368)	£1100	£1200
F34		1f. lake and yellow-green (No. 306)	£1100	£1200
F29/F34 Set of 6			£2750	£2750

The 5c., 10c., 15c., 20c., 1pi. on 25c., 40c., 2pi. on 50c. and 4pi. on 1f. of French Post Offices in the Turkish Empire with this overprint were prepared but not issued.

On 21 August 1920 the French forces withdrew and the island was occupied by the Italians.

B. ITALIAN OCCUPATION

100 Centesimi=1 Lira

In accordance with the Treaty of Sèvres on 10 August 1920 Castelrosso was awarded to Italy. After a temporary transference to Italian naval administration on 1 March 1921, it came later under the rule of the Governor of the Dodecanese Islands and Castelrosso.

CASTELROSSO
(1)   2

1922 (11 July). Contemporary stamps of Italy (various portraits of Victor Emmanuel III) optd with T **1**.

1	37	5c. green	7·00	29·00
2	38	10c. rose-red	3·25	29·00
3	37	15c. slate	5·00	29·00
4	41	20c. orange (No. 105)	3·25	29·00
5	39	25c. blue	3·25	29·00
6	40	40c. brown	70·00	34·00
7		50c. violet	70·00	34·00
8	39	60c. carmine-red	70·00	48·00
9		85c. red-brown	7·00	60·00
1/9 Set of 9			£225	£300

1923 (Jan). Typo. Wmk Crown. P 14.

10	2	5c. green	5·25	30·00
11		10c. carmine	5·25	30·00
12		25c. blue	5·25	30·00
13		50c. dull purple	5·25	30·00
14		1l. brown	5·25	30·00
10/14 Set of 5			24·00	£140

CASTELROSSO
(3)   (4)

1924 (Mar). Contemporary stamps of Italy optd with T **3**.

15	37	5c. green	2·75	34·00
16	38	10c. rose-red	2·75	34·00
17	37	15c. slate	2·75	47·00
18	41	20c. orange (No. 105)	2·75	47·00
19	39	25c. blue	2·75	36·00
20	40	40c. brown	2·75	36·00
21		50c. violet	2·75	47·00
22	39	60c. carmine-red	2·75	55·00
23		85c. red-brown	3·25	65·00
24	34	1l. brown and green	3·25	65·00
15/24 Set of 10			26·00	£425

1930 (20 Oct). Ferrucci issue of Italy (colours changed) optd with T **4**.

25	114	20c. bright violet (R.)	9·50	8·75
26	115	25c. deep green (R.)	9·50	18·00
27		50c. black (R.)	9·50	8·75
28		1l.25 blue (R.)	9·50	20·00
29	116	5l. +2l. carmine-red (B.)	44·00	90·00
25/29 Set of 5			75·00	£130

See also Dodecanese Islands Nos. 35/39.

1931 (28 Aug). Types **128/129** and similar types (Garibaldi) of Italy with colours changed optd with T **4**.

30		10c. sepia (R.)	39·00	65·00
31		20c. lake-brown (B.)	39·00	65·00
32		25c. green (R.)	39·00	65·00

33	30c. slate-blue (R.)		39·00	65·00
34	50c. purple (B.)		39·00	65·00
35	75c. lake (B.)		39·00	65·00
36	1l.25c. deep blue (R.)		39·00	65·00
37	1l.75 +25c. sepia (R.)		39·00	65·00
38	2l.55 +50c. orange-vermilion (B.)		39·00	65·00
39	5l. +1l. violet (R.)		39·00	65·00
30/39	Set of 10		£350	£600

Designs: Horiz—10c. Garibaldi's birthplace, Nice; 20c., 30c. T **128**; 25c., 50c. Here we make Italy or die; 75c. Death of Anita (Garibaldi's wife); 1l.25, Garibaldi's tomb; 1l.75, Quarto Rock. Vert—2l.55, Garibaldi's statue, Rome; 5l. T **129**.
See also Dodecanese Islands Nos. 89/98.

Castelrosso was transferred to Greece with the Dodecanese Islands by the Treaty of Paris, which came into force on 15 September 1947. It is now called Kastellorizon.

Crete

After many rebellions against Turkish rule, Crete was made autonomous, under Turkish suzerainty, in November 1898, and British, French, Italian and Russian troops were stationed in four separate zones there until July 1908. On 7 October 1908, the Cretan Assembly proclaimed union with Greece, but this was not recognised until Turkey ceded the island by the Treaty of London on 30 May 1913.

Crete, formerly part of the Turkish Empire, was made autonomous, under Turkish suzerainty, in November 1898 with British, French, Italian and Russian troops stationed in separate zones to keep the peace.

I. BRITISH ADMINISTRATION

CANDIA PROVINCE (HERAKLEION)

(Now Iraklion)

(Currency. 40 paras = 1 piastre)

The British postal service operated from 25 November 1898 until the end of 1899.

Overseas mail franked with Nos. B1/B5 was forwarded through the Austrian post office at Canea, being additionally franked with stamps of the Austro-Hungarian Post Offices in the Turkish Empire.

B 1 B 2

1998 (25 Nov). Handstruck locally. Imperf.
B1 B **1** 20pa. bright violet £450 £225

1998 (3 Dec). Litho by M. Grundmann, Athens. P 11½.
B2 B **2** 10pa. blue .... 11·00 25·00
  a. Imperf (pair) £250
B3   20pa. green .... 20·00 23·00
  a. Imperf (pair) £250

1899. P 11½.
B4 B **2** 10pa. brown .... 11·00 35·00
  a. Imperf (pair) £250
B5   20pa. rose .... 20·00 19·00
  a. Imperf (pair) £250

Forgeries exist of Nos. B1/B5. Note that genuine examples of T B **2** show a full circle in the ornament above the figures of value. Forgeries with a broken circle in this position are frequently met with.

The British postal service closed at the end of 1899.

After many rebellions against Turkish rule, Crete was made autonomous, under Turkish suzerainty, in November 1898, and British, French, Italian and Russian troops were stationed in four separate zones there until July 1908. On 7 October 1908, the Cretan Assembly proclaimed union with Greece, but this was not recognised until Turkey ceded the island by the Treaty of London on 30 May 1913.

II. RUSSIAN ADMINISTRATION

RETHYMNON PROVINCE

4 Metallik = 1 Grosion (Turkish piastre)

The Russian postal service operated from 1 May to 29 July 1899.

R 1 R 2

CRETE / Russian Administration / Provisional Government of Crete

1899 (May). Handstruck (block of four) locally and with violet or blue control handstamp. Laid paper. Imperf.

R1	R 1	1m. blue (1.5.99)	95·00	65·00
		a. Wove paper	£120	65·00
R2	R 2	1m. green	14·50	6·25
		a. Wove paper	14·50	6·50
R3		2m. rose (1.5.99)	£300	£200
		a. Wove paper	£275	£190
R4		2m. green-black	13·50	6·00
		a. Wove paper	14·50	6·50

R 3　　　　　　　R 4

(Litho Grohmann & Stangel, Athens)

1899 (27 May–8 June). Control mark of Russian double eagle in a circle, in violet. P 11½.

(a) Without stars in oval (27.5.99)

R5	R 3	1m. rose	£200	£130
R6		2m. rose	£200	£130
R7		1g. rose	£200	£130
R8		1m. blue	£200	£130
R9		2m. blue	£200	£130
R10		1g. blue	£200	£130
R11		1m. green	£200	£130
R12		2m. green	£200	£130
R13		1g. green	£200	£130
R14		1m. claret	£200	£130
R15		2m. claret	£200	£130
R16		1g. claret	£200	£130
R17		1m. orange	£200	£130
R18		2m. orange	£200	£130
R19		1g. orange	£200	£130
R20		1m. yellow	£200	£130
R21		2m. yellow	£200	£130
R22		1g. yellow	£200	£130
R23		1m. black	£1300	£1200
R24		2m. black	£1300	£1200
R25		1g. black	£1300	£1200
		a. Perf 10½×10½×12×12		

Nos. R23/R25 may not have been authorised for issue, but used examples are known.

(b) Star at each side. Figures at foot shaded (8.6.99)

R26	R 4	1m. rose	£140	75·00
R27		2m. rose	16·00	13·50
R28		1g. rose	16·00	11·50
R29		1m. blue	43·00	32·00
R30		2m. blue	16·00	13·50
R31		1g. blue	16·00	11·50
R32		1m. green	43·00	32·00
R33		2m. green	16·00	13·50
R34		1g. green	16·00	11·50
R35		1m. claret	43·00	32·00
R36		2m. claret	16·00	13·50
R37		1g. claret	16·00	11·50

Many of the above can be supplied unused without the control mark.

Dangerous forgeries exist.

III. PROVISIONAL GOVERNMENT OF CRETE

High Commissioner: Prince George of Greece

21 December 1898–25 September 1906

100 Lepta = 1 Drachma

1 Hermes　　　**2** Hera　　　**3** Prince George of Greece

4 Talos　　　**5** Minos　　　**6** St George and the Dragon

(Recess Bradbury Wilkinson)

1900 (1 Mar). P 14.

(a) Without opt

1	1	1l. chocolate	65	45
2	2	5l. green	2·50	45
3	3	10l. scarlet	2·10	55
4	2	20l. rose	7·25	1·60

ΠΡΟΣΩΡΙΝΟΝ

7 ('Provisional')

(b) Optd with T 7. P 14

A. In vermilion

5A	3	25l. blue	2·20	1·20
6A	1	50l. deep lilac	3·25	1·50
7A	4	1d. indigo-violet	15·00	15·00
8A	5	2d. brown	38·00	31·00
9A	6	5d. black and green	£190	£190

B. In black

5B	3	25l. blue	3·00	95
6B	1	50l. deep lilac	3·00	2·20
7B	4	1d. indigo-violet	13·00	7·50
		a. Opt inverted	£375	
8B	5	2d. brown	33·00	23·00
9B	6	5d. black and green	£100	£100

I ΔΡΑΧΜΗ

D **8**　　　　　　(D **9**)

(Litho Bradbury Wilkinson)

1901 (Feb). POSTAGE DUE. P 14.

D10	D 8	1l. red	40	40
D11		5l. red	65	40
D12		10l. red	90	50
D13		20l. red	1·30	65
D14		40l. red	12·50	12·50
D15		50l. red	12·50	12·50
D16		1d. red	25·00	25·00
D17		2d. red	16·00	12·50

1901 (June). POSTAGE DUE. Surch with T D **9**.

D18	D 8	1d. on 1d. red	12·50	10·50

ΠΡΟΣΩΡΙΝΟΝ　5　5

(8)　　　　　(9)

1901. Optd locally with T **8**.

10	3	25l. blue (Grey-Blk.)	31·00	1·30
		a. First letter of opt inverted	£450	£300
11		25l. blue (Blk.)	31·00	1·30
		a. 'S' of opt omitted	£190	90·00

1901. Without opt. Colours changed. P 14.

12	1	1l. olive-yellow	1·30	1·40
13	2	20l. orange	3·75	1·20
14	1	50l. ultramarine	15·00	15·00

No. 12 is a revenue stamp which was authorised for postal use for about 14 days in 1901 and again in 1904. Other values in olive-yellow are revenue stamps without postal validity.

1901–02. As Nos. 5/9 but without opt.

15	3	25l. blue	12·50	65
16	1	50l. deep lilac	44·00	31·00
17	4	1d. indigo-violet	50·00	31·00
18	5	2d. brown	16·00	13·00
19	6	5d. black and green	20·00	15·00

CRETE / Provisional Government of Crete

1904 (Dec). No. 13 surch with T **9**.
20	**2**	5l. on 20l. orange	3·75	1·30
		a. '5' with straight top	£190	£190

10 Rhea   **11** Europa   **12** Prince George of Greece

13 Miletus   **14** Triton   **15** Ariadne

16 Europa and Jupiter   **17** Minos Ruins

18 View of Mount Ida, etc.

(Recess Bradbury Wilkinson)

1905 (9 Feb). P 14.
21	**10**	2l. slate-lilac	1·90	25
22	**11**	5l. green	2·50	25
23	**12**	10l. red	2·50	1·30
24	**13**	20l. blue-green	7·00	75
25	**14**	25l. ultramarine	8·75	1·30
26	**15**	50l. brown	10·00	3·75
27	**16**	1d. sepia and carmine	75·00	50·00
28	**17**	3d. black and orange	44·00	35·00
29	**18**	5d. black and olive-green	20·00	20·00

Date quoted is that of earliest use seen.

High Commissioner: Alexander Zaimis
25 September 1906

19 High Commissioner A. T. A. Zaimis

20 Landing of Prince George of Greece at Suda

(Recess Bradbury Wilkinson)

1907 (28 Aug). P 14.
30	**19**	25l. black and blue	50·00	1·30
31	**20**	1d. black and green	12·50	8·75

O **21**   O **22**

(Litho Bradbury Wilkinson)

1908 (14 Jan). OFFICIAL. P 14.
O32	O **21**	10l. dull claret	25·00	1·30
O33	O **22**	30l. slate-blue	50·00	1·30

ΕΛΛΑΣ

21 Hermes   (**22**)

Varieties

A. 'Σ' inverted reading 'ΕΛΛΑΕ'
B. 'Δ' instead of 'Α', reading 'ΕΛΛΔΣ'
C. 'Ε' omitted, reading 'ΛΛΑΣ'
D. 'Α' and 'Λ' transposed, reading 'ΕΛΑΛΣ'
E. First 'Λ' omitted, reading 'Ε ΛΑΣ'
F. 'Σ' omitted, reading 'ΕΛΛΑ'

1908 (21 Sept). Optd with T **22** ('GREECE').
32	**1**	1l. chocolate (No. 1)	75	50
		a. Variety A	15·00	15·00
		b. Variety B	15·00	15·00
		g. Opt inverted	31·00	31·00
33	**10**	2l. slate-lilac (No. 21)	75	50
		a. Variety A	19·00	19·00
		b. Variety B	19·00	19·00
		h. Opt double		
		i. Pair, one without opt	75·00	75·00
34	**11**	5l. green (No. 22)	75	50
		a. Variety A	19·00	19·00
		b. Variety B	19·00	19·00
		c. Variety C	£150	£150
		d. Variety D	£180	£180
		e. Variety E	£150	£150
		g. Opt inverted		
		i. Pair, one without opt		
35	**3**	10l. scarlet (No. 3)	1·50	1·00
		c. Variety C	90·00	90·00
		d. Variety D	90·00	90·00
		f. Variety F		
		g. Opt inverted		
36	**21**	10l. dull carmine	3·75	1·00
		a. Variety A	23·00	23·00
		b. Variety B	23·00	23·00
		i. Pair, one without opt	£130	£130
37	**13**	20l. blue-green (No. 24)	3·75	1·30
		f. Variety F		
		i. Pair, one without opt		
38	**19**	25l. black and blue (No. 30)	10·00	2·50
		d. Variety D		
		f. Variety F		
39	**15**	50l. brown (No. 26)	14·00	5·00
		g. Opt inverted	£300	£300
40	**16**	1d. sepia and carmine (No. 27)	£100	75·00
		f. Variety F		
41	**5**	2d. brown (No. 18)	12·50	10·00
		f. Variety F		
42	**17**	3d. black and orange (No. 28)	44·00	41·00
43	**18**	5d. black and olive-green (No. 29)	38·00	38·00

The above were issued before the (unrecognised) proclamation of union with Greece.

Varieties

A. 'Σ' inverted, reading 'ΕΛΛΑ Ε'
B. 'Δ' instead of 'Α' reading 'ΕΛΛΔΣ'
C. 'Α' inverted, reading 'ΕΛΛΑΣ'
D. 'Σ' omitted, reading 'ΕΛΛΑ'

1908 (Sept). POSTAGE DUE. Optd with T **22**.
D44	D **8**	1l. red	40	40
		a. Variety A		
		c. Variety C		
		d. Variety D		
		e. Opt inverted		

CRETE / Provisional Government of Crete / Revolutionary Assembly

D45		f. Pair, one without opt		
		5l. red	75	75
		a. Variety A		
		d. Variety D		
		e. Opt inverted		
D46		10l. red	75	75
		a. Variety A		
		e. Opt inverted		
		f. Pair, one without opt		
D47		20l. red	1·90	1·90
		a. Variety A		
D48		40l. red	8·75	7·50
		a. Variety A	£110	£110
		b. Variety B	75·00	75·00
		e. Opt inverted		
D49		50l. red	11·50	10·00
		e. Opt inverted		
		f. Pair, one without opt		
D50		1d. red (No. D16)	£375	£375
		b. Variety B		
		f. Pair, one without opt		
D51		1d. on 1d. red (No. D18)	12·50	10·00
		a. Variety A	£150	£150
		b. Variety B	£150	£150
		e. Opt inverted		
D52		2d. red	20·00	12·50
		a. Variety A	£150	£150
		b. Variety B	£150	£150
		e. Opt inverted		

1908. OFFICIAL. Optd with T **22**.
O44	O **21**	10l. dull claret	19·00	1·30
		a. 'Σ' inverted	75·00	31·00
		b. 'Δ' for 'Λ'	75·00	31·00
O45	O **22**	30l. slate-blue	38·00	1·30
		a. Opt inverted	£190	£190
		b. 'Σ' inverted	£110	55·00
		c. 'Δ' for 'Λ'	£110	55·00

ΕΛΛΑΣ
(23)

ΠΡΟΣΩΡΙΝΟΝ
(24)

2
ΠΡΟΣΩΡΙΝΟΝ
(25)

ΕΛΛΑΣ
ΕΛΛΑΣ

5 **5**
ΠΡΟΣΩΡΙΝΟΝ
(26)

1909. Optd or surch with Types **23/26** for postal use.
44	23	1l. olive-yellow (No. 12)	3·50	3·50
45		1l. red (No. D10)	1·90	1·50
46	24	2l. on 20l. red (No. D47)	1·90	1·50
		a. Surch inverted	95·00	
		b. 'D' for first 'P'	55·00	55·00
47	25	2l. on 20l. red (No. D13)	1·90	1·60
48	26	5l. on 20l. rose (No. 4)	£200	£200
49		5l. on 20l. orange (No. 13)	1·90	1·60

ΕΛΛΑΣ
(27)

ΕΛΛΑΣ
(28)

ΕΛΛΑΣ
(29)

ΕΛΛΑΣ
(30)

1909. Optd with Types **27/29**.
50	27	10l. dull carmine (Type **21**)	3·75	1·30
		a. Opt inverted	£120	
51		20l. blue-green (No. 24)	6·25	1·30
52	29	25l. black and blue (No. 30)	6·25	2·50
53	27	50l. brown (No. 26)	10·00	5·00
54	28	1d. black and green (No. 31)	15·00	8·75
55	27	2d. brown (No. 18)	15·00	12·50
56	28	3d. black and orange (No. 28)	£130	£120
57	29	5d. black and olive-green (No. 29)	50·00	50·00

1909 (Mar)–**10**. Optd as T **30**.
58		1l. chocolate (R.) (No. 1)	50	25
59		2l. slate-lilac (R.) (No. 21)	50	40
60		5l. green (R.) (No. 22)	50	40
61		10l. dull carmine (Type **21**)	75	75
62		20l. blue-green (R.) (No. 24) (1.2.10)	2·00	75
63		25l. ultramarine (R.) (No. 25) (1.2.10)	3·25	75
64		50l. brown (R.) (No. 26) (1.2.10)	7·50	1·80
65		1d. sepia and carmine (No. 27) (5.10)	90·00	90·00
66		3d. black and orange (R.) (No. 28) (5.10)	75·00	75·00
67		5d. black and olive-green (R.) (No. 29) (5.10)	50·00	50·00

1910 (Feb). OFFICIAL. Optd as T **30**.
O68	O **21**	10l. dull claret	2·50	1·30
O69	O **22**	30l. slate-blue	2·50	1·30

1910 (April). POSTAGE DUE. Optd as T **30**.
D70	D **8**	1l. red	50	40
D71		5l. red	1·30	40
D72		10l. red	1·30	50
D73		20l. red	3·25	1·90
D74		40l. red	12·50	5·75
D75		50l. red	19·00	12·50
D76		1d. red	31·00	31·00
D77		2d. red	31·00	31·00

The 1l. is found overprinted 'ΧΑΡΤΟΣΗΜΟΝ', = Revenue, and has no postal significance.

After Greece officially took over Crete on 10 December 1913, Greek stamps were placed on sale. The remainders of Cretan stamps were overprinted and issued in Greece in 1923 (see Greece Nos. 358/402).

During the Italian Occupation of the eastern part of Crete in 1941–1943 stamps of the Dodecanese Islands were used there.

IV. REVOLUTIONARY ASSEMBLY

March-November, 1905

In March, 1905, a revolt in favour of union with Greece began, organised by Venizelos with Headquarters at Theriso, south of Canea. The revolt collapsed in November, 1905.

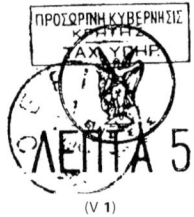

(V **1**)

(Handstamped by Kokinakis, Stangel, Athens)

1905 (1 Sept). T V **1** and similar type, but with Greek characters meaning 'drachma' for No. R5.
V1		5l. carmine-rose and blue-green	19·00	10·00
V2		10l. green and rose	19·00	10·00
V3		20l. blue and carmine-rose	19·00	10·00
V4		50l. green and violet	19·00	10·00
V5		1d. carmine-rose and blue	19·00	10·00

Many varieties are to be found such as 'tête-bêche', 'semi-tête-bêche', 'without the circular control', 'control inverted, 'stamps overlapping', 'double print', etc, etc. We believe that most of these are bogus varieties.

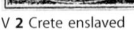

V **2** Crete enslaved   V **3** King George of Greece

(Litho Kokinakis, Athens)

1905 (5 Oct). P 11½.
V6	V **2**	5l. orange	1·00	1·00
V7		10l. grey	1·00	1·00
V8		20l. mauve	1·00	1·00
V9		50l. blue	2·00	2·00
V10	V **3**	1d. violet and red	5·00	5·00
V11		2d. brown and green	7·50	7·50

These stamps imperf are reprints.

V **4** Map of Crete

1905. Imperf.
V12	V **4**	5l. green	19·00
V13		10l. red	19·00
V14		20l. blue	38·00

The above were prepared but not issued. They also exist tête-bêche.

AUSTRO-HUNGARIAN POST OFFICES

Postal agencies opened by the Austrian Lloyd Company at Canea, Candia and Rethymnon had by the 1890s become Post Offices. Stamps issued for Lombardy and Venetia and for Austro-Hungarian Post Offices in the Turkish Empire (the latter denominated in either Turkish or French currency) were used in these offices but such use can only be identified by the postmarks. For listings of these stamps see *Austria & Hungary* or *Central Asia* of this catalogue.

These post offices closed on 15 December 1914.

FRENCH POST OFFICES

100 Centimes = 1 Franc
25 Centimes = 1 Piastre

French Post Offices were opened at Canea, Rethymnon, Candia, San Nicolo (Ayios Nikolaus). Sitia and Hierapetra in July 1897.

T **10** of France unoverprinted was used at first, cancelled with datestamps. No. 4 of French Post Offices in Turkish Empire was also used in Crete.

French stamps overprinted or surcharged.

1902 (Oct)–**03**. Blanc (T **11**), Mouchon (T **14**) and Merson (T **13**), types of France, inscr CRETE. P 14×13½.
1	**11**	1c. grey	3·25	2·30
2		2c. claret	1·90	2·00
3		3c. orange-red	2·50	2·75
4		4c. brown	3·25	3·75
5		5c. green	2·75	2·30
6	**14**	10c. carmine (12.02)	3·75	2·75
7		15c. pale red (2.03)	4·25	4·75
8		20c. purple-brown (3.03)	4·75	5·25
9		25c. blue (9.03)	7·00	4·00
10		30c. mauve (5.03)	8·00	16·00
11	**13**	40c. red and pale blue	19·00	24·00
12		50c. brown and lavender	20·00	24·00
13		1f. lake and yellow-green	29·00	26·00
14		2f. deep lilac and buff	50·00	60·00
		a. Imperf	£150	
15		5f. deep blue and buff	75·00	70·00
1/15 Set of 15			£200	£225

1903 (Feb–Mar). Nos. 9 and 12/15, surch with values in Turkish currency, as T **1** (No. 16) or T **2** (others).
16	**14**	1pi. on 25c. blue (3.03)	70·00	60·00
17	**13**	2pi. on 50c. brown and lavender	85·00	70·00
18		4pi. on 1f. lake and green	£130	£140
19		8pi. on 2f. deep lilac and buff	£160	£160
20		20pi. on 5f. deep blue and buff	£250	£250
16/20 Set of 5			£600	£600

The French post offices at Ayios Nikolaos, Sitia and Hierapetra were closed in December 1899 and the three others on 13 October 1914.

ITALIAN POST OFFICES

1900. 40 Paras = 1 Piastre
1906. 100 Centesimi = 1 Lira

A military post office using unoverprinted Italian stamps operated in 1899. A civil post office opened 15 January 1900 and closed 31 December 1914.

Italian stamps surcharged or overprinted

1900 (10 July). Stamp of 1893 (Umberto I) surch as T **1** but without 'LA CANEA'.
1	27	1pi. on 25c. blue (R.)	14·50	£100

1901 (1 July). Stamp of 1901 (Victor Emmanuel III) surch with T **1**.
2	33	1pi. on 25c. blue	8·25	16·00

1906 (5 Nov). EXPRESS LETTER. No. E73 optd with T **2**.
E1	E 35	25c. rose	12·50	28·00

1906 (15 Nov). Stamps of 1901 and 1905 (Arms (T **30**) or portraits of Victor Emmanuel III (others)) optd with T **2**.
3	30	1c. brown	3·25	5·00
		a. Opt double	£425	
		b. Pair, one with opt	£1500	
4	31	2c. orange-brown	3·25	5·00
		a. Opt double	£425	
		b. Pair, one with opt	£2250	
5	32	5c. green	4·50	5·00
6	33	10c. lake	£350	£225
7		15c. on 20c. orange (No. 73)	6·25	5·00
8		25c. blue	15·00	20·00
9		40c. brown	15·00	20·00
10		45c. grey-green	15·00	20·00
11		50c. mauve	15·00	20·00
12	34	1l. brown and green	80·00	95·00
13		5l. blue and rose	£475	£425
3/13 Set of 11			£900	£750

1907–12. Stamps of 1906–1909 (portraits of Victor Emmanuel III) optd with T **2**.
14	37	5c. green (7.07)	3·25	3·75
		a. Opt inverted	£400	
15	38	10c. rose (3.07)	3·25	3·75
		a. Opt double		
16	41	15c. slate-black (V.) (1.12)	7·50	6·25
17	39	25c. blue (4.09)	7·50	12·50
18	40	40c. pale brown (1910)	39·00	50·00
19		50c. mauve (6.09)	7·50	12·50
14/19 Set of 6			60·00	80·00

Dodecanese Islands

A. ITALIAN OCCUPATION

These islands (literally, in Greek, the '12 Islands') consist of 12 small islands in the south-east Aegean Sea, with the larger island of Rhodes. In 1912 they declared their independence from Turkey, but they were occupied by Italy in May of that year, during the Turco-Italian War; her possession of them was not recognised until the Greco-Italian Agreement of 10 August 1920. Castelrosso was placed under the same administration in 1921.

100 Centesimi = 1 Lira

1912 (22 Sept). Nos. 77 and 79 of Italy optd 'EGEO'.

1	39	25c. blue	70·00	44·00
		a. Opt inverted	£300	£300
2	40	50c. violet	70·00	44·00
		a. Opt inverted	£300	£300

1912 (1 Dec)–**22**. Stamps of Italy (Arms (T **31**) or various portraits of Victor Emmanuel III (others)) optd for the individual islands (in capitals on Nos. 6 and 10, in upper and lower case on others).

A. Calimno

3A	31	2c. orange-brown	10·00	8·75
4A	37	5c. green	4·00	8·25
5A	38	10c. rose-red	1·20	8·25
6A	49	15c. slate (No. 90, no wmk) (V.)	50·00	24·00
7A	37	15c. slate (No. 104, wmkd) (10.21)	7·00	60·00
8A	49	20c. on 15c. slate (No. 100) (1.1.16)	25·00	44·00
9A	41	20c. orange (No. 101, no wmk) (6.17)	£130	£200
10A		20c. orange (No. 105, wmkd) (9.21)	7·00	60·00
11A	39	25c. blue	10·00	8·75
12A	40	40c. brown	1·20	8·75
13A		50c. violet	1·20	22·00
3A/13A Set of 11			£225	£400

B. Caso

3B	31	2c. orange-brown	10·00	9·50
4B	37	5c. green	4·00	9·50
5B	38	10c. rose-red	1·20	9·50
6B	49	15c. slate (No. 90, no wmk) (V.)	60·00	24·00
7B	37	15c. slate (No. 104, wmkd) (10.21)	7·00	55·00
8B	49	20c. on 15c. slate (No. 100) (1.1.16)	2·50	44·00
9B	41	20c. orange (No. 101, no wmk) (6.17)	£180	£200
10B		20c. orange (No. 105, wmkd) (9.21)	7·00	55·00
11B	39	25c. blue	1·20	9·50
12B	40	40c. brown	1·20	9·50
13B		50c. violet	1·20	22·00
3B/13B Set of 11			£250	£400

C. Cos

3C	31	2c. orange-brown	10·00	9·50
4C	37	5c. green	£110	9·50
5C	38	10c. rose-red	5·50	9·50
6C	49	15c. slate (No. 90, no wmk) (V.)	70·00	24·00
7C	37	15c. slate (No. 104, wmkd) (10.21)	7·00	60·00
8C	49	20c. on 15c. slate (No. 100) (1.1.16)	25·00	48·00
9C	41	20c. orange (No. 101, no wmk) (6.17)	80·00	£200
10C		20c. orange (No. 105, wmkd) (9.21)	7·00	55·00
11C	39	25c. blue	47·00	9·50
12C	40	40c. brown	1·20	9·50
13C		50c. violet	1·20	22·00
3C/13C Set of 11			£325	£400

D. Karki

3D	31	2c. orange-brown	10·00	9·50
4D	37	5c. green	3·75	9·50
5D	38	10c. rose-red	1·20	9·50
6D	49	15c. slate (No. 90, no wmk) (V.)	60·00	24·00
7D	37	15c. slate (No. 104, wmkd) (10.21)	7·00	55·00
8D	49	20c. on 15c. slate (No. 100) (1.1.16)	3·75	38·00
9D	41	20c. orange (No. 101, no wmk) (6.17)	£180	£200
10D		20c. orange (No. 105, wmkd) (9.21)	7·00	55·00
11D	39	25c. blue	1·20	9·50
12D	40	40c. brown	1·20	9·50
13D		50c. violet	1·20	22·00
3D/13D Set of 11			£250	£400

E. Leros

3E	31	2c. orange-brown	12·00	9·50
4E	37	5c. green	8·50	9·50
5E	38	10c. rose-red	2·50	9·50
6E	49	15c. slate (No. 90, no wmk) (V.)	£100	24·00
7E	37	15c. slate (No. 104, wmkd) (10.21)	7·00	55·00
8E	49	20c. on 15c. slate (No. 100) (1.1.16)	25·00	44·00
9E	41	20c. orange (No. 101, no wmk) (6.17)	80·00	£225
10E		20c. orange (No. 105, wmkd) (9.21)	£225	£150
11E	39	25c. blue	65·00	9·50
12E	40	40c. brown	7·00	9·50
13E		50c. violet	1·20	22·00
3E/13E Set of 11			£475	£500

F. Lipso

3F	31	2c. orange-brown	10·00	9·50
4F	37	5c. green	3·75	9·50
5F	38	10c. rose-red	2·50	9·50
6F	49	15c. slate (No. 90, no wmk) (V.)	60·00	24·00
7F	37	15c. slate (No. 104, wmkd) (10.21)	7·00	55·00
8F	49	20c. on 15c. slate (No. 100) (1.1.16)	2·50	40·00
9F	41	20c. orange (No. 101, no wmk) (6.17)	£110	£200
10F		20c. orange (No. 105, wmkd) (9.21)	7·50	55·00
11F	39	25c. blue	1·20	9·50
12F	40	40c. brown	1·20	9·50
13F		50c. violet	1·20	22·00
3F/13F Set of 11			£190	£400

G. Nisiros

3G	31	2c. orange-brown	10·00	9·50
4G	37	5c. green	3·75	9·50
5G	38	10c. rose-red	1·20	9·50
6G	49	15c. slate (No. 90, no wmk) (V.)	55·00	24·00
7G	37	15c. slate (No. 104, wmkd) (10.21)	38·00	60·00
8G	49	20c. on 15c. slate (No. 100) (1.1.16)	2·50	38·00
9G	41	20c. orange (No. 101, no wmk) (6.17)	£190	£200
10G		20c. orange (No. 105, wmkd) (9.21)	£140	£150
11G	39	25c. blue	3·25	7·25
12G	40	40c. brown	1·20	7·25
13G		50c. violet	6·25	21·00
3G/13G Set of 11			£400	£475

H. Patmos

3H	31	2c. orange-brown	10·00	9·50
4H	37	5c. green	4·00	9·50
5H	38	10c. rose-red	3·50	9·50
6H	49	15c. slate (No. 90, no wmk) (V.)	55·00	24·00
7H	37	15c. slate (No. 104, wmkd) (10.21)	7·00	60·00
8H	49	20c. on 15c. slate (No. 100) (1.1.16)	25·00	48·00
9H	41	20c. orange (No. 101, no wmk) (6.17)	£120	£200
10H		20c. orange (No. 105, wmkd) (9.21)	£225	£225
11H	39	25c. blue	1·50	9·50
12H	40	40c. brown	5·75	9·50
13H		50c. violet	1·30	21·00
3H/13H Set of 11			£400	£550

I. Piscopi

3I	31	2c. orange-brown	10·00	9·50
4I	37	5c. green	4·00	9·50
5I	38	10c. rose-red	1·20	9·50
6I	49	15c. slate (No. 90, no wmk) (V.)	60·00	24·00
7I	37	15c. slate (No. 104, wmkd) (10.21)	25·00	60·00
8I	49	20c. on 15c. slate (No. 100) (1.1.16)	2·50	40·00
9I	41	20c. orange (No. 101, no wmk) (6.17)	£110	£200
10I		20c. orange (No. 105, wmkd) (9.21)	75·00	90·00
11I	39	25c. blue	1·20	9·50
12I	40	40c. brown	1·20	9·50
13I		50c. violet	1·20	21·00
3I/13I Set of 11			£250	£425

J. Rodi*

3J	31	2c. orange-brown	1·30	9·50
4J	37	5c. green	4·00	9·50
5J	38	10c. rose-red	1·20	9·50
6J	49	15c. slate (No. 90, no wmk) (V.)	60·00	24·00
7J	37	15c. slate (No. 104, wmkd) (10.21)	£225	85·00
8J	49	20c. on 15c. slate (No. 100) (1.1.16)	£190	£200
9J	41	20c. orange (No. 101, no wmk) (6.17)	£275	£200
10J		20c. orange (No. 105, wmkd) (9.21)	10·00	25·00
11J	39	25c. blue	4·00	9·50
12J	40	40c. brown	6·00	9·50
13J		50c. violet	1·20	22·00
3J/13J Set of 11			£700	£550

* Dates of issue of Nos. 7, 9 and 10 with the 'Rodi' overprint were 4.22, 5.17 and 8.19 respectively.

K. Scarpanto

3K	31	2c. orange-brown	10·00	9·50
4K	37	5c. green	4·00	9·50
5K	38	10c. rose-red	1·20	9·50
6K	49	15c. slate (No. 90, no wmk) (V.)	47·00	24·00
7K	37	15c. slate (No. 104, wmkd) (10.21)	25·00	46·00
8K	49	20c. on 15c. slate (No. 100) (1.1.16)	2·50	46·00
9K	41	20c. orange (No. 101, no wmk) (6.17)	£180	£200
10K		20c. orange (No. 105, wmkd) (9.21)	75·00	70·00
11K	39	25c. blue	10·00	9·50
12K	40	40c. brown	1·20	9·50
13K		50c. violet	3·50	22·00
3K/13K Set of 11			£325	£400

1916 DODECANESE ISLANDS / Italian Occupation

L. Simi

3L	31	2c. orange-brown	16·00	9·50
4L	37	5c. green	30·00	9·50
5L	38	10c. rose-red	1·20	9·50
6L	49	15c. slate (No. 90, no wmk) (V.)	80·00	24·00
7L	37	15c. slate (No. 104, wmkd) (10.21)	£180	90·00
8L	49	20c. on 15c. slate (No. 100) (1.1.16)	16·00	33·00
9L	41	20c. orange (No. 101, no wmk) (6.17)	95·00	£140
10L		20c. orange (No. 105, wmkd) (9.21)	95·00	49·00
11L	39	25c. blue	6·25	9·50
12L	40	40c. brown	1·20	9·50
13L		50c. violet	1·20	22·00
3L/13L Set of 11			£475	£375

M. Stampalia

3M	31	2c. orange-brown	10·00	9·50
4M	37	5c. green	1·20	9·50
5M	38	10c. rose-red	1·20	9·50
6M	49	15c. slate (No. 90, no wmk) (V.)	55·00	24·00
7M	37	15c. slate (No. 104, wmkd) (10.21)	17·00	46·00
8M	49	20c. on 15c. slate (No. 100) (1.1.16)	2·50	31·00
9M	41	20c. orange (No. 101, no wmk) (6.17)	£120	£140
10M		20c. orange (No. 105, wmkd) (9.21)	65·00	70·00
11M	39	25c. blue	1·90	9·50
12M	40	40c. brown	6·25	9·50
13M		50c. violet	1·20	22·00
3M/13M Set of 11			£250	£350

1916–24. Nos. 66, 110 and 71 of Italy optd 'Rodi'.

14	33	20c. orange (1.16)	5·00	12·50
15	39	85c. red-brown (9.22)	£100	£150
16	34	1l. brown and green (1924)	5·75	

1 Rhodian Windmill

2 Knight kneeling before the Holy City

(Des F. Di Fausto. Litho (A) by Bestelli & Tuminelli, Milan, (B) by Govt Ptg Wks, Rome)

1929 (19 May)–**32**. King of Italy's Visit to the Aegean Islands. Types **1/2** (and similar types).

A. Without printers' imprint. No wmk. P 11

17A		5c. claret	16·00	2·75
18A		10c. sepia	16·00	2·75
19A		20c. scarlet	16·00	1·30
20A		25c. green	16·00	1·30
21A		30c. deep blue	44·00	1·30
22A		50c. chocolate	16·00	1·10
23A		1l.25 deep blue	16·00	2·75
24A		5l. claret	£110	£150
25A		10l. olive-green	£375	£400
17A/25A Set of 9			£550	£500

B. With imprint (8.32). Wmk Crown. P 14

17B		5c. claret	2·00	30
18B		10c. sepia	2·00	30
19B		20c. scarlet	2·00	30
20B		25c. green	2·00	30
21B		30c. deep blue	2·00	30
22B		50c. chocolate	2·00	30
23B		1l.25 deep blue	2·00	30
24B		5l. claret	2·00	3·25
25B		10l. olive-green	4·00	7·50
17B/25B Set of 9			18·00	11·50

Designs: Vert—5c. T **1**; 10c. Galley of Knights of St John; 20c., 25c. Knight defending Christianity; 50c., 1l.25, A Knight's tomb. As T **2**: 30c., 5l., 10l.

Although these stamps are inscribed 'RODI' they were issued for general use in all the Dodecanese Islands.

Nos. 17B/25B and 124/127 were also used in eastern Crete during its Italian occupation, 1941–1943.

XXI Congresso Idrologico (3) ISOLE ITALIANE DELL'EGEO (4)

1930 (25 Sept). 21st Hydrological Congress. Nos. 17A/25A optd with T **3**.

26	5c. claret	25·00	38·00
27	10c. sepia	28·00	38·00
28	20c. scarlet	31·00	40·00
29	25c. green	50·00	40·00
30	30c. deep blue	31·00	40·00
31	50c. chocolate	£1100	90·00
32	1l.25 deep blue	£750	£160
33	5l. claret	£650	£600
34	10l. olive-green	£650	£750
26/34 Set of 9		£3000	£1600

1930 (20 Oct). Ferrucci issue of Italy (colours changed), optd in capital letters for the individual islands.

A. CALINO	F. LISSO
B. CASO	G. NISIRO
C. COO	H. PATMO
D. CALCHI	I. PISCOPI
E. LERO	J. RODI
	K. SCARPANTO
	L. SIMI
	M. STAMPALIA

Same prices for each island

35	114	20c. bright violet (R.)	5·75	10·50
36	115	25c. deep green (R.)	5·75	10·50
37		50c. black (R.)	5·75	18·00
38		1l.25 blue (R.)	5·75	18·00
39	116	5l. +2l. carmine-red (B.)	9·00	30·00
35/39 Set of 5			29·00	80·00

See also Castelrosso Nos. 25/29.

1930 (20 Oct). AIR. Ferrucci air stamps of Italy (colours changed), optd with T **4**.

40	117	50c. purple (B.)	16·00	31·00
41		1l. deep blue (R.)	16·00	31·00
42		5l. +2l. carmine-red (B.)	34·00	75·00
40/42 Set of 3			60·00	£120

ISOLE ITALIANE DELL'EGEO (5)   1931 CONGRESSO EUCARISTICO ITALIANO (6)

1930 (1 Dec). Virgil. Nos. 290/302 of Italy optd as T **5**. Colours changed.

(a) POSTAGE. As T **118**

43	15c. slate-violet (R.)	2·75	23·00
44	20c. chestnut (B.)	2·75	23·00
45	25c. blue-green (R.)	2·75	11·00
46	30c. brown (B.)	2·75	11·00
47	50c. purple (R.)	2·75	11·00
48	75c. carmine-red (R.)	2·75	24·00
49	1l.25 greenish blue (R.)	2·75	31·00
50	5l. +1l.50 purple (R.)	8·50	60·00
51	10l. +2l.50 brown (B.)	8·50	60·00

(b) AIR. T **119**

52	50c. blue-green (R.)	3·75	47·00
53	1l. carmine-red (R.)	3·75	47·00
54	7l.70 +1l.30 brown (R.)	7·25	47·00
55	9l. +2l. slate-blue (R.)	7·25	90·00
43/55 Set of 13		50·00	£425

Designs: 15c. T **118**; 20c. The passing legions, *Aeneid* VI; 25c. Landing of Aeneas, *Aeneid* VII; 30c. Earth's bounties, *Georgics* II; 50c. Harvesting, *Georgics* II; 75c. Rural life, *Georgics* II; 1l.25, Aeneas sights Italy, *Aeneid* III; 5l. A shepherd's hut, *Bucolics* VII; 10l. Turnus, King of the Rutuli, *Aeneid* XI. Nos. 52/55, T **119**.

1931 (16 Sept). Italian Eucharistic Congress. Nos. 17A/23A optd with T **6**.

56	5c. claret (B.)	9·75	23·00
57	10c. sepia (R.)	9·75	23·00
58	20c. scarlet (B.)	9·75	30·00
	a. Opt inverted	£300	
59	25c. green (R.)	9·75	30·00
60	30c. deep blue (R.)	9·75	30·00
61	50c. chocolate (R.)	80·00	70·00
62	1l.25 deep blue (R.)	65·00	£110
56/62 Set of 7		£170	£275

1932 (21 Feb). Types **121/122** and similar types of Italy (St Anthony) optd as T **4**. Colours changed.

63	20c. slate-purple (B.)	39·00	30·00
64	25c. green (R.)	39·00	30·00
65	30c. red-brown (B.)	39·00	30·00
66	50c. purple (B.)	39·00	30·00
67	75c. carmine-rose (B.)	39·00	37·00
68	1l.25 light blue (R.)	39·00	41·00
69	5l. +2l.50 orange (B.)	39·00	£150
63/69 Set of 7		£250	£325

Designs: Horiz—20c. T **121**; 25c. Sermon to the Fish; 30c. Hermitage of Olivares; 50c. Basilica of the Saint at Padua; 75c. Death of St Antony; 1l.25, St Antony liberating prisoners. Vert—5l.+2l., T **122**.

ISOLE DELL' ITALIANE EGEO (7)

DODECANESE ISLANDS / Italian Occupation 1932

1932 (May–Nov). Dante. Nos. 314/332 of Italy optd as T **7**. Colours changed.

*(a) POSTAGE. As T **124***

70		10c. olive-green	2·30	5·00
71		15c. violet-slate	2·30	5·00
72		20c. chestnut	2·30	5·00
73		25c. green	2·30	5·00
74		30c. orange-vermilion	2·30	5·00
75		50c. purple	2·30	3·75
76		75c. carmine-red	2·30	6·25
77		1l.25 blue	2·30	6·25
78		1l.75 sepia	3·50	8·75
79		2l.75 carmine	3·50	8·75
80		5l. +2l. bright violet	4·00	23·00
81		10l. +2l.50 chocolate	4·00	55·00
70/81	Set of 12		30·00	£120

(b) AIR

82	**125**	50c. carmine	2·40	6·25
83	**126**	1l. green	2·40	6·25
84		3l. purple	2·40	6·25
85		5l. orange-vermilion	2·40	6·25
86	**125**	7l.70 +2l. sepia	5·50	27·00
87	**126**	10l. +2l.50 deep blue	5·50	34·00

Inscr 'ISOLE ITALIANE DELL'EGEO'

88	**127**	100l. olive-green and blue (11.32)	31·00	£160
82/88	Set of 7		46·00	£225

Designs: 10c. Giovanni Boccaccio (writer); 15c. Niccolò Machiavelli (statesman); 20c. Fra Paolo Sarpi (philosopher); 25c. Vittorio Alfieri (poet); 30c. Ugo Foscolo (writer); 50c. Giacomo Leopardi (poet); 75c. Giosuè Carducci (poet); 1l.25, Carlo Botta (historian); 1l.75, Torquato Tasso (poet); 2l.75, Francesco Petrarch (poet); 5l. Ludovico Ariosto (poet); 10l.+2l.50, T **124**.

1932 (28 Aug). Garibaldi issue (Types **128/129** and similar types) of Italy, optd in capital letters for the individual islands. Colours changed.

A. CALINO	F. LISSO	J. RODI
B. CASO	G. NISIRO	K. SCARPANTO
C. COO	H. PATMO	L. SIMI
D. CALCHI	I. PISCOPI	M. STAMPALIA
E. LERO		

Same prices for each island

89	10c. sepia (R.)	25·00	39·00
90	20c. lake-brown (B.)	25·00	39·00
91	25c. green (R.)	25·00	39·00
92	30c. slate-blue (R.)	25·00	39·00
93	50c. purple (R.)	25·00	39·00
94	75c. lake (B.)	25·00	39·00
95	1l.25. deep blue (R.)	25·00	39·00
96	1l.75 +25c. sepia (R.)	25·00	39·00
97	2l.55 +50c. orange-vermilion (B.)	25·00	39·00
98	5l. +1l. deep violet (R.)	25·00	39·00
89/98	Set of 10	£225	£350

See also Castelrosso Nos. 30/39.

1932 (28 Aug). AIR. Garibaldi air stamps as T **130** optd as T **4**. Colours changed.

99	50c. olive-green (R.)	80·00	£170
100	80c. lake (B.)	80·00	£170
101	1l. +25c. deep blue (R.)	80·00	£170
102	2l. +50c. lake-brown (B.)	80·00	£170
103	5l. +1l. slate (R.)	80·00	£170
99/103	Set of 5	£350	£750

Designs: Vert—50c., 1l. T **130**; 80c. The Ravenna hut; 2l. Anita; 5l. Garibaldi.

1932 (28 Aug). AIR EXPRESS. Garibaldi Air Express stamps as T **131** optd as T **4**. Colours changed.

E104	2l.25 +1l. carmine and blue (B.)	£120	£225
E105	4l.50 +1l.50 grey and yellow (Y.)	£120	£225

 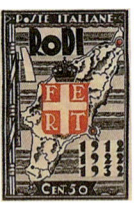

8   9

(Litho Bestelli & Tuminelli, Milan)

1932 (Oct). 20th Anniversary of Italian Occupation of Dodecanese Islands. Wmk Crown. P 11.

106	**8**	5c. scarlet, black and emerald	9·00	20·00
107		10c. scarlet, black and blue	9·00	15·00
108		20c. scarlet, black and yellow	9·00	15·00
109		25c. scarlet, black and violet	9·00	15·00
110		30c. scarlet, black and rose	9·00	15·00
111	**9**	50c. scarlet, black and pale blue	9·00	15·00
112		1l.25 scarlet, maroon and pale blue	9·00	33·00
113		5l. scarlet, blue and pale blue	23·00	80·00
114		10l. scarlet, green and pale blue	65·00	£140
115		25l. scarlet, chocolate and pale blue	£550	£1400
106/115	Set of 10		£650	£1600

10 Airship *Graf Zeppelin*   **11** Wing from the Arms of Francesco Sans

(Des G. Rondini. Photo)

1933 (12 May). AIR. Wmk Crown. P 14.

116	**10**	3l. brown	£110	£275
117		5l. purple	£110	£325
118		10l. blue-green	£110	£500
119		12l. blue	£110	£550
120		15l. carmine	£110	£550
121		20l. black	£110	£550
116/121	Set of 6		£600	£2500

1933 (20 May). AIR. Balbo Transatlantic Mass Formation Flight. As Types **135/136** of Italy, without the pilot's name, optd as T **5** (smaller) on both left and right sides. Centres in slate-blue.

122	**135**	5l.25 +19l.75 scarlet and green/green/scarlet	£100	£200
123	**136**	5l.25 +44l.75 green and scarlet/scarlet/green	£100	£200

(Des B. Bramanti. Typo)

1934 (Jan). AIR. Wmk Crown. P 14.

124	**11**	50c. black and yellow	75	45
125		80c. black and carmine	5·75	5·75
126		1l. black and green	3·75	1·30
127		5l. black and magenta	12·50	14·00
124/127	Set of 4		20·00	19·00

See note below No. 25.

1934 (15 June). World Football Championship. As Nos. 413/421 of Italy optd 'ISOLE ITALIANE DELL'EGEO' as T **5**, but smaller. Colours changed.

(a) POSTAGE

128	20c. lake-red	£100	£110
129	25c. green (R.)	£100	£110
130	50c. bright violet (R.)	£450	65·00
131	1l.25 deep blue (R.)	£100	£225
132	5l. +2l.50 bright blue (R.)	£100	£500
128/132	Set of 5	£750	£900

Designs: Horiz—20c. T **143**; 25c., 50c., 1l.25, Two footballers. Vert—5l. Heading the ball.

(b) AIR

133	50c. brown (R.)	14·00	90·00
134	75c. carmine-red	14·00	90·00
135	5l. +2l.50 orange-vermilion	38·00	£180
136	10l. +5l. green (R.)	38·00	£190
133/136	Set of 4	95·00	£525

Designs (Marina Fiat MF.5 flying boat over): Horiz—50c. Mussolini Stadium, Turin; 5l. Stadium, Rome. Vert—75c. T **144**; 10l. Littoral Stadium, Bologna.

P **12** Galley and Rose

P **13** Stag and St Paul's Gate, Rhodes

(Des B. Bramanti. Photo)

1934 (1 July). PARCEL POST. Wmk Crown. P 13½.

			Used	Used
		Un pair	pair	half
P137	P **12** 5c. orange	6·25	8·00	4·00
P138	10c. scarlet	6·25	8·00	4·00
P139	20c. green	6·25	8·00	4·00

1934 DODECANESE ISLANDS / Italian Occupation

P140	25c. bright violet		6·25	8·00	4·00
P141	50c. deep blue		6·25	8·00	4·00
P142	60c. black		6·25	8·00	4·00
P143	P 13	1l. orange	6·25	8·00	4·00
P144		2l. scarlet	6·25	8·00	4·00
P145		3l. green	6·25	8·00	4·00
P146		4l. bright violet	6·25	8·00	4·00
P147		10l. deep blue	6·25	8·00	4·00
P137/P147 Set of 11			60·00	80·00	40·00

The left-hand portion is affixed to the packet-card, the right-hand portion to the receipt. Prices in the first column are for unused complete pairs, in the second column for used pairs (usually cancelled-to-order) and in the third column for the left half used.

D **14** Badge of the Knights of St John

D **15** Immortelle

(Des B. Bramanti. Photo)

1934 (1 July). POSTAGE DUE. Wmk Crown. P 14.

D148	D **14**	5c. orange	4·25	5·00
D149		10c. scarlet	4·25	5·00
D150		20c. green	4·25	5·00
D151		30c. bright violet	4·25	5·00
D152		40c. deep blue	4·25	6·25
D153	D **15**	50c. orange	4·25	6·25
D154		60c. scarlet	4·25	12·50
D155		1l. green	4·25	12·50
D156		2l. bright violet	4·25	8·75
D148/D156 Set of 9			34·00	60·00

1934 (Dec). Military Medal Centenary. As Nos. 424/441 and E442/E443 of Italy, optd 'ISOLE ITALIANE DELL'EGEO' as T **5**, but smaller. Colours changed.

(a) POSTAGE

157	10c. slate (R.)	65·00	£110
158	15c. brown	65·00	£110
159	20c. orange-vermilion	65·00	£110
160	25c. green (R.)	65·00	£110
161	30c. claret	65·00	£110
162	50c. olive-green	65·00	£110
163	75c. carmine-red	65·00	£110
164	1l.25 blue (R.)	65·00	£110
165	1l.75 +1l. bright violet (R.)	65·00	£110
166	2l.55 +2l. lake	65·00	£110
167	2l.75 +2l. chestnut	65·00	£110
157/167 Set of 11		£650	£1000

Designs: Vert—10c. T **146**; 25c. Mountaineers; 1l.75, Cavalry. Horiz—15c., 50c. Barbed-wire cutter; 20c. Throwing hand-grenade; 30c. Wielding crutch; 75c. Artillery; 1l.25, Soldiers cheering; 2l.55, Sapper; 2l.75, First aid.

(b) AIR

168	25c. green	85·00	£130
169	50c. brown-black (R.)	85·00	£130
170	75c. rose-carmine	85·00	£130
171	80c. brown	85·00	£130
172	1l. +50c. olive-green	75·00	£130
173	2l. +1l. blue (R.)	75·00	£130
174	3l. +2l. bright violet (R.)	75·00	£130
168/174 Set of 7		£500	£825

Designs: Horiz—25c., 80c. T **147**; 50c., 75c. Naval launch; 1l. Caproni Ca 101 aeroplane and troops in desert; 2l. Pomilio PC type biplane and troops. Vert—3l. Unknown soldier's tomb.

(c) AIR EXPRESS

E175	2l. +1l.25 blue	75·00	£130
E176	4l.50 +2l. green	75·00	£130
E175/E176 Set of 9		£650	£1100

Design: Horiz—2l., 4l.50, Caproni Ca 101 aeroplane over triumphal arch.

16 E **17**

(Des B. Bramanti. Photo)

1935 (Apr). Holy Year. Wmk Crown. P 14.

177	**16**	5c. orange	30·00	42·00
178		10c. brown	30·00	42·00
179		20c. carmine	30·00	42·00
180		25c. green	30·00	42·00
181		30c. purple	30·00	42·00
182		50c. chestnut	30·00	42·00
183		1l.25 blue	30·00	£130
177/183 Set of 7			£190	£350

A 5l. value was prepared but not issued (*Price* £325 *un*).

(Des B. Bramanti. Photo)

1935 (6 Dec). EXPRESS LETTER. Wmk Crown. P 14.

E184	E **17**	1l.25 green	4·00	3·50
E185		2l.50 orange	8·25	8·25

ISOLE ITALIANE DELL'ECEO
(**18**)

1938 (10 May). Augustus Bimillenary. As Nos. 506/520 of Italy, optd with T **18**. Colours changed.

(a) POSTAGE

186	10c. olive-brown (B.)	4·75	8·25
187	15c. bright violet (R.)	4·75	8·25
188	20c. red-brown (B.)	4·75	8·25
189	25c. grey-green (R.)	4·75	8·25
190	30c. purple (B.)	4·75	8·25
191	50c. deep blue-green (R.)	4·75	14·00
192	75c. carmine (R.)	4·75	14·00
193	1l.25 deep blue (R.)	4·75	14·00
194	1l.75 +1l. orange (B.)	7·75	33·00
195	2l.55 +2l. sepia (R.)	7·75	33·00
186/195 Set of 10		48·00	£130

Designs: 10c. T **163**; 15c. Military trophies; 20c. Reconstructing temples of Rome; 25c. Census (with reference to birth of Jesus Christ); 30c. Statue of Julius Caesar; 50c. Election of Augustus as Emperor; 75c. Conquest of Ethiopia; 1l.25, Constructing a new fleet; 1l.75, Building the Altar of Peace; 2l.55, The Capitol.

(b) AIR

196	25c. slate-violet (R.)	5·50	11·00
197	50c. green (R.)	5·50	11·00
198	80c. blue (R.)	5·50	23·00
199	1l. +1l. purple (B.)	10·50	34·00
200	5l. +1l. scarlet (B.)	14·50	65·00
196/200 Set of 5		37·00	£130

Designs: 25c. Agriculture; 50c. Prosperity of the Romans; 80c. Horses of the Sun Chariot; 1l. Staff and Map of Roman Empire; 5l. T **164**.

1938 (20 Aug). 600th Death Anniversary of Giotto (painter). Nos. 527 and 530 of Italy optd with T **18**.

201	1l.25 blue (R.)	2·50	3·75
202	2l.75 +2l. brown (R.)	2·50	14·00

19 Dante House, Rhodes   **20** Roman Wolf Statue

21 Crown and Maltese Cross   **22** Savoia Marchetti S. M.75 over Statues, Rhodes Harbour

(Des G. Rondini. Photo)

1940 (3 June). Colonial Exhibition. Types **19/22** and similar design inscr 'TRIENNALE D'OLTREMARE'. Wmk Crown. P 14.

(a) POSTAGE

203	**20**	5c. brown	75	1·90
204	**21**	10c. orange	75	1·90

DODECANESE ISLANDS / Italian Occupation / Island Committee for Union with Greece / Greek Military Administration

205	19	25c. green		1·60	2·50
206	20	50c. violet		1·60	2·50
207	21	75c. carmine		1·60	4·50
208	19	1l.25 blue		1·60	4·50
209	21	2l. +75c. pink		1·60	24·00
203/209 Set of 7				5·50	35·00

(b) AIR

210	22	50c. sepia		2·50	4·50
211	–	1l. violet		2·50	4·50
212	22	2l. +75c. deep blue		2·50	9·50
213	–	5l. +2l.50 red-brown		2·50	18·00
210/213 Set of 4				9·00	30·00

Design: Horiz—1l., 5l. Savoia Marchetti SM.75 aeroplane and Government House, Rhodes.

(23)   (E 24)

1943 (15 Nov). Relief Fund.

(a) POSTAGE. Nos. 17B/24B surch with premium as T 23

214	5c. +5c. claret		4·00	4·75
215	10c. +10c. sepia		4·00	4·75
216	20c. +20c. scarlet		4·00	4·75
217	25c. +25c. green		4·25	4·75
	a. Inverted opt		70·00	
218	30c. +30c. deep blue (R.)		6·25	5·50
219	50c. +50c. chocolate		6·25	5·50
220	1l.25 +1l.25 deep blue (R.)		7·75	8·25
221	5l. +5l. claret		£170	£200
214/221 Set of 8			£190	£225

(b) EXPRESS. Surch with premium as T E 24

E222	E 17	1l.25 +1l.25 green (R.)		90·00	80·00
E223		2l.50 +2l.50 orange (R.)		£120	£110

(25)   (E 26)

1944 (16 July). War Victims' Relief. Nos. 17B/20B and 22B/23B surch with premium as T 25.

224	5c. +3l. claret		3·75	7·75
225	10c. +3l. sepia (R.)		3·75	7·75
226	20c. +3l. scarlet		3·75	7·75
227	25c. +3l. green (R.)		3·75	7·75
228	50c. +3l. chocolate (R.)		3·75	7·75
229	1l.25 +5l. deep blue (R.)		55·00	65·00
224/229 Set of 6			65·00	95·00

1944. EXPRESS LETTER. Nos. 19B/20B surch as T E 26.

E230	1l.25 on 25c. green		1·50	3·25
E231	2l.50 on 20c. scarlet		1·50	3·25

PRO
SINISTRATI
DI
GVERRA

£ 2

(27)

10
FEBBRAIO
1945

(28)

1944 (11 Oct). AIR. War Victims' Relief. Surch with premium as T 27, in silver.

232	11	50c. +2l. black and yellow	20·00	7·50
233		80c. +2l. black and carmine	22·00	15·00
234		1l. +2l. black and green	28·00	19·00
235		5l. +2l. black and magenta	£120	£130
232/235 Set of 4			£170	£150

1945 (18 Feb). Red Cross Fund. Nos. 24B/25B surch with premium as T 28.

236	+10l. on 5l. claret (R.)	19·00	31·00
237	+10l. on 10l. olive-green (R.)	19·00	31·00

In October 1944 the Dodecanese Islands were occupied by the British and Great Britain stamps overprinted 'MEF' were used (see British Occupation of Italian Colonies in *Commonwealth & British Empire* catalogue until 31 March 1947 when they were transferred to Greek administration.

The islands are now known as Kalimnos, Kasos, Kos, Khalki, Leros, Lipsoi, Nisiros, Patmos, Tilos (Piskopi), Rhodes (Rodos), Karpathos, Simi and Astipalaia.

B. ISLAND COMMITTEE FOR UNION WITH GREECE

100 Lepta = 1 Drachma

K **1** Apollo
(Litho Aspiotis)

1912 (21 May). Serrated roul 13½.

K1	K **1**	1l. blue-green	4·50	44·00
K2		5l. deep blue	4·50	44·00
K3		10l. red	4·50	44·00
K1/K3 Set of 3			12·00	£120

This issue was prepared by the Island Committee for Union with Greece but the Italian Military Administration in Rhodes forbade its use. However, it was placed on sale in Kalimnos and a few postally used copies are known. Copies are known cancelled by favour from Kasos, Leros, Patmos, Simi and Astipalaia and forged postmarks exist. This design appears on the Greek issue of 1947 commemorating the transfer of the Dodecanese Islands to Greece.

C. GREEK MILITARY ADMINISTRATION

100 Lepta = 1 Drachma

The Dodecanese Islands were transferred to Greek administration on 31 March 1947.

1947. Optd 'ΣΔΔ'.

(a) Horiz, in silver or red on Nos. 623, 625 and 627 of Greece

G1	10d. on 2000d. blue (Sil.) (1.4.47)	2·00	2·10
G2	10d. on 2000d. blue (R.) (2.4.47)	2·00	2·10
G3	20d. on 500d. olive-brown (R.)	2·00	2·10
G4	30d. on 5d. blue-green (R.)	2·00	2·10
	a. On No. 627a	39·00	41·00

(b) Vert, in black, on stamps as Nos. 642/643 of Greece, but with T 118 within a narrow frame also in black

G5	50d. on 1d. green (20.4.47)	2·20	2·20
	a. Surch inverted	£130	
G6	250d. on 3d. red-brown (20.4.47)	2·20	2·20
	a. Surch inverted	£130	

Nos. G1/G2 although surcharged '10' were sold at and had a franking value of 100 drachmas.

(G 1)

1947 (21 Sept). Stamps of Greece surch as T G **1**.

G7	50d. on 2d. reddish brown (No. 573)	1·00	1·60
G8	250d. on 10d. red-brown (No. 510)	1·30	2·10
G9	400d. on 15d. blue-green (No. 511) (R.)	2·00	3·25
	a. Surch inverted	£110	
G10	1000d. on 200d. ultramarine (No. 581) (R.)	1·70	2·75
	a. On No. 581a	20·00	32·00
G7/G10 Set of 4		5·50	8·75

The islands came under Greek sovereignty on 15 September 1947.

Stamps of Greece have been used since 20 November 1947.

Thrace

A. GREEK OCCUPATION, 1913

Dedeagatz was occupied by Greek troops during the Second Balkan War from 11 July to 21 August and from 1 September to 1 October 1913. Gumultsina was occupied from 16 July to 8 August 1913.

ISSUES FOR DEDEAGATZ
(Now Alexandroupolis)

ΕΛΛΗΝΙΚΗ
ΔΙΟΙΚΗΣΙΣ
ΔΕΔΕΑΓΑΤΣ
ΔΕΚΑ ΛΕΠΤΑ
(1) (10l.)

ΕΛΛΗΝΙΚΗ
ΔΙΟΙΚΗΣΙΣ
ΔΕΔΕΑΓΑΤΣ
10
ΛΕΠΤΑ
(2)

(Trans: 'Greek Administration Dedeagatz')

1913 (18 July). Type-set as T **1**. Circular control cachet with Greek inscription, crown and anchor in carmine (only part on each stamp). No gum. P 11½.
1		ΠΕΝΤΕ l. = 5l. black.............................	75·00	44·00
2		ΛΕΚΑ l. = 10l. black.............................	8·75	6·25
		a. *Tête-bêche*.............................	75·00	50·00
		b. Second 'l' of second word omitted.............................	75·00	50·00
3		25l. black.............................	10·00	8·75

This issue was printed in sheets of eight, containing one 5l., four 10l. (incl. one *tête-bêche* pair) and three 25l. with one blank space (*Price* £225 *unused*, £150 *used*).

1913 (24 July). Stamps of Bulgaria, 1911, surch as T **2**.
4	23	5l. on 1st. myrtle-green (R.)...............	£100	55·00
5	27	10l. on 10st. black and red (B.)...............	44·00	28·00
6	26	25l. on 5st. black and green (B.)...............	55·00	35·00
7	24	50l. on 2st. black and carmine (B.)........	£100	65·00
8	29	1d. on 25st. black and ultramarine (R.)	£140	80·00

The above were overprinted in a setting of eight, the value being altered for each. In position 6 there is a Greek 'L' instead of 'D' for the third letter of the third word.

The 25l. was applied in error to eight copies of the 25st. of Bulgaria, No. 165, of which only three copies are known.

ΠΡΟΣΩΡΙΝΟΝ
ΕΛΛΗΝΙΚΗ
ΔΙΟΙΚΗΣΙΣ
ΔΕΔΕΑΓΑΤΣ
2 ΛΕΠΤΑ 2
(3)

ΠΡΟΣΩΡΙΝΟΝ
ΕΛΛΗΝΙΚΗ
ΔΙΟΙΚΗΣΙΣ
ΔΕΔΕΑΓΑΤΣ
1 ΛΕΠΤΟΝ 1
(4)

1913 (15 Sept). Type-set as T **3** on white paper. Ungummed. Circular control cachet in blue. P 11½.
9		1l. blue.............................	£375	£110
10		2l. blue.............................	£375	£110
11		3l. blue.............................	£375	£110
12		5l. blue.............................	£375	£110
13		10l. blue.............................	£375	£110
14		25l. blue.............................	£375	£110
15		40l. blue.............................	£375	£110
16		50l. blue.............................	£375	£110

Printed in sheets of eight, one of each value (*Price* £3500 *unused*, £1300 *used*).

1913 (25 Sept). Type-set as T **4** on bluish paper. Ungummed. Circular control cachet in blue. P 11½.
17		1l. blue/*blue*.............................	£275	90·00
18		5l. blue/*blue*.............................	£275	90·00
19		10l. blue/*blue*.............................	£275	90·00
20		25l. blue/*blue*.............................	£275	90·00
21		30l. blue/*blue*.............................	£275	90·00
22		50l. blue/*blue*.............................	£275	90·00

Printed in sheets of six, one of each value (*Price* £2500 *unused*, £700 *used*).

For French Post Offices in Dedeagatz (Dédéagh), see under French Post Offices in the Turkish Empire in *French Colonies* or *Central Asia* of this catalogue.

ISSUE FOR GUMULTSINA
(Now Komotini)

(1)

1913 (7 Aug). Stamps of Turkey, 1909–1910, surch as T **1**.
1	28	10l. on 20pa. rose-carmine (B.)...............	70·00	70·00
2		25l. on 10pa. green (R.)...............	£100	£110
3		25l. on 20pa. rose-carmine (B.)...............	£100	£110
4		25l. on 1pi. ultramarine (R.)...............	£150	£150

B. AUTONOMOUS GOVERNMENT OF WESTERN THRACE

The area known as Western Thrace was the territory bounded by the Rhodope Mountains, the Aegean Sea and the Nestos and Evros (formerly Maritza) Rivers. In Turkey until 1912, it was occupied by Bulgarian troops in the First Balkan War that year.

In October 1913 the Moslem inhabitants of Western Thrace drove out the Bulgarian troops and set up an autonomous régime.

40 Paras = 1 Piastre or Grush

1

1913 (Oct). Litho. Imperf.

(a) Size 23×27 mm. (11.11.13)
1	**1**	1pi. blue.............................	25·00	19·00
2		2pi. violet.............................	25·00	19·00

(b) Size 19½×29½ mm
3	**1**	10pa. vermilion.............................	44·00	31·00
4		20pa. blue.............................	44·00	31·00
5		1pi. violet.............................	55·00	38·00

Nos. 1/2 were impressed on envelopes handed in by the public and are known with or without control mark.

(2)   **(3)**

1913 (Oct). Stamps of Turkey (GPO, Constantinople) surch with T **2**.
6	30	1pi. on 2pa. olive-green (R.)...............	38·00	38·00
		a. Surch in black.............................	38·00	38·00
7		1pi. on 5pa. bistre.............................	38·00	38·00
		a. Surch in red.............................	38·00	38·00
8		1pi. on 20pa. rose.............................	44·00	44·00
9		1pi. on 5pi. purple (R.)...............	95·00	95·00
		a. Surch in black.............................	95·00	95·00

THRACE / Autonomous Government of Western Thrace / Allied Occupation / Greek Occupation

10		1pi. on 10pi. vermilion	£150	£150
11		1pi. on 25pi. deep green	£700	£700

1913 (Oct). Stamps of Greece handstamped as T **3** for use in Dedeagatz.

(a) No. 252

12	**35**	10pa. on 1l. brown (B.)	38·00	38·00
13		20pa. on 1l. brown (B.)	38·00	38·00
14		1pi. on 1l. brown (B.)	38·00	38·00

(b) 1911 issue (recess)

15	**29**	10pa. on 1l. green (R.)	31·00	31·00
		a. Surch in blue	31·00	31·00
16	**30**	10pa. on 25l. ultramarine	50·00	50·00
17		20pa. on 2l. carmine (B.)	31·00	31·00
18	**29**	1pi. on 3l. vermilion (B.)	31·00	31·00
19	**31**	2pi. on 5l. green (R.)	90·00	90·00
20	**29**	2½pi. on 10l. carmine (B.)	90·00	90·00
21	**30**	5pi. on 40l. deep blue (R.)	£160	£160

1913 (10 Oct). Stamps of Bulgaria, 1911, handstamped as T **3** for use in Gumultsina.

22	**23**	10pa. on 1st. myrtle-green (R.)	31·00	31·00
23	**24**	20pa. on 2st. black and carmine (B.)	31·00	31·00
24	**26**	1pi. on 5st. black and green (R.)	31·00	31·00
25	**25**	2pi. on 3st. black and lake (B.)	44·00	44·00
26	**27**	2½pi. on 10st. black and red (B.)	55·00	55·00
27	**28**	5pi. on 15st. bistre (B.)	£100	£100

By the Treaty of Bucharest, 1913, Bulgaria acquired Western Thrace.

C. ALLIED OCCUPATION, 1919–1920

After the defeat of Bulgaria in October 1918, Allied troops occupied Western Thrace.

100 Stotinki = 1 Leva

THRACE INTERALLIÉE (4)   THRACE INTERALLIEE (5)

1920 (7 Jan). Stamps of Bulgaria handstamped with T **4**, sideways reading up on 5st. to 25st. and 1l.

28	**49**	1st. black (R.)	40	40
29		2st. olive	40	40
30	**50**	5st. green	40	40
31		10st. rose	40	40
32		15st. violet	40	40
33	**29**	25st. black and deep blue	40	40
34	**32**	1l. deep brown	6·25	6·25
35	**43**	2l. chestnut	10·00	10·00
36	**44**	3l. claret	15·00	15·00
28/36 Set of 9			30·00	30·00

1920 (9 Jan). POSTAGE DUE. Postage Due stamps of Bulgaria handstamped with T **4**, sideways reading up. P 12×11½.

D37	D **37**	5st. bright green	65	65
D38		10st. dull violet	1·30	1·30
D39		50st. deep blue	3·75	2·50
D37/D39 Set of 3			5·25	4·00

Minor varieties occur in the opt, T **4**: Second 'L' of 'INTERALLIEE' inverted: 'INTERALLIEF'.

1920 (11 Jan). Contemporary stamps of Bulgaria handstamped diagonally inverted with T **5**.

40	**49**	1st. black	3·75	2·50
41		2st. olive	3·75	2·50
42	**50**	5st. green	1·30	65
43		10st. rose	1·30	65
44		15st. violet	1·30	65
45	**29**	25st. black and deep blue	1·30	65
40/45 Set of 6			11·50	6·75

THRACE Interalliée (6)   THRACE OCCIDENTALE (7)

1920 (10 Apr). Stamps of Bulgaria optd with T **6**.

46	**50**	5st. green	40	40
47		10st. rose	40	40
48		15st. violet	40	40
49		50st. yellow-brown	1·90	1·90
		a. Opt reading down	31·00	38·00
46/49 Set of 4			2·75	2·75

Varieties 'r' for 'n' in 'Interalliée' and last 'e' inverted occur in this overprint.

1920 (19 Apr). Stamps of Bulgaria optd as T **7**, but 15½ mm. between lines, P 11½, or imperf (30st.).

50	**50**	5st. green	40	40
		a. Opt inverted	50·00	
51		10st. rose	40	40
52		15st. violet	40	40
53		25st. blue	40	40
54		30st. chocolate	1·90	1·90
55		50st. yellow-brown	40	40
50/55 Set of 6			3·50	3·50

1920 (21 Apr). POSTAGE DUE. Postage Due stamps of Bulgaria optd with T **7**.

(a) Imperf

D56	D **37**	5st. bright green	40	40
D57		10st. dull violet	2·50	2·50
D58		20st. red-orange	65	65
D59		50st. deep blue	1·90	1·90

(b) P 12×11½

D60	D **37**	10st. dull violet	1·50	1·00
D56/D60 Set of 5			6·25	6·25

Except for No. D60 the above were supplied to Thrace imperforate. All values are known perforated (including the 10st. in gauges other than that listed) but their status is uncertain.

D. GREEK OCCUPATION, 1920

At the Spa Conference Greece was given a mandate to administer both Western and Eastern Thrace.

The area known as Eastern Thrace was the territory bounded by the Bulgarian frontier of 1913, the Black Sea, the Chataldja lines to the west of Constantinople (Istanbul), the Sea of Marmora and the Evros River (formerly Maritza). It included the city of Adrianople (now Edirne), the Gallipoli peninsula and the island of Imbros (now Imroz).

100 Lepta = 1 Drachma

Διοίκησις Δυτικῆς Θράκης (8)   ΔΙΟΙΚΗΣΙΣ ΔΥΤΙΚΗΣ ΘΡΑΚΗΣ (9)

('Administration of Western Thrace')

1920 (May). Stamps of Greece optd with T **8** or T **9** (25d.).

(a) On issue of 1911, recess

61	**30**	2l. carmine	1·30	
62	**29**	3l. vermilion	1·30	
63	**32**	1d. ultramarine	38·00	
64		2d. vermilion	55·00	
65		3d. carmine	75·00	
66		5d. grey-blue	30·00	
67		10d. deep blue	30·00	
68	**33**	25d. deep blue	75·00	

Nos. 61/68 are not know used.

(b) On issue of 1913, lithographed

69	**29**	1l. green	40	1·00
70	**30**	2l. carmine	40	65
71	**29**	3l. vermilion	40	65
72	**31**	5l. green	40	65
73	**29**	10l. carmine	65	1·30
74	**30**	15l. dull blue	40	65
75		25l. ultramarine	65	1·30
76	**31**	30l. carmine-red		
77	**30**	40l. deep blue	1·90	3·75
78	**31**	50l. brown-purple	1·90	2·50
79	**32**	1d. ultramarine	10·00	12·50
80		2d. vermilion	38·00	44·00

Faked overprints have appeared on the 20l. value.

(c) On Royalist issue of 1916 with 'E.T.' and Crown overprint

81	**29**	1l. green	6·25	
82	**30**	2l. rose-red	40	65
83	**29**	10l. carmine	65	1·00
84	**30**	20l. purple-grey	65	1·00
85	**31**	30l. carmine-red (No. 276)	65	1·00
86	**32**	2d. vermilion	45·00	
87		3d. carmine	60·00	38·00
88		5d. grey-blue	55·00	
89		10d. deep blue	38·00	

Double and inverted overprint errors occur in the above issue.

THRACE / Greek Occupation / MACEDONIA

Διοικησις
Θράκης
(T **10** 'Administration of Thrace')

Ὑπάτη Ἁρμοστεία
Θράκης
5 Λεπτά **5**
(T **11** Trans 'High Commission of Thrace')

1920 (July). Stamps of Greece optd with T **10**.

(a) On 1911 issue, recess

89a	30	2l. carmine	2·50	
90	29	3l. vermilion	2·50	
91	30	20l. lilac	7·50	
92	33	25d. deep blue	75·00	

(b) On 1913 issue, lithographed

93	29	1l. green	40	1·30
94	30	2l. carmine	40	65
95	29	3l. vermilion	40	65
96	31	5l. green	40	65
97	29	10l. carmine	65	1·00
98	30	20l. purple-grey	65	1·00
99		25l. ultramarine	1·30	1·90
100		40l. deep blue	1·90	3·75
101	31	50l. brown-purple	1·90	2·50
102	32	1d. ultramarine	19·00	25·00
103		2d. vermilion	38·00	44·00

(c) On Royalist issue of 1916 with 'E.T.' and Crown overprint

103a	29	1l. green	12·50	
104	30	2l. rose-red	40	65
105	31	5l. green	10·00	
106	30	20l. purple-grey	40	65
107	31	30l. carmine-red (No. 276)	40	65
108	32	3d. carmine	16·00	25·00
109		5d. grey-blue	31·00	
110		10d. deep blue	50·00	

Double and inverted overprint errors occur in the above issue. Other stamps exist with this overprint but were not issued in Thrace.

1920 (Aug). Occupation of Adrianople. Stamps of Turkey surch as T **11** (vert downwards on 1d. and 3d.).

111	72	1l. on 5pa. orange (No. 917a) (B.)	65	65
112	40	5l. on 3pi. blue (No. 965)	65	65
113	38	20l. on 1pi. deep blue-green (No. 964)	90	90
114	69	25l. on 5pi. on 2pa. greenish blue (No. 923) (R.)	90	90
115	78	50l. on 5pi. sepia and greenish blue (No. 922a) (R.)	6·25	6·25
116	74	1d. on 20pa. carmine (No. 948) (B.)	3·25	2·50
117	30	2d. on 10pa. on 2pa. olive-green (No. 946) (R.)	3·25	3·25
118	85	3d. on 1pi. indigo (No. 940) (R.)	15·00	15·00
119	31	5d. on 20pa. red	12·50	12·50

By the Treaty of Sèvres, 10 August 1920, all of Thrace was incorporated into Greece. After the Greek defeat by the Turks in Asia Minor in 1922 Eastern Thrace was returned to Turkey by the Treaty of Lausanne, 24 July 1923; Western Thrace remained part of Greece.

Macedonia

Formerly part of the Turkish Empire, the area of Macedonia was, after the Balkan Wars of 1912–1913, divided among Serbia, Bulgaria and Greece. In 1918, when the Kingdom of the Serbs, Croats and Slovenes (later Yugoslavia) was set up, Serbia incorporated its section as South Serbia.

A. GERMAN OCCUPATION, 1944

During the Second World War Bulgaria, in April 1941, occupied Yugoslav Macedonia as far as a line running south and east of Bela Palanka, Lescovac and Gnjilane; this included Pirot, Skopje, Prilep, Bitola and Ohrid. Stamps of Bulgaria were used.
On 8 September 1944 Bulgaria, which had occupied Macedonia, signed an armistice and Macedonia was occupied by German troops and declared its independence, which lasted until German troops left on 13 November.

100 Stotinki = 1 Lev

(1)   (2)

1944 (28 Oct). Stamps of Bulgaria, 1940–1944, surch.

*(a) As T **1***

1	**140**	1l. on 10st. orange (B.)	5·75	26·00
2	–	3l. on 15st. blue (No. 450) (R.)	5·75	26·00

*(b) As T **2***

3	–	6l. on 10st. blue (No. 469) (R.)	7·25	39·00
4	–	9l. on 15st. deep blue-green (No. 470) (R.)	7·25	39·00
5	–	9l. on 15st. blackish olive (No. 471) (R.)	11·00	46·00
6	–	15l. on 4l. olive-black (No. 504) (R.)	38·00	90·00
7	**156**	20l. on 7l. blue (R.)	55·00	£100
8	**157**	30l. on 14l. brown (B.)	65·00	£170
1/8	*Set of 8*		£180	£475

Designs: No. 2 Beehive; No. 3 Threshing; Nos. 4 and 5 Ploughing with Oxen; No. 6 Hoisting the Flag.
Numerous errors and varieties occur in these surcharges including two types of '9' in '1944' and the 20l. on 7l. with or without bar over the original face value.
Nos. 1/8 are known with genuine postmarks of Skopje and Kumanovo from 28 October to early November 1944.

On the reconstitution of Yugoslavia as a Federal People's Republic in 1945, Serbian Macedonia became a constituent republic.

B. INDEPENDENT REPUBLIC

The former Yugoslav republic of Macedonia was declared independent, following a referendum, on 8 September 1991.

1991. 100 Paras = 1 Dinar
1992. 100 Deni (de.) = 1 Denar (d.)

> **SURCHARGED STAMPS.** Yugoslav definitive issues exist surcharged '1991–1992', 'Macedonia' in Cyrillic letters and new value. There is no evidence that these were official issues.

   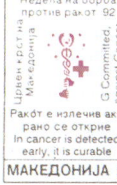

1 Trumpeters   **2** Emblems and Inscriptions

MACEDONIA 1991

(Litho Institute for the Production of Bank Notes, Belgrade)

1991 (30 Dec). OBLIGATORY TAX. Independence. P 13½.

1	**1**	2d.50 brownish black and yellow-orange	80	75

No. 1 was in use throughout Macedonia between 30 December 1991 and 8 September 1992 and from rural post offices until the end of March 1993. Covers exist showing the stamp cancelled with a Skopje postmark dated 8 September 1991, the actual date of Independence.

(Des Zh. Matejevic. Litho)

1992 (1 Mar). OBLIGATORY TAX. Anti-cancer Week. P 10.

*(a) T **2** and similar vert designs showing Red Cross symbol at bottom left*

2	5d. magenta, blue and black	90	80
	a. Block of 4. Nos. 2/5	3·75	
3	5d. multicoloured	90	80
4	5d. multicoloured	90	80
5	5d. multicoloured	90	80
2/5 Set of 4		3·25	3·00

Designs: No. 2, T **2**; No. 3, Flowers, columns and scanner; No. 4, Scanner and couch; No. 5, Computer trolley.

*(b) As T **2** but with right-hand inscr reading down instead of up, and similar vert designs without Red Cross symbol*

6	5d. magenta, blue and black	35	30
	a. Block of 4. Nos. 6/9	1·50	
7	5d. multicoloured (as No. 3)	35	30
8	5d. multicoloured (as No. 4)	35	30
9	5d. multicoloured (as No. 5)	35	30
6/9 Set of 4		1·30	1·10

Nos. 2/5 and 6/9 were each issued together in *se-tenant* blocks of four within their sheets. Nos. 6/9 also exist as perforate and imperforate miniature sheets containing a *se-tenant* block of four.

For compulsory use from 1 to 8 March.

New Currency
100 Deni (de.) = 1 Denar (d.)

3 Red Cross Aircraft dropping Supplies

1992 (8 May). OBLIGATORY TAX. Red Cross Week. T **3** and similar horiz designs. Multicoloured. Litho. P 10.

10	10d. Red Cross slogans (dated 08–15 MAJ 1992)	25	25
	a. Block of 4. Nos. 10/13	1·10	
11	10d. Type **3**	25	25
12	10d. Treating road accident victim	25	25
13	10d. Evacuating casualties from ruined building	25	25
10/13 Set of 4		90	90

Nos. 10/13 were issued together in *se-tenant* blocks of four within the sheet; the three pictoral designs are taken from children's paintings. They also exist as perforate and imperforate miniature sheets containing a *se-tenant* block of four.

For compulsory use from 8 to 15 May.

4 Skopje Earthquake

(Des Zh. Matejevic. Litho)

1992 (1 June). OBLIGATORY TAX. Solidarity Week. T **4** and similar vert designs. P 10.

14	20d. black and magenta	25	25
	a. Block of 4. Nos. 14/17	1·10	
15	20d. multicoloured	25	25
16	20d. multicoloured	25	25
17	20d. multicoloured	25	25
14/17 Set of 4		90	90

Designs: No. 14, T **4**; No. 15, Red Cross nurse with child; No. 16, Mothers carrying toddlers at airport; No. 17, Family at airport.

Nos. 14/17 were issued together in *se-tenant* blocks of four within the sheet. They were accompanied by perforate and imperforate 130d. miniature sheets showing a woman and child in front of a control tower.

For compulsory use from 1 to 7 June.

5 Wood-carvers Petar and Makarie (icon), St Joven Bigorski Monastery, Debar

6 Nurse with Baby

(Des M. Dameski. Litho)

1992 (8 Sept). First Anniversary of Independence. P 13½×13.

18	**5**	30d. multicoloured	75	70

For 40d. in same design see No. 33.

1992 (14 Sept). OBLIGATORY TAX. Anti-tuberculosis Week. T **6** and similar vert designs. Multicoloured. Litho. P 10.

19	20d. Anti-tuberculosis slogans (dated 14–21.IX.1992)	30	25
	a. Block of 4. Nos. 19/22	1·30	
20	20d. Type **6**	30	25
21	20d. Nurse giving oxygen	30	25
22	20d. Baby in cot	30	25
19/22 Set of 4		1·10	90

Nos. 19/22 were issued together in *se-tenant* blocks of four within the sheet. They were accompanied by perforate and imperforate 200d. miniature sheets showing a child undergoing treatment; these sheets exist with country name and top marginal inscription in magenta or red.

For compulsory use from 14 to 21 September.

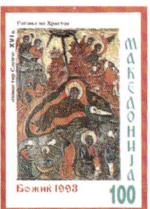

7 The Nativity (fresco, Slepce Monastery)

8 Mixed Bouquet

(Des M. Dameski. Litho)

1992 (10 Dec). Christmas. T **7** and similar vert design. Multicoloured. P 13×13½.

23	100d. Type **7**	1·70	1·60
24	500d. Madonna and Child (fresco), Zrze Monastery	4·00	3·75

(Des A. Popovski and N. Tozi. Litho)

1993 (1 Feb). OBLIGATORY TAX. Red Cross Fund. T **8** and similar horiz designs. Multicoloured with country name (Nos. 25/28) and background (Nos. 26/28) in gold. P 10.

25	20d. Red Cross slogans	30	25
	a. Block of 4. Nos. 25/28	1·30	
26	20d. Marguerites	30	25
27	20d. Carnations	30	25
28	20d. Type **8**	30	25
25/28 Set of 4		1·10	90

Nos. 25/28 were issued together in *se-tenant* blocks of four within the sheet. They were accompanied by a 500d. miniature sheet, perforate or imperforate, containing a *se-tenant* block of four with country name (Nos. 25/28) and background (Nos. 26/28) in either gold or silver.

For compulsory use from 1 February to 31 March.

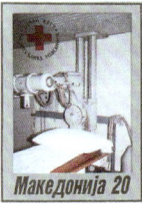

9 Radiography Equipment

10 Macedonian Flag

1993 (1 Mar). OBLIGATORY TAX. Anti-cancer Week. T **9** and similar vert designs. Multicoloured with country name (No. 29) and background (Nos. 30/32) in silver. Litho. P 10.

29	20d. Anti-cancer slogans (dated 1–8 MART 1993)		30	25
	a. Block of 4. Nos. 29/32		1·30	
30	20d. Type **9**		30	25
31	20d. Overhead treatment unit		30	25
32	20d. Scanner		30	25
29/32 Set of 4			1·10	90

Nos. 29/32 were issued together in *se-tenant* blocks of four within the sheet. They also exist as 500d. miniature sheets, perforate or imperforate, containing a *se-tenant* block of four with the country inscription (as No. 29) and background (as Nos. 30/32) in gold.
For compulsory use from 1 to 8 March.

1993 (15 Mar). As No. 18 but changed face value shown in black. P 10.

33	**5**	40d. multicoloured	80	70

(Des M. Dameski. Litho)

1993 (15 Mar). P 13½×13.

34	**10**	10d. multicoloured	45	40
35		40d. multicoloured	1·70	1·60
36		50d. multicoloured	2·20	2·00
34/36 Set of 3			4·00	3·50

11 Macedonian Roach (*Rutilus macedonicus*)

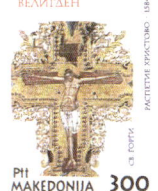
12 Crucifix, St George's Monastery

(Des M. Dameski. Litho)

1993 (15 Mar). Fish from Lake Ohrid. T **11** and similar horiz design. Multicoloured. P 10.

37		50d. Type **11**	30	25
38		100d. Ohrid Salmon (*Salmothymus ochridanus*)	45	40
39		1000d. Type **11**	4·25	4·00
40		2000d. As No. 38	5·75	5·50
37/40 Set of 4			9·75	9·25

(Des M. Dameski. Litho)

1993 (16 Apr). Easter. P 10.

41	**12**	300d. multicoloured	3·75	3·50

13 Diagram of Telecommunications Cable and Map

14 Red Cross Worker with Baby

(Des M. Dameski. Litho)

1993 (6 May). Opening of Trans-Balkan Telecommunications Line. P 10.

42	**13**	500d. new blue, black and lemon	1·90	1·80

1993 (8 May). OBLIGATORY TAX. Red Cross Week. T **14** and similar horiz designs. Multicoloured with country name (No. 43) or frame (others) in silver. Litho. P 10.

43		50d. Red Cross inscriptions (dated 08–15 MAJ 1993)	30	25
		a. Block of 4. Nos. 43/46	1·30	
44		50d. Type **14**	30	25
45		50d. Physiotherapist and child in wheelchair	30	25
46		50d. Stretcher party	30	25
43/46 Set of 4			1·10	90

Nos. 43/46 were issued together in *se-tenant* blocks of four within the sheet. They were accompanied by a 700d. miniature sheet, perforate or imperforate, containing a *se-tenant* block of four with inscription (as No. 43) or frames (others) in yellow.
For compulsory use from 8 to 15 May.
For 1d. value in T **14**, see No. 73.

Currency Reform

1 (new) denar = 100 (old) denar

15 Unloading UNICEF Supplies from Lorry

1993 (1 June). OBLIGATORY TAX. Solidarity Week. T **15** and similar horiz designs. Litho. P 10.

47		– 50de. black, magenta and silver	30	25
		a. Block of 4. Nos. 47/50	1·30	
48	**15**	50de. multicoloured (silver frame)	30	25
49		– 50de. multicoloured (silver frame)	30	25
50		– 50de. multicoloured (silver frame)	30	25
47/50 Set of 4			1·10	90

Designs: No. 47, Skopje Earthquake; No. 49, Labelling parcels in warehouse; No. 50, Consignment of parcels on fork-lift truck.
Nos. 47/50 were issued together in *se-tenant* blocks of four within the sheet. They were accompanied by a 7d. miniature sheet, perforate or imperforate, containing a *se-tenant* block of four with country name (as No. 47) or frames (others) in gold.
For compulsory use from 1 to 7 June.
For 1d. value as No. 50, see No. 72.

16 UN Emblem and Rainbow

(Des R. Lazeska. Litho)

1993 (28 July). Admission to United Nations Organisation. P 10.

51	**16**	10d. multicoloured	1·70	1·60
		a. Inscription in gold		

17 Insurrection (detail, B. Lazeski)

18 Children in Meadow

1993 (2 Aug). 90th Anniversary of Macedonian Insurrection. Litho. P 10.

52	**17**	10d. multicoloured	1·70	1·60
MS53	116×73 mm. Type **17** 30d. multicoloured. Imperf		5·00	4·75

(Des R. Shapkar. Litho)

1993 (14 Sept). OBLIGATORY TAX. Anti-tuberculosis Week. T **18** and similar horiz designs. Multicoloured. P 10.

54		50de. Anti-tuberculosis slogans (dated 14–21.09.1993)	30	25
		a. Block of 4. Nos. 54/57	1·30	
		ab. Block of 4. Yellow omitted	2·50	
55		50de. Type **18**	30	25
56		50de. Bee on flower	30	25
57		50de. Goat behind boulder	30	25
54/57 Set of 4			1·10	90

Nos. 54/57 were issued together in *se-tenant* blocks of four within the sheet. They were accompanied by a 15d. miniature sheet, perforate or imperforate, containing a *se-tenant* block of four with designer's name omitted from designs as Nos. 55/57.
For compulsory use from 14 to 21 September.
For 1d. value in T **18** see No. 71.

MACEDONIA 1993

19 Tapestry **20** The Nativity (fresco from St George's Monastery, Rajcica)

(Des A. Jordanova and M. Dameski. Litho)

1993 (4 Nov). Centenary of Founding of Inner Macedonia Revolutionary Organisation. T **19** and similar multicoloured design. P 10.

58		4d. Type **19**	75	70
MS59	90×75 mm. 40d. Two motifs as Type **19**. Imperf		5·00	4·75

(Des M. Dameski. Litho A. D. Printers)

1993 (31 Dec). Christmas. T **20** and similar square design. Multicoloured. P 10.

60	2d. Type **20**	75	70
61	20d. The Three Kings (fresco from Slepce Monastery)	5·00	4·75

21 Lily   (**22**)

(Des R. Shapkar. Litho)

1994 (1 Mar). OBLIGATORY TAX. Anti-cancer Week. T **21** and similar horiz designs. Multicoloured with background (No. 62) or frame (others) in silver. P 10.

62		1d. Red Cross and anti-cancer emblems	30	25
		a. Block of 4. Nos. 62/65	1·30	
63		1d. Type **21**	30	25
64		1d. Caesar's Mushroom	30	25
65		1d. Mute Swans on lake	30	25
62/65 Set of 4			1·10	90

Nos. 62/65 were issued together in *se-tenant* blocks of four within the sheet. They were accompanied by a 20d. miniature sheet, perforate or imperforate, containing a *se-tenant* block of four without the silver.

For compulsory use from 1 to 8 March.

1994 (2 Apr). Nos. 1, 18 and 34 surch as T **22**.

66	**5**	2d. on 30d. multicoloured	30	25
67	**1**	8d. on 2d.50 brownish black and yellow-orange	1·00	95
68	**10**	15d. on 10d. multicoloured	2·20	2·00
66/68 Set of 3			3·25	3·00

Nos. 67/68 show smaller numerals in the surcharge with the 8d. including an oblong over the original value.

See also Nos. 95/96.

23 Decorated Eggs **24** Kosta Racin (writer)

(Des M. Serafimovski. Litho)

1994 (29 Apr). Easter. P 10.

| 69 | **23** | 2d. multicoloured | 75 | 70 |

1994 (8 May). OBLIGATORY TAX. Red Cross Week. As previous designs but values, and date (No. 70), changed. Multicoloured. Litho. P 10.

70		1d. Red Cross inscriptions (dated '8–15 MAJ 1994')	30	25
		a. Block of 4. Nos. 70/73	1·30	
71		1d. Type **18**	30	25
72		1d. As No. 50	30	25
73		1d. Type **14**	30	25
70/73 Set of 4			1·10	90

Nos. 70/73 were issued together in *se-tenant* blocks of four within the sheet. They were accompanied by a 30d. miniature sheet, perforate or imperforate, containing a *se-tenant* block of four with face values removed.

For compulsory use from 8 to 15 May.

(Des M. Dameski. Litho)

1994 (23 May). Revolutionaries. T **24** and similar vert designs showing portraits by Dimitar Kondovski. Multicoloured. P 10.

74	8d. Type **24**	75	70
75	15d. Grigor Prlicev (writer)	1·50	1·40
76	20d. Nikola Vaptsarov (Bulgarian poet)	2·20	2·00
77	50d. Goce Delcev (founder of Internal Macedonian–Odrin Revolutionary Organisation)	5·00	4·75
74/77 Set of 4		8·50	8·00

25 Skopje Earthquake   **26** Tree and Family

(Des Zh. Matejevik. Litho)

1994 (1 June). OBLIGATORY TAX. Solidarity Week. P 10.

| 78 | **25** | 1d. black, bright scarlet and silver | 45 | 40 |

For compulsory use from 1 to 7 June.

1994 (21 June). Census. Litho. P 10.

| 79 | **26** | 2d. multicoloured | 75 | 70 |

27 St Prohor Pcinski Monastery (venue)   **28** Swimmer

1994 (2 Aug). 50th Anniversary of Macedonian National Liberation Council. Litho. P 10.

80	**27**	5d. multicoloured	75	70
MS81	108×73 mm. 50d. Aerial view of Monastery. Imperf		5·00	4·75

1994 (22 Aug). Swimming Marathon, Ohrid. Litho. P 10.

| 82 | **28** | 8d. multicoloured | 1·00 | 95 |

29 Turkish Cancellation and 1992 30d. Stamp on Cover   **30** Mastheads

(Des M. Stefanovska and M. Serafimovski. Litho)

1994 (12 Sept). 150th Anniversary (1993) of Postal Service in Macedonia. P 10.
83	**29**	2d. multicoloured	1·50	1·40

(Des M. Veljkovik-Misho. Litho)

1994 (13 Sept). 50th Anniversaries of *Nova Makedonija, Mlad Borec* and *Makedonka* (newspapers). P 10.
84	**30**	2d. multicoloured	1·50	1·40

31 Open Book

(Des K. Fidanovski. Litho)

1994 (29 Sept). 50th Anniversary of St Clement of Ohrid Library. T **31** and similar multicoloured design. P 10.
85		2d. Type **31**	35	35
86		10d. Page of manuscript (*vert*)	1·70	1·60

 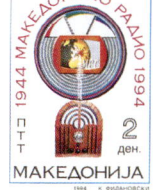

32 Globe   **33** Wireless and Gramophone Record

1994 (1 Dec). OBLIGATORY TAX. Anti-AIDS Week. T **32** and similar horiz designs. Litho. P 10.
87		2d. scarlet and black	30	25
		a. Block of 4. Nos. 87/90	1·30	
88		2d. black, scarlet and bright blue	30	25
89		2d. black, greenish yellow and scarlet	30	25
90		2d. black and scarlet	30	25
87/90 Set of 4			1·10	90

Designs: No. 87, Inscriptions in Cyrillic (dated '01–08.12.1994'); No. 88, T **32**; No. 89, Exclamation mark in warning triangle; No. 90, Safe sex campaign emblem.

Nos. 87/90 were issued together in *se-tenant* blocks of four stamps within the sheet. They were accompanied by a 40d. miniature sheet, perforate or imperforate, depicting the motif in T **32**.

For compulsory use from 1 to 8 December.

(Des K. Fidanovski. Litho)

1994 (26 Dec). 50th Anniversary of Macedonian Radio. P 10.
91	**33**	2d. multicoloured	75	70

34 Macedonian Pine (*Pinus peluse*)   (**35**)   **36** Emblems and Inscriptions

(Des R. Lezeska. Litho)

1994 (26 Dec). Flora and Fauna. T **34** and similar horiz design. Multicoloured. P 10.
92		5d. Type **34**	75	70
93		10d. Lynx (*Lynx lynx martinoi*)	1·50	1·40

1995 (13 Mar). Nos. 35 and 33 surch with T **35** (No. 94) or as T **22** (Nos. 95/96).
94	**10**	2d. on 40d. multicoloured	1·50	1·40
95		2d. on 40d. multicoloured	1·50	1·40
96	**5**	5d. on 40d. multicoloured (Gold)	75	70
94/96 Set of 3			3·50	3·25

(Des V. Pulevski. Litho)

1995 (10 Apr). OBLIGATORY TAX. Anti-cancer Week. T **36** and similar vert designs. Multicoloured. P 10.
97		1d. Type **36**	30	25
		a. Block of 4. Nos. 97/100	1·30	
98		1d. White Lilies	30	25
99		1d. Red Lilies	30	25
100		1d. Red Roses	30	25
97/100 Set of 4			1·10	90

Nos. 97/100 were issued together in *se-tenant* blocks of four within the sheet. They were accompanied by a 30d. miniature sheet, perforate or imperforate, containing designs as T **36** and No. 100 but with country inscription, face value and dates omitted.

For compulsory use from 10 to 16 April. The stamps are however dated 01-08 MART 1995.

37 Fresco

(Des M. Dameski. Litho 11 Oktombri)

1995 (23 Apr). Easter. P 10.
101	**37**	4d. multicoloured	75	70

No. 101 was issued in sheets of 24 stamps and one label.

38 Voluntary Workers   **39** Troops on Battlefield

(Des Zh. Matejevik and V. Pulevski. Litho)

1995 (8 May). OBLIGATORY TAX. Red Cross Week. T **38** and similar vert designs. Multicoloured. P 10.
102		1d. Cross and inscriptions in Cyrillic (dated 8–15 MAJ 1995)	30	25
		a. Horiz strip of 4. Nos. 102/105	1·30	
103		1d. Type **38**	30	25
104		1d. Volunteers in t-shirts	30	25
105		1d. Globe, red cross and red crescent	30	25
102/105 Set of 4			1·10	90

Nos. 102/105 were issued together in horizontal *se-tenant* strips of four stamps within the sheet. They were accompanied by a 30d. miniature sheet, perforate or imperforate, containing design as No. 105 but with inscriptions replacing date and face value.

For compulsory use from 8 to 15 May.

(Des T. Ivanovski and M. Dameski. Litho 11 Oktombri)

1995 (9 May). 50th Anniversary of End of Second World War. P 10.
106	**39**	2d. multicoloured	1·50	1·40

40 Anniversary Emblem   **41** Röntgen and X-Ray Lamp

1995 (20 May). 50th Anniversary of Macedonian Red Cross. Litho. P 10.
107	**40**	2d. multicoloured	1·50	1·40

(Des M. Dameski. Litho 11 Oktombri)

1995 (31 May). Centenary of Discovery of X-Rays by Wilhelm Röntgen. P 10.
108	**41**	2d. multicoloured	1·70	1·60

MACEDONIA 1995

42 Skopje Earthquake

43 Cernodrinski (dramatist)

(Des Zh. Matejevik and V. Puleski. Litho)

1995 (1 June). OBLIGATORY TAX. Solidarity Week. P 10.
109 **42** 1d. black, vermilion and gold 30 25
No. 109 was accompanied by a 30d. miniature sheet, perforate or imperforate, containing design as T **42** but without bottom panel.
For compulsory use from 1 to 7 June.

(Des M. Dameski. Litho 11 Oktombri)

1995 (8 June). 50th Anniversary of Vojdan Cernodrinski Theatre Festival. P 10.
110 **43** 10d. multicoloured .... 1·50 1·40

44 Kraljevic (fresco, Markov Monastery, Skopje)

(Des M. Dameski. Litho 11 Oktombri)

1995 (22 June). 600th Death Anniversary of Marko Kraljevic (Serbian Prince). P 10.
111 **44** 20d. multicoloured .... 1·90 1·80

45 Puleski

46 Manuscript, Bridge and Emblem

(Des M. Dameski. Litho 11 Oktombri)

1995 (8 July). Death Centenary of Gorgi Puleski (linguist and revolutionary). P 10.
112 **45** 2d. multicoloured .... 1·50 1·40

(Des M. Dameski. Litho 11 Oktombri)

1995 (23 Aug). Writers' Festival, Struga. P 10.
113 **46** 2d. multicoloured .... 1·50 1·40

47 Robert Koch (discoverer of tubercule bacillus)

48 Child holding Parents' Hands

(Des V. Pulevski and Zh. Matejevik. Litho)

1995 (14 Sept). OBLIGATORY TAX. Anti-tuberculosis Week. P 10.
114 **47** 1d. orange-brown, black and scarlet-vermilion 45 40
No. 114 was accompanied by a 30d. miniature sheet, perforate or imperforate, containing design as T **47** but without top inscription, country name or face value.
For compulsory use from 14 to 21 September.

1995 (2 Oct). OBLIGATORY TAX. Children's Week. Litho. Self-adhesive. Die-cut.
115 **48** 2d. ultramarine 45 40
For compulsory use from 2 to 8 October.

49 Maleshevija

50 Interior of Mosque

(Des M. Dameski and P. Namichev. Litho 11 Oktombri)

1995 (4 Oct). Buildings. T **49** and similar square design. Multicoloured. P 10.
116 2d. Type **49** 30 25
117 20d. Krakornica .... 1·50 1·40

(Des M. Dameski. Litho 11 Oktombri)

1995 (4 Oct). Tetovo Mosque. P 10.
118 **50** 15d. multicoloured .... 1·50 1·40

51 Lumière Brothers (inventors of cine-camera)

(Des M. Dameski. Litho 11 Oktombri)

1995 (6 Oct). Centenary of Motion Pictures. T **51** and similar horiz design. Multicoloured. P 10 (3 sides).
119 10d. Type **51** .... 1·50 1·40
  a. Horiz pair. Nos. 119/120 .... 3·25 3·00
120 10d. Milton and Janaki Manaki (Macedonian cinematographers) .... 1·50 1·40
Nos. 119/120 were issued together in horizontal *se-tenant* pairs within the sheet, each pair forming a composite design. The outer vertical edges of the pair are imperforate giving stamps with one side imperf.

52 Globe in Nest within Frame

53 Male and Female Symbols

(Des M. Dameski. Litho 11 Oktombri)

1995 (24 Oct). 50th Anniversary of United Nations Organisation. T **52** and similar horiz design. Multicoloured. P 10.
121 20d. Type **52** .... 1·20 1·10
122 50d. Sun within frame .... 3·25 3·00

(Des Zh. Matejevik and V. Pulevski. Litho)

1995 (1 Dec). OBLIGATORY TAX. Anti-AIDS Week. P 10.
123 **53** 1d. multicoloured 45 40
No. 123 was accompanied by a 30d. miniature sheet, perforate or imperforate, containing design as T **53** but without top inscription, country name or face value.
For compulsory use from 1 to 7 December.

54 Madonna and Child

55 Dalmatian Pelican (*Pelecanus crispus*)

(Des B. Damevska. Litho 11 Oktombri)

1995 (13 Dec). Christmas. P 10.
124 **54** 15d. multicoloured .... 1·70 1·60

1995 MACEDONIA

(Des B. Damevska. Litho 11 Oktombri)

1995 (14 Dec). Birds. T **55** and similar horiz design. Multicoloured. P 10.

125		15d. Type **55**	1·50	1·40
126		40d. Lammergeier (*Gypaetus barbatus*)	3·00	2·75

56 Letters of Alphabet and Jigsaw Pieces

57 St Clement of Ohrid (detail of fresco)

(Des S. Kozhukharova. Litho 11 Oktombri)

1995 (18 Dec). 50th Anniversary of Alphabet Reform. P 10.

127	**56**	5d. multicoloured	75	70

(Des M. Dameski. Litho 11 Oktombri)

1995 (19 Dec). 700th Anniversary of Fresco, St Bogorodica's Church, Ohrid. P 10.

128	**57**	8d. multicoloured	85	80
MS129	85×67 mm. **57**	50d. multicoloured. Imperf	75·00	70·00

58 Postal Headquarters, Skopje

59 Zip joining Flags

1995 (27 Dec). Second Anniversary of Membership of Universal Postal Union. Litho. P 10.

130	**58**	10d. multicoloured	85	80

(Des S. Kozhukharova, Stankoski and M. Dameski. Litho 11 Oktombri)

1995 (27 Dec). Entry to Council of Europe and Organisation for Security and Co-operation in Europe. P 10.

131	**59**	20d. multicoloured	2·00	1·90

60 Hand holding out Apple

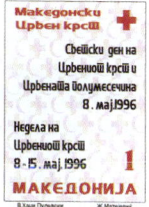
61 Inscriptions

(Des V. Pulevski. Litho)

1996 (1 Mar). OBLIGATORY TAX. Anti-cancer Week. P 10.

132	**60**	1d. bright scarlet, black and yellowish green	45	40

No. 132 was accompanied by a 30d. miniature sheet, perforate or imperforate, containing design as T **60** but without top inscription and bottom panel.

For compulsory use from 1 to 8 March.

(Des V. Pulevski and Zh. Matejevik. Litho)

1996 (8 May). OBLIGATORY TAX. Red Cross Week. T **61** and similar vert designs. Each bright scarlet, black and lemon. P 10.

133		1d. Type **61**	30	25
		a. Strip of 5. Nos. 133/137	1·60	
134		1d. Red Cross principles in Macedonian	30	25
135		1d. Red Cross principles in English	30	25
136		1d. Red Cross principles in French	30	25
137		1d. Red Cross principles in Spanish	30	25
133/137	Set of 5		1·40	1·10

Nos. 133/137 were issued together in *se-tenant* strips of five stamps within the sheet. They were accompanied by a 30d. miniature sheet, perforate or imperforate, containing a design combining the motifs of Nos. 133/137.

For compulsory use from 8 to 15 May.

62 Canoeing

63 Skopje Earthquake

(Des B. Damevska. Litho 11 Oktombri)

1996 (20 May). Olympic Games, Atlanta. T **62** and similar multicoloured designs showing statue of discus thrower and sport. P 10.

138		2d. Type **62**	45	40
139		8d. Basketball (*vert*)	60	55
140		15d. Swimming	1·00	95
141		20d. Wrestling	1·60	1·50
142		40d. Boxing (*vert*)	3·25	3·00
143		50d. Running (*vert*)	4·00	3·75
138/143	Set of 6		9·75	9·25

(Des V. Pulevski and Zh. Matejevik. Litho)

1996 (1 June). OBLIGATORY TAX. Solidarity Week. P 10.

144	**63**	1d. gold, bright rose-red and black	45	40

No. 144 was accompanied by a 30d. miniature sheet, perforate or imperforate, containing design as T **63** but without country name and face value.

For compulsory use from 1 to 7 June.

64 Scarecrow Drug Addict

65 Boy

(Des M. Dameski. Litho 11 Oktombri)

1996 (11 July). United Nations Anti-drugs Decade. Litho. P 10.

145	**64**	20d. multicoloured	1·50	1·40

1996 (15 July). Children's Week. T **65** and similar vert design showing children's drawings. Multicoloured. Litho. P 10.

146		2d. Type **65**	30	25
147		8d. Girl	60	55

66 Fragment from Tomb and Tsar Samuel (after Dimitar Kondovski)

67 Petrov

1996 (19 July). Millenary of Crowning of Tsar Samuel (ruler of Bulgaria and Macedonia). Litho. P 10.

148	**66**	40d. multicoloured	2·50	2·40

(Des M. Dameski. Litho 11 Oktombri)

1996 (2 Aug). 75th Death Anniversary of Gorce Petrov (revolutionary). P 10.

149	**67**	20d. multicoloured	1·50	1·40

MACEDONIA 1996

68 Ohrid Seal, 1903, and State Flag

69 Lungs on Globe

(Des M. Dameski. Litho 11 Oktombri)

1996 (8 Sept). Fifth Anniversary of Independence. P 10.
150	**68**	10d. multicoloured	75	70

(Des V. Pulevski. Litho)

1996 (14 Sept). OBLIGATORY TAX. Anti-tuberculosis Week. P 10.
151	**69**	1d. bright scarlet, blue and black	60	55

No. 151 was accompanied by a 30d. miniature sheet, perforate or imperforate, containing design as T **69** but without all inscriptions.
For compulsory use from 14 to 21 September.

70 Vera Čiriviri-Trena (freedom fighter)

71 Hand holding Syringe

(Des S. Kozhukharova (20d.), B. Damevska (40d.). Litho BNF)

1996 (22 Nov). Europa. Famous Women. T **70** and similar vert design. Multicoloured. P 13×13½.
152		20d. Type **70**	10·00	9·50
153		40d. Mother Teresa (Nobel Peace Prize winner and founder of Missionaries of Charity)	14·50	13·50

(Des V. Pulevski. Litho)

1996 (1 Dec). OBLIGATORY TAX. Anti-AIDS Week. P 10.
154	**71**	1d. black, scarlet and yellow	45	40

No. 154 was accompanied by a 30d. miniature sheet, perforate or imperforate, containing design as T **71** but without bottom panel and inscription.
For compulsory use from 1 to 7 December.

72 Candle, Nuts and Fruit

73 Daniel in the Lions' Den

1996 (14 Dec). Christmas. T **72** and similar vert design. Multicoloured. Litho. P 10.
155		10d. Type **72**	85	80
		a. Pair. Nos. 155/156	1·80	1·70
156		10d. Tree and carol singers	85	80

Nos. 155/156 were issued together in *se-tenant* pairs within the sheet.

1996 (19 Dec). Early Christian Terracotta Reliefs. T **73** and similar vert designs. Litho. P 10.

(a) Yellow-olive backgrounds
157		4d. Type **73**	30	25
		a. Block of 4. Nos. 157/160	6·00	
158		8d. St Christopher and St George	45	40
159		20d. Joshua and Caleb	1·50	1·40
160		50d. Unicorn	3·50	3·25
157/160 Set of 4			5·00	4·75

(b) Turquoise-blue backgrounds
161		4d. Type **73**	30	25
		a. Block of 4. Nos. 161/164	6·00	
162		8d. As No. 158	45	40
163		20d. As No. 159	1·50	1·40
164		50d. As No. 160	3·50	3·25
161/164 Set of 4			5·00	4·75

Nos. 157/160 and 161/164 respectively were issued together in *se-tenant* blocks of four stamps within their sheets.

74 Nistrovo

75 *Pseudochazara cingovskii*

(Litho 11 Oktombri)

1996 (20–25 Dec). Traditional Houses. T **74** and similar square designs. Multicoloured. P 10.
165		2d. Type **74** (25.12.96)	30	25
166		8d. Brodec	75	70
167		10d. Nivište (25.12.96)	1·00	95
165/167 Set of 3			1·80	1·70

(Des S. Kozhukharova. Litho 11 Oktombri)

1996 (21 Dec). Butterflies. T **75** and similar horiz design. Multicoloured. P 10.
168		4d. Type **75**	30	25
169		40d. Danube Clouded Yellow (*Colias balcanica*)	3·25	3·00

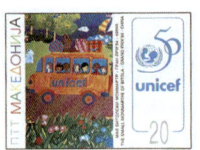

76 UNICEF Coach

(Des M. Dameski (40d.). Litho Courvoisier)

1996 (31 Dec). 50th Anniversaries. T **76** and similar horiz design. Multicoloured. P 14½×15.
170		20d. Type **76** (United Nations Children's Fund)	1·50	1·40
171		40d. Church in Mtskheta, Georgia (United Nations Educational, Scientific and Cultural Organisation)	3·00	2·75

77 Skier

(Des M. Dameski. Litho 11 Oktombri)

1997 (7 Feb). 50 Years of Ski Championships at Šar Planina. P 10.
172	**77**	20d. multicoloured	1·70	1·60

78 Bell

79 Family and Healthy Foodstuffs

(Des Lj. Ivanovski. Litho 11 Oktombri)

1997 (12 Mar). 150th Birth Anniversary of Alexander Graham Bell (telephone pioneer). P 10.

173	**78**	40d. multicoloured	3·00	2·75

(Des V. Pulevski. Litho)

1997 (1 Mar). OBLIGATORY TAX. Anti-cancer Week. P 10.

174	**79**	1d. multicoloured	1·70	1·60

For compulsory use from 1 to 8 March.

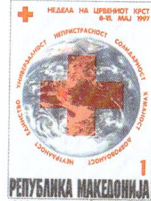

80 Hound   **81** Red Cross on Globe

(Des M. Dameski. Litho 11 Oktombri)

1997 (26 Mar). Roman Mosaics from Heraklia. T **80** and similar horiz designs. Multicoloured. P 10.

175		2d. Type **80**	30	25
176		8d. Steer	75	70
177		20d. Lion	1·70	1·60
178		40d. Leopard with prey	3·00	2·75
175/178		*Set of 4*	5·25	4·75
MS179		85×60 mm. 50d. Deer and plant tub. Imperf	5·75	5·50

(Des V. Pulevski. Litho)

1997 (8 May). OBLIGATORY TAX. Red Cross Week. P 10.

180	**81**	1d. multicoloured (orange cross)	45	40
		a. Red cross	45	40

For compulsory use from 8 to 15 May.

82 Gold Plate   **83** Schoolchildren

(Des F. Unkovski and D. Drakalski. Litho 11 Oktombri)

1997 (24 May). 1100th Anniversary of Cyrillic Alphabet. T **82** and similar horiz design. Multicoloured.

181		10d. Type **82**	85	80
		a. Pair. Nos. 181/182	1·80	1·70
182		10d. Sts Cyril and Methodius	85	80

(Des V. Pulevski. Litho)

1997 (1 June). OBLIGATORY TAX. Solidarity Week. P 10.

183	**83**	1d. multicoloured (orange cross)	45	40
		a. Red cross	45	40

For compulsory use from 1 to 7 June.

84 Mountain Flowers   **85** Itar Pejo

(Des. A. Jankovik. Litho 11 Oktombri)

1997 (5 June). Fifth Anniversary of Ecological Association. P 10.

184	**84**	15d. multicoloured	1·50	1·40

(Des B. Damevska. Litho Courvoisier)

1997 (6 June). Europa. Tales and Legends. T **85** and similar vert design. Multicoloured. P 15×14½.

185		20d. Type **85**	8·75	8·00
186		40d. Stork-men	16·00	15·00

86 St Naum and St Naum's Church, Ohrid   **87** Diseased Lungs

(Des Lj. Ivanovski. Litho 11 Oktombri)

1997 (3 July). 1100th Birth Anniversary of St Naum. P 10.

187	**86**	15d. multicoloured	1·50	1·40

(Des V. Pulevski. Litho 11 Oktombri)

1997 (14 Sept). OBLIGATORY TAX. Anti-tuberculosis Week. P 10.

188	**87**	1d. multicoloured	45	40

For compulsory use from 14 to 21 September.

88 Stibnite   **89** Dove and Sun above Child in Open Hand

(Des B. Damevska. Litho 11 Oktombri)

1997 (10 Oct). Minerals. T **88** and similar vert designs. Multicoloured. P 10.

189		27d. Type **88**	2·20	2·00
190		40d. Lorandite	3·00	2·75

(Des M. Veljkovik. Litho 11 Oktombri)

1997 (11 Oct). International Children's Day. P 10.

191	**89**	27d. multicoloured	2·00	1·90

90 Chanterelle (*Cantharellus cibarius*)   **91** Group of Children

(Des I. Stevkovski. Litho 11 Oktombri)

1997 (7 Nov). Fungi. T **90** and similar horiz designs. Multicoloured. P 10.

192		2d. Type **90**	45	40
193		15d. Bronze Boletus (*Boletus aereus*)	1·00	95
194		27d. Caesar's Mushroom (*Amanita caesarea*)	1·90	1·80
195		50d. Morchella conica	3·25	3·00
192/195		*Set of 4*	6·00	5·50

(Des V. Pulevski. Litho 11 Oktombri)

1998 (14 Jan). OBLIGATORY TAX. Anti-AIDS Week. P 10.

196	**91**	1d. multicoloured	45	40

For compulsory use from 14 to 21 January.

MACEDONIA 1998

92 Mahatma Gandhi

93 Formula of Pythagoras's Theory

(Des M. Dameski. Litho 11 Oktombri)

1998 (4 Feb). 50th Death Anniversary of Mahatma Gandhi (Indian independence campaigner). P 13½.
197	**92**	30d. multicoloured...............................		1·70	1·60

(Des D. Unkovski. Litho 11 Oktombri)

1998 (6 Feb). 2500th Death Anniversary of Pythagoras (philosopher and mathematician). P 13½.
198	**93**	16d. multicoloured...............................		1·00	95

94 Alpine Skiing   **95** Novo Selo

(Des I. Stevkovski. Litho 11 Oktombri)

1998 (7 Feb). Winter Olympic Games, Nagano, Japan. T **94** and similar horiz design. Multicoloured. P 13½.
199		4d. Type **94**...............................		30	25
200		30d. Cross-country skiing...............		1·50	1·40

(Des M. Dameski (1d., 4d., 5d., 30d.), I. Stevkovski (6d.), Lj. Ivanovski (16d.), L. Zhivkovska (others). Litho 11 Oktombri)

1998 (9 Feb)–**02**. Traditional Houses. T **95** and similar square designs. Multicoloured. P 13½.
201	1d. Bogomila (5.11.99)......................		15	15
202	2d. Type **95**......................................		15	15
203	3d. Jachintse (5.11.02)........................		20	20
204	4d. Jablanica..		30	25
205	4d. Svekani (1.2.99).............................		30	25
206	5d. Teovo (25.2.99)..............................		35	35
207	6d. Zdunje (28.7.00).............................		45	40
208	6d. Mitrasinci (25.6.01).......................		45	40
209	9d. Ratevo (5.11.02).............................		60	55
210	16d. Kiselica (10.6.98).........................		85	80
211	20d. Konopnica (12.2.98)....................		1·00	95
212	30d. Ambar...		1·50	1·40
213	50d. Galicnik (12.2.98)........................		3·00	2·75
201/213 *Set of* 13...			8·50	7·75

96 *Exodus* (Kole Manev)

97 *Proportions of Man* (Leonardo da Vinci)

(Des M. Dameski. Litho 11 Oktombri)

1998 (11 Feb). 50th Anniversary of Exodus of Children during Greek Civil War. P 13½.
215	**96**	30d. multicoloured...............................		1·70	1·60

(Des V. Pulevski. Litho 11 Oktombri)

1998 (1 Mar). OBLIGATORY TAX. Anti-cancer Week. P 13½.
216	**97**	1d. multicoloured...............................		45	40

For compulsory use from 1 to 8 March.

98 Bowl supported by Animal

99 Football Pitch

(Des M. Dameski. Litho 11 Oktombri)

1998 (27 Apr). Archaeological Finds from Nedit. T **98** and similar horiz designs. Multicoloured. P 13½.
217	4d. Carafes..		30	25
218	18d. Type **98**.....................................		75	70
219	30d. Sacred female figurine..............		1·50	1·40
220	60d. Stemmed cup..............................		3·25	3·00
217/220 *Set of* 4...			5·25	4·75

(Des A. Prilepchanski. Litho 11 Oktombri)

1998 (30 Apr). World Cup Football Championship, France. T **99** and similar horiz design. Multicoloured. P 13½.
221	4d. Type **99**.....................................		30	25
222	30d. Globe and football pitch..........		1·70	1·60

100 Folk Dance

101 Profiles

(Des T. Pocevska and A. Stojkovik. Litho 11 Oktombri)

1998 (5 May). Europa. National Festivals. T **100** and similar horiz design. Multicoloured. P 13½.
223	30d. Type **100**.................................		3·75	3·50
224	40d. Carnival......................................		5·00	4·75

(Des V. Pulevski. Litho 11 Oktombri)

1998 (8 May). OBLIGATORY TAX. Red Cross Week. P 13½.
225	**101**	2d. multicoloured...............................		45	40

For compulsory use from 8 to 15 May.

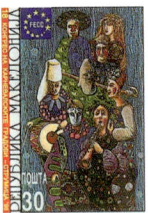
102 Carnival Procession

103 Hands and Red Cross

(Des A. Mikhailov. Litho 11 Oktombri)

1998 (10 May). 18th Congress of Carnival Towns, Strumica. P 13½.
226	**102**	30d. multicoloured...............................		1·70	1·60

(Des V. Pulevski. Litho 11 Oktombri)

1998 (1 June). OBLIGATORY TAX. Solidarity Week. P 13½.
227	**103**	2d. multicoloured...............................		45	40

For compulsory use from 1 to 7 June.

104 Flower

105 Dimitrija Čupovski

1998 MACEDONIA

(Des D. Drakalski (4d.); D. Mikhajlov (30d.).
Litho 11 Oktombri)

1998 (5 June). Environmental Protection. T **104** and similar vert design. Multicoloured. P 13½.

228	4d. Type **104**		30	25
229	30d. Polluting chimney uprooting tree		1·50	1·40

(Des D. Andonova. Litho 11 Oktombri)

1998 (30 June). 120th Birth Anniversary of Dimitrija Čupovski. P 13½.

230	**105**	16d. multicoloured	85	80

106 Steam Locomotive and Station

107 Doctor and Patient

(Des D. Isailovski (30d.); S. Sharovik (60d.).
Litho 11 Oktombri)

1997 (9 Aug). 150th Anniversary of Railways in Macedonia. T **106** and similar multicoloured design. P 13½.

231	30d. Type **106**		2·20	2·00
232	60d. Steam locomotive, 1873 (*horiz*)		4·25	4·00

(Des V. Pulevski. Litho 11 Oktombri)

1998 (14 Sept). OBLIGATORY TAX. Anti-tuberculosis Week. P 13½.

233	**107**	2d. multicoloured	45	40

108 *Ursus spelaeus*

109 Atanos Badev (composer) and Score

(Des P. Namičev. Litho 11 Oktombri)

1998 (17 Sept). Fossilised Skulls. T **108** and similar horiz designs. Multicoloured. P 13½.

234	4d. Type **108**	30	25
235	8d. *Mesopithecus pentelici*	45	40
236	18d. *Tragoceros*	1·00	95
237	30d. *Aceratherium incsivum*	1·70	1·60
234/237	Set of 4	3·00	3·00

(Des I. Markovska. Litho 11 Oktombri)

1998 (21 Sept). Centenary of Zlatoustova Liturgy. P 13½.

238	**109**	25d. multicoloured	1·50	1·40

110 Child with Kite

111 *Cerambyx cerdo* (Longhorn Beetle)

(Des G. Bliznakovski. Litho 11 Oktombri)

1998 (5 Oct). Children's Day. P 13½.

239	**110**	30d. multicoloured	1·70	1·60

(Des Lj. Ivanovski. Litho 11 Oktombri)

1998 (20 Oct). Insects. T **111** and similar horiz designs. Multicoloured. P 13½.

240	4d. Type **111**	30	25
241	8d. Alpine Longhorn Beetle (*Rosalia alpina*)	45	40
242	20d. European Rhinoceros Beetle (*Oryctes nasicornis*)	1·20	1·10
243	40d. Stag Beetle (*Lucanus cervus*)	2·30	2·20
240/243	Set of 4	3·75	3·50

112 Reindeer and Snowflakes

113 Ribbon and Gender Symbols

(Des L. Zhivkovska (4d.), A. Bartling (30d.).
Litho 11 Oktombri)

1998 (20 Nov). Christmas and New Year. T **112** and similar horiz design. Multicoloured. P 13½.

244	**112**	4d. Type **112**	30	25
245		30d. Bread and Oak leaves	1·70	1·60

(Des V. Pulevski. Litho 11 Oktombri)

1998 (1 Dec). OBLIGATORY TAX. Anti-AIDS Week. P 13½.

246	**113**	2d. multicoloured	45	40

114 Stylised Couple

115 Sharplaninec

(Des V. Pulevski and S. Sharovik. Litho 11 Oktombri)

1998 (10 Dec). 50th Anniversary of Universal Declaration of Human Rights. P 13½.

247	**114**	30d. multicoloured	1·70	1·60

(Des I. Stevkovski. Litho 11 Oktombri)

1999 (20 Jan). Dogs. P 13½.

248	**115**	15d. multicoloured	1·50	1·40

116 Girl's Face

117 The Annunciation (Demir Hisar, Slepce Monastery)

(Des V. Pulevski. Litho 11 Oktombri)

1999 (1 Mar). OBLIGATORY TAX. Anti-cancer Week. P 13½.

249	**116**	2d. multicoloured	45	40

For compulsory use from 1 to 8 March.

(Des Lj. Ivanovski. Photo Courvoisier)

1999 (3 Mar). Icons. T **117** and similar vert designs. Multicoloured. P 11½.

250	4d. Type **117**	35	35
251	8d. Saints (St Nicholas's Church, Ohrid)	60	55
252	18d. Madonna and Child (Demir Hisar, Slepce Monastery)	1·00	95
253	30d. Christ the Redeemer (Zrze Monastery, Prilep)	1·60	1·50
250/253	Set of 4	3·25	3·00
MS254	53×74 mm. 50d. Christ and Archangels (Archangel Michael Church, Lesnovo Monastery, Probištip)	3·75	3·50

391

MACEDONIA 1999

118 Dimitar Pandilov and *Hay Harvest*

119 Telegraph Apparatus

(Des M. Dameski. Litho 11 Oktombri)

1999 (14 Mar). Birth Centenary of Dimitar Pandilov (painter). P 13½.
255   **118**   4d. multicoloured 30   25

(Des G. Bliznakovski. Litho 11 Oktombri)

1999 (22 Apr). Centenary of the Telegraph in Macedonia. P 13½.
256   **119**   4d. multicoloured 30   25

120 University and Sts Cyril and Methodius

121 Anniversary Emblem and Map of Europe

(Des I. Stevkovski. Litho 11 Oktombri)

1999 (24 Apr). 50th Anniversary of Sts Cyril and Methodius University. P 13½.
257   **120**   8d. multicoloured 45   40

(Des A. Bartling. Litho 11 Oktombri)

1999 (5 May). 50th Anniversary of Council of Europe. P 13½.
258   **121**   30d. multicoloured .... 1·90   1·80

122 Pelister National Park

123 Figures linking Raised Arms

(Des Lj. Ivanovski. Litho 11 Oktombri)

1999 (5 May). Europa. Parks and Gardens. T **122** and similar horiz design. Multicoloured. P 13½.
259   30d. Type **122** .... 3·75   3·50
260   40d. Mavrovo National Park .... 5·00   4·75

(Des V. Pulevski. Litho 11 Oktombri)

1999 (8 May). OBLIGATORY TAX. Red Cross Week. P 13½.
261   **123**   2d. multicoloured 60   55
       For compulsory use from 8 to 15 May.

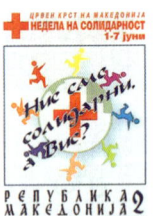

124 People running round Globe

125 Tree

(Des V. Pulevski. Litho 11 Oktombri)

1999 (1 June). OBLIGATORY TAX. Solidarity Week. P 13½.
262   **124**   2d. multicoloured 60   55
       For compulsory use from 1 to 7 June.

(Des M. Markovska. Litho 11 Oktombri)

1999 (5 June). Environmental Protection. P 13½.
263   **125**   30d. multicoloured .... 1·70   1·60

126 Tsar Petur Delyan

1999 (25 June). Medieval Rulers of Macedonia. T **126** and similar horiz designs. Multicoloured. Litho. P 13½.
264   4d. Type **126** 30   25
         a. Block of 4. Nos. 264/267 .... 3·25
265   8d. Prince Gjorgji Vojteh 45   40
266   18d. Prince Dobromir Hrs 85   80
267   30d. Prince Strez .... 1·50   1·40
264/267 Set of 4 .... 2·75   2·50
       Nos. 264/267 were issued together in *se-tenant* blocks of four stamps within the sheet, each block forming a composite design.

127 Kuzman Shaikarev (author)

(Des S. Sharovik. Litho 11 Oktombri)

1999 (1 Sept). 125th Anniversary of First Macedonian Language Primer. P 13½.
268   **127**   4d. multicoloured 30   25

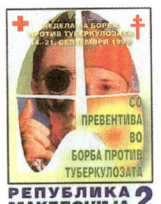

128 Faces in Outline of Lungs

129 *Crocus scardicus*

(Des V. Pulevski. Litho 11 Oktombri)

1999 (14 Sept). OBLIGATORY TAX. Anti-tuberculosis Week. P 13½.
269   **128**   2d. multicoloured 60   55
       For compulsory use from 14 to 21 September.

(Des I. Stevkovski. Litho 11 Oktombri)

1999 (16 Sept). Flowers. T **129** and similar vert designs. Multicoloured. P 13½.
270   4d. Type **129** 30   30
271   8d. *Astragalus mayeri* 45   40
272   18d. *Campanula formanekiana* .... 1·10   1·00
273   30d. *Viola kosaninii* .... 1·80   1·70
270/273 Set of 4 .... 3·25   3·00

130 Child

131 Emblem

(Des A. Stojkovik. Litho 11 Oktombri)

1999 (4 Oct). Children's Week. P 13½.
274   **130**   30d. multicoloured .... 1·80   1·70

(Des T. Pocevska. Litho 11 Oktombri)

1999 (9 Oct). 125th Anniversary of Universal Postal Union. T **131** and similar horiz design. Multicoloured. P 13½.
275   5d. Type **131** 40   35
276   30d. Emblem (*different*) .... 1·80   1·70

1999 MACEDONIA

132 Men on Horseback
133 Krste Petkov Misirkov

(Des I. Stevkovski. Litho 11 Oktombri)

1999 (27 Oct). 1400th Anniversary of Slavs in Macedonia. P 13½.
277	**132**	5d. multicoloured	40	35

(Des L. Zhivkovska. Litho 11 Oktombri)

1999 (18 Nov). 125th Birth Anniversary (2000) of Krste Petkov Misirkov (writer). P 13½.
278	**133**	5d. multicoloured	40	35

134 Pine Needles
135 Stylised Figures supporting Globe

(Des T. Pocevska (5d.), I. Stevkovski (30d.). Litho 11 Oktombri)

1999 (24 Nov). Christmas. T **134** and similar multicoloured design. P 13½.
279	5d. Type **134**		40	35
280	30d. Traditional pastry (*vert*)		1·80	1·70

(Des V. Khadzipulevski. Litho 11 Oktombri)

1999 (1 Dec). OBLIGATORY TAX. Anti-AIDS Week. P 13½.
281	**135**	2d.50 multicoloured	60	55

For compulsory use from 1 to 7 December.

136 Altar Cross (19th-century), St Nikita Monastery
137 '2000'

(Litho 11 Oktombri)

2000 (19 Jan). Bimillenary of Christianity. T **136** and similar multicoloured designs. P 13½.
282	5d. Type **136**		40	35
283	10d. Akathist of the Holy Mother of God (14th-century fresco), Marko's Monastery (*horiz*)		75	70
284	15d. St Clement (14th-century icon), Ohrid		90	85
285	30d. Paul the Apostle (14th-century fresco), St Andrew's Monastery		1·70	1·50
282/285	Set of 4		3·50	3·00
MS286	70×50 mm. 50d. Cathedral Church of St Sophia (11th-century), Ohrid (29×31 *mm*)		3·00	2·75

The stamp in No. **MS**286 has the top edge imperforate.

(Des G. Bliznakovski. Litho 11 Oktombri)

2000 (16 Feb). New Year. T **137** and similar horiz design. Multicoloured. P 13½.
287	5d. Type **137**		40	35
	a. Pair. Nos. 287/288		2·00	1·90
288	30d. Religious symbols		1·50	1·40

Nos. 287/288 were issued together in *se-tenant* pairs within the sheetlet.

138 Globe Unravelling and Medical Symbols
139 Jewelled Brooch with Icon, Orhid

(Des V. Pulevski. Litho 11 Oktombri)

2000 (1 Mar). OBLIGATORY TAX. Anti-Cancer Week. P 13½.
289	**138**	1d.50 multicoloured	60	55

For compulsory use from 1 to 8 March.

(Des T. Potsevska. Litho 11 Oktombri)

2000 (1 Mar). Jewellery. T **139** and similar vert designs. Multicoloured. P 13½.
290	5d. Type **139**		40	35
291	10d. Bracelet, Bitola		45	40
292	20d. Earrings, Ohrid		1·10	1·00
293	30d. Butterfly brooch, Bitola		1·80	1·70
290/293	Set of 4		3·50	3·00

140 Magnifying Glass and Perforation Gauge
141 Globe and Emblem

(Des T. Potsevska. Litho 11 Oktombri)

2000 (19 Mar). 50th Anniversary of Philately in Macedonia. P 13½.
294	**140**	5d. multicoloured	40	35

(Des I. Stevkovski. Litho 11 Oktombri)

2000 (23 Mar). 50th Anniversary of World Meteorological Organisation. P 13½.
295	**141**	30d. multicoloured	1·80	1·70

142 Men with Easter Eggs
143 Stylised Figures

(Litho 11 Oktombri)

2000 (21 Apr). Easter. P 13½.
296	**142**	5d. multicoloured	40	35

(Des V. Pulevski. Litho 11 Oktombri)

2000 (8 May). OBLIGATORY TAX. Red Cross Week. P 13½.
297	**143**	2d.50 multicoloured	60	55

For compulsory use from 8 to 15 May.

144 Building Europe
145 Running

MACEDONIA 2000

(Des J.-P. Cousin. Litho)

2000 (9 May). Europa. P 14.
298   144   30d. multicoloured .... 3·75   3·50

(Des I. Stevkovski. Litho 11 Oktombri)

2000 (17 May). Olympic Games, Sydney. T **145** and similar horiz designs. Multicoloured. P13½.
299   5d. Type **145** 40   35
300   30d. Wrestling .... 1·80   1·70

146 Cupped Hands   **147** Flower and Globe

(Des. V. Pulevski. Litho 11 Oktombri)

2000 (1 June). OBLIGATORY TAX. Solidarity Week. P 13½.
301   146   2d.50 multicoloured 60   55
For compulsory use from 1 to 7 June.

(Des K. Zarkovska. Litho 11 Oktombri)

2000 (5 June). International Environmental Protection Day. P 13½.
302   147   5d. multicoloured 40   35

148 Teodosija Sinaitski (printing pioneer)   **149** Mother Teresa

(Des T. Potsevska. Litho 11 Oktombri)

2000 (28 July). Printing. T **148** and similar vert design. Multicoloured. P 13½.
303   6d. Type **148** 40   35
304   30d. Johannes Gutenberg (inventor of printing press) .... 1·80   1·70

(Des I. Stevkovski. Photo 11 Oktombri)

2000 (28 Aug). Third Death Anniversary of Mother Teresa (founder of Order of Missionaries of Charity). P 13½.
305   149   6d. multicoloured 40   35

150 Faces and Hands   **151** Little Egret (*Egretta garzetta*)

(Des V. Pulevski. Litho 11 Oktombri)

2000 (14 Sept). OBLIGATORY TAX. Red Cross Week. P 13½.
306   150   3d. multicoloured 60   55
For compulsory use from 14 to 21 September.

(Des I. Stevkovski. Litho 11 Oktombri)

2000 (14 Sept). Birds. T **151** and similar vert designs. Multicoloured. P 13½.
307   6d. Type **151** 45   40
308   10d. Grey Heron (*Ardea cinerea*) 60   55
309   20d. Purple Heron (*Adrea purpurea*) .... 1·40   1·30
310   30d. Glossy Ibis (*Plegadis falcinellus*) .... 2·10   2·00
307/310 Set of 4 .... 4·00   3·75

152 Children and Tree   **153** Dimo Dimov

(Des K. Zarkovska. Litho 11 Oktombri)

2000 (2 Oct). Children's Week. P 13½.
311   152   6d. multicoloured 40   35

(Des I. Stevkovski. Litho 11 Oktombri)

2000 (20 Oct). 125th Birth Anniversary of Dimo Hadži Dimov (revolutionary). P 13½.
312   153   6d. multicoloured 40   35

154 Emblem   **155** Church and Frontispiece

(Des T. Pocevska. Litho 11 Oktombri)

2000 (1 Nov). 50th Anniversary of Faculty of Economics, St Cyril and St Methodius University, Skopje. P 13½.
313   154   6d. multicoloured 40   35

(Des Lj. Ivanovski. Litho 11 Oktombri)

2000 (8 Nov). 250th Birth Anniversary of Joakim Kržovski (writer). P 13½.
314   155   6d. multicoloured .... 1·20   1·10

156 Nativity   **157** Hand holding Condom

(Des Lj. Ivanovski. Litho 11 Oktombri)

2000 (22 Nov). Christmas. P 13½.
315   156   30d. multicoloured .... 1·80   1·70

(Des V. Pulevski. Litho 11 Oktombri)

2000 (1 Dec). OBLIGATORY TAX. Anti-AIDS Week. P 13½.
316   157   3d. multicoloured 60   55
For compulsory use from 1 to 7 December.

158 Handprints and Emblem   **159** Imperial Eagle on Branch

(Des K. Zarkovska. Litho 11 Oktombri)

2001 (10 Jan). 50th Anniversary of United Nations Commissioner for Human Rights. T **158** and similar multicoloured design. P 13½.
317   6d. Type **158** 45   40
318   30d. Hands forming Globe (*vert*) .... 2·00   1·90

2001 (1 Feb). Endangered Species. The Imperial Eagle (*Aquila heliaca*). T **159** and similar horiz designs. Multicoloured. P 14.

319	6d. Type **159**		45	40
	a. Block of 4. Nos. 319/322		3·50	
320	8d. With chick		50	50
321	10d. Flying		70	65
322	30d. Head		1·70	1·60
319/322	Set of 4		3·00	2·75

Nos. 319/322 were issued together in *se-tenant* blocks of four stamps, within sheets of eight.

160 Partenja Zografski
161 Emblem

(Des T. Pocevska. Litho 11 Oktombri)

2001 (6 Feb). 125th Death Anniversary of Partenja Zografski (historian). P 13½.
323 **160** 6d. multicoloured 45 40

(Des V. Pulevski. Litho 11 Oktombri)

2001 (1 Mar). OBLIGATORY TAX. Anti-Cancer Week. P 13½.
324 **161** 3d. multicoloured 70 65
For compulsory use from 1 to 8 March.

162 Woman in Costume

2001 (1 Mar). Regional Costumes. T **162** and similar vert designs. Multicoloured. P 13½.

325	6d. Type **162**		45	40
326	12d. Couple in costume		85	80
327	18d. Woman in costume		1·20	1·10
328	30d. Couple in costume		1·70	1·60
325/328	Set of 4		3·75	3·50
MS329	76×64 mm. 50d. Women working (30×30 mm). Imperf		3·50	3·25

163 Landscape

2001 (26 Mar). Birth Centenary of Lazar Licenoski (artist). Litho. P 13½.
330 **163** 6d. multicoloured 45 40

164 Text
165 Jesus and Sick Man

2001 (1 Apr). 50th Anniversary of State Archives. Litho. P 13½.
331 **164** 6d. multicoloured 45 40

2001 (15 Apr). Easter. Litho. P 13½.
332 **165** 6d. multicoloured 45 40

166 Children
167 Lake and Island (left side)

2001 (8 May). OBLIGATORY TAX. Red Cross Week. Litho. P 13½.
333 **166** 3d. multicoloured 70 65
For compulsory use from 8 to 15 May.

2001 (16 May). Europa. Water Resources. T **167** and similar horiz design. Multicoloured. Paper with fluorescent fibres. Litho. P 13½.

334	18d. Type **167**		1·40	1·30
	a. Pair. Nos. 334/335		4·75	4·25
335	36d. Right-side of lake and island		3·00	2·75

Nos. 334/335 were issued together in horizontal *se-tenant* pairs within the sheet, each pair forming a composite design.

168 Dimitri Berovski (nationalist leader) and Flag
169 Man carrying Red Cross Boxes

2001 (20 May). 125th Anniversary of Razlovci Village Uprising. Litho. P 13½.
336 **168** 6d. multicoloured 45 40

2001 (1 June). OBLIGATORY TAX. Red Cross Week. Litho. P 13½.
337 **169** 3d. multicoloured 50 50
For compulsory use from 1 to 7 June.

170 Championship Emblem
171 Boats on Lake

2001 (1 June). Second Individual European Chess Championship, Ohrid. Litho. P 13½.
338 **170** 36d. multicoloured 2·50 2·40

2001 (5 June). Environment Protection. Lake Dojran. Litho. P 13½.
339 **171** 6d. multicoloured 45 40

172 Emblem
173 Juniper (*Juniperus exelsa*)

2001 (8 Sept). Tenth Anniversary of Independence. Litho. P 13½.
340 **172** 6d. multicoloured 45 40

2001 (12 Sept). Trees. T **173** and similar horiz designs. Multicoloured. Litho. P 13½.
341 6d. Type **173** 45 40

MACEDONIA 2001

342	12d. Macedonian Oak (*Quercus macedonica*)		85	80
343	24d. Strawberry Tree (*Arbutus andrachne*).......		1·50	1·40
344	36d. Kermes Oak (*Quercus coccifera*)		2·20	2·10
341/344	*Set of 4*...		4·50	4·25

174 Man with raised Arms

175 Stylised Woman with Basket

2001 (14 Sept). OBLIGATORY TAX. Anti-Tuberculosis Week. Litho. P 13½.
345 **174** 3d. multicoloured 70 65
For compulsory use from 14 to 21 September.

2001 (1 Oct). Children's Day. Litho. P 13½.
346 **175** 6d. multicoloured 45 40

176 Children encircling Globe

177 Fox and Cubs

(Urska Golob. Litho)
2001 (9 Oct). United Nations Year of Dialogue among Civilisations. P 13½.
347 **176** 36d. multicoloured .... 3·00 2·75

2001 (26 Oct). 75th Anniversary of Zoological Museum. Litho. P 13½.
348 **177** 6d. multicoloured 70 65

178 Icon

179 Faces

2001 (22 Nov). Christmas. Litho. P 13½.
349 **178** 6d. multicoloured 70 65

2001 (1 Dec). OBLIGATORY TAX. Anti-AIDS Week. Litho. P 13½.
350 **179** 3d. multicoloured 70 65
For compulsory use from 1 to 7 December.

180 Alfred Nobel

181 Skier

2001 (10 Dec). Centenary of First Nobel Prize. Litho. P 13½.
351 **180** 36d. multicoloured .... 2·50 2·40

2002 (16 Jan). Winter Olympic Games, Salt Lake City, USA. T **181** and similar horiz design. Multicoloured. Litho. P 14.
352   6d. Type **181** 50 50
353   36d. Skier (*different*) .... 2·00 1·90

182 Sunrise

183 Likej (coin)

2002 (1 Mar). OBLIGATORY TAX. Anti-Cancer Week. Litho. P 13½.
354 **182** 3d. multicoloured 70 65
For compulsory use from 1 to 8 March.

2002 (1 Mar). Ancient Coins. T **183** and similar horiz designs showing coins. Multicoloured. Litho. P 14.
355   6d. Type **183** 50 50
356   12d. Alexander III tetradrachm............................ 85 80
357   24d. Lichnidos... 1·50 1·40
358   36d. Philip II gold coin (stater)............................ 2·20 2·10
355/358 *Set of 4*... 4·50 4·25
MS359 85×62 mm. 50d. Coin... 4·25 4·00

184 Painting and Petar Mazev

185 The Risen Christ

2002 (15 Apr). Artists Birth Anniversaries. T **184** and similar horiz designs. Multicoloured. Litho. P 14.
360   6d. Type **184** (75th anniversary)........................ 70 65
361   6d. Triptych, 1978 (Dimitar Kondovski, 75th anniversary)... 70 65
362   36d. *Mona Lisa* (La Gioconda) and Leonardo da Vinci (550th anniversary)........................ 2·50 2·40
360/362 *Set of 3*... 3·50 3·25

2002 (24 Apr). Easter. P 14.
363 **185** 6d. multicoloured 70 65

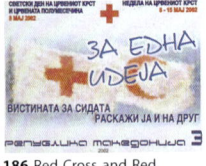
186 Red Cross and Red Crescent Flags

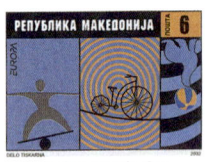
187 Acrobat, Bicycle, Sea Lion and Ball

2002 (8 May). OBLIGATORY TAX. Red Cross Week. Litho. P 13½.
364 **186** 3d. multicoloured 70 65
For compulsory use from 8 to 15 May.

2002 (9 May). Europa. Circus. T **187** and similar horiz design. Multicoloured. Litho. P 14.
365   6d. Type **187** 70 65
366   36d. Circles, bicycle and ball............................... 2·50 2·40

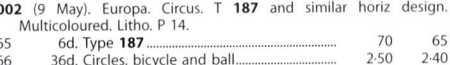

188 Championship Emblem, Ball and Player

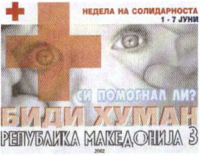
189 Red Cross and Face

2002 (15 May). World Cup Football Championship, Japan and South Korea. Litho. P 14.
367 **188** 6d. multicoloured .... 3·00 3·00

2002 (1 June). OBLIGATORY TAX. Solidarity Week. Litho. P 13½.
368   **189**   3d. multicoloured 70   65
For compulsory use from 1 to 7 June.

190 Tree containing Shapes

191 1595 Korenic Neonic Coat of Arms

2002 (5 June). Environment Protection. Litho. P 14.
369   **190**   6d. multicoloured 70   65

2002 (19 June). National Arms. T **191** and similar vert design. Multicoloured. P 14.
370   10d. Type **191** 85   80
371   36d. 1620 Coat of Arms .... 2·50   2·40

192 House, Kruševo

193 Metodija Andonov-Cento

2002 (28 June). City Architecture. T **192** and similar horiz design. Multicoloured. Litho. P 13½.
372   36d. Type **192** .... 1·70   1·60
373   50d. House, Bitola .... 3·50   3·25

(Des I. Stevkovski. Litho)
2002 (18 Aug). Birth Centenary of Metodija Andonov-Cento (first Macedonian president). P 13½.
374   **193**   6d. multicoloured 70   65

194 Nikola Karev

195 Grey Partridge (*Perdix perdix*)

(Des L. Ž. Donev. Litho)
2002 (18 Aug). 125th Birth Anniversary of Nikola Karev (revolutionary leader). P 13½.
375   **194**   18d. multicoloured .... 1·40   1·30

(Des I. Stevkovski. Litho)
2002 (11 Sept). Fauna. T **195** and similar horiz designs. Multicoloured. P 14.
376   6d. Type **195** 50   50
         a. Block of 4. Nos. 376/379 .... 4·25
377   12d. Wild Pig (*Sus scrofa*) 70   65
378   24d. Chamois (*Rupicapra rupicapra*) .... 1·20   1·10
379   36d. Rock Partridge (*Alectoris graeca*) .... 1·70   1·60
376/379 Set of 4 .... 3·75   3·50
Nos. 376/379 were issued in *se-tenant* blocks of four stamps within the sheet.

196 Face

197 House and People (child's drawing)

2002 (14 Sept). OBLIGATORY TAX. Anti-Tuberculosis Week. Litho. P 13½.
380   **196**   3d. multicoloured 70   65
For compulsory use from 14 to 21 September.

(Des L. Žhivkovska Donev. Litho)
2002 (1 Oct). Children's Day. P 14.
381   **197**   6d. multicoloured 70   65

198 Mary and Jesus (14th-century icon)

199 Clock, Numbers and Face

2002 (20 Nov). Christmas. P 13½.
382   **198**   9d. multicoloured 70   65

2002 (1 Dec). OBLIGATORY TAX. Anti-AIDS Week. Litho. P 13½.
383   **199**   3d. multicoloured 70   65
For compulsory use from 1 to 7 December.

200 Andreja Damjanov and Building Façade

201 Gajga

2003 (2 Jan). 125th Death Anniversary of Andreja Damjanov (architect). Litho. P 13½.
384   **200**   36d. multicoloured .... 2·50   2·40

2003 (18 Feb). Traditional Musical Instruments. T **201** and similar vert designs. Multicoloured. Litho. P 13½.
385   9d. Type **201** 65   60
386   10d. Tambura 70   65
387   20d. Kemene .... 1·70   1·60
388   50d. Tapan .... 3·50   3·25
385/388 Set of 4 .... 6·00   5·50

202 Scouts and Campsite

203 Face surrounded by Petals

2003 (22 Feb). 50th Anniversary of Scouting in Macedonia. P 13½.
389   **202**   9d. multicoloured 70   65

2003 (1 Mar). OBLIGATORY TAX. Anti-Cancer Week. Litho. P 13½.
390   **203**   4d. multicoloured 70   65
For compulsory use from 1 to 8 March.

204 Krste Petkov Misirkov (founder)

MACEDONIA 2003

2003 (5 Mar). 50th Anniversary of Krste Petkov Misirkov Macedonian Language Institute. P 13½.

| 391 | **204** | 9d. multicoloured | 70 | 65 |

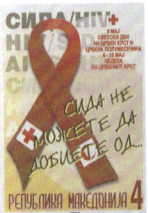

205 Red Ribbon with Red Cross and Red Crescent Emblems

2003 (8 May). OBLIGATORY TAX. Red Cross Week. Litho. P 13½.

| 392 | **205** | 3d. multicoloured | 70 | 65 |

For compulsory use from 8 to 15 May.

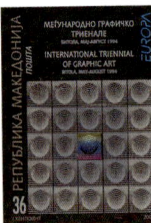 

206 International Graphic Art Triennial, Bitola (1994)

207 Outstretched Hand

2003 (9 May). Europa. Poster Art. T **206** and similar vert design. Multicoloured. P 13½.

| 393 | 36d. Type **206** | 2·50 | 2·40 |
| 394 | 36d. Ohrider Sommer (1966) | 2·50 | 2·40 |

2003 (1 June). OBLIGATORY TAX. Solidarity Week. Litho. P 13½.

| 395 | **207** | 4d. multicoloured | 70 | 65 |

For compulsory use from 1 to 7 June.

208 Brown Bear (*Ursus arctos*)

2003 (5 June). P 13½.

| 396 | **208** | 9d. multicoloured | 70 | 65 |

2003 (16 June). City Architecture. Horiz designs as T **192**. Multicoloured. Litho. P 13½.

| 397 | 10d. House, Skopje | 70 | 65 |
| 398 | 20d. House, Resen | 1·40 | 1·30 |

2003 (23 June). National Arms. Vert designs as T **191**. Multicoloured. Litho. P 14.

| 399 | 9d. 17th-century Arms | 70 | 65 |
| 400 | 36d. 1694 Coat of Arms | 2·75 | 2·50 |

209 Handball Player

210 Seal and Revolutionaries

2003 (30 July). World Youth Handball Championships. P 13½.

| 401 | **209** | 36d. multicoloured | 2·50 | 2·40 |

2003 (2 Aug). Centenary of Ilinden Uprising. T **210** and similar horiz designs. Multicoloured. Litho. P 13½.

402	9d. Type **210**	70	65
403	36d. Leaders and Mechen Kamen monument	2·75	2·50
MS404	60×75 mm. 50d. Revolutionaries (*different*)	3·50	3·25

211 *Self Portrait* (Nikola Martinovski) (½ *size illustration*)

2003 (18 Aug). Artists' Anniversaries. T **211** and similar multicoloured design. Litho. P 13½.

| 405 | 9d. Type **211** (birth centenary) | 70 | 65 |
| 406 | 36d. *Moulin de Galette* (Vincent van Gogh) (150th birth anniversary) (*horiz*) | 2·40 | 2·20 |

212 Stylised Figure

213 Colchicum (*Colchicum macedonicum*)

2003 (14 Sept). OBLIGATORY TAX. Anti-Tuberculosis Week. Litho. P 13½.

| 407 | **212** | 4d. multicoloured | 70 | 65 |

For compulsory use from 14 to 21 September.

2003 (25 Sept). Flowers. T **213** and similar vert designs. Multicoloured. Litho. P 13½.

408	9d. Type **213**	1·00	95
409	20d. *Viola* (*Viola allchariensis*)	2·00	1·90
410	36d. *Tulipa mariannae*	3·25	3·00
411	50d. *Thymus oehmianus*	5·00	4·75
408/411	Set of 4	10·00	9·50

214 Said Najdeni

215 Family sheltering under Umbrella

2003 (30 Sept). Death Centenaries. T **214** and similar horiz design. Multicoloured. P 13½.

| 412 | 9d. Type **214** (Albanian writer and reformer) | 1·00 | 95 |
| 413 | 9d. Jeronim de Rada (Italian-Albanian writer) | 1·00 | 95 |

(Des L. Žhivkovska. Litho)

2003 (6 Oct). Children's Day. P 13½.

| 414 | **215** | 9d. multicoloured | 1·00 | 95 |

2003 MACEDONIA

216 Seal and Armed Revolutionaries

2003 (17 Oct). 125th of Kresna Uprising. Litho. P 13½.
415	216	9d. multicoloured	1·00	95

217 Dimitir Vlahov

2003 (8 Nov). 50th Death Anniversary of Dimitir Vlahov (politician). Litho. P 13½.
416	217	9d. multicoloured	1·00	95

218 Mary and Jesus (fresco)   **219** Ribbon

2003 (19 Nov). Christmas. Litho. P 13½.
417	218	9d. multicoloured	1·00	95

2003 (1 Dec). OBLIGATORY TAX. Anti-AIDS Week. Litho. P 13½.
418	219	4d. scarlet vermilion	1·00	95

For compulsory use from 1 to 7 December.

220 19th-century Jug, Smojmirovo   **221** Wilbur and Orville Wright and Wright *Flyer*

2003 (16 Dec)–**06**. Cultural Artifacts. T **220** and similar horiz designs. Multicoloured. P 13½.
419		3d. Amphora (4.6.04)	50	50
420		3d. 18th/19th-century lidded jug (P 13) (30.8.06)	50	50
421		4d. 19th-century coffee pot (*horiz*) (P 13) (30.11.06)	65	60
422		5d. Tassel, Vrutok (25.1.04)	75	70
423		5d. 20th-century circular flask (P 13) (30.11.06)	75	70
424		6d. 18th/19th-century jug and ewer (P 13) (30.8.06)	90	85
425		9d. Type **220**	1·00	95
426		10d. Kettle, Ohrid (20.1.04)	1·00	95
427		10d. 18th-century hand-bell (P 13) (30.11.06)	1·00	95
428		12d. Albastron (alabaster incense pot) (4.6.04)	1·30	1·20
429		12d. 18th/19th-century pot with cover (P 13) (30.11.06)	1·30	1·20
430		20d. Chest decoration, Galicnik (25.1.04)	2·30	2·20
419/430		*Set of* 12	11·00	10·00

Numbers have been left for additions to this series.

2003 (17 Dec). Centenary of Powered Flight. P 13½.
440	221	50d. multicoloured	5·00	4·75

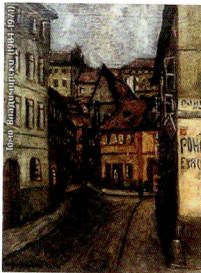 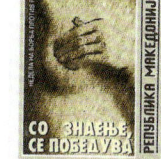

222 Street Scene (Tomo Vladimirski)   **223** Breast Examination

2004 (14 Feb). Artists' Birth Centenaries. T **222** and similar multicoloured design. Litho. P 13½.
441		9d. Type **222**	1·00	95
442		9d. Ohrid Street (Vangel Kodzoman)	1·00	95

2004 (1 Mar). OBLIGATORY TAX. Anti-Cancer Week. Litho. P 13½.
443	223	4d. multicoloured	75	70

For compulsory use from 1 to 8 March.

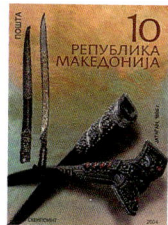 

224 Knives and Armour   **225** Carpet

2004 (10 Mar). Cultural Heritage. Weapons. T **224** and similar vert designs. Multicoloured. Litho. P 13½.
444		10d. Type **224**	1·00	95
445		20d. 19th-century sword	2·00	1·90
446		36d. 18th-century pistol	3·00	3·00
447		50d. 18th-century rifle	4·00	3·75
444/447		*Set of* 4	9·00	8·75

2004 (24 Mar). Traditional Carpets. T **225** and similar vert design. Multicoloured. Litho. P 13½.
448		36d. Type **225**	3·00	3·00
449		50d. Carpet (*different*)	4·50	4·25

226 Kostandin Kristoforidhi (writer)   **227** House, Kratovo

2004 (19 Apr). Centenary of Publication of First Albanian Dictionary in Macedonia. Litho. P 13½.
450	226	36d. multicoloured	3·50	3·25

2004 (23 Apr). City Architecture. Litho. P 13½.
451	227	20d. multicoloured	2·00	1·90

MACEDONIA 2004

228 Parasol and Woman Reading

229 Profiles

2004 (7 May). Europa. Holidays. T **228** and similar vert design. Multicoloured. Litho. P 13½.
452	50d. Type **228**	4·75	4·50
	a. Pair. Nos. 452/453	9·75	9·25
453	50d. Yacht and island	4·75	4·50

Nos. 452/453 were issued in *se-tenant* pairs within the sheet, each pair forming a composite design of a beach scene.

2004 (8 May). OBLIGATORY TAX. Red Cross Week. Litho. P 13½.
454	**229** 4d. multicoloured	75	70

For compulsory use from 8 to 15 May.

230 Stars

231 Hands enclosing Globe

2004 (9 May). Application to join European Union. Litho. P 13½.
455	**230** 36d. multicoloured	3·50	3·25

2004 (1 June). OBLIGATORY TAX. Solidarity Week. Litho. P 13½.
456	**231** 6d. multicoloured	75	70

For compulsory use from 1 to 7 June.

232 Pelican and Lake

233 Flags as Interlocking Rings

2004 (5 June). Prespa National Park. Litho. P 13½.
457	**232** 36d. multicoloured	3·50	3·25

2004 (16 June). Olympic Games, Athens. T **233** and similar horiz design. Multicoloured. Litho. P 13½.
458	50d. Type **233**	4·25	4·00
	a. Pair. Nos. 458/459	8·75	8·25
459	50d. Rings (*different*)	4·25	4·00

Nos. 458/459 were issued in horizontal *se-tenant* pairs within the sheet, each pair forming a composite design of Olympic rings.

234 Sami Frasheri

235 Emblem, Feet and Ball

2004 (18 June). Death Centenary of Sami Frasheri (Albanian writer). Litho. P 13½.
460	**234** 12d. multicoloured	1·30	1·20

2004 (3 July). Centenary of FIFA (Fédèration Internationale de Football Association). Litho. P 13½.
461	**235** 100d. multicoloured	8·75	8·50

236 Marko Cepenkov

237 Child blowing Bubbles

2004 (1 Sept). Anniversaries. T **236** and similar multicoloured design. Litho. P 13½.
462	12d. Type **236** (writer) (175th birth)	1·30	1·20
463	12d. Vasil Glavinov (politician) (75th death) (*vert*)	1·30	1·20

2004 (14 Sept). OBLIGATORY TAX. Anti-Tuberculosis Week. Litho. P 13½.
464	**237** 4d. multicoloured	75	70

For compulsory use from 14 to 21 September.

238 Bohemian Waxwing (*Bombycilla garrulous*)

239 Children

2004 (25 Sept). Birds. T **238** and similar vert designs. Multicoloured. Litho. P 13½.
465	12d. Type **238**	1·30	1·20
466	24d. Woodchat Shrike (*Lanius senator*)	2·30	2·20
467	36d. Rock Thrush (*Monticola saxatilis*)	3·25	3·00
468	48d. Northern Bullfinch (*Pyrrhula pyrrhula*) ...	4·50	4·25
465/468	*Set of 4*	10·00	9·50
MS469	86×61 mm. 60d. Wallcreeper (*Tichodroma muraria*) Imperf	6·25	6·00

2004 (4 Oct). Children's Day. Litho. P 13½.
470	**239** 12d. multicoloured	1·30	1·20

240 Binary Code

241 Manuscript

2004 (16 Oct). World Summit on Information Technology Society (WSIS). Litho. P 13½.
471	**240** 36d. multicoloured	3·50	3·25

2004 (27 Oct). Millenary of Publication of Asseman Gospel (Glagolitic (early Slavonic language) liturgical gospel). Litho. P 13½.
472	**241** 12d. multicoloured	1·30	1·20

242 Marco Polo

243 Star, Ribbons, Snowflakes and Holly

2004 (10 Nov). 750th Birth Anniversary of Marco Polo (traveller). Litho. P 13½.
473 242 36d. multicoloured .... 3·50 3·25

2004 (24 Nov). Christmas. Litho. P 13½.
474 243 12d. multicoloured .... 1·30 1·20

244 Hands

245 Konstantin Miladinov

2004 (1 Dec). OBLIGATORY TAX. Anti-AIDS Week. Litho. P 13½.
475 244 6d. multicoloured 75 70
For compulsory use from 1 to 7 December.

2005 (4 Feb). 175th Birth Anniversary of Konstantin Miladinov (writer). Litho. P 13½.
476 245 36d. multicoloured .... 3·75 3·50

246 Ash Tray

247 Manuscript (16th/17th-century)

2005 (1 Mar). OBLIGATORY TAX. Anti-Cancer Week. Litho. P 13½.
477 246 6d. multicoloured 75 70
For compulsory use from 1 to 8 March.

2005 (9 Mar). Illuminated Manuscripts. T **247** and similar vert designs. Multicoloured. Litho. P 13½.
478 12d. Type **247** .... 1·30 1·20
479 24d. Illustration (16th-century) .... 2·30 2·20

248 Embroidered Cloth (19th-century)

2005 (9 Mar). Embroidery. T **248** and similar horiz design. Multicoloured. Litho. P 13½.
480 36d. Type **248** .... 3·00 3·00
481 50d. Embroidery (20th-century) .... 4·50 4·25

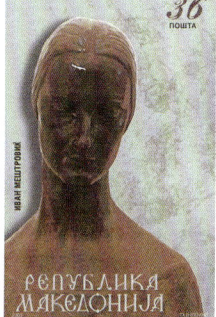
249 Woman's Head (sculpture) (Ivan Mestrovic)

250 Fragment

2005 (6 Apr). Art. T **249** and similar multicoloured design. Litho. P 13½.
482 36d. Type **249** .... 3·00 3·00
483 50d. Portrait of Woman (painting) (Paja Jovanovic) (*horiz*) .... 4·50 4·25

2005 (27 Apr). 450th Anniversary of *The Missal* by Gjon Buzuku (first book written and published in Albanian. Litho. P 13½.
484 250 12d. multicoloured .... 1·30 1·20

251 Skanderbeg

252 Henry Dunant (Red Cross founder)

2005 (27 Apr). 600th Birth Anniversary of Gjergj Kastrioti (Skanderbeg) (Albanian leader). Litho. P 13½.
485 251 36d. multicoloured .... 3·00 3·00

2004 (8 May). OBLIGATORY TAX. Red Cross Week. Litho. P 13½.
486 252 6d. multicoloured 75 70
For compulsory use from 8 to 15 May.

253 Grain, Cake and Bread

254 Building and Script

2005 (9 May). Europa. Gastronomy. T **253** and similar horiz design. Multicoloured. Litho. P 13½.
487 36d. Type **253** .... 3·00 3·00
  a. Horiz pair. Nos. 487/488 .... 8·75 8·50
488 60d. Roasted meat with peppers .... 5·50 5·25
Nos. 487/488 were issued in horizontal *se-tenant* pairs within the sheet.

2005 (23 May). Centenary of National Day of Vlachs (Aromanians) (imperial decree, issued by Ottoman Sultan Abdual Hamid II, which gave Vlachs their first collective rights). Litho. P 13½.
489 254 12d. multicoloured .... 1·30 1·20

No. 490 and T **255** have been left for OBLIGATORY TAX. Solidarity Week issued 1 June not yet received.

256 Globe as Tree

257 Figure (16th-century)

2005 (5 June). Environmental Protection. Litho. P 13½.
491 256 36d. multicoloured .... 3·00 3·00

2005 (8 June). Carvings. T **257** and similar vert designs. Multicoloured. Litho. P 13½.
492 3d. Type **257** 50 50
493 4d. Ten-sided stars shape (15th-century) 65 60
494 6d. Winged Serpents (16th-century) 75 70
495 8d. Diamond shaped design (1883–1884) ... 90 85
496 12d. Figure, Snake and animals (16th-century) .... 1·30 1·20
492/496 Set of 5 .... 3·75 3·50

MACEDONIA 2005

258 Ford (1905)

2005 (15 June). Transport Anniversaries. T **258** and similar horiz design. Multicoloured. Litho. P 13½.
497	12d. Type **258** (centenary of first car)..............		1·00	95
498	36d. Glider (50th anniversary of Macedonia aircraft)..		3·00	3·00

259 Albert Einstein and Emblem

260 Cross of Lorraine

2005 (30 June). International Year of Physics. Centenary of Publication of *Theory of Special Relativity*. Litho. P 13½.
499	**259**	60d. multicoloured............................	5·00	4·75

2005 (14 Sept). OBLIGATORY TAX. Anti-Tuberculosis Week. Litho. P 13½.
500	**260**	6d. multicoloured..................................	75	70

For compulsory use from 14 to 21 September.

261 *Malus* (Apples)

262 Smolarski Waterfall

2005 (14 Sept). Fruit. T **261** and similar multicoloured designs. P 13½.
501	12d. Type **261**	1·00	95
502	24d. *Prunus persica* (Peaches)...........................	2·00	1·90
503	36d. *Prunus avium*	3·00	3·00
504	48d. *Prunus* (Plums)..	4·00	3·75
501/504 *Set of 4*..		9·00	8·75
MS505 97×65 mm. 100d. *Pyrus* (Pears) (*vert*)...........		8·75	8·50

2005 (14 Sept). Litho. P 13½.
506	**262**	24d. multicoloured...............................	2·00	1·90

263 Hans Christian Andersen

2005 (3 Oct). Birth Bicentenary of Hans Christian Andersen (writer). Litho. P 13½.
507	**263**	12d. multicoloured.............................	1·00	95

264 Kozjak Dam

2005 (25 Oct). Litho. P 13½.
508	**264**	12d. multicoloured.............................	1·00	95

265 '1880–8'

266 Delegates

2005 (25 Oct). 125th Anniversary of Brsjai Rebellion. Litho. P 13½.
509	**265**	12d. multicoloured.............................	1·00	95

2005 (28 Oct). Centenary of Rila Congress. Litho. P 13½.
510	**266**	12d. multicoloured.............................	1·00	95

267 2002 36d. Stamp (as T **187**)

268 Candle

2005 (14 Nov). 50th Anniversary of Europa Stamps. T **267** and similar horiz designs. Multicoloured. Litho. P 13½.
511	60d. Type **267**	5·00	4·75
	a. Block of 4. Nos. 511/514...............................	70·00	
512	170d. 1999 30d. stamp (as Type **122**)................	12·50	12·00
513	250d. 1997 20d. stamp (as Type **85**).................	20·00	19·00
514	350d. 1996 40d. stamp (as No. **153**)................	25·00	24·00
511/514 *Set of 4*..		55·00	55·00
MS515 66×132 mm. Nos. 511/514...............................		90·00	85·00

Nos. 511/514 were issued in *se-tenant* blocks of four stamps within the sheet.

2005 (23 Nov). Christmas. Litho. P 13½.
516	**268**	12d. multicoloured.............................	1·00	95

269 White Water Kayaking

270 Hand holding Condom

2005 (23 Nov). Litho. P 13½.
517	**269**	36d. multicoloured.............................	3·00	3·00

2005 (1 Dec). OBLIGATORY TAX. Anti-AIDS Week. Litho. P 13½.
518	**270**	6d. multicoloured...............................	75	70

For compulsory use from 1 to 7 December.

271 Postal Emblem

272 Skier

2005 (14 Dec). Litho. P 13½.
519	**271**	12d. multicoloured.............................	1·00	95

2006 (25 Jan). Winter Olympic Games, Turin. T **272** and similar vert design. Multicoloured. Litho. P 13½.
520	36d. Type **272**	3·00	3·00
521	60d. Ice hockey player.....................................	5·00	4·75

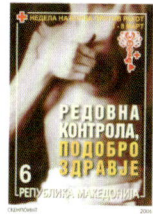 

273 Woman examining Breast   **274** Fresco, Monastic Church, Matejce

2006 (1 Mar). OBLIGATORY TAX. Anti-Cancer Week. Litho. P 13½.
522   **273**   6d. multicoloured 75   70
For compulsory use from 1 to 8 March.

2006 (8 Mar). Cultural Heritage. T **274** and similar vert design. Multicoloured. Litho. P 13½.
523   12d. Type **274** .... 1·00   95
524   24d. Isaac Celebi Mosque, Bitola .... 2·00   1·90

275 Leopold Senghor   **276** Wooden Pattens

2006 (20 Mar). Birth Centenary of Leopold Sedar Senghor (Senegalese politician). Litho. P 13½.
525   **275**   36d. multicoloured .... 3·00   3·00

2006 (22 Mar). Craftwork. Mother of Pearl Inlays. T **276** and similar vert design. Multicoloured. Litho. P 13½.
526   12d. Type **276** .... 1·00   95
527   24d. Pipes .... 2·00   1·90

277 Woodcarving, Church of the Holy Saviour, Skopje   **278** Cupola

2006 (5 Apr). Birth Bicentenary of Makarie Negriev Frčkovski. Litho. P 13½.
528   **277**   12d. multicoloured .... 1·00   95

2006 (5 Apr). 450th Anniversary of Cupola, Church of St Peter, Rome. P 13½.
529   **278**   36d. multicoloured .... 3·00   3·00

279 Zhivko Firkov   **280** Mozart, Score and Violins

2006 (26 Apr). Birth Centenary of Zhivko Firkov (composer). P 13½.
530   **279**   24d. multicoloured .... 2·00   1·90

2006 MACEDONIA

2006 (26 Apr). 250th Birth Anniversary of Wolfgang Amadeus Mozart (composer). P 13½.
531   **280**   60d. multicoloured .... 5·00   4·75

281 Stylised Figure   **282** Coloured Balls

2006 (8 May). OBLIGATORY TAX. Red Cross Week. Litho. P 13½.
532   **281**   6d. multicoloured 75   70
For compulsory use from 8 to 15 May.

2006 (9 May). Europa. Integration. T **282** and similar vert design. Multicoloured. Litho. P 13½.
533   36d. Type **282** .... 3·00   3·00
534   60d. Coloured building blocks .... 5·00   4·75

283 Pope John Paul II   **284** Greenery running to Sand through Hourglass

2006 (9 May). Tenth Anniversary of Europa Stamps in Macedonia. Sheet 80×70 mm containing T **283** and similar vert design. Multicoloured. Litho. P 13½.
MS535   60d.×2, Type **283**; Mother Teresa .... 10·50   10·00

2006 (5 June). International Year of Deserts and Desertification. Litho. P 13½.
536   **284**   12d. multicoloured .... 1·00   95

285 Chequered Flag   **286** Nikola Tesla

2006 (14 June). Centenary of Grand Prix Motor Race. Litho. P 13½.
537   **285**   36d. multicoloured .... 3·00   3·00

2006 (28 June). 150th Birth Anniversary of Nikola Tesla (inventor). Litho. P 13½.
538   **286**   24d. multicoloured .... 2·00   1·90

287 Santa Maria   **288** Ancylus scalariformis

2006 (28 June). 500th Death Anniversary of Christopher Columbus. Litho. P 13½.
539   **287**   36d. multicoloured .... 3·00   3·00

2006 (6 Sept). Shells. T **288** and similar vert designs. Multicoloured. Litho. P 13½.

540		12d. Type **288**	1·00	95
541		24d. *Macedopyrgula pavlovici*	2·00	1·90
542		36d. *Gyraulus trapezoides*	3·00	3·00
543		48d. *Valvata hirsutecostata*	4·00	3·75
540/543		Set of 4	9·00	8·75
MS544		80×70 mm. 72d. *Ochridopyrgula macedonica*	6·25	6·00

289 Child

290 Girl drawing

2006 (14 Sept). OBLIGATORY TAX. Anti-Tuberculosis Week. Litho. P 13½.

545	**289**	6d. multicoloured	75	70

For compulsory use from 14 to 21 September.

2006 (2 Oct). 60th Anniversary of UNICEF. Litho. P 13½.

546	**290**	12d. multicoloured	1·00	95

291 National Park, Galicica

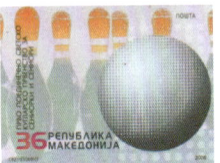
292 Ball and Pins

2006 (2 Oct). Litho. P 13½.

547	**291**	24d. multicoloured	2·00	1·90

2006 (20 Oct). World Ten-Pin Bowling Championship, Skopje. Litho. P 13½.

548	**292**	36d. multicoloured	3·00	3·00

293 Frang Bardhi (author of the first Albanian dictionary)

294 Stars

2006 (25 Oct). Personalities. T **293** and similar vert designs. Multicoloured. Litho. P 13½.

549		12d. Type **293**	1·00	95
550		12d. Boris Trajkovski (president, 1999–2004)	1·00	95
551		24d. Mustafa Kemel Attatürk (founder of Turkish Republic)	2·00	1·90
552		24d. Dositheus II (Metropolitan of Macedonia)	2·00	1·90
549/552		Set of 4	5·50	5·25

2006 (22 Nov). Christmas. Litho. P 13½.

553	**294**	12d. multicoloured	1·00	95

295 Emblem

296 Carved Stone

2006 (1 Dec). OBLIGATORY TAX. Anti-AIDS Week. Litho. P 13½.

554	**295**	6d. multicoloured	75	70

For compulsory use from 1 to 7 December.

2007 (31 Jan). Kokino Megalithic Observatory. T **296** and similar vert design. Multicoloured. Litho. P 13½.

555		12d. Type **296**	1·00	95
556		36d. Sunrise	3·00	3·00

297 Slivnik Monastery (400th Anniversary)

298 18th/19th-century Metal Cap

2007 (31 Jan). Monasteries' Anniversaries. T **297** and multicoloured design. Litho. P 13½.

557		12d. Type **297**	1·00	95
558		36d. St Nikita (700th anniversary) (*vert*)	3·00	3·00

2007 (14 Feb). Crafts. T **298** and horiz design. Multicoloured. Litho. P 13½.

559		12d. Type **297**	1·00	95
560		36d. 19th-century decorated box	3·00	3·00

299 *Cobitis vardarensis*

299a Woman

(Des I. Stefkovski. Litho)

2006 (28 Feb). Fish. T **299** and horiz design. Multicoloured. P 13½.

561		12d. Type **299**	1·00	95
562		36d. *Zingel balcanicus*	3·00	3·00
563		60d. *Chondrostoma vardarense*	5·00	4·75
564		100d. *Barbus macedonicus*	8·25	8·00
561/564		Set of 4	16·00	15·00
MS565		60×71 mm. 100d. *Leuciscus cephalus*	8·75	8·50

2007 (1 Mar). OBLIGATORY TAX. Anti-Cancer Week. Litho. P 13½.

565a	**299a**	6d. multicoloured	75	70

For compulsory use from 1 to 8 March.

300 *Epos of Freedom* (mosaic, detail) (Borko Lazeski)

(Des I. Stefkovski. Litho)

2007 (14 Mar). Art. Centenary of Cubism. T **300** and similar multicoloured design. Litho. P 13½.

566		36d. Type **300**	3·00	3·00
567		100d. *Head of a Woman* (Pablo Picasso) (*vert*)	8·25	8·00

301 Emblem and People talking

(Des I. Stefkovski. Litho)

2007 (20 Mar). International Day of Francophonie (Organisation of French speaking communities). P 13½.

568	**301**	12d. multicoloured	1·00	95

302 Cat   **302a** Hands and Globe

(Des G. Boev. Litho)

2007 (9 Apr). Pets. P 13½.
569   302   12d. multicoloured .... 1·00   95

2007 (8 May). OBLIGATORY TAX. Red Cross Week. Litho. P 13½.
569a   302a   6d. multicoloured 75   70
For compulsory use from 8 to 15 May.

303 Camp   **303a** Fresco, Basilica of San Clemente (detail)

(Des I. Stefkovski. Litho)

2006 (9 May). Europa. Centenary of Scouting. T **303** and similar multicoloured designs. P 13½.
570   60d. Type **303** .... 6·50   6·25
571   100d. Scout (vert) .... 9·75   9·25
MS572 60×70 mm. 160d. Emblem............. 55·00   55·00

(Des Igor Stevkovski)

2007 (23 May). 150th Anniversary of Discovery of St Cyril's Grave. P 13½.
572a   303a   50d. multicoloured .... 4·25   4·00

304 Globe, Chimneys and Clock   **305** Dimitri Ivanovich Mendeleev

(Des I. Najdenovski Litho)

2007 (5 June). Pollution Awareness. P 13½.
573   304   12d. multicoloured .... 1·00   95

(Des M. Georgievski. Litho)

2007 (20 June). Scientific Personalities. T **305** and similar multicoloured design. P 13½.
574   36d. Type **305** (chemist and creator of first periodic tables) (death centenary) .... 3·00   3·00
575   36d. Carl von Linné (Linnaeus) (scientist and plant and animal classification deviser) (300th birth anniversary) (vert)   3·00   3·00

306 NATO and EPAC Emblems   **307** Yachts

(Des L. Živkovska Donev. Litho)

2007 (28 June). Euro–Atlantic Security Forum, Ohrid. P 13½.
576   306   60d. multicoloured .... 5·00   4·75

(Des I. Stevkovski. Litho)

2007 (31 July). Centenary of Yacht Racing Union. P 13½.
577   307   36d. multicoloured .... 3·00   3·00

308 Child and Dandelion   **309** Maminska River Waterfall

2007 (14 Sept). OBLIGATORY TAX. Anti-Tuberculosis Week. Litho. P 13½.
578   308   6d. multicoloured 75   70
For compulsory use from 14 to 21 September.

(Des L. Živkovska Donev. Litho)

2007 (19 Sept). Natural Heritage. P 13½.
579   309   12d. multicoloured .... 1·00   95

310 Dhimitër Pasko (Mitrush Kuteli)   **311** Drawings and Child

(Des I. Stevkovski. Litho)

2007 (25 Sept). Personalities. T **310** and similar vert design. Multicoloured. P 13½.
580   12d. Type **310** (writer) (birth centenary) .... 1·00   95
581   12d. Theofan (Fan) Stilian Noli (nationalist) (125th birth anniversary)................ 1·00   95

(Des I. Stevkovski. Litho)

2007 (1 Oct). Children's Day. P 13½.
582   311   12d. multicoloured .... 1·00   95

312 Sputnik   **313** Petre Prlicko

(Des I. Stevkovski. Litho)

2007 (4 Oct). 50th Anniversary of Space Exploration. P 13½.
583   312   36d. multicoloured .... 3·00   3·00

(Des I. Stevkovski. Litho)

2007 (31 Oct). Petre Prlicko (actor) Commemoration. P 13½.
584   313   12d. multicoloured .... 1·00   95

314 Jordan Dzinot   **315** Textile

MACEDONIA 2007

(Des L. Živkovska Donev. Litho)

2007 (31 Oct). Jordan Hadzi-Konstantinov Dzinot (educator) Commemoration. P 13½.
585 **314** 12d. multicoloured .... 1·00 95

(Des L. Živkovska Donev)

2007 (9 Nov). P 13½.
586 **315** 12d. multicoloured .... 1·00 95

316 Santa Claus   **317** AIDS Ribbon

(Des I. Stevkovski. Litho)

2007 (21 Nov). Christmas. P 13½.
587 **316** 12d. multicoloured .... 1·00 95

2007 (1 Dec). OBLIGATORY TAX. Anti-AIDS Week. Litho. P 13½.
588 **317** 6d. multicoloured 75 70
For compulsory use from 1 to 7 December.

318 Tose Proeski   **319** Earrings

(Des D. Moraitov and I. Stevkovski)

2007 (15 Dec). Tose Proeski (singer) Commemoration. P 13½.
589 **318** 12d. multicoloured .... 1·00 95

(Des L. Živkovska Donev)

2008 (23 Jan). Cultural Heritage. Jewellery. T **319** and similar multicoloured design. P 13½.
590 12d. Type **319** .... 1·30 1·20
591 24d. Lion headed earring (vert) .... 2·50 2·40

320 Launching of Satellite *Explorer 1*   **321** Train

(Des I. Stevkovski. Litho)

2008 (31 Jan). 50th Anniversary of Space Exploration. P 13½.
592 **320** 24d. multicoloured .... 2·50 2·40

(Des D. Milanovski)

2008 (27 Feb). Transportation. P 13½.
593 **321** 100d. multicoloured .... 10·00 9·50

322 Child and Cigarette

2008 (1 Mar). OBLIGATORY TAX. Anti-Cancer Week. Litho. P 13½.
594 **322** 6d. multicoloured 75 70
For compulsory use from 1 to 8 March.

323 Hoopoe

(Des Igor Stevkovski)

2008 (28 Mar). Hoopoe (*Upupa epops*). T **323** and similar horiz designs. Multicoloured. P 13½.
595 12d. Type **323** .... 1·30 1·20
  a. Block of 4. Nos. 595/598.............................. 16·00
596 24d. Head... 2·50 2·40
597 48d. Facing left.. 5·00 4·75
598 60d. Facing right... 6·25 6·00
595/598 Set of 4.. 13·50 13·00
Nos. 595/598 were issued in *se-tenant* blocks of four stamps within the sheet.

324 Bull Dog   **325** Envelope and Globe

(Des Igor Stevkovski)

2008 (16 Apr). Pets. P 13½.
599 **324** 30d. multicoloured .... 3·00 3·00

(Des Igor Stevkovski)

2008 (2 May). Europa. The Letter. T **325** and similar horiz designs. Multicoloured, background colours given. P 13½.
600 50d. Type **325** .... 5·00 4·75
  a. Pair. Nos. 600/601..................................... 10·50 9·75
  b. Block of 4. Nos. 600/603........................... 16·00
601 50d. Envelopes and globe................................... 5·00 4·75
602 50d. As Type **325** (cobalt)................................... 5·00 4·75
  a. Pair. Nos. 602/603..................................... 10·50 9·75
603 50d. As No. 601 (cobalt)..................................... 5·00 4·75
604 50d. As Type **325** (deep grey-blue).................... 5·00 4·75
  a. Pair. Nos. 604/605..................................... 16·00 14·50
605 100d. As No. 601 (deep grey-blue)..................... 10·00 9·50
600/605 Set of 6.. 32·00 30·00
Nos. 600/601, 602/603 and 604/605, respectively were printed in horizontal *se-tenant* pairs, each pair forming a composite design.
No. 600b has blue margins.

326 Stylised Figures and Globe as Jigsaw Puzzle   **327** Robert Schuman (one of founders of EU)

2008 (8 May). OBLIGATORY TAX. Red Cross Week. Litho. P 13½.
606 **326** 6d. multicoloured 75 70
For compulsory use from 8 to 15 May.

(Des I. Stevkovski. Litho)

2008 (22 May). European Union. T **327** and similar multicoloured designs. P 13½.
607 36d. Type **327** .... 3·75 3·50
608 50d. Eiffel Tower (*horiz*)...................................... 5·00 4·75
609 50d. Ljublijana (*horiz*).. 5·00 4·75
607/609 Set of 3.. 12·50 11·50

2008 MACEDONIA

328 Cupped Hands and Water

329 Rudolf Diesel

333a Figure

334 Ubava Cave

(Des I. Stevkovski. Litho)

2008 (5 June). Environmental Protection. P 13½.
610   **328**   12d. multicoloured .... 1·30   1·20

(Des I. Stevkovski. Litho)

2008 (18 June). 150th Birth Anniversary of Rudolf Diesel (German engineer and inventor of the diesel engine). P 13½.
611   **329**   30d. multicoloured .... 3·00   3·00

330 Sailing

(Des M. Micova)

2008 (25 June). Olympic Games, Beijing. T **330** and similar horiz designs showing stylised athletes. Multicoloured. P 13½.
612   12d. Type **330** .... 1·30   1·20
613   18d. Gymnastics .... 1·80   1·70
614   20d. Tennis .... 2·00   1·90
615   36d. Equestrian .... 3·75   3·50
612/615 Set of 4 .... 8·00   7·50

331 Eqrem Cabej

(Des I. Stevkovski. Litho)

2008 (6 Aug). Birth Centenary of Eqrem Cabej. P 13½.
616   **331**   12d. multicoloured .... 1·30   1·20

332 Helichrysum zivojinii

333 St Sava and Religious Sites in Ohrid

(Des I. Stevkovski. Litho)

2008 (10 Sept). Flora. T **332** and similar multicoloured designs. P 13½.
617   1d. Type **332** 15   10
618   12d. Pulsatilla halleri (horiz) .... 1·30   1·20
619   50d. Stachysi va griseb (horiz) .... 5·00   4·75
620   72d. Fritillaria macedonica .... 6·75   6·50
617/620 Set of 4 .... 12·00   11·50
MS621 59×70 mm. 72d. Centaurea grbavacensis .... 7·50   7·25

(Des L. Ž. Donev)

2008 (10 Sept). International Congress of Slavists, Ohrid. Symbols of the congress. Multicoloured. P 13½.
622   **333**   12d. multicoloured .... 1·30   1·20

2008 (14 Sept). OBLIGATORY TAX. Anti-Tuberculosis Week. Litho. P 13½.
622a   **333a**   6d. multicoloured 75   70
For compulsory use from 14 to 21 September.

(Des I. Stevkovski. Litho)

2008 (24 Sept). Natural beauty. P 13½.
623   **334**   12d. multicoloured .... 1·30   1·20

335 Child and Jigsaw

336 Stylised Players

(Des L. Živkovska Donev)

2008 (6 Oct). Children's Day. P 13½.
624   **335**   12d. multicoloured .... 1·30   1·20

(Des I. Stevkovski. Litho)

2008 (15 Oct). European Women's Handball Championship, Macedonia. P 13½.
625   **336**   30d. multicoloured .... 3·00   3·00

337 Annotation

338 Giacomo Puccini and Score

(Des M. Velichovska)

2008 (22 Oct). 700th Anniversary of Eucharistic Song by Saint John Kukuzel. P 13½.
626   **337**   12d. multicoloured .... 1·30   1·20

(Des R. Gilafi)

2008 (22 Oct). 150th Birth Anniversary of Giacomo Puccini (composer). P 13½.
627   **338**   100d. multicoloured .... 8·75   8·50

339 Kosta Racin

340 Congress Members, Buildings and Script

(Des L. Živkovska Donev)

2008 (5 Nov). Birth Centenary of Kosta Solev (Kosta Racin) (revolutionary and poet). P 13½.
628   **339**   12d. multicoloured .... 1·30   1·20

MACEDONIA 2008

2008 (14 Nov). Centenary of Congress of Monastir (to decide on the use of Latin script for written Albanian). P 13½.
629   340   12d. multicoloured .... 1·30   1·20

341 Baubles

341a Emblem

(Des I. Stevkovski)

2008 (19 Nov). Christmas and New Year. P 13½.
630   341   12d. multicoloured .... 1·00   95

2008 (1 Dec). OBLIGATORY TAX. Anti-Cancer Week. Litho. P 13½.
630*a*   **341a**   6d. multicoloured 75   70
For compulsory use from 1 to 8 December.

342 Street, Ohrid

343 Lech Walesa

2008 (4 Dec). Architecture. T **342** and similar vert designs. P 13½.
631   12d. brown, salmon and black..................... 1·00   95
632   12d. indigo, new blue and black................. 1·00   95
633   12d. indigo, greenish slate and black .... 1·00   95
634   12d. deep yellow-green and scarlet-
              vermilion.. 1·00   95
635   12d. black and bright green .... 1·00   95
631/635 *Set of 5*.. 4·50   4·25
Designs: No. 631, T **342**; No. 632, Street, Bitola; No. 633, Bridge, Skopje; No. 634, Building, Tetobo; No. 635, Building, Stip.

2008 (8 Dec). Macedonia–Poland Friendship. P 13½.
636   343   50d. multicoloured .... 4·25   4·00

344 Anvil

345 Yuri Gagarin

(Des L. Ž. Donev and L. Kufalo)

2009 (21 Jan). Cultural Heritage. T **344** and similar multicoloured design. P 13½.
637   10d. Type **344** .... 1·00   95
638   20d. Hand made Horse shoe .... 2·00   1·90

(Des L. Ž. Donev)

2009 (4 Feb). 75th Birth Anniversary of Yuri Alekseyevich Gagarin (cosmonaut and first man in space). P 13½.
639   **345**   50d. multicoloured .... 4·25   4·00

345a Figure

346 Diana, the Huntress

2009 (1 Mar). OBLIGATORY TAX. AIDS Awareness Week. Litho. P 13½.
639*a*   **345a**   6d. multicoloured 75   70
For compulsory use from 1 to 8 March.

(Des I. Stevkovski)

2009 (2 Mar). Breast Cancer Awareness. P 13½.
640   **346**   15d. multicoloured .... 1·30   1·20
Design as T **2342** of USA.

347 Trajko Prokopiev and Todor Skalovski

348 Chestnut

(Des L. Živkovska Donev)

2009 (18 Mar). Composers Anniversaries. T **347** and similar horiz design. Multicoloured. P 13½.
641   12d. Type **347** (birth centenaries) .... 1·00   95
642   60d. George Frideric Handel (150th death
              anniversary) and Franz Josef Haydn
              (death bicentenary) .... 5·00   4·75

(Des I. Stevkovski)

2009 (15 Apr). Horses. T **348** and similar vert design. Multicoloured. P 13½.
643   20d. Type **348** .... 1·80   1·70
644   50d. Bay cantering .... 4·25   4·00

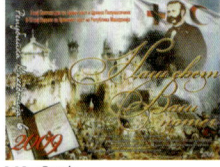
348a Battle

349 Macedonian Folklore Constellations (Hen and chicks)

2009 (1 May). OBLIGATORY TAX. 150th Anniversary of Battle of Solferino (witnessed by Henry Dunant who instigated campaign resulting in establishment of Geneva Conventions and Red Cross). Litho. P 13½.
644*a*   **348a**   6d. multicoloured 75   70
For compulsory use from 1 to 8 May.

(Des L. Kufalo)

2009 (6 May). Europa. Astronomy. T **349** and similar multicoloured design. P 13½.
645   50d. Type **349** .... 8·75   8·50
646   100d. Macedonian folklore constellations
              (Plough) .... 16·00   16·00
MS647 57×77 mm 150d. Macedonian folklore
    constellations (Rooster) (*vert*) .... 38·00   36·00

350 Prague

351 Vrelo

(Des L. Ž. Donev)

2009 (9 May). Macedonia in Europe. T **350** and similar multicoloured design. P 13½.
648   10d. Type **350** .... 1·00   95
649   60d. Pippi Longstocking (Swedish children's
              book character) and European flag
              (*vert*) .... 5·00   4·75

(Des L. Ž. Donev)

2009 (5 June). Caves. P 13½.
650   **351**   12d. multicoloured .... 1·00   95

2009 MACEDONIA

352 Charles Darwin (evolutionary theorist) and Anthropoid Progress

353 Galeb

(Des I. Stevkovski)

2009 (17 June). Science. Birth Bicentenaries. T **352** and similar horiz design. P 13½.
651		18d. multicoloured	1·50	1·40
652		18d. black, scarlet-vermilion and orange	1·50	1·40

Designs: No. 651, T **352**; No. 652, Louis Braille (inventor of Braille writing for the blind) and Braille letters

(Des I. Stevkovski)

2009 (24 June). Ships. P 13½.
653	**353**	18d. multicoloured	1·50	1·40

354 Ship's Prow

355 Bell Tower, Prilep

(Des L. Kufalo)

2009 (24 June). Ships. P 13½.
654	**354**	18d. multicoloured	1·50	1·40

(Des I. Stevkovski)

2009 (27 July). Cities. P 13.
655	**355**	18d. brown-purple, azure and black	1·50	1·40

(Des L. Ž. Donev)

2009 (7 Aug). Cities. Vert design as T **355**. Grey-black, dull orange and black. P 13.
656		16d. Town Hall, Strumica	1·30	1·20

356 Player, Emblem and Flag

357 Cyclist

(Des I. Stevkovski)

2009 (12 Aug). Centenary of Football in Macedonia. P 13½.
657	**356**	18d. multicoloured	1·50	1·40

(Des I.Stevkovski (No. 658) or L. Kufalo (No. 659))

2009 (2 Sept). Centenary of Giro d'Italia (cycle race). T **357** and similar multicoloured design. P 13½.
658		18d. Type **357**	1·50	1·40
659		18d. Chain wheel and pedal (horiz)	1·50	1·40

 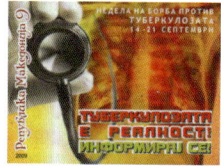

358 Pelobates syriacus balcanicus (Balkan Spadefoot Toad)

358a

(Des L. Živkovska Donev)

2009 (9 Sept). Fauna. T **358** and similar multicoloured designs. P 13½.
660		2d. Type **358**	25	25
661		3d. *Salmo letnica* (Ohrid Trout)	35	30
662		6d. *Austropotamobius torrentium macedonicus* (Macedonian Stone Crayfish)	65	60
663		8d. *Triturus macedonicus* (Macedonian Crested Newt)	75	70
660/663	Set of 4		1·80	1·70
MS664	60×70 mm. 100d. Dr. Stanko Karaman and Crustaceans (vert)		8·75	8·50

2009 (14 Sept). Obligatory Tax. Anti-Tuberculosis Week. P 13½.
665	**358a**	6d. multicoloured	75	70

For compulsory use from 14 to 21 September.

359 Paintings

360

(Des I. Stevkovski)

2009 (30 Sept). 150th Birth Anniversary of Dimitar Andonov Papradishki (artist). P 13½.
666	**359**	16d. multicoloured	1·50	1·40

(Des I. Stevkovski)

2009 (14 Oct). Centenary of Elbasan High School. P 13½.
667	**360**	16d. multicoloured	1·50	1·40

361 Filip Shiroka

362 Krume Kepeski

(Des L. Kufalo)

2009 (4 Nov). 150th Birth Anniversary of Filip Shiroka (poet). P 13½.
668	**361**	16d. multicoloured	1·50	1·40

(Des L. Živkovska Donev)

2009 (4 Nov). Birth Centenary of Krume Kepeski (linguist). P 13½.
669	**362**	16d. multicoloured	1·50	1·40

 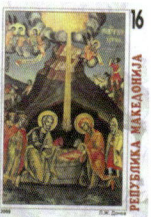

363 Petre M. Andreevski

364 The Nativity

(Des I. Stevkovski)

2009 (4 Nov). 75th Birth Anniversary of Petre M. Andreevski (poet, novelist, short story writer and playwright). P 13½.
670	**363**	16d. multicoloured	1·50	1·40

(Des I. Stevkovski, L. Ž. Donev and L. Kufalo)

2009 (11 Nov). Cities. Vert designs as T **355**. P 13.
671		16d. olive-green and turquoise-blue	1·50	1·40
672		16d. orange-brown and dull ultramarine	1·50	1·40
673		16d. deep turquoise-green and bistre-brown	1·50	1·40
674		16d. dull ultramarine and bright crimson	1·50	1·40

MACEDONIA 2009

675	16d. olive-sepia and black		1·50	1·40
676	16d. orange-brown and black		1·50	1·40
671/676 Set of 6			8·00	7·50

Designs: No. 671 Kicevo; No. 672 Gostivar; No. 673 Delcevo; No. 674 Struga; No. 675 Kumanovo; No. 676 Resen.

(Des L. Ž. Donev)

2009 (18 Nov). Christmas. P 13½.

677	364	16d. multicoloured	1·50	1·40

365 Profiles and Emblem

(Litho)

2009 (1 Dec). Obligatory Tax. AIDS Awareness Week. P 13½.

678	365	8d. muulticoloured	75	70

For compulsory use from 1 to 8 December.

366 Helicopter

(Des I. Stevkovski)

2010 (12 Feb). Transport. P 13½.

679	366	50d. multicoloured	4·25	4·00

367 Ski Jump and Stone Emblem   367a Profile, Hands and Emblem

(Des I. Stevkovski)

2010 (12 Feb). Winter Olympic Games, Vancouver. T **367** and similar vert design. Multicoloured. P 13½.

680	50d. Type **367**	4·25	4·00
681	100d. Hockey and emblem	8·25	8·00

2010 (1 Mar). Obligatory Tax. AIDS Awareness Week. P 13½.

681a	367a	8d. multicoloured	75	70

368 Deep Pink Peony   369 Frescoes

(Des I. Stevkovski)

2010 (8 Mar). Centenary of International Women's Day. Sheet 80×65 mm containing T **368** and similar vert design. Multicoloured. P 13½.

MS682	18d.×2, Type **368**; Pale pink Peony from below	3·25	3·00

2010 (25 Mar). 650th Anniversary of St Peter's Church, Golem Grad. P 13½.

683	369	18d. multicoloured	1·50	1·40

370 Budgerigar   370a Globe and Symbols of Habitation

(Des I. Stevkovski)

2010 (14 Apr). Pets. Birds. T **370** and similar design. Multicoloured. P 13½.

684	20d. Type **370**	1·80	1·70
685	40d. Macaw (horiz)	3·50	3·25

2010 (8 May). Obligatory Tax. Red Cross–Urban Life. P 13½.

685a	370a	8d. multicoloured	75	70

 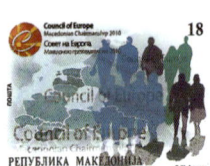

371 Peter Pan   372 Map of Europe and Silhouettes

(Des I. Stevkovski)

2010 (5 May). Europa. Children's Books. P 13½.

686	371	100d. multicoloured	14·00	13·00

(Des L. Ž. Donev)

2010 (8 May). Macedonian Chairmanship of Council of Europe. P 13½.

687	372	18d. multicoloured	2·00	1·90

373 EU Headquarters, Brussels

(Des I. Stevkovski)

2010 (8 May). Macedonia in the EU. T **373** and similar horiz design. Multicoloured. P 13½.

688	20d. Type **373**	1·80	1·70
689	50d. Palacio de Comunicaciones, Madrid	4·25	4·00

(Des I. Stevkovski)

2010 (8 May). Cities. Vert designs as T **355**. Multicoloured. P 13.

689a	16d. House, Debar	1·50	1·40
689b	16d. Terrace, Gevgelija	1·50	1·40
689c	16d. Bridge, Kratovo	1·50	1·40
689d	18d. Clock Tower, Veles	1·60	1·60
689e	18d. House, Kruševo	1·60	1·60
689a/689e Set of 5		7·00	6·75

374 Chestnut and Tree

(Des L. Ž. Donev)

2010 (5 June). Environmental Protection. Sweet Chestnut (*Castanea sativa*). P 13½.

690	374	20d. multicoloured	1·80	1·70

2010 MACEDONIA

375 Robert Schumann, Piano Keys and Musical Score

376 Frédéric Chopin

(Des I. Stevkovski)
2010 (8 June). Birth Bicentenary of Robert Alexander Schumann (composer). P 13½.
691 **375** 50d. black, azure and orange-vermilion ...... 4·25 4·00

(Des L. Ž. Donev)
2010 (8 June). Birth Bicentenary of Frédéric François Chopin (composer). P 13½.
692 **376** 60d. multicoloured ...... 5·00 4·75

377 Football in Net

378 Church St Sophia, Ohrid

(Des I. Stevkovski)
2010 (11 June). World Cup Football Championships, South Africa. T **377** and similar multicoloured designs. P 13½.
693 50d. Type **377** ...... 4·25 4·00
694 100d. Football on centre line (vert) ...... 8·25 8·00
MS695 70×60 mm. 150d. Championship emblem and football ...... 13·00 12·50

(Des L. Ž. Donev)
2010 (30 June). 50th Ohrid Summer Festival. P 13½.
696 **378** 18d. multicoloured ...... 1·50 1·40

379 Mother Teresa

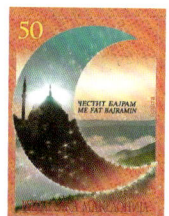
380 Crescent Moon and Mosque

(Des H. Ademi)
2010 (26 Aug). Birth Centenary of Mother Teresa (Agnes Gonxha Bojaxhiu) (founder of Missionaries of Charity in Calcutta). P 13½.
697 **379** 60d. multicoloured ...... 5·00 4·75
Stamps of a similar design were issued by Albanis and Kosovo.

(Des I. Stevkovski)
2010 (9 Sept). Bayram Festival. P 13½.
698 **380** 50d. multicoloured ...... 4·25 4·00

381 Chara ohridana (Algae)

382 Laurel Wreath and Hand writing Poem

(Des L. Ž. Donev or I. Stevkovski)
2010 (10 Sept). Flora and Fauna of Lake Ohrid. T **381** and vert designs. Multicoloured. P 13½.
699 18d. Type **381** ...... 1·50 1·40
700 20d. *Gocea ohridana* (Water Snail) ...... 1·80 1·70
701 44d. *Surirella spiralis* (Algae) ...... 3·75 3·50
702 100d. *Ochridaspongia rotunda* Arndt (Sponge) ...... 8·25 8·00
699/702 Set of 4 ...... 14·00 13·00

(Des I. Stevkovski)
2010 (10 Sept). 150th Anniversary of Award of Laurel Wreath to Grigor Prlicev (first prize for best poem in literary competition held every year in Athens) for his Poem. P 13½.
703 **382** 100d. multicoloured ...... 8·25 8·00

383 Joyful Figures

384 Henry Dunant

(Litho)
2010 (14 Sept). Obligatory Tax. Anti-Tuberculosis Week. P 13½.
704 **383** 8d. multicoloured 75 70
For compulsory use from 14 to 21 September.

(Des L. Kufalo)
2010 (20 Oct). Death Centenary of Henry Dunant (instigator of Red Cross movement). P 13½.
705 **384** 10d. scarlet-vermilion and black ...... 1·00 95

385 Jacques Cousteau

386 Robert Koch

(Des I. Stevkovski)
2010 (20 Oct). Birth Centenary of Jacques-Yves Cousteau (marine explorer, ecologist, filmmaker, and writer). P 13½.
706 **385** 20d. multicoloured ...... 1·80 1·70

(Des L. Ž. Donev)
2010 (20 Oct). Death Centenary of Heinrich Hermann Robert Koch (isolator of anthrax, cholera and TB bacilli and winner of 1905, Nobel Prize for Medicine). P 13½.
707 **386** 20d. multicoloured ...... 1·80 1·70

387 St Naum (icon)

388 Dimitar Miladinov

(Des L. Ž. Donev)
2010 (Oct). 1100th Death Anniversary of St Naum of Ohrid (educator and one of founders of Macedonian Orthodox Church). P 13½.
708 **387** 18d. multicoloured ...... 1·50 1·40

(Des L. Kufalo)
2010 (5 Nov). Birth Bicentenary of Dimitar Miladinov (poet and folklorist). P 13½.
709 **388** 18d. multicoloured ...... 1·50 1·40

MACEDONIA 2010

389 Skyline, Family and Voting Form

390 Marin Barleti

(Des L. Ž. Donev)

2010 (11 Nov). 20th Anniversary of Multi-Party Elections. P 13½.
710   **389**   16d. multicoloured .... 1·50   1·40

(Des I. Stevkovski)

2010 (15 Nov). 550th Birth Anniversary of Marin Barleti (historian and Catholic priest). P 13½.
711   **390**   20d. multicoloured .... 1·80   1·70

391 Seated Figure

392 Emaciated Figures

(Des L. Ž. Donev)

2010 (15 Nov). Birth Centenary of Dimce Koco (artist). P 13½.
712   **391**   50d. multicoloured .... 4·25   4·00

(Des I. Stevkovski)

2010 (15 Nov). Birth Centenary of Dimo Todorovski (sculptor). P 13½.
713   **392**   50d. multicoloured .... 4·25   4·00

393 Christmas Baskets

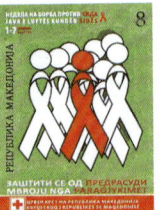
393a Ribbons

(Des I. Stevkovski)

2010 (22 Nov). Christmas. P 13½.
714   **393**   16d. multicoloured .... 1·50   1·40

2010 (1 Dec). Obligatory Tax. AIDS Awareness Week. P 13½.
714a   **393a**   8d. multicoloured 75   70
For compulsory use from 1 to 7 December.

(Des I. Stevkovski, L. Ž. Donev and L. Kufalo)

2010 (11 Dec). Cities. Vert designs as T **355**. P 13.
715   16d. Kavadarci .... 1·50   1·40
716   16d. Kriva Planka .... 1·50   1·40
717   16d. Negotin .... 1·50   1·40
718   16d. Probištip .... 1·50   1·40
719   18d. Koščani .... 1·60   1·60
720   18d. Radoviš (*horiz*) .... 1·60   1·60
721   18d. Sveti Nikole .... 1·60   1·60
715/721 Set of 7... 9·75   8·25

394 Prince Konstantin Dragaš Coin, 1371–1395

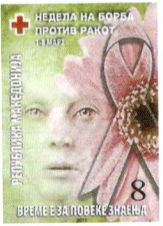
394a Face, Flower and AIDS Ribbon

(Des I. Stevkovski)

2011 (28 Feb). Cultural Heritage. Coins. P 13½.
722   **394**   50d. multicoloured .... 4·25   4·00

2011 (1 Mar). Obligatory Tax. AIDS Awareness Week. P 13½.
722a   **394a**   8d. multicoloured 75   70
For compulsory use from 1 to 8 March.

395 Space Walk

396 Menorah

(Des I. Stevkovski)

2011 (4 Mar). 50th Anniversary of First Manned Space Flight. P 13½.
723   **395**   40d. multicoloured .... 23·00   22·00

(Des L. Ž. Donev)

2011 (8 Mar). Holocaust Memorial Centre for Jews of Macedonia, Skopje. P 13½.
724   **396**   100d. ultramarine, chrome yellow and black .... 8·25   8·00

397 Karaman (Macedonian Shepherd Dog)

398 Princess Diana

(Des I. Stevkovski)

2011 (11 Apr). Pets. Dog. P 13½.
725   **397**   50d. multicoloured .... 4·25   4·00

(Des L. Kufalo)

2011 (12 Apr). 50th Birth Anniversary of Princess Diana. P 13½.
726   **398**   100d. multicoloured .... 8·25   8·00

399 Distillation and Periodic Tables

400 Benz Patent-Motorwagen, 1886

(Des I. Stevkovski)

2011 (13 Apr). International Year of Chemistry. P 13½.
727   **399**   60d. multicoloured .... 5·00   4·75

(Des L. Kufalo)

2011 (15 Apr). Transport. 125th Anniversary of First Automobile (20d.) or Centenary of First Automobile in Skopje (70d.). T **400** and similar multicoloured design. P 13½.
728   20d. Type **400** .... 1·80   1·70
729   70d. First car in Skopje (*vert*) .... 5·75   5·50

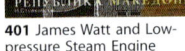
401 James Watt and Low-pressure Steam Engine

402 Warsaw

(Des I. Stevkovski)
2011 (20 Apr). Science. 275th Birth Anniversary of James Watt. P 13½.
730   401   60d. multicoloured .... 5·00   4·75

(Des I. Stevkovski)
2011 (1 May). Macedonia in EU. T **402** and similar horiz design. Multicoloured. P 13½.
731   40d. Type **402** .... 3·25   3·00
732   40d. Budapest .... 3·25   3·00

403 Woods in Autumn

404 Heart-shaped Labyrinth containing Red Cross

(Des I. Stevkovski)
2011 (5 May). Europa. Forests. T **403** and similar horiz designs. Multicoloured. P 13½.
733   50d. Type **403** .... 5·00   4·75
734   100d. Woods in winter .... 10·00   9·50
MS735   70×60 mm. 100d. Woods in spring .... 12·50 12·00

2011 (8 May). Obligatory Tax. Red Cross. P 13½.
736   404   8d. scarlet-vermilion and black 75   70
For compulsory use from 8 to 15 May.

405 Front Page of *Shkupi*

406 Book

(Des L. Ž. Donev)
2011 (10 June). Centenary of *Shkupi* (newspaper). P 13½.
737   405   60d. multicoloured .... 5·00   4·75

(Des I. Stevkovski)
2011 (15 June). 50th Anniversary of Poetry Evenings. P 13½.
738   406   40d. multicoloured .... 3·50   3·25

407 Emperor Justinian

(Des L. Kufalo)
2011 (1 July). 60th Anniversary of Faculty of Law. Sheet 110×42 mm. P 13½.
MS739   407   100d. multicoloured .... 8·75   8·50

2011 (27 July). Cities. Multicoloured. P 13.
739a   10d. Vinca .... 1·00   95
T **407a** is unavailable.

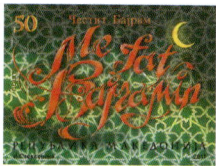
408 Emblem

409 Ball, Crowd and Emblem

(Des I. Stevkovski)
2011 (30 Aug). Bayram Festival. P 13½.
740   408   50d. multicoloured .... 4·25   4·00

(Des L. Ž. Donev)
2011 (31 Aug). European Basketball Championship. P 13½.
741   409   70d. multicoloured .... 5·75   5·50
No. 741 was perforated in a circle contained in an outer perforated square.

410 Sunrise

410a Lungs

(Des L. Ž. Donev)
2011 (9 Sept). 20th Anniversary of Independence. P 13½.
742   410   20d. multicoloured .... 1·80   1·70

(Des Mijov Branko. Litho)
2011 (14 Sept). Obligatory Tax. Anti-Tuberculosis Week. P 13½.
742a   410a   8d. multicoloured 75   70
For compulsory use from 14 to 21 September.

411 Landscape with Houses

412 Franz Liszt

(Des L. Kufalo)
2011 (14 Sept). Birth Centenary of Ljubomir Belogaski (artist). P 13½.
743   411   20d. multicoloured .... 1·80   1·70

(Des I. Stevkovski)
2011 (21 Sept). Birth Bicentenary of Franz Liszt (composer). P 13½.
744   412   50d. black .... 4·25   4·00

413 Ernest Hemingway

(Des I. Stevkovski)
2011 (11 Oct). 50th Death Anniversary of Ernest Miller Hemingway (writer). P 13½.
745   413   50d. multicoloured .... 4·25   4·00

414 Migjeni

(Des L. Ž. Donev)
2011 (19 Oct). Birth Centenary of Millosh Gjergj Nikolla (Migjeni) (writer). P 13½.
746   414   20d. multicoloured .... 1·80   1·70

MACEDONIA 2011

415 Archbishop Angelarios   **415a** Demi Hisar   **415b** Dojran

(Des I. Stevkovski)

2011 (26 Oct). Birth Centenary of Archbishop Angelarios. P 13½.
747   415   40d. multicoloured ....   3·50   3·25

(Des L. Kufalo. Litho)

2011 (10 Nov). Cities. P 13.
747a   415a   16d. multicoloured ....   1·50   1·40
747b   415b   18d. multicoloured ....   1·60   1·60

416 Emblem and Globe   **417** *Spermophilus citellus*

(Des Mijov Branko)

2011 (1 Dec). Obligatory Tax. AIDS Awareness Week. P 13½.
748   416   8d. multicoloured   75   70
    For compulsory use from 1 to 7 December.

(Des L. Ž. Donev)

2011 (13 Dec). Endangered Species. European Ground Squirrel (*Spermophilus citellus*). T **417** and similar vert designs. Multicoloured. P 13½.
749   12d. Type **417** ....   1·00   95
            a. Block of 4. Nos. 749/752 ....   12·50
750   24d. Adult holding food and young ....   2·00   1·90
751   48d. Adult facing right ....   4·00   3·75
752   60d. Group of adults facing right ....   5·00   4·75
749/752 Set of 4 ....   11·00   10·00
    Nos. 749/752 were printed, *se-tenant*, in blocks of four stamps within the sheet.

418 *Parnassius apollo*

(Des L. Ž. Donev)

2011 (19 Dec). Butterflies. T **418** and similar horiz designs. Multicoloured. P 13½.
753   12d. Type **418** ....   1·00   95
754   24d. *Zerynthia polyxena* ....   2·00   1·90
755   48d. *Parnassius mnemosyne* ....   4·00   3·75
756   60d. *Elphinstonia penia* ....   5·00   4·75
753/756 Set of 4 ....   11·00   10·00

419 Oak Leaves, Acorns, Christmas Bun and Fruit

(Des L. Ž. Donev)

2011 (20 Dec). Christmas. P 13½.
757   419   18d. multicoloured ....   1·50   1·40

420 Gjerasim Kiriazi   **421** Woven Rug

(Des L. Ž. Donev)

2011 (28 Dec). Gjerasim Kiriazi (preacher and educator) Commemoration. P 13½.
758   420   20d. multicoloured ....   1·80   1·70

(Des L. Kufalo)

2012 (20 Feb). Cultural Heritage. Weaving. P 13½.
759   421   20d. multicoloured ....   1·80   1·70

422 Stylised Figures   **423** Tortoise

2012 (1 Mar). Obligatory Tax. AIDS Awareness Week. P 13½.
760   422   8d. multicoloured   75   70
    For compulsory use from 1 to 8 March.

(Des L. Ž. Donev)

2012 (3 Apr). Pets. Tortoise. P 13½.
761   423   100d. multicoloured ....   8·25   8·00
    No. 761 is inscribed 'Pet Turtle'.

424 In Flight   **425** Telegraph Transmitter and Samuel Morse (inventor)

(Des L. Ž. Donev (40d.) or L. Kufalo (60d.))

2012 (4 Apr). Transport. Aircraft. T **423** and similar horiz design. Multicoloured. P 13½.
762   40d. Type **424** (country name incorrect) ....   28·00   27·00
            a. Country name corrected ....   3·75   3·50
763   60d. In flight, front ....   5·00   4·75
    No. 762 was reissued on 4 April 2013.

(Des L. Kufalo)

2012 (5 Apr). 175th Anniversary of Invention of the Telegraph. P 13½.
764   425   100d. multicoloured ....   8·25   8·00

426 Nicosia   **427** House and Aerial View of Ohrid

2012 MACEDONIA

(Des L. Ž. Donev)

2012 (9 Apr). Macedonia in EU. T **426** and similar vert design. Multicoloured. P 13½.
765	20d. Type **426** (country name incorrect)........		15·00	14·50
	a. Country name corrected		1·80	1·70
766	40d. Copenhagen (country name incorrect)........		30·00	29·00
	a. Country name corrected		3·75	3·50

(Des L. Ž. Donev)

2012 (13 Apr). Europa. Visit Macedonia. T **427** and similar horiz designs. Multicoloured. P 13½.
767	20d. Type **427**		2·50	2·40
768	100d. *Alexander the Great* (statue), Skopje		11·50	11·00
MS769	108×48 mm. 100d. Vardar River Bridge, Skopje		14·00	13·00

428 Titanic

429 '20' enclosing One Dinar Coin

(Des L. Ž. Donev)

2012 (17 Apr). Centenary of *Titanic* Disaster. P 13½.
770	**428**	100d. multicoloured	8·25	8·00

(Des L. Ž. Donev)

2012 (26 Apr). 20th Anniversary of Monetary Independence. P 13½.
771	**429**	50d. multicoloured	4·25	4·00

430 People on Earth, Red Cross and Red Crescent Symbols

431 Early Orchestra

(Des L. Ž. Donev)

2012 (8 May). Obligatory Tax. Red Cross. P 13½.
772	**430**	8d. multicoloured	75	70

For compulsory use from 8 to 15 May.

(Des L. Ž. Donev)

2012 (12 June). Centenary of Zani and Maleve Orchestra. P 13½.
773	**431**	40d. multicoloured	3·50	3·25

(Des L. Ž. Donev)

2012 (4 July). Cities. Vert designs as T **355**. P 13.
774	2d. Berovo		25	25
775	16d. Valandovo		1·50	1·40
776	18d. Makedonska Kamenica...............................		1·60	1·60
774/776	Set of 3		3·00	3·00

432 Hurdler

433 Praying and Mosque

(Des L. Ž. Donev)

2012 (24 July). Olympic Games, London. T **432** and similar horiz design. Multicoloured. P 13½.
777	50d. Type **432**		4·25	4·00
778	100d. Wrestling		8·25	8·00

(Des L. Ž. Donev)

2012 (30 Aug). Bayram Festival. P 13½.
779	**433**	50d. multicoloured	4·25	4·00

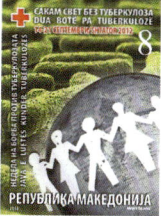

434 Bacillus, Globe and Cut-out Figures

435a *Rhinolophus euryale* (Mediterranean Horseshoe Bat)

(Des Mijov Branko)

2012 (14 Sept). Obligatory Tax. Anti-Tuberculosis Week. P 13½.
780	**434**	8d. multicoloured	75	70

For compulsory use from 14 to 21 September.

(Des L. Kufalo)

2012 (18 Sept). Fauna. Bats. T **435a** and similar horiz designs. Multicoloured. P 13½.
781	10d. Type **435a**..		1·00	95
782	20d. *Rhinolophus ferrumequinum* (Greater Horseshoe Bat)...		1·80	1·70
783	50d. *Rhinolophus hipposideros* (Lesser Horseshoe Bat)...		4·25	4·00
784	100d. *Miniopterus schreibersi* (Common Bent-wing Bat)		8·25	8·00
781/784	Set of 4		14·00	13·00

436a Interior of La Scala, Milan

437 Kole Nedelkovski

(Des Larisa Ž. Donev)

2012 (19 Sept). 125th Anniversary of First Performance of *Otello* (opera by Giuseppe Verdi). P 13½.
785	**436a**	40d. multicoloured	3·50	3·25

(Des Larisa Ž. Donev)

2012 (16 Oct). Birth Centenary of Kole Nedelkovski (revolutionary and poet). P 13½.
786	**437**	50d. multicoloured	4·25	4·00

438 Archbishop Gavril

439 AIDS Ribbons

(Des L. Kufalo)

2012 (16 Oct). Birth Centenary of Gavril II, Archbishop of Ohrid and Macedonia (George Milosheva Gavril). P 13½.
787	**438**	60d. multicoloured	5·00	4·75

2012 (1 Dec). Obligatory Tax. AIDS Awareness Week. P 13½.
788	**439**	8d. multicoloured	75	70

For compulsory use from 1 to 7 December.

440 The Elves and the Shoemaker

441 The Nativity

(Des L. Kufalo. Litho)

2012 (3 Dec). Bicentenary of Grimm's Fairy Tales. P 13.
789 440 20d. multicoloured .... 1·80 1·70

(Des Larisa Ž. Donev)

2012 (11 Dec). Christmas. P 13½.
790 441 50d. multicoloured .... 4·25 4·00

442 Covered Dish

443 AIDS Ribbons as Figures

(Des Larisa Ž. Donev)

2013 (27 Feb). Cultural Heritage. T **442** and similar horiz design. Multicoloured. P 13½.
791 40d. Type **442** .... 3·25 3·00
792 50d. Large platter .... 4·25 4·00

(Des V. Mujov)

2013 (1 Mar). Obligatory Tax. AIDS Awareness Week. P 13½.
793 443 8d. multicoloured 75 70
For compulsory use from 1 to 8 March.

444 White Rabbit

445 Inscr 'MOTORI'

(Des Larisa Ž. Donev)

2013 (14 Mar). Pets. Rabbit. P 13½.
794 444 60d. multicoloured .... 5·00 4·75

(Des L. Kufalo)

2013 (21 Mar). Transport. Motorcycle. P 13½.
795 445 50d. multicoloured .... 4·25 4·00

446 John Dunlop and Tyres

447 Dublin

(Des L. Ž. Donev)

2013 (3 Apr). Science. Anniversaries. T **446** and similar horiz design. Multicoloured. P 13½.
796 40d. Type **446** (125th anniversary of patent for inflated tyres) .... 3·25 3·00
797 50d. Vladimir Zworykin (inventor of TV transmitting and receiving system using cathode ray tubes) (125th birth anniversary) .... 4·25 4·00

(Des L. Ž. Donev)

2013 (17 Apr). Macedonia in EU. T **447** and similar horiz design. Multicoloured. P 13½.
798 40d. Type **447** .... 3·25 3·00
799 60d. Vilnius .... 5·00 4·75

448 Large Mercedes Post Van

449 Henry Dunant

(Des L. Ž. Donev)

2013 (22 Apr). Europa. Postal Transport. T **448** and similar horiz designs. Multicoloured. P 13½.
800 40d. Type **448** .... 4·50 4·25
801 60d. Smaller VW post van .... 6·75 6·50
MS802 60×80 mm. 100d. Mercedes post lorry and VW Caddy post van .... 11·50 11·00

2013 (8 May). Obligatory Tax. Red Cross. 150th Anniversary of Red Cross. P 13½.
803 449 8d. multicoloured 75 70
For compulsory use from 8 to 15 May.

450 Ali Riza Ulqinaku

451 Rexhep Mitrovica

(Des L. Kufalo)

2013 (10 June). Death Centenary of Ali Riza Ulqinaku (teacher). P 13½.
804 450 16d. multicoloured .... 1·30 1·20

(Des Larisa Ž. Donev)

2013 (10 June). 125th Birth Anniversary of Rexhep Mitrovica (politician and nationalist). P 13½.
805 451 18d. multicoloured .... 1·50 1·40

452 St Cyril and St Methodius

(Des L. Ž. Donev)

2013 (24 June). 1150th Anniversary of Arrival of St Cyril and St Methodius to Great Moravia. P 13½.
806 452 40d. multicoloured .... 3·25 3·00

452a Demir Kapija

452b Makedonski Brod

2013 (5 July). Cities. P 13.
806*a* 452a 16d. multicoloured .... 1·50 1·40

(Des L. Ž. Donev. Litho)

2013 (18 July). Cities. P 13.
806*b* 452b 16d. multicoloured .... 1·50 1·40

2013 MACEDONIA

453 Damaged Building   **454** Mosque

(Des L. Ž. Donev)

2013 (26 July). 50th Anniversary of Skopje Earthquake. P 13½.
807   **453**   100d. multicoloured .... 8·25   8·00

(Des L. Ž. Donev)

2013 (30 July). Bayram Festival. P 13½.
808   **454**   40d. multicoloured .... 3·25   3·00

455 Vasil Chekalarov   **456** Kokaleski

(Des L. Ž. Donev. Litho)

2013 (10 Sept). Death Centenary of Vasil Chekalarov (revolutionary). P 13.
809   **455**   16d. multicoloured .... 1·30   1·20

(Des L. Ž. Donev. Litho)

2013 (11 Sept). 150th Death Anniversary of Gjurchin Kokaleski (nationalist leader and writer of the first known Macedonian autobiography). P 13.
810   **456**   18d. multicoloured .... 1·50   1·40

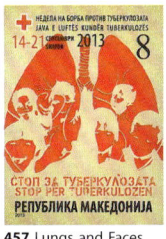 

457 Lungs and Faces   **458** Demonstrator

(Des Mijov Branko)

2013 (14 Sept). Obligatory Tax. Anti-Tuberculosis Week. P 13½.
811   **457**   8d. multicoloured 75   70

For compulsory use from 14 to 21 September.

(Des L. Ž. Donev. Litho)

2013 (19 Sept). Centenary of Ohrid-Debar Uprising. P 13.
812   **458**   60d. multicoloured .... 5·00   4·75

459 Player   **460** St Cyril and St Methodius, National Flags and Confucius

(Des L. Ž. Donev)

2013 (20 Sept). European Basketball Championship, Slovenia. P 13½.
813   **459**   90d. multicoloured .... 7·50   7·25

No. 813 was perforated in a circle contained in an outer perforated square.

(Des L. Ž. Donev. Litho)

2013 (15 Oct). 20th Anniversary of Macedonia–China Diplomatic Relations. P 13.
814   **460**   100d. multicoloured .... 8·25   8·00

461 *Boletus satanas*   **462** Petre Bogdanov-Kocko

(Des L. Ž. Donev. Litho)

2013 (16 Oct). Fungi. T **461** and similar vert designs. Multicoloured. P 13.
815   10d. Type **461** .... 1·00   95
     a. Strip of 4. Nos. 815/818 .... 16·00
816   20d. *Myriostoma coliforme* .... 1·80   1·70
817   50d. *Calocypha fulgens* .... 4·25   4·00
818   100d. *Terana caerulea* .... 8·25   8·00
815/818 Set of 4 .... 14·00   13·00

Nos. 815/818 were printed, *se-tenant*, in horizontal strips of four stamps within the sheet.

(Des L. Kufalo. Litho)

2013 (13 Nov). Birth Centenary of Petre Bogdanov-Kocko (singer). P 13.
819   **462**   20d. multicoloured .... 1·80   1·70

463 Richard Wagner   **464** Symbols of AIDS as Ribbon

(Des L. Kufalo. Litho)

2013 (14 Nov). Birth Bicentenary of Richard Wagner. P 13.
820   **463**   40d. multicoloured .... 3·25   3·00

(Des V. Mujov)

2013 (1 Dec). Obligatory Tax. AIDS Awareness Week. P 13½.
821   **464**   8d. multicoloured 75   70

For compulsory use from 1 to 7 December.

465 The Nativity

(Des L. Ž. Donev. Litho)

2013 (22 Dec). Christmas. P 13.
822   **465**   40d. multicoloured .... 3·25   3·00

466 Tomatoes

(Des L. Ž. Donev. Litho)

2013 (28 Dec). Vegetables. T **466** and similar vert design. Multicoloured. P 13.
823   8d. Type **466** 65   60
824   10d. Aubergine 75   70

MACEDONIA 2014

467 Cash Register

468 Profiles and Ribbon

(Des L. Kufalo. Litho)

2014 (13 Jan). State Lottery. T 467 and similar vert design. Multicoloured. P 13.
| 825 | 8d. Type 467 | 65 | 60 |
| 826 | 8d. Shopping trolley | 65 | 60 |

(Des V. Mujov)

2014 (1 Mar). Obligatory Tax. AIDS Awareness Week. P 13½.
| 827 | 468 | 8d. multicoloured | 75 | 70 |

For compulsory use from 1 to 8 March.

469 People from Many Nations

470 Filigree Belt

(Des V. Mujov)

2014 (8 May). Obligatory Tax. Red Cross. P 13½.
| 828 | 469 | 8d. multicoloured | 75 | 70 |

For compulsory use from 8 to 15 May.

(Des L. Kufalo (24d.) or L. Ž. Donev (40d.))

2014 (22 May). Cultural Heritage. Filigree Jewellery. T 470 and similar multicoloured design. P 13½.
| 829 | 24d. Type 470 | 2·30 | 2·20 |
| 830 | 40d. Pafta: part of belt (*vert*) | 3·75 | 3·50 |

471 Ice Hockey Player

472 Michelangelo

(Des L. Ž. Donev. Litho)

2014 (22 May). Winter Olympic Games, Sochi, Russia. T 471 and similar design. Multicoloured. P 13½.
| 831 | 50d. Type 471 | 4·50 | 4·25 |
| 832 | 100d. Ski jumper | 9·25 | 9·00 |

Nos. 831/832 were each perforated in a circle contained in an outer perforated square.

(Des L. Kufalo. Litho)

2014 (27 May). 450th Death Anniversary of Michelangelo Buonarroti. P 13½.
| 833 | 472 | 144d. multicoloured | 13·50 | 12·50 |

473 Cabbage

474 Goldfish

(Des L. Ž. Donev. Litho)

2014 (28 May–20 June). Vegetables. T 473 and similar vert designs. Multicoloured. P 13.
884	6d. Type 473	50	50
885	16d. Beans (13.6.14)	1·50	1·40
886	18d. Cauliflower (20.6.14)	1·80	1·70
884/886	Set of 3	3·50	3·25

(Des L. Ž. Donev (21d.) or L. Kufalo (60d.))

2014 (28 May). Pets. Goldfish. I 474 and similar horiz design. Multicoloured. P 13½.
| 887 | 21d. Type 474 | 2·00 | 1·90 |
| 888 | 60d. Goldfish (*different*) | 5·50 | 5·25 |

Nos. 887/888 are inscribed 'Carassius auratus'.

475 Volvo FH16 Artic

476 Galileo Galilei and the Sun

(Des L. Ž. Donev)

2014 (29 May). Transport. Lorries. P 13½.
| 889 | 475 | 50d. multicoloured | 4·50 | 4·25 |

(Des L. Kufalo)

2014 (30 May). Science. 450th Birth Anniversary of Galileo Galilei. P 13½.
| 890 | 476 | 20d. multicoloured | 2·00 | 1·90 |

477 George Stephenson and Killingworth Colliery Locomotive, 1816

478 Parthenon, Acropolis, Athens

(Des L. Ž. Donev)

2014 (30 May). Bicentenary of First Steam Locomotive constructed by George Stephenson. P 13½.
| 891 | 477 | 40d. multicoloured | 3·75 | 3·50 |

(Des L. Ž. Donev)

2014 (3 June). Macedonia in EU. T 478 and similar horiz design. Multicoloured. P 13½.
| 892 | 40d. Type 478 | 3·75 | 3·50 |
| 893 | 60d. Colosseum, Rome | 5·50 | 5·25 |

479 Zurla (woodwind)

480 Caver and Emblem

(Des L. Ž. Donev)

2014 (4 June). Europa. Musical Instruments. T 479 and similar horiz designs. Multicoloured. P 13½.
894	40d. Type 479	3·75	3·50
895	50d. Neolithic ocarina (circular flute)	4·50	4·25
MS896	95×75 mm. 50d.×4, Tanbur; Chifteli; Kemane; Bagpipe (National Musical Instruments)	19·00	18·00
MS897	83×60 mm. 60d. Tapan (drum)	5·75	5·50

No. MS896 was issued in a folder.

(Des L. Kufalo)

2014 (4 June). 50th Anniversary of Peoni Speleological (scientific study of caves and other karst features) Association. P 13½.
| 898 | 480 | 80d. multicoloured | 7·50 | 7·25 |

2014 MACEDONIA

481 Stylised Trophy

(Des L. Kufalo)

2014 (12 June). World Cup Football Championships, Brazil. T **481** and similar vert design. Multicoloured. P 13½.
899		50d. Type **481**	4·50	4·25
900		100d. Stylised *Christ the Redeemer*, emblem and stylised trophy	9·25	9·00

482 Mosque, Tetovo

(Des L. Ž. Donev)

2014 (15 June). Bayram Festival. P 13½.
901	**482**	40d. multicoloured	3·75	3·50

483 Death of Samuel, Emperor of Bulgaria (detail, 14th-century Vatican manuscript)   **484** Taško Karadza

(Des L. Kufalo)

2014 (29 June). Millenary of Battle of Belasitsa (Kleidion). P 13½.
902	**483**	50d. multicoloured	4·50	4·25

(Des L. Ž. Donev)

2015 (21 Apr). Personalities. Birth Centenaries. T **484** and similar vert designs. Multicoloured. P 13½.
903		16d. Type **484** (Communist leader)................	1·30	1·20
904		18d. Ivan Točko (writer)..................................	1·50	1·40
905		20d. Nedzat Agoli (jurist and politician)..........	1·80	1·70
906		24d. Sterjo Spasse (literary critic).....................	2·30	2·20
903/906 Set of 4...			6·25	5·75

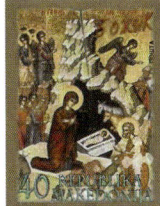

485 The Nativity   **486** Vladimir Komarov and Voskhod

(Des Larisa Ž. Donev. Litho)

2015 (21 Apr). Christmas. P 13.
907	**485**	40d. multicoloured	3·75	3·50

No. 907 has '2014' imprint date.

(Des L. Ž. Donev)

2015 (21 Apr). 50th Anniversary of Launch of Spacecraft Voskhod, piloted by Vladimir Komarov. P 13½.
908	**486**	50d. multicoloured	4·50	4·25

487 Charlie Chaplin

(Des Larisa Ž. Donev)

2015 (21 Apr). 125th Birth Anniversary of Charlie Chaplin. P 13½.
909	**487**	50d. multicoloured	4·50	4·25

488 Common Wood Pigeon (*Columba palumbus*)

(Des L. Kufalo)

2015 (22 Apr). Pigeons. T **488** and similar horiz designs. Multicoloured. P 13½.
910		11d. Type **488**	1·00	95
		a. Strip of 4. Nos. 910/913	18·00	
911		20d. Stock Dove (*Columba oenas*)	1·80	1·70
912		50d. Rock Pigeon (*Columba livia*)....................	4·50	4·25
913		100d. Messenger Pigeon (*Columba livia forma domestica*)..	9·25	9·00
910/913 Set of 4...			15·00	14·50

Nos. 910/913 were printed, *se-tenant*, in vertical strips of four stamps within the sheet.

489 Player   **490** European Goldfinch (*Carduelis carduelis*)

(Des L. Ž. Donev)

2015 (22 Apr). World Men's Handball Championships, Qatar. P 13½.
914	**489**	100d. multicoloured	9·25	9·00

(Des L. Ž. Donev. Litho)

2015 (23 Apr). Domesticated Songbirds. T **490** and similar vert design. Multicoloured. P 13.
915		31d. Type **490**	2·75	2·75
916		50d. Canary (*Serinus canaria domestica*)..........	4·50	4·25

491 Stomna (water vessel) (20th-century)   **492** Battle Scene

(Des L. Ž. Donev. Litho)

2015 (24 Apr). Cultural Heritage. Pottery. P 13½.
917	**491**	50d. multicoloured	4·50	4·25

MACEDONIA 2015

(Des L. Ž. Donev)
2015 (27 Apr). Centenary of Battle of Çanakkale, Turkey. P 13½.
918   492   70d. multicoloured .... 6·50   6·25

493 Grand Ducal Palace, Luxembourg
494 Saxaphone

(Des L. Ž. Donev. Litho)
2015 (29 Apr). Macedonia in EU. T **493** and similar horiz design. Multicoloured. P 13½.
919   40d. Type **493** .... 3·75   3·50
920   60d. Old City, Riga, Latvia .... 5·50   5·25

(Des L. Ž. Donev. Litho)
2015 (29 Apr). 175th Anniversary of Saxaphone. P 13½.
920a   494   44d. multicoloured .... 4·00   3·75

495 Benjamin Franklin
496 Pyotr Tchaikovsky

(Des L. Ž. Donev. Litho)
2015 (29 Apr). 225th Death Anniversary Benjamin Franklin (scientist and diplomat). P 13½.
921   495   60d. multicoloured .... 5·50   5·25

(Des L. Ž. Donev. Litho)
2015 (29 Apr). 175th Birth Anniversary of Pyotr Ilyich Tchaikovsky. P 13½.
922   496   100d. multicoloured .... 9·25   9·00

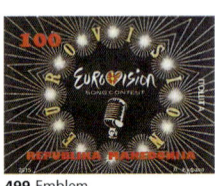

497 Bicycle
498 Yoyo

(Des L. Ž. Donev. Litho)
2015 (29 Apr). Transport. Bicycle. P 13½.
923   497   100d. multicoloured .... 9·25   9·00

(Des L. Ž. Donev. Litho)
2015 (6 May). Europa. Old Toys. T **498** and similar horiz deigns. Multicoloured. P 13½.
924   50d. Type **498** .... 4·50   4·25
925   100d. Rocking Horse .... 9·25   9·00
MS926 84×59 mm. 150d. Spinning top .... 14·50   14·00

499 Emblem
499a Principles

(Des L. Kufalo. Litho)
2015 (7 May). Eurovision Song Contest, Austria. Sheet 84×59 mm. P 13½.
MS927   499   100d. multicoloured .... 9·50   9·00

(Des V. Mujov)
2015 (8 May). Obligatory Tax. Red Cross. 50th Anniversary of the Red Cross Fundamental Principles. P 13½.
927u   499a   8d. multicoloured 75   70
For compulsory use from 8 to 15 May.

500 Carrots
501 Symbols of Festival

(Des L. Kufalo. Litho)
2015 (2 July). Vegetables. P 13.
928   500   2d. multicoloured 25   25

(Des L. Ž. Donev. Litho)
2015 (15 July). Bayram Festival. P 13½.
929   501   40d. multicoloured .... 3·75   3·50

502 Players and Emblem
502a Stylised Figures and Lungs

(Des L. Ž. Donev. Litho)
2015 (4 Sept). European Basketball Championship, Slovenia. P 13½.
930   502   50d. multicoloured .... 4·75   4·50

2015 (14 Sept). Obligatory Tax. Anti-Tuberculosis Week. P 13½.
930a   502a   9d. multicoloured 75   70
For compulsory use from 14 to 21 September.

503 Mirče Acev
504 *Thymus serpyllum*

(Des L. Ž. Donev. Litho)
2015 (17 Sept). Personalities. T **503** and similar multicoloured designs. P 13½.
931   16d. Type **503** (Macedonian national activist, participant in National Liberation War) (birth centenary) .... 1·50   1·40
932   16d. Ibrahim Temo (Ottoman Albanian politician and revolutionary) (150th birth anniversary) .... 1·50   1·40
933   18d. Jane Sandanski (Macedonian duke and the head of Macedonian revolutionary organisation) (death centenary) .... 1·80   1·70
934   18d. Ali Pasha Tepelena (Muslim Albanian ruler during Ottoman Empire) (275th birth anniversary) .... 1·80   1·70
935   20d. Arthur Miller (American writer) (birth centenary) .... 2·00   1·90
931/935 Set of 5 .... 7·75   7·25

(Des L. Ž. Donev)

2015 (14 Oct). Flora. T **504** and similar vert designs. Multicoloured. P 13½.
936	11d. Type **504**		75	70
	a. Block of 4. Nos. 936/939		18·00	
937	20d. Calendula officinalis		1·80	1·70
938	50d. Hypericum perforatum		4·75	4·50
939	100d. Urtica dioica		9·25	9·00
936/939	Set of 4		15·00	14·50

Nos. 936/939 were printed, se-tenant, in blocks of four stamps within the sheet.

505 Symbols of Christmas

506 Shar Mountain, Popova Shapka and Brezovica

(Des L. Ž. Donev. Litho)

2015 (8 Dec). Christmas. P 13.
940	**505**	40d. multicoloured	3·75	3·50

(Des M. Kufalo. Litho)

2016 (23 Mar). Mountain Tourism. Sheet 85×80 mm. P 13½.
MS941	**506**	144d. multicoloured	14·00	13·00

No. **MS**941 also contains a stamp-size label.

507 St Clement

508 Hamster

(Des L. Kufalo. Litho)

2016 (25 Apr). 1100th Death Anniversary of St Clement. P 13½.
942	**507**	18d. multicoloured	1·80	1·70

(Des L. Ž. Donev. Litho)

2016 (26 Apr). Pets. Hamster. P 13½.
943	**508**	81d. multicoloured	7·50	7·25

509 Donatello and *David*

509a Electric Locomotive

(Des L. Ž. Donev. Litho)

2016 (26 Apr). 500th Birth Anniversary of Donato di Niccolò di Betto Bardi (Donatello). P 13½.
944	**509**	40d. multicoloured	3·75	3·50

(Des L. Ž. Donev. Litho)

2016 (28 Apr). Transport. Railways. P 13½.
944a	**509a**	44d. multicoloured	4·00	3·75

510 Avenue Damrak, Netherlands

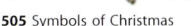
510a Stylised Cell

(Des L. Ž. Donev. Litho)

2016 (29 Apr). Macedonia in EU. T **510** and similar horiz design. Multicoloured. P 13½.
945	40d. Type **510**		3·75	3·50
946	60d. Bratislava Castle, Slovakia		5·50	5·25

2016 (8 May). Obligatory Tax. Red Cross and Red Crescent Day. P 13½.
946a	**510**	8d. multicoloured	75	70

For compulsory use from 8 to 15 May.

511 Fauna on Povardarie Mountain

512 Garlic

(Des L. Ž. Donev)

2016 (10 May). Europa. Think Green. T **511** and similar multicoloured designs. P 13½.
947	50d. Type **511**		4·75	4·50
948	100d. Dojran, Matka and Ohrid landscape montage		9·25	9·00
MS949	95×75 mm. 50d.×4, Dojran and Prespa Lake; Lakeside; Lake and pier; Stork and lakeside		20·00	19·00
MS950	63×82 mm. 144d. Bear (vert)		14·50	14·00

The stamps and margins of Nos. **MS**949/**MS**950 form composite designs.

(Des L. Kufalo. Litho)

2016 (13 May). Vegetables. T **512** and similar vert designs. Multicoloured. P 13.
951	3d. Type **512**		25	25
952	6d. Beetroot		50	50
953	13d. Chilli Peppers		1·30	1·20
951/953	Set of 3		1·80	1·80

T **513** is vacant.

514 Minaret

(Des L. Kufalo. Litho)

2016 (9 June). Bayram Festival. P 13½.
955	**514**	44d. multicoloured	4·00	3·75

515 Player

(Des L. Kufalo. Litho)

2016 (10 June). European Football Championship, France. P 13½.
956	**515**	101d. multicoloured	9·25	9·00

516 René Laennec

MACEDONIA 2016

(Des L. Ž. Donev)

2016 (12 July). Science. Anniversaries. T **516** and similar horiz design. Multicoloured. P 13½.

957	40d. Type **516** (bicentenary (2019) of discovery of the stethoscope)		3·75	3·50
958	50d. Claude Shannon (mathematician) (birth centenary)		4·75	4·50

517 Wrestling

518 Educational Document and a Class

(Des L. Ž. Donev. Litho)

2016 (5 Aug). Olympic Games, Rio 2016, Brazil. T **517** and similar multicoloured design. P 13½.

959	40d. Type **377**		3·75	3·50
960	60d. Judo		5·50	5·25
MS961	87×60 mm. 50d. Emblem (*vert*)		5·00	4·75

(Des L. Kufalo. Litho)

2016 (7 Sept). 75th Anniversary of First Basic Schools in Albanian Language in Macedonia. P 13½.

962	**518**	50d. multicoloured	4·75	4·50

519 '25'

520 Lawrence Anthony

(Des L. Ž. Donev. Litho)

2016 (8 Sept). 25th Anniversary of Independence. P 13½.

963	**519**	18d. multicoloured	1·80	1·70

(Des L. Kufalo. Litho)

2016 (12 Sept). Personalities. T **520** and similar multicoloured design. P 13½.

964	20d. Type **520** (25th death anniversary)	1·90	1·80
965	40d. Antonio Vivaldi (275th death anniversary) (*horiz*)	3·75	3·50

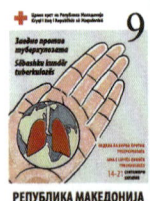
520a Hand holding Lungs

521 Tajar Zavalani

(Des V. Mujov)

2016 (14 Sept). Obligatory Tax. Anti-Tuberculosis Week. P 13½.

965*a*	**520a**	9d. multicoloured	75	70

For compulsory use from 14 to 21 September.

(Des L. Kufalo. Litho)

2016 (20 Sept). Personalities. T **521** and similar multicoloured designs. P 13½.

966	18d. Type **521** (Albanian historian, publicist, and writer) (50th death anniversary)	1·80	1·70
967	18d. Jordan Nikolov (leader of the labour movement) (birth centenary)	1·80	1·70
968	50d. Walt Disney and characters (50th death anniversary) (*horiz*)	4·75	4·50
966/968	*Set of* 3	7·50	7·00

522 European Badger (*Meles meles*)

523 Symbols of Christmas

(Des L. Kufalo)

2016 (20 Oct). Fauna. T **522** and similar horiz designs. Multicoloured. P 13½.

969	11d. Type **522**		75	70
	a. Strip of 4. Nos. 969/972		18·00	
970	20d. Marbled Polecat (*Vormela peregusna*)		1·80	1·70
971	50d. Weasel (*Mustela nivalis*)		4·75	4·50
972	100d. Eurasian Otter (*Lutra lutra*)		9·25	9·00
969/972	*Set of* 4		15·00	14·50

Nos. 969/972 were printed, *se-tenant*, in vertical strips of four stamps within the sheet.

(Des L. Ž. Donev. Litho)

2016 (7 Nov). Christmas. P 13.

973	**523**	40d. multicoloured	3·75	3·50

523a Spinach

524 AIDS Ribbon

(Des L. Ž. Donev. Litho)

2016 (16 Nov). Vegetables. P 13.

973*a*	**523a**	18d. multicoloured	1·80	1·70

(Des V. Mujov)

2016 (1 Dec). Obligatory Tax. AIDS Awareness Week. P 13½.

974	**524**	9d. scarlet and black	75	70

For compulsory use from 1 to 7 December.

525 Holy Trinity Cathedral, Saint Petersburg

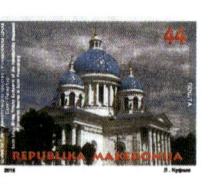
525a Globe, Ribbon and Couple

(Des L. Kufalo)

2016 (23 Dec). Cultural Heritage. Churches. T **525** and similar horiz design. Multicoloured. P 13½.

975	44d. Type **525**	3·75	3·50
	a. Pair. Nos. 975/976	13·50	13·00
976	100d. Church of the Holy Apostle John the theologian, Ohrid	9·25	9·00

Nos. 975/976 were printed, *se-tenant*, in horizontal pairs within the sheet.

Stamps of a similar design were issued by Russia.

2017 (Mar 1). OBLIGATORY TAX Red Cross 2017 Anti Cancer Week. P 13½.

976*a*	**525a**	9d. multicoloured	75	70

For compulsory use from 1 to 8 March.

526 Courgettes

527 Potatoes

2017 MACEDONIA

2017 (15 Mar). Vegetables. P 13.
(Des L. Ž. Donev. Litho)
977 526 18d. multicoloured .... 1·80 1·70

2017 (22 Mar). Vegetables. P 13.
(Des L. Ž. Donev. Litho)
978 527 18d. multicoloured .... 1·80 1·70

528 Mosque

(Des L. Ž. Donev)
2017 (27 Apr). 525th Anniversary of Mustafa Pasha Mosque. P 13½.
979 528 18d. multicoloured .... 1·80 1·70

529 Player

(Des L. Ž. Donev)
2017 (27 Apr). World Men's Handball Championships, France. P 13½.
980 529 86d. multicoloured .... 8·00 7·75

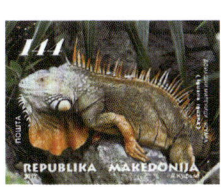 

530 Iguana **530a** Globe and Cut-out Figures

(Des L. Ž. Donev)
2017 (27 Apr). Pets. Green Iguana. P 13½.
981 530 144d. multicoloured .... 13·50 12·50

2017 (May 8). Obligatory Tax. Red Cross and Red Crescent Day. P 13½.
981a 530a 9d. multicoloured 75 70
For compulsory use from 8 to 15 May.

531 Edmond Halley **532** 17th-century Barque

(Des L. Ž. Donev)
2017 (28 Apr). 275th Death Anniversary of Edmond Halley (astronomer). P 13½.
982 531 88d. multicoloured .... 8·25 8·00

(Des L. Ž. Donev. Litho)
2017 (4 May). Transport. Old Ships. P 13½.
983 532 144d. multicoloured .... 13·50 12·50

533 Big Ben, London **534** Skopje Fortress

(Des L. Kufalo. Litho)
2017 (5 May). Macedonia in EU. T **533** and similar multicoloured design. P 13½.
984 32d. Type **533** .... 3·00 3·00
985 32d. Valletta, Malta (horiz) .... 3·00 3·00

(Des L. Ž. Donev)
2017 (8 May). Europa. Castles. T **534** and similar horiz designs. Multicoloured. P 13½.
986 73d. Type **534** .... 6·75 6·50
987 73d. Samuel's Fortress, Ohrid .... 6·75 6·50
MS988 116×56 mm. 144d. Medieval Skopje Fortress (Lithography attributed to the Dutch printer Jacobus Harevin) .... 14·00 13·00

535 Bee, Honeycomb and Sunflower

(Des L. Ž. Donev)
2017 (5 June). Fauna. Bees. T **535** and similar horiz design. Multicoloured. P 13½.
989 18d. Type **535** .... 1·80 1·70
990 72d. Hive, swarm and Bee .... 6·75 6·50

536 Arasta Mosque, Skopje

(Des L. Ž. Donev. Litho)
2017 (23 June). Bayram Festival. P 13½.
991 536 18d. multicoloured .... 1·80 1·70

537 Cvetan Dimov **538** Anniversary Emblem

(Des L. Ž. Donev. Litho)
2017 (6 July). Personalities. T **537** and similar vert designs. Multicoloured. P 13½.
992 18d. Type **537** (Macedonian Communist activist and martyr) (75th death anniversary) .... 1·80 1·70
993 18d. Faik Konica (Albanian cultural and political figure) (75th death anniversary) .... 1·80 1·70
994 73d. Michael Faraday (British scientific pioneer) (150th death anniversary) .... 6·75 6·50
992/994 Set of 3 .... 9·25 9·00

MACEDONIA 2017

(Des L. Ž. Donev. Litho)
2017 (18 Aug). 25th Anniversary of Macedonian Army. P 13½.
995 538 18d. multicoloured .... 1·80 1·70

539 Player
540 Muhammad Ali

(Des L. Ž. Donev. Litho)
2017 (31 Aug). European Basketball Championship, France. P 13½.
996 539 86d. multicoloured .... 8·00 7·75

(Des L. Ž. Donev)
2017 (12 Sept). 75th Birth Anniversary of Muhammad Ali. P 13½.
997 540 86d. multicoloured .... 8·00 7·75

541 Arturo Toscanini
542 Auguste Rodin and *The Thinker*

(Des L. Kufalo)
2017 (21 Sept). 150th Birth Anniversary of Arturo Toscanini (compsoer). P 13½.
998 541 72d. multicoloured .... 6·75 6·50

(Des L. Ž. Donev)
2017 (28 Sept). Death Centenary of Auguste Rodin (sculptor). P 13½.
999 542 88d. multicoloured .... 8·25 8·00

543 Children's Hands and Emblem
544 Emblem and Building

(Des L. Kufalo)
2017 (4 Oct). Rare Disease Day. P 13½.
1000 543 48d. multicoloured .... 4·50 4·25

(Des L. Ž. Donev)
2017 (9 Oct). 50th Anniversary of Macedonian Academy Arts and Sciences. P 13½.
1001 544 18d. multicoloured .... 1·80 1·70

545 Cannabis (*Caninbis sativa*)
546 Mary and the Infant Jesus

(Des L. Ž. Donev)
2017 (19 Oct). Flora. T **545** and similar square designs showing plants. Multicoloured. P 13½.
1002   11d. Type **545** 75   70
         a. Strip of 4. Nos. 1002/1005 .... 17·00

1003   20d. Cotton (*Gossypium hirsutum*) .... 1·80 1·70
1004   50d. Tobacco (*Nicotiana tabacum*) .... 4·50 4·25
1005   100d. Poppy (*Papaver somniferum*) .... 9·00 8·75
1002/1005 *Set of* 4 .... 14·50 14·00
Nos. 1002/1005 were perforated in a circle around the design, enclosed in an outer perforated square, and were printed, *se-tenant*, in strips of four stamps within the sheet.

(Des L. Ž. Donev. Litho)
2017 (22 Nov). Christmas. P 13.
1006 546 18d. multicoloured .... 1·80 1·70

547 St Clement's Church
548 Mata Canyon

(Des L. Ž. Donev)
2017 (12 Dec). 50th Anniversary of Restoration of Ohrid Archbishopric. P 13½.
1007 547 18d. multicoloured .... 1·80 1·70

(Des L. Kufalo)
2017 (19 Dec). Tourism. P 13½.
1008 548 48d. multicoloured .... 4·50 4·25

549 Kiro Gligorov
550 Onions

(Des L. Ž. Donev. Litho)
2017 (22 Dec). Birth Centenary of President Kiro Gligorov. P 13.
1009 549 18d. multicoloured .... 1·80 1·70

(Des L. Kufalo. Litho)
2017 (Dec). Vegetables. T **550** and similar vert designs. Multicoloured. P 13.
1010   18d. Type **550** .... 1·80 1·70
1011   18d. Radish .... 1·80 1·70
1012   18d. Squash .... 1·80 1·70
1013   18d. Celery .... 1·80 1·70
1010/1013 *Set of* 4 .... 6·50 6·00

551 Skanderbeg
552 Figure Skating

(Des L. Ž. Donev. Litho)
2018 (10 Jan). 550th Death Anniversary of George Kastrioti (Skanderbeg) (national hero). P 13½.
1014 551 18d. multicoloured .... 1·80 1·70

(Des L. Kufalo)
2018 (6 Feb). Winter Olympic Games, Pyeongchang. T **552** and similar horiz design. Multicoloured. P 13½.
1015   72d. Type **552** .... 6·75 6·50
1016   73d. Luge .... 6·75 6·50

2018 MACEDONIA

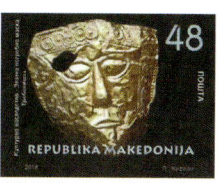

553 Golden Funeral Mask, from Trebenište

553a Symbols of Work of Red Cross

(Des L. Kufalo)

2018 (8 Feb). Cultural Heritage. Funeral Masks. P 13½.
1017   553   48d. multicoloured .... 4·50   4·25

2018 (1 Mar). Obligatory Tax. Red Cross and Red Crescent Day. P 13½.
1017a   553a   9d. multicoloured 85   80
For compulsory use from 8 to 15 May.

554 Ram

555 Capsule

(Des L. Kufalo. Litho)

2018 (7 Mar). Domestic Animals. Sheep. T **554** and similar horiz design. Multicoloured. P 13½.
1018   72d. Type **554** .... 6·75   6·50
1019   86d. Ewes .... 8·00   7·75

(Des L. Kufalo)

2018 (14 Mar). Science. Anniversaries. T **555** and similar horiz design. Multicoloured. P 13½.
1020   48d. Type **555** (75th anniversary of discovery of Streptomycin, antibiotic against tuberculosis) .... 4·50   4·25
1021   86d. James Prescott Joule (studied the nature of heat, and discovered its relationship to mechanical work) (birth bicentenary) .... 8·00   7·75

556 Copernicus

557 Old Locomotive on Kicevo Line

(Des L. Kufalo)

2018 (28 Mar). 475th Birth Anniversary of Nicolaus Copernicus (astronomer). P 13½.
1022   **556**   73d. multicoloured .... 6·75   6·50
MS1023 77×57 mm. 102d. As Type **556** .... 9·75   9·25

(Des L. Ž. Donev. Litho)

2018 (4 Apr). Transport. Trains. P 13½.
1024   **557**   144d. multicoloured .... 13·50   13·00

558 St Nedelya Eastern Orthodox Church in Sofia, Bulgaria

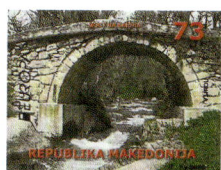

559 Old Bridge over Babuna River, Veles

(Des L. Kufalo. Litho)

2018 (25 Apr). Macedonia in EU. T **558** and similar horiz design. Multicoloured. P 13½.
1025   72d. Type **558** .... 4·50   4·25
1026   48d. Schönbrunn Palace, Vienna, Austria .... 4·50   4·25

(Des L. Kufalo)

2018 (2 May). Europa. Bridges. T **559** and similar horiz design. Multicoloured. P 13½.
1027   73d. Type **559** .... 6·75   6·50
1028   80d. Stone arch bridge over Gradeska River, Mariovo village, Zovic .... 7·50   7·00
MS1029 105×75 mm. 50d.×4, Gorenica bridge on the Radika River (*different*); As Type **559**; As No. 1028; Elenski skok bridge, Mogorche .... 20·00   19·00
MS1030 70×90 mm. 144d. Gorenica bridge on the Radika River, near Debar, dismantled due to the construction of the reservoir Spilje .... 14·00   13·50
No. **MS**1029 was sold in a folder.

560 Teapot, cups and cakes

561 Stylised trophy and football

(Des L. Ž. Donev)

2018 (3 June). Bayram Festival. Horiz design showing food and drink. Multicoloured. P 13½.
1031   18d. Type **560** .... 1·70   1·60

(Des L. Ž. Donev)

2018 (5 June). World Cup Football Championships, Russia. Two vert designs showing emblem. Multicoloured. P 13½.
1032   72d. Type **561** .... 6·75   6·50
1033   88d. Stylised trophy with pitch and goal net behind .... 8·25   7·75

562 Kočo Racin

562a Crowd with Exposed Lungs

(Des L. Ž. Donev)

2018 (13 June). 75th Death Anniversary of Kočo Racin (Kosta Apostolov Solev) (writer and partisan). P 13½.
1034   18d. multicoloured .... 1·70   1·60

2018 (14 Spet). Obligatory Tax. Anti-Tuberculosis Week. P 13½.
1034a   562a   18d. multicoloured 85   80
For compulsory use from 14 to 21 September.

563 Symbols of Transportation

(Des T Pochevska)

2018 (19 Sept). 75th Anniversary of the Holocaust in Macedonia. P 13½.
1035   **563**   50d. multicoloured .... 4·75   4·50

425

(Des L. Ž. Donev)

2018 (9 Oct). 25th Anniversary of Macedonia's Membership of UPU. Vert design showing emblems. Multicoloured. P 13½.
1036   73d. UPU and Macedonia Post emblems .... 6·75 6·50
T **564** is unavailable.

565 Milan Firfov   **566** Jacobo Tintoretto

(Des L. Ž. Donev)

2018 (17 Oct). Music Anniversaries. T **565** and similar vert design. P 13½.
1037   48d. Type **564** (75th birth anniversary) .... 4·50 4·25
1038   80d. Claude Debusy (death centenary) .... 7·50 7·00

(Des L. Ž. Donev)

2018 (5 Nov). Art Anniversaries. T **566** and similar multicoloured design. P 13½.
1039   72d. Type **566** (500th birth anniversary) .... 6·75 6·50
1040   88d. Ibrahim Kodra (birth centenary)
        (30×40 *mm*) .... 8·25 7·75

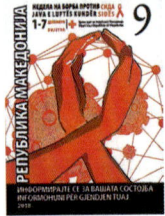 

567 AIDS Ribbon and Virus   **568** Madonna and Child

2018 (1 Dec). Obligatory Tax. AIDS Awareness Week. P 13½.
1041 **567**   9d. multicoloured 85 80
For compulsory used from 1 to 7 December.

2018 (4 Dec). Christmas. P 13½.
1042 **568**   18d. multicoloured .... 1·75 1·60

Dear Catalogue User,

As a collector and Stanley Gibbons catalogue user for many years myself, I am only too aware of the need to provide you with the information you seek in an accurate, timely and easily accessible manner. Naturally, I have my own views on where changes could be made, but one thing I learned long ago is that we all have different opinions and requirements.

I would therefore be most grateful if you would complete the form overleaf and return it to me. Please contact Lorraine Holcombe (lholcombe@stanleygibbons.com) if you would like to be emailed the questionnaire.

Very many thanks for your help.

Yours sincerely,

Hugh Jefferies,
Editor.

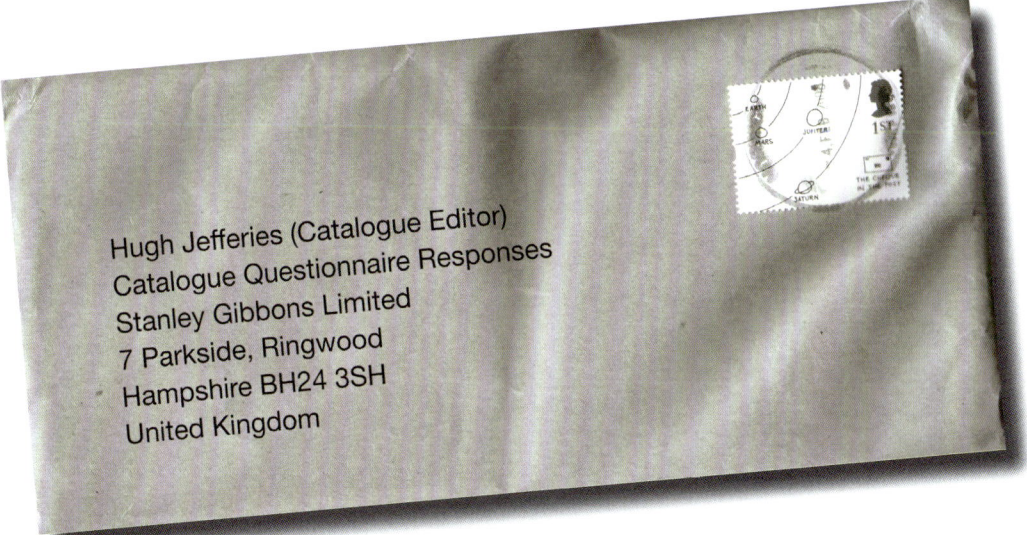

Questionnaire

2019 Southern Balkans

1. **Level of detail**
   Do you feel that the level of detail in this catalogue is:
   a. too specialised   ○
   b. about right   ○
   c. inadequate   ○

2. **Frequency of issue**
   How often would you purchase a new edition of this catalogue?
   a. Annually   ○
   b. Every two years   ○
   c. Every three to five years   ○
   d. Less frequently   ○

3. **Design and Quality**
   How would you describe the layout and appearance of this catalogue?
   a. Excellent   ○
   b. Good   ○
   c. Adequate   ○
   d. Poor   ○

4. How important to you are the prices given in the catalogue:
   a. Important   ○
   b. Quite important   ○
   c. Of little interest   ○
   d. Of no interest   ○

5. Would you be interested in an online version of this catalogue?
   a. Yes   ○
   b. No   ○

6. Do you like the new format?
   a. Yes   ○
   b. No   ○

7. What changes would you suggest to improve the catalogue? E.g. Which other indices would you like to see included?
   ....
   ....
   ....
   ....

8. Which other Stanley Gibbons Catalogues do you buy?
   ....
   ....
   ....
   ....

9. Would you like us to let you know when the next edition of this catalogue is due to be published?
   a. Yes   ○
   b. No   ○
   If so please give your contact details below.
   Name: ....
   Address: ....
   ....
   ....
   ....
   Email: ....
   Telephone: ....

10. Which other Stanley Gibbons Catalogues are you interested in?
    a. ....
    b. ....
    c. ....

Many thanks for your comments.

Please complete and return it to: Hugh Jefferies (Catalogue Editor)
Stanley Gibbons Limited, 7 Parkside, Ringwood, Hampshire BH24 3SH, United Kingdom
or email: lholcombe@stanleygibbons.com to request a soft copy

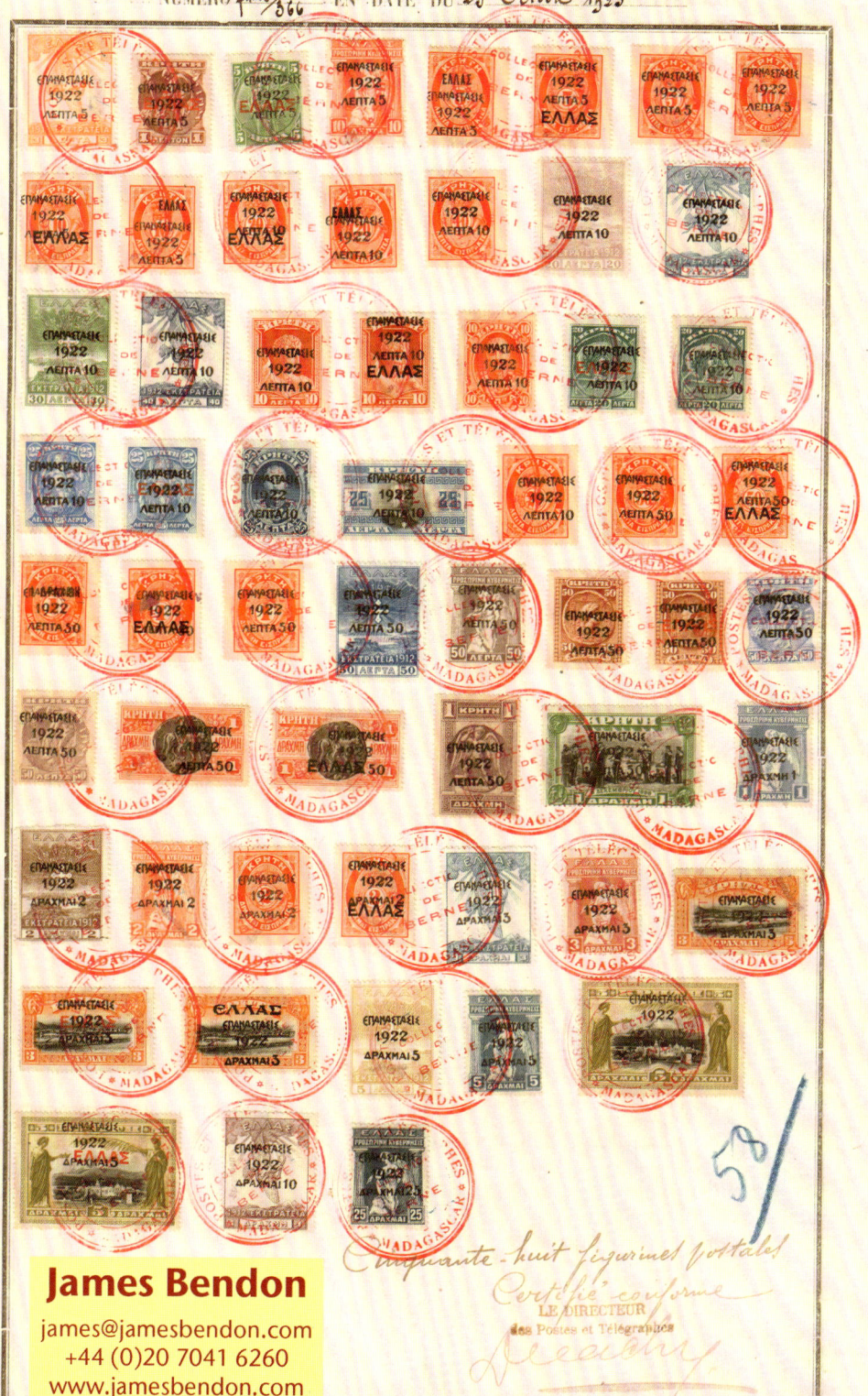

Southern Balkans Order Form

YOUR ORDER

Stanley Gibbons account number

Condition (mint/UM/used)	Country	SG No.	Description	Price	Office use only
			POSTAGE & PACKING	£3.60	
			TOTAL		

The lowest price charged for individual stamps or sets purchased from Stanley Gibbons Ltd, is £1.

Payment & address details

Name
Address (We cannot deliver to PO Boxes)

Postcode
Tel No.
Email

PLEASE NOTE Overseas customers MUST quote a telephone number or the order cannot be dispatched. Please complete ALL sections of this form to allow us to process the order.

☐ Cheque (made payable to Stanley Gibbons Ltd)
☐ I authorise you to charge my
  Mastercard   Visa   Diners   Amex   Maestro

Card No.
Valid from   Expiry date   Issue No. (Maestro only)   CVC No. (4 if Amex)   (Maestro only)
CVC No. is the last three digits on the back of your card (4 if Amex)

Signature   Date

4 EASY WAYS TO ORDER

Post to
Mark Pegg,
Stamp Mail Order
Department, Stanley
Gibbons Ltd, 399
Strand, London,
WC2R 0LX, England

Call
020 7836 8444
+44 (0)20 7836 8444

Fax
020 7557 4499
+44 (0)20 7557 4499

Click
mpegg@stanleygibbons.com

Like What You See?
Take Your 1st £55 worth FREE

Announcing
UPA's Next £1.8 Million Auction

Universal's 20,000± lot
October/January/April/ July Auction
Catalogue will soon be available
NO Buyer's Premium, All Lots Guaranteed

START NOW
Simply Request Your Next FREE Catalogue below

New Client Auction Offer: Yes, I'd like to See Stamps like these I can win in auction. Send / Airmail Me Your Your Next *FREE Secret Weapon UPA Auction Catalogue* **Worth £20**, PLUS 1st £55 Auction Winnings FREE OFFER When I Win Stamps Worth £75+.
I understand I am under NO obligation whatsoever

1 ➜ *Request Free £20 'Secret Weapon' catalogue NOW*:
   www.upastampauctions.co.uk **Go to Auctions**

2 ➜ *Call My Team to Collect Your SECRET WEAPON:* 01451 861111
   Fax Your Request: 01451 861297

3 ➜ *Write:* **Universal Philatelic Auctions**, **UPA** (SG Balk 6/19),
   4, The Old Coalyard, West End, Northleach, Glos GL54 3HE England